AMERICAN POLITICAL LEADERS 1789–2005

AMERICAN POLITICAL LEADERS 1789–2005

CQ PRESS

A Division of Congressional Quarterly Inc.
Washington, D.C.

CQ Press
1255 22nd Street, NW, Suite 400
Washington, DC 20037

Phone, 202-729-1900; toll-free, 1-866-427-7737 (1-866-4CQ-PRESS)

Web: www.cqpress.com

Cover design: Ion Graphic Design Works

Cover photos: George W. Bush (AP Photos); Charles Rangel and Raul Grijalva (http://www.house.gov); Abraham Lincoln, Ruth Bader Ginsburg, Ronald Reagan, Francis Perkins, Sandra Day O'Connor, John F. Kennedy, Theodore Roosevelt, and Bill Clinton (Library of Congress); George Pataki (http://www.state.ny.us/governor); Daniel Inouye (http://www.senate.gov); and Colin Powell (http://www.state.gov).

∞ The paper used in this publication exceeds the requirements of the American National Standard for Information Sciences—Permanence of Paper for Printed Library Materials, ANSI Z39.48-1992.

Printed and bound in the United States of America

09   08   07   06   05   1   2   3   4   5

Library of Congress Cataloging-in-Publication Data

American political leaders, 1789–2005.
    p. cm.
  Rev. ed. of: American political leaders, 1789–2000. c2000.
  Includes indexes.
  ISBN 1-56802-967-5 (hardcover: alk. paper)
  1. Politicians—United States—Biography—Dictionaries. 2. United States—Biography—Dictionaries. I. American political leaders, 1789–2000. II. Title.

E176.A513 2005
973'.09'9–dc22

                                                                2005007732

Contents

AMERICAN POLITICAL LEADERS 1789–2005

Presidents

The president has emerged as the focal point of the U.S. system of government. The Founders, however, left little indication in the Constitution of the type of person they believed would be best suited for the office of president of the United States. The qualifications clause—in Article II, Section 1—states: "No person except a natural born Citizen, or a Citizen of the United States, at the time of the Adoption of this Constitution, shall be eligible to the Office of President; neither shall any person be eligible to that Office who shall not have attained to the Age of thirty five Years, and been fourteen Years a Resident within the United States." More than anything, these stipulations reflect the issues at hand at the time the Founders devised them.

The citizenship requirement was tied to contemporary politics. Rumors had spread while the Constitutional Convention was meeting that the delegates were going to install a European monarch as president. The practice of importing foreign rulers was not unheard of among the European monarchies of the day. The delegates knew the imposition of an independent executive would be met with suspicion; opponents feared the president would be a latent monarchy. Requiring that the president be a natural born citizen, the delegates reasoned, would at least squelch the foreign king rumors.

The residency requirement was designed to eliminate from consideration as president both British sympathizers who had fled to England during the American Revolution and popular foreign military leaders who had emigrated to the United States to fight in the Revolution. The Founders were concerned that the new nation not be made unduly vulnerable to foreign influences. The length of residency—fourteen years—was reduced from the initially proposed requirement of twenty-one years because the longer requirement would have barred three of the convention's delegates from the presidency.

The age requirement had two obvious justifications. First, the Founders wanted to ensure maturity in the president. Second, age left a record for voters to assess.

The Constitution does not contain property or class qualifications for president. The delegates apparently could not agree on property requirements acceptable to all. Some argued against the very idea of them. A desire also existed that the United States government not take on the aristocratic bent of the British government, which made high social class a prerequisite for membership in the House of Lords and property a requirement for voting and hence inclusion in the House of Commons.

Selecting a President

The method of selecting a president was the subject of long debate at the Constitutional Convention of 1787. Several plans were proposed and rejected before the convention adopted a compromise solution, which has been modified only slightly since then.

Facing the convention when it opened May 25 was the question of whether the chief executive should be chosen by direct popular election, by Congress, by state legislatures, or by intermediate electors. Direct election was opposed because it was felt generally that the people lacked sufficient knowledge of the character and qualifications of possible candidates to make an intelligent choice. Many delegates also feared that the people of the various states would be unlikely to agree on a single person, usually casting their votes for favorite-son candidates well known to them.

The possibility of giving Congress the power to choose the president also received consideration. However, this plan was rejected, largely because of concern that it would jeopardize the principle of executive independence. Similarly, a plan favored by many delegates, to let state legislatures choose the president, was turned down because it was feared that the president might feel so indebted to the states as to allow them to encroach on federal authority.

Unable to agree on a plan, the convention on Aug. 31 appointed a "Committee of 11" to propose a solution. The committee Sept. 4 suggested a compromise under which each state would appoint presidential electors equal to the total number of its representatives and senators. The electors, chosen in a manner set forth by each state legislature, would meet in their states and each cast votes for two persons. The votes would be counted in Congress, with the candidate receiving a majority elected president and the second-highest candidate becoming vice president.

No distinction was made between ballots for president and vice president. Moreover, the development of national political parties and the nomination of tickets for president and vice president created further confusion. All the electors of one party tended to cast ballots for their two

Presidential Disability and the Line of Succession

Congressional concern over the question of presidential disability was eased in 1967 by ratification of the Twenty-fifth Amendment to the Constitution. The amendment for the first time provided for continuity in carrying out the functions of the presidency in the event of presidential disability and for filling a vacancy in the vice presidency.

The ambiguity of the language of the disability clause (Article II, Section 1) of the Constitution had provoked occasional debate ever since the Constitutional Convention of 1787. The section provided that Congress should decide who was to succeed to the presidency if both the president and the vice president died, resigned, or became disabled. But it never had been decided how far the term "disability" extended or who would be the judge of it.

Not until the Twenty-fifth Amendment did a procedure exist to determine when a president was disabled, even though eleven presidents who served before 1967 were disabled during at least part of their administration. The most seriously afflicted were James A. Garfield, shot in 1881 and confined to his bed until he died two and a half months later, and Woodrow Wilson, who suffered a stroke in 1919 that incapacitated him during most of his final year and a half in office. In neither case did the vice president assume any duties of the president for fear he would appear to be usurping the powers of the office.

As for the vice presidency, before passage of the Twenty-fifth Amendment the United States had been without a vice president sixteen times for a total of thirty-seven years, after the elected vice president succeeded to the presidency, died, or resigned. The possibility that a vice president would not be available to succeed to the president was not regarded as intolerable until after the assassination of President John F. Kennedy in 1963. The absence of a vice president during the first fourteen months of Lyndon Johnson's presidency seemed especially distressing because the next two offices in line of succession were occupied by weak and ill members of Congress. The amendment was introduced less than three weeks after Kennedy's assassination.

The Twenty-fifth Amendment provided that the vice president should become acting president under either of two circumstances. If the president informed Congress that he was unable to perform his duties, the vice president would become acting president until the president could resume his office. If the vice president and a majority of the cabinet, or another body chosen by Congress (to prevent the president from simply firing the cabinet), found the president to be incapacitated, the vice president would become acting president until the president informed Congress that his disability had ended. Congress had twenty-one days to resolve any dispute over the president's disability; a two-thirds vote of both chambers was required to overrule the president's declaration that he no longer was incapacitated.

When a vacancy occurred in the vice presidency, the Twenty-fifth Amendment empowered the president to nominate a vice president, whose nomination was to be confirmed by a majority vote of both houses of Congress. As of March 2005, the power of the president to appoint a new vice president had been used twice. In 1973, when Vice President Spiro T. Agnew resigned, President Richard Nixon nominated Gerald R. Ford as vice president. Ford was confirmed by both houses of Congress and sworn in Dec. 6, 1973. On Nixon's resignation Aug. 9, 1974, Ford succeeded to the presidency, becoming the first president in American history who had not been elected to either the presidency or the vice presidency. Ford chose Nelson A. Rockefeller as his vice president.

Reagan Assassination Attempt

In the aftermath of the attempted assassination of President Ronald Reagan in March 1981, Vice President George Bush and members of the cabinet decided not to invoke the Twenty-fifth Amendment. However, some

party nominees. But with no distinction between the presidential and vice presidential nominees, the danger arose of a tie vote between the two. That happened in 1800, when the Democratic Republican electors inadvertently caused a tie in the electoral college by casting equal numbers of votes for Thomas Jefferson, whom they wished to elect president, and Aaron Burr, whom they wished to elect vice president. The election was thrown into the House of Representatives, and thirty-six ballots were re-

quired before Jefferson was finally elected president. The Twelfth Amendment, ratified in 1804, sought to prevent a recurrence by providing that the electors should vote separately for president and vice president.

The compromise plan constituted a great concession to the less populous states, given that they were assured of three votes (two for their two senators and at least one for their representative) however small their populations might be. The plan also left important powers with the

of the public statements made by administration officials immediately after the shooting reflected continuing confusion over the issue of who is in charge when the president temporarily is unable to function. In a televised press briefing, Secretary of State Alexander M. Haig Jr. confirmed that Reagan was in surgery and under anesthesia. Attempting to reassure the country, Haig stated that he was "in control" at the White House pending the return of Bush, who was in Texas.

This assertion was followed by a question from the press about who was making administrative decisions. Haig responded, erroneously, "Constitutionally, gentlemen, you have the president, the vice president, and the secretary of state in that order, and should the president decide he wants to transfer the helm to the vice president, he will do so. He has not done that." The law applicable in the 1981 shooting was the Presidential Succession Act of 1947 as modified. Haig's response reflected the law in effect before 1947. Congress has enacted succession laws three times. The act of March 1, 1792, provided for succession (after the vice president) of the president pro tempore of the Senate and then of the House Speaker; if either one became president a special election was to be held to choose a new president. That law stood until the passage of the Presidential Succession Act of Jan. 19, 1886, which changed the line of succession to run from the vice president to the secretary of state, secretary of the Treasury, and so on through the cabinet in order of rank. Congress was to decide whether a special election was to be held. Pursuant to the 1947 act amendments, the line of succession as of 2005 was the vice president, the Speaker of the House, the president pro tempore of the Senate, the secretaries of state, Treasury, defense, the attorney general, the secretaries of interior, agriculture, commerce, labor, health and human services, housing and urban development, transportation, energy, education, veterans affairs, and homeland security. The successor president was to serve until the end of the presidential term.

Major Surgery and the Presidency

The first time the Twenty-fifth Amendment was applied to a temporarily incapacitated president was on July 13, 1985, when Reagan underwent cancer surgery. Reagan transferred his powers to Bush just before receiving anesthesia for the surgery and signed papers reclaiming them almost as soon as he awoke, seven hours and fifty-four minutes later. During that time, Bush served as acting president.

Because of the delicate wording of Reagan's official letter of notification, it remains unclear whether the Twenty-fifth Amendment was actually invoked. Reagan stated in his letter that "I am mindful of the provisions" of the Twenty-fifth Amendment. But he added that "I do not believe that the drafters of this amendment intended its application" to situations such as his. Even though Reagan avoided designating Bush as acting president, White House officials acknowledged that Bush played that role while Reagan was in the operating room.

George W. Bush became the second president to invoke the amendment when he underwent a colonoscopy that required anesthesia on June 29, 2002. In a letter citing his upcoming operation, he temporarily transferred his powers to Vice President Richard B. Cheney: "In view of present circumstances, I have determined to transfer temporarily my Constitutional powers and duties to the Vice President during the brief period of the procedure and recovery." Two hours after the operation, he transmitted a second letter announcing the resumption of the powers and duties of his office: "In accordance with the provisions of Section 3 of the Twenty-Fifth Amendment to the United States Constitution, this letter shall constitute my written declaration that I am presently able to resume the discharge of the Constitutional powers and duties of the office of President of the United States."

states by giving complete discretion to state legislatures to determine the method of choosing electors.

The only part of the committee's plan that aroused serious opposition was a provision giving the Senate the right to decide presidential elections in which no candidate received a majority of electoral votes. Some delegates feared that the Senate, which already had been given treaty approval powers and the responsibility to "advise and consent" on all important executive appointments, might become too powerful. Therefore, a counterproposal was made and accepted to let the House decide in instances when the electors failed to give a majority of their votes to a single candidate. The interests of the small states were preserved by giving each state's delegation only one vote in the House on roll calls to elect a president.

The system adopted by the Constitutional Convention was a compromise born out of problems involving diverse state voting requirements, the slavery problem, big-state versus small-state rivalries, and the complexities of the balance of power among different branches of the government. It also apparently was as close to a direct popular election as those who wrote the Constitution thought possible and appropriate at the time.

Only once since ratification of the Constitution has an amendment—the Twelfth Amendment—been adopted that substantially altered the method of electing the president. Other changes in the system, however, evolved over the years. The authors of the Constitution, for example, had intended that each state choose its most distinguished citizens as electors and that they would deliberate and vote as individuals in electing the president. But as strong political parties began to appear, the electors came to be chosen merely as representatives of the parties; independent voting by electors disappeared almost entirely.

Common Characteristics

All presidents have shared several important characteristics. First, all have been men. Through the 2004 election, no woman had been nominated for president by a major political party.

Second, each of the forty-two descended from northern European ancestors, with the vast majority tracing their roots to the British Isles. *(See box, Nationalities of the Presidents, p. 5.)*

Third, no one had reached the presidency without significant experience as a public servant or military officer. Most presidents had served in at least one elective office at the national or state level. Twenty-four presidents had previously served in Congress; twenty had been colonial, state, or territorial governors; and fourteen had been vice presidents. Presidents have also served as cabinet members, diplomats, state legislators, mayors, judges, sheriffs, and prosecutors on their way to higher office. *(See box, Members of Congress Who Became President, p. 58.)*

Beyond these three characteristics common to each of the first forty-two presidents, two others have dominated: marriage and Protestantism. All presidents but James Buchanan were married at least once; and only one, Ronald Reagan, was divorced and remarried. An overwhelming majority have belonged to Protestant denominations. *(See box, Religious Affiliations of the Presidents, p. 6.)*

Backgrounds

Presidents have come into office with a variety of backgrounds, although there have been some distinct trends in the selection process.

Secretary of State

In the earliest days of the republic the job of secretary of state seemed to pave the way to the presidency. The secretary of state was considered the preeminent cabinet officer and thus the most important person in the executive branch after the president.

George Washington's first secretary of state was Jefferson. Although Jefferson left the cabinet early in Washington's second term, he went on to become leader of the newly formed Democratic Republican Party and its candidate for president in 1796, 1800, and 1804. Losing to John Adams in 1796, Jefferson came back to win the next two elections.

In turn, Jefferson's secretary of state for two terms, James Madison, won the presidency in 1808. During his first term, President Madison appointed fellow Virginian James Monroe as his secretary of state. Monroe went on to be elected to the presidency and served two terms (1817–25).

Throughout Monroe's terms, the secretary of state was John Quincy Adams, son of former president John Adams. When Monroe's second term was nearing its end, five major candidates, including Adams, entered the race to succeed him. None of the candidates managed to acquire a majority in the electoral college, and the House then chose Secretary of State Adams.

Adams was the last secretary of state to go directly from his cabinet post to the White House. After him, only two secretaries of state made it to the White House—Martin Van Buren and James Buchanan.

Military

After these early presidents, one of the most prevalent backgrounds was the military. Andrew Jackson, who ran in 1824 (unsuccessfully), 1828, and 1832, was a general in the War of 1812, gaining near-heroic stature by his defeat of the British at the Battle of New Orleans in January 1815. Like most military officers who have risen to the presidency, however, Jackson was only a part-time military man.

Other candidates after Jackson who were or had been military officers included William Henry Harrison, a Whig candidate in 1836 and 1840; Zachary Taylor, the Whig candidate in 1848; Winfield Scott, the Whig candidate in 1852; Franklin Pierce, the Democratic nominee in 1852; and John Charles Fremont, the Republican Party's first presidential candidate in 1856. Thus, from 1824 through 1856, all but one presidential election featured a major candidate with a military background.

The smoldering political conflicts of the 1840s and 1850s probably contributed to the nomination of military men for the presidency. Generals had usually escaped involvement in national politics and had avoided taking stands on the issues that divided the country—slavery, expansion, the currency, and the tariff.

Later on, the nature of the Civil War almost automatically led at least one of the parties to choose a military officer as presidential standard-bearer every four years. To have been on the "right" side during the war—fighting to save the Union and destroy slavery—was a major political asset in the North and Middle West, where tens of thousands of war veterans were effectively organized in the Grand Army of the Republic (GAR). The GAR became part of the backbone of the Republican Party during the last third of the nineteenth century.

Consequently, it became customary for Republicans to have a Civil War officer at the head of their ticket. Except

Nationalities of the Presidents

Listed below are the presidents and their nationalities. Eight presidents, marked with an asterisk (*), were born British subjects.

President	Nationality
George Washington*	English
John Adams*	English
Thomas Jefferson*	Welsh
James Madison*	English
James Monroe*	Scotch
John Quincy Adams*	English
Andrew Jackson*	Scotch-Irish
Martin Van Buren	Dutch
William Henry Harrison*	English
John Tyler	English
James K. Polk	Scotch-Irish
Zachary Taylor	English
Millard Fillmore	English
Franklin Pierce	English
James Buchanan	Scotch-Irish
Abraham Lincoln	English
Andrew Johnson	English
Ulysses S. Grant	English-Scotch
Rutherford B. Hayes	Scotch
James A. Garfield	English
Chester A. Arthur	Scotch-Irish
Grover Cleveland	English-Irish
Benjamin Harrison	English
William McKinley	Scotch-Irish
Theodore Roosevelt	Dutch
William Howard Taft	English
Woodrow Wilson	Scotch-Irish
Warren G. Harding	English-Scotch-Irish
Calvin Coolidge	English
Herbert Hoover	Swiss-German
Franklin D. Roosevelt	Dutch
Harry S. Truman	English-Scotch-Irish
Dwight D. Eisenhower	Swiss-German
John F. Kennedy	Irish
Lyndon B. Johnson	English
Richard Nixon	English-Scotch-Irish
Gerald R. Ford	English
Jimmy Carter	English-Scotch-Irish
Ronald Reagan	English-Scotch-Irish
George Bush	English
Bill Clinton	English
George W. Bush	English

Sources: Joseph Nathan Kane, *Facts about the Presidents: A Compilation of Biographical and Historical Information,* 6th ed. (New York: Wilson, 1993); Congressional Quarterly.

for James G. Blaine in 1884, every Republican presidential nominee from 1868 to 1900 had served as an officer in the Union Army during the Civil War. Of all the Republican nominees, however, only Ulysses S. Grant, who was elected president in 1868 and 1872, was a professional military man. The others—Rutherford B. Hayes in

Religious Affiliations of the Presidents

Listed below are the presidents and their religious affiliations. Although three presidents claimed no religious affiliation, all presidents have professed a belief in God.

President	Religious Affiliation
George Washington	Episcopalian
John Adams	Unitarian
Thomas Jefferson	none
James Madison	Episcopalian
James Monroe	Episcopalian
John Quincy Adams	Unitarian
Andrew Jackson	Presbyterian
Martin Van Buren	Dutch Reformed
William Henry Harrison	Episcopalian
John Tyler	Episcopalian
James K. Polk	Presbyterian
Zachary Taylor	Episcopalian
Millard Fillmore	Unitarian
Franklin Pierce	Episcopalian
James Buchanan	Presbyterian
Abraham Lincoln	none
Andrew Johnson	none
Ulysses S. Grant	Methodist
Rutherford B. Hayes	Methodist
James A. Garfield	Disciples of Christ
Chester A. Arthur	Episcopalian
Grover Cleveland	Presbyterian
Benjamin Harrison	Presbyterian
William McKinley	Methodist
Theodore Roosevelt	Dutch Reformed
William Howard Taft	Unitarian
Woodrow Wilson	Presbyterian
Warren G. Harding	Baptist
Calvin Coolidge	Congregationalist
Herbert Hoover	Society of Friends (Quaker)
Franklin D. Roosevelt	Episcopalian
Harry S. Truman	Baptist
Dwight D. Eisenhower	Presbyterian
John F. Kennedy	Roman Catholic
Lyndon B. Johnson	Disciples of Christ
Richard Nixon	Society of Friends (Quaker)
Gerald R. Ford	Episcopalian
Jimmy Carter	Baptist
Ronald Reagan	Episcopalian
George Bush	Episcopalian
Bill Clinton	Baptist
George W. Bush	Episcopalian/Methodist

Sources: Joseph Nathan Kane, *Facts about the Presidents: A Compilation of Biographical and Historical Information,* 6th ed. (New York: Wilson, 1993); Congressional Quarterly.

1876, James A. Garfield in 1880, Benjamin Harrison in 1888 and 1892, and William McKinley in 1896 and 1900—were civilians who volunteered for service in the Civil War.

The Democrats, who split over the war, had few prominent military veterans from which to choose. Only twice between 1860 and 1900 did the Democrats pick a Civil War officer as their nominee, and neither was elected. In 1864, during the Civil War, the Democrats nominated Gen. George B. McClellan, the Union military commander who had fallen out with President Abraham Lincoln. In 1880 Gen. Winfield Scott Hancock of Pennsylvania was the Democrats' choice.

Swing State

Democrats tended to favor governors or former governors of New York. Their 1868 nominee was Horatio Seymour, who had been governor of New York from 1853 to 1855 and again from 1863 to 1865. In 1876 they chose Samuel J. Tilden, New York's reform governor who was battling Tammany Hall. And in 1884 Grover Cleveland, another New York reform governor, captured the Democratic nomination. He went on to become the first Democrat to win the White House in twenty-eight years. Cleveland was the Democratic nominee again in 1888, but he lost. However, he was renominated and won in 1892, becoming the only president to serve two nonconsecutive terms.

Besides being the most populous state, New York was a swing state in presidential politics. During the period from Reconstruction through the turn of the century, most Southern states voted Democratic, while the Republicans usually carried Pennsylvania, the Midwest, and New England. A New Yorker appeared as the nominee for president or vice president of at least one of the major parties in every single election from 1868 through 1892.

This tradition generally continued through the candidacy of Thomas E. Dewey, Republican governor of New York, in 1948. Only twice between 1896 and 1948 was there no New Yorker on the national ticket of at least one of the major parties—for president or vice president. Once, in 1944, both major party presidential nominees, Democrat Franklin D. Roosevelt and Republican Dewey, were from New York.

From 1952 through 2004, however, no New Yorkers were nominated by a major party for president and only three for vice president. The latter were Rep. William E. Miller, R (1951–65), in 1964; Rep. Geraldine A. Ferraro, D (1979–85), in 1984; and Rep. Jack Kemp, R (1971–89) in 1996. Dwight D. Eisenhower in 1952 and Richard Nixon in 1968 were technically residents of New York, but they were generally identified with other states. Gerald R. Ford's vice president, Nelson Rockefeller, was a former governor of New York, but he was appointed to the vice presidency. He was not asked to be on the ticket when Ford ran for reelection in 1976.

Another major swing state in the years from the Civil War through World War I was Indiana. In most elections, a prominent Indianan found his way onto one of the major party's national tickets. In the thirteen presidential elections between 1868 and 1916, an Indianan appeared ten times on at least one of the major parties' national tickets. Since 1916 one Indianan, Wendell Willkie in 1940, has been a major party's presidential nominee, and another Indianan, Dan Quayle in 1988, was elected vice president.

Governors

Governors generally—not only those representing New York—have been popular choices for presidential tickets. Through the 2004 election, twenty presidents had been governors of either a state, colony, or territory before assuming office. The sixteen state governors were Van Buren, Cleveland, Theodore Roosevelt, and Franklin Roosevelt from New York; Monroe and John Tyler from Virginia; James K. Polk and Andrew Johnson from Tennessee; Hayes and McKinley from Ohio; and Woodrow Wilson from New Jersey, Calvin Coolidge from Massachusetts, Jimmy Carter from Georgia, Reagan from California, Bill Clinton from Arkansas, and George W. Bush from Texas. In addition, Jefferson served as governor of colonial Virginia; Jackson and William Henry Harrison were territorial governors of Florida and Indiana, respectively; and William Howard Taft served as provisional governor of the Philippines.

In recent years gubernatorial experience has almost become a prerequisite for winning the White House. Between 1976 and 2004 governors or former governors won seven out of eight presidential elections. Carter in 1976 and Reagan in 1980 were former governors. Clinton in 1992 and Bush in 2000 were sitting governors, the only two since Franklin Roosevelt was elected in 1932.

Other governors had also contended for their party's nomination. Reagan came close in 1976 to depriving incumbent Ford of the Republican presidential nomination. In that same election, Carter faced a dramatic last-minute challenge for the Democratic nomination from the governor of California, Edmund G. "Jerry" Brown Jr. Brown challenged Carter for the nomination again in 1980; also throwing his hat into the ring that year was former Texas governor John B. Connally. In 1984 former Florida governor Reubin Askew vied unsuccessfully for the Democratic presidential nomination. Another governor, Michael Dukakis of Massachusetts, captured the Democratic presidential nomination in 1988; former Arizona governor Bruce Babbitt also had made a run for the nomination. Former Delaware governor Pierre S. "Pete" du Pont IV was a contender for the GOP nomination in 1988. Before Clinton secured the top spot on the Democratic ticket in 1992, Virginia governor L. Douglas Wilder had made an early bid for the nomination, and Jerry Brown ran an innovative campaign throughout the primary season and into the convention. Former Tennessee governor Lamar Alexander campaigned for the GOP nomination in the 1996 and 2000 races. In the 2004 campaign, two governors joined the crowded Democratic field: former Florida governor and sitting senator Daniel Robert "Bob" Graham and Vermont governor Howard Dean. Dean became the early Democratic front-runner before losing the nomination to Massachusetts senator John F. Kerry, who had also served previously as lieutenant governor.

Vice Presidents

The vice presidency has also been a presidential training ground. Fourteen of the forty-two presidents previously were vice presidents. Of these, only five first got to the Oval Office by being elected to it and the others made it because of the death or resignation of the president. *(See box, From VP to President, p. 19.)*

Of the five elevated by election, two—John Adams and Jefferson—were elected when there was no direct

A Biographical Summary of the First Ladies

As the president's wife, the first lady is one of the most prominent women in the country. Yet she holds no official position—the Constitution does not mention her—and earns no salary. The modern first lady has a varied, demanding role. She acts as manager of the White House and hostess at receptions, parties, and formal dinners. She also plays a political role and participates in social causes on behalf of her husband's administration, while fulfilling her responsibilities as wife and mother. *(See box, White House Hostesses, p. 11.)*

The wives of four presidents were not first ladies because they died before their husbands reached the White House: Martha Jefferson (Oct. 19, 1748–Sept. 6, 1782), Rachel Jackson (June 15, 1767–Dec. 22, 1828), Hannah Van Buren (March 8, 1783–Feb. 5, 1819), and Ellen Arthur (Aug. 30, 1837–Jan. 12, 1880). Theodore Roosevelt's second wife served as first lady when he was in office; his first wife, Alice Hathaway Lee Roosevelt (July 29, 1861–Feb. 14, 1884), had died at age twenty-two. Ronald Reagan had divorced his first wife, Jane Wyman (born Sarah Jane Fulks, Jan. 14, 1914–), in 1949.

This biographical summary lists, alphabetically, all the first ladies since 1789. The material is organized as follows: name; relationship to presidents, vice presidents, members of Congress, Supreme Court justices, and governors; date of birth; date of death (if applicable); time as first lady; and elective office.

Under the Constitution, presidential terms from 1789 to 1933 were from March 4 to March 4; since 1934, the four-year term has been from Jan. 20 to Jan. 20. Exact dates are cited when service began or ended in midterm.

The major source of information for this list was *Guide to the Presidency*, 3rd ed. (Washington, D.C.: CQ Press, 2002). Additional data were obtained from Joseph Nathan Kane, *Facts about the Presidents: A Compilation of Biographical and Historical Information*, 6th ed. (New York: Wilson, 1993); and various newspapers.

Adams, Abigail Smith (wife of John Adams, mother of Pres. John Quincy Adams, grandmother of Rep. Charles Francis Adams) Nov. 11, 1744–Oct. 28, 1818; first lady 1797–1801.

Adams, Louisa Catherine Johnson (wife of John Quincy Adams, daughter-in-law of Pres. John Adams) Feb. 12, 1775–May 15, 1852; first lady 1825–29.

Bush, Barbara Pierce (wife of George Herbert Walker Bush, mother of Pres. George W. Bush of Texas and Gov. Jeb Bush of Fla., daughter-in-law of Sen. Prescott Sheldon Bush) June 8, 1925– ; first lady 1989–93.

Bush, Laura (wife of George W. Bush, daughter-in-law of Pres. George Herbert Walker Bush) November 4, 1946– ; first lady 2001– .

Carter, Rosalynn Smith (wife of James Earl "Jimmy" Carter Jr.) Aug. 18, 1927– ; first lady 1977–81.

Cleveland, Frances Folsom (wife of Stephen Grover Cleveland) July 21, 1864–Oct. 29, 1947; first lady, June 2, 1886–89, 1893–97.

Clinton, Hillary Rodham (wife of William Jefferson "Bill" Clinton) Oct. 26, 1947– ; first lady 1993–2001; Senate 2001– .

Coolidge, Grace Anna Goodhue (wife of John Calvin Coolidge) Jan. 3, 1879–July 8, 1957; first lady Aug. 3, 1923–29.

Eisenhower, Marie Geneva Doud "Mamie" (wife of Dwight David Eisenhower) Nov. 14, 1896–Nov. 1, 1979; first lady 1953–61.

Fillmore, Abigail Powers (wife of Millard Fillmore) March 13, 1798–March 30, 1853; first lady July 10, 1850–53.

Ford, Elizabeth Bloomer Warren "Betty" (wife of Gerald Rudolph Ford Jr.) April 8, 1918– ; first lady Aug. 9, 1974–77.

Garfield, Lucretia Rudolph (wife of James Abram Garfield) April 19, 1832–March 14, 1918; first lady March 4–Sept. 19, 1881.

Grant, Julia Boggs Dent (wife of Ulysses Simpson Grant) Jan. 26, 1826–Dec. 14, 1902; first lady 1869–77.

---

mass participation in the presidential nomination or election process. Martin Van Buren was elected directly to the presidency in 1836, as was George Bush in 1988. Richard Nixon narrowly lost his bid to move up from the vice presidency in 1960 but was elected president eight years later.

Of those who assumed the office after the death or resignation of a president, five—Theodore Roosevelt, Coolidge, Harry S. Truman, Lyndon B. Johnson, and Ford—subsequently were nominated by their parties for a full term as president, and all but Ford were elected.

In addition to Nixon, Johnson, Ford, and Bush, other vice presidents in modern times to be nominated included Hubert H. Humphrey in 1968, Walter F. Mondale in 1984, and Al Gore in 2000. None of the three advanced to the presidency. Vice President Spiro T. Agnew had been the leading contender for the 1976 Republican presidential nomination before his resignation. Bush's vice president, Quayle, considered running for the GOP nomination in 1996 and 2000 but pulled out early when he failed to generate enough support.

Even a vice presidential nomination has become a springboard of sorts. Six of the losing vice presidential candidates since 1956 later showed support in presidential nominating contests: Henry Cabot Lodge Jr. in 1964, Edmund S. Muskie in 1972, Sargent Shriver in 1976,

Harding, Florence Kling DeWolfe (wife of Warren Gamaliel Harding) Aug. 15, 1860–Nov. 21, 1924; first lady 1921–Aug. 2, 1923.

Harrison, Anna Symmes (wife of William Henry Harrison, mother of Rep. John Scott Harrison, grandmother of Benjamin Harrison, great-great-grandmother of Rep. William Henry Harrison, sister-in-law of Rep. Carter Basset Harrison) July 25, 1775–Feb. 25, 1864; first lady March 4–April 4, 1841.

Harrison, Caroline Lavinia Scott (wife of Benjamin Harrison, grandmother of Rep. William Henry Harrison, daughter-in-law of Rep. John Scott Harrison) Oct. 1, 1832–Oct. 25, 1892; first lady 1889–Oct. 25, 1892.

Hayes, Lucy Ware Webb (wife of Rutherford Birchard Hayes) Aug. 28, 1831–June 25, 1889; first lady 1877–81.

Hoover, Lou Henry (wife of Herbert Clark Hoover) March 29, 1874–Jan. 7, 1944; first lady 1929–33.

Johnson, Claudia Alta Taylor "Lady Bird" (wife of Lyndon Baines Johnson, mother-in-law of Sen. Charles S. Robb) Dec. 22, 1912– ; first lady Nov. 22, 1963–69.

Johnson, Eliza McCardle (wife of Andrew Johnson, mother-in-law of Sen. David Trotter Patterson) Oct. 4, 1810–Jan. 15, 1876; first lady April 15, 1865–69.

Kennedy, Jacqueline Lee Bouvier (wife of John Fitzgerald Kennedy, sister-in-law of Sens. Edward Moore Kennedy and Robert Francis Kennedy, aunt of Reps. Joseph Patrick Kennedy II and Patrick J. Kennedy) July 28, 1929–May 19, 1994; first lady 1961–Nov. 22, 1963.

Lincoln, Mary Todd (wife of Abraham Lincoln) Dec. 13, 1818–July 16, 1882; first lady 1861–April 15, 1865.

Madison, Dorothea Payne Todd "Dolley" (wife of James Madison) May 20, 1768–July 12, 1849; first lady 1809–17.

McKinley, Ida Saxton (wife of William McKinley Jr.) June 8, 1847–May 26, 1907; first lady 1897–Sept. 14, 1901.

Monroe, Elizabeth Kortright (wife of James Monroe, aunt of Rep. James Monroe) July 30, 1768–Sept. 23, 1830; first lady 1817–25.

Nixon, Thelma Catherine Ryan "Pat" (wife of Richard Milhous Nixon) March 16, 1912–June 22, 1993; first lady 1969–Aug. 9, 1974.

Pierce, Jane Means Appleton (wife of Franklin Pierce) March 12, 1806–Dec. 2, 1863; first lady 1853–57.

Polk, Sarah Childress (wife of James Knox Polk, sister-in-law of Rep. William Hawkins Polk) Sept. 4, 1803–Aug. 14, 1891; first lady 1845–49.

Reagan, Nancy Davis (born Anne Frances Robbins) (second wife of Ronald Wilson Reagan) July 6, 1923– ; first lady 1981–89.

Roosevelt, Anna Eleanor Roosevelt (wife of Franklin Delano Roosevelt, mother of Reps. Franklin D. Roosevelt Jr. and James Roosevelt, niece of Theodore Roosevelt) Oct. 11, 1884–Nov. 7, 1962; first lady 1933–April 12, 1945.

Roosevelt, Edith Kermit Carow (second wife of Theodore Roosevelt) Aug. 6, 1861–Sept. 30, 1948; first lady Sept. 14, 1901–09.

Taft, Helen Herron (wife of William Howard Taft, mother of Sen. Robert Alphonso Taft, grandmother of Sen. Robert A. Taft Jr., great-grandmother of Gov. Robert A. Taft II of Ohio, sister-in-law of Rep. Charles Phelps Taft) June 2, 1861–May 22, 1943; first lady 1909–13.

Taylor, Margaret Mackall Smith (wife of Zachary Taylor) Sept. 21, 1788–Aug. 18, 1852; first lady 1849–July 9, 1850.

Truman, Elizabeth Virginia Wallace "Bess" (wife of Harry S. Truman) Feb. 13, 1885–Oct. 18, 1982; first lady April 12, 1945–53.

Tyler, Julia Gardiner (second wife of John Tyler, mother of Rep. David Gardiner Tyler, daughter-in-law of Gov. John Tyler of Va.) May 4, 1820–July 10, 1889; first lady June 26, 1844–45.

Tyler, Letitia Christian (first wife of John Tyler, daughter-in-law of Gov. John Tyler of Va.) Nov. 12, 1790–Sept. 10, 1842; first lady April 6, 1841–Sept. 10, 1842.

Washington, Martha Dandridge Custis (wife of George Washington, aunt of Assoc. Justice Bushrod Washington) June 21, 1731–May 22, 1802; first lady April 30, 1789–97.

Wilson, Edith Bolling Galt (second wife of Thomas Woodrow Wilson) Oct. 15, 1872–Dec. 28, 1961; first lady Dec. 18, 1915–21.

Wilson, Ellen Louise Axson (first wife of Thomas Woodrow Wilson) May 15, 1860–Aug. 16, 1914; first lady 1913–Aug. 16, 1914.

Robert J. "Bob" Dole in 1980 and 1996, Mondale in 1984, and Joseph I. Lieberman in 2004. Mondale and Dole (in 1996) won their party's nomination.

Congress

More than half of the presidents—twenty-four through the 2004 election—previously served in Congress. Nine served in the House only, six in the Senate only, and nine in both chambers. Only eight of the total served in the White House in the twentieth and twenty-first centuries. *(See box, Members of Congress Who Became President, p. 58.)*

The year 1960 marked only the second time in the twentieth century that an incumbent U.S. senator was nominated for the presidency—John F. Kennedy, the Democratic candidate. Warren G. Harding, in 1920, was the earlier senator. There would be only two more in the twentieth century. In the nineteenth century the phenomenon also was rare, with National Republican Henry Clay in 1832, Democrat Lewis Cass in 1848, and Democrat Stephen A. Douglas in 1860 the only incumbent senators nominated for president by official party conventions. Republican Garfield was a senator-elect at the time of his election in 1880.

Senators dominated presidential campaigns from 1960 to 1972. In that period every major party nominee was a senator or former senator: Kennedy and Nixon in 1960; Lyndon Johnson and Barry Goldwater in 1964; Nixon and Humphrey in 1968; and Nixon and George McGovern in 1972. (In addition to Kennedy, Goldwater and McGovern were incumbent senators.)

Only three senators secured the top spot on a major party ticket between 1976 and 2004—Mondale in 1984, Dole in 1996, and Kerry in 2004. However, several senators were tapped as vice presidential running mates: Mondale with Carter and Dole with Ford in 1976; Lloyd Bentsen with Dukakis and Quayle with Bush in 1988; Gore with Clinton in 1992 and 1996; and John Edwards with Kerry in 2004. Numerous senators or former senators pursued the presidential nomination, including Birch Bayh, Robert C. Byrd, Frank Church, and Henry M. Jackson in 1976; Dole, Howard H. Baker Jr., and Edward M. Kennedy in 1980; McGovern, Alan Cranston, John Glenn, Gary Hart, and Ernest F. Hollings in 1984; Dole, Gore, Hart, Joseph R. Biden Jr., and Paul Simon in 1988; Tom Harkin, Bob Kerrey, and Paul E. Tsongas in 1992; Phil Gramm and Richard Lugar in 1996; Gore, Bill Bradley, Orrin Hatch, and John McCain in 2000; and Edwards, Graham, Kerry, Lieberman, and Carol Moseley-Braun in 2004. Along with the five senators competing for the Democratic nomination in 2004 were two members of the House of Representatives, Richard A. Gephardt and Dennis J. Kucinich.

Recent Changes

Since 1960 the pool from which presidential and vice presidential candidates have emerged has grown wider. Barriers have been broken, allowing for deviations from the stereotypical candidate described as male, middle-aged, white, Protestant, a lawyer, and hailing from a large, northern industrial state.

Geraldine Ferraro, Walter Mondale's vice presidential running mate, in 1984 became the first woman nominated to a major party's national ticket. Elizabeth Hanford Dole's campaign to head the 2000 Republican ticket was seen by many as the most serious presidential bid to date by a woman. She dropped out of the race early, however, citing a lack of campaign funds. Dole, the wife of 1996 GOP presidential nominee Bob Dole, previously had served in the Reagan and Bush administrations and had been president of the American Red Cross. She was elected to the Senate from her home state of North Carolina in 2002.

Black candidate Jesse Jackson launched serious pursuits for the Democratic presidential nomination in 1984 and 1988, in the latter campaign finishing second out of a field of eight candidates who began the primary and caucus season. In 1960 Kennedy became the first Catholic elected president. By profession, Presidents Johnson, Carter, Reagan, George Bush, and George W. Bush were not lawyers. Four southerners have been elected president—Johnson in 1964, Carter in 1976, Clinton in 1992 and 1996, and George W. Bush in 2000 and 2004. (Bush Sr. claimed Texas as his legal residence but was more strongly associated with New England states.)

Political experience of the nominees remains important to the electorate. Candidates short on such experience have stressed their leadership in other areas. For example, Carter augmented his short political résumé—two years as a state legislator and four years as governor—with entries of nuclear engineer, farmer, and businessman. Reagan often mentioned his term as the head of the Screen Actors Guild to augment his political experience as California governor. Jesse Jackson, who had held no elective office, stressed his role in civil rights activities and as head of a civil rights organization. Texas billionaire H. Ross Perot, who ran as an independent in 1992 and on the Reform Party ticket in 1996, cited his executive business experience. Similarly, publishing magnate Malcolm S. "Steve" Forbes Jr., who sought the Republican nomination in 1996 and again in 2000, championed the fact that he was an outsider and not a professional politician. Another candidate who promoted his outsider status was George W. Bush, whose only political experience was as governor of Texas, having also been owner of a small oil company and managing general partner of the Texas Rangers baseball team.

Since the onset of the nuclear age, added emphasis has also been placed on foreign policy expertise. Although not as important to many voters as domestic policy, experience in foreign affairs often will be cited by candidates as another advantage over opponents.

Party ties have become weaker in recent years. Political campaigns now tend to stress the candidate instead of the candidate's party identification. Some candidates have even switched parties without political fall-out—Reagan was a Democrat for most of his adult life before switching to the GOP in 1964. Clinton overcame voters' distrust of parties by depicting himself as a "new Democrat" and borrowed a number of popular Republican positions along the way. But parties still offer candidates nationwide networks of support and significant campaign assistance.

The personal traits of candidates have come under increased scrutiny. Campaigns have self-destructed when candidates failed to exhibit certain moral qualities. Edward Kennedy, in his 1980 pursuit of the Democratic presidential nomination, could not overcome questions about his behavior following a 1969 automobile accident at Chappaquiddick, Mass., in which a woman passenger was killed. In 1988 Hart's campaign collapsed, and his front-runner status with it, when newspaper reports appeared alleging adultery. In something of a turnabout, Clinton in 1992 was able to defuse negative stories about his suspected extramarital affairs and claims that he had dodged the draft. In 1996 Clinton again managed to overcome negative media coverage of a sexual harassment lawsuit against him, controversy over White House fundraising practices, and an investigation into the Clintons' investment in a failed real estate venture in Arkansas, known as Whitewater. George W. Bush in 2000 and 2004 had to face questions about his National Guard service during the Vietnam War. Kerry, Bush's 2004 opponent, also had to defend his Vietnam War record against personal attacks.

White House Hostesses

During the course of the American presidency, particularly between 1828 and 1868, many presidents' wives have refused or have been unable, usually for health reasons, to fulfill the social duties of first lady. Other presidents were widowers or never married. Thus, substitutes carried out the social responsibilities of the first lady when the wife of the president was not available. *(See box, First Ladies, pp. 8–9.)*

The following is a list of the women who served as White House hostesses since 1789. The major source of information for this list was *Guide to the Presidency,* 3rd ed. (Washington, D.C.: CQ Press, 2002). Additional data were obtained from Joseph Nathan Kane, *Facts about the Presidents: A Compilation of Biographical and Historical Information,* 6th ed. (New York: Wilson, 1993).

Rose Cleveland. Sister of Grover Cleveland, who entered the White House in 1885 as a bachelor. Cleveland married Frances Folsom in 1886.

Mary Scott Lord Dimmick. Niece of Benjamin Harrison's first wife, Caroline Scott Harrison, who became an invalid and died near the end of Harrison's presidency. Harrison married Dimmick after leaving office.

Emily Donelson. Niece of Andrew Jackson, whose wife, Rachel Jackson, died between his election and inauguration as president in 1829.

Mary Abigail Fillmore. Daughter of Millard Fillmore, whose wife, Abigail Fillmore, lacked the health or desire to act as first lady.

Jane Irwin Harrison. Daughter-in-law of William Henry Harrison, whose wife, Anna Symmes Harrison, was in poor health.

Harriet Lane. Niece of James Buchanan, who never married.

Mary Arthur McElroy. Sister of Chester A. Arthur, who had been a widower for eighteen months before succeeding to the presidency in 1881.

Abby Kent Means. Longtime friend of Franklin Pierce's wife, Jane Pierce, and wife of Jane's uncle. Means assumed the role of White House hostess while Jane was in mourning following the death of her only remaining child. Means was assisted in her duties by Varina Davis, wife of Pierce's secretary of war, Jefferson Davis.

Mrs. Louis More. Sister of William Howard Taft's wife, Helen Herron Taft, who was ill during part of Taft's administration.

Martha Johnson Patterson. Daughter of Andrew Johnson, whose wife, Eliza Johnson, suffered from tuberculosis.

Martha Jefferson Randolph. Daughter of Thomas Jefferson, who had been a widower for eighteen years when he became president in 1801. Future First Lady Dolley Madison, wife of Jefferson's secretary of state, James Madison, also served as hostess for Jefferson.

Mary Elizabeth Taylor. Daughter of Zachary Taylor, whose wife, Margaret Taylor, lacked the health or desire to act as first lady.

Priscilla Cooper Tyler. Daughter-in-law of John Tyler, whose first wife, Letitia Tyler, was a semi-invalid who died two years into Tyler's presidency. John Tyler married Julia Gardiner in 1844.

Angelica Singleton Van Buren. Daughter-in-law of Martin Van Buren, who had been a widower for nineteen years before entering the White House in 1837.

Margaret Wilson. Daughter of Woodrow Wilson, whose first wife, Ellen Louise Axson Wilson, died two years into Wilson's presidency. Wilson married Edith Bolling Galt in 1915.

Presidential contenders also have had to fight perceptions of weakness. Michigan governor George Romney, a strong contender for the 1968 Republican nomination, dropped out early in the face of negative reaction to his statement that he had been "brainwashed" by generals about the U.S. role in the Vietnam War. Sen. Muskie's 1972 campaign faltered when he appeared to cry as he issued an attack against the tactics of the *Manchester Union Leader.* George Bush had to overcome the label of "wimp."

Other Presidential Facts

Presidents have worked in all types of professions before starting their careers in public service. Twenty-five of the forty-two men who have occupied the Oval Office were, by profession, lawyers. More than half of the presidents had some experience in agriculture, either as a plantation owner, dirt farmer, rancher, field worker, or son of a farming family. Others have been teachers, professional soldiers, merchants, and journalists. Twenty-seven served in the military.

The youngest elected president was Kennedy, who was inaugurated at the age of forty-three. Theodore Roosevelt, however, became the youngest man ever to serve as president when, at forty-two, he succeeded McKinley, who was assassinated. Clinton, at forty-six, was the third youngest person to enter the White House; he also was the first person born after World War II to be elected president and the first president who was a Rhodes scholar. The oldest president was Ronald Reagan. He was nearly seventy when he took his first oath of office in 1981 and just a few weeks away from his seventy-eighth birthday when he left the White House.

Franklin Roosevelt was president the longest, having served twelve years and thirty-nine days, from March 4, 1933, until his death on April 12, 1945. Shortly thereafter the Twenty-second Amendment, ratified in 1951, limited a president to two terms. William Henry Harrison served as president for the shortest period of time—thirty-two days—from March 4, 1841, through April 4, 1841.

Four presidents died of natural causes while in office: William Henry Harrison, Taylor, Harding, and Franklin Roosevelt. Four presidents were assassinated in office: Lincoln, Garfield, McKinley, and Kennedy. Five others were victims of failed assassination attempts: Andrew Jackson, Franklin Roosevelt, Truman, Ford (twice), and Reagan. Reagan was the only one of the five injured; he recovered and served two terms in office.

Two presidents have been impeached by the House of Representatives: Andrew Johnson and Clinton. Both were acquitted by the Senate. Nixon was the only person to resign the presidency, which he did effective Aug. 9, 1974.

Presidents: Biographies

This biographical summary lists, alphabetically, all the presidents of the United States since 1789. The material is organized as follows: name; relationship to other presidents, vice presidents, members of Congress, Supreme Court justices, or governors; party (at the time of service as president) and state elected from; date of birth; date of death (if applicable); period of service as president; congressional service (including representing territories), service as vice president, cabinet member, Supreme Court justice, governor, delegate to the Continental Congress, House or Senate majority leader, House or Senate minority leader, Speaker of the House of Representatives, president pro tempore of the Senate (when elected), chair of standing congressional committees (since 1947), or chair of the Democratic National Committee or the Republican National Committee. *(See Party Abbreviations, p. 324.)*

Under the Constitution, presidential terms from 1789 to 1933 were from March 4 to March 4; since 1934, the four-year term has been from Jan. 20 to Jan. 20. If a president began or ended his service in midterm, exact dates are shown.

For congressional terms, only the years are given for beginning and ending dates if the standard terms were served. From 1789 to 1933 terms of service were from March 4 to March 4; since 1934, service has been from Jan. 3 to Jan. 3.

The major source of information for this list was *Congressional Quarterly's Guide to U.S. Elections,* 4th ed. (Washington, D.C.: CQ Press, 2001). Additional data were obtained from Joseph Nathan Kane, *Facts about the Presidents: A Compilation of Biographical and Historical Information,* 6th ed. (New York: Wilson, 1993); and various newspapers.

Adams, John (father of John Quincy Adams, grandfather of Rep. Charles Francis Adams) (F Mass.) Oct. 30, 1735–July 4, 1826; president 1797–1801; Cont. Cong. 1774–77; vice president April 21, 1789–97.

Adams, John Quincy (son of John Adams, father of Rep. Charles Francis Adams) (DR Mass.) July 11, 1767–Feb. 23, 1848; president 1825–29; Senate 1803–08 (Federalist); secretary of state Sept. 22, 1817–March 3, 1825; House 1831–Feb. 23, 1848 (Federalist).

Arthur, Chester Alan (R N.Y.) Oct. 5, 1829–Nov. 18, 1886; president Sept. 20, 1881–85 (succeeded James Abram Garfield, who was assassinated); vice president March 4–Sept. 20, 1881.

Buchanan, James (D Pa.) April 23, 1791–June 1, 1868; president 1857–61; House 1821–31 (no party); Senate Dec. 6, 1834–March 5, 1845; secretary of state March 10, 1845–March 7, 1849.

Bush, George Herbert Walker (son of Sen. Prescott Sheldon Bush, father of George W. Bush and Gov. John Ellis "Jeb" Bush of Fla.) (R Texas) June 12, 1924– ; president 1989–93; House 1967–71; vice president 1981–89; chair Rep. Nat. Comm. Jan. 1973–Sept. 1974.

Bush, George W. (son of George Herbert Walker Bush, grandson of Sen. Prescott Sheldon Bush, brother of Gov. John Ellis "Jeb" Bush of Fla.) (R Texas) July 6, 1946– ; president 2001– ; Gov. Jan. 17, 1995–Dec. 20, 2000.

Carter, James Earl "Jimmy" Jr. (D Ga.) Oct. 1, 1924– ; president 1977–81; Gov. Jan. 12, 1971–Jan. 14, 1975.

Cleveland, Stephen Grover (D N.Y.) March 18, 1837–June 24, 1908; president 1885–89, 1893–97; Gov. Jan. 1, 1883–Jan. 6, 1885.

Clinton, William Jefferson "Bill" (born William Jefferson Blythe IV) (husband of Sen. Hillary Rodham Clinton) (D Ark.) Aug. 19, 1946– ; president 1993–2001; Gov. Jan. 9, 1979–Jan. 19, 1981, Jan. 11, 1983–Dec. 12, 1992.

Coolidge, John Calvin (cousin of Gov. William Wallace Stickney of Vt.) (R Mass.) July 4, 1872–Jan. 5, 1933; president Aug. 3, 1923–29 (succeeded Warren Gamaliel Harding, who died in office); Gov. Jan. 2, 1919–Jan. 6, 1921; vice president 1921–Aug. 3, 1923.

Eisenhower, Dwight David (born David Dwight Eisenhower) (R N.Y.) Oct. 14, 1890–March 28, 1969; president 1953–61.

Fillmore, Millard (W N.Y.) Jan. 7, 1800–March 8, 1874; president July 10, 1850–53 (succeeded Zachary Taylor, who died in office); House 1833–35, 1837–43; vice president 1849–July 10, 1850.

Ford, Gerald Rudolph Jr. (born Leslie Lynch King Jr.) (R Mich.) July 14, 1913– ; president Aug. 9, 1974–77; House 1949–Dec. 6,

1973; House minority leader 1965–Dec. 6, 1973; vice president Dec. 6, 1973–Aug. 9, 1974.

Garfield, James Abram (R Ohio) Nov. 19, 1831–Sept. 19, 1881; president March 4–Sept. 19, 1881 (assassinated); House 1863–Nov. 8, 1880.

Grant, Ulysses Simpson (born Hiram Ulysses Grant) (R Ill.) April 27, 1822–July 23, 1885; president 1869–77.

Harding, Warren Gamaliel (R Ohio) Nov. 2, 1865–Aug. 2, 1923; president 1921–Aug. 2, 1923 (died in office); Senate 1915–Jan. 13, 1921.

Harrison, Benjamin (grandson of William Henry Harrison, son of Rep. John Scott Harrison, grandfather of Rep. William Henry Harrison) (R Ind.) Aug. 20, 1833–March 13, 1901; president 1889–93; Senate 1881–87.

Harrison, William Henry (father of Rep. John Scott Harrison, brother of Rep. Carter Basset Harrison, grandfather of Benjamin Harrison, great-great-grandfather of Rep. William Henry Harrison) (W Ohio) Feb. 9, 1773–April 4, 1841; president March 4–April 4, 1841 (died in office); House (Terr. del.) 1799–May 14, 1800, (Rep.) Oct. 8, 1816–19; Senate 1825–May 20, 1828 (no party); Gov. (Ind. Terr.) 1801–13.

Hayes, Rutherford Birchard (R Ohio) Oct. 4, 1822–Jan. 17, 1893; president 1877–81; House 1865–July 20, 1867; Gov. Jan. 13, 1868–Jan. 8, 1872, Jan. 10, 1876–March 2, 1877.

Hoover, Herbert Clark (R Calif.) Aug. 10, 1874–Oct. 20, 1964; president 1929–33; secretary of commerce March 5, 1921–Aug. 21, 1928.

Jackson, Andrew (D Tenn.) March 15, 1767–June 8, 1845; president 1829–37; Gov. (Fla. Terr.) March 10–July 18, 1821; House Dec. 5, 1796–Sept. 1797 (no party); Senate Sept. 26, 1797–April 1798, 1823–Oct. 14, 1825 (Republican).

Jefferson, Thomas (father-in-law of Gov. Thomas Mann Randolph of Va.) (DR Va.) April 13, 1743–July 4, 1826; president 1801–09; Cont. Cong. 1775–76, 1783–84; Gov. (Colonial) 1779–June 1781; secretary of state March 22, 1790–Dec. 31, 1793; vice president 1797–1801.

Johnson, Andrew (father-in-law of Sen. David Trotter Patterson) (R Tenn.) Dec. 29, 1808–July 31, 1875; president April 15, 1865–69 (succeeded Abraham Lincoln, who was assassinated); House 1843–53 (Democrat); Gov. Oct. 17, 1853–Nov. 3, 1857 (Democrat), March 12, 1862–March 4, 1865 (Military Gov.); Senate Oct. 8, 1857–March 4, 1862 (Democrat), March 4–July 31, 1875; vice president March 4–April 15, 1865.

Johnson, Lyndon Baines (father-in-law of Sen. Charles S. Robb) (D Texas) Aug. 27, 1908–Jan. 22, 1973; president Nov. 22, 1963–69 (succeeded John Fitzgerald Kennedy, who was assassinated); House April 10, 1937–49; Senate 1949–Jan. 3, 1961; Senate minority leader 1953–55; Senate majority leader 1955–61; chair Senate Aeronautical and Space Sciences 1958–61; vice president 1961–Nov. 22, 1963.

Kennedy, John Fitzgerald (brother of Sens. Edward Moore Kennedy and Robert Francis Kennedy, grandson of Rep. John Francis Fitzgerald, uncle of Reps. Joseph Patrick Kennedy II and Patrick J. Kennedy) (D Mass.) May 29, 1917–Nov. 22, 1963; president 1961–Nov. 22, 1963 (assassinated); House 1947–53; Senate 1953–Dec. 22, 1960.

Lincoln, Abraham (R Ill.) Feb. 12, 1809–April 15, 1865; president 1861–April 15, 1865 (assassinated); House 1847–49 (Whig).

Madison, James (DR Va.) March 16, 1751–June 28, 1836; president 1809–17; Cont. Cong. 1780–83, 1787–88; House 1789–97 (1789–95 no party, 1795–97 Republican); secretary of state May 2, 1801–March 3, 1809.

McKinley, William Jr. (R Ohio) Jan. 29, 1843–Sept. 14, 1901; president 1897–Sept. 14, 1901 (assassinated); House 1877–May 27, 1884, 1885–91; Gov. Jan. 11, 1892–Jan. 13, 1896.

Monroe, James (uncle of Rep. James Monroe) (DR Va.) April 28, 1758–July 4, 1831; president 1817–25; Cont. Cong. 1783–86; Senate Nov. 9, 1790–May 27, 1794 (no party); Gov. Dec. 1, 1799–Dec. 1, 1802, Jan. 16–April 3, 1811; secretary of state April 6, 1811–Sept. 30, 1814, Feb. 28, 1815–March 3, 1817; secretary of war Oct. 1, 1814–Feb. 28, 1815.

Nixon, Richard Milhous (R Calif.) Jan. 9, 1913–April 22, 1994; president 1969–Aug. 9, 1974 (resigned); House 1947–Nov. 30, 1950; Senate Dec. 1, 1950–Jan. 1, 1953; vice president 1953–61.

Pierce, Franklin (D N.H.) Nov. 23, 1804–Oct. 8, 1869; president 1853–57; House 1833–37; Senate 1837–Feb. 28, 1842.

Polk, James Knox (brother of Rep. William Hawkins Polk) (D Tenn.) Nov. 2, 1795–June 15, 1849; president 1845–49; House 1825–39 (1825–27 no party, 1827–37 Jacksonian, 1837–39 Democrat); Speaker Dec. 7, 1835–37, Sept. 4, 1837–39; Gov. Oct. 14, 1839–Oct. 15, 1841.

Reagan, Ronald Wilson (R Calif.) Feb. 6, 1911–June 5, 2004; president 1981–89; Gov. Jan. 5, 1967–Jan. 6, 1975.

Roosevelt, Franklin Delano (father of Reps. Franklin D. Roosevelt Jr. and James Roosevelt) (D N.Y.) Jan. 30, 1882–April 12, 1945; president 1933–April 12, 1945 (died in office); Gov. Jan. 1, 1929–Jan. 1, 1933.

Roosevelt, Theodore (R N.Y.) Oct. 27, 1858–Jan. 6, 1919; president Sept. 14, 1901–09 (succeeded William McKinley Jr., who was assassinated); Gov. Jan. 1, 1899–Jan. 1, 1901; vice president March 4–Sept. 14, 1901.

Taft, William Howard (father of Sen. Robert Alphonso Taft, grandfather of Sen. Robert A. Taft Jr., great-grandfather of Gov. Robert A. Taft II of Ohio, brother of Rep. Charles Phelps Taft) (R Ohio) Sept. 15, 1857–March 8, 1930; president 1909–13; Provisional Gov. of Philippines 1901–04; secretary of war Feb. 1, 1904–June 30, 1908; chief justice July 11, 1921–Feb. 3, 1930.

Taylor, Zachary (W La.) Nov. 24, 1784–July 9, 1850; president 1849–July 9, 1850 (died in office).

Truman, Harry S. (D Mo.) May 8, 1884–Dec. 26, 1972; president April 12, 1945–53 (succeeded Franklin Delano Roosevelt, who died in office); Senate 1935–Jan. 17, 1945; vice president Jan. 20–April 12, 1945.

Tyler, John (son of Gov. John Tyler of Va., father of Rep. David Gardiner Tyler) (W Va.) March 29, 1790–Jan. 18, 1862; president April 6, 1841–45 (succeeded William Henry Harrison, who died in office); House Dec. 16, 1817–21 (Republican); Gov. Dec. 10, 1825–March 4, 1827 (Democratic Republican); Senate 1827–Feb. 29, 1836 (Republican); elected pres. pro tempore March 3, 1835; vice president March 4–April 6, 1841.

Van Buren, Martin (half-brother of Rep. James Isaac Van Alen) (D N.Y.) Dec. 5, 1782–July 24, 1862; president 1837–41; Senate 1821–Dec. 20, 1828 (no party); Gov. Jan. 1–March 12, 1829 (Jeffersonian Republican); secretary of state March 28, 1829–March 23, 1831; vice president 1833–37.

Washington, George (uncle of Assoc. Justice Bushrod Washington) (F Va.) Feb. 22, 1732–Dec. 14, 1799; president April 30, 1789–97; Cont. Cong. 1774–75.

Wilson, Thomas Woodrow (D N.J.) Dec. 28, 1856–Feb. 3, 1924; president 1913–21; Gov. Jan. 17, 1911–March 1, 1913.

Vice Presidents

Throughout much of its history the office of the vice president has had little esteem and a lot of ridicule. "The vice presidency isn't worth a pitcher of warm spit," said John Nance Garner, an active vice president who served during the first two terms of Franklin D. Roosevelt's administration, in what is probably the most frequently quoted assessment of the office. Others have been equally unkind. John Adams, the first to hold the job, once complained, "My country has in its wisdom contrived for me the most insignificant office that ever the invention of man contrived or his imagination conceived." More than a century later Thomas R. Marshall, Woodrow Wilson's vice president, expressed a similarly dismal view: "Once there were two brothers. One ran away to sea; the other was elected Vice President. And nothing was ever heard of either of them again."

Constitutionally the vice presidency was born weak. To a large extent, the roles and resources the vice president does enjoy are delegated—and can be revoked—at the discretion of the president. Accordingly, the activities and influence of individual vice presidents vary considerably from administration to administration.

But what is sometimes lost in the jokes and disparagement of the office is an appreciation of how significant the position can be. The vice presidency is most important when it provides a successor to the president. Nine vice presidents, one-fifth of those who have served in the office, have become president when the incumbent chief executive died or resigned. Collectively, they led the nation for forty-two years. Besides its long-standing role as presidential successor, the vice presidency has also become an important electoral springboard to the presidency. The vice president is not only a presumptive candidate for president but the presumptive front-runner as well. *(See box, From VP to President, p. 19.)*

Moreover, after the end of World War II through the beginning of the twenty-first century, the office and responsibilities of the vice president grew substantially. The advent of nuclear weapons capable of mass destruction, the cold war with the Soviet Union, and the rise of world terrorism led many Americans to insist that the vice president be sufficiently competent and informed so that, if the need for a presidential succession should arise, no lapse in national leadership would occur.

Certain kinds of vice presidential activities now are taken for granted, including regular private meetings with the president and attendance at many other important presidential meetings, membership on the National Security Council, full national security briefings, diplomatic missions, public advocacy of the president's leadership and programs, and a party leadership role.

History of the Office

The original Constitution provided that the vice presidency be awarded to the person who received the second-highest number of electoral votes for president. If two or more candidates finished in a second-place tie, the Senate would choose among them. The vice president's only ongoing responsibility was to preside over the Senate, casting tie-breaking votes. The most important duty of the vice president was to stand by as successor to the presidency in the case of the president's death, impeachment, resignation, or "inability to discharge the Powers and Duties" of the office.

The Constitution, however, was vague both about whether the vice president was to assume the office of the president or only its powers and duties and about whether the succession was to last until the end of the departed president's four-year term or until a special election could be held to choose a new president. The Constitution also left the term "inability" undefined and provided no procedure for the vice president to take power in the event the president became disabled. Finally, by giving the vice president both legislative and executive responsibilities, the office was deprived of solid moorings in either Congress or the presidency.

It did not take long for the system of choosing the president and the vice president to run into trouble. Dissatisfied with the divided partisan result of the 1796 election—Federalist John Adams won the presidency; Democratic Republican Thomas Jefferson, the vice presidency—each party nominated a complete ticket in 1800, instructing its electors to cast their two votes for its presidential and vice presidential candidates. The intention was that both would be elected; the result was that neither was. The electors having voted as instructed, Jefferson and his vice presidential running mate, Aaron Burr, ended up with an equal number of votes for president. Under the Constitution, the House of Representatives was called upon to vote for president, and, after thirty-six ballots and Federalist interferences, it finally chose Jefferson. Burr was elected vice president.

15

The experience of 1800 showed that something had to be done about the electoral college so that it could accommodate the existence of party competition. Burr's nomination indicated that the parties had begun to use the vice presidency as a device to balance the ticket. In 1804 motions were made in Congress to abolish the vice presidency instead of continuing it in a form degraded from its original constitutional status as the position awarded to the second-most-qualified person to be president. Suggestions to require the electors to vote separately for president and vice president were criticized because the vice president would no longer be perceived as being on the same level as the president. Nevertheless, the Twelfth Amendment became part of the Constitution in 1804, providing that electors "shall name in their ballots the person voted for as President, and in distinct ballots the person voted for as Vice-President." If no one received a majority vote for vice president, the choice would be thrown to the Senate. The amendment's final provision regarding the vice presidency extended the Constitution's original age, citizenship, and residency qualifications to the vice president.

The rise of political parties and the enactment of the Twelfth Amendment further weakened the vice presidency. Party leaders, not presidential candidates, chose the nominees for vice president. It was a formula that did not foster trust or respect between the president and vice president. The vice presidential nominee was supposed to placate the region or faction of the party that had been most dissatisfied with the presidential choice, and the nominee should be able to carry a swing state in the general election where the presidential candidate was not popular.

Because ticket balancing was the main basis for selection as vice president, a stigma became attached to the office. Many politicians were unwilling to accept a nomination. Daniel Webster, declining the vice presidential slot on the Whig Party ticket in 1848, said, "I do not propose to be buried until I am dead." Those who were nominated and elected found that political problems four years later invariably led the party leaders to balance the ticket differently. No first-term vice president in the nineteenth century was renominated for a second term by a party convention.

The roster of nineteenth-century vice presidents is a virtual rogues' gallery of personal and political failures. Because the office was so unappealing, an unusual number of those who could be enticed to run were old and in bad health. Six died in office, all of natural causes: George Clinton, Elbridge Gerry, William R. King, Henry Wilson, Thomas A. Hendricks, and Garret A. Hobart. Daniel D. Tompkins, Schuyler Colfax, and Wilson became embroiled in financial scandals. Tompkins and Andrew Johnson were heavy drinkers. Richard M. Johnson kept a series of slave mistresses and while vice president left Washington, D.C., for a year to run a tavern. Clinton, John C. Calhoun, and Chester A. Arthur each publicly expressed his dislike for the president.

The history of the nineteenth-century vice presidency did settle one controversy. The succession question arose in 1841, when William Henry Harrison became the first president to die in office. Vice President John Tyler laid claim to both the office and the balance of Harrison's term. This was accepted with little debate, setting a precedent that the next successor president, Vice President Millard Fillmore, was able to follow without rancor.

Issues of succession and disability as related to the vice presidency remained unresolved in the nineteenth century, however. Taken together, six vice presidential deaths, one vice presidential resignation, and four presidential deaths left the nation without a vice president during eleven of the century's twenty-five presidential terms. (Between July 1850 and March 1857, the vice presidency was vacant for all but one month in 1853.) And during times of presidential disability, vice presidential action was uncertain. Not wanting to appear a usurper, Vice President Arthur stood by helplessly for eighty days while President James A. Garfield lay incapacitated before dying from an assassin's bullet.

The rise of national news media, a new style of active presidential campaigning, and alterations in the vice presidential nominating process enhanced the status of the vice presidency during the first half of the twentieth century. In 1900 Theodore Roosevelt became the first vice presidential candidate to campaign vigorously nationwide. The national reputation he gained through travel and the media stood him in good stead when he succeeded to the presidency after William McKinley was assassinated. Unlike Tyler, Fillmore, Andrew Johnson, and Arthur, Roosevelt was nominated by his party to run for a full term as president, in 1904, thus setting a precedent for Calvin Coolidge in 1924, Harry S. Truman in 1948, Lyndon B. Johnson in 1964, and Gerald R. Ford in 1976. Starting with James S. Sherman in 1912, every first-term vice president in the twentieth century who sought a second term was nominated for reelection, reversing the nineteenth-century practice.

The enhanced political status of the vice presidency soon began to make it a more attractive office to some able and experienced political leaders, including Nobel Prize winner Charles Dawes, Senate majority leader Charles Curtis, and Speaker of the House Garner. And, with somewhat more talent to offer, vice presidents were given more responsibilities by the presidents they served.

Garner, Franklin Roosevelt's vice president during his first two terms, broke the mold in many respects. Even though the conservative Texan had been imposed on him at the 1932 Democratic convention, Roosevelt came to rely on him heavily. Most significant, Garner served as a liaison between Roosevelt and Congress. Garner also undertook a good-will mission to Mexico at Roosevelt's behest, another innovation that virtually all later presidents continued.

During Roosevelt's second administration, he had a falling out with Garner. This rupture set the stage for an important modification of the vice presidential selection process to foster greater harmony between presidents and vice presidents. In 1936, at Roosevelt's insistence, the Democrats had abolished their two-thirds rule for presidential nominations, which meant that candidates for president no longer had to tolerate as much trading of vice presidential nominees and other administration posts to win at the convention. They also got rid of the two-thirds rule for vice presidential nominations, reducing the degree of consensus needed for that choice as well. In 1940 Roosevelt completed his coup by seizing the party leaders' traditional prerogative to determine nominations for vice president and making it his own. His tactic was simple: He threatened that unless the convention nominated Henry A. Wallace for vice president, which it did not want to do, he would not accept the nomination for president. Since then, presidential nominees have all handpicked their running mates, the only exception being in 1956 when Democrat Adlai E. Stevenson left the choice up to the convention.

To meet the post–World War II expectations about vice presidential quality, most modern presidential candidates have paid considerable attention to experience, ability, and political compatibility in selecting their running mates. Winning votes on election day is as much the goal as in the days of old-style ticket balancing, but presidential nominees realize that voters now care more about competence and loyalty—a vice presidential candidate's ability to succeed to the presidency ably and to carry on the departed president's policies faithfully—than they do about having all regions of the country or factions of the party represented on the ticket. This has helped to create a climate for a more influential vice presidency.

The modern era also has been marked by an almost complete absence of ideologically opposed running mates. Those vice presidential candidates who have differed even slightly on the issues with the heads of their tickets have played down past disagreements and denied that any still exist.

Vice Presidential Roles

The vice presidency has become institutionalized, both in the narrow sense that it is organizationally larger and more complex than it used to be and in the broader sense that certain kinds of vice presidential activities now are taken for granted. The variety of roles the modern vice president performs can be grouped into four categories: constitutional, statutory, advisory, and representative.

Constitutional Roles

The original Constitution assigned two roles to the vice president: to serve as president of the Senate, voting only to break ties, and to succeed to the presidency in the event of a presidential death, resignation, removal, or disability. In 1967 the Twenty-fifth Amendment clarified the vice president's responsibilities as presidential successor and as acting president during periods of presidential disability. The amendment also made the vice president the central figure in determining whether the president is disabled. *(See box, Presidential Disability and the Line of Succession, pp. 2–3.)*

In the early years, when the Senate was small and relatively informal, the vice president's role as president of the Senate allowed him to influence the Senate's agenda, steer debate, name the members of its committees, and

frequently cast tie-breaking votes. In contrast, modern vice presidents spend little time performing their constitutional role in the Senate. Because the Senate, too, has become more institutionalized, the powers of the presiding officer are circumscribed and largely ceremonial—the vice president is expected to follow the advice of the Senate's parliamentarian, not to lead independently. Because the Senate is so much larger today, tie votes rarely occur. For example, John Adams and John C. Calhoun decided twenty-nine and twenty-eight tie votes, respectively. In recent decades Walter F. Mondale cast only one tie-breaking vote; George Bush, seven; Dan Quayle, none; Al Gore, four; Richard B. Cheney, six (by the end of 2004). The diminution of the vice president's role in the Senate contributed to the vice presidency being associated more with the presidency than with Congress.

Vice President Tyler's actions in the wake of President William Henry Harrison's death in 1841 set the pattern for future successions by claiming the office for the balance of Harrison's unexpired term. The Twenty-fifth Amendment codified this precedent. The amendment also set forth procedures for determining when a presidential disability existed, something the original Constitution failed to do. Presidents now are empowered to declare themselves disabled. If a disabled president is unwilling or unable to make such a declaration, the vice president and a majority of the cabinet can make the determination. Congress has the authority to replace the cabinet with some other body, but it cannot remove the vice president from the decision-making process. The Twenty-fifth Amendment also stipulated that during a presidential disability, the vice president serves as acting president until the president is able to resume the duties of office.

Statutory Roles

The vice president has only two statutory roles: member of the National Security Council (NSC) and member of the Board of Regents of the Smithsonian Institution.

The vice president was added to the NSC by Congress in 1949. As the only council member whom the president cannot command or remove from office, the vice president is entitled to attend all NSC meetings for the entire term. Few presidents, however, have wanted to feel obligated to involve the vice president in important foreign policy deliberations. As a result, most either have called a limited number of NSC meetings or used the meetings as forums to announce, instead of make, policy.

Advisory Roles

Every vice president since Garner has regularly attended cabinet meetings at the invitation of the president. A few earlier presidents asked their vice presidents to take part in cabinet meetings, but only on rare occasions. For all its symbolic value, cabinet membership seldom has been a position of real influence for the vice president—the exceptions being Garner and Richard Nixon, who presided over nineteen cabinet meetings during President Dwight D. Eisenhower's various illnesses. One reason is that cabinet meetings themselves have become

Vice Presidents Who Served in Congress

Listed below are the thirty-three vice presidents who served in Congress and the chambers in which they were members. Eleven served only in the House of Representatives; eight served only in the Senate; fourteen served in both chambers. Daniel D. Tompkins, who was vice president under James Monroe, was elected to the House but resigned before the beginning of his term to accept an appointment as associate justice of the New York state supreme court.

Three other vice presidents—John Adams, Thomas Jefferson, and George Clinton—served in the Continental Congress, as did Elbridge Gerry, who also served in the House and is included below.

House Only	**Senate Only**
Elbridge Gerry	Aaron Burr
Millard Fillmore	Martin Van Buren
Schuyler Colfax	George M. Dallas
William A. Wheeler	Henry Wilson
Levi P. Morton	Charles W. Fairbanks
Adlai E. Stevenson	Harry S. Truman
James S. Sherman	Hubert H. Humphrey
John Nance Garner	Walter F. Mondale
Gerald R. Ford	
George Bush	
Richard B. Cheney	

Both Chambers

John C. Calhoun	Thomas A. Hendricks
Richard M. Johnson	Charles Curtis
John Tyler	Alben W. Barkley
William R. King	Richard Nixon
John C. Breckinridge	Lyndon B. Johnson
Hannibal Hamlin	Dan Quayle
Andrew Johnson	Al Gore

Source: *Congressional Quarterly's Guide to U.S. Elections,* 4th ed. (Washington, D.C.: CQ Press, 2001).

less important in recent years. In addition, most vice presidents have felt bound to sit in near silence at the meetings while the president and department heads discuss administrative matters.

Eisenhower was the first president to appoint his vice president to chair a presidential commission, a practice that most of his successors have followed. Typically, presidents have created commissions to symbolize their concern for an issue or constituency; they name their vice presidents as chairs because the vice presidency is a visible and prestigious office and because they want to convince the public that the vice president is actively involved in the business of government. Seldom, however, do presidents entrust commissions with substantive powers and responsibilities.

For a long time, being chair of a commission was thought to be more of a burden than a blessing for the vice president. Vice President Mondale went so far as to ask President Jimmy Carter to refrain from assigning him commission duties so he could be free to serve the president as general adviser and troubleshooter. Mondale argued that commissions inevitably rouse the ire of the agencies of the bureaucracy whose activities they study, that neither commissions nor the vice president have any authority to enact any goals, that commission assignments demean the vice presidency by wasting the vice president's time, and that the vice president lacks the staff to do an effective job as commission chair. Carter granted Mondale's request. But several of Mondale's successors discovered that some commissions offered a great deal of clout. Vice President Quayle used commission assignments to influence the direction of the space program and federal regulatory activity, and Gore enthusiastically chaired a commission aimed at

From VP to President

Fourteen vice presidents (VPs) had become president as of March 2005: John Adams, Thomas Jefferson, Martin Van Buren, John Tyler, Millard Fillmore, Andrew Johnson, Chester A. Arthur, Theodore Roosevelt, Calvin Coolidge, Harry S. Truman, Richard Nixon, Lyndon B. Johnson, Gerald R. Ford, and George Bush.

Adams, Jefferson, Van Buren, Nixon, and Bush first became president by being elected to the office, while the others assumed the office on the death or resignation of their predecessor. Four of the vice presidents who succeeded to the presidency—Roosevelt, Coolidge, Truman, and Lyndon Johnson—subsequently were elected to a full term as president. Ford received his party's nomination but lost in the general election.

Vice presidents who were nominated by a major party in the twentieth and twenty-first centuries but lost the election included:

• Nixon, Republican vice president under Dwight D. Eisenhower from 1953 to 1961, was the GOP nominee in 1960. (But he won in 1968.)
• Hubert H. Humphrey, Democratic vice president under Lyndon Johnson from 1965 to 1969, was the Democratic nominee in 1968.
• Walter F. Mondale, Democratic vice president under Jimmy Carter from 1977 to 1981, was the Democratic nominee in 1984.
• Al Gore, Democratic vice president under Bill Clinton from 1993 to 2001, was the Democratic nominee in 2000.

In addition, Henry A. Wallace, Democratic vice president under Franklin D. Roosevelt from 1941 to 1945, was the Progressive Party nominee in 1948.

Source: *Congressional Quarterly's Guide to U.S. Elections,* 4th ed. (Washington, D.C.: CQ Press, 2001).

"reinventing government" to make it more modern and efficient.

Some vice presidents have been sought out by the president for advice and counsel. But, until modern times, these vice presidents were the exception. Before Franklin Roosevelt won for presidential candidates the right to name their running mates, presidents typic`ally took office with little personal trust in their vice presidents, much less a willingness to rely on them for political or policy advice. Most recent presidents have turned to their vice presidents for advice on matters about which they are knowledgeable or experienced. Mondale extended the vice president's role as presidential adviser beyond all previous limits. Reagan made good use of George Bush's experience in foreign policy, and Bush in turn asked Quayle for advice on political and congressional strategy. Bill Clinton brought Gore into his inner circle of advisers and sought his views on all major issues. Cheney, under George W. Bush, may have wielded the most power as vice president in U.S. history. Cheney's years of experience in the federal government—including his service as chief of staff to President Ford and defense secretary to Bush's father when the senior Bush was president—allowed Cheney to function in elevated roles. He led the presidential transition team in 2000, took charge of the administration's energy policies in 2001, and functioned as key advisor in the

wars on terrorism and Iraq during the remainder of Bush's first term.

Representative Roles

In recent years, presidents have asked their vice presidents to represent their administrations to a variety of constituencies. Even though the vice president's Senate responsibilities have declined in importance and the office of the vice presidency has grown more affiliated with the executive branch, vice presidents have developed a new role on Capitol Hill—as legislative liaison. Since 1933, twelve of fifteen vice presidents have had experience as members of Congress. Seven of them served presidents who lacked federal legislative experience. Not surprisingly, then, vice presidents have passed information and advice between representatives and senators on one end of Pennsylvania Avenue and the president on the other, working in conjunction with the White House staff's team of legislative lobbyists.

Since Franklin Roosevelt's time, presidents have called on vice presidents to serve as their special envoys, making official trips abroad as representatives of the United States. Many, perhaps most, special envoy assignments have been almost entirely symbolic in nature—the president simply wished to demonstrate the good will of the United States toward the visited country without having to undertake a trip personally. But sometimes the vice president has carried an important message to a foreign government, affirmed U.S. support for a beleaguered regime, or negotiated on a small diplomatic matter. Even relatively inconsequential trips are of political value to vice presidents, who gain greater-than-usual press coverage and reinforce their image among voters as knowledgeable world leaders.

The role of administration defender is one that the vice president must perform vigorously, enthusiastically, and with unquestioned loyalty. The role offers significant benefits to those who perform it well. It builds trust between the vice president and the president and the White House staff, endears the vice president to the party faithful, and increases the vice president's political visibility. Taken together, these benefits usually give the vice president the inside track for a subsequent presidential run. The role has its dangers, however. Vice presidents may appear to be narrow, divisive figures, especially when defending the administration involves attacking its critics. They can also come across as weak and parrot-like, always defending the ideas of another while submerging their own thoughts and expertise.

Vice Presidential Facts

Most of those who became vice president came to the office with a career in public service. Thirty-three had served as members of Congress. Fifteen had been governors of a state or territory. Of those, six were governors of the state of New York—George Clinton, Tompkins, Martin Van Buren, Levi P. Morton, Theodore Roosevelt, and Nelson Rockefeller. Jefferson (colonial) and Tyler governed Virginia; Gerry and Coolidge, Massachusetts; Hendricks and Marshall, Indiana; Hannibal Hamlin, Maine; Andrew Johnson, Tennessee; and Spiro Agnew, Maryland. All except Morton served as governors before their tenure as vice president. Johnson served one of his terms as military governor. *(See box, Vice Presidents Who Served in Congress, p. 18.)*

The youngest man to become vice president was John C. Breckinridge at age thirty-six. Alben W. Barkley was the oldest vice president. He was seventy-one at the time of his inauguration in 1949.

Of the nine vice presidents who succeeded to office on the death or resignation of the president under whom they were serving, Tyler, Fillmore, Coolidge, and Truman assumed office after the natural death of the president. Andrew Johnson, Arthur, Theodore Roosevelt, and Lyndon Johnson succeeded to the presidency after the assassination of the president; and Ford became president after the resignation of the president.

Five vice presidents became president after having been elected in their own right—John Adams, Jefferson, Van Buren, Nixon, and George Bush. *(See box, From VP to President, p. 19.)*

King held the office of vice president for the shortest length of time. King, who served during the Franklin Pierce administration, was vice president from March 24, 1853, until he died less than a month later on April 18. (King also was the only executive officer of the United States to take the oath of office on foreign soil—Cuba.) George Clinton and Calhoun were the only vice presidents to have served under two different presidents; Clinton under Jefferson and James Madison, Calhoun under John Quincy Adams and Andrew Jackson. Two vice presidents, Ford and Rockefeller, were appointed under the provisions of the Twenty-fifth Amendment.

Seven vice presidents died in office—George Clinton, Gerry, Hendricks, Hobart, King, Sherman, and Wilson. Two—Calhoun and Agnew—resigned.

Quayle, who served with George Bush, was the first vice president born after World War II, in the "baby boom" generation.

Only one woman has received a major party's nomination for the vice presidency—Democrat Geraldine A. Ferraro of New York in 1984.

Vice Presidents: Biographies

This biographical summary lists, alphabetically, all the vice presidents of the United States since 1789. The material is organized as follows: name; relationship to other vice presidents, presidents, members of Congress, Supreme Court justices, or governors; party (at time of service as vice president) and state; date of birth; date of death (if applicable); period of service as vice president; congressional service (including representing territories), service as president, cabinet member, Supreme Court justice, governor, delegate to the Continental Congress, House or Senate majority leader, House or Senate minority leader, Speaker of the House of Representatives, president pro tempore of the Senate (when elected), chair of standing congressional committees (since 1947), or chair of the Democratic National Committee or the Republican National Committee. *(See Party Abbreviations, p. 324.)*

Under the Constitution, terms of service from 1789 to 1933 were from March 4 to March 4; since 1934, service has been from Jan. 20 to Jan. 20. If a vice president began or ended his service in midterm, exact dates are shown.

For congressional terms, only the years are given for beginning and ending dates if the standard terms were served. From 1789 to 1933 terms of service were from March 4 to March 4; since 1934, service has been from Jan. 3 to Jan. 3.

The major source of information for this list was *Congressional Quarterly's Guide to U.S. Elections,* 4th ed. (Washington, D.C.: CQ Press, 2001). Additional data were obtained from Joseph Nathan Kane, *Facts about the Presidents: A Compilation of Biographical and Historical Information,* 6th ed. (New York: Wilson, 1993).

Adams, John (father of Pres. John Quincy Adams, grandfather of Rep. Charles Francis Adams) (F Mass.) Oct. 30, 1735–July 4, 1826; vice president April 21, 1789–97; Cont. Cong. 1774–77; president 1797–1801.

Agnew, Spiro Theodore (R Md.) Nov. 9, 1918–Sept. 17, 1996; vice president 1969–Oct. 10, 1973 (resigned); Gov. Jan. 25, 1967–Jan. 7, 1969.

Arthur, Chester Alan (R N.Y.) Oct. 5, 1830–Nov. 18, 1886; vice president March 4–Sept. 20, 1881; president Sept. 20, 1881–85 (succeeded James Abram Garfield, who was assassinated).

Barkley, Alben William (D Ky.) Nov. 24, 1877–April 30, 1956; vice president 1949–53; House 1913–27; Senate 1927–Jan. 19, 1949, 1955–April 30, 1956; Senate majority leader July 22, 1937–47; Senate minority leader 1947–49.

Breckinridge, John Cabell (grandson of Sen. John Breckinridge, father of Rep. Clifton Rodes Breckinridge, cousin of Rep. Henry Donnel Foster) (D Ky.) Jan. 21, 1821–May 17, 1875; vice president 1857–61; House 1851–55; Senate March 4–Dec. 4, 1861.

Burr, Aaron (cousin of Rep. Theodore Dwight, father-in-law of Gov. Joseph Alston of S.C.) (DR N.Y.) Feb. 6, 1756–Sept. 14, 1836; vice president 1801–05; Senate 1791–97 (Democrat).

Bush, George Herbert Walker (son of Sen. Prescott Sheldon Bush, father of Pres. George W. Bush and Gov. John Ellis "Jeb" Bush of Fla.) (R Texas) June 12, 1924– ; vice president 1981–89; House 1967–71; chair Rep. Nat. Comm. Jan. 1973–Sept. 1974; president 1989–93.

Calhoun, John Caldwell (cousin of Sen. John Ewing Colhoun and Rep. Joseph Calhoun) (DR S.C.) March 18, 1782–March 31, 1850; vice president 1825–Dec. 28, 1832 (resigned); House 1811–Nov. 3, 1817 (Republican); secretary of war Oct. 8, 1817–March 7, 1825; Senate Dec. 29, 1832–43 (Republican), Nov. 26, 1845–March 31, 1850 (Republican); secretary of state April 1, 1844–March 10, 1845.

Cheney, Richard Bruce "Dick" (R. Wyo.) Jan. 30, 1941– ; vice president Jan. 20, 2001– ; secretary of defense 1989–93; House Jan. 3, 1979–March 17, 1989.

Clinton, George (father of Rep. George Clinton, uncle of Rep. James Graham Clinton and Gov. De Witt Clinton of N.Y.) (DR N.Y.) July 26, 1739–April 20, 1812; vice president 1805–April 20, 1812 (died in office); Cont. Cong. 1775–76; Gov. July 30, 1777–June 30, 1795, July 1, 1801–July 1, 1804.

Colfax, Schuyler (R Ind.) March 23, 1823–Jan. 13, 1885; vice president 1869–73; House 1855–69; Speaker Dec. 7, 1863–65, Dec. 4, 1865–67, March 4, 1867–March 2, 1869.

Coolidge, John Calvin (cousin of Gov. William Wallace Stickney of Vt.) (R Mass.) July 4, 1872–Jan. 5, 1933; vice president 1921–Aug. 3, 1923; Gov. Jan. 2, 1919–Jan. 6, 1921; president Aug. 3, 1923–29 (succeeded Warren G. Harding, who died in office).

Curtis, Charles (R Kan.) Jan. 25, 1860–Feb. 8, 1936; vice president 1929–33; House 1893–Jan. 28, 1907; Senate Jan. 29, 1907–13, 1915–29; elected pres. pro tempore Dec. 4, 1911 (to serve Dec. 4–Dec. 12, 1911); Senate majority leader Nov. 28, 1924–29.

Dallas, George Mifflin (great-great-great-uncle of Claiborne de Borda Pell) (D Pa.) July 10, 1792–Dec. 31, 1864; vice president 1845–49; Senate Dec. 13, 1831–33.

Dawes, Charles Gates (son of Rep. Rufus Dawes, brother of Rep. Beman Gates Dawes) (R Ill.) Aug. 27, 1865–April 23, 1951; vice president 1925–29.

Fairbanks, Charles Warren (R Ind.) May 11, 1852–June 4, 1918; vice president 1905–09; Senate 1897–1905.

Fillmore, Millard (W N.Y.) Jan. 7, 1800–March 8, 1874; vice president 1849–July 10, 1850; House 1833–35, 1837–43; president July 10, 1850–53 (succeeded Zachary Taylor, who died in office).

Ford, Gerald Rudolph Jr. (R Mich.) July 14, 1913– ; vice president Dec. 6, 1973–Aug. 9, 1974; House 1949–Dec. 6, 1973; House minority leader 1965–Dec. 6, 1973; president Aug. 9, 1974–77 (succeeded Richard M. Nixon, who resigned).

Garner, John Nance (D Texas) Nov. 22, 1868–Nov. 7, 1967; vice president 1933–Jan. 20, 1941; House 1903–33; House minority leader 1929–31; Speaker Dec. 7, 1931–33.

Gerry, Elbridge (great-grandfather of Sen. Peter Goelet Gerry, grandfather of Rep. Elbridge Gerry) (DR Mass.) July 17, 1744–Nov. 23, 1814; vice president 1813–Nov. 23, 1814 (died in office); Cont. Cong. 1776–80, 1783–85; House 1789–93 (no party); Gov. June 2, 1810–June 5, 1812 (Democratic Republican).

Gore, Albert Arnold "Al" Jr. (son of Sen. Albert Arnold Gore) (D Tenn.) March 31, 1948– ; vice president 1993–2001; House 1977–85; Senate 1985–Jan. 2, 1993.

Hamlin, Hannibal (R Maine) Aug. 27, 1809–July 4, 1891; vice president 1861–65; House 1843–47 (Democrat); Senate June 8,

1848–Jan. 7, 1857 (Democrat), 1857–Jan. 17, 1861 (Republican), 1869–81 (Republican); Gov. Jan. 8–Feb. 25, 1857 (Republican).

Hendricks, Thomas Andrews (nephew of Sen. William Hendricks) (D Ind.) Sept. 7, 1819–Nov. 25, 1885; vice president March 4–Nov. 25, 1885 (died in office); House 1851–55; Senate 1863–69; Gov. Jan. 13, 1873–Jan. 8, 1877.

Hobart, Garret Augustus (R N.J.) June 3, 1844–Nov. 21, 1899; vice president 1897–Nov. 21, 1899 (died in office).

Humphrey, Hubert Horatio Jr. (husband of Sen. Muriel Buck Humphrey) (D Minn.) May 27, 1911–Jan. 13, 1978; vice president 1965–69; Senate 1949–Dec. 29, 1964, 1971–Jan. 13, 1978.

Jefferson, Thomas (father-in-law of Gov. Thomas Mann Randolph of Va.) (DR Va.) April 13, 1743–July 4, 1826; vice president 1797–1801; Cont. Cong. 1775–76, 1783–84; Gov. (Colonial) 1779–June 1781; secretary of state March 22, 1790–Dec. 31, 1793; president 1801–09.

Johnson, Andrew (father-in-law of Sen. David Trotter Patterson) (R Tenn.) Dec. 29, 1808–July 31, 1875; vice president March 4–April 15, 1865; House 1843–53 (Democrat); Gov. Oct. 17, 1853–Nov. 3, 1857 (Democrat), March 12, 1862–March 4, 1865 (Military Gov.); Senate Oct. 8, 1857–March 4, 1862 (Democrat), March 4–July 31, 1875; president April 15, 1865–69 (succeeded Abraham Lincoln, who was assassinated).

Johnson, Lyndon Baines (father-in-law of Sen. Charles S. Robb) (D Texas) Aug. 27, 1908–Jan. 22, 1973; vice president 1961–Nov. 22, 1963; House April 10, 1937–49; Senate 1949–Jan. 3, 1961; Senate minority leader 1953–55; Senate majority leader 1955–61; chair Senate Aeronautical and Space Sciences 1958–61; president Nov. 22, 1963–69 (succeeded John F. Kennedy, who was assassinated).

Johnson, Richard Mentor (brother of Reps. James Johnson and John Telemachus Johnson, uncle of Sen. Robert Ward Johnson) (D Ky.) Oct. 17, 1780–Nov. 19, 1850; vice president 1837–41; House 1807–19 (Republican), 1829–37 (Republican); Senate Dec. 10, 1819–29 (Republican).

King, William Rufus deVane (D Ala.) April 7, 1786–April 18, 1853; vice president March 24–April 18, 1853 (died in office); House 1811–Nov. 4, 1816 (no party N.C.); Senate Dec. 14, 1819–April 15, 1844 (Dec. 14, 1819–21 Republican, 1821–April 15, 1844 Republican/Jacksonian), July 1, 1848–Dec. 20, 1852 (Democrat); elected pres. pro tempore July 1, 1836, Jan. 28, 1837, March 7, 1837, Oct. 13, 1837, July 2, 1838, Feb. 25, 1839, July 3, 1840, March 3, 1841, March 4, 1841, May 6, 1850, July 11, 1850.

Marshall, Thomas Riley (D Ind.) March 14, 1854–June 1, 1925; vice president 1913–21; Gov. Jan. 11, 1909–Jan. 13, 1913.

Mondale, Walter Frederick "Fritz" (D Minn.) Jan. 5, 1928– ; vice president 1977–81; Senate Dec. 30, 1964–Dec. 30, 1976.

Morton, Levi Parsons (R N.Y.) May 16, 1824–May 16, 1920; vice president 1889–93; House 1879–March 21, 1881; Gov. Jan. 1, 1895–Jan. 1, 1897.

Nixon, Richard Milhous (R Calif.) Jan. 9, 1913–April 22, 1994; vice president 1953–61; House 1947–Nov. 30, 1950; Senate Dec. 1, 1950–Jan. 1, 1953; president 1969–Aug. 9, 1974 (resigned).

Quayle, James Danforth "Dan" (R Ind.) Feb. 4, 1947– ; vice president 1989–93; House 1977–81; Senate 1981–Jan. 3, 1989.

Rockefeller, Nelson Aldrich (brother of Gov. Winthrop Rockefeller of Ark., uncle of Sen. John Davison "Jay" Rockefeller IV, nephew of Rep. Richard Steere Aldrich, grandson of Sen. Nelson Wilmarth Aldrich) (R N.Y.) July 8, 1908–Jan. 26, 1979; vice president Dec. 19, 1974–77; Gov. Jan. 1, 1959–Dec. 18, 1973.

Roosevelt, Theodore (R N.Y.) Oct. 27, 1858–Jan. 6, 1919; vice president March 4–Sept. 14, 1901; Gov. Jan. 1, 1899–Jan. 1, 1901; president Sept. 14, 1901–09 (succeeded William McKinley Jr., who was assassinated).

Sherman, James Schoolcraft (R N.Y.) Oct. 24, 1855–Oct. 30, 1912; vice president 1909–Oct. 30, 1912 (died in office); House 1887–91, 1893–1909.

Stevenson, Adlai Ewing (grandfather of Gov. Adlai Ewing Stevenson II of Ill., great-grandfather of Sen. Adlai Ewing Stevenson III) (D Ill.) Oct. 23, 1835–June 14, 1914; vice president 1893–97; House 1875–77, 1879–81.

Tompkins, Daniel D. (DR N.Y.) June 21, 1774–June 11, 1825; vice president 1817–25; Gov. July 1, 1807–Feb. 24, 1817.

Truman, Harry S. (D Mo.) May 8, 1884–Dec. 26, 1972; vice president Jan. 20–April 12, 1945; Senate 1935–Jan. 17, 1945; president April 12, 1945–53 (succeeded Franklin Delano Roosevelt, who died in office).

Tyler, John (son of Gov. John Tyler of Va., father of Rep. David Gardiner Tyler) (W Va.) March 29, 1790–Jan. 18, 1862; vice president March 4–April 6, 1841; Gov. Dec. 10, 1825–March 4, 1827 (Democratic Republican); House Dec. 16, 1817–21 (Republican); Senate 1827–Feb. 29, 1936 (Republican); elected pres. pro tempore March 3, 1835; president April 6, 1841–45 (succeeded William Henry Harrison, who died in office).

Van Buren, Martin (half-brother of Rep. James Isaac Van Alen) (D N.Y.) Dec. 5, 1782–July 24, 1862; vice president 1833–37; Senate 1821–Dec. 20, 1828 (no party); Gov. Jan. 1–March 12, 1829 (Jeffersonian Republican); secretary of state March 28, 1829–March 23, 1831; president 1837–41.

Wallace, Henry Agard (D Iowa) Oct. 7, 1888–Nov. 18, 1965; vice president 1941–45; secretary of agriculture March 4, 1933–Sept. 4, 1940; secretary of commerce March 2, 1945–Sept. 20, 1946.

Wheeler, William Almon (R N.Y.) June 30, 1819–June 4, 1887; vice president 1877–81; House 1861–63, 1869–77.

Wilson, Henry (R Mass.) Feb. 16, 1812–Nov. 22, 1875; vice president 1873–Nov. 22, 1875 (died in office); Senate Jan. 31, 1855–73 (1855–59 Free-Soiler/American Party/Democrat).

Cabinet Members

Although some presidents consulted their top executive officers often, cabinets for the most part have been a sidelight of the presidency. Neither the Constitution nor statutory law provided for the cabinet. George Washington initiated the practice of meeting with the secretaries of state, Treasury, and war, as well as his attorney general, to seek their advice on domestic and foreign policy. Today fifteen executive department heads make up the cabinet, and the vice president routinely sits in on cabinet meetings. Other officials—for example, the director of the Office of Management and Budget—may be invited to join the cabinet as well. Elevation to cabinet rank is at a president's discretion.

Origin and Development

The members of the Constitutional Convention discussed providing the president with an advisory council. Gouverneur Morris and Charles Cotesworth Pinckney, the first delegates to use the term "cabinet" at the convention, proposed creation of a council of state, composed of the executive department heads, to advise the president. The idea of a cabinet did not win approval, however, because the Founders feared the president would become overburdened with unnecessary advisory councils.

Having no constitutional or statutory mandate for the institution of a cabinet, presidents have relied on the provision that allows them to seek the advice of their principal executive branch officers. Under the Articles of Confederation, several executive departments already existed. Thus, Washington's first cabinet evolved out of an established executive pattern that began in the early 1780s. Washington understood that the constitutional language about the responsibilities of the departments was ambiguous. When he was inaugurated in 1789, he consulted with Alexander Hamilton, James Madison, and others on the powers and duties of the presidency and permanently settled the matter by instituting the foundation of the modern cabinet. Early in his administration, Washington took the view that department heads should be assistants to the president, not Congress.

Seeking both administrative and advisory help in his new administration, Washington asked Congress to create three executive departments to oversee, respectively, foreign affairs, military affairs, and fiscal matters. For more than two months Congress debated the proper es-

tablishment of these departments. Primarily concerned with the relationship of each department to Congress and believing that not all departments should be alike in these relationships, most members of Congress preferred that the departments concerned with foreign affairs and war be primarily under the control of the executive. The Treasury, however, had some legislative purposes and thus should fall more under the control of Congress. Part of the rationale for requiring the secretary of the Treasury to report fiscal matters directly to Congress was the constitutional requirement that revenue bills originate in the House of Representatives.

Hamilton, appointed the first Treasury secretary by Washington, did much to increase the prestige and independence of the cabinet. Although Treasury had been created as an extension of Congress's authority, Hamilton made it a stronghold of executive power.

Washington initially believed that the Senate would fill the role of advisory council, but that hope faded in August 1790 when he went to the Senate floor, accompanied by Secretary of War Henry Knox, to get advice on an American Indian treaty. The senators made clear that they were uncomfortable meeting with the president and that they would not serve in the capacity of an advisory council. As a result, Washington gradually began to rely on the advice of his department heads, the attorney general, Vice President John Adams, and Chief Justice John Jay.

At first Washington consulted with each individually, both in person and in writing. Later, in 1791, when he was preparing to leave the capital for a few days, he authorized his vice president, chief justice, and the secretaries to meet and discuss government matters in his absence. In the following year, he conferred frequently with his department heads and the attorney general, omitting the vice president and chief justice.

Washington had hoped that his advisers would consult with one another and work together harmoniously. A personal and political rift between Hamilton and Secretary of State Thomas Jefferson eventually made that impossible. Both left the service of the administration, and Washington replaced them with men of cooler heads but lesser talent, whose advice he did not value as much.

John Adams, Washington's successor, experienced a similar disillusionment with the workings of his cabinet. Yet during his administration the formal cabinet remained the president's principal official advisory unit.

Fifteen Executive Departments

Fifteen executive departments existed as of January 2005: State, Treasury, Defense, Justice, Interior, Agriculture, Commerce, Labor, Health and Human Services, Education, Housing and Urban Development, Transportation, Energy, Veterans Affairs, and Homeland Security.

The first executive department—the Department of Foreign Affairs—was created by Congress in legislation enacted July 27, 1789. Two months later Congress changed the name to the Department of State. During George Washington's administration, two more departments were established on his request: War and Treasury, authorized in acts of Aug. 7, 1789, and Sept. 2, 1789, respectively. Washington also had at his service an attorney general, whose position and office were created by the Judiciary Act of Sept. 24, 1789. It was not until June 22, 1870, however, that the Department of Justice, with the attorney general at the helm, was established.

Many efforts were made in the early nineteenth century to form a "home" department. They finally were successful in March 1849, when legislation was signed into law that provided for the Department of the Interior. The idea of having an agriculture agency in the federal government was with the nation at its inception, when farmers made up 90 percent of the population. It was not until 1862, however, that the Department of Agriculture was established and not until 1889 did it gain cabinet status.

The Department of Commerce and Labor was created by legislation enacted Feb. 14, 1903. Ten years later the department was split in two. The Department of Labor was established by legislation enacted March 4, 1913, and the Department of Commerce and Labor became the Department of Commerce.

Numerous bills were introduced in Congress between 1921 and 1945 aimed at unifying the armed forces. The National Security Act of 1947 was signed into law July 26, 1947. It created the National Military Establishment, which combined the War Department and the Navy Department (established in 1798) under the loose supervision of a secretary of defense. However, because the secretary had not been given any real authority, administrative problems arose. These were resolved by the National Security Act Amendments of 1949, which reorganized the National Military Establishment into the Department of Defense and consolidated authority in the secretary of defense. Thus, the office predates the department by two years.

The Department of Health, Education and Welfare (HEW) evolved from a series of presidential reorganization plans and laws that became effective between 1939 and 1953. HEW formally came into being April 11, 1953. Further reorganizations eventually resulted in the consolidation of the education functions of HEW into a separate department. Legislation signed Oct. 17, 1979, provided for the Department of Education, with the

---

The role of the cabinet under Washington and Adams established a pattern of ambiguity that has endured throughout the history of the presidency.

The first part of the nineteenth century witnessed a gradual decline in importance of the cabinet. Few cabinets got along well, and few presidents relied on their cabinets as advisory groups. Because the selection of cabinet members became more and more dictated by political and geographic considerations, presidents increasingly appointed cabinet members whom they did not know personally or necessarily trust.

Andrew Jackson was the first president to largely ignore his formal cabinet. During his first two years in office, he called no cabinet meetings, and he convened his cabinet only sixteen times during the entire eight years of his presidency. Jackson preferred the intimacy of his "kitchen cabinet," a group of close personal advisers (many of whom were newspapermen who kept him in touch with public opinion).

Abraham Lincoln appointed strong political leaders, many of them his political antagonists, to his cabinet, which has been described as overly ambitious. Cabinet officers during the Lincoln administration were known for their intrigues. Secretary of State William H. Seward, for example, considered himself Lincoln's prime minister. Salmon P. Chase, secretary of the Treasury, schemed with a few members of the Senate to remove Seward and increase his own influence. Lincoln's strong leadership, however, allowed him to retain control of his cabinet and use it for his own ends. The critical decisions were his alone, but he usually sought cabinet endorsement.

During the latter part of the nineteenth century an attempt was made to move responsibility for the cabinet from the White House to Congress, thereby giving Congress considerable access to information on the executive branch. Legislation was introduced to allow department heads to occupy seats on the House floor. The proposal was never voted into law.

Early in the twentieth century the cabinet grew in size but continued to play only a modest role as an advisory body. President Woodrow Wilson, for example, rarely met with his cabinet. Even during World War I, Wilson

remaining HEW responsibilities vested in the renamed Department of Health and Human Services. The changes became effective May 4, 1980.

President John F. Kennedy's 1961 proposal for a department of housing was controversial. He and then his successor, Lyndon B. Johnson, lobbied Congress for four years before it acted. Legislation signed Sept. 9, 1965, provided for the Department of Housing and Urban Development, which became a cabinet-level department at midnight Nov. 8, 1965.

Johnson also pursued the idea of establishing a transportation department, and Congress acceded to his wishes in 1966. The Department of Transportation officially began operation on April 1, 1967.

President Richard Nixon Aug. 12, 1970, signed the most comprehensive postal legislation since the founding of the republic. Effective July 1, 1971, the law provided that the U.S. Postal Service be established as an independent federal agency and take over the powers and duties of the Post Office Department. In addition, the postmaster general no longer held cabinet status. The roots of the postal service go back to the Second Continental Congress of 1777.

The 1973–74 Arab oil embargo brought evidence that the U.S. government needed to formulate a more coherent and comprehensive energy policy to centralize its energy-related programs. On Aug. 4, 1977, a bill was signed into law that created a Department of Energy, which came into existence on Oct. 1, 1977.

Bills to elevate the Veterans Administration to cabinet-level status had been introduced in at least seventeen successive Congresses before the Department of Veterans Affairs finally was established in legislation signed into law Oct. 25, 1988. The Department of Veterans Affairs officially opened its doors March 15, 1989. By January 2005 the department employed more than 220,000 workers, making it second only to the Defense Department in size.

In response to the September 11, 2001, terrorist attacks on the World Trade Center and the Pentagon, President George W. Bush signed the Homeland Security Act of 2002 into law on November 25, 2002, creating the Department of Homeland Security. This department combined all or part of twenty-two federal agencies—totaling about 180,000 employees—responsible for homeland security and counterterrorism efforts. The consolidation was the largest reorganization of the federal bureaucracy since the creation of the Defense Department in 1949. The Department of Homeland Security became the fifteenth executive department when it began operating on March 1, 2003.

did not consult his cabinet about the 1915 sinking of the *Lusitania* or his 1917 call for Congress to declare war. Instead, he relied on advice from his Council of National Defense, which was created in 1916 and composed of the secretaries of war, navy, interior, agriculture, commerce, and labor.

The cabinet in the middle and latter part of the twentieth century continued to function largely according to the predilection and personality of the chief executive. Under Franklin D. Roosevelt, cabinet meetings remained more of a forum for discussion than a decision-making body. He customarily went around the table and asked each cabinet member what was on his or her mind. Important matters were not often discussed and never in detail. Roosevelt also often interceded in the activities of his cabinet members.

Harry S. Truman believed the cabinet should operate similar to a board of directors. He called for a strong, active cabinet. Unlike Roosevelt, he asked his cabinet to vote on some major issues. Toward the end of his administration, however, Truman backed away from the board

of directors approach. For example, when North Korea attacked South Korea in 1950 he did not convene his cabinet to discuss the matter. He relied instead on an informal group—consisting of the secretaries of defense and state, the Joint Chiefs of Staff, and some of his closest aides—to advise him on the entry of the United States into the war. Throughout his administration, Truman reserved the most difficult decisions for himself.

Dwight D. Eisenhower took his cabinet more seriously than any other twentieth-century president. He established a cabinet secretariat—one of the department heads set the agenda and served as liaison between the president and the other cabinet members—and he charged the cabinet with both advising him on major issues and seeing that decisions were carried out.

Eisenhower expanded cabinet meetings to include not only department secretaries but also important aides such as the U.S. ambassador to the United Nations, the budget director, the White House chief of staff, and the national security affairs assistant. Vice presidents routinely took part in cabinet meetings since Franklin Roosevelt's administration, but Eisenhower was the first president to effectively use his vice president in the cabinet. He made his vice president, Richard Nixon, chairman of several cabinet committees and acting chairman of the cabinet if he was unable to attend a meeting. Twenty or more people participated in Eisenhower's cabinet meetings, which were weekly and often lasted three or more hours. Although Eisenhower accepted responsibility for final decisions, he attempted to make the cabinet more than just a body of advisers by including wide-ranging, important issues on the agenda.

John F. Kennedy did not follow the Eisenhower style. He seldom held cabinet meetings, although he did meet individually with department heads. Because he believed few subjects warranted discussion by the entire cabinet, Kennedy preferred to spend his time with the aides and secretaries most concerned with a specific issue.

Although Lyndon B. Johnson used his cabinet more than Kennedy did, cabinet meetings were mostly for show and contained little in the way of substantive discussion. Johnson used the meetings to create the impression of a consensus within his administration. He gave little credit to the cabinet as a consultative body, keeping many of his cabinet officers at a distance.

Although Nixon, as vice president under Eisenhower, wielded a great deal of influence from the cabinet, when he became president he relegated his cabinet to a position of lesser importance than that of most of his White House staff. The Watergate revelations forced him to promise to deal regularly and openly with the cabinet, but his resignation prevented him from making good on that promise. Convinced that Watergate resulted from Nixon's carelessness in allowing his personal aides to gain too much power at the expense of his cabinet, Nixon's successor, Gerald R. Ford, restored the cabinet secretariat established by Eisenhower. Ford's cabinet became a meaningful advisory group. A cabinet secretary would draw up formal agendas for cabinet meetings, which often were used to gauge the views of the department heads on different issues.

Both Jimmy Carter and Ronald Reagan met less and less with their respective cabinets as their tenure in office progressed. Reagan, however, was more successful in employing the cabinet as an advisory group. His cabinet was divided into seven councils, each addressing a specific substantive area: economic affairs, commerce and trade, food and agriculture, human resources, natural resources, legal policy, and management and administration. Under this system, cabinet members could concentrate on matters germane to them and not to the cabinet as a whole. In some respects this system restored the advisory function that the cabinet performed during the Eisenhower administration.

When George Bush came into office, he put some of his oldest and most trusted friends into his cabinet and turned to well-respected figures in Washington for several other cabinet slots. In the early years of his presidency, he gave his cabinet a greater policy role than Reagan's cabinet had had. But major policy decisions still were made by the president and a few senior advisers.

Bill Clinton selected a mix of old friends, congressional allies, and professional experts for his cabinet. But an overriding concern in the selection process was diversity. Emphasizing that he wanted a cabinet that "looks like America," Clinton named more women and minorities to the cabinet than ever before. Clinton's tendency to micromanage policy, however, contributed to the centralizing of policy making within the White House. Major policy decisions were made by Clinton and his advisers rather than the executive departments.

George W. Bush followed Clinton's precedent by assembling a demographically diverse group of individuals in his cabinet. Considerably less hands on than Clinton, Bush embraced a more controlled, corporate style of top-down governing that delegated authority to trusted administration officials. Major policy decisions still emanated from the White House rather than the executive departments. Bush strove to avoid internal clashes by removing cabinet members who disagreed with him, and he rewarded loyalists with top cabinet positions at the start of his second term.

Role and Function

Most presidents have come to expect little from their cabinets except the opportunity to exchange information. Use of the cabinet as a source of advice has been rare. Even when presidents emphasized the importance of their cabinets early in their administrations, commitment to a strong cabinet soon diminished. As administrations mature, daily administrative matters and domestic and international crises often take more and more of a president's time. Moreover, presidential programs and goals become fixed, and cabinet secretaries find themselves competing for scarce resources. Cabinet meetings thus become less frequent, less enthusiastic, and less cordial.

The role of presidential adviser still is considered the ideal one for the cabinet. Many presidents, however, have intentionally avoided placing their cabinets in such a position. They are not willing to delegate the decision-making power needed to make the cabinet an effective advisory board. Many presidents feel that doing so might challenge their power. Moreover, a strong, institutionalized cabinet with its own staff might put the president at a disadvantage in the control of resources and information.

The presidential reluctance to use cabinets as advisory groups also stems from situations in which presidents are forced to choose cabinet appointees who may be weak or who may not represent the goals of the administration. Most cabinet selections are influenced heavily by political considerations.

Because presidents have not associated closely with their cabinet officers, they have tended to rely on their White House staffs for advice. With their closer proximity to the Oval Office, these staffers have more access to the president than the cabinet. Moreover, they often are longtime personal friends of the president and exhibit loyalty not necessarily found among members of the cabinet.

Particularly strong or assertive presidents may be less likely to use their cabinets as vital advisory bodies. Pres-

Cabinet Holdovers

In the history of presidential cabinets, holdover members have been common. And from the time of John Adams's presidency, cabinet members appointed by one administration have been passed to the next.

The majority of holdovers are retained between terms of the same president. In addition, when a president died in office, his successor often kept the cabinet intact. When Lyndon B. Johnson was elected in his own right in 1964, he held on to eight cabinet members originally appointed by John F. Kennedy.

Holdover cabinet members do not need to be reconfirmed. "Nowhere in the Constitution is there a specific termination date" for cabinet secretaries, a Senate legal adviser explained. "They are appointed for an indefinite period of time, and unless they are dismissed by the president [or resign], they are not subject to reconfirmation."

In 1989 George Bush retained three cabinet members from the Reagan administration—Treasury Secretary Nicholas F. Brady, Education Secretary Lauro F. Cavazos, and Attorney General Richard Thornburgh. Bush's action marked the first time since Herbert Hoover took over from Calvin Coolidge that a completely new administration retained department heads named by a former president. This was in part because it was the first time since 1929 that a "friendly takeover" of the White House had taken place.

idents also may use cabinet meetings more to generate enthusiasm or display administration unity than to carefully examine and debate complex problems.

Appointment Process

The cabinet secretary's job is a difficult one. Cabinet officers must have the management skills necessary to administer a large public bureaucracy as well as some knowledge of the subject area of their departments. Some highly qualified individuals may not be willing to make the financial sacrifice necessary to enter public service, however.

Selection of the department secretaries is an indication of the policy direction and credibility of the new administration. Cabinet appointments provide presidents with their best early opportunity to show their leadership. And the first step toward a successful administration likely is the wise and prudent selection of the cabinet.

Ideally, cabinet appointees should be able to demonstrate that they are uniquely qualified to head a major department of the federal government, and the president should be able to make appointments to cabinet positions based on the administrative qualifications of the nominee. In practice, however, presidents do not make appointments based exclusively on administrative ability. Instead, they also consider such factors as personal loyalty, political party loyalty, ideological compatibility, acceptability to Congress, geographic representation, constituent group representation, reputation, expertise, and previous government experience.

Although the criteria that presidents use in filling cabinet positions often call for certain selections, the appointment process itself can impose additional restrictions on their ability to choose the best possible cabinet. Unlike some presidential appointments, cabinet appoint-

ments must be approved by the Senate. Some nominees are unwilling to submit to the scrutiny that accompanies the Senate confirmation procedure, which can be long and demanding.

A notably contentious recent case involved George Bush's first nominee for secretary of defense, John Tower, former Republican senator from Texas. Tower's professional and personal life were the subject of discussion and debate during Senate Armed Services Committee confirmation hearings in 1989. A reputation as a womanizer, FBI reports alleging a long record of alcohol abuse, and fears of potential conflicts of interest because of his consulting work for defense contractors were enough to sink Tower's nomination. Supporters contended that the full Senate's rejection of Tower was a partisan act and politically motivated.

Clinton in 1993 had to drop his first two choices for attorney general after questions arose over their use of illegal immigrants as domestic workers. Similarly George W. Bush's first choice for labor secretary in 2001 and his choice for homeland security secretary in 2004 both withdrew after disclosing that they had hired illegal immigrants for domestic help.

Cabinet Member Facts

Eight presidents had served as executive department heads: Thomas Jefferson, James Madison, John Quincy Adams, Martin Van Buren, and James Buchanan as secretary of state; James Monroe as secretary of state and secretary of war; William Howard Taft as secretary of war; and Herbert Hoover as secretary of commerce.

Five vice presidents had cabinet experience: Jefferson and Van Buren as secretary of state; John C. Calhoun as secretary of state and secretary of war; Henry A. Wallace as secretary of agriculture and secretary of commerce;

and Richard B. Cheney as secretary of defense. Calhoun served as war secretary and Wallace as commerce secretary subsequent to their tenure as vice president.

Twenty-two members of the Supreme Court held cabinet posts, nine of which were attorney general.

The only president who did not see a change in his cabinet membership during his administration was Franklin Pierce.

James Wilson served longest as a cabinet member. He was secretary of agriculture from March 6, 1897, to March 5, 1913, under the administrations of William McKinley, Theodore Roosevelt, William Howard Taft, and Woodrow Wilson.

The greatest number of cabinet posts—four—was held by Elliot Richardson, who served as secretary of health, education and welfare; secretary of defense; attorney general; and secretary of commerce. Four other men served three positions each: George Cortelyou (commerce and labor, Treasury, and postmaster general), Walter Gresham (Treasury, postmaster general, and state), Timothy Pickering (postmaster general, war, and state), and George P. Shultz (Treasury, labor, and state).

The first woman appointed to a cabinet post was Frances Perkins in 1933. She served as secretary of labor. Johnson appointed the first black—Robert C. Weaver as the first secretary of housing and urban development. Lauro F. Cavazos became the first Hispanic member of a president's cabinet. He was appointed by Ronald Reagan in 1988 as secretary of education. Clinton appointed women for the first time to the two top cabinet positions: Janet Reno as attorney general in 1993, and Madeleine Albright as secretary of state in 1997. For secretary of state, George W. Bush appointed the first black, Colin L. Powell, in 2001 and the first black women, Condoleeza Rice, in 2005. Bush also appointed the first Hispanic—Alberto Gonzales—as attorney general in 2005.

Cabinet Members: Biographies

This biographical summary lists, alphabetically, all executive department heads since 1789. The material is organized as follows: name; state from; date of birth; date of death (if applicable); period of service as cabinet member; service as president, vice president, Supreme Court justice, governor, delegate to the Continental Congress, member of Congress, House or Senate minority leader, House or Senate majority leader, Speaker of the House of Representatives, president pro tempore of the Senate (when elected), chair of standing congressional committees (since 1947), or chairman of the Democratic National Committee or the Republican National Committee.

This list does not include those appointed for ad interim terms.

Specific dates of service are provided where available. For presidential, vice presidential, and congressional terms, only the years are given for beginning and ending dates if the standard terms were served. Presidential and vice presidential terms from 1789 to 1933 were from March 4 to March 4; since 1934, the four-year term has been from Jan. 20 to Jan. 20. Terms of service for representatives and senators from 1789 to 1933 were from March 4 to March 4; since 1934, service has been from Jan. 3 to Jan. 3.

The major source of information for this list was the executive departments. Additional data were obtained from the *Biographical Directory of the American Congress, 1774–1996* (Alexandria, Va.: CQ Staff Directories, 1997); Michael Nelson, ed., *Guide to the Presidency,* 3rd ed. (Washington, D.C.: CQ Press, 2002); Robert Sobel, ed., *Biographical Directory of the United States Executive Branch, 1774–1977* (Westport, Conn.: Greenwood Press, 1977); the *Weekly Compilation of Presidential Documents; CQ Weekly;* and various newspapers.

Abraham, Spencer (Mich.) June 12, 1952– ; secretary of energy Jan. 20, 2001–Feb. 1, 2005; Senate 1995–2001 (Republican).

Acheson, Dean Gooderham (Conn.) April 11, 1893–Oct. 12, 1971; secretary of state Jan. 21, 1949–Jan. 20, 1953.

Adams, Brockman "Brock" (Wash.) Jan. 13, 1927– ; secretary of transportation Jan. 23, 1977–July 22, 1979; House 1965–Jan. 22, 1977 (Democrat); Senate 1987–93 (Democrat).

Adams, Charles Francis (Mass.) Aug. 2, 1866–June 10, 1954; secretary of the navy March 5, 1929–March 4, 1933.

Adams, John Quincy (Mass.) July 11, 1767–Feb. 23, 1848; secretary of state Sept. 22, 1817–March 3, 1825; Senate 1803–June 8, 1808 (Federalist); president 1825–29 (Democratic Republican); House 1831–Feb. 23, 1848 (Federalist).

Akerman, Amos Tappan (Ga.) Feb. 23, 1821–Dec. 21, 1880; attorney general June 23, 1870–Jan. 10, 1872.

Albright, Madeleine K. (D.C.) May 15, 1937– ; secretary of state Jan. 23, 1997–Jan. 20, 2001.

Alexander, Joshua Willis (Mo.) Jan. 22, 1852–Feb. 27, 1936; secretary of commerce Dec. 16, 1919–March 4, 1921; House 1907–Dec. 15, 1919 (Democrat).

Alexander, Lamar (Tenn.) July 3, 1940– ; secretary of education March 22, 1991–Jan. 20, 1993; Senate 2003– (Republican); Gov. Jan. 17, 1979–Jan. 17, 1987 (Republican).

Alger, Russell Alexander (Mich.) Feb. 27, 1836–Jan. 24, 1907; secretary of war March 5, 1897–Aug. 1, 1899; Senate Sept. 27, 1902–Jan. 24, 1907 (Republican); Gov. Jan. 1, 1885–Jan. 1, 1887 (Republican).

Anderson, Clinton Presba (N.M.) Oct. 23, 1895–Nov. 11, 1975; secretary of agriculture June 30, 1945–May 10, 1948; House 1941–June 30, 1945 (Democrat); Senate 1949–73 (Democrat).

Anderson, Robert Bernard (Conn.) June 4, 1910–Aug. 14, 1989; secretary of the Treasury July 29, 1957–Jan. 20, 1961.

Andrus, Cecil Dale (Idaho) Aug. 25, 1931– ; secretary of the interior Jan. 23, 1977–Jan. 20, 1981; Gov. Jan. 4, 1971–Jan. 24, 1977 (Democrat), Jan. 5, 1987–Jan. 2, 1995 (Democrat).

Armstrong, John Jr. (N.Y.) Nov. 25, 1758–April 1, 1843; secretary of war Jan. 13, 1813–Sept. 27, 1814; Senate Nov. 6, 1800–Feb. 5, 1802, Nov. 10, 1803–June 30, 1804 (no party).

Ashcroft, John (Ill.) May 9, 1942– ; attorney general Feb. 1, 2001– Feb. 3, 2005; Senate 1995–2001; Gov. Jan. 14, 1985–Jan. 11, 1993.

Aspin, Leslie "Les" (Wis.) July 21, 1938–May 21, 1995; secretary of defense Jan. 22, 1993–Feb. 2, 1994; House 1971–Jan. 20, 1993 (Democrat); chair House Armed Services 1985–93.

Babbitt, Bruce Edward (Ariz.) June 27, 1938– ; secretary of the interior Jan. 22, 1993–Jan. 2, 2001; Gov. March 4, 1978–Jan. 5, 1987 (Democrat).

Bacon, Robert (N.Y.) July 5, 1860–May 29, 1919; secretary of state Jan. 27–March 5, 1909.

Badger, George Edmund (N.C.) April 17, 1795–May 11, 1866; secretary of the navy March 6–Sept. 11, 1841; Senate Nov. 25, 1846–55 (Whig).

Baker, James Addison III (Texas) April 28, 1930– ; secretary of the Treasury Feb. 4, 1985–Aug. 17, 1988; secretary of state Jan. 27, 1989–Aug. 23, 1992.

Baker, Newton Diehl (Ohio) Dec. 3, 1871–Dec. 25, 1937; secretary of war March 9, 1916–March 4, 1921.

Baldrige, Malcolm (Conn.) Oct. 4, 1922–July 25, 1987; secretary of commerce Jan. 20, 1981–July 25, 1987.

Ballinger, Richard Achilles (Wash.) July 9, 1858–June 6, 1922; secretary of the interior March 6, 1909–March 12, 1911.

Bancroft, George (Mass.) Oct. 3, 1800–Jan. 17, 1891; secretary of the navy March 11, 1845–Sept. 9, 1846.

Barbour, James (Va.) June 10, 1775–June 7, 1842; secretary of war March 7, 1825–May 23, 1828; Gov. Jan. 3, 1812–Dec. 1, 1814 (Anti-Democrat/State Rights Party); Senate Jan. 2, 1815–March 7, 1825 (Anti-Democrat/State Rights Party); elected pres. pro tempore Feb. 15, 1819.

Barr, Joseph Walker (Ind.) Jan. 17, 1918–Feb. 23, 1996; secretary of the Treasury Dec. 21, 1968–Jan. 20, 1969; House 1959–61 (Democrat).

Barr, William Pelham (Va.) May 23, 1950–; attorney general Nov. 26, 1991–Jan. 15, 1993.

Barry, William Taylor (Ky.) Feb. 5, 1784–Aug. 30, 1835; postmaster general April 6, 1829–April 30, 1835; House Aug. 8, 1810–11 (Republican); Senate Dec. 16, 1814–May 1, 1816 (Republican).

Bates, Edward (Mo.) Sept. 4, 1793–March 25, 1869; attorney general March 5, 1861–Sept. 1864; House 1827–29 (no party).

Bayard, Thomas Francis Sr. (Del.) Oct. 29, 1828–Sept. 28, 1898; secretary of state March 7, 1885–March 6, 1889; Senate

1869–March 6, 1885 (Democrat); elected pres. pro tempore Oct. 10, 1881.

Belknap, William Worth (Iowa) Sept. 22, 1829–Oct. 13, 1890; secretary of war Oct. 25, 1869–March 2, 1876.

Bell, Griffin Boyette (Ga.) Oct. 31, 1918– ; attorney general Jan. 26, 1977–Aug. 16, 1979.

Bell, John (Tenn.) Feb. 15, 1797–Sept. 10, 1869; secretary of war March 5–Sept. 13, 1841; House 1827–41 (no party); Speaker June 2, 1834–35; Senate Nov. 22, 1847–59 (Whig).

Bell, Terrel Howard (Utah) Nov. 11, 1921–June 22, 1996; secretary of education Jan. 23, 1981–Dec. 31, 1984.

Bennett, William John (D.C.) July 31, 1943– ; secretary of education Feb. 6, 1985–Sept. 20, 1988.

Benson, Ezra Taft (Utah) Aug. 4, 1899–May 30, 1994; secretary of agriculture Jan. 21, 1953–Jan. 20, 1961.

Bentsen, Lloyd Millard Jr. (Texas) Feb. 11, 1921– ; secretary of the Treasury Jan. 22, 1993–Dec. 22, 1994; House Dec. 4, 1948–55 (Democrat); Senate 1971–Jan. 20, 1993 (Democrat); chair Senate Finance 1987–93.

Bergland, Robert Selmer (Minn.) July 22, 1928– ; secretary of agriculture Jan. 23, 1977–Jan. 20, 1981; House 1971–Jan. 22, 1977 (Democrat).

Berrien, John Macpherson (Ga.) Aug. 23, 1781–Jan. 1, 1856; attorney general March 9, 1829–July 20, 1831; Senate 1825–March 9, 1829 (Jacksonian), 1841–May 1845 (Whig), Nov. 13, 1845–May 28, 1852 (Whig).

Bibb, George Mortimer (Ky.) Oct. 30, 1776–April 14, 1859; secretary of the Treasury July 4, 1844–March 7, 1845; Senate 1811–Aug. 23, 1814 (no party), 1829–35 (Jacksonian).

Biddle, Francis Beverley (Pa.) May 9, 1886–Oct. 4, 1968; attorney general Sept. 15, 1941–June 30, 1945.

Bissell, Wilson Shannon (N.Y.) Dec. 31, 1847–Oct. 6, 1903; postmaster general March 8, 1893–April 3, 1895.

Black, Jeremiah Sullivan (Pa.) Jan. 10, 1810–Aug. 19, 1883; attorney general March 6, 1857–Dec. 17, 1860; secretary of state Dec. 17, 1860–March 5, 1861.

Blaine, James Gillespie (Maine) Jan. 31, 1830–Jan. 27, 1893; secretary of state March 7–Dec. 19, 1881, March 7, 1889–June 4, 1892; House 1863–July 10, 1876 (Republican); Speaker 1869–73, Dec. 1, 1873–75; Senate July 10, 1876–March 5, 1881 (Republican).

Blair, Montgomery (D.C.) May 10, 1813–July 27, 1883; postmaster general March 9, 1861–Sept. 30, 1864.

Bliss, Cornelius Newton (N.Y.) Jan. 28, 1833–Oct. 9, 1911; secretary of the interior March 6, 1897–Feb. 19, 1899.

Block, John Rusling (Ill.) Feb. 15, 1935– ; secretary of agriculture Jan. 23, 1981–Feb. 14, 1986.

Blount, Winton Malcolm (Ala.) Feb. 1, 1921– ; postmaster general Jan. 22, 1969–Jan. 12, 1971.

Blumenthal, Werner Michael (Mich.) Jan. 3, 1926– ; secretary of the Treasury Jan. 23, 1977–Aug. 4, 1979.

Bodman, Samuel Wright (Mass.) Nov. 26, 1938– ; secretary of energy Feb. 1, 2005– .

Bonaparte, Charles Joseph (Md.) June 9, 1851–June 28, 1921; attorney general Dec. 17, 1906–March 4, 1909; secretary of the navy July 1, 1905–Dec. 16, 1906.

Borie, Adolph Edward (Pa.) Nov. 25, 1809–Feb. 5, 1880; secretary of the navy March 9–June 25, 1869.

Boutwell, George Sewel (Mass.) Jan. 28, 1818–Feb. 27, 1905; secretary of the Treasury March 12, 1869–March 16, 1873; Gov. Jan. 11, 1851–Jan. 14, 1853 (Democrat); House 1863–March 12, 1869 (Republican); Senate March 17, 1873–77 (Republican).

Bowen, Otis Ray (Ind.) Feb. 26, 1918– ; secretary of health and human services Dec. 13, 1985–Jan. 20, 1989; Gov. Jan. 8, 1973–Jan. 12, 1981 (Republican).

Boyd, Alan Stephenson (Fla.) July 20, 1922– ; secretary of transportation Jan. 23, 1967–Jan. 20, 1969.

Bradford, William (Pa.) Sept. 14, 1755–Aug. 23, 1795; attorney general Jan. 27, 1794–Aug. 23, 1795.

Brady, Nicholas Frederick (N.J.) April 11, 1930– ; secretary of the Treasury Sept. 16, 1988–Jan. 19, 1993; Senate April 12–Dec. 20, 1982 (Republican).

Branch, John (N.C.) Nov. 4, 1782–Jan. 3, 1863; secretary of the navy March 9, 1829–May 12, 1831; Gov. Dec. 6, 1817–Dec. 7, 1820 (Democratic Republican); Senate 1823–March 9, 1829 (Democrat); House May 12, 1831–33 (Democrat).

Brannan, Charles Franklin (Colo.) Aug. 23, 1903–July 2, 1992; secretary of agriculture June 2, 1948–Jan. 20, 1953.

Breckinridge, John (Ky.) Dec. 2, 1760–Dec. 14, 1806; attorney general Aug. 7, 1805–Dec. 14, 1806; Senate 1801–Aug. 7, 1805 (Republican).

Brennan, Peter Joseph (N.Y.) May 24, 1918–Oct. 2, 1996; secretary of labor Feb. 2, 1973–March 15, 1975.

Brewster, Benjamin Harris (Pa.) Oct. 13, 1816–April 4, 1888; attorney general Jan. 2, 1882–March 5, 1885.

Brinegar, Claude Stout (Calif.) Dec. 16, 1926– ; secretary of transportation Feb. 2, 1973–Feb. 1, 1975.

Bristow, Benjamin Helm (Ky.) June 20, 1832–June 22, 1896; secretary of the Treasury June 4, 1874–June 20, 1876.

Brock, William Emerson III (Tenn.) Nov. 23, 1930– ; secretary of labor April 29, 1985–Oct. 31, 1987; House 1963–71 (Republican); Senate 1971–77 (Republican); chair Rep. Nat. Comm. Jan. 1977–Jan. 1981.

Brown, Aaron Venable (Tenn.) Aug. 15, 1795–March 8, 1859; postmaster general March 7, 1857–March 8, 1859; House 1839–45 (Democrat); Gov. Oct. 14, 1845–Oct. 16, 1847 (Democrat).

Brown, Harold (N.Y.) Sept. 19, 1927– ; secretary of defense Jan. 21, 1977–Jan. 20, 1981.

Brown, Jesse (Ill.) March 27, 1944–Aug. 15, 2002; secretary of veterans affairs Jan. 22, 1993–July 1, 1997.

Brown, Ronald Harmon (D.C.) Aug. 1, 1941–April 3, 1996; secretary of commerce Jan. 22, 1993–April 3, 1996; chair Dem. Nat. Comm. 1989–92.

Brown, Walter Folger (Ohio) May 31, 1869–Jan. 26, 1961; postmaster general March 5, 1929–March 5, 1933.

Brownell, Herbert Jr. (N.Y.) Feb. 20, 1904–May 1, 1996; attorney general Jan. 21, 1953–Nov. 8, 1957; chair Rep. Nat. Comm. 1944–46.

Browning, Orville Hickman (Ill.) Feb. 10, 1806–Aug. 10, 1881; secretary of the interior Sept. 1, 1866–March 4, 1869; Senate June 26, 1861–Jan. 12, 1863 (Republican).

Bryan, William Jennings (Neb.) March 19, 1860–July 26, 1925; secretary of state March 5, 1913–June 9, 1915; House 1891–95 (Democrat).

Buchanan, James (Pa.) April 23, 1791–June 1, 1868; secretary of state March 10, 1845–March 7, 1849; House 1821–31 (no party); Senate Dec. 6, 1834–March 5, 1845 (Democrat); president 1857–61 (Democrat).

Burleson, Albert Sidney (Texas) June 7, 1863–Nov. 24, 1937; postmaster general March 5, 1913–March 4, 1921; House 1899–March 6, 1913 (Democrat).

Burnley, James Horace IV (Va.) July 30, 1948– ; secretary of transportation Dec. 3, 1987–Jan. 30, 1989.

Butler, Benjamin Franklin (N.Y.) Dec. 17, 1795–Nov. 8, 1858; attorney general Nov. 15, 1833–Sept. 1, 1838.

Butz, Earl Lauer (Ind.) July 3, 1909– ; secretary of agriculture Dec. 2, 1971–Oct. 4, 1976.

Byrnes, James Francis (S.C.) May 2, 1879–April 9, 1972; secretary of state July 3, 1945–Jan. 21, 1947; House 1911–25 (Democrat);

Senate 1931–July 8, 1941 (Democrat); assoc. justice July 8, 1941–Oct. 3, 1942; Gov. Jan. 16, 1951–Jan. 18, 1955 (Democrat).

Calhoun, John Caldwell (S.C.) March 18, 1782–March 31, 1850; secretary of war Oct. 8, 1817–March 7, 1825; secretary of state April 1, 1844–March 10, 1845; House 1811–Nov. 3, 1817 (Republican); vice president 1825–Dec. 28, 1832 (Democratic Republican); Senate Dec. 29, 1832–43 (Republican), Nov. 26, 1845–March 31, 1850 (Republican).

Califano, Joseph Anthony Jr. (N.Y.) May 15, 1931– ; secretary of health, education and welfare Jan. 25, 1977–Aug. 3, 1979.

Cameron, James Donald (Pa.) May 14, 1833–Aug. 30, 1918; secretary of war May 22, 1876–March 3, 1877; Senate March 20, 1877–97 (Republican); chair Rep. Nat. Comm. 1879–80.

Cameron, Simon (Pa.) March 8, 1799–June 26, 1889; secretary of war March 5, 1861–Jan. 14, 1862; Senate March 13, 1845–49 (no party), 1857–March 4, 1861 (Republican), 1867–March 12, 1877 (Republican).

Campbell, George Washington (Tenn.) Feb. 9, 1769–Feb. 17, 1848; secretary of the Treasury Feb. 9–Oct. 5, 1814; House 1803–09 (Republican); Senate Oct. 8, 1811–Feb. 11, 1814 (Republican), Oct. 10, 1815–April 20, 1818 (Republican).

Campbell, James (Pa.) Sept. 1, 1812–Jan. 1893; postmaster general March 8, 1853–March 6, 1857.

Card, Andrew Hill Jr. (Mass.) May 10, 1947– ; secretary of transportation Feb. 24, 1992–Jan. 20, 1993.

Carlisle, John Griffin (Ky.) Sept. 5, 1835–July 31, 1910; secretary of the Treasury March 7, 1893–March 5, 1897; House 1877–May 26, 1890 (Democrat); Speaker Dec. 3, 1883–85, Dec. 7, 1885–87, Dec. 5, 1887–89; Senate May 26, 1890–Feb. 4, 1893 (Democrat).

Carlucci, Frank Charles III (Va.) Oct. 18, 1930– ; secretary of defense Nov. 23, 1987–Jan. 20, 1989.

Cass, Lewis (Mich.) Oct. 9, 1782–June 17, 1866; secretary of war Aug. 1, 1831–Oct. 5, 1836; secretary of state March 6, 1857–Dec. 14, 1860; Gov. (Mich. Terr.) 1813–31; Senate 1845–May 29, 1848 (Democrat), 1849–57 (Democrat); elected pres. pro tempore Dec. 4, 1854.

Cavazos, Lauro Fred (Texas) Jan. 4, 1927– ; secretary of education Sept. 20, 1988–Dec. 12, 1990.

Celebrezze, Anthony Joseph (Ohio) Sept. 4, 1910–Oct. 29, 1998; secretary of health, education and welfare July 31, 1962–Aug. 17, 1965.

Chandler, William Eaton (N.H.) Dec. 28, 1835–Nov. 30, 1917; secretary of the navy April 16, 1882–March 6, 1885; Senate June 14, 1887–89 (Republican), June 18, 1889–1901 (Republican).

Chandler, Zachariah (Mich.) Dec. 10, 1813–Nov. 1, 1879; secretary of the interior Oct. 19, 1875–March 11, 1877; Senate 1857–75 (Republican), Feb. 22–Nov. 1, 1879 (Republican); chair Rep. Nat. Comm. 1876–79.

Chao, Elaine L. (Ky.) March 26, 1953– ; secretary of labor Jan. 31, 2001– .

Chapin, Roy Dikeman (Mich.) Feb. 23, 1880–Feb. 16, 1936; secretary of commerce Aug. 8, 1932–March 3, 1933.

Chapman, Oscar Littleton (Colo.) Oct. 22, 1896–Feb. 8, 1978; secretary of the interior Dec. 1, 1949–Jan. 20, 1953.

Chase, Salmon Portland (Ohio) Jan. 13, 1808–May 7, 1873; secretary of the Treasury March 7, 1861–June 30, 1864; Senate 1849–55 (Free-Soiler), March 4–6, 1861 (Republican); Gov. Jan. 14, 1856–Jan. 9, 1860 (Republican); chief justice Dec. 15, 1864–May 7, 1873.

Cheney, Richard Bruce (Wyo.) Jan. 30, 1941– ; secretary of defense March 21, 1989–Jan. 20, 1993; House 1979–March 17, 1989 (Republican); vice president 2001– (Republican).

Chertoff, Michael (N.J.) Nov. 28, 1953– ; secretary of homeland security March 3, 2005– .

Christopher, Warren Minor (Calif.) Oct. 27, 1925– ; secretary of state Jan. 22, 1993–Jan. 20, 1997.

Cisneros, Henry Gabriel (Texas) June 11, 1947– ; secretary of housing and urban development Jan. 22, 1993–Jan. 17, 1997.

Civiletti, Benjamin Richard (Md.) July 17, 1935– ; attorney general Aug. 16, 1979–Jan. 19, 1981.

Clark, Thomas Campbell (Texas) Sept. 23, 1899–June 13, 1977; attorney general July 1, 1945–Aug. 24, 1949; assoc. justice Aug. 24, 1949–June 12, 1967.

Clark, William Patrick (Calif.) Oct. 23, 1931– ; secretary of the interior Nov. 18, 1983–Feb. 7, 1985.

Clark, William Ramsey (Texas) Dec. 18, 1927– ; attorney general March 2, 1967–Jan. 20, 1969.

Clay, Henry (Ky.) April 12, 1777–June 29, 1852; secretary of state March 7, 1825–March 3, 1829; Senate Nov. 19, 1806–07 (no party), Jan. 4, 1810–11 (no party), Nov. 10, 1831–March 31, 1842 (Whig), 1849–June 29, 1852 (Whig); House 1811–Jan. 19, 1814 (Republican), 1815–21 (Republican), 1823–March 6, 1825 (Republican); Speaker Nov. 4, 1811–13, May 24, 1813–Jan. 19, 1814, Dec. 4, 1815–17, Dec. 1, 1817–19, Dec. 6, 1819–Oct. 28, 1820, Dec. 1, 1823–25.

Clayton, John Middleton (Del.) July 24, 1796–Nov. 9, 1856; secretary of state March 8, 1849–July 22, 1850; Senate 1829–Dec. 29, 1836 (no party), 1845–Feb. 23, 1849 (Whig), 1853–Nov. 9, 1856 (Whig).

Clifford, Clark McAdams (Md.) Dec. 25, 1906–Oct. 10, 1998; secretary of defense March 1, 1968–Jan. 20, 1969.

Clifford, Nathan (Maine) Aug. 18, 1803–July 25, 1881; attorney general Oct. 17, 1846–March 17, 1848; House 1839–43 (Democrat); assoc. justice Jan. 21, 1858–July 25, 1881.

Cobb, Howell (Ga.) Sept. 7, 1815–Oct. 9, 1868; secretary of the Treasury March 7, 1857–Dec. 8, 1860; House 1843–51 (Democrat), 1855–57 (Democrat); Speaker Dec. 22, 1849–51; Gov. Nov. 5, 1851–Nov. 9, 1853 (Union Democrat).

Cohen, Wilbur Joseph (Md.) June 10, 1913–May 17, 1987; secretary of health, education and welfare May 16, 1968–Jan. 20, 1969.

Cohen, William Sebastian (Maine) Aug. 28, 1940– ; secretary of defense Jan. 24, 1997–Jan. 20, 2001; House 1973–79; Senate 1979–97 (Republican).

Colby, Bainbridge (N.Y.) Dec. 22, 1869–April 11, 1950; secretary of state March 23, 1920–March 4, 1921.

Coleman, William Thaddeus Jr. (Pa.) July 7, 1920– ; secretary of transportation March 7, 1975–Jan. 20, 1977.

Collamer, Jacob (Vt.) Jan. 8, 1791–Nov. 9, 1865; postmaster general March 8, 1849–July 22, 1850; House 1843–49 (Whig); Senate 1855–Nov. 9, 1865 (Republican).

Colman, Norman Jay (Mo.) May 16, 1827–Nov. 3, 1911; secretary of agriculture Feb. 15–March 6, 1889.

Connally, John Bowden (Texas) Feb. 27, 1917–June 15, 1993; secretary of the Treasury Feb. 11, 1971–June 12, 1972; Gov. Jan. 15, 1963–Jan. 21, 1969 (Democrat).

Connor, John Thomas (N.J.) Nov. 3, 1914–Oct. 6, 2000; secretary of commerce Jan. 18, 1965–Jan. 31, 1967.

Conrad, Charles Magill (La.) Dec. 24, 1804–Feb. 11, 1878; secretary of war Aug. 15, 1850–March 7, 1853; Senate April 14, 1842–43 (Whig); House 1849–Aug. 17, 1850 (Whig).

Cortelyou, George Bruce (N.Y.) July 26, 1862–Oct. 23, 1940; secretary of commerce and labor Feb. 18, 1903–June 30, 1904; secretary of the Treasury March 4, 1907–March 7, 1909; postmaster general March 7, 1905–March 3, 1907; chair Rep. Nat. Comm. 1904–07.

Corwin, Thomas (Ohio) July 29, 1794–Dec. 18, 1865; secretary of the Treasury July 23, 1850–March 6, 1853; House 1831–May 30, 1840 (Whig), 1859–March 12, 1861 (Republican); Gov. Dec. 16, 1840–Dec. 14, 1842 (Whig); Senate 1845–July 20, 1850 (Whig).

Cox, Jacob Dolson (Ohio) Oct. 27, 1828–Aug. 4, 1900; secretary of the interior March 5, 1869–Oct. 31, 1870; Gov. Jan. 8, 1866–Jan. 13, 1868 (Republican); House 1877–79 (Republican).

Crawford, George Washington (Ga.) Dec. 22, 1798–July 27, 1872; secretary of war March 8, 1849–July 23, 1850; House Jan. 7–March 3, 1843 (Whig); Gov. Nov. 8, 1943–Nov. 3, 1847 (Whig).

Crawford, William Harris (Ga.) Feb. 24, 1772–Sept. 15, 1834; secretary of war Aug. 1, 1815–Oct. 22, 1816; secretary of the Treasury Oct. 22, 1816–March 6, 1825; Senate Nov. 7, 1807–March 23, 1813 (no party); elected pres. pro tempore March 24, 1812.

Creswell, John Angel James (Md.) Nov. 18, 1828–Dec. 23, 1891; postmaster general March 6, 1869–July 6, 1874; House 1863–65 (Republican); Senate March 9, 1865–67 (Republican).

Crittenden, John Jordan (Ky.) Sept. 10, 1786–July 26, 1863; attorney general March 5–Sept. 13, 1841, July 22, 1850–March 3, 1853; Senate 1817–19 (no party), 1835–41 (Whig), March 31, 1842–June 12, 1848 (Whig), 1855–61 (Whig); Gov. June 1, 1848–July 1850 (Whig); House 1861–63 (Unionist).

Crowninshield, Benjamin Williams (Mass.) Dec. 27, 1772–Feb. 3, 1851; secretary of the navy Jan. 16, 1815–Sept. 30, 1818; House 1823–31 (no party).

Cummings, Homer Stille (Conn.) April 30, 1870–Sept. 10, 1956; attorney general March 4, 1933–Jan. 2, 1939; chair Dem. Nat. Comm. 1919–20.

Cuomo, Andrew (N.Y.) Dec. 6, 1957– ; secretary of housing and urban development Jan. 30, 1997–Jan. 20, 2001.

Cushing, Caleb (Mass.) Jan. 17, 1800–Jan. 2, 1879; attorney general March 7, 1853–March 3, 1857; House 1835–43 (Whig).

Daley, William (Ill.) Aug. 9, 1949– ; secretary of commerce Jan. 30, 1997–July 19, 2000.

Dallas, Alexander James (Pa.) June 21, 1759–Jan. 16, 1817; secretary of the Treasury Oct. 6, 1814–Oct. 21, 1816.

Daniels, Josephus (N.C.) May 18, 1862–Jan. 15, 1948; secretary of the navy March 5, 1913–March 5, 1921.

Daugherty, Harry Micajah (Ohio) Jan. 26, 1860–Oct. 12, 1941; attorney general March 5, 1921–March 28, 1924.

Davis, Dwight Filley (Mo.) July 5, 1879–Nov. 28, 1945; secretary of war Oct. 14, 1925–March 5, 1929.

Davis, James John (Pa.) Oct. 27, 1873–Nov. 22, 1947; secretary of labor March 5, 1921–Nov. 30, 1930; Senate Dec. 2, 1930–45 (Republican).

Davis, Jefferson Finis (Miss.) June 3, 1808–Dec. 6, 1889; secretary of war March 7, 1853–March 6, 1857; House 1845–June 1846 (Democrat); Senate Aug. 10, 1847–Sept. 23, 1851 (Democrat), 1857–Jan. 21, 1861 (Democrat).

Day, James Edward (Calif.) Oct. 11, 1914–Oct. 29, 1996; postmaster general Jan. 21, 1961–Aug. 9, 1963.

Day, William Rufus (Ohio) April 17, 1849–July 9, 1923; secretary of state April 28–Sept. 16, 1898; assoc. justice March 2, 1903–Nov. 13, 1922.

Dearborn, Henry (Mass.) Feb. 23, 1751–June 6, 1829; secretary of war March 5, 1801–March 7, 1809; House 1793–97 (1793–95 no party, 1795–97 Republican).

Delano, Columbus (Ohio) June 4, 1809–Oct. 23, 1896; secretary of the interior Nov. 1, 1870–Sept. 30, 1875; House 1845–47 (Whig), 1865–67 (Republican), June 3, 1868–69 (Republican).

Denby, Edwin (Mich.) Feb. 18, 1870–Feb. 8, 1929; secretary of the navy March 6, 1921–March 10, 1924; House 1905–11 (Republican).

Dennison, William Jr. (Ohio) Nov. 23, 1815–June 15, 1882; postmaster general Oct. 1, 1864–July 16, 1866; Gov. Jan. 9, 1860–Jan. 13, 1862 (Republican).

Dent, Frederick Baily (S.C.) Aug. 17, 1922– ; secretary of commerce Feb. 2, 1973–March 26, 1975.

Dern, George Henry (Utah) Sept. 8, 1872–Aug. 27, 1936; secretary of war March 4, 1933–Aug. 27, 1936; Gov. Jan. 5, 1925–Jan. 2, 1933.

Derwinski, Edward Joseph (Ill.) Sept. 15, 1926– ; secretary of veterans affairs March 15, 1989–Sept. 26, 1992; House 1959–83 (Republican).

Devens, Charles (Mass.) April 4, 1820–Jan. 7, 1891; attorney general March 12, 1877–March 6, 1881.

Dexter, Samuel (Mass.) May 14, 1761–May 4, 1816; secretary of war May 13–Dec. 31, 1800; secretary of the Treasury Jan. 1–May 13, 1801; House 1793–95 (no party); Senate 1799–May 30, 1800 (Federalist).

Dickerson, Mahlon (N.J.) April 17, 1770–Oct. 5, 1853; secretary of the navy July 1, 1834–June 30, 1838; Gov. Oct. 26, 1815–Feb. 1, 1817 (Republican); Senate 1817–Jan. 30, 1829 (Republican).

Dickinson, Donald McDonald (Mich.) Jan. 17, 1846–Oct. 15, 1917; postmaster general Jan. 17, 1888–March 5, 1889.

Dickinson, Jacob McGavock (Tenn.) Jan. 30, 1851–Dec. 13, 1928; secretary of war March 12, 1909–May 21, 1911.

Dillon, Clarence Douglas (N.J.) April 21, 1909–Jan. 10, 2003; secretary of the Treasury Jan. 21, 1961–April 1, 1965.

Dix, John Adams (N.Y.) July 24, 1798–April 21, 1879; secretary of the Treasury Jan. 15–March 6, 1861; Senate Jan. 27, 1845–49 (Democrat); Gov. Jan. 1, 1873–Jan. 1, 1875 (Republican).

Doak, William Nuckles (Va.) Dec. 12, 1882–Oct. 23, 1933; secretary of labor Dec. 9, 1930–March 4, 1933.

Dobbin, James Cochrane (N.C.) Jan. 17, 1814–Aug. 4, 1857; secretary of the navy March 8, 1853–March 6, 1857; House 1845–47 (Democrat).

Dole, Elizabeth Hanford (Kan.) July 29, 1936– ; secretary of transportation Feb. 7, 1983–Sept. 30, 1987; secretary of labor Jan. 30, 1989–Nov. 23, 1990; Senate 2003– .

Donaldson, Jesse Monroe (Mo.) Aug. 17, 1885–March 25, 1970; postmaster general Dec. 16, 1947–Jan. 20, 1953.

Donovan, Raymond James (N.J.) Aug. 31, 1930– ; secretary of labor Feb. 4, 1981–March 15, 1985.

Duane, William John (Pa.) May 9, 1780–Sept. 27, 1865; secretary of the Treasury May 29–Sept. 22, 1833.

Dulles, John Foster (N.Y.) Feb. 25, 1888–May 24, 1959; secretary of state Jan. 21, 1953–April 22, 1959; Senate July 7–Nov. 8, 1949 (Republican).

Duncan, Charles William Jr. (Texas) Sept. 9, 1926– ; secretary of energy Aug. 24, 1979–Jan. 20, 1981.

Dunlop, John Thomas (Mass.) July 5, 1914–Oct. 2, 2003; secretary of labor March 18, 1975–Jan. 31, 1976.

Durkin, Martin Patrick (Md.) March 18, 1894–Nov. 13, 1955; secretary of labor Jan. 21–Sept. 10, 1953.

Eagleburger, Lawrence Sidney (Fla.) Aug. 1, 1930– ; secretary of defense Dec. 8, 1992–Jan. 19, 1993.

Eaton, John Henry (Tenn.) June 18, 1790–Nov. 17, 1856; secretary of war March 9, 1829–June 18, 1831; Senate Sept. 5, 1818–21 (Republican), Sept. 27, 1821–March 9, 1829 (Republican); Gov. (Fla. Terr.) 1834–36.

Edison, Charles (N.J.) Aug. 3, 1890–July 31, 1969; secretary of the navy Jan. 2–June 24, 1940; Gov. Jan. 21, 1941–Jan. 18, 1944 (Democrat).

Edwards, James Burrows (S.C.) June 24, 1927– ; secretary of energy Jan. 23, 1981–Nov. 5, 1982; Gov. Jan. 21, 1975–Jan. 10, 1979.

Elkins, Stephen Benton (W.Va.) Sept. 26, 1841–Jan. 4, 1911; secretary of war Dec. 17, 1891–March 5, 1893; House (Terr. Del. N.M.) 1873–77; Senate 1895–Jan. 4, 1911 (Republican).

Endicott, William Crowninshield (Mass.) Nov. 19, 1826–May 6, 1900; secretary of war March 5, 1885–March 5, 1889.

Espy, Albert Michael "Mike" (Miss.) Nov. 30, 1953– ; secretary of agriculture Jan. 22, 1993–Dec. 31, 1994; House 1987–Jan. 22, 1993 (Democrat).

Eustis, William (Mass.) June 10, 1753–Feb. 6, 1825; secretary of war March 7, 1809–Jan. 13, 1813; House 1801–05 (Republican), Aug. 21, 1820–23 (Republican); Gov. May 31, 1823–Feb. 6, 1825 (Republican).

Evans, Donald L. (Texas) July 27, 1946– ; secretary of commerce Jan. 20, 2001–Feb. 7, 2005.

Evarts, William Maxwell (N.Y.) Feb. 6, 1818–Feb. 28, 1901; attorney general July 15, 1868–March 3, 1869; secretary of state March 12, 1877–March 7, 1881; Senate 1885–91 (Republican).

Everett, Edward (Mass.) April 11, 1794–Jan. 15, 1865; secretary of state Nov. 6, 1852–March 3, 1853; House 1825–35 (no party); Gov. Jan. 13, 1836–Jan. 18, 1840 (Whig); Senate 1853–June 1, 1854 (Whig).

Ewing, Thomas (Ohio) Dec. 28, 1789–Oct. 26, 1871; secretary of the Treasury March 4–Sept. 11, 1841; secretary of the interior March 8, 1849–July 22, 1850; Senate 1831–37 (Whig), July 20, 1850–51 (Whig).

Fairchild, Charles Stebbins (N.Y.) April 30, 1842–Nov. 24, 1924; secretary of the Treasury April 1, 1887–March 6, 1889.

Fall, Albert Bacon (N.M.) Nov. 26, 1861–Nov. 30, 1944; secretary of the interior March 5, 1921–March 4, 1923; Senate March 27, 1912–March 4, 1921 (Republican).

Farley, James Aloysius (N.Y.) May 30, 1888–June 9, 1976; postmaster general March 6, 1933–Aug. 31, 1940; chair Dem. Nat. Comm. 1932–40.

Fessenden, William Pitt (Maine) Oct. 16, 1806–Sept. 8, 1869; secretary of the Treasury July 5, 1864–March 3, 1865; House 1841–43 (Whig); Senate Feb. 10, 1854–July 1, 1864 (Feb. 10, 1854–59 Whig, 1859–July 1, 1864 Republican), 1865–Sept. 8, 1869 (Republican).

Finch, Robert Hutchinson (Calif.) Oct. 9, 1925–Oct. 10, 1995; secretary of health, education and welfare Jan. 21, 1969–June 23, 1970.

Fish, Hamilton (N.Y.) Aug. 3, 1808–Sept. 7, 1893; secretary of state March 17, 1869–March 12, 1877; House 1843–45 (Whig); Gov. Jan. 1, 1849–Jan. 1, 1851 (Whig); Senate 1851–57 (Whig).

Fisher, Walter Lowrie (Ill.) July 4, 1862–Nov. 9, 1935; secretary of the interior March 13, 1911–March 5, 1913.

Flemming, Arthur Sherwood (Ohio) June 12, 1905–Sept. 7, 1996; secretary of health, education and welfare Aug. 1, 1958–Jan. 19, 1961.

Floyd, John Buchanan (Va.) June 1, 1806–Aug. 26, 1863; secretary of war March 6, 1857–Dec. 29, 1860; Gov. Jan. 1, 1849–Jan. 16, 1852 (Democrat).

Folger, Charles James (N.Y.) April 16, 1818–Sept. 4, 1884; secretary of the Treasury Nov. 14, 1881–Sept. 4, 1884.

Folsom, Marion Bayard (N.Y.) Nov. 23, 1893–Sept. 27, 1976; secretary of health, education and welfare Aug. 1, 1955–July 31, 1958.

Forrestal, James Vincent (N.Y.) Feb. 15, 1892–May 22, 1949; secretary of the navy May 19, 1944–Sept. 17, 1947; secretary of defense Sept. 17, 1947–March 27, 1949.

Forsyth, John (Ga.) Oct. 22, 1780–Oct. 21, 1841; secretary of state July 1, 1834–March 3, 1841; House 1813–Nov. 23, 1818 (Republican), 1823–Nov. 7, 1827 (Republican); Senate Nov. 23, 1818–Feb. 17, 1819 (Republican), Nov. 9, 1829–June 27, 1834 (Jacksonian); Gov. Nov. 7, 1827–Nov. 4, 1829 (Democratic Republican).

Forward, Walter (Pa.) Jan. 24, 1786–Nov. 24, 1852; secretary of the Treasury Sept. 13, 1841–March 1, 1843; House Oct. 8, 1822–25 (no party).

Foster, Charles (Ohio) April 12, 1828–Jan. 9, 1904; secretary of the Treasury Feb. 25, 1891–March 6, 1893; Gov. Jan. 12, 1880–Jan. 14, 1884 (Republican); House 1871–79 (Republican).

Foster, John Watson (Ind.) March 2, 1836–Nov. 15, 1917; secretary of state June 29, 1892–Feb. 23, 1893.

Fowler, Henry Hamill (Va.) Sept. 5, 1908–Jan. 3, 2000; secretary of the Treasury April 1, 1965–Dec. 20, 1968.

Francis, David Rowland (Mo.) Oct. 1, 1850–Jan. 15, 1927; secretary of the interior Sept. 3, 1896–March 5, 1897; Gov. Jan. 14, 1889–Jan. 9, 1893 (Democrat).

Franklin, Barbara Hackman (Pa.) March 19, 1940– ; secretary of commerce Feb. 27, 1992–Jan. 20, 1993.

Freeman, Orville Lothrop (Minn.) May 9, 1918–Feb. 20, 2003; secretary of agriculture Jan. 21, 1961–Jan. 20, 1969; Gov. Jan. 5, 1955–Jan. 2, 1961 (Democrat Farmer Labor).

Frelinghuysen, Frederick Theodore (N.J.) Aug. 4, 1817–May 20, 1885; secretary of state Dec. 19, 1881–March 6, 1885; Senate Nov. 12, 1866–69 (Republican), 1871–77 (Republican).

Gage, Lyman Judson (Ill.) June 28, 1836–Jan. 26, 1927; secretary of the Treasury March 6, 1897–Jan. 31, 1902.

Gallatin, Albert (Pa.) Jan. 29, 1761–Aug. 12, 1849; secretary of the Treasury May 14, 1801–Feb. 8, 1814; Senate Dec. 2, 1793–Feb. 28, 1794 (no party); House 1795–1801 (no party).

Gardner, John William (N.Y.) Oct. 8, 1912–Feb. 16, 2002; secretary of health, education and welfare Aug. 18, 1965–March 1, 1968.

Garfield, James Rudolph (Ohio) Oct. 17, 1865–March 24, 1950; secretary of the interior March 5, 1907–March 5, 1909.

Garland, Augustus Hill (Ark.) June 11, 1832–Jan. 26, 1899; attorney general March 6, 1885–March 5, 1889; Gov. Nov. 12, 1874–Jan. 11, 1877 (Democrat); Senate 1877–March 6, 1885 (Democrat).

Garrison, Lindley Miller (N.J.) Nov. 28, 1864–Oct. 19, 1932; secretary of war March 5, 1913–Feb. 10, 1916.

Gary, James Albert (Md.) Oct. 22, 1833–Oct. 31, 1920; postmaster general March 6, 1897–April 22, 1898.

Gates, Thomas Sovereign Jr. (Pa.) April 10, 1906– ; secretary of defense Dec. 2, 1959–Jan. 20, 1961.

Gilmer, Thomas Walker (Va.) April 6, 1802–Feb. 28, 1844; secretary of the navy Feb. 19–Feb. 28, 1844; Gov. March 31, 1840–March 1, 1841 (Whig); House 1841–Feb. 16, 1844 (1841–43 Whig, 1843–Feb. 16, 1844 Democrat).

Gilpin, Henry Dilworth (Pa.) April 14, 1801–Jan. 29, 1860; attorney general Jan. 11, 1840–March 4, 1841.

Glass, Carter (Va.) Jan. 4, 1858–May 28, 1946; secretary of the Treasury Dec. 16, 1918–Feb. 1, 1920; House Nov. 4, 1902–Dec. 16, 1918 (Democrat); Senate Feb. 2, 1920–May 28, 1946 (Democrat); elected pres. pro tempore July 10, 1941, Jan. 5, 1943.

Glickman, Daniel R. (Kan.) Nov. 24, 1944– ; secretary of agriculture March 30, 1995–Jan. 19, 2001; House 1977–95 (Democrat).

Goff, Nathan Jr. (W.Va.) Feb. 9, 1843–April 24, 1920; secretary of the navy Jan. 7–March 6, 1881; House 1883–89 (Republican); Senate April 1, 1913–19 (Republican).

Goldberg, Arthur Joseph (D.C.) Aug. 8, 1908–Jan. 18, 1990; secretary of labor Jan. 21, 1961–Sept. 20, 1962; assoc. justice Oct. 1, 1962–July 25, 1965.

Goldschmidt, Neil (Ore.) June 16, 1940– ; secretary of transportation July 27, 1979–Jan. 20, 1981; Gov. Jan. 12, 1987–Jan. 14, 1991 (Democrat).

Gonzales, Alberto R. (Texas) Aug. 4, 1955– ; attorney general Feb. 3, 2005– .

Good, James William (Iowa) Sept. 24, 1866–Nov. 18, 1929; secretary of war March 6–Nov. 18, 1929; House 1909–June 15, 1921 (Republican).

Gore, Howard Mason (W.Va.) Oct. 12, 1877–June 20, 1947; secretary of agriculture Nov. 22, 1924–March 4, 1925; Gov. March 4, 1925–March 4, 1929 (Republican).

Graham, William Alexander (N.C.) Sept. 5, 1804–Aug. 11, 1875; secretary of the navy Aug. 2, 1850–July 25, 1852; Senate Nov. 25, 1840–43 (Whig); Gov. Jan. 1, 1845–Jan. 1, 1849 (Whig).

Granger, Francis (N.Y.) Dec. 1, 1792–Aug. 31, 1868; postmaster general March 8–Sept. 13, 1841; House 1835–37 (Whig), 1839–March 5, 1841 (Whig), Nov. 27, 1841–43 (Whig).

Granger, Gideon (Conn.) Sept. 19, 1767–Dec. 31, 1822; postmaster general Nov. 28, 1801–Feb. 25, 1814.

Gregory, Thomas Watt (Texas) Nov. 6, 1861–Feb. 26, 1933; attorney general Sept. 3, 1914–March 4, 1919.

Gresham, Walter Quintin (Ind.) March 7, 1832–May 28, 1895; secretary of the Treasury Sept. 5–Oct. 30, 1884; postmaster general April 11, 1883–Sept. 24, 1884; secretary of state March 7, 1893–May 28, 1895.

Griggs, John William (N.J.) July 10, 1849–Nov. 28, 1927; attorney general June 25, 1898–March 29, 1901; Gov. Jan. 21, 1896–Jan. 31, 1898 (Republican).

Gronouski, John A. Jr. (Wis.) Oct. 26, 1919–Jan. 7, 1996; postmaster general Sept. 30, 1963–Nov. 2, 1965.

Grundy, Felix (Tenn.) Sept. 11, 1777–Dec. 19, 1840; attorney general Sept. 1, 1838–Dec. 1, 1839; House 1811–14 (Republican); Senate Oct. 19, 1829–July 4, 1838 (Jacksonian), Nov. 19, 1839–Dec. 19, 1840 (Democrat).

Guthrie, James (Ky.) Dec. 5, 1792–March 13, 1869; secretary of the Treasury March 7, 1853–March 6, 1857; Senate 1865–Feb. 7, 1868 (Democrat).

Gutierrez, Carlos (Mich.) Nov. 4, 1953– ; secretary of commerce Feb. 7, 2005– .

Habersham, Joseph (Ga.) July 28, 1751–Nov. 17, 1815; postmaster general July 1, 1795–Nov. 2, 1801.

Haig, Alexander Meigs Jr. (Conn.) Dec. 2, 1924– ; secretary of state Jan. 22, 1981–July 5, 1982.

Hall, Nathan Kelsey (N.Y.) March 28, 1810–March 2, 1874; postmaster general July 23, 1850–Sept. 13, 1852; House 1847–49 (Whig).

Hamilton, Alexander (N.Y.) Jan. 11, 1757–July 12, 1804; secretary of the Treasury Sept. 11, 1789–Jan. 31, 1795.

Hamilton, Paul (S.C.) Oct. 16, 1762–June 30, 1816; secretary of the navy May 15, 1809–Dec. 31, 1812; Gov. Dec. 7, 1804–Dec. 9, 1806 (Democratic Republican).

Hannegan, Robert Emmet (Mo.) June 30, 1903–Oct. 6, 1949; postmaster general July 1, 1945–Dec. 15, 1947; chair Dem. Nat. Comm. 1944–47.

Hardin, Clifford Morris (Neb.) Oct. 9, 1915– ; secretary of agriculture Jan. 21, 1969–Nov. 17, 1971.

Harlan, James (Iowa) Aug. 26, 1820–Oct. 5, 1899; secretary of the interior May 15, 1865–Aug. 31, 1866; Senate Dec. 31, 1855–Jan. 12, 1857 (Free-Soiler), Jan. 29, 1857–May 15, 1865 (Republican), 1867–73 (Republican).

Harmon, Judson (Ohio) Feb. 3, 1846–Feb. 22, 1927; attorney general June 8, 1895–March 5, 1897; Gov. Jan. 11, 1909–Jan. 13, 1913 (Democrat).

Harriman, William Averell (N.Y.) Nov. 15, 1891–July 26, 1986; secretary of commerce Oct. 7, 1946–April 22, 1948; Gov. Jan 1, 1955–Jan. 1, 1959.

Harris, Patricia Roberts (Ill.) May 31, 1924–March 23, 1985; secretary of housing and urban development Jan. 23, 1977–Aug. 3, 1979; secretary of health, education and welfare Aug. 3, 1979–May 4, 1980; secretary of health and human services May 4, 1980–Jan. 20, 1981.

Hathaway, Stanley Knapp (Wyo.) July 19, 1924– ; secretary of the interior June 12–Oct. 9, 1975; Gov. Jan. 2, 1967–Jan. 6, 1975 (Republican).

Hatton, Frank (Iowa) April 28, 1846–April 30, 1894; postmaster general Oct. 15, 1884–March 6, 1885.

Hay, John Milton (D.C.) Oct. 8, 1838–July 1, 1905; secretary of state Sept. 30, 1898–July 1, 1905.

Hays, William Harrison (Ind.) Nov. 5, 1879–March 7, 1954; postmaster general March 5, 1921–March 3, 1922; chair Rep. Nat. Comm. 1918–21.

Heckler, Margaret Mary O'Shaughnessy (Mass.) June 21, 1931– ; secretary of health and human services March 9, 1983–Dec. 13, 1985; House 1967–83 (Republican).

Henshaw, David (Mass.) April 2, 1791–Nov. 11, 1852; secretary of the navy July 24, 1843–Feb. 18, 1844.

Herbert, Hilary Abner (Ala.) March 12, 1834–March 6, 1919; secretary of the navy March 7, 1893–March 5, 1897; House 1877–93 (Democrat).

Herman, Alexis (Ala.) July 16, 1947– ; secretary of labor May 1, 1997–Jan. 20, 2001.

Herrington, John Stewart (Calif.) May 31, 1939– ; secretary of energy Feb. 11, 1985–Jan. 20, 1989.

Herter, Christian Archibald (Mass.) March 28, 1895–Dec. 30, 1966; secretary of state April 22, 1959–Jan. 20, 1961; House 1943–53 (Republican); Gov. Jan. 8, 1953–Jan. 3, 1957 (Republican).

Hickel, Walter Joseph (Alaska) Aug. 18, 1919– ; secretary of the interior Jan. 24, 1969–Nov. 25, 1970; Gov. Dec. 5, 1966–Jan. 29, 1969 (Democrat), Dec. 3, 1990–Dec. 5, 1994 (Independent).

Hills, Carla Anderson (Calif.) Jan. 3, 1934– ; secretary of housing and urban development March 10, 1975–Jan. 20, 1977.

Hitchcock, Ethan Allen (Mo.) Sept. 19, 1835–April 9, 1909; secretary of the interior Feb. 20, 1899–March 4, 1907.

Hitchcock, Frank Harris (Mass.) Oct. 5, 1867–Aug. 25, 1935; postmaster general March 6, 1909–March 4, 1913; chair Rep. Nat. Comm. 1908–09.

Hoar, Ebenezer Rockwood (Mass.) Feb. 21, 1816–Jan. 31, 1895; attorney general March 5, 1869–June 23, 1870; House 1873–75 (Republican).

Hobby, Oveta Culp (Texas) Jan. 19, 1905–Aug. 16, 1995; secretary of health, education and welfare April 11, 1953–July 31, 1955.

Hodel, Donald Paul (Ore.) May 23, 1935– ; secretary of the interior Feb. 8, 1985–Jan. 20, 1989; secretary of energy Nov. 5, 1982–Feb. 7, 1985.

Hodges, Luther Hartwell (N.C.) March 9, 1898–Oct. 6, 1974; secretary of commerce Jan. 21, 1961–Jan. 15, 1965; Gov. Nov. 7, 1954–Jan. 5, 1961 (Democrat).

Hodgson, James Day (Minn.) Dec. 3, 1915– ; secretary of labor July 2, 1970–Feb. 1, 1973.

Holt, Joseph (Ky.) Jan. 6, 1807–Aug. 1, 1894; postmaster general March 14, 1859–Dec. 31, 1860; secretary of war Jan. 18–March 5, 1861.

Hoover, Herbert Clark (Calif.) Aug. 10, 1874–Oct. 20, 1964; secretary of commerce March 5, 1921–Aug. 21, 1928; president 1929–33 (Republican).

Hopkins, Harry Lloyd (N.Y.) Aug. 17, 1890–Jan. 29, 1946; secretary of commerce Dec. 24, 1938–Sept. 18, 1940.

Houston, David Franklin (Mo.) Feb. 17, 1866–Sept. 2, 1940; secretary of the Treasury Feb. 2, 1920–March 3, 1921; secretary of agriculture March 6, 1913–Feb. 2, 1920.

Howe, Timothy Otis (Wis.) Feb. 24, 1816–March 25, 1883; postmaster general Jan. 5, 1882–March 25, 1883; Senate 1861–79 (Republican).

Hubbard, Samuel Dickinson (Conn.) Aug. 10, 1799–Oct. 8, 1855; postmaster general Sept. 14, 1852–March 7, 1853; House 1845–49 (Whig).

Hufstedler, Shirley Mount (Calif.) Aug. 24, 1925– ; secretary of education Dec. 6, 1979–Jan. 19, 1981.

Hughes, Charles Evans (N.Y.) April 11, 1862–Aug. 27, 1948; secretary of state March 5, 1921–March 4, 1925; Gov. Jan. 1, 1907–Oct. 6, 1910 (Republican); assoc. justice Oct. 10, 1910–June 10, 1916; chief justice Feb. 24, 1930–July 1, 1941.

Hull, Cordell (Tenn.) Oct. 2, 1871–July 23, 1955; secretary of state March 4, 1933–Nov. 30, 1944; House 1907–21 (Democrat), 1923–31 (Democrat); chair Dem. Nat. Comm. 1921–24; Senate 1931–March 3, 1933 (Democrat).

Humphrey, George Magoffin (Ohio) March 8, 1890–Jan. 20, 1970; secretary of the Treasury Jan. 21, 1953–July 29, 1957.

Hunt, William Henry (La.) June 12, 1823–Feb. 27, 1884; secretary of the navy March 7, 1881–April 16, 1882.

Hurley, Patrick Jay (Okla.) Jan. 8, 1883–July 30, 1963; secretary of war Dec. 9, 1929–March 3, 1933.

Hyde, Arthur Mastick (Mo.) July 12, 1877–Oct. 17, 1947; secretary of agriculture March 6, 1929–March 4, 1933; Gov. Jan. 10, 1921–Jan. 12, 1925 (Republican).

Ickes, Harold LeClair (Ill.) March 15, 1874–Feb. 3, 1952; secretary of the interior March 4, 1933–Feb. 15, 1946.

Ingham, Samuel Delucenna (Pa.) Sept. 16, 1779–June 5, 1860; secretary of the Treasury March 6, 1829–June 20, 1831; House 1813–July 6, 1818 (Republican), Oct. 8, 1822–29 (Republican).

Jackson, Alphonso Roy (Texas) Sept. 9, 1945– ; secretary of housing and urban development April 1, 2004– .

Jackson, Robert Houghwout (N.Y.) Feb. 13, 1892–Oct. 9, 1954; attorney general Jan. 18, 1940–July 10, 1941; assoc. justice July 11, 1941–Oct. 9, 1954.

James, Thomas Lemuel (N.Y.) March 29, 1831–Sept. 11, 1916; postmaster general March 8, 1881–Jan. 4, 1882.

Jardine, William Marion (Kan.) Jan. 16, 1879–Jan. 17, 1955; secretary of agriculture March 5, 1925–March 4, 1929.

Jay, John (N.Y.) Dec. 12, 1745–May 17, 1829; secretary of Foreign Affairs 1784–89; Cont. Cong. 1774–76, 1778–79 (president); Gov. July 1, 1795–June 30, 1801 (Federalist); chief justice Oct. 19, 1789–June 29, 1795.

Jefferson, Thomas (Va.) April 13, 1743–July 4, 1826; secretary of state March 22, 1790–Dec. 31, 1793; Cont. Cong. 1775–76, 1783–84; Gov. (Colonial) 1779–June 1781; vice president 1797–1801 (Democratic Republican); president 1801–09 (Democratic Republican).

Jewell, Marshall (Conn.) Oct. 20, 1825–Feb. 10, 1883; postmaster general Sept. 1, 1874–July 12, 1876; Gov. May 5, 1869–May 4, 1870 (Republican), May 16, 1871–May 7, 1873 (Republican); chair Rep. Nat. Comm. 1880–83.

Johanns, Mike (Neb.) June 18, 1950– ; secretary of agriculture Jan. 21, 2005– ; Gov. Jan. 7, 1999–Jan. 20, 2005 (Republican).

Johnson, Cave (Tenn.) Jan. 11, 1793–Nov. 23, 1866; postmaster general March 7, 1845–March 5, 1849; House 1829–37 (Jacksonian), 1839–45 (Democrat).

Johnson, Louis Arthur (W.Va.) Jan. 10, 1891–April 24, 1956; secretary of defense March 28, 1949–Sept. 19, 1950.

Johnson, Reverdy (Md.) May 21, 1796–Feb. 10, 1876; attorney general March 8, 1849–July 20, 1850; Senate 1845–March 7, 1849 (Whig), 1863–July 10, 1868 (Democrat).

Jones, Jesse Holman (Texas) April 5, 1874–June 1, 1956; secretary of commerce Sept. 19, 1940–March 1, 1945.

Jones, William (Pa.) 1760–Sept. 6, 1831; secretary of the navy Jan. 19, 1813–Dec. 1, 1814; House 1801–03 (Republican).

Kantor, Michael "Mickey" (Calif.) Aug. 7, 1939– ; secretary of commerce, April 12, 1996–Jan. 21, 1997.

Katzenbach, Nicholas de Belleville (D.C.) Jan. 17, 1922– ; attorney general Feb. 11, 1965–Oct. 2, 1966.

Kellogg, Frank Billings (Minn.) Dec. 22, 1856–Dec. 21, 1937; secretary of state March 5, 1925–March 28, 1929; Senate 1917–23 (Republican).

Kemp, Jack French (N.Y.) July 13, 1935– ; secretary of housing and urban development Feb. 13, 1989–Jan. 20, 1993; House 1971–89 (Republican).

Kendall, Amos (Ky.) Aug. 16, 1789–Nov. 12, 1869; postmaster general May 1, 1835–May 25, 1840.

Kennedy, David Matthew (Utah) July 21, 1905–May 1, 1996; secretary of the Treasury Jan. 22, 1969–Feb. 10, 1971.

Kennedy, John Pendleton (Md.) Oct. 25, 1795–Aug. 18, 1870; secretary of the navy July 26, 1852–March 7, 1853; House April 25, 1838–39 (Whig), 1841–45 (Whig).

Kennedy, Robert Francis (N.Y.) Nov. 20, 1925–June 6, 1968; attorney general Jan. 21, 1961–Sept. 3, 1964; Senate 1965–June 6, 1968 (Democrat).

Key, David McKendree (Tenn.) Jan. 27, 1824–Feb. 3, 1900; postmaster general March 13, 1877–Aug. 24, 1880; Senate Aug. 18, 1875–Jan. 19, 1877 (Democrat).

King, Horatio (Maine) June 21, 1811–May 20, 1897; postmaster general Feb. 12–March 9, 1861.

Kirkwood, Samuel Jordan (Iowa) Dec. 20, 1813–Sept. 1, 1894; secretary of the interior March 8, 1881–April 17, 1882; Gov. Jan. 11, 1860–Jan. 14, 1864 (Republican), Jan. 13, 1876–Feb. 1, 1877 (Republican); Senate Jan. 13, 1866–67 (Republican), 1877–March 7, 1881 (Republican).

Kissinger, Henry Alfred (D.C.) May 27, 1923– ; secretary of state Sept. 22, 1973–Jan. 20, 1977.

Kleindienst, Richard Gordon (Ariz.) Aug. 5, 1923–Feb. 3, 2000; attorney general June 12, 1972–May 24, 1973.

Kleppe, Thomas Savig (N.D.) July 1, 1919– ; secretary of the interior Oct. 17, 1975–Jan. 20, 1977; House 1967–71 (Republican).

Klutznick, Philip M. (Ill.) July 9, 1907–Aug. 14, 1999; secretary of commerce Jan. 9, 1980–Jan. 19, 1981.

Knebel, John Albert (Va.) Oct. 4, 1936– ; secretary of agriculture Nov. 4, 1976–Jan. 20, 1977.

Knox, Henry (Mass.) July 25, 1750–Oct. 21, 1806; secretary of war Sept. 12, 1789–Dec. 31, 1794.

Knox, Philander Chase (Pa.) May 6, 1853–Oct. 12, 1921; attorney general April 5, 1901–June 30, 1904; secretary of state March 6, 1909–March 5, 1913; Senate June 10, 1904–March 4, 1909 (Republican), 1917–Oct. 12, 1921 (Republican).

Knox, William Franklin "Frank" (Ill.) Jan. 1, 1874–April 28, 1944; secretary of the navy July 11, 1940–April 28, 1944.

Kreps, Juanita Morris (Ky.) Jan. 11, 1921– ; secretary of commerce Jan. 23, 1977–Oct. 31, 1979.

Krug, Julius Albert (Wis.) Nov. 23, 1907–March 26, 1970; secretary of the interior March 18, 1946–Dec. 1, 1949.

Laird, Melvin Robert (Wis.) Sept. 1, 1922– ; secretary of defense Jan. 22, 1969–Jan. 29, 1973; House 1953–Jan. 21, 1969 (Republican).

Lamar, Lucius Quintus Cincinnatus (Miss.) Sept. 17, 1825–Jan. 23, 1893; secretary of the interior March 6, 1885–Jan. 10, 1888; House 1857–Dec. 1860 (Democrat), 1873–77 (Democrat); Senate 1877–March 6, 1885 (Democrat); assoc. justice Jan. 18, 1888–Jan. 23, 1893.

Lamont, Daniel Scott (N.Y.) Feb. 9, 1851–July 23, 1905; secretary of war March 5, 1893–March 5, 1897.

Lamont, Robert Patterson (Ill.) Dec. 1, 1867–Feb. 20, 1948; secretary of commerce March 5, 1929–Aug. 7, 1932.

Landrieu, Maurice Edwin "Moon" (La.) July 23, 1930– ; secretary of housing and urban development Sept. 24, 1979–Jan. 20, 1981.

Lane, Franklin Knight (Calif.) July 15, 1864–May 18, 1921; secretary of the interior March 6, 1913–Feb. 29, 1920.

Lansing, Robert (N.Y.) Oct. 17, 1864–Oct. 30, 1928; secretary of state June 24, 1915–Feb. 13, 1920.

Leavitt, Michael Okerlund (Utah) Feb. 11, 1951– ; secretary of health and human services Jan. 26, 2005– ; Gov. Jan. 3, 1993–Nov. 5, 2003 (Republican).

Lee, Charles (Va.) July 1758–June 24, 1815; attorney general Dec. 10, 1795–Feb. 18, 1801.

Legare, Hugh Swinton (S.C.) Jan. 2, 1797–June 20, 1843; attorney general Sept. 13, 1841–June 20, 1843; House 1837–39 (Democrat).

Levi, Edward Hirsh (Ill.) June 26, 1911–March 7, 2000; attorney general Feb. 6, 1975–Jan. 20, 1977.

Lewis, Andrew Lindsay "Drew" Jr. (N.Y.) Nov. 3, 1931– ; secretary of transportation Jan. 23, 1981–Feb. 1, 1983.

Lincoln, Levi (Mass.) May 15, 1749–April 14, 1820; attorney general March 5, 1801–March 3, 1805; House Dec. 15, 1800–March 5, 1801 (Republican); Gov. Dec. 10, 1808–May 1, 1809 (Democratic Republican); Cont. Cong. (elected but did not attend) 1781.

Lincoln, Robert Todd (Ill.) Aug. 1, 1843–July 25, 1926; secretary of war March 5, 1881–March 5, 1885.

Livingston, Edward (La.) May 28, 1764–May 23, 1836; secretary of state May 24, 1831–May 29, 1833; House 1795–1801 (no party N.Y.), 1823–29 (no party); Senate 1829–May 24, 1831 (no party).

Long, John Davis (Mass.) Oct. 27, 1838–Aug. 28, 1915; secretary of the navy March 6, 1897–April 30, 1902; Gov. Jan. 8, 1880–Jan. 4, 1883 (Republican); House 1883–89 (Republican).

Lovett, Robert Abercrombie (N.Y.) Sept. 14, 1895–May 7, 1986; secretary of defense Sept. 17, 1951–Jan. 20, 1953.

Lujan, Manuel Jr. (N.M.) May 12, 1928– ; secretary of the interior Feb. 8, 1989–Jan. 20, 1993; House 1969–89.

Lyng, Richard Edmund (Calif.) June 29, 1918–Feb. 1, 2003; secretary of agriculture March 7, 1986–Jan. 20, 1989.

Lynn, James Thomas (Ohio) Feb. 27, 1927– ; secretary of housing and urban development Feb. 2, 1973–Feb. 10, 1975.

MacVeagh, Franklin (Ill.) Nov. 22, 1837–July 6, 1934; secretary of the Treasury March 8, 1909–March 5, 1913.

MacVeagh, Wayne (Pa.) April 19, 1833–Jan. 11, 1917; attorney general March 7–Oct. 24, 1881.

Madigan, Edward Rell (Ill.) Jan. 13, 1936–Dec. 7, 1994; secretary of agriculture March 12, 1991–Jan. 20, 1993; House 1973–March 8, 1991.

Madison, James (Va.) March 16, 1751–June 28, 1836; secretary of state May 2, 1801–March 3, 1809; Cont. Cong. 1780–83, 1787–88; House 1789–97 (1789–95 no party, 1795–97 Republican); president 1809–17 (Democratic Republican).

Manning, Daniel (N.Y.) Aug. 16, 1831–Dec. 24, 1887; secretary of the Treasury March 8, 1885–March 31, 1887.

Marcy, William Learned (N.Y.) Dec. 12, 1786–July 4, 1857; secretary of war March 6, 1845–March 4, 1849; secretary of state March 8, 1853–March 6, 1857; Senate 1831–Jan. 1, 1833 (Jacksonian); Gov. Jan. 1, 1833–Jan. 1, 1839 (Jacksonian).

Marshall, Freddie Ray (La.) Aug. 22, 1928– ; secretary of labor Jan. 27, 1977–Jan. 20, 1981.

Marshall, George Catlett (Pa.) Dec. 31, 1880–Oct. 16, 1959; secretary of state Jan. 21, 1947–Jan. 20, 1949; secretary of defense Sept. 21, 1950–Sept. 12, 1951.

Marshall, James William (Va.) Aug. 14, 1822–Feb. 5, 1910; postmaster general July 7–Aug. 31, 1874.

Marshall, John (Va.) Sept. 24, 1755–July 6, 1835; secretary of state June 6, 1800–Feb. 4, 1801; House 1799–June 7, 1800 (Federalist); chief justice Feb. 4, 1801–July 6, 1835.

Martin, Lynn Morley (Ill.) Dec. 26, 1939– ; secretary of labor Feb. 22, 1991–Jan. 20, 1993; House 1981–91 (Republican).

Martinez, Melquiades Rafael "Mel" (Fla.) Oct. 23, 1946– ; secretary of housing and urban development Jan. 24, 2001–Dec. 9, 2003; Senate 2005– .

Mason, John Young (Va.) April 18, 1799–Oct. 3, 1859; secretary of the navy March 26, 1844–March 10, 1845, Sept. 10, 1846–March 7, 1849; attorney general March 11, 1845–Sept. 9, 1846; House 1831–Jan. 11, 1837 (Jacksonian).

Matthews, Forrest David (Ala.) Dec. 6, 1935– ; secretary of health, education and welfare Aug. 8, 1975–Jan. 20, 1977.

Maynard, Horace (Tenn.) Aug. 30, 1814–May 3, 1882; postmaster general Aug. 25, 1880–March 7, 1881; House 1857–63 (1857–59 American Party, 1859–61 Opposition Party, 1861–63 Unionist), July 24, 1866–75 (July 24, 1866–67 Unconditional Unionist, 1867–75 Republican).

McAdoo, William Gibbs (Calif.) Oct. 31, 1863–Feb. 1, 1941; secretary of the Treasury March 6, 1913–Dec. 15, 1918; Senate 1933–Nov. 8, 1938 (Democrat).

McClelland, Robert (Mich.) Aug. 1, 1807–Aug. 30, 1880; secretary of the interior March 8, 1853–March 9, 1857; House 1843–49 (Democrat); Gov. Jan. 1, 1851–March 7, 1853 (Democrat).

McCrary, George Washington (Iowa) Aug. 29, 1835–June 23, 1890; secretary of war March 12, 1877–Dec. 10, 1879; House 1869–77 (Republican).

McCulloch, Hugh (Ind.) Dec. 7, 1808–May 24, 1895; secretary of the Treasury March 9, 1865–March 3, 1869, Oct. 31, 1884–March 7, 1885.

McElroy, Neil Hosler (Ohio) Oct. 30, 1904–Nov. 30, 1972; secretary of defense Oct. 9, 1957–Dec. 1, 1959.

McGranery, James Patrick (Pa.) July 8, 1895–Dec. 23, 1962; attorney general May 27, 1952–Jan. 20, 1953; House 1937–Nov. 17, 1943 (Democrat).

McGrath, James Howard (R.I.) Nov. 28, 1903–Sept. 2, 1966; attorney general Aug. 24, 1949–April 7, 1952; Gov. Jan. 7, 1941–Oct. 6, 1945 (Democrat); Senate 1947–Aug. 23, 1949 (Democrat); chair Dem. Nat. Comm. 1947–49.

McHenry, James (Md.) Nov. 16, 1753–May 3, 1816; secretary of war Jan. 27, 1796–May 13, 1800.

McKay, Douglas James (Ore.) June 24, 1893–July 22, 1959; secretary of the interior Jan. 21, 1953–April 15, 1956; Gov. Jan. 10, 1949–Dec. 27, 1952 (Republican).

McKenna, Joseph (Calif.) Aug. 10, 1843–Nov. 21, 1926; attorney general March 5, 1897–Jan. 25, 1898; House 1885–March 28, 1892 (Republican); assoc. justice Jan. 26, 1898–Jan. 5, 1925.

McKennan, Thomas McKean Thompson (Pa.) March 31, 1794–July 9, 1852; secretary of the interior Aug. 15–Aug. 26, 1850; House 1831–39 (Anti-Masonic), May 30, 1842–43 (Whig).

McLane, Louis (Del.) May 28, 1786–Oct. 7, 1857; secretary of the Treasury Aug. 8, 1831–May 28, 1833; secretary of state May 29, 1833–June 30, 1834; House 1817–27 (no party); Senate 1827–April 16, 1829 (no party).

McLaughlin, Ann Dore (D.C.) Nov. 18, 1941– ; secretary of labor Dec. 17, 1987–Jan. 20, 1989.

McLean, John (Ohio) March 11, 1785–April 4, 1861; postmaster general July 1, 1823–March 9, 1829; House 1813–16 (Republican); assoc. justice Jan. 11, 1830–April 4, 1861.

McNamara, Robert Strange (Mich.) June 9, 1916– ; secretary of defense Jan. 21, 1961–Feb. 29, 1968.

McReynolds, James Clark (Tenn.) Feb. 3, 1862–Aug. 24, 1946; attorney general March 5, 1913–Aug. 29, 1914; assoc. justice Oct. 12, 1914–Jan. 31, 1941.

Meese, Edwin III (Calif.) Dec. 2, 1931– ; attorney general Feb. 25, 1985–Aug. 12, 1988.

Meigs, Return Jonathan Jr. (Ohio) Nov. 17, 1764–March 29, 1825; postmaster general April 11, 1814–June 30, 1823; Senate Dec. 12, 1808–May 1, 1810 (Republican); Gov. Dec. 8, 1810–March 24, 1814 (Democratic Republican).

Mellon, Andrew William (Pa.) March 24, 1855–Aug. 26, 1937; secretary of the Treasury March 4, 1921–Feb. 12, 1932.

Meredith, Edwin Thomas (Iowa) Dec. 23, 1876–June 17, 1928; secretary of agriculture Feb. 2, 1920–March 4, 1921.

Meredith, William Morris (Pa.) June 8, 1799–Aug. 17, 1873; secretary of the Treasury March 8, 1849–July 22, 1850.

Metcalf, Victor Howard (Calif.) Oct. 10, 1853–Feb. 20, 1936; secretary of commerce and labor July 1, 1904–Dec. 16, 1906; secretary of the navy Dec. 17, 1906–Nov. 30, 1908; House 1899–July 1, 1904 (Republican).

Meyer, George von Lengerke (Mass.) June 24, 1858–March 9, 1918; postmaster general March 4, 1907–March 5, 1909; secretary of the navy March 6, 1909–March 4, 1913.

Miller, George William (R.I.) March 9, 1925– ; secretary of the Treasury Aug. 7, 1979–Jan. 20, 1981.

Miller, William Henry Harrison (Ind.) Sept. 6, 1840–May 25, 1917; attorney general March 5, 1889–March 6, 1893.

Mills, Ogden Livingston (N.Y.) Aug. 23, 1884–Oct. 11, 1937; secretary of the Treasury Feb. 13, 1932–March 4, 1933; House 1921–27 (Republican).

Mineta, Norman Yoshio (Calif.) Nov. 12, 1941– ; secretary of commerce July 21, 2000–Jan. 19, 2001; secretary of transportation Jan. 25, 2001– ; House 1975–Oct. 10, 1995 (Democrat).

Mitchell, James Paul (N.J.) Nov. 12, 1900–Oct. 19, 1964; secretary of labor Oct. 9, 1953–Jan. 20, 1961.

Mitchell, John Newton (N.Y.) Sept. 15, 1913–Nov. 9, 1988; attorney general Jan. 21, 1969–March 1, 1972.

Mitchell, William DeWitt (Minn.) Sept. 9, 1874–Aug. 24, 1955; attorney general March 5, 1929–March 3, 1933.

Monroe, James (Va.) April 28, 1758–July 4, 1831; secretary of state April 6, 1811–Sept. 30, 1814, Feb. 28, 1815–March 3, 1817; secretary of war Oct. 1, 1814–Feb. 28, 1815; Cont. Cong. 1783–86; Senate Nov. 9, 1790–May 27, 1794 (no party); Gov. Dec. 1, 1799–Dec. 1, 1802 (Democratic Republican), Jan. 16–April 3, 1811 (Democratic Republican); president 1817–25 (Democratic Republican).

Moody, William Henry (Mass.) Dec. 23, 1853–July 2, 1917; secretary of the navy May 1, 1902–June 30, 1904; attorney general July 1, 1904–Dec. 17, 1906; House Nov. 5, 1895–May 1, 1902 (Republican); assoc. justice Dec. 17, 1906–Nov. 20, 1910.

Morgenthau, Henry Jr. (N.Y.) May 11, 1891–Feb. 6, 1967; secretary of the Treasury Jan. 1, 1934–July 22, 1945.

Morrill, Lot Myrick (Maine) May 3, 1813–Jan. 10, 1883; secretary of the Treasury July 7, 1876–March 9, 1877; Gov. Jan. 8, 1858–Jan. 2, 1861 (Republican); Senate Jan. 17, 1861–69 (Republican), Oct. 30, 1869–July 7, 1876 (Republican).

Morton, Julius Sterling (Neb.) April 22, 1832–April 27, 1902; secretary of agriculture March 7, 1893–March 5, 1897.

Morton, Paul (Ill.) May 22, 1857–Feb. 19, 1911; secretary of the navy July 1, 1904–July 1, 1905.

Morton, Rogers Clark Ballard (Md.) Sept. 19, 1914–April 19, 1979; secretary of the interior Jan. 29, 1971–April 30, 1975; secretary of commerce May 1, 1975–Feb. 2, 1976; House 1963–Jan. 29, 1971 (Republican); chair Rep. Nat. Comm. April 1969–Jan. 1971.

Mosbacher, Robert Adam (Texas) March 11, 1927– ; secretary of commerce Feb. 3, 1989–Jan. 15, 1992.

Mueller, Frederick Henry (Mich.) Nov. 22, 1893–Aug. 31, 1976; secretary of commerce Aug. 10, 1959–Jan. 19, 1961.

Murphy, Francis William (Mich.) April 13, 1890–July 19, 1949; attorney general Jan. 17, 1939–Jan. 18, 1940; Gov. Jan. 1, 1937–Jan. 1, 1939 (Democrat); assoc. justice Feb. 5, 1940–July 19, 1949.

Muskie, Edmund Sixtus (Maine) March 28, 1914–March 26, 1996; secretary of state May 8, 1980–Jan. 18, 1981; Gov. Jan. 5, 1955–Jan. 3, 1959 (Democrat); Senate 1959–May 7, 1980 (Democrat).

Nagel, Charles (Mo.) Aug. 9, 1849–June 5, 1940; secretary of commerce and labor March 6, 1909–March 4, 1913.

Nelson, John (Md.) June 1, 1794–Jan. 18, 1860; attorney general July 1, 1843–March 3, 1845; House 1821–23 (no party).

New, Harry Stewart (Ind.) Dec. 31, 1858–May 9, 1937; postmaster general March 4, 1923–March 5, 1929; chair Rep. Nat. Comm. 1907–08; Senate 1917–23 (Republican).

Newberry, Truman Handy (Mich.) Nov. 5, 1864–Oct. 3, 1945; secretary of the navy Dec. 1, 1908–March 5, 1909; Senate 1919–Nov. 18, 1922 (Republican).

Nicholson, Jim (Colo.) Feb. 4, 1938– ; secretary of veterans affairs Jan. 26, 2005– ; chair Rep. Nat. Comm. 1997–2001.

Niles, John Milton (Conn.) Aug. 20, 1787–May 31, 1856; postmaster general May 26, 1840–March 3, 1841; Senate Dec. 21, 1835–39 (Democrat), 1843–49 (Democrat).

Noble, John Willock (Mo.) Oct. 26, 1831–March 22, 1912; secretary of the interior March 7, 1889–March 6, 1893.

Norton, Gale A. (Kans.) March 11, 1954– ; secretary of the interior Jan. 31, 2001– .

O'Brien, Lawrence Francis (Mass.) July 7, 1917–September 27, 1990; postmaster general Nov. 3, 1965–April 26, 1968; chair Dem. Nat. Comm. 1968–69, 1970–72.

O'Leary, Hazel Rollins (Minn.) May 17, 1937– ; secretary of energy Jan. 22, 1993–Jan. 20, 1997.

Olney, Richard (Mass.) Sept. 15, 1835–April 8, 1917; attorney general March 6, 1893–June 7, 1895; secretary of state June 10, 1895–March 5, 1897.

O'Neill, Paul H. (Mo.) Dec. 4, 1935– ; secretary of the Treasury Jan. 20, 2001–Dec. 31, 2002.

Osgood, Samuel (Mass.) Feb. 3, 1748–Aug. 12, 1813; postmaster general Sept. 26, 1789–Aug. 18, 1791.

Paige, Rod (Miss.) June 17, 1933– ; secretary of education Jan. 24, 2001–Jan. 20, 2005.

Palmer, Alexander Mitchell (Pa.) May 4, 1872–May 11, 1936; attorney general March 5, 1919–March 5, 1921; House 1909–15 (Democrat).

Patterson, Robert Porter (N.Y.) Feb. 12, 1891–Jan. 22, 1952; secretary of war Sept. 27, 1945–July 18, 1947.

Paulding, James Kirke (N.Y.) Aug. 22, 1778–April 6, 1860; secretary of the navy July 1, 1838–March 3, 1841.

Payne, Henry Clay (Wis.) Nov. 23, 1843–Oct. 4, 1904; postmaster general Jan. 15, 1902–Oct. 4, 1904; chair Rep. Nat. Comm. 1904.

Payne, John Barton (Ill.) Jan. 26, 1855–Jan. 24, 1935; secretary of the interior March 15, 1920–March 4, 1921.

Pena, Federico Fabian (Colo.) March 15, 1947– ; secretary of transportation Jan. 22, 1993–Feb. 14, 1997; secretary of energy March 12, 1997–June 30, 1998.

Perkins, Frances (N.Y.) April 10, 1882–May 14, 1965; secretary of labor March 4, 1933–June 30, 1945.

Perry, William James (Calif.) Oct. 11, 1927– ; secretary of defense Feb. 3, 1994–Jan. 22, 1997.

Peterson, Peter George (Neb.) June 5, 1926– ; secretary of commerce Feb. 29, 1972–Feb. 1, 1973.

Pickering, Timothy (Mass.) July 17, 1745–Jan. 29, 1829; postmaster general Aug. 19, 1791–Jan. 2, 1795; secretary of war Jan. 2–Dec. 10, 1795; secretary of state Dec. 10, 1795–May 12, 1800; Senate 1803–11 (Federalist); House 1813–17 (Federalist).

Pierce, Samuel Riley Jr. (N.Y.) Sept. 8, 1922–Oct. 31, 2000; secretary of housing and urban development Jan. 23, 1981–Jan. 20, 1989.

Pierrepont, Edwards (N.Y.) March 4, 1817–March 6, 1892; attorney general May 15, 1875–May 22, 1876.

Pinkney, William (Md.) March 17, 1764–Feb. 25, 1822; attorney general Dec. 11, 1811–Feb. 10, 1814; House March 4–Nov. 1791 (no party), 1815–April 18, 1816 (no party); Senate Dec. 21, 1819–Feb. 25, 1822 (Republican).

Poinsett, Joel Roberts (S.C.) March 2, 1779–Dec. 12, 1851; secretary of war March 7, 1837–March 5, 1841; House 1821–March 7, 1825 (Democrat).

Porter, James Madison (Pa.) Jan. 6, 1793–Nov. 11, 1862; secretary of war March 8, 1843–Jan. 30, 1844.

Porter, Peter Buell (N.Y.) Aug. 14, 1773–March 20, 1844; secretary of war May 26, 1828–March 9, 1829; House 1809–13 (Republican), 1815–Jan. 23, 1816 (Republican).

Powell, Colin L. (N.Y.) April 5, 1937– ; secretary of state Jan. 20, 2001–Jan. 26, 2005.

Preston, William Ballard (Va.) Nov. 25, 1805–Nov. 16, 1862; secretary of the navy March 8, 1849–July 22, 1850; House 1847–49 (Whig).

Principi, Anthony J. (N.Y.) April 16, 1944– ; secretary of veterans affairs Jan. 24, 2001–Jan. 24, 2005.

Proctor, Redfield (Vt.) June 1, 1831–March 4, 1908; secretary of war March 5, 1889–Nov. 5, 1891; Gov. Oct. 3, 1878–Oct. 7, 1880 (Republican); Senate Nov. 2, 1891–March 4, 1908 (Republican).

Ramsey, Alexander (Minn.) Sept. 8, 1815–April 22, 1903; secretary of war Dec. 10, 1879–March 5, 1881; House 1843–47 (Whig Pa.); Gov. April 2, 1849–53 (Minn. Terr.), Jan. 2, 1860–July 10, 1863 (Republican); Senate 1863–75 (Republican).

Randall, Alexander Williams (Wis.) Oct. 31, 1819–July 26, 1872; postmaster general July 25, 1866–March 4, 1869; Gov. Jan. 4, 1858–Jan. 6, 1862 (Republican).

Randolph, Edmund Jennings (Va.) Aug. 10, 1753–Sept. 13, 1813; attorney general Sept. 26, 1789–Jan. 2, 1794; secretary of state Jan. 2, 1794–Aug. 20, 1795.

Rawlins, John Aaron (Ill.) Feb. 13, 1831–Sept. 6, 1869; secretary of war March 13–Sept. 6, 1869.

Redfield, William Cox (N.Y.) June 18, 1858–June 13, 1932; secretary of commerce March 5, 1913–Oct. 31, 1919; House 1911–13 (Democrat).

Regan, Donald Thomas (N.J.) Dec. 21, 1918–June 10, 2003; secretary of the Treasury Jan. 22, 1981–Feb. 1, 1985.

Reich, Robert Bernard (Mass.) June 24, 1946– ; secretary of labor Jan. 22, 1993–Jan. 10, 1997.

Reno, Janet (Fla.) July 21, 1938– ; attorney general March 12, 1993–Jan. 20, 2001.

Ribicoff, Abraham Alexander (Conn.) April 9, 1910–Feb. 22, 1998; secretary of health, education and welfare Jan. 21, 1961–July 13, 1962; House 1949–53 (Democrat); Gov. Jan. 5, 1955–Jan. 21, 1961 (Democrat); Senate 1963–81 (Democrat).

Rice, Condoleeza (D.C.) Nov. 14, 1954– ; secretary of state Jan. 26, 2005– .

Richardson, Elliot Lee (Mass.) July 20, 1920–Dec. 31, 1999; secretary of health, education and welfare June 24, 1970–Jan. 29, 1973; secretary of defense Jan. 30–May 24, 1973; attorney general May 25–Oct. 20, 1973; secretary of commerce Feb. 2, 1976–Jan. 20, 1977.

Richardson, William Adams (Mass.) Nov. 2, 1821–Oct. 19, 1896; secretary of the Treasury March 17, 1873–June 3, 1874.

Richardson, William Blaine (N.M.) Nov. 15, 1947– ; secretary of energy Aug. 18, 1998–Jan. 20, 2001; House 1983–Feb. 13, 1997; Gov. Jan. 1, 2003– .

Ridge, Thomas Joseph (Penn.) Aug. 26, 1945– ; secretary of homeland security Jan. 24, 2003–Feb. 1, 2005; Gov. Jan. 17, 1995–Oct. 5, 2001 (Republican).

Riley, Richard Wilson (S.C.) Jan. 2, 1933– ; secretary of education Jan. 22, 1993–Jan. 20, 2001; Gov. Jan. 10, 1979–Jan. 14, 1987 (Democrat).

Robeson, George Maxwell (N.J.) March 16, 1829–Sept. 27, 1897; secretary of the navy June 26, 1869–March 12, 1877; House 1879–83 (Republican).

Rodney, Caesar Augustus (Del.) Jan. 4, 1772–June 10, 1824; attorney general Jan. 20, 1807–Dec. 11, 1811; House 1803–05 (Republican), 1821–Jan. 24, 1822 (Republican); Senate Jan. 24, 1822–Jan. 29, 1823 (Republican).

Rogers, William Pierce (Md.) June 23, 1913–Jan. 2, 2001; attorney general Nov. 8, 1957–Jan. 20, 1961; secretary of state Jan. 22, 1969–Sept. 3, 1973.

Romney, George Wilcken (Mich.) July 8, 1907–July 26, 1995; secretary of housing and urban development Jan. 20, 1969–Feb. 2, 1973; Gov. Jan. 1, 1963–Jan. 22, 1969 (Republican).

Root, Elihu (N.Y.) Feb. 15, 1845–Feb. 7, 1937; secretary of war Aug. 1, 1899–Jan. 31, 1904; secretary of state July 19, 1905–Jan. 27, 1909; Senate 1909–15 (Republican).

Roper, Daniel Calhoun (S.C.) April 1, 1867–April 11, 1943; secretary of commerce March 4, 1933–Dec. 23, 1938.

Royall, Kenneth Claiborne (N.C.) July 24, 1894–May 27, 1971; secretary of war July 19–Sept. 17, 1947.

Rubin, Robert (N.Y.) Aug. 29, 1938– ; secretary of the Treasury Jan. 10, 1995–July 2, 1999.

Rumsfeld, Donald Henry (Ill.) July 9, 1932– ; secretary of defense Nov. 20, 1975–Jan. 20, 1977, Jan. 20, 2001– ; House 1963–May 25, 1969 (Republican).

Rush, Richard (Pa.) Aug. 29, 1780–July 30, 1859; attorney general Feb. 10, 1814–Nov. 13, 1817; secretary of the Treasury March 7, 1825–March 5, 1829.

Rusk, David Dean (N.Y.) Feb. 9, 1909–Dec. 20, 1994; secretary of state Jan. 21, 1961–Jan. 20, 1969.

Rusk, Jeremiah McLain (Wis.) June 17, 1830–Nov. 21, 1893; secretary of agriculture March 6, 1889–March 6, 1893; House 1871–77 (Republican); Gov. Jan. 2, 1882–Jan. 7, 1889 (Republican).

Sargent, John Garibaldi (Vt.) Oct. 13, 1860–March 5, 1939; attorney general March 17, 1925–March 5, 1929.

Sawyer, Charles (Ohio) Feb. 10, 1887–April 7, 1979; secretary of commerce May 6, 1948–Jan. 20, 1953.

Saxbe, William Bart (Ohio) June 24, 1916– ; attorney general Jan. 4, 1974–Feb. 3, 1975; Senate 1969–Jan. 3, 1974.

Schlesinger, James Rodney (Va.) Feb. 15, 1929– ; secretary of defense July 2, 1973–Nov. 19, 1975; secretary of energy Aug. 6, 1977–Aug. 23, 1979.

Schofield, John McAllister (Ill.) Sept. 29, 1831–March 4, 1906; secretary of war June 1, 1868–March 13, 1869.

Schurz, Carl (Mo.) March 2, 1829–May 14, 1906; secretary of the interior March 12, 1877–March 7, 1881; Senate 1869–75 (Republican).

Schweiker, Richard Schultz (Pa.) June 1, 1926– ; secretary of health and human services Jan. 22, 1981–Feb. 3, 1983; House 1961–69 (Republican); Senate 1969–81 (Republican).

Schwellenbach, Lewis Baxter (Wash.) Sept. 20, 1894–June 10, 1948; secretary of labor July 1, 1945–June 10, 1948; Senate 1935–Dec. 16, 1940 (Democrat).

Seaton, Frederick Andrew (Neb.) Dec. 11, 1909–Jan. 16, 1974; secretary of the interior June 8, 1956–Jan. 20, 1961; Senate Dec. 10, 1951–Nov. 4, 1952 (Republican).

Seward, William Henry (N.Y.) May 16, 1801–Oct. 10, 1872; secretary of state March 6, 1861–March 4, 1869; Gov. Jan. 1, 1839–Jan. 1, 1843 (Whig); Senate 1849–61 (1849–55 Whig, 1855–61 Republican).

Shalala, Donna Edna (Wis.) Feb. 14, 1941– ; secretary of health and human services Jan. 22, 1993–Jan. 20, 2001.

Shaw, Leslie Mortier (Iowa) Nov. 2, 1848–March 28, 1932; secretary of the Treasury Feb. 1, 1902–March 3, 1907; Gov. Jan. 13, 1898–Jan. 16, 1902 (Republican).

Sherman, John (Ohio) May 10, 1823–Oct. 22, 1900; secretary of the Treasury March 10, 1877–March 3, 1881; secretary of state March 6, 1897–April 27, 1898; House 1855–March 21, 1861 (Republican); Senate March 21, 1861–March 8, 1877 (Republican), 1881–March 4, 1897 (Republican); elected pres. pro tempore Dec. 7, 1885.

Sherman, William Tecumseh (Ohio) Feb. 8, 1820–Feb. 14, 1891; secretary of war Sept. 11–Oct. 25, 1869.

Shultz, George Pratt (Calif.) Dec. 13, 1920– ; secretary of labor (Ill.) Jan. 22, 1969–July 1, 1970; secretary of the Treasury (Ill.) June 12, 1972–May 8, 1974; secretary of state July 16, 1982–Jan. 20, 1989.

Simon, William Edward (N.J.) Nov. 27, 1927–June 3, 2000; secretary of the Treasury May 8, 1974–Jan. 20, 1977.

Skinner, Samuel Knox (Ill.) June 10, 1938– ; secretary of transportation Feb. 6, 1989–Dec. 16, 1991.

Slater, Rodney (Ark.) Feb. 23, 1955– ; secretary of transportation Feb. 14, 1997–Jan. 20, 2001.

Smith, Caleb Blood (Ind.) April 16, 1808–Jan. 7, 1864; secretary of the interior March 5, 1861–Dec. 31, 1862; House 1843–49 (Whig).

Smith, Charles Emory (Pa.) Feb. 18, 1842–Jan. 19, 1908; postmaster general April 23, 1898–Jan. 14, 1902.

Smith, Cyrus Rowlett (N.Y.) Sept. 9, 1899–April 4, 1990; secretary of commerce March 6, 1968–Jan. 19, 1969.

Smith, Hoke (Ga.) Sept. 2, 1855–Nov. 27, 1931; secretary of the interior March 6, 1893–Sept. 1, 1896; Gov. June 29, 1907–June 26, 1909 (Democrat), July 1–Nov. 16, 1911 (Democrat); Senate Nov. 16, 1911–21 (Democrat).

Smith, Robert (Md.) Nov. 3, 1757–Nov. 26, 1842; secretary of the navy July 27, 1801–March 7, 1809; secretary of state March 6, 1809–April 1, 1811.

Smith, William French (Calif.) Aug. 26, 1917–Oct. 29, 1990; attorney general Jan. 23, 1981–Feb. 24, 1985.

Snow, John W. (Ohio) Aug. 2, 1939– ; secretary of the Treasury Feb. 3, 2003– .

Snyder, John Wesley (Mo.) June 21, 1895–Oct. 8, 1985; secretary of the Treasury June 25, 1946–Jan. 20, 1953.

Southard, Samuel Lewis (N.J.) June 9, 1787–June 26, 1842; secretary of the navy Sept. 16, 1823–March 3, 1829; Senate Jan. 26, 1821–23 (Republican), 1833–June 26, 1842 (Whig); elected pres. pro tempore March 11, 1841; Gov. Oct. 26, 1832–Feb. 27, 1833 (Republican).

Speed, James (Ky.) March 11, 1812–June 25, 1887; attorney general Dec. 2, 1864–July 17, 1866.

Spellings, Margaret (Va.) Nov. 30, 1957– ; secretary of education Jan. 20, 2005– .

Spencer, John Canfield (N.Y.) Jan. 8, 1788–May 18, 1855; secretary of war Oct. 12, 1841–March 3, 1843; secretary of the Treasury March 8, 1843–May 2, 1844; House 1817–19 (Republican).

Stanberry, Henry (Ohio) Feb. 20, 1803–June 26, 1881; attorney general July 23, 1866–March 12, 1868.

Stans, Maurice Hubert (N.Y.) March 22, 1908–April 14, 1998; secretary of commerce Jan. 21, 1969–Feb. 15, 1972.

Stanton, Edwin McMasters (Pa.) Dec. 19, 1814–Dec. 24, 1869; attorney general Dec. 20, 1860–March 3, 1861; secretary of war Jan. 20, 1862–May 28, 1868.

Stettinius, Edward Reilly Jr. (Va.) Oct. 22, 1900–Oct. 31, 1949; secretary of state Dec. 1, 1944–June 27, 1945.

Stimson, Henry Lewis (N.Y.) Sept. 21, 1867–Oct. 20, 1950; secretary of war May 22, 1911–March 4, 1913, July 10, 1940–Sept. 21, 1945; secretary of state March 28, 1929–March 4, 1933.

Stoddert, Benjamin (Md.) 1751–Dec. 18, 1813; secretary of the navy June 18, 1798–March 31, 1801.

Stone, Harlan Fiske (N.Y.) Oct. 11, 1872–April 22, 1946; attorney general April 7, 1924–March 2, 1925; assoc. justice March 2, 1925–July 2, 1941, chief justice July 3, 1941–April 22, 1946.

Straus, Oscar Solomon (N.Y.) Dec. 23, 1850–Jan. 11, 1931; secretary of commerce and labor Dec. 17, 1906–March 5, 1909.

Stuart, Alexander Hugh Holmes (Va.) April 2, 1807–Feb. 13, 1891; secretary of the interior Sept. 12, 1850–March 7, 1853; House 1841–43 (Whig).

Sullivan, Louis Wade (Ga.) Nov. 3, 1933– ; secretary of health and human services March 10, 1989–Jan. 20, 1993.

Summerfield, Arthur Ellsworth (Mich.) March 17, 1899–April 26, 1972; postmaster general Jan. 21, 1953–Jan. 20, 1961; chair Rep. Nat. Comm. 1952–53.

Summers, Lawrence H. (Md.) Nov. 30, 1954– ; secretary of the Treasury July 2, 1999–Jan. 20, 2001.

Swanson, Claude Augustus (Va.) March 31, 1862–July 7, 1939; secretary of the navy March 4, 1933–July 7, 1939; House 1893–Jan. 30, 1906 (Democrat); Gov. Feb. 1, 1906–Feb. 1, 1910 (Democrat); Senate Aug. 1, 1910–33 (Democrat).

Taft, Alphonso (Ohio) Nov. 5, 1810–May 21, 1891; secretary of war March 8–May 22, 1876; attorney general May 22, 1876–March 11, 1877.

Taft, William Howard (Ohio) Sept. 15, 1857–March 8, 1930; secretary of war Feb. 1, 1904–June 30, 1908; Gov. (prov.) 1901–04 (Philippines); president 1909–13 (Republican); chief justice July 11, 1921–Feb. 3, 1930.

Taney, Roger Brooke (Md.) March 17, 1777–Oct. 12, 1864; secretary of the Treasury Sept. 23, 1833–June 25, 1834; attorney general July 20, 1831–Sept. 24, 1833; chief justice March 28, 1836–Oct. 12, 1864.

Teller, Henry Moore (Colo.) May 23, 1830–Feb. 23, 1914; secretary of the interior April 18, 1882–March 3, 1885; Senate Nov. 15, 1876–April 17, 1882 (Republican), 1885–1909 (1885–97 Republican, 1897–1903 Silver Republican, 1903–09 Democrat).

Thomas, Philip Francis (Md.) Sept. 12, 1810–Oct. 2, 1890; secretary of the Treasury Dec. 12, 1860–Jan. 14, 1861; House 1839–41 (Democrat), 1875–77 (Democrat); Gov. Jan. 3, 1848–Jan. 6, 1851 (Democrat).

Thompson, Jacob (Miss.) May 15, 1810–March 24, 1885; secretary of the interior March 10, 1857–Jan. 8, 1861; House 1839–51 (Democrat).

Thompson, Richard Wigginton (Ind.) June 9, 1809–Feb. 9, 1900; secretary of the navy March 13, 1877–Dec. 20, 1880; House 1841–43 (Whig), 1847–49 (Whig).

Thompson, Smith (N.Y.) Jan. 17, 1768–Dec. 18, 1843; secretary of the navy Jan. 1, 1819–Aug. 31, 1823; assoc. justice Feb. 10, 1824–Dec. 18, 1843.

Thompson, Tommy George (Wisc.) Nov. 19, 1941– ; secretary of health and human services Feb. 2, 2001–Jan. 26, 2005; Gov. Jan. 5, 1987–Feb. 1, 2001 (Republican).

Thornburgh, Richard Lewis (Pa.) July 16, 1932– ; attorney general Aug. 12, 1988–Aug. 9, 1991; Gov. Jan. 16, 1979–Jan. 20, 1987 (Republican).

Tobin, Maurice Joseph (Mass.) May 22, 1901–July 19, 1953; secretary of labor Aug. 13, 1948–Jan. 20, 1953; Gov. Jan. 3, 1945–Jan. 2, 1947 (Democrat).

Toucey, Isaac (Conn.) Nov. 15, 1792–July 30, 1869; attorney general June 21, 1848–March 3, 1849; secretary of the navy March 7, 1857–March 6, 1861; Gov. May 6, 1846–May 5, 1847 (Democrat); House 1835–39 (Democrat); Senate May 12, 1852–57 (Democrat).

Tracy, Benjamin Franklin (N.Y.) April 26, 1830–Aug. 6, 1915; secretary of the navy March 6, 1889–March 6, 1893.

Trowbridge, Alexander Buel (D.C.) Dec. 12, 1929– ; secretary of commerce June 14, 1967–March 1, 1968.

Tyner, James Noble (Ind.) Jan. 17, 1826–Dec. 5, 1904; postmaster general July 13, 1876–March 12, 1877; House 1869–75 (Republican).

Udall, Stewart Lee (Ariz.) Jan. 31, 1920– ; secretary of the interior Jan. 21, 1961–Jan. 20, 1969; House 1955–Jan. 18, 1961 (Democrat).

Upshur, Abel Parker (Va.) June 17, 1790–Feb. 28, 1844; secretary of state July 24, 1843–Feb. 28, 1844; secretary of the navy Oct. 11, 1841–July 23, 1843.

Usery, William Julian Jr. (Ga.) Dec. 21, 1923– ; secretary of labor Feb. 10, 1976–Jan. 20, 1977.

Usher, John Palmer (Ind.) Jan. 9, 1816–April 13, 1889; secretary of the interior Jan. 1, 1863–May 15, 1865.

Van Buren, Martin (N.Y.) Dec. 5, 1782–July 24, 1862; secretary of state March 28, 1829–March 23, 1831; Senate 1821–Dec. 20, 1828 (no party); Gov. Jan. 1–March 12, 1829 (Jeffersonian Republican); vice president 1833–37 (Democrat); president 1837–41 (Democrat).

Vance, Cyrus Roberts (W.Va.) March 27, 1917–Jan. 12, 2002; secretary of state Jan. 23, 1977–April 28, 1980.

Veneman, Ann M. (Calif.) June 29, 1949– ; secretary of agriculture Jan. 20, 2001–Jan. 20, 2005.

Verity, Calvin William Jr. (Ohio) Jan. 26, 1917– ; secretary of commerce Oct. 19, 1987–Jan. 20, 1989.

Vilas, William Freeman (Wis.) July 9, 1840–Aug. 27, 1908; postmaster general March 7, 1885–Jan. 16, 1888; secretary of the interior Jan. 16, 1888–March 6, 1889; Senate 1891–97 (Democrat).

Vinson, Frederick Moore (Ky.) Jan. 22, 1890–Sept. 8, 1953; secretary of the Treasury July 23, 1945–June 23, 1946; House Jan. 12, 1924–29 (Democrat), 1931–May 12, 1938 (Democrat); chief justice June 24, 1946–Sept. 8, 1953.

Volpe, John Anthony (Mass.) Dec. 8, 1908–Nov. 11, 1994; secretary of transportation Jan. 22, 1969–Feb. 1, 1973; Gov. Jan. 5, 1961–Jan. 3, 1963 (Republican), Jan. 7, 1965–Jan. 22, 1969 (Republican).

Walker, Frank Comerford (Pa.) May 30, 1886–Sept. 13, 1959; postmaster general Sept. 11, 1940–June 30, 1945; chair Dem. Nat. Comm. 1943–44.

Walker, Robert John (Miss.) July 19, 1801–Nov. 11, 1869; secretary of the Treasury March 8, 1845–March 5, 1849; Senate 1835–March 5, 1845 (Democrat); Gov. (Kan. Terr.) April–Dec. 1857.

Wallace, Henry Agard (Iowa) Oct. 7, 1888–Nov. 18, 1965; secretary of agriculture March 4, 1933–Sept. 4, 1940; secretary of commerce March 2, 1945–Sept. 20, 1946; vice president 1941–45 (Democrat).

Wallace, Henry Cantwell (Iowa) May 11, 1866–Oct. 25, 1924; secretary of agriculture March 5, 1921–Oct. 25, 1924.

Wanamaker, John (Pa.) July 11, 1838–Dec. 12, 1922; postmaster general March 6, 1889–March 7, 1893.

Washburne, Elihu Benjamin (Ill.) Sept. 23, 1816–Oct. 23, 1887; secretary of state March 5–March 16, 1869; House 1853–March 6, 1869 (1853–55 Whig, 1855–March 6, 1869 Republican).

Watkins, James David (Calif.) March 7, 1927– ; secretary of energy March 9, 1989–Jan. 20, 1993.

Watson, William Marvin (Texas) June 6, 1924– ; postmaster general April 26, 1968–Jan. 20, 1969.

Watt, James Gaius (Colo.) Jan. 31, 1938– ; secretary of the interior Jan. 23, 1981–Nov. 8, 1983.

Weaver, Robert Clifton (D.C.) Dec. 29, 1907–July 17, 1997; secretary of housing and urban development Jan. 18, 1966–Dec. 3, 1968.

Webster, Daniel (Mass.) Jan. 18, 1782–Oct. 24, 1852; secretary of state March 6, 1841–May 8, 1843, July 23, 1850–Oct. 24, 1852; House 1813–17 (Federalist N.H.), 1823–May 30, 1827 (Federalist); Senate May 30, 1827–Feb. 22, 1841 (1827–33 Federalist, 1833–Feb. 22, 1841 Whig), 1845–July 22, 1850 (Whig).

Weeks, Charles Sinclair (Mass.) June 15, 1893–Feb. 7, 1972; secretary of commerce Jan. 21, 1953–Nov. 10, 1958; Senate Feb. 8–Dec. 19, 1944 (Republican).

Weeks, John Wingate (Mass.) April 11, 1860–July 12, 1926; secretary of war March 5, 1921–Oct. 13, 1925; House 1905–March 4, 1913 (Republican); Senate 1913–19 (Republican).

Weinberger, Caspar Willard (Calif.) Aug. 18, 1917– ; secretary of health, education and welfare Feb. 12, 1973–Aug. 8, 1975; secretary of defense Jan. 21, 1981–Nov. 21, 1987.

Welles, Gideon (Conn.) July 1, 1802–Feb. 11, 1878; secretary of the navy March 7, 1861–March 3, 1869.

West, Roy Owen (Ill.) Oct. 27, 1868–Nov. 29, 1958; secretary of the interior July 25, 1928–March 4, 1929.

West, Togo D. Jr. (D.C.) 1942– ; secretary of veterans affairs May 5, 1998–July 24, 2000.

Whiting, William Fairfield (Mass.) July 20, 1864–Aug. 31, 1936; secretary of commerce Aug. 22, 1928–March 4, 1929.

Whitney, William Collins (N.Y.) July 5, 1841–Feb. 2, 1902; secretary of the navy March 7, 1885–March 5, 1889.

Wickard, Claude Raymond (Ind.) Feb. 28, 1893–April 29, 1967; secretary of agriculture Sept. 5, 1940–June 29, 1945.

Wickersham, George Woodward (N.Y.) Sept. 19, 1858–Jan. 26, 1936; attorney general March 5, 1909–March 5, 1913.

Wickliffe, Charles Anderson (Ky.) June 8, 1788–Oct. 31, 1869; postmaster general Oct. 13, 1841–March 6, 1845; House 1823–33 (1823–27 no party, 1827–33 Jacksonian), 1861–63 (Unionist); Gov. Oct. 5, 1839–June 1, 1840 (Whig).

Wilbur, Curtis Dwight (Calif.) May 10, 1867–Sept. 8, 1954; secretary of the navy March 19, 1924–March 4, 1929.

Wilbur, Ray Lyman (Calif.) April 13, 1875–June 26, 1949; secretary of the interior March 5, 1929–March 4, 1933.

Wilkins, William (Pa.) Dec. 20, 1779–June 23, 1865; secretary of war Feb. 15, 1844–March 4, 1845; Senate 1831–June 30, 1834 (Jacksonian); House 1843–Feb. 14, 1844 (Democrat).

Williams, George Henry (Ore.) March 26, 1823–April 4, 1910; attorney general Jan. 10, 1872–May 15, 1875; Senate 1865–71 (Republican).

Wilson, Charles Erwin (Mich.) July 18, 1890–Sept. 26, 1961; secretary of defense Jan. 28, 1953–Oct. 8, 1957.

Wilson, James (Iowa) Aug. 16, 1835–Aug. 26, 1920; secretary of agriculture March 6, 1897–March 5, 1913; House 1873–77 (Republican), 1883–85 (Republican).

Wilson, William Bauchop (Pa.) April 2, 1862–May 25, 1934; secretary of labor March 4, 1913–March 4, 1921; House 1907–13 (Democrat).

Wilson, William Lyne (W.Va.) May 3, 1843–Oct. 17, 1900; postmaster general April 4, 1895–March 5, 1897; House 1883–95 (Democrat).

Windom, William (Minn.) May 10, 1827–Jan. 29, 1891; secretary of the Treasury March 8–Nov. 13, 1881, March 7, 1889–Jan. 29, 1891; House 1859–69 (Republican); Senate July 15, 1870–Jan. 22, 1871 (Republican), March 4, 1871–March 7, 1881 (Republican), Nov. 15, 1881–83 (Republican).

Wirt, William (Va.) Nov. 8, 1772–Feb. 18, 1834; attorney general Nov. 13, 1817–March 3, 1829.

Wirtz, William Willard (Ill.) March 14, 1912– ; secretary of labor Sept. 25, 1962–Jan. 20, 1969.

Wolcott, Oliver Jr. (Conn.) Jan. 11, 1760–June 1, 1833; secretary of the Treasury Feb. 3, 1795–Dec. 31, 1800; Gov. May 8, 1817–May 2, 1827 (Democratic Republican).

Woodbury, Levi (N.H.) Dec. 22, 1789–Sept. 4, 1851; secretary of the navy May 23, 1831–June 30, 1834; secretary of the Treasury July 1, 1834–March 3, 1841; Gov. June 5, 1823–June 2, 1824 (Democratic Republican); Senate March 16, 1825–31 (no party), 1841–Nov. 20, 1845 (Democrat); assoc. justice Sept. 23, 1845–Sept. 4, 1851.

Woodin, William Hartman (N.Y.) May 27, 1868–May 3, 1934; secretary of the Treasury March 5–Dec. 31, 1933.

Woodring, Harry Hines (Kan.) May 31, 1890–Sept. 9, 1967; secretary of war Sept. 25, 1936–June 20, 1940; Gov. Jan. 12, 1931–Jan. 9, 1933 (Democrat).

Work, Hubert (Colo.) July 3, 1860–Dec. 14, 1942; postmaster general March 4, 1922–March 4, 1923; secretary of the interior March 5, 1923–July 24, 1928; chair Rep. Nat. Comm. 1928–29.

Wright, Luke Edward (Tenn.) Aug. 29, 1846–Nov. 17, 1922; secretary of war July 1, 1908–March 11, 1909.

Wynne, Robert John (Pa.) Nov. 18, 1851–March 11, 1922; postmaster general Oct. 10, 1904–March 4, 1905.

Yeutter, Clayton Keith (Neb.) Dec. 10, 1930– ; secretary of agriculture Feb. 16, 1989–March 1, 1991; chair Rep. Nat. Comm. March 1991–Jan. 1992.

Supreme Court Justices

The Supreme Court is one of the most exclusive governing bodies in the world. No constitutional or statutory qualifications exist for serving on the Supreme Court. The Constitution simply states that "the judicial power of the United States shall be vested in one Supreme Court" as well as any lower federal courts Congress may establish (Article III) and that the president "by and with the Advice and Consent of the Senate, shall appoint . . . Judges of the Supreme Court" (Article II). No age limitation exists; no requirement that appointees have a legal background. The Constitution also makes no stipulation that the Supreme Court justices be native-born Americans, which means presidents are free to name foreign-born members to the Court. (Six justices were born outside the United States: James Wilson, James Iredell, William Paterson, David Brewer, George Sutherland, and Felix Frankfurter.)

Informal criteria for membership quickly developed. Every nominee to the Court has been a lawyer—although it was not until the twentieth century that most justices were law school graduates. Over the years many other factors have entered into the process of presidential selection. Some of them became long-lasting traditions with virtually the force of a formal requirement. Others were as fleeting as the personal friendship between president and the nominee.

The First Justices

George Washington, as the first president of the United States, had the responsibility of choosing the original six justices of the Supreme Court. The type of men he chose and the reasons he chose them foreshadowed the process of selection carried out by his successors.

In naming the first justices, Washington paid close attention to their politics, which at that time meant primarily loyalty to the new Constitution. Of the six original appointees, three had attended the Philadelphia convention that formulated the Constitution, and the other three had supported its adoption. John Jay, the first chief justice, was coauthor with Alexander Hamilton and James Madison of *The Federalist,* a series of influential essays published in New York supporting ratification of the Constitution.

During his two terms of office, Washington had occasion to make five additional Supreme Court appointments. All were staunch supporters of the Constitution and the new federal government.

Another of Washington's major considerations was geographical. The new states were a disparate group that had barely held together during the fight for independence and the confederation government of the 1780s. To help bind them more closely together, Washington consciously tried to represent each geographical area of the country in the nation's new supreme tribunal.

His first six appointees consisted of three northerners—Chief Justice John Jay from New York and Associate Justices William Cushing of Massachusetts and James Wilson of Pennsylvania—and three southerners—John Blair of Virginia, James Iredell of North Carolina, and John Rutledge of South Carolina. The five later appointees were Oliver Ellsworth of Connecticut, Thomas Johnson and Samuel Chase of Maryland, William Paterson of New Jersey, and Rutledge, appointed a second time. By the time Washington left office, nine of the original thirteen states had achieved representation on the Supreme Court.

Appointment Opportunities

With a total of eleven, Washington still holds the record for the number of Supreme Court appointments made by any president. The second-highest total—nine—belongs to President Franklin D. Roosevelt, the only president to serve more than two terms. Roosevelt also came closest since Washington to naming the entire membership of the Court—only two justices who served before the Roosevelt years were still on the Court at the time of his death. One of the two—Harlan Fiske Stone—Roosevelt elevated from associate justice to chief justice.

Presidents Andrew Jackson and William Howard Taft had the next highest number of justices appointed with six each. Taft holds the record for a one-term president. Next in order are Abraham Lincoln and Dwight D. Eisenhower; each made five appointments.

Five presidents made no appointments to the Supreme Court. William Henry Harrison and Zachary Taylor both died in office before any vacancies occurred.

Andrew Johnson, who served just six weeks short of a full term, had no chance to make a Supreme Court appointment because of his rancorous political battle with Congress over Reconstruction. So bitter did the struggle

Sixteen Chief Justices

Listed below, in chronological order, are the sixteen chief justices who have served in the history of the United States as of March 2005.

John Jay
John Rutledge
Oliver Ellsworth
John Marshall
Roger B. Taney
Salmon P. Chase
Morrison R. Waite
Melville W. Fuller
Edward D. White
William Howard Taft
Charles Evans Hughes
Harlan Fiske Stone
Frederick M. Vinson
Earl Warren
Warren E. Burger
William H. Rehnquist

become that Congress in effect took away Johnson's power of appointment by passing legislation in 1866 to reduce the Court from ten to seven members as vacancies occurred.

The legislation was occasioned by the death of Justice John Catron in 1865 and Johnson's nomination in 1866 of Henry Stanbery to replace him. The Senate took no action on Stanbery's nomination and instead passed the bill reducing the size of the Court. When Justice James Wayne died in 1867, the membership of the Court automatically dropped to eight. In 1869, when the Republicans had recaptured the White House, they enacted legislation increasing the Court to nine seats, allowing President Ulysses S. Grant to make a nomination.

Jimmy Carter and George W. Bush (as of March 2005) have been the only full-term presidents to be denied the opportunity of appointing someone to the Court. No deaths or resignations occurred during Carter's tenure or Bush's first term. At the start of Bush's second term, however, four out of nine justices were in their seventies or eighties, several of whom had been ailing. It appeared likely that Bush would have the opportunity of making one or two Supreme Court appointments before he left the White House.

Nonpartisan Appointments

As political parties became an established fact of American political life, the major parties sought to have members appointed to the Supreme Court who would espouse their view of what the federal government should and should not do. As Washington had appointed supporters of the new Constitution, so most presidents have selected nominees with whom they were philosophically and politically in accord. It is an exception when a president goes to the opposite political party to find a nominee.

The first clear-cut instance of a president of one party appointing a member of the other to the Supreme Court was Republican Lincoln's selection of Democrat Stephen J. Field of California in 1863. President John Tyler, elected vice president as a Whig in 1840, had appointed Democrat Samuel Nelson to the Court in 1845, but by that time Tyler was no longer identified with either major political party.

After Lincoln's example, Republican presidents occasionally appointed Democrats to the Court. President Benjamin Harrison selected Democrat Howell Jackson of Tennessee in 1893; Warren G. Harding appointed Democrat Pierce Butler in 1922; Herbert Hoover appointed Democrat Benjamin Cardozo in 1932; Eisenhower appointed Democrat William J. Brennan Jr. in 1956; and Richard Nixon appointed Democrat Lewis F. Powell Jr. in 1971. Republican Taft was the only president to appoint more than one member of the opposite party to the Court. Three of his six nominees to the Court were Democrats—Edward D. White, whom Taft elevated from associate justice to chief justice, and Horace Lurton and Joseph R. Lamar, southern Democrats appointed in 1909 and 1910, respectively.

The only two Democrats ever to appoint Republicans to the Supreme Court were Franklin Roosevelt and Harry S. Truman. Roosevelt elevated Republican Stone from associate justice to chief justice in 1941. Truman appointed Republican senator Harold H. Burton of Ohio, an old friend and colleague from Truman's Senate days, in 1945.

Lobbying for a Nomination

Before a president finally decides whom to nominate, a process of balancing and sifting usually goes on, sometimes involving many participants and sometimes only a few. But occasionally a president's choice has all but been made by overwhelming pressure for a particular nominee.

One of the more dramatic instances of this process occurred in 1853, when President Franklin Pierce nominated John A. Campbell of Alabama for a seat on the Court. Campbell was a forty-one-year-old lawyer who had such a brilliant reputation that the Supreme Court justices decided they wanted him as a colleague. As a result, the entire membership of the Court wrote to Pierce requesting Campbell's nomination. To emphasize their point, they sent two justices to the president to deliver the letters in person. Pierce complied, and Campbell was confirmed within four days.

In 1862 Lincoln was looking for a new justice from the Midwest. The Iowa congressional delegation began pressing for the appointment of Samuel Miller, a doctor and lawyer who had helped form the Iowa Republican Party and had a strong reputation for moral and intellectual integrity. The movement grew rapidly until 129 of

140 House members and all but four senators had signed a petition for Miller's nomination. With such massive and unprecedented congressional support, Miller received Lincoln's approval despite his lack of any judicial experience. He became the first justice from west of the Mississippi River.

In 1932 a strong national movement began for the appointment of Cardozo, chief judge of the New York court of appeals, to the Supreme Court. Cardozo was a Democrat, while the president who was to make the appointment, Hoover, was a Republican. Furthermore, Cardozo was Jewish and one Jew already was seated on the Court, Louis D. Brandeis. Under these circumstances, it was considered unlikely Hoover would make the nomination.

But Cardozo's record was so impressive that a groundswell of support arose for him. Deans and faculty members of the nation's leading law schools, chief judges of other state courts, labor and business leaders, and powerful senators all urged Hoover to choose Cardozo. Despite his desire to appoint a western Republican, Hoover finally yielded and nominated Cardozo, who was confirmed without opposition.

Geographical Factors

George Washington's weighing of geographical factors in appointing the first justices continued as a tradition for more than a century. It was reinforced by the justices' duty under the Judiciary Act of 1789 to ride and preside over circuit court sessions. Presidents strove not only for geographical balance in their appointments but also considered it important that each justice be a native of the circuit over which he presided.

But the burdensome attendance requirement was curtailed by legislation during the nineteenth century until it became optional in 1891 and was abolished altogether in 1911. In the twentieth century, geography became less and less a consideration in Supreme Court nominations, although as recently as 1970 President Nixon made an issue of it after the Senate refused to confirm Clement Haynsworth Jr. and G. Harrold Carswell to the Court. Nixon claimed the Senate would not confirm a conservative southerner and turned to Minnesotan Harry A. Blackmun instead.

In its heyday, the geographical factor was sometimes almost sacrosanct. The most enduring example was the so-called New England seat, which was occupied by a New Englander, usually from Massachusetts, from 1789 to 1932. There also was a seat for a New Yorker from 1806 to 1894 and a Maryland-Virginia seat from 1789 to 1860. *(See box, Geographical Considerations in Appointments, p. 44.)*

Geography had strong political ramifications as well, especially for the South. With the growth of sectional differences, particularly over the slavery issue, before the Civil War, the South felt on the defensive. One of the ways it sought to defend its interests was to gain a majority on the Supreme Court. Five of the nine justices in 1860 were from slaveholding states.

With the coming of the Civil War, the sectional balance of power shifted. Four of the five southern justices

died between 1860 and 1867, and another—Justice John A. Campbell of Alabama—resigned to join the Confederate cause.

Not one of these justices was replaced by a southerner. Thus by 1870 every Supreme Court seat was held by a northerner or westerner. But with the gradual decline of bitterness over the war, southern members again began to appear on the Court. President Rutherford B. Hayes, who sought to reconcile relations between the North and South, made the first move by appointing William B. Woods of Georgia in 1880. Woods was not a native southerner, having migrated there after the Civil War. But despite this "carpetbagger" background, he was never identified with the corruption and profligacy associated with the Reconstruction era. As a federal judge for the Fifth Circuit—the deep South—he gained the respect of his neighbors for his fairness and honesty.

The first native southerner appointed to the Court after the Civil War was Woods's successor, Lucius Q. C. Lamar of Mississippi, confirmed in 1888. Lamar had personally drafted Mississippi's ordinance of secession in 1861 and had served the Confederacy both as a military officer and as a diplomatic envoy to Europe. So his accession to the Court was an even more significant symbol of reconciliation between the sections than Woods's appointment eight years earlier.

Thirty-one states have contributed justices to the Supreme Court. New York has by far the highest total, with fourteen, followed by Ohio and Massachusetts with nine each, and Virginia with seven. Several major states have had only one justice, including Texas, Indiana, and Missouri—as have such small states as Utah, Maine, and Wyoming.

Of the nineteen states that have never had a native on the Court, most are smaller western states. Only six of the nineteen are east of the Mississippi River. The largest state never to have had a justice is Florida.

The lack of representation on the Court from some of the less densely populated states resulted in a controversy during the 1950s when North Dakota's outspoken maverick senator, Republican William Langer, began opposing all non–North Dakotan Supreme Court nominees as a protest against big-state nominees. Langer was chairman of the Senate Judiciary Committee during the 83rd Congress (1953–55). In 1954 he joined in delaying tactics against the nomination of Earl Warren as chief justice, managing to hold off confirmation for two months. He continued his struggle until his death in 1959.

Only Lawyers

All of Washington's appointees were lawyers, and no president has deviated from this precedent. The legal education of the justices has changed radically over the years, however. Until the midnineteenth century, it was traditional for aspiring lawyers to study privately in a law office until they had learned the law sufficiently to pass the bar. There were no law schools as such in the early years, although some universities had courses in law. John Marshall, for example, attended a course of law lectures at William and Mary College in the 1770s. Two of the

Geographical Considerations in Appointments

Geography was a prime consideration in the appointment of Supreme Court justices throughout the nineteenth century. Presidents found it expedient to have each of the expanding nation's rival sections represented on the Court. Whenever a justice died or resigned, his replacement usually came from the same state or a neighboring one. In addition, the justices' circuit duties, which required them to attend court sessions in their circuits periodically, made it desirable for each justice to be a native of the circuit over which he presided.

The 'New England Seat'

The most notable instance of geographical continuity was the seat traditionally held by a New Englander. William Cushing of Massachusetts was appointed an associate justice by President George Washington in 1789. From then until 1932, the seat was held by a New England appointee, usually from Massachusetts.

When Cushing died after twenty-one years on the Court, President James Madison looked to New England for a successor. He offered the post to both former attorney general Levi Lincoln and John Quincy Adams, both from Massachusetts, but they declined. After Madison's nomination of Alexander Wolcott of Connecticut was turned down by the Senate, the president turned back to Massachusetts and selected Joseph Story, at thirty-two the youngest justice ever chosen. Story served nearly thirty-four years, dying in 1845. President James K. Polk chose to continue the New England tradition of holding the seat by appointing Levi Woodbury of New Hampshire.

Woodbury's tenure lasted six years, and it fell to President Millard Fillmore to find a successor. He chose Benjamin Curtis, another Massachusetts native. Curtis resigned in 1857, largely because of his acrimonious relations with other members of the Taney court. President James Buchanan, mindful of the continued need for a New Englander on the Court, chose Nathan Clifford of Maine.

Clifford served until his death in July 1881, shortly after President James A. Garfield was shot. When Garfield died in September, his successor, Chester A. Arthur, chose the chief justice of the Massachusetts Supreme Court, Horace Gray, as the new justice from New England. Gray served until 1902, when he was succeeded by another Massachusetts Supreme Court chief justice, Oliver Wendell Holmes, appointed by President Theodore Roosevelt.

By the time of Holmes's appointment, however, the significance of geography had declined as a qualification for selection to the Supreme Court. President Theodore Roosevelt, in particular, was disdainful of such a prerequisite, and it was mostly accidental that Holmes came from Massachusetts. Nevertheless, his selection extended for another twenty-nine years the tradition of the "New England seat." After Holmes's resignation in 1932, President Herbert Hoover chose as his successor Benjamin Cardozo, chief judge of New York state's highest court, thus ending the Supreme Court's longest-lasting geographical tradition. Although Cardozo's

earliest justices—John Rutledge and John Blair—received their legal education in England, at the Inns of Court. A modern justice, Frank Murphy, also studied there.

Sixty-one justices (including Rutledge and Blair) went to law school. The largest number (seventeen) attended Harvard; Yale taught nine justices law and Columbia six. Counted twice in this tally is Ruth Bader Ginsburg, who attended Harvard for two years, then completed her law school education at Columbia. The first justice to receive a law degree from an American university was Benjamin Curtis, who graduated from Harvard in 1832.

But it was not until 1957 that the Supreme Court was composed, for the first time, entirely of law school graduates. Before that, many had attended law school but had not received degrees. The last justice never to have attended law school was James F. Byrnes, who served from 1941 to 1942. The son of poor Irish immigrants, Byrnes never even graduated from high school. He left school at

age fourteen, worked as a law clerk, and eventually became a court stenographer. Reading law in his spare time, Byrnes passed the bar at age twenty-four.

The last justice not to have a law degree was Stanley F. Reed, who served from 1938 to 1957. He attended both the University of Virginia and Columbia law schools but received a degree from neither.

Precourt Experience

Most justices have been active either in politics or in judicial office before coming to the Supreme Court. In fact, only one justice—George Shiras Jr.—had never engaged in political or judicial activities before his appointment.

Judges

A total of sixty-seven justices had some judicial experience—federal or state—before coming to the Supreme Court. Surprisingly, many more had experi-

successor, Felix Frankfurter, was a resident of Massachusetts, that fact apparently played no role in his selection.

The 'New York Seat'

New York was another longtime holder of a specific seat on the Supreme Court. With the appointment of Justice Henry Brockholst Livingston by President Thomas Jefferson in 1806, a tradition began that continued until New Yorkers themselves ended it in 1894 by their internal quarreling.

Livingston served until his death in 1823. President James Monroe offered the post indirectly to Martin Van Buren, then a U.S. senator, but received a noncommittal response. The president then chose Smith Thompson of New York, his secretary of the navy. Thompson served for twenty years. His death in 1843 came at an inopportune moment politically: President John Tyler was disliked by both Democrats and Whigs and had little political leverage. His attempts to choose a successor to Thompson met with repeated failure, the Senate defeating one nominee and forcing another to withdraw. Finally, at the last moment before leaving office in 1845, Tyler found a New Yorker acceptable to the Senate for the post. He was Justice Samuel Nelson, who continued to serve until his resignation in November 1872.

Two more New Yorkers held the seat after Nelson's retirement, Ward Hunt from 1873 to 1882 and Samuel Blatchford from 1882 to 1893. But then a bitter quarrel between New Yorkers over the seat ended the tradition. The two main New York antagonists were President Grover Cleveland and Sen. David B. Hill, old political enemies. Cleveland twice nominated a New Yorker for the post, and twice Hill used senatorial courtesy to object to the nominees. In both cases, the Senate followed its own tradition of honoring a senator's objection to a nominee of his own party from his own state and rejected Cleveland's choices. Cleveland then abandoned New York and chose U.S. Senator Edward D. White of Louisiana, who was confirmed immediately.

The 'Virginia-Maryland Seat'

Virginia and Maryland shared a seat on the Supreme Court from the first appointments in 1789 until the Civil War. John Blair of Virginia, appointed by Washington, served until 1796. Washington chose as his successor Samuel Chase of Maryland. After Chase's death in 1811, another Marylander, Gabriel Duval, was given the seat. After Duval's resignation in 1835, the seat went back to Virginia, with Philip Barbour holding it from 1836 to 1841 and Peter V. Daniel from 1842 to 1860. With the coming of the Civil War, there was a realignment of circuits as well as the desire of the new Republican administration to appoint more northerners and westerners to the Court. The Maryland-Virginia tradition was ended when Iowan Samuel Miller was appointed as Daniel's successor by President Abraham Lincoln.

ence on the state level (forty-four) than on the federal level (thirty-one). (An overlap in the figures exists because eight justices held both federal and state judicial offices.)

All except two of Washington's appointees had state judicial experience. Washington believed such experience was important for justices of the new federal court. But not until 1826 was a federal judge appointed to the Court. Robert Trimble had served nine years as a U.S. district judge before being appointed to the Supreme Court.

Even after Trimble's appointment, judges with federal judicial experience continued to be a rarity on the Supreme Court. By 1880 only two other federal judges—Philip P. Barbour in 1836 and Peter V. Daniel in 1842—had made it to the Court. After 1880, when federal circuit judge William B. Woods was appointed, the pace picked up, and federal judicial experience became an increasingly important criterion for appointment to the Supreme Court.

Politicians

Many justices have come from a political background, serving in Congress, as governors, or as members of a cabinet. One president, Taft, was later appointed to the Court, as chief justice, in 1921. One-fourth of all justices—twenty-seven—held congressional office before their elevation to the Court. An additional six justices sat in the Continental Congress in the 1770s or 1780s.

The first justice who had a congressional background was William Paterson, who had served in the Senate from 1789 to 1790. Chief Justice John Marshall was the first justice with cabinet experience, having held the post of secretary of state from 1800 to 1801.

Despite the number of justices with a congressional background, few incumbent members have been nominated directly to the Supreme Court. Only one incumbent House member, James M. Wayne in 1835, has ever been named to the Court, and six incumbent senators: Oliver Ellsworth in 1796, John McKinley in 1837, Levi

Catholic and Jewish Justices

The Supreme Court has been overwhelmingly Protestant. The first time the Protestant tradition was broken was in 1835, when Andrew Jackson nominated Roger B. Taney, a Roman Catholic, for chief justice. Taney's religion raised no controversy; instead, Taney's close alliance with Jackson, whom he served as attorney general and Treasury secretary, was the main focus of attention.

Not until 1894—nearly thirty years after Taney's death—was the second Catholic, Edward D. White of Louisiana, appointed, by Grover Cleveland. More than sixteen years later, William Howard Taft made White chief justice. White's religion was not an issue. Both Taney and White were from traditional Catholic areas and had long been engaged in American politics without any religion bias. In 1897 William McKinley chose Joseph McKenna, his attorney general and a Catholic, as an associate justice. In that appointment, geography was the overriding factor; McKenna came from California, as did his predecessor, Stephen J. Field.

Pierce Butler was the next Catholic appointee. President Warren G. Harding named him to the bench in 1922, largely because of Butler's political base. He was a Democrat, and Harding wanted to make a show of bipartisanship. On Butler's death in 1939, Franklin D. Roosevelt picked as his successor Frank Murphy, an Irish Catholic politician who had been mayor of Detroit, governor of Michigan, and was then serving as Roosevelt's attorney general. In 1949, when Murphy died, Harry S. Truman broke the continuity of a Catholic seat on the Court by naming Protestant Tom C. Clark. For the first time since 1894, no Catholic sat on the Court.

Of all the Catholic appointments, Dwight D. Eisenhower's 1956 choice of William J. Brennan Jr. attracted the most notice, although it, too, was relatively noncontroversial. Republicans were making a strong appeal in election year 1956 to normally Democratic Catholic voters in the big cities. Some saw the appointment as part of GOP strategy, but Eisenhower insisted it was made purely on merit.

Ronald Reagan named two Catholics to the Court: Antonin Scalia and Anthony M. Kennedy.

Much more controversial than any of the Catholic nominees was Louis D. Brandeis, the first Jewish justice, named by Woodrow Wilson in 1916. Brandeis was already a figure of great controversy because of his views on social and economic matters. Conservatives bitterly fought his nomination, and an element of anti-Semitism existed in some of the opposition.

Herbert Hoover's 1932 nomination of Benjamin Cardozo established a so-called Jewish seat on the Supreme Court. Felix Frankfurter replaced Cardozo in 1939. He in turn was replaced by Arthur J. Goldberg in 1962. When Goldberg resigned, Lyndon B. Johnson chose Abe Fortas to replace him. But with Fortas's resignation in 1969, Richard Nixon broke the tradition of a Jewish seat by choosing Harry A. Blackmun of Minnesota, a Protestant. No Jewish justice sat on the Court again until Bill Clinton chose Ruth Bader Ginsburg in 1993 to fill the vacancy caused by the retirement of Byron R. White. Clinton's second appointee, Stephen G. Breyer, also was Jewish. He filled the seat vacated by Blackmun in 1994.

Clarence Thomas was an Episcopalian when named to the Court in 1991, but in 1996 he announced that he had returned to Catholicism, the faith of his youth. That personal decision made history: for the first time, a majority of the justices were not Protestant. Thomas, Scalia, and Kennedy were Catholic; Breyer and Ginsburg, Jewish.

Woodbury in 1845, Edward D. White in 1894, Hugo L. Black in 1937, and Harold Burton in 1945.

The Senate traditionally has confirmed its members without much debate. But in January 1853, when lame-duck president Millard Fillmore nominated Whig senator George Badger of North Carolina to the Court, the Democratic Senate postponed the nomination until the close of the congressional session in March. Then the new Democratic president, Franklin Pierce, was able to nominate his own justice. The postponement of Badger's nomination was a polite way of defeating a colleague's nomination, avoiding an outright rejection.

Senator White's nomination came about after a bitter quarrel between President Grover Cleveland and Sen. David B. Hill of New York that resulted in the Senate's rejection of two Cleveland nominees from New York. Cleveland then turned to the Senate for one of its own members, White, and that body quickly accepted the choice.

Sen. Hugo Black's 1937 nomination was surrounded by controversy. Sen. Joseph T. Robinson of Arkansas, the Senate majority leader who had led the fight for President Franklin Roosevelt's so-called "court-packing" plan, was expected to get the nomination but died suddenly. So Roosevelt picked Black, one of the few southern senators other than Robinson who had championed the president in the Court battle. Black's support of the controversial bill—plus what some felt was his general lack of qualifications for the Supreme Court—led to a brief but acrimonious fight over his nomination. After he was confirmed, publicity grew over his one-time membership in the Ku Klux Klan, and charges were made that he was still a member. But in a nationwide radio address, Black denied any racial or religious intolerance on his part and defused the criticism.

The last Supreme Court appointee with any previous congressional service was Sherman Minton in 1949. He had served as a U.S. senator from Indiana from 1935 to 1941, then was appointed to a circuit court of appeals judgeship. Since the retirement of Black in 1971, no Supreme Court member has had any congressional experience.

Cabinet Members

Twenty members of the Supreme Court previously held cabinet-level posts, including Charles Evans Hughes, who was secretary of state in between his two terms on the Court. In addition to these twenty, James F. Byrnes served as secretary of state after leaving the Court.

Nine attorneys general, including seven incumbents, have been appointed to the Court, four secretaries of state (not including John Jay, who was secretary of foreign affairs), four secretaries of the Treasury, and three secretaries of the navy. Included twice in these tallies are Roger Brooke Taney, who served as attorney general and Treasury secretary; Levi Woodbury, who served as Treasury secretary and navy secretary; and William Henry Moody, who served as navy secretary and attorney general.

One postmaster general, one secretary of the interior, one secretary of war, and one secretary of labor also were appointed to the Court.

The appointment of incumbent attorneys general has been largely a twentieth-century phenomenon: six of the seven appointments took place after 1900. The other was made just before that, when President William McKinley appointed his attorney general, Joseph McKenna. The twentieth-century incumbents named to the Court were William H. Moody, appointed by Theodore Roosevelt in 1906; James C. McReynolds (Woodrow Wilson, 1914); Harlan Fiske Stone (Calvin Coolidge, 1925); Frank Murphy (Franklin Roosevelt, 1940); Robert H. Jackson (Roosevelt, 1941); and Tom C. Clark (Truman, 1949).

In the nineteenth century two men who had served as attorney general eventually were elevated to the Supreme Court. They were Roger Brooke Taney, appointed chief justice by Jackson in 1835, after serving as Jackson's attorney general from 1831 to 1833, and Nathan Clifford, appointed to the Court by James Buchanan in 1857, after serving as James K. Polk's attorney general from 1846 to 1848.

The last Supreme Court justice with cabinet experience was Arthur Goldberg, John F. Kennedy's secretary of labor.

Governors

Only six governors or former governors have ever been appointed to the Supreme Court. The first was

Women Justices

At the beginning of 2005, the Supreme Court had 108 members in its entire history, all except two of whom were male. The first woman justice, Sandra Day O'Connor, was nominated by President Ronald Reagan, who called her "a person for all seasons." She won unanimous confirmation, 99–0, from the Senate on Sept. 21, 1981. Ruth Bader Ginsburg, who had pioneered legal advocacy for women's rights, joined O'Connor on the high bench in 1993, becoming the second female associate justice. Ginsburg had been nominated by President Bill Clinton and was confirmed 96–3 on Aug. 3. Three conservative Republicans cast the negative votes.

William Paterson, who served as governor of New Jersey from 1790 to 1793. The most recent was California governor Earl Warren, appointed chief justice by Eisenhower in 1953. Warren had a long political career behind him, having served as attorney general of California before winning three terms as governor of his state. In 1948 he was the Republican nominee for vice president and was briefly a candidate for the presidential nomination in 1952.

Charles Evans Hughes of New York was appointed to the Supreme Court by Taft in 1910. Hughes was a reform governor who had conducted investigations into fraudulent insurance practices in New York before being elected governor in 1906. He left the Court in 1916 to run for president on the Republican ticket, losing narrowly to Wilson. Later he served as secretary of state under Harding and Coolidge and returned to the Court in 1930 as chief justice.

The three other former governors appointed to the Supreme Court were Levi Woodbury of New Hampshire in 1845 (governor, 1823–24), Salmon P. Chase of Ohio in 1864 (governor, 1856–60), and Frank Murphy of Michigan in 1940 (governor, 1937–39).

John Jay resigned as the first chief justice to become governor of New York. James F. Byrnes left the bench after serving sixteen months to serve in other positions in federal and state government, the last of which was governor of South Carolina.

Generation Gaps

The age at which justices joined the Court has varied widely. The oldest person ever initially appointed was Horace H. Lurton, who was sixty-five when he went on the Court in 1910. Two justices were older than that when they achieved the office of chief justice. When he was named chief justice in 1941, Harlan Fiske Stone was sixty-eight; and Charles Evans Hughes was sixty-seven when he returned to the Court to be chief justice in 1930.

Representing the younger generation, Justices William Johnson and Joseph Story were both only thirty-two when they were appointed in 1804 and 1811, respectively. Story was younger than Johnson by about a month.

Only two other justices were under forty when appointed: Bushrod Washington, nephew of the president, who was thirty-six when appointed in 1798, and James Iredell, who was thirty-eight when appointed in 1790. Iredell also was the youngest justice to die on the Court—forty-eight when he died in 1799.

The youngest justice in the twentieth century was William O. Douglas, who was forty when appointed in 1939. The oldest justice ever on the Court was Oliver Wendell Holmes, who retired at ninety in 1932, the Court's only nonagenarian. The second-oldest member, Chief Justice Roger Taney, was eighty-seven when he died in 1864. All previous justices who had served past the age of eighty had retired from the bench and had not died in office. They were Harry A. Blackmun (eighty-five), William Brennan (eighty-four), Thurgood Marshall (eighty-three), Louis Brandeis (eighty-two), Gabriel Duval (eighty-two), Joseph McKenna (eighty-one), Stephen Field (eighty-one), and Samuel Nelson (eighty). At the start of 2005, two justices serving were in their eighties: William Rehnquist (eighty) and John Paul Stevens (eighty-four).

The youngest member ever to leave the Court was Benjamin Curtis, who resigned in 1857 at forty-seven. Others who left the Court before the age of fifty were Justices Iredell, dead at forty-eight, Alfred Moore, who retired at forty-eight, and John Jay and John A. Campbell, who retired at forty-nine. Jay also holds the record for number of years survived after leaving the Court—thirty-four years. In modern times, Justice James F. Byrnes lived twenty-nine years after resigning from the Court in 1942.

Longevity

Length of service on the Court has also varied greatly, from six months to thirty-six years. Justice Thomas Johnson served on the Court for only six months after taking the judicial oath on Aug. 6, 1792. Although he retired because of ill health on March 4, 1793, he lived another twenty-six years, dying at the age of eighty-seven. In more recent times, Justice Byrnes served the shortest time, taking the judicial oath July 8, 1941, and then resigning on Oct. 3, 1942, to become director of the World War II Office of Economic Stabilization.

Edwin Stanton, the controversial secretary of war during the Lincoln and Andrew Johnson administrations, was nominated for the Supreme Court by Grant. The Senate confirmed him on Dec. 20, 1869, but Stanton died of a heart attack on Dec. 24. Because he did not have a chance to begin his service on the Court, he is not considered to have been a justice.

In January 1974 Justice William Douglas broke the old longevity record for service on the Court, held since

December 1897 by Stephen Field, who had served thirty-four years and six months when he resigned. Douglas went on to serve until November 1975, when he resigned after thirty-six years and seven months on the Court. Chief Justice John Marshall established the first longevity record by serving for thirty-four years and five months between 1801 and 1835. That record held until Field broke it in 1897. In January 2005 Chief Justice Rehnquist marked his thirty-third year on the Court.

Other justices who served thirty years or longer include Hugo Black (thirty-four years, one month), the first John Marshall Harlan (thirty-three years, ten months), Brennan (thirty-three years, nine months), Story (thirty-three years, seven months), James Wayne (thirty-two years, six months), John McLean (thirty-one years, three months), Byron R. White (thirty-one years, two months), Bushrod Washington (thirty years, ten months), and William Johnson (thirty years, three months).

The long terms of Black and Douglas spanned an era of such changing membership on the Court that they each served with more than a quarter of the Court's entire membership throughout its history.

Four or five years is usually the longest the Court goes without a change in justices. The longest period during which the Court kept the same membership intact was eleven years—from 1812, when Joseph Story was sworn in, to 1823, when Justice Henry Brockholst Livingston died. However, by 2005, the record was ready to fall. In March 2005 it had been more than ten years, seven months since the last change on the court—Bill Clinton's appointment of Steven G. Breyer in Aug. 1994.

Infirmity

Longevity of service sometimes leads to questions of disability, as justices age and are no longer capable of carrying a full load of casework. By early 1870 Justice Robert C. Grier was nearly seventy-six. His mental and physical powers were obviously impaired, and he often seemed confused and feeble. Grier complied when a committee of his fellow justices approached him to urge his resignation. He died eight months later.

Among the justices urging Grier's retirement was Stephen Field. Ironically, a quarter of a century later, Field found himself in the same position as Grier. His powers had visibly declined, and he was taking less and less part in Court proceedings. The other justices began hinting strongly that Field resign. But Field insisted on staying on the Court long enough to break Chief Justice John Marshall's record for length of service.

In 1880 an especially infirm set of justices manned the Court; three of the nine were incapacitated. Justice Ward Hunt had suffered a paralytic stroke in 1879 and took no further part in Court proceedings, but he refused to resign because he was not eligible for a full pension under the law then in effect. After three years, Congress passed a special law exempting Hunt from the terms of the pension law, granting him retirement at full pay if he would resign within thirty days of enactment of the exemption. Hunt resigned the same day.

Longest Vacancies in the Court's History

The longest vacancy in the Supreme Court's history lasted for two years, three months, and eighteen days. During that period the Senate rejected four nominations by two presidents, and James Buchanan, who would serve as the fifteenth president of the United States, declined three invitations to fill the vacancy.

When Justice Henry Baldwin died April 21, 1844, John Tyler was president. Elected vice president on the Whig ticket in 1840, Tyler broke with the party after he had become president on William Henry Harrison's death in 1841. From then on, he was a president essentially without a party or personal popularity. At the time of Baldwin's death, one Tyler nomination to the Court had already been rejected and a second was pending. Tyler first offered the Baldwin vacancy to Buchanan, who, like Baldwin, was a Pennsylvanian. When he declined, the president nominated Philadelphia attorney Edward King to the seat.

Followers of Henry Clay, however, who controlled the Senate, thought Clay would win the presidency in that year's election, and they voted in June 1844 to postpone consideration of both King's nomination and Tyler's pending appointment of Reuben H. Walworth to the second vacancy. Tyler resubmitted King's name in December. Again the Senate refused to act, and Tyler was forced to withdraw the appointment.

By this time, Tyler was a lame-duck president, and Clay had lost the election to Democrat James K. Polk. Nonetheless, Tyler in February 1845 named John M. Read, a Philadelphia attorney who had support among the Democrats and the Clay Whigs in the Senate. But the Senate failed to act on the nomination before adjournment, and the vacancy was left for Polk to fill.

Polk had only slightly better luck with his appointments. After six months in office he offered the position to Buchanan, who again refused it. Another few months passed before Polk formally nominated George W. Woodward to the Baldwin vacancy in December 1845. Woodward turned out to be a hapless choice. He was opposed by one of the senators from his home state, Pennsylvania, and his extreme "American nativist" views made him unpopular with many other senators. His nomination was rejected on a 20–29 vote in January 1846. Polk then asked Buchanan once again to take the seat. Buchanan at first accepted but later changed his mind and declined a third time. The president then turned to Robert C. Grier, a district court judge from Pennsylvania who proved acceptable to almost everyone. The Senate confirmed him Aug. 4, 1846, the day following his nomination. He was sworn in Aug. 10.

The second-longest vacancy lasted almost as long as the first—two years, one month, and twenty days. It occurred when Justice Peter V. Daniel of Virginia died May 31, 1860. At this point four of the remaining justices were northerners; four were from the South. Naturally, the South wanted then-President James Buchanan to replace Daniel with another southerner; the North urged a nomination from one of its states.

Buchanan took a long time making up his mind. In February 1861, eight months after the vacancy occurred, he nominated Secretary of State Jeremiah S. Black, a former chief justice of the Pennsylvania Supreme Court and U.S. attorney general. Black might have proved acceptable to southern senators, but many of them had already resigned from the Senate to join the Confederacy. Though he supported the Union, Black was not an abolitionist, and his nomination drew criticism from the northern antislavery press. Black also was opposed by Democrat Stephen A. Douglas, who had just lost the presidential election to Abraham Lincoln. Finally, Republicans in the Senate were not anxious to help fill a vacancy that they could leave open for the incoming Republican president. Had Buchanan acted earlier, it is likely that Black would have been confirmed. As it was, the Senate rejected his nomination by a one-vote margin, 25–26.

Buchanan made no further attempt to fill the Daniel vacancy. Lincoln, who soon had two more seats on the Court to fill, did not name anyone to the Daniel seat until July 1862—more than a year after his inauguration. His choice was Samuel F. Miller, a well-respected Iowa attorney. Miller's nomination had been urged by a majority of both the House and Senate and by other politicians and members of the legal profession. The Senate confirmed his nomination within half an hour of receiving it July 16, 1862. He was sworn in five days later.

Sources: Henry J. Abraham, *Justices and Presidents: A Political History of Appointments to the Supreme Court* (New York: Oxford University Press, 1974); and Charles Warren, *The Supreme Court in United States History,* rev. ed., 2 vols. (Boston: Little, Brown, 1922, 1926).

Justice Nathan Clifford also had suffered a stroke that prevented him from participating in Court activities. But Clifford also refused to resign, hoping to live long enough for a Democratic president to name a successor. At the time, Clifford was the only Democrat left on the Court who had been named by a Democratic president. But he died while Republicans were still in power.

While Hunt and Clifford were both incapacitated, Justice Noah Swayne's mental acuity was noticeably declining. He was persuaded to resign by President Hayes, with the promise that Swayne's friend and fellow Ohioan Stanley Matthews would be chosen as his successor.

The most recent case of a Court disability was that of Justice William Douglas, who suffered a stroke in January 1975. At first, Douglas attempted to continue his duties, but in November 1975 he resigned, citing pain and physical disability.

Controversial Justices

The only time a justice clearly has been driven from the Court by outside pressure occurred in 1969, when Justice Abe Fortas resigned. The resignation followed by less than eight months a successful Senate filibuster against President Lyndon B. Johnson's nomination of Fortas to be chief justice. Fortas's departure from the Court climaxed a furor brought on by the disclosure early in May 1969 that he had received and held for eleven months a $20,000 fee from the family foundation of a man later imprisoned for illegal stock manipulation.

A year after Fortas's resignation, an attempt was made to bring impeachment charges against Justice Douglas. General dissatisfaction with Douglas's liberal views and controversial lifestyle—combined with frustration over the Senate's rejection of two of President Nixon's conservative southern nominees—seemed to spark the action. House Republican leader Gerald R. Ford of Michigan, who led the attempt to impeach Douglas, charged among other things that the justice had practiced law in violation of federal law, had failed to disqualify himself in cases in which he had an interest, and violated standards of good behavior by allegedly advocating revolution. A special House Judiciary subcommittee created to investigate the charges found no grounds for impeachment.

The only Supreme Court justice ever to be impeached was Samuel Chase. A staunch Federalist who had rankled Jeffersonians with his partisan political statements and his vigorous prosecution of the Alien and Sedition Act, Chase was impeached by the House in 1804. But his critics failed to achieve the necessary two-thirds majority in the Senate for conviction.

Other, less heralded cases of questionable behavior have occurred from time to time. One early controversy surfaced in 1857, when the nation was awaiting the Court's decision in the *Dred Scott* case. Justices Robert C. Grier and John Catron wrote privately to the incoming president, James Buchanan, detailing the Court's discussions and foretelling the final decision. Buchanan was glad of the news and was able to say in his inaugural address that the decision was expected to come soon and that he and all Americans should acquiesce in it. But divulging the Court's decision before it is publicly announced is generally considered to be unethical.

Another controversy arose fourteen years later in the so-called *Legal Tender Cases*. The Court, with two vacancies, had found the Civil War legal tender acts unconstitutional. After President Grant named two justices to fill the vacancies, the Court voted to rehear the case. With the two new justices—William Strong and Joseph P. Bradley—voting with the majority, the Court now found the legal tender acts constitutional. It was charged that Grant had appointed the two knowing in advance that they would vote to reverse the Court's previous decision. But historians have not turned up any evidence that any explicit arrangement was involved.

Although political activity by Supreme Court justices usually has been frowned upon, several justices in the nineteenth century showed a keen interest in their party's presidential nomination. Justice John McLean entertained presidential ambitions throughout his long Supreme Court career and flirted with several political parties at various stages. In 1856 he received 190 votes on an informal first ballot at the first Republican national convention. He also sought the Republican presidential nomination in 1860.

Chief Justice Salmon Chase had aspired to the presidency before going on the bench, losing the Republican nomination to Lincoln in 1860. In 1864, while serving as Lincoln's secretary of the Treasury, he allowed himself to become the focus of an anti-Lincoln group within the Republican Party. During his service on the Court, in both 1868 and 1872, he made no secret of his still-burning presidential ambitions and allowed friends to maneuver politically for him.

In 1877 the Supreme Court was thrust into the election process when a dispute arose as to the outcome of the 1876 presidential election. To resolve the problem, Congress created a special electoral commission that included five Supreme Court justices. Each house of Congress also chose five members; the Democratic House choosing five Democrats and the Republican Senate choosing five Republicans.

The five justices were supposed to be divided evenly politically—two Democrats, Nathan Clifford and Stephen J. Field; two Republicans, Samuel Miller and William Strong; and one independent, David Davis. Davis, however, withdrew from consideration because he had been elected a U.S. senator from Illinois. Justice Joseph P. Bradley, a Republican, was substituted for Davis, making the overall lineup on the commission eight to seven in favor of the Republicans.

The three Republican justices loyally supported the claims of Republican presidential aspirant Rutherford B. Hayes on all questions, and the two Democratic justices backed Democratic nominee Samuel J. Tilden. The result was the election of Hayes. Justice Clifford, the chairman of the commission, was so contemptuous of the outcome that he called Hayes an illegitimate president and refused to enter the White House during his term.

A controversial recent case surrounded the 1991 confirmation of Clarence Thomas, George Bush's choice to fill the vacancy caused by Thurgood Marshall's resignation. Marshall, whose six-decade legal career shaped the country's civil rights struggles and liberal activism, was the Court's first African American justice. Thomas, also an African American, was by contrast notably conservative. But his conservative stance and controversy over other issues were eclipsed during the confirmation process by allegations that he had sexually harassed a former employee. Three days of dramatic hearings on national television failed to resolve the charges and Thomas won confirmation by a vote of 52–48, the closest Supreme Court confirmation vote in more than a century.

In late 2000 the Court stepped in and decided the outcome of another presidential election. The close presidential race between Texas governor George W. Bush and outgoing Vice President Al Gore came down to who won the state of Florida. After the first statewide machine recount, Bush led in Florida by only a few hundred votes. As Democrats pressed for a hand recount in four counties, Republicans took the issue to court. The case quickly rose to the Supreme Court, which handed down a decision five weeks after the election. Voting 5–4 along party lines, the Court ruled in favor of halting the hand recount, effectively giving the election to Bush. Some felt the Court should have found a way of abstaining from deciding a presidential election, perhaps by sending the matter back to Florida. Many felt that the highly political ruling tarnished the Court's reputation as standing above partisan politics.

Supreme Court Justices: Biographies

This biographical summary lists, alphabetically, all the justices of the Supreme Court since 1789. The material is organized as follows: name; relationship to other justices, presidents, and vice presidents; state; date of birth; date of death (if applicable); nominating president; date of confirmation, date of swearing in (recess appointment noted, if applicable); date of confirmation, date of swearing in as chief justice (if applicable); date of resignation (in cases where the justice left the Court before death); service as president, vice president, cabinet member, governor, delegate to the Continental Congress, member of Congress, House or Senate majority leader, House or Senate minority leader, Speaker of the House of Representatives, president pro tempore of the Senate (when elected), chair of standing congressional committees (since 1947), or chair of the Democratic National Committee or the Republican National Committee.

Specific dates of service are provided where available. For presidential, vice presidential, and congressional terms, only the years are given for beginning and ending dates if the standard terms were served. Presidential and vice presidential terms from 1789 to 1933 were from March 4 to March 4; since 1934, the four-year term has been from Jan. 20 to Jan. 20. Congressional terms from 1789 to 1933 were from March 4 to March 4; since 1934, service has been from Jan. 3 to Jan. 3.

The major sources of information for this list were David G. Savage, *Guide to U.S. Supreme Court,* 4th ed. (Washington, D.C.: CQ Press, 2004); the U.S. Supreme Court; and various newspapers.

Baldwin, Henry (Pa.) Jan. 14, 1780–April 21, 1844; nominated by Andrew Jackson; confirmed Jan. 6, 1830, sworn in Jan. 18, 1830; House 1817–May 8, 1822 (no party).

Barbour, Philip Pendleton (Va.) May 25, 1783–Feb. 25, 1841; nominated by Andrew Jackson; confirmed March 15, 1836, sworn in May 12, 1836; House Sept. 19, 1814–25 (Republican), 1827–Oct. 15, 1830 (1827–29 Republican, 1829–Oct. 15, 1830 Jacksonian); Speaker Dec. 4, 1821–23.

Black, Hugo Lafayette (Ala.) Feb. 27, 1886–Sept. 25, 1971; nominated by Franklin D. Roosevelt; confirmed Aug. 17, 1937, sworn in Aug. 19, 1937, resigned Sept. 17, 1971; Senate 1927–Aug. 19, 1937 (Democrat).

Blackmun, Harry Andrew (Minn.) Nov. 12, 1908–March 4, 1999; nominated by Richard Nixon; confirmed May 12, 1970, sworn in June 9, 1970, resigned Aug. 3, 1994.

Blair, John Jr. (Va.) 1732–Aug. 31, 1800; nominated by George Washington; confirmed Sept. 26, 1789, sworn in Feb. 2, 1790, resigned Jan. 27, 1796.

Blatchford, Samuel (N.Y.) March 9, 1820–July 7, 1893; nominated by Chester A. Arthur; confirmed March 27, 1882, sworn in April 3, 1882.

Bradley, Joseph P. (N.J.) March 14, 1813–Jan. 22, 1892; nominated by Ulysses S. Grant; confirmed March 21, 1870, sworn in March 23, 1870.

Brandeis, Louis Dembitz (Mass.) Nov. 13, 1856–Oct. 5, 1941; nominated by Woodrow Wilson; confirmed June 1, 1916, sworn in June 5, 1916, resigned Feb. 13, 1939.

Brennan, William Joseph Jr. (N.J.) April 25, 1906–July 24, 1997; nominated by Dwight D. Eisenhower; confirmed March 19, 1957, sworn in Oct. 16, 1956 (recess appointment), resigned July 20, 1990.

Brewer, David Josiah (nephew of Assoc. Justice Stephen Johnson Field) (Kan.) June 20, 1837–March 28, 1910; nominated by Benjamin Harrison; confirmed Dec. 18, 1889, sworn in Jan. 6, 1890.

Breyer, Stephen Gerald (Mass.) Aug. 15, 1938– ; nominated by Bill Clinton; confirmed July 29, 1994, sworn in Aug. 3, 1994.

Brown, Henry Billings (Mich.) March 2, 1836–Sept. 4, 1913; nominated by Benjamin Harrison; confirmed Dec. 29, 1890, sworn in Jan. 5, 1891, resigned May 28, 1906.

Burger, Warren Earl (Minn.) Sept. 17, 1907–June 25, 1995; nominated by Richard Nixon; confirmed as chief justice June 9, 1969, sworn in June 23, 1969, resigned Sept. 26, 1986.

Burton, Harold Hitz (Ohio) June 22, 1888–Oct. 28, 1964; nominated by Harry S. Truman; confirmed Sept. 19, 1945, sworn in Oct.

1, 1945, resigned Oct. 13, 1958; Senate 1941–Sept. 30, 1945 (Republican).

Butler, Pierce (Minn.) March 17, 1866–Nov. 16, 1939; nominated by Warren G. Harding; confirmed Dec. 21, 1922, sworn in Jan. 2, 1923.

Byrnes, James Francis (S.C.) May 2, 1879–April 9, 1972; nominated by Franklin D. Roosevelt; confirmed June 12, 1941, sworn in July 8, 1941, resigned Oct. 3, 1942; House 1911–25 (Democrat); Senate 1931–July 8, 1941 (Democrat); secretary of state July 3, 1945–Jan. 21, 1947; Gov. Jan. 16, 1951–Jan. 18, 1955 (Democrat).

Campbell, John Archibald (Ala.) June 24, 1811–March 12, 1889; nominated by Franklin Pierce; confirmed March 25, 1853, sworn in April 11, 1853, resigned April 30, 1861.

Cardozo, Benjamin Nathan (N.Y.) May 24, 1870–July 9, 1938; nominated by Herbert Hoover; confirmed Feb. 24, 1932, sworn in March 14, 1932.

Catron, John (Tenn.) 1786–May 30, 1865; nominated by Andrew Jackson; confirmed March 8, 1837, sworn in May 1, 1837.

Chase, Salmon Portland (Ohio) Jan. 13, 1808–May 7, 1873; nominated by Abraham Lincoln; confirmed as chief justice Dec. 6, 1864, sworn in Dec. 15, 1864; Senate 1849–55 (Free-Soiler), March 4–6, 1861 (Republican); Gov. Jan. 14, 1856–Jan. 9, 1860 (Republican); secretary of the Treasury March 7, 1861–June 30, 1864.

Chase, Samuel (Md.) April 17, 1741–June 19, 1811; nominated by George Washington; confirmed Jan. 27, 1796, sworn in Feb. 4, 1796; Cont. Cong. 1774–78.

Clark, Thomas Campbell (Texas) Sept. 23, 1899–June 13, 1977; nominated by Harry S. Truman; confirmed Aug. 18, 1949, sworn in Aug. 24, 1949, resigned June 12, 1967; attorney general July 1, 1945–Aug. 24, 1949.

Clarke, John Hessin (Ohio) Sept. 18, 1857–March 22, 1945; nominated by Woodrow Wilson; confirmed July 24, 1916, sworn in Oct. 9, 1916, resigned Sept. 18, 1922.

Clifford, Nathan (Maine) Aug. 18, 1803–July 25, 1881; nominated by James Buchanan; confirmed Jan. 12, 1858, sworn in Jan. 21, 1858; House 1839–43 (Democrat); attorney general Oct. 17, 1846–March 17, 1848.

Curtis, Benjamin Robbins (Mass.) Nov. 4, 1809–Sept. 15, 1874; nominated by Millard Fillmore; confirmed Dec. 29, 1851 (recess appointment), sworn in Oct. 10, 1851, resigned Sept. 30, 1857.

Cushing, William (Mass.) March 1, 1732–Sept. 13, 1810; nominated by George Washington; confirmed Sept. 26, 1789, sworn in Feb. 2, 1790.

Daniel, Peter Vivian (Va.) April 24, 1784–May 31, 1860; nominated by Martin Van Buren; confirmed March 2, 1841, sworn in Jan. 10, 1842.

Davis, David (Ill.) March 9, 1815–June 26, 1886; nominated by Abraham Lincoln; confirmed Dec. 8, 1862, sworn in Dec. 10, 1862, resigned March 4, 1877; Senate 1877–83 (Independent); elected pres. pro tempore Oct. 13, 1881.

Day, William Rufus (Ohio) April 17, 1849–July 9, 1923; nominated by Theodore Roosevelt; confirmed Feb. 23, 1903, sworn in March 2, 1903, resigned Nov. 13, 1922; secretary of state April 28–Sept. 16, 1898.

Douglas, William Orville (Conn.) Oct. 16, 1898–Jan. 19, 1980; nominated by Franklin D. Roosevelt; confirmed April 4, 1939, sworn in April 17, 1939, resigned Nov. 12, 1975.

Duvall, Gabriel (Md.) Dec. 6, 1752–March 6, 1844; nominated by James Madison; confirmed Nov. 18, 1811, sworn in Nov. 23, 1811, resigned Jan. 14, 1835; House Nov. 11, 1794–March 28, 1796 (Nov. 11, 1794–95 no party, 1795–March 28, 1796 Republican).

Ellsworth, Oliver (Conn.) April 29, 1745–Nov. 26, 1807; nominated by George Washington; confirmed as chief justice March 4, 1796, sworn in March 8, 1796, resigned Dec. 15, 1800; Cont. Cong. 1778–83; Senate 1789–March 8, 1796 (no party).

Field, Stephen Johnson (uncle of Assoc. Justice David Josiah Brewer) (Calif.) Nov. 4, 1816–April 9, 1899; nominated by Abraham Lincoln; confirmed March 10, 1863, sworn in May 20, 1863, resigned Dec. 1, 1897.

Fortas, Abe (D.C.) June 19, 1910–April 5, 1982; nominated by Lyndon B. Johnson; confirmed Aug. 11, 1965, sworn in Oct. 4, 1965, resigned May 14, 1969.

Frankfurter, Felix (Mass.) Nov. 15, 1882–Feb. 22, 1965; nominated by Franklin D. Roosevelt; confirmed Jan. 17, 1939, sworn in Jan. 30, 1939, resigned Aug. 28, 1962.

Fuller, Melville Weston (Ill.) Feb. 11, 1833–July 4, 1910; nominated by Grover Cleveland; confirmed as chief justice July 20, 1888, sworn in Oct. 8, 1888.

Ginsburg, Ruth Bader (D.C.) March 15, 1933– ; nominated by Bill Clinton; confirmed Aug. 3, 1993, sworn in Aug. 10, 1993.

Goldberg, Arthur Joseph (Ill.) Aug. 8, 1908–Jan. 18, 1990; nominated by John F. Kennedy; confirmed Sept. 25, 1962, sworn in Oct. 1, 1962, resigned July 25, 1965; secretary of labor Jan. 21, 1961–Sept. 25, 1962.

Gray, Horace (son-in-law of Assoc. Justice Stanley Matthews) (Mass.) March 24, 1828–Sept. 15, 1902; nominated by Chester A. Arthur; confirmed Dec. 20, 1881, sworn in Jan. 9, 1882.

Grier, Robert Cooper (Pa.) March 5, 1794–Sept. 25, 1870; nominated by James K. Polk; confirmed Aug. 4, 1846, sworn in Aug. 10, 1846, resigned Jan. 31, 1870.

Harlan, John Marshall (grandfather of Assoc. Justice John Marshall Harlan) (Ky.) June 1, 1833–Oct. 14, 1911; nominated by Rutherford B. Hayes; confirmed Nov. 29, 1877, sworn in Dec. 10, 1877.

Harlan, John Marshall (grandson of Assoc. Justice John Marshall Harlan) (N.Y.) May 20, 1899–Dec. 29, 1971; nominated by Dwight D. Eisenhower; confirmed March 16, 1955, sworn in March 28, 1955, resigned Sept. 23, 1971.

Holmes, Oliver Wendell Jr. (Mass.) March 8, 1841–March 6, 1935; nominated by Theodore Roosevelt; confirmed Dec. 4, 1902, sworn in Dec. 8, 1902, resigned Jan. 12, 1932.

Hughes, Charles Evans (N.Y.) April 11, 1862–Aug. 27, 1948; nominated by William Howard Taft; confirmed May 2, 1910, sworn in Oct. 10, 1910, resigned June 10, 1916; nominated as chief justice by Herbert Hoover; confirmed as chief justice Feb. 13, 1930, sworn in Feb. 24, 1930, resigned July 1, 1941; Gov. Jan. 1, 1907–Oct. 6, 1910 (Republican); secretary of state March 5, 1921–March 4, 1925.

Hunt, Ward (N.Y.) June 14, 1810–March 24, 1886; nominated by Ulysses S. Grant; confirmed Dec. 11, 1872, sworn in Jan. 9, 1873, resigned Jan. 27, 1882.

Iredell, James (N.C.) Oct. 5, 1751–Oct. 20, 1799; nominated by George Washington; confirmed Feb. 10, 1790, sworn in May 12, 1790.

Jackson, Howell Edmunds (Tenn.) April 8, 1832–Aug. 8, 1895; nominated by Benjamin Harrison; confirmed Feb. 18, 1893, sworn in March 4, 1893; Senate 1881–April 14, 1886.

Jackson, Robert Houghwout (N.Y.) Feb. 13, 1892–Oct. 9, 1954; nominated by Franklin D. Roosevelt; confirmed July 7, 1941, sworn in July 11, 1941; attorney general Jan. 18, 1940–July 10, 1941.

Jay, John (brother-in-law of Assoc. Justice Henry Brockholst Livingston) (N.Y.) Dec. 12, 1745–May 17, 1829; nominated by George Washington; confirmed as chief justice Sept. 26, 1789, sworn in Oct. 19, 1789, resigned June 29, 1795; Cont. Cong. 1774–76, 1778–79 (president); secretary of foreign affairs 1784–89; Gov. July 1, 1795–June 30, 1801 (Federalist).

Johnson, Thomas (Md.) Nov. 4, 1732–Oct. 26, 1819; nominated by George Washington; confirmed Nov. 7, 1791, sworn in Aug. 6, 1792, resigned March 4, 1793; Cont. Cong. 1774–76.

Johnson, William (S.C.) Dec. 27, 1771–Aug. 4, 1834; nominated by Thomas Jefferson; confirmed March 24, 1804, sworn in May 7, 1804.

Kennedy, Anthony McLeod (Calif.) July 23, 1936– ; nominated by Ronald Reagan; confirmed Feb. 3, 1988, sworn in Feb. 18, 1988.

Lamar, Joseph Rucker (cousin of Assoc. Justice Lucius Quintus Cincinnatus Lamar) (Miss.) Oct. 14, 1857–Jan. 2, 1916; nominated by William Howard Taft; confirmed Dec. 15, 1910, sworn in Jan. 3, 1911.

Lamar, Lucius Quintus Cincinnatus (cousin of Assoc. Justice Joseph Rucker Lamar) (Miss.) Sept. 17, 1825–Jan. 23, 1893; nominated by Grover Cleveland; confirmed Jan. 16, 1888, sworn in Jan. 18, 1888; House 1857–Dec. 1860, 1873–77 (Democrat); Senate 1877–March 6, 1885 (Democrat); secretary of the interior March 6, 1885–Jan. 10, 1888.

Livingston, Henry Brockholst (brother-in-law of Chief Justice John Jay, father-in-law of Assoc. Justice Smith Thompson) (N.Y.) Nov. 25, 1757–March 18, 1823; nominated by Thomas Jefferson; confirmed Dec. 17, 1806, sworn in Jan. 20, 1807.

Lurton, Horace Harmon (Tenn.) Feb. 26, 1844–July 12, 1914; nominated by William Howard Taft; confirmed Dec. 20, 1909, sworn in Jan. 3, 1910.

Marshall, John (Va.) Sept. 24, 1755–July 6, 1835; nominated by John Adams; confirmed as chief justice Jan. 27, 1801, sworn in Feb. 4, 1801; House 1799–June 7, 1800 (Federalist); secretary of state June 6, 1800–Feb. 4, 1801.

Marshall, Thurgood (N.Y.) July 2, 1908–Jan. 24, 1993; nominated by Lyndon B. Johnson; confirmed Aug. 30, 1967, sworn in Oct. 2, 1967, resigned Oct. 1, 1991.

Matthews, Stanley (father-in-law of Assoc. Justice Horace Gray) (Ohio) July 21, 1824–March 22, 1889; nominated by Rutherford B. Hayes; confirmed May 12, 1881, sworn in May 17, 1881; Senate March 21, 1877–79 (Republican).

McKenna, Joseph (Calif.) Aug. 10, 1843–Nov. 21, 1926; nominated by William McKinley; confirmed Jan. 21, 1898, sworn in Jan. 26, 1898, resigned Jan. 5, 1925; House 1885–March 28, 1892 (Republican); attorney general March 5, 1897–Jan. 25, 1898.

McKinley, John (Ala.) May 1, 1780–July 19, 1852; nominated by Martin Van Buren; confirmed Sept. 25, 1837, sworn in Jan. 9, 1838; Senate Nov. 27, 1826–31 (no party), March 4–April 22, 1837 (Jacksonian); House 1833–35 (Jacksonian).

McLean, John (Ohio) March 11, 1785–April 4, 1861; nominated by Andrew Jackson; confirmed March 7, 1829, sworn in Jan. 11, 1830; House 1813–16 (Republican); postmaster general July 1, 1823–March 9, 1829.

McReynolds, James Clark (Tenn.) Feb. 3, 1862–Aug. 24, 1946; nominated by Woodrow Wilson; confirmed Aug. 29, 1914, sworn in Oct. 12, 1914, resigned Jan. 31, 1941; attorney general March 5, 1913–Aug. 29, 1914.

Miller, Samuel Freeman (Iowa) April 5, 1816–Oct. 13, 1890; nominated by Abraham Lincoln; confirmed July 16, 1862, sworn in July 21, 1862.

Minton, Sherman (Ind.) Oct. 20, 1890–April 9, 1965; nominated by Harry S. Truman; confirmed Oct. 4, 1949, sworn in Oct. 12, 1949, resigned Oct. 15, 1956; Senate 1935–41 (Democrat).

Moody, William Henry (Mass.) Dec. 23, 1853–July 2, 1917; nominated by Theodore Roosevelt; confirmed Dec. 12, 1906, sworn in Dec. 17, 1906, resigned Nov. 20, 1910; House Nov. 5, 1895–May 1, 1902 (Republican); secretary of the navy May 1, 1902–June 30, 1904; attorney general July 1, 1904–Dec. 17, 1906.

Moore, Alfred (N.C.) May 21, 1755–Oct. 15, 1810; nominated by John Adams; confirmed Dec. 10, 1799, sworn in April 21, 1800, resigned Jan. 26, 1804.

Murphy, Francis William (Mich.) April 13, 1890–July 19, 1949; nominated by Franklin D. Roosevelt; confirmed Jan. 15, 1940, sworn in Feb. 5, 1940; Gov. Jan. 1, 1937–Jan. 1, 1939 (Democrat); attorney general Jan. 17, 1939–Jan. 18, 1940.

Nelson, Samuel (N.Y.) Nov. 10, 1792–Dec. 13, 1873; nominated by John Tyler; confirmed Feb. 14, 1845, sworn in Feb. 27, 1845, resigned Nov. 28, 1872.

O'Connor, Sandra Day (Ariz.) March 26, 1930– ; nominated by Ronald Reagan; confirmed Sept. 21, 1981, sworn in Sept. 25, 1981.

Paterson, William (N.J.) Dec. 24, 1745–Sept. 9, 1806; nominated by George Washington; confirmed March 4, 1793, sworn in March 11, 1793; Cont. Cong. (elected but did not attend) 1780, 1787; Senate 1789–Nov. 13, 1790 (no party); Gov. Oct. 30, 1790–March 4, 1793 (Federalist).

Peckham, Rufus Wheeler (N.Y.) Nov. 8, 1838–Oct. 24, 1909; nominated by Grover Cleveland; confirmed Dec. 9, 1895, sworn in Jan. 6, 1896.

Pitney, Mahlon (N.J.) Feb. 5, 1858–Dec. 9, 1924; nominated by William Howard Taft; confirmed March 13, 1912, sworn in March 18, 1912, resigned Dec. 31, 1922; House 1895–Jan. 10, 1899 (Republican).

Powell, Lewis Franklin Jr. (Va.) Sept. 19, 1907–Aug. 24, 1998; nominated by Richard Nixon; confirmed Dec. 6, 1971, sworn in Jan. 7, 1972, resigned June 26, 1987.

Reed, Stanley Forman (Ky.) Dec. 31, 1884–April 2, 1980; nominated by Franklin D. Roosevelt; confirmed Jan. 25, 1938, sworn in Jan. 31, 1938, resigned Feb. 25, 1957.

Rehnquist, William Hubbs (Ariz.) Oct. 1, 1924– ; nominated by Richard Nixon; confirmed Dec. 10, 1971, sworn in Jan. 7, 1972; nominated as chief justice by Ronald Reagan; confirmed as chief justice Sept. 17, 1986, sworn in Sept. 26, 1986.

Roberts, Owen Josephus (Pa.) May 2, 1875–May 17, 1955; nominated by Herbert Hoover; confirmed May 20, 1930, sworn in June 2, 1930, resigned July 31, 1945.

Rutledge, John (S.C.) Sept. 1739–July 18, 1800; nominated by George Washington; confirmed Sept. 26, 1789, sworn in May 12, 1790, resigned March 5, 1791; nominated as chief justice by George Washington, sworn in as chief justice Aug. 12, 1795 (recess appointment, nomination not confirmed, service ended Dec. 15, 1795); Cont. Cong. 1774–75, 1782–83.

Rutledge, Wiley Blount (Iowa) July 20, 1894–Sept. 10, 1949; nominated by Franklin D. Roosevelt; confirmed Feb. 8, 1943, sworn in Feb. 15, 1943.

Sanford, Edward Terry (Tenn.) July 23, 1865–March 8, 1930; nominated by Warren G. Harding; confirmed Jan. 29, 1923, sworn in Feb. 19, 1923.

Scalia, Antonin (D.C.) March 11, 1936– ; nominated by Ronald Reagan; confirmed Sept. 17, 1986, sworn in Sept. 26, 1986.

Shiras, George Jr. (Pa.) Jan. 26, 1832–Aug. 2, 1924; nominated by Benjamin Harrison; confirmed July 26, 1892, sworn in Oct. 10, 1892, resigned Feb. 23, 1903.

Souter, David H. (N.H.) Sept. 17, 1939– ; nominated by George Bush; confirmed Oct. 2, 1990, sworn in Oct. 9, 1990.

Stevens, John Paul (Ill.) April 20, 1920– ; nominated by Gerald R. Ford; confirmed Dec. 17, 1975, sworn in Dec. 19, 1975.

Stewart, Potter (Ohio) Jan. 23, 1915–Dec. 7, 1985; nominated by Dwight D. Eisenhower; confirmed May 5, 1959, sworn in Oct. 14, 1958 (recess appointment), resigned July 3, 1981.

Stone, Harlan Fiske (N.Y.) Oct. 11, 1872–April 22, 1946; nominated by Calvin Coolidge; confirmed Feb. 5, 1925, sworn in March 2, 1925; nominated as chief justice by Franklin D. Roosevelt; confirmed as chief justice June 27, 1941, sworn in July 3, 1941; attorney general April 7, 1924–March 2, 1925.

Story, Joseph (Mass.) Sept. 18, 1779–Sept. 10, 1845; nominated by James Madison; confirmed Nov. 18, 1811, sworn in Feb. 3, 1812; House May 23, 1808–09 (Republican).

Strong, William (Pa.) May 6, 1808–Aug. 19, 1895; nominated by Ulysses S. Grant; confirmed Feb. 18, 1870, sworn in March 14, 1870, resigned Dec. 14, 1880; House 1847–51 (Democrat).

Sutherland, George (Utah) March 25, 1862–July 18, 1942; nominated by Warren G. Harding; confirmed Sept. 5, 1922, sworn in Oct. 2, 1922, resigned Jan. 17, 1938; House 1901–03 (Republican); Senate 1905–17 (Republican).

Swayne, Noah Haynes (Ohio) Dec. 7, 1804–June 8, 1884; nominated by Abraham Lincoln; confirmed Jan. 24, 1862, sworn in Jan. 27, 1862, resigned Jan. 24, 1881.

Taft, William Howard (Ohio) Sept. 15, 1857–March 8, 1930; nominated by Warren G. Harding; confirmed as chief justice June 30, 1921, sworn in July 11, 1921, resigned Feb. 3, 1930; president 1909–13 (Republican); secretary of war Feb. 1, 1904–June 30, 1908; Provisional Gov. of Philippines 1901–04.

Taney, Roger Brooke (Md.) March 17, 1777–Oct. 12, 1864; nominated as chief justice by Andrew Jackson; confirmed as chief justice March 15, 1836, sworn in March 28, 1836; attorney general July 20, 1831–Sept. 24, 1833; secretary of the Treasury Sept. 23, 1833–June 25, 1834.

Thomas, Clarence (Va.) June 23, 1948– ; nominated by George Bush; confirmed Oct. 15, 1991, sworn in Oct. 23, 1991.

Thompson, Smith (son-in-law of Assoc. Justice Henry Brockholst Livingston) (N.Y.) Jan. 17, 1768–Dec. 18, 1843; nominated by James Monroe; confirmed Dec. 19, 1823, sworn in Feb. 10, 1824; secretary of navy Jan. 1, 1819–Aug. 31, 1823.

Todd, Thomas (Ky.) Jan. 23, 1765–Feb. 7, 1826; nominated by Thomas Jefferson; confirmed March 3, 1807, sworn in May 4, 1807.

Trimble, Robert (Ky.) Nov. 17, 1776–Aug. 25, 1828; nominated by John Quincy Adams; confirmed May 9, 1826, sworn in June 16, 1826.

Van Devanter, Willis (Wyo.) April 17, 1859–Feb. 8, 1941; nominated by William Howard Taft; confirmed Dec. 15, 1910, sworn in Jan. 3, 1911, resigned June 2, 1937.

Vinson, Frederick Moore (Ky.) Jan. 22, 1890–Sept. 8, 1953; nominated by Harry S. Truman; confirmed as chief justice June 20, 1946, sworn in June 24, 1946; House Jan. 12, 1924–29, 1931–May 12, 1938 (Democrat); secretary of the Treasury July 23, 1945–June 23, 1946.

Waite, Morrison Remick (Ohio) Nov. 29, 1816–March 23, 1888; nominated by Ulysses S. Grant; confirmed as chief justice Jan. 21, 1874, sworn in March 4, 1874.

Warren, Earl (Calif.) March 19, 1891–July 9, 1974; nominated by Dwight D. Eisenhower; confirmed as chief justice March 1, 1954, sworn in Oct. 5, 1953 (recess appointment), resigned June 23, 1969; Gov. Jan. 4, 1943–Oct. 5, 1953.

Washington, Bushrod (nephew of Pres. George Washington) (Va.) June 5, 1762–Nov. 26, 1829; nominated by John Adams; confirmed Dec. 20, 1798, sworn in Feb. 4, 1799.

Wayne, James Moore (Ga.) 1790–July 5, 1867; nominated by Andrew Jackson; confirmed Jan. 9, 1835, sworn in Jan. 14, 1835; House 1829–Jan. 13, 1835 (Jacksonian).

White, Byron Raymond (Colo.) June 8, 1917–April 15, 2002; nominated by John F. Kennedy; confirmed April 11, 1962, sworn in April 16, 1962, resigned June 28, 1993.

White, Edward Douglas (La.) Nov. 3, 1845–May 19, 1921; nominated by Grover Cleveland; confirmed Feb. 19, 1894, sworn in March 12, 1894; nominated as chief justice by William Howard Taft; confirmed as chief justice Dec. 12, 1910, sworn in Dec. 19, 1910; Senate 1891–March 12, 1894 (Democrat).

Whittaker, Charles Evans (Mo.) Feb. 22, 1901–Nov. 26, 1973; nominated by Dwight D. Eisenhower; confirmed March 19, 1957, sworn in March 25, 1957, resigned March 31, 1962.

Wilson, James (Pa.) Sept. 14, 1742–Aug. 21, 1798; nominated by George Washington; confirmed Sept. 26, 1789, sworn in Oct. 5, 1789; Cont. Cong. 1775–77, 1783, 1785–86.

Woodbury, Levi (N.H.) Dec. 22, 1789–Sept. 4, 1851; nominated by James K. Polk; confirmed Jan. 3, 1846, sworn in Sept. 23, 1845 (recess appointment); Gov. June 5, 1823–June 2, 1824 (Democratic Republican); Senate March 16, 1825–31 (no party), 1841–Nov. 20, 1845 (Democrat); secretary of the navy May 23, 1831–June 30, 1834; secretary of the Treasury July 1, 1834–March 3, 1841.

Woods, William Burnham (Ga.) Aug. 3, 1824–May 14, 1887; nominated by Rutherford B. Hayes; confirmed Dec. 21, 1880, sworn in Jan. 5, 1881.

Members of Congress

Independence from Great Britain had brought new problems for the newly formed United States. Americans' allegiance still was directed toward their own states. The former colonists were reluctant to yield state sovereignty to any superior governmental power. The Articles of Confederation, the first basic law of the new nation, reflected this widespread distrust of centralized power. Under the Articles, the United States was little more than a league of independent states, bickering and feuding among themselves. The states retained control over most essential government functions, and Congress—in which each state had one vote—was the sole organ of central government. So limited were its powers that it could not levy taxes or regulate trade, and it had no sanction to enforce any of its decisions.

Calls for change became louder, and the Constitutional Convention opened in Philadelphia in the summer of 1787. The task facing the fifty-five convention delegates was to devise a system of government that would bind the thirteen sovereign and rival states into one firm union without compromising on the principles of representative government and personal freedom to which Americans had become wedded. The delegates' early decision that a national government, if formed, should consist of three branches—legislative, executive, and judicial—was undisputed. The concept of government by consent of the governed formed the basic principle of the Constitution. The rights of the people were to be protected by diffusing power among rival interests. The Constitution strengthened central authority, but national powers were carefully enumerated; all other powers were reserved to the states and the people.

Structure of Congress

Both the Continental Congress and the Congress of the Articles of Confederation had been unicameral. But once the convention decided to abandon the Articles, there was little doubt that the new Congress should be bicameral. A legislature of two houses, patterned after the English Parliament, had been set up by most of the colonial governments and retained by ten of the thirteen original states.

The nationalists insisted that the new government rest on the consent of the people instead of on the state legislatures. So they held it as essential that the members of the House, at least, be elected directly by the people.

Those who were suspicious of a national government preferred election of the House by the state legislatures. The convention voted to support the nationalists' view.

A proposal was made that the House elect the Senate from persons nominated by the state legislatures. But there was little support for this plan because it would have made the Senate subservient to the House. Most delegates agreed that the function of the Senate should be to check the doings of the House. The concept of the Senate's role as that of representing the states emerged later, after the decision in favor of equal representation. Delegates preferred election of senators by the state legislatures to popular election as provided for House members. (Senators were elected by state legislatures until the Constitution was amended by the Seventeenth Amendment, ratified April 8, 1913, which provided for the direct election of senators.)

A plan calling for representation of the states in both the House and Senate in proportion to their wealth or free population was also put forward. This proposal led to a revolt by the small states, which was eventually resolved by a vote for equal representation of the states in the Senate. Although the principle of proportional representation in the House was never seriously challenged, the idea of basing it on wealth or the free population raised questions that led to adoption of important qualifications.

To retain southern support for the initial proposal for proportional representation in the Senate, a proposal was made that the House be apportioned according to a count of the whole number of free citizens and three-fifths of all others (meaning slaves), excluding American Indians not paying taxes. This formula was adopted. Then the convention decided that the new Congress should have the power to determine the number of representatives based on the wealth and population of the states. Because southerners regarded slaves as property, northerners who wanted representation in the House to be based on population alone were led to ask why slaves should be counted at all.

Gouverneur Morris proposed that the power of Congress to apportion the House according to wealth and numbers be subject to a proviso "that direct taxation shall be in proportion to representation." The proviso was adopted without debate. The slave issue now appeared in a different light given that the Morris proviso seemed to mean that the South would have to pay additional taxes for any increases in representation it gained by counting

Members of Congress Who Became President

Twenty-four presidents entered the White House with previous service in the House of Representatives or the Senate or both.

Following is a list of these presidents and the chambers in which they served. Three other presidents—George Washington, John Adams, and Thomas Jefferson—had served in the Continental Congress, as had two of those included below, James Madison and James Monroe.

James A. Garfield was elected to the Senate in January 1880 for a term beginning March 4, 1881, but declined to accept in December 1880 because he had been elected president. John Quincy Adams served in the House for seventeen years after he had been president, and Andrew Johnson returned to the Senate five months before he died.

House Only

James Madison
James K. Polk
Millard Fillmore
Abraham Lincoln
Rutherford B. Hayes
James A. Garfield
William McKinley
Gerald R. Ford
George Bush

Senate Only

James Monroe
John Quincy Adams
Martin Van Buren
Benjamin Harrison
Warren G. Harding
Harry S. Truman

Both Chambers

Andrew Jackson
William Henry Harrison
John Tyler
Franklin Pierce
James Buchanan

Andrew Johnson
John F. Kennedy
Lyndon B. Johnson
Richard Nixon

slaves. So the northerners dropped their opposition to the three-fifths count demanded by the southerners.

The word "wealth" was dropped from the provision, thus leaving House representation based solely on population (counting all whites and three-fifths of the blacks). This solution to the issue gave five free voters in a slave state a voice in the House equivalent to that of seven free voters in a nonslave state.

The convention committee that recommended equal representation in the Senate also proposed that each state have one vote in the House for every 40,000 inhabitants. This proposal precipitated the debate on representation, during which it was decided to let Congress regulate the future size of the House so as to allow for population changes and the admission of new states. After reflection by the delegates, however, it was feared that under such an arrangement a majority in Congress would be able to block a reapportionment plan or change the basis of representation for slaves. Thus northerners and southerners agreed that the periods between reapportionments and the rules for revising representation in the House ought to be fixed by the Constitution.

A regular census was proposed, and the convention adopted a plan, finally incorporated in Article I, Section 2, linking the apportionment of representatives to an "enumeration" every ten years of the "whole number of free persons . . . and three fifths of all others." It was decided that the number of representatives would be set at one for every 30,000. (After the reapportionment following the 2000 census, House districts averaged about 647,000 constituents.) Until the first census was taken, the size of the House was fixed at sixty-five representatives, allotted as provided in Article I. (In 1911 the size of the House was set at 435 members, where it has remained ever since except for a brief period after Alaska and Hawaii became states. In addition to the 435 members, the House has five nonvoting representatives from the District of Columbia, Puerto Rico, the Virgin Islands, Guam, and American Samoa.)

The size of the Senate was fixed at two members from each state. A proposal to allow each state three senators had been turned down on the ground that it would penalize poorer and more distant states and that too large a membership would hamper quick action by the body.

Attempts at Limiting Terms

Proposals to set term limits for elected officials became popular in the early 1990s. But by the beginning of the twenty-first century—after state efforts to limit federal terms had been declared unconstitutional and congressional attempts to limit terms through a constitutional amendment had failed—the momentum for term limits had stalled.

The term limits movement began in 1990 when Colorado became the first state to seek to limit the number of terms that members of Congress could serve. A referendum approved by more than two-thirds of Colorado voters limited House members to six two-year terms and senators to two six-year terms. The measure also set term limits on state legislators and statewide elected offices.

By 1995 advocates of term limits had won ballot initiatives or laws in at least twenty-three states. That same year the Supreme Court ruled in *U.S. Term Limits v. Thornton* and *Bryant v. Hill* that states could not impose limits on congressional terms. The rulings left term limits supporters only one solution: a constitutional amendment. But amendments are difficult to pass: they must receive a two-thirds majority vote from both chambers of Congress and then be ratified by three-fourths (thirty-eight) of the states.

Term limits supporters argued that mandatory retirement after twelve years was necessary to bring new people and viewpoints into Congress, to reduce the constant pressure to get reelected, and to control federal spending, which they said resulted from career politicians getting too close to special interest groups seeking federal funds.

Opponents countered that term limits would strip Congress of experienced legislators, diminish the political power of less populated states that were helped by their members gaining seniority, and would speed up, not solve, the problem of legislators getting too friendly with special interest groups. Depriving voters of the right to vote for an incumbent would be undemocratic, opponents added.

Efforts in the 1990s to pass a constitutional amendment failed in both the House and Senate. The House rejected an amendment in 1995 when backers failed to muster a two-thirds majority and the Senate was unable to cut off a filibuster against an amendment the following year. The House made another attempt in 1997 but once again failed to obtain the two-thirds vote needed for passage.

The idea that senators should vote individually instead of as a delegation came from Elbridge Gerry, who wanted to "prevent the delays and inconveniences" that had occurred in Congress under the Articles of Confederation's allocation of one vote per state. Although this provision was at odds with the decision that the states should be equally represented in the Senate, it was accepted with little objection and included in Article I, Section 3.

Although the delegates had a strong attachment to the tradition of annual elections, it was successfully argued that representatives needed more time to become informed about the office and the national interests. At first the convention adopted a plan that called for House elections every three years. Many delegates continued to press for more frequent elections, however. The convention reconsidered the question and compromised on biennial elections and a two-year term for representatives.

The delegates also changed their minds about the Senate, agreeing first to a term of seven years, although the terms of state senators varied from two years to a maximum of five. When this decision was reviewed, alternatives of four, six, and nine years were considered. Having decided on biennial elections for the House, the convention voted to make the Senate term six years, with one-third of the membership to be elected every two years.

The convention decided on a minimum age of thirty for senators and twenty-five for representatives. Two additional qualifications were later instituted: U.S. citizenship (seven years for the House, nine for the Senate) and residence within the state to be represented. Some delegates wanted to require residence in a state for a minimum time—from one to seven years. But those proposals were voted down.

The convention debated the desirability of a property qualification. Most of the state constitutions required members of their legislatures to own certain amounts of property. A proposal was offered and rejected, and no further efforts were made to include a property qualification.

Delegates were even less disposed to include a religious qualification, although all of the states except New York and Virginia imposed such a qualification on state representatives. The convention's outlook on this point was made clear when, in debating a proposed oath of office, the delegates adopted without dissent a proviso (which became a part of Article VI) that "no religious test shall ever be required as a qualification to any office or public trust under the United States." Thus the only qualifications established by the Constitution for election to Congress were those of age, citizenship, and residence.

The delegates decided to forgo any restrictions on the eligibility of representatives or senators for reelection. Under the Articles of Confederation, no one could serve for more than three years in any six-year period. Critics of the rule charged that it deprived Congress of some of its better members. *(See box, Attempts at Limiting Terms, p. 59.)*

Whether members of Congress should be eligible to hold other offices was debated at much greater length. After negotiating and compromising, the delegates decided that no member could be appointed during his term to a federal office created during his term or to a federal office for which the pay was increased during the member's term, and no one holding federal office could be a member of Congress at the same time. The provision, incorporated in Section 6 of Article I, made no reference to state office or to ineligibility following expiration of a member's term.

Characteristics of Congress

The American electorate makes its decision on a new Congress on the first Tuesday after the first Monday in November of even-numbered years. Early the following January the elected representatives and senators gather at the Capitol to begin their first session. Many new members may be sworn in. But whether the turnover is large or small, a certain uniformity pervades Congress.

Congress has been dominated since its beginning by middle-aged white men with backgrounds in law or business. Their levels of income and education have consistently been above the national average. Since the 1970s members for the most part have been career politicians, due in part to ethics rules limiting the income that can be earned outside of Congress and also to the fact that serving in Congress has become a full-time job. In 2005, 494 members or 92 percent of Congress had at least a bachelor's degree.

Ever so slowly, other changes have crept into the makeup of Congress. The numbers of women, African Americans, and Hispanic Americans have increased in recent decades, although still not in proportion to their share of the total population. Of the 535 members at the beginning of the 109th Congress (2005–2007), seventy-nine were women, forty-one were black, twenty-five were Hispanic, five were of Asian or Pacific Islands descent, and one was of Native American heritage. In addition, of the five nonvoting delegates sent to the House, three were women, two were black, one was Hispanic, and one was Pacific Island descent.

As an institution, Congress has suffered public criticism almost since the nation's beginnings. An early but still familiar critique of Congress was written in the 1830s by Alexis de Tocqueville, the French aristocrat, scholar, and astute observer of America. After he had seen both chambers in session, de Tocqueville wrote the following in *Democracy in America*:

> On entering the House of Representatives at Washington, one is struck by the vulgar demeanor of that great assembly. Often there is not a distinguished man in the whole number. Its members are almost all obscure individuals, whose names bring no associations to mind. They are mostly village lawyers, men in trade, or even persons belonging to the lower classes of society. In a country in which education is very general, it is said that the representatives of the people do not always know how to write correctly.
>
> At a few yards' distance is the door of the Senate, which contains within a small space a large proportion of the celebrated men of America. Scarcely an individual is to be seen in it who has not had an active and illustrious career: the Senate is composed of eloquent advocates, distinguished generals, wise magistrates, and statesmen of note, whose arguments would do honor to the most remarkable parliamentary debates of Europe.

The modern view of Congress as a whole probably is not much more charitable than de Tocqueville's opinion of the House. Gallup polls assessing the amount of trust and confidence that Americans have in various institutions have found Congress consistently ranking third among the three branches of government. But, paradoxically, election results often have indicated that although Congress as an institution might not be held in high regard, voters were more generous in returning the incumbents who represented them.

In the modern era the power of incumbency for the most part remained strong with the turnover rate averaging about 10 percent or less—historically a low level. But in the early 1990s incumbents' hold weakened enough to allow for a change in the political party controlling Congress. The landmark 1994 elections swept Republicans to power in both chambers. Democrats had controlled either the House or Senate, and usually both, since 1955. From 1933—when the Great Depression realigned political power—to 1995, Republicans had managed to control both chambers only twice—in the 80th Congress (1947–49) and the 83rd Congress (1953–55). Republicans also held a Senate majority from 1981 to 1987. Beginning in 1995, Republicans maintained control of both houses—except when they lost hold of the Senate from June 6, 2001 to January 3, 2003—through to the start of the 109th Congress in 2005.

Characteristics of Members

Age. The average age of members of Congress went up substantially between the post–Civil War period and the 1950s and then remained fairly constant until the mid-1970s. In the 41st Congress (1869–71), the average age of members was 44.6 years; by the 85th Congress (1957–59), the average had increased by more than nine years, to 53.8. During the next eighteen years, the average fluctuated only slightly. But when the 94th Congress (1975–77) met in January 1975, the average had dropped to 50.9 years. The difference was made in the House, where ninety-two freshman members reduced the average age of representatives to 49.8 years, the first time since World War II that the average in either chamber had fallen below 50 years. *(See box, Age Structure of Congress, p. 61.)*

The 96th Congress (1979–81) was the youngest since 1949; the overall average age for both chambers had slipped to 49.5 years. It dropped again in the next Congress, when the House had eight members under 30 years, the most since World War II. The younger trend bottomed out in 1983 when the average age hit 47 years.

After that came a gradual increase, continuing through the beginning of the 109th Congress in 2005, when the average age climbed to a record-high 56 years. The average for senators in 2005 was 60.4 years, also a record. That aging trend was partly attributable to the aging trend of the nation's population. But low turnover in Congress was also a big factor. The youngest Congress of the 1990s was the 104th (1995–97), when the Republicans took control of both houses for the first time in forty years. The average age for House members in 1995 was 50.9 years. By January 2005 the average was a record 55 years.

Occupations. The legal profession was long the dominant occupational background of members of Congress since its beginning. In the First Congress, more than one-third of the House members had legal training. The proportion of members with a legal background crested at 70 percent in 1840 but remained high. From 1950 to the mid-1970s it was in the 55–60 percent range.

The first significant decline in members with a law background began with the 96th Congress. Although sixty-five of the 100 senators were lawyers in 1979, lawyers in the House made up less than a majority for the first time in at least thirty years. The situation continued through the 1990s. When the 109th Congress convened in January 2005, 178 representatives and sixty-four senators were lawyers, or about 45 percent of both chambers. For the first time, business or banking, which had long been the second most listed category by members, overtook law in 2005. In the 109th Congress, 205 representatives and forty senators claimed a business or banking background, or nearly 46 percent. *(See box, Members' Occupations, 109th Congress, p. 62.)*

However, another category (some members listed overlapping backgrounds) topped both law and business in 2005 and highlighted the trend toward career politicians. In the 109th Congress, 254 members, or 47 percent, listed backgrounds in public service or politics. Additionally, out of the 535 members, 274—more than half—had previous experience as state legislators. This trend became possible when states and localities in the 1970s began to think of political positions as full-time jobs and raised salaries accordingly. Moreover, the demands of modern political campaigns have left less time for the pursuit of other careers.

The number of members with military experience declined dramatically into the twenty-first century. At the start of the 91st Congress in 1969, 73 percent of members were military veterans. By 1991 the percentage of veterans in Congress dropped to 52 percent. At the start of the 109th Congress in 2005, only 140, or 26 percent, cited military service. This in part reflected the advent of the all-volunteer army in 1973.

Other fields represented by members of the 109th Congress included real estate (forty-two), agriculture (thirty-four), medicine/physician (twenty), and journalism (eighteen). Members of the clergy continue to be un-

Age Structure of Congress

The following chart lists average ages of members at the beginning of the first session of each Congress.

Year	House	Senate	Congress
1949	51.0	58.5	53.8
1951	52.0	56.6	53.0
1953	52.0	56.6	53.0
1955	51.4	57.2	52.2
1957	52.9	57.9	53.8
1959	51.7	57.1	52.7
1961	52.2	57.0	53.2
1963	51.7	56.8	52.7
1965	50.5	57.7	51.9
1967	50.8	57.7	52.1
1969	52.2	56.6	53.0
1971	51.9	56.4	52.7
1973	51.1	55.3	52.0
1975	49.8	55.5	50.9
1977	49.3	54.7	50.3
1979	48.8	52.7	49.5
1981	48.4	52.5	49.2
1983	45.5	53.4	47.0
1985	49.7	54.2	50.5
1987	50.7	54.4	52.5
1989	52.1	55.6	52.8
1991	52.8	57.2	53.6
1993	51.7	58.0	52.9
1995	50.9	58.4	52.2
1997	51.6	57.5	52.7
1999	52.6	58.3	53.7
2001	54.4	59.8	55.4
2003	54.0	59.7	55.5
2005	55.0	60.4	56.0

Source: Congressional Quarterly.

derrepresented in Congress. Only a handful of Protestant ministers have served in Congress, and no Catholic priest had done so until 1971, when Rep. Robert F. Drinan, D-Mass., a Jesuit, took a House seat. (Father Gabriel Richard was the nonvoting delegate of the Territory of Michigan from 1823 to 1825.) Drinan did not seek a sixth term in 1980 after Pope John Paul II that year ordered priests not to hold public office. The pope's directive also prompted Robert J. Cornell, a Catholic priest and former House member, to halt his political comeback bid in Wisconsin. Cornell, a Democrat elected in 1974, served two terms before he was defeated in 1978. Only three members of the House listed their occupation as clergy in the 109th Congress.

Religious Affiliations. Among religious groups, Protestants have made up nearly two-thirds of the mem-

Members' Occupations, 109th Congress

The following chart lists occupations of the members of the 109th Congress at the start of the first session in January 2005. Because some members cite more than one occupation, totals are larger than the number of members.

Occupation	House			Senate			Congress
	D	R	Total	D	R	Total	Total
Actor/entertainer	1	2	3	0	0	0	3
Aeronautics	0	2	2	0	0	0	2
Agriculture	9	20	29	1	4	5	34
Artistic/creative	1[a]	1	2	0	0	0	2
Business	65	140	205	14	26	40	245
Clergy	2	1	3	0	0	0	3
Education	52[a]	39	91	6	7	13	104
Engineering	1	3	4	0	1	1	5
Health care	4	2	6	0	0	0	6
Homemaker/domestic	2	2	4	0	0	0	4
Journalism	3[a]	8	11	2	5	7	18
Labor/blue collar	4	5	9	1	2	3	12
Law	90	88	178	30[a]	34	64	242
Law enforcement	6	3	9	1	0	1	10
Medicine	4	12	16	0	4	4	20
Military	0	3	3	0	1	1	4
Other occupations	44[a]	114	158	5	20	25	183
Professional sports	0	2	2	0	1	1	3
Public service/politics	116	93	209	23	22	45	254
Real estate	3	36	39	1	2	3	42
Science	2	4	6	0	0	0	6
Technical/skilled labor	1	2	3	0	0	0	3
Miscellaneous	1	2	3	0	0	0	3

a. Includes two independents in Congress, both from Vermont: Sen. James M. Jeffords and Rep. Bernard Sanders. Both caucused with the Democrats.

Source: Congressional Quarterly.

bership of both houses in recent years. However, Roman Catholics form the biggest single religious group—a distinction they had held since taking the lead from Methodists in 1965.

At the beginning of the 109th Congress, there were 153 Catholics. Among Protestant denominations, Baptists were most numerous (seventy-two), followed by Methodists (sixty-two), Presbyterians (fifty), Episcopalians (forty-two), and Lutherans (twenty-one). There were thirty-seven Jewish members. In all, members listed affiliations with some twenty religious groups. Thirty-eight simply listed "Protestant," and only six did not specify a religious preference.

Women in Congress

A total of 223 women had been elected or appointed to Congress by January 2005. Of these, 220 actually served—189 in the House only, twenty-four in the Senate only, and seven in both chambers. *(See box, Number of Women Members in Congress, 1947–2005, p. 63. For a roster of all women who have served in Congress, see appendix, p. 375.)*

The first woman to be a member of Congress was Rep. Jeannette Rankin, R-Mont., elected in 1916. Her state gave women the right to vote before the Nineteenth Amendment to the Constitution enfranchising women was ratified in 1920.

The first female senator, Rebecca L. Felton, was a member of the Senate for only one day. The Georgia Democrat, appointed in 1922 to fill a vacancy, stepped aside the day after she was sworn in to make way for a man who had been elected to fill the vacancy.

More than eighty years after Rankin took her seat in the House, the 109th Congress opened in 2005 with an all-time high of seventy-nine women (sixty-five in the House—not including nonvoting delegates—and fourteen in the Senate).

The climb in women's membership had been long and slow. Rankin's election was not followed by a surge of women members, even after women received the vote. The first notable increase came in the 71st Congress (1929–31), when nine women served in the House. The number had scarcely more than doubled by the 87th Congress (1961–63), when twenty women—two senators and eighteen representatives—were members.

Women's membership declined slightly after that and did not reach twenty again until the 95th Congress (1977–79). The total went down to seventeen in the next Congress but was up to twenty-three in the 97th Congress (1981–83). Since then, the number has increased in all but two Congresses, and in those two the total remained the same as in the previous Congress.

The elections of 1992—dubbed the "Year of the Woman"—found record numbers of women running for and being elected to Congress. The 103rd Congress (1993–95) opened with forty-seven women in the House and six in the Senate. (A seventh woman joined the Senate later in 1993.) Several factors contributed to the success of women candidates in 1992. Many capitalized on an unusually large number of retirements to run for open seats. They also benefited from reapportionment, which created dozens of opportunities for newcomers in the South and West. Another factor was public dissatisfaction with Congress, which allowed women to portray themselves positively as outsiders. The Senate's questioning of law professor Anita F. Hill's accusations of sexual harassment in the 1991 confirmation hearings of Supreme Court Justice Clarence Thomas also had an impact. The televised image of an all-male Senate Judiciary panel sharply questioning Hill brought home dramatically to many women their lack of representation in Congress.

The number of women elected to full Senate terms increased dramatically beginning in the 1990s. Up to that time, only six women had ever won election to full Senate terms. By 2005, however, a record fourteen women serving in the Senate had all been elected to full terms, and three states—California, Maine, and Washington—were represented in the Senate solely by women.

In the past many women had gotten their start in Congress by way of the "widow's mandate." According to this custom, widows were appointed to replace their husbands who had died in office. This practice allowed state leaders extra time to choose a successor or hold a special election. Sometimes a widow was chosen by her late husband's party to run for his seat on the theory that a strong sympathy vote would sweep her into office.

Although many women elected to Congress on the basis of the "widow's mandate" served only the remainder of the husband's term, others have stayed to build strong political reputations for themselves. Edith Nourse Rogers, a Massachusetts Republican, entered the House after her husband died in 1925 and remained there until her death in 1960. Maine Republican Margaret Chase Smith filled her late husband's House seat in 1940 and

Number of Women Members in Congress, 1947–2005

Listed below by Congress is the number of women members of the Senate and House of Representatives from the 80th Congress through the beginning of the first session of the 109th Congress. Totals are for an entire Congress. They include women elected in general and special elections as well as those who were appointed to office. Members sworn in after the adjournment of a Congress are not counted in the total for that Congress. House totals exclude nonvoting delegates. The total for the 109th Congress is through January 31, 2005. *(See appendix, p. 375, for roster of all women who have served in Congress.)*

Congress		Senate	House
80th	(1947–1949)	1	7
81st	(1949–1951)	1	9
82nd	(1951–1953)	1	10
83rd	(1953–1955)	3	11
84th	(1955–1957)	1	15
85th	(1957–1959)	1	15
86th	(1959–1961)	1	16
87th	(1961–1963)	2	18
88th	(1963–1965)	2	12
89th	(1965–1967)	2	11
90th	(1967–1969)	1	11
91st	(1969–1971)	1	10
92nd	(1971–1973)	2	13
93rd	(1973–1975)	0	16
94th	(1975–1977)	0	17
95th	(1977–1979)	2	18
96th	(1979–1981)	1	16
97th	(1981–1983)	2	21
98th	(1983–1985)	2	22
99th	(1985–1987)	2	23
100th	(1987–1989)	2	23
101st	(1989–1991)	2	28
102nd	(1991–1993)	3	28
103rd	(1993–1995)	7	47
104th	(1995–1997)	9	48
105th	(1997–1999)	9	54
106th	(1999–2001)	9	56
107th	(2001–2003)	14	60
108th	(2003–2005)	14	60
109th	(2005–2007)	14	66

Source: Congressional Quarterly.

Number of Black Members in Congress, 1947–2005

Listed below by Congress is the number of black members of the Senate and House of Representatives from the 80th Congress through the beginning of the first session of the 109th Congress. Totals are for an entire Congress. They include blacks elected in general and special elections as well as those who were appointed to office. Members sworn in after the adjournment of a Congress are not counted in the total for that Congress. House totals exclude nonvoting delegates. The total for the 109th Congress is through January 31, 2005. *(See appendix, p. 378, for roster of all blacks who have served in Congress.)*

Congress		Senate	House
80th	(1947–1949)	0	2
81st	(1949–1951)	0	2
82nd	(1951–1953)	0	2
83rd	(1953–1955)	0	2
84th	(1955–1957)	0	3
85th	(1957–1959)	0	4
86th	(1959–1961)	0	4
87th	(1961–1963)	0	4
88th	(1963–1965)	0	5
89th	(1965–1967)	0	6
90th	(1967–1969)	1	5
91st	(1969–1971)	1	10
92nd	(1971–1973)	1	12
93rd	(1973–1975)	1	15
94th	(1975–1977)	1	16
95th	(1977–1979)	1	16
96th	(1979–1981)	0	16
97th	(1981–1983)	0	18
98th	(1983–1985)	0	21
99th	(1985–1987)	0	21
100th	(1987–1989)	0	23
101st	(1989–1991)	0	24
102nd	(1991–1993)	0	26
103rd	(1993–1995)	1	39
104th	(1995–1997)	1	38
105th	(1997–1999)	1	38
106th	(1999–2001)	0	37
107th	(2001–2003)	0	37
108th	(2003–2005)	0	37
109th	(2005–2007)	1	40

Source: Congressional Quarterly.

Democrat, who was appointed to the Senate seat of her late husband in 1931, was returned to Congress by Arkansas voters in 1932 and 1938.

As women have become more active in politics at all levels, the congressional tradition of the widow's mandate has faded. By the 109th Congress, only four women held the House seats of their late husbands. In 1978 Republican Nancy Landon Kassebaum of Kansas became the first woman ever elected to the Senate without being preceded in Congress by her husband.

Marriages have also linked members of Congress. Rep. Emily Taft Douglas, D-Ill., was elected to Congress in 1944, four years before her husband, Sen. Paul H. Douglas, D-Ill. Another woman, Rep. Martha Keys, D-Kan., married Rep. Andrew Jacobs, D-Ind., in 1976. This marriage between colleagues was the first of its kind in congressional history. Rep. Olympia J. Snowe, R-Maine, in 1989 married Maine Gov. John R. McKernan Jr., a former U.S. representative. Rep. Marjorie Margolies-Mezvinsky, D-Pa., was the wife of former Iowa representative Edward M. Mezvinsky when she was elected to Congress in 1992. Reps. Susan Molinari, R-N.Y., and Bill Paxon, R-N.Y., were married in 1994. Kassebaum, after she left office in 1997, married former senator Howard Baker (R-Tenn.). Beginning her first term in 2003, Sen. Elizabeth Dole (R-N.C.) was the wife of former senate majority leader Robert J. Dole (R-Kan.).

Blacks in Congress

By the start of 2005, a total of 112 African Americans had served in Congress—five in the Senate and 107 in the House. *(See box, Number of Black Members in Congress, 1947–2005, left. For a roster of all blacks who have served in Congress, see appendix, p. 378.)*

The first black elected to Congress was John W. Menard, R-La., who won election in 1868 to an unexpired term in the 40th Congress (1867–69). Menard's election was disputed, however, and the House denied him a seat. Thus the distinction of being the first black to serve in Congress went to Hiram R. Revels, R-Miss., who served in the Senate from February 1870 to March 1871. The first black to serve in the House was Joseph H. Rainey, R-S.C., from December 1870 to March 1879.

These men were elected during the post–Civil War Reconstruction era (1865–77), when many white voters were disenfranchised and Confederate veterans were barred from holding office. During that period sixteen black men were sent to Congress from the South. But from the end of Reconstruction until the end of the century, only seven black men were elected to Congress. They, like their predecessors, were Republicans from the South.

As federal controls were lifted in the South, literacy tests, poll taxes, and sometimes threats of violence eroded black voting rights. From the time Blanche K. Bruce, R-Miss.—the second black elected to the Senate—left in 1881, there was no other black in the Senate until Edward W. Brooke III, R-Mass., who was elected in 1966.

The last black person elected to the House in the nineteenth century was George Henry White, R-N.C., who

stayed there until 1948, when she won the first of four terms in the Senate. Hattie W. Caraway, an Arkansas

won election in 1896 and 1898 but did not seek renomination in 1900.

For nearly three decades no blacks served in Congress. In 1928 Rep. Oscar De Priest, R-Ill., became the first black member elected in the twentieth century. Only three more blacks were elected during the next twenty-five years, all to the House. All three were Democrats representing big-city constituencies in Chicago (Arthur W. Mitchell and William L. Dawson) and New York (Adam Clayton Powell Jr.).

Only two blacks were added in the 1950s—Reps. Charles C. Diggs Jr., D-Mich., and Robert N.C. Nix, D-Pa.—but after that the pace quickened. Five more were elected in the 1960s, fourteen in the 1970s, and fifteen in the 1980s. The number of black Americans elected to Congress more than doubled during the 1990s—thirty-six were elected to the House and one to the Senate. When the 109th Congress opened in 2005, there were forty blacks in the House and one in the Senate. All were Democrats. Only four black representatives in the twentieth century had been Republicans, including J. C. Watts Jr. (R-Okla.), who left the House in 2003. Sen. Barack Obama (D-Ill.), elected in 2004, was the first black senator elected since the first black woman senator in U.S. history, Carol Moseley-Braun (D-Ill.), lost reelection to the Senate in 1996. Obama was also the fifth black to serve in the Senate.

The Supreme Court's "one person, one vote" rulings in the early 1960s, ratification of the Twenty-fourth Amendment in 1964, and enactment of the 1965 Voting Rights Act are credited with opening up the polls to black voters as never before.

The Voting Rights Act provided for federal oversight in jurisdictions where black registration and voting were exceptionally low; the Twenty-fourth Amendment outlawed poll taxes and similar restrictions on voting; and the courts eventually ended a southern practice of diluting black voting power by gerrymandering voting districts. As black voter turnouts increased, so did black representation in Congress.

Along with that increased representation came a number of milestones. In 1968 Rep. Shirley Chisholm, D-N.Y., became the first black woman to be elected to Congress. Southern voters, who had last elected an African American in 1898, broke the long dry spell in 1972. In that year Democrats Barbara Jordan of Texas and Andrew Young Jr. of Georgia won seats in the House. Both Georgia and Texas later sent other black representatives, who were joined by black House members from Tennessee, Mississippi, and Louisiana. In addition to Moseley-Braun's becoming the first black women ever elected to the Senate, the 1992 elections sent to Congress House delegations from Alabama, Florida, North Carolina, South Carolina, and Virginia that for the first time since Reconstruction had black members.

The dramatic gains for African Americans in the 1992 elections were in large measure a result of redistricting aimed at increasing minority strength in Congress—a legacy of the civil rights era. This effort to draw so-called majority-minority districts, however, came under heated attack as the decade of the 1990s wore on. By 2005 the Supreme Court in a number of decisions had set new standards that greatly limited this method of increasing black representation in Congress.

Hispanics in Congress

The fast-expanding population of Hispanic Americans sparked predictions that they would emerge as a powerful bloc. The 2000 census listed Hispanics as making up 12.5 percent of the U.S. population, up from 9 percent in 1990. However, as of 2005, Hispanic voter turnouts traditionally fell well below the national average. Hispanic activists blamed low participation on poverty, lack of education, language barriers, immigration status, and alienation resulting from discrimination. Age was seen as another factor diminishing Hispanic political clout, with the median age of the Hispanic population substantially younger than the national median age. Also, many Hispanic immigrants remained attached to their homeland.

Although the 109th Congress opened with a record number of members claiming Hispanic heritage—twenty-five—that represented less than 5 percent of Congress. By 2005, a total of forty-eight Hispanics had served in Congress—two in the Senate, two in both the Senate and the House, and forty-four in the House only.

The growth of Hispanic representation in the House was in large part the result of judicial interpretations of the Voting Rights Act requiring that minorities be given maximum opportunity to elect members of their own group to Congress. After the 1990 census, congressional district maps in states with significant Hispanic populations were redrawn with the aim of sending more Hispanics to Congress, a goal furthered by the 1992 elections. Eight new Hispanic representatives were elected that year.

In 2005 for the first time two Hispanic members joined the Senate: Ken Salazar (D-Colo.) and Mel Martinez (R-Fla.). No Hispanic candidate had been elected to the Senate since 1970, when Joseph Montoya, D-N.M., won his second and last term. Dennis Chavez, his fellow Democrat from New Mexico, was the first Hispanic to serve in the Senate (1935–62). Salazar's brother, John Salazar (D-Colo.), also began serving in the House in 2005, making the brothers one of three pairs serving in Congress. A second Hispanic pair of brothers were Lincoln Diaz-Balart (R-Fla.) and Mario Diaz-Balart (R-Fla.). Two other Hispanic siblings, Linda Sanchez (D-Calif.) and Loretta Sanchez (D-Calif.), made history in 2003 when they became the first sisters ever to serve in Congress.

Rep. Romualdo Pacheco, R-Calif., was the first Hispanic to serve in the House (1877–78; 1879–83), as well as the only Hispanic in Congress during the nineteenth century. No other Hispanic was elected to Congress until 1912. After that, only in 1927–31 and 1941–43 was Congress without any Hispanic American member. *(See box, Number of Hispanic Members in Congress, 1947–2005, p. 66. For a roster of all Hispanics who have served in Congress, see appendix, p. 380.)*

Turnover in Membership

Congress experienced high turnover rates in the nineteenth and early twentieth centuries, primarily in the

Number of Hispanic Members in Congress, 1947–2005

Listed below by Congress is the number of Hispanic members of the Senate and House of Representatives from the 80th Congress through the beginning of the first session of the 109th Congress. Totals are for an entire Congress. They include Hispanics elected in general and special elections as well as those who were appointed to office. Members sworn in after the adjournment of a Congress are not counted in the total for that Congress. House totals exclude nonvoting delegates. The total for the 109th Congress is through January 31, 2005. *(See appendix, p. 380, for roster of all Hispanics who have served in Congress.)*

Congress		Senate	House
80th	(1947–1949)	1	1
81st	(1949–1951)	1	1
82nd	(1951–1953)	1	1
83rd	(1953–1955)	1	1
84th	(1955–1957)	1	1
85th	(1957–1959)	1	1
86th	(1959–1961)	1	1
87th	(1961–1963)	1	2
88th	(1963–1965)	0	3
89th	(1965–1967)	1	4
90th	(1967–1969)	1	4
91st	(1969–1971)	1	5
92nd	(1971–1973)	1	6
93rd	(1973–1975)	1	6
94th	(1975–1977)	1	6
95th	(1977–1979)	0	5
96th	(1979–1981)	0	6
97th	(1981–1983)	0	7
98th	(1983–1985)	0	10
99th	(1985–1987)	0	11
100th	(1987–1989)	0	11
101st	(1989–1991)	0	11
102nd	(1991–1993)	0	11
103rd	(1993–1995)	0	17
104th	(1995–1997)	0	17
105th	(1997–1999)	0	18
106th	(1999–2001)	0	19
107th	(2001–2003)	0	19
108th	(2003–2005)	0	23
109th	(2005–2007)	2	23

Source: Congressional Quarterly.

House. The Senate membership was more stable because its members had six-year terms and because state legislatures tended to reelect the same men to the Senate. In 1869, for example, only 98 of 243 House members had served in previous Congresses. The Senate's turnover rate began to increase only after the direct election of senators was instituted by the Seventeenth Amendment in 1913.

In the middle decades of the twentieth century, congressional turnover held steady at a relatively low rate. In the quarter century after World War II, each Congress had an average of about seventy-eight new members—sixty-five in the House and thirteen in the Senate. An increase began in the 1970s; more than one hundred new members entered Congress in 1975. Turnover remained fairly high through the early 1980s, and then came a spell in the House of strong incumbency and relatively low turnover that lasted into the 1990s. There was enough fluctuation in the Senate to allow for a change in party control—from Republicans to Democrats—in 1986 and the highest incumbent reelection rate in the 1990 election—96.9 percent—since direct elections began in the Senate. The 1990s were a tumultuous decade, with control of both chambers changing from the Democrats to the Republicans.

Several factors contributed to the increased turnover in the 1970s and early 1980s. The elections of 1972 and 1974 were affected by redistricting that followed the 1970 census; many House veterans had decided to retire instead of facing strong new opposition. Those two elections also were the first in which eighteen-year-olds were allowed to vote. In 1974 probably the chief reason for change was the Watergate scandal, which put an end to the Nixon administration and badly damaged the Republican party. The Democrats gained forty-three seats in the House, and seventy-five of the ninety-two freshman representatives at the beginning of the 94th Congress (1975–77) were Democrats.

Most of those Democrats managed to hold on to their seats in the 1976 elections. The upheaval in that year's elections took place in the Senate. Eighteen new senators were sworn in when Congress convened in January 1977, marking the largest turnover in the Senate since 1959.

An even larger Senate turnover came in the 1978 elections. It resulted in a 1979 freshman class of twenty senators, the biggest since the twenty-three-member class of 1947. In 1978 ten incumbents retired, more than in any year since World War II. Three incumbents were beaten in primaries, the most in a decade. And seven incumbents were defeated for reelection, the second-highest number in twenty years. On the House side, a record number of fifty-eight seats were open due to retirements, deaths, primary defeats, and other causes. With the defeat of nineteen incumbents in the general election, the House ended up with a freshman class of seventy-seven in 1979.

The 97th Congress opened in 1981 with ninety-two freshmen—eighteen in the Senate and seventy-four in the House. In 1980, when Ronald Reagan won the White House, Republicans won Senate control for the first time since 1952, ending the longest one-party dominance of the Senate in history. They also netted the largest increase in the House since 1966—thirty-three seats.

The 1982 elections resulted in eighty-one new members in the House, fifty-seven of them Democrats. Republicans lost twenty-six seats in the House, half of them held by freshmen. Only three other elections in the past thirty years had brought in so many freshman Democrats. As in the 1972 and 1974 elections, redistricting played a major part. The 1980 census shifted seventeen seats from the Northeast and Midwest to the Sun Belt states of the South and West. The Democrats took ten of these seats. With only five new senators, the turnover was the smallest in the sixty-eight-year history of popular Senate elections.

In 1984 the Republicans gained fourteen House seats and Democrats picked up two Senate seats in an election that resulted in little turnover. There were forty-three newcomers in the House and only seven in the Senate when the 99th Congress opened. On only four previous occasions since 1914 had there been fewer than ten Senate newcomers.

In 1986 Democrats recaptured the Senate, electing eleven of the thirteen freshman senators. The 1986 House elections were extraordinarily good for incumbents of both parties. Only six House members lost in the general election; two had lost in the primaries. But enough other seats were open from retirement and death to yield a freshman class of fifty members—twenty-three Republicans and twenty-seven Democrats.

In 1988 George Bush was not only the first Republican since 1928 to hold the White House for his party for a third consecutive term but also the first candidate since John F. Kennedy to win the presidential election while his party lost seats in the House. Seven House incumbents were defeated at the polls—six in the general election and one in a primary election—which was a new post–World War II low for total number of defeated members. The House freshman class numbered thirty-three (seventeen Democrats, sixteen Republicans), making it smaller than any class in the 1980s. In 1988 Senate races one Democratic and three Republican incumbents were defeated. A freshman class of ten—five Democrats and five Republicans—entered the Senate in January 1989.

In the 1990 Senate elections, the Republicans suffered a net loss of one seat, the only incumbent defeated. The 1990 Senate incumbent reelection rate of 96.9 percent was the highest since direct elections began. The freshman class numbered four (one Democrat, three Republicans) in the Senate and forty-three (twenty-five Democrats, eighteen Republicans) in the House. For the third straight election, the Democrats gained House seats (nine). That feat had not been accomplished since the Democrats' string of victories in 1954, 1956, and 1958.

In 1992, for only the second time in U.S. history, the incumbent president lost while his party gained seats in the House. The nine-seat gain by the GOP was modest, however. Republican strategists' hopes to end the Democrats' thirty-eight-year run as House majority party fell short. Ethical scandals, including overdrafts at the House bank, combined with a weak economy and the post-census reapportionment that moved seats from Democratic

Congressional Service

The record for the longest service in Congress—nearly fifty-seven years—was held by Carl Hayden, D-Ariz., who retired from the Senate in 1969 at the age of ninety-one. Hayden gave up his job as a county sheriff to become Arizona's first representative in 1912. He was sworn in Feb. 19, 1912, five days after Arizona became a state, and served in the House for fifteen years. In 1927 he moved to the Senate where he served seven six-year terms. When Hayden retired, he was president pro tempore of the Senate and chair of the Senate Appropriations Committee.

The runner-up, Jamie L. Whitten, D-Miss., served in the House for fifty-three years. Whitten entered the House Nov. 4, 1941, when he was thirty-one years old, and left in 1995 at the age of eighty-four. As chair of the Appropriations Committee from 1979 to 1993, Whitten was sometimes referred to as "the last of the New Dealers."

At the start of the 109th Congress in 2005, two members of Congress were closing in on the service record. In the Senate, eighty-seven-year-old Robert Byrd of West Virginia started his fifty-third year in Congress. Before he became senator in 1959, Byrd spent six years in the House. The longest serving member of the House was seventy-eight-year-old John D. Dingell, D-Mich., who began his fiftieth year of consecutive service in 2005.

regions to the more Republican Sun Belt contributed to the defeat of twenty-four House incumbents. All this tumult resulted in an influx of freshmen exceeding anything Washington had seen in more than forty years. In total, 110 new House members were elected and eleven new senators. Two Democratic and two Republican incumbent senators were defeated.

The midterm elections of 1994 brought even more upheaval as the Republicans gained control of both the House and Senate for the first time since 1955. The GOP tide was attributed to the Democrats' difficulty in motivating their core constituency, as well as continued Republican gains from redistricting and the fund-raising advantages of some GOP challengers. Republicans gained fifty-two House seats. Seventy-three freshman Republicans were elected and all 157 GOP incumbents who ran were reelected. On the Democratic side, thirteen freshmen were elected, 191 incumbents reelected, and thirty-four incumbents defeated. (Four other representatives—three Democrats and one Republican—lost primary elections.) Republicans also swept the Senate in 1994, after eight years in the minority. The GOP captured all nine open seats and ousted two Democratic incumbents. The incoming Senate freshman class had eleven Republicans and no Democrats. There had never been an all-GOP Senate freshman class since popular elections of senators began in 1914.

The 1996 elections also ended up in the record books. Never before had voters reelected a Democratic president and at the same time entrusted both the House and the Senate to the Republican Party. Republicans won their first back-to-back majority in the House since the 1920s. But Democrats did manage to cut into the GOP's numbers, with a net gain of nine seats. Of the twenty House incumbents defeated, all but three were Republicans. (Two additional members—one Democrat and one Republican—lost renomination bids.) The heaviest toll in 1996 was among the mainly conservative and contentious GOP freshman class—eleven freshman Republicans were defeated. In the Senate, Republicans built on their gains in the previous election, picking up two seats and giving them a 55–45 majority over the Democrats. That was the Republicans' highest total in the Senate following any election since 1928. But unlike the 1994 election this time there were Democrats in the freshman class—six—along with nine freshman Republicans. Only one incumbent senator was defeated, a Republican.

By 1998 the turnover in Congress had slowed down. All but seven of the 402 House members seeking reelection in November were returned to office—a 98.3 percent success rate. The Democrats picked up five House seats, which left the Republicans with a twelve-seat majority. Just three of the thirty senators up for reelection in 1998 were defeated, or a 90 percent success rate. Eight Senate freshmen—four Democrats and four Republicans—and forty new members of the House joined the 106th Congress.

In 2000 the GOP won a fourth term in the majority, but it was also the third straight election in which the Republicans lost House seats. The election resulted in a 221–212 party split in the House, with two independents. The nine-seat difference was the closest after a House election since 1952. The GOP slim majority in the Senate fell to an exact tie: fifty Democrats and fifty Republicans. However, the Republicans retained control because their party won back the White House, which allowed Richard B. Cheney, the incoming vice president and presiding Senate officer, to vote to break a tie. This rare arrangement was short-lived, however, as moderate Republican James Jeffords of Vermont left the GOP to become an Independent in June 2001, giving majority control of the Senate to the Democrats for the first time since 1994.

The Republicans regained control of both houses in the 2002 elections. For only the third time in a century,

and the first time since 1934, the party in control of the White House won seats in a midterm election. The GOP regained the Senate by winning two seats and expanded its majority in the House by picking up six seats. Only sixteen of the 398 incumbents seeking reelection to the House were defeated, giving House incumbents a success rate of 96 percent. Incumbents in the Senate had an 85.7 percent success rate as four incumbents out of the twenty-eight seeking reelection lost.

In 2004 the Republicans held onto the White House while picking up seats in both houses of Congress. In the Senate the GOP gained four seats to widen their majority to fifty-five versus forty-four Democrats and one Independent. In the House the GOP added three seats to increase their majority to 232 versus 202 Democrats and one Independent. Incumbents continued to be returned to Congress at a high rate. In the House 97.8 percent of those incumbents seeking reelection won. Only one incumbent in the Senate lost reelection while twenty-five won—a 96.2 percent success rate. The 109th Congress began with nine new senators and forty-one new representatives.

Shifts between Chambers

From the early days of Congress, members have shifted from one chamber to another. But far fewer former senators have gone to the House than vice versa. In the 1790s, nineteen former representatives became senators and three former senators moved to the House. That same pattern continued through the nineteenth century and into the twentieth. By the end of the twentieth century, it was common to find House members running for the Senate, but senators rarely, if ever, moved to the House. The greatest number of former senators to become House members in any one decade was nine in the years 1810 to 1820.

Although both chambers are equal under the law, for some representatives the Senate has distinct advantages. They find appealing the stability of a six-year term, the larger Senate staffs and more generous perquisites, the opportunity for increased effectiveness in a chamber of only 100 members, the Senate's greater role in foreign affairs, and the prestige of statewide constituencies.

Perhaps the most notable shift from the Senate to the House was that of Henry Clay, Ky., who gave up his Senate seat in 1811 to assume a House seat, which he held for most of the next fifteen years. In his first term in the House, Clay was elected Speaker—an office he used successfully to help push the country into the War of 1812. Clay left the House in 1825 and returned to the Senate in 1831. Another prominent House member who had once been a senator was John Quincy Adams, Whig-Mass., who also was one of only two former presidents to serve in Congress. (Andrew Johnson was the other.) *(See box, Members of Congress Who Became President, p. 58.)*

Members of Congress: Biographies

This biographical summary lists, alphabetically, all men and women who served in Congress as senators, representatives, delegates, resident commissioners, or territorial delegates from March 4, 1789, through March 10, 2005—from the First Congress to the beginning of the 109th Congress.

The material is organized as follows: name; relationship to other members, presidents, or vice presidents; party (at time of service), state (of service); date of birth; date of death (if applicable); congressional service; service as House or Senate majority leader, House or Senate minority leader, Speaker of the House, or president pro tempore of the Senate (when elected); chair of standing congressional committees (since 1947), service as president, vice president, cabinet member, Supreme Court justice, governor, delegate to the Continental Congress, or chair of the Democratic National Committee or the Republican National Committee.

If a member changed parties during his or her congressional service, party designation appearing after the member's name is that which applied at the end of such service and further breakdown is included after dates of congressional service. Party designation is multiple only if the member was elected by two or more parties at the same time. Where service date is left open, the member was serving in the 109th Congress. *(See Party Abbreviations, p. 324.)*

Dates of service are inclusive and may cover more than one term—six years for senators and two years for representatives. Under the Constitution, terms of service from 1789 to 1933 were from March 4 to March 4; since 1934, service has been from Jan. 3 to Jan. 3. In actual practice, members often have been sworn in on other dates at the beginning of a Congress. The exact date is shown (where available) only if a member began or ended his or her service in midterm.

For Senate presidents pro tempore, only the dates of their election are included, not the dates of their complete service. Until March 12, 1890, the appointment or election of the president pro tempore was for the occasion only, resulting in more than one president pro tempore appearing per session or none at all. Since then, the president pro tempore serves until the Senate orders otherwise.

Presidential and vice presidential terms from 1789 to 1933 were from March 4 to March 4; since 1934, the four-year term has been from Jan. 20 to Jan. 20.

The primary source of information for this list was the *Biographical Directory of the American Congress, 1774–1996* (Alexandria, Va.: CQ Staff Directories, 1997). Additional data were obtained from the files of the Joint Committee on Printing; the House Historian; the Senate Historian; Congressional Quarterly's *Guide to Congress,* 5th ed. (Washington, D.C.: Congressional Quarterly, 2000); *Congressional Quarterly's Guide to U.S. Elections,* 4th ed. (Washington, D.C.: CQ Press, 2001); *CQ Weekly*; and various newspapers and Web sites.

Aandahl, Fred George (R N.D.) April 9, 1897–April 7, 1966; House 1951–53; Gov. Jan. 4, 1945–Jan. 3, 1951.

Abbitt, Watkins Moorman (D Va.) May 21, 1908–July 13, 1998; House Feb. 17, 1948–73.

Abbot, Joel (R Ga.) March 17, 1776–Nov. 19, 1826; House 1817–25.

Abbott, Amos (W Mass.) Sept. 10, 1786–Nov. 2, 1868; House 1843–49.

Abbott, Joseph (D Texas) Jan. 15, 1840–Feb. 11, 1908; House 1887–97.

Abbott, Joseph Carter (R N.C.) July 15, 1825–Oct. 8, 1881; Senate July 14, 1868–71.

Abbott, Josiah Gardner (D Mass.) Nov. 1, 1814–June 2, 1891; House July 28, 1876–77.

Abbott, Nehemiah (R Maine) March 29, 1804–July 26, 1877; House 1857–59.

Abdnor, James (R S.D.) Feb. 13, 1923– ; House 1973–81; Senate 1981–87.

Abel, Hazel Hempell (R Neb.) July 10, 1888–July 30, 1966; Senate Nov. 8–Dec. 31, 1954.

Abele, Homer E. (R Ohio) Nov. 21, 1916–May 12, 2000; House 1963–65.

Abercrombie, James (UW Ala.) 1795–July 2, 1861; House 1851–55.

Abercrombie, John William (D Ala.) May 17, 1866–July 2, 1940; House 1913–17.

Abercrombie, Neil (D Hawaii) June 26, 1938– ; House Sept. 23, 1986–87, 1991– .

Abernethy, Charles Laban (D N.C.) March 18, 1872–Feb. 23, 1955; House Nov. 7, 1922–35.

Abernethy, Thomas Gerstle (D Miss.) May 16, 1903–June 11, 1998; House 1943–73.

Abourezk, James George (D S.D.) Feb. 24, 1931– ; House 1971–73; Senate 1973–79.

Abraham, Spencer (R Mich.) June 12, 1952– ; Senate 1995–2000; secretary of energy Jan. 20, 2001–Feb. 1, 2005.

Abzug, Bella Savitzky (D N.Y.) July 24, 1920–March 31, 1998; House 1971–77.

Acevedo-Vilá, Anibal (D P.R.) Feb. 13, 1962– ; House (Res. Comm.) 2001–2005.

Acheson, Ernest Francis (R Pa.) Sept. 19, 1855–May 16, 1917; House 1895–1909.

Acker, Ephraim Leister (D Pa.) Jan. 11, 1827–May 12, 1903; House 1871–73.

Ackerman, Ernest Robinson (R N.J.) June 17, 1863–Oct. 18, 1931; House 1919–Oct. 18, 1931.

Ackerman, Gary Leonard (D N.Y.) Nov. 19, 1942– ; House March 1, 1983– .

Acklen, Joseph Hayes (D La.) May 20, 1850–Sept. 28, 1938; House Feb. 20, 1878–81.

Adair, Edwin Ross (R Ind.) Dec. 14, 1907–May 5, 1983; House 1951–71.

Adair, Jackson Leroy (D Ill.) Feb. 23, 1887–Jan. 19, 1956; House 1933–37.

Adair, John (J Ky.) Jan. 9, 1757–May 19, 1840; Senate Nov. 8, 1805–Nov. 18, 1806 (no party); House 1831–33; Gov. June 1, 1820–June 1, 1824 (Democratic Republican).

Adair, John Alfred McDowell (D Ind.) Dec. 22, 1864–Oct. 5, 1938; House 1907–17.

Adams, Alva Blanchard (D Colo.) Oct. 29, 1875–Dec. 1, 1941; Senate May 17, 1923–Nov. 30, 1924, 1933–Dec. 1, 1941.

Adams, Benjamin (F Mass.) Dec. 16, 1764–March 28, 1837; House Dec. 2, 1816–21.

Adams, Brockman "Brock" (D Wash.) Jan. 13, 1927–Sept. 10, 2004; House 1965–Jan. 22, 1977; chair House Budget 1975–77; Senate 1987–93; secretary of transportation Jan. 23, 1977–July 22, 1979.

Adams, Charles Francis (son of John Quincy Adams, grandson of Pres. John Adams) (R Mass.) Aug. 18, 1807–Nov. 21, 1886; House 1859–May 1, 1861.

Adams, Charles Henry (R N.Y.) April 10, 1824–Dec. 15, 1902; House 1875–77.

Adams, George Everett (R Ill.) June 18, 1840–Oct. 5, 1917; House 1883–91.

Adams, George Madison (nephew of Green Adams) (D Ky.) Dec. 20, 1837–April 6, 1920; House 1867–75.

Adams, Green (uncle of George Madison Adams) (O Ky.) Aug. 20, 1812–Jan. 18, 1884; House 1847–49 (Whig), 1859–61.

Adams, Henry Cullen (R Wis.) Nov. 28, 1850–July 9, 1906; House 1903–July 9, 1906.

Adams, John (J N.Y.) Aug. 26, 1778–Sept. 25, 1854; House March 4–Dec. 26, 1815 (Republican), 1833–35.

Adams, John Joseph (D N.Y.) Sept. 16, 1848–Feb. 16, 1919; House 1883–87.

Adams, John Quincy (son of Pres. John Adams, father of Charles Francis Adams) (F Mass.) July 11, 1767–Feb. 23, 1848; Senate 1803–June 8, 1808; House 1831–Feb. 23, 1848; secretary of state Sept. 22, 1817–March 3, 1825; president 1825–29 (Democratic Republican).

Adams, Parmenio (– N.Y.) Sept. 9, 1776–Feb. 19, 1832; House Jan. 7, 1824–27.

Adams, Robert Jr. (R Pa.) Feb. 26, 1849–June 1, 1906; House Dec. 19, 1893–June 1, 1906.

Adams, Robert Huntington (J Miss.) 1792–July 2, 1830; Senate Jan. 6, 1830–July 2, 1830.

Adams, Sherman (R N.H.) Jan. 8, 1899–Oct. 27, 1986; House 1945–47; Gov. Jan. 6, 1949–Jan. 1, 1953.

Adams, Silas (R Ky.) Feb. 9, 1839–May 5, 1896; House 1893–95.

Adams, Stephen (D Miss.) Oct. 17, 1807–May 11, 1857; House 1845–47; Senate March 17, 1852–57.

Adams, Wilbur Louis (D Del.) Oct. 23, 1884–Dec. 4, 1937; House 1933–35.

Adamson, William Charles (D Ga.) Aug. 13, 1854–Jan. 3, 1929; House 1897–Dec. 18, 1917.

Addabbo, Joseph Patrick (D N.Y.) March 17, 1925–April 10, 1986; House 1961–April 10, 1986.

Addams, William (D Pa.) April 11, 1777–May 30, 1858; House 1825–29.

Addonizio, Hugh Joseph (D N.J.) Jan. 31, 1914–Feb. 2, 1981; House 1949–June 30, 1962.

Aderholt, Robert B. (R Ala.) July 22, 1965– ; House 1997– .

Adgate, Asa (R N.Y.) Nov. 17, 1767–Feb. 15, 1832; House June 7, 1815–17.

Adkins, Charles (R Ill.) Feb. 7, 1863–March 31, 1941; House 1925–33.

Adrain, Garnett Bowditch (ALD N.J.) Dec. 15, 1815–Aug. 17, 1878; House 1857–61 (1857–59 Democrat).

Ahl, John Alexander (D Pa.) Aug. 16, 1813–April 25, 1882; House 1857–59.

Aiken, David Wyatt (father of Wyatt Aiken, cousin of William Aiken) (D S.C.) March 17, 1828–April 6, 1887; House 1877–87.

Aiken, George David (R Vt.) Aug. 20, 1892–Nov. 19, 1984; Senate Jan. 10, 1941–75; chair Senate Expenditures in the Exec. Depts. 1947–49; chair Senate Agriculture and Forestry 1953–55; Gov. Jan. 7, 1937–Jan. 9, 1941.

Aiken, William (cousin of David Wyatt Aiken) (D S.C.) Jan. 28, 1806–Sept. 7, 1887; House 1851–57; Gov. 1844–46.

Aiken, Wyatt (son of David Wyatt Aiken) (D S.C.) Dec. 14, 1863–Feb. 6, 1923; House 1903–17.

Ainey, William David Blakeslee (R Pa.) April 8, 1864–Sept. 4, 1932; House Nov. 7, 1911–15.

Ainslie, George (D Idaho) Oct. 30, 1838–May 19, 1913; House (Terr. Del.) 1879–83.

Ainsworth, Lucien Lester (D Iowa) June 21, 1831–April 19, 1902; House 1875–77.

Aitken, David Demerest (R Mich.) Sept. 5, 1853–May 26, 1930; House 1893–97.

Akaka, Daniel Kahikina (D Hawaii) Sept. 11, 1924– ; House 1977–May 16, 1990; Senate May 16, 1990– .

Akers, Thomas Peter (AP Mo.) Oct. 4, 1828–April 3, 1877; House Aug. 18, 1856–57.

Akin, Theron (PR N.Y.) May 23, 1855–March 26, 1933; House 1911–13.

Akin, W. Todd (R Mo.) July 5, 1947– ; House 2001– .

Albaugh, Walter Hugh (R Ohio) Jan. 2, 1890–Jan. 21, 1942; House Nov. 8, 1938–39.

Albert, Carl Bert (cousin of Charles Wesley Vursell) (D Okla.) May 10, 1908–Feb. 4, 2000; House 1947–77; House majority leader Jan. 10, 1962–71; Speaker Jan. 21, 1971–75, Jan. 14, 1975–77.

Albert, William Julian (R Md.) Aug. 4, 1816–March 29, 1879; House 1873–75.

Albertson, Nathaniel (D Ind.) June 10, 1800–Dec. 16, 1863; House 1849–51.

Albosta, Donald Joseph (D Mich.) Dec. 5, 1925– ; House 1979–85.

Albright, Charles (R Pa.) Dec. 13, 1830–Sept. 28, 1880; House 1873–75.

Albright, Charles Jefferson (R Ohio) May 9, 1816–Oct. 21, 1883; House 1855–57.

Alcorn, James Lusk (R Miss.) Nov. 4, 1816–Dec. 19, 1894; Senate Dec. 1, 1871–77; Gov. March 10, 1870–Nov. 30, 1871.

Alderson, John Duffy (D W.Va.) Nov. 29, 1854–Dec. 5, 1910; House 1889–95.

Aldrich, Cyrus (R Minn.) June 18, 1808–Oct. 5, 1871; House 1859–63.

Aldrich, James Franklin (son of William Aldrich) (R Ill.) April 6, 1853–March 8, 1933; House 1893–97.

Aldrich, Nelson Wilmarth (father of Richard Steere Aldrich, cousin of William Aldrich, great-grandfather of John Davidson "Jay" Rockefeller IV, grandfather of Vice Pres. Nelson Aldrich Rockefeller and Gov. Winthrop Rockefeller of Ark.) (R R.I.) Nov. 6, 1841–April 16, 1915; House 1879–Oct. 4, 1881; Senate Oct. 5, 1881–1911.

Aldrich, Richard Steere (son of Nelson Wilmarth Aldrich, great-uncle of John Davison "Jay" Rockefeller IV, uncle of Vice Pres. Nelson Aldrich Rockefeller and Gov. Winthrop Rockefeller of Ark.) (R R.I.) Feb. 29, 1884–Dec. 25, 1941; House 1923–33.

Aldrich, Truman Heminway (brother of William Farrington Aldrich) (R Ala.) Oct. 17, 1848–April 28, 1932; House June 9, 1896–97.

Aldrich, William (father of James Franklin Aldrich, cousin of Nelson Wilmarth Aldrich) (R Ill.) Jan. 19, 1820–Dec. 3, 1885; House

1877–83.

Aldrich, William Farrington (brother of Truman Heminway Aldrich) (R Ala.) March 11, 1853–Oct. 30, 1925; House March 13, 1896–97, Feb. 9, 1898–99, March 8, 1900–01.

Aleshire, Arthur William (D Ohio) Feb. 15, 1900–March 11, 1940; House 1937–39.

Alexander, Adam Rankin (F Tenn.) ?–?; House 1823–27.

Alexander, Armstead Milton (D Mo.) May 26, 1834–Nov. 7, 1892; House 1883–85.

Alexander, De Alva Stanwood (R N.Y.) July 17, 1846–Jan. 30, 1925; House 1897–1911.

Alexander, Evan Shelby (cousin of Nathaniel Alexander) (R N.C.) about 1767–Oct. 28, 1809; House Feb. 24, 1806–09.

Alexander, Henry Porteous (W N.Y.) Sept. 13, 1801–Feb. 22, 1867; House 1849–51.

Alexander, Hugh Quincy (D N.C.) Aug. 7, 1911–Sept. 17, 1989; House 1953–63.

Alexander, James Jr. (W Ohio) Oct. 17, 1789–Sept. 5, 1846; House 1837–39.

Alexander, John (R Ohio) April 16, 1777–June 28, 1848; House 1813–17.

Alexander, John Grant (R Minn.) July 16, 1893–Dec. 8, 1971; House 1939–41.

Alexander, Joshua Willis (D Mo.) Jan. 22, 1852–Feb. 27, 1936; House 1907–Dec. 15, 1919; secretary of commerce Dec. 16, 1919–March 4, 1921.

Alexander, Lamar (R Tenn.) July 3, 1940– ; Senate 2003– ; secretary of education March 22, 1991–Jan. 20, 1993; Gov. Jan. 17, 1979–Jan. 17, 1987.

Alexander, Mark (J Va.) Feb. 7, 1792–Oct. 7, 1883; House 1819–33 (1819–29 no party).

Alexander, Nathaniel (cousin of Evan Shelby Alexander) (R N.C.) March 5, 1756–March 7, 1808; House 1803–Nov. 1805; Gov. Dec. 10, 1805–Dec. 1, 1807 (Democratic Republican).

Alexander, Rodney (R La.) Dec. 5, 1946– ; House 2003– (2003–Aug. 9, 2004 Democrat).

Alexander, Syndenham Benoni (cousin of Adlai Ewing Stevenson and John Sharp Williams) (D N.C.) Dec. 8, 1840–June 14, 1921; House 1891–95.

Alexander, William Vollie Jr. (D Ark.) Jan. 16, 1934– ; House 1969–93.

Alford, Julius Caesar (W Ga.) May 10, 1799–Jan. 1, 1863; House Jan. 2–March 3, 1837 (State Rights Party), 1839–Oct. 1, 1841.

Alford, Thomas Dale (ID Ark.) Jan. 28, 1916–Jan. 25, 2000; House 1959–63.

Alger, Bruce Reynolds (R Texas) June 12, 1918– ; House 1955–65.

Alger, Russell Alexander (R Mich.) Feb. 27, 1836–Jan. 24, 1907; Senate Sept. 27, 1902–Jan. 24, 1907; Gov. Jan. 1, 1885–Jan. 1, 1887; secretary of war March 5, 1897–Aug. 1, 1899.

Allan, Chilton (W Ky.) April 6, 1786–Sept. 3, 1858; House 1831–37 (1831–35 Anti-Jacksonian).

Allard, Wayne (R Colo.) Dec. 2, 1943– ; House 1991–97; Senate 1997– .

Allee, James Frank (R Del.) Dec. 2, 1857–Oct. 12, 1938; Senate March 2, 1903–07.

Allen, Alfred Gaither (D Ohio) July 23, 1867–Dec. 9, 1932; House 1911–17.

Allen, Amos Lawrence (R Maine) March 17, 1837–Feb. 20, 1911; House Nov. 6, 1899–Feb. 20, 1911.

Allen, Asa Leonard (D La.) Jan. 5, 1891–Jan. 5, 1969; House 1937–53.

Allen, Charles (son of Joseph Allen, great-nephew of Samuel Adams) (FS Mass.) Aug. 9, 1797–Aug. 6, 1869; House 1849–53.

Allen, Charles Herbert (R Mass.) April 15, 1848–April 20, 1934; House 1885–89.

Allen, Clarence Emir (R Utah) Sept. 8, 1852–July 9, 1932; House Jan. 4, 1896–97.

Allen, Clifford Robertson (D Tenn.) Jan. 6, 1912–June 18, 1978; House Nov. 25, 1975–June 18, 1978.

Allen, Edward Payson (R Mich.) Oct. 28, 1839–Nov. 25, 1909; House 1887–91.

Allen, Elisha Hunt (son of Samuel Clesson Allen) (W Maine) Jan. 28, 1804–Jan. 1, 1883; House 1841–43.

Allen, George Felix (R Va.) March 8, 1952– ; House Nov. 12, 1991–93; Senate 2001– ; Gov. Jan. 15, 1994–Jan. 17, 1998.

Allen, Heman (W Vt.) June 14, 1777–Dec. 11, 1844; House 1831–39 (1831–35 no party).

Allen, Heman (R Vt.) Feb. 23, 1779–April 7, 1852; House 1817–April 20, 1818.

Allen, Henry Crosby (R N.J.) May 13, 1872–March 7, 1942; House 1905–07.

Allen, Henry Dixon (D Ky.) June 24, 1854–March 9, 1924; House 1899–1903.

Allen, Henry Justin (R Kan.) Sept. 11, 1868–Jan. 17, 1950; Senate April 1, 1929–Nov. 30, 1930; Gov. Jan. 13, 1919–Jan. 8, 1923.

Allen, James Browning (husband of Maryon Pittman Allen) (D Ala.) Dec. 28, 1912–June 1, 1978; Senate 1969–June 1, 1978.

Allen, James Cameron (D Ill.) Jan. 29, 1822–Jan. 30, 1912; House 1853–July 18, 1856, Nov. 4, 1856–57, 1863–65.

Allen, John (father of John William Allen) (F Conn.) June 12, 1763–July 31, 1812; House 1797–99.

Allen, John Beard (R Wash.) May 18, 1845–Jan. 28, 1903; House (Terr. Del.) March 4–Nov. 11, 1889; Senate Nov. 20, 1889–93.

Allen, John Clayton (R Ill.) Feb. 14, 1860–Jan. 12, 1939; House 1925–33.

Allen, John James (brother of Robert Allen) (AJ Va.) Sept. 25, 1797–Sept. 18, 1871; House 1833–35.

Allen, John Joseph Jr. (R Calif.) Nov. 27, 1899–March 7, 1995; House 1947–59.

Allen, John Mills (D Miss.) July 8, 1846–Oct. 30, 1917; House 1885–1901.

Allen, John William (son of John Allen) (W Ohio) Aug. 1802–Oct. 5, 1887; House 1837–41.

Allen, Joseph (father of Charles Allen, nephew of Samuel Adams) (F Mass.) Sept. 2, 1749–Sept. 2, 1827; House Oct. 8, 1810–11.

Allen, Judson (D N.Y.) April 3, 1797–Aug. 6, 1880; House 1839–41.

Allen, Leo Elwood (R Ill.) Oct. 5, 1898–Jan. 19, 1973; House 1933–61; chair House Rules 1947–49, 1953–55.

Allen, Maryon Pittman (wife of James Browning Allen) (D Ala.) Nov. 30, 1925– ; Senate June 8–Nov. 7, 1978.

Allen, Nathaniel (father-in-law of Robert Lawson Rose) (– N.Y.) 1780–Dec. 22, 1832; House 1819–21.

Allen, Philip (D R.I.) Sept. 1, 1785–Dec. 16, 1865; Senate July 20, 1853–59; Gov. May 6, 1851–July 20, 1853.

Allen, Robert (– Tenn.) June 19, 1778–Aug. 19, 1844; House 1819–27.

Allen, Robert (brother of John James Allen) (J Va.) July 30, 1794–Dec. 30, 1859; House 1827–33.

Allen, Robert Edward Lee (D W.Va.) Nov. 28, 1865–Jan. 28, 1951; House 1923–25.

Allen, Robert Gray (D Pa.) Aug. 24, 1902–Aug. 9, 1963; House 1937–41.

Allen, Samuel Clesson (father of Elisha Hunt Allen) (F Mass.) Jan. 5, 1772–Feb. 8, 1842; House 1817–29.

Allen, Thomas (D Mo.) Aug. 29, 1813–April 8, 1882; House 1881–April 8, 1882.

Allen, Thomas H. (D Maine) April 16, 1945– ; House 1997– .

Allen, William (D Ohio) Dec. 18 or Dec. 27, 1803–July 11, 1879; House 1833–35 (Jacksonian); Senate 1837–49; Gov. Jan. 12, 1874–Jan. 10, 1876.

Allen, William (D Ohio) Aug. 13, 1827–July 6, 1881; House 1859–63.

Allen, William Franklin (D Del.) Jan. 19, 1883–June 14, 1946; House 1937–39.

Allen, William Joshua (son of Willis Allen) (D Ill.) June 9, 1829–Jan. 26, 1901; House June 2, 1862–65.

Allen, William Vincent (P Neb.) Jan. 28, 1847–Jan. 2, 1924; Senate 1893–99, Dec. 13, 1899–March 28, 1901.

Allen, Willis (father of William Joshua Allen) (D Ill.) Dec. 15, 1806–April 15, 1859; House 1851–55.

Alley, John Bassett (R Mass.) Jan. 7, 1817–Jan. 19, 1896; House 1859–67.

Allgood, Miles Clayton (D Ala.) Feb. 22, 1878–March 4, 1977; House 1923–35.

Allison, James Jr. (father of John Allison) (– Pa.) Oct. 4, 1772–June 17, 1854; House 1823–25.

Allison, John (son of James Allison Jr.) (W Pa.) Aug. 5, 1812–March 23, 1878; House 1851–53, 1855–57.

Allison, Robert (AMas. Pa.) March 10, 1777–Dec. 2, 1840; House 1831–33.

Allison, William Boyd (R Iowa) March 2, 1829–Aug. 4, 1908; House 1863–71; Senate 1873–Aug. 4, 1908.

Allott, Gordon Llewellyn (R Colo.) Jan. 2, 1907–Jan. 17, 1989; Senate 1955–73.

Almon, Edward Berton (D Ala.) April 18, 1860–June 22, 1933; House 1915–June 22, 1933.

Almond, James Lindsay Jr. (D Va.) June 15, 1898–April 14, 1986; House Jan. 22, 1946–April 17, 1948; Gov. Jan. 11, 1958–Jan. 13, 1962.

Alston, Lemuel James (R S.C.) 1760–1836; House 1807–11.

Alston, William Jeffreys (W Ala.) Dec. 31, 1800–June 10, 1876; House 1849–51.

Alston, Willis (nephew of Nathaniel Macon) (J N.C.) 1769–April 10, 1837; House 1799–1815 (Republican), 1825–31 (1825–29 Republican).

Alvord, James Church (W Mass.) April 14, 1808–Sept. 27, 1839; House 1839–Sept. 27, 1839.

Ambler, Jacob A. (R Ohio) Feb. 18, 1829–Sept. 22, 1906; House 1869–73.

Ambro, Jerome Anthony Jr. (D N.Y.) June 27, 1928–March 4, 1993; House 1975–81.

Amerman, Lemuel (D Pa.) Oct. 29, 1846–Oct. 7, 1897; House 1891–93.

Ames, Adelbert (father of Butler Ames, son-in-law of Benjamin Franklin Butler) (R Miss.) Oct. 31, 1835–April 12, 1933; Senate Feb. 23, 1870–Jan. 10, 1874; Gov. June 15, 1868–March 10, 1870 (Military), Jan. 4, 1874–March 20, 1876.

Ames, Butler (son of Adelbert Ames, grandson of Benjamin Franklin Butler) (R Mass.) Aug. 22, 1871–Nov. 6, 1954; House 1903–13.

Ames, Fisher (F Mass.) April 9, 1758–July 4, 1808; House 1789–97 (1789–95 no party).

Ames, Oakes (R Mass.) Jan. 10, 1804–May 8, 1873; House 1863–73.

Amlie, Thomas Ryum (Prog. Wis.) April 17, 1897–Aug. 22, 1973; House Oct. 13, 1931–33 (Republican), 1935–39.

Ammerman, Joseph Scofield (D Pa.) July 14, 1924–Oct. 14, 1993; House 1977–79.

Ancona, Sydenham Elnathan (D Pa.) Nov. 20, 1824–June 20, 1913; House 1861–67.

Andersen, Herman Carl (R Minn.) Jan. 27, 1897–July 26, 1978; House 1939–63.

Anderson, Albert Raney (IR Iowa) Nov. 8, 1837–Nov. 17, 1898; House 1887–89.

Anderson, Alexander Outlaw (son of Joseph Anderson) (D Tenn.) Nov. 10, 1794–May 23, 1869; Senate Feb. 26, 1840–41.

Anderson, Carl Carey (D Ohio) Dec. 2, 1877–Oct. 1, 1912; House 1909–Oct. 1, 1912.

Anderson, Chapman Levy (D Miss.) March 15, 1845–April 27, 1924; House 1887–91.

Anderson, Charles Arthur (D Mo.) Sept. 26, 1899–April 26, 1977; House 1937–41.

Anderson, Charles Marley (D Ohio) Jan. 5, 1845–Dec. 28, 1908; House 1885–87.

Anderson, Clinton Presba (D N.M.) Oct. 23, 1895–Nov. 11, 1975; House 1941–June 30, 1945; Senate 1949–73; chair Senate Interior and Insular Affairs 1961–63; chair Senate Aeronautical and Space Sciences 1963–73; secretary of agriculture June 30, 1945–May 10, 1948.

Anderson, George Alburtus (D Ill.) March 11, 1853–Jan. 31, 1896; House 1887–89.

Anderson, George Washington (R Mo.) May 22, 1832–Feb. 26, 1902; House 1865–69.

Anderson, Glenn Malcolm (D Calif.) Feb. 21, 1913–Dec. 13, 1994; House 1969–93; chair House Public Works and Transportation 1988–91.

Anderson, Hugh Johnston (D Maine) May 10, 1801–May 31, 1881; House 1837–41; Gov. Jan. 5, 1844–May 12, 1847.

Anderson, Isaac (R Pa.) Nov. 23, 1760–Oct. 27, 1838; House 1803–07.

Anderson, James Patton (D Wash.) Feb. 16, 1822–Sept. 20, 1872; House (Terr. Del.) 1855–57.

Anderson, John (J Maine) July 30, 1792–Aug. 21, 1853; House 1825–33 (1825–29 no party).

Anderson, John Alexander (R Kan.) June 26, 1834–May 18, 1892; House 1879–91 (1879–87 Republican, 1887–89 Independent Republican).

Anderson, John Bayard (R Ill.) Feb. 15, 1922– ; House 1961–81.

Anderson, John Zuinglius (R Calif.) March 22, 1904–Feb. 9, 1981; House 1939–53.

Anderson, Joseph (father of Alexander Outlaw Anderson) (– Tenn.) Nov. 5, 1757–April 17, 1837; Senate Sept. 26, 1797–1815; elected pres. pro tempore Jan. 15, 1805, Feb. 28, 1805, March 2, 1805.

Anderson, Joseph Halstead (D N.Y.) Aug. 25, 1800–June 23, 1870; House 1843–47.

Anderson, Josiah McNair (W Tenn.) Nov. 29, 1807–Nov. 8, 1861; House 1849–51.

Anderson, LeRoy Hagen (D Mont.) Feb. 2, 1906–Sept. 25, 1991; House 1957–61.

Anderson, Lucian (UU Ky.) June 23, 1824–Oct. 18, 1898; House 1863–65.

Anderson, Richard Clough Jr. (R Ky.) Aug. 4, 1788–July 24, 1826; House 1817–21.

Anderson, Samuel (– Pa.) 1773–Jan. 17, 1850; House 1827–29.

Anderson, Simeon H. (father of William Clayton Anderson) (W Ky.) March 2, 1802–Aug. 11, 1840; House 1839–Aug. 11, 1840.

Anderson, Sydney (R Minn.) Sept. 18, 1881–Oct. 8, 1948; House 1911–25.

Anderson, Thomas Lilbourne (ID Mo.) Dec. 8, 1808–March 6, 1885; House 1857–61 (1857–59 American Party).

Anderson, Wendell Richard (D Minn.) Feb. 1, 1933– ; Senate Dec. 30, 1976–Dec. 29, 1978; Gov. Jan. 4, 1971–Dec. 29, 1976.

Anderson, William (R Pa.) 1762–Dec. 16, 1829; House 1809–15, 1817–19.

Anderson, William Black (I Ill.) April 2, 1830–Aug. 28, 1901; House 1875–77.

Anderson, William Clayton (son of Simeon H. Anderson, nephew of Albert Gallatin Talbott) (O Ky.) Dec. 26, 1826–Dec. 23, 1861; House 1859–61.

Anderson, William Coleman (R Tenn.) July 10, 1853–Sept. 8, 1902; House 1895–97.

Anderson, William Robert (D Tenn.) June 17, 1921– ; House 1965–73.

Andresen, August Herman (R Minn.) Oct. 11, 1890–Jan. 14, 1958; House 1925–33, 1935–Jan. 14, 1958.

Andrew, Abram Piatt Jr. (R Mass.) Feb. 12, 1873–June 3, 1936; House Sept. 27, 1921–June 3, 1936.

Andrew, John Forrester (D Mass.) Nov. 26, 1850–May 30, 1895; House 1889–93.

Andrews, Arthur Glenn (R Ala.) Jan. 15, 1909– ; House 1965–67.

Andrews, Charles (D Maine) Feb. 11, 1814–April 30, 1852; House 1851–April 30, 1852.

Andrews, Charles Oscar (D Fla.) March 7, 1877–Sept. 18, 1946; Senate Nov. 4, 1936–Sept. 18, 1946.

Andrews, Elizabeth Bullock (widow of George William Andrews) (D Ala.) Feb. 12, 1911–Dec. 2, 2002; House April 4, 1972–73.

Andrews, George Rex (W N.Y.) Sept. 21, 1808–Dec. 5, 1873; House 1849–51.

Andrews, George William (husband of Elizabeth Bullock Andrews) (D Ala.) Dec. 12, 1906–Dec. 25, 1971; House March 14, 1944–Dec. 25, 1971.

Andrews, Ike Franklin (D N.C.) Sept. 2, 1925– ; House 1973–85.

Andrews, John Tuttle (D N.Y.) May 29, 1803–June 11, 1894; House 1837–39.

Andrews, Landaff Watson (W Ky.) Feb. 12, 1803–Dec. 23, 1887; House 1839–43.

Andrews, Mark (R N.D.) May 19, 1926– ; House Oct. 22, 1963–81; Senate 1981–87.

Andrews, Michael Allen (D Texas) Feb. 7, 1944– ; House 1983–95.

Andrews, Robert E. (D N.J.) Aug. 4, 1957– ; House Nov. 6, 1990– .

Andrews, Samuel George (R N.Y.) Oct. 16, 1796–June 11, 1863; House 1857–59.

Andrews, Sherlock James (W Ohio) Nov. 17, 1801–Feb. 11, 1880; House 1841–43.

Andrews, Thomas H. (D Maine) March 22, 1953– ; House 1991–95.

Andrews, Walter Gresham (R N.Y.) July 16, 1889–March 5, 1949; House 1931–49; chair House Armed Services 1947–49.

Andrews, William Ezekiel (R Neb.) Dec. 17, 1854–Jan. 19, 1942; House 1895–97, 1919–23.

Andrews, William Henry (R N.M.) Jan. 14, 1846–Jan. 16, 1919; House (Terr. Del.) 1905–Jan. 7, 1912.

Andrews, William Noble (R Md.) Nov. 13, 1876–Dec. 27, 1937; House 1919–21.

Andrus, John Emory (R N.Y.) Feb. 16, 1841–Dec. 26, 1934; House 1905–13.

Anfuso, Victor L'Episcopo (D N.Y.) March 10, 1905–Dec. 28, 1966; House 1951–53, 1955–63.

Angel, William G. (J N.Y.) July 17, 1790–Aug. 13, 1858; House 1825–27 (no party), 1829–33.

Angell, Homer Daniel (R Ore.) Jan. 12, 1875–March 31, 1968; House 1939–55.

Ankeny, Levi (R Wash.) Aug. 1, 1844–March 29, 1921; Senate 1903–09.

Annunzio, Frank (D Ill.) Jan. 12, 1915–April 8, 2001; House 1965–93; chair House Administration 1985–91.

Ansberry, Timothy Thomas (D Ohio) Dec. 24, 1871–July 5, 1943; House 1907–Jan. 9, 1915.

Ansorge, Martin Charles (R N.Y.) Jan. 1, 1882–Feb. 4, 1967; House 1921–23.

Anthony, Beryl Franklin Jr. (D Ark.) Feb. 21, 1938– ; House 1979–93.

Anthony, Daniel Read Jr. (R Kan.) Aug. 22, 1870–Aug. 4, 1931; House May 23, 1907–29.

Anthony, Henry Bowen (R R.I.) April 1, 1815–Sept. 2, 1884; Senate 1859–Sept. 2, 1884; elected pres. pro tempore March 23, 1869, April 9, 1869, May 28, 1870, July 1, 1870, July 14, 1870, March 10, 1871, April 17, 1871, May 23, 1871, Dec. 21, 1871, Feb. 23, 1872, June 8, 1872, Dec. 4, 1872, Dec. 13, 1872, Dec. 20, 1872, Jan. 24, 1873, Jan. 23, 1875, Feb. 15, 1875; Gov. May 1, 1849–May 6, 1851 (Whig).

Anthony, Joseph Biles (J Pa.) June 19, 1795–Jan. 10, 1851; House 1833–37.

Antony, Edwin Le Roy (D Texas) Jan. 5, 1852–Jan. 16, 1913; House June 14, 1892–93.

Aplin, Henry Harrison (R Mich.) April 15, 1841–July 23, 1910; House Oct. 20, 1901–03.

Appleby, Stewart Hoffman (son of Theodore Frank Appleby) (R N.J.) May 17, 1890–Jan. 12, 1964; House Nov. 3, 1925–27.

Appleby, Theodore Frank (father of Stewart Hoffman Appleby) (R N.J.) Oct. 10, 1864–Dec. 15, 1924; House 1921–23.

Applegate, Douglas Earl (D Ohio) March 27, 1928– ; House 1977–95.

Appleton, John (D Maine) Feb. 11, 1815–Aug. 22, 1864; House 1851–53.

Appleton, Nathan (cousin of William Appleton) (W Mass.) Oct. 6, 1779–July 14, 1861; House 1831–33 (Anti-Jacksonian), June 9–Sept. 28, 1842.

Appleton, William (cousin of Nathan Appleton) (Const U Mass.) Nov. 16, 1786–Feb. 15, 1862; House 1851–55 (Whig), March 4–Sept. 27, 1861.

Apsley, Lewis Dewart (R Mass.) Sept. 29, 1852–April 11, 1925; House 1893–97.

Archer, John (father of Stevenson Archer, grandfather of Stevenson Archer born in 1827) (R Md.) May 5, 1741–Sept. 28, 1810; House 1801–07.

Archer, Stevenson (son of John Archer, father of Stevenson Archer, below) (R Md.) Oct. 11, 1786–June 26, 1848; House Oct. 26, 1811–17, 1819–21.

Archer, Stevenson (son of Stevenson Archer, above, grandson of John Archer) (D Md.) Feb. 28, 1827–Aug. 2, 1898; House 1867–75.

Archer, William Reynolds Jr. "Bill" (R Texas) March 22, 1928– ; House 1971–2001; chair House Ways and Means 1995–2001.

Archer, William Segar (nephew of Joseph Eggleston) (W Va.) March 5, 1789–March 28, 1855; House Jan. 3, 1820–35 (no party); Senate 1841–47.

Arends, Leslie Cornelius (R Ill.) Sept. 27, 1895–July 17, 1985; House 1935–Dec. 31, 1974.

Arens, Henry Martin (FL Minn.) Nov. 21, 1873–Oct. 6, 1963; House 1933–35.

Arentz, Samuel Shaw "Ulysses" (R Nev.) Jan. 8, 1879–June 17, 1934; House 1921–23, 1925–33.

Armey, Richard Keith "Dick" (R Texas) July 7, 1940– ; House 1985–2003; House majority leader 1995–2003.

Armfield, Robert Franklin (D N.C.) July 9, 1829–Nov. 9, 1898; House 1879–83.

Armstrong, David Hartley (D Mo.) Oct. 21, 1812–March 18, 1893; Senate Sept. 29, 1877–Jan. 26, 1879.

Armstrong, James (brother of John Armstrong Jr.) (– Pa.) Aug. 29, 1748–May 6, 1828; House 1793–95.

Armstrong, John Jr. (brother of James Armstrong) (– N.Y.) Nov. 25, 1758–April 1, 1843; Senate Nov. 6, 1800–Feb. 5, 1802, Nov. 10, 1803–June 30, 1804; secretary of war Jan. 13, 1813–Sept. 27, 1814.

Armstrong, Moses Kimball (D Dakota) Sept. 19, 1832–Jan. 11, 1906; House (Terr. Del.) 1871–75.

Armstrong, Orland Kay (R Mo.) Oct. 2, 1893–April 15, 1987; House 1951–53.

Armstrong, William (D Va.) Dec. 23, 1782–May 10, 1865; House 1825–33.

Armstrong, William Hepburn (R Pa.) Sept. 7, 1824–May 14, 1919; House 1869–71.

Armstrong, William Lester (R Colo.) March 16, 1937– ; House 1973–79; Senate 1979–91.

Arnell, Samuel Mayes (R Tenn.) May 3, 1833–July 20, 1903; House July 24, 1866–71 (July 24, 1866–67 Unconditional Unionist).

Arnold, Benedict (brother-in-law of Matthias J. Bovee) (– N.Y.) Oct. 5, 1780–March 3, 1849; House 1829–31.

Arnold, Isaac Newton (R Ill.) Nov. 30, 1815–April 24, 1884; House 1861–65.

Arnold, Laurence Fletcher (D Ill.) June 8, 1891–Dec. 6, 1966; House 1937–43.

Arnold, Lemuel Hastings (great-great-uncle of Theodore Francis Green) (W R.I.) Jan. 29, 1792–June 27, 1852; House 1845–47; Gov. May 4, 1831–May 1, 1833 (Democratic Republican).

Arnold, Marshall (D Mo.) Oct. 21, 1845–June 12, 1913; House 1891–95.

Arnold, Samuel (D Conn.) June 1, 1806–May 5, 1869; House 1857–59.

Arnold, Samuel Greene (great-uncle of Theodore Francis Green) (R R.I.) April 12, 1821–Feb. 14, 1880; Senate Dec. 1, 1862–63.

Arnold, Samuel Washington (R Mo.) Sept. 21, 1879–Dec. 18, 1961; House 1943–49.

Arnold, Thomas Dickens (W Tenn.) May 3, 1798–May 26, 1870; House 1831–33 (Anti-Jacksonian), 1841–43.

Arnold, Warren Otis (R R.I.) June 3, 1839–April 1, 1910; House 1887–91, 1895–97.

Arnold, William Carlile (R Pa.) July 15, 1851–March 20, 1906; House 1895–99.

Arnold, William Wright (D Ill.) Oct. 14, 1877–Nov. 23, 1957; House 1923–Sept. 16, 1935.

Arnot, John Jr. (D N.Y.) March 11, 1831–Nov. 20, 1886; House 1883–Nov. 20, 1886.

Arrington, Archibald Hunter (uncle of Archibald Hunter Arrington Williams) (D N.C.) Nov. 13, 1809–July 20, 1872; House 1841–45.

Arthur, William Evans (D Ky.) March 3, 1825–May 18, 1897; House 1871–75.

Ash, Michael Woolston (J Pa.) March 5, 1789–Dec. 14, 1858; House 1835–37.

Ashbrook, Jean Spencer (widow of John Milan Ashbrook, daughter-in-law of William Albert Ashbrook) (R Ohio) Sept. 21, 1934– ; House July 12, 1982–83.

Ashbrook, John Milan (husband of Jean Spencer Ashbrook, son of William Albert Ashbrook) (R Ohio) Sept. 21, 1928–April 24, 1982; House 1961–April 24, 1982.

Ashbrook, William Albert (father of John Milan Ashbrook, father-in-law of Jean Spencer Ashbrook) (D Ohio) July 1, 1867–Jan. 1, 1940; House 1907–21, 1935–Jan. 1, 1940.

Ashcroft, John (R Mo.) May 9, 1942– ; Senate 1995–2001; attorney general Feb. 1, 2001–Feb. 3, 2005; Gov. Jan. 14, 1985–Jan. 11, 1993.

Ashe, John Baptista (uncle of John Baptista Ashe of Tenn., Thomas Samuel Ashe, and William Shepperd Ashe) (F N.C.) 1748–Nov. 27, 1802; House March 24, 1790–93; Cont. Cong. 1787.

Ashe, John Baptista (brother of William Shepperd Ashe, nephew of John Baptista Ashe of N.C., cousin of Thomas Samuel Ashe) (W Tenn.) 1810–Dec. 29, 1857; House 1843–45.

Ashe, Thomas Samuel (nephew of John Baptista Ashe of N.C., cousin of John Baptista Ashe of Tenn., William Shepperd Ashe) (D N.C.) July 19, 1812–Feb. 4, 1887; House 1873–77.

Ashe, William Shepperd (brother of John Baptista Ashe of Tenn., nephew of John Baptista Ashe of N.C., cousin of Thomas Samuel Ashe) (D N.C.) Sept. 14, 1814–Sept. 14, 1862; House 1849–55.

Ashley, Chester (D Ark.) June 1, 1790–April 29, 1848; Senate Nov. 8, 1844–April 29, 1848.

Ashley, Delos Rodeyn (R Nev.) Feb. 19, 1828–July 18, 1873; House 1865–69.

Ashley, Henry (– N.Y.) Feb. 19, 1778–Jan. 14, 1829; House 1825–27.

Ashley, James Mitchell (great-grandfather of Thomas William Ludlow Ashley) (R Ohio) Nov. 14, 1824–Sept. 16, 1896; House 1859–69; Gov. (Mont. Terr.) 1869–70.

Ashley, Thomas William Ludlow (great-grandson of James Mitchell Ashley) (D Ohio) Jan. 11, 1923– ; House 1955–81.

Ashley, William Henry (J Mo.) 1778–March 26, 1838; House Oct. 31, 1831–37.

Ashmore, John Durant (cousin of Robert Thomas Ashmore) (D S.C.) Aug. 18, 1819–Dec. 5, 1871; House 1859–Dec. 21, 1860.

Ashmore, Robert Thomas (cousin of John Durant Ashmore) (D S.C.) Feb. 22, 1904–Oct. 4, 1989; House June 2, 1953–69.

Ashmun, Eli Porter (father of George Ashmun) (– Mass.) June 24, 1770–May 10, 1819; Senate June 12, 1816–May 10, 1818.

Ashmun, George (son of Eli Porter Ashmun) (W Mass.) Dec. 25, 1804–July 16, 1870; House 1845–51.

Ashurst, Henry Fountain (D Ariz.) Sept. 13, 1874–May 31, 1962; Senate March 27, 1912–41.

Asper, Joel Funk (R Mo.) April 20, 1822–Oct. 1, 1872; House 1869–71.

Aspin, Leslie "Les" (D Wis.) July 21, 1938–May 21, 1995; House 1971–Jan. 20, 1993; chair House Armed Services 1985–93; secretary of defense Jan. 22, 1993–Feb. 2, 1994.

Aspinall, Wayne Norviel (D Colo.) April 3, 1896–Oct. 9, 1983; House 1949–73; chair House Interior and Insular Affairs 1959–73.

Aswell, James Benjamin (D La.) Dec. 23, 1869–March 16, 1931; House 1913–March 16, 1931.

Atchison, David Rice (W Mo.) Aug. 11, 1807–Jan. 26, 1886; Senate Oct. 14, 1843–55; elected pres. pro tempore Aug. 8, 1846, Jan. 11, 1847, March 3, 1847, Feb. 2, 1848, June 1, 1848, June 26, 1848, July 29, 1848, Dec. 26, 1848, March 2, 1849, March 5, 1849, March 16, 1849, Dec. 20, 1852, March 4, 1853.

Atherton, Charles Gordon (son of Charles Humphrey Atherton) (D N.H.) July 4, 1804–Nov. 15, 1853; House 1837–43; Senate 1843–49 (also elected for the term beginning 1853 but never qualified).

Atherton, Charles Humphrey (father of Charles Gordon Atherton) (F N.H.) Aug. 14, 1773–Jan. 8, 1853; House 1815–17.

Atherton, Gibson (D Ohio) Jan. 19, 1831–Nov. 10, 1887; House 1879–83.

Atkeson, William Oscar (R Mo.) Aug. 24, 1854–Oct. 16, 1931; House 1921–23.

Atkins, Chester Greenough (D Mass.) April 14, 1948– ; House 1985–93.

Atkins, John DeWitt Clinton (D Tenn.) June 4, 1825–June 2, 1908; House 1857–59, 1873–83.

Atkinson, Archibald (D Va.) Sept. 15, 1792–Jan. 7, 1872; House 1843–49.

Atkinson, Eugene Vincent (D Pa.) April 5, 1927– ; House 1979–83 (Oct. 14, 1981–83 Republican).

Atkinson, George Wesley (R W.Va.) June 29, 1845–April 4, 1925; House Feb. 26, 1890–91; Gov. March 4, 1897–March 4, 1901.

Atkinson, Louis Evans (R Pa.) April 16, 1841–Feb. 5, 1910; House 1883–93.

Atkinson, Richard Merrill (D Tenn.) Feb. 6, 1894–April 29, 1947; House 1937–39.

Atwater, John Wilbur (IP N.C.) Dec. 27, 1840–July 4, 1910; House 1899–1901.

Atwood, David (R Wis.) Dec. 15, 1815–Dec. 11, 1889; House Feb. 23, 1870–71.

Atwood, Harrison Henry (R Mass.) Aug. 26, 1863–Oct. 22, 1954; House 1895–97.

Auchincloss, James Coats (R N.J.) Jan. 19, 1885–Oct. 2, 1976; House 1943–65.

AuCoin, Les (D Ore.) Oct. 21, 1942– ; House 1975–93.

Auf der Heide, Oscar Louis (D N.J.) Dec. 8, 1874–March 29, 1945; House 1925–35.

Austin, Albert Elmer (stepfather of Clare Boothe Luce) (R Conn.) Nov. 15, 1877–Jan. 26, 1942; House 1939–41.

Austin, Archibald (R Va.) Aug. 11, 1772–Oct. 16, 1837; House 1817–19.

Austin, Richard Wilson (R Tenn.) Aug. 26, 1857–April 20, 1919; House 1909–19.

Austin, Warren Robinson (R Vt.) Nov. 12, 1877–Dec. 25, 1962; Senate April 1, 1931–Aug. 2, 1946.

Averett, Thomas Hamlet (D Va.) July 10, 1800–June 30, 1855; House 1849–53.

Averill, John Thomas (R Minn.) March 1, 1825–Oct. 3, 1889; House 1871–75.

Avery, Daniel (R N.Y.) Sept. 18, 1766–Jan. 30, 1842; House 1811–15, Sept. 30, 1816–17.

Avery, John (R Mich.) Feb. 29, 1824–Jan. 21, 1914; House 1893–97.

Avery, William Henry (R Kan.) Aug. 11, 1911– ; House 1955–65; Gov. Jan. 11, 1965–Jan. 9, 1967.

Avery, William Tecumsah (D Tenn.) Nov. 11, 1819–May 22, 1880; House 1857–61.

Avis, Samuel Brashear (R W.Va.) Feb. 19, 1872–June 8, 1924; House 1913–15.

Axtell, Samuel Beach (D Calif.) Oct. 14, 1819–Aug. 6, 1891; House 1867–71; Gov. (Utah Terr.) 1874–June 1875; Gov. (N.M. Terr.) 1875–78.

Aycrigg, John Bancker (W N.J.) July 9, 1798–Nov. 8, 1856; House 1837–39, 1841–43.

Ayer, Richard Small (R Va.) Oct. 9, 1829–Dec. 14, 1896; House Jan. 31, 1870–71.

Ayers, Roy Elmer (D Mont.) Nov. 9, 1882–May 23, 1955; House 1933–37; Gov. Jan. 4, 1937–Jan. 6, 1941.

Ayres, Steven Beckwith (ID N.Y.) Oct. 27, 1861–June 1, 1929; House 1911–13.

Ayres, William Augustus (D Kan.) April 19, 1867–Feb. 17, 1952; House 1915–21, 1923–Aug. 22, 1934.

Ayres, William Hanes (R Ohio) Feb. 5, 1916–Dec. 20, 2000; House 1951–71.

Babbitt, Clinton (D Wis.) Nov. 16, 1831–March 11, 1907; House 1891–93.

Babbitt, Elijah (R Pa.) July 29, 1795–Jan. 9, 1887; House 1859–63.

Babcock, Alfred (W N.Y.) April 15, 1805–May 16, 1871; House 1841–43.

Babcock, Joseph Weeks (grandson of Joseph Weeks) (R Wis.) March 6, 1850–April 27, 1909; House 1893–1907.

Babcock, Leander (D N.Y.) March 1, 1811–Aug. 18, 1864; House 1851–53.

Babcock, William (AMas. N.Y.) 1785–Oct. 20, 1838; House 1831–33.

Babka, John Joseph (D Ohio) March 16, 1884–March 22, 1937; House 1919–21.

Baca, Joseph (D Calif.) Jan. 23, 1947– ; House 1999– .

Bacchus, James (D Fla.) June 21, 1949– ; House 1991–95.

Bacharach, Isaac (R N.J.) Jan. 5, 1870–Sept. 5, 1956; House 1915–37.

Bachman, Nathan Lynn (D Tenn.) Aug. 2, 1878–April 23, 1937; Senate Feb. 28, 1933–April 23, 1937.

Bachman, Reuben Knecht (D Pa.) Aug. 6, 1834–Sept. 19, 1911; House 1879–81.

Bachmann, Carl George (R W.Va.) May 14, 1890–Jan. 22, 1980; House 1925–33.

Bachus, Spencer (R Ala.) Dec. 28, 1947– ; House 1993– .

Bacon, Augustus Octavius (cousin of William Schley Howard) (D Ga.) Oct. 20, 1839–Feb. 14, 1914; Senate 1895–Feb. 14, 1914; elected pres. pro tempore Jan. 15, 1912 (to serve Jan. 15–Jan. 17, March 11–March 12, April 8, May 10, May 30–June 3, June 13–July 5, Aug. 1–Aug. 10, Aug. 27–Dec. 15, 1912, Jan. 5–Jan. 18, Feb. 2–Feb. 15, 1913).

Bacon, Ezekiel (son of John Bacon, father of William Johnson Bacon) (R Mass.) Sept. 1, 1776–Oct. 18, 1870; House Sept. 16, 1807–13.

Bacon, Henry (D N.Y.) March 14, 1846–March 25, 1915; House Dec. 6, 1886–89, 1891–93.

Bacon, John (father of Ezekiel Bacon, grandfather of William Johnson Bacon) (R Mass.) April 5, 1738–Oct. 25, 1820; House 1801–03.

Bacon, Mark Reeves (R Mich.) Feb. 29, 1852–Aug. 20, 1941; House March 4–Dec. 13, 1917.

Bacon, Robert Low (R N.Y.) July 23, 1884–Sept. 12, 1938; House 1923–Sept. 12, 1938.

Bacon, William Johnson (son of Ezekiel Bacon, grandson of John Bacon) (R N.Y.) Feb. 18, 1803–July 3, 1889; House 1877–79.

Badger, De Witt Clinton (D Ohio) Aug. 7, 1858–May 20, 1926; House 1903–05.

Badger, George Edmund (W N.C.) April 17, 1795–May 11, 1866; Senate Nov. 25, 1846–55; secretary of the navy March 6–Sept. 11, 1841.

Badger, Luther (– N.Y.) April 10, 1785–1869; House 1825–27.

Badham, Robert Edward (R Calif.) June 9, 1929– ; House 1977–89.

Badillo, Herman (D N.Y.) Aug. 21, 1929– ; House 1971–Dec. 31, 1977.

Baer, George Jr. (F Md.) 1763–April 3, 1834; House 1797–1801, 1815–17.

Baer, John Miller (R N.D.) March 29, 1886–Feb. 18, 1970; House July 10, 1917–21.

Baesler, Scotty (D Ky.) July 9, 1941– ; House 1993–99.

Bafalis, Louis Arthur (R Fla.) Sept. 28, 1929– ; House 1973–83.

Bagby, Arthur Pendleton (D Ala.) 1794–Sept. 21, 1858; Senate Nov. 24, 1841–June 16, 1848; Gov. Nov. 21, 1837–Nov. 22, 1841.

Bagby, John Courts (D Ill.) Jan. 24, 1819–April 4, 1896; House 1875–77.

Bagley, George Augustus (R N.Y.) July 22, 1826–May 12, 1915; House 1875–79.

Bagley, John Holroyd Jr. (D N.Y.) Nov. 26, 1832–Oct. 23, 1902; House 1875–77, 1883–85.

Bailey, Alexander Hamilton (R N.Y.) Aug. 14, 1817–April 20, 1874; House Nov. 30, 1867–71.

Bailey, Cleveland Monroe (D W.Va.) July 15, 1886–July 13, 1965; House 1945–47, 1949–63.

Bailey, David Jackson (D Ga.) March 11, 1812–June 14, 1897; House 1851–55 (1851–53 State Rights Party).

Bailey, Donald Allen (D Pa.) July 21, 1945– ; House 1979–83.

Bailey, Goldsmith Fox (R Mass.) July 17, 1823–May 8, 1862; House 1861–May 8, 1862.

Bailey, James Edmund (D Tenn.) Aug. 15, 1822–Dec. 29, 1885; Senate Jan. 19, 1877–81.

Bailey, Jeremiah (W Maine) May 1, 1773–July 6, 1853; House 1835–37.

Bailey, John (– Mass.) 1786–June 26, 1835; House Dec. 13, 1824–31.

Bailey, John Mosher (R N.Y.) Aug. 24, 1838–Feb. 21, 1916; House Nov. 5, 1878–81.

Bailey, Joseph (D Pa.) March 18, 1810–Aug. 26, 1885; House 1861–65.

Bailey, Joseph Weldon (father of Joseph Weldon Bailey Jr.) (D Texas) Oct. 6, 1862–April 13, 1929; House 1891–1901; Senate 1901–Jan. 3, 1913.

Bailey, Joseph Weldon Jr. (son of Joseph Weldon Bailey) (D Texas) Dec. 15, 1892–July 17, 1943; House 1933–35.

Bailey, Josiah William (D N.C.) Sept. 14, 1873–Dec. 15, 1946; Senate 1931–Dec. 15, 1946.

Bailey, Ralph Emerson (R Mo.) July 14, 1878–April 8, 1948; House 1925–27.

Bailey, Theodorus (– N.Y.) Oct. 12, 1758–Sept. 6, 1828; House 1793–97, 1799–1801, Oct. 6, 1801–03; Senate 1803–Jan. 16, 1804.

Bailey, Warren Worth (D Pa.) Jan. 8, 1855–Nov. 9, 1928; House 1913–17.

Bailey, Wendell (R Mo.) July 30, 1940– ; House 1981–83.

Bailey, Willis Joshua (R Kan.) Oct. 12, 1854–May 19, 1932; House 1899–1901; Gov. Jan. 12, 1903–Jan. 9, 1905.

Baird, Brian (D Wash.) March 7, 1956– ; House 1999– .

Baird, David (father of David Baird Jr.) (R N.J.) April 7, 1839–Feb. 25, 1927; Senate Feb. 23, 1918–19.

Baird, David Jr. (son of David Baird) (R N.J.) Oct. 10, 1881–Feb. 28, 1955; Senate Nov. 30, 1929–Dec. 2, 1930.

Baird, Joseph Edward (R Ohio) Nov. 12, 1865–June 14, 1942; House 1929–31.

Baird, Samuel Thomas (D La.) May 5, 1861–April 22, 1899; House 1897–April 22, 1899.

Baker, Caleb (– N.Y.) 1762–June 26, 1849; House 1819–21.

Baker, Charles Simeon (R N.Y.) Feb. 18, 1839–April 21, 1902; House 1885–91.

Baker, David Jewett (D Ill.) Sept. 7, 1792–Aug. 6, 1869; Senate Nov. 12–Dec. 11, 1830.

Baker, Edward Dickinson (R Ore.) Feb. 24, 1811–Oct. 21, 1861; House 1845–Jan. 15, 1847 (Whig Ill.), 1849–51 (Whig Ill.); Senate Oct. 2, 1860–Oct. 21, 1861.

Baker, Ezra (R N.J.) ?–?; House 1815–17.

Baker, Henry Moore (R N.H.) Jan. 11, 1841–May 30, 1912; House 1893–97.

Baker, Howard Henry (husband of Irene Bailey Baker, father of Howard Henry Baker Jr.) (R Tenn.) Jan. 12, 1902–Jan. 7, 1964; House 1951–Jan. 7, 1964.

Baker, Howard Henry Jr. (son of Howard Henry Baker, stepson of Irene Bailey Baker, son-in-law of Everett McKinley Dirksen) (R Tenn.) Nov. 15, 1925– ; Senate 1967–85; Senate minority leader 1977–81; Senate majority leader 1981–85.

Baker, Irene Bailey (widow of Howard Henry Baker, stepmother of Howard Henry Baker Jr.) (R Tenn.) Nov. 17, 1901–April 2, 1994; House March 10, 1964–65.

Baker, Jacob Thompson (D N.J.) April 13, 1847–Dec. 7, 1919; House 1913–15.

Baker, Jehu (D Ill.) Nov. 4, 1822–March 1, 1903; House 1865–69 (Republican), 1887–89 (Republican), 1897–99.

Baker, John (F Va.) ?–Aug. 18, 1823; House 1811–13.

Baker, John Harris (brother of Lucien Baker) (R Ind.) Feb. 28, 1832–Oct. 21, 1915; House 1875–81.

Baker, LaMar (R Tenn.) Dec. 29, 1915–June 20, 2003; House 1971–75.

Baker, Lucien (brother of John Harris Baker) (R Kan.) June 8, 1846–June 21, 1907; Senate 1895–1901.

Baker, Osmyn (W Mass.) May 18, 1800–Feb. 9, 1875; House Jan. 14, 1840–45.

Baker, Richard Hugh (R La.) May 22, 1948– ; House 1987– .

Baker, Robert (D N.Y.) April 1862–June 15, 1943; House 1903–05.

Baker, Stephen (R N.Y.) Aug. 12, 1819–June 9, 1875; House 1861–63.

Baker, William (P Kan.) April 29, 1831–Feb. 11, 1910; House 1891–97.

Baker, William Benjamin (R Md.) July 22, 1840–May 17, 1911; House 1895–1901.

Baker, William Henry (R N.Y.) Jan. 17, 1827–Nov. 25, 1911; House 1875–79.

Baker, William P. "Bill" (R Calif.) June 14, 1940– ; House 1993–97.

Bakewell, Charles Montague (R Conn.) April 24, 1867–Sept. 19, 1957; House 1933–35.

Bakewell, Claude Ignatius (R Mo.) Aug. 9, 1912–March 18, 1987; House 1947–49, March 9, 1951–53.

Baldacci, John E. (D Maine) Jan. 30, 1955– ; House 1995–2003; Gov. Jan. 8, 2003– .

Baldrige, Howard Malcolm (R Neb.) June 23, 1894–Jan. 19, 1985; House 1931–33.

Baldus, Alvin James (D Wis.) April 27, 1926– ; House 1975–81.

Baldwin, Abraham (F Ga.) Nov. 22, 1754–April 4, 1807; House 1789–99; Senate 1799–April 4, 1807; elected pres. pro tempore Dec. 7, 1801, April 17, 1802; Cont. Cong. 1785, 1787–88.

Baldwin, Augustus Carpenter (UD Mich.) Dec. 24, 1817–Jan. 21, 1903; House 1863–65.

Baldwin, Harry Streett (D Md.) Aug. 21, 1894–Oct. 19, 1952; House 1943–47.

Baldwin, Henry (– Pa.) Jan. 14, 1780–April 21, 1844; House 1817–May 8, 1822; assoc. justice Jan. 18, 1830–April 21, 1844.

Baldwin, Henry Alexander (R Hawaii) Jan. 12, 1871–Oct. 8, 1946; House (Terr. Del.) March 25, 1922–23.

Baldwin, Henry Porter (R Mich.) Feb. 22, 1814–Dec. 31, 1892; Senate Nov. 17, 1879–81; Gov. Jan. 6, 1869–Jan. 1, 1873.

Baldwin, John (– Conn.) April 5, 1772–March 27, 1850; House 1825–29.

Baldwin, John Denison (R Mass.) Sept. 28, 1809–July 8, 1883; House 1863–69.

Baldwin, John Finley Jr. (R Calif.) June 28, 1915–March 9, 1966; House 1955–March 9, 1966.

Baldwin, Joseph Clark (R N.Y.) Jan. 11, 1897–Oct. 27, 1957; House March 11, 1941–47.

Baldwin, Melvin Riley (D Minn.) April 12, 1838–April 15, 1901; House 1893–95.

Baldwin, Raymond Earl (R Conn.) Aug. 31, 1893–Oct. 4, 1986; Senate Dec. 27, 1946–Dec. 16, 1949; Gov. Jan. 4, 1939–Jan. 8, 1941, Jan. 6, 1943–Dec. 27, 1946.

Baldwin, Roger Sherman (son of Simeon Baldwin) (W Conn.) Jan. 4, 1793–Feb. 19, 1863; Senate Nov. 11, 1847–51; Gov. May 1844–May 6, 1846.

Baldwin, Simeon (father of Roger Sherman Baldwin) (F Conn.) Dec. 14, 1761–May 26, 1851; House 1803–05.

Baldwin, Tammy (D Wis.) Feb. 11, 1962– ; House 1999– .

Ball, Edward (W Ohio) Nov. 6, 1811–Nov. 22, 1872; House 1853–57.

Ball, Joseph Hurst (R Minn.) Nov. 3, 1905–Dec. 18, 1993; Senate Oct. 14, 1940–Nov. 17, 1942, 1943–49.

Ball, Lewis Heisler (R Del.) Sept. 21, 1861–Oct. 18, 1932; House 1901–03; Senate March 3, 1903–05, 1919–25.

Ball, Thomas Henry (D Texas) Jan. 14, 1859–May 7, 1944; House 1897–Nov. 16, 1903.

Ball, Thomas Raymond (R Conn.) Feb. 12, 1896–June 16, 1943; House 1939–41.

Ball, William Lee (R Va.) Jan. 2, 1781–Feb. 28, 1824; House 1817–Feb. 28, 1824.

Ballance, Frank W. (D N.C.) Feb. 15, 1952– ; House 2003–June 11, 2004.

Ballenger, Cass (great-great-grandson of Lewis Cass) (R N.C.) Dec. 6, 1926– ; House 1987–2005.

Ballentine, John Goff (D Tenn.) May 20, 1825–Nov. 23, 1915; House 1883–87.

Ballou, Latimer Whipple (R R.I.) March 1, 1812–May 9, 1900; House 1875–81.

Baltz, William Nicolas (D Ill.) Feb. 5, 1860–Aug. 22, 1943; House 1913–15.

Bandstra, Bert Andrew (D Iowa) Jan. 25, 1922–Oct. 23, 1995; House 1965–67.

Bankhead, John Hollis (father of John Hollis Bankhead II and William Brockman Bankhead, grandfather of Walter Will Bankhead) (D Ala.) Sept. 13, 1842–March 1, 1920; House 1887–1907; Senate June 18, 1907–March 1, 1920.

Bankhead, John Hollis II (son of John Hollis Bankhead, brother of William Brockman Bankhead, father of Walter Will Bankhead) (D Ala.) July 8, 1872–June 12, 1946; Senate 1931–June 12, 1946.

Bankhead, Walter Will (son of John Hollis Bankhead II, grandson of John Hollis Bankhead, nephew of William Brockman Bankhead) (D Ala.) July 21, 1897–Nov. 24, 1988; House Jan. 3–Feb. 1, 1941.

Bankhead, William Brockman (son of John Hollis Bankhead, brother of John Hollis Bankhead II, uncle of Walter Will Bankhead) (D Ala.) April 12, 1874–Sept. 15, 1940; House 1917–Sept. 15, 1940; House majority leader 1935–June 4, 1936; Speaker June 4, 1936–37, Jan. 5, 1937–Sept. 15, 1940.

Banks, John (AMas. Pa.) Oct. 17, 1793–April 3, 1864; House 1831–36.

Banks, Linn (D Va.) Jan. 23, 1784–Jan. 13, 1842; House April 28, 1838–Dec. 6, 1841.

Banks, Nathaniel Prentice (R Mass.) Jan. 30, 1816–Sept. 1, 1894; House 1853–Dec. 24, 1857, Dec. 4, 1865–73, 1875–79, 1889–91 (1853–55 Democrat, 1855–57 American Party, March 4–Dec. 24, 1857 Republican, Dec. 4, 1865–67 Union Republican, 1867–73 Republican, 1875–77 Independent); Speaker Feb. 2, 1856–57; Gov. Jan. 6, 1858–Jan. 2, 1861.

Banning, Henry Blackstone (D Ohio) Nov. 10, 1836–Dec. 10, 1881; House 1873–79 (1873–75 Liberal Republican).

Bannon, Henry Towne (R Ohio) June 5, 1867–Sept. 6, 1950; House 1905–09.

Banta, Parke Monroe (R Mo.) Nov. 21, 1891–May 12, 1970; House 1947–49.

Barber, Hiram Jr. (R Ill.) March 24, 1835–Aug. 5, 1924; House 1879–81.

Barber, Isaac Ambrose (R Md.) Jan. 26, 1852–March 1, 1909; House 1897–99.

Barber, Joel Allen (R Wis.) Jan. 17, 1809–June 17, 1881; House 1871–75.

Barber, Laird Howard (D Pa.) Oct. 25, 1848–Feb. 16, 1928; House 1899–1901.

Barber, Levi (R Ohio) Oct. 16, 1777–April 23, 1833; House 1817–19, 1821–23.

Barber, Noyes (uncle of Edwin Barbour Morgan and Christopher Morgan) (– Conn.) April 28, 1781–Jan. 3, 1844; House 1821–35.

Barbour, Henry Ellsworth (R Calif.) March 8, 1877–March 21, 1945; House 1919–33.

Barbour, James (brother of Philip Pendleton Barbour, cousin of John Strode Barbour) (AD/SR Va.) June 10, 1775–June 7, 1842; Senate Jan. 2, 1815–March 7, 1825; elected pres. pro tempore Feb. 15, 1819; Gov. Jan. 3, 1812–Dec. 1, 1814; secretary of war March 7, 1825–May 23, 1828.

Barbour, John Strode (father of John Strode Barbour Jr., cousin of James Barbour and Philip Pendleton Barbour) (J Va.) Aug. 8, 1790–Jan. 12, 1855; House 1823–33 (1823–27 no party).

Barbour, John Strode Jr. (son of John Strode Barbour) (D Va.) Dec. 29, 1820–May 14, 1892; House 1881–87; Senate 1889–May 14, 1892.

Barbour, Lucien (R Ind.) March 4, 1811–July 19, 1880; House 1855–57.

Barbour, Philip Pendleton (brother of James Barbour, cousin of John Strode Barbour) (J Va.) May 25, 1783–Feb. 25, 1841; House Sept. 19, 1814–25 (Republican), 1827–Oct. 15, 1830 (1827–29 Republican); Speaker Dec. 4, 1821–23; assoc. justice May 12, 1836–Feb. 25, 1841.

Barbour, William Warren (R N.J.) July 31, 1888–Nov. 22, 1943; Senate Dec. 1, 1931–37, Nov. 9, 1938–Nov. 22, 1943.

Barca, Peter W. (D Wis.) Aug. 7, 1955– ; House June 8, 1993–95.

Barchfeld, Andrew Jackson (R Pa.) May 18, 1863–Jan. 28, 1922; House 1905–17.

Barcia, James A. (D Mich.) Feb. 25, 1952– ; House 1993–2003.

Barclay, Charles Frederick (R Pa.) May 9, 1844–March 9, 1914; House 1907–11.

Barclay, David (D Pa.) 1823–Sept. 10, 1889; House 1855–57.

Bard, David (R Pa.) 1744–March 12, 1815; House 1795–99, 1803–March 12, 1815.

Bard, Thomas Robert (R Calif.) Dec. 8, 1841–March 5, 1915; Senate Feb. 7, 1900–05.

Barden, Graham Arthur (D N.C.) Sept. 25, 1896–Jan. 29, 1967; House 1935–61; chair House Education and Labor 1950–53, 1955–61.

Barham, John All (R Calif.) July 17, 1843–Jan. 22, 1926; House 1895–1901.

Baring, Walter Stephan Jr. (D Nev.) Sept. 9, 1911–July 13, 1975; House 1949–53, 1957–73.

Barker, Abraham Andrews (UR Pa.) March 30, 1816–March 18, 1898; House 1865–67.

Barker, David Jr. (– N.H.) Jan. 8, 1797–April 1, 1834; House 1827–29.

Barker, Joseph (R Mass.) Oct. 19, 1751–July 5, 1815; House 1805–09.

Barkley, Alben William (D Ky.) Nov. 24, 1877–April 30, 1956; House 1913–27; Senate 1927–Jan. 19, 1949, 1955–April 30, 1956; Senate majority leader July 22, 1937–47; Senate minority leader 1947–49; vice president 1949–53.

Barkley, Dean (I Minn.) Aug. 31, 1950– ; Senate Nov. 12, 2002–03.

Barksdale, Ethelbert (brother of William Barksdale) (D Miss.) Jan. 4, 1824–Feb. 17, 1893; House 1883–87.

Barksdale, William (brother of Ethelbert Barksdale) (D Miss.) Aug. 21, 1821–July 2, 1863; House 1853–Jan. 12, 1861.

Barlow, Bradley (G Vt.) May 12, 1814–Nov. 6, 1889; House 1879–81.

Barlow, Charles Averill (P Calif.) March 17, 1858–Oct. 3, 1927; House 1897–99.

Barlow, Stephen (– Pa.) June 13, 1779–Aug. 24, 1845; House 1827–29.

Barlow, Tom (D Ky.) Aug. 7, 1940– ; House 1993–95.

Barnard, Daniel Dewey (W N.Y.) July 16, 1797–April 24, 1861; House 1827–29 (no party), 1839–45.

Barnard, Druie Douglas Jr. (D Ga.) March 20, 1922– ; House 1977–93.

Barnard, Isaac Dutton (J Pa.) July 18, 1791–Feb. 28, 1834; Senate 1827–Dec. 6, 1831.

Barnard, William Oscar (R Ind.) Oct. 25, 1852–April 8, 1939; House 1909–11.

Barnes, Demas (D N.Y.) April 4, 1827–May 1, 1888; House 1867–69.

Barnes, George Thomas (D Ga.) Aug. 14, 1833–Oct. 24, 1901; House 1885–91.

Barnes, James Martin (D Ill.) Jan. 9, 1899–June 8, 1958; House 1939–43.

Barnes, Lyman Eddy (D Wis.) June 30, 1855–Jan. 16, 1904; House 1893–95.

Barnes, Michael Darr (D Md.) Sept. 3, 1943– ; House 1979–87.

Barnett, William (R Ga.) March 4, 1761–April 1832; House Oct. 5, 1812–15.

Barney, John (F Md.) Jan. 18, 1785–Jan. 26, 1857; House 1825–29.

Barney, Samuel Stebbins (R Wis.) Jan. 31, 1846–Dec. 31, 1919; House 1895–1903.

Barnhart, Henry A. (D Ind.) Sept. 11, 1858–March 26, 1934; House Nov. 3, 1908–19.

Barnitz, Charles Augustus (AMas. Pa.) Sept. 11, 1780–Jan. 8, 1850; House 1833–35.

Barnum, William Henry (D Conn.) Sept. 17, 1818–April 30, 1889; House 1867–May 18, 1876; Senate May 18, 1876–79; chair Dem. Nat. Comm. 1877–89.

Barnwell, Robert (father of Robert Woodward Barnwell) (F S.C.) Dec. 21, 1761–Oct. 24, 1814; House 1791–93; Cont. Cong. 1789.

Barnwell, Robert Woodward (son of Robert Barnwell) (– S.C.) Aug. 10, 1801–Nov. 5, 1882; House 1829–33; Senate June 4–Dec. 8, 1850.

Barr, Bob (R Ga.) Nov. 5, 1948– ; House 1995–2003.

Barr, Joseph Walker (D Ind.) Jan. 17, 1918–Feb. 23, 1996; House 1959–61; secretary of the Treasury Dec. 21, 1968–Jan. 20, 1969.

Barr, Samuel Fleming (R Pa.) June 15, 1829–May 29, 1919; House 1881–85.

Barr, Thomas Jefferson (ID N.Y.) 1812–March 27, 1881; House Jan. 17, 1859–61.

Barrere, Granville (nephew of Nelson Barrere) (R Ill.) July 11, 1829–Jan. 13, 1889; House 1873–75.

Barrere, Nelson (uncle of Granville Barrere) (W Ohio) April 1, 1808–Aug. 20, 1883; House 1851–53.

Barret, John Richard (D Mo.) Aug. 21, 1825–Nov. 2, 1903; House 1859–June 8, 1860, Dec. 3, 1860–61.

Barrett, Frank Aloysius (R Wyo.) Nov. 10, 1892–May 30, 1962; House 1943–Dec. 31, 1950; Senate 1953–59; Gov. Jan. 1, 1951–Jan. 3, 1953.

Barrett, James Gresham (R S.C.) Feb. 14, 1961– ; House 2003– .

Barrett, Thomas M. (D Wis.) Dec. 8, 1953– ; House 1993–2003.

Barrett, William Aloysius (D Pa.) Aug. 14, 1896–April 12, 1976; House 1945–47, 1949–April 12, 1976.

Barrett, William E. (R Neb.) Feb. 9, 1929– ; House 1991–2001.

Barrett, William Emerson (R Mass.) Dec. 29, 1858–Feb. 12, 1906; House 1895–99.

Barringer, Daniel Laurens (uncle of Daniel Moreau Barringer) (– N.C.) Oct. 1, 1788–Oct. 16, 1852; House Dec. 4, 1826–35.

Barringer, Daniel Moreau (nephew of Daniel Laurens Barringer) (W N.C.) July 30, 1806–Sept. 1, 1873; House 1843–49.

Barrow, Alexander (W La.) March 27, 1801–Dec. 29, 1846; Senate 1841–Dec. 29, 1846.

Barrow, John (D Ga.) Oct. 31, 1955– ; House 2005– .

Barrow, Middleton Pope (grandson of Wilson Lumpkin) (D Ga.) Aug. 1, 1839–Dec. 23, 1903; Senate Nov. 15, 1882–83.

Barrow, Washington (W Tenn.) Oct. 5, 1807–Oct. 19, 1866; House 1847–49.

Barrows, Samuel June (R Mass.) May 26, 1845–April 21, 1909; House 1897–99.

Barry, Alexander Grant (R Ore.) Aug. 23, 1892–Dec. 28, 1952; Senate Nov. 9, 1938–39.

Barry, Frederick George (D Miss.) Jan. 12, 1845–May 7, 1909; House 1885–89.

Barry, Henry W. (R Miss.) April 1840–June 7, 1875; House Feb. 23, 1870–75.

Barry, Robert Raymond (R N.Y.) May 15, 1915–June 14, 1988; House 1959–65.

Barry, William Bernard (D N.Y.) July 21, 1902–Oct. 20, 1946; House Nov. 5, 1935–Oct. 20, 1946.

Barry, William Taylor (R Ky.) Feb. 5, 1784–Aug. 30, 1835; House Aug. 8, 1810–11; Senate Dec. 16, 1814–May 1, 1816; postmaster general April 6, 1829–April 30, 1835.

Barry, William Taylor Sullivan (D Miss.) Dec. 10, 1821–Jan. 29, 1868; House 1853–55.

Barstow, Gamaliel Henry (AMas. N.Y.) July 20, 1784–March 30, 1865; House 1831–33.

Barstow, Gideon (– Mass.) Sept. 7, 1783–March 26, 1852; House 1821–23.

Bartholdt, Richard (R Mo.) Nov. 2, 1855–March 19, 1932; House 1893–1915.

Bartine, Horace Franklin (R Nev.) March 21, 1848–Aug. 27, 1918; House 1889–93.

Bartlett, Bailey (F Mass.) Jan. 29, 1750–Sept. 9, 1830; House Nov. 27, 1797–1801.

Bartlett, Charles Lafayette (D Ga.) Jan. 31, 1853–April 21, 1938; House 1895–1915.

Bartlett, Dewey Follett (R Okla.) March 28, 1919–March 1, 1979; Senate 1973–79; Gov. Jan. 9, 1967–Jan. 11, 1971.

Bartlett, Edward Lewis "Bob" (D Alaska) April 20, 1904–Dec. 11, 1968; House (Terr. Del.) 1945–59; Senate 1959–Dec. 11, 1968.

Bartlett, Franklin (D N.Y.) Sept. 10, 1847–April 23, 1909; House 1893–97.

Bartlett, George Arthur (D Nev.) Nov. 30, 1869–June 1, 1951; House 1907–11.

Bartlett, Harry Stephen "Steve" (R Texas) Sept. 19, 1947– ; House 1983–March 11, 1991.

Bartlett, Ichabod (– N.H.) July 24, 1786–Oct. 19, 1853; House 1823–29.

Bartlett, Josiah Jr. (son of Gov. Josiah Bartlett of N.H.) (R N.H.) Aug. 29, 1768–April 16, 1838; House 1811–13.

Bartlett, Roscoe G. (R Md.) June 3, 1926– ; House 1993– .

Bartlett, Thomas Jr. (D Vt.) June 18, 1808–Sept. 12, 1876; House 1851–53.

Bartley, Mordecai (– Ohio) Dec. 16, 1783–Oct. 10, 1870; House 1823–31; Gov. Dec. 3, 1844–Dec. 12, 1846 (Whig).

Barton, Bruce (R N.Y.) Aug. 5, 1886–July 5, 1967; House Nov. 2, 1937–41.

Barton, David (– Mo.) Dec. 14, 1783–Sept. 28, 1837; Senate Aug. 10, 1821–31.

Barton, Joe Linus (R Texas) Sept. 15, 1949– ; House 1985– ; chair House Energy and Commerce Feb. 16, 2004– .

Barton, Richard Walker (W Va.) 1800–March 15, 1859; House 1841–43.

Barton, Samuel (J N.Y.) July 27, 1785–Jan. 29, 1858; House 1835–37.

Barton, Silas Reynolds (R Neb.) May 21, 1872–Nov. 7, 1916; House 1913–15.

Barton, William Edward (cousin of Courtney Walker Hamlin) (D Mo.) April 11, 1868–July 29, 1955; House 1931–33.

Barwig, Charles (D Wis.) March 19, 1837–Feb. 15, 1912; House 1889–95.

Bashford, Coles (I Ariz.) Jan. 24, 1816–April 25, 1878; House (Terr. Del.) 1867–69; Gov. March 25, 1856–Jan. 4, 1858 (Republican Wis.).

Bass, Lyman Kidder (R N.Y.) Nov. 13, 1836–May 11, 1889; House 1873–77.

Bass, Charles F. (son of Perkins Bass, grandson of Gov. Robert P. Bass of N.H.) (R N.H.) Jan. 8, 1952– ; House 1995– .

Bass, Perkins (son of Gov. Robert P. Bass of N.H., father of Charles F. Bass) (R N.H.) Oct. 6, 1912– ; House 1955–63.

Bass, Ross (D Tenn.) March 17, 1918–Jan. 1, 1993; House 1955–Nov. 3, 1964; Senate Nov. 4, 1964–Jan. 2, 1967.

Bassett, Burwell (R Va.) March 18, 1764–Feb. 26, 1841; House 1805–13, 1815–19, 1821–29.

Bassett, Edward Murray (D N.Y.) Feb. 7, 1863–Oct. 27, 1948; House 1903–05.

Bassett, Richard (grandfather of Richard Henry Bayard and James Asheton Bayard Jr., father-in-law of Joshua Clayton) (– Del.) April 2, 1745–Aug. 15, 1815; Senate 1789–93; Gov. Jan. 9, 1799–March 3, 1801 (Federalist).

Bate, William Brimage (D Tenn.) Oct. 7, 1826–March 9, 1905; Senate 1887–March 9, 1905; Gov. Jan. 15, 1883–Jan. 17, 1887.

Bateman, Ephraim (– N.J.) July 9, 1780–Jan. 28, 1829; House 1815–23; Senate Nov. 10, 1826–Jan. 12, 1829.

Bateman, Herbert Harvell (R Va.) Aug. 7, 1928–Sept. 11, 2000; House 1983–Sept. 11, 2000.

Bates, Arthur Laban (nephew of John Milton Thayer) (R Pa.) June 6, 1859–Aug. 26, 1934; House 1901–13.

Bates, Edward (brother of James Woodson Bates) (– Mo.) Sept. 4, 1793–March 25, 1869; House 1827–29; attorney general March 5, 1861–Sept. 1864.

Bates, George Joseph (father of William Henry Bates) (R Mass.) Feb. 25, 1891–Nov. 1, 1949; House 1937–Nov. 1, 1949.

Bates, Isaac Chapman (W Mass.) Jan. 23, 1779–March 16, 1845; House 1827–35 (no party); Senate Jan. 13, 1841–March 16, 1845.

Bates, James (J Maine) Sept. 24, 1789–Feb. 25, 1882; House 1831–33.

Bates, James Woodson (brother of Edward Bates) (– Ark.) Aug. 25, 1788–Dec. 26, 1846; House (Terr. Del.) Dec. 21, 1819–23.

Bates, Jim (D Calif.) July 21, 1941– ; House 1983–91.

Bates, Joseph Bengal (D Ky.) Oct. 29, 1893–Sept. 10, 1965; House June 4, 1938–53.

Bates, Martin Waltham (D Del.) Feb. 24, 1786–Jan. 1, 1869; Senate Jan. 14, 1857–59.

Bates, William Henry (son of George Joseph Bates) (R Mass.) April 26, 1917–June 22, 1969; House Feb. 14, 1950–June 22, 1969.

Bathrick, Elsworth Raymond (D Ohio) Jan. 6, 1863–Dec. 23, 1917; House 1911–15, March 4–Dec. 23, 1917.

Battin, James Franklin (R Mont.) Feb. 13, 1925–Sept. 27, 1996; House 1961–Feb. 27, 1969.

Battle, Laurie Calvin (D Ala.) May 10, 1912–May 2, 2000; House 1947–55.

Baucus, Max Sieben (D Mont.) Dec. 11, 1941– ; House 1975–Dec. 14, 1978; Senate Dec. 15, 1978– ; chair Senate Environment and Public Works 1993–95, Senate Finance Jan. 3, 2001–Jan. 20, 2001, June 6, 2001–03.

Bauman, Robert Edmund (R Md.) April 4, 1937– ; House Aug. 21, 1973–81.

Baumhart, Albert David Jr. (R Ohio) June 15, 1908–Jan. 23, 2001; House 1941–Sept. 2, 1942, 1955–61.

Baxter, Portus (R Vt.) Dec. 4, 1806–March 4, 1868; House 1861–67.

Bay, William Van Ness (D Mo.) Nov. 23, 1818–Feb. 10, 1894; House 1849–51.

Bayard, James Asheton (father of Richard Henry Bayard and James Asheton Bayard Jr., grandfather of Thomas Francis Bayard, great-grandfather of Thomas Francis Bayard Jr.) (F Del.) July 28, 1767–Aug. 6, 1815; House 1797–1803; Senate Nov. 13, 1804–13.

Bayard, James Asheton Jr. (son of James Asheton Bayard, brother of Richard Henry Bayard, grandson of Richard Bassett, father of Thomas Francis Bayard, grandfather of Thomas Francis Bayard Jr.) (D Del.) Nov. 15, 1799–June 13, 1880; Senate 1851–Jan. 29, 1864, April 5, 1867–69.

Bayard, Richard Henry (son of James Asheton Bayard, brother of James Asheton Bayard Jr., grandson of Richard Bassett) (W Del.) Sept. 26, 1796–March 4, 1868; Senate June 17, 1836–Sept. 19, 1839, Jan. 12, 1841–45.

Bayard, Thomas Francis (son of James Asheton Bayard Jr., father of Thomas Francis Bayard Jr.) (D Del.) Oct. 29, 1828–Sept. 28, 1898; Senate 1869–March 6, 1885; elected pres. pro tempore Oct. 10, 1881; secretary of state March 7, 1885–March 6, 1889.

Bayard, Thomas Francis Jr. (son of Thomas Francis Bayard, grandson of James Ashton Bayard Jr.) (D Del.) June 4, 1868–July 12, 1942; Senate Nov. 8, 1922–29.

Bayh, Birch Evan (father of Evan Bayh) (D Ind.) Jan. 22, 1928– ; Senate 1963–81; chair Senate Select Intelligence Activities 1978–81.

Bayh, Evan (son of Birch Evan Bayh) (D Ind.) Dec. 26, 1955– ; Senate 1999– ; Gov. Jan. 9, 1989–Jan. 13, 1997.

Baylies, Francis (brother of William Baylies) (– Mass.) Oct. 16, 1783–Oct. 28, 1852; House 1821–27.

Baylies, William (brother of Francis Baylies) (J Mass.) Sept. 15, 1776–Sept. 27, 1865; House March 4–June 28, 1809, 1813–17 (1809–17 Federalist), 1833–35 (Anti-Jacksonian).

Baylor, Robert Emmett Bledsoe (nephew of Jesse Bledsoe) (J Ala.) May 10, 1793–Jan. 6, 1874; House 1829–31.

Bayly, Thomas (F Md.) Sept. 13, 1775–1829; House 1817–23.

Bayly, Thomas Henry (son of Thomas Monteagle Bayly) (D Va.) Dec. 11, 1810–June 23, 1856; House May 6, 1844–June 23, 1856.

Bayly, Thomas Monteagle (father of Thomas Henry Bayly) (F Va.) March 26, 1775–Jan. 7, 1834; House 1813–15.

Bayne, Thomas McKee (R Pa.) June 14, 1836–June 16, 1894; House 1877–91.

Beach, Clifton Bailey (R Ohio) Sept. 16, 1845–Nov. 15, 1902; House 1895–99.

Beach, Lewis (D N.Y.) March 30, 1835–Aug. 10, 1886; House 1881–Aug. 10, 1886.

Beakes, Samuel Willard (D Mich.) Jan. 11, 1861–Feb. 9, 1927; House 1913–March 3, 1917, Dec. 13, 1917–19.

Beale, Charles Lewis (R N.Y.) March 5, 1824–Jan. 29, 1900; House 1859–61.

Beale, James Madison Hite (D Va.) Feb. 7, 1786–Aug. 2, 1866; House 1833–37 (Jacksonian), 1849–53.

Beale, Joseph Grant (R Pa.) March 26, 1839–May 21, 1915; House 1907–09.

Beale, Richard Lee Turberville (D Va.) May 22, 1819–April 21, 1893; House 1847–49, Jan. 23, 1879–81.

Beales, Cyrus William (R Pa.) Dec. 16, 1877–Nov. 14, 1927; House 1915–17.

Beall, James Andrew "Jack" (D Texas) Oct. 25, 1866–Feb. 12, 1929; House 1903–15.

Beall, James Glenn (father of John Glenn Beall Jr.) (R Md.) June 5, 1894–Jan. 14, 1971; House 1943–53; Senate 1953–65.

Beall, John Glenn Jr. (son of James Glenn Beall) (R Md.) June 19, 1927– ; House 1969–71; Senate 1971–77.

Beall, Reasin (R Ohio) Dec. 3, 1769–Feb. 20, 1843; House April 20, 1813–June 7, 1814.

Beam, Harry Peter (D Ill.) Nov. 23, 1892–Dec. 31, 1967; House 1931–Dec. 6, 1942.

Beaman, Fernando Cortez (R Mich.) June 28, 1814–Sept. 27, 1882; House 1861–71.

Beamer, John Valentine (R Ind.) Nov. 17, 1896–Sept. 8, 1964; House 1951–59.

Bean, Benning Moulton (J N.H.) Jan. 9, 1782–Feb. 6, 1866; House 1833–37.

Bean, Curtis Coe (R Ariz.) Jan. 4, 1828–Feb. 1, 1904; House (Terr. Del.) 1885–87.

Bean, Melissa (D Ill.) Jan. 22, 1962– ; House 2005– .

Beard, Edward Peter (D R.I.) Jan. 20, 1940– ; House 1975–81.

Beard, Robin Leo Jr. (R Tenn.) Aug. 21, 1939– ; House 1973–83.

Beardsley, Samuel (D N.Y.) Feb. 6, 1790–May 6, 1860; House 1831–March 29, 1836 (Jacksonian), 1843–Feb. 29, 1844.

Beatty, John (– N.J.) Dec. 10, 1749–May 30, 1826; House 1793–95; Cont. Cong. 1784–85.

Beatty, John (R Ohio) Dec. 16, 1828–Dec. 21, 1914; House Feb. 5, 1868–73.

Beatty, William (D Pa.) 1787–April 12, 1851; House 1837–41.

Beaty, Martin (AJ Ky.) ?–?; House 1833–35.

Beaumont, Andrew (J Pa.) Jan. 24, 1790–Sept. 30, 1853; House 1833–37.

Beauprez, Robert Lewis "Bob" (R Colo.) Sept. 22, 1948– ; House 2003– .

Becerra, Xavier (D Calif.) Jan. 26, 1958– ; House 1993– .

Beck, Erasmus Williams (D Ga.) Oct. 21, 1833–July 22, 1898; House Dec. 2, 1872–73.

Beck, James Burnie (D Ky.) Feb. 13, 1822–May 3, 1890; House 1867–75; Senate 1877–May 3, 1890.

Beck, James Montgomery (R Pa.) July 9, 1861–April 12, 1936; House Nov. 8, 1927–Sept. 30, 1934.

Beck, Joseph David (R Wis.) March 14, 1866–Nov. 8, 1936; House 1921–29.

Becker, Frank John (R N.Y.) Aug. 27, 1899–Sept. 4, 1981; House 1953–65.

Beckham, John Crepps Wickliffe (grandson of Charles Anderson Wickliffe, cousin of Robert Charles Wickliffe) (D Ky.) Aug. 5, 1869–Jan. 9, 1940; Senate 1915–21; Gov. Feb. 3, 1900–Dec. 10, 1907.

Beckner, William Morgan (D Ky.) June 19, 1841–March 14, 1910; House Dec. 3, 1894–95.

Beckwith, Charles Dyer (R N.J.) Oct. 22, 1838–March 27, 1921; House 1889–91.

Beckworth, Lindley Garrison "Gary" Sr. (D Texas) June 30, 1913–March 9, 1984; House 1939–53, 1957–67.

Bede, James Adam (R Minn.) Jan. 13, 1856–April 11, 1942; House 1903–09.

Bedell, Berkley Warren (D Iowa) March 5, 1921– ; House 1975–87.

Bedinger, George Michael (uncle of Henry Bedinger) (R Ky.) Dec. 10, 1756–Dec. 7, 1843; House 1803–07.

Bedinger, Henry (nephew of George Michael Bedinger) (D Va.) Feb. 3, 1812–Nov. 26, 1858; House 1845–49.

Bee, Carlos (D Texas) July 8, 1867–April 20, 1932; House 1919–21.

Beebe, George Monroe (D N.Y.) Oct. 28, 1836–March 1, 1927; House 1875–79.

Beecher, Philemon (– Ohio) 1775–Nov. 30, 1839; House 1817–21, 1823–29.

Beedy, Carroll Lynwood (R Maine) Aug. 3, 1880–Aug. 30, 1947; House 1921–35.

Beekman, Thomas (– N.Y.) ?–?; House 1829–31.

Beeman, Joseph Henry (D Miss.) Nov. 17, 1833–July 31, 1909; House 1891–93.

Beermann, Ralph Frederick (R Neb.) Aug. 13, 1912–Feb. 17, 1977; House 1961–65.

Beers, Cyrus (D N.Y.) June 21, 1786–June 5, 1850; House Dec. 3, 1838–39.

Beers, Edward McMath (R Pa.) May 27, 1877–April 21, 1932; House 1923–April 21, 1932.

Beeson, Henry White (D Pa.) Sept. 14, 1791–Oct. 28, 1863; House May 31, 1841–43.

Begg, James Thomas (R Ohio) Feb. 16, 1877–March 26, 1963; House 1919–29.

Begich, Nicholas Joseph (D Alaska) April 6, 1932–?; House 1971–72. (Disappeared on an airplane flight Oct. 16, 1972, and presumed dead; congressional seat declared vacant Dec. 29, 1972.)

Begole, Josiah Williams (R Mich.) Jan. 20, 1815–June 5, 1896; House 1873–75; Gov. Jan. 1, 1883–Jan. 1, 1885.

Beidler, Jacob Atlee (R Ohio) Nov. 2, 1852–Sept. 13, 1912; House 1901–07.

Beilenson, Anthony Charles (D Calif.) Oct. 26, 1932– ; House 1977–97; chair House Select Intelligence 1989–91.

Beirne, Andrew (D Va.) 1771–March 16, 1845; House 1837–41.

Beiter, Alfred Florian (D N.Y.) July 7, 1894–March 11, 1974; House 1933–39, 1941–43.

Belcher, Hiram (W Maine) Feb. 23, 1790–May 6, 1857; House 1847–49.

Belcher, Nathan (D Conn.) June 23, 1813–June 2, 1891; House 1853–55.

Belcher, Page Henry (R Okla.) April 21, 1899–Aug. 2, 1980; House 1951–73.

Belden, George Ogilvie (– N.Y.) March 28, 1797–Oct. 9, 1833; House 1827–29.

Belden, James Jerome (R N.Y.) Sept. 30, 1825–Jan. 1, 1904; House Nov. 8, 1887–95, 1897–99.

Belford, James Burns (cousin of Joseph McCrum Belford) (R Colo.) Sept. 28, 1837–Jan. 10, 1910; House Oct. 3, 1876–Dec. 13, 1877, 1879–85.

Belford, Joseph McCrum (cousin of James Burns Belford) (R N.Y.) Aug. 5, 1852–May 3, 1917; House 1897–99.

Belknap, Charles Eugene (R Mich.) Oct. 17, 1846–Jan. 16, 1929; House 1889–91, Nov. 3, 1891–93.

Belknap, Hugh Reid (R Ill.) Sept. 1, 1860–Nov. 12, 1901; House Dec. 27, 1895–99.

Bell, Alphonzo (R Calif.) Sept. 19, 1914–April 25, 2004; House 1961–77.

Bell, Charles Henry (nephew of Samuel Bell, cousin of James Bell) (R N.H.) Nov. 18, 1823–Nov. 11, 1893; Senate March 13–June 18, 1879; Gov. June 2, 1881–June 7, 1883.

Bell, Charles Jasper (D Mo.) Jan. 16, 1885–Jan. 21, 1978; House 1935–49.

Bell, Charles Keith (nephew of Reese Bowen Brabson) (D Texas) April 18, 1853–April 21, 1913; House 1893–97.

Bell, Charles Webster (PR Calif.) June 11, 1857–April 19, 1927; House 1913–15.

Bell, R. Christopher "Chris" (R Texas) Nov. 23, 1959– ; House 2003–05.

Bell, Hiram (W Ohio) April 22, 1808–Dec. 21, 1855; House 1851–53.

Bell, Hiram Parks (D Ga.) Jan. 19, 1827–Aug. 17, 1907; House 1873–75, March 13, 1877–79.

Bell, James (son of Samuel Bell, uncle of Samuel Newell Bell, cousin of Charles Henry Bell) (R N.H.) Nov. 13, 1804–May 26, 1857; Senate July 30, 1855–May 26, 1857.

Bell, James Martin (AJ Ohio) Oct. 16, 1796–April 4, 1849; House 1833–35.

Bell, John (W Ohio) June 19, 1796–May 4, 1869; House Jan. 7–March 3, 1851.

Bell, John (W Tenn.) Feb. 15, 1797–Sept. 10, 1869; House 1827–41 (no party); Speaker June 2, 1834–35; Senate Nov. 22, 1847–59; secretary of war March 5–Sept. 13, 1841.

Bell, John Calhoun (P Colo.) Dec. 11, 1851–Aug. 12, 1933; House 1893–1903.

Bell, John Junior (D Texas) May 15, 1910–Jan. 24, 1963; House 1955–57.

Bell, Joshua Fry (W Ky.) Nov. 26, 1811–Aug. 17, 1870; House 1845–47.

Bell, Peter Hansbrough (D Texas) May 12, 1812–March 8, 1898; House 1853–57; Gov. Dec. 21, 1849–Nov. 23, 1853.

Bell, Samuel (father of James Bell, grandfather of Samuel Newell Bell, uncle of Charles Henry Bell) (W N.H.) Feb. 9, 1770–Dec. 23, 1850; Senate 1823–35 (1823–34 no party); Gov. June 3, 1819–June 5, 1823 (Democratic Republican).

Bell, Samuel Newell (grandson of Samuel Bell, nephew of James Bell) (D N.H.) March 25, 1829–Feb. 8, 1889; House 1871–73, 1875–77.

Bell, Theodore Arlington (D Calif.) July 25, 1872–Sept. 4, 1922; House 1903–05.

Bell, Thomas Montgomery (D Ga.) March 17, 1861–March 18, 1941; House 1905–31.

Bellamy, John Dillard (D N.C.) March 24, 1854–Sept. 25, 1942; House 1899–1903.

Bellinger, Joseph (R S.C.) 1773–Jan. 10, 1830; House 1817–19.

Bellmon, Henry Louis (R Okla.) Sept. 3, 1921– ; Senate 1969–81; Gov. Jan. 14, 1963–Jan. 9, 1967, Jan. 12, 1987–Jan. 14, 1991.

Belmont, Oliver Hazard Perry (brother of Perry Belmont) (D N.Y.) Nov. 12, 1858–June 10, 1908; House 1901–03.

Belmont, Perry (brother of Oliver Hazard Perry Belmont) (D N.Y.) Dec. 28, 1851–May 25, 1947; House 1881–Dec. 1, 1888.

Belser, James Edwin (D Ala.) Dec. 22, 1805–Jan. 16, 1859; House 1843–45.

Beltzhoover, Frank Eckels (D Pa.) Nov. 6, 1841–June 2, 1923; House 1879–83, 1891–95.

Bender, George Harrison (R Ohio) Sept. 29, 1896–June 18, 1961; House 1939–49, 1951–Dec. 15, 1954; Senate Dec. 16, 1954–57.

Benedict, Charles Brewster (D N.Y.) Feb. 7, 1828–Oct. 3, 1901; House 1877–79.

Benedict, Cleveland Keith (R W.Va.) March 21, 1935– ; House 1981–83.

Benedict, Henry Stanley (R Calif.) Feb. 20, 1878–July 10, 1930; House Nov. 7, 1916–17.

Benet, Christie (D S.C.) Dec. 26, 1879–March 30, 1951; Senate July 6–Nov. 5, 1918.

Benham, John Samuel (R Ind.) Oct. 24, 1863–Dec. 11, 1935; House 1919–23.

Benitez, Jaime (PD P.R.) Oct. 29, 1908–May 30, 2001; House (Res. Comm.) 1973–77.

Benjamin, Adam Jr. (D Ind.) Aug. 6, 1935–Sept. 7, 1982; House 1977–Sept. 7, 1982.

Benjamin, John Forbes (R Mo.) Jan. 23, 1817–March 8, 1877; House 1865–71.

Benjamin, Judah Philip (D La.) Aug. 6, 1811–May 6, 1884; Senate 1853–Feb. 4, 1861 (1853–59 Whig).

Benner, George Jacob (D Pa.) April 13, 1859–Dec. 30, 1930; House 1897–99.

Bennet, Augustus Witschief (son of William Stiles Bennet) (R N.Y.) Oct. 7, 1897–June 5, 1983; House 1945–47.

Bennet, Benjamin (R N.J.) Oct. 31, 1764–Oct. 8, 1840; House 1815–19.

Bennet, Hiram Pitt (CR Colo.) Sept. 2, 1826–Nov. 11, 1914; House (Terr. Del.) Aug. 19, 1861–65.

Bennet, William Stiles (father of Augustus Witschief Bennet) (R N.Y.) Nov. 9, 1870–Dec. 1, 1962; House 1905–11, Nov. 2, 1915–17.

Bennett, Charles Edward (D Fla.) Dec. 2, 1910–Sept. 6, 2003; House 1949–93; chair House Standards of Official Conduct 1977–81.

Bennett, Charles Goodwin (R N.Y.) Dec. 11, 1863–May 25, 1914; House 1895–99.

Bennett, David Smith (R N.Y.) May 3, 1811–Nov. 6, 1894; House 1869–71.

Bennett, Granville Gaylord (R Dakota) Oct. 9, 1833–June 28, 1910; House (Terr. Del.) 1879–81.

Bennett, Hendley Stone (D Miss.) April 7, 1807–Dec. 15, 1891; House 1855–57.

Bennett, Henry (R N.Y.) Sept. 29, 1808–May 10, 1868; House 1849–59 (1849–57 Whig).

Bennett, John Bonifas (R Mich.) Jan. 10, 1904–Aug. 9, 1964; House 1943–45, 1947–Aug. 9, 1964.

Bennett, Joseph Bentley (R Ky.) April 21, 1859–Nov. 7, 1923; House 1905–11.

Bennett, Marion Tinsley (son of Philip Allen Bennett) (R Mo.) June 6, 1914–Sept. 6, 2000; House Jan. 12, 1943–49.

Bennett, Philip Allen (father of Marion Tinsley Bennett) (R Mo.) March 5, 1881–Dec. 7, 1942; House 1941–Dec. 7, 1942.

Bennett, Risden Tyler (D N.C.) June 18, 1840–July 21, 1913; House 1883–87.

Bennett, Robert Foster (son of Wallace Foster Bennett) (R Utah) Sept. 18, 1933– ; Senate 1993– .

Bennett, Thomas Warren (I Idaho) Feb. 16, 1831–Feb. 2, 1893; House (Terr. Del.) 1875–June 23, 1876; Gov. (Idaho Terr.) Sept. 1871–Dec. 4, 1875.

Bennett, Wallace Foster (father of Robert Foster Bennett) (R Utah) Nov. 13, 1898–Dec. 19, 1993; Senate 1951–Dec. 20, 1974.

Benny, Allan (D N.J.) July 12, 1867–Nov. 6, 1942; House 1903–05.

Benson, Alfred Washburn (R Kan.) July 15, 1843–Jan. 1, 1916; Senate June 11, 1906–Jan. 23, 1907.

Benson, Carville Dickinson (D Md.) Aug. 24, 1872–Feb. 8, 1929; House Nov. 5, 1918–21.

Benson, Egbert (F N.Y.) June 21, 1746–Aug. 24, 1833; House 1789–93 (no party), March 4–Aug. 2, 1813; Cont. Cong. 1784, 1787–88.

Benson, Elmer Austin (FL Minn.) Sept. 22, 1895–March 13, 1985; Senate Dec. 27, 1935–Nov. 3, 1936; Gov. Jan. 4, 1937–Jan. 2, 1939.

Benson, Samuel Page (R Maine) Nov. 28, 1804–Aug. 12, 1876; House 1853–57 (1853–55 Whig).

Bentley, Alvin Morell (R Mich.) Aug. 30, 1918–April 10, 1969; House 1953–61.

Bentley, Helen Delich (R Md.) Nov. 28, 1923– ; House 1985–95.

Bentley, Henry Wilbur (D N.Y.) Sept. 30, 1838–Jan. 27, 1907; House 1891–93.

Benton, Charles Swan (D N.Y.) July 12, 1810–May 4, 1882; House 1843–47.

Benton, Jacob (R N.H.) Aug. 19, 1814–Sept. 29, 1892; House 1867–71.

Benton, Lemuel (great-grandfather of George William Dargan) (R S.C.) 1754–May 18, 1818; House 1793–99 (1793–95 no party).

Benton, Maecenas Eason (D Mo.) Jan. 29, 1848–April 27, 1924; House 1897–1905.

Benton, Thomas Hart (father-in-law of John Charles Fremont) (D Mo.) March 14, 1782–April 10, 1858; Senate Aug. 10, 1821–51; House 1853–55.

Benton, William (D Conn.) April 1, 1900–March 18, 1973; Senate Dec. 17, 1949–53.

Bentsen, Ken (nephew of Lloyd Bentsen) (D Texas) June 3, 1959– ; House 1995–2003.

Bentsen, Lloyd Millard Jr. (uncle of Ken Bentsen) (D Texas) Feb. 11, 1921– ; House Dec. 4, 1948–55; Senate 1971–Jan. 20, 1993; chair Senate Finance 1987–93; secretary of the Treasury Jan. 22, 1993–Dec. 22, 1994.

Bereuter, Douglas K. (R Neb.) Oct. 6, 1939– ; House 1979–Aug. 31, 2004.

Bergen, Christopher Augustus (R N.J.) Aug. 2, 1841–Feb. 18, 1905; House 1889–93.

Bergen, John Teunis (second cousin of Teunis Garret Bergen) (J N.Y.) 1786–March 9, 1855; House 1831–33.

Bergen, Teunis Garret (second cousin of John Teunis Bergen) (D N.Y.) Oct. 6, 1806–April 24, 1881; House 1865–67.

Berger, Victor Luitpold (Soc. Wis.) Feb. 28, 1860–Aug. 7, 1929; House 1911–13, 1923–29.

Bergland, Robert Selmer (D Minn.) July 22, 1928– ; House 1971–Jan. 22, 1977; secretary of agriculture Jan. 23, 1977–Jan. 20, 1981.

Berkley, Shelley (D Nev.) Jan. 20, 1951– ; House 1999– .

Berlin, William Markle (D Pa.) March 29, 1880–Oct. 14, 1962; House 1933–37.

Berman, Howard Lawrence (D Calif.) April 15, 1941– ; House 1983– .

Bernard, John Toussaint (FL Minn.) March 6, 1893–Aug. 6, 1983; House 1937–39.

Bernhisel, John Milton (W Utah) July 23, 1799–Sept. 28, 1881; House (Terr. Del.) 1851–59, 1861–63.

Berrien, John Macpherson (W Ga.) Aug. 23, 1781–Jan. 1, 1856; Senate 1825–March 9, 1829 (Jacksonian), 1841–May 1845, Nov. 13, 1845–May 28, 1852; attorney general March 9, 1829–July 20, 1831.

Berry, Albert Seaton (D Ky.) May 13, 1836–Jan. 6, 1908; House 1893–1901.

Berry, Campbell Polson (cousin of James Henderson Berry) (D Calif.) Nov. 7, 1834–Jan. 8, 1901; House 1879–83.

Berry, Ellis Yarnal (R S.D.) Oct. 6, 1902–April 1, 1999; House 1951–71.

Berry, George Leonard (D Tenn.) Sept. 12, 1882–Dec. 4, 1948; Senate May 6, 1937–Nov. 8, 1938.

Berry, James Henderson (cousin of Campbell Polson Berry) (D Ark.) May 15, 1841–Jan. 30, 1913; Senate March 20, 1885–1907; Gov. Jan. 13, 1883–Jan. 17, 1885.

Berry, John (D Ohio) April 26, 1833–May 18, 1879; House 1873–75.

Berry, Robert Marion (D Ark.) Aug. 27, 1942– ; House 1997– .

Beshlin, Earl Hanley (D/Prohib. Pa.) April 28, 1870–July 12, 1971; House Nov. 8, 1917–19.

Bethune, Edwin Ruthvin Jr. (R Ark.) Dec. 19, 1935– ; House 1979–85.

Bethune, Lauchlin (J N.C.) April 15, 1785–Oct. 10, 1874; House 1831–33.

Bethune, Marion (R Ga.) April 8, 1816–Feb. 20, 1895; House Dec. 22, 1870–71.

Betton, Silas (F N.H.) Aug. 26, 1768–Jan. 22, 1822; House 1803–07.

Betts, Jackson Edward (R Ohio) May 26, 1904–Aug. 13, 1993; House 1951–73.

Betts, Samuel Rossiter (R N.Y.) June 8, 1787–Nov. 2, 1868; House 1815–17.

Betts, Thaddeus (W Conn.) Feb. 4, 1789–April 7, 1840; Senate 1839–April 7, 1840.

Beveridge, Albert Jeremiah (R Ind.) Oct. 6, 1862–April 27, 1927; Senate 1899–1911.

Beveridge, John Lourie (R Ill.) July 6, 1824–May 3, 1910; House Nov. 7, 1871–Jan. 4, 1873; Gov. Jan. 23, 1873–Jan. 8, 1877.

Bevill, Tom (D Ala.) March 27, 1921– ; House 1967–97.

Biaggi, Mario (D N.Y.) Oct. 26, 1917– ; House 1969–Aug. 8, 1988.

Bibb, George Mortimer (J Ky.) Oct. 30, 1776–April 14, 1859; Senate 1811–Aug. 23, 1814 (no party), 1829–35; secretary of the Treasury July 4, 1844–March 7, 1845.

Bibb, William Wyatt (R Ga.) Oct. 2, 1781–July 9, 1820; House Jan. 26, 1807–Nov. 6, 1813; Senate Nov. 6, 1813–Nov. 9, 1816; Gov. Nov. 9, 1819–July 10, 1820 (Democratic Republican Ala.).

Bibighaus, Thomas Marshal (W Pa.) March 17, 1817–June 18, 1853; House 1851–53.

Bible, Alan Harvey (D Nev.) Nov. 20, 1909–Sept. 12, 1988; Senate Dec. 2, 1954–Dec. 17, 1974; chair Senate District of Columbia 1959–69; chair Senate Select Small Business 1969–75.

Bicknell, Bennet (D N.Y.) Nov. 14, 1781–Sept. 15, 1841; House 1837–39.

Bicknell, George Augustus (D Ind.) Feb. 6, 1815–April 11, 1891; House 1877–81.

Biddle, Charles John (nephew of Richard Biddle) (D Pa.) April 30, 1819–Sept. 28, 1873; House July 2, 1861–63.

Biddle, John (– Mich.) March 2, 1792–Aug. 25, 1859; House (Terr. Del.) 1829–Feb. 21, 1831.

Biddle, Joseph Franklin (R Pa.) Sept. 14, 1871–Dec. 3, 1936; House Nov. 8, 1932–33.

Biddle, Richard (uncle of Charles John Biddle) (AMas. Pa.) March 25, 1796–July 6, 1847; House 1837–40.

Biden, Joseph Robinette Jr. (D Del.) Nov. 20, 1942– ; Senate 1973– ; chair Senate Judiciary 1987–95; chair Senate Foreign Relations June 6, 2001–03.

Bidlack, Benjamin Alden (D Pa.) Sept. 8, 1804–Feb. 6, 1849; House 1841–45.

Bidwell, Barnabas (R Mass.) Aug. 23, 1763–July 27, 1833; House 1805–July 13, 1807.

Bidwell, John (R Calif.) Aug. 5, 1819–April 4, 1900; House 1865–67.

Biemiller, Andrew John (D Wis.) July 23, 1906–April 3, 1982; House 1945–47, 1949–51.

Biermann, Frederick Elliott (D Iowa) March 20, 1884–July 1, 1968; House 1933–39.

Biery, James Soloman (R Pa.) March 2, 1839–Dec. 3, 1904; House 1873–75.

Biester, Edward George Jr. (R Pa.) Jan. 5, 1931– ; House 1967–77.

Bigby, John Summerfield (R Ga.) Feb. 13, 1832–March 28, 1898; House 1871–73.

Bigelow, Abijah (F Mass.) Dec. 5, 1775–April 5, 1860; House Oct. 8, 1810–15.

Bigelow, Herbert Seely (D Ohio) Jan. 4, 1870–Nov. 11, 1951; House 1937–39.

Bigelow, Lewis (F Mass.) Aug. 18, 1785–Oct. 2, 1838; House 1821–23.

Biggert, Judy (R Ill.) Aug. 15, 1936– ; House 1999– .

Biggs, Asa (D N.C.) Feb. 4, 1811–March 6, 1878; House 1845–47; Senate 1855–May 5, 1858.

Biggs, Benjamin Thomas (D Del.) Oct. 1, 1821–Dec. 25, 1893; House 1869–73; Gov. Jan. 18, 1887–Jan. 20, 1891.

Biggs, Marion (D Calif.) May 2, 1823–Aug. 2, 1910; House 1887–91.

Bigler, William (brother of Gov. John Bigler of Calif.) (D Pa.) Jan. 1, 1814–Aug. 9, 1880; Senate Jan. 14, 1856–61; Gov. Jan. 20, 1852–Jan. 16, 1855.

Bilbo, Theodore Gilmore (D Miss.) Oct. 13, 1877–Aug. 21, 1947; Senate 1935–Aug. 21, 1947; Gov. Jan. 18, 1916–Jan. 20, 1920, Jan. 17, 1928–Jan. 19, 1932.

Bilbray, Brian P. (nephew of James Hubert Bilbray) (R Calif.) Jan. 28, 1951– ; House 1995–2001.

Bilbray, James Hubert (uncle of Brian P. Bilbray) (D Nev.) May 19, 1938– ; House 1987–95.

Bilirakis, Michael (R Fla.) July 16, 1930– ; House 1983– .

Billinghurst, Charles (R Wis.) July 27, 1818–Aug. 18, 1865; House 1855–59.

Billmeyer, Alexander (D Pa.) Jan. 7, 1841–May 24, 1924; House Nov. 4, 1902–03.

Binderup, Charles Gustav (D Neb.) March 5, 1873–Aug. 19, 1950; House 1935–39.

Bines, Thomas (R N.J.) ?–April 9, 1826; House Nov. 2, 1814–15.

Bingaman, Jesse Francis Jr. "Jeff" (D N.M.) Oct. 3, 1943– ; Senate 1983– ; chair Senate Energy and Natural Resources, June 6, 2001–03.

Bingham, Henry Harrison (R Pa.) Dec. 4, 1841–March 22, 1912; House 1879–March 22, 1912.

Bingham, Hiram (father of Jonathan Brewster Bingham) (R Conn.) Nov. 19, 1875–June 6, 1956; Senate Dec. 17, 1924–33; Gov. Jan. 7–Jan. 8, 1925.

Bingham, John Armor (R Ohio) Jan. 21, 1815–March 19, 1900; House 1855–63, 1865–73.

Bingham, Jonathan Brewster (son of Hiram Bingham) (D N.Y.) April 24, 1914–July 3, 1986; House 1965–83.

Bingham, Kinsley Scott (R Mich.) Dec. 16, 1808–Oct. 5, 1861; House 1847–51 (Democrat); Senate 1859–Oct. 5, 1861; Gov. Jan. 3, 1855–Jan. 5, 1859.

Bingham, William (F Pa.) March 8, 1752–Feb. 7, 1804; Senate 1795–1801; elected pres. pro tempore Feb. 16, 1797; Cont. Cong. 1786–88.

Binney, Horace (AJ Pa.) Jan. 4, 1780–Aug. 12, 1875; House 1833–35.

Birch, William Fred (R N.J.) Aug. 30, 1870–Jan. 25, 1946; House Nov. 5, 1918–19.

Bird, John (F N.Y.) Nov. 22, 1768–Feb. 2, 1806; House 1799–July 25, 1801.

Bird, John Taylor (D N.J.) Aug. 16, 1829–May 6, 1911; House 1869–73.

Bird, Richard Ely (R Kan.) Nov. 4, 1878–Jan. 10, 1955; House 1921–23.

Birdsall, Ausburn (D N.Y.) ?–July 10, 1903; House 1847–49.

Birdsall, Benjamin Pixley (R Iowa) Oct. 26, 1858–May 26, 1917; House 1903–09.

Birdsall, James (R N.Y.) 1783–July 20, 1856; House 1815–17.

Birdsall, Samuel (D N.Y.) May 14, 1791–Feb. 8, 1872; House 1837–39.

Birdseye, Victory (W N.Y.) Dec. 25, 1782–Sept. 16, 1853; House 1815–17 (Republican), 1841–43.

Bisbee, Horatio Jr. (R Fla.) May 1, 1839–March 27, 1916; House 1877–Feb. 20, 1879, Jan. 22–March 3, 1881, June 1, 1882–85.

Bishop, Cecil William "Runt" (R Ill.) June 29, 1890–Sept. 21, 1971; House 1941–55.

Bishop, James (W N.J.) May 11, 1816–May 10, 1895; House 1855–57.

Bishop, Phanuel (R Mass.) Sept. 3, 1739–Jan. 6, 1812; House 1799–1807.

Bishop, Robert (R Utah) July 13, 1951– ; House 2003– .

Bishop, Roswell Peter (R Mich.) Jan. 6, 1843–March 4, 1920; House 1895–1907.

Bishop, Sanford D. Jr. (D Ga.) Feb. 4, 1947– ; House 1993– .

Bishop, Timothy H. (D N.Y.) June 1, 1950– ; House 2003– .

Bishop, William Darius (D Conn.) Sept. 14, 1827–Feb. 4, 1904; House 1857–59.

Bissell, William Harrison (ID Ill.) April 25, 1811–March 18, 1860; House 1849–55 (1849–53 Democrat); Gov. Jan. 12, 1857–March 18, 1860 (Republican).

Bixler, Harris Jacob (R Pa.) Sept. 16, 1870–March 29, 1941; House 1921–27.

Black, Edward Junius (father of George Robison Black) (D Ga.) Oct. 30, 1806–Sept. 1, 1846; House 1839–41 (Whig), Jan. 3, 1842–45.

Black, Eugene (D Texas) July 2, 1879–May 22, 1975; House 1915–29.

Black, Frank Swett (R N.Y.) March 8, 1853–March 22, 1913; House 1895–Jan. 7, 1897; Gov. Jan. 1, 1897–Jan. 1, 1899.

Black, George Robison (son of Edward Junius Black) (D Ga.) March 24, 1835–Nov. 3, 1886; House 1881–83.

Black, Henry (W Pa.) Feb. 25, 1783–Nov. 28, 1841; House June 28–Nov. 28, 1841.

Black, Hugo Lafayette (D Ala.) Feb. 27, 1886–Sept. 25, 1971; Senate 1927–Aug. 19, 1937; assoc. justice Aug. 19, 1937–Sept. 17, 1971.

Black, James (D Pa.) March 6, 1793–June 21, 1872; House Dec. 5, 1836–37 (Jacksonian), 1843–47.

Black, James Augustus (D S.C.) 1793–April 3, 1848; House 1843–April 3, 1848.

Black, James Conquest Cross (D Ga.) May 9, 1842–Oct. 1, 1928; House 1893–March 4, 1895, Oct. 2, 1895–97.

Black, John (W Miss.) ?–Aug. 29, 1854; Senate Nov. 12, 1832–March 3, 1833 (no party), Nov. 22, 1833–Jan. 22, 1838.

Black, John Charles (D Ill.) Jan. 27, 1839–Aug. 17, 1915; House 1893–Jan. 12, 1895.

Black, Loring Milton Jr. (D N.Y.) May 17, 1886–May 21, 1956; House 1923–35.

Blackburn, Benjamin Bentley (R Ga.) Feb. 14, 1927– ; House 1967–75.

Blackburn, Edmond Spencer (R N.C.) Sept. 22, 1868–March 10, 1912; House 1901–03, 1905–07.

Blackburn, Joseph Clay Stiles (D Ky.) Oct. 1, 1838–Sept. 12, 1918; House 1875–85; Senate 1885–97, 1901–07.

Blackburn, Marsha (R Tenn.) June 6, 1952– ; House 2003– .

Blackburn, Robert E. Lee (R Ky.) April 9, 1870–Sept. 20, 1935; House 1929–31.

Blackburn, William Jasper (R La.) July 24, 1820–Nov. 10, 1899; House July 18, 1868–69.

Blackledge, William (father of William Salter Blackledge) (R N.C.) ?–Oct. 19, 1828; House 1803–09, 1811–13.

Blackledge, William Salter (son of William Blackledge) (– N.C.) 1793–March 21, 1857; House Feb. 7, 1821–23.

Blackmar, Esbon (W N.Y.) June 19, 1805–Nov. 19, 1857; House Dec. 4, 1848–49.

Blackmon, Fred Leonard (D Ala.) Sept. 15, 1873–Feb. 8, 1921; House 1911–Feb. 8, 1921.

Blackney, William Wallace (R Mich.) Aug. 28, 1876–March 14, 1963; House 1935–37, 1939–53.

Blackwell, Julius W. (D Tenn.) ?–?; House 1839–41, 1843–45.

Blackwell, Lucien E. (D Pa.) Aug. 1, 1931–Jan. 24, 2003; House Nov. 13, 1991–95.

Blagojevich, Rod R. (D Ill.) Dec. 10, 1956– ; House 1997–2003; Gov. Jan. 13, 2003– .

Blaine, James Gillespie (R Maine) Jan. 31, 1830–Jan. 27, 1893; House 1863–July 10, 1876; Speaker 1869–73, Dec. 1, 1873–75; Senate July 10, 1876–March 5, 1881; secretary of state March 7–Dec. 19, 1881, March 7, 1889–June 4, 1892.

Blaine, John James (R Wis.) May 4, 1875–April 16, 1934; Senate 1927–33; Gov. Jan. 3, 1921–Jan. 3, 1927.

Blair, Austin (R Mich.) Feb. 8, 1818–Aug. 6, 1894; House 1867–73; Gov. Jan. 2, 1861–Jan. 4, 1865.

Blair, Bernard (W N.Y.) May 24, 1801–May 7, 1880; House 1841–43.

Blair, Francis Preston Jr. (D Mo.) Feb. 19, 1821–July 8, 1875; House 1857–59 (Republican), June 8–25, 1860, 1861–July 1862, 1863–June 10, 1864; Senate Jan. 20, 1871–73.

Blair, Henry William (R N.H.) Dec. 6, 1834–March 14, 1920; House 1875–79, 1893–95; Senate June 20, 1879–85, March 10, 1885–91.

Blair, Jacob Beeson (UU W.Va.) April 11, 1821–Feb. 12, 1901; House Dec. 2, 1861–63 (U Va.), Dec. 7, 1863–65.

Blair, James (J S.C.) 1790–April 1, 1834; House 1821–May 8, 1822 (no party), 1829–April 1, 1834.

Blair, James Gorrall (LR Mo.) Jan. 1, 1825–March 1, 1904; House 1871–73.

Blair, John (J Tenn.) Sept. 13, 1790–July 9, 1863; House 1823–35 (1823–25 no party).

Blair, Samuel Steel (R Pa.) Dec. 5, 1821–Dec. 8, 1890; House 1859–63.

Blaisdell, Daniel (F N.H.) Jan. 22, 1762–Jan. 10, 1833; House 1809–11.

Blake, Harrison Gray Otis (R Ohio) March 17, 1818–April 16, 1876; House Oct. 11, 1859–63.

Blake, John Jr. (R N.Y.) Dec. 5, 1762–Jan. 13, 1826; House 1805–09.

Blake, John Lauris (R N.J.) March 25, 1831–Oct. 10, 1899; House 1879–81.

Blake, Thomas Holdsworth (– Ind.) June 14, 1792–Nov. 28, 1849; House 1827–29.

Blakeney, Albert Alexander (R Md.) Sept. 28, 1850–Oct. 15, 1924; House 1901–03, 1921–23.

Blakley, William Arvis (D Texas) Nov. 17, 1898–Jan. 5, 1976; Senate Jan. 15–April 28, 1957, Jan. 3–June 14, 1961.

Blanchard, George Washington (R Wis.) Jan. 26, 1884–Oct. 2, 1964; House 1933–35.

Blanchard, James Johnston (D Mich.) Aug. 8, 1942– ; House 1975–83; Gov. Jan. 1, 1983–91.

Blanchard, John (W Pa.) Sept. 30, 1787–March 9, 1849; House 1845–49.

Blanchard, Newton Crain (D La.) Jan. 29, 1849–June 22, 1922; House 1881–March 12, 1894; Senate March 12, 1894–97; Gov. May 10, 1904–May 18, 1908.

Bland, Oscar Edward (R Ind.) Nov. 21, 1877–Aug. 3, 1951; House 1917–23.

Bland, Richard Parks (D Mo.) Aug. 19, 1835–June 15, 1899; House 1873–95, 1897–June 15, 1899.

Bland, Schuyler Otis (D Va.) May 4, 1872–Feb. 16, 1950; House July 2, 1918–Feb. 16, 1950; chair House Merchant Marine and Fisheries 1949–50.

Bland, Theodorick (– Va.) March 21, 1742–June 1, 1790; House 1789–June 1, 1790; Cont. Cong. 1780–83.

Bland, William Thomas (grandson of John George Jackson, cousin of James Monroe Jackson) (D Mo.) Jan. 21, 1861–Jan. 15, 1928; House 1919–21.

Blanton, Leonard Ray (D Tenn.) April 10, 1930–Nov. 22, 1996; House 1967–73; Gov. Jan. 18, 1975–Jan. 17, 1979.

Blanton, Thomas Lindsay (D Texas) Oct. 25, 1872–Aug. 11, 1957; House 1917–29, May 20, 1930–37.

Blatnik, John Anton (D Minn.) Aug. 17, 1911–Dec. 17, 1991; House 1947–Dec. 31, 1974; chair House Public Works 1971–75.

Blaz, Ben Garrido (R Guam) Feb. 14, 1928– ; House (Del.) 1985–93.

Bleakley, Orrin Dubbs (R Pa.) May 15, 1854–Dec. 3, 1927; House March 4–April 3, 1917.

Blease, Coleman Livingston (D S.C.) Oct. 8, 1868–Jan. 19, 1942; Senate 1925–31; Gov. Jan. 17, 1911–Jan. 14, 1915.

Bledsoe, Jesse (uncle of Robert Emmett Bledsoe Baylor) (R Ky.) April 6, 1776–June 25, 1836; Senate 1813–Dec. 24, 1814.

Bleecker, Harmanus (F N.Y.) Oct. 9, 1779–July 19, 1849; House 1811–13.

Bliley, Thomas Jerome Jr. (R Va.) Jan. 28, 1932– ; House 1981–2001; chair House Commerce 1995–2000.

Bliss, Aaron Thomas (R Mich.) May 22, 1837–Sept. 16, 1906; House 1889–91; Gov. Jan. 1, 1901–Jan. 1, 1905.

Bliss, Archibald Meserole (D N.Y.) Jan. 25, 1838–March 19, 1923; House 1875–83, 1885–89.

Bliss, George (D Ohio) Jan. 1, 1813–Oct. 24, 1868; House 1853–55, 1863–65.

Bliss, Philemon (R Ohio) July 28, 1813–Aug. 25, 1889; House 1855–59.

Blitch, Iris Faircloth (D Ga.) April 25, 1912–Aug. 19, 1993; House 1955–63.

Blodgett, Rufus (D N.J.) Oct. 9, 1834–Oct. 3, 1910; Senate 1887–93.

Bloodworth, Timothy (– N.C.) 1736–Aug. 24, 1814; House April 6, 1790–91; Senate 1795–1801; Cont. Cong. 1786.

Bloom, Isaac (– N.Y.) 1716–April 26, 1803; House March 4–April 26, 1803.

Bloom, Sol (D N.Y.) March 9, 1870–March 7, 1949; House 1923–March 7, 1949.

Bloomfield, Joseph (R N.J.) Oct. 18, 1753–Oct. 3, 1823; House 1817–21; Gov. Oct. 31, 1801–Oct. 28, 1802, Oct. 29, 1803–Oct. 29, 1812.

Blouin, Michael Thomas (D Iowa) Nov. 7, 1945– ; House 1975–79.

Blount, James Henderson (D Ga.) Sept. 12, 1837–March 8, 1903; House 1873–93.

Blount, Thomas (brother of William Blount, uncle of William Grainger Blount) (R N.C.) May 10, 1759–Feb. 7, 1812; House 1793–99 (1793–95 no party), 1805–09, 1811–Feb. 7, 1812.

Blount, William (father of William Grainger Blount, brother of Thomas Blount) (– Tenn.) March 26, 1749–March 21, 1800; Senate Aug. 2, 1796–July 8, 1797; Cont. Cong. 1782–83, 1786–87 (N.C.).

Blount, William Grainger (son of William Blount, nephew of Thomas Blount) (R Tenn.) 1784–May 21, 1827; House Dec. 8, 1815–19.

Blow, Henry Taylor (R Mo.) July 15, 1817–Sept. 11, 1875; House 1863–67 (1863–65 Unconditional Unionist).

Blue, Richard Whiting (R Kan.) Sept. 8, 1841–Jan. 28, 1907; House 1895–97.

Blumenauer, Earl (D Ore.) Aug. 16, 1949– ; House May 30, 1996– .

Blunt, Roy (father of Gov. Matt Blunt of Mo.) (R Mo.) Jan. 10, 1950– ; House 1997– .

Blute, Peter I. (R Mass.) Jan. 28, 1956– ; House 1993–97.

Boardman, Elijah (father of William Whiting Boardman) (D Conn.) March 7, 1760–Aug. 18, 1823; Senate 1821–Aug. 18, 1823.

Boardman, William Whiting (son of Elijah Boardman) (W Conn.) Oct. 10, 1794–Aug. 27, 1871; House Dec. 7, 1840–43.

Boarman, Alexander "Aleck" (LR La.) Dec. 10, 1839–Aug. 30, 1916; House Dec. 3, 1872–73.

Boatner, Charles Jahleal (D La.) Jan. 23, 1849–March 21, 1903; House 1889–95, June 10, 1896–97.

Bockee, Abraham (J N.Y.) Feb. 3, 1784–June 1, 1865; House 1829–31, 1833–37.

Bocock, Thomas Stanley (D Va.) May 18, 1815–Aug. 5, 1891; House 1847–61.

Boden, Andrew (R Pa.) ?–Dec. 20, 1835; House 1817–21.

Bodine, Robert Nall (D Mo.) Dec. 17, 1837–March 16, 1914; House 1897–99.

Bodle, Charles (J N.Y.) 1787–Oct. 31, 1835; House 1833–35.

Boehlert, Sherwood Louis (R N.Y.) June 28, 1936– ; House 1983– ; chair House Science 2001– .

Boehne, John William (father of John William Boehne Jr.) (D Ind.) Oct. 28, 1856–Dec. 27, 1946; House 1909–13.

Boehne, John William Jr. (son of John William Boehne) (D Ind.) March 2, 1895–July 5, 1973; House 1931–43.

Boehner, John A. (R Ohio) Nov. 7, 1949– ; House 1991– ; chair House Education and the Workforce 2001– .

Boen, Haldor Erickson (P Minn.) Jan. 2, 1851–July 23, 1912; House 1893–95.

Boggs, Corinne Claiborne "Lindy" (widow of Thomas Hale Boggs Sr.) (D La.) March 13, 1916– ; House March 20, 1973–91.

Boggs, James Caleb (R Del.) May 15, 1909–March 26, 1993; House 1947–53; Senate 1961–73; Gov. Jan. 20, 1953–Dec. 30, 1960.

Boggs, Thomas Hale Sr. (husband of Corinne Claiborne Boggs) (D La.) Feb. 15, 1914–?; House 1941–43, 1947–73; House majority leader 1971–73. (Disappeared on an airplane flight Oct. 16,

1972, and presumed dead; congressional seat declared vacant Jan. 3, 1973.)

Bogy, Lewis Vital (D Mo.) April 9, 1813–Sept. 20, 1877; Senate 1873–Sept. 20, 1877.

Bohn, Frank Probasco (R Mich.) July 14, 1866–June 1, 1944; House 1927–33.

Boies, William Dayton (R Iowa) Jan. 3, 1857–May 31, 1932; House 1919–29.

Boileau, Gerald John (Prog. Wis.) Jan. 15, 1900–Jan. 30, 1981; House 1931–39 (1931–35 Republican).

Bokee, David Alexander (W N.Y.) Oct. 6, 1805–March 15, 1860; House 1849–51.

Boland, Edward Patrick (D Mass.) Oct. 1, 1911–Nov. 4, 2001; House 1953–89; chair House Select Intelligence 1977–85.

Boland, Patrick Joseph (husband of Veronica Grace Boland) (D Pa.) Jan. 6, 1880–May 18, 1942; House 1931–May 18, 1942.

Boland, Veronica Grace (widow of Patrick Joseph Boland) (D Pa.) March 18, 1899–June 19, 1982; House Nov. 19, 1942–43.

Boles, Thomas (R Ark.) July 16, 1837–March 13, 1905; House June 22, 1868–71, Feb. 9, 1872–73.

Bolles, Stephen (R Wis.) June 25, 1866–July 8, 1941; House 1939–July 8, 1941.

Bolling, Richard Walker (great-great-grandson of John Williams Walker, great-great-nephew of Percy Walker) (D Mo.) May 17, 1916–April 21, 1991; House 1949–83; chair House Rules 1979–83.

Bolton, Chester Castle (husband of Frances Payne Bolton, father of Oliver Payne Bolton) (R Ohio) Sept. 5, 1882–Oct. 29, 1939; House 1929–37, Jan. 3–Oct. 29, 1939.

Bolton, Frances Payne (widow of Chester Castle Bolton, granddaughter of Henry B. Payne, mother of Oliver Payne Bolton) (R Ohio) March 29, 1885–March 9, 1977; House Feb. 27, 1940–69.

Bolton, Oliver Payne (son of Chester Castle Bolton and Frances Payne Bolton, great-grandson of Henry B. Payne) (R Ohio) Feb. 22, 1917–Dec. 13, 1972; House 1953–57, 1963–65.

Bolton, William P. (D Md.) July 2, 1885–Nov. 22, 1964; House 1949–51.

Bond, Charles Grosvenor (nephew of Charles Henry Grosvenor) (R N.Y.) May 29, 1877–Jan. 10, 1974; House 1921–23.

Bond, Christopher Samuel "Kit" (R Mo.) March 6, 1939– ; Senate 1987– ; chair Senate Small Business and Entrepreneurship 1995–Jan. 3, 2001, Jan. 20, 2001–June 6, 2001; Gov. Jan. 8, 1973–Jan. 10, 1977, Jan. 12, 1981–Jan. 14, 1985.

Bond, Shadrack (– Ill.) Nov. 24, 1773–April 12, 1832; House (Terr. Del.) Dec. 3, 1812–Aug. 2, 1813; Gov. Oct. 6, 1818–Dec. 5, 1822 (Democratic Republican).

Bond, William Key (W Ohio) Oct. 2, 1792–Feb. 17, 1864; House 1835–41.

Bone, Homer Truett (D Wash.) Jan. 25, 1883–March 11, 1970; Senate 1933–Nov. 13, 1944.

Boner, William Hill (D Tenn.) Feb. 14, 1945– ; House 1979–Oct. 5, 1987.

Bonham, Milledge Luke (D S.C.) Dec. 25, 1813–Aug. 27, 1890; House 1857–Dec. 21, 1860; Gov. Dec. 17, 1862–Dec. 20, 1864 (Confederate Democrat).

Bonilla, Henry (R Texas) Jan. 2, 1954– ; House 1993– .

Bonin, Edward John (R Pa.) Dec. 23, 1904–Dec. 20, 1990; House 1953–55.

Bonior, David Edward (D Mich.) June 6, 1945– ; House 1977–2003.

Bonker, Don Leroy (D Wash.) March 7, 1937– ; House 1975–89.

Bonner, Herbert Covington (D N.C.) May 16, 1891–Nov. 7, 1965; House Nov. 5, 1940–Nov. 7, 1965; chair House Merchant Marine and Fisheries 1955–66.

Bonner, Josiah Robbins Jr. "Jo" (R Ala.) Nov. 19, 1959– ; House 2003– .

Bono, Mary (widow of Sonny Bono) (R Calif.) Oct. 24, 1961– ; House April 21, 1998– .

Bono, Sonny (husband of Mary Bono) (R Calif.) Feb. 16, 1935–Jan. 5, 1998; House 1995–Jan. 5, 1998.

Bonynge, Robert William (R Colo.) Sept. 8, 1863–Sept. 22, 1939; House Feb. 16, 1904–09.

Boody, Azariah (W N.Y.) April 21, 1815–Nov. 18, 1885; House March 4–Oct. 1853.

Boody, David Augustus (D N.Y.) Aug. 13, 1837–Jan. 20, 1930; House March 4–Oct. 13, 1891.

Booher, Charles Ferris (D Mo.) Jan. 31, 1848–Jan. 21, 1921; House Feb. 19–March 3, 1889, 1907–Jan. 21, 1921.

Booker, George William (C Va.) Dec. 5, 1821–June 4, 1883; House Jan. 26, 1870–71.

Boon, Ratliff (D Ind.) Jan. 18, 1781–Nov. 20, 1844; House 1825–27 (no party), 1829–39 (1829–37 Jacksonian); Gov. Sept. 12–Dec. 5, 1822 (Democrat).

Boone, Andrew Rechmond (D Ky.) April 4, 1831–Jan. 26, 1886; House 1875–79.

Booth, Newton (AM Calif.) Dec. 30, 1825–July 14, 1892; Senate 1875–81; Gov. Dec. 8, 1871–Feb. 27, 1875 (Republican).

Booth, Walter (FS Conn.) Dec. 8, 1791–April 30, 1870; House 1849–51.

Boothman, Melvin Morella (R Ohio) Oct. 16, 1846–March 5, 1904; House 1887–91.

Booze, William Samuel (R Md.) Jan. 9, 1862–Dec. 6, 1933; House 1897–99.

Boozman, John (R Ark.) Dec. 10, 1950– ; House Nov. 20, 2001– .

Borah, William Edgar (R Idaho) June 29, 1865–Jan. 19, 1940; Senate 1907–Jan. 19, 1940.

Borchers, Charles Martin (D Ill.) Nov. 18, 1869–Dec. 2, 1946; House 1913–15.

Bordallo, Madeleine Z. (D Guam) May 13, 1933– ; House (Del.) 2003– .

Borden, Nathaniel Briggs (W Mass.) April 15, 1801–April 10, 1865; House 1835–39 (1835–37 Jacksonian, 1837–39 Democrat), 1841–43.

Boreing, Vincent (R Ky.) Nov. 24, 1839–Sept. 16, 1903; House 1899–Sept. 16, 1903.

Boreman, Arthur Inghram (R W.Va.) July 24, 1823–April 19, 1896; Senate 1869–75; Gov. June 20, 1863–Feb. 26, 1869.

Boren, Daniel David (son of David Lyle Boren, grandson of Lyle H. Boren) (D Okla.) Aug. 2, 1973– ; House 2005– .

Boren, David Lyle (son of Lyle H. Boren, father of Daniel David Boren) (D Okla.) April 21, 1941– ; Senate 1979–Nov. 15, 1994; chair Senate Select Intelligence Activities 1987–92; Gov. Jan. 13, 1975–Jan. 3, 1979.

Boren, Lyle H. (father of David Lyle Boren, grandfather of Daniel David Boren) (D Okla.) May 11, 1909–July 2, 1992; House 1937–47.

Borland, Charles Jr. (– N.Y.) June 29, 1786–Feb. 23, 1852; House Nov. 8, 1821–23.

Borland, Solon (D Ark.) Sept. 21, 1808–Jan. 1, 1864; Senate March 30, 1848–April 3, 1853.

Borland, William Patterson (D Mo.) Oct. 14, 1867–Feb. 20, 1919; House 1909–Feb. 20, 1919.

Borski, Robert Anthony Jr. (D Pa.) Oct. 20, 1948– ; House 1983–2003.

Borst, Peter I. (J N.Y.) April 24, 1797–Nov. 14, 1848; House 1829–31.

Bosch, Albert Henry (R N.Y.) Oct. 30, 1908– ; House 1953–Dec. 31, 1960.

Boschwitz, Rudolf Eli "Rudy" (R Minn.) Nov. 7, 1930– ; Senate Dec. 30, 1978–91.

Bosco, Douglas Harry (D Calif.) July 28, 1946– ; House 1983–91.

Bosone, Reva Zilpha Beck (D Utah) April 2, 1895–July 21, 1983; House 1949–53.

Boss, John Linscom Jr. (F R.I.) Sept. 7, 1780–Aug. 1, 1819; House 1815–19.

Bossier, Pierre Evariste John Baptiste (D La.) March 22, 1797–April 24, 1844; House 1843–April 24, 1844.

Boswell, Leonard L. (D Iowa) Jan. 10, 1934– ; House 1997– .

Boteler, Alexander Robinson (O Va.) May 16, 1815–May 8, 1892; House 1859–61.

Botkin, Jeremiah Dunham (P Kan.) April 24, 1849–Dec. 29, 1921; House 1897–99.

Botts, John Minor (W Va.) Sept. 16, 1802–Jan. 8, 1869; House 1839–43, 1847–49.

Bottum, Joseph H. (R S.D.) Aug. 7, 1903–July 4, 1984; Senate July 11, 1962–63.

Boucher, Frederick C. "Rick" (D Va.) Aug. 1, 1946– ; House 1983– .

Bouck, Gabriel (nephew of Joseph Bouck) (D Wis.) Dec. 16, 1828–Feb. 21, 1904; House 1877–81.

Bouck, Joseph (uncle of Gabriel Bouck) (J N.Y.) July 22, 1788–March 30, 1858; House 1831–33.

Boude, Thomas (F Pa.) May 17, 1752–Oct. 24, 1822; House 1801–03.

Boudinot, Elias (– N.J.) May 2, 1740–Oct. 24, 1821; House 1789–95; Cont. Cong. 1778, 1781–83.

Bouldin, James Wood (brother of Thomas Tyler Bouldin) (D Va.) 1792–March 30, 1854; House March 15, 1834–39 (March 15, 1834–37 Jacksonian).

Bouldin, Thomas Tyler (brother of James Wood Bouldin) (J Va.) 1781–Feb. 11, 1834; House 1829–33, Aug. 26, 1833–Feb. 11, 1834.

Bouligny, Charles Dominique Joseph (uncle of John Edward Bouligny) (– La.) Aug. 22, 1773–March 4, 1833; Senate Nov. 19, 1824–29.

Bouligny, John Edward (nephew of Charles Dominique Joseph Bouligny) (AP La.) Feb. 5, 1824–Feb. 20, 1864; House 1859–61.

Boulter, Eldon Beau (R Texas) Feb. 23, 1942– ; House 1985–89.

Bound, Franklin (R Pa.) April 9, 1829–Aug. 8, 1910; House 1885–89.

Bouquard, Marilyn Laird Lloyd. (See Lloyd, Marilyn Laird.)

Bourne, Benjamin (F R.I.) Sept. 9, 1755–Sept. 17, 1808; House Aug. 31, 1790–96 (Aug. 31, 1790–95 no party).

Bourne, Jonathan Jr. (R Ore.) Feb. 23, 1855–Sept. 1, 1940; Senate 1907–13.

Bourne, Shearjasub (– Mass.) June 14, 1746–March 11, 1806; House 1791–95.

Boustany, Charles W. Jr. (R La.) Feb. 21, 1956– ; House 2005– .

Boutell, Henry Sherman (R Ill.) March 14, 1856–March 11, 1926; House Nov. 23, 1897–1911.

Boutelle, Charles Addison (R Maine) Feb. 9, 1839–May 21, 1901; House 1883–1901.

Boutwell, George Sewel (R Mass.) Jan. 28, 1818–Feb. 27, 1905; House 1863–March 12, 1869; Senate March 17, 1873–77; Gov. Jan. 11, 1851–Jan. 14, 1853 (Democrat); secretary of the Treasury March 12, 1869–March 16, 1873.

Bovee, Matthias Jacob (brother-in-law of Benedict Arnold) (J N.Y.) July 24, 1793–Sept. 12, 1872; House 1835–37.

Bow, Frank Townsend (R Ohio) Feb. 20, 1901–Nov. 13, 1972; House 1951–Nov. 13, 1972.

Bowden, George Edwin (nephew of Lemuel Jackson Bowden) (R Va.) July 6, 1852–Jan. 22, 1908; House 1887–91.

Bowden, Lemuel Jackson (uncle of George Edwin Bowden) (R Va.) Jan. 16, 1815–Jan. 2, 1864; Senate 1863–Jan. 2, 1864.

Bowdle, Stanley Eyre (D Ohio) Sept. 4, 1868–April 6, 1919; House 1913–15.

Bowdon, Franklin Welsh (uncle of Sydney Johnston Bowie) (D Ala.) Feb. 17, 1817–June 8, 1857; House Dec. 7, 1846–51.

Bowen, Christopher Columbus (R S.C.) Jan. 5, 1832–June 23, 1880; House July 20, 1868–71.

Bowen, David Reece (D Miss.) Oct. 21, 1932– ; House 1973–83.

Bowen, Henry (son of Rees Tate Bowen, nephew of John Warfield Johnston, cousin of William Bowen Campbell) (R Va.) Dec. 26, 1841–April 29, 1915; House 1883–85 (Readjuster), 1887–89.

Bowen, John Henry (R Tenn.) Sept. 1780–Sept. 25, 1822; House 1813–15.

Bowen, Rees Tate (father of Henry Bowen) (D Va.) Jan. 10, 1809–Aug. 29, 1879; House 1873–75.

Bowen, Thomas Mead (R Colo.) Oct. 26, 1835–Dec. 30, 1906; Senate 1883–89; Gov. (Idaho Terr.) 1871.

Bower, Gustavus Miller (D Va.) Dec. 12, 1790–Nov. 17, 1864; House 1843–45.

Bower, William Horton (D N.C.) June 6, 1850–May 11, 1910; House 1893–95.

Bowers, Eaton Jackson (D Miss.) June 17, 1865–Oct. 26, 1939; House 1903–11.

Bowers, George Meade (R W.Va.) Sept. 13, 1863–Dec. 7, 1925; House May 9, 1916–23.

Bowers, John Myer (F N.Y.) Sept. 25, 1772–Feb. 24, 1846; House May 26–Dec. 20, 1813.

Bowers, William Wallace (R Calif.) Oct. 20, 1834–May 2, 1917; House 1891–97.

Bowersock, Justin De Witt (R Kan.) Sept. 19, 1842–Oct. 27, 1922; House 1899–1907.

Bowie, Richard Johns (W Md.) June 23, 1807–March 12, 1888; House 1849–53.

Bowie, Sydney Johnston (nephew of Franklin Welsh Bowdon) (D Ala.) July 26, 1865–May 7, 1928; House 1901–07.

Bowie, Thomas Fielder (great-nephew of Walter Bowie, brother-in-law of Reverdy Johnson) (D Md.) April 7, 1808–Oct. 30, 1869; House 1855–59.

Bowie, Walter (great-uncle of Thomas Fielder Bowie) (R Md.) 1748–Nov. 9, 1810; House March 24, 1802–05.

Bowler, James Bernard (D Ill.) Feb. 5, 1875–July 18, 1957; House July 7, 1953–July 18, 1957.

Bowles, Chester Bliss (D Conn.) April 5, 1901–May 25, 1986; House 1959–61; Gov. Jan. 5, 1949–Jan. 3, 1951.

Bowles, Henry Leland (R Mass.) Jan. 6, 1866–May 17, 1932; House Sept. 29, 1925–29.

Bowlin, James Butler (D Mo.) Jan. 16, 1804–July 19, 1874; House 1843–51.

Bowling, William Bismarck (D Ala.) Sept. 24, 1870–Dec. 27, 1946; House Dec. 14, 1920–Aug. 16, 1928.

Bowman, Charles Calvin (R Pa.) Nov. 14, 1852–July 3, 1941; House 1911–Dec. 12, 1912.

Bowman, Frank Llewellyn (R W.Va.) Jan. 21, 1879–Sept. 15, 1936; House 1925–33.

Bowman, Selwyn Zadock (R Mass.) May 11, 1840–Sept. 30, 1928; House 1879–83.

Bowman, Thomas (D Iowa) May 25, 1848–Dec. 1, 1917; House 1891–93.

Bowne, Obadiah (W N.Y.) May 19, 1822–April 27, 1874; House 1851–53.

Bowne, Samuel Smith (D N.Y.) April 11, 1800–July 9, 1865; House 1841–43.

Bowring, Eva Kelly (R Neb.) Jan. 9, 1892–Jan. 8, 1985; Senate April 16–Nov. 7, 1954.

Box, John Calvin (D Texas) March 28, 1871–May 17, 1941; House 1919–31.

Boxer, Barbara (D Calif.) Nov. 11, 1940– ; House 1983–93; Senate 1993– .

Boyce, William Henry (D Del.) Nov. 28, 1855–Feb. 6, 1942; House 1923–25.

Boyce, William Waters (D S.C.) Oct. 24, 1818–Feb. 3, 1890; House 1853–Dec. 21, 1860.

Boyd, Adam (R N.J.) March 21, 1746–Aug. 15, 1835; House 1803–05, March 8, 1808–13.

Boyd, Alexander (F N.Y.) Sept. 14, 1764–April 8, 1857; House 1813–15.

Boyd, F. Allen Jr. (D Fla.) June 6, 1945– ; House 1997– .

Boyd, John Frank (R Neb.) Aug. 8, 1853–May 28, 1945; House 1907–09.

Boyd, John Huggins (W N.Y.) July 31, 1799–July 2, 1868; House 1851–53.

Boyd, Linn (D Ky.) Nov. 22, 1800–Dec. 17, 1859; House 1835–37 (Jacksonian), 1839–55; Speaker Dec. 1, 1851–53, Dec. 5, 1853–55.

Boyd, Sempronius Hamilton (R Mo.) May 28, 1828–June 22, 1894; House 1863–65 (Unconditional Unionist), 1869–71.

Boyd, Thomas Alexander (R Ill.) June 25, 1830–May 28, 1897; House 1877–81.

Boyden, Nathaniel (C N.C.) Aug. 16, 1796–Nov. 20, 1873; House 1847–49 (Whig), July 13, 1868–69.

Boyer, Benjamin Markley (D Pa.) Jan. 22, 1823–Aug. 16, 1887; House 1865–69.

Boyer, Lewis Leonard (D Ill.) May 19, 1886–March 12, 1944; House 1937–39.

Boykin, Frank William (D Ala.) Feb. 21, 1885–March 12, 1969; House July 30, 1935–63.

Boylan, John Joseph (D N.Y.) Sept. 20, 1878–Oct. 5, 1938; House 1923–Oct. 5, 1938.

Boyle, Charles Augustus (D Ill.) Aug. 13, 1907–Nov. 4, 1959; House 1955–Nov. 4, 1959.

Boyle, Charles Edmund (D Pa.) Feb. 4, 1836–Dec. 15, 1888; House 1883–87.

Boyle, John (R Ky.) Oct. 28, 1774–Feb. 28, 1835; House 1803–09.

Brabson, Reese Bowen (uncle of Charles Keith Bell) (O Tenn.) Sept. 16, 1817–Aug. 16, 1863; House 1859–61.

Brace, Jonathan (F Conn.) Nov. 12, 1754–Aug. 26, 1837; House Dec. 3, 1798–1800.

Brackenridge, Henry Marie (W Pa.) May 11, 1786–Jan. 18, 1871; House Oct. 13, 1840–41.

Bradbury, George (F Mass.) Oct. 10, 1770–Nov. 7, 1823; House 1813–17.

Bradbury, James Ware (D Maine) June 10, 1802–Jan. 6, 1901; Senate 1847–53.

Bradbury, Theophilus (F Mass.) Nov. 13, 1739–Sept. 6, 1803; House 1795–July 24, 1797.

Brademas, John (D Ind.) March 2, 1927– ; House 1959–81.

Bradford, Allen Alexander (R Colo.) July 23, 1815–March 12, 1888; House (Terr. Del.) 1865–67, 1869–71.

Bradford, Taul (grandson of Micah Taul) (D Ala.) Jan. 20, 1835–Oct. 28, 1883; House 1875–77.

Bradford, William (– R.I.) Nov. 4, 1729–July 6, 1808; Senate 1793–Oct. 1797; elected pres. pro tempore July 6, 1797; Cont. Cong. (elected but did not attend) 1776.

Bradley, Edward (D Mich.) April 1808–Aug. 5, 1847; House March 4–Aug. 5, 1847.

Bradley, Frederick Van Ness (R Mich.) April 12, 1898–May 24, 1947; House 1939–May 24, 1947; chair House Merchant Marine and Fisheries 1947.

Bradley, Jeb E. (R N.H.) Oct. 20, 1953– ; House 2003– .

Bradley, Michael Joseph (D Pa.) May 24, 1897–Nov. 27, 1979; House 1937–47.

Bradley, Nathan Ball (R Mich.) May 28, 1831–Nov. 8, 1906; House 1873–77.

Bradley, Stephen Row (father of William Czar Bradley) (– Vt.) Feb. 20, 1754–Dec. 9, 1830; Senate Oct. 17, 1791–95, Oct. 15, 1801–13; elected pres. pro tempore Dec. Dec. 14, 1802, Feb. 25, 1803, March 2, 1803, Dec. 28, 1808.

Bradley, Thomas Joseph (D N.Y.) Jan. 2, 1870–April 1, 1901; House 1897–1901.

Bradley, Thomas Wilson (R N.Y.) April 6, 1844–May 30, 1920; House 1903–13.

Bradley, William Czar (son of Stephen Row Bradley) (– Vt.) March 23, 1782–March 3, 1867; House 1813–15 (Republican), 1823–27.

Bradley, William O'Connell (R Ky.) March 18, 1847–May 23, 1914; Senate 1909–May 23, 1914; Gov. Dec. 10, 1895–Dec. 12, 1899.

Bradley, William Warren "Bill" (D N.J.) July 28, 1943– ; Senate 1979–97.

Bradley, Willis Winter (R Calif.) June 28, 1884–Aug. 27, 1954; House 1947–49.

Bradshaw, Samuel Carey (W Pa.) June 10, 1809–June 9, 1872; House 1855–57.

Brady, James Dennis (R Va.) April 3, 1843–Nov. 30, 1900; House 1885–87.

Brady, James Henry (R Idaho) June 12, 1862–Jan. 13, 1918; Senate Feb. 6, 1913–Jan. 13, 1918; Gov. Jan. 4, 1909–Jan. 2, 1911.

Brady, Jasper Ewing (W Pa.) March 4, 1797–Jan. 26, 1871; House 1847–49.

Brady, Kevin (R Texas) April 11, 1955– ; House 1997– .

Brady, Nicholas Frederick (R N.J.) April 11, 1930– ; Senate April 12–Dec. 20, 1982; secretary of the Treasury Sept. 15, 1988–93.

Brady, Robert A. (D Pa.) April 7, 1945– ; House May 21, 1998– .

Bragg, Edward Stuyvesant (D Wis.) Feb. 20, 1827–June 20, 1912; House 1877–83, 1885–87.

Bragg, John (D Ala.) Jan. 14, 1806–Aug. 10, 1878; House 1851–53.

Bragg, Thomas (D N.C.) Nov. 9, 1810–Jan. 21, 1872; Senate 1859–March 6, 1861; Gov. Jan. 1, 1855–Jan. 1, 1859.

Brainerd, Lawrence (FS Vt.) March 16, 1794–May 9, 1870; Senate Oct. 14, 1854–55.

Brainerd, Samuel Myron (R Pa.) Nov. 13, 1842–Nov. 21, 1898; House 1883–85.

Bramblett, Ernest King (R Calif.) April 25, 1901–Dec. 27, 1966; House 1947–55.

Branch, John (uncle of Lawrence O'Bryan Branch, great-uncle of William Augustus Blount Branch) (D N.C.) Nov. 4, 1782–Jan. 3, 1863; Senate 1823–March 9, 1829; House May 12, 1831–33; Gov. Dec. 6, 1817–Dec. 7, 1820 (Democratic Republican); secretary of the navy March 9, 1829–March 12, 1831.

Branch, Lawrence O'Bryan (father of William Augustus Blount Branch, nephew of John Branch) (D N.C.) Nov. 28, 1820–Sept. 17, 1862; House 1855–61.

Branch, William Augustus Blount (son of Lawrence O'Bryan Branch, great-nephew of John Branch) (D N.C.) Feb. 26, 1847–Nov. 18, 1910; House 1891–95.

Brand, Charles (R Ohio) Nov. 1, 1871–May 23, 1966; House 1923–33.

Brand, Charles Hillyer (D Ga.) April 20, 1861–May 17, 1933; House 1917–May 17, 1933.

Brandegee, Augustus (father of Frank Bosworth Brandegee) (R Conn.) July 15, 1828–Nov. 10, 1904; House 1863–67.

Brandegee, Frank Bosworth (son of Augustus Brandegee) (R Conn.) July 8, 1864–Oct. 14, 1924; House Nov. 5, 1902–May 10, 1905; Senate May 10, 1905–Oct. 14, 1924; elected pres. pro tempore May 25, 1912 (to serve May 25, 1912).

Brantley, William Gordon (D Ga.) Sept. 18, 1860–Sept. 11, 1934; House 1897–1913.

Brasco, Frank James (D N.Y.) Oct. 15, 1932–Oct. 19, 1998; House 1967–75.

Bratton, John (– S.C.) March 7, 1831–Jan. 12, 1898; House Dec. 8, 1884–85.

Bratton, Robert Franklin (D Md.) May 3, 1845–May 10, 1894; House 1893–May 10, 1894.

Bratton, Sam Gilbert (D N.M.) Aug. 19, 1888–Sept. 22, 1963; Senate 1925–June 24, 1933.

Brawley, William Huggins (cousin of John James Hemphill, great-uncle of Robert Witherspoon Hemphill) (D S.C.) May 13, 1841–Nov. 15, 1916; House 1891–Feb. 12, 1894.

Braxton, Elliott Muse (D Va.) Oct. 8, 1823–Oct. 2, 1891; House 1871–73.

Bray, William Gilmer (R Ind.) June 17, 1903–June 4, 1979; House 1951–75.

Brayton, William Daniel (R R.I.) Nov. 6, 1815–June 30, 1887; House 1857–61.

Breaux, John Berlinger (D La.) March 1, 1944– ; House Sept. 30, 1972–87; Senate 1987–2005.

Breazeale, Phanor (D La.) Dec. 29, 1858–April 29, 1934; House 1899–1905.

Breck, Daniel (brother of Samuel Breck) (W Ky.) Feb. 12, 1788–Feb. 4, 1871; House 1849–51.

Breck, Samuel (brother of Daniel Breck) (– Pa.) July 17, 1771–Aug. 31, 1862; House 1823–25.

Breckinridge, Clifton Rodes (son of John Cabell Breckinridge, great-grandson of John Breckinridge) (D Ark.) Nov. 22, 1846–Dec. 3, 1932; House 1883–Sept. 5, 1890, Nov. 4, 1890–Aug. 14, 1894.

Breckinridge, James (brother of John Breckinridge, great-great-great-uncle of John Bayne Breckinridge, cousin of John Brown of Va. and Ky., James Brown, and Francis Preston) (F Va.) March 7, 1763–May 13, 1833; House 1809–17.

Breckinridge, James Douglas (– Ky.) ?–May 6, 1849; House Nov. 21, 1821–23.

Breckinridge, John (brother of James Breckinridge, grandfather of John Cabell Breckinridge and William Campbell Preston Breckinridge, great-grandfather of Clifton Rodes Breckinridge, great-great-grandfather of John Bayne Breckinridge, cousin of John Brown of Va. and Ky., James Brown, and Francis Preston) (R Ky.) Dec. 2, 1760–Dec. 14, 1806; Senate 1801–Aug. 7, 1805; attorney general Aug. 7, 1805–Dec. 14, 1806.

Breckinridge, John Bayne (great-great-grandson of John Breckinridge, great-great-great-nephew of James Breckinridge, great-nephew of William Campbell Preston Breckinridge) (D Ky.) Nov. 29, 1913–July 29, 1979; House 1973–79.

Breckinridge, John Cabell (grandson of John Breckinridge, father of Clifton Rodes Breckinridge, cousin of Henry Donnel Foster)

(D Ky.) Jan. 21, 1821–May 17, 1875; House 1851–55; Senate March 4–Dec. 4, 1861; vice president 1857–61.

Breckinridge, William Campbell Preston (grandson of John Breckinridge, uncle of Levin Irving Handy, great-uncle of John Bayne Breckinridge) (D Ky.) Aug. 28, 1837–Nov. 18, 1904; House 1885–95.

Breeding, James Floyd (D Kan.) Sept. 28, 1901–Oct. 17, 1977; House 1957–63.

Breen, Edward G. (D Ohio) June 10, 1908–May 8, 1991; House 1949–Oct. 1, 1951.

Breese, Sidney (D Ill.) July 15, 1800–June 27, 1878; Senate 1843–49.

Brehm, Walter Ellsworth (R Ohio) May 25, 1892–Aug. 24, 1971; House 1943–53.

Breitung, Edward (R Mich.) Nov. 10, 1831–March 3, 1887; House 1883–85.

Bremner, Robert Gunn (D N.J.) Dec. 17, 1874–Feb. 5, 1914; House 1913–Feb. 5, 1914.

Brengle, Francis (W Md.) Nov. 26, 1807–Dec. 10, 1846; House 1843–45.

Brennan, Joseph Edward (D Maine) Nov. 2, 1934– ; House 1987–91; Gov. Jan. 3, 1979–Jan. 7, 1987.

Brennan, Martin Adlai (D Ill.) Sept. 21, 1879–July 4, 1941; House 1933–37.

Brennan, Vincent Morrison (R Mich.) April 22, 1890–Feb. 4, 1959; House 1921–23.

Brenner, John Lewis (D Ohio) Feb. 2, 1832–Nov. 1, 1906; House 1897–1901.

Brent, Richard (uncle of William Leigh Brent, nephew of Daniel Carroll) (– Va.) 1757–Dec. 30, 1814; House 1795–99, 1801–03; Senate 1809–Dec. 30, 1814.

Brent, William Leigh (nephew of Richard Brent) (– La.) Feb. 20, 1784–July 7, 1848; House 1823–29.

Brentano, Lorenzo (R Ill.) Nov. 4, 1813–Sept. 18, 1891; House 1877–79.

Brenton, Samuel (R Ind.) Nov. 22, 1810–March 29, 1857; House 1851–53 (Whig), 1855–March 29, 1857.

Brents, Thomas Hurley (R Wash.) Dec. 24, 1840–Oct. 23, 1916; House (Terr. Del.) 1879–85.

Bretz, John Lewis (D Ind.) Sept. 21, 1852–Dec. 25, 1920; House 1891–95.

Brevard, Joseph (– S.C.) July 19, 1766–Oct. 11, 1821; House 1819–21.

Brewer, Francis Beattie (R N.Y.) Oct. 8, 1820–July 29, 1892; House 1883–85.

Brewer, John Hart (R N.J.) March 29, 1844–Dec. 21, 1900; House 1881–85.

Brewer, Mark Spencer (R Mich.) Oct. 22, 1837–March 18, 1901; House 1877–81, 1887–91.

Brewer, Willis (D Ala.) March 15, 1844–Oct. 30, 1912; House 1897–1901.

Brewster, Daniel Baugh (D Md.) Nov. 23, 1923– ; House 1959–63; Senate 1963–69.

Brewster, David P. (D N.Y.) June 15, 1801–Feb. 20, 1876; House 1839–43.

Brewster, Henry Colvin (R N.Y.) Sept. 7, 1845–Jan. 29, 1928; House 1895–99.

Brewster, Ralph Owen (R Maine) Feb. 22, 1888–Dec. 25, 1961; House 1935–41; Senate 1941–Dec. 31, 1952; Gov. Jan. 8, 1925–Jan. 2, 1929.

Brewster, William (D Okla.) Nov. 8, 1941– ; House 1991–97.

Brice, Calvin Stewart (D Ohio) Sept. 17, 1845–Dec. 15, 1898; Senate 1891–97; chair Dem. Nat. Comm. 1889–92.

Brick, Abraham Lincoln (R Ind.) May 27, 1860–April 7, 1908; House 1899–April 7, 1908.

Bricker, John William (R Ohio) Sept. 6, 1893–March 22, 1986; Senate 1947–59; chair Senate Interstate and Foreign Commerce 1953–55; Gov. Jan. 9, 1939–Jan. 8, 1945.

Brickner, George H. (D Wis.) Jan. 21, 1834–Aug. 12, 1904; House 1889–95.

Bridges, George Washington (– Tenn.) Oct. 9, 1825–March 16, 1873; House Feb. 25–March 3, 1863.

Bridges, Henry Styles (R N.H.) Sept. 9, 1898–Nov. 26, 1961; Senate 1937–Nov. 26, 1961; chair Senate Appropriations 1947–49, 1953–55; Senate minority leader Jan. 8, 1952–53; elected pres. pro tempore Jan. 3, 1953; Gov. Jan. 3, 1935–Jan. 7, 1937.

Bridges, Samuel Augustus (D Pa.) Jan. 27, 1802–Jan. 14, 1884; House March 6, 1848–49, 1853–55, 1877–79.

Briggs, Clay Stone (D Texas) Jan. 8, 1876–April 29, 1933; House 1919–April 29, 1933.

Briggs, Frank Obadiah (son of James Frankland Briggs) (R N.J.) Aug. 12, 1851–May 8, 1913; Senate 1907–13.

Briggs, Frank Parks (D Mo.) Feb. 25, 1894–Sept. 23, 1992; Senate Jan. 18, 1945–47.

Briggs, George (R N.Y.) May 6, 1805–June 1, 1869; House 1849–53 (Whig), 1859–61.

Briggs, George Nixon (W Mass.) April 12, 1796–Sept. 11, 1861; House 1831–43 (1831–35 Anti-Jacksonian); Gov. Jan. 3, 1844–Jan. 11, 1851.

Briggs, James Frankland (father of Frank Obadiah Briggs) (R N.H.) Oct. 23, 1827–Jan. 21, 1905; House 1877–83.

Brigham, Elbert Sidney (R Vt.) Oct. 19, 1877–July 5, 1962; House 1925–31.

Brigham, Elijah (F Mass.) July 7, 1751–Feb. 22, 1816; House 1811–Feb. 22, 1816.

Brigham, Lewis Alexander (R N.J.) Jan. 2, 1831–Feb. 19, 1885; House 1879–81.

Bright, Jesse David (D Ind.) Dec. 18, 1812–May 20, 1875; Senate 1845–Feb. 5, 1862; elected pres. pro tempore Dec. 5, 1854, June 11, 1856, June 12, 1860.

Bright, John Morgan (D Tenn.) Jan. 20, 1817–Oct. 3, 1911; House 1871–81.

Brinkerhoff, Henry Roelif (cousin of Jacob Brinkerhoff) (D Ohio) Sept. 23, 1787–April 30, 1844; House 1843–April 30, 1844.

Brinkerhoff, Jacob (cousin of Henry Roelif Brinkerhoff) (D Ohio) Aug. 31, 1810–July 19, 1880; House 1843–47.

Brinkley, Jack Thomas (D Ga.) Dec. 22, 1930– ; House 1967–83.

Brinson, Samuel Mitchell (D N.C.) March 20, 1870–April 13, 1922; House 1919–April 13, 1922.

Brisbin, John (D Pa.) July 13, 1818–Feb. 3, 1880; House Jan. 13–March 3, 1851.

Bristow, Francis Marion (O Ky.) Aug. 11, 1804–June 10, 1864; House Dec. 4, 1854–55 (Whig), 1859–61.

Bristow, Henry (R N.Y.) June 5, 1840–Oct. 11, 1906; House 1901–03.

Bristow, Joseph Little (R Kan.) July 22, 1861–July 14, 1944; Senate 1909–15.

Britt, Charles Robin (D N.C.) June 29, 1942– ; House 1983–85.

Britt, James Jefferson (R N.C.) March 4, 1861–Dec. 26, 1939; House 1915–17, March 1, 1919–March 3, 1919.

Britten, Frederick Albert (R Ill.) Nov. 18, 1871–May 4, 1946; House 1913–35.

Broadhead, James Overton (D Mo.) May 29, 1819–Aug. 7, 1898; House 1883–85.

Brock, Lawrence (D Neb.) Aug. 16, 1906–Aug. 28, 1968; House 1959–61.

Brock, William Emerson (grandfather of William Emerson Brock III) (D Tenn.) March 14, 1872–Aug. 5, 1950; Senate Sept. 2, 1929–31.

Brock, William Emerson III (grandson of William Emerson Brock) (R Tenn.) Nov. 23, 1930– ; House 1963–71; Senate 1971–77; chair Rep. Nat. Comm. 1977–81; secretary of labor April 29, 1985–Oct. 31, 1987.

Brockenbrough, William Henry (D Fla.) Feb. 23, 1812–Jan. 28, 1850; House Jan. 24, 1846–47.

Brockson, Franklin (D Del.) Aug. 6, 1865–March 16, 1942; House 1913–15.

Brockway, John Hall (W Conn.) Jan. 31, 1801–July 29, 1870; House 1839–43.

Brodbeck, Andrew R. (D Pa.) April 11, 1860–Feb. 27, 1937; House 1913–15, 1917–19.

Broderick, Case (cousin of David Colbreth Broderick and Andrew Kennedy) (R Kan.) Sept. 23, 1839–April 1, 1920; House 1891–99.

Broderick, David Colbreth (cousin of Andrew Kennedy and Case Broderick) (D Calif.) Feb. 4, 1820–Sept. 16, 1859; Senate 1857–Sept. 16, 1859.

Brodhead, John (J N.H.) Oct. 5, 1770–April 7, 1838; House 1829–33.

Brodhead, John Curtis (D N.Y.) Oct. 27, 1780–Jan. 2, 1859; House 1831–33 (Jacksonian), 1837–39.

Brodhead, Joseph Davis (son of Richard Brodhead) (– Pa.) Jan. 12, 1859–April 23, 1920; House 1907–09.

Brodhead, Richard (father of Joseph Brodhead) (D Pa.) Jan. 5, 1811–Sept. 16, 1863; House 1843–49; Senate 1851–57.

Brodhead, William McNulty (D Mich.) Sept. 12, 1941– ; House 1975–83.

Brogden, Curtis Hooks (R N.C.) Nov. 6, 1816–Jan. 5, 1901; House 1877–79; Gov. July 11, 1874–Jan. 1, 1877.

Bromberg, Frederick George (LR Ala.) June 19, 1837–Sept. 4, 1930; House 1873–75.

Bromwell, Henry Pelham Holmes (R Ill.) Aug. 26, 1823–Jan. 7, 1903; House 1865–69.

Bromwell, Jacob Henry (R Ohio) May 11, 1848–June 4, 1924; House Dec. 3, 1894–1903.

Bromwell, James Edward (R Iowa) March 26, 1920– ; House 1961–65.

Bronson, David (W Maine) Feb. 8, 1800–Nov. 20, 1863; House May 31, 1841–43.

Bronson, Isaac Hopkins (D N.Y.) Oct. 16, 1802–Aug. 13, 1855; House 1837–39.

Broocks, Moses Lycurgus (D Texas) Nov. 1, 1864–May 27, 1908; House 1905–07.

Brooke, Edward William III (R Mass.) Oct. 26, 1919– ; Senate 1967–79.

Brooke, Walker (W Miss.) Dec. 25, 1813–Feb. 18, 1869; Senate Feb. 18, 1852–53.

Brookhart, Smith Wildman (R Iowa) Feb. 2, 1869–Nov. 15, 1944; Senate Nov. 7, 1922–April 12, 1926, 1927–33 (Nov. 7, 1922–25 Progressive Republican).

Brooks, Charles Wayland (R Ill.) March 8, 1897–Jan. 14, 1957; Senate Nov. 22, 1940–49; chair Senate Rules and Administration 1947–49.

Brooks, David (F N.Y.) 1756–Aug. 30, 1838; House 1797–99.

Brooks, Edward Schroeder (R Pa.) June 14, 1867–July 12, 1957; House 1919–23.

Brooks, Edwin Bruce (cousin of Edmund Howard Hinshaw) (R Ill.) Sept. 20, 1868–Sept. 18, 1933; House 1919–23.

Brooks, Franklin Eli (R Colo.) Nov. 19, 1860–Feb. 7, 1916; House 1903–07.

Brooks, George Merrick (R Mass.) July 26, 1824–Sept. 22, 1893; House Nov. 2, 1869–May 13, 1872.

Brooks, Jack Bascom (D Texas) Dec. 18, 1922– ; House 1953–95; chair House Government Operations 1975–89; chair House Judiciary 1989–95.

Brooks, James (D N.Y.) Nov. 10, 1810–April 30, 1873; House 1849–53 (Whig), 1863–April 7, 1866, 1867–April 30, 1873.

Brooks, Joshua Twing (D Pa.) Feb. 27, 1884–Feb. 7, 1956; House 1933–37.

Brooks, Micah (R N.Y.) May 14, 1775–July 7, 1857; House 1815–17.

Brooks, Overton (nephew of John Holmes Overton) (D La.) Dec. 21, 1897–Sept. 16, 1961; House 1937–Sept. 16, 1961; chair House Science and Astronautics 1959–61.

Brooks, Preston Smith (D S.C.) Aug. 5, 1819–Jan. 27, 1857; House 1853–July 15, 1856, Aug. 1, 1856–Jan. 27, 1857.

Brookshire, Elijah Voorhees (D Ind.) Aug. 15, 1856–April 14, 1936; House 1889–95.

Broom, Jacob (son of James Madison Broom) (AP Pa.) July 25, 1808–Nov. 28, 1864; House 1855–57.

Broom, James Madison (father of Jacob Broom) (F Del.) 1776–Jan. 15, 1850; House 1805–07.

Broomall, John Martin (R Pa.) Jan. 19, 1816–June 3, 1894; House 1863–69.

Broomfield, William S. (R Mich.) April 28, 1922– ; House 1957–93.

Brophy, John Charles (R Wis.) Oct. 8, 1901–Dec. 26, 1976; House 1947–49.

Brosius, Marriott (R Pa.) March 7, 1843–March 16, 1901; House 1889–March 16, 1901.

Brotzman, Donald Glenn (R Colo.) June 28, 1922–Sept. 15, 2004; House 1963–65, 1967–75.

Broughton, Joseph Melville (D N.C.) Nov. 17, 1888–March 6, 1949; Senate Dec. 31, 1948–March 6, 1949; Gov. Jan. 9, 1941–Jan. 4, 1945.

Broussard, Edwin Sidney (brother of Robert Foligny Broussard) (D La.) Dec. 4, 1874–Nov. 19, 1934; Senate 1921–33.

Broussard, Robert Foligny (brother of Edwin Sidney Broussard) (D La.) Aug. 17, 1864–April 12, 1918; House 1897–1915; Senate 1915–April 12, 1918.

Browder, Glen (D Ala.) Jan. 15, 1943– ; House April 18, 1989–97.

Brower, John Morehead (R N.C.) July 19, 1845–Aug. 5, 1913; House 1887–91.

Brown, Aaron Venable (D Tenn.) Aug. 15, 1795–March 8, 1859; House 1839–45; Gov. Oct. 14, 1845–Oct. 16, 1847; postmaster general March 7, 1857–March 8, 1859.

Brown, Albert Gallatin (D Miss.) May 31, 1813–June 12, 1880; House 1839–41, 1847–53; Senate Jan. 7, 1854–Jan. 12, 1861; Gov. Jan. 10, 1844–Jan. 10, 1848.

Brown, Anson (W N.Y.) 1800–June 14, 1840; House 1839–June 14, 1840.

Brown, Arthur (R Utah) March 8, 1843–Dec. 12, 1906; Senate Jan 22, 1896–97.

Brown, Bedford (D N.C.) June 6, 1795–Dec. 6, 1870; Senate Dec. 9, 1829–Nov. 16, 1840.

Brown, Benjamin (nephew of John Brown) (F Mass.) Sept. 23, 1756–Sept. 17, 1831; House 1815–17.

Brown, Benjamin Gratz (grandson of John Brown of Va. and Ky.) (UU Mo.) May 28, 1826–Dec. 13, 1885; Senate Nov. 13, 1863–67; Gov. Jan. 9, 1871–Jan. 8, 1873 (Liberal Republican).

Brown, Charles (D Pa.) Sept. 23, 1797–Sept. 4, 1883; House 1841–43, 1847–49.

Brown, Charles Elwood (R Ohio) July 4, 1834–May 22, 1904; House 1885–89.

Brown, Charles Harrison (D Mo.) Oct. 22, 1920– ; House 1957–61.

Brown, Clarence J. (father of Clarence J. Brown Jr.) (R Ohio) July 14, 1893–Aug. 23, 1965; House 1939–Aug. 23, 1965.

Brown, Clarence J. Jr. (son of Clarence J. Brown) (R Ohio) June 18, 1927– ; House Nov. 2, 1965–83.

Brown, Corrine (D Fla.) Nov. 11, 1946– ; House 1993– .

Brown, Elias (J Md.) May 9, 1793–July 7, 1857; House 1829–31.

Brown, Ernest S. (R Nev.) Sept. 25, 1903–July 23, 1965; Senate Oct. 1–Dec. 1, 1954.

Brown, Ethan Allen (– Ohio) July 4, 1776–Feb. 24, 1852; Senate Jan. 3, 1822–25; Gov. Dec. 14, 1818–Jan. 4, 1822 (Democratic Republican).

Brown, Foster Vincent (father of Joseph Edgar Brown) (R Tenn.) Dec. 24, 1852–March 26, 1937; House 1895–97.

Brown, Fred Herbert (D N.H.) April 12, 1879–Feb. 3, 1955; Senate 1933–39; Gov. Jan. 4, 1923–Jan. 1, 1925.

Brown, Garry Eldridge (R Mich.) Aug. 12, 1923–Aug. 15, 1998; House 1967–79.

Brown, George Edward Jr. (D Calif.) March 6, 1920–July 15, 1999; House 1963–71, 1973–July 15, 1999; chair House Science, Space, and Technology 1991–95.

Brown, George Hanks (Hank) (R Colo.) Feb. 12, 1940– ; House 1981–91; Senate 1991–97.

Brown, George Houston (W N.J.) Feb. 12, 1810–Aug. 1, 1865; House 1851–53.

Brown, Henry E. Jr. (R S.C.) Dec. 20, 1935– ; House 2001– .

Brown, James (brother of John Brown of Va. and Ky., cousin of John Breckinridge, James Breckinridge, and Francis Preston) (– La.) Sept. 11, 1776–April 7, 1835; Senate Feb. 5, 1813–17, 1819–Dec. 10, 1823.

Brown, James Sproat (D Wis.) Feb. 1, 1824–April 15, 1878; House 1863–65.

Brown, James W. (son-in-law of Thomas Marshall Howe) (IR Pa.) July 14, 1844–Oct. 23, 1909; House 1903–05.

Brown, Jason Brevoort (D Ind.) Feb. 26, 1839–March 10, 1898; House 1889–95.

Brown, Jeremiah (W Pa.) April 14, 1785–March 2, 1858; House 1841–45.

Brown, John (uncle of Benjamin Brown, grandfather of John Brown Francis) (F R.I.) Jan. 27, 1736–Sept. 20, 1803; House 1799–1801; Cont. Cong. (elected but did not attend) 1784, 1785.

Brown, John (R Md.) ?–Dec. 13, 1815; House 1809–10.

Brown, John (brother of James Brown, grandfather of Benjamin Gratz Brown, cousin of John Breckinridge, James Breckinridge, and Francis Preston) (– Va./Ky.) Sept. 12, 1757–Aug. 29, 1837; House 1789–June 1, 1792 (Ky. district of Va.); Senate June 18, 1792–1805 (Ky.); elected pres. pro tempore Oct. 17, 1803, Jan. 23, 1804; Cont. Cong. (Ky. district of Va.) 1787–88.

Brown, John (– Pa.) Aug. 12, 1772–Oct. 12, 1845; House 1821–25.

Brown, John Brewer (D Md.) May 13, 1836–May 16, 1898; House Nov. 8, 1892–93.

Brown, John Robert (R Va.) Jan. 14, 1842–Aug. 4, 1927; House 1887–89.

Brown, John W. (J N.Y.) Oct. 11, 1796–Sept. 6, 1875; House 1833–37.

Brown, John Young (nephew of Bryan Rust Young and William Singleton Young) (D Ky.) June 28, 1835–Jan. 11, 1904; House 1859–61, 1873–77; Gov. Sept. 1, 1891–Dec. 10, 1895.

Brown, John Young (D Ky.) Feb. 1, 1900–June 16, 1985; House 1933–35.

Brown, Joseph Edgar (son of Foster Vincent Brown) (R Tenn.) Feb. 11, 1880–June 13, 1939; House 1921–23.

Brown, Joseph Emerson (D Ga.) April 15, 1821–Nov. 30, 1894; Senate May 26, 1880–91; Gov. Nov. 6, 1857–June 17, 1865.

Brown, Lathrop (D N.Y.) Feb. 26, 1883–Nov. 28, 1959; House 1913–15.

Brown, Milton (W Tenn.) Feb. 28, 1804–May 15, 1883; House 1841–47.

Brown, Norris (R Neb.) May 2, 1863–Jan. 5, 1960; Senate 1907–13.

Brown, Paul (D Ga.) March 31, 1880–Sept. 24, 1961; House July 5, 1933–61.

Brown, Prentiss Marsh (D Mich.) June 18, 1889–Dec. 19, 1973; House 1933–Nov. 18, 1936; Senate Nov. 19, 1936–43.

Brown, Robert (R Pa.) Dec. 25, 1744–Feb. 26, 1823; House Dec. 4, 1798–1815.

Brown, Seth W. (R Ohio) Jan. 4, 1841–Feb. 24, 1923; House 1897–1901.

Brown, Sherrod (D Ohio) Nov. 9, 1952– ; House 1993– .

Brown, Titus (– N.H.) Feb. 11, 1786–Jan. 29, 1849; House 1825–29.

Brown, Webster Everett (R Wis.) July 16, 1851–Dec. 14, 1929; House 1901–07.

Brown, William (– Ky.) April 19, 1779–Oct. 6, 1833; House 1819–21.

Brown, William Gay (father of William Gay Brown Jr.) (UU W.Va.) Sept. 25, 1800–April 19, 1884; House 1845–49 (Democrat Va.), 1861–63 (Unionist Va.), Dec. 7, 1863–65.

Brown, William Gay Jr. (son of William Gay Brown) (D W.Va.) April 7, 1856–March 9, 1916; House 1911–March 9, 1916.

Brown, William John (D Ind.) Aug. 15, 1805–March 18, 1857; House 1843–45, 1849–51.

Brown, William Ripley (R Kan.) July 16, 1840–March 3, 1916; House 1875–77.

Brown, William Wallace (R Pa.) April 22, 1836–Nov. 4, 1926; House 1883–87.

Brownback, Sam (R Kan.) Sept. 12, 1956– ; House 1995–Nov. 6, 1996; Senate Nov. 27, 1996– .

Browne, Charles (D N.J.) Sept. 28, 1875–Aug. 17, 1947; House 1923–25.

Browne, Edward Everts (R Wis.) Feb. 16, 1868–Nov. 23, 1945; House 1913–31.

Browne, George Huntington (D/Const U R.I.) Jan. 6, 1811–Sept. 26, 1885; House 1861–63.

Browne, Thomas Henry Bayly (R Va.) Feb. 8, 1844–Aug. 27, 1892; House 1887–91.

Browne, Thomas McLelland (R Ind.) April 19, 1829–July 17, 1891; House 1877–91.

Browning, Gordon Weaver (D Tenn.) Nov. 22, 1889–May 23, 1976; House 1923–35; Gov. Jan. 15, 1937–Jan. 16, 1939, Jan. 17, 1949–Jan. 15, 1953.

Browning, Orville Hickman (R Ill.) Feb. 10, 1806–Aug. 10, 1881; Senate June 26, 1861–Jan. 12, 1863; secretary of the interior Sept. 1, 1866–March 4, 1869.

Browning, William John (R N.J.) April 11, 1850–March 24, 1920; House Nov. 7, 1911–March 24, 1920.

Brownlow, Walter Preston (nephew of William Gannaway Brownlow) (R Tenn.) March 27, 1851–July 8, 1910; House 1897–July 8, 1910.

Brownlow, William Gannaway (uncle of Walter Preston Brownlow) (R Tenn.) Aug. 29, 1805–April 29, 1877; Senate 1869–75; Gov. April 5, 1865–Feb. 25, 1869.

Brownson, Charles Bruce (R Ind.) Feb. 5, 1914–Aug. 4, 1988; House 1951–59.

Brown-Waite, Ginny (R Fla.) Oct. 5, 1943– ; House 2003– .

Broyhill, James Thomas (R N.C.) Aug. 19, 1927– ; House 1963–July 14, 1986; Senate July 14–Nov. 10, 1986.

Broyhill, Joel Thomas (R Va.) Nov. 4, 1919– ; House 1953–Dec. 31, 1974.

Bruce, Blanche Kelso (R Miss.) March 1, 1841–March 17, 1898; Senate 1875–81.

Bruce, Donald Cogley (R Ind.) April 27, 1921–Aug. 31, 1969; House 1961–65.

Bruce, Phineas (F Mass.) June 7, 1762–Oct. 4, 1809; elected to the House for the term beginning 1803 but did not serve.

Bruce, Terry L. (D Ill.) March 25, 1944– ; House 1985–93.

Bruce, William Cabell (D Md.) March 12, 1860–May 9, 1946; Senate 1923–29.

Brucker, Ferdinand (D Mich.) Jan. 8, 1858–March 3, 1904; House 1897–99.

Bruckner, Henry (D N.Y.) June 17, 1871–April 14, 1942; House 1913–Dec. 31, 1917.

Brumbaugh, Clement Laird (D Ohio) Feb. 28, 1863–Sept. 28, 1921; House 1913–21.

Brumbaugh, David Emmert (R Pa.) Oct. 8, 1894–April 22, 1977; House Nov. 2, 1943–47.

Brumm, Charles Napoleon (father of George Franklin Brumm) (R Pa.) June 9, 1838–Jan. 11, 1917; House 1881–89 (1881–85 Greenbacker); 1895–99, Nov. 6, 1906–Jan. 4, 1909.

Brumm, George Franklin (son of Charles Napoleon Brumm) (R Pa.) Jan. 24, 1880–May 29, 1934; House 1923–27, 1929–May 29, 1934.

Brundidge, Stephen Jr. (D Ark.) Jan. 1, 1857–Jan. 14, 1938; House 1897–1909.

Brunner, David B. (D Pa.) March 7, 1835–Nov. 29, 1903; House 1889–93.

Brunner, William Frank (D N.Y.) Sept. 15, 1887–April 23, 1965; House 1929–Sept. 27, 1935.

Brunsdale, Clarence Norman (R N.D.) July 9, 1891–Jan. 27, 1978; Senate Nov. 19, 1959–Aug. 7, 1960; Gov. Jan. 3, 1951–Jan. 9, 1957.

Brush, Henry (– Ohio) June 1778–Jan. 19, 1855; House 1819–21.

Bruyn, Andrew DeWitt (D N.Y.) Nov. 18, 1790–July 27, 1838; House 1837–July 27, 1838.

Bryan, Guy Morrison (D Texas) Jan. 12, 1821–June 4, 1901; House 1857–59.

Bryan, Henry H. (– Tenn.) ?–May 7, 1835; House 1819–21 (elected for the term beginning 1821 but did not serve).

Bryan, James Wesley (Prog. Wash.) March 11, 1874–Aug. 26, 1956; House 1913–15.

Bryan, John Heritage (– N.C.) Nov. 4, 1798–May 19, 1870; House 1825–29.

Bryan, Joseph (R Ga.) Aug. 18, 1773–Sept. 12, 1812; House 1803–06.

Bryan, Joseph Hunter (R N.C.) ?–?; House 1815–19.

Bryan, Nathan (R N.C.) 1748–June 4, 1798; House 1795–June 4, 1798.

Bryan, Nathan Philemon (brother of William James Bryan) (D Fla.) April 23, 1872–Aug. 8, 1935; Senate 1911–17.

Bryan, Richard H. (D Nev.) July 16, 1937– ; Senate 1989–2001; Gov. Jan. 3, 1983–Jan. 3, 1989; chair Senate Select Ethics 1993–95.

Bryan, William James (brother of Nathan Philemon Bryan) (D Fla.) Oct. 10, 1876–March 22, 1908; Senate Dec. 26, 1907–March 22, 1908.

Bryan, William Jennings (father of Ruth Bryan Owen) (D Neb.) March 19, 1860–July 26, 1925; House 1891–95; secretary of state March 5, 1913–June 9, 1915.

Bryant, Ed (R Tenn.) Sept. 7, 1948– ; House 1995–2003.

Bryant, John Wiley (D Texas) Feb. 22, 1947– ; House 1983–97.

Bryce, Lloyd Stephens (D N.Y.) Sept. 4, 1851–April 2, 1917; House 1887–89.

Bryson, Joseph Raleigh (D S.C.) Jan. 18, 1893–March 10, 1953; House 1939–March 10, 1953.

Buchanan, Andrew (D Pa.) April 8, 1780–Dec. 2, 1848; House 1835–39 (1835–37 Jacksonian).

Buchanan, Frank (D Ill.) June 14, 1862–April 18, 1930; House 1911–17.

Buchanan, Frank (husband of Vera Daerr Buchanan) (D Pa.) Dec. 1, 1902–April 27, 1951; House May 21, 1946–April 27, 1951.

Buchanan, Hugh (D Ga.) Sept. 15, 1823–June 11, 1890; House 1881–85.

Buchanan, James (D Pa.) April 23, 1791–June 1, 1868; House 1821–31 (no party); Senate Dec. 6, 1834–March 5, 1845; secretary of state March 10, 1845–March 7, 1849; president 1857–61.

Buchanan, James (R N.J.) June 17, 1839–Oct. 30, 1900; House 1885–93.

Buchanan, James Paul (cousin of Edward William Pou) (D Texas) April 30, 1867–Feb. 22, 1937; House April 5, 1913–Feb. 22, 1937.

Buchanan, John Alexander (D Va.) Oct. 7, 1843–Sept. 2, 1921; House 1889–93.

Buchanan, John Hall Jr. (R Ala.) March 19, 1928– ; House 1965–81.

Buchanan, Vera Daerr (widow of Frank Buchanan) (D Pa.) July 20, 1902–Nov. 26, 1955; House July 24, 1951–Nov. 26, 1955.

Bucher, John Conrad (J Pa.) Dec. 28, 1792–Oct. 15, 1851; House 1831–33.

Buck, Alfred Eliab (R Ala.) Feb. 7, 1832–Dec. 4, 1902; House 1869–71.

Buck, Charles Francis (D La.) Nov. 5, 1841–Jan. 19, 1918; House 1895–97.

Buck, Clayton Douglass (great-great-nephew of John Middleton Clayton) (R Del.) March 21, 1890–Jan. 27, 1965; Senate 1943–49; chair Senate District of Columbia 1947–49; Gov. Jan. 15, 1929–Jan. 19, 1937.

Buck, Daniel (father of Daniel Azro Ashley Buck) (F Vt.) Nov. 9, 1753–Aug. 16, 1816; House 1795–97.

Buck, Daniel Azro Ashley (son of Daniel Buck) (– Vt.) April 19, 1789–Dec. 24, 1841; House 1823–25, 1827–29.

Buck, Ellsworth Brewer (R N.Y.) July 3, 1892–Aug. 14, 1970; House June 6, 1944–49.

Buck, Frank Henry (D Calif.) Sept. 23, 1887–Sept. 17, 1942; House 1933–Sept. 17, 1942.

Buck, John Ransom (R Conn.) Dec. 6, 1835–Feb. 6, 1917; House 1881–83, 1885–87.

Buckalew, Charles Rollin (D Pa.) Dec. 28, 1821–May 19, 1899; Senate 1863–69; House 1887–91.

Buckbee, John Theodore (R Ill.) Aug. 1, 1871–April 23, 1936; House 1927–April 23, 1936.

Buckingham, William Alfred (R Conn.) May 28, 1804–Feb. 5, 1875; Senate 1869–Feb. 5, 1875; Gov. May 5, 1858–May 2, 1866.

Buckland, Ralph Pomeroy (R Ohio) Jan. 20, 1812–May 27, 1892; House 1865–69.

Buckler, Richard Thompson (FL Minn.) Oct. 27, 1865–Jan. 23, 1950; House 1935–43.

Buckley, Charles Anthony (D N.Y.) June 23, 1890–Jan. 22, 1967; House 1935–65; chair House Public Works 1951–53, 1955–65.

Buckley, Charles Waldron (R Ala.) Feb. 18, 1835–Dec. 4, 1906; House July 21, 1868–73.

Buckley, James Lane (C N.Y.) March 9, 1923– ; Senate 1971–77.

Buckley, James Richard (D Ill.) Nov. 18, 1870–June 22, 1945; House 1923–25.

Buckley, James Vincent (D Ill.) May 15, 1894–July 30, 1954; House 1949–51.

Buckman, Clarence Bennett (R Minn.) April 1, 1851–March 1, 1917; House 1903–07.

Buckner, Alexander (– Mo.) 1785–June 6, 1833; Senate 1831–June 6, 1833.

Buckner, Aylett Hawes (nephew of Aylett Hawes, cousin of Richard Hawes and Albert Gallatin Hawes) (D Mo.) Dec. 14, 1816–Feb. 5, 1894; House 1873–85.

Buckner, Aylette (son of Richard Aylett Buckner) (W Ky.) July 21, 1806–July 3, 1869; House 1847–49.

Buckner, Richard Aylett (father of Aylette Buckner) (– Ky.) July 16, 1763–Dec. 8, 1847; House 1823–29.

Budd, James Herbert (D Calif.) May 18, 1851–July 30, 1908; House 1883–85; Gov. Jan. 11, 1895–Jan. 3, 1899.

Budge, Hamer Harold (R Idaho) Nov. 21, 1910–July 22, 2003; House 1951–61.

Buechner, John William "Jack" (R Mo.) June 6, 1940– ; House 1987–91.

Buel, Alexander Woodruff (D Mich.) Dec. 13, 1813–April 19, 1868; House 1849–51.

Buell, Alexander Hamilton (D N.Y.) July 14, 1801–Jan. 29, 1853; House 1851–Jan. 29, 1853.

Buffett, Howard Homan (R Neb.) Aug. 13, 1903–April 30, 1964; House 1943–49, 1951–53.

Buffington, James (R Mass.) March 16, 1817–March 7, 1875; House 1855–63, 1869–March 7, 1875.

Buffington, Joseph (W Pa.) Nov. 27, 1803–Feb. 3, 1872; House 1843–47.

Buffum, Joseph Jr. (– N.H.) Sept. 23, 1784–Feb. 24, 1874; House 1819–21.

Bugg, Robert Malone (W Tenn.) Jan. 20, 1805–Feb. 18, 1887; House 1853–55.

Bulkeley, Morgan Gardner (cousin of Edwin Denison Morgan) (R Conn.) Dec. 26, 1837–Nov. 6, 1922; Senate 1905–11; Gov. Jan. 10, 1889–Jan. 4, 1893.

Bulkley, Robert Johns (D Ohio) Oct. 8, 1880–July 21, 1965; House 1911–15; Senate Dec. 1, 1930–39.

Bull, John (– Mo.) 1803–Feb. 1863; House 1833–35.

Bull, Melville (R R.I.) Sept. 29, 1854–July 5, 1909; House 1895–1903.

Bullard, Henry Adams (W La.) Sept. 9, 1788–April 17, 1851; House 1831–Jan. 4, 1834 (Anti-Jacksonian), Dec. 5, 1850–51.

Bulloch, William Bellinger (R Ga.) 1777–May 6, 1852; Senate April 8–Nov. 6, 1813.

Bullock, Robert (D Fla.) Dec. 8, 1828–July 27, 1905; House 1889–93.

Bullock, Stephen (F Mass.) Oct. 10, 1735–Feb. 2, 1816; House 1797–99.

Bullock, Wingfield (– Ky.) ?–Oct. 13, 1821; House 1821–Oct. 13, 1821.

Bulow, William John (D S.D.) Jan. 13, 1869–Feb. 26, 1960; Senate 1931–43; Gov. Jan. 4, 1927–Jan. 6, 1931.

Bulwinkle, Alfred Lee (D N.C.) April 21, 1883–Aug. 31, 1950; House 1921–29, 1931–Aug. 31, 1950.

Bumpers, Dale Leon (D Ark.) Aug. 12, 1925– ; Senate 1975–99; chair Senate Small Business 1987–95; Gov. Jan. 12, 1971–Jan. 2, 1975.

Bunch, Samuel (White supporter Tenn.) Dec. 4, 1786–Sept. 5, 1849; House 1833–37 (1833–35 Jacksonian).

Bundy, Hezekiah Sanford (R Ohio) Aug. 15, 1817–Dec. 12, 1895; House 1865–67, 1873–75, Dec. 4, 1893–95.

Bundy, Solomon (R N.Y.) May 22, 1823–Jan. 13, 1889; House 1877–79.

Bunker, Berkeley Lloyd (D Nev.) Aug. 12, 1906–June 21, 1999; Senate Nov. 27, 1940–Dec. 6, 1942; House 1945–47.

Bunn, Benjamin Hickman (D N.C.) Oct. 19, 1844–Aug. 25, 1907; House 1889–95.

Bunn, Jim (R Ore.) Dec. 12, 1956– ; House 1995–97.

Bunnell, Frank Charles (R Pa.) March 19, 1842–Sept. 11, 1911; House Dec. 24, 1872–73 (no party), 1885–89.

Bunner, Rudolph (– N.Y.) Aug. 17, 1779–July 16, 1837; House 1827–29.

Bunning, James Paul David (R Ky.) Oct. 23, 1931– ; House 1987–99; Senate 1999– .

Bunting, Thomas Lathrop (D N.Y.) April 24, 1844–Dec. 27, 1898; House 1891–93.

Burch, John Chilton (D Calif.) Feb. 1, 1826–Aug. 31, 1885; House 1859–61.

Burch, Thomas Granville (D Va.) July 3, 1869–March 20, 1951; House 1931–May 31, 1946; Senate May 31–Nov. 5, 1946.

Burchard, Horatio Chapin (R Ill.) Sept. 22, 1825–May 14, 1908; House Dec. 6, 1869–79.

Burchard, Samuel Dickinson (D Wis.) July 17, 1836–Sept. 1, 1901; House 1875–77.

Burchill, Thomas Francis (D N.Y.) Aug. 3, 1882–March 28, 1960; House 1943–45.

Burd, George (– Pa.) 1793–Jan. 13, 1844; House 1831–35.

Burdett, Samuel Swinfin (R Mo.) Feb. 21, 1836–Sept. 24, 1914; House 1869–73.

Burdick, Clark (R R.I.) Jan. 13, 1868–Aug. 27, 1948; House 1919–33.

Burdick, Jocelyn Birch (widow of Quentin Northrop Burdick, daughter-in-law of Usher Lloyd Burdick, sister-in-law of Robert Woodrow Levering) (D N.D.) Feb. 6, 1922– ; Senate Sept. 16–Dec. 14, 1992.

Burdick, Quentin Northrop (husband of Jocelyn Birch Burdick, son of Usher Lloyd Burdick, brother-in-law of Robert Woodrow Levering) (D N.D.) June 19, 1908–Sept. 8, 1992; House 1959–Aug. 8, 1960; Senate Aug. 8, 1960–Sept. 8, 1992; chair Senate Environment and Public Works 1987–92.

Burdick, Theodore Weld (R Iowa) Oct. 7, 1836–July 16, 1898; House 1877–79.

Burdick, Usher Lloyd (father of Quentin Northrop Burdick, father-in-law of Jocelyn Birch Burdick, father-in-law of Robert Woodrow Levering) (R N.D.) Feb. 21, 1879–Aug. 19, 1960; House 1935–45, 1949–59.

Burgener, Clair Walter (R Calif.) Dec. 5, 1921– ; House 1973–83.

Burges, Dempsey (R N.C.) 1751–Jan. 13, 1800; House 1795–99.

Burges, Tristam (great-great-uncle of Theodore Francis Green) (AJ R.I.) Feb. 26, 1770–Oct. 13, 1853; House 1825–35 (1825–31 no party).

Burgess, George Farmer (D Texas) Sept. 21, 1861–Dec. 31, 1919; House 1901–17.

Burgess, Michael (R Texas) Dec. 23, 1950– ; House 2003– .

Burgin, William Olin (D N.C.) July 28, 1877–April 11, 1946; House 1939–April 11, 1946.

Burk, Henry (R Pa.) Sept. 26, 1850–Dec. 5, 1903; House 1901–Dec. 5, 1903.

Burke, Aedanus (– S.C.) June 16, 1743–March 30, 1802; House 1789–91.

Burke, Charles Henry (R S.D.) April 1, 1861–April 7, 1944; House 1899–1907, 1909–15.

Burke, Edmund (D N.H.) Jan. 23, 1809–Jan. 25, 1882; House 1839–45.

Burke, Edward Raymond (D Neb.) Nov. 28, 1880–Nov. 4, 1968; House 1933–35; Senate 1935–41.

Burke, Frank Welsh (D Ky.) June 1, 1920– ; House 1959–63.

Burke, J. Herbert (R Fla.) Jan. 14, 1913–June 16, 1993; House 1967–79.

Burke, James Anthony (D Mass.) March 30, 1910–Oct. 13, 1983; House 1959–79.

Burke, James Francis (R Pa.) Oct. 21, 1867–Aug. 8, 1932; House 1905–15.

Burke, John Harley (D Calif.) June 2, 1894–May 14, 1951; House 1933–35.

Burke, Michael Edmund (D Wis.) Oct. 15, 1863–Dec. 12, 1918; House 1911–17.

Burke, Raymond Hugh (R Ohio) Nov. 4, 1881–Aug. 18, 1954; House 1947–49.

Burke, Robert Emmet (D Texas) Aug. 1, 1847–June 5, 1901; House 1897–June 5, 1901.

Burke, Thomas A. (D Ohio) Oct. 30, 1898–Dec. 5, 1971; Senate Nov. 10, 1953–Dec. 2, 1954.

Burke, Thomas Henry (D Ohio) May 6, 1904–Sept. 12, 1959; House 1949–51.

Burke, William Joseph (R Pa.) Sept. 25, 1862–Nov. 7, 1925; House 1919–23.

Burke, Yvonne Brathwaite (D Calif.) Oct. 5, 1932– ; House 1973–79.

Burkett, Elmer Jacob (R Neb.) Dec. 1, 1867–May 23, 1935; House 1899–March 4, 1905; Senate 1905–11.

Burkhalter, Everett Glen (D Calif.) Jan. 19, 1897–May 24, 1975; House 1963–65.

Burleigh, Edwin Chick (R Maine) Nov. 27, 1843–June 16, 1916; House June 21, 1897–1911; Senate 1913–June 16, 1916; Gov. Jan. 2, 1889–Jan. 4, 1893.

Burleigh, Henry Gordon (R N.Y.) June 2, 1832–Aug. 10, 1900; House 1883–87.

Burleigh, John Holmes (son of William Burleigh) (R Maine) Oct. 9, 1822–Dec. 5, 1877; House 1873–77.

Burleigh, Walter Atwood (R Dakota) Oct. 25, 1820–March 7, 1896; House (Terr. Del.) 1865–69.

Burleigh, William (father of John Holmes Burleigh) (– Maine) Oct. 24, 1785–July 2, 1827; House 1823–July 2, 1827.

Burleson, Albert Sidney (D Texas) June 7, 1863–Nov. 24, 1937; House 1899–March 6, 1913; postmaster general March 5, 1913–March 4, 1921.

Burleson, Omar Truman (D Texas) March 19, 1906–May 14, 1991; House 1947–Dec. 31, 1978; chair House Administration 1955–68.

Burlingame, Anson (R Mass.) Nov. 14, 1820–Feb. 23, 1870; House 1855–61 (1855–57 American Party).

Burlison, William Dean (D Mo.) March 15, 1933– ; House 1969–81.

Burnell, Barker (W Mass.) Jan. 30, 1798–June 15, 1843; House 1841–June 15, 1843.

Burnes, Daniel Dee (D Mo.) Jan. 4, 1851–Nov. 2, 1899; House 1893–95.

Burnes, James Nelson (D Mo.) Aug. 22, 1827–Jan. 23, 1889; House 1883–Jan. 23, 1889.

Burnet, Jacob (F N.J.) Feb. 22, 1770–May 10, 1853; Senate Dec. 10, 1828–31.

Burnett, Edward (D Mass.) March 16, 1849–Nov. 5, 1925; House 1887–89.

Burnett, Henry Cornelius (D Ky.) Oct. 5, 1825–Oct. 1, 1866; House 1855–Dec. 3, 1861.

Burnett, John Lawson (D Ala.) Jan. 20, 1854–May 13, 1919; House 1899–May 13, 1919.

Burney, William Evans (D Colo.) Sept. 11, 1893–Jan. 29, 1969; House Nov. 5, 1940–41.

Burnham, Alfred Avery (R Conn.) March 8, 1819–April 11, 1879; House 1859–63.

Burnham, George (R Calif.) Dec. 28, 1868–June 28, 1939; House 1933–37.

Burnham, Henry Eben (R N.H.) Nov. 8, 1844–Feb. 8, 1917; Senate 1901–13.

Burns, Conrad (R Mont.) Jan. 25, 1935– ; Senate 1989– .

Burns, John Anthony (D Hawaii) March 30, 1909–April 5, 1975; House (Terr. Del.) 1957–Aug. 21, 1959; Gov. Dec. 3, 1962–Dec. 2, 1974.

Burns, Joseph (J Ohio) March 11, 1800–May 12, 1875; House 1857–59.

Burns, Max (R Ga.) Nov. 8, 1948– ; House 2003–05.

Burns, Robert (D N.H.) Dec. 12, 1792–June 26, 1866; House 1833–37.

Burnside, Ambrose Everett (R R.I.) May 23, 1824–Sept. 13, 1881; Senate 1875–Sept. 13, 1881; Gov. May 29, 1866–May 25, 1869.

Burnside, Maurice Gwinn (D W.Va.) Aug. 23, 1902–Feb. 2, 1991; House 1949–53, 1955–57.

Burnside, Thomas (R Pa.) July 28, 1782–March 25, 1851; House Oct. 10, 1815–April 1816.

Burr, Aaron (cousin of Theodore Dwight, father-in-law of Gov. Joseph Alston of S.C.) (D N.Y.) Feb. 6, 1756–Sept. 14, 1836; Senate 1791–97; vice president 1801–05.

Burr, Albert George (D Ill.) Nov. 8, 1829–June 10, 1882; House 1867–71.

Burr, Richard M. (R N.C.) Nov. 30, 1955– ; House 1995–2005; Senate 2005– .

Burrell, Orlando (R Ill.) July 26, 1826–June 7, 1921; House 1895–97.

Burrill, James Jr. (great-grandfather of Theodore Francis Green) (– R.I.) April 25, 1772–Dec. 25, 1820; Senate 1817–Dec. 25, 1820.

Burroughs, Sherman Everett (R N.H.) Feb. 6, 1870–Jan. 27, 1923; House June 7, 1917–Jan. 27, 1923.

Burroughs, Silas Mainville (R N.Y.) July 16, 1810–June 3, 1860; House 1857–June 3, 1860.

Burrows, Daniel (uncle of Lorenzo Burrows) (– Conn.) Oct. 26, 1766–Jan. 23, 1858; House 1821–23.

Burrows, Joseph Henry (G Mo.) May 15, 1840–April 28, 1914; House 1881–83.

Burrows, Julius Caesar (R Mich.) Jan. 9, 1837–Nov. 16, 1915; House 1873–75, 1879–83, 1885–Jan. 23, 1895; Senate Jan. 24, 1895–1911.

Burrows, Lorenzo (nephew of Daniel Burrows) (W N.Y.) March 15, 1805–March 6, 1885; House 1849–53.

Bursum, Holm Olaf (R N.M.) Feb. 10, 1867–Aug. 7, 1953; Senate March 11, 1921–25.

Burt, Armistead (D S.C.) Nov. 13, 1802–Oct. 30, 1883; House 1843–53.

Burtness, Olger Burton (R N.D.) March 14, 1884–Jan. 20, 1960; House 1921–33.

Burton, Charles Germman (R Mo.) April 4, 1846–Feb. 25, 1926; House 1895–97.

Burton, Clarence Godber (D Va.) Dec. 14, 1886–Jan. 18, 1982; House Nov. 2, 1948–53.

Burton, Danny Lee (R Ind.) June 21, 1938– ; House 1983– ; chair House Government Reform 1997–2003.

Burton, Harold Hitz (R Ohio) June 22, 1888–Oct. 28, 1964; Senate 1941–Sept. 30, 1945; assoc. justice Oct. 1, 1945–Oct. 13, 1958.

Burton, Hiram Rodney (R Del.) Nov. 13, 1841–June 17, 1927; House 1905–09.

Burton, Hutchins Gordon (– N.C.) 1782–April 21, 1836; House Dec. 6, 1819–March 23, 1824; Gov. Dec. 7, 1824–Dec. 8, 1827 (Federalist).

Burton, John Lowell (brother of Phillip Burton, brother-in-law of Sala Burton) (D Calif.) Dec. 15, 1932– ; House June 25, 1974–83.

Burton, Joseph Ralph (R Kan.) Nov. 16, 1850–Feb. 27, 1923; Senate 1901–June 4, 1906.

Burton, Laurence Junior (R Utah) Oct. 30, 1926– ; House 1963–71.

Burton, Phillip (brother of John Lowell Burton, husband of Sala Burton) (D Calif.) June 1, 1926–April 10, 1983; House Feb. 18, 1964–April 10, 1983.

Burton, Sala (widow of Phillip Burton, sister-in-law of John Lowell Burton) (D Calif.) April 1, 1925–Feb. 1, 1987; House June 21, 1983–Feb. 1, 1987.

Burton, Theodore Elijah (R Ohio) Dec. 20, 1851–Oct. 28, 1929; House 1889–91, 1895–1909, 1921–Dec. 15, 1928; Senate 1909–15, Dec. 15, 1928–Oct. 28, 1929.

Burwell, William Armisted (R Va.) March 15, 1780–Feb. 16, 1821; House Dec. 1, 1806–Feb. 16, 1821.

Busbey, Fred Ernst (R Ill.) Feb. 8, 1895–Feb. 11, 1966; House 1943–45, 1947–49, 1951–55.

Busby, George Henry (D Ohio) June 10, 1794–Aug. 22, 1869; House 1851–53.

Busby, Thomas Jefferson (D Miss.) July 26, 1884–Oct. 18, 1964; House 1923–35.

Busey, Samuel Thompson (D Ill.) Nov. 16, 1835–Aug. 12, 1909; House 1891–93.

Bush, Alvin Ray (R Pa.) June 4, 1893–Nov. 5, 1959; House 1951–Nov. 5, 1959.

Bush, George Herbert Walker (son of Prescott Sheldon Bush, father of Pres. George W. Bush and Gov. John Ellis "Jeb" Bush of Fla.) (R Texas) June 12, 1924– ; House 1967–71; president 1989–93; vice president 1981–89; chair Rep. Nat. Comm. Jan. 1973–Sept. 1974.

Bush, Prescott Sheldon (father of George Herbert Walker Bush; grandfather of Pres. George W. Bush and Gov. John Ellis "Jeb" Bush of Fla.) (R Conn.) May 15, 1895–Oct. 8, 1972; Senate Nov. 4, 1952–Jan. 2, 1963.

Bushfield, Harlan John (husband of Vera Cahalan Bushfield) (R S.D.) Aug. 6, 1882–Sept. 27, 1948; Senate 1943–Sept. 27, 1948; Gov. Jan. 3, 1939–Jan. 5, 1943.

Bushfield, Vera Cahalan (widow of Harlan John Bushfield) (R S.D.) Aug. 9, 1889–April 16, 1976; Senate Oct. 6–Dec. 26, 1948.

Bushnell, Allen Ralph (D Wis.) July 18, 1833–March 29, 1909; House 1891–93.

Bushong, Robert Grey (grandson of Anthony Ellmaker Roberts) (R Pa.) June 10, 1883–April 6, 1951; House 1927–29.

Bustamante, Albert Garza (D Texas) April 8, 1935– ; House 1985–93.

Butler, Andrew Pickens (son of William Butler born in 1759, brother of William Butler born in 1790, uncle of Matthew Calbraith Butler) (SRD S.C.) Nov. 18, 1796–May 25, 1857; Senate Dec. 4, 1846–May 25, 1857.

Butler, Benjamin Franklin (grandfather of Butler Ames, father-in-law of Adelbert Ames) (R Mass.) Nov. 5, 1818–Jan. 11, 1893; House 1867–75, 1877–79; Gov. Jan. 4, 1883–Jan. 3, 1884 (Democrat/Greenback).

Butler, Chester Pierce (W Pa.) March 21, 1798–Oct. 5, 1850; House 1847–Oct. 5, 1850.

Butler, Ezra (R Vt.) Sept. 24, 1763–July 12, 1838; House 1813–15; Gov. Oct. 13, 1826–Oct. 10, 1828 (Democratic Republican).

Butler, Hugh Alfred (R Neb.) Feb. 28, 1878–July 1, 1954; Senate 1941–July 1, 1954; chair Senate Public Lands 1947–48; chair Senate Interior and Insular Affairs 1948–49, 1953–54.

Butler, James Joseph (D Mo.) Aug. 29, 1862–May 31, 1917; House 1901–June 28, 1902, Nov. 4, 1902–Feb. 26, 1903, 1903–05.

Butler, John Cornelius (R N.Y.) July 2, 1887–Aug. 13, 1953; House April 22, 1941–49, 1951–53.

Butler, John Marshall (R Md.) July 21, 1897–March 14, 1978; Senate 1951–63.

Butler, Josiah (R N.H.) Dec. 4, 1779–Oct. 27, 1854; House 1817–23.

Butler, Manley Caldwell (R Va.) June 2, 1925– ; House Nov. 7, 1972–83.

Butler, Marion (P N.C.) May 20, 1863–June 3, 1938; Senate 1895–1901.

Butler, Matthew Calbraith (son of William Butler born in 1790, grandson of William Butler born in 1759, nephew of Andrew Pickens Butler) (D S.C.) March 8, 1836–April 14, 1909; Senate 1877–95.

Butler, Mounce Gore (D Tenn.) May 11, 1849–Feb. 13, 1917; House 1905–07.

Butler, Pierce (D S.C.) July 11, 1744–Feb. 15, 1822; Senate 1789–Oct. 25, 1796, Nov. 4, 1802–Nov. 21, 1804; Cont. Cong. 1787.

Butler, Robert Reyburn (grandson of Roderick Randum Butler) (R Ore.) Sept. 24, 1881–Jan. 7, 1933; House Nov. 6, 1928–Jan. 7, 1933.

Butler, Roderick Randum (grandfather of Robert Reyburn Butler) (R Tenn.) April 9, 1827–Aug. 18, 1902; House 1867–75, 1887–89.

Butler, Sampson Hale (D S.C.) Jan. 3, 1803–March 16, 1848; House 1839–Sept. 27, 1842.

Butler, Thomas (R La.) April 14, 1785–Aug. 7, 1847; House Nov. 16, 1818–21.

Butler, Thomas Belden (W Conn.) Aug. 22, 1806–June 8, 1873; House 1849–51.

Butler, Thomas Stalker (R Pa.) Nov. 4, 1855–May 26, 1928; House 1897–May 26, 1928 (1897–99 Independent Republican).

Butler, Walter Halben (D Iowa) Feb. 13, 1852–April 24, 1931; House 1891–93.

Butler, William (father of Andrew Pickens Butler and William Butler, below, grandfather of Matthew Calbraith Butler) (R S.C.) Dec. 17, 1759–Nov. 15, 1821; House 1801–13.

Butler, William (son of William Butler, above, brother of Andrew Pickens Butler, father of Matthew Calbraith Butler) (W S.C.) Feb. 1, 1790–Sept. 25, 1850; House 1841–43.

Butler, William Morgan (R Mass.) Jan. 29, 1861–March 29, 1937; Senate Nov. 13, 1924–Dec. 6, 1926; chair Rep. Nat. Comm. 1924–28.

Butler, William Orlando (D Ky.) April 19, 1791–Aug. 6, 1880; House 1839–43.

Butman, Samuel (– Maine) 1788–Oct. 9, 1864; House 1827–31.

Butterfield, George K. (D N.C.) April 27, 1947– ; House July 20, 2004– .

Butterfield, Martin (R N.Y.) Dec. 8, 1790–Aug. 6, 1866; House 1859–61.

Butterworth, Benjamin (R Ohio) Oct. 22, 1837–Jan. 16, 1898; House 1879–83, 1885–91.

Button, Daniel Evan (R N.Y.) Nov. 1, 1917– ; House 1967–71.

Buttz, Charles Wilson (R S.C.) Nov. 16, 1837–July 20, 1913; House Nov. 7, 1876–77.

Buyer, Steve (R Ind.) Nov. 26, 1958– ; House 1993– ; chair House Veterans Affairs 2005– .

Bynum, Jesse Atherton (D N.C.) May 23, 1797–Sept. 23, 1868; House 1833–41 (1833–37 Jacksonian).

Bynum, William Dallas (D Ind.) June 26, 1846–Oct. 21, 1927; House 1885–95.

Byrd, Adam Monroe (D Miss.) July 6, 1859–June 21, 1912; House 1903–11.

Byrd, Harry Flood (father of Harry Flood Byrd Jr., nephew of Henry De La Warr Flood and Joel West Flood) (D Va.) June 10, 1887–Oct. 20, 1966; Senate 1933–Nov. 10, 1965; chair Senate Finance 1955–65; Gov. Feb. 1, 1926–Jan. 15, 1930.

Byrd, Harry Flood Jr. (son of Harry Flood Byrd) (I Va.) Dec. 20, 1914– ; Senate Nov. 12, 1965–83 (1965–71 Democrat).

Byrd, Robert Carlyle (D W.Va.) Nov. 20, 1917– ; House 1953–59; Senate 1959– ; Senate majority leader 1977–81, 1987–89; Senate minority leader 1981–87; elected pres. pro tempore Jan. 3, 1989–1995, June 6, 2001–03; chair Senate Appropriations 1989–95, Jan. 3, 2001–Jan. 20, 2001, June 6, 2001–03.

Byrne, Emmet Francis (R Ill.) Dec. 6, 1896–Sept. 25, 1974; House 1957–59.

Byrne, James Aloysius (D Pa.) June 22, 1906–Sept. 3, 1980; House 1953–73.

Byrne, Leslie L. (D Va.) Oct. 27, 1946– ; House 1993–95.

Byrne, William Thomas (D N.Y.) March 6, 1876–Jan. 27, 1952; House 1937–Jan. 27, 1952.

Byrnes, James Francis (D S.C.) May 2, 1879–April 9, 1972; House 1911–25; Senate 1931–July 8, 1941; assoc. justice July 8, 1941–Oct. 3, 1942; secretary of state July 3, 1945–Jan. 21, 1947; Gov. Jan. 16, 1951–Jan. 18, 1955.

Byrnes, John William (R Wis.) June 12, 1913–Jan. 12, 1985; House 1945–73.

Byrns, Joseph Wellington (father of Joseph Wellington Byrns Jr.) (D Tenn.) July 20, 1869–June 4, 1936; House 1909–June 4, 1936; House majority leader 1933–35; Speaker 1935–June 4, 1936.

Byrns, Joseph Wellington Jr. (son of Joseph Wellington Byrns) (D Tenn.) Aug. 15, 1903–March 8, 1973; House 1939–41.

Byrns, Samuel (D Mo.) March 4, 1848–July 9, 1914; House 1891–93.

Byron, Beverly Barton Butcher (widow of Goodloe Edgar Byron, daughter-in-law of Katharine Edgar Byron and William Devereaux Byron) (D Md.) July 26, 1932– ; House 1979–93.

Byron, Goodloe Edgar (son of Katharine Edgar Byron and William Devereaux Byron, great-grandson of Louis Emory McComas, husband of Beverly Barton Butcher Byron) (D Md.) June 22, 1929–Oct. 11, 1978; House 1971–Oct. 11, 1978.

Byron, Katharine Edgar (widow of William Devereaux Byron, mother of Goodloe Edgar Byron, granddaughter of Louis Emory McComas, mother-in-law of Beverly Barton Butcher Byron) (D Md.) Oct. 25, 1903–Dec. 28, 1976; House May 27, 1941–43.

Byron, William Devereaux (husband of Katharine Edgar Byron, father of Goodloe Edgar Byron, father-in-law of Beverly Barton Butcher Byron) (D Md.) May 15, 1895–Feb. 27, 1941; House 1939–Feb. 27, 1941.

Cabaniss, Thomas Banks (cousin of Thomas Chipman McRae) (D Ga.) Aug. 31, 1835–Aug. 14, 1915; House 1893–95.

Cabell, Earle (D Texas) Oct. 27, 1906–Sept. 24, 1975; House 1965–73.

Cabell, Edward Carrington (W Fla.) Feb. 5, 1816–Feb. 28, 1896; House Oct. 6, 1845–Jan. 24, 1846 (no party), 1847–53.

Cabell, George Craighead (D Va.) Jan. 25, 1836–June 23, 1906; House 1875–87.

Cabell, Samuel Jordan (R Va.) Dec. 15, 1756–Aug. 4, 1818; House 1795–1803.

Cable, Benjamin Taylor (D Ill.) Aug. 11, 1853–Dec. 13, 1923; House 1891–93.

Cable, John Levi (great-grandson of Joseph Cable) (R Ohio) April 15, 1884–Sept. 15, 1971; House 1921–25, 1929–33.

Cable, Joseph (great-grandfather of John Levi Cable) (D Ohio) April 17, 1801–May 1, 1880; House 1849–53.

Cabot, George (great-grandfather of Henry Cabot Lodge, great-great-grandfather of Henry Cabot Lodge Jr.) (– Mass.) Dec. 3, 1752–April 18, 1823; Senate 1791–June 9, 1796.

Cadmus, Cornelius Andrew (D N.J.) Oct. 7, 1844–Jan. 20, 1902, House 1891–95.

Cadwalader, John (D Pa.) April 1, 1805–Jan. 26, 1879; House 1855–57.

Cadwalader, Lambert (– N.J.) 1742–Sept. 13, 1823; House 1789–91, 1793–95; Cont. Cong. 1785–87.

Cady, Claude Ernest (D Mich.) May 28, 1878–Nov. 30, 1953; House 1933–35.

Cady, Daniel (uncle of John Watts Cady) (F N.Y.) April 29, 1773–Oct. 31, 1859; House 1815–17.

Cady, John Watts (nephew of Daniel Cady) (– N.Y.) June 28, 1790–Jan. 5, 1854; House 1823–25.

Caffery, Donelson (grandfather of Patrick Thomson Caffery) (D La.) Sept. 10, 1835–Dec. 30, 1906; Senate Dec. 31, 1892–1901.

Caffery, Patrick Thomson (grandson of Donelson Caffery) (D La.) July 6, 1932– ; House 1969–73.

Cage, Harry (J Miss.) ?–1859; House 1833–35.

Cahill, William Thomas (R N.J.) June 25, 1912–July 1, 1996; House 1959–Jan. 19, 1970; Gov. Jan. 20, 1970–Jan. 15, 1974.

Cahoon, William (AMas. Vt.) Jan. 12, 1774–May 30, 1833; House 1829–33.

Cain, Harry Pulliam (R Wash.) Jan. 10, 1906–March 3, 1979; Senate Dec. 26, 1946–53.

Cain, Richard Harvey (R S.C.) April 12, 1825–Jan. 18, 1887; House 1873–75, 1877–79.

Caine, John Thomas (PP Utah) Jan. 8, 1829–Sept. 20, 1911; House (Terr. Del.) Nov. 7, 1882–93 (1882–89 Democrat).

Cake, Henry Lutz (R Pa.) Oct. 6, 1827–Aug. 26, 1899; House 1867–71.

Calder, William Musgrave (R N.Y.) March 3, 1869–March 3, 1945; House 1905–15; Senate 1917–23.

Calderhead, William Alexander (R Kan.) Sept. 26, 1844–Dec. 18, 1928; House 1895–97, 1899–1911.

Caldwell, Alexander (R Kan.) March 1, 1830–May 19, 1917; Senate 1871–March 24, 1873.

Caldwell, Andrew Jackson (D Tenn.) July 22, 1837–Nov. 22, 1906; House 1883–87.

Caldwell, Ben Franklin (D Ill.) Aug. 2, 1848–Dec. 29, 1924; House 1899–1905, 1907–09.

Caldwell, Charles Pope (D N.Y.) June 18, 1875–July 31, 1940; House 1915–21.

Caldwell, George Alfred (D Ky.) Oct. 18, 1814–Sept. 17, 1866; House 1843–45, 1849–51.

Caldwell, Greene Washington (D N.C.) April 13, 1806–July 10, 1864; House 1841–43.

Caldwell, James (R Ohio) Nov. 30, 1770–May 1838; House 1813–17.

Caldwell, John Alexander (R Ohio) April 21, 1852–May 24, 1927; House 1889–May 4, 1894.

Caldwell, John Henry (D Ala.) April 4, 1826–Sept. 4, 1902; House 1873–77.

Caldwell, John William (D Ky.) Jan. 15, 1837–July 4, 1903; House 1877–83.

Caldwell, Joseph Pearson (W N.C.) March 5, 1808–June 30, 1853; House 1849–53.

Caldwell, Millard Fillmore (D Fla.) Feb. 6, 1897–Oct. 23, 1984; House 1933–41; Gov. Jan. 2, 1945–Jan. 4, 1949.

Caldwell, Patrick Calhoun (D S.C.) March 10, 1801–Nov. 22, 1855; House 1841–43.

Caldwell, Robert Porter (D Tenn.) Dec. 16, 1821–March 12, 1885; House 1871–73.

Caldwell, William Parker (D Tenn.) Nov. 8, 1832–June 7, 1903; House 1875–79.

Cale, Thomas (I Alaska) Sept. 17, 1848–Feb. 3, 1941; House (Terr. Del.) 1907–09.

Calhoon, John (W Ky.) 1797–?; House 1835–39.

Calhoun, John Caldwell (cousin of John Ewing Colhoun and Joseph Calhoun) (R S.C.) March 18, 1782–March 31, 1850; House 1811–Nov. 3, 1817; Senate Dec. 29, 1832–43, Nov. 26, 1845–March 31, 1850; vice president 1825–Dec. 28, 1832 (Democratic Republican); secretary of war Oct. 8, 1817–March 7, 1825; secretary of state April 1, 1844–March 10, 1845.

Calhoun, Joseph (cousin of John Caldwell Calhoun and John Ewing Colhoun) (R S.C.) Oct. 22, 1750–April 14, 1817; House June 2, 1807–11.

Calhoun, William Barron (W Mass.) Dec. 29, 1796–Nov. 8, 1865; House 1835–43.

Calkin, Hervey Chittenden (D N.Y.) March 23, 1828–April 20, 1913; House 1869–71.

Calkins, William Henry (R Ind.) Feb. 18, 1842–Jan. 29, 1894; House 1877–Oct. 20, 1884.

Call, Jacob (– Ind.) ?–April 20, 1826; House Dec. 23, 1824–25.

Call, Richard Keith (uncle of Wilkinson Call) (– Fla.) Oct. 24, 1792–Sept. 14, 1862; House (Terr. Del.) 1823–25; Gov. (Fla. Terr.) 1835–40, 1841–44.

Call, Wilkinson (nephew of Richard Keith Call, cousin of James David Walker) (D Fla.) Jan. 9, 1834–Aug. 24, 1910; Senate 1879–97.

Callahan, Herbert Leon "Sonny" (R Ala.) Sept. 11, 1932– ; House 1985–2003.

Callahan, James Yancy (FSil. Okla.) Dec. 19, 1852–May 3, 1935; House (Terr. Del.) 1897–99.

Callan, Clair Armstrong (D Neb.) March 20, 1920– ; House 1965–67.

Callaway, Howard Hollis "Bo" (R Ga.) April 2, 1927– ; House 1965–67.

Callaway, Oscar (D Texas) Oct. 2, 1872–Jan. 31, 1947; House 1911–17.

Callis, John Benton (R Ala.) Jan. 3, 1828–Sept. 24, 1898; House July 21, 1868–69.

Calvert, Charles Benedict (U Md.) Aug. 24, 1808–May 12, 1864; House 1861–63.

Calvert, Ken (R Calif.) June 8, 1953– ; House 1993– .

Calvin, Samuel (W Pa.) July 30, 1811–March 12, 1890; House 1849–51.

Cambreleng, Churchill Caldom (D N.Y.) Oct. 24, 1786–April 30, 1862; House 1821–39 (1821–29 no party, 1829–37 Jacksonian).

Camden, Johnson Newlon (father of Johnson Newlon Camden Jr.) (D W.Va.) March 6, 1828–April 25, 1908; Senate 1881–87, Jan. 25, 1893–95.

Camden, Johnson Newlon Jr. (son of Johnson Newlon Camden) (D Ky.) Jan. 5, 1865–Aug. 16, 1942; Senate June 16, 1914–15.

Cameron, Angus (R Wis.) July 4, 1826–March 30, 1897; Senate 1875–81, March 14, 1881–85.

Cameron, James Donald (son of Simon Cameron) (R Pa.) May 14, 1833–Aug. 30, 1918; Senate March 20, 1877–97; secretary of war May 22, 1876–March 3, 1877; chair Rep. Nat. Comm. 1879–80.

Cameron, Ralph Henry (R Ariz.) Oct. 21, 1863–Feb. 12, 1953; House (Terr. Del.) 1909–Feb. 18, 1912; Senate 1921–27.

Cameron, Ronald Brooks (D Calif.) Aug. 16, 1927– ; House 1963–67.

Cameron, Simon (father of James Donald Cameron) (R Pa.) March 8, 1799–June 26, 1889; Senate March 13, 1845–49 (no party), 1857–March 4, 1861, 1867–March 12, 1877; secretary of war March 5, 1861–Jan. 14, 1862.

Caminetti, Anthony (D Calif.) July 30, 1854–Nov. 17, 1923; House 1891–95.

Camp, Albert Sidney (D Ga.) July 26, 1892–July 24, 1954; House Aug. 1, 1939–July 24, 1954.

Camp, David (R Mich.) July 9, 1953– ; House 1991– .

Camp, John Henry (R N.Y.) April 4, 1840–Oct. 12, 1892; House 1877–83.

Camp, John Newbold Happy (R Okla.) May 11, 1908–Sept. 27, 1987; House 1969–75.

Campbell, Albert James (D Mont.) Dec. 12, 1857–Aug. 9, 1907; House 1899–1901.

Campbell, Alexander (R Ohio) 1779–Nov. 5, 1857; Senate Dec. 11, 1809–13.

Campbell, Alexander (I Ill.) Oct. 4, 1814–Aug. 8, 1898; House 1875–77.

Campbell, Ben Nighthorse (R Colo.) April 13, 1933– ; House 1987–93 (Democrat); Senate 1993–2005 (1993–March 3, 1995 Democrat); chair Senate Indian Affairs 1995–Jan. 3, 2001, Jan. 20, 2001–June 6, 2001, 2003–05.

Campbell, Brookins (D Tenn.) 1808–Dec. 25, 1853; House March 4–Dec. 25, 1853.

Campbell, Carroll Ashmore Jr. (R S.C.) July 24, 1940– ; House 1979–87; Gov. Jan. 14, 1987–Jan. 11, 1995.

Campbell, Courtney Warren (D Fla.) April 29, 1895–Dec. 22, 1971; House 1953–55.

Campbell, Ed Hoyt (R Iowa) March 6, 1882–April 26, 1969; House 1929–33.

Campbell, Felix (D N.Y.) Feb. 28, 1829–Nov. 8, 1902; House 1883–91.

Campbell, George Washington (R Tenn.) Feb. 9, 1769–Feb. 17, 1848; House 1803–09; Senate Oct. 8, 1811–Feb. 11, 1814, Oct. 10, 1815–April 20, 1818; secretary of the Treasury Feb. 9–Oct. 5, 1814.

Campbell, Guy Edgar (R Pa.) Oct. 9, 1871–Feb. 17, 1940; House 1917–33 (1917–23 Democrat).

Campbell, Howard Edmond (R Pa.) Jan. 4, 1890–Jan. 6, 1971; House 1945–47.

Campbell, Jacob Miller (R Pa.) Nov. 20, 1821–Sept. 27, 1888; House 1877–79, 1881–87.

Campbell, James Edwin (nephew of Lewis Davis Campbell) (D Ohio) July 7, 1843–Dec. 18, 1924; House June 20, 1884–89; Gov. Jan. 13, 1890–Jan. 11, 1892.

Campbell, James Hepburn (W Pa.) Feb. 8, 1820–April 12, 1895; House 1855–57, 1859–63.

Campbell, James Romulus (D Ill.) May 4, 1853–Aug. 12, 1924; House 1897–99.

Campbell, John (F Md.) Sept. 11, 1765–June 23, 1828; House 1801–11.

Campbell, John (brother of Robert Blair Campbell) (D S.C.) ?–May 19, 1845; House 1829–31 (Jacksonian), 1837–45 (1837–39 Nullifier).

Campbell, John Goulder (D Ariz.) June 25, 1827–Dec. 22, 1903; House (Terr. Del.) 1879–81.

Campbell, John Hull (AP Pa.) Oct. 10, 1800–Jan. 19, 1868; House 1845–47.

Campbell, John Pierce Jr. (AP Ky.) Dec. 8, 1820–Oct. 29, 1888; House 1855–57.

Campbell, John Wilson (R Ohio) Feb. 23, 1782–Sept. 24, 1833; House 1817–27.

Campbell, Lewis Davis (uncle of James Edwin Campbell) (D Ohio) Aug. 9, 1811–Nov. 26, 1882; House 1849–May 25, 1858 (1849–55 Whig, 1855–57 American Party, 1857–May 25, 1858 Republican), 1871–73.

Campbell, Philip Pitt (R Kan.) April 25, 1862–May 26, 1941; House 1903–23.

Campbell, Robert Blair (brother of John Campbell of S.C.) (N S.C.) ?–July 12, 1862; House 1823–25 (no party), Feb. 27, 1834–37.

Campbell, Samuel (– N.Y.) July 11, 1773–June 2, 1853; House 1821–23.

Campbell, Thomas Jefferson (W Tenn.) 1786–April 13, 1850; House 1841–43.

Campbell, Thompson (D Ill.) 1811–Dec. 6, 1868; House 1851–53.

Campbell, Timothy John (D N.Y.) Jan. 8, 1840–April 7, 1904; House Nov. 3, 1885–89, 1891–95.

Campbell, Tom (R Calif.) Aug. 14, 1952– ; House 1989–93; House Dec. 15, 1995–2001.

Campbell, William Bowen (cousin of Henry Bowen) (U Tenn.) Feb. 1, 1807–Aug. 19, 1867; House 1837–43 (Whig), July 24, 1866–67; Gov. Oct. 16, 1851–Oct. 16, 1853 (Whig).

Campbell, William W. (AP N.Y.) June 10, 1806–Sept. 7, 1881; House 1845–47.

Campbell, William Wildman (R Ohio) April 2, 1853–Aug. 13, 1927; House 1905–07.

Canady, Charles T. (R Fla.) June 22, 1954– ; House 1993–2001.

Canby, Richard Sprigg (W Ohio) Sept. 30, 1808–July 27, 1895; House 1847–49.

Candler, Allen Daniel (cousin of Ezekiel Samuel Candler Jr. and Milton Anthony Candler) (D Ga.) Nov. 4, 1834–Oct. 26, 1910; House 1883–91; Gov. Oct. 29, 1898–Oct. 25, 1902.

Candler, Ezekiel Samuel Jr. (nephew of Milton Anthony Candler, cousin of Allen Daniel Candler) (D Miss.) Jan. 18, 1862–Dec. 18, 1944; House 1901–21.

Candler, John Wilson (R Mass.) Feb. 10, 1828–March 16, 1903; House 1881–83, 1889–91.

Candler, Milton Anthony (uncle of Ezekiel Samuel Candler Jr., cousin of Allen Daniel Candler) (D Ga.) Jan. 11, 1837–Aug. 8, 1909; House 1875–79.

Canfield, Gordon (R N.J.) April 15, 1898–June 20, 1972; House 1941–61.

Canfield, Harry Clifford (D Ind.) Nov. 22, 1875–Feb. 9, 1945; House 1923–33.

Cannon, Arthur Patrick (D Fla.) May 22, 1904–Jan. 23, 1966; House 1939–47.

Cannon, Christopher (R Utah) Oct. 20, 1950– ; House 1997– .

Cannon, Clarence Andrew (D Mo.) April 11, 1879–May 12, 1964; House 1923–May 12, 1964; chair House Appropriations 1949–53, 1955–64.

Cannon, Frank Jenne (son of George Quayle Cannon) (R Utah) Jan. 25, 1859–July 25, 1933; House (Terr. Del.) 1895–Jan. 4, 1896; Senate Jan. 22, 1896–99.

Cannon, George Quayle (father of Frank Jenne Cannon) (R Utah) Jan. 11, 1827–April 12, 1901; House (Terr. Del.) 1873–81.

Cannon, Howard Walter (D Nev.) Jan. 26, 1912–March 5, 2002; Senate 1959–83; chair Senate Rules and Administration 1973–77; chair Senate Select Standards and Conduct 1975–77; chair Senate Commerce, Science, and Transportation 1978–81.

Cannon, Joseph Gurney (R Ill.) May 7, 1836–Nov. 12, 1926; House 1873–91, 1893–1913, 1915–23; Speaker Nov. 9, 1903–05, Dec. 4, 1905–07, Dec. 2, 1907–09, March 15, 1909–11.

Cannon, Marion (P Calif.) Oct. 30, 1834–Aug. 27, 1920; House 1893–95.

Cannon, Newton (R Tenn.) May 22, 1781–Sept. 16, 1841; House Sept. 16, 1814–17, 1819–23; Gov. Oct. 12, 1835–Oct. 14, 1839 (Whig).

Cannon, Raymond Joseph (D Wis.) Aug. 26, 1894–Nov. 25, 1951; House 1933–39.

Cantor, Eric I. (R Va.) June 6, 1963– ; House 2001– .

Cantor, Jacob Aaron (D N.Y.) Dec. 6, 1854–July 2, 1921; House Nov. 4, 1913–15.

Cantrill, James Campbell (D Ky.) July 9, 1870–Sept. 2, 1923; House 1909–Sept. 2, 1923.

Cantwell, Maria (D Wash.) Oct. 13, 1958– ; House 1993–95; Senate 2001– .

Capehart, Homer Earl (R Ind.) June 6, 1897–Sept. 3, 1979; Senate 1945–63; chair Senate Banking and Currency 1953–55.

Capehart, James (D W.Va.) March 7, 1847–April 28, 1921; House 1891–95.

Caperton, Allen Taylor (son of Hugh Caperton) (D W.Va.) Nov. 21, 1810–July 26, 1876; Senate 1875–July 26, 1876.

Caperton, Hugh (father of Allen Taylor Caperton) (F Va.) April 17, 1781–Feb. 9, 1847; House 1813–15.

Capito, Shelley Moore (daughter of Gov. Arch Alfred Moore Jr. of W.Va.) (R W.Va.) Nov. 26, 1953– ; House 2001– .

Capozzoli, Louis Joseph (D N.Y.) March 6, 1901–Oct. 8, 1982; House 1941–45.

Capper, Arthur (R Kan.) July 14, 1865–Dec. 19, 1951; Senate 1919–49; chair Senate Agriculture and Forestry 1947–49; Gov. Jan. 11, 1915–Jan. 13, 1919.

Capps, Lois D. (widow of Walter Capps) (D Calif.) Jan. 10, 1938– ; House March 17, 1998– .

Capps, Walter (husband of Lois D. Capps) (D Calif.) May 5, 1934–Oct. 28, 1997; House 1997–Oct. 28, 1997.

Capron, Adin Ballou (R R.I.) Jan. 9, 1841–March 17, 1911; House 1897–1911.

Capstick, John Henry (R N.J.) Sept. 2, 1856–March 17, 1918; House 1915–March 17, 1918.

Capuano, Michael Everett (R Mass.) Jan. 9, 1952– ; House 1999– .

Caputo, Bruce Faulkner (R N.Y.) Aug. 7, 1943– ; House 1977–79.

Caraway, Hattie Wyatt (widow of Thaddeus Horatius Caraway) (D Ark.) Feb. 1, 1878–Dec. 21, 1950; Senate Nov. 13, 1931–Jan. 2, 1945.

Caraway, Thaddeus Horatius (husband of Hattie Wyatt Caraway) (D Ark.) Oct. 17, 1871–Nov. 6, 1931; House 1913–21; Senate 1921–Nov. 6, 1931.

Carden, Cap Robert (D Ky.) Dec. 17, 1866–June 13, 1935; House 1931–June 13, 1935.

Cardin, Benjamin Louis (D Md.) Oct. 5, 1943– ; House 1987– .

Cardoza, Dennis (D Calif.) March 31, 1959– ; House 2003– .

Carew, John Francis (nephew of Thomas Francis Magner) (D N.Y.) April 16, 1873–April 10, 1951; House 1913–Dec. 28, 1929.

Carey, Hugh Leo (D N.Y.) April 11, 1919– ; House 1961–Dec. 31, 1974; Gov. Jan. 1, 1975–Jan. 1, 1983.

Carey, John (R Ohio) April 5, 1792–March 17, 1875; House 1859–61.

Carey, Joseph Maull (father of Robert Davis Carey) (R Wyo.) Jan. 19, 1845–Feb. 5, 1924; House (Terr. Del.) 1885–July 10, 1890; Senate Nov. 15, 1890–95; Gov. Jan. 2, 1911–Jan. 4, 1915.

Carey, Robert Davis (son of Joseph Maull Carey) (R Wyo.) Aug. 12, 1878–Jan. 17, 1937; Senate Dec. 1, 1930–37; Gov. Jan. 6, 1919–Jan. 1, 1923.

Carleton, Ezra Child (D Mich.) Sept. 6, 1838–July 24, 1911; House 1883–87.

Carleton, Peter (R N.H.) Sept. 19, 1755–April 29, 1828; House 1807–09.

Carley, Patrick J. (D N.Y.) Feb. 2, 1866–Feb. 25, 1936; House 1927–35.

Carlile, John Snyder (U Va.) Dec. 16, 1817–Oct. 24, 1878; House 1855–57 (American Party), March 4–July 9, 1861; Senate July 9, 1861–65.

Carlin, Charles Creighton (D Va.) April 8, 1866–Oct. 14, 1938; House Nov. 5, 1907–19.

Carlisle, John Griffin (D Ky.) Sept. 5, 1835–July 31, 1910; House 1877–May 26, 1890; Speaker Dec. 3, 1883–85, Dec. 7, 1885–87, Dec. 5, 1887–89; Senate May 26, 1890–Feb. 4, 1893; secretary of the Treasury March 7, 1893–March 5, 1897.

Carlson, Cliffard Dale (R Ill.) Dec. 30, 1915–Aug. 28, 1977; House April 4, 1972–73.

Carlson, Frank (R Kan.) Jan. 23, 1893–May 30, 1987; House 1935–47; Senate Nov. 29, 1950–69; chair Senate Post Office and Civil Service 1953–55; Gov. Jan. 13, 1947–Nov. 28, 1950.

Carlton, Henry Hull (D Ga.) May 14, 1835–Oct. 26, 1905; House 1887–91.

Carlyle, Frank Ertel (D N.C.) April 7, 1897–Oct. 2, 1960; House 1949–57.

Carmack, Edward Ward (D Tenn.) Nov. 5, 1858–Nov. 9, 1908; House 1897–1901; Senate 1901–07.

Carman, Gregory Wright (R N.Y.) Jan. 31, 1937– ; House 1981–83.

Carmichael, Archibald Hill (D Ala.) June 17, 1864–July 15, 1947; House Nov. 14, 1933–37.

Carmichael, Richard Bennett (J Md.) Dec. 25, 1807–Oct. 21, 1884; House 1833–35.

Carnahan, Albert Sidney Johnson (grandfather of Russ Carnahan, father-in-law of Jean Carnahan) (D Mo.) Jan. 9, 1897–March 24, 1968; House 1945–47, 1949–61.

Carnahan, Jean (daughter-in-law of Albert Sidney Johnson Carnahan, mother of Russ Carnahan) (D Mo.) Dec. 20, 1933– ; Senate Jan. 3, 2001–Nov. 25, 2002.

Carnahan, Russ (son of Gov. Mel Eugene Carnahan of Mo. and Jean Carnahan, grandson of Albert Sidney Johnson Carnahan) (D Mo.) July 10, 1958– ; House 2005– .

Carnes, Thomas Petters (– Ga.) 1762–May 5, 1822; House 1793–95.

Carney, Charles Joseph (D Ohio) April 17, 1913–Oct. 7, 1987; House Nov. 3, 1970–79.

Carney, William (R N.Y.) July 1, 1942– ; House 1979–87.

Carpenter, Cyrus Clay (R Iowa) Nov. 24, 1829–May 29, 1898; House 1879–83; Gov. Jan. 11, 1872–Jan. 13, 1876.

Carpenter, Davis (W N.Y.) Dec. 25, 1799–Oct. 22, 1878; House Nov. 8, 1853–55.

Carpenter, Edmund Nelson (R Pa.) June 27, 1865–Nov. 4, 1952; House 1925–27.

Carpenter, Levi D. (D N.Y.) Aug. 21, 1802–Oct. 27, 1856; House Nov. 5, 1844–45.

Carpenter, Lewis Cass (R S.C.) Feb. 20, 1836–March 6, 1908; House Nov. 3, 1874–75.

Carpenter, Matthew Hale (R Wis.) Dec. 22, 1824–Feb. 24, 1881; Senate 1869–75, 1879–Feb. 24, 1881; elected pres. pro tempore March 12, 1873, March 26, 1873, Dec. 11, 1873, Dec. 23, 1874.

Carpenter, Terry McGovern (D Neb.) March 28, 1900–April 27, 1978; House 1933–35.

Carpenter, William Randolph (D Kan.) April 24, 1894–July 26, 1956; House 1933–37.

Carper, Thomas Richard (D Del.) Jan. 23, 1947– ; House 1983–93; Senate 2001– ; Gov. Jan. 19, 1993–Jan. 3, 2001.

Carr, Francis (father of James Carr) (R Mass.) Dec. 6, 1751–Oct. 6, 1821; House April 6, 1812–13.

Carr, James (son of Francis Carr) (F Mass.) Sept. 9, 1777–Aug. 24, 1818; House 1815–17.

Carr, John (D Ind.) April 9, 1793–Jan. 20, 1845; House 1831–37 (Jacksonian), 1839–41.

Carr, Milton Robert "Bob" (D Mich.) March 27, 1943– ; House 1975–81, 1983–95.

Carr, Nathan Tracy (D Ind.) Dec. 25, 1833–May 28, 1885; House Dec. 5, 1876–77.

Carr, Wooda Nicholas (D Pa.) Feb. 6, 1871–June 28, 1953; House 1913–15.

Carrier, Chester Otto (R Ky.) May 5, 1897–Sept. 24, 1980; House Nov. 30, 1943–45.

Carrigg, Joseph Leonard (R Pa.) Feb. 23, 1901–Feb. 6, 1989; House Nov. 6, 1951–59.

Carroll, Charles (cousin of Daniel Carroll) (– Md.) Sept. 19, 1737–Nov. 14, 1832; Senate 1789–Nov. 30, 1792; Cont. Cong. 1776–78.

Carroll, Charles Holker (W N.Y.) May 4, 1794–June 8, 1865; House 1843–47.

Carroll, Daniel (uncle of Richard Brent, cousin of Charles Carroll) (– Md.) July 22, 1730–May 7, 1796; House 1789–91; Cont. Cong. 1781–83.

Carroll, James (D Md.) Dec. 2, 1791–Jan. 16, 1873; House 1839–41.

Carroll, John Albert (D Colo.) July 30, 1901–Aug. 31, 1983; House 1947–51; Senate 1957–63.

Carroll, John Michael (D N.Y.) April 27, 1823–May 8, 1901; House 1871–73.

Carson, Brad R. (D Okla.) March 11, 1967– ; House 2001–05.

Carson, Henderson Haverfield (R Ohio) Oct. 25, 1893–Oct. 5, 1971; House 1943–45, 1947–49.

Carson, Julia (D Ind.) July 8, 1938– ; House 1997– .

Carson, Samuel Price (– N.C.) Jan. 22, 1798–Nov. 2, 1838; House 1825–33.

Carss, William Leighton (FL Minn.) Feb. 15, 1865–May 31, 1931; House 1919–21 (Union Laborite), 1925–29.

Carter, Albert Edward (R Calif.) July 5, 1881–Aug. 8, 1964; House 1925–45.

Carter, Charles David (D Okla.) Aug. 16, 1868–April 9, 1929; House Nov. 16, 1907–27.

Carter, John (J S.C.) Sept. 10, 1792–June 20, 1850; House Dec. 11, 1822–29 (Dec. 11, 1822–27 no party).

Carter, John Rice (R Texas) Nov. 6, 1941– ; House 2003– .

Carter, Luther Cullen (R N.Y.) Feb. 25, 1805–Jan. 3, 1875; House 1859–61.

Carter, Steven V. (D Iowa) Oct. 8, 1915–Nov. 4, 1959; House Jan. 3–Nov. 4, 1959.

Carter, Thomas Henry (R Mont.) Oct. 30, 1854–Sept. 17, 1911; House (Terr. Del.) March 4–Nov. 7, 1889, (Rep.) Nov. 8, 1889–91; Senate 1895–1901, 1905–11; chair Rep. Nat. Comm. 1892–96.

Carter, Tim Lee (R Ky.) Sept. 2, 1910–March 27, 1987; House 1965–81.

Carter, Timothy Jarvis (D Maine) Aug. 18, 1800–March 14, 1838; House Sept. 4, 1837–March 14, 1838.

Carter, Vincent Michael (R Wyo.) Nov. 6, 1891–Dec. 30, 1972; House 1929–35.

Carter, William Blount (W Tenn.) Oct. 22, 1792–April 17, 1848; House 1835–41.

Carter, William Henry (R Mass.) June 15, 1864–April 23, 1955; House 1915–19.

Cartter, David Kellogg (D Ohio) June 22, 1812–April 16, 1887; House 1849–53.

Cartwright, Wilburn (D Okla.) Jan. 12, 1892–March 14, 1979; House 1927–43.

Caruth, Asher Graham (D Ky.) Feb. 7, 1844–Nov. 25, 1907; House 1887–95.

Caruthers, Robert Looney (W Tenn.) July 31, 1800–Oct. 2, 1882; House 1841–43.

Caruthers, Samuel (D Mo.) Oct. 13, 1820–July 20, 1860; House 1853–59 (1853–57 Whig).

Carville, Edward Peter (D Nev.) May 14, 1885–June 27, 1956; Senate July 25, 1945–47; Gov. Jan. 2, 1939–July 24, 1945.

Cary, George (– Ga.) Aug. 7, 1789–Sept. 10, 1843; House 1823–27.

Cary, George Booth (D Va.) 1811–March 5, 1850; House 1841–43.

Cary, Glover H. (D Ky.) May 1, 1885–Dec. 5, 1936; House 1931–Dec. 5, 1936.

Cary, Jeremiah Eaton (D N.Y.) April 30, 1803–June 1888; House 1843–45.

Cary, Samuel Fenton (IR Ohio) Feb. 18, 1814–Sept. 29, 1900; House Nov. 21, 1867–69.

Cary, Shepard (D Maine) July 3, 1805–Aug. 9, 1866; House May 10, 1844–45.

Cary, William Joseph (R Wis.) March 22, 1865–Jan. 2, 1934; House 1907–19.

Case, Charles (R Ind.) Dec. 21, 1817–June 30, 1883; House Dec. 7, 1857–61.

Case, Clifford Philip (R N.J.) April 16, 1904–March 5, 1982; House 1945–Aug. 16, 1953; Senate 1955–79.

Case, Edward E. "Ed" (D Hawaii) Sept. 27, 1952– ; House Nov. 30, 2002– .

Case, Francis Higbee (R S.D.) Dec. 9, 1896–June 22, 1962; House 1937–51; Senate 1951–June 22, 1962; chair Senate District of Columbia 1953–55.

Case, Walter (– N.Y.) 1776–Oct. 7, 1859; House 1819–21.

Casey, John Joseph (D Pa.) May 26, 1875–May 5, 1929; House 1913–17, 1919–21, 1923–25, 1927–May 5, 1929.

Casey, Joseph (W Pa.) Dec. 17, 1814–Feb. 10, 1879; House 1849–51.

Casey, Joseph Edward (D Mass.) Dec. 27, 1898–Sept. 1, 1980; House 1935–43.

Casey, Levi (R S.C.) about 1752–Feb. 3, 1807; House 1803–Feb. 3, 1807.

Casey, Lyman Rufus (R N.D.) May 6, 1837–Jan. 26, 1914; Senate Nov. 25, 1889–93.

Casey, Robert Randolph (D Texas) July 27, 1915–April 17, 1986; House 1959–Jan. 22, 1976.

Casey, Samuel Lewis (U Ky.) Feb. 12, 1821–Aug. 25, 1902; House March 10, 1862–63.

Casey, Zadoc (ID Ill.) March 7, 1796–Sept. 4, 1862; House 1833–43 (1833–37 Jacksonian, 1837–41 Democrat).

Caskie, John Samuels (D Va.) Nov. 8, 1821–Dec. 16, 1869; House 1851–59.

Cason, Thomas Jefferson (R Ind.) Sept. 13, 1828–July 10, 1901; House 1873–77.

Cass, Lewis (great-great-grandfather of Cass Ballenger) (D Mich.) Oct. 9, 1782–June 17, 1866; Senate 1845–May 29, 1848, 1849–57; elected pres. pro tempore Dec. 4, 1854; Gov. (Mich. Terr.) 1813–31; secretary of war Aug. 1, 1831–Oct. 5, 1836; secretary of state March 6, 1857–Dec. 14, 1860.

Cassedy, George (– N.J.) Sept. 16, 1783–Dec. 31, 1842; House 1821–27.

Cassel, Henry Burd (R Pa.) Oct. 19, 1855–April 28, 1926; House Nov. 5, 1901–09.

Casserly, Eugene (D Calif.) Nov. 13, 1820–June 14, 1883; Senate 1869–Nov. 19, 1873.

Cassidy, George Williams (D Nev.) April 25, 1836–June 24, 1892; House 1881–85.

Cassidy, James Henry (R Ohio) Oct. 28, 1869–Aug. 23, 1926; House April 20, 1909–11.

Cassingham, John Wilson (D Ohio) June 22, 1840–March 14, 1930; House 1901–05.

Castellow, Bryant Thomas (D Ga.) July 29, 1876–July 23, 1962; House Nov. 8, 1932–37.

Castle, Curtis Harvey (P Calif.) Oct. 4, 1848–July 12, 1928; House 1897–99.

Castle, James Nathan (D Minn.) May 23, 1836–Jan. 2, 1903; House 1891–93.

Castle, Michael Newbold (R Del.) July 2, 1939– ; House 1993– ; Gov. Jan. 15, 1985–Dec. 31, 1992.

Castor, George Albert (R Pa.) Aug. 6, 1855–Feb. 19, 1906; House Feb. 16, 1904–Feb. 19, 1906.

Caswell, Lucien Bonaparte (R Wis.) Nov. 27, 1827–April 26, 1919; House 1875–83, 1885–91.

Catchings, Thomas Clendinen (D Miss.) Jan. 11, 1847–Dec. 24, 1927; House 1885–1901.

Cate, George Washington (D Wis.) Sept. 17, 1825–March 7, 1905; House 1875–77.

Cate, William Henderson (D Ark.) Nov. 11, 1839–Aug. 23, 1899; House 1889–March 5, 1890, 1891–93.

Cathcart, Charles William (D Ind.) July 24, 1809–Aug. 22, 1888; House 1845–49; Senate Dec. 6, 1852–53.

Catlin, George Smith (D Conn.) Aug. 24, 1808–Dec. 26, 1851; House 1843–45.

Catlin, Theron Ephron (R Mo.) May 16, 1878–March 19, 1960; House 1911–Aug. 12, 1912.

Catron, Thomas Benton (R N.M.) Oct. 6, 1840–May 15, 1921; House (Terr. Del.) 1895–97; Senate March 27, 1912–17.

Cattell, Alexander Gilmore (R N.J.) Feb. 12, 1816–April 8, 1894; Senate Sept. 19, 1866–71.

Caulfield, Bernard Gregory (D Ill.) Oct. 18, 1828–Dec. 19, 1887; House Feb. 1, 1875–77.

Caulfield, Henry Stewart (R Mo.) Dec. 9, 1873–May 11, 1966; House 1907–09; Gov. Jan. 14, 1929–Jan. 9, 1933.

Causey, John Williams (D Del.) Sept. 19, 1841–Oct. 1, 1908; House 1891–95.

Causin, John M. S. (W Md.) 1811–Jan. 30, 1861; House 1843–45.

Cavalcante, Anthony (D Pa.) Feb. 6, 1897–Oct. 29, 1966; House 1949–51.

Cavanaugh, James Michael (D Mont.) July 4, 1823–Oct. 30, 1879; House May 11, 1858–59 (Minn.), 1867–71 (Terr. Del.).

Cavanaugh, John Joseph III (D Neb.) Aug. 1, 1945– ; House 1977–81.

Cavicchia, Peter Angelo (R N.J.) May 22, 1879–Sept. 11, 1967; House 1931–37.

Cederberg, Elford Alfred (R Mich.) March 6, 1918– ; House 1953–Dec. 31, 1978.

Celler, Emanuel (D N.Y.) May 6, 1888–Jan. 15, 1981; House 1923–73; chair House Judiciary 1949–53, 1955–73.

Cessna, John (R Pa.) June 29, 1821–Dec. 13, 1893; House 1869–71, 1873–75.

Chabot, Steve (R Ohio) Jan. 22, 1953– ; House 1995– .

Chace, Jonathan (R R.I.) July 22, 1829–June 30, 1917; House 1881–Jan. 26, 1885; Senate Jan. 20, 1885–April 9, 1889.

Chadwick, E. Wallace (R Pa.) Jan. 17, 1884–Aug. 18, 1969; House 1947–49.

Chafee, John Hubbard (father of Lincoln Chaffee) (R R.I.) Oct. 22, 1922–Oct. 24, 1999; Senate Dec. 29, 1976–Oct. 24, 1999; Gov. Jan. 1, 1963–Jan. 7, 1969; chair Senate Environment and Public Works 1995–Oct. 24, 1999.

Chafee, Lincoln (son of John Hubbard Chaffee) (R R.I.) March 26, 1953– ; Senate Nov. 4, 1999– .

Chaffee, Calvin Clifford (AP Mass.) Aug. 28, 1811–Aug. 8, 1896; House 1855–59.

Chaffee, Jerome Bunty (R Colo.) April 17, 1825–March 9, 1886; House (Terr. Del.) 1871–75; Senate Nov. 15, 1876–79.

Chalmers, James Ronald (son of Joseph Williams Chalmers) (I Miss.) Jan. 12, 1831–April 9, 1898; House 1877–April 29, 1882 (Democrat), June 25, 1884–85.

Chalmers, Joseph Williams (father of James Ronald Chalmers) (D Miss.) 1807–June 16, 1853; Senate Nov. 3, 1845–47.

Chalmers, William Wallace (R Ohio) Nov. 1, 1861–Oct. 1, 1944; House 1921–23, 1925–31.

Chamberlain, Charles Ernest (R Mich.) July 22, 1917–Nov. 25, 2002; House 1957–Dec. 31, 1974.

Chamberlain, Ebenezer Mattoon (D Ind.) Aug. 20, 1805–March 14, 1861; House 1853–55.

Chamberlain, George Earle (D Ore.) Jan. 1, 1854–July 9, 1928; Senate 1909–21; Gov. Jan. 14, 1903–Feb. 28, 1909.

Chamberlain, Jacob Payson (R N.Y.) Aug. 1, 1802–Oct. 5, 1878; House 1861–63.

Chamberlain, John Curtis (F N.H.) June 5, 1772–Dec. 8, 1834; House 1809–11.

Chamberlain, William (F Vt.) April 27, 1755–Sept. 27, 1828; House 1803–05, 1809–11.

Chambers, David (– Ohio) Nov. 25, 1780–Aug. 8, 1864; House Oct. 9, 1821–23.

Chambers, Ezekiel Forman (– Md.) Feb. 28, 1788–Jan. 30, 1867; Senate Jan. 24, 1826–Dec. 20, 1834.

Chambers, George (AMas. Pa.) Feb. 24, 1786–March 25, 1866; House 1833–37.

Chambers, Henry H. (– Ala.) Oct. 1, 1790–Jan. 24, 1826; Senate 1825–Jan. 24, 1826.

Chambers, John (W Ky.) Oct. 6, 1780–Sept. 21, 1852; House Dec. 1, 1828–29 (no party), 1835–39; Gov. (Iowa Terr.) 1841–45.

Chambliss, Saxby (R Ga.) Nov. 10, 1943– ; House 1995–2003; Senate 2003– ; chair Senate Agriculture, Nutrition, and Forestry 2005– .

Champion, Edwin Van Meter (D Ill.) Sept. 18, 1890–Feb. 11, 1976; House 1937–39.

Champion, Epaphroditus (F Conn.) April 6, 1756–Dec. 22, 1834; House 1807–17.

Champlin, Christopher Grant (F R.I.) April 12, 1768–March 18, 1840; House 1797–1801; Senate June 26, 1809–Oct. 2, 1811.

Chandler, Albert Benjamin "Happy" (D Ky.) July 14, 1898–June 15, 1991; Senate Oct. 10, 1939–Nov. 1, 1945; Gov. Dec. 10, 1935–Oct. 9, 1939, Dec. 13, 1955–Dec. 8, 1959.

Chandler, Albert Benjamin "Ben" (D Ky.) Sept. 12, 1959– ; House Feb. 23, 2004– .

Chandler, John (brother of Thomas Chandler, uncle of Zachariah Chandler) (R Maine) Feb. 1, 1762–Sept. 25, 1841; House 1805–09 (Mass.); Senate June 14, 1820–29.

Chandler, Joseph Ripley (W Pa.) Aug. 22, 1792–July 10, 1880; House 1849–55.

Chandler, Rod Dennis (great-great-great-nephew of Zachariah Chandler) (R Wash.) July 13, 1942– ; House 1983–93.

Chandler, Thomas (brother of John Chandler, uncle of Zachariah Chandler) (J N.H.) Aug. 10, 1772–Jan. 28, 1866; House 1829–33.

Chandler, Thomas Alberter (R Okla.) July 26, 1871–June 22, 1953; House 1917–19, 1921–23.

Chandler, Walter "Clift" (D Tenn.) Oct. 5, 1887–Oct. 1, 1967; House 1935–Jan. 2, 1940.

Chandler, Walter Marion (R N.Y.) Dec. 8, 1867–March 16, 1935; House 1913–19 (1913–17 Progressive), 1921–23.

Chandler, William Eaton (R N.H.) Dec. 28, 1835–Nov. 30, 1917; Senate June 14, 1887–89, June 18, 1889–1901; secretary of the navy April 16, 1882–March 6, 1885.

Chandler, Zachariah (nephew of John Chandler and Thomas Chandler, grandfather of Frederick Hale, great-great-great-uncle of Rod Dennis Chandler) (R Mich.) Dec. 10, 1813–Nov. 1, 1879; Senate 1857–75, Feb. 22, 1879–Nov. 1, 1879; secretary of the interior Oct. 19, 1875–March 11, 1877; chair Rep. Nat. Comm. 1876–79.

Chaney, John (D Ohio) Jan. 12, 1790–April 10, 1881; House 1833–39 (1833–37 Jacksonian).

Chaney, John Crawford (R Ind.) Feb. 1, 1853–April 26, 1940; House 1905–09.

Chanler, John Winthrop (father of William Astor Chanler) (D N.Y.) Sept. 14, 1826–Oct. 19, 1877; House 1863–69.

Chanler, William Astor (son of John Winthrop Chanler) (D N.Y.) June 11, 1867–March 4, 1934; House 1899–1901.

Chapin, Alfred Clark (grandfather of Hamilton Fish Jr. born in 1926) (D N.Y.) March 8, 1848–Oct. 2, 1936; House Nov. 3, 1891–Nov. 16, 1892.

Chapin, Chester Williams (D Mass.) Dec. 16, 1798–June 10, 1883; House 1875–77.

Chapin, Graham Hurd (J N.Y.) Feb. 10, 1799–Sept. 8, 1843; House 1835–37.

Chapman, Andrew Grant (son of John Grant Chapman) (D Md.) Jan. 17, 1839–Sept. 25, 1892; House 1881–83.

Chapman, Augustus Alexandria (D Va.) March 9, 1803–June 7, 1876; House 1843–47.

Chapman, Bird Beers (D Neb.) Aug. 24, 1821–Sept. 21, 1871; House (Terr. Del.) 1855–57.

Chapman, Charles (W Conn.) June 21, 1799–Aug. 7, 1869; House 1851–53.

Chapman, Henry (D Pa.) Feb. 4, 1804–April •11, 1891; House 1857–59.

Chapman, Jim (D Texas) March 8, 1945– ; House Aug. 3, 1985–97.

Chapman, John (F Pa.) Oct. 18, 1740–Jan. 27, 1800; House 1797–1799.

Chapman, John Grant (father of Andrew Grant Chapman) (W Md.) July 5, 1798–Dec. 10, 1856; House 1845–49.

Chapman, Pleasant Thomas (R Ill.) Oct. 8, 1854–Jan. 31, 1931; House 1905–11.

Chapman, Reuben (D Ala.) July 15, 1799–May 16, 1882; House 1835–47 (1835–37 Jacksonian); Gov. Dec. 16, 1847–Dec. 17, 1849.

Chapman, Virgil Munday (D Ky.) March 15, 1895–March 8, 1951; House 1925–29, 1931–49; Senate 1949–March 8, 1951.

Chapman, William Williams (D Iowa) Aug. 11, 1808–Oct. 18, 1892; House (Terr. Del.) Sept. 10, 1838–Oct. 27, 1840.

Chappell, Absalom Harris (cousin of Lucius Quintus Cincinnatus Lamar) (W Ga.) Dec. 18, 1801–Dec. 11, 1878; House Oct. 2, 1843–45.

Chappell, John Joel (R S.C.) Jan. 19, 1782–May 23, 1871; House 1813–17.

Chappell, William Venroe Jr. (D Fla.) Feb. 3, 1922–March 30, 1989; House 1969–89.

Chappie, Eugene A. (R Calif.) March 28, 1920–May 31, 1992; House 1981–87.

Charles, William Barclay (R N.Y.) April 3, 1861–Nov. 25, 1950; House 1915–17.

Charlton, Robert Milledge (D Ga.) Jan. 19, 1807–Jan. 18, 1854; Senate May 31, 1852–53.

Chase, Dudley (uncle of Salmon Portland Chase and Dudley Chase Denison) (R Vt.) Dec. 30, 1771–Feb. 23, 1846; Senate 1813–Nov. 3, 1817 (Jefferson Democrat), 1825–31.

Chase, George William (W N.Y.) ?–April 17, 1867; House 1853–55.

Chase, Jackson Burton (R Neb.) Aug. 19, 1890–May 4, 1974; House 1955–57.

Chase, James Mitchell (R Pa.) Dec. 19, 1891–Jan. 1, 1945; House 1927–33.

Chase, Lucien Bonaparte (D Tenn.) Dec. 5, 1817–Dec. 4, 1864; House 1845–49.

Chase, Ray P. (R Minn.) March 12, 1880–Sept. 18, 1948; House 1933–35.

Chase, Salmon Portland (nephew of Dudley Chase, cousin of Dudley Chase Denison) (R Ohio) Jan. 13, 1808–May 7, 1873; Senate 1849–55 (Free-Soiler), March 4, 1861–March 6, 1861; Gov. Jan. 14, 1856–Jan. 9, 1860; secretary of the Treasury March 7, 1861–June 30, 1864; chief justice Dec. 15, 1864–May 7, 1873.

Chase, Samuel (– N.Y.) ?–Aug. 3, 1838; House 1827–29.

Chastain, Elijah Webb (D Ga.) Sept. 25, 1813–April 9, 1874; House 1851–55 (1851–53 Unionist).

Chatham, Richard Thurmond (D N.C.) Aug. 16, 1896–Feb. 5, 1957; House 1949–57.

Chaves, Jose Francisco (R N.M.) June 27, 1833–Nov. 26, 1904; House (Terr. Del.) 1865–67, Feb. 20, 1869–71.

Chavez, Dennis (D N.M.) April 8, 1888–Nov. 18, 1962; House 1931–35; Senate May 11, 1935–Nov. 18, 1962; chair Senate Public Works 1949–53, 1955–62.

Cheadle, Joseph Bonaparte (R Ind.) Aug. 14, 1842–May 28, 1904; House 1887–91.

Cheatham, Henry Plummer (R N.C.) Dec. 27, 1857–Nov. 29, 1935; House 1889–93.

Cheatham, Richard (W Tenn.) Feb. 20, 1799–Sept. 9, 1845; House 1837–39.

Chelf, Frank Leslie (D Ky.) Sept. 22, 1907–Sept. 1, 1982; House 1945–67.

Cheney, Person Colby (R N.H.) Feb. 25, 1828–June 19, 1901; Senate Nov. 24, 1886–June 14, 1887; Gov. June 10, 1875–June 6, 1877.

Cheney, Richard Bruce (R Wyo.) Jan. 30, 1941– ; House 1979–March 17, 1989; secretary of defense March 21, 1989–Jan. 20, 1993; vice president 2001– .

Chenoweth, Helen (R Idaho) Jan. 27, 1938– ; House 1995–2001.

Chenoweth, John Edgar (R Colo.) Aug. 17, 1897–Jan. 2, 1986; House 1941–49, 1951–65.

Chesney, Chester Anton (D Ill.) March 9, 1916–Sept. 20, 1986; House 1949–51.

Chesnut, James Jr. (D S.C.) Jan. 18, 1815–Feb. 1, 1885; Senate Dec. 3, 1858–Nov. 10, 1860.

Chetwood, William (W N.J.) June 17, 1771–Dec. 17, 1857; House Dec. 5, 1836–37.

Cheves, Langdon (R S.C.) Sept. 17, 1776–June 26, 1857; House Dec. 31, 1810–15; Speaker Jan. 19, 1814–15.

Chickering, Charles Addison (R N.Y.) Nov. 26, 1843–Feb. 13, 1900; House 1893–Feb. 13, 1900.

Chilcott, George Miles (R Colo.) Jan. 2, 1828–March 6, 1891; House (Terr. Del.) 1867–69; Senate April 17, 1882–Jan. 27, 1883.

Child, Thomas Jr. (W N.Y.) March 22, 1818–March 9, 1869; elected to the House for the term beginning 1855 but never qualified or attended session owing to illness.

Childs, Robert Andrew (R Ill.) March 22, 1845–Dec. 19, 1915; House 1893–95.

Childs, Timothy (W N.Y.) 1785–Nov. 8, 1847; House 1829–31 (Anti-Mason), 1835–39, 1841–43.

Chiles, Lawton Mainor Jr. (D Fla.) April 3, 1930–Dec. 12, 1998; Senate 1971–89; chair Senate Budget 1987–89; Gov. Jan. 8, 1991–Dec. 12, 1998.

Chilton, Horace (grandson of Thomas Chilton) (D Texas) Dec. 29, 1853–June 12, 1932; Senate June 10, 1891–March 22, 1892, 1895–1901.

Chilton, Samuel (W Va.) Sept. 7, 1804–Jan. 14, 1867; House 1843–45.

Chilton, Thomas (grandfather of Horace Chilton) (AJ Ky.) July 30, 1798–Aug. 15, 1854; House Dec. 22, 1827–31 (no party), 1833–35.

Chilton, William Edwin (D W.Va.) March 17, 1858–Nov. 7, 1939; Senate 1911–17.

Chindblom, Carl Richard (R Ill.) Dec. 21, 1870–Sept. 12, 1956; House 1919–33.

Chinn, Joseph William (J Va.) Nov. 16, 1798–Dec. 5, 1840; House 1831–35.

Chinn, Thomas Withers (cousin of Robert Enoch Withers) (W La.) Nov. 22, 1791–May 22, 1852; House 1839–41.

Chiperfield, Burnett Mitchell (father of Robert Bruce Chiperfield) (R Ill.) June 14, 1870–June 24, 1940; House 1915–17, 1929–33.

Chiperfield, Robert Bruce (son of Burnett Mitchell Chiperfield) (R Ill.) Nov. 20, 1899–April 9, 1971; House 1939–63; chair House Foreign Affairs 1953–55.

Chipman, Daniel (brother of Nathaniel Chipman, great-uncle of John Logan Chipman) (F Vt.) Oct. 22, 1765–April 23, 1850; House 1815–May 5, 1816.

Chipman, John Logan (grandson of Nathaniel Chipman, great-nephew of Daniel Chipman) (D Mich.) June 5, 1830–Aug. 17, 1893; House 1887–Aug. 17, 1893.

Chipman, John Smith (D Mich.) Aug. 10, 1800–July 27, 1869; House 1845–47.

Chipman, Nathaniel (brother of Daniel Chipman, grandfather of John Logan Chipman) (F Vt.) Nov. 15, 1752–Feb. 13, 1843; Senate Oct. 17, 1797–1803.

Chipman, Norton Parker (R D.C.) March 7, 1836–Feb. 1, 1924; House (Del.) April 21, 1871–75.

Chisholm, Shirley Anita (D N.Y.) Nov. 30, 1924–Jan. 1, 2005; House 1969–83.

Chittenden, Martin (F Vt.) March 12, 1763–Sept. 5, 1840; House 1803–13; Gov. Oct. 23, 1813–Oct. 14, 1815.

Chittenden, Simeon Baldwin (R N.Y.) March 29, 1814–April 14, 1889; House Nov. 3, 1874–81 (Nov. 3, 1874–77 Independent Republican).

Chittenden, Thomas Cotton (W N.Y.) Aug. 30, 1788–Aug. 22, 1866; House 1839–43.

Choate, Rufus (W Mass.) Oct. 1, 1799–July 13, 1859; House 1831–June 30, 1834; Senate Feb. 23, 1841–45.

Chocola, Joseph Christopher "Chris" (R Ind.) Feb. 24, 1962– ; House 2003– .

Chrisman, James Stone (D Ky.) Sept. 14, 1818–July 29, 1881; House 1853–55.

Christensen, Donna M. C. (elected initially as Donna Christian-Green) (D V.I.) Sept. 19, 1945– ; House (Del.) 1997– .

Christensen, Jon (R Neb.) Feb. 20, 1963– ; House 1995–99.

Christgau, Victor Laurence August (R Minn.) Sept. 20, 1894–Oct. 10, 1991; House 1929–33.

Christiancy, Isaac Peckham (R Mich.) March 12, 1812–Sept. 8, 1890; Senate 1875–Feb. 10, 1879.

Christianson, Theodore (R Minn.) Sept. 12, 1883–Dec. 9, 1948; House 1933–37; Gov. Jan. 6, 1925–Jan. 6, 1931.

Christie, Gabriel (R Md.) 1755–April 1, 1808; House 1793–97 (no party), 1799–1801.

Christopher, George Henry (D Mo.) Dec. 9, 1888–Jan. 23, 1959; House 1949–51, 1955–Jan. 23, 1959.

Christopherson, Charles Andrew (R S.D.) July 23, 1871–Nov. 2, 1951; House 1919–33.

Chrysler, Dick (R Mich.) April 29, 1942– ; House 1995–97.

Chudoff, Earl (D Pa.) Nov. 15, 1907–May 17, 1993; House 1949–Jan. 5, 1958.

Church, Denver Samuel (D Calif.) Dec. 11, 1862–Feb. 21, 1952; House 1913–19, 1933–35.

Church, Frank Forrester (D Idaho) July 25, 1924–April 7, 1984; Senate 1957–81; chair Senate Foreign Relations 1979–81.

Church, Marguerite Stitt (widow of Ralph Edwin Church) (R Ill.) Sept. 13, 1892–May 26, 1990; House 1951–63.

Church, Ralph Edwin (husband of Marguerite Stitt Church) (R Ill.) May 5, 1883–March 21, 1950; House 1935–41, 1943–March 21, 1950.

Churchill, George Bosworth (R Mass.) Oct. 24, 1866–July 1, 1925; House March 4–July 1, 1925.

Churchill, John Charles (R N.Y.) Jan. 17, 1821–June 4, 1905; House 1867–71.

Churchwell, William Montgomery (D Tenn.) Feb. 20, 1826–Aug. 18, 1862; House 1851–55.

Cilley, Bradbury (uncle of Jonathan Cilley and Joseph Cilley) (F N.H.) Feb. 1, 1760–Dec. 17, 1831; House 1813–17.

Cilley, Jonathan (nephew of Bradbury Cilley, brother of Joseph Cilley) (D Maine) July 2, 1802–Feb. 24, 1838; House 1837–Feb. 24, 1838.

Cilley, Joseph (nephew of Bradbury Cilley, brother of Jonathan Cilley) (D N.H.) Jan. 4, 1791–Sept. 16, 1887; Senate June 13, 1846–47.

Citron, William Michael (D Conn.) Aug. 29, 1896–June 7, 1976; House 1935–39.

Claflin, William (R Mass.) March 6, 1818–Jan. 5, 1905; House 1877–81; Gov. Jan. 7, 1869–Jan. 4, 1872; chair Rep. Nat. Comm. 1868–72.

Clagett, Clifton (R N.H.) Dec. 3, 1762–Jan. 25, 1829; House 1803–05 (Federalist), 1817–21.

Clagett, William Horace (uncle of Samuel Barrett Pettengill) (R Mont.) Sept. 21, 1838–Aug. 3, 1901; House (Terr. Del.) 1871–73.

Clague, Frank (R Minn.) July 13, 1865–March 25, 1952; House 1921–33.

Claiborne, James Robert (D Mo.) June 22, 1882–Feb. 16, 1944; House 1933–37.

Claiborne, John (son of Thomas Claiborne born in 1749, brother of Thomas Claiborne born in 1780) (R Va.) 1777–Oct. 9, 1808; House 1805–Oct. 9, 1808.

Claiborne, John Francis Hamtramck (nephew of William Charles Cole Claiborne and Nathaniel Herbert Claiborne, great-great-grandfather of Claiborne de Borda Pell, great-nephew of Thomas Claiborne born in 1749, great-grandfather of Herbert Claiborne Pell Jr., great-great-great-uncle of Corinne Claiborne Boggs) (J Miss.) April 24, 1807–May 17, 1884; House 1835–37, July 18, 1837–Feb. 5, 1838.

Claiborne, Nathaniel Herbert (brother of William Charles Cole Claiborne, nephew of Thomas Claiborne born in 1749, uncle of John Francis Hamtramck Claiborne, great-great-great-great-uncle of Corinne Claiborne Boggs) (AJ Va.) Nov. 14, 1777–Aug. 15, 1859; House 1825–37 (1825–31 Jacksonian).

Claiborne, Thomas (father of John Claiborne and Thomas Claiborne born in 1780, uncle of Nathaniel Herbert Claiborne, great-uncle of John Francis Hamtramck Claiborne, great-great-great-great-great-uncle of Corinne Claiborne Boggs) (R Va.) Feb. 1, 1749–1812; House 1793–99, 1801–05.

Claiborne, Thomas (son of Thomas Claiborne born in 1749, brother of John Claiborne) (R Tenn.) May 17, 1780–Jan. 7, 1856; House 1817–19.

Claiborne, William Charles Cole (brother of Nathaniel Herbert Claiborne, nephew of Thomas Claiborne born in 1749, uncle of John Francis Hamtramck Claiborne, great-great-great-great-uncle of Corinne Claiborne Boggs) (D La.) 1775–Nov. 23, 1817; House 1797–1801; Senate March 4–Nov. 23, 1817; Gov. 1801–03 (Miss. Terr.), 1804–12 (Orleans Terr.), July 30, 1812–Dec. 16, 1816 (Democratic Republican).

Clancy, Donald Daniel (R Ohio) July 24, 1921– ; House 1961–77.

Clancy, John Michael (D N.Y.) May 7, 1837–July 25, 1903; House 1889–95.

Clancy, John Richard (D N.Y.) March 8, 1859–April 21, 1932; House 1913–15.

Clancy, Robert Henry (R Mich.) March 14, 1882–April 23, 1962; House 1923–25 (Democrat), 1927–33.

Clapp, Asa William Henry (D Maine) March 6, 1805–March 22, 1891; House 1847–49.

Clapp, Moses Edwin (R Minn.) May 21, 1851–March 6, 1929; Senate Jan. 23, 1901–17.

Clardy, John Daniel (D Ky.) Aug. 30, 1828–Aug. 20, 1918; House 1895–99.

Clardy, Kit Francis (R Mich.) June 17, 1892–Sept. 5, 1961; House 1953–55.

Clardy, Martin Linn (D Mo.) April 26, 1844–July 5, 1914; House 1879–89.

Clark, Abraham (– N.J.) Feb. 15, 1726–Sept. 15, 1794; House 1791–Sept. 15, 1794; Cont. Cong. 1776–78, 1780–83, 1786–88.

Clark, Alvah Augustus (cousin of James Nelson Pidcock) (D N.J.) Sept. 13, 1840–Dec. 27, 1912; House 1877–81.

Clark, Ambrose Williams (R N.Y.) Feb. 19, 1810–Oct. 13, 1887; House 1861–65.

Clark, Amos Jr. (R N.J.) Nov. 8, 1828–Oct. 31, 1912; House 1873–75.

Clark, Charles Benjamin (R Wis.) Aug. 24, 1844–Sept. 10, 1891; House 1887–91.

Clark, Charles Nelson (R Mo.) Aug. 21, 1827–Oct. 4, 1902; House 1895–97.

Clark, Christopher Henderson (brother of James Clark, uncle of John Bullock Clark, great-uncle of John Bullock Clark Jr.) (R Va.) 1767–Nov. 21, 1828; House Nov. 5, 1804–July 1, 1806.

Clark, Clarence Don (R Wyo.) April 16, 1851–Nov. 18, 1930; House Dec. 1, 1890–93; Senate Jan. 23, 1895–1917.

Clark, Daniel (– Orleans) about 1766–Aug. 16, 1813; House (Terr. Del.) Dec. 1, 1806–09.

Clark, Daniel (R N.H.) Oct. 24, 1809–Jan. 2, 1891; Senate June 27, 1857–July 27, 1866; elected pres. pro tempore April 26, 1864, Feb. 9, 1865.

Clark, David Worth (D Idaho) April 2, 1902–June 19, 1955; House 1935–39; Senate 1939–45.

Clark, Ezra Jr. (R Conn.) Sept. 12, 1813–Sept. 26, 1896; House 1855–59 (1855–57 American Party).

Clark, Frank (D Fla.) March 28, 1860–April 14, 1936; House 1905–25.

Clark, Frank Monroe (D Pa.) Dec. 24, 1915– ; House 1955–Dec. 31, 1974.

Clark, Franklin (D Maine) Aug. 2, 1801–Aug. 24, 1874; House 1847–49.

Clark, Henry Alden (R Pa.) Jan. 7, 1850–Feb. 15, 1944; House 1917–19.

Clark, Henry Selby (D N.C.) Sept. 9, 1809–Jan. 8, 1869; House 1845–47.

Clark, Horace Francis (ALD N.Y.) Nov. 29, 1815–June 19, 1873; House 1857–61 (1857–59 Democrat).

Clark, James (brother of Christopher Henderson Clark, uncle of John Bullock Clark, great-uncle of John Bullock Clark Jr.) (R Ky.) Jan. 16, 1770–Sept. 27, 1839; House 1813–16, Aug. 1, 1825–31; Gov. June 1, 1836–Sept. 27, 1839 (Whig).

Clark, James Beauchamp "Champ" (father of Joel Bennett Clark) (D Mo.) March 7, 1850–March 2, 1921; House 1893–95, 1897–March 2, 1921; House minority leader 1908–11, 1919–21; Speaker April 4, 1911–13, April 7, 1913–15, Dec. 6, 1915–17, April 2, 1917–19.

Clark, James West (R N.C.) Oct. 15, 1779–Dec. 20, 1843; House 1815–17.

Clark, Jerome Bayard (D N.C.) April 5, 1882–Aug. 26, 1959; House 1929–49.

Clark, Joel Bennett (son of James Beauchamp Clark) (D Mo.) Jan. 8, 1890–July 13, 1954; Senate Feb. 3, 1933–45.

Clark, John Bullock (father of John Bullock Clark Jr., nephew of Christopher Henderson Clark and James Clark) (D Mo.) April 17, 1802–Oct. 29, 1885; House Dec. 7, 1857–July 13, 1861.

Clark, John Bullock Jr. (son of John Bullock Clark, great-nephew of Christopher Henderson Clark and James Clark) (D Mo.) Jan. 14, 1831–Sept. 7, 1903; House 1873–83.

Clark, John Chamberlain (W N.Y.) Jan. 14, 1793–Oct. 25, 1852; House 1827–29 (no party), 1837–43 (1837–39 Democrat).

Clark, Joseph Sill (D Pa.) Oct. 21, 1901–Jan. 12, 1990; Senate 1957–69.

Clark, Lincoln (D Iowa) Aug. 9, 1800–Sept. 16, 1886; House 1851–53.

Clark, Linwood Leon (R Md.) March 21, 1876–Nov. 18, 1965; House 1929–31.

Clark, Lot (– N.Y.) May 23, 1788–Dec. 18, 1862; House 1823–25.

Clark, Richard Clarence "Dick" (D Iowa) Sept. 14, 1929– ; Senate 1973–79.

Clark, Robert (– N.Y.) June 12, 1777–Oct. 1, 1837; House 1819–21.

Clark, Rush (R Iowa) Oct. 1, 1834–April 29, 1879; House 1877–April 29, 1879.

Clark, Samuel (D Mich.) Jan. 1800–Oct. 2, 1870; House 1833–35 (J N.Y.), 1853–55.

Clark, Samuel Mercer (R Iowa) Oct. 11, 1842–Aug. 11, 1900; House 1895–99.

Clark, William (AMas. Pa.) Feb. 18, 1774–March 28, 1851; House 1833–37.

Clark, William Andrews (D Mont.) Jan. 8, 1839–March 2, 1925; Senate Dec. 4, 1899–May 15, 1900, 1901–07.

Clark, William Thomas (R Texas) June 29, 1831–Oct. 12, 1905; House March 31, 1870–May 13, 1872.

Clarke, Archibald Smith (brother of Staley Nichols Clarke) (R N.Y.) 1788–Dec. 4, 1821; House Dec. 2, 1816–17.

Clarke, Bayard (W N.Y.) March 17, 1815–June 20, 1884; House 1855–57.

Clarke, Beverly Leonidas (D Ky.) Feb. 11, 1809–March 17, 1860; House 1847–49.

Clarke, Charles Ezra (W N.Y.) April 8, 1790–Dec. 29, 1863; House 1849–51.

Clarke, Frank Gay (R N.H.) Sept. 10, 1850–Jan. 9, 1901; House 1897–Jan. 9, 1901.

Clarke, Freeman (R N.Y.) March 22, 1809–June 24, 1887; House 1863–65, 1871–75.

Clarke, James McClure (D N.C.) June 12, 1917–April 13, 1999; House 1983–85, 1987–91.

Clarke, James Paul (D Ark.) Aug. 18, 1854–Oct. 1, 1916; Senate 1903–Oct. 1, 1916; elected pres. pro tempore March 13, 1913, Dec. 6, 1915; Gov. Jan. 18, 1895–Jan. 12, 1897.

Clarke, John Blades (D Ky.) April 14, 1833–May 23, 1911; House 1875–79.

Clarke, John Davenport (husband of Marian Williams Clarke) (R N.Y.) Jan. 15, 1873–Nov. 5, 1933; House 1921–25, 1927–Nov. 5, 1933.

Clarke, John Hopkins (W R.I.) April 1, 1789–Nov. 23, 1870; Senate 1847–53.

Clarke, Marian Williams (widow of John Davenport Clarke) (R N.Y.) July 29, 1880–April 8, 1953; House Dec. 28, 1933–35.

Clarke, Reader Wright (R Ohio) May 18, 1812–May 23, 1872; House 1865–69.

Clarke, Richard Henry (D Ala.) Feb. 9, 1843–Sept. 26, 1906; House 1889–97.

Clarke, Sidney (R Kan.) Oct. 16, 1831–June 18, 1909; House 1865–71.

Clarke, Staley Nichols (brother of Archibald Smith Clarke) (W N.Y.) May 24, 1794–Oct. 14, 1860; House 1841–43.

Clason, Charles Russell (R Mass.) Sept. 3, 1890–July 7, 1985; House 1937–49.

Classon, David Guy (R Wis.) Sept. 27, 1870–Sept. 6, 1930; House 1917–23.

Clausen, Don Holst (R Calif.) April 27, 1923– ; House Jan. 22, 1963–83.

Clawson, Delwin Morgan (R Calif.) Jan. 11, 1914–May 5, 1992; House June 11, 1963–Dec. 31, 1978.

Clawson, Isaiah Dunn (R N.J.) March 30, 1822–Oct. 9, 1879; House 1855–59 (1855–57 Whig).

Clay, Alexander Stephens (D Ga.) Sept. 25, 1853–Nov. 13, 1910; Senate 1897–Nov. 13, 1910.

Clay, Brutus Junius (U Ky.) July 1, 1808–Oct. 11, 1878; House 1863–65.

Clay, Clement Claiborne Jr. (son of Clement Comer Clay) (D Ala.) Dec. 13, 1816–Jan. 3, 1882; Senate Nov. 29, 1853–Jan. 21, 1861.

Clay, Clement Comer (father of Clement Claiborne Clay Jr.) (D Ala.) Dec. 17, 1789–Sept. 7, 1866; House 1829–35 (no party); Senate June 19, 1837–Nov. 15, 1841; Gov. Nov. 21, 1835–July 17, 1837.

Clay, Henry (father of James Brown Clay) (W Ky.) April 12, 1777–June 29, 1852; Senate Nov. 19, 1806–07 (no party), Jan. 4, 1810–11 (no party), Nov. 10, 1831–March 31, 1842, 1849–June 29, 1852; House 1811–Jan. 19, 1814 (Republican), 1815–21 (Republican), 1823–March 6, 1825 (Republican); Speaker Nov. 4, 1811–13, May 24, 1813–Jan. 19, 1814, Dec. 4, 1815–17, Dec. 1, 1817–19, Dec. 6, 1819–Oct. 28, 1820, Dec. 1, 1823–25; secretary of state March 7, 1825–March 3, 1829.

Clay, James Brown (son of Henry Clay) (D Ky.) Nov. 9, 1817–Jan. 26, 1864; House 1857–59.

Clay, James Franklin (D Ky.) Oct. 29, 1840–Aug. 17, 1921; House 1883–85.

Clay, Joseph (R Pa.) July 24, 1769–Aug. 27, 1811; House 1803–08.

Clay, Matthew (R Va.) March 25, 1754–May 27, 1815; House 1797–1813, March 4–May 27, 1815.

Clay, William Lacy Jr. (son of William Lacy Clay Sr.) (D Mo.) July 27, 1956– ; House 2001– .

Clay, William Lacy Sr. (father of William Lacy Clay Jr.) (D Mo.) April 30, 1931– ; House 1969–2001; chair House Post Office and Civil Service 1991–95.

Claypool, Harold Kile (son of Horatio Clifford Claypool, cousin of John Barney Peterson) (D Ohio) June 2, 1886–Aug. 2, 1958; House 1937–43.

Claypool, Horatio Clifford (father of Harold Kile Claypool, cousin of John Barney Peterson) (D Ohio) Feb. 9, 1859–Jan. 19, 1921; House 1911–15, 1917–19.

Clayton, Augustin Smith (J Ga.) Nov. 27, 1783–June 21, 1839; House Jan. 21, 1832–35.

Clayton, Bertram Tracy (brother of Henry De Lamar Clayton) (D N.Y.) Oct. 19, 1862–May 30, 1918; House 1899–1901.

Clayton, Charles (R Calif.) Oct. 5, 1825–Oct. 4, 1885; House 1873–75.

Clayton, Eva (D N.C.) Sept. 16, 1934– ; House Nov. 4, 1992–2003.

Clayton, Henry De Lamar (brother of Bertram Tracy Clayton) (D Ala.) Feb. 10, 1857–Dec. 21, 1929; House 1897–May 25, 1914.

Clayton, John Middleton (nephew of Joshua Clayton, cousin of Thomas Clayton, great-great-uncle of Clayton Douglass Buck) (W Del.) July 24, 1796–Nov. 9, 1856; Senate 1829–Dec. 29, 1836 (no party), 1845–Feb. 23, 1849, 1853–Nov. 9, 1856; secretary of state March 8, 1849–July 22, 1850.

Clayton, Joshua (father of Thomas Clayton, uncle of John Middleton Clayton, son-in-law of Richard Bassett) (– Del.) July 20, 1744–Aug. 11, 1798; Senate Jan. 19–Aug. 11, 1798; Gov. June 2, 1789–Jan. 13, 1796 (Federalist).

Clayton, Powell (R Ark.) Aug. 7, 1833–Aug. 25, 1914; Senate 1871–77; Gov. July 2, 1868–March 17, 1871.

Clayton, Thomas (son of Joshua Clayton, cousin of John Middleton Clayton) (W Del.) July 1777–Aug. 21, 1854; House 1815–17 (Federalist); Senate Jan. 8, 1824–27 (no party), Jan. 9, 1837–47.

Cleary, William Edward (D N.Y.) July 20, 1849–Dec. 20, 1932; House March 5, 1918–21, 1923–27.

Cleaver, Emanuel II (D Mo.) Oct. 26, 1944– ; House 2005– .

Cleland, Max (D Ga.) Aug. 24, 1942– ; Senate 1997–2003.

Clemens, Jeremiah (D Ala.) Dec. 28, 1814–May 21, 1865; Senate Nov. 30, 1849–53.

Clemens, Sherrard (D Va.) April 28, 1820–June 30, 1881; House Dec. 6, 1852–53, 1857–61.

Clement, Robert Nelson (D Tenn.) Sept. 23, 1943– ; House Jan. 25, 1988–2003.

Clemente, Louis Gary (D N.Y.) June 10, 1908–May 13, 1968; House 1949–53.

Clements, Andrew Jackson (U Tenn.) Dec. 23, 1832–Nov. 7, 1913; House 1861–63.

Clements, Earle Chester (D Ky.) Oct. 22, 1896–March 12, 1985; House 1945–Jan. 6, 1948; Senate Nov. 27, 1950–57; Gov. Dec. 9, 1947–Nov. 27, 1950.

Clements, Isaac (R Ill.) March 31, 1837–May 31, 1909; House 1873–75.

Clements, Judson Claudius (D Ga.) Feb. 12, 1846–June 18, 1917; House 1881–91.

Clements, Newton Nash (D Ala.) Dec. 23, 1837–Feb. 20, 1900; House Dec. 8, 1880–81.

Clendenin, David (R Ohio) ?–?; House Oct. 11, 1814–17.

Cleveland, Chauncey Fitch (D Conn.) Feb. 16, 1799–June 6, 1887; House 1849–53; Gov. May 4, 1842–May 1844.

Cleveland, James Colgate (R N.H.) June 13, 1920–Dec. 3, 1995; House 1963–81.

Cleveland, Jesse Franklin (D Ga.) Oct. 25, 1804–June 22, 1841; House Oct. 5, 1835–39 (Oct. 5, 1835–37 Jacksonian).

Cleveland, Orestes (D N.J.) March 2, 1829–March 30, 1896; House 1869–71.

Clevenger, Cliff (R Ohio) Aug. 20, 1885–Dec. 13, 1960; House 1939–59.

Clevenger, Raymond Francis (D Mich.) June 6, 1926– ; House 1965–67.

Clever, Charles P. (D N.M.) Feb. 23, 1830–July 8, 1874; House (Terr. Del.) Sept. 2, 1867–Feb. 20, 1869.

Clifford, Nathan (D Maine) Aug. 18, 1803–July 25, 1881; House 1839–43; attorney general Oct. 17, 1846–March 17, 1848; assoc. justice Jan. 21, 1858–July 25, 1881.

Clift, Joseph Wales (R Ga.) Sept. 30, 1837–May 2, 1908; House July 25, 1868–69.

Clinch, Duncan Lamont (W Ga.) April 6, 1787–Nov. 27, 1849; House Feb. 15, 1844–45.

Cline, Cyrus (D Ind.) July 12, 1856–Oct. 5, 1923; House 1909–17.

Clinger, William Floyd Jr. (R Pa.) April 4, 1929– ; House 1979–97; chair House Government Reform and Oversight 1995–97.

Clingman, Thomas Lanier (D N.C.) July 27, 1812–Nov. 3, 1897; House 1843–45 (Whig), 1847–May 7, 1858 (Whig); Senate May 7, 1858–March 28, 1861.

Clinton, De Witt (half-brother of James Graham Clinton, cousin of George Clinton, nephew of Vice Pres. George Clinton) (R N.Y.) March 2, 1769–Feb. 11, 1828; Senate Feb. 9, 1802–Nov. 4, 1803; Gov. July 1, 1817–Jan. 1, 1823, Jan. 1, 1825–Feb. 11, 1828.

Clinton, George (cousin of De Witt Clinton and James Graham Clinton, son of Vice Pres. George Clinton) (R N.Y.) June 6, 1771–Sept. 16, 1809; House Feb. 14, 1805–09.

Clinton, Hillary Rodham (wife of Pres. William Jefferson "Bill" Clinton) Oct. 26, 1947– ; Senate 2001– ; first lady 1993–2001.

Clinton, James Graham (half-brother of De Witt Clinton, cousin of George Clinton, nephew of Vice Pres. George Clinton) (D N.Y.) Jan. 2, 1804–May 28, 1849; House 1841–45.

Clippinger, Roy (R Ill.) Jan. 13, 1886–Dec. 24, 1962; House Nov. 6, 1945–49.

Clopton, David (D Ala.) Sept. 29, 1820–Feb. 5, 1892; House 1859–Jan. 21, 1861.

Clopton, John (R Va.) Feb. 7, 1756–Sept. 11, 1816; House 1795–99, 1801–Sept. 11, 1816.

Clouse, Wynne F. (R Tenn.) Aug. 29, 1883–Feb. 19, 1944; House 1921–23.

Clover, Benjamin Hutchinson (P Kan.) Dec. 22, 1837–Dec. 30, 1899; House 1891–93.

Clowney, William Kennedy (N S.C.) March 21, 1797–March 12, 1851; House 1833–35, 1837–39.

Cluett, Ernest Harold (R N.Y.) July 13, 1874–Feb. 4, 1954; House 1937–43.

Clunie, Thomas Jefferson (D Calif.) March 25, 1852–June 30, 1903; House 1889–91.

Clyburn, James E. (D S.C.) July 21, 1940– ; House 1993– .

Clymer, George (– Pa.) March 16, 1739–Jan. 23, 1813; House 1789–91; Cont. Cong. 1776–77, 1780–82.

Clymer, Hiester (nephew of William Hiester, cousin of Isaac Ellmaker Hiester) (D Pa.) Nov. 3, 1827–June 12, 1884; House 1873–81.

Coad, Merwin (D Iowa) Sept. 28, 1924– ; House 1957–63.

Coady, Charles Pearce (D Md.) Feb. 22, 1868–Feb. 16, 1934; House Nov. 4, 1913–21.

Coats, Daniel Ray (R Ind.) May 16, 1943– ; House 1981–Jan. 1, 1989; Senate 1989–99.

Cobb, Amasa (R Wis.) Sept. 27, 1823–July 5, 1905; House 1863–71.

Cobb, Clinton Levering (R N.C.) Aug. 25, 1842–April 30, 1879; House 1869–75.

Cobb, David (– Mass.) Sept. 14, 1748–April 17, 1830; House 1793–95.

Cobb, George Thomas (D N.J.) Oct. 13, 1813–Aug. 12, 1870; House 1861–63.

Cobb, Howell (uncle of Howell Cobb, below) (R Ga.) Aug. 3, 1772–May 26, 1818; House 1807–12.

Cobb, Howell (nephew of Howell Cobb, above) (D Ga.) Sept. 7, 1815–Oct. 9, 1868; House 1843–51, 1855–57; Speaker Dec. 22, 1849–51; Gov. Nov. 5, 1851–Nov. 9, 1853 (Union Democrat); secretary of the Treasury March 7, 1857–Dec. 8, 1860.

Cobb, James Edward (– Ala.) Oct. 5, 1835–June 2, 1903; House 1887–April 21, 1896.

Cobb, Seth Wallace (D Mo.) Dec. 5, 1838–May 22, 1909; House 1891–97.

Cobb, Stephen Alonzo (R Kan.) June 17, 1833–Aug. 24, 1878; House 1873–75.

Cobb, Thomas Reed (D Ind.) July 2, 1828–June 23, 1892; House 1877–87.

Cobb, Thomas Willis (– Ga.) 1784–Feb. 1, 1830; House 1817–21, 1823–Dec. 6, 1824; Senate Dec. 6, 1824–28.

Cobb, Williamson Robert Winfield (D Ala.) June 8, 1807–Nov. 1, 1864; House 1847–Jan. 30, 1861.

Cobey, William Wilfred Jr. (R N.C.) May 13, 1939– ; House 1985–87.

Coble, Howard (R N.C.) March 18, 1931– ; House 1985– .

Coburn, Frank Potter (D Wis.) Dec. 6, 1858–Nov. 2, 1932; House 1891–93.

Coburn, John (R Ind.) Oct. 27, 1825–Jan. 28, 1908; House 1867–75.

Coburn, Stephen (R Maine) Nov. 11, 1817–July 4, 1882; House Jan. 2–March 3, 1861.

Coburn, Thomas Allen (R Okla.) March 14, 1948– ; House 1995–2001; Senate 2005– .

Cochran, Alexander Gilmore (D Pa.) March 20, 1846–May 1, 1928; House 1875–77.

Cochran, Charles Fremont (D Mo.) Sept. 27, 1846–Dec. 19, 1906; House 1897–1905.

Cochran, James (grandfather of James Cochrane Dobbin) (R N.C.) about 1767–April 7, 1813; House 1809–13.

Cochran, James (F N.Y.) Feb. 11, 1769–Nov. 7, 1848; House 1797–99.

Cochran, John Joseph (D Mo.) Aug. 11, 1880–March 6, 1947; House Nov. 2, 1926–47.

Cochran, Thomas Cunningham (R Pa.) Nov. 30, 1877–Dec. 10, 1957; House 1927–35.

Cochran, William Thad (R Miss.) Dec. 7, 1937– ; House 1973–Dec. 26, 1978; Senate Dec. 27, 1978– ; chair Senate Agriculture, Nutrition, and Forestry 2003–05; chair Senate Appropriations 2005– .

Cochrane, Aaron Van Schaick (nephew of Isaac Whitbeck Van Schaick) (R N.Y.) March 14, 1858–Sept. 7, 1943; House 1897–1901.

Cochrane, Clark Betton (uncle of George Cochrane Hazelton and Gerry Whiting Hazelton) (R N.Y.) May 31, 1815–March 5, 1867; House 1857–61.

Cochrane, John (D N.Y.) Aug. 27, 1813–Feb. 7, 1898; House 1857–61.

Cocke, John (son of William Cocke, uncle of William Michael Cocke) (– Tenn.) 1772–Feb. 16, 1854; House 1819–27.

Cocke, William (father of John Cocke, grandfather of William Michael Cocke) (R Tenn.) 1748–Aug. 22, 1828; Senate Aug. 2, 1796–March 3, 1797, April 22–Sept. 26, 1797, 1799–1805.

Cocke, William Michael (grandson of William Cocke, nephew of John Cocke) (W Tenn.) July 16, 1815–Feb. 6, 1896; House 1845–49.

Cockerill, Joseph Randolph (D Ohio) Jan. 2, 1818–Oct. 23, 1875; House 1857–59.

Cockran, William Bourke (D N.Y.) Feb. 28, 1854–March 1, 1923; House 1887–89, Nov. 3, 1891–95, Feb. 23, 1904–09, 1921–March 1, 1923.

Cockrell, Francis Marion (brother of Jeremiah Vardaman Cockrell) (D Mo.) Oct. 1, 1834–Dec. 13, 1915; Senate 1875–1905.

Cockrell, Jeremiah Vardaman (brother of Francis Marion Cockrell) (D Texas) May 7, 1832–March 18, 1915; House 1893–97.

Cocks, William Willets (brother of Frederick Cocks Hicks) (R N.Y.) July 24, 1861–May 24, 1932; House 1905–11.

Codd, George Pierre (R Mich.) Dec. 7, 1869–Feb. 16, 1927; House 1921–23.

Codding, James Hodge (R Pa.) July 8, 1849–Sept. 12, 1919; House Nov. 5, 1895–99.

Coelho, Anthony Lee "Tony" (D Calif.) June 15, 1942– ; House 1979–June 15, 1989.

Coffee, Harry Buffington (D Neb.) March 16, 1890–Oct. 3, 1972; House 1935–43.

Coffee, John (J Ga.) Dec. 3, 1782–Sept. 25, 1836; House 1833–Sept. 25, 1836.

Coffee, John Main (D Wash.) Jan. 23, 1897–June 3, 1983; House 1937–47.

Coffeen, Henry Asa (D Wyo.) Feb. 14, 1841–Dec. 9, 1912; House 1893–95.

Coffey, Robert Lewis Jr. (D Pa.) Oct. 21, 1918–April 20, 1949; House Jan. 3–April 20, 1949.

Coffin, Charles Dustin (W Ohio) Sept. 9, 1805–Feb. 28, 1880; House Dec. 20, 1837–39.

Coffin, Charles Edward (R Md.) July 18, 1841–May 24, 1912; House Nov. 6, 1894–97.

Coffin, Frank Morey (D Maine) July 11, 1919– ; House 1957–61.

Coffin, Howard Aldridge (R Mich.) June 11, 1877–Feb. 28, 1956; House 1947–49.

Coffin, Peleg Jr. (– Mass.) Nov. 3, 1756–March 6, 1805; House 1793–95.

Coffin, Thomas Chalkley (D Idaho) Oct. 25, 1887–June 8, 1934; House 1933–June 8, 1934.

Coffroth, Alexander Hamilton (D Pa.) May 18, 1828–Sept. 2, 1906; House 1863–65, Feb. 19–July 18, 1866, 1879–81.

Coghlan, John Maxwell (R Calif.) Dec. 8, 1835–March 26, 1879; House 1871–73.

Cogswell, William (R Mass.) Aug. 23, 1838–May 22, 1895; House 1887–May 22, 1895.

Cohelan, Jeffrey (D Calif.) June 24, 1914–Feb. 15, 1999; House 1959–71.

Cohen, John Sanford (D Ga.) Feb. 26, 1870–May 13, 1935; Senate April 25, 1932–Jan. 11, 1933.

Cohen, William Sebastian (R Maine) Aug. 28, 1940– ; House 1973–79; Senate 1979–97; secretary of defense Jan. 24, 1997–Jan. 20, 2001.

Cohen, William Wolfe (D N.Y.) Sept. 6, 1874–Oct. 12, 1940; House 1927–29.

Coit, Joshua (F Conn.) Oct. 7, 1758–Sept. 5, 1798; House 1793–Sept. 5, 1798 (1793–95 no party).

Coke, Richard (nephew of Richard Coke Jr.) (D Texas) March 13, 1829–May 14, 1897; Senate 1877–95; Gov. Jan. 15, 1874–Dec. 1, 1876.

Coke, Richard Jr. (uncle of Richard Coke) (J Va.) Nov. 16, 1790–March 31, 1851; House 1829–33.

Colcock, William Ferguson (D S.C.) Nov. 5, 1804–June 13, 1889; House 1849–53.

Colden, Cadwallader David (– N.Y.) April 4, 1769–Feb. 7, 1834; House Dec. 12, 1821–23.

Colden, Charles J. (D Calif.) Aug. 24, 1870–April 15, 1938; House 1933–April 15, 1938.

Cole, Albert McDonald (R Kan.) Oct. 13, 1901–June 5, 1994; House 1945–53.

Cole, Cornelius (R Calif.) Sept. 17, 1822–Nov. 3, 1924; House 1863–65 (Union Republican); Senate 1867–73.

Cole, Cyrenus (R Iowa) Jan. 13, 1863–Nov. 14, 1939; House July 19, 1921–33.

Cole, George Edward (D Wash.) Dec. 23, 1826–Dec. 3, 1906; House (Terr. Del.) 1863–65; Gov. (Wash. Terr.) Nov. 1866–March 4, 1867.

Cole, Nathan (R Mo.) July 26, 1825–March 4, 1904; House 1877–79.

Cole, Orsamus (W Wis.) Aug. 23, 1819–May 5, 1903; House 1849–51.

Cole, Ralph Dayton (brother of Raymond Clinton Cole) (R Ohio) Nov. 30, 1873–Oct. 15, 1932; House 1905–11.

Cole, Raymond Clinton (brother of Ralph Dayton Cole) (R Ohio) Aug. 21, 1870–Feb. 8, 1957; House 1919–25.

Cole, Thomas J. (R Okla.) April 28, 1949– ; House 2003– .

Cole, William Clay (R Mo.) Aug. 29, 1897–Sept. 23, 1965; House 1943–49, 1953–55.

Cole, William Hinson (D Md.) Jan. 11, 1837–July 8, 1886; House 1885–July 8, 1886.

Cole, William Purington Jr. (D Md.) May 11, 1889–Sept. 22, 1957; House 1927–29, 1931–Oct. 26, 1942.

Cole, William Sterling (R N.Y.) April 18, 1904–March 15, 1987; House 1935–Dec. 1, 1957.

Coleman, Earl Thomas (R Mo.) May 29, 1943– ; House Nov. 2, 1976–93.

Coleman, Hamilton Dudley (R La.) May 12, 1845–March 16, 1926; House 1889–91.

Coleman, Nicholas Daniel (J Ky.) April 22, 1800–May 11, 1874; House 1829–31.

Coleman, Norm R. (R Minn.) Aug. 17, 1949– ; Senate 2003– .

Coleman, Ronald D'Emory (D Texas) Nov. 29, 1941– ; House 1983–97.

Coleman, William Henry (R Pa.) Dec. 28, 1871–June 3, 1943; House 1915–17.

Colerick, Walpole Gillespie (D Ind.) Aug. 1, 1845–Jan. 11, 1911; House 1879–83.

Coles, Isaac (father of Walter Coles) (R Va.) March 2, 1747–June 3, 1813; House 1789–91 (no party), 1793–97 (1793–95 no party).

Coles, Walter (son of Isaac Coles) (D Va.) Dec. 8, 1790–Nov. 9, 1857; House 1835–45 (1835–37 Jacksonian).

Colfax, Schuyler (R Ind.) March 23, 1823–Jan. 13, 1885; House 1855–69; Speaker Dec. 7, 1863–65, Dec. 4, 1865–67, March 4, 1867–March 2, 1869; vice president 1869–73.

Colhoun, John Ewing (cousin of John Caldwell Calhoun and Joseph Calhoun) (R S.C.) about 1749–Oct. 26, 1802; Senate 1801–Oct. 26, 1802.

Collamer, Jacob (R Vt.) Jan. 8, 1791–Nov. 9, 1865; House 1843–49 (Whig); Senate 1855–Nov. 9, 1865; postmaster general March 8, 1849–July 22, 1850.

Collier, Harold Reginald (R Ill.) Dec. 12, 1915– ; House 1957–75.

Collier, James William (D Miss.) Sept. 28, 1872–Sept. 28, 1933; House 1909–33.

Collier, John Allen (great-great-grandfather of Edwin Arthur Hall) (AMas. N.Y.) Nov. 13, 1787–March 24, 1873; House 1831–33.

Collin, John Francis (D N.Y.) April 30, 1802–Sept. 16, 1889; House 1845–47.

Collins, Barbara-Rose (D Mich.) April 13, 1939– ; House 1991–97.

Collins, Cardiss (widow of George Washington Collins) (D Ill.) Sept. 24, 1931– ; House June 5, 1973–97.

Collins, Ela (father of William Collins) (– N.Y.) Feb. 14, 1786–Nov. 23, 1848; House 1823–25.

Collins, Francis Dolan (D Pa.) March 5, 1841–Nov. 21, 1891; House 1875–79.

Collins, George Washington (husband of Cardiss Collins) (D Ill.) March 5, 1925–Dec. 8, 1972; House Nov. 3, 1970–Dec. 8, 1972.

Collins, James Mitchell (R Texas) April 29, 1916–July 21, 1989; House Aug. 24, 1968–83.

Collins, Michael A. "Mac" (R Ga.) Oct. 15, 1944– ; House 1993–2005.

Collins, Patrick Andrew (D Mass.) March 12, 1844–Sept. 13, 1905; House 1883–89.

Collins, Ross Alexander (D Miss.) April 25, 1880–July 14, 1968; House 1921–35, 1937–43.

Collins, Samuel LaFort (R Calif.) Aug. 6, 1895–June 26, 1965; House 1933–37.

Collins, Susan (R Maine) Dec. 7, 1952– ; Senate 1997– ; chair Senate Governmental Affairs 2003–05; chair Senate Homeland Security and Governmental Affairs 2005– .

Collins, William (son of Ela Collins) (D N.Y.) Feb. 22, 1818–June 18, 1878; House 1847–49.

Colmer, William Meyers (D Miss.) Feb. 11, 1890–Sept. 9, 1980; House 1933–73; chair House Rules 1967–73.

Colorado, Antonio J. (D P.R.) Sept. 8, 1939– ; House (Res. Comm.) March 4, 1992–Jan. 3, 1993.

Colquitt, Alfred Holt (son of Walter Terry Colquitt) (D Ga.) April 20, 1824–March 26, 1894; House 1853–55 (no party); Senate 1883–March 26, 1894; Gov. Jan. 12, 1877–Nov. 4, 1882.

Colquitt, Walter Terry (father of Alfred Holt Colquitt) (D Ga.) Dec. 27, 1799–May 7, 1855; House 1839–July 21, 1840 (Whig), Jan. 3, 1842–43 (Van Buren Democrat); Senate 1843–Feb. 1848.

Colson, David Grant (R Ky.) April 1, 1861–Sept. 27, 1904; House 1895–99.

Colston, Edward (F Va.) Dec. 25, 1786–April 23, 1852; House 1817–19.

Colt, LeBaron Bradford (R R.I.) June 25, 1846–Aug. 18, 1924; Senate 1913–Aug. 18, 1924.

Colton, Don Byron (R Utah) Sept. 15, 1876–Aug. 1, 1952; House 1921–33.

Combest, Larry Ed (R Texas) March 20, 1945– ; House 1985–May 31, 2003; chair House Select Intelligence 1995–97; chair House Agriculture 1999–2003.

Combs, George Hamilton Jr. (D Mo.) May 2, 1899–Nov. 29, 1977; House 1927–29.

Combs, Jesse Martin (D Texas) July 7, 1889–Aug. 21, 1953; House 1945–53.

Comegys, Joseph Parsons (W Del.) Dec. 29, 1813–Feb. 1, 1893; Senate Nov. 19, 1856–Jan. 14, 1857.

Comer, Braxton Bragg (D Ala.) Nov. 7, 1848–Aug. 15, 1927; Senate March 5–Nov. 2, 1920; Gov. Jan. 14, 1907–Jan. 17, 1911.

Comingo, Abram (D Mo.) Jan. 9, 1820–Nov. 10, 1889; House 1871–75.

Comins, Linus Bacon (R Mass.) Nov. 29, 1817–Oct. 14, 1892; House 1855–59 (1855–57 American Party).

Compton, Barnes (great-grandson of Philip Key) (D Md.) Nov. 16, 1830–Dec. 4, 1898; House 1885–March 20, 1890, 1891–May 15, 1894.

Compton, C. H. Ranulf (R Conn.) Sept. 16, 1878–Jan. 26, 1974; House 1943–45.

Comstock, Charles Carter (D Mich.) March 5, 1818–Feb. 20, 1900; House 1885–87.

Comstock, Daniel Webster (R Ind.) Dec. 16, 1840–May 19, 1917; House March 4–May 19, 1917.

Comstock, Oliver Cromwell (R N.Y.) March 1, 1780–Jan. 11, 1860; House 1813–19.

Comstock, Solomon Gilman (R Minn.) May 9, 1842–June 3, 1933; House 1889–91.

Conable, Barber Benjamin Jr. (R N.Y.) Nov. 2, 1922–Nov. 30, 2003; House 1965–85.

Conard, John (R Pa.) Nov. 1773–May 9, 1857; House 1813–15.

Conaway, K. Michael "Mike" (R Texas) June 11, 1948– ; House 2005– .

Condict, Lewis (R N.J.) March 3, 1772–May 26, 1862; House 1811–17, 1821–33.

Condit, Gary (D Calif.) April 21, 1948– ; House Sept. 20, 1989–2003.

Condit, John (father of Silas Condit) (R N.J.) July 8, 1755–May 4, 1834; House 1799–1803, March 4–Nov. 4, 1819; Senate Sept. 1, 1803– March 3, 1809, March 21, 1809–17.

Condit, Silas (son of John Condit) (AJ N.J.) Aug. 18, 1778–Nov. 29, 1861; House 1831–33.

Condon, Francis Bernard (D R.I.) Nov. 11, 1891–Nov. 23, 1965; House Nov. 4, 1930–Jan. 10, 1935.

Condon, Robert Likens (D Calif.) Nov. 10, 1912–June 3, 1976; House 1953–55.

Conger, Edwin Hurd (R Iowa) March 7, 1843–May 18, 1907; House 1885–Oct. 3, 1890.

Conger, Harmon Sweatland (W N.Y.) April 9, 1816–Oct. 22, 1882; House 1847–51.

Conger, James Lockwood (W Mich.) Feb. 18, 1805–April 10, 1876; House 1851–53.

Conger, Omar Dwight (R Mich.) April 1, 1818–July 11, 1898; House 1869–81; Senate 1881–87.

Conkling, Alfred (father of Frederick Augustus Conkling and Roscoe Conkling) (– N.Y.) Oct. 12, 1789–Feb. 5, 1874; House 1821–23.

Conkling, Frederick Augustus (son of Alfred Conkling, brother of Roscoe Conkling) (R N.Y.) Aug. 22, 1816–Sept. 18, 1891; House 1861–63.

Conkling, Roscoe (son of Alfred Conkling, brother of Frederick Augustus Conkling) (R N.Y.) Oct. 30, 1829–April 18, 1888; House 1859–63, 1865–March 4, 1867; Senate March 4, 1867–May 16, 1881.

Conlan, John Bertrand (R Ariz.) Sept. 17, 1930– ; House 1973–77.

Conn, Charles Gerard (D Ind.) Jan. 29, 1844–Jan. 5, 1931; House 1893–95.

Connally, Thomas Terry "Tom" (D Texas) Aug. 19, 1877–Oct. 28, 1963; House 1917–29; Senate 1929–53; chair Senate Foreign Relations 1949–53.

Connell, Charles Robert (son of William Connell) (R Pa.) Sept. 22, 1864–Sept. 26, 1922; House 1921–Sept. 26, 1922.

Connell, Richard Edward (D N.Y.) Nov. 6, 1857–Oct. 30, 1912; House 1911–Oct. 30, 1912.

Connell, William (father of Charles Robert Connell) (R Pa.) Sept. 10, 1827–March 21, 1909; House 1897–1903, Feb. 10, 1904–05.

Connell, William James (R Neb.) July 6, 1846–Aug. 16, 1924; House 1889–91.

Connelly, John Robert (D Kan.) Feb. 27, 1870–Sept. 9, 1940; House 1913–19.

Conner, James Perry (R Iowa) Jan. 27, 1851–March 19, 1924; House Dec. 4, 1900–09.

Conner, John Coggswell (D Texas) Oct. 14, 1842–Dec. 10, 1873 House March 31, 1870–73.

Conner, Samuel Shepard (R Mass.) about 1783–Dec. 17, 1820 House 1815–17.

Connery, Lawrence Joseph (brother of William Patrick Connery Jr.) (D Mass.) Oct. 17, 1895–Oct. 19, 1941; House Sept. 28 1937–Oct. 19, 1941.

Connery, William Patrick Jr. (brother of Lawrence Joseph Connery) (D Mass.) Aug. 24, 1888–June 15, 1937; House 1923–June 15 1937.

Conness, John (UR Calif.) Sept. 22, 1821–Jan. 10, 1909; Senate 1863–69 (elected as Douglas Democrat).

Connolly, Daniel Ward (D Pa.) April 24, 1847–Dec. 4, 1894; House 1883–85.

Connolly, James Austin (R Ill.) March 8, 1843–Dec. 15, 1914; House 1895–99.

Connolly, James Joseph (R Pa.) Sept. 24, 1881–Dec. 10, 1952; House 1921–35.

Connolly, Maurice (D Iowa) March 13, 1877–May 28, 1921; House 1913–15.

Connor, Henry William (D N.C.) Aug. 5, 1793–Jan. 6, 1866; House 1821–41 (1821–33 no party, 1833–37 Jacksonian).

Conover, Simon Barclay (R Fla.) Sept. 23, 1840–April 19, 1908; Senate 1873–79.

Conover, William Sheldrick II (R Pa.) Aug. 27, 1928– ; House April 25, 1972–73.

Conrad, Charles Magill (W La.) Dec. 24, 1804–Feb. 11, 1878; Senate April 14, 1842–43; House 1849–Aug. 17, 1850; secretary of war Aug. 15, 1850–March 7, 1853.

Conrad, Frederick (R Pa.) 1759–Aug. 3, 1827; House 1803–07.

Conrad, Kent (D N.D.) March 12, 1948– ; Senate 1987– ; chair Senate Budget Jan. 3, 2001–Jan. 20, 2001, June 6, 2001–03.

Conry, Joseph Aloysius (D Mass.) Sept. 12, 1868–June 22, 1943; House 1901–03.

Conry, Michael Francis (D N.Y.) April 2, 1870–March 2, 1917; House 1909–March 2, 1917.

Constable, Albert (D Md.) June 3, 1805–Sept. 18, 1855; House 1845–47.

Conte, Silvio Otto (R Mass.) Nov. 9, 1921–Feb. 8, 1991; House 1959–Feb. 8, 1991.

Contee, Benjamin (uncle of Alexander Contee Hanson, great-uncle of Thomas Contee Worthington) (– Md.) 1755–Nov. 30, 1815; House 1789–91; Cont. Cong. 1788.

Converse, George Leroy (D Ohio) June 4, 1827–March 30, 1897; House 1879–85.

Conway, Henry Wharton (cousin of Ambrose Hundley Sevier) (– Ark.) March 18, 1793–Nov. 9, 1827; House (Terr. Del.) 1823–Nov. 9, 1827.

Conway, Martin Franklin (R Kan.) Nov. 19, 1827–Feb. 15, 1882; House Jan. 29, 1861–63.

Conyers, John Jr. (D Mich.) May 16, 1929– ; House 1965– ; chair House Government Operations 1989–95.

Cook, Burton Chauncey (R Ill.) May 11, 1819–Aug. 18, 1894; House 1865–Aug. 26, 1871.

Cook, Daniel Pope (– Ill.) 1794–Oct. 16, 1827; House 1819–27.

Cook, George Washington (R Colo.) Nov. 10, 1851–Dec. 18, 1916; House 1907–09.

Cook, Joel (R Pa.) March 20, 1842–Dec. 15, 1910; House Nov. 5, 1907–Dec. 15, 1910.

Cook, John Calhoun (D Iowa) Dec. 26, 1846–June 7, 1920; House March 3, 1883, Oct. 9, 1883–85.

Cook, John Parsons (W Iowa) Aug. 31, 1817–April 17, 1872; House 1853–55.

Cook, Marlow Webster (R Ky.) July 27, 1926– ; Senate Dec. 17, 1968–Dec. 27, 1974.

Cook, Merrill (R Utah) May 6, 1946– ; House 1997–2001.

Cook, Orchard (R Mass.) March 24, 1763–Aug. 12, 1819; House 1805–11.

Cook, Philip (D Ga.) July 30, 1817–May 24, 1894; House 1873–83.

Cook, Robert Eugene (D Ohio) May 19, 1920–Nov. 28, 1988; House 1959–63.

Cook, Samuel Andrew (R Wis.) Jan. 28, 1849–April 4, 1918; House 1895–97.

Cook, Samuel Ellis (D Ind.) Sept. 30, 1860–Feb. 22, 1946; House 1923–25.

Cook, Zadock (R Ga.) Feb. 18, 1769–Aug. 3, 1863; House Dec. 2, 1816–19.

Cooke, Bates (AMas. N.Y.) Dec. 23, 1787–May 31, 1841; House 1831–33.

Cooke, Edmund Francis (R N.Y.) April 13, 1885–May 13, 1967; House 1929–33.

Cooke, Edward Dean (R Ill.) Oct. 17, 1849–June 24, 1897; House 1895–June 24, 1897.

Cooke, Eleutheros (AJ Ohio) Dec. 25, 1787–Dec. 27, 1864; House 1831–33.

Cooke, Thomas Burrage (R N.Y.) Nov. 21, 1778–Nov. 20, 1853; House 1811–13.

Cooksey, John (R L.A.) Aug. 20, 1941– ; House 1997–2003.

Cooley, Harold Dunbar (D N.C.) July 26, 1897–Jan. 15, 1974; House July 7, 1934–67; chair House Agriculture 1949–53, 1955–67.

Cooley, Wes (R Ore.) March 28, 1932– ; House 1995–97.

Coolidge, Frederick Spaulding (father of Marcus Allen Coolidge) (D Mass.) Dec. 7, 1841–June 8, 1906; House 1891–93.

Coolidge, Marcus Allen (son of Frederick Spaulding Coolidge) (D Mass.) Oct. 6, 1865–Jan. 23, 1947; Senate 1931–37.

Coombs, Frank Leslie (R Calif.) Dec. 27, 1853–Oct. 5, 1934; House 1901–03.

Coombs, William Jerome (D N.Y.) Dec. 24, 1833–Jan. 12, 1922; House 1891–95.

Coon, Samuel Harrison (R Ore.) April 15, 1903–May 8, 1980; House 1953–57.

Cooney, James (D Mo.) July 28, 1848–Nov. 16, 1904; House 1897–1903.

Cooper, Allen Foster (R Pa.) June 16, 1862–April 20, 1917; House 1903–11.

Cooper, Charles Merian (D Fla.) Jan. 16, 1856–Nov. 14, 1923; House 1893–97.

Cooper, Edmund (brother of Henry Cooper) (U Tenn.) Sept. 11, 1821–July 21, 1911; House July 24, 1866–67.

Cooper, Edward (R W.Va.) Feb. 26, 1873–March 1, 1928; House 1915–19.

Cooper, George Byran (D Mich.) June 6, 1808–Aug. 29, 1866; House 1859–May 15, 1860.

Cooper, George William (D Ind.) May 21, 1851–Nov. 27, 1899; House 1889–95.

Cooper, Henry (brother of Edmund Cooper) (D Tenn.) Aug. 22, 1827–Feb. 4, 1884; Senate 1871–77.

Cooper, Henry Allen (R Wis.) Sept. 8, 1850–March 1, 1931; House 1893–1919, 1921–March 1, 1931.

Cooper, James (W Pa.) May 8, 1810–March 28, 1863; House 1839–43; Senate 1849–55.

Cooper, James Haynes Shofner "Jim" (son of Gov. William Prentice Cooper of Tenn.) (D Tenn.) June 19, 1954– ; House 1983–95, 2003– .

Cooper, Jere (D Tenn.) July 20, 1893–Dec. 18, 1957; House 1929–Dec. 18, 1957; chair House Ways and Means 1955–57.

Cooper, John Gordon (R Ohio) April 27, 1872–Jan. 7, 1955; House 1915–37.

Cooper, John Sherman (R Ky.) Aug. 23, 1901–Feb. 21, 1991; Senate Nov. 6, 1946–49, Nov. 5, 1952–55, Nov. 7, 1956–73.

Cooper, Mark Anthony (cousin of Eugenius Aristides Nisbet) (D Ga.) April 20, 1800–March 17, 1885; House 1839–41 (Whig), Jan. 3, 1842–June 26, 1843.

Cooper, Richard Matlack (– N.J.) Feb. 29, 1768–March 10, 1843; House 1829–33.

Cooper, Samuel Bronson (D Texas) May 30, 1850–Aug. 21, 1918; House 1893–1905, 1907–09.

Cooper, Thomas (F Del.) 1764–1829; House 1813–17.

Cooper, Thomas Buchecker (D Pa.) Dec. 29, 1823–April 4, 1862; House 1861–April 4, 1862.

Cooper, William (F N.Y.) Dec. 2, 1754–Dec. 22, 1809; House 1795–97, 1799–1801.

Cooper, William Craig (R Ohio) Dec. 18, 1832–Aug. 29, 1902; House 1885–91.

Cooper, William Raworth (D N.J.) Feb. 20, 1793–Sept. 22, 1856; House 1839–41.

Copeland, Oren Sturman (R Neb.) March 16, 1887–April 10, 1958; House 1941–43.

Copeland, Royal Samuel (D N.Y.) Nov. 7, 1868–June 17, 1938; Senate 1923–June 17, 1938.

Copley, Ira Clifton (nephew of Richard Henry Whiting) (R Ill.) Oct. 25, 1864–Nov. 1, 1947; House 1911–23 (1915–17 Progressive).

Coppersmith, Sam (D Ariz.) May 22, 1955– ; House 1993–95.

Corbett, Henry Winslow (UR Ore.) Feb. 18, 1827–March 31, 1903; Senate 1867–73.

Corbett, Robert James (R Pa.) Aug. 25, 1905–April 25, 1971; House 1939–41, 1945–April 25, 1971.

Corcoran, Thomas Joseph (R Ill.) May 23, 1939– ; House 1977–85.

Cordon, Guy (R Ore.) April 24, 1890–June 8, 1969; Senate March 4, 1944–55; chair Senate Interior and Insular Affairs 1954–55.

Cordova, Jorge Luis (New Prog. P.R.) April 20, 1907–Sept. 16, 1994; House (Res. Comm.) 1969–73.

Corker, Stephen Alfestus (D Ga.) May 7, 1830–Oct. 18, 1879; House Dec. 22, 1870–71.

Corlett, William Wellington (R Wyo.) April 10, 1842–July 22, 1890; House (Terr. Del.) 1877–79.

Corley, Manuel Simeon (R S.C.) Feb. 10, 1823–Nov. 20, 1902; House July 25, 1868–69.

Corliss, John Blaisdell (R Mich.) June 7, 1851–Dec. 24, 1929; House 1895–1903.

Corman, James Charles (D Calif.) Oct. 20, 1920–Dec. 30, 2000; House 1961–81.

Cornell, Robert John (D Wis.) Dec. 16, 1919– ; House 1975–79.

Cornell, Thomas (R N.Y.) Jan. 27, 1814–March 30, 1890; House 1867–69, 1881–83.

Corning, Erastus (grandfather of Parker Corning) (D N.Y.) Dec. 14, 1794–April 9, 1872; House 1857–59, 1861–Oct. 5, 1863.

Corning, Parker (grandson of Erastus Corning) (D N.Y.) Jan. 22, 1874–May 24, 1943; House 1923–37.

Cornish, Johnston (D N.J.) June 13, 1858–June 26, 1920; House 1893–95.

Cornwell, David Lance (D Ind.) June 14, 1945– ; House 1977–79.

Cornyn, John (R Texas) Feb. 2, 1952– ; Senate Dec. 2, 2002– .

Corrada-del Rio, Baltasar (New Prog. P.R.) April 10, 1935– ; House (Res. Comm.) 1977–85.

Corwin, Franklin (nephew of Moses Bledso Corwin and Thomas Corwin) (R Ill.) Jan. 12, 1818–June 15, 1879; House 1873–75.

Corwin, Moses Bledso (brother of Thomas Corwin, uncle of Franklin Corwin) (W Ohio) Jan. 5, 1790–April 7, 1872; House 1849–51, 1853–55.

Corwin, Thomas (brother of Moses Bledso Corwin, uncle of Franklin Corwin) (R Ohio) July 29, 1794–Dec. 18, 1865; House 1831–May 30, 1840 (Whig), 1859–March 12, 1861; Senate 1845–July 20, 1850 (Whig); Gov. Dec. 16, 1840–Dec. 14, 1841 (Whig); secretary of the Treasury July 23, 1850–March 6, 1853.

Corzine, Jon Stevens (D N.J.) Jan. 1, 1947– ; Senate 2001– .

Cosden, Jeremiah (– Md.) 1768–Dec. 5, 1824; House 1821–March 19, 1822.

Cosgrove, John (D Mo.) Sept. 12, 1839–Aug. 15, 1925; House 1883–85.

Costa, Jim (D Calif.) April 13, 1952– ; House 2005– .

Costello, Jerry Francis (D Ill.) Sept. 25, 1949– ; House Aug. 11, 1988– .

Costello, John Martin (D Calif.) Jan. 15, 1903–Aug. 28, 1976; House 1935–45.

Costello, Peter Edward (R Pa.) June 27, 1854–Oct. 23, 1935; House 1915–21.

Costigan, Edward Prentiss (D Colo.) July 1, 1874–Jan. 17, 1939; Senate 1931–37.

Cothran, James Sproull (D S.C.) Aug. 8, 1830–Dec. 5, 1897; House 1887–91.

Cotter, William Ross (D Conn.) July 18, 1926–Sept. 8, 1981; House 1971–Sept. 8, 1981.

Cottman, Joseph Stewart (IW Md.) Aug. 16, 1803–Jan. 28, 1863; House 1851–53.

Cotton, Aylett Rains (R Iowa) Nov. 29, 1826–Oct. 30, 1912; House 1871–75.

Cotton, Norris H. (R N.H.) May 11, 1900–Feb. 24, 1989; House 1947–Nov. 7, 1954; Senate Nov. 8, 1954–Dec. 31, 1974, Aug. 8–Sept. 18, 1975.

Cottrell, James La Fayette (D Ala.) Aug. 25, 1808–Sept. 7, 1885; House Dec. 7, 1846–47.

Coudert, Frederick René Jr. (R N.Y.) May 7, 1898–May 21, 1972; House 1947–59.

Coudrey, Harry Marcy (R Mo.) Feb. 28, 1867–July 5, 1930; House June 23, 1906–11.

Coughlin, Clarence Dennis (uncle of Robert Lawrence Coughlin) (R Pa.) July 27, 1883–Dec. 15, 1946; House 1921–23.

Coughlin, Robert Lawrence (nephew of Clarence Dennis Coughlin) (R Pa.) April 11, 1929–Nov. 30, 2001; House 1969–93.

Coulter, Richard (J Pa.) March 1788–April 21, 1852; House 1827–35 (1827–29 no party).

Courter, James Andrew (R N.J.) Oct. 14, 1941– ; House 1979–91.

Courtney, William Wirt (D Tenn.) Sept. 7, 1889–April 6, 1961; House May 11, 1939–49.

Cousins, Robert Gordon (R Iowa) Jan. 31, 1859–June 20, 1933; House 1893–1909.

Couzens, James (R Mich.) Aug. 26, 1872–Oct. 22, 1936; Senate Nov. 29, 1922–Oct. 22, 1936.

Coverdell, Paul (R Ga.) Jan. 20, 1939–July 18, 2000; Senate 1993–July 18, 2000.

Covert, James Way (D N.Y.) Sept. 2, 1842–May 16, 1910; House 1877–81, 1889–95.

Covington, George Washington (D Md.) Sept. 12, 1838–April 6, 1911; House 1881–85.

Covington, James Harry (D Md.) May 3, 1870–Feb. 4, 1942; House 1909–Sept. 30, 1914.

Covington, Leonard (R Md.) Oct. 30, 1768–Nov. 14, 1813; House 1805–07.

Covode, John (R Pa.) March 17, 1808–Jan. 11, 1871; House 1855–63 (1855–57 Whig), 1867–69, Feb. 9, 1870–Jan. 11, 1871.

Cowan, Edgar (R Pa.) Sept. 19, 1815–Aug. 31, 1885; Senate 1861–67.

Cowan, Jacob Pitzer (D Ohio) March 20, 1823–July 9, 1895; House 1875–77.

Cowen, Benjamin Sprague (W Ohio) Sept. 27, 1793–Sept. 27, 1860; House 1841–43.

Cowen, John Kissig (D Md.) Oct. 28, 1844–April 26, 1904; House 1895–97.

Cowger, William Owen (R Ky.) Jan. 1, 1922–Oct. 2, 1971; House 1967–71.

Cowgill, Calvin (R Ind.) Jan. 7, 1819–Feb. 10, 1903; House 1879–81.

Cowherd, William Strother (D Mo.) Sept. 1, 1860–June 20, 1915; House 1897–1905.

Cowles, Charles Holden (nephew of William Henry Harrison Cowles) (R N.C.) July 16, 1875–Oct. 2, 1957; House 1909–11.

Cowles, George Washington (R N.Y.) Dec. 6, 1823–Jan. 20, 1901; House 1869–71.

Cowles, Henry Booth (– N.Y.) March 18, 1798–May 17, 1873; House 1829–31.

Cowles, William Henry Harrison (uncle of Charles Holden Cowles) (D N.C.) April 22, 1840–Dec. 30, 1901; House 1885–93.

Cox, C. Christopher (R Calif.) Oct. 16, 1952– ; House 1989– ; chair House Homeland Security 2003– .

Cox, Edward Eugene (D Ga.) April 3, 1880–Dec. 24, 1952; House 1925–Dec. 24, 1952.

Cox, Isaac Newton (D N.Y.) Aug. 1, 1846–Sept. 28, 1916; House 1891–93.

Cox, Jacob Dolson (R Ohio) Oct. 27, 1828–Aug. 4, 1900; House 1877–79; Gov. Jan. 8, 1866–Jan. 13, 1868; secretary of the interior March 5, 1869–Oct. 31, 1870.

Cox, James (R N.J.) June 14, 1753–Sept. 12, 1810; House 1809–Sept. 12, 1810.

Cox, James Middleton (D Ohio) March 31, 1870–July 15, 1957; House 1909–Jan. 12, 1913; Gov. Jan. 13, 1913–Jan. 11, 1915, Jan. 8, 1917–Jan. 10, 1921.

Cox, John W. Jr. (D Ill.) July 10, 1947– ; House 1991–93.

Cox, Leander Martin (AP Ky.) May 7, 1812–March 19, 1865; House 1853–57 (1853–55 Whig).

Cox, Nicholas Nichols (D Tenn.) Jan. 6, 1837–May 2, 1912; House 1891–1901.

Cox, Samuel Sullivan (D N.Y.) Sept. 30, 1824–Sept. 10, 1889; House 1857–65 (Ohio), 1869–73, Nov. 4, 1873–May 20, 1885, Nov. 2, 1886–Sept. 10, 1889.

Cox, William Elijah (D Ind.) Sept. 6, 1861–March 11, 1942; House 1907–19.

Cox, William Ruffin (D N.C.) March 11, 1831–Dec. 26, 1919; House 1881–87.

Coxe, William Jr. (F N.J.) May 3, 1762–Feb. 25, 1831; House 1813–15.

Coyle, William Radford (R Pa.) July 10, 1878–Jan. 30, 1962; House 1925–27, 1929–33.

Coyne, James Kitchenman III (R Pa.) Nov. 17, 1946– ; House 1981–83.

Coyne, William Joseph (D Pa.) Aug. 24, 1936– ; House 1981–2003.

Crabb, George Whitfield (W Ala.) Feb. 22, 1804–Aug. 15, 1846; House Sept. 4, 1838–41.

Crabb, Jeremiah (F Md.) 1760–1800; House 1795–96.

Craddock, John Durrett (R Ky.) Oct. 26, 1881–May 20, 1942; House 1929–31.

Cradlebaugh, John (– Nev.) Feb. 22, 1819–Feb. 22, 1872; House (Terr. Del.) Dec. 2, 1861–63.

Crafts, Samuel Chandler (– Vt.) Oct. 6, 1768–Nov. 19, 1853; House 1817–25; Senate April 23, 1842–43; Gov. Oct. 10, 1828–Oct. 18, 1831 (National Republican).

Cragin, Aaron Harrison (R N.H.) Feb. 3, 1821–May 10, 1898; House 1855–59 (1855–57 American Party); Senate 1865–77.

Crago, Thomas Spencer (R Pa.) Aug. 8, 1866–Sept. 12, 1925; House 1911–13, 1915–21, Sept. 20, 1921–23.

Craig, Alexander Kerr (D Pa.) Feb. 21, 1828–July 29, 1892; House Feb. 26–July 29, 1892.

Craig, George Henry (R Ala.) Dec. 25, 1845–Jan. 26, 1923; House Jan. 9–March 3, 1885.

Craig, Hector (J N.Y.) 1775–Jan. 31, 1842; House 1823–25 (no party), 1829–July 12, 1830.

Craig, James (D Mo.) Feb. 28, 1818–Oct. 22, 1888; House 1857–61.

Craig, Larry Edwin (R Idaho) July 20, 1945– ; House 1981–91; Senate 1991– ; chair Senate Veterans' Affairs 2005– .

Craig, Robert (D Va.) 1792–Nov. 25, 1852; House 1829–33 (Jacksonian), 1835–41.

Craig, Samuel Alfred (R Pa.) Nov. 19, 1839–March 17, 1920; House 1889–91.

Craig, William Benjamin (D Ala.) Nov. 2, 1877–Nov. 27, 1925; House 1907–11.

Craige, Francis Burton (D N.C.) March 13, 1811–Dec. 30, 1875; House 1853–61.

Craik, William (F Md.) Oct. 31, 1761–prior to 1814; House Dec. 5, 1796–1801.

Crail, Joe (R Calif.) Dec. 25, 1877–March 2, 1938; House 1927–33.

Crain, William Henry (D Texas) Nov. 25, 1848–Feb. 10, 1896; House 1885–Feb. 10, 1896.

Craley, Nathaniel Nieman Jr. (D Pa.) Nov. 17, 1927– ; House 1965–67.

Cramer, John (J N.Y.) May 17, 1779–June 1, 1870; House 1833–37.

Cramer, Robert E. "Bud" Jr. (D Ala.) Aug. 22, 1947– ; House 1991– .

Cramer, William Cato (R Fla.) Aug. 4, 1922–Oct. 18, 2003; House 1955–71.

Cramton, Louis Convers (R Mich.) Dec. 2, 1875–June 23, 1966; House 1913–31.

Crane, Daniel Bever (brother of Philip Miller Crane) (R Ill.) Jan. 10, 1936– ; House 1979–85.

Crane, Joseph Halsey (W Ohio) Aug. 31, 1782–Nov. 13, 1851; House 1829–37 (1829–33 no party, 1833–35 Anti-Jacksonian).

Crane, Philip Miller (brother of Daniel Bever Crane) (R Ill.) Nov. 3, 1930– ; House Nov. 25, 1969–2005.

Crane, Winthrop Murray (R Mass.) April 23, 1853–Oct. 2, 1920; Senate Oct. 12, 1904–13; Gov. Jan. 4, 1900–Jan. 8, 1903.

Cranford, John Walter (D Texas) 1862–March 3, 1899; House 1897–March 3, 1899.

Cranston, Alan (D Calif.) June 19, 1914–Dec. 31, 2000; Senate 1969–93; chair Senate Veterans' Affairs 1977–81, 1987–93.

Cranston, Henry Young (brother of Robert Bennie Cranston) (W R.I.) Oct. 9, 1789–Feb. 12, 1864; House 1843–47 (1843–45 Law & Order).

Cranston, Robert Bennie (brother of Henry Young Cranston) (W R.I.) Jan. 14, 1791–Jan. 27, 1873; House 1837–43, 1847–49.

Crapo, Michael D. (R Idaho) May 20, 1951– ; House 1993–99; Senate 1999– .

Crapo, William Wallace (R Mass.) May 16, 1830–Feb. 28, 1926; House Nov. 2, 1875–83.

Crary, Isaac Edwin (D Mich.) Oct. 2, 1804–May 8, 1854; House Jan. 26, 1837–41 (Jan. 26–March 3, 1837 Jacksonian).

Cravens, James Addison (second cousin of James Harrison Cravens) (D Ind.) Nov. 4, 1818–June 20, 1893; House 1861–65.

Cravens, James Harrison (second cousin of James Addison Cravens) (W Ind.) Aug. 2, 1802–Dec. 4, 1876; House 1841–43.

Cravens, Jordan Edgar (cousin of William Ben Cravens) (D Ark.) Nov. 7, 1830–April 8, 1914; House 1877–83 (1877–79 Independent Democrat).

Cravens, William Ben (father of William Fadjo Cravens, cousin of Jordan Edgar Cravens) (D Ark.) Jan. 17, 1872–Jan. 13, 1939; House 1907–13, 1933–Jan. 13, 1939.

Cravens, William Fadjo (son of William Ben Cravens) (D Ark.) Feb. 15, 1889–April 16, 1974; House Sept. 12, 1939–49.

Crawford, Coe Isaac (R S.D.) Jan. 14, 1858–April 25, 1944; Senate 1909–15; Gov. Jan. 8, 1907–Jan. 5, 1909.

Crawford, Fred Lewis (R Mich.) May 5, 1888–April 13, 1957; House 1935–53.

Crawford, George Washington (W Ga.) Dec. 22, 1798–July 27, 1872; House Jan. 7–March 3, 1843; Gov. Nov. 8, 1843–Nov. 3, 1847; secretary of war March 8, 1849–July 23, 1850.

Crawford, Joel (R Ga.) June 15, 1783–April 5, 1858; House 1817–21.

Crawford, Martin Jenkins (D Ga.) March 17, 1820–July 23, 1883; House 1855–Jan. 23, 1861.

Crawford, Thomas Hartley (J Pa.) Nov. 14, 1786–Jan. 27, 1863; House 1829–33.

Crawford, William (R Pa.) 1760–Oct. 23, 1823; House 1809–17.

Crawford, William Harris (– Ga.) Feb. 24, 1772–Sept. 15, 1834; Senate Nov. 7, 1807–March 23, 1813; elected pres. pro tempore March 24, 1812; secretary of war Aug. 1, 1815–Oct. 22, 1816; secretary of the Treasury Oct. 22, 1816–March 6, 1825.

Crawford, William Thomas (D N.C.) June 1, 1856–Nov. 16, 1913; House 1891–95, 1899–May 10, 1900, 1907–09.

Creager, Charles Edward (R Okla.) April 28, 1873–Jan. 11, 1964; House 1909–11.

Creal, Edward Wester (D Ky.) Nov. 20, 1883–Oct. 13, 1943; House Nov. 5, 1935–Oct. 13, 1943.

Creamer, Thomas James (D N.Y.) May 26, 1843–Aug. 4, 1914; House 1873–75, 1901–03.

Crebs, John Montgomery (D Ill.) April 9, 1830–June 26, 1890; House 1869–73.

Creely, John Vaudain (IR Pa.) Nov. 14, 1839–Sept. 28, 1900; House 1871–73.

Creighton, William Jr. (R Ohio) Oct. 29, 1778–Oct. 1, 1851; House May 4, 1813–17, 1827–28, 1829–33.

Cremeans, Frank A. (R Ohio) April 5, 1943–Jan. 2, 2003; House 1995–97.

Crenshaw, Ander (R Fla.) Sept. 1, 1944– ; House 2001– .

Creswell, John Angel James (R Md.) Nov. 18, 1828–Dec. 23, 1891; House 1863–65; Senate March 9, 1865–67; postmaster general March 6, 1869–July 6, 1874.

Cretella, Albert William (R Conn.) April 22, 1897–May 24, 1979; House 1953–59.

Crippa, Edward David (R Wyo.) April 8, 1899–Oct. 20, 1960; Senate June 24–Nov. 28, 1954.

Crisfeld, John Woodland (U Md.) Nov. 8, 1806–Jan. 12, 1897; House 1847–49 (Whig), 1861–63.

Crisp, Charles Frederick (father of Charles Robert Crisp) (D Ga.) Jan. 29, 1845–Oct. 23, 1896; House 1883–Oct. 23, 1896; Speaker Dec. 8, 1891–93, Aug. 7, 1893–95.

Crisp, Charles Robert (son of Charles Frederick Crisp) (D Ga.) Oct. 19, 1870–Feb. 7, 1937; House Dec. 19, 1896–97, 1913–Oct. 7, 1932.

Crist, Henry (R Ky.) Oct. 20, 1764–Aug. 11, 1844; House 1809–11.

Critcher, John (D Va.) March 11, 1820–Sept. 27, 1901; House 1871–73.

Crittenden, John Jordan (uncle of Thomas Theodore Crittenden) (U Ky.) Sept. 10, 1786–July 26, 1863; Senate 1817–19 (no party), 1835–41 (Whig), March 31, 1842–June 12, 1848 (Whig), 1855–61 (Whig); House 1861–63; Gov. June 1, 1848–July 1850 (Whig); attorney general March 5–Sept. 13, 1841, July 22, 1850–March 3, 1853.

Crittenden, Thomas Theodore (nephew of John Jordan Crittenden) (D Mo.) Jan. 1, 1832–May 29, 1909; House 1873–75, 1877–79; Gov. Jan. 10, 1881–Jan. 12, 1885.

Crocheron, Henry (brother of Jacob Crocheron) (R N.Y.) Dec. 26, 1772–Nov. 8, 1819; House 1815–17.

Crocheron, Jacob (brother of Henry Crocheron) (J N.Y.) Aug. 23, 1774–Dec. 27, 1849; House 1829–31.

Crocker, Alvah (R Mass.) Oct. 14, 1801–Dec. 26, 1874; House Jan. 2, 1872–Dec. 26, 1874.

Crocker, Samuel Leonard (W Mass.) March 31, 1804–Feb. 10, 1883; House 1853–55.

Crockett, David (father of John Wesley Crockett) (AJ Tenn.) Aug. 17, 1786–March 6, 1836; House 1827–31 (no party), 1833–35.

Crockett, George William Jr. (D Mich.) Aug. 10, 1909–Sept. 7, 1997; House Nov. 12, 1980–91.

Crockett, John Wesley (son of David Crockett) (W Tenn.) July 10, 1807–Nov. 24, 1852; House 1837–41.

Croft, George William (father of Theodore Gaillard Croft) (D S.C.) Dec. 20, 1846–March 10, 1904; House 1903–March 10, 1904.

Croft, Theodore Gaillard (son of George William Croft) (D S.C.) Nov. 26, 1874–March 23, 1920; House May 17, 1904–05.

Croll, William Martin (D Pa.) April 9, 1866–Oct. 21, 1929; House 1923–25.

Cromer, George Washington (R Ind.) May 13, 1856–Nov. 8, 1936; House 1899–1907.

Cronin, Paul William (R Mass.) March 14, 1938–April 5, 1997; House 1973–75.

Crook, Thurman Charles (D Ind.) July 18, 1891–Oct. 23, 1981; House 1949–51.

Crooke, Philip Schuyler (R N.Y.) March 2, 1810–March 17, 1881; House 1873–75.

Crosby, Charles Noel (D Pa.) Sept. 29, 1876–Jan. 26, 1951; House 1933–39.

Crosby, John Crawford (D Mass.) June 15, 1859–Oct. 14, 1943; House 1891–93.

Cross, Edward (D Ark.) Nov. 11, 1798–April 6, 1887; House 1839–45.

Cross, Oliver Harlan (D Texas) July 13, 1868–April 24, 1960; House 1929–37.

Crosser, Robert (D Ohio) June 7, 1874–June 3, 1957; House 1913–19, 1923–55; chair House Interstate and Foreign Commerce 1949–53.

Crossland, Edward (D Ky.) June 30, 1827–Sept. 11, 1881; House 1871–75.

Crouch, Edward (R Pa.) Nov. 9, 1764–Feb. 2, 1827; House Oct. 12, 1813–15.

Crounse, Lorenzo (R Neb.) Jan. 27, 1834–May 13, 1909; House 1873–77; Gov. Jan. 13, 1893–Jan. 3, 1895.

Crouse, George Washington (R Ohio) Nov. 23, 1832–Jan. 5, 1912; House 1887–89.

Crow, Charles Augustus (R Mo.) March 31, 1873–March 20, 1938; House 1909–11.

Crow, William Evans (father of William Josiah Crow) (R Pa.) March 10, 1870–Aug. 2, 1922; Senate Oct. 24, 1921–Aug. 2, 1922.

Crow, William Josiah (son of William Evans Crow) (R Pa.) Jan. 22, 1902–Oct. 13, 1974; House 1947–49.

Crowe, Eugene Burgess (D Ind.) Jan. 5, 1878–May 12, 1970; House 1931–41.

Crowell, John (– Ala.) Sept. 18, 1780–June 25, 1846; House (Terr. Del.) Jan. 29, 1818–19, (Rep.) Dec. 14, 1819–21.

Crowell, John (W Ohio) Sept. 15, 1801–March 8, 1883; House 1847–51.

Crowley, Joseph (D N.Y.) March 16, 1962– ; House 1999– .

Crowley, Joseph Burns (D Ohio) July 19, 1858–June 25, 1931; House 1899–1905.

Crowley, Miles (D Texas) Feb. 22, 1859–Sept. 22, 1921; House 1895–97.

Crowley, Richard (R N.Y.) Dec. 14, 1836–July 22, 1908; House 1879–83.

Crowninshield, Benjamin Williams (brother of Jacob Crowninshield) (– Mass.) Dec. 27, 1772–Feb. 3, 1851; House 1823–31; secretary of the navy Jan. 16, 1815–Sept. 30, 1818.

Crowninshield, Jacob (brother of Benjamin Williams Crowninshield) (R Mass.) March 31, 1770–April 15, 1808; House 1803–April 15, 1808.

Crowther, Frank (R N.Y.) July 10, 1870–July 20, 1955; House 1919–43.

Crowther, George Calhoun (R Mo.) Jan. 26, 1849–March 18, 1914; House 1895–97.

Croxton, Thomas (D Va.) March 8, 1822–July 3, 1903; House 1885–87.

Crozier, John Hervey (W Tenn.) Feb. 10, 1812–Oct. 25, 1889; House 1845–49.

Crozier, Robert (R Kan.) Oct. 13, 1827–Oct. 2, 1895; Senate Nov. 24, 1873–Feb. 12, 1874.

Crudup, Josiah (– N.C.) Jan. 13, 1791–May 20, 1872; House 1821–23.

Cruger, Daniel (R N.Y.) Dec. 22, 1780–July 12, 1843; House 1817–19.

Crump, Edward Hull (D Tenn.) Oct. 2, 1874–Oct. 16, 1954; House 1931–35.

Crump, George William (– Va.) Sept. 26, 1786–Oct. 1, 1848; House Jan. 21, 1826–27.

Crump, Rousseau Owen (R Mich.) May 20, 1843–May 1, 1901; House 1895–May 1, 1901.

Crumpacker, Edgar Dean (father of Maurice Edgar Crumpacker, cousin of Shepard J. Crumpacker Jr.) (R Ind.) May 27, 1851–May 19, 1920; House 1897–1913.

Crumpacker, Maurice Edgar (son of Edgar Dean Crumpacker, cousin of Shepard J. Crumpacker Jr.) (R Ore.) Dec. 19, 1886–July 24, 1927; House 1925–July 24, 1927.

Crumpacker, Shepard J. Jr. (cousin of Edgar Dean Crumpacker and Maurice Edgar Crumpacker) (R Ind.) Feb. 13, 1917–Oct. 14, 1986; House 1951–57.

Crutchfield, William (R Tenn.) Nov. 16, 1824–Jan. 24, 1890; House 1873–75.

Cubin, Barbara (R Wyo.) Nov. 30, 1946– ; House 1995– .

Cuellar, Henry Roberto (D Texas) Sept. 19, 1955– ; House 2005– .

Culberson, Charles Allen (son of David Browning Culberson) (D Texas) June 10, 1855–March 19, 1925; Senate 1899–1923; Gov. Jan. 15, 1895–Jan. 17, 1899.

Culberson, David Browning (father of Charles Allen Culberson, great-great uncle of John A. Culberson) (D Texas) Sept. 29, 1830–May 7, 1900; House 1875–97.

Culberson, John A. (R Texas) (great-great nephew of David Browning Culberson) Aug. 24, 1956– ; House 2001– .

Culbertson, William Constantine (R Pa.) Nov. 25, 1825–May 24, 1906; House 1889–91.

Culbertson, William Wirt (R Ky.) Sept. 22, 1835–Oct. 31, 1911; House 1883–85.

Culbreth, Thomas (R Md.) April 13, 1786–April 16, 1843; House 1817–21.

Culkin, Francis Dugan (R N.Y.) Nov. 10, 1874–Aug. 4, 1943; House Nov. 6, 1928–Aug. 4, 1943.

Cullen, Elisha Dickerson (AP Del.) April 23, 1799–Feb. 8, 1862; House 1855–57.

Cullen, Thomas Henry (D N.Y.) March 29, 1868–March 1, 1944; House 1919–March 1, 1944.

Cullen, William (R Ill.) March 4, 1826–Jan. 17, 1914; House 1881–85.

Cullom, Alvan (brother of William Cullom, uncle of Shelby Moore Cullom) (D Tenn.) Sept. 4, 1797–July 20, 1877; House 1843–47.

Cullom, Shelby Moore (nephew of Alvan Cullom and William Cullom) (R Ill.) Nov. 22, 1829–Jan. 28, 1914; House 1865–71; Senate 1883–1913; Senate majority leader 1911–13; Gov. Jan. 8, 1877–Feb. 8, 1883.

Cullom, William (brother of Alvan Cullom, uncle of Shelby Moore Cullom) (W Tenn.) June 4, 1810–Dec. 6, 1896; House 1851–55.

Cullop, William Allen (D Ind.) March 28, 1853–Oct. 9, 1927; House 1909–17.

Culpepper, John (F N.C.) 1761–Jan. 1841; House 1807–Jan. 2, 1808, Feb. 23, 1808–09, 1813–17, 1819–21, 1823–25, 1827–29.

Culver, Charles Vernon (R Pa.) Sept. 6, 1830–Jan. 10, 1909; House 1865–67.

Culver, Erastus Dean (W N.Y.) March 15, 1803–Oct. 13, 1889; House 1845–47.

Culver, John Chester (D Iowa) Aug. 8, 1932– ; House 1965–75; Senate 1975–81.

Cumback, William (R Ind.) March 24, 1829–July 31, 1905; House 1855–57.

Cumming, Thomas William (D N.Y.) 1814 or 1815–Oct. 13, 1855; House 1853–55.

Cummings, Amos Jay (D N.Y.) May 15, 1841–May 2, 1902; House 1887–89, Nov. 5, 1889–Nov. 21, 1894, Nov. 5, 1895–May 2, 1902.

Cummings, Elijah E. (D Md.) Jan. 18, 1951– ; House April 25, 1996– .

Cummings, Fred Nelson (D Colo.) Sept. 18, 1864–Nov. 10, 1952; House 1933–41.

Cummings, Henry Johnson Brodhead (R Iowa) May 21, 1831–April 16, 1909; House 1877–79.

Cummings, Herbert Wesley (D Pa.) July 13, 1873–March 4, 1956; House 1923–25.

Cummins, Albert Baird (R Iowa) Feb. 15, 1850–July 30, 1926; Senate Nov. 24, 1908–July 30, 1926; elected pres. pro tempore May 19, 1919, March 7, 1921; Gov. Jan. 16, 1902–Nov. 24, 1908.

Cummins, John D. (D Ohio) 1791–Sept. 11, 1849; House 1845–49.

Cunningham, Francis Alanson (D Ohio) Nov. 9, 1804–Aug. 16, 1864; House 1845–47.

Cunningham, Glenn Clarence (R Neb.) Sept. 10, 1912–Dec. 18, 1988; House 1957–71.

Cunningham, John Edward III (R Wash.) March 27, 1931– ; House May 17, 1977–79.

Cunningham, Paul Harvey (R Iowa) June 15, 1890–July 16, 1961; House 1941–59.

Cunningham, Randall "Duke" (R Calif.) Dec. 8, 1941– ; House 1991– .

Curley, Edward Walter (D N.Y.) May 23, 1873–Jan. 6, 1940; House Nov. 5, 1935–Jan. 6, 1940.

Curley, James Michael (D Mass.) Nov. 20, 1874–Nov. 12, 1958; House 1911–Feb. 4, 1914, 1943–47; Gov. Jan. 3, 1935–Jan. 7, 1937.

Curlin, William Prather Jr. (D Ky.) Nov. 30, 1933– ; House Dec. 4, 1971–73.

Currie, Gilbert Archibald (R Mich.) Sept. 19, 1882–June 5, 1960; House 1917–21.

Currier, Frank Dunklee (R N.H.) Oct. 30, 1853–Nov. 25, 1921; House 1901–13.

Curry, Charles Forrest (father of Charles Forrest Curry Jr.) (R Calif.) March 14, 1858–Oct. 10, 1930; House 1913–Oct. 10, 1930.

Curry, Charles Forrest Jr. (son of Charles Forrest Curry) (R Calif.) Aug. 13, 1893–Oct. 7, 1972; House 1931–33.

Curry, George (R N.M.) April 3, 1861–Nov. 27, 1947; House Jan. 8, 1912–13; Gov. (N.M. Terr.) 1907–11.

Curry, Jabez Lamar Monroe (D Ala.) June 5, 1825–Feb. 12, 1903; House 1857–Jan. 21, 1861.

Curtin, Andrew Gregg (D Pa.) April 22, 1815–Oct. 7, 1894; House 1881–87; Gov. Jan. 15, 1861–Jan. 15, 1867 (Republican).

Curtin, Willard Sevier (R Pa.) Nov. 18, 1905–Feb. 4, 1996; House 1957–67.

Curtis, Carl Thomas (R Neb.) March 15, 1905–Jan. 24, 2000; House 1939–Dec. 31, 1954; Senate Jan. 1, 1955–79.

Curtis, Carlton Brandaga (R Pa.) Dec. 17, 1811–March 17, 1883; House 1851–55 (Democrat), 1873–75.

Curtis, Charles (R Kan.) Jan. 25, 1860–Feb. 8, 1936; House 1893–Jan. 28, 1907; Senate Jan. 29, 1907–13, 1915–29; elected pres. pro tempore Dec. 4, 1911 (to serve Dec. 4–Dec. 12, 1911); Senate majority leader Nov. 28, 1924–29; vice president 1929–33.

Curtis, Edward (W N.Y.) Oct. 25, 1801–Aug. 2, 1856; House 1837–41.

Curtis, George Martin (R Iowa) April 1, 1844–Feb. 9, 1921; House 1895–99.

Curtis, Laurence (R Mass.) Sept. 3, 1893–July 11, 1989; House 1953–63.

Curtis, Newton Martin (R N.Y.) May 21, 1835–Jan. 8, 1910; House Nov. 3, 1891–97.

Curtis, Samuel Ryan (R Iowa) Feb. 3, 1805–Dec. 25, 1866; House 1857–Aug. 4, 1861.

Curtis, Thomas Bradford (R Mo.) May 14, 1911–Jan. 10, 1993; House 1951–69.

Cusack, Thomas (D Ill.) Oct. 5, 1858–Nov. 19, 1926; House 1899–1901.

Cushing, Caleb (W Mass.) Jan. 17, 1800–Jan. 2, 1879; House 1835–43; attorney general March 7, 1853–March 3, 1857.

Cushman, Francis Wellington (R Wash.) May 8, 1867–July 6, 1909; House 1899–July 6, 1909.

Cushman, John Paine (F N.Y.) March 8, 1784–Sept. 16, 1848; House 1817–19.

Cushman, Joshua (– Maine) April 11, 1761–Jan. 27, 1834; House 1819–21 (Mass.), 1821–25.

Cushman, Samuel (D N.H.) June 8, 1783–May 20, 1851; House 1835–39 (1835–37 Jacksonian).

Cutcheon, Byron M. (R Mich.) May 11, 1836–April 12, 1908; House 1883–91.

Cuthbert, Alfred (brother of John Alfred Cuthbert) (R Ga.) Dec. 23, 1785–July 9, 1856; House Dec. 13, 1813–Nov. 9, 1816, 1821–27; Senate Jan. 12, 1835–43.

Cuthbert, John Alfred (brother of Alfred Cuthbert) (– Ga.) June 3, 1788–Sept. 22, 1881; House 1819–21.

Cutler, Augustus William (D N.J.) Oct. 22, 1827–Jan. 1, 1897; House 1875–79.

Cutler, Manasseh (F Mass.) May 13, 1742–July 28, 1823; House 1801–05.

Cutler, William Parker (R Ohio) July 12, 1812–April 11, 1889; House 1861–63.

Cutting, Bronson Murray (R N.M.) June 23, 1888–May 6, 1935; Senate Dec. 29, 1927–Dec. 6, 1928, 1929–May 6, 1935.

Cutting, Francis Brockholst (D N.Y.) Aug. 6, 1804–June 26, 1870; House 1853–55.

Cutting, John Tyler (R Calif.) Sept. 7, 1844–Nov. 24, 1911; House 1891–93.

Cutts, Charles (F N.H.) Jan. 31, 1769–Jan. 25, 1846; Senate June 21, 1810–March 3, 1813, April 2–June 10, 1813.

Cutts, Marsena Edgar (R Iowa) May 22, 1833–Sept. 1, 1883; House 1881–Sept. 1, 1883.

Cutts, Richard (R Mass.) June 28, 1771–April 7, 1845; House 1801–13.

Daddario, Emilio Quincy (D Conn.) Sept. 24, 1918– ; House 1959–71.

Daggett, David (F Conn.) Dec. 31, 1764–April 12, 1851; Senate May 13, 1813–19.

Daggett, Rollin Mallory (R Nev.) Feb. 22, 1831–Nov. 12, 1901; House 1879–81.

Dague, Paul Bartram (R Pa.) May 19, 1898–Dec. 2, 1974; House 1947–67.

Dahle, Herman Bjorn (R Wis.) March 30, 1855–April 25, 1920; House 1899–1903.

Daily, Samuel Gordon (R Neb.) 1823–Aug. 15, 1866; House (Terr. Del.) May 18, 1860–65.

Dale, Harry Howard (D N.Y.) Dec. 3, 1868–Nov. 17, 1935; House 1913–Jan. 6, 1919.

Dale, Porter Hinman (R Vt.) March 1, 1867–Oct. 6, 1933; House 1915–Aug. 11, 1923; Senate Nov. 7, 1923–Oct. 6, 1933.

Dale, Thomas Henry (R Pa.) June 12, 1846–Aug. 21, 1912; House 1905–07.

D'Alesandro, Thomas Jr. (father of Nancy Pelosi) (D Md.) Aug. 1, 1903–Aug. 23, 1987; House 1939–May 16, 1947.

Dallas, George Mifflin (great-great-great-uncle of Claiborne de Borda Pell) (D Pa.) July 10, 1792–Dec. 31, 1864; Senate Dec. 13, 1831–33; vice president 1845–49.

Dallinger, Frederick William (R Mass.) Oct. 2, 1871–Sept. 5, 1955; House 1915–25, Nov. 2, 1926–Oct. 1, 1932.

Dalton, Tristram (– Mass.) May 28, 1738–May 30, 1817; Senate 1789–91; Cont. Cong. (elected but did not attend) 1783, 1784.

Daly, John Burrwood (D Pa.) Feb. 13, 1872–March 12, 1939; House 1935–March 12, 1939.

Daly, William Davis (D N.J.) June 4, 1851–July 31, 1900; House 1899–July 31, 1900.

Dalzell, John (R Pa.) April 19, 1845–Oct. 2, 1927; House 1887–1913.

D'Amato, Alfonse Marcello (R N.Y.) Aug. 1, 1937– ; Senate 1981–99; chair Senate Banking, Housing, and Urban Affairs 1995–99.

D'Amours, Norman Edward (D N.H.) Oct. 14, 1937– ; House 1975–85.

Damrell, William Shapleigh (R Mass.) Nov. 29, 1809–May 17, 1860; House 1855–59 (1855–57 American Party).

Dana, Amasa (D N.Y.) Oct. 19, 1792–Dec. 24, 1867; House 1839–41, 1843–45.

Dana, Judah (D Maine) April 25, 1772–Dec. 27, 1845; Senate Dec. 7, 1836–37.

Dana, Samuel (R Mass.) June 26, 1767–Nov. 20, 1835; House Sept. 22, 1814–15.

Dana, Samuel Whittlesey (F Conn.) Feb. 13, 1760–July 21, 1830; House Jan. 3, 1797–May 10, 1810 (no party); Senate May 10, 1810–21.

Danaher, John Anthony (R Conn.) Jan. 9, 1899–Sept. 22, 1990; Senate 1939–45.

Dane, Joseph (– Maine) Oct. 25, 1778–May 1, 1858; House Nov. 6, 1820–23.

Danford, Lorenzo (R Ohio) Oct. 18, 1829–June 19, 1899; House 1873–79, 1895–June 19, 1899.

Danforth, Henry Gold (R N.Y.) June 14, 1854–April 8, 1918; House 1911–17.

Danforth, John Claggett (R Mo.) Sept. 5, 1936– ; Senate Dec. 27, 1976–95; chair Senate Commerce, Science, and Transportation 1985–87.

Daniel, Charles Ezra (D S.C.) Nov. 11, 1895–Sept. 13, 1964; Senate Sept. 6–Dec. 23, 1954.

Daniel, Henry (J Ky.) March 15, 1786–Oct. 5, 1873; House 1827–33.

Daniel, John Reeves Jones (D N.C.) Jan. 13, 1802–June 22, 1868; House 1841–53.

Daniel, John Warwick (D Va.) Sept. 5, 1842–June 29, 1910; House 1885–87; Senate 1887–June 29, 1910.

Daniel, Price Marion (D Texas) Oct. 10, 1910–Aug. 25, 1988; Senate 1953–Jan. 14, 1957; Gov. Jan. 15, 1957–Jan. 15, 1963.

Daniel, Robert Williams Jr. (R Va.) March 17, 1936– ; House 1973–83.

Daniel, Wilbur Clarence "Dan" (D Va.) May 12, 1914–Jan. 23, 1988; House 1969–Jan. 23, 1988.

Daniell, Warren Fisher (D N.H.) June 26, 1826–July 30, 1913; House 1891–93.

Daniels, Charles (R N.Y.) March 24, 1825–Dec. 20, 1897; House 1893–97.

Daniels, Dominick Vincent (D N.J.) Oct. 18, 1908–July 17, 1987; House 1959–77.

Daniels, Milton John (R Calif.) April 18, 1838–Dec. 1, 1914; House 1903–05.

Danielson, George Elmore (D Calif.) Feb. 20, 1915–Sept. 12, 1998; House 1971–March 9, 1982.

Dannemeyer, William Edwin (R Calif.) Sept. 22, 1929– ; House 1979–93.

Danner, Joel Buchanan (D Pa.) 1804–July 29, 1885; House Dec. 2, 1850–51.

Danner, Patsy Ann "Pat" (D Mo.) Jan. 13, 1934– ; House 1993–2001.

Darby, Ezra (R N.J.) June 7, 1768–Jan. 27, 1808; House 1805–Jan. 27, 1808.

Darby, Harry (R Kan.) Jan. 23, 1895–Jan. 17, 1987; Senate Dec. 2, 1949–Nov. 28, 1950.

Darby, John Fletcher (W Mo.) Dec. 10, 1803–May 11, 1882; House 1851–53.

Darden, Colgate Whitehead Jr. (D Va.) Feb. 11, 1897–June 9, 1981; House 1933–37, 1939–March 1, 1941; Gov. Jan. 21, 1942–Jan. 16, 1946.

Darden, George "Buddy" (D Ga.) Nov. 22, 1943– ; House Nov. 8, 1983–95.

Dargan, Edmund Strother (D Ala.) April 15, 1805–Nov. 22, 1879; House 1845–47.

Dargan, George William (great-grandson of Lemuel Benton) (D S.C.) May 11, 1841–June 29, 1898; House 1883–91.

Darling, Mason Cook (D Wis.) May 18, 1801–March 12, 1866; House June 9, 1848–49.

Darling, William Augustus (R N.Y.) Dec. 27, 1817–May 26, 1895; House 1865–67.

Darlington, Edward (cousin of Isaac Darlington and William Darlington, second cousin of Smedley Darlington) (AMas. Pa.) Sept. 17, 1795–Nov. 21, 1884; House 1833–39.

Darlington, Isaac (cousin of Edward Darlington and William Darlington, second cousin of Smedley Darlington) (F Pa.) Dec. 13, 1781–April 27, 1839; House 1817–19.

Darlington, Smedley (second cousin of Edward Darlington, Isaac Darlington, and William Darlington) (R Pa.) Dec. 24, 1827–June 24, 1899; House 1887–91.

Darlington, William (cousin of Edward Darlington and Isaac Darlington, second cousin of Smedley Darlington) (R Pa.) April 28, 1782–April 23, 1863; House 1815–17, 1819–23.

Darragh, Archibald Bard (R Mich.) Dec. 23, 1840–Feb. 21, 1927; House 1901–09.

Darragh, Cornelius (W Pa.) 1809–Dec. 22, 1854; House March 26, 1844–47.

Darrall, Chester Bidwell (R La.) June 24, 1842–Jan. 1, 1908; House 1869–Feb. 20, 1878, 1881–83.

Darrow, George Potter (R Pa.) Feb. 4, 1859–June 7, 1943; House 1915–37, 1939–41.

Daschle, Thomas Andrew (D S.D.) Dec. 9, 1947– ; House 1979–87; Senate 1987–2005; Senate minority leader 1995–June 6, 2001, 2003–05; Senate majority leader June 6, 2001–03.

Daub, Harold John "Hal" Jr. (R Neb.) April 23, 1941– ; House 1981–89.

Daugherty, James Alexander (D Mo.) Aug. 30, 1847–Jan. 26, 1920; House 1911–13.

Daughton, Ralph Hunter (D Va.) Sept. 23, 1885–Dec. 22, 1958; House Nov. 7, 1944–47.

Davee, Thomas (D Maine) Dec. 9, 1797–Dec. 9, 1841; House 1837–41.

Davenport, Franklin (F N.J.) Sept. 1755–July 27, 1832; Senate Dec. 5, 1798–99; House 1799–1801.

Davenport, Frederick Morgan (R N.Y.) Aug. 27, 1866–Dec. 26, 1956; House 1925–33.

Davenport, Harry James (D Pa.) Aug. 28, 1902–Dec. 19, 1977; House 1949–51.

Davenport, Ira (R N.Y.) June 28, 1841–Oct. 6, 1904; House 1885–89.

Davenport, James (brother of John Davenport of Conn.) (F Conn.) Oct. 12, 1758–Aug. 3, 1797; House Dec. 5, 1796–Aug. 3, 1797.

Davenport, James Sanford (D Okla.) Sept. 21, 1864–Jan. 3, 1940; House Nov. 16, 1907–09, 1911–17.

Davenport, John (brother of James Davenport) (F Conn.) Jan. 16, 1752–Nov. 28, 1830; House 1799–1817.

Davenport, John (– Ohio) Jan. 9, 1788–July 18, 1855; House 1827–29.

Davenport, Samuel Arza (R Pa.) Jan. 15, 1834–Aug. 1, 1911; House 1897–1901.

Davenport, Stanley Woodward (D Pa.) July 21, 1861–Sept. 26, 1921; House 1899–1901.

Davenport, Thomas (AJ Va.) ?–Nov. 18, 1838; House 1825–35 (1825–29 no party, 1829–33 Jacksonian).

Davey, Martin Luther (D Ohio) July 25, 1884–March 31, 1946; House Nov. 5, 1918–21, 1923–29; Gov. Jan. 14, 1935–Jan. 9, 1939.

Davey, Robert Charles (D La.) Oct. 22, 1853–Dec. 26, 1908; House 1893–95, 1897–Dec. 26, 1908.

Davidson, Alexander Caldwell (D Ala.) Dec. 26, 1826–Nov. 6, 1897; House 1885–89.

Davidson, Irwin Delmore (D/L N.Y.) Jan. 2, 1906–Aug. 1, 1981; House 1955–Dec. 31, 1956.

Davidson, James Henry (R Wis.) June 18, 1858–Aug. 6, 1918; House 1897–1913, 1917–Aug. 6, 1918.

Davidson, Robert Hamilton McWhorta (D Fla.) Sept. 23, 1832–Jan. 18, 1908; House 1877–91.

Davidson, Thomas Green (D La.) Aug. 3, 1805–Sept. 11, 1883; House 1855–61.

Davidson, William (F N.C.) Sept. 12, 1778–Sept. 16, 1857; House Dec. 2, 1818–21.

Davies, Edward (AMas. Pa.) Nov. 1779–May 18, 1853; House 1837–41.

Davies, John Clay (D N.Y.) May 1, 1920– ; House 1949–51.

Davila, Felix Cordova (U P.R.) Nov. 20, 1878–Dec. 3, 1938; House (Res. Comm.) Aug. 7, 1917–April 11, 1932.

Davis, Alexander Mathews (D Va.) Jan. 17, 1833–Sept. 25, 1889; House 1873–March 5, 1874.

Davis, Amos (brother of Garrett Davis) (AJ Ky.) Aug. 15, 1794–June 11, 1835; House 1833–35.

Davis, Artur (D Ala.) Oct. 9, 1967– ; House 2003– .

Davis, Charles Russell (R Minn.) Sept. 17, 1849–July 29, 1930; House 1903–25.

Davis, Clifford (D Tenn.) Nov. 18, 1897–June 8, 1970; House Feb. 15, 1940–65.

Davis, Cushman Kellogg (R Minn.) June 16, 1838–Nov. 27, 1900; Senate 1887–Nov. 27, 1900; Gov. Jan. 7, 1874–Jan. 7, 1876.

Davis, Danny K. (D Ill.) Sept. 6, 1941– ; House 1997– .

Davis, David (cousin of Henry Winter Davis) (I Ill.) March 9, 1815–June 26, 1886; Senate 1877–83; elected pres. pro tempore Oct. 13, 1881; assoc. justice Dec. 10, 1862–March 4, 1877.

Davis, Ewin Lamar (D Tenn.) Feb. 5, 1876–Oct. 23, 1949; House 1919–33.

Davis, Garrett (brother of Amos Davis) (D Ky.) Sept. 10, 1801–Sept. 22, 1872; House 1839–47 (Whig); Senate Dec. 10, 1861–Sept. 22, 1872 (1861–67 Unionist).

Davis, Geoffrey C. "Geoff" (R Ky.) Oct. 26, 1958– ; House 2005– .

Davis, George Royal (R Ill.) Jan. 3, 1840–Nov. 25, 1899; House 1879–85.

Davis, George Thomas (W Mass.) Jan. 12, 1810–June 17, 1877; House 1851–53.

Davis, Glenn Robert (R Wis.) Oct. 28, 1914–Sept. 21, 1988; House April 22, 1947–57, 1965–Dec. 31, 1974.

Davis, Henry Gassaway (brother of Thomas Beall Davis, grandfather of Davis Elkins) (D W.Va.) Nov. 16, 1823–March 11, 1916; Senate 1871–83.

Davis, Henry Winter (cousin of David Davis) (UU Md.) Aug. 16, 1817–Dec. 30, 1865; House 1855–61 (American Party), 1863–65.

Davis, Horace (R Calif.) March 16, 1831–July 12, 1916; House 1877–81.

Davis, Jack (R Ill.) Sept. 6, 1935– ; House 1987–89.

Davis, Jacob Cunningham (D Ill.) Sept. 16, 1820–Dec. 25, 1883; House Nov. 4, 1856–57.

Davis, Jacob Erastus (D Ohio) Oct. 31, 1905–Feb. 28, 2003; House 1941–43.

Davis, James Curran (D Ga.) May 17, 1895–Dec. 18, 1981; House 1947–63.

Davis, James Harvey "Cyclone" (D Texas) Dec. 24, 1853–Jan. 31, 1940; House 1915–17.

Davis, James John (R Pa.) Oct. 27, 1873–Nov. 22, 1947; Senate Dec. 2, 1930–45; secretary of labor March 5, 1921–Nov. 30, 1930.

Davis, Jeff (D Ark.) May 6, 1862–Jan. 3, 1913; Senate 1907–Jan. 3, 1913; Gov. Jan. 8, 1901–Jan. 8, 1907.

Davis, Jefferson Finis (D Miss.) June 3, 1808–Dec. 6, 1889; House 1845–June 1846; Senate Aug. 10, 1847–Sept. 23, 1851, 1857–Jan. 21, 1861; secretary of war March 7, 1853–March 6, 1857.

Davis, Jim (D Fla.) Oct. 11, 1957– ; House 1997– .

Davis, Jo Ann S. (R Va.) June 29, 1950– ; House 2001– .

Davis, John (W Mass.) Jan. 13, 1787–April 19, 1854; House 1825–Jan. 14, 1834 (no party); Senate 1835–Jan. 5, 1841, March 24, 1845–53; Gov. Jan. 9, 1834–March 1, 1835, Jan. 7, 1841–Jan. 17, 1843.

Davis, John (D Pa.) Aug. 7, 1788–April 1, 1878; House 1839–41.

Davis, John (P Kan.) Aug. 9, 1826–Aug. 1, 1901; House 1891–95.

Davis, John Givan (ALD Ind.) Oct. 10, 1810–Jan. 18, 1866; House 1851–55 (Democrat), 1857–61 (1857–59 Democrat).

Davis, John James (father of John William Davis of W.Va.) (ID W.Va.) May 5, 1835–March 19, 1916; House 1871–75 (1871–73 Democrat).

Davis, John Wesley (D Ind.) April 16, 1799–Aug. 22, 1859; House 1835–37 (Jacksonian), 1839–41, 1843–47; Speaker Dec. 1, 1845–47; Gov. (Ore. Terr.) 1853, 1854.

Davis, John William (son of John James Davis) (D W.Va.) April 13, 1873–March 24, 1955; House 1911–Aug. 29, 1913.

Davis, John William (D Ga.) Sept. 12, 1916–Oct. 3, 1992; House 1961–75.

Davis, Joseph Jonathan (D N.C.) April 13, 1828–Aug. 7, 1892; House 1875–81.

Davis, Lincoln (D Tenn.) Sept. 13, 1943– ; House 2003– .

Davis, Lowndes Henry (D Mo.) Dec. 13, 1836–Feb. 4, 1920; House 1879–85.

Davis, Mendel Jackson (D S.C.) Oct. 23, 1942– ; House April 27, 1971–81.

Davis, Noah (R N.Y.) Sept. 10, 1818–March 20, 1902; House 1869–July 15, 1870.

Davis, Reuben (D Miss.) Jan. 18, 1813–Oct. 14, 1890; House 1857–Jan. 12, 1861.

Davis, Richard David (D N.Y.) 1799–June 17, 1871; House 1841–45.

Davis, Robert Lee (R Pa.) Oct. 29, 1893–May 5, 1967; House Nov. 8, 1932–33.

Davis, Robert Thompson (R Mass.) Aug. 28, 1823–Oct. 29, 1906; House 1883–89.

Davis, Robert William (R Mich.) July 31, 1932– ; House 1979–93.

Davis, Robert Wyche (D Fla.) March 15, 1849–Sept. 15, 1929; House 1897–1905.

Davis, Roger (R Pa.) Oct. 2, 1762–Nov. 20, 1815; House 1811–15.

Davis, Samuel (F Mass.) 1774–April 20, 1831; House 1813–15.

Davis, Susan A. (D Calif.) April 13, 1944– ; House 2001– .

Davis, Thomas (D R.I.) Dec. 18, 1806–July 26, 1895; House 1853–55.

Davis, Thomas Beall (brother of Henry Gassaway Davis) (D W.Va.) April 25, 1828–Nov. 26, 1911; House June 6, 1905–07.

Davis, Thomas M. III (R Va.) Jan. 5, 1949– ; House 1995– ; chair House Government Reform 2003– .

Davis, Thomas Terry (R Ky.) ?–Nov. 15, 1807; House 1797–1803.

Davis, Thomas Treadwell (grandson of Thomas Tredwell) (R N.Y.) Aug. 22, 1810–May 2, 1872; House 1863–67 (1863–65 Unionist).

Davis, Timothy (R Iowa) March 29, 1794–April 27, 1872; House 1857–59.

Davis, Timothy (R Mass.) April 12, 1821–Oct. 23, 1888; House 1855–59 (1855–57 American Party).

Davis, Warren Ransom (N S.C.) May 8, 1793–Jan. 29, 1835; House 1827–Jan. 29, 1835 (1827–31 Jacksonian).

Davis, William Morris (R Pa.) Aug. 16, 1815–Aug. 5, 1891; House 1861–63.

Davison, George Mosby (R Ky.) March 23, 1855–Dec. 18, 1912; House 1897–99.

Davy, John Madison (R N.Y.) June 29, 1835–April 21, 1909; House 1875–77.

Dawes, Beman Gates (son of Rufus Dawes, brother of Vice Pres. Charles Gates Dawes) (R Ohio) Jan. 14, 1870–May 15, 1953; House 1905–09.

Dawes, Henry Laurens (R Mass.) Oct. 30, 1816–Feb. 5, 1903; House 1857–75 (no party); Senate 1875–93.

Dawes, Rufus (father of Vice Pres. Charles Gates Dawes and Beman Gates Dawes) (R Ohio) July 4, 1838–Aug. 2, 1899; House 1881–83.

Dawson, Albert Foster (R Iowa) Jan. 26, 1872–March 9, 1949; House 1905–11.

Dawson, John (R Va.) 1762–March 31, 1814; House 1797–March 31, 1814; Cont. Cong. 1788.

Dawson, John Bennett (D La.) March 17, 1798–June 26, 1845; House 1841–June 26, 1845.

Dawson, John Littleton (D Pa.) Feb. 7, 1813–Sept. 18, 1870; House 1851–55, 1863–67.

Dawson, William (D Mo.) March 17, 1848–Oct. 12, 1929; House 1885–87.

Dawson, William Adams (R Utah) Nov. 5, 1903–Nov. 7, 1981; House 1947–49, 1953–59.

Dawson, William Crosby (W Ga.) Jan. 4, 1798–May 5, 1856; House Nov. 7, 1836–Nov. 13, 1841 (Nov. 7, 1836–37 State Rights Party); Senate 1849–55.

Dawson, William Johnson (– N.C.) ?–1798; House 1793–95.

Dawson, William Levi (D Ill.) April 26, 1886–Nov. 9, 1970; House 1943–Nov. 9, 1970; chair House Expenditures in the Executive Departments 1949–52; chair House Government Operations 1952–53, 1955–71.

Day, Rowland (J N.Y.) March 6, 1779–Dec. 23, 1853; House 1823–25 (no party), 1833–35.

Day, Stephen Albion (R Ill.) July 13, 1882–Jan. 5, 1950; House 1941–45.

Day, Timothy Crane (R Ohio) Jan. 8, 1819–April 15, 1869; House 1855–57.

Dayan, Charles (J N.Y.) July 8, 1792–Dec. 25, 1877; House 1831–33.

Dayton, Alston Gordon (R W.Va.) Oct. 18, 1857–July 30, 1920; House 1895–March 16, 1905.

Dayton, Mark (D Minn.) Jan. 26, 1947– ; Senate 2001– .

Dayton, Jonathan (F N.J.) Oct. 16, 1760–Oct. 9, 1824; House 1791–99 (no party); Speaker Dec. 7, 1795–97, May 15, 1797–99; Senate 1799–1805; Cont. Cong. 1787–88.

Dayton, William Lewis (W N.J.) Feb. 17, 1807–Dec. 1, 1864; Senate July 2, 1842–51.

Deal, Joseph Thomas (D Va.) Nov. 19, 1860–March 7, 1942; House 1921–29.

Deal, Nathan (R Ga.) Aug. 25, 1942– ; House 1993– (1993–April 10, 1995 Democrat).

Dean, Benjamin (D Mass.) Aug. 14, 1824–April 9, 1897; House March 28, 1878–79.

Dean, Ezra (D Ohio) April 9, 1795–Jan. 25, 1872; House 1841–45.

Dean, Gilbert (D N.Y.) Aug. 14, 1819–Oct. 12, 1870; House 1851–July 3, 1854.

Dean, Josiah (R Mass.) March 6, 1748–Oct. 14, 1818; House 1807–09.

Dean, Sidney (R Conn.) Nov. 16, 1818–Oct. 29, 1901; House 1855–59 (1855–57 American Party).

Deane, Charles Bennett (D N.C.) Nov. 1, 1898–Nov. 24, 1969; House 1947–57.

Dear, Cleveland (D La.) Aug. 22, 1888–Dec. 30, 1950; House 1933–37.

Dearborn, Henry (father of Henry Alexander Scammell Dearborn) (D Mass.) Feb. 23, 1751–June 6, 1829; House 1793–97 (1793–95 no party); secretary of war March 5, 1801–March 7, 1809.

Dearborn, Henry Alexander Scammell (son of Henry Dearborn) (AJ Mass.) March 3, 1783–July 29, 1851; House 1831–33.

De Armond, David Albaugh (D Mo.) March 18, 1844–Nov. 23, 1909; House 1891–Nov. 23, 1909.

Deberry, Edmund (W N.C.) Aug. 14, 1787–Dec. 12, 1859; House 1829–31 (no party), 1833–45 (1833–35 Anti-Jacksonian), 1849–51.

Deboe, William Joseph (R Ky.) June 30, 1849–June 15, 1927; Senate 1897–1903.

De Bolt, Rezin A. (D Mo.) Jan. 20, 1828–Oct. 30, 1891; House 1875–77.

Deckard, Huey Joel (R Ind.) March 7, 1942– ; House 1979–83.

Decker, Perl D. (D Mo.) Sept. 10, 1875–Aug. 22, 1934; House 1913–19.

Deconcini, Dennis Webster (D Ariz.) May 8, 1937– ; Senate 1977–95; chair Senate Select Intelligence Activities 1993–95.

Deemer, Elias (R Pa.) Jan. 3, 1838–March 29, 1918; House 1901–07.

Deen, Braswell Drue (D Ga.) June 28, 1893–Nov. 28, 1981; House 1933–39.

Deering, Nathaniel Cobb (R Iowa) Sept. 2, 1827–Dec. 11, 1887; House 1877–83.

DeFazio, Peter Anthony (D Ore.) May 27, 1947– ; House 1987– .

De Forest, Henry Schermerhorn (R N.Y.) Feb. 16, 1847–Feb. 13, 1917; House 1911–13.

De Forest, Robert Elliott (D Conn.) Feb. 20, 1845–Oct. 1, 1924; House 1891–95.

Defrees, Joseph Hutton (R Ind.) May 13, 1812–Dec. 21, 1885; House 1865–67.

Degener, Edward (R Texas) Oct. 20, 1809–Sept. 11, 1890; House March 31, 1870–71.

Degetau, Frederico (R P.R.) Dec. 5, 1862–Jan. 20, 1914; House (Res. Comm.) 1901–05.

DeGette, Diana (D Colo.) July 29, 1957– ; House 1997– .

De Graff, John Isaac (D N.Y.) Oct. 2, 1783–July 26, 1848; House 1827–29 (no party), 1837–39.

De Graffenreid, Reese Calhoun (D Texas) May 7, 1859–Aug. 29, 1902; House 1897–Aug. 29, 1902.

Degraffenried, Edward (D Ala.) June 30, 1899–Nov. 5, 1974; House 1949–53.

De Haven, John Jefferson (R Calif.) March 12, 1849–Jan. 26, 1913; House 1889–Oct. 1, 1890.

Deitrick, Frederick Simpson (D Mass.) April 9, 1875–May 24, 1948; House 1913–15.

De Jarnette, Daniel Coleman (ID Va.) Oct. 18, 1822–Aug. 20, 1881; House 1859–61.

De Lacy, Emerson Hugh (D Wash.) May 9, 1910–Aug. 19, 1986; House 1945–47.

De la Garza, Eligio "Kika" II (D Texas) Sept. 22, 1927– ; House 1965–97; chair House Agriculture 1981–95.

Delahunt, William D. (D Mass.) July 18, 1941– ; House 1997– .

De la Matyr, Gilbert (G Ind.) July 8, 1825–May 17, 1892; House 1879–81.

De la Montanya, James (D N.Y.) March 20, 1798–April 29, 1849; House 1839–41.

Delaney, James Joseph (D N.Y.) March 19, 1901–May 24, 1987; House 1945–47, 1949–Dec. 31, 1978; chair House Rules 1977–78.

Delaney, John Joseph (D N.Y.) Aug. 21, 1878–Nov. 18, 1948; House March 5, 1918–19, 1931–Nov. 18, 1948.

Delano, Charles (R Mass.) June 24, 1820–Jan. 23, 1883; House 1859–63.

Delano, Columbus (R Ohio) June 4, 1809–Oct. 23, 1896; House 1845–47 (Whig), 1865–67, June 3, 1868–69; secretary of the interior Nov. 1, 1870–Sept. 30, 1875.

De Lano, Milton (R N.Y.) Aug. 11, 1844–Jan. 2, 1922; House 1887–91.

Delaplaine, Isaac Clason (D N.Y.) Oct. 27, 1817–July 17, 1866; House 1861–63.

De Large, Robert Carlos (R S.C.) March 15, 1842–Feb. 14, 1874; House 1871–Jan. 24, 1873.

DeLauro, Rosa (D Conn.) March 2, 1943– ; House 1991– .

DeLay, Thomas Dale (R Texas) April 8, 1947– ; House 1985– ; House majority leader 2003– .

Delgado, Francisco Afan (Nat. P.I.) Jan. 25, 1886–Oct. 27, 1964; House (Res. Comm.) 1935–Feb. 14, 1936.

Dellay, Vincent John (D N.J.) June 23, 1907–April 16, 1999; House 1957–59 (1957 Republican).

Dellenback, John Richard (R Ore.) Nov. 6, 1918–Dec. 7, 2002; House 1967–75.

Dellet, James (W Ala.) Feb. 18, 1788–Dec. 21, 1848; House 1839–41, 1843–45.

Dellums, Ronald Vernie (D Calif.) Nov. 24, 1935– ; House 1971–Feb. 6, 1998; chair House District of Columbia 1979–93; chair House Armed Services 1993–95.

De Lugo, Ron (D V.I.) Aug. 2, 1930– ; House (Del.) 1973–79, 1981–95.

Deming, Benjamin F. (AMas. Vt.) 1790–July 11, 1834; House 1833–July 11, 1834.

Deming, Henry Champion (R Conn.) May 23, 1815–Oct. 8, 1872; House 1863–67.

DeMint, James (R S.C.) Sept. 2, 1951– ; House 1999–2005; Senate 2005– .

De Mott, John (D N.Y.) Oct. 7, 1790–July 31, 1870; House 1845–47.

De Motte, Mark Lindsey (R Ind.) Dec. 28, 1832–Sept. 23, 1908; House 1881–83.

Dempsey, John Joseph (D N.M.) June 22, 1879–March 11, 1958; House 1935–41, 1951–March 11, 1958; Gov. Jan. 1, 1943–Jan. 1, 1947.

Dempsey, Stephen Wallace (R N.Y.) May 8, 1862–March 1, 1949; House 1915–31.

De Muth, Peter Joseph (D Pa.) Jan. 1, 1892–April 3, 1993; House 1937–39.

DeNardis, Lawrence Joseph (R Conn.) March 18, 1938– ; House 1981–83.

Denby, Edwin (grandson of Graham Newell Fitch) (R Mich.) Feb. 18, 1870–Feb. 8, 1929; House 1905–11; secretary of the navy March 6, 1921–March 10, 1924.

Deneen, Charles Samuel (R Ill.) May 4, 1863–Feb. 5, 1940; Senate Feb. 26, 1925–31; Gov. Jan. 9, 1905–Feb. 3, 1913.

Denholm, Frank Edward (D S.D.) Nov. 29, 1923– ; House 1971–75.

Denison, Charles (nephew of George Denison) (D Pa.) Jan. 23, 1818–June 27, 1867; House 1863–June 27, 1867.

Denison, Dudley Chase (nephew of Dudley Chase, cousin of Salmon Portland Chase) (R Vt.) Sept. 13, 1819–Feb. 10, 1905; House 1875–79 (1875–77 Independent Republican).

Denison, Edward Everett (R Ill.) Aug. 28, 1873–June 17, 1953; House 1915–31.

Denison, George (uncle of Charles Denison) (– Pa.) Feb. 22, 1790–Aug. 20, 1831; House 1819–23.

De Nivernais, Edward James. (See Livernash, Edward James.)

Denney, Robert Vernon (R Neb.) April 11, 1916–June 26, 1981; House 1967–71.

Denning, William (– N.Y.) April 1740–Oct. 30, 1819; House 1809–10.

Dennis, David Worth (R Ind.) June 7, 1912–Jan. 6, 1999; House 1969–75.

Dennis, George Robertson (D Md.) April 8, 1822–Aug. 13, 1882; Senate 1873–79.

Dennis, John (father of John Dennis, below, uncle of Littleton Purnell Dennis) (F Md.) Dec. 17, 1771–Aug. 17, 1806; House 1797–1805.

Dennis, John (son of John Dennis, above) (W Md.) 1807–Nov. 1, 1859; House 1837–41.

Dennis, Littleton Purnell (nephew of John Dennis born in 1771, cousin of John Dennis born in 1807) (AJ Md.) July 21, 1786–April 14, 1834; House 1833–April 14, 1834.

Dennison, David Short (R Ohio) July 29, 1918–Sept. 21, 2001; House 1957–59.

Denny, Arthur Armstrong (R Wash.) June 20, 1822–Jan. 9, 1899; House (Terr. Del.) 1865–67.

Denny, Harmar (great-grandfather of Harmar Denny Denny Jr.) (AMas. Pa.) May 13, 1794–Jan. 29, 1852; House Dec. 15, 1829–37.

Denny, Harmar Denny Jr. (great-grandson of Harmar Denny) (R Pa.) July 2, 1886–Jan. 6, 1966; House 1951–53.

Denny, James William (D Md.) Nov. 20, 1838–April 12, 1923; House 1899–1901, 1903–05.

Denny, Walter McKennon (D Miss.) Oct. 28, 1853–Nov. 5, 1926; House 1895–97.

Denoyelles, Peter (R N.Y.) 1766–May 6, 1829; House 1813–15.

Denson, William Henry (D Ala.) March 4, 1846–Sept. 26, 1906; House 1893–95.

Dent, Charles W. (R Pa.) May 24, 1960– ; House 2005– .

Dent, George (F Md.) 1756–Dec. 2, 1813; House 1793–1801 (1793–95 no party).

Dent, John Herman (D Pa.) March 10, 1908–April 9, 1988; House Jan. 21, 1958–79.

Dent, Stanley Hubert Jr. (D Ala.) Aug. 16, 1869–Oct. 6, 1938; House 1909–21.

Dent, William Barton Wade (D Ga.) Sept. 8, 1806–Sept. 7, 1855; House 1853–55.

Denton, George Kirkpatrick (father of Winfield Kirkpatrick Denton) (D Ind.) Nov. 17, 1864–Jan. 4, 1926; House 1917–19.

Denton, Jeremiah Andrew Jr. (R Ala.) July 15, 1924– ; Senate Jan. 2, 1981–87.

Denton, Winfield Kirkpatrick (son of George Kirkpatrick Denton) (D Ind.) Oct. 28, 1896–Nov. 2, 1971; House 1949–53, 1955–67.

Denver, James William (father of Matthew Rombach Denver) (D Calif.) Oct. 23, 1817–Aug. 9, 1892; House 1855–57; Gov. (Kansas Terr.) June 7, 1857–58.

Denver, Matthew Rombach (son of James William Denver) (D Ohio) Dec. 21, 1870–May 13, 1954; House 1907–13.

Depew, Chauncey Mitchell (R N.Y.) April 23, 1834–April 5, 1928; Senate 1899–1911.

De Priest, Oscar (R Ill.) March 9, 1871–May 12, 1951; House 1929–35.

De Rouen, René Louis (D La.) Jan. 7, 1874–March 27, 1942; House Aug. 23, 1927–41.

Derounian, Steven Boghos (R N.Y.) April 6, 1918– ; House 1953–65.

Derrick, Butler Carson Jr. (D S.C.) Sept. 30, 1936– ; House 1975–95.

Dershem, Franklin Lewis (D Pa.) March 5, 1865–Feb. 14, 1950; House 1913–15.

Derwinski, Edward Joseph (R Ill.) Sept. 15, 1926– ; House 1959–83; secretary of veterans affairs March 15, 1989–Sept. 26, 1992.

De Saussure, William Ford (D S.C.) Feb. 22, 1792–March 13, 1870; Senate May 10, 1852–53.

Desha, Joseph (brother of Robert Desha) (R Ky.) Dec. 9, 1768–Oct. 11, 1842; House 1807–19; Gov. June 1, 1824–June 1, 1828 (Democratic Republican).

Desha, Robert (brother of Joseph Desha) (J Tenn.) Jan. 14, 1791–Feb. 6, 1849; House 1827–31.

Destrehan, Jean Noel (– La.) 1754–1823; Senate Sept. 3–Oct. 1, 1812.

Deuster, Peter Victor (D Wis.) Feb. 13, 1831–Dec. 31, 1904; House 1879–85.

Deutsch, Peter (D Fla.) April 1, 1957– ; House 1993–2005.

Devereux, James Patrick Sinnott (R Md.) Feb. 20, 1903–Aug. 5, 1988; House 1951–59.

De Veyra, Jaime Carlos (Nat. P.I.) Nov. 4, 1873–March 7, 1963; House (Res. Comm.) 1917–23.

Devine, Samuel Leeper (R Ohio) Dec. 21, 1915–June 27, 1997; House 1959–81.

Devitt, Edward James (R Minn.) May 5, 1911–March 2, 1992; House 1947–49.

De Vries, Marion (D Calif.) Aug. 15, 1865–Sept. 11, 1939; House 1897–Aug. 20, 1900.

Dewalt, Arthur Granville (D Pa.) Oct. 11, 1854–Oct. 26, 1931; House 1915–21.

Dewart, Lewis (father of William Lewis Dewart) (J Pa.) Nov. 14, 1780–April 26, 1852; House 1831–33.

D'Ewart, Wesley Abner (R Mont.) Oct. 1, 1889–Sept. 2, 1973; House June 5, 1945–55.

Dewart, William Lewis (son of Lewis Dewart) (D Pa.) June 21, 1821–April 19, 1888; House 1857–59.

Deweese, John Thomas (R N.C.) June 4, 1835–July 4, 1906; House July 6, 1868–Feb. 28, 1870.

Dewey, Charles Schuveldt (R Ill.) Nov. 10, 1880–Dec. 27, 1980; House 1941–45.

Dewey, Daniel (F Mass.) Jan. 29, 1766–May 26, 1815; House 1813–Feb. 24, 1814.

DeWine, Michael (R Ohio) Jan. 5, 1947– ; House 1983–91; Senate 1995– .

De Witt, Alexander (AP Mass.) April 2, 1798–Jan. 13, 1879; House 1853–57 (1853–55 Free-Soiler).

De Witt, Charles Gerrit (J N.Y.) Nov. 7, 1789–April 12, 1839; House 1829–31.

De Witt, David Miller (D N.Y.) Nov. 25, 1837–June 23, 1912; House 1873–75.

De Witt, Francis Byron (R Ohio) March 11, 1849–March 21, 1929; House 1895–97.

De Witt, Jacob Hasbrouck (– N.Y.) Oct. 2, 1784–Jan. 30, 1867; House 1819–21.

De Wolf, James (R R.I.) March 18, 1764–Dec. 21, 1837; Senate 1821–Oct. 31, 1825.

Dexter, Samuel (F Mass.) May 14, 1761–May 4, 1816; House 1793–95 (no party); Senate 1799–May 30, 1800; secretary of war May 13–Dec. 31, 1800; secretary of the Treasury Jan. 1–May 13, 1801.

Dezendorf, John Frederick (R Va.) Aug. 10, 1834–June 22, 1894; House 1881–83.

Dial, Nathaniel Barksdale (D S.C.) April 24, 1862–Dec. 11, 1940; Senate 1919–25.

Diaz-Balart, Lincoln (brother of Mario Diaz-Balart) (R Fla.) Aug. 13, 1954– ; House 1993– .

Diaz-Balart, Mario (brother of Lincoln Diaz-Balart) (R Fla.) Sept. 25, 1961– ; House 2003– .

Dibble, Samuel (D S.C.) Sept. 16, 1837–Sept. 16, 1913; House June 9, 1881–May 31, 1882, 1883–91.

Dibrell, George Gibbs (D Tenn.) April 12, 1822–May 9, 1888; House 1875–85.

Dick, Charles William Frederick (R Ohio) Nov. 3, 1858–March 13, 1945; House Nov. 8, 1898–March 23, 1904; Senate March 23, 1904–11.

Dick, John (father of Samuel Bernard Dick) (R Pa.) June 17, 1794–May 29, 1872; House 1853–59 (1853–55 Whig).

Dick, Samuel Bernard (son of John Dick) (R Pa.) Oct. 26, 1836–May 10, 1907; House 1879–81.

Dickens, Samuel (R N.C.) ?–1840; House Dec. 2, 1816–17.

Dickerman, Charles Heber (D Pa.) Feb. 3, 1843–Dec. 17, 1915; House 1903–05.

Dickerson, Mahlon (brother of Philemon Dickerson) (R N.J.) April 17, 1770–Oct. 5, 1853; Senate 1817–Jan. 30, 1829; Gov. Oct. 26, 1815–Feb. 1, 1817; secretary of the navy July 1, 1834–June 30, 1838.

Dickerson, Philemon (brother of Mahlon Dickerson) (D N.J.) Jan. 11, 1788–Dec. 10, 1862; House 1833–Nov. 3, 1836 (Jacksonian), 1839–41; Gov. Nov. 3, 1836–Oct. 27, 1837 (Democrat).

Dickerson, William Worth (D Ky.) Nov. 29, 1851–Jan. 31, 1923; House June 21, 1890–93.

Dickey, Henry Luther (D Ohio) Oct. 29, 1832–May 23, 1910; House 1877–81.

Dickey, Jay (R Ark.) Dec. 14, 1939– ; House 1993–2001.

Dickey, Jesse Column (W Pa.) Feb. 27, 1808–Feb. 19, 1890; House 1849–51.

Dickey, John (father of Oliver James Dickey) (W Pa.) June 23, 1794–March 14, 1853; House 1843–45, 1847–49.

Dickey, Oliver James (son of John Dickey) (R Pa.) April 6, 1823–April 21, 1876; House Dec. 7, 1868–73.

Dickinson, Clement Cabell (D Mo.) Dec. 6, 1849–Jan. 14, 1938; House Feb. 1, 1910–21, 1923–29, 1931–35.

Dickinson, Daniel Stevens (D N.Y.) Sept. 11, 1800–April 12, 1866; Senate Nov. 30, 1844–51.

Dickinson, David W. (nephew of William Hardy Murfree) (W Tenn.) June 10, 1808–April 27, 1845; House 1833–35 (Jacksonian), 1843–45.

Dickinson, Edward (W Mass.) Jan. 1, 1803–June 16, 1874; House 1853–55.

Dickinson, Edward Fenwick (D Ohio) Jan. 21, 1829–Aug. 25, 1891; House 1869–71.

Dickinson, John Dean (– N.Y.) June 28, 1767–Jan. 28, 1841; House 1819–23, 1827–31.

Dickinson, Lester Jesse (cousin of Fred Dickinson Letts) (R Iowa) Oct. 29, 1873–June 4, 1968; House 1919–31; Senate 1931–37.

Dickinson, Philemon (– N.J.) April 5, 1739–Feb. 4, 1809; Senate Nov. 23, 1790–93; Cont. Cong. 1782–83 (Del.).

Dickinson, Rodolphus (D Ohio) Dec. 28, 1797–March 20, 1849; House 1847–March 20, 1849.

Dickinson, William Louis (R Ala.) June 5, 1925– ; House 1965–93.

Dicks, Norman DeValois (D Wash.) Dec. 16, 1940– ; House 1977– .

Dickson, David (W Miss.) ?–July 31, 1836; House 1835–July 31, 1836.

Dickson, Frank Stoddard (R Ill.) Oct. 6, 1876–Feb. 24, 1953; House 1905–07.

Dickson, John (AMas. N.Y.) June 1, 1783–Feb. 22, 1852; House 1831–35.

Dickson, Joseph (F N.C.) April 1745–April 14, 1825; House 1799–1801.

Dickson, Samuel (W N.Y.) March 29, 1807–May 3, 1858; House 1855–57.

Dickson, William (R Tenn.) May 5, 1770–Feb. 1816; House 1801–07.

Dickson, William Alexander (D Miss.) July 20, 1861–Feb. 25, 1940; House 1909–13.

Dickstein, Samuel (D N.Y.) Feb. 5, 1885–April 22, 1954; House 1923–Dec. 30, 1945.

Diekema, Gerrit John (R Mich.) March 27, 1859–Dec. 20, 1930; House March 17, 1908–11.

Dies, Martin (father of Martin Dies Jr.) (D Texas) March 13, 1870–July 13, 1922; House 1909–19.

Dies, Martin Jr. (son of Martin Dies) (D Texas) Nov. 5, 1900–Nov. 14, 1972; House 1931–45, 1953–59.

Dieterich, William Henry (D Ill.) March 31, 1876–Oct. 12, 1940; House 1931–33; Senate 1933–39.

Dietrich, Charles Elmer (D Pa.) July 30, 1889–May 20, 1942; House 1935–37.

Dietrich, Charles Henry (R Neb.) Nov. 26, 1853–April 10, 1924; Senate March 28, 1901–05; Gov. Jan. 3–May 1, 1901.

Dietz, William (– N.Y.) June 28, 1778–Aug. 24, 1848; House 1825–27.

Difenderfer, Robert Edward (D Pa.) June 7, 1849–April 25, 1923; House 1911–15.

Diggs, Charles Coles Jr. (D Mich.) Dec. 2, 1922–Aug. 24, 1998; House 1955–June 3, 1980; chair House District of Columbia 1973–79.

Dill, Clarence Cleveland (D Wash.) Sept. 21, 1884–Jan. 14, 1978; House 1915–19; Senate 1923–35.

Dillingham, Paul Jr. (father of William Paul Dillingham) (D Vt.) Aug. 10, 1799–July 26, 1891; House 1843–47; Gov. Oct. 13, 1865–Oct. 13, 1867 (Republican).

Dillingham, William Paul (son of Paul Dillingham Jr.) (R Vt.) Dec. 12, 1843–July 12, 1923; Senate Oct. 18, 1900–July 12, 1923; Gov. Oct. 4, 1888–Oct. 2, 1890.

Dillon, Charles Hall (R S.D.) Dec. 18, 1853–Sept. 15, 1929; House 1913–19.

Dilweg, LaVern Ralph (D Wis.) Nov. 1, 1903–Jan. 2, 1968; House 1943–45.

Dimmick, Milo Melankthon (brother of William Harrison Dimmick) (D Pa.) Oct. 30, 1811–Nov. 22, 1872; House 1849–53.

Dimmick, William Harrison (brother of Milo Melankthon Dimmick) (D Pa.) Dec. 20, 1815–Aug. 2, 1861; House 1857–61.

Dimock, Davis Jr. (D Pa.) Sept. 17, 1801–Jan. 13, 1842; House 1841–Jan. 13, 1842.

Dimond, Anthony Joseph (D Alaska) Nov. 30, 1881–May 28, 1953; House (Terr. Del.) 1933–45.

Dingell, John David (father of John David Dingell Jr.) (D Mich.) Feb. 2, 1894–Sept. 19, 1955; House 1933–Sept. 19, 1955.

Dingell, John David Jr. (son of John David Dingell) (D Mich.) July 8, 1926– ; House Dec. 13, 1955– ; chair House Energy and Commerce 1981–95.

Dingley, Nelson Jr. (R Maine) Feb. 15, 1832–Jan. 13, 1899; House Sept. 12, 1881–Jan. 13, 1899; Gov. Jan. 7, 1874–Jan. 5, 1876.

Dinsmoor, Samuel (R N.H.) July 1, 1766–March 15, 1835; House 1811–13; Gov. June 2, 1831–June 5, 1834 (Jacksonian).

Dinsmore, Hugh Anderson (D Ark.) Dec. 24, 1850–May 2, 1930; House 1893–1905.

Dioguardi, Joseph J. (R N.Y.) Sept. 20, 1940– ; House 1985–89.

Dirksen, Everett McKinley (father-in-law of Howard H. Baker Jr.) (R Ill.) Jan. 4, 1896–Sept. 7, 1969; House 1933–49; chair House District of Columbia 1947–49; Senate 1951–Sept. 7, 1969; Senate minority leader 1959–Sept. 7, 1969.

Disney, David Tiernan (D Ohio) Aug. 25, 1803–March 14, 1857; House 1849–55.

Disney, Wesley Ernest (D Okla.) Oct. 31, 1883–March 26, 1961; House 1931–45.

Ditter, John William (R Pa.) Sept. 5, 1888–Nov. 21, 1943; House 1933–Nov. 21, 1943.

Diven, Alexander Samuel (R N.Y.) Feb. 10, 1809–June 11, 1896; House 1861–63.

Dix, John Adams (son-in-law of John Jordan Morgan) (D N.Y.) July 24, 1798–April 21, 1879; Senate Jan. 27, 1845–49; secretary of the Treasury Jan. 15–March 6, 1861; Gov. Jan. 1, 1873–Jan. 1, 1875 (Republican).

Dixon, Alan John (D Ill.) July 7, 1927– ; Senate 1981–93.

Dixon, Archibald (W Ky.) April 2, 1802–April 23, 1876; Senate Sept. 1, 1852–55.

Dixon, Henry Aldous (R Utah) June 29, 1890–Jan. 22, 1967; House 1955–61.

Dixon, James (R Conn.) Aug. 5, 1814–March 27, 1873; House 1845–49 (Whig); Senate 1857–69.

Dixon, Joseph (R N.C.) April 9, 1828–March 3, 1883; House Dec. 5, 1870–71.

Dixon, Joseph Andrew (D Ohio) June 3, 1879–July 4, 1942; House 1937–39.

Dixon, Joseph Moore (R Mont.) July 31, 1867–May 22, 1934; House 1903–07; Senate 1907–13; Gov. Jan. 3, 1921–Jan. 4, 1925.

Dixon, Julian Carey (D Calif.) Aug. 8, 1934–Dec. 8, 2000; House 1979–Dec. 8, 2000; chair House Standards of Official Conduct 1985–91.

Dixon, Lincoln (D Ind.) Feb. 9, 1860–Sept. 16, 1932; House 1905–19.

Dixon, Nathan Fellows (grandfather of Nathan Fellows Dixon born in 1847, father of Nathan Fellows Dixon, below) (W R.I.) Dec. 13, 1774–Jan. 29, 1842; Senate 1839–Jan. 29, 1842.

Dixon, Nathan Fellows (son of Nathan Fellows Dixon, above, father of Nathan Fellows Dixon, below) (R R.I.) May 1, 1812–April 11, 1881; House 1849–51 (Whig), 1863–71.

Dixon, Nathan Fellows (son of Nathan Fellows Dixon, above, grandson of Nathan Fellows Dixon born in 1774) (R R.I.) Aug. 28, 1847–Nov. 8, 1897; House Feb. 12–March 3, 1885; Senate April 10, 1889–95.

Dixon, William Wirt (D Mont.) June 3, 1838–Nov. 13, 1910; House 1891–93.

Doan, Robert Eachus (R Ohio) July 23, 1831–Feb. 24, 1919; House 1891–93.

Doan, William (D Ohio) April 4, 1792–June 22, 1847; House 1839–43.

Dobbin, James Cochrane (grandson of James Cochran of North Carolina) (D N.C.) Jan. 17, 1814–Aug. 4, 1857; House 1845–47; secretary of the navy March 8, 1853–March 6, 1857.

Dobbins, Donald Claude (D Ill.) March 20, 1878–Feb. 14, 1943; House 1933–37.

Dobbins, Samuel Atkinson (R N.J.) April 14, 1814–May 26, 1886; House 1873–77.

Dockery, Alexander Monroe (D Mo.) Feb. 11, 1845–Dec. 26, 1926; House 1883–99; Gov. Jan. 14, 1901–Jan. 9, 1905.

Dockery, Alfred (father of Oliver Hart Dockery) (W N.C.) Dec. 11, 1797–Dec. 7, 1875; House 1845–47, 1851–53.

Dockery, Oliver Hart (son of Alfred Dockery) (R N.C.) Aug. 12, 1830–March 21, 1906; House July 13, 1868–71.

Dockweiler, John Francis (D Calif.) Sept. 19, 1895–Jan. 31, 1943; House 1933–39.

Dodd, Christopher John (son of Thomas Joseph Dodd) (D Conn.) May 27, 1944– ; House 1975–81; Senate 1981– ; general chair Dem. Nat. Comm. 1994–97; chair Senate Rules and Administration Jan. 3, 2001–Jan. 20, 2001, June 6, 2001–03.

Dodd, Edward (R N.Y.) Aug. 25, 1805–March 1, 1891; House 1855–59 (1855–57 Whig).

Dodd, Thomas Joseph (father of Christopher John Dodd) (D Conn.) May 15, 1907–May 24, 1971; House 1953–57; Senate 1959–Jan. 2, 1971.

Doddridge, Philip (– Va.) May 17, 1773–Nov. 19, 1832; House 1829–Nov. 19, 1832.

Dodds, Francis Henry (R Mich.) June 9, 1858–Dec. 23, 1940; House 1909–13.

Dodds, Ozro John (D Ohio) March 22, 1840–April 18, 1882; House Oct. 8, 1872–73.

Dodge, Augustus Caesar (son of Henry Dodge) (D Iowa) Jan. 2, 1812–Nov. 20, 1883; House (Terr. Del.) Oct. 28, 1840–Dec. 28, 1846; Senate Dec. 7, 1848–Feb. 22, 1855.

Dodge, Grenville Mellen (R Iowa) April 12, 1831–Jan. 3, 1916; House 1867–69.

Dodge, Henry (father of Augustus Caesar Dodge) (D Wis.) Oct. 12, 1782–June 19, 1867; House (Terr. Del.) 1841–45; Senate June 8, 1848–57; Gov. (Wis. Terr.) 1836–41, 1845–48.

Dodge, William Earle (R N.Y.) Sept. 4, 1805–Feb. 9, 1883; House April 7, 1866–67.

Doe, Nicholas Bartlett (W N.Y.) June 16, 1786–Dec. 6, 1856; House Dec. 7, 1840–41.

Doggett, Lloyd (D Texas) Oct. 6, 1946– ; House 1995– .

Doig, Andrew Wheeler (D N.Y.) July 24, 1799–July 11, 1875; House 1839–43.

Dole, Elizabeth Hanford (wife of Robert Joseph "Bob" Dole) (R N.C.) July 29, 1936– ; Senate 2003– ; secretary of transportation Feb. 7, 1983–Sept. 30, 1987; secretary of labor Jan. 30, 1989–Nov. 23, 1990.

Dole, Robert Joseph "Bob" (husband of Elizabeth Hanford Dole) (R Kan.) July 22, 1923– ; House 1961–69; Senate 1969–June 11, 1996; chair Senate Finance 1981–85; Senate majority leader 1985–87, 1995–June 11, 1996; Senate minority leader 1987–95; chair Rep. Nat. Comm. Jan. 1971–Jan. 1973.

Dollinger, Isidore (D N.Y.) Nov. 13, 1903–Jan. 30, 2000; House 1949–Dec. 31, 1959.

Dolliver, James Isaac (nephew of Jonathan Prentiss Dolliver) (R Iowa) Aug. 31, 1894–Dec. 10, 1978; House 1945–57.

Dolliver, Jonathan Prentiss (uncle of James Isaac Dolliver) (R Iowa) Feb. 6, 1858–Oct. 15, 1910; House 1889–Aug. 22, 1900; Senate Aug. 22, 1900–Oct. 15, 1910.

Dolph, Joseph Norton (uncle of Frederick William Mulkey) (R Ore.) Oct. 19, 1835–March 10, 1897; Senate 1883–95.

Domengeaux, James (D La.) Jan. 6, 1907–April 11, 1988; House 1941–April 15, 1944, Nov. 7, 1944–49.

Domenici, Peter Vichi (R N.M.) May 7, 1932– ; Senate 1973– ; chair Senate Budget 1981–87, 1995–Jan. 3, 2001, Jan. 20, 2001–June 6, 2001; chair Senate Energy and Natural Resources 2003– .

Dominick, Frederick Haskell (D S.C.) Feb. 20, 1877–March 11, 1960; House 1917–33.

Dominick, Peter Hoyt (nephew of Howard Alexander Smith) (R Colo.) July 7, 1915–March 18, 1981; House 1961–63; Senate 1963–75.

Donahey, Alvin Victor (D Ohio) July 7, 1873–April 8, 1946; Senate 1935–41; Gov. Jan. 8, 1923–Jan. 14, 1929.

Dondero, George Anthony (R Mich.) Dec. 16, 1883–Jan. 29, 1968; House 1933–57; chair House Public Works 1947–49, 1953–55.

Donley, Joseph Benton (R Pa.) Oct. 10, 1838–Jan. 23, 1917; House 1869–71.

Donnan, William G. (R Iowa) June 30, 1834–Dec. 4, 1908; House 1871–75.

Donnell, Forrest C. (R Mo.) Aug. 20, 1884–March 3, 1980; Senate 1945–51; Gov. Jan. 13, 1941–Jan. 8, 1945.

Donnell, Richard Spaight (grandson of Richard Dobbs Spaight, nephew of Richard Dobbs Spaight Jr.) (W N.C.) Sept. 20, 1820–June 3, 1867; House 1847–49.

Donnelly, Brian Joseph (D Mass.) March 2, 1946– ; House 1979–93.

Donnelly, Ignatius (R Minn.) Nov. 3, 1831–Jan. 1, 1901; House 1863–69.

Donohoe, Michael (D Pa.) Feb. 22, 1864–Jan. 17, 1958; House 1911–15.

Donohue, Harold Daniel (D Mass.) June 18, 1901–Nov. 4, 1984; House 1947–Dec. 31, 1974.

Donovan, Dennis D. (D Ohio) Jan. 31, 1859–April 21, 1941; House 1891–95.

Donovan, James George (D N.Y.) Dec. 15, 1898–April 6, 1987; House 1951–57.

Donovan, Jeremiah (D Conn.) Oct. 18, 1857–April 22, 1935; House 1913–15.

Donovan, Jerome Francis (D N.Y.), Feb. 1, 1872–Nov. 2, 1949; House March 5, 1918–21.

Dooley, Calvin (D Calif.) Jan. 11, 1954– ; House 1991–2005.

Dooley, Edwin Benedict (R N.Y.) April 13, 1905–Jan. 25, 1982; House 1957–63.

Dooling, Peter Joseph (D N.Y.) Feb. 15, 1857–Oct. 18, 1931; House 1913–21.

Doolittle, Dudley (D Kan.) June 21, 1881–Nov. 14, 1957; House 1913–19.

Doolittle, James Rood (R Wis.) Jan. 3, 1815–July 23, 1897; Senate 1857–69.

Doolittle, John T. (R Calif.) Oct. 30, 1950– ; House 1991– .

Doolittle, William Hall (R Wash.) Nov. 6, 1848–Feb. 26, 1914; House 1893–97.

Doremus, Frank Ellsworth (D Mich.) Aug. 31, 1865–Sept. 4, 1947; House 1911–21.

Dorgan, Byron Leslie (D N.D.) May 14, 1942– ; House 1981–Dec. 15, 1992; Senate Dec. 15, 1992– .

Dorn, Francis Edwin (R N.Y.) April 18, 1911–Sept. 17, 1987; House 1953–61.

Dorn, William Jennings Bryan (D S.C.) April 14, 1916– ; House 1947–49, 1951–Dec. 31, 1974; chair House Veterans' Affairs 1973–75.

Dornan, Robert Kenneth (R Calif.) April 3, 1933– ; House 1977–83, 1985–97.

Dorr, Charles Phillips (R W.Va.) Aug. 12, 1852–Oct. 8, 1914; House 1897–99.

Dorsey, Clement (– Md.) 1778–Aug. 6, 1848; House 1825–31.

Dorsey, Frank Joseph Gerard (D Pa.) April 26, 1891–July 13, 1949; House 1935–39.

Dorsey, George Washington Emery (R Neb.) Jan. 25, 1842–June 12, 1911; House 1885–91.

Dorsey, John Lloyd Jr. (D Ky.) Aug. 10, 1891–March 22, 1960; House Nov. 4, 1930–31.

Dorsey, Stephen Wallace (R Ark.) Feb. 28, 1842–March 20, 1916; Senate 1873–79.

Dorsheimer, William (D N.Y.) Feb. 5, 1832–March 26, 1888; House 1883–85.

Doty, James Duane (cousin of Morgan Lewis Martin) (ID Wis.) Nov. 5, 1799–June 13, 1865; House (Terr. Del.) Jan. 14, 1839–41 (Democrat), (Rep.) 1849–53 (1849–51 Democrat); Gov. (Wis. Terr.) 1841–44, (Utah Terr.) 1863–65.

Doubleday, Ulysses Freeman (J N.Y.) Dec. 15, 1792–March 11, 1866; House 1831–33, 1835–37.

Dougherty, Charles (D Fla.) Oct. 15, 1850–Oct. 11, 1915; House 1885–89.

Dougherty, Charles Francis (R Pa.) June 26, 1937– ; House 1979–83.

Dougherty, John (D Mo.) Feb. 25, 1857–Aug. 1, 1905; House 1899–1905.

Doughton, Robert Lee (D N.C.) Nov. 7, 1863–Oct. 1, 1954; House 1911–53; chair House Ways and Means 1949–53.

Douglas, Albert (R Ohio) April 25, 1852–March 14, 1935; House 1907–11.

Douglas, Beverly Browne (D Va.) Dec. 21, 1822–Dec. 22, 1878; House 1875–Dec. 22, 1878.

Douglas, Charles Gwynn III "Chuck" (R N.H.) Dec. 2, 1942– ; House 1989–91.

Douglas, Emily Taft (wife of Paul Howard Douglas) (D Ill.) April 10, 1899–Jan. 28, 1994; House 1945–47.

Douglas, Fred James (R N.Y.) Sept. 14, 1869–Jan. 1, 1949; House 1937–45.

Douglas, Helen Gahagan (D Calif.) Nov. 25, 1900–June 28, 1980; House 1945–51.

Douglas, Lewis Williams (D Ariz.) July 2, 1894–March 7, 1974; House 1927–March 4, 1933.

Douglas, Paul Howard (husband of Emily Taft Douglas) (D Ill.) March 26, 1892–Sept. 24, 1976; Senate 1949–67.

Douglas, Stephen Arnold (D Ill.) April 23, 1813–June 3, 1861; House 1843–47; Senate 1847–June 3, 1861.

Douglas, William Harris (R N.Y.) Dec. 5, 1853–Jan. 27, 1944; House 1901–05.

Douglass, John Joseph (D Mass.) Feb. 9, 1873–April 5, 1939; House 1925–35.

Doutrich, Isaac Hoffer (R Pa.) Dec. 19, 1871–May 28, 1941; House 1927–37.

Dovener, Blackburn Barrett (R W.Va.) April 20, 1842–May 9, 1914; House 1895–1907.

Dow, John Goodchild (D N.Y.) May 6, 1905–March 11, 2003; House 1965–69, 1971–73.

Dowd, Clement (D N.C.) Aug. 27, 1832–April 15, 1898; House 1881–85.

Dowdell, James Ferguson (D Ala.) Nov. 26, 1818–Sept. 6, 1871; House 1853–59.

Dowdney, Abraham (D N.Y.) Oct. 31, 1841–Dec. 10, 1886; House 1885–Dec. 10, 1886.

Dowdy, Charles Wayne (D Miss.) July 27, 1943– ; House July 9, 1981–89.

Dowdy, John Vernard (D Texas) Feb. 11, 1912–April 12, 1995; House Sept. 23, 1952–73.

Dowell, Cassius Clay (R Iowa) Feb. 29, 1864–Feb. 4, 1940; House 1915–35, 1937–Feb. 4, 1940.

Downey, Sheridan (son of Stephen Wheeler Downey) (D Calif.) March 11, 1884–Oct. 25, 1961; Senate 1939–Nov. 30, 1950.

Downey, Stephen Wheeler (father of Sheridan Downey) (R Wyo.) July 25, 1839–Aug. 3, 1902; House (Terr. Del.) 1879–81.

Downey, Thomas Joseph (D N.Y.) Jan. 28, 1949– ; House 1975–93.

Downing, Charles (– Fla.) ?–1845; House (Terr. Del.) 1837–41.

Downing, Finis Ewing (D Ill.) Aug. 24, 1846–March 8, 1936; House 1895–June 5, 1896.

Downing, Thomas Nelms (D Va.) Feb. 1, 1919–Oct. 23, 2001; House 1959–77.

Downs, Le Roy Donnelly (D Conn.) April 11, 1900–Jan. 18, 1970; House 1941–43.

Downs, Solomon Weathersbee (D La.) 1801–Aug. 14, 1854; Senate 1847–53.

Dowse, Edward (– Mass.) Oct. 22, 1756–Sept. 3, 1828; House 1819–May 26, 1820.

Dox, Peter Myndert (grandson of John Nicholas) (D Ala.) Sept. 11, 1813–April 2, 1891; House 1869–73.

Doxey, Charles Taylor (R Ind.) July 13, 1841–April 30, 1898; House Jan. 17–March 3, 1883.

Doxey, Wall (D Miss.) Aug. 8, 1892–March 2, 1962; House 1929–Sept. 28, 1941; Senate Sept. 29, 1941–43.

Doyle, Clyde Gilman (D Calif.) July 11, 1887–March 14, 1963; House 1945–47, 1949–March 14, 1963.

Doyle, Mike (D Pa.) Aug. 5, 1953– ; House 1995– .

Doyle, Thomas Aloysius (D Ill.) Jan. 9, 1886–Jan. 29, 1935; House Nov. 6, 1923–31.

Drake, Charles Daniel (R Mo.) April 11, 1811–April 1, 1892; Senate 1867–Dec. 19, 1870.

Drake, John Reuben (R N.Y.) Nov. 28, 1782–March 21, 1857; House 1817–19.

Drake, Thelma Sawyers (R Va.) Nov. 20, 1949– ; House 2005– .

Drane, Herbert Jackson (D Fla.) June 20, 1863–Aug. 11, 1947; House 1917–33.

Draper, Joseph (J Va.) Dec. 25, 1794–June 10, 1834; House Dec. 6, 1830–31, Dec. 6, 1832–33.

Draper, William Franklin (R Mass.) April 9, 1842–Jan. 28, 1910; House 1893–97.

Draper, William Henry (R N.Y.) June 24, 1841–Dec. 7, 1921; House 1901–13.

Drayton, William (J S.C.) Dec. 30, 1776–May 24, 1846; House May 17, 1825–33 (May 17, 1825–27 no party).

Dreier, David Timothy (R Calif.) July 5, 1952– ; House 1981– ; chair House Rules 1999– .

Dresser, Solomon Robert (R Pa.) Feb. 1, 1842–Jan. 21, 1911; House 1903–07.

Drew, Ira Walton (D Pa.) Aug. 31, 1878–Feb. 12, 1972; House 1937–39.

Drew, Irving Webster (R N.H.) Jan. 8, 1845–April 10, 1922; Senate Sept. 2–Nov. 5, 1918.

Drewry, Patrick Henry (D Va.) May 24, 1875–Dec. 21, 1947; House April 27, 1920–Dec. 21, 1947.

Driggs, Edmund Hope (D N.Y.) May 2, 1865–Sept. 27, 1946; House Dec. 6, 1897–1901.

Driggs, John Fletcher (R Mich.) March 8, 1813–Dec. 17, 1877; House 1863–69.

Drinan, Robert Frederick (D Mass.) Nov. 15, 1920– ; House 1971–81.

Driscoll, Daniel Angelus (D N.Y.) March 6, 1875–June 5, 1955; House 1909–17.

Driscoll, Denis Joseph (D Pa.) March 27, 1871–Jan. 18, 1958; House 1935–37.

Driscoll, Michael Edward (R N.Y.) Feb. 9, 1851–Jan. 19, 1929; House 1899–1913.

Driver, William Joshua (D Ark.) March 2, 1873–Oct. 1, 1948; House 1921–39.

Dromgoole, George Coke (uncle of Alexander Dromgoole Sims) (D Va.) May 15, 1797–April 27, 1847; House 1835–41 (1835–37 Jacksonian), 1843–April 27, 1847.

Drukker, Dow Henry (R N.J.) Feb. 7, 1872–Jan. 11, 1963; House April 7, 1914–19.

Drum, Augustus (D Pa.) Nov. 26, 1815–Sept. 15, 1858; House 1853–55.

Dryden, John Fairfield (R N.J.) Aug. 7, 1839–Nov. 24, 1911; Senate Jan. 29, 1902–07.

Dubois, Fred Thomas (D Idaho) May 29, 1851–Feb. 14, 1930; House (Terr. Del.) 1887–July 3, 1890; Senate 1891–97, 1901–07 (1887–97 Republican, 1901 Silver Republican).

Du Bose, Dudley McIver (D Ga.) Oct. 28, 1834–March 2, 1883; House 1871–73.

Dudley, Charles Edward (– N.Y.) May 23, 1780–Jan. 23, 1841; Senate Jan. 15, 1829–33.

Dudley, Edward Bishop (– N.C.) Dec. 15, 1789–Oct. 30, 1855; House Nov. 10, 1829–31; Gov. Dec. 31, 1836–Jan. 1, 1841 (Whig).

Duell, Rodolphus Holland (R N.Y.) Dec. 20, 1824–Feb. 11, 1891; House 1859–63, 1871–75.

Duer, William (W N.Y.) May 25, 1805–Aug. 25, 1879; House 1847–51.

Duff, James Henderson (R Pa.) Jan. 21, 1883–Dec. 20, 1969; Senate Jan. 18, 1951–57; Gov. Jan. 21, 1947–Jan. 16, 1951.

Duffey, Warren Joseph (D Ohio) Jan. 24, 1886–July 7, 1936; House 1933–July 7, 1936.

Duffy, Francis Ryan (D Wis.) June 23, 1888–Aug. 16, 1979; Senate 1933–39.

Duffy, James Patrick Bernard (D N.Y.) Nov. 25, 1878–Jan. 8, 1969; House 1935–37.

Dugro, Philip Henry (D N.Y.) Oct. 3, 1855–March 1, 1920; House 1881–83.

Duke, Richard Thomas Walker (C Va.) June 6, 1822–July 2, 1898; House Nov. 8, 1870–73.

Dulles, John Foster (R N.Y.) Feb. 25, 1888–May 24, 1959; Senate July 7–Nov. 8, 1949; secretary of state Jan. 21, 1953–April 22, 1959.

Dulski, Thaddeus Joseph (D N.Y.) Sept. 27, 1915–Oct. 11, 1988; House 1959–Dec. 31, 1974; chair House Post Office and Civil Service 1967–75.

Dumont, Ebenezer (U Ind.) Nov. 23, 1814–April 16, 1871; House 1863–67.

Dunbar, James Whitson (R Ind.) Oct. 17, 1860–May 19, 1943; House 1919–23, 1929–31.

Dunbar, William (D La.) 1805–March 18, 1861; House 1853–55.

Duncan, Alexander (D Ohio) 1788–March 23, 1853; House 1837–41, 1843–45.

Duncan, Daniel (W Ohio) July 22, 1806–May 18, 1849; House 1847–49.

Duncan, James (– Pa.) 1756–June 24, 1844; elected to the House for the term beginning 1821 but resigned before Congress assembled.

Duncan, James Henry (W Mass.) Dec. 5, 1793–Feb. 8, 1869; House 1849–53.

Duncan, John James (father of John J. "Jimmy" Duncan Jr.) (R Tenn.) March 24, 1919–June 21, 1988; House 1965–June 21, 1988.

Duncan, John J. "Jimmy" Jr. (son of John James Duncan) (R Tenn.) July 21, 1947 – ; House Nov. 8, 1988– .

Duncan, Joseph (J Ill.) Feb. 22, 1794–Jan. 15, 1844; House 1827–Sept. 21, 1834; Gov. Dec. 3, 1834–Dec. 7, 1838 (Whig).

Duncan, Richard Meloan (D Mo.) Nov. 10, 1889–Aug. 1, 1974; House 1933–43.

Duncan, Robert Blackford (D Ore.) Dec. 4, 1920– ; House 1963–67, 1975–81.

Duncan, William Addison (D Pa.) Feb. 2, 1836–Nov. 14, 1884; House 1883–Nov. 14, 1884.

Duncan, William Garnett (W Ky.) March 2, 1800–May 25, 1875; House 1847–49.

Dungan, James Irvine (D Ohio) May 29, 1844–Dec. 28, 1931; House 1891–93.

Dunham, Cyrus Livingston (D Ind.) Jan. 16, 1817–Nov. 21, 1877; House 1849–55.

Dunham, Ransom Williams (R Ill.) March 21, 1838–Aug. 19, 1896; House 1883–89.

Dunlap, George Washington (U Ky.) Feb. 22, 1813–June 6, 1880; House 1861–63.

Dunlap, Robert Pinkney (D Maine) Aug. 17, 1794–Oct. 20, 1859; House 1843–47; Gov. Jan. 1, 1834–Jan. 3, 1838.

Dunlap, William Claiborne (J Tenn.) Feb. 25, 1798–Nov. 16, 1872; House 1833–37.

Dunn, Aubert Culberson (D Miss.) Nov. 20, 1896–Jan. 4, 1987; House 1935–37.

Dunn, George Grundy (R Ind.) Dec. 20, 1812–Sept. 4, 1857; House 1847–49 (Whig), 1855–57.

Dunn, George Hedford (W Ind.) Nov. 15, 1794–Jan. 12, 1854; House 1837–39.

Dunn, James Whitney (R Mich.) July 21, 1943– ; House 1981–83.

Dunn, Jennifer (R Wash.) July 29, 1941– ; House 1993–2005.

Dunn, John Thomas (D N.J.) June 4, 1838–Feb. 22, 1907; House 1893–95.

Dunn, Matthew Anthony (D Pa.) Aug. 15, 1886–Feb. 13, 1942; House 1933–41.

Dunn, Poindexter (D Ark.) Nov. 3, 1834–Oct. 12, 1914; House 1879–89.

Dunn, Thomas Byrne (R N.Y.) March 16, 1853–July 2, 1924; House 1913–23.

Dunn, William McKee (R Ind.) Dec. 12, 1814–July 24, 1887; House 1859–63.

Dunnell, Mark Hill (R Minn.) July 2, 1823–Aug. 9, 1904; House 1871–83, 1889–91.

Dunphy, Edward John (D N.Y.) May 12, 1856–July 29, 1926; House 1889–95.

Dunwell, Charles Tappan (R N.Y.) Feb. 13, 1852–June 12, 1908; House 1903–June 12, 1908.

Du Pont, Henry Algernon (cousin of Thomas Coleman du Pont) (R Del.) July 30, 1838–Dec. 31, 1926; Senate June 13, 1906–17.

Du Pont, Pierre Samuel "Pete" IV (R Del.) Jan. 22, 1935– ; House 1971–77; Gov. Jan. 18, 1977–Jan. 15, 1985.

Du Pont, Thomas Coleman (cousin of Henry Algernon du Pont) (R Del.) Dec. 11, 1863–Nov. 11, 1930; Senate July 7, 1921–Nov. 7, 1922, 1925–Dec. 9, 1928.

Dupre, Henry Garland (D La.) July 28, 1873–Feb. 21, 1924; House Nov. 8, 1910–Feb. 21, 1924.

Durand, George Harman (D Mich.) Feb. 21, 1838–June 8, 1903; House 1875–77.

Durbin, Richard Joseph (D Ill.) Nov. 21, 1944– ; House 1983–97; Senate 1997– .

Durborow, Allan Cathcart Jr. (D Ill.) Nov. 10, 1857–March 10, 1908; House 1891–95.

Durell, Daniel Meserve (R N.H.) July 20, 1769–April 29, 1841; House 1807–09.

Durenberger, David Ferdinand (R Minn.) Aug. 19, 1934– ; Senate Nov. 8, 1978–95; chair Senate Select Intelligence Activities 1985–87.

Durey, Cyrus (R N.Y.) May 16, 1864–Jan. 4, 1933; House 1907–11.

Durfee, Job (– R.I.) Sept. 20, 1790–July 26, 1847; House 1821–25.

Durfee, Nathaniel Briggs (R R.I.) Sept. 29, 1812–Nov. 9, 1872; House 1855–59 (1855–57 American Party).

Durgan, George Richard (D Ind.) Jan. 20, 1872–Jan. 13, 1942; House 1933–35.

Durham, Carl Thomas (D N.C.) Aug. 28, 1892–April 29, 1974; House 1939–61.

Durham, Milton Jameson (D Ky.) May 16, 1824–Feb. 12, 1911; House 1873–79.

Durkee, Charles (R Wis.) Dec. 10, 1805–Jan. 14, 1870; House 1849–53 (Free-Soiler); Senate 1855–61; Gov. (Utah Terr.) 1865–69.

Durkin, John Anthony (D N.H.) March 29, 1936– ; Senate Sept. 18, 1975–Dec. 29, 1980.

Durno, Edwin Russell (R Ore.) Jan. 26, 1899–Nov. 20, 1976; House 1961–63.

Duval, Isaac Harding (R W.Va.) Sept. 1, 1824–July 10, 1902; House 1869–71.

Duval, William Pope (R Ky.) 1784–March 19, 1854; House 1813–15; Gov. (Fla. Terr.) 1822–34.

Duvall, Gabriel (R Md.) Dec. 6, 1752–March 6, 1844; House Nov. 11, 1794–March 28, 1796 (Nov. 11, 1794–95 no party); assoc. justice Nov. 23, 1811–Jan. 14, 1835.

Dwight, Henry Williams (– Mass.) Feb. 26, 1788–Feb. 21, 1845; House 1821–31.

Dwight, Jeremiah Wilbur (father of John Wilbur Dwight) (R N.Y.) April 17, 1819–Nov. 26, 1885; House 1877–83.

Dwight, John Wilbur (son of Jeremiah Wilbur Dwight) (R N.Y.) May 24, 1859–Jan. 19, 1928; House Nov. 2, 1902–13.

Dwight, Theodore (cousin of Aaron Burr) (F Conn.) Dec. 15, 1764–June 12, 1846; House Dec. 1, 1806–07.

Dwight, Thomas (F Mass.) Oct. 29, 1758–Jan. 2, 1819; House 1803–05.

Dwinell, Justin (– N.Y.) Oct. 28, 1785–Sept. 17, 1850; House 1823–25.

Dworshak, Henry Clarence (R Idaho) Aug. 29, 1894–July 23, 1962; House 1939–Nov. 5, 1946; Senate Nov. 6, 1946–49, Oct. 14, 1949–July 23, 1962.

Dwyer, Bernard James (D N.J.) Jan. 24, 1921–Oct. 31, 1998; House 1981–93.

Dwyer, Florence Price (R N.J.) July 4, 1902–Feb. 29, 1976; House 1957–73.

Dyal, Kenneth Warren (D Calif.) July 9, 1910–May 12, 1978; House 1965–67.

Dyer, David Patterson (uncle of Leonidas Carstarphen Dyer) (R Mo.) Feb. 12, 1838–April 29, 1924; House 1869–71.

Dyer, Leonidas Carstarphen (nephew of David Patterson Dyer) (R Mo.) June 11, 1871–Dec. 15, 1957; House 1911–June 19, 1914, 1915–33.

Dymally, Mervyn Malcolm (D Calif.) May 12, 1926– ; House 1981–93.

Dyson, Royden Patrick "Roy" (D Md.) Nov. 15, 1948– ; House 1981–91.

Eagan, John Joseph (D N.J.) Jan. 22, 1872–June 13, 1956; House 1913–21, 1923–25.

Eager, Samuel Watkins (R N.Y.) April 8, 1789–Dec. 23, 1860; House Nov. 2, 1830–31.

Eagle, Joe Henry (D Texas) Jan. 23, 1870–Jan. 10, 1963; House 1913–21, Jan. 28, 1933–37.

Eagleton, Thomas Francis (D Mo.) Sept. 4, 1929– ; Senate Dec. 28, 1968–87; chair Senate District of Columbia 1971–77.

Eames, Benjamin Tucker (R R.I.) June 4, 1818–Oct. 6, 1901; House 1871–79.

Earhart, Daniel Scofield (D Ohio) May 28, 1907–Jan. 2, 1976; House Nov. 3, 1936–37.

Earle, Elias (uncle of Samuel Earle and John Baylis Earle, great-grandfather of John Laurens Manning Irby and Joseph Haynsworth Earle) (R S.C.) June 19, 1762–May 19, 1823; House 1805–07, 1811–15, 1817–21.

Earle, John Baylis (nephew of Elias Earle, cousin of Samuel Earle) (R S.C.) Oct. 23, 1766–Feb. 3, 1863; House 1803–05.

Earle, Joseph Haynsworth (great-grandson of Elias Earle, cousin of John Laurens Manning Irby, nephew of William Lowndes Yancey) (D S.C.) April 30, 1847–May 20, 1897; Senate March 4–May 20, 1897.

Earle, Samuel (nephew of Elias Earle, cousin of John Baylis Earle) (R S.C.) Nov. 28, 1760–Nov. 24, 1833; House 1795–97.

Earll, Jonas Jr. (cousin of Nehemiah Hezekiah Earll) (J N.Y.) 1786–Oct. 28, 1846; House 1827–31.

Earll, Nehemiah Hezekiah (cousin of Jonas Earll Jr.) (D N.Y.) Oct. 5, 1787–Aug. 26, 1872; House 1839–41.

Early, Joseph Daniel (D Mass.) Jan. 31, 1933– ; House 1975–93.

Early, Peter (R Ga.) June 20, 1773–Aug. 15, 1817; House Jan. 10, 1803–07; Gov. Nov. 5, 1813–Nov. 10, 1815 (Democratic Republican).

Earnshaw, Manuel (I P.I.) Nov. 19, 1862–Feb. 13, 1936; House (Res. Comm.) 1913–17.

Earthman, Harold Henderson (D Tenn.) April 13, 1900–Feb. 26, 1987; House 1945–47.

East, John Porter (R N.C.) May 5, 1931–June 29, 1986; Senate 1981–June 29, 1986.

Eastland, James Oliver (D Miss.) Nov. 28, 1904–Feb. 19, 1986; Senate June 30–Sept. 28, 1941, 1943–Dec. 27, 1978; chair Senate Judiciary 1956–78; elected pres. pro tempore July 28, 1972.

Eastman, Ben C. (D Wis.) Oct. 24, 1812–Feb. 2, 1856; House 1851–55.

Eastman, Ira Allen (nephew of Nehemiah Eastman) (D N.H.) Jan. 1, 1809–March 21, 1881; House 1839–43.

Eastman, Nehemiah (uncle of Ira Allen Eastman) (– N.H.) June 16, 1782–Jan. 11, 1856; House 1825–27.

Easton, Rufus (– Mo.) May 4, 1774–July 5, 1834; House (Terr. Del.) Sept. 17, 1814–Aug. 5, 1816.

Eaton, Charles Aubrey (uncle of William Robb Eaton) (R N.J.) March 29, 1868–Jan. 23, 1953; House 1925–53; chair House Foreign Affairs 1947–49.

Eaton, John Henry (R Tenn.) June 18, 1790–Nov. 17, 1856; Senate Sept. 5, 1818–21, Sept. 27, 1821–March 9, 1829; secretary of war March 9, 1829–June 18, 1831; Gov. (Fla. Terr.) 1834–36.

Eaton, Lewis (– N.Y.) ?–?; House 1823–25.

Eaton, Thomas Marion (R Calif.) Aug. 3, 1896–Sept. 16, 1939; House Jan. 3–Sept. 16, 1939.

Eaton, William Robb (nephew of Charles Aubrey Eaton) (R Colo.) Dec. 17, 1877–Dec. 16, 1942; House 1929–33.

Eaton, William Wallace (D Conn.) Oct. 11, 1816–Sept. 21, 1898; Senate Feb. 5, 1875–81; House 1883–85.

Eberharter, Herman Peter (D Pa.) April 29, 1892–Sept. 9, 1958; House 1937–Sept. 9, 1958.

Echols, Leonard Sidney (R W.Va.) Oct. 30, 1871–May 9, 1946; House 1919–23.

Eckart, Dennis Edward (D Ohio) April 6, 1950– ; House 1981–93.

Eckert, Charles Richard (D Pa.) Jan. 20, 1868–Oct. 26, 1959; House 1935–39.

Eckert, Fred J. (R N.Y.) May 6, 1941– ; House 1985–87.

Eckert, George Nicholas (W Pa.) July 4, 1802–June 28, 1865; House 1847–49.

Eckhardt, Robert Christian (cousin of Richard Mifflin Kleberg Sr., great-nephew of Rudolph Kleberg, nephew of Harry McLeary Wurzbach) (D Texas) July 16, 1913–Nov. 13, 2001; House 1967–81.

Eckley, Ephraim Ralph (R Ohio) Dec. 9, 1811–March 27, 1908; House 1863–69.

Ecton, Zales Nelson (R Mont.) April 1, 1898–March 3, 1961; Senate 1947–53.

Eddy, Frank Marion (R Minn.) April 1, 1856–Jan. 13, 1929; House 1895–1903.

Eddy, Norman (D Ind.) Dec. 10, 1810–Jan. 28, 1872; House 1853–55.

Eddy, Samuel (– R.I.) March 31, 1769–Feb. 3, 1839; House 1819–25.

Edelstein, Morris Michael (D N.Y.) Feb. 5, 1888–June 4, 1941; House Feb. 6, 1940–June 4, 1941.

Eden, John Rice (D Ill.) Feb. 1, 1826–June 9, 1909; House 1863–65, 1873–79, 1885–87.

Edgar, Robert William (D Pa.) May 29, 1943– ; House 1975–87.

Edge, Walter Evans (R N.J.) Nov. 20, 1873–Oct. 29, 1956; Senate 1919–Nov. 21, 1929; Gov. Jan. 15, 1917–May 16, 1919, Jan. 18, 1944–Jan. 21, 1947.

Edgerton, Alfred Peck (brother of Joseph Ketchum Edgerton) (D Ohio) Jan. 11, 1813–May 14, 1897; House 1851–55.

Edgerton, Alonzo Jay (R Minn.) June 7, 1827–Aug. 9, 1896; Senate March 12–Oct. 30, 1881.

Edgerton, Joseph Ketchum (brother of Alfred Peck Edgerton) (D Ind.) Feb. 16, 1818–Aug. 25, 1893; House 1863–65.

Edgerton, Sidney (R Ohio) Aug. 17, 1818–July 19, 1900; House 1859–63; Gov. (Mont. Terr.) 1865, 1866.

Edie, John Rufus (W Pa.) Jan. 14, 1814–Aug. 27, 1888; House 1855–59.

Edmands, John Wiley (W Mass.) March 1, 1809–Jan. 31, 1877; House 1853–55.

Edmiston, Andrew (D W.Va.) Nov. 13, 1892–Aug. 28, 1966; House Nov. 28, 1933–43.

Edmond, William (F Conn.) Sept. 28, 1755–Aug. 1, 1838; House Nov. 13, 1797–1801.

Edmonds, George Washington (R Pa.) Feb. 22, 1864–Sept. 28, 1939; House 1913–25, 1933–35.

Edmondson, Edmond Augustus (brother of James Howard Edmondson) (D Okla.) April 7, 1919–Dec. 8, 1990; House 1953–73.

Edmondson, James Howard (brother of Edmond Augustus Edmondson) (D Okla.) Sept. 27, 1925–Nov. 17, 1971; Senate Jan. 7, 1963–Nov. 3, 1964; Gov. Jan. 12, 1959–Jan. 6, 1963.

Edmunds, George Franklin (R Vt.) Feb. 1, 1828–Feb. 27, 1919; Senate April 3, 1866–Nov. 1, 1891; elected pres. pro tempore March 3, 1883, Jan. 14, 1884.

Edmunds, Paul Carrington (D Va.) Nov. 1, 1836–March 12, 1899; House 1889–95.

Edmundson, Henry Alonzo (D Va.) June 14, 1814–Dec. 16, 1890; House 1849–61.

Edsall, Joseph E. (D N.J.) 1789–1865; House 1845–49.

Edwards, Benjamin (father of Ninian Edwards, grandfather of Benjamin Edwards Grey) (– Md.) Aug. 12, 1753–Nov. 13, 1829; House Jan. 2–March 3, 1795.

Edwards, Caldwell (P Mont.) Jan. 8, 1841–July 23, 1922; House 1901–03.

Edwards, Charles Gordon (D Ga.) July 2, 1878–July 13, 1931; House 1907–17, 1925–July 13, 1931.

Edwards, Don (D Calif.) Jan. 6, 1915– ; House 1963–95.

Edwards, Don Calvin (R Ky.) July 13, 1861–Sept. 19, 1938; House 1905–11.

Edwards, Edward Irving (D N.J.) Dec. 1, 1863–Jan. 26, 1931; Senate 1923–29; Gov. Jan. 20, 1920–Jan. 15, 1923.

Edwards, Edwin Washington (husband of Elaine Schwartzenburg Edwards) (D La.) Aug. 7, 1927– ; House Oct. 18, 1965–May 9, 1972; Gov. May 9, 1972–March 10, 1980, March 12, 1984–May 14, 1988, Jan. 8, 1992–Jan. 8, 1996.

Edwards, Elaine Schwartzenburg (wife of Edwin Washington Edwards) (D La.) March 8, 1929– ; Senate Aug. 1–Nov. 13, 1972.

Edwards, Francis Smith (AP N.Y.) May 28, 1817–May 20, 1899; House 1855–Feb. 28, 1857.

Edwards, Henry Waggaman (– Conn.) Oct. 1779–July 22, 1847; House 1819–23; Senate Oct. 8, 1823–27; Gov. May 4, 1833–May 7, 1834, May 6, 1835–May 2, 1838.

Edwards, John (– Ky.) 1748–1837; Senate June 18, 1792–95.

Edwards, John (D N.Y.) Aug. 6, 1781–Dec. 28, 1850; House 1837–39.

Edwards, John (great-uncle of John Edwards Leonard) (W Pa.) 1786–June 26, 1843; House 1839–43 (1839–41 AMas.).

Edwards, John (LR Ark.) Oct. 24, 1805–April 8, 1894; House 1871–Feb. 9, 1872.

Edwards, John (D N.C.) June 10, 1953– ; Senate 1999–2005.

Edwards, John Cummins (D Mo.) June 24, 1804–Sept. 14, 1888; House 1841–43; Gov. Nov. 20, 1844–Nov. 27, 1848.

Edwards, Marvin Henry "Mickey" (R Okla.) July 12, 1937– ; House 1977–93.

Edwards, Ninian (son of Benjamin Edwards) (R Ill.) March 17, 1775–July 20, 1833; Senate Dec. 3, 1818–24; Gov. 1809–18 (Ill. Terr.), Dec. 6, 1826–Dec. 6, 1830.

Edwards, Samuel (– Pa.) March 12, 1785–Nov. 21, 1850; House 1819–27.

Edwards, Thomas Chester "Chet" (D Texas) Nov. 24, 1951– ; House 1991– .

Edwards, Thomas McKey (R N.H.) Dec. 16, 1795–May 1, 1875; House 1859–63.

Edwards, Thomas Owen (W Ohio) March 29, 1810–Feb. 5, 1876; House 1847–49.

Edwards, Weldon Nathaniel (R N.C.) Jan. 25, 1788–Dec. 18, 1873; House Feb. 7, 1816–27.

Edwards, William Jackson "Jack" (R Ala.) Sept. 20, 1928– ; House 1965–85.

Edwards, William Posey (R Ga.) Nov. 9, 1835–June 28, 1900; House July 25, 1868–69.

Efner, Valentine (J N.Y.) May 5, 1776–Nov. 20, 1865; House 1835–37.

Egbert, Albert Gallatin (D Pa.) April 13, 1828–March 28, 1896; House 1875–77.

Egbert, Joseph (D N.Y.) April 10, 1807–July 7, 1888; House 1841–43.

Ege, George (F Pa.) March 9, 1748–Dec. 14, 1829; House Dec. 8, 1796–Oct. 1797.

Eggleston, Benjamin (R Ohio) Jan. 3, 1816–Feb. 9, 1888; House 1865–69.

Eggleston, Joseph (uncle of William Segar Archer) (R Va.) Nov. 24, 1754–Feb. 13, 1811; House Dec. 3, 1798–1801.

Ehlers, Vernon J. (R Mich.) Feb. 6, 1934– ; House Jan. 25, 1994– .

Ehrlich, Robert L. Jr. (R Md.) Nov. 25, 1957– ; House 1995–2003; Gov. Jan. 15, 2003– .

Eicher, Edward Clayton (D Iowa) Dec. 16, 1878–Nov. 29, 1944; House 1933–Dec. 2, 1938.

Eickhoff, Anthony (D N.Y.) Sept. 11, 1827–Nov. 5, 1901; House 1877–79.

Eilberg, Joshua (D Pa.) Feb. 12, 1921–March 24, 2004; House 1967–79.

Einstein, Edwin (R N.Y.) Nov. 18, 1842–Jan. 24, 1905; House 1879–81.

Ekwall, William Alexander (R Ore.) June 14, 1887–Oct. 16, 1956; House 1935–37.

Ela, Jacob Hart (R N.H.) July 18, 1820–Aug. 21, 1884; House 1867–71.

Elam, Joseph Barton (D La.) June 12, 1821–July 4, 1885; House 1877–81.

Elder, James Walter (D La.) Oct. 5, 1882–Dec. 16, 1941; House 1913–15.

Eldredge, Charles Augustus (D Wis.) Feb. 27, 1820–Oct. 26, 1896; House 1863–75.

Eldredge, Nathaniel Buel (D Mich.) March 28, 1813–Nov. 27, 1893; House 1883–87.

Eliot, Samuel Atkins (great-grandfather of Thomas Hopkinson Eliot) (W Mass.) March 5, 1798–Jan. 29, 1862; House Aug. 22, 1850–51.

Eliot, Thomas Dawes (R Mass.) March 20, 1808–June 14, 1870; House April 17, 1854–55 (Whig), 1859–69.

Eliot, Thomas Hopkinson (great-grandson of Samuel Atkins Eliot) (D Mass.) June 14, 1907–Oct. 14, 1991; House 1941–43.

Elizalde, Joaquin Miguel (– P.I.) Aug. 2, 1896–Feb. 9, 1965; House (Res. Comm.) Sept. 29, 1938–Aug. 9, 1944.

Elkins, Davis (son of Stephen Benton Elkins, grandson of Henry Gassaway Davis) (R W.Va.) Jan. 24, 1876–Jan. 5, 1959; Senate Jan. 9–Jan. 31, 1911, 1919–25.

Elkins, Stephen Benton (father of Davis Elkins) (R W.Va.) Sept. 26, 1841–Jan. 4, 1911; House (Terr. Del. N.M.) 1873–77; Senate 1895–Jan. 4, 1911; secretary of war Dec. 17, 1891–March 5, 1893.

Ellenbogen, Henry (D Pa.) April 3, 1900–July 4, 1985; House 1933–Jan. 3, 1938.

Ellender, Allen Joseph (D La.) Sept. 24, 1890–July 27, 1972; Senate 1937–July 27, 1972; chair Senate Agriculture and Forestry 1951–53, 1955–71; elected pres. pro tempore Jan. 22, 1971; chair Senate Appropriations 1971–72.

Ellerbe, James Edwin (D S.C.) Jan. 12, 1867–Oct. 24, 1917; House 1905–13.

Ellery, Christopher (R R.I.) Nov. 1, 1768–Dec. 2, 1840; Senate May 6, 1801–05.

Ellett, Henry Thomas (D Miss.) March 8, 1812–Oct. 15, 1887; House Jan. 26–March 3, 1847.

Ellett, Tazewell (D Va.) Jan. 1, 1856–May 19, 1914; House 1895–97.

Ellicott, Benjamin (R N.Y.) April 17, 1765–Dec. 10, 1827; House 1817–19.

Elliott, Alfred James (D Calif.) June 1, 1895–Jan. 17, 1973; House May 4, 1937–49.

Elliott, Carl Atwood (D Ala.) Dec. 20, 1913–Jan. 9, 1999; House 1949–65.

Elliott, Douglas Hemphill (R Pa.) June 3, 1921–June 19, 1960; House April 26–June 19, 1960.

Elliott, James (F Vt.) Aug. 18, 1775–Nov. 10, 1839; House 1803–09.

Elliott, James Thomas (R Ark.) April 22, 1823–July 28, 1875; House Jan. 13–March 3, 1869.

Elliott, John (– Ga.) Oct. 24, 1773–Aug. 9, 1827; Senate 1819–25.

Elliott, John Milton (D Ky.) May 20, 1820–March 26, 1879; House 1853–59.

Elliott, Mortimer Fitzland (D Pa.) Sept. 24, 1839–Aug. 5, 1920; House 1883–85.

Elliott, Richard Nash (R Ind.) April 25, 1873–March 21, 1948; House June 26, 1917–31.

Elliott, Robert Brown (R S.C.) Aug. 11, 1842–Aug. 9, 1884; House 1871–Nov. 1, 1874.

Elliott, William (D S.C.) Sept. 3, 1838–Dec. 7, 1907; House 1887–Sept. 23, 1890, 1891–93, 1895–June 4, 1896, 1897–1903.

Ellis, Caleb (F N.H.) April 16, 1767–May 6, 1816; House 1805–07.

Ellis, Chesselden (D N.Y.) 1808–May 10, 1854; House 1843–45.

Ellis, Clyde Taylor (D Ark.) Dec. 21, 1908–Feb. 9, 1980; House 1939–43.

Ellis, Edgar Clarence (R Mo.) Oct. 2, 1854–March 15, 1947; House 1905–09, 1921–23, 1925–27, 1929–31.

Ellis, Ezekiel John (D La.) Oct. 15, 1840–April 25, 1889; House 1875–85.

Ellis, Hubert Summers (R W.Va.) July 6, 1887–Dec. 3, 1959; House 1943–49.

Ellis, Powhatan (– Miss.) Jan. 17, 1790–March 18, 1863; Senate Sept. 28, 1825–Jan. 28, 1826, 1827–July 16, 1832.

Ellis, William Cox (– Pa.) May 5, 1787–Dec. 13, 1871; House (elected to the term beginning 1821 but resigned before Congress assembled), 1823–25.

Ellis, William Russell (R Ore.) April 23, 1850–Jan. 18, 1915; House 1893–99, 1907–11.

Ellis, William Thomas (D Ky.) July 24, 1845–Jan. 8, 1925; House 1889–95.

Ellison, Andrew (D Ohio) 1812–about 1860; House 1853–55.

Ellison, Daniel (R Md.) Feb. 14, 1886–Aug. 20, 1960; House 1943–45.

Ellmaker, Amos (– Pa.) Feb. 2, 1787–Nov. 28, 1851; elected to the House for the term beginning 1815 but did not qualify.

Ellsberry, William Wallace (D Ohio) Dec. 18, 1833–Sept. 7, 1894; House 1885–87.

Ellsworth, Charles Clinton (R Mich.) Jan. 29, 1824–June 25, 1899; House 1877–79.

Ellsworth, Franklin Fowler (R Minn.) July 10, 1879–Dec. 23, 1942; House 1915–21.

Ellsworth, Matthew Harris (R Ore.) Sept. 17, 1899–Feb. 7, 1986; House 1943–57.

Ellsworth, Oliver (father of William Wolcott Ellsworth) (– Conn.) April 29, 1745–Nov. 26, 1807; Senate 1789–March 8, 1796; Cont. Cong. 1778–83; chief justice March 8, 1796–Dec. 15, 1800.

Ellsworth, Robert Fred (R Kan.) June 11, 1926– ; House 1961–67.

Ellsworth, Samuel Stewart (D N.Y.) Oct. 13, 1790–June 4, 1863; House 1845–47.

Ellsworth, William Wolcott (son of Oliver Ellsworth) (– Conn.) Nov. 10, 1791–Jan. 15, 1868; House 1829–July 8, 1834; Gov. May 2, 1838–May 4, 1842 (Whig).

Ellwood, Reuben (R Ill.) Feb. 21, 1821–July 1, 1885; House 1883–July 1, 1885.

Ellzey, Lawrence Russell (D Miss.) March 20, 1891–Dec. 7, 1977; House March 15, 1932–35.

Elmendorf, Lucas Conrad (R N.Y.) 1758–Aug. 17, 1843; House 1797–1803.

Elmer, Ebenezer (brother of Jonathan Elmer, father of Lucius Quintius Cincinnatus Elmer) (R N.J.) Aug. 23, 1752–Oct. 18, 1843; House 1801–07.

Elmer, Jonathan (brother of Ebenezer Elmer, uncle of Lucius Quintius Cincinnatus Elmer) (– N.J.) Nov. 29, 1745–Sept. 3, 1817; Senate 1789–91; Cont. Cong. 1777–78, 1781–83, 1787–88.

Elmer, Lucius Quintius Cincinnatus (son of Ebenezer Elmer, nephew of Jonathan Elmer) (D N.J.) Feb. 3, 1793–March 11, 1883; House 1843–45.

Elmer, William Price (R Mo.) March 2, 1871–May 11, 1956; House 1943–45.

Elmore, Franklin Harper (D S.C.) Oct. 15, 1799–May 29, 1850; House Dec. 10, 1836–39 (State Rights Democrat); Senate April 11–May 28, 1850.

Elsaesser, Edward Julius (R N.Y.) March 10, 1904–Jan. 7, 1983; House 1945–49.

Elston, Charles Henry (R Ohio) Aug. 1, 1891–Sept. 25, 1980; House 1939–53.

Elston, John Arthur (R Calif.) Feb. 10, 1874–Dec. 15, 1921; House 1915–Dec. 15, 1921 (1915–17 Progressive).

Eltse, Ralph Roscoe (R Calif.) Sept. 13, 1885–March 18, 1971; House 1933–35.

Elvins, Politte (R Mo.) March 16, 1878–Jan. 14, 1943; House 1909–11.

Ely, Alfred (R N.Y.) Feb. 15, 1815–May 18, 1892; House 1859–63.

Ely, Frederick David (R Mass.) Sept. 24, 1838–Aug. 6, 1921; House 1885–87.

Ely, John (D N.Y.) Oct. 8, 1774–Aug. 20, 1849; House 1839–41.

Ely, Smith Jr. (D N.Y.) April 17, 1825–July 1, 1911; House 1871–73, 1875–Dec. 11, 1876.

Ely, William (F Mass.) Aug. 14, 1765–Oct. 9, 1817; House 1805–15.

Emanuel, Rahm (D Ill.) Nov. 29, 1959– ; House 2003– .

Embree, Elisha (W Ind.) Sept. 28, 1801–Feb. 28, 1863; House 1847–49.

Emerich, Martin (D Ill.) April 27, 1846–Sept. 27, 1922; House 1903–05.

Emerson, Henry Ivory (R Ohio) March 15, 1871–Oct. 28, 1953; House 1915–21.

Emerson, Jo Ann (widow of Norvell William "Bill" Emerson) (R Mo.) Sept. 16, 1950– ; House Nov. 5, 1996– .

Emerson, Louis Woodard (R N.Y.) July 25, 1857–June 10, 1924; House 1899–1903.

Emerson, Norvell William "Bill" (husband of Jo Ann Emerson) (R Mo.) Jan. 1, 1938–June 22, 1996; House 1981–June 22, 1996.

Emery, David Farnham (R Maine) Sept. 1, 1948– ; House 1975–83.

Emott, James (F N.Y.) March 9, 1771–April 7, 1850; House 1809–13.

Emrie, Jonas Reece (R Ohio) April 25, 1812–June 5, 1869; House 1855–57.

Engel, Albert Joseph (R Mich.) Jan. 1, 1888–Dec. 2, 1959; House 1935–51.

Engel, Eliot L. (D N.Y.) Feb. 18, 1947– ; House 1989– .

England, Edward Theodore (R W.Va.) Sept. 29, 1869–Sept. 9, 1934; House 1927–29.

Engle, Clair (D Calif.) Sept. 21, 1911–July 30, 1964; House Aug. 31, 1943–59; chair House Interior and Insular Affairs 1955–59; Senate 1959–July 30, 1964.

Englebright, Harry Lane (son of William Fellows Englebright) (R Calif.) Jan. 2, 1884–May 13, 1943; House Aug. 31, 1926–May 13, 1943.

Englebright, William Fellows (father of Harry Lane Englebright) (R Calif.) Nov. 23, 1855–Feb. 10, 1915; House Nov. 6, 1906–11.

English, Glenn Lee Jr. (D Okla.) Nov. 30, 1940– ; House 1975–Jan. 7, 1994.

English, James Edward (D Conn.) March 13, 1812–March 2, 1890; House 1861–65; Senate Nov. 27, 1875–May 17, 1876; Gov. May 1, 1867–May 5, 1869, May 4, 1870–May 16, 1871.

English, Karan (D Ariz.) March 23, 1949– ; House 1993–95.

English, Phil (R Pa.) June 20, 1956– ; House 1995– .

English, Thomas Dunn (D N.J.) June 29, 1819–April 1, 1902; House 1891–95.

English, Warren Barkley (D Calif.) May 1, 1840–Jan. 9, 1913; House April 4, 1894–95.

English, William Eastin (son of William Hayden English) (D Ind.) Nov. 3, 1850–April 29, 1926; House May 22, 1884–85.

English, William Hayden (father of William Eastin English) (D Ind.) Aug. 27, 1822–Feb. 7, 1896; House 1853–61.

Enloe, Benjamin Augustine (D Tenn.) Jan. 18, 1848–July 8, 1922; House 1887–95.

Enochs, William Henry (R Ohio) March 29, 1842–July 13, 1893; House 1891–July 13, 1893.

Ensign, John (R Nev.) March 25, 1958– ; House 1995–99; Senate 2001– .

Enzi, Michael B. (R Wyo.) Feb. 1, 1944– ; Senate 1997– ; chair Senate Health, Education, Labor, and Pensions 2005– .

Epes, James Fletcher (cousin of Sydney Parham Epes) (D Va.) May 23, 1842–Aug. 24, 1910; House 1891–95.

Epes, Sydney Parham (cousin of James Fletcher Epes and William Bacon Oliver) (D Va.) Aug. 20, 1865–March 3, 1900; House 1897–March 23, 1898 (no party), 1899–March 3, 1900.

Eppes, John Wayles (R Va.) April 7, 1773–Sept. 13, 1823; House 1803–11, 1813–15; Senate 1817–Dec. 4, 1819.

Erdahl, Arlen Ingolf (R Minn.) Feb. 27, 1931– ; House 1979–83.

Erdman, Constantine Jacob (grandson of Jacob Erdman) (D Pa.) Sept. 4, 1846–Jan. 15, 1911; House 1893–97.

Erdman, Jacob (grandfather of Constantine Jacob Erdman) (D Pa.) Feb. 22, 1801–July 20, 1867; House 1845–47.

Erdreich, Ben (D Ala.) Dec. 9, 1938– ; House 1983–93.

Erickson, John Edward (D Mont.) March 14, 1863–May 25, 1946; Senate March 13, 1933–Nov. 6, 1934; Gov. Jan. 5, 1925–March 13, 1933.

Erk, Edmund Frederick (R Pa.) April 17, 1872–Dec. 14, 1953; House Nov. 4, 1930–33.

Erlenborn, John Neal (R Ill.) Feb. 8, 1927– ; House 1965–85.

Ermentrout, Daniel (D Pa.) Jan. 24, 1837–Sept. 17, 1899; House 1881–89, 1897–Sept. 17, 1899.

Ernst, Richard Pretlow (R Ky.) Feb. 28, 1858–April 13, 1934; Senate 1921–27.

Errett, Russell (R Pa.) Nov. 10, 1817–April 7, 1891; House 1877–83.

Ertel, Allen Edward (D Pa.) Nov. 7, 1936– ; House 1977–83.

Ervin, James (R S.C.) Oct. 17, 1778–July 7, 1841; House 1817–21.

Ervin, Joseph Wilson (brother of Samuel James Ervin Jr.) (D N.C.) March 3, 1901–Dec. 25, 1945; House Jan. 3–Dec. 25, 1945.

Ervin, Samuel James Jr. (brother of Joseph Wilson Ervin) (D N.C.) Sept. 27, 1896–April 23, 1985; House Jan. 22, 1946–47; Senate June 5, 1954–Dec. 31, 1974; chair Senate Government Operations 1972–74.

Esch, John Jacob (R Wis.) March 20, 1861–April 27, 1941; House 1899–1921.

Esch, Marvin Lionel (R Mich.) Aug. 4, 1927– ; House 1967–77.

Eshleman, Edwin Duing (R Pa.) Dec. 4, 1920–Jan. 10, 1985; House 1967–77.

Eshoo, Anna G. (D Calif.) Dec. 13, 1942– ; House 1993– .

Eslick, Edward Everett (husband of Willa McCord Blake Eslick) (D Tenn.) April 19, 1872–June 14, 1932; House 1925–June 14, 1932.

Eslick, Willa McCord Blake (widow of Edward Everett Eslick) (D Tenn.) Sept. 8, 1878–Feb. 18, 1961; House Aug. 4, 1932–33.

Espy, Albert Michael "Mike" (D Miss.) Nov. 30, 1953– ; House 1987–Jan. 22, 1993; secretary of agriculture Jan. 22, 1993–Dec. 31, 1994.

Essen, Frederick (R Mo.) April 22, 1863–Aug. 18, 1946; House Nov. 5, 1918–19.

Estabrook, Experience (– Neb.) April 30, 1813–March 26, 1894; House (Terr. Del.) 1859–May 18, 1860.

Estep, Harry Allison (R Pa.) Feb. 1, 1884–Feb. 28, 1968; House 1927–33.

Esterly, Charles Joseph (R Pa.) Feb. 8, 1888–Sept. 3, 1940; House 1925–27, 1929–31.

Estil, Benjamin (– Va.) March 13, 1780–July 14, 1853; House 1825–27.

Estopinal, Albert (D La.) Jan. 30, 1845–April 28, 1919; House Nov. 3, 1908–April 28, 1919.

Esty, Constantine Canaris (R Mass.) Dec. 26, 1824–Dec. 27, 1912; House Dec. 2, 1872–73.

Etheridge, Bob R. (D N.C.) Aug. 7, 1941– ; House 1997– .

Etheridge, Emerson (O Tenn.) Sept. 28, 1819–Oct. 21, 1902; House 1853–57 (1853–55 Whig, 1855–57 American Party), 1859–61.

Eustis, George Jr. (brother of James Biddle Eustis) (AP La.) Sept. 28, 1828–March 15, 1872; House 1855–59.

Eustis, James Biddle (brother of George Eustis Jr.) (D La.) Aug. 27, 1834–Sept. 9, 1899; Senate Jan. 12, 1876–79, 1885–91.

Eustis, William (R Mass.) June 10, 1753–Feb. 6, 1825; House 1801–05, Aug. 21, 1820–23; secretary of war March 7, 1809–Jan. 13, 1813; Gov. May 31, 1823–Feb. 6, 1825.

Evans, Alexander (W Md.) Sept. 13, 1818–Dec. 5, 1888; House 1847–53.

Evans, Alvin (R Pa.) Oct. 4, 1845–June 19, 1906; House 1901–05.

Evans, Billy Lee (D Ga.) Nov. 10, 1941– ; House 1977–83.

Evans, Charles Robley (D Nev.) Aug. 9, 1866–Nov. 30, 1954; House 1919–21.

Evans, Daniel Jackson (R Wash.) Oct. 16, 1925– ; Senate Sept. 12, 1983–89; Gov. Jan. 11, 1965–Jan. 12, 1977.

Evans, David Ellicott (– N.Y.) March 19, 1788–May 17, 1850; House March 4–May 2, 1827.

Evans, David Reid (R S.C.) Feb. 20, 1769–March 8, 1843; House 1813–15.

Evans, David Walter (D Ind.) Aug. 17, 1946– ; House 1975–83.

Evans, Frank Edward (D Colo.) Sept. 6, 1923– ; House 1965–79.

Evans, George (W Maine) Jan. 12, 1797–April 6, 1867; House July 20, 1829–41 (no party); Senate 1841–47.

Evans, Henry Clay (R Tenn.) June 18, 1843–Dec. 12, 1921; House 1889–91.

Evans, Hiram Kinsman (R Iowa) March 17, 1863–July 9, 1941; House June 4, 1923–25.

Evans, Isaac Newton (R Pa.) July 29, 1827–Dec. 3, 1901; House 1877–79, 1883–87.

Evans, James La Fayette (R Ind.) March 27, 1825–May 28, 1903; House 1875–79.

Evans, John Morgan (D Mont.) Jan. 7, 1863–March 12, 1946; House 1913–21, 1923–33.

Evans, Joshua Jr. (J Pa.) Jan. 20, 1777–Oct. 2, 1846; House 1829–33.

Evans, Josiah James (D S.C.) Nov. 27, 1786–May 6, 1858; Senate 1853–May 6, 1858.

Evans, Lane Allen (D Ill.) Aug. 4, 1951– ; House 1983– .

Evans, Lemuel Dale (AP Texas) Jan. 8, 1810–July 1, 1877; House 1855–57.

Evans, Lynden (D Ill.) June 28, 1858–May 6, 1926; House 1911–13.

Evans, Marcellus Hugh (D N.Y.) Sept. 22, 1884–Nov. 21, 1953; House 1935–41.

Evans, Melvin Herbert (R V.I.) Aug. 7, 1917–Nov. 27, 1984; House (Del.) 1979–81.

Evans, Nathan (W Ohio) June 24, 1804–Sept. 27, 1879; House 1847–51.

Evans, Robert Emory (R Neb.) July 15, 1856–July 8, 1925; House 1919–23.

Evans, Thomas (F Va.) ?–?; House 1797–1801.

Evans, Thomas Beverley Jr. (R Del.) Nov. 5, 1931– ; House 1977–83.

Evans, Thomas Cooper (R Iowa) May 26, 1924– ; House 1981–87.

Evans, Walter (nephew of Burwell Clark Ritter) (R Ky.) Sept. 18, 1842–Dec. 30, 1923; House 1895–99.

Evans, William Elmer (R Calif.) Dec. 14, 1877–Nov. 12, 1959; House 1927–35.

Evarts, William Maxwell (grandson of Roger Sherman) (R N.Y.) Feb. 6, 1818–Feb. 28, 1901; Senate 1885–91; attorney general July 15, 1868–March 3, 1869; secretary of state March 12, 1877–March 7, 1881.

Everett, Edward (father of William Everett) (W Mass.) April 11, 1794–Jan. 15, 1865; House 1825–35 (no party); Senate 1853–June 1, 1854; Gov. Jan. 13, 1836–Jan. 18, 1840; secretary of state Nov. 6, 1852–March 3, 1853.

Everett, Horace (W Vt.) July 17, 1779–Jan. 30, 1851; House 1829–43 (1829–35 no party).

Everett, Robert Ashton (D Tenn.) Feb. 24, 1915–Jan. 26, 1969; House Feb. 1, 1958–Jan. 26, 1969.

Everett, Robert Terry (R Ala.) Feb. 15, 1937– ; House 1993– .

Everett, Robert William (D Ga.) March 3, 1839–Feb. 27, 1915; House 1891–93.

Everett, William (son of Edward Everett) (D Mass.) Oct. 10, 1839–Feb. 16, 1910; House April 25, 1893–95.

Everhart, James Bowen (son of William Everhart) (R Pa.) July 26, 1821–Aug. 23, 1888; House 1883–87.

Everhart, William (father of James Bowen Everhart) (W Pa.) May 17, 1785–Oct. 30, 1868; House 1853–55.

Evins, John Hamilton (D S.C.) July 18, 1830–Oct. 20, 1884; House 1877–Oct. 20, 1884.

Evins, Joseph Landon (D Tenn.) Oct. 24, 1910–March 31, 1984; House 1947–77; chair House Select Small Business 1963–75; chair House Small Business 1975–77.

Ewart, Hamilton Glover (R N.C.) Oct. 23, 1849–April 28, 1918; House 1889–91.

Ewing, Andrew (brother of Edwin Hickman Ewing) (D Tenn.) June 17, 1813–June 16, 1864; House 1849–51.

Ewing, Edwin Hickman (brother of Andrew Ewing) (W Tenn.) Dec. 2, 1809–April 24, 1902; House 1845–47.

Ewing, John (W Ind.) May 19, 1789–April 6, 1858; House 1833–35 (no party), 1837–39.

Ewing, John Hoge (W Pa.) Oct. 5, 1796–June 9, 1887; House 1845–47.

Ewing, Presley Underwood (W Ky.) Sept. 1, 1822–Sept. 27, 1854; House 1851–Sept. 27, 1854.

Ewing, Thomas (father of Thomas Ewing, below) (W Ohio) Dec. 28, 1789–Oct. 26, 1871; Senate 1831–37, July 20, 1850–51; secretary of the Treasury March 4–Sept. 11, 1841; secretary of the interior March 8, 1849–July 22, 1850.

Ewing, Thomas (son of Thomas Ewing, above) (D Ohio) Aug. 7, 1829–Jan. 21, 1896; House 1877–81.

Ewing, Thomas W. (R Ill.) Sept. 19, 1935– ; House July 10, 1991–2001.

Ewing, William Lee Davidson (– Ill.) Aug. 31, 1795–March 25, 1846; Senate Dec. 30, 1835–37; Gov. Nov. 17–Dec. 3, 1834.

Exon, John James (D Neb.) Aug. 9, 1921– ; Senate 1979–97; Gov. Jan. 7, 1971–Jan. 3, 1979.

Faddis, Charles Isiah (D Pa.) June 13, 1890–April 1, 1972; House 1933–Dec. 4, 1942.

Fair, James Graham (D Nev.) Dec. 3, 1831–Dec. 28, 1894; Senate 1881–87.

Fairbanks, Charles Warren (R Ind.) May 11, 1852–June 4, 1918; Senate 1897–1905; vice president 1905–09.

Fairchild, Benjamin Lewis (R N.Y.) Jan. 5, 1863–Oct. 25, 1946; House 1895–97, 1917–19, 1921–23, Nov. 6, 1923–27.

Fairchild, George Winthrop (R N.Y.) May 6, 1854–Dec. 31, 1924; House 1907–19.

Faircloth, Duncan McLauchlin "Lauch" (R N.C.) Jan. 14, 1928– ; Senate 1993–99.

Fairfield, John (D Maine) Jan. 30, 1797–Dec. 24, 1847; House 1835–Dec. 24, 1838; Senate 1843–Dec. 24, 1847; Gov. Jan. 2, 1839–Jan. 6, 1841, Jan. 5, 1842–March 7, 1843.

Fairfield, Louis William (R Ind.) Oct. 15, 1858–Feb. 20, 1930; House 1917–25.

Faison, John Miller (D N.C.) April 17, 1862–April 21, 1915; House 1911–15.

Falconer, Jacob Alexander (Prog. Wash.) Jan. 26, 1869–July 1, 1928; House 1913–15.

Faleomavaega, Eni F. H. (D Am. Samoa) Aug. 15, 1943– ; House (Del.) 1989– .

Fall, Albert Bacon (R N.M.) Nov. 26, 1861–Nov. 30, 1944; Senate March 27, 1912–March 4, 1921; secretary of the interior March 5, 1921–March 4, 1923.

Fallon, George Hyde (D Md.) July 24, 1902–March 21, 1980; House 1945–71; chair House Public Works 1965–71.

Fannin, Paul Jones (R Ariz.) Jan. 29, 1907–Jan. 13, 2002; Senate 1965–77; Gov. Jan. 5, 1959–Jan. 4, 1965.

Faran, James John (D Ohio) Dec. 29, 1808–Dec. 12, 1892; House 1845–49.

Farbstein, Leonard (D N.Y.) Oct. 12, 1902–Nov. 9, 1993; House 1957–71.

Faris, George Washington (R Ind.) June 9, 1854–April 17, 1914; House 1895–1901.

Farlee, Isaac Gray (– N.J.) May 18, 1787–Jan. 12, 1855; House 1843–45.

Farley, Ephraim Wilder (W Maine) Aug. 29, 1817–April 3, 1880; House 1853–55.

Farley, James Indus (D Ind.) Feb. 24, 1871–June 16, 1948; House 1933–39.

Farley, James Thompson (D Calif.) Aug. 6, 1829–Jan. 22, 1886; Senate 1879–85.

Farley, Michael Francis (D N.Y.) March 1, 1863–Oct. 8, 1921; House 1915–17.

Farlin, Dudley (J N.Y.) Sept. 2, 1777–Sept. 26, 1837; House 1835–37.

Farnsley, Charles Rowland Peaslee (D Ky.) March 28, 1907–June 19, 1990; House 1965–67.

Farnsworth, John Franklin (R Ill.) March 27, 1820–July 14, 1897; House 1857–61, 1863–73.

Farnum, Billie Sunday (D Mich.) April 11, 1916–Nov. 18, 1979; House 1965–67.

Farquhar, John Hanson (R Ind.) Dec. 20, 1818–Oct. 1, 1873; House 1865–67.

Farquhar, John McCreath (R N.Y.) April 17, 1832–April 24, 1918; House 1885–91.

Farr, Evarts Worcester (R N.H.) Oct. 10, 1840–Nov. 30, 1880; House 1879–Nov. 30, 1880.

Farr, John Richard (R Pa.) July 18, 1857–Dec. 11, 1933; House 1911–19, Feb. 25–March 3, 1921.

Farr, Sam (D Calif.) July 4, 1941– ; House June 16, 1993– .

Farrelly, John Wilson (son of Patrick Farrelly) (W Pa.) July 7, 1809–Dec. 20, 1860; House 1847–49.

Farrelly, Patrick (father of John Wilson Farrelly) (– Pa.) 1770–Jan. 12, 1826; House 1821–Jan. 12, 1826.

Farrington, James (D N.H.) Oct. 1, 1791–Oct. 29, 1859; House 1837–39.

Farrington, Joseph Rider (husband of Mary Elizabeth Pruett Farrington) (R Hawaii) Oct. 15, 1897–June 19, 1954; House (Terr. Del.) 1943–June 19, 1954.

Farrington, Mary Elizabeth Pruett (widow of Joseph Rider Farrington) (R Hawaii) May 30, 1898–July 21, 1984; House (Terr. Del.) July 31, 1954–57.

Farrow, Samuel (R S.C.) 1759–Nov. 18, 1824; House 1813–15.

Farwell, Charles Benjamin (R Ill.) July 1, 1823–Sept. 23, 1903; House 1871–May 6, 1876, 1881–83; Senate Jan. 19, 1887–91.

Farwell, Nathan Allen (cousin of Owen Lovejoy) (R Maine) Feb. 24, 1812–Dec. 9, 1893; Senate Oct. 27, 1864–65.

Farwell, Sewall Spaulding (R Iowa) April 26, 1834–Sept. 21, 1909; House 1881–83.

Fary, John George (D Ill.) April 11, 1911–June 7, 1984; House July 8, 1975–83.

Fascell, Dante Bruno (D Fla.) March 9, 1917–Nov. 28, 1998; House 1955–93; chair House Foreign Affairs 1984–93.

Fassett, Jacob Sloat (– N.Y.) Nov. 13, 1853–April 21, 1924; House 1905–11.

Fattah, Chaka (D Pa.) Nov. 21, 1956– ; House 1995– .

Faulkner, Charles James (father of Charles James Faulkner, below) (D W.Va.) July 6, 1806–Nov. 1, 1884; House 1851–59 (1851–55 Whig) (Va.), 1875–77.

Faulkner, Charles James (son of Charles James Faulkner, above) (D W.Va.) Sept. 21, 1847–Jan. 13, 1929; Senate 1887–99.

Fauntroy, Walter Edward (D D.C.) Feb. 6, 1933– ; House (Del.) March 23, 1971–91.

Faust, Charles Lee (R Mo.) April 24, 1879–Dec. 17, 1928; House 1921–Dec. 17, 1928.

Favrot, George Kent (D La.) Nov. 26, 1868–Dec. 26, 1934; House 1907–09, 1921–25.

Fawell, Harris Walter (R Ill.) March 25, 1929– ; House 1985–99.

Fay, Francis Ball (W Mass.) June 12, 1793–Oct. 6, 1876; House Dec. 13, 1852–53.

Fay, James Herbert (D N.Y.) April 29, 1899–Sept. 10, 1948; House 1939–41, 1943–45.

Fay, John (– N.Y.) Feb. 10, 1773–June 21, 1855; House 1819–21.

Fazio, Victor Herbert Jr. (D Calif.) Oct. 11, 1942– ; House 1979–99.

Fearing, Paul (F N.W. Terr.) Feb. 28, 1762–Aug. 21, 1822; House (Terr. Del.) 1801–03.

Featherston, Winfield Scott (D Miss.) Aug. 8, 1820–May 28, 1891; House 1847–51.

Featherstone, Lewis Porter (Lab. Ark.) July 28, 1851–March 14, 1922; House March 5, 1890–91.

Feazel, William Crosson (D La.) June 10, 1895–March 16, 1965; Senate May 18–Dec. 30, 1948.

Feely, John Joseph (D Ill.) Aug. 1, 1875–Feb. 15, 1905; House 1901–03.

Feeney, Tom C. (R Fla.) May 21, 1958– ; House 2003– .

Feighan, Edward Farrell (nephew of Michael Aloysius Feighan) (D Ohio) Oct. 22, 1947– ; House 1983–93.

Feighan, Michael Aloysius (uncle of Edward Farrell Feighan) (D Ohio) Feb. 16, 1905–March 19, 1992; House 1943–71.

Feingold, Russell D. (D Wis.) March 2, 1953– ; Senate 1993– .

Feinstein, Dianne (D Calif.) June 22, 1933– ; Senate Nov. 10, 1992– .

Felch, Alpheus (D Mich.) Sept. 28, 1804–June 13, 1896; Senate 1847–53; Gov. Jan. 5, 1846–March 3, 1847.

Felder, John Myers (N S.C.) July 7, 1782–Sept. 1, 1851; House 1831–35 (1831–33 Jacksonian).

Fellows, Frank (R Maine) Nov. 7, 1889–Aug. 27, 1951; House 1941–Aug. 27, 1951.

Fellows, John R. (D N.Y.) July 29, 1832–Dec. 7, 1896; House 1891–Dec. 31, 1893.

Felton, Charles Norton (R Calif.) Jan. 1, 1828–Sept. 13, 1914; House 1885–89; Senate March 19, 1891–93.

Felton, Rebecca Latimer (wife of William Harrell Felton) (D Ga.) June 10, 1835–Jan. 24, 1930; Senate Nov. 21–Nov. 22, 1922.

Felton, William Harrell (husband of Rebecca Latimer Felton) (ID Ga.) June 1, 1823–Sept. 24, 1909; House 1875–81.

Fenerty, Clare Gerald (R Pa.) July 25, 1895–July 1, 1952; House 1935–37.

Fenn, Edward Hart (R Conn.) Sept. 12, 1856–Feb. 23, 1939; House 1921–31.

Fenn, Stephen Southmyd (D Idaho) March 28, 1820–April 13, 1892; House (Terr. Del.) June 23, 1876–79.

Fenner, James (R R.I.) Jan. 22, 1771–April 17, 1846; Senate 1805–Sept. 1807; Gov. May 6, 1807–May 1, 1811 (Democratic Republican), May 5, 1824–May 4, 1831 (Democratic Republican), May 2, 1843–May 6, 1845 (Law & Order Whig).

Fenton, Ivor David (R Pa.) Aug. 3, 1889–Oct. 23, 1986; House 1939–63.

Fenton, Lucien Jerome (R Ohio) May 7, 1844–June 28, 1922; House 1895–99.

Fenton, Reuben Eaton (R N.Y.) July 4, 1819–Aug. 25, 1885; House 1853–55 (Democrat), 1857–Dec. 20, 1864 (Democrat); Senate 1869–75; Gov. Jan. 1, 1865–Jan. 1, 1869 (Union Republican).

Fenwick, Millicent Hammond (R N.J.) Feb. 25, 1910–Sept. 16, 1992; House 1975–83.

Ferdon, John William (R N.Y.) Dec. 13, 1826–Aug. 5, 1884; House 1879–81.

Ferguson, Fenner (D Neb.) April 25, 1814–Oct. 11, 1859; House (Terr. Del.) 1857–59.

Ferguson, Homer (R Mich.) Feb. 25, 1889–Dec. 17, 1982; Senate 1943–55.

Ferguson, Michael "Mike" (R N.J.) July 22, 1970– ; House 2001– .

Ferguson, Phillip Colgan (D Okla.) Aug. 15, 1903–Aug. 8, 1978; House 1935–41.

Fergusson, Harvey Butler (D N.M.) Sept. 9, 1848–June 10, 1915; House (Terr. Del.) 1897–99, (Rep.) Jan. 8, 1912–15.

Fernald, Bert Manfred (R Maine) April 3, 1858–Aug. 23, 1926; Senate Sept. 12, 1916–Aug. 23, 1926; Gov. Jan. 6, 1909–Jan. 4, 1911.

Fernandez, Antonio Manuel (D N.M.) Jan. 17, 1902–Nov. 7, 1956; House 1943–Nov. 7, 1956.

Fernandez, Joachim Octave (D La.) Aug. 14, 1896–Aug. 8, 1978; House 1931–41.

Fernos-Isern, Antonio (PD P.R.) May 10, 1895–Jan. 19, 1974; House (Res. Comm.) Sept. 11, 1946–65.

Ferraro, Geraldine Anne (D N.Y.) Aug. 26, 1935– ; House 1979–85.

Ferrell, Thomas Merrill (D N.J.) June 20, 1844–Oct. 20, 1916; House 1883–85.

Ferris, Charles Goadsby (D N.Y.) about 1796–June 4, 1848; House Dec. 1, 1834–35 (Jacksonian), 1841–43.

Ferris, Scott (D Okla.) Nov. 3, 1877–June 8, 1945; House Nov. 16, 1907–21.

Ferris, Woodbridge Nathan (D Mich.) Jan. 6, 1853–March 23, 1928; Senate 1923–March 23, 1928; Gov. Jan. 1, 1913–Jan. 1, 1917.

Ferriss, Orange (R N.Y.) Nov. 26, 1814–April 11, 1894; House 1867–71.

Ferry, Orris Sanford (LR/D Conn.) Aug. 15, 1823–Nov. 21, 1875; House 1859–61 (Republican); Senate 1867–Nov. 21, 1875 (1867–73 Republican).

Ferry, Thomas White (R Mich.) June 10, 1827–Oct. 13, 1896; House 1865–71; Senate 1871–83; elected pres. pro tempore March 9, 1875, March 19, 1875, Dec. 20, 1875, March 5, 1877, Feb. 26, 1878, April 17, 1878, March 3, 1879.

Fess, Simeon Davison (R Ohio) Dec. 11, 1861–Dec. 23, 1936; House 1913–23; Senate 1923–35; chair Rep. Nat. Comm. 1930–32.

Fessenden, Samuel Clement (brother of Thomas Amory Deblois Fessenden and William Pitt Fessenden) (R Maine) March 7, 1815–April 18, 1882; House 1861–63.

Fessenden, Thomas Amory Deblois (brother of Samuel Clement Fessenden and William Pitt Fessenden) (R Maine) Jan. 23, 1826–Sept. 28, 1868; House Dec. 1, 1862–63.

Fessenden, William Pitt (brother of Samuel Clement Fessenden and Thomas Amory Deblois Fessenden) (R Maine) Oct. 16, 1806–Sept. 8, 1869; House 1841–43 (Whig); Senate Feb. 10, 1854–July 1, 1864 (Feb. 10, 1854–59 Whig), 1865–Sept. 8, 1869; secretary of the Treasury July 5, 1864–March 3, 1865.

Few, William (– Ga.) June 8, 1748–July 16, 1828; Senate 1789–93; Cont. Cong. 1780–82, 1786–88.

Ficklin, Orlando Bell (D Ill.) Dec. 16, 1808–May 5, 1886; House 1843–49, 1851–53.

Fiedler, Roberta Frances "Bobbi" (née Horowitz) (R Calif.) April 22, 1937– ; House 1981–87.

Fiedler, William Henry Frederick (D N.J.) Aug. 25, 1847–Jan. 1, 1919; House 1883–85.

Field, David Dudley (D N.Y.) Feb. 13, 1805–April 13, 1894; House Jan. 11–March 3, 1877.

Field, Moses Whelock (R Mich.) Feb. 10, 1828–March 14, 1889; House 1873–75.

Field, Richard Stockton (son of Richard Stockton) (R N.J.) Dec. 31, 1803–May 25, 1870; Senate Nov. 21, 1862–Jan. 14, 1863.

Field, Scott (D Texas) Jan. 26, 1847–Dec. 20, 1931; House 1903–07.

Field, Walbridge Abner (R Mass.) April 26, 1833–July 15, 1899; House 1877–March 28, 1878 (no party), 1879–81.

Fielder, George Bragg (D N.J.) July 24, 1842–Aug. 14, 1906; House 1893–95.

Fields, Cleo (D La.) Nov. 22, 1962– ; House 1993–97.

Fields, Jack Milton Jr. (R Texas) Feb. 3, 1952– ; House 1981–97.

Fields, William Craig (R N.Y.) Feb. 13, 1804–Oct. 27, 1882; House 1867–69.

Fields, William Jason (D Ky.) Dec. 29, 1874–Oct. 21, 1954; House 1911–Dec. 11, 1923; Gov. Dec. 11, 1923–Dec. 13, 1927.

Fiesinger, William Louis (D Ohio) Oct. 25, 1877–Sept. 11, 1953; House 1931–37.

Fillmore, Millard (W N.Y.) Jan. 7, 1800–March 8, 1874; House 1833–35, 1837–43; vice president 1849–July 10, 1850; president July 10, 1850–53.

Filner, Bob (D Calif.) Sept. 4, 1942– ; House 1993– .

Finch, Isaac (– N.Y.) Oct. 13, 1783–June 23, 1845; House 1829–31.

Finck, William Edward (D Ohio) Sept. 1, 1822–Jan. 25, 1901; House 1863–67, Dec. 7, 1874–75.

Findlay, James (brother of John Findlay and William Findlay) (J Ohio) Oct. 12, 1770–Dec. 28, 1835; House 1825–33 (1825–29 no party).

Findlay, John (brother of James Findlay and William Findlay) (– Pa.) March 31, 1766–Nov. 5, 1838; House Oct. 9, 1821–27.

Findlay, John Van Lear (D Md.) Dec. 21, 1839–April 19, 1907; House 1883–87.

Findlay, William (brother of James Findlay and John Findlay) (R Pa.) June 20, 1768–Nov. 12, 1846; Senate Dec. 10, 1821–27; Gov. Dec. 16, 1817–Dec. 19, 1820 (Democratic Republican).

Findley, Paul (R Ill.) June 23, 1921– ; House 1961–83.

Findley, William (R Pa.) 1741 or 1742–April 4, 1821; House 1791–99 (1791–95 no party), 1803–17.

Fine, John (D N.Y.) Aug. 26, 1794–Jan. 4, 1867; House 1839–41.

Fine, Sidney Asher (D N.Y.) Sept. 14, 1903–April 13, 1982; House 1951–Jan. 2, 1956.

Finerty, John Frederick (ID Ill.) Sept. 10, 1846–June 10, 1908; House 1883–85.

Fingerhut, Eric D. (D Ohio) May 6, 1959– ; House 1993–95.

Finkelnburg, Gustavus Adolphus (LR Mo.) April 6, 1837–May 18, 1908; House 1869–73 (1869–71 Republican).

Finley, Charles (son of Hugh Franklin Finley) (R Ky.) March 26, 1865–March 18, 1941; House Feb. 15, 1930–33.

Finley, David Edward (D S.C.) Feb. 28, 1861–Jan. 26, 1917; House 1899–Jan. 26, 1917.

Finley, Ebenezer Byron (nephew of Stephen Ross Harris) (D Ohio) July 31, 1833–Aug. 22, 1916; House 1877–81.

Finley, Hugh Franklin (father of Charles Finley) (R Ky.) Jan. 18, 1833–Oct. 16, 1909; House 1887–91.

Finley, Jesse Johnson (D Fla.) Nov. 18, 1812–Nov. 6, 1904; House April 19, 1876–77, Feb. 20–March 3, 1879, 1881–June 1, 1882.

Finnegan, Edward Rowan (D Ill.) June 5, 1905–Feb. 2, 1971; House 1961–Dec. 6, 1964.

Finney, Darwin Abel (R Pa.) Aug. 11, 1814–Aug. 25, 1868; House 1867–Aug. 25, 1868.

Fino, Paul Albert (R N.Y.) Dec. 15, 1913– ; House 1953–Dec. 31, 1968.

Fischer, Israel Frederick (R N.Y.) Aug. 17, 1858–March 16, 1940; House 1895–99.

Fish, Hamilton (father of Hamilton Fish, below, grandfather of Hamilton Fish born in 1888, great-grandfather of Hamilton Fish Jr. born in 1926) (W N.Y.) Aug. 3, 1808–Sept. 7, 1893; House 1843–45; Senate 1851–57; Gov. Jan. 1, 1849–Jan. 1, 1851; secretary of state March 17, 1869–March 12, 1877.

Fish, Hamilton (son of Hamilton Fish, above, father of Hamilton Fish born in 1888, grandfather of Hamilton Fish Jr. born in 1926) (R N.Y.) April 17, 1849–Jan. 15, 1936; House 1909–11.

Fish, Hamilton (son of Hamilton Fish born in 1849, father of Hamilton Fish Jr., below, grandson of Hamilton Fish born in 1808) (R N.Y.) Dec. 7, 1888–Jan. 18, 1991; House Nov. 2, 1920–45.

Fish, Hamilton Jr. (son of Hamilton Fish born in 1888, above, grandson of Hamilton Fish born in 1849, great-grandson of Hamilton Fish born in 1808) (R N.Y.) June 3, 1926–July 23, 1996; House 1969–95.

Fishburne, John Wood (cousin of Fontaine Maury Maverick) (D Va.) March 8, 1868–June 24, 1937; House 1931–33.

Fisher, Charles (R N.C.) Oct. 20, 1789–May 7, 1849; House Feb. 11, 1819–21, 1839–41.

Fisher, David (W Ohio) Dec. 3, 1794–May 7, 1886; House 1847–49.

Fisher, George (– N.Y.) March 17, 1788–March 26, 1861; House 1829–Feb. 5, 1830.

Fisher, George Purnell (U Del.) Oct. 13, 1817–Feb. 10, 1899; House 1861–63.

Fisher, Horatio Gates (R Pa.) April 21, 1838–May 8, 1890; House 1879–83.

Fisher, Hubert Frederick (D Tenn.) Oct. 6, 1877–June 16, 1941; House 1917–31.

Fisher, John (R N.Y.) March 13, 1806–March 28, 1882; House 1869–71.

Fisher, Joseph Lyman (D Va.) Jan. 11, 1914–Feb. 19, 1992; House 1975–81.

Fisher, Ovie Clark (D Texas) Nov. 22, 1903–Dec. 9, 1994; House 1943–Dec. 31, 1974.

Fisher, Spencer Oliver (D Mich.) Feb. 3, 1843–June 1, 1919; House 1885–89.

Fisk, James (R Vt.) Oct. 4, 1763–Nov. 17, 1844; House 1805–09, 1811–15; Senate Nov. 4, 1817–Jan. 8, 1818.

Fisk, Jonathan (R N.Y.) Sept. 26, 1778–July 13, 1832; House 1809–11, 1813–March 1815.

Fitch, Asa (F N.Y.) Nov. 10, 1765–Aug. 24, 1843; House 1811–13.

Fitch, Ashbel Parmelee (D N.Y.) Oct. 8, 1838–May 4, 1904; House 1887–Dec. 26, 1893 (1887–89 Republican).

Fitch, Graham Newell (grandfather of Edwin Denby) (D Ind.) Dec. 5, 1809–Nov. 29, 1892; House 1849–53; Senate Feb. 4, 1857–61.

Fitch, Thomas (R Nev.) Jan. 27, 1838–Nov. 12, 1923; House 1869–71.

Fite, Samuel McClary (D Tenn.) June 12, 1816–Oct. 23, 1875; House March 4–Oct. 23, 1875.

Fithian, Floyd James (D Ind.) Nov. 3, 1928–June 27, 2003; House 1975–83.

Fithian, George Washington (D Ill.) July 4, 1854–Jan. 21, 1921; House 1889–95.

Fitzgerald, Frank Thomas (D N.Y.) May 4, 1857–Nov. 25, 1907; House March 4–Nov. 4, 1889.

Fitzgerald, John Francis (grandfather of John Fitzgerald Kennedy, Robert Francis Kennedy and Edward Moore Kennedy, great-grandfather of Joseph Patrick Kennedy II) (D Mass.) Feb. 11, 1863–Oct. 2, 1950; House 1895–1901, March 4–Oct. 23, 1919.

Fitzgerald, John Joseph (D N.Y.) March 10, 1872–May 13, 1952; House 1899–Dec. 31, 1917.

Fitzgerald, Peter G. (R Ill.) Oct. 20, 1960– ; Senate 1999–2005.

Fitzgerald, Roy Gerald (R Ohio) Aug. 25, 1875–Nov. 16, 1962; House 1921–31.

Fitzgerald, Thomas (D Mich.) April 10, 1796–March 25, 1855; Senate June 8, 1848–49.

Fitzgerald, William (J Tenn.) Aug. 6, 1799–March 1864; House 1831–33.

Fitzgerald, William Joseph (D Conn.) March 2, 1887–May 6, 1947; House 1937–39, 1941–43.

Fitzgerald, William Thomas (R Ohio) Oct. 13, 1858–Jan. 12, 1939; House 1925–29.

Fitzgibbons, John (D N.Y.) July 10, 1868–Aug. 4, 1941; House 1933–35.

Fitzhenry, Louis (D Ill.) June 13, 1870–Nov. 18, 1935; House 1913–15.

Fitzpatrick, Benjamin (D Ala.) June 30, 1802–Nov. 21, 1869; Senate Nov. 25, 1848–Nov. 30, 1849, Jan. 14, 1853–55, Nov. 26, 1855–Jan. 21, 1861; elected pres. pro tempore Dec. 7, 1857, March 29, 1858, June 14, 1858, Jan. 25, 1859, March 9, 1859, Dec. 19, 1859, Feb. 20, 1860, June 26, 1860; Gov. Nov. 22, 1841–Dec. 10, 1845.

Fitzpatrick, James Martin (D N.Y.) June 27, 1869–April 10, 1949; House 1927–45.

Fitzpatrick, Michael G. (R Pa.) June 28, 1963– ; House 2005– .

Fitzpatrick, Morgan Cassius (D Tenn.) Oct. 29, 1868–June 25, 1908; House 1903–05.

Fitzpatrick, Thomas Young (D Ky.) Sept. 20, 1850–Jan. 21, 1906; House 1897–1901.

Fitzsimons, Thomas (– Pa.) 1741–Aug. 26, 1811; House 1789–95; Cont. Cong. 1782–83.

Fjare, Orvin Benonie (R Mont.) April 16, 1918– ; House 1955–57.

Flack, William Henry (R N.Y.) March 22, 1861–Feb. 2, 1907; House 1903–Feb. 2, 1907.

Flagler, Thomas Thorn (W N.Y.) Oct. 12, 1811–Sept. 6, 1897; House 1853–57.

Flaherty, Lawrence James (R Calif.) July 4, 1878–June 13, 1926; House 1925–June 13, 1926.

Flaherty, Thomas Aloysius (D Mass.) Dec. 21, 1898–April 27, 1965; House Dec. 14, 1937–43.

Flake, Floyd Harold (D N.Y.) Jan. 30, 1945– ; House 1987–Nov. 15, 1997.

Flake, Jeff (R Ariz.) Dec. 31, 1962– ; House 2001– .

Flanagan, De Witt Clinton (D N.J.) Dec. 28, 1870–Jan. 15, 1946; House June 18, 1902–03.

Flanagan, James Winright (R Texas) Sept. 5, 1805–Sept. 28, 1887; Senate March 30, 1870–75.

Flanagan, Michael Patrick (R Ill.) Nov. 9, 1962– ; House 1995–97.

Flanders, Alvan (R Wash.) Aug. 2, 1825–March 14, 1884; House (Terr. Del.) 1867–69; Gov. (Wash. Terr.) 1869–70.

Flanders, Benjamin Franklin (U La.) Jan. 26, 1816–March 13, 1896; House Dec. 3, 1862–63; Military Gov. June 6, 1867–Jan. 8, 1868.

Flanders, Ralph Edward (R Vt.) Sept. 28, 1880–Feb. 19, 1970; Senate Nov. 1, 1946–59.

Flannagan, John William Jr. (D Va.) Feb. 20, 1885–April 27, 1955; House 1931–49.

Flannery, John Harold (D Pa.) April 19, 1898–June 3, 1961; House 1937–Jan. 3, 1942.

Fleeger, George Washington (R Pa.) March 13, 1839–June 25, 1894; House 1885–87.

Fleetwood, Frederick Gleed (R Vt.) Sept. 27, 1868–Jan. 28, 1938; House 1923–25.

Fleger, Anthony Alfred (D Ohio) Oct. 21, 1900–July 16, 1963; House 1937–39.

Fleming, William Bennett (D Ga.) Oct. 29, 1803–Aug. 19, 1886; House Feb. 10–March 3, 1879.

Fleming, William Henry (D Ga.) Oct. 18, 1856–June 9, 1944; House 1897–1903.

Fletcher, Charles Kimball (R Calif.) Dec. 15, 1902–Sept. 29, 1985; House 1947–49.

Fletcher, Duncan Upshaw (D Fla.) Jan. 6, 1859–June 17, 1936; Senate 1909–June 17, 1936.

Fletcher, Ernest L. "Ernie" (R Ky.) Nov. 12, 1952– ; House 1999–Dec. 8, 2003; Gov. 2003– .

Fletcher, Isaac (D Vt.) Nov. 22, 1784–Oct. 19, 1842; House 1837–41.

Fletcher, Loren (R Minn.) April 10, 1833–April 15, 1919; House 1893–1903, 1905–07.

Fletcher, Richard (W Mass.) Jan. 8, 1788–June 21, 1869; House 1837–39.

Fletcher, Thomas (R Ky.) Oct. 21, 1779–?; House Dec. 2, 1816–17.

Fletcher, Thomas Brooks (D Ohio) Oct. 10, 1879–July 1, 1945; House 1925–29, 1933–39.

Flick, James Patton (R Iowa) Aug. 28, 1845–Feb. 25, 1929; House 1889–93.

Flint, Frank Putnam (R Calif.) July 15, 1862–Feb. 11, 1929; Senate 1905–11.

Flippo, Ronnie Gene (D Ala.) Aug. 15, 1937– ; House 1977–91.

Flood, Daniel John (D Pa.) Nov. 26, 1903–May 28, 1994; House 1945–47, 1949–53, 1955–Jan. 31, 1980.

Flood, Henry De La Warr (brother of Joel West Flood, uncle of Harry Flood Byrd) (D Va.) Sept. 2, 1865–Dec. 8, 1921; House 1901–Dec. 8, 1921.

Flood, Joel West (brother of Henry De La Warr Flood, uncle of Harry Flood Byrd) (D Va.) Aug. 2, 1894–April 27, 1964; House Nov. 8, 1932–33.

Flood, Thomas Schmeck (R N.Y.) April 12, 1844–Oct. 28, 1908; House 1887–91.

Florence, Elias (W Ohio) Feb. 15, 1797–Nov. 21, 1880; House 1843–45.

Florence, Thomas Birch (D Pa.) Jan. 26, 1812–July 3, 1875; House 1851–61.

Florio, James Joseph (D N.J.) Aug. 29, 1937– ; House 1975–Jan. 16, 1990; Gov. Jan. 16, 1990–Jan. 18, 1994.

Flournoy, Thomas Stanhope (W Va.) Dec. 15, 1811–March 12, 1883; House 1847–49.

Flower, Roswell Pettibone (D N.Y.) Aug. 7, 1835–May 12, 1899; House Nov. 8, 1881–83, 1889–Sept. 16, 1891; Gov. Jan. 1, 1892–Jan. 1, 1895.

Flowers, Walter (D Ala.) April 12, 1933–April 12, 1984; House 1969–79.

Floyd, Charles Albert (D N.Y.) 1791–Feb. 20, 1873; House 1841–43.

Floyd, John (– Ga.) Oct. 3, 1769–June 24, 1839; House 1827–29.

Floyd, John (R Va.) April 24, 1783–Aug. 17, 1837; House 1817–29; Gov. March 4, 1830–March 31, 1834 (Democrat).

Floyd, John Charles (D Ark.) April 14, 1858–Nov. 4, 1930; House 1905–15.

Floyd, John Gelston (grandson of William Floyd) (D N.Y.) Feb. 5, 1806–Oct. 5, 1881; House 1839–43, 1851–53.

Floyd, William (grandfather of John Gelston Floyd) (– N.Y.) Dec. 17, 1734–Aug. 4, 1821; House 1789–91; Cont. Cong. 1774–76, 1779–83.

Flye, Edwin (R Maine) March 4, 1817–July 12, 1886; House Dec. 4, 1876–77.

Flynn, Dennis Thomas (R Okla.) Feb. 13, 1861–June 19, 1939; House (Terr. Del.) 1893–97, 1899–1903.

Flynn, Gerald Thomas (D Wis.) Oct. 7, 1910–May 14, 1990; House 1959–61.

Flynn, Joseph Vincent (D N.Y.) Sept. 2, 1883–Feb. 6, 1940; House 1915–19.

Flynt, John James Jr. (D Ga.) Nov. 8, 1914– ; House Nov. 2, 1954–79; chair House Standards of Official Conduct 1975–77.

Focht, Benjamin Kurtz (R Pa.) March 12, 1863–March 27, 1937; House 1907–13, 1915–23, 1933–March 27, 1937.

Foelker, Otto Godfrey (R N.Y.) Dec. 29, 1875–Jan. 18, 1943; House Nov. 3, 1908–11.

Foerderer, Robert Hermann (R Pa.) May 16, 1860–July 26, 1903; House 1901–July 26, 1903.

Fogarty, John Edward (D R.I.) March 23, 1913–Jan. 10, 1967; House 1941–Dec. 7, 1944, Feb. 7, 1945–Jan. 10, 1967.

Fogg, George Gilman (R N.H.) May 26, 1813–Oct. 5, 1881; Senate Aug. 31, 1866–67.

Foglietta, Thomas Michael (D Pa.) Dec. 3, 1928–Nov. 13, 2004; House 1981–Nov. 12, 1997 (1981–83 Independent).

Foley, James Bradford (D Ind.) Oct. 18, 1807–Dec. 5, 1886; House 1857–59.

Foley, John Robert (D Md.) Oct. 16, 1917–Nov. 11, 2001; House 1959–61.

Foley, Mark (R Fla.) Sept. 8, 1954– ; House 1995– .

Foley, Thomas Stephen (D Wash.) March 6, 1929– ; House 1965–95; chair House Agriculture 1975–81; House majority leader 1987–June 6, 1989; Speaker June 6, 1989–95.

Folger, Alonzo Dillard (brother of John Hamlin Folger) (D N.C.) July 9, 1888–April 30, 1941; House 1939–April 30, 1941.

Folger, John Hamlin (brother of Alonzo Dillard Folger) (D N.C.) Dec. 18, 1880–July 19, 1963; House June 14, 1941–49.

Folger, Walter Jr. (R Mass.) June 12, 1765–Sept. 8, 1849; House 1817–21.

Follett, John Fassett (D Ohio) Feb. 18, 1831–April 15, 1902; House 1883–85.

Fong, Hiram Leong (R Hawaii) Oct. 1, 1907–Aug. 18, 2004; Senate Aug. 21, 1959–77.

Foot, Samuel Augustus (– Conn.) Nov. 8, 1780–Sept. 15, 1846; House 1819–21, 1823–25, 1833–May 9, 1834; Senate 1827–33; Gov. May 7, 1834–May 6, 1835 (Whig).

Foot, Solomon (R Vt.) Nov. 19, 1802–March 28, 1866; House 1843–47 (Whig); Senate 1851–March 28, 1866 (1851–57 Whig); elected pres. pro tempore Feb. 16, 1861, March 23, 1861, July 18, 1861, Jan. 15, 1862, March 31, 1862, June 19, 1862, Feb. 18, 1863, March 4, 1863, Dec. 18, 1863, Feb. 23, 1864, April 11, 1864.

Foote, Charles Augustus (– N.Y.) April 15, 1785–Aug. 1, 1828; House 1823–25.

Foote, Ellsworth Bishop (R Conn.) Jan. 12, 1898–Jan. 18, 1977; House 1947–49.

Foote, Henry Stuart (D Miss.) Feb. 28, 1804–May 19, 1880; Senate 1847–Jan. 8, 1852; Gov. Jan. 10, 1852–Jan. 5, 1854.

Foote, Wallace Turner Jr. (R N.Y.) April 7, 1864–Dec. 17, 1910; House 1895–99.

Foraker, Joseph Benson (R Ohio) July 5, 1846–May 10, 1917; Senate 1897–1909; Gov. Jan. 11, 1886–Jan. 13, 1890.

Foran, Martin Ambrose (D Ohio) Nov. 11, 1844–June 28, 1921; House 1883–89.

Forand, Aime Joseph (D R.I.) May 23, 1895–Jan. 18, 1972; House 1937–39, 1941–61.

Forbes, J. Randy (R Va.) Feb. 17, 1952– ; House June 19, 2001– .

Forbes, Michael P. (D N.Y.) July 16, 1952– ; House 1995–2001 (1995–99 Republican).

Ford, Aaron Lane (D Miss.) Dec. 21, 1903–July 8, 1983; House 1935–43.

Ford, George (D Ind.) Jan. 11, 1846–Aug. 30, 1917; House 1885–87.

Ford, Gerald Rudolph Jr. (R Mich.) July 14, 1913– ; House 1949–Dec. 6, 1973; House minority leader 1965–Dec. 6, 1973; vice president Dec. 6, 1973–Aug. 9, 1974; president Aug. 9, 1974–77.

Ford, Harold Eugene (D Tenn.) (father of Harold Eugene Ford Jr.) May 20, 1945– ; House 1975–97.

Ford, Harold Eugene Jr. (D Tenn.) (son of Harold Eugene Ford) May 11, 1970– ; House 1997– .

Ford, James (J Pa.) May 4, 1783–Aug. 18, 1859; House 1829–33.

Ford, Leland Merritt (R Calif.) March 8, 1893–Nov. 27, 1965; House 1939–43.

Ford, Melbourne Haddock (D Mich.) June 30, 1849–April 20, 1891; House 1887–89, March 4–April 20, 1891.

Ford, Nicholas (G Mo.) June 21, 1833–June 18, 1897; House 1879–83.

Ford, Thomas Francis (D Calif.) Feb. 18, 1873–Dec. 26, 1958; House 1933–45.

Ford, Wendell Hampton (D Ky.) Sept. 8, 1924– ; Senate Dec. 28, 1974–99; chair Senate Rules and Administration 1987–95; Gov. Dec. 7, 1971–Dec. 28, 1974.

Ford, William David (D Mich.) Aug. 6, 1927–Aug. 14, 2004; House 1965–95; chair House Post Office and Civil Service 1981–91; chair House Education and Labor 1991–95.

Ford, William Donnison (D N.Y.) 1779–Oct. 1, 1833; House 1819–21.

Fordney, Joseph Warren (R Mich.) Nov. 5, 1853–Jan. 8, 1932; House 1899–1923.

Foreman, Edgar Franklin (R N.M.) Dec. 22, 1933– ; House 1963–65 (Texas), 1969–71.

Forester, John B. (White supporter Tenn.) ?–Aug. 31, 1845; House 1833–37 (1833–35 Jacksonian).

Forker, Samuel Carr (D N.J.) March 16, 1821–Feb. 10, 1900; House 1871–73.

Forman, William St. John (D Ill.) Jan. 20, 1847–June 10, 1908; House 1889–95.

Fornance, Joseph (D Pa.) Oct. 18, 1804–Nov. 24, 1852; House 1839–43.

Fornes, Charles Vincent (D N.Y.) Jan. 22, 1844–May 22, 1929; House 1907–13.

Forney, Daniel Munroe (son of Peter Forney, uncle of William Henry Forney) (R N.C.) May 1784–Oct. 15, 1847; House 1815–18.

Forney, Peter (father of Daniel Munroe Forney, grandfather of William Henry Forney) (R N.C.) April 21, 1756–Feb. 1, 1834; House 1813–15.

Forney, William Henry (grandson of Peter Forney, nephew of Daniel Munroe Forney) (D Ala.) Nov. 9, 1823–Jan. 16, 1894; House 1875–93.

Forrest, Thomas (– Pa.) 1747–March 20, 1825; House 1819–21, Oct. 8, 1822–23.

Forrest, Uriah (– Md.) 1756–July 6, 1805; House 1793–Nov. 8, 1794; Cont. Cong. 1787.

Forrester, Elijah Lewis (D Ga.) Aug. 16, 1896–March 19, 1970; House 1951–65.

Forsyth, John (J Ga.) Oct. 22, 1780–Oct. 21, 1841; House 1813–Nov. 23, 1818 (Republican), 1823–Nov. 7, 1827 (Republican); Senate Nov. 23, 1818–Feb. 17, 1819 (Republican), Nov. 9, 1829–June 27, 1834; Gov. Nov. 7, 1827–Nov. 4, 1829 (Democratic Republican); secretary of state July 1, 1834–March 3, 1841.

Forsythe, Albert Palaska (G Ill.) May 24, 1830–Sept. 2, 1906; House 1879–81.

Forsythe, Edwin Bell (R N.J.) Jan. 17, 1916–March 29, 1984; House Nov. 3, 1970–March 29, 1984.

Fort, Franklin William (R N.J.) March 30, 1880–June 20, 1937; House 1925–31.

Fort, Greenbury Lafayette (R Ill.) Oct. 17, 1825–Jan. 13, 1883; House 1873–81.

Fort, Tomlinson (– Ga.) July 14, 1787–May 11, 1859; House 1827–29.

Fortenberry, Jeff (R Neb.) Dec. 27, 1960– ; House 2005– .

Fortuno, Luis G. (R P.R.) Oct. 31, 1960– ; House (Res. Comm.) 2005– .

Forward, Chauncey (brother of Walter Forward) (J Pa.) Feb. 4, 1793–Oct. 19, 1839; House Dec. 4, 1826–31 (Dec. 4, 1826–29 no party).

Forward, Walter (brother of Chauncey Forward) (– Pa.) Jan. 24, 1786–Nov. 24, 1852; House Oct. 8, 1822–25; secretary of the Treasury Sept. 13, 1841–March 1, 1843.

Fosdick, Nicoll (– N.Y.) Nov. 9, 1785–May 7, 1868; House 1825–27.

Foss, Eugene Noble (brother of George Edmund Foss) (D Mass.) Sept. 24, 1858–Sept. 13, 1939; House March 22, 1910–Jan. 4, 1911; Gov. Jan. 5, 1911–Jan. 8, 1914.

Foss, Frank Herbert (R Mass.) Sept. 20, 1865–Feb. 15, 1947; House 1925–35.

Foss, George Edmund (brother of Eugene Noble Foss) (R Ill.) July 2, 1863–March 15, 1936; House 1895–1913, 1915–19.

Fossella, Vito J. Jr. (great-grandson of James O' Leary) (R N.Y.) March 9, 1965– ; House Nov. 5, 1997– .

Foster, A. Lawrence (W N.Y.) ?–?; House 1841–43.

Foster, Abiel (F N.H.) Aug. 8, 1735–Feb. 6, 1806; House 1789–91 (no party), 1795–1803; Cont. Cong. 1783–85.

Foster, Addison Gardner (R Wash.) Jan. 28, 1837–Jan. 16, 1917; Senate 1899–1905.

Foster, Charles (R Ohio) April 12, 1828–Jan. 9, 1904; House 1871–79; Gov. Jan. 12, 1880–Jan. 14, 1884; secretary of the Treasury Feb. 25, 1891–March 6, 1893.

Foster, David Johnson (R Vt.) June 27, 1857–March 21, 1912; House 1901–March 21, 1912.

Foster, Dwight (brother of Theodore Foster) (F Mass.) Dec. 7, 1757–April 29, 1823; House 1793–June 6, 1800 (no party); Senate June 6, 1800–March 2, 1803.

Foster, Ephraim Hubbard (W Tenn.) Sept. 17, 1794–Sept. 6, 1854; Senate Sept. 17, 1838–39; Oct. 17, 1843–45.

Foster, George Peter (D Ill.) April 3, 1858–Nov. 11, 1928; House 1899–1905.

Foster, Henry Allen (D N.Y.) May 7, 1800–May 11, 1889; House 1837–39; Senate Nov. 30, 1844–Jan. 27, 1845.

Foster, Henry Donnel (cousin of John Cabell Breckinridge) (D Pa.) Dec. 19, 1808–Oct. 16, 1880; House 1843–47, 1871–73.

Foster, Israel Moore (R Ohio) Jan. 12, 1873–June 10, 1950; House 1919–25.

Foster, John Hopkins (R Ind.) Jan. 31, 1862–Sept. 5, 1917; House May 16, 1905–09.

Foster, Lafayette Sabine (R Conn.) Nov. 22, 1806–Sept. 19, 1880; Senate 1855–67; elected pres. pro tempore March 7, 1865.

Foster, Martin David (D Ill.) Sept. 3, 1861–Oct. 20, 1919; House 1907–19.

Foster, Murphy James (cousin of Jared Young Sanders) (D La.) Jan. 12, 1849–June 12, 1921; Senate 1901–13; Gov. May 16, 1892–May 21, 1900 (Anti-Lottery Democrat).

Foster, Nathaniel Greene (AP Ga.) Aug. 25, 1809–Oct. 19, 1869; House 1855–57 (affiliated with the Democratic Party).

Foster, Stephen Clark (R Maine) Dec. 24, 1799–Oct. 5, 1872; House 1857–61.

Foster, Theodore (brother of Dwight Foster) (F R.I.) April 29, 1752–Jan. 13, 1828; Senate June 7, 1790–1803.

Foster, Thomas Flournoy (W Ga.) Nov. 23, 1790–Sept. 14, 1848; House 1829–35 (no party), 1841–43.

Foster, Wilder De Ayr (R Mich.) Jan. 8, 1819–Sept. 20, 1873; House Dec. 4, 1871–Sept. 20, 1873.

Fouke, Philip Bond (D Ill.) Jan. 23, 1818–Oct. 3, 1876; House 1859–63.

Foulkes, George Ernest (D Mich.) Dec. 25, 1878–Dec. 13, 1960; House 1933–35.

Foulkrod, William Walker (R Pa.) Nov. 22, 1846–Nov. 13, 1910; House 1907–Nov. 13, 1910.

Fountain, Lawrence H. (D N.C.) April 23, 1913–Oct. 10, 2002; House 1953–83.

Fowler, Charles Newell (R N.J.) Nov. 2, 1852–May 27, 1932; House 1895–1911.

Fowler, Hiram Robert (D Ill.) Feb. 7, 1851–Jan. 5, 1926; House 1911–15.

Fowler, John (R Ky.) 1755–Aug. 22, 1840; House 1797–1807.

Fowler, John Edgar (P N.C.) Sept. 8, 1866–July 4, 1930; House 1897–99.

Fowler, Joseph Smith (U Tenn.) Aug. 31, 1820–April 1, 1902; Senate July 24, 1866–71.

Fowler, Orin (W Mass.) July 19, 1791–Sept. 3, 1852; House 1849–Sept. 3, 1852.

Fowler, Samuel (grandfather of Samuel Fowler, below) (J N.J.) Oct. 30, 1779–Feb. 20, 1844; House 1833–37.

Fowler, Samuel (grandson of Samuel Fowler, above) (D N.J.) March 22, 1851–March 17, 1919; House 1889–93.

Fowler, Tillie (R Fla.) Dec. 23, 1942–March 2, 2005; House 1993–2001.

Fowler, Wyche Jr. (D Ga.) Oct. 6, 1940– ; House April 6, 1977–87; Senate 1987–93.

Fox, Andrew Fuller (D Miss.) April 26, 1849–Aug. 29, 1926; House 1897–1903.

Fox, John (D N.Y.) June 30, 1835–Jan. 17, 1914; House 1867–71.

Fox, Jon D. (R Pa.) April 22, 1947– ; House 1995–99.

Foxx, Virginia Ann (R N.C.) June 29, 1943– ; House 2005– .

Frahm, Sheila (R Kan.) March 22, 1945– ; Senate June 11, 1996–Nov. 27, 1996.

France, Joseph Irvin (R Md.) Oct. 11, 1873–Jan. 26, 1939; Senate 1917–23.

Franchot, Richard (R N.Y.) June 2, 1816–Nov. 23, 1875; House 1861–63.

Francis, George Blinn (R N.Y.) Aug. 12, 1883–May 20, 1967; House 1917–19.

Francis, John Brown (grandson of John Brown of R.I.) (W R.I.) May 31, 1791–Aug. 9, 1864; Senate Jan. 25, 1844–45; Gov. May 1, 1833–May 2, 1838 (Democrat).

Francis, William Bates (D Ohio) Oct. 25, 1860–Dec. 5, 1954; House 1911–15.

Frank, Augustus (nephew of William Patterson of N.Y. and George Washington Patterson) (R N.Y.) July 17, 1826–April 29, 1895; House 1859–65.

Frank, Barney (D Mass.) March 31, 1940– ; House 1981– .

Frank, Nathan (R Mo.) Feb. 23, 1852–April 5, 1931; House 1889–91.

Frankhauser, William Horace (R Mich.) March 5, 1863–May 9, 1921; House March 4–May 9, 1921.

Franklin, Benjamin Joseph (D Mo.) March 1839–May 18, 1898; House 1875–79; Gov. (Ariz. Terr.) April 18, 1896–July 29, 1897.

Franklin, Jesse (brother of Meshack Franklin) (R N.C.) March 24, 1760–Aug. 31, 1823; House 1795–97 (no party); Senate 1799–1805, 1807–13; elected pres. pro tempore March 10, 1804; Gov. Dec. 7, 1820–Dec. 7, 1821 (Democratic Republican).

Franklin, John Rankin (W Md.) May 6, 1820–Jan. 11, 1878; House 1853–55.

Franklin, Meshack (brother of Jesse Franklin) (R N.C.) 1772–Dec. 18, 1839; House 1807–15.

Franklin, William Webster (R Miss.) Dec. 13, 1941– ; House 1983–87.

Franks, Gary (R Conn.) Feb. 9, 1953– ; House 1991–97.

Franks, Robert Douglas "Bob" (R N.J.) Sept. 21, 1951– ; House 1993–2001.

Franks, Trent (R Ariz.) June 19, 1957– ; House 2003– .

Fraser, Donald MacKay (DFL Minn.) Feb. 20, 1924– ; House 1963–79.

Frazer, Victor O. (I V.I.) May 24, 1943– ; House (Del.) 1995–97.

Frazier, James Beriah (father of James Beriah Frazier Jr.) (D Tenn.) Oct. 18, 1856–March 28, 1937; Senate March 21, 1905–11; Gov. Jan. 19, 1903–March 21, 1905.

Frazier, James Beriah Jr. (son of James Beriah Frazier) (D Tenn.) June 23, 1890–Oct. 30, 1978; House 1949–63.

Frazier, Lynn Joseph (R N.D.) Dec. 21, 1874–Jan. 11, 1947; Senate 1923–41; Gov. Jan. 3, 1917–Nov. 23, 1921.

Frear, James Archibald (R Wis.) Oct. 24, 1861–May 28, 1939; House 1913–35.

Frear, Joseph Allen Jr. (D Del.) March 7, 1903–Jan. 15, 1993; Senate 1949–61.

Frederick, Benjamin Todd (D Iowa) Oct. 5, 1834–Nov. 3, 1903; House 1885–87.

Fredericks, John Donnan (R Calif.) Sept. 10, 1869–Aug. 26, 1945; House May 1, 1923–27.

Free, Arthur Monroe (R Calif.) Jan. 15, 1879–April 1, 1953; House 1921–33.

Freedley, John (W Pa.) May 22, 1793–Dec. 8, 1851; House 1847–51.

Freeman, Chapman (R Pa.) Oct. 8, 1832–March 22, 1904; House 1875–79.

Freeman, James Crawford (R Ga.) April 1, 1820–Sept. 3, 1885; House 1873–75.

Freeman, John D. (U Miss.) ?–Jan. 17, 1886; House 1851–53.

Freeman, Jonathan (uncle of Nathaniel Freeman Jr.) (F N.H.) March 21, 1745–Aug. 20, 1808; House 1797–1801.

Freeman, Nathaniel Jr. (nephew of Jonathan Freeman) (R Mass.) May 1, 1766–Aug. 22, 1800; House 1795–99 (1795–97 Federalist).

Freeman, Richard Patrick (R Conn.) April 24, 1869–July 8, 1944; House 1915–33.

Freer, Romeo Hoyt (R W.Va.) Nov. 9, 1846–May 9, 1913; House 1899–1901.

Frelinghuysen, Frederick (father of Theodore Frelinghuysen, great-uncle of Frederick Theodore Frelinghuysen, great-great-great-grandfather of Peter Hood Ballantine Frelinghuysen Jr., great-great-great-grandfather of Rodney P. Frelinghuysen) (– N.J.) April 13, 1753–April 13, 1804; Senate 1793–Nov. 12, 1796; Cont. Cong. 1779.

Frelinghuysen, Frederick Theodore (nephew and adopted son of Theodore Frelinghuysen, great-nephew of Frederick Frelinghuysen, uncle of Joseph Sherman Frelinghuysen, great-grandfather of Peter Hood Ballantine Frelinghuysen Jr., great-great-grandfather of Rodney P. Frelinghuysen) (R N.J.) Aug. 4, 1817–May 20, 1885; Senate Nov. 12, 1866–69, 1871–77; secretary of state Dec. 19, 1881–March 6, 1885.

Frelinghuysen, Joseph Sherman (nephew of Frederick Theodore Frelinghuysen, cousin of Peter Hood Ballantine Frelinghuysen Jr.) (R N.J.) March 12, 1869–Feb. 8, 1948; Senate 1917–23.

Frelinghuysen, Peter Hood Ballantine Jr. (father of Rodney P. Frelinghuysen, cousin of Joseph Sherman Frelinghuysen, great-grandson of Frederick Theodore Frelinghuysen, great-great-nephew of Theodore Frelinghuysen, great-great-great-grandson of Frederick Frelinghuysen) (R N.J.) Jan. 17, 1916– ; House 1953–75.

Frelinghuysen, Rodney P. (son of Peter Hood Ballantine Frelinghuysen Jr., great-great-grandson of Frederick Theodore Frelinghuysen, great-great-great-great-grandson of Frederick Frelinghuysen) (R N.J.) April 29, 1946– ; House 1995– .

Frelinghuysen, Theodore (son of Frederick Frelinghuysen, uncle and adoptive father of Frederick Theodore Frelinghuysen, great-great-uncle of Peter Hood Ballantine Frelinghuysen Jr.) (N.J.) March 28, 1787–April 12, 1862; Senate 1829–35.

Fremont, John Charles (son-in-law of Thomas Hart Benton) (D Calif.) Jan. 21, 1813–July 13, 1890; Senate Sept. 9, 1850–51; Gov. (Ariz. Terr.) 1878–81.

French, Burton Lee (R Idaho) Aug. 1, 1875–Sept. 12, 1954; House 1903–09, 1911–15, 1917–33.

French, Carlos (D Conn.) Aug. 6, 1835–April 14, 1903; House 1887–89.

French, Ezra Bartlett (R Maine) Sept. 23, 1810–April 24, 1880; House 1859–61.

French, John Robert (R N.C.) May 28, 1819–Oct. 2, 1890; House July 6, 1868–69.

French, Richard (D Ky.) June 20, 1792–May 1, 1854; House 1835–37 (Jacksonian), 1843–45, 1847–49.

Frenzel, William Eldridge (R Minn.) July 31, 1928– ; House 1971–91.

Frey, Louis Jr. (R Fla.) Jan. 11, 1934– ; House 1969–79.

Frey, Oliver Walter (D Pa.) Sept. 7, 1887–Aug. 26, 1939; House Nov. 7, 1933–39.

Frick, Henry (W Pa.) March 17, 1795–March 1, 1844; House 1843–March 1, 1844.

Friedel, Samuel Nathaniel (D Md.) April 18, 1898–March 21, 1979; House 1953–71; chair House Administration 1968–71.

Fries, Frank William (D Ill.) May 1, 1893–July 17, 1980; House 1937–41.

Fries, George (D Ohio) 1799–Nov. 13, 1866; House 1845–49.

Frisa, Daniel (R N.Y.) April 27, 1955– ; House 1995–97.

Frist, Bill (R Tenn.) Feb. 22, 1952– ; Senate 1995– ; Senate majority leader 2003– .

Froehlich, Harold Vernon (R Wis.) May 12, 1932– ; House 1973–75.

Fromentin, Eligius (R La.) ?–Oct. 6, 1822; Senate 1813–19.

Frost, Joel (– N.Y.) ?–Sept. 11, 1827; House 1823–25.

Frost, Jonas Martin (D Texas) Jan. 1, 1942– ; House 1979–2005.

Frost, Richard Graham (D Mo.) Dec. 29, 1851–Feb. 1, 1900; House 1879–March 2, 1883.

Frost, Rufus Smith (R Mass.) July 18, 1826–March 6, 1894; House 1875–July 28, 1876.

Frothingham, Louis Adams (R Mass.) July 13, 1871–Aug. 23, 1928; House 1921–Aug. 23, 1928.

Fry, Jacob Jr. (D Pa.) June 10, 1802–Nov. 28, 1866; House 1835–39 (1835–37 Jacksonian).

Fry, Joseph Jr. (J Pa.) Aug. 4, 1781–Aug. 15, 1860; House 1827–31 (1827–29 no party).

Frye, William Pierce (grandfather of Wallace Humphrey White Jr.) (R Maine) Sept. 2, 1830–Aug. 8, 1911; House 1871–March 17, 1881; Senate March 18, 1881–Aug. 8, 1911; elected pres. pro tempore Feb. 7, 1896, March 7, 1901, Dec. 5, 1907.

Fugate, Thomas Bacon (D Va.) April 10, 1899–Sept. 22, 1980; House 1949–53.

Fulbright, James Franklin (D Mo.) Jan. 24, 1877–April 5, 1948; House 1923–25, 1927–29, 1931–33.

Fulbright, James William (D Ark.) April 9, 1905–Feb. 9, 1995; House 1943–45; Senate 1945–Dec. 31, 1974; chair Senate Banking and Currency 1955–59; chair Senate Foreign Relations 1959–75.

Fulkerson, Abram (D Va.) May 13, 1834–Dec. 17, 1902; House 1881–83 (elected as Readjuster Democrat).

Fulkerson, Frank Ballard (R Mo.) March 5, 1866–Aug. 30, 1936; House 1905–07.

Fuller, Alvan Tufts (R Mass.) Feb. 27, 1878–April 30, 1958; House 1917–Jan. 5, 1921 (1917–19 Independent Republican); Gov. Jan. 8, 1925–Jan. 3, 1929.

Fuller, Benoni Stinson (D Ind.) Nov. 13, 1825–April 14, 1903; House 1875–79.

Fuller, Charles Eugene (R Ill.) March 31, 1849–June 25, 1926; House 1903–13, 1915–June 25, 1926.

Fuller, Claude Albert (D Ark.) Jan. 20, 1876–Jan. 8, 1968; House 1929–39.

Fuller, George (D Pa.) Nov. 7, 1802–Nov. 24, 1888; House Dec. 2, 1844–45.

Fuller, Hawden Carlton (R N.Y.) Aug. 28, 1895–Jan. 29, 1990; House Nov. 2, 1943–49.

Fuller, Henry Mills (W Pa.) Jan. 3, 1820–Dec. 26, 1860; House 1851–53, 1855–57.

Fuller, Philo Case (W N.Y.) Aug. 14, 1787–Aug. 16, 1855; House 1833–Sept. 2, 1836 (1833–35 Anti-Mason).

Fuller, Thomas James Duncan (D Maine) March 17, 1808–Feb. 13, 1876; House 1849–57.

Fuller, Timothy (R Mass.) July 11, 1778–Oct. 1, 1835; House 1817–25.

Fuller, William Elijah (R Iowa) March 30, 1846–April 23, 1918; House 1885–89.

Fuller, William Kendall (J N.Y.) Nov. 24, 1792–Nov. 11, 1883; House 1833–37.

Fullerton, David (uncle of David Fullerton Robison) (– Pa.) Oct. 4, 1772–Feb. 1, 1843; House 1819–May 15, 1820.

Fulmer, Hampton Pitts (husband of Willa Lybrand Fulmer) (D S.C.) June 23, 1875–Oct. 19, 1944; House 1921–Oct. 19, 1944.

Fulmer, Willa Lybrand (widow of Hampton Pitts Fulmer) (D S.C.) Feb. 3, 1884–May 13, 1968; House Nov. 7, 1944–45.

Fulton, Andrew Steele (brother of John Hall Fulton) (W Va.) Sept. 29, 1800–Nov. 22, 1884; House 1847–49.

Fulton, Charles William (brother of Elmer Lincoln Fulton) (R Ore.) Aug. 24, 1853–Jan. 27, 1918; Senate 1903–09.

Fulton, Elmer Lincoln (brother of Charles William Fulton) (D Okla.) April 22, 1865–Oct. 4, 1939; House Nov. 16, 1907–09.

Fulton, James Grove (R Pa.) March 1, 1903–Oct. 6, 1971; House 1945–Oct. 6, 1971.

Fulton, John Hall (brother of Andrew Steele Fulton) (J Va.) ?–Jan. 28, 1836; House 1833–35.

Fulton, Richard Harmon (D Tenn.) Jan. 27, 1927– ; House 1963–Aug. 14, 1975.

Fulton, William Savin (D Ark.) June 2, 1795–Aug. 15, 1844; Senate Sept. 18, 1836–Aug. 15, 1844; Gov. (Ark. Terr.) 1835–36.

Funderburk, David (R N.C.) April 28, 1944– ; House 1995–97.

Funk, Benjamin Franklin (father of Frank Hamilton Funk) (R Ill.) Oct. 17, 1838–Feb. 14, 1909; House 1893–95.

Funk, Frank Hamilton (son of Benjamin Franklin Funk) (R Ill.) April 5, 1869–Nov. 24, 1940; House 1921–27.

Funston, Edward Hogue (R Kan.) Sept. 16, 1836–Sept. 10, 1911; House March 21, 1884–Aug. 2, 1894.

Fuqua, Don (D Fla.) Aug. 20, 1933– ; House 1963–87; chair House Science and Technology 1979–87.

Furcolo, Foster (D Mass.) July 29, 1911–July 25, 1995; House 1949–Sept. 30, 1952; Gov. Jan. 3, 1957–Jan. 5, 1961.

Furlong, Robert Grant (D Pa.) Jan. 4, 1886–March 19, 1973; House 1943–45.

Furlow, Allen John (R Minn.) Nov. 9, 1890–Jan. 29, 1954; House 1925–29.

Furse, Elizabeth (D Ore.) Oct. 13, 1936– ; House 1993–99.

Fuster, Jaime B. (D P.R.) Jan. 12, 1941– ; House (Res. Comm.) 1985–March 4, 1992.

Fyan, Robert Washington (D Mo.) March 11, 1835–July 28, 1896; House 1883–85, 1891–95.

Gabaldon, Isauro (Nat. P.I.) Dec. 8, 1875–Dec. 21, 1942; House (Res. Comm.) 1920–July 16, 1928.

Gage, Joshua (R Mass.) Aug. 7, 1763–Jan. 24, 1831; House 1817–19.

Gahn, Harry Conrad (R Ohio) April 26, 1880–Nov. 2, 1962; House 1921–23.

Gaillard, John (uncle of Theodore Gaillard Hunt) (R S.C.) Sept. 5, 1765–Feb. 26, 1826; Senate Dec. 6, 1804–Feb. 26, 1826; elected pres. pro tempore Feb. 28, 1810, April 17, 1810, April 18, 1814, Nov. 25, 1814, March 6, 1817, March 31, 1818, Jan. 25, 1820, Feb. 1, 1822, Feb. 19, 1823, May 21, 1824, March 9, 1825.

Gaines, John Pollard (W Ky.) Sept. 22, 1795–Dec. 9, 1857; House 1847–49; Gov. (Ore. Terr.) 1850–53.

Gaines, John Wesley (D Tenn.) Aug. 24, 1860–July 4, 1926; House 1897–1909.

Gaines, Joseph Holt (R W.Va.) Sept. 3, 1864–April 12, 1951; House 1901–11.

Gaines, William Embre (R Va.) Aug. 30, 1844–May 4, 1912; House 1887–89.

Gaither, Nathan (J Ky.) Sept. 15, 1788–Aug. 12, 1862; House 1829–33.

Galbraith, John (D Pa.) Aug. 2, 1794–June 15, 1860; House 1833–37 (Jacksonian), 1839–41.

Gale, George (father of Levin Gale) (– Md.) June 3, 1756–Jan. 2, 1815; House 1789–91.

Gale, Levin (son of George Gale) (– Md.) April 24, 1784–Dec. 18, 1834; House 1827–29.

Gale, Richard Pillsbury (R Minn.) Oct. 30, 1900–Dec. 4, 1973; House 1941–45.

Galifianakis, Nick (D N.C.) July 22, 1928– ; House 1967–73.

Gallagher, Cornelius Edward (D N.J.) March 2, 1921– ; House 1959–73.

Gallagher, James A. (R Pa.) Jan. 16, 1869–Dec. 8, 1957; House 1943–45, 1947–49.

Gallagher, Thomas (D Ill.) July 6, 1850–Feb. 24, 1930; House 1909–21.

Gallagher, William James (D Minn.) May 13, 1875–Aug. 13, 1946; House 1945–Aug. 13, 1946.

Gallatin, Albert (– Pa.) Jan. 29, 1761–Aug. 12, 1849; Senate Dec. 2, 1793–Feb. 28, 1794; House 1795–1801; secretary of the Treasury May 14, 1801–Feb. 8, 1814.

Gallegly, Elton William (R Calif.) March 7, 1944– ; House 1987– .

Gallegos, José Manuel (D N.M.) Oct. 30, 1815–April 21, 1875; House (Terr. Del.) 1853–July 23, 1856, 1871–73.

Gallinger, Jacob Harold (R N.H.) March 28, 1837–Aug. 17, 1918; House 1885–89; Senate 1891–Aug. 17, 1918; Senate minority leader 1913–Aug. 17, 1918; elected pres. pro tempore Feb. 12, 1912 (to serve Feb. 12–Feb. 14, April 26–April 27, May 7, July 6–July 31, Aug. 12–Aug. 26, 1912, Dec. 16, 1912–Jan. 4, 1913, Jan. 19–Feb. 1, Feb. 16–March 3, 1913).

Gallivan, James Ambrose (D Mass.) Oct. 22, 1866–April 3, 1928; House April 7, 1914–April 3, 1928.

Gallo, Dean Anderson (R N.J.) Nov. 23, 1935–Nov. 6, 1994; House 1985–Nov. 6, 1994.

Galloway, Samuel (R Ohio) March 20, 1811–April 5, 1872; House 1855–57.

Gallup, Albert (D N.Y.) Jan. 30, 1796–Nov. 5, 1851; House 1837–39.

Gamble, James (D Pa.) Jan. 28, 1809–Feb. 22, 1883; House 1851–55.

Gamble, John Rankin (brother of Robert Jackson Gamble, uncle of Ralph Abernethy Gamble) (R S.D.) Jan. 15, 1848–Aug. 14, 1891; House March 4–Aug. 14, 1891.

Gamble, Ralph Abernethy (son of Robert Jackson Gamble, nephew of John Rankin Gamble) (R N.Y.) May 6, 1885–March 4, 1959; House Nov. 2, 1937–57.

Gamble, Robert Jackson (brother of John Rankin Gamble, father of Ralph Abernethy Gamble) (R S.D.) Feb. 7, 1851–Sept. 22, 1924; House 1895–97, 1899–1901; Senate 1901–13.

Gamble, Roger Lawson (W Ga.) 1787–Dec. 20, 1847; House 1833–35 (Jacksonian); 1841–43.

Gambrell, David Henry (D Ga.) Dec. 20, 1929– ; Senate Feb. 1, 1971–Nov. 7, 1972.

Gambrill, Stephen Warfield (D Md.) Oct. 2, 1873–Dec. 19, 1938; House Nov. 4, 1924–Dec. 19, 1938.

Gammage, Robert Alton (D Texas) March 13, 1938– ; House 1977–79.

Gandy, Harry Luther (D S.D.) Aug. 13, 1881–Aug. 15, 1957; House 1915–21.

Ganly, James Vincent (D N.Y.) Sept. 13. 1878–Sept. 7, 1923; House 1919–21, March 4–Sept. 7, 1923.

Gannett, Barzillai (R Mass.) June 17, 1764–1832; House 1809–12.

Ganske, Greg (R Iowa) March 31, 1949– ; House 1995–2003.

Ganson, John (D N.Y.) Jan. 1, 1818–Sept. 28, 1874; House 1863–65.

Gantz, Martin Kissinger (D Ohio) Jan. 28, 1862–Feb. 10, 1916; House 1891–93.

Garber, Harvey Cable (D Ohio) July 6, 1866–March 23, 1938; House 1903–07.

Garber, Jacob Aaron (R Va.) Jan. 25, 1879–Dec. 2, 1953; House 1929–31.

Garber, Milton Cline (R Okla.) Nov. 30, 1867–Sept. 12, 1948; House 1923–33.

Garcia, Robert (D N.Y.) Jan. 9, 1933– ; House Feb. 21, 1978–Jan. 7, 1990 (in Feb. 21, 1978, special election, registered as Democrat but elected as Republican-Liberal).

Gard, Warren (D Ohio) July 2, 1873–Nov. 1, 1929; House 1913–21.

Gardenier, Barent (F N.Y.) ?–Jan. 10, 1822; House 1807–11.

Gardner, Augustus Peabody (uncle of Henry Cabot Lodge Jr. and John Davis Lodge) (R Mass.) Nov. 5, 1865–Jan. 14, 1918; House Nov. 3, 1902–May 15, 1917.

Gardner, Edward Joseph (D Ohio) Aug. 7, 1898–Dec. 7, 1950; House 1945–47.

Gardner, Francis (R N.H.) Dec. 27, 1771–June 25, 1835; House 1807–09.

Gardner, Frank (D Ind.) May 8, 1872–Feb. 1, 1937; House 1923–29.

Gardner, Gideon (R Mass.) May 30, 1759–March 22, 1832; House 1809–11.

Gardner, James Carson (R N.C.) April 8, 1933– ; House 1967–69.

Gardner, John James (R N.J.) Oct. 17, 1845–Feb. 7, 1921; House 1893–1913.

Gardner, Mills (R Ohio) Jan. 30, 1830–Feb. 20, 1910; House 1877–79.

Gardner, Obadiah (D Maine) Sept. 13, 1852–July 24, 1938; Senate Sept. 23, 1911–13.

Gardner, Washington (R Mich.) Feb. 16, 1845–March 31, 1928; House 1899–1911.

Garfield, James Abram (R Ohio) Nov. 19, 1831–Sept. 19, 1881; House 1863–Nov. 8, 1880; president March 4–Sept. 19, 1881.

Garfielde, Selucius (R Wash.) Dec. 8, 1822–April 13, 1881; House (Terr. Del.) 1869–73.

Garland, Augustus Hill (D Ark.) June 11, 1832–Jan. 26, 1899; Senate 1877–March 6, 1885; Gov. Nov. 12, 1874–Jan. 11, 1877; Atty. General March 6, 1885–March 5, 1889.

Garland, David Shepherd (R Va.) Sept. 27, 1769–Oct. 7, 1841; House Jan. 17, 1810–11.

Garland, James (C Va.) June 6, 1791–Aug. 8, 1885; House 1835–41 (1835–37 Jacksonian, 1837–39 Democrat).

Garland, Mahlon Morris (R Pa.) May 4, 1856–Nov. 19, 1920; House 1915–Nov. 19, 1920.

Garland, Peter Adams (R Maine) June 16, 1923– ; House 1961–63.

Garland, Rice (W La.) about 1795–1861; House April 28, 1834–July 21, 1840 (April 28, 1834–35 no party, 1835–37 Anti-Jacksonian).

Garmatz, Edward Alexander (D Md.) Feb. 7, 1903–July 22, 1986; House July 15, 1947–73; chair House Merchant Marine and Fisheries 1966–73.

Garn, Edwin Jacob "Jake" (R Utah) Oct. 12, 1932– ; Senate Dec. 21, 1974–93; chair Senate Banking, Housing, and Urban Affairs 1981–87.

Garner, Alfred Buckwalter (R Pa.) March 4, 1873–July 30, 1930; House 1909–11.

Garner, John Nance (D Texas) Nov. 22, 1868–Nov. 7, 1967; House 1903–33; House minority leader 1929–31; Speaker Dec. 7, 1931–33; vice president 1933–Jan. 20, 1941.

Garnett, James Mercer (brother of Robert Selden Garnett, grandfather of Muscoe Russell Hunter Garnett, cousin of Charles Fenton Mercer) (R Va.) June 8, 1770–April 23, 1843; House 1805–09.

Garnett, Muscoe Russell Hunter (grandson of James Mercer Garnett) (D Va.) July 25, 1821–Feb. 14, 1864; House Dec. 1, 1856–61.

Garnett, Robert Selden (brother of James Mercer Garnett, cousin of Charles Fenton Mercer) (R Va.) April 26, 1789–Aug. 15, 1840; House 1817–27.

Garnsey, Daniel Greene (– N.Y.) June 17, 1779–May 11, 1851; House 1825–29.

Garrett, Abraham Ellison (D Tenn.) March 6, 1830–Feb. 14, 1907; House 1871–73.

Garrett, Clyde Leonard (D Texas) Dec. 16, 1885–Dec. 18, 1959; House 1937–41.

Garrett, Daniel Edward (D Texas) April 28, 1869–Dec. 13, 1932; House 1913–15, 1917–19, 1921–Dec. 13, 1932.

Garrett, E. Scott (R N.J.) July 9, 1959– ; House 2003– .

Garrett, Finis James (D Tenn.) Aug. 26, 1875–May 25, 1956; House 1905–29; House minority leader 1923–29.

Garrison, Daniel (– N.J.) April 3, 1782–Feb. 13, 1851; House 1823–27.

Garrison, George Tankard (D Va.) Jan. 14, 1835–Nov. 14, 1889; House 1881–83, March 20, 1884–85.

Garrow, Nathaniel (– N.Y.) April 25, 1780–March 3, 1841; House 1827–29.

Garth, William Willis (D Ala.) Oct. 28, 1828–Feb. 25, 1912; House 1877–79.

Gartner, Fred Christian (R Pa.) March 14, 1896–Sept. 1, 1972; House 1939–41.

Gartrell, Lucius Jeremiah (uncle of Choice Boswell Randell) (D Ga.) Jan. 7, 1821–April 7, 1891; House 1857–Jan. 23, 1861.

Garvin, William Swan (D Pa.) July 25, 1806–Feb. 20, 1883; House 1845–47.

Gary, Frank Boyd (D S.C.) March 9, 1860–Dec. 7, 1922; Senate March 6, 1908–09.

Gary, Julian Vaughan (D Va.) Feb. 25, 1892–Sept. 6, 1973; House March 6, 1945–65.

Gasque, Allard Henry (husband of Elizabeth "Bessie" Hawley Gasque) (D S.C.) March 8, 1873–June 17, 1938; House 1923–June 17, 1938.

Gasque, Elizabeth "Bessie" Hawley (widow of Allard Henry Gasque) (Mrs. A. J. Van Exem) (D S.C.) Feb. 26, 1896–Nov. 2, 1989; House Sept. 13, 1938–39.

Gassaway, Percy Lee (D Okla.) Aug. 30, 1885–May 15, 1937; House 1935–37.

Gaston, Athelston (D Pa.) April 24, 1838–Sept. 23, 1907; House 1899–1901.

Gaston, William (F N.C.) Sept. 19, 1778–Jan. 23, 1844; House 1813–17.

Gates, Seth Merrill (W N.Y.) Oct. 10, 1800–Aug. 24, 1877; House 1839–43.

Gathings, Ezekiel Candler (D Ark.) Nov. 10, 1903–May 2, 1979; House 1939–69.

Gatlin, Alfred Moore (– N.C.) April 20, 1790–?; House 1823–25.

Gause, Lucien Coatsworth (D Ark.) Dec. 25, 1836–Nov. 5, 1880; House 1875–79.

Gavagan, Joseph Andrew (D N.Y.) Aug. 20, 1892–Oct. 18, 1968; House Nov. 5, 1929–Dec. 30, 1943.

Gavin, Leon Harry (R Pa.) Feb. 25, 1893–Sept. 15, 1963; House 1943–Sept. 15, 1963.

Gay, Edward James (grandfather of Edward James Gay, below) (D La.) Feb. 3, 1816–May 30, 1889; House 1885–May 30, 1889.

Gay, Edward James (grandson of Edward James Gay, above) (D La.) May 5, 1878–Dec. 1, 1952; Senate Nov. 6, 1918–21.

Gaydos, Joseph Matthew (D Pa.) July 3, 1926– ; House Nov. 5, 1968–93.

Gayle, John (W Ala.) Sept. 11, 1792–July 21, 1859; House 1847–49; Gov. Nov. 26, 1831–Nov. 21, 1835 (Democrat).

Gayle, June Ward (D Ky.) Feb. 22, 1865–Aug. 5, 1942; House Jan. 15, 1900–01.

Gaylord, James Madison (– Ohio) May 29, 1811–June 14, 1874; House 1851–53.

Gazlay, James William (– Ohio) July 23, 1784–June 8, 1874; House 1823–25.

Gear, John Henry (R Iowa) April 7, 1825–July 14, 1900; House 1887–91, 1893–95; Senate 1895–July 14, 1900; Gov. Jan. 17, 1878–Jan. 12, 1882.

Gearhart, Bertrand Wesley (R Calif.) May 31, 1890–Oct. 11, 1955; House 1935–49.

Gearin, John McDermeid (D Ore.) Aug. 15, 1851–Nov. 12, 1930; Senate Dec. 13, 1905–Jan. 23, 1907.

Geary, Thomas J. (D Calif.) Jan. 18, 1854–July 6, 1929; House Dec. 9, 1890–95.

Gebhard, John (– N.Y.) Feb. 22, 1782–Jan. 3, 1854; House 1821–23.

Geddes, George Washington (D Ohio) July 16, 1824–Nov. 9, 1892; House 1879–87.

Geddes, James (F N.Y.) July 22, 1763–Aug. 19, 1838; House 1813–15.

Geelan, James Patrick (D Conn.) Aug. 11, 1901–Aug. 10, 1982; House 1945–47.

Gehrmann, Bernard John (Prog. Wis.) Feb. 13, 1880–July 12, 1958; House 1935–43.

Geissenhainer, Jacob Augustus (D N.J.) Aug. 28, 1839–July 20, 1917; House 1889–95.

Gejdenson, Samuel (D Conn.) May 20, 1948– ; House 1981–2001.

Gekas, George William (R Pa.) April 14, 1930– ; House 1983–2003.

Gensman, Lorraine Michael (R Okla.) Aug. 26, 1878–May 27, 1954; House 1921–23.

Gentry, Brady Preston (D Texas) March 25, 1896–Nov. 9, 1966; House 1953–57.

Gentry, Meredith Poindexter (W Tenn.) Sept. 15, 1809–Nov. 2, 1866; House 1839–43, 1845–53.

George, Henry Jr. (D N.Y.) Nov. 3, 1862–Nov. 14, 1916; House 1911–15.

George, James Zachariah (D Miss.) Oct. 20, 1826–Aug. 14, 1897; Senate 1881–Aug. 14, 1897.

George, Melvin Clark (R Ore.) May 13, 1849–Feb. 22, 1933; House 1881–85.

George, Myron Virgil (R Kan.) Jan. 6, 1900–April 11, 1972; House Nov. 7, 1950–59.

George, Newell Adolphus (D Kan.) Sept. 24, 1904–Oct. 22, 1992; House 1959–61.

George, Walter Franklin (D Ga.) Jan. 29, 1878–Aug. 4, 1957; Senate Nov. 22, 1922–57; chair Senate Finance 1949–53; elected pres. pro tempore Jan. 5, 1955; chair Senate Foreign Relations 1955–57.

Gephardt, Richard A. (D Mo.) Jan. 31, 1941– ; House 1977–2005; House majority leader June 14, 1989–95; House minority leader 1995–2003.

Geran, Elmer Hendrickson (D N.J.) Oct. 24, 1875–Jan. 12, 1954; House 1923–25.

Geren, Presten M. "Pete" (D Texas) Jan. 29, 1952– ; House Sept. 20, 1989–97.

Gerlach, Charles Lewis (R Pa.) Sept. 14, 1895–May 5, 1947; House 1939–May 5, 1947.

Gerlach, James W. "Jim" (R Pa.) Feb. 25, 1955– ; House 2003– .

German, Obadiah (R N.Y.) April 22, 1766–Sept. 24, 1842; Senate 1809–15.

Gernerd, Fred Benjamin (R Pa.) Nov. 22, 1879–Aug. 7, 1948; House 1921–23.

Gerry, Elbridge (great-grandfather of Peter Goelet Gerry, grandfather of Elbridge Gerry, below) (– Mass.) July 17, 1744–Nov. 23, 1814; House 1789–93; Cont. Cong. 1776–80, 1783–85; Gov. June 2, 1810–June 5, 1812 (Democratic Republican); vice president 1813–Nov. 23, 1814 (Democratic Republican).

Gerry, Elbridge (grandson of Elbridge Gerry, above) (D Maine) Dec. 6, 1813–April 10, 1886; House 1849–51.

Gerry, James (D Pa.) Aug. 14, 1796–July 19, 1873; House 1839–43.

Gerry, Peter Goelet (great-grandson of Elbridge Gerry) (D R.I.) Sept. 18, 1879–Oct. 31, 1957; House 1913–15; Senate 1917–29, 1935–47.

Gest, William Harrison (R Ill.) Jan. 7, 1838–Aug. 9, 1912; House 1887–91.

Gettys, Thomas Smithwick (D S.C.) June 19, 1912–June 8, 2003; House Nov. 3, 1964–Dec. 31, 1974.

Getz, James Lawrence (D Pa.) Sept. 14, 1821–Dec. 25, 1891; House 1867–73.

Geyer, Henry Sheffie (W Mo.) Dec. 9, 1790–March 5, 1859; Senate 1851–57.

Geyer, Lee Edward (D Calif.) Sept. 9, 1888–Oct. 11, 1941; House 1939–Oct. 11, 1941.

Gholson, James Herbert (AJ Va.) 1798–July 2, 1848; House 1833–35.

Gholson, Samuel Jameson (D Miss.) May 19, 1808–Oct. 16, 1883; House Dec. 1, 1836–37 (Jacksonian), July 18, 1837–Feb. 5, 1838.

Gholson, Thomas Jr. (R Va.) ?–July 4, 1816; House Nov. 7, 1808–July 4, 1816.

Giaimo, Robert Nicholas (D Conn.) Oct. 15, 1919– ; House 1959–81; chair House Budget 1977–81.

Gibbons, James A. "Jim" (R Nev.) Dec. 16, 1944– ; House 1997– .

Gibbons, Sam Melville (D Fla.) Jan. 20, 1920– ; House 1963–97; chair House Ways and Means 1994–95.

Gibbs, Florence Reville (widow of Willis Benjamin Gibbs) (D Ga.) April 4, 1890–Aug. 19, 1964; House Oct. 1, 1940–41.

Gibbs, Willis Benjamin (husband of Florence Reville Gibbs) (D Ga.) April 15, 1889–Aug. 7, 1940; House 1939–Aug. 7, 1940.

Gibson, Charles Hopper (cousin of Henry Richard Gibson) (D Md.) Jan. 19, 1842–March 31, 1900; House 1885–91; Senate Nov. 19, 1891–97.

Gibson, Ernest Willard (father of Ernest William Gibson Jr.) (R Vt.) Dec. 29, 1872–June 20, 1940; House Nov. 6, 1923–Oct. 19, 1933; Senate Nov. 21, 1933–June 20, 1940.

Gibson, Ernest William Jr. (son of Ernest Willard Gibson) (R Vt.) March 6, 1901–Nov. 4, 1969; Senate June 24, 1940–41; Gov. Jan. 9, 1947–Jan. 16, 1950.

Gibson, Eustace (D W.Va.) Oct. 4, 1842–Dec. 10, 1900; House 1883–87.

Gibson, Henry Richard (cousin of Charles Hopper Gibson) (R Tenn.) Dec. 24, 1837–May 25, 1938; House 1895–1905.

Gibson, James King (C Va.) Feb. 18, 1812–March 30, 1879; House Jan. 28, 1870–71.

Gibson, John Strickland (D Ga.) Jan. 3, 1893–Oct. 19, 1960; House 1941–47.

Gibson, Paris (D Mont.) July 1, 1830–Dec. 16, 1920; Senate March 7, 1901–05.

Gibson, Randall Lee (D La.) Sept. 10, 1832–Dec. 15, 1892; House 1875–83; Senate 1883–Dec. 15, 1892.

Giddings, De Witt Clinton (D Texas) July 18, 1827–Aug. 19, 1903; House May 13, 1872–75, 1877–79.

Giddings, Joshua Reed (R Ohio) Oct. 6, 1795–May 27, 1864; House Dec. 3, 1838–March 22, 1842 (Whig); Dec. 5, 1842–59 (Dec. 5, 1842–49 Whig, 1849–55 Free-Soiler).

Giddings, Napoleon Bonaparte (D Neb.) Jan. 2, 1816–Aug. 3, 1897; House (Terr. Del.) Jan. 5–March 3, 1855.

Gifford, Charles Laceille (R Mass.) March 15, 1871–Aug. 23, 1947; House Nov. 7, 1922–Aug. 23, 1947.

Gifford, Oscar Sherman (R S.D.) Oct. 20, 1842–Jan. 16, 1913; House (Terr. Del. Dakota) 1885–89, (Rep.) Nov. 2, 1889–91.

Gilbert, Abijah (R Fla.) June 18, 1806–Nov. 23, 1881; Senate 1869–75.

Gilbert, Edward (D Calif.) about 1819–Aug. 2, 1852; House Sept. 11, 1850–51.

Gilbert, Ezekiel (F N.Y.) March 25, 1756–July 17, 1841; House 1793–97 (1793–95 no party).

Gilbert, George Gilmore (father of Ralph Waldo Emerson Gilbert) (D Ky.) Dec. 24, 1849–Nov. 9, 1909; House 1899–1907.

Gilbert, Jacob H. (D N.Y.) June 17, 1920–Feb. 27, 1981; House March 8, 1960–71.

Gilbert, Newton Whiting (R Ind.) May 24, 1862–July 5, 1939; House 1905–Nov. 6, 1906.

Gilbert, Ralph Waldo Emerson (son of George Gilmore Gilbert) (D Ky.) Jan. 17, 1882–July 30, 1939; House 1921–29, 1931–33.

Gilbert, Sylvester (R Conn.) Oct. 20, 1755–Jan. 2, 1846; House Nov. 16, 1818–19.

Gilbert, William Augustus (W N.Y.) Jan. 25, 1815–May 25, 1875; House 1855–Feb. 27, 1857.

Gilchrest, Wayne T. (R Md.) April 15, 1946– ; House 1991– .

Gilchrist, Fred Cramer (R Iowa) June 2, 1868–March 10, 1950; House 1931–45.

Gildea, James Hilary (D Pa.) Oct. 21, 1890–June 5, 1988; House 1935–39.

Giles, William Branch (R Va.) Aug. 12, 1762–Dec. 4, 1830; House Dec. 7, 1790–Oct. 2, 1798 (no party), 1801–03; Senate Aug. 11, 1804–15; Gov. March 4, 1827–March 4, 1830.

Giles, William Fell (D Md.) April 8, 1807–March 21, 1879; House 1845–47.

Gilfillan, Calvin Willard (R Pa.) Feb. 20, 1832–Dec. 2, 1901; House 1869–71.

Gilfillan, John Bachop (R Minn.) Feb. 11, 1835–Aug. 19, 1924; House 1885–87.

Gilhams, Clarence Chauncey (R Ind.) April 11, 1860–June 5, 1912; House Nov. 6, 1906–09.

Gill, John Jr. (D Md.) June 9, 1850–Jan. 27, 1918; House 1905–11.

Gill, Joseph John (R Ohio) Sept. 21, 1846–May 22, 1920; House Dec. 4, 1899–Oct. 31, 1903.

Gill, Michael Joseph (D Mo.) Dec. 5, 1864–Nov. 1, 1918; House June 19, 1914–15.

Gill, Patrick Francis (D Mo.) Aug. 16, 1868–May 21, 1923; House 1909–11, Aug. 12, 1912–13.

Gill, Thomas Ponce (D Hawaii) April 21, 1922– ; House 1963–65.

Gillen, Courtland Craig (D Ind.) July 3, 1880–Sept. 1, 1954; House 1931–33.

Gillespie, Dean Milton (R Colo.) May 3, 1884–Feb. 2, 1949; House March 7, 1944–47.

Gillespie, Eugene Pierce (D Pa.) Sept. 24, 1852–Dec. 16, 1899; House 1891–93.

Gillespie, James (R N.C.) ?–Jan. 11, 1805; House 1793–99 (1793–95 no party), 1803–Jan. 11, 1805.

Gillespie, James Frank (D Ill.) April 18, 1869–Nov. 26, 1954; House 1933–35.

Gillespie, Oscar William (D Texas) June 20, 1858–Aug. 23, 1927; House 1903–11.

Gillet, Charles William (R N.Y.) Nov. 26, 1840–Dec. 31, 1908; House 1893–1905.

Gillet, Ransom Hooker (D N.Y.) Jan. 27, 1800–Oct. 24, 1876; House 1833–37.

Gillett, Frederick Huntington (R Mass.) Oct. 16, 1851–July 31, 1935; House 1893–1925; Speaker May 19, 1919–21, April 11, 1921–23, Dec. 3, 1923–25; Senate 1925–31.

Gillett, James Norris (R Calif.) Sept. 20, 1860–April 20, 1937; House 1903–Nov. 4, 1906; Gov. Jan. 8, 1907–Jan. 3, 1911.

Gillette, Edward Hooker (son of Francis Gillette) (G Iowa) Oct. 1, 1840–Aug. 14, 1918; House 1879–81.

Gillette, Francis (father of Edward Hooker Gillette) (FS Conn.) Dec. 14, 1807–Sept. 30, 1879; Senate May 24, 1854–55.

Gillette, Guy Mark (D Iowa) Feb. 3, 1879–March 3, 1973; House 1933–Nov. 3, 1936; Senate Nov. 4, 1936–45, 1949–55.

Gillette, Wilson Darwin (R Pa.) July 1, 1880–Aug. 7, 1951; House Nov. 4, 1941–Aug. 7, 1951.

Gillie, George W. (R Ind.) Aug. 15, 1880–July 3, 1963; House 1939–49.

Gilligan, John Joyce (D Ohio) March 22, 1921– ; House 1965–67; Gov. Jan. 11, 1971–Jan. 13, 1975.

Gillis, James Lisle (D Pa.) Oct. 2, 1792–July 8, 1881; House 1857–59.

Gillmor, Paul E. (R Ohio) Feb. 1, 1939– ; House 1989– .

Gillon, Alexander (– S.C.) 1741–Oct. 6, 1794; House 1793–Oct. 6, 1794; Cont. Cong. (elected but did not attend) 1784.

Gilman, Benjamin Arthur (R N.Y.) Dec. 6, 1922– ; House 1973–2003; chair House International Relations 1995–2001.

Gilman, Charles Jervis (great-nephew of John Taylor Gilman and Nicholas Gilman) (R Maine) Feb. 26, 1824–Feb. 5, 1901; House 1857–59.

Gilman, Nicholas (brother of John Taylor Gilman and great-uncle of Charles Jervis Gilman) (R N.H.) Aug. 3, 1755–May 2, 1814; House 1789–97 (no party); Senate 1805–May 2, 1814; Cont. Cong. 1787–89.

Gilmer, George Rockingham (J Ga.) April 11, 1790–Nov. 16, 1859; House 1821–23 (no party), Oct. 1, 1827–29 (no party), 1833–35; Gov. Nov. 4, 1829–Nov. 9, 1831 (Jacksonian), Nov. 8, 1837–Nov. 6, 1839 (Whig).

Gilmer, John Adams (O N.C.) Nov. 4, 1805–May 14, 1868; House 1857–61 (1857–59 American Party).

Gilmer, Thomas Walker (D Va.) April 6, 1802–Feb. 28, 1844; House 1841–Feb. 16, 1844 (1841–43 Whig); Gov. March 31, 1840–March 1, 1841 (Whig); secretary of the navy Feb. 19–Feb. 28, 1844.

Gilmer, William Franklin "Dixie" (D Okla.) June 7, 1901–June 9, 1954; House 1949–51.

Gilmore, Alfred (son of John Gilmore) (D Pa.) June 9, 1812–June 29, 1890; House 1849–53.

Gilmore, Edward (D Mass.) Jan. 4, 1867–April 10, 1924; House 1913–15.

Gilmore, John (father of Alfred Gilmore) (J Pa.) Feb. 18, 1780–May 11, 1845; House 1829–33.

Gilmore, Samuel Louis (D La.) July 30, 1859–July 18, 1910; House March 30, 1909–July 18, 1910.

Gingery, Don (D Pa.) Feb. 19, 1884–Oct. 15, 1961; House 1935–39.

Gingrey, John Philip "Phil" (R Ga.) July 10, 1942– ; House 2003– .

Gingrich, Newt (R Ga.) June 17, 1943– ; House 1979–99; Speaker 1995–99.

Ginn, Ronald "Bo" Bryan (D Ga.) May 31, 1934–Jan. 6, 2005; House 1973–83.

Gist, Joseph (– S.C.) Jan. 12, 1775–March 8, 1836; House 1821–27.

Gittins, Robert Henry (D N.Y.) Dec. 14, 1869–Dec. 25, 1957; House 1913–15.

Glascock, John Raglan (D Calif.) Aug. 25, 1845–Nov. 10, 1913; House 1883–85.

Glascock, Thomas (D Ga.) Oct. 21, 1790–May 19, 1841; House Oct. 5, 1835–39 (Oct. 5, 1835–37 Jacksonian).

Glasgow, Hugh (R Pa.) Sept. 8, 1769–Jan. 31, 1818; House 1813–17.

Glass, Carter (D Va.) Jan. 4, 1858–May 28, 1946; House Nov. 4, 1902–Dec. 16, 1918; Senate Feb. 2, 1920–May 28, 1946; elected pres. pro tempore July 10, 1941, Jan. 5, 1943; secretary of the Treasury Dec. 16, 1918–Feb. 1, 1920.

Glass, Presley Thornton (D Tenn.) Oct. 18, 1824–Oct. 9, 1902; House 1885–89.

Glatfelter, Samuel Feiser (D Pa.) April 7, 1858–April 23, 1927; House 1923–25.

Glen, Henry (F N.Y.) July 13, 1739–Jan. 6, 1814; House 1793–1801 (1793–95 no party).

Glenn, John Herschel Jr. (D Ohio) July 18, 1921– ; Senate Dec. 24, 1974–99; chair Senate Governmental Affairs 1987–95.

Glenn, Milton Willits (R N.J.) June 18, 1903–Dec. 14, 1967; House Nov. 5, 1957–65.

Glenn, Otis Ferguson (R Ill.) Aug. 27, 1879–March 11, 1959; Senate Dec. 3, 1928–33.

Glenn, Thomas Louis (P Idaho) Feb. 2, 1847–Nov. 18, 1918; House 1901–03.

Glickman, Daniel Robert (D Kan.) Nov. 24, 1944– ; House 1977–95; chair House Select Intelligence 1993–95; secretary of agriculture March 20, 1995–Jan. 19, 2001.

Gloninger, John (F Pa.) Sept. 19, 1758–Jan. 22, 1836; House March 4–Aug. 2, 1813.

Glossbrenner, Adam John (D Pa.) Aug. 31, 1810–March 1, 1889; House 1865–69.

Glover, David Delano (D Ark.) Jan. 18, 1868–April 5, 1952; House 1929–35.

Glover, John Milton (nephew of John Montgomery Glover) (D Mo.) June 23, 1852–Oct. 20, 1929; House 1885–89.

Glover, John Montgomery (uncle of John Milton Glover) (D Mo.) Sept. 4, 1822–Nov. 15, 1891; House 1873–79.

Glynn, James Peter (R Conn.) Nov. 12, 1867–March 6, 1930; House 1915–23, 1925–March 6, 1930.

Glynn, Martin Henry (D N.Y.) Sept. 27, 1871–Dec. 14, 1924; House 1899–1901; Gov. Oct. 17, 1913–Jan. 1, 1915.

Goddard, Calvin (F Conn.) July 17, 1768–May 2, 1842; House May 14, 1801–05.

Godshalk, William (R Pa.) Oct. 25, 1817–Feb. 6, 1891; House 1879–83.

Godwin, Hannibal Lafayette (D N.C.) Nov. 3, 1873–June 9, 1929; House 1907–21.

Goebel, Herman Philip (R Ohio) April 5, 1853–May 4, 1930; House 1903–11.

Goeke, John Henry (D Ohio) Oct. 28, 1869–March 25, 1930; House 1911–15.

Goff, Abe McGregor (R Idaho) Dec. 21, 1899–Nov. 23, 1984; House 1947–49.

Goff, Guy Despard (son of Nathan Goff, father of Louise Goff Reece, father-in-law of Brazilla Carroll Reece) (R W.Va.) Sept. 13, 1866–Jan. 7, 1933; Senate 1925–31.

Goff, Nathan Jr. (father of Guy Despard Goff, grandfather of Louise Goff Reece) (R W.Va.) Feb. 9, 1843–April 24, 1920; House 1883–89; Senate April 1, 1913–19; secretary of the navy Jan. 7–March 6, 1881.

Goggin, William Leftwich (W Va.) May 31, 1807–Jan. 3, 1870; House 1839–43, April 25, 1844–45, 1847–49.

Gohmert, Louis "Louie" (R Texas) Aug. 18, 1953– ; House 2005– .

Gold, Thomas Ruggles (F N.Y.) Nov. 4, 1764–Oct. 24, 1827; House 1809–13, 1815–17.

Golden, James Stephen (R Ky.) Sept. 10, 1891–Sept. 6, 1971; House 1949–55.

Golder, Benjamin Martin (R Pa.) Dec. 23, 1891–Dec. 30, 1946; House 1925–33.

Goldfogle, Henry Mayer (D N.Y.), May 23, 1856–June 1, 1929; House 1901–15, 1919–21.

Goldsborough, Charles (great-grandfather of Thomas Alan Goldsborough and Winder Laird Henry) (F Md.) July 15, 1765–Dec. 13, 1834; House 1805–17; Gov. Jan. 8–Dec. 20, 1819.

Goldsborough, Phillips Lee (R Md.) Aug. 6, 1865–Oct. 22, 1946; Senate 1929–35; Gov. Jan. 10, 1912–Jan. 12, 1916.

Goldsborough, Robert Henry (great-grandfather of Winder Laird Henry) (W Md.) Jan. 4, 1779–Oct. 5, 1836; Senate May 21, 1813–19 (Federalist), Jan. 13, 1835–Oct. 5, 1836.

Goldsborough, Thomas Alan (great-grandson of Charles Goldsborough) (D Md.) Sept. 16, 1877–June 16, 1951; House 1921–April 5, 1939.

Goldthwaite, George Thomas (D Ala.) Dec. 10, 1809–March 16, 1879; Senate 1871–77.

Goldwater, Barry Morris (father of Barry Morris Goldwater Jr.) (R Ariz.) Jan. 1, 1909–May 29, 1998; Senate 1953–65, 1969–87; chair Senate Select Intelligence Activities 1981–85; chair Senate Armed Services 1985–87.

Goldwater, Barry Morris Jr. (son of Barry Morris Goldwater) (R Calif.) July 15, 1938– ; House April 29, 1969–83.

Goldzier, Julius (D Ill.) Jan. 20, 1854–Jan. 20, 1925; House 1893–95.

Golladay, Edward Isaac (brother of Jacob Shall Golladay) (D Tenn.) Sept. 9, 1830–July 11, 1897; House 1871–73.

Golladay, Jacob Shall (brother of Edward Isaac Golladay) (D Ky.) Jan. 19, 1819–May 20, 1887; House Dec. 5, 1867–Feb. 28, 1870.

Gonzalez, Charles A. "Charlie" (son of Henry Barbosa Gonzalez) (D Texas) May 5, 1945– ; House 1999– .

Gonzalez, Henry Barbosa (father of Charles A. Gonzalez) (D Texas) May 3, 1916–Nov. 28, 2000; House Nov. 4, 1961–99; chair House Banking, Housing, and Urban Affairs 1989–95.

Gooch, Daniel Linn (D Ky.) Oct. 28, 1853–April 12, 1913; House 1901–05.

Gooch, Daniel Wheelwright (R Mass.) Jan. 8, 1820–Nov. 11, 1891; House Jan. 31, 1858–Sept. 1, 1865, 1873–75.

Good, James William (R Iowa) Sept. 24, 1866–Nov. 18, 1929; House 1909–June 15, 1921; secretary of war March 6–Nov. 18, 1929.

Goodall, Louis Bertrand (R Maine) Sept. 23, 1851–June 26, 1935; House 1917–21.

Goode, John Jr. (D Va.) May 27, 1829–July 14, 1909; House 1875–81.

Goode, Patrick Gaines (W Ohio) May 10, 1798–Oct. 17, 1862; House 1837–43.

Goode, Samuel (– Va.) March 21, 1756–Nov. 14, 1822; House 1799–1801.

Goode, Virgil (R Va.) Oct. 17, 1946– ; House 1997– (1997–Jan. 24, 2000 Democrat, Jan. 24, 2000–Sept. 30, 2002 Independent).

Goode, William Osborne (D Va.) Sept. 16, 1798–July 3, 1859; House 1841–43, 1853–July 3, 1859.

Goodell, Charles Ellsworth (R N.Y.) March 16, 1926–Jan. 21, 1987; House May 26, 1959–Sept. 9, 1968; Senate Sept. 10, 1968–71.

Goodenow, John Milton (– Ohio) 1782–July 20, 1838; House 1829–April 9, 1830.

Goodenow, Robert (brother of Rufus King Goodenow) (W Maine) April 19, 1800–May 15, 1874; House 1851–53.

Goodenow, Rufus King (brother of Robert Goodenow) (W Maine) April 24, 1790–March 24, 1863; House 1849–51.

Goodhue, Benjamin (F Mass.) Sept. 20, 1748–July 28, 1814; House 1789–June 1796 (no party); Senate June 11, 1796–Nov. 8, 1800.

Goodin, John Randolph (D Kan.) Dec. 14, 1836–Dec. 18, 1885; House 1875–77.

Gooding, Frank Robert (R Idaho) Sept. 16, 1859–June 24, 1928; Senate Jan. 15, 1921–June 24, 1928; Gov. Jan. 2, 1905–Jan. 4, 1908.

Goodlatte, Robert W. (R Va.) Sept. 22, 1952– ; House 1993– ; chair House Agriculture 2003– .

Goodling, George Atlee (father of William Franklin Goodling) (R Pa.) Sept. 26, 1896–Oct. 17, 1982; House 1961–65, 1967–75.

Goodling, William Franklin (son of George Atlee Goodling) (R Pa.) Dec. 5, 1927– ; House 1975–2001; chair House Education and the Workforce 1995–2001.

Goodnight, Isaac Herschel (D Ky.) Jan. 31, 1849–July 24, 1901; House 1889–95.

Goodrich, Chauncey (brother of Elizur Goodrich) (F Conn.) Oct. 20, 1759–Aug. 18, 1815; House 1795–1801; Senate Oct. 25, 1807–May 1813.

Goodrich, Elizur (brother of Chauncey Goodrich) (F Conn.) March 24, 1761–Nov. 1, 1849; House 1799–1801.

Goodrich, John Zacheus (W Mass.) Sept. 27, 1804–April 19, 1885; House 1851–55.

Goodrich, Milo (R N.Y.) Jan. 3, 1814–April 15, 1881; House 1871–73.

Goodwin, Angier Louis (R Mass.) Jan. 30, 1881–June 20, 1975; House 1943–55.

Goodwin, Forrest (R Maine) June 14, 1862–May 28, 1913; House March 4–May 28, 1913.

Goodwin, Godfrey Gummer (R Minn.) Jan. 11, 1873–Feb. 16, 1933; House 1925–Feb. 16, 1933.

Goodwin, Henry Charles (R N.Y.) June 25, 1824–Nov. 12, 1860; House Nov. 7, 1854–55 (Whig), 1857–59.

Goodwin, John Noble (R Ariz.) Oct. 18, 1824–April 29, 1887; House (Rep. Maine) 1861–63, (Terr. Del.) 1865–67; Gov. (Ariz. Terr.) 1863–65.

Goodwin, Philip Arnold (R N.Y.) Jan. 20, 1882–June 6, 1937; House 1933–June 6, 1937.

Goodwin, Robert Kingman (R Iowa) May 23, 1905–Feb. 21, 1983; House March 5, 1940–41.

Goodwin, William Shields (D Ark.) May 2, 1866–Aug. 9, 1937; House 1911–21.

Goodwyn, Albert Taylor (P Ala.) Dec. 17, 1842–July 2, 1931; House April 22, 1896–97.

Goodwyn, Peterson (R Va.) 1745–Feb. 21, 1818; House 1803–Feb. 21, 1818.

Goodyear, Charles (D N.Y.) April 26, 1804–April 9, 1876; House 1845–47, 1865–67.

Goodykoontz, Wells (R W.Va.) June 3, 1872–March 2, 1944; House 1919–23.

Gordon, Barton Jennings (D Tenn.) Jan. 24, 1949– ; House 1985– .

Gordon, George Washington (D Tenn.) Oct. 5, 1836–Aug. 9, 1911; House 1907–Aug. 9, 1911.

Gordon, James (– N.Y.) Oct. 31, 1739–Jan. 17, 1810; House 1791–95.

Gordon, James (– Miss.) Dec. 6, 1833–Nov. 28, 1912; Senate Dec. 27, 1909–Feb. 22, 1910.

Gordon, John Brown (D Ga.) Feb. 6, 1832–Jan. 9, 1904; Senate 1873–May 26, 1880, 1891–97; Gov. Nov. 9, 1886–Nov. 8, 1890.

Gordon, Robert Bryarly (D Ohio) Aug. 6, 1855–Jan. 3, 1923; House 1899–1903.

Gordon, Samuel (D N.Y.) April 28, 1802–Oct. 28, 1873; House 1841–43, 1845–47.

Gordon, Thomas Sylvy (D Ill.) Dec. 17, 1893–Jan. 22, 1959; House 1943–59; chair House Foreign Affairs 1957–59.

Gordon, William (F N.H.) April 12, 1763–May 8, 1802; House 1797–June 12, 1800.

Gordon, William (D Ohio) Dec. 15, 1862–Jan. 16, 1942; House 1913–19.

Gordon, William Fitzhugh (J Va.) Jan. 13, 1787–Aug. 28, 1858; House Jan. 25, 1830–35.

Gore, Albert Arnold (father of Albert Arnold Gore Jr.) (D Tenn.) Dec. 26, 1907–Dec. 5, 1998; House 1939–Dec. 4, 1944, 1945–53; Senate 1953–71.

Gore, Albert Arnold Jr. (son of Albert Arnold Gore) (D Tenn.) March 31, 1948– ; House 1977–85; Senate 1985–Jan. 2, 1993; vice president 1993–2001.

Gore, Christopher (F Mass.) Sept. 21, 1758–March 1, 1827; Senate May 5, 1813–May 30, 1816; Gov. May 1, 1809–June 2, 1810.

Gore, Thomas Pryor (D Okla.) Dec. 10, 1870–March 16, 1949; Senate Dec. 11, 1907–21, 1931–37.

Gorham, Benjamin (AJ Mass.) Feb. 13, 1775–Sept. 27, 1855; House Nov. 6, 1820–23 (no party), July 23, 1827–31 (no party), 1833–35.

Gorman, Arthur Pue (D Md.) March 11, 1839–June 4, 1906; Senate 1881–99, 1903–June 4, 1906.

Gorman, George Edmund (D Ill.) April 13, 1873–Jan. 13, 1935; House 1913–15.

Gorman, James Sedgwick (D Mich.) Dec. 28, 1850–May 27, 1923; House 1891–95.

Gorman, John Jerome (R Ill.) June 2, 1883–Feb. 24, 1949; House 1921–23, 1925–27.

Gorman, Willis Arnold (D Ind.) Jan. 12, 1816–May 20, 1876; House 1849–53; Gov. (Minn. Terr.) 1853–57.

Gorski, Chester Charles (D N.Y.) June 22, 1906–April 25, 1975; House 1949–51.

Gorski, Martin (D Ill.) Oct. 30, 1886–Dec. 4, 1949; House 1943–Dec. 4, 1949.

Gorton, Thomas Slade III (R Wash.) Jan. 8, 1928– ; Senate 1981–87, 1989–2001.

Goss, Edward Wheeler (R Conn.) April 27, 1893–Dec. 27, 1972; House Nov. 4, 1930–35.

Goss, James Hamilton (R S.C.) Aug. 9, 1820–Oct. 31, 1886; House July 18, 1868–69.

Goss, Porter (R Fla.) Nov. 26, 1938– ; House 1989–Sept. 23, 2004; chair House Select Intelligence 1997–Aug. 25, 2004.

Gossett, Charles Clinton (D Idaho) Sept. 2, 1888–Sept. 20, 1974; Senate Nov. 17, 1945–47; Gov. Jan. 1–Nov. 17, 1945.

Gossett, Ed Lee (D Texas) Jan. 27, 1902–Nov. 6, 1990; House 1939–July 31, 1951.

Gott, Daniel (W N.Y.) July 10, 1794–July 6, 1864; House 1847–51.

Gould, Arthur Robinson (R Maine) March 16, 1857–July 24, 1946; Senate Nov. 30, 1926–31.

Gould, Herman Day (W N.Y.) Jan. 16, 1799–Jan. 26, 1852; House 1849–51.

Gould, Norman Judd (grandson of Norman Buel Judd) (R N.Y.) March 15, 1877–Aug. 20, 1964; House Nov. 2, 1915–23.

Gould, Samuel Wadsworth (D Maine) Jan. 1, 1852–Dec. 19, 1935; House 1911–13.

Goulden, Joseph Aloysius (D N.Y.) Aug. 1, 1844–May 3, 1915; House 1903–11, 1913–May 3, 1915.

Gourdin, Theodore (R S.C.) March 20, 1764–Jan. 17, 1826; House 1813–15.

Govan, Andrew Robison (– S.C.) Jan. 13, 1794–June 27, 1841; House Dec. 4, 1822–27.

Gove, Samuel Francis (R Ga.) March 9, 1822–Dec. 3, 1900; House June 25, 1868–69.

Grabowski, Bernard Francis (D Conn.) June 11, 1923– ; House 1963–67.

Gradison, Willis David Jr. (R Ohio) Dec. 28, 1928– ; House 1975–Jan. 31, 1993.

Grady, Benjamin Franklin (D N.C.) Oct. 10, 1831–March 6, 1914; House 1891–95.

Graff, Joseph Verdi (R Ill.) July 1, 1854–Nov. 10, 1921; House 1895–1911.

Graham, Daniel Robert "Bob" (D Fla.) Nov. 9, 1936– ; Senate 1987–2005; chair Senate Select Intelligence Activities June 6, 2001–03; Gov. Jan. 2, 1979–Jan. 3, 1987.

Graham, Frank Porter (D N.C.) Oct. 14, 1886–Feb. 16, 1972; Senate March 29, 1949–Nov. 26, 1950.

Graham, George Scott (R Pa.) Sept. 13, 1850–July 4, 1931; House 1913–July 4, 1931.

Graham, James (brother of William Alexander Graham) (W N.C.) Jan. 7, 1793–Sept. 25, 1851; House 1833–March 29, 1836 (1833–35 no party), Dec. 5, 1836–43, 1845–47.

Graham, James Harper (R N.Y.) Sept. 18, 1812–June 23, 1881; House 1859–61.

Graham, James McMahon (D Ill.) April 14, 1852–Oct. 23, 1945; House 1909–15.

Graham, John Hugh (D N.Y.) April 1, 1835–July 11, 1895; House 1893–95.

Graham, Lindsey (R S.C.) July 9, 1955– ; House 1995–2003; Senate 2003– .

Graham, Louis Edward (R Pa.) Aug. 4, 1880–Nov. 9, 1965; House 1939–55.

Graham, William (W Ind.) March 16, 1782–Aug. 17, 1858; House 1837–39.

Graham, William Alexander (brother of James Graham) (W N.C.) Sept. 5, 1804–Aug. 11, 1875; Senate Nov. 25, 1840–43; Gov. Jan. 1, 1845–Jan. 1, 1849; secretary of the navy Aug. 2, 1850–July 25, 1852.

Graham, William Harrison (R Pa.) Aug. 3, 1844–March 2, 1923; House Nov. 29, 1898–1903, 1905–11.

Graham, William Johnson (R Ill.) Feb. 7, 1872–Nov. 10, 1937; House 1917–June 7, 1924.

Gramm, Phil (R Texas) July 8, 1942– ; House 1979–Jan. 5, 1983, Feb. 22, 1983–85 (1979–Jan. 5, 1983, Democrat); Senate 1985–Nov. 30, 2002; chair Senate Banking, Housing, and Urban Affairs 1999–2001.

Grammer, Elijah Sherman (R Wash.) April 3, 1868–Nov. 19, 1936; Senate Nov. 22, 1932–33.

Grams, Rodney (R Minn.) Feb. 4, 1948– ; House 1993–95; Senate 1995–2001.

Granahan, Kathryn Elizabeth (widow of William Thomas Granahan) (D Pa.) Dec. 7, 1906–July 10, 1979; House Nov. 6, 1956–63.

Granahan, William Thomas (husband of Kathryn Elizabeth Granahan) (D Pa.) July 26, 1895–May 25, 1956; House 1945–47, 1949–May 25, 1956.

Granata, Peter Charles (R Ill.) Oct. 28, 1898–Sept. 29, 1973; House 1931–April 5, 1932.

Grandy, Frederick Lawrence (R Iowa) June 29, 1948– ; House 1987–95.

Granfield, William Joseph (D Mass.) Dec. 18, 1889–May 28, 1959; House Feb. 11, 1930–37.

Granger, Amos Phelps (cousin of Francis Granger) (R N.Y.) June 3, 1789–Aug. 20, 1866; House 1855–59 (1855–57 Whig).

Granger, Bradley Francis (R Mich.) March 12, 1825–Nov. 4, 1882; House 1861–63.

Granger, Daniel Larned Davis (D R.I.) May 30, 1852–Feb. 14, 1909; House 1903–Feb. 14, 1909.

Granger, Francis (cousin of Amos Phelps Granger) (W N.Y.) Dec. 1, 1792–Aug. 31, 1868; House 1835–37, 1839–March 5, 1841, Nov. 27, 1841–43; postmaster general March 8–Sept. 13, 1841.

Granger, Kay (R Texas) Jan. 18, 1943– ; House 1997– .

Granger, Miles Tobey (D Conn.) Aug. 12, 1817–Oct. 21, 1895; House 1887–89.

Granger, Walter Keil (D Utah) Oct. 11, 1888–April 21, 1978; House 1941–53.

Grant, Abraham Phineas (D N.Y.) April 5, 1804–Dec. 11, 1871; House 1837–39.

Grant, George McInvale (D Ala.) July 11, 1897–Nov. 4, 1982; House June 14, 1938–65.

Grant, James William (R Fla.) Feb. 21, 1943– ; House 1987–91 (1987–Feb. 21, 1989 Democrat).

Grant, John Gaston (R N.C.) Jan. 1, 1858–June 21, 1923; House 1909–11.

Grant, Robert Allen (R Ind.) July 31, 1905–March 2, 1998; House 1939–49.

Grantland, Seaton (D Ga.) June 8, 1782–Oct. 18, 1864; House 1835–39 (1835–37 Jacksonian).

Grassley, Charles Ernest (R Iowa) Sept. 17, 1933– ; House 1975–81; Senate 1981– ; chair Senate Finance Jan. 20, 2001–June 6, 2001, 2003– .

Grasso, Ella Tambussi (D Conn.) May 10, 1919–Feb. 5, 1981; House 1971–75; Gov. Jan. 8, 1975–Dec. 31, 1980.

Gravel, Maurice Robert "Mike" (D Alaska) May 13, 1930– ; Senate 1969–Jan. 2, 1981.

Gravely, Joseph Jackson (R Mo.) Sept. 25, 1828–April 28, 1872; House 1867–69.

Graves, Alexander (D Mo.) Aug. 25, 1844–Dec. 23, 1916; House 1883–85.

Graves, Dixie Bibb (wife of Gov. David Bibb Graves of Ala.) (D Ala.) July 26, 1882–Jan. 21, 1965; Senate Aug. 20, 1937–Jan. 10, 1938.

Graves, Samuel B. "Sam" (R Mo.) Nov. 7, 1963– ; House 2001– .

Graves, William Jordan (W Ky.) 1805–Sept. 27, 1848; House 1835–41.

Gray, Edward Winthrop (R N.J.) Aug. 18, 1870–June 10, 1942; House 1915–19.

Gray, Edwin (F Va.) July 18, 1743–?; House 1799–1813.

Gray, Finly Hutchinson (D Ind.) July 21, 1863–May 8, 1947; House 1911–17, 1933–39.

Gray, George (D Del.) May 4, 1840–Aug. 7, 1925; Senate March 18, 1885–99.

Gray, Hiram (D N.Y.) July 10, 1801–May 6, 1890; House 1837–39.

Gray, John Cowper (– Va.) 1783–May 18, 1823; House Aug. 28, 1820–21.

Gray, Joseph Anthony (D Pa.) Feb. 25, 1884–May 8, 1966; House 1935–39.

Gray, Kenneth James (D Ill.) Nov. 14, 1924– ; House 1955–Dec. 31, 1974, 1985–89.

Gray, Oscar Lee (D Ala.) July 2, 1865–Jan. 2, 1936; House 1915–19.

Gray, William Herbert III (D Pa.) Aug. 20, 1941– ; House 1979–Sept. 11, 1991; chair House Budget 1985–89.

Grayson, William (father of William John Grayson, uncle of Alexander Dalrymple Orr) (– Va.) about 1740–March 12, 1790; Senate 1789–March 12, 1790; Cont. Cong. 1785–87.

Grayson, William John (son of William Grayson, cousin of Alexander Dalrymple Orr) (N S.C.) Nov. 2, 1788–Oct. 4, 1863; House 1833–37.

Greeley, Horace (W N.Y.) Feb. 3, 1811–Nov. 29, 1872; House Dec. 4, 1848–49.

Green, Al (D Texas) Sept. 1, 1947– ; House 2005– .

Green, Bryam (– N.Y.) April 15, 1786–Oct. 18, 1865; House 1843–45.

Green, Edith Starrett (D Ore.) Jan. 17, 1910–April 21, 1987; House 1955–Dec. 31, 1975.

Green, Frederick William (D Ohio) Feb. 18, 1816–June 18, 1879; House 1851–55.

Green, Henry Dickinson (D Pa.) May 3, 1857–Dec. 29, 1929; House Nov. 7, 1899–1903.

Green, Innis (J Pa.) Feb. 26, 1776–Aug. 4, 1839; House 1827–31 (1827–29 no party).

Green, Isaiah Lewis (R Mass.) Dec. 28, 1761–Dec. 5, 1841; House 1805–09, 1811–13.

Green, James Stephen (D Mo.) Feb. 28, 1817–Jan. 19, 1870; House 1847–51; Senate Jan. 12, 1857–61.

Green, Mark (R Wis.) June 1, 1960– ; House 1999– .

Green, Raymond Eugene "Gene" (D Texas) Oct. 17, 1947– ; House 1993– .

Green, Robert Alexis (D Fla.) Feb. 10, 1892–Feb. 9, 1973; House 1925–Nov. 25, 1944.

Green, Robert Stockton (D N.J.) March 25, 1831–May 7, 1895; House 1885–Jan. 17, 1887; Gov. Jan. 18, 1887–Jan. 21, 1890.

Green, Sedgwick William "Bill" (R N.Y.) Oct. 16, 1929–Oct. 14, 2002; House Feb. 21, 1978–93.

Green, Theodore Francis (great-nephew of Samuel Greene Arnold, great-great-nephew of Tristam Burges, great-grandson of James Burrill Jr., great-great-grandson of Jonathan Arnold, great-great-nephew of Lemuel Hastings Arnold) (D R.I.) Oct. 2, 1867–May 19, 1966; Senate 1937–61; chair Senate Rules and Administration 1955–57; chair Senate Foreign Relations 1957–59; Gov. Jan. 3, 1933–Jan. 5, 1937.

Green, Wharton Jackson (grandson of Jesse Wharton, cousin of Matt Whitaker Ransom) (D N.C.) Feb. 28, 1831–Aug. 6, 1910; House 1883–87.

Green, William Joseph III (son of William Joseph Green Jr.) (D Pa.) June 24, 1938– ; House April 28, 1964–77.

Green, William Joseph Jr. (father of William Joseph Green III) (D Pa.) March 5, 1910–Dec. 21, 1963; House 1945–47, 1949–Dec. 21, 1963.

Green, William Raymond (R Iowa) Nov. 7, 1856–June 11, 1947; House June 5, 1911–March 31, 1928.

Green, Willis (W Ky.) ?–?; House 1839–45.

Greene, Albert Collins (W R.I.) April 15, 1792–Jan. 8, 1863; Senate 1845–51.

Greene, Frank Lester (R Vt.) Feb. 10, 1870–Dec. 17, 1930; House July 30, 1912–23; Senate 1923–Dec. 17, 1930.

Greene, George Woodward (D N.Y.) July 4, 1831–July 21, 1895; House 1869–Feb. 17, 1870.

Greene, Ray (F R.I.) Feb. 2, 1765–Jan. 11, 1849; Senate Nov. 13, 1797–March 5, 1801.

Greene, Thomas Marston (– Miss.) Feb. 26, 1758–Feb. 7, 1813; House (Terr. Del.) Dec. 6, 1802–03.

Greene, William Laury (P Neb.) Oct. 3, 1849–March 11, 1899; House 1897–March 11, 1899.

Greene, William Stedman (R Mass.) April 28, 1841–Sept. 22, 1924; House May 31, 1898–Sept. 22, 1924.

Greenhalge, Frederic Thomas (R Mass.) July 19, 1842–March 5, 1896; House 1889–91; Gov. Jan. 3, 1894–March 5, 1896.

Greenleaf, Halbert Stevens (D N.Y.) April 12, 1827–Aug. 25, 1906; House 1883–85, 1891–93.

Greenman, Edward Whitford (D N.Y.) Jan. 26, 1840–Aug. 3, 1908; House 1887–89.

Greenup, Christopher (R Ky.) 1750–April 27, 1818; House Nov. 9, 1792–97 (Nov. 9, 1792–95 no party); Gov. June 1, 1804–June 1, 1808.

Greenway, Isabella Selmes (later Mrs. Harry Orland King) (D Ariz.) March 22, 1886–Dec. 18, 1953; House Oct. 3, 1933–37.

Greenwood, Alfred Burton (D Ark.) July 11, 1811–Oct. 4, 1889; House 1853–59.

Greenwood, Arthur Herbert (D Ind.) Jan. 31, 1880–April 26, 1963; House 1923–39.

Greenwood, Ernest (D N.Y.) Nov. 25, 1884–June 15, 1955; House 1951–53.

Greenwood, James Charles (R Pa.) May 4, 1951– ; House 1993–2005.

Greever, Paul Ranous (D Wyo.) Sept. 28, 1891–Feb. 16, 1943; House 1935–39.

Gregg, Alexander White (D Texas) Jan. 31, 1855–April 30, 1919; House 1903–19.

Gregg, Andrew (grandfather of James Xavier McLanahan) (R Pa.) June 10, 1755–May 20, 1835; House 1791–1807 (no party); Senate 1807–13; elected pres. pro tempore June 26, 1809.

Gregg, Curtis Hussey (D Pa.) Aug. 9, 1865–Jan. 18, 1933; House 1911–13.

Gregg, James Madison (D Ind.) June 26, 1806–June 16, 1869; House 1857–59.

Gregg, Judd Alan (son of Gov. Hugh Gregg of N.H.) (R N.H.) Feb. 14, 1947– ; House 1981–89; Senate 1993– ; chair Senate Health, Education, Labor, and Pensions 2003–05; chair Senate Budget 2005– ; Gov. Jan. 4, 1989–Jan. 7, 1993.

Gregory, Dudley Sanford (W N.J.) Feb. 5, 1800–Dec. 8, 1874; House 1847–49.

Gregory, Noble Jones (brother of William Voris Gregory) (D Ky.) Aug. 30, 1897–Sept. 26, 1971; House 1937–59.

Gregory, William Voris (brother of Noble Jones Gregory) (D Ky.) Oct. 21, 1877–Oct. 10, 1936; House 1927–Oct. 10, 1936.

Greig, John (W N.Y.) Aug. 6, 1779–April 9, 1858; House May 21–Sept. 25, 1841.

Greigg, Stanley Lloyd (D Iowa) May 7, 1931–June 13, 2002; House 1965–67.

Grennell, George Jr. (W Mass.) Dec. 25, 1786–Nov. 19, 1877; House 1829–39 (1829–31 no party, 1831–35 Anti-Jacksonian).

Gresham, Walter (D Texas) July 22, 1841–Nov. 6, 1920; House 1893–95.

Grey, Benjamin Edwards (grandson of Benjamin Edwards) (W Ky.) ?–?; House 1851–55.

Grider, George William (D Tenn.) Oct. 1, 1912–March 20, 1991; House 1965–67.

Grider, Henry (D Ky.) July 16, 1796–Sept. 7, 1866; House 1843–47 (Whig), 1861–Sept. 7, 1866 (1861–65 Unionist).

Griest, William Walton (R Pa.) Sept. 22, 1858–Dec. 5, 1929; House 1909–Dec. 5, 1929.

Griffin, Anthony Jerome (D N.Y.) April 1, 1866–Jan. 13, 1935; House March 5, 1918–Jan. 13, 1935.

Griffin, Charles Hudson (great-great-grandson of Isaac Griffin) (D Miss.) May 9, 1926–Sept. 10, 1989; House March 12, 1968–73.

Griffin, Daniel Joseph (D N.Y.) March 26, 1880–Dec. 11, 1926; House 1913–Dec. 31, 1917.

Griffin, Isaac (great-grandfather of Eugene McLanahan Wilson, great-great-grandfather of Charles Hudson Griffin) (R Pa.) Feb. 27, 1756–Oct. 12, 1827; House May 24, 1813–17.

Griffin, John King (D S.C.) Aug. 13, 1789–Aug. 1, 1841; House 1831–41 (1831–39 Nullifier).

Griffin, Levi Thomas (D Mich.) May 23, 1837–March 17, 1906; House Dec. 4, 1893–95.

Griffin, Michael (R Wis.) Sept. 9, 1842–Dec. 29, 1899; House Nov. 5, 1894–99.

Griffin, Robert Paul (R Mich.) Nov. 6, 1923– ; House 1957–May 10, 1966; Senate May 11, 1966–Jan. 2, 1979.

Griffin, Samuel (– Va.) ?–Nov. 3, 1810; House 1789–95.

Griffin, Thomas (F Va.) 1773–Oct. 7, 1837; House 1803–05.

Griffith, Francis Marion (D Ind.) Aug. 21, 1849–Feb. 8, 1927; House Dec. 6, 1897–1905.

Griffith, John Keller (D La.) Oct. 16, 1882–Sept. 25, 1942; House 1937–41.

Griffith, Samuel (D Pa.) Feb. 14, 1816–Oct. 1, 1893; House 1871–73.

Griffiths, Martha Wright (D Mich.) Jan. 29, 1912–April 22, 2003; House 1955–Dec. 31, 1974.

Griffiths, Percy Wilfred (R Ohio) March 30, 1893–June 12, 1983; House 1943–49.

Griggs, James Mathews (D Ga.) March 29, 1861–Jan. 5, 1910; House 1897–Jan. 5, 1910.

Grigsby, George Barnes (D Alaska) Dec. 2, 1874–May 9, 1962; House (Terr. Del.) June 3, 1920–March 1, 1921.

Grijalva, Raul M. (D Ariz.) Feb. 19, 1948– ; House 2003– .

Grimes, James Wilson (R Iowa) Oct. 20, 1816–Feb. 7, 1872; Senate 1859–Dec. 6, 1869; Gov. Dec. 9, 1854–Jan. 13, 1858 (Whig).

Grimes, Thomas Wingfield (D Ga.) Dec. 18, 1844–Oct. 28, 1905; House 1887–91.

Grinnell, Joseph (brother of Moses Hicks Grinnell) (W Mass.) Nov. 17, 1788–Feb. 7, 1885; House Dec. 7, 1843–51.

Grinnell, Josiah Bushnell (R Iowa) Dec. 22, 1821–March 31, 1891; House 1863–67.

Grinnell, Moses Hicks (brother of Joseph Grinnell) (W N.Y.) March 3, 1803–Nov. 24, 1877; House 1839–41.

Grisham, Wayne Richard (R Calif.) Jan. 10, 1923– ; House 1979–83.

Griswold, Dwight Palmer (R Neb.) Nov. 27, 1893–April 12, 1954; Senate Nov. 5, 1952–April 12, 1954; Gov. Jan. 9, 1941–Jan. 9, 1947.

Griswold, Gaylord (F N.Y.) Dec. 18, 1767–March 1, 1809; House 1803–05.

Griswold, Glenn Hasenfratz (D Ind.) Jan. 20, 1890–Dec. 5, 1940; House 1931–39.

Griswold, Harry Wilbur (R Wis.) May 19, 1886–July 4, 1939; House Jan. 3–July 4, 1939.

Griswold, John Ashley (D N.Y.) Nov. 18, 1822–Feb. 22, 1902; House 1869–71.

Griswold, John Augustus (R N.Y.) Nov. 11, 1822–Oct. 31, 1872; House 1863–69 (1863–65 Democrat).

Griswold, Matthew (grandson of Roger Griswold) (R Pa.) June 6, 1833–May 19, 1919; House 1891–93, 1895–97.

Griswold, Roger (grandfather of Matthew Griswold) (F Conn.) May 21, 1762–Oct. 25, 1812; House 1795–1805; Gov. May 9, 1811–Oct. 25, 1812.

Griswold, Stanley (– Ohio) Nov. 14, 1763–Aug. 21, 1815; Senate May 18–Dec. 11, 1809.

Groesbeck, William Slocum (D Ohio) July 24, 1815–July 7, 1897; House 1857–59.

Gronna, Asle Jorgenson (R N.D.) Dec. 10, 1858–May 4, 1922; House 1905–Feb. 2, 1911; Senate Feb. 2, 1911–21.

Groome, James Black (D Md.) April 4, 1838–Oct. 5, 1893; Senate 1879–85; Gov. March 4, 1874–Jan. 12, 1876.

Gross, Chester Heilman (R Pa.) Oct. 13, 1888–Jan. 9, 1973; House 1939–41, 1943–49.

Gross, Ezra Carter (– N.Y.) July 11, 1787–April 9, 1829; House 1819–21.

Gross, Harold Royce (R Iowa) June 30, 1899–Sept. 22, 1987; House 1949–75.

Gross, Samuel (– Pa.) Nov. 10, 1776–March 19, 1839; House 1819–23.

Grosvenor, Charles Henry (uncle of Charles Grosvenor Bond) (R Ohio) Sept. 20, 1833–Oct. 30, 1917; House 1885–91, 1893–1907.

Grosvenor, Thomas Peabody (F N.Y.) Dec. 20, 1778–April 24, 1817; House Jan. 29, 1813–17.

Grotberg, John E. (R Ill.) March 23, 1925–Nov. 15, 1986; House 1985–Nov. 15, 1986.

Grout, Jonathan (– Mass.) July 23, 1737–Sept. 8, 1807; House 1789–91.

Grout, William Wallace (R Vt.) May 24, 1836–Oct. 7, 1902; House 1881–83, 1885–1901.

Grove, William Barry (F N.C.) Jan. 15, 1764–March 30, 1818; House 1791–1803 (1791–1801 no party).

Grover, Asa Porter (D Ky.) Feb. 18, 1819–July 20, 1887; House 1867–69.

Grover, James Russell Jr. (R N.Y.) March 5, 1919– ; House 1963–75.

Grover, La Fayette (D Ore.) Nov. 29, 1823–May 10, 1911; House Feb. 15–March 3, 1859; Senate 1877–83; Gov. Sept. 14, 1870–Feb. 1, 1877.

Grover, Martin (D N.Y.) Oct. 20, 1811–Aug. 23, 1875; House 1845–47.

Grow, Galusha Aaron (R Pa.) Aug. 31, 1823–March 31, 1907; House 1851–63 (1851–57 Democrat), Feb. 26, 1894–1903; Speaker July 4, 1861–63.

Gruening, Ernest (D Alaska) Feb. 6, 1887–June 26, 1974; Senate 1959–69; Gov. (Alaska Terr.) 1939–53.

Grundy, Felix (D Tenn.) Sept. 11, 1777–Dec. 19, 1840; House 1811–14 (Republican); Senate Oct. 19, 1829–July 4, 1838 (Jacksonian), Nov. 19, 1839–Dec. 19, 1840; attorney general Sept. 1–Dec. 1, 1838.

Grundy, Joseph Ridgway (R Pa.) Jan. 13, 1863–March 3, 1961; Senate Dec. 11, 1929–Dec. 1, 1930.

Guarini, Frank Joseph Jr. (D N.J.) Aug. 20, 1924– ; House 1979–93.

Gubser, Charles Samuel (R Calif.) Feb. 1, 1916– ; House 1953–Dec. 31, 1974.

Gude, Gilbert (R Md.) March 9, 1923– ; House 1967–77.

Gudger, James Madison Jr. (father of Katherine Gudger Langley, father-in-law of John Wesley Langley) (D N.C.) Oct. 22, 1855–Feb. 29, 1920; House 1903–07, 1911–15.

Gudger, Vonno Lamar Jr. (D N.C.) April 30, 1919– ; House 1977–81.

Guenther, Richard William (R Wis.) Nov. 30, 1845–April 5, 1913; House 1881–89.

Guernsey, Frank Edward (R Maine) Oct. 15, 1866–Jan. 1, 1927; House Nov. 3, 1908–17.

Guevara, Pedro (Nat. P.I.) Feb. 23, 1879–Jan. 19, 1937; House (Res. Comm.) 1923–Feb. 14, 1936.

Guffey, Joseph F. (D Pa.) Dec. 29, 1870–March 6, 1959; Senate 1935–47.

Guggenheim, Simon (R Colo.) Dec. 30, 1867–Nov. 2, 1941; Senate 1907–13.

Guill, Ben Hugh (R Texas) Sept. 8, 1909–Jan. 15, 1994; House May 6, 1950–51.

Guion, Walter (D La.) April 3, 1849–Feb. 7, 1927; Senate April 22–Nov. 5, 1918.

Gunckel, Lewis B. (R Ohio) Oct. 15, 1826–Oct. 3, 1903; House 1873–75.

Gunderson, Steven Craig (R Wis.) May 10, 1951– ; House 1981–97.

Gunn, James (– Ga.) March 13, 1753–July 30, 1801; Senate 1789–1801; Cont. Cong. (elected but did not attend) 1787.

Gunn, James (– Idaho) March 6, 1843–Nov. 5, 1911; House 1897–99.

Gunter, Thomas Montague (D Ark.) Sept. 18, 1826–Jan. 12, 1904; House June 16, 1874–83.

Gunter, William Dawson Jr. (D Fla.) July 16, 1934– ; House 1973–75.

Gurley, Henry Hosford (– La.) May 20, 1788–March 16, 1833; House 1823–31.

Gurley, John Addison (R Ohio) Dec. 9, 1813–Aug. 19, 1863; House 1859–63.

Gurney, Edward John (R Fla.) Jan. 12, 1914–May 14, 1996; House 1963–69; Senate 1969–Dec. 31, 1974.

Gurney, John Chandler "Chan" (R S.D.) May 21, 1896–March 9, 1985; Senate 1939–51; chair Senate Armed Services 1947–49.

Gustine, Amos (D Pa.) 1789–March 3, 1844; House May 4, 1841–43.

Guthrie, James (D Ky.) Dec. 5, 1792–March 13, 1869; Senate 1865–Feb. 7, 1868; secretary of the Treasury March 7, 1853–March 6, 1857.

Gutierrez, Luis Vincente (D Ill.) Dec. 10, 1954– ; House 1993– .

Gutknecht, Gil (R Minn.) March 20, 1951– ; House 1995– .

Guyer, Tennyson (R Ohio) Nov. 29, 1913–April 12, 1981; House 1973–April 12, 1981.

Guyer, Ulysses Samuel (R Kan.) Dec. 13, 1868–June 5, 1943; House Nov. 4, 1924–25, 1927–June 5, 1943.

Guyon, James Jr. (– N.Y.) Dec. 24, 1778–March 9, 1846; House Jan. 14, 1820–21.

Gwin, William McKendree (D Calif.) Oct. 9, 1805–Sept. 3, 1885; House 1841–43 (Miss.); Senate Sept. 9, 1850–55, Jan. 13, 1857–61.

Gwinn, Ralph Waldo (R N.Y.) March 29, 1884–Feb. 27, 1962; House 1945–59.

Gwynne, John William (R Iowa) Oct. 20, 1889–July 5, 1972; House 1935–49.

Habersham, Richard Wylly (W Ga.) Dec. 1786–Dec. 2, 1842; House 1839–Dec. 2, 1842.

Hackett, Richard Nathaniel (D N.C.) Dec. 4, 1866–Nov. 22, 1923; House 1907–09.

Hackett, Thomas C. (D Ga.) ?–Oct. 8, 1851; House 1849–51.

Hackley, Aaron Jr. (–N.Y.) May 6, 1783–Dec. 28, 1868; House 1819–21.

Hackney, Thomas (D Mo.) Dec. 11, 1861–Dec. 24, 1946; House 1907–09.

Hadley, Lindley Hoag (R Wash.) June 19, 1861–Nov. 1, 1948; House 1915–33.

Hadley, William Flavius Lester (R Ill.) June 15, 1847–April 25, 1901; House Dec. 2, 1895–97.

Hagan, George Elliott (D Ga.) May 24, 1916–Dec. 26, 1990; House 1961–73.

Hagans, John Marshall (R W.Va.) Aug. 13, 1838–June 17, 1900; House 1873–75.

Hagedorn, Thomas Michael (R Minn.) Nov. 27, 1943– ; House 1975–83.

Hagel, Charles Timothy "Chuck" (R Neb.) Oct. 4, 1946– ; Senate 1997– .

Hagen, Harlan Francis (D Calif.) Oct. 8, 1914–Nov. 25, 1990; House 1953–67.

Hagen, Harold Christian (R Minn.) Nov. 10, 1901–March 19, 1957; House 1943–55 (1943–45 Farmer Laborite).

Hager, Alva Lysander (R Iowa) Oct. 29, 1850–Jan. 29, 1923; House 1893–99.

Hager, John Sharpenstein (D Calif.) March 12, 1818–March 19, 1890; Senate Dec. 23, 1873–75.

Haggott, Warren Armstrong (R Colo.) May 18, 1864–April 29, 1958; House 1907–09.

Hahn, John (R Pa.) Oct. 30, 1776–Feb. 26, 1823; House 1815–17.

Hahn, Michael (R La.) Nov. 24, 1830–March 15, 1886; House Dec. 3, 1862–63 (Unionist), 1885–March 15, 1886; Gov. March 4, 1864–March 3, 1865 (State Rights Free-Trader).

Haight, Charles (D N.J.) Jan. 4, 1838–Aug. 1, 1891; House 1867–71.

Haight, Edward (D N.Y.) March 26, 1817–Sept. 15, 1885; House 1861–63.

Haile, William (– Miss.) 1797–March 7, 1837; House July 10, 1826–Sept. 12, 1828.

Hailey, John (D Idaho) Aug. 29, 1835–April 10, 1921; House (Terr. Del.) 1873–75, 1885–87.

Hainer, Eugene Jerome (R Neb.) Aug. 16, 1851–March 17, 1929; House 1893–97.

Haines, Charles Delemere (D N.Y.) June 9, 1856–April 11, 1929; House 1893–95.

Haines, Harry Luther (D Pa.) Feb. 1, 1880–March 29, 1947; House 1931–39, 1941–43.

Haldeman, Richard Jacobs (D Pa.) May 19, 1831–Oct. 1, 1886; House 1869–73.

Hale, Artemas (W Mass.) Oct. 20, 1783–Aug. 3, 1882; House 1845–49.

Hale, Eugene (father of Frederick Hale) (R Maine) June 9, 1836–Oct. 27, 1918; House 1869–79; Senate 1881–1911.

Hale, Fletcher (R N.H.) Jan. 22, 1883–Oct. 22, 1931; House 1925–Oct. 22, 1931.

Hale, Frederick (son of Eugene Hale, grandson of Zachariah Chandler, cousin of Robert Hale) (R Maine) Oct. 7, 1874–Sept. 28, 1963; Senate 1917–41.

Hale, James Tracy (R Pa.) Oct. 14, 1810–April 6, 1865; House 1859–65.

Hale, John Blackwell (D Mo.) Feb. 27, 1831–Feb. 1, 1905; House 1885–87.

Hale, John Parker (FS N.H.) March 31, 1806–Nov. 19, 1873; House 1843–45 (Democrat); Senate 1847–53, July 30, 1855–65.

Hale, Nathan Wesley (R Tenn.) Feb. 11, 1860–Sept. 16, 1941; House 1905–09.

Hale, Robert (cousin of Frederick Hale) (R Maine) Nov. 29, 1889–Nov. 30, 1976; House 1943–59.

Hale, Robert Safford (R N.Y.) Sept. 24, 1822–Dec. 14, 1881; House Dec. 3, 1866–67, 1873–75.

Hale, Salma (R N.H.) March 7, 1787–Nov. 19, 1866; House 1817–19.

Hale, William (F N.H.) Aug. 6, 1765–Nov. 8, 1848; House 1809–11, 1813–17.

Haley, Elisha (D Conn.) Jan. 21, 1776–Jan. 22, 1860; House 1835–39 (1835–37 Jacksonian).

Haley, James Andrew (D Fla.) Jan. 4, 1899–Aug. 6, 1981; House 1953–77; chair House Interior and Insular Affairs 1973–77.

Hall, Albert Richardson (R Ind.) Aug. 27, 1884–Nov. 29, 1969; House 1925–31.

Hall, Augustus (D Iowa) April 29, 1814–Feb. 1, 1861; House 1855–57.

Hall, Benton Jay (D Iowa) Jan. 13, 1835–Jan. 5, 1894; House 1885–87.

Hall, Bolling (R Ga.) Dec. 25, 1767–Feb. 25, 1836; House 1811–17.

Hall, Chapin (R Pa.) July 12, 1816–Sept. 12, 1879; House 1859–61.

Hall, Darwin Scott (R Minn.) Jan. 23, 1844–Feb. 23, 1919; House 1889–91.

Hall, David McKee (D N.C.) May 16, 1918–Jan. 29, 1960; House 1959–Jan. 29, 1960.

Hall, Durward Gorham (R Mo.) Sept. 14, 1910–March 15, 2001; House 1961–73.

Hall, Edwin Arthur (great-grandson of John Allen Collier) (R N.Y.) Feb. 11, 1909– ; House Nov. 7, 1939–53.

Hall, George (– N.Y.) May 12, 1770–March 20, 1840; House 1819–21.

Hall, Hiland (W Vt.) July 20, 1795–Dec. 18, 1885; House Jan. 1, 1833–43 (Jan. 1–Jan. 3, 1833 no party, 1833–35 Anti-Jacksonian); Gov. Oct. 10, 1858–Oct. 12, 1860 (Republican).

Hall, Homer William (R Ill.) July 22, 1870–Sept. 22, 1954; House 1927–33.

Hall, James Knox Polk (D Pa.) Sept. 30, 1844–Jan. 5, 1915; House 1899–Nov. 29, 1902.

Hall, Joseph (J Maine) June 26, 1793–Dec. 31, 1859; House 1833–37.

Hall, Joshua Gilman (R N.H.) Nov. 5, 1828–Oct. 31, 1898; House 1879–83.

Hall, Katie Beatrice Green (D Ind.) April 3, 1938– ; House Nov. 2, 1982–85.

Hall, Lawrence Washington (D Ohio) 1819–Jan. 18, 1863; House 1857–59.

Hall, Leonard Wood (R N.Y.) Oct. 2, 1900–June 2, 1979; House 1939–Dec. 31, 1952; chair Rep. Nat. Comm. April 1953–Feb. 1957.

Hall, Nathan Kelsey (W N.Y.) March 28, 1810–March 2, 1874; House 1847–49; postmaster general July 23, 1850–Sept. 13, 1852.

Hall, Norman (D Pa.) Nov. 17, 1829–Sept. 29, 1917; House 1887–89.

Hall, Obed (R N.H.) Dec. 23, 1757–April 1, 1828; House 1811–13.

Hall, Osee Matson (D Minn.) Sept. 10, 1847–Nov. 26, 1914; House 1891–95.

Hall, Philo (R S.D.) Dec. 31, 1865–Oct. 7, 1938; House 1907–09.

Hall, Ralph Moody (R Texas) May 3, 1923– ; House 1981– (1981–Jan. 5, 2004 Democrat).

Hall, Robert Bernard (R Mass.) Jan. 28, 1812–April 15, 1868; House 1855–59 (1855–57 American Party).

Hall, Robert Samuel (D Miss.) March 10, 1879–June 10, 1941; House 1929–33.

Hall, Sam Blakeley Jr. (D Texas) Jan. 11, 1924–April 10, 1994; House June 19, 1976–May 27, 1985.

Hall, Thomas (R N.D.) June 6, 1869–Dec. 4, 1958; House Nov. 4, 1924–33.

Hall, Thomas H. (J N.C.) June 1773–June 30, 1853; House 1817–25 (Republican), 1827–35 (1827–29 no party).

Hall, Tim Lee (D Ill.) June 11, 1925– ; House 1975–77.

Hall, Tony Patrick (D Ohio) Jan. 16, 1942– ; House 1979–Sept. 9, 2002.

Hall, Uriel Sebree (son of William Augustus Hall, nephew of Willard Preble Hall) (D Mo.) April 12, 1852–Dec. 30, 1932; House 1893–97.

Hall, Willard (R Del.) Dec. 24, 1780–May 10, 1875; House 1817–Jan. 22, 1821.

Hall, Willard Preble (brother of William Augustus Hall, uncle of Uriel Sebree Hall) (D Mo.) May 9, 1820–Nov. 3, 1882; House 1847–53; Gov. Jan. 31, 1864–Jan. 2, 1865 (Unionist).

Hall, William (J Tenn.) Feb. 11, 1775–Oct. 7, 1856; House 1831–33; Gov. April 16–Oct. 1, 1829 (Democratic Republican).

Hall, William Augustus (father of Uriel Sebree Hall, brother of Willard Preble Hall) (D Mo.) Oct. 15, 1815–Dec. 15, 1888; House Jan. 20, 1862–65.

Hall, Wilton Earle (D S.C.) March 11, 1901–Feb. 25, 1980; Senate Nov. 20, 1944–45.

Halleck, Charles Abraham (R Ind.) Aug. 22, 1900–March 3, 1986; House Jan. 29, 1935–69; House majority leader 1947–49, 1953–55; House minority leader 1959–65.

Hallock, John Jr. (D N.Y.) July 1783–Dec. 6, 1840; House 1825–29.

Halloway, Ransom (W N.Y.) about 1793–April 6, 1851; House 1849–51.

Hallowell, Edwin (D Pa.) April 2, 1844–Sept. 13, 1916; House 1891–93.

Halpern, Seymour (R N.Y.) Nov. 19, 1913–Jan. 10, 1997; House 1959–73.

Halsell, John Edward (D Ky.) Sept. 11, 1826–Dec. 26, 1899; House 1883–87.

Halsey, George Armstrong (R N.J.) Dec. 7, 1827–April 1, 1894; House 1867–69, 1871–73.

Halsey, Jehiel Howell (son of Silas Halsey, brother of Nicoll Halsey) (– N.Y.) Oct. 7, 1788–Dec. 5, 1867; House 1829–31.

Halsey, Nicoll (son of Silas Halsey, brother of Jehiel Howell Halsey) (J N.Y.) March 8, 1782–March 3, 1865; House 1833–35.

Halsey, Silas (father of Jehiel Howell Halsey and Nicoll Halsey) (R N.Y.) Oct. 6, 1743–Nov. 19, 1832; House 1805–07.

Halsey, Thomas Jefferson (R Mo.) May 4, 1863–March 17, 1951; House 1929–31.

Halstead, William (W N.J.) June 4, 1794–March 4, 1878; House 1837–39, 1841–43.

Halterman, Frederick (R Pa.) Oct. 22, 1831–March 22, 1907; House 1895–97.

Halvorson, Kittel (P Minn.) Dec. 15, 1846–July 12, 1936; House 1891–93.

Hambleton, Samuel (D Md.) Jan. 8, 1812–Dec. 9, 1886; House 1869–73.

Hamburg, Daniel Eugene (D Calif.) Oct. 6, 1948– ; House 1993–95.

Hamer, Thomas Lyon (uncle of Thomas Ray Hamer) (D Ohio) July 1800–Dec. 2, 1846; House 1833–39 (1833–37 Jacksonian).

Hamer, Thomas Ray (nephew of Thomas Lyon Hamer) (R Idaho) May 4, 1864–Dec. 22, 1950; House 1909–11.

Hamill, James Alphonsus (D N.J.) March 30, 1877–Dec. 15, 1941; House 1907–21.

Hamill, Patrick (D Md.) April 28, 1817–Jan. 15, 1895; House 1869–71.

Hamilton, Andrew Holman (D Ind.) June 7, 1834–May 9, 1895; House 1875–79.

Hamilton, Andrew Jackson (brother of Morgan Calvin Hamilton) (ID Texas) Jan. 28, 1815–April 11, 1875; House 1859–61; Military Gov. 1862–65; Provisional Gov. June 17, 1865–Aug. 9, 1866.

Hamilton, Charles Mann (R N.Y.) Jan. 23, 1874–Jan. 3, 1942; House 1913–19.

Hamilton, Charles Memorial (R Fla.) Nov. 1, 1840–Oct. 22, 1875; House July 1, 1868–71.

Hamilton, Cornelius Springer (R Ohio) Jan. 2, 1821–Dec. 22, 1867; House March 4–Dec. 22, 1867.

Hamilton, Daniel Webster (D Iowa) Dec. 20, 1861–Aug. 21, 1936; House 1907–09.

Hamilton, Edward La Rue (R Mich.) Dec. 9, 1857–Nov. 2, 1923; House 1897–1921.

Hamilton, Finley (D Ky.) June 19, 1886–Jan. 10, 1940; House 1933–35.

Hamilton, James Jr. (– S.C.) May 8, 1786–Nov. 15, 1857; House Dec. 13, 1822–29; Gov. Dec. 9, 1830–Dec. 13, 1832 (State Rights Democrat).

Hamilton, John (R Pa.) Nov. 25, 1754–Aug. 22, 1837; House 1805–07.

Hamilton, John M. (D W.Va.) March 16, 1855–Dec. 27, 1916; House 1911–13.

Hamilton, John Taylor (D Iowa) Oct. 16, 1843–Jan. 25, 1925; House 1891–93.

Hamilton, Lee Herbert (D Ind.) April 20, 1931– ; House 1965–99; chair House Select Intelligence 1985–87; chair House Foreign Affairs 1993–95.

Hamilton, Morgan Calvin (brother of Andrew Jackson Hamilton) (R Texas) Feb. 25, 1809–Nov. 21, 1893; Senate March 31, 1870–77.

Hamilton, Norman Rond (D Va.) Nov. 13, 1877–March 26, 1964; House 1937–39.

Hamilton, Robert (D N.J.) Dec. 9, 1809–March 14, 1878; House 1873–77.

Hamilton, William Thomas (D Md.) Sept. 8, 1820–Oct. 26, 1888; House 1849–55; Senate 1869–75; Gov. Jan. 14, 1880–Jan. 9, 1884.

Hamlin, Courtney Walker (cousin of William Edward Barton) (D Mo.) Oct. 27, 1858–Feb. 16, 1950; House 1903–05, 1907–19.

Hamlin, Edward Stowe (W Ohio) July 6, 1808–Nov. 23, 1894; House Oct. 8, 1844–45.

Hamlin, Hannibal (R Maine) Aug. 27, 1809–July 4, 1891; House 1843–47 (Democrat); Senate June 8, 1848–Jan. 7, 1857 (Democrat), 1857–Jan. 17, 1861, 1869–81; Gov. Jan. 8–Feb. 25, 1857; vice president 1861–65.

Hamlin, Simon Moulton (D Maine) Aug. 10, 1866–July 27, 1939; House 1935–37.

Hammer, William Cicero (D N.C.) March 24, 1865–Sept. 26, 1930; House 1921–Sept. 26, 1930.

Hammerschmidt, John Paul (R Ark.) May 4, 1922– ; House 1967–93.

Hammett, William Henry (D Miss.) March 25, 1799–July 9, 1861; House 1843–45.

Hammond, Edward (D Md.) March 17, 1812–Oct. 19, 1882; House 1849–53.

Hammond, Jabez Delno (R N.Y.) Aug. 2, 1778–Aug. 18, 1855; House 1815–17.

Hammond, James Henry (D S.C.) Nov. 15, 1807–Nov. 13, 1864; House 1835–Feb. 26, 1836 (Nullifier); Senate Dec. 7, 1857–Nov. 11, 1860; Gov. Dec. 8, 1842–Dec. 7, 1844 (Democrat).

Hammond, John (R N.Y.) Aug. 17, 1827–May 28, 1889; House 1879–83.

Hammond, Nathaniel Job (D Ga.) Dec. 26, 1833–April 20, 1899; House 1879–87.

Hammond, Peter Francis (D Ohio) June 30, 1887–April 2, 1971; House Nov. 3, 1936–37.

Hammond, Robert Hanna (D Pa.) April 28, 1791–June 2, 1847; House 1837–41.

Hammond, Samuel (R Ga.) Sept. 21, 1757–Sept. 11, 1842; House 1803–Feb. 2, 1805; Gov. (Upper La. Terr.) 1805–24.

Hammond, Thomas (D Ind.) Feb. 27, 1843–Sept. 21, 1909; House 1893–95.

Hammond, Winfield Scott (D Minn.) Nov. 17, 1863–Dec. 30, 1915; House 1907–Jan. 6, 1915; Gov. Jan. 7–Dec. 30, 1915.

Hammons, David (D Maine) May 12, 1808–Nov. 7, 1888; House 1847–49.

Hammons, Joseph (J N.H.) March 3, 1787–March 29, 1836; House 1829–33.

Hampton, James Giles (W N.J.) June 13, 1814–Sept. 22, 1861; House 1845–49.

Hampton, Moses (W Pa.) Oct. 28, 1803–June 27, 1878; House 1847–51.

Hampton, Wade (grandfather of Wade Hampton, below) (R S.C.) 1752–Feb. 4, 1835; House 1795–97, 1803–05.

Hampton, Wade (grandson of Wade Hampton, above, son-in-law of George McDuffie) (D S.C.) March 28, 1818–April 11, 1902; Senate 1879–91; Gov. Dec. 14, 1876–Feb. 26, 1879.

Hanback, Lewis (R Kan.) March 27, 1839–Sept. 7, 1897; House 1883–87.

Hanbury, Harry Alfred (R N.Y.) Jan. 1, 1863–Aug. 22, 1940; House 1901–03.

Hance, Kent Ronald (D Texas) Nov. 14, 1942– ; House 1979–85.

Hanchett, Luther (R Wis.) Oct. 25, 1825–Nov. 24, 1862; House 1861–Nov. 24, 1862.

Hancock, Clarence Eugene (R N.Y.) Feb. 13, 1885–Jan. 3, 1948; House Nov. 8, 1927–47.

Hancock, Franklin Wills Jr. (D N.C.) Nov. 1, 1894–Jan. 23, 1969; House Nov. 4, 1930–39.

Hancock, George (– Va.) June 13, 1754–July 18, 1820; House 1793–97.

Hancock, John (D Texas) Oct. 24, 1824–July 19, 1893; House 1871–77, 1883–85.

Hancock, Milton D. "Mel" (R Mo.) Sept. 14, 1929– ; House 1989–97.

Hand, Augustus Cincinnatus (D N.Y.) Sept. 4, 1803–March 8, 1878; House 1839–41.

Hand, Thomas Millet (R N.J.) July 7, 1902–Dec. 26, 1956; House 1945–Dec. 26, 1956.

Handley, William Anderson (D Ala.) Dec. 15, 1834–June 23, 1909; House 1871–73.

Handy, Levin Irving (nephew of William Campbell Preston Breckenridge) (D Del.) Dec. 24, 1861–Feb. 3, 1922; House 1897–99.

Hanks, James Millander (D Ark.) Feb. 12, 1833–May 24, 1909; House 1871–73.

Hanley, James Michael (D N.Y.) July 19, 1920–Oct. 16, 2003; House 1965–81; chair House Post Office and Civil Service 1979–81.

Hanly, James Franklin (R Ind.) April 4, 1863–Aug. 1, 1920; House 1895–97; Gov. Jan. 9, 1905–Jan. 11, 1909.

Hanna, John (R Ind.) Sept. 3, 1827–Oct. 24, 1882; House 1877–79.

Hanna, John Andre (grandfather of Archibald McAllister) (R Pa.) 1762–July 23, 1805; House 1797–July 23, 1805.

Hanna, Louis Benjamin (R N.D.) Aug. 9, 1861–April 23, 1948; House 1909–Jan. 7, 1913; Gov. Jan. 8, 1913–Jan. 3, 1917.

Hanna, Marcus Alonzo (father of Ruth Hanna McCormick) (R Ohio) Sept. 24, 1837–Feb. 15, 1904; Senate March 5, 1897–Feb. 15, 1904; chair Rep. Nat. Comm. 1896–1904.

Hanna, Richard Thomas (D Calif.) June 9, 1914–June 9, 2001; House 1963–Dec. 31, 1974.

Hanna, Robert (W Ind.) April 6, 1786–Nov. 16, 1858; Senate Aug. 19, 1831–Jan. 3, 1832.

Hannaford, Mark Warren (D Calif.) Feb. 7, 1925–June 2, 1985; House 1975–79.

Hannegan, Edward Allen (D Ind.) June 25, 1807–Feb. 25, 1859; House 1833–37; Senate 1843–49.

Hanrahan, Robert Paul (R Ill.) Feb. 25, 1934– ; House 1973–75.

Hansbrough, Henry Clay (R N.D.) Jan. 30, 1848–Nov. 16, 1933; House Nov. 2, 1889–91; Senate 1891–1909.

Hansen, Clifford Peter (R Wyo.) Oct. 16, 1912– ; Senate 1967–Dec. 31, 1978; Gov. Jan. 6, 1963–Jan. 2, 1967.

Hansen, George Vernon (R Idaho) Sept. 14, 1930– ; House 1965–69, 1975–85.

Hansen, James Vear (R Utah) Aug. 14, 1932– ; House 1981–2003; chair House Standards of Official Conduct 1997–99; chair House Resources 2001–03.

Hansen, John Robert (D Iowa) Aug. 24, 1901–Sept. 23, 1974; House 1965–67.

Hansen, Julia Butler (D Wash.) June 14, 1907–May 3, 1988; House Nov. 8, 1960–Dec. 31, 1974.

Hansen, Orval Howard (R Idaho) Aug. 3, 1926– ; House 1969–75.

Hanson, Alexander Contee (F Md.) Feb. 27, 1786–April 23, 1819; House 1813–16; Senate Dec. 20, 1816–April 23, 1819.

Haralson, Hugh Anderson (D Ga.) Nov. 13, 1805–Sept. 25, 1854; House 1843–51.

Haralson, Jeremiah (R Ala.) April 1, 1846–about 1916; House 1875–77.

Hard, Gideon (W N.Y.) April 29, 1797–April 27, 1885; House 1833–37 (1833–35 Anti-Mason).

Hardeman, Thomas Jr. (D Ga.) Jan. 12, 1825–March 6, 1891; House 1859–Jan. 23, 1861 (Opposition), 1883–85.

Harden, Cecil Murray (R Ind.) Nov. 21, 1894–Dec. 5, 1984; House 1949–59.

Hardenbergh, Augustus Albert (D N.J.) May 18, 1830–Oct. 5, 1889; House 1875–79, 1881–83.

Hardin, Benjamin (cousin of Martin Davis Hardin) (W Ky.) Feb. 29, 1784–Sept. 24, 1852; House 1815–17 (Republican), 1819–23 (Republican), 1833–37 (1833–35 Anti-Jacksonian).

Hardin, John J. (son of Martin Davis Hardin) (W Ill.) Jan. 6, 1810–Feb. 23, 1847; House 1843–45.

Hardin, Martin Davis (cousin of Benjamin Hardin, father of John J. Hardin) (F Ky.) June 21, 1780–Oct. 8, 1823; Senate Nov. 13, 1816–17.

Harding, Aaron (D Ky.) Feb. 20, 1805–Dec. 24, 1875; House 1861–67 (1861–65 Unionist).

Harding, Abner Clark (R Ill.) Feb. 10, 1807–July 19, 1874; House 1865–69.

Harding, Benjamin Franklin (D Ore.) Jan. 4, 1823–June 16, 1899; Senate Sept. 12, 1862–65.

Harding, John Eugene (R Ohio) June 27, 1877–July 26, 1959; House 1907–09.

Harding, Ralph R. (D Idaho) Sept. 9, 1929– ; House 1961–65.

Harding, Warren Gamaliel (R Ohio) Nov. 2, 1865–Aug. 2, 1923; Senate 1915–Jan. 13, 1921; president 1921–Aug. 2, 1923.

Hardwick, Thomas William (D Ga.) Dec. 9, 1872–Jan. 31, 1944; House 1903–Nov. 2, 1914; Senate Nov. 4, 1914–19; Gov. June 25, 1921–June 30, 1923.

Hardy, Alexander Merrill (R Ind.) Dec. 16, 1847–Aug. 31, 1927; House 1895–97.

Hardy, Guy Urban (R Colo.) April 4, 1872–Jan. 26, 1947; House 1919–33.

Hardy, John (D N.Y.) Sept. 19, 1835–Dec. 9, 1913; House Dec. 5, 1881–85.

Hardy, Porter Jr. (D Va.) June 1, 1903–April 19, 1995; House 1947–69.

Hardy, Rufus (D Texas) Dec. 16, 1855–March 13, 1943; House 1907–23.

Hare, Butler Black (father of James Butler Hare) (D S.C.) Nov. 25, 1875–Dec. 30, 1967; House 1925–33, 1939–47.

Hare, Darius Dodge (D Ohio) Jan. 9, 1843–Feb. 10, 1897; House 1891–95.

Hare, James Butler (son of Butler Black Hare) (D S.C.) Sept. 4, 1918–July 16, 1966; House 1949–51.

Hare, Silas (D Texas) Nov. 13, 1827–Nov. 26, 1907; House 1887–91.

Hargis, Denver David (D Kan.) July 22, 1921–March 16, 1989; House 1959–61.

Harkin, Thomas Richard (D Iowa) Nov. 19, 1939– ; House 1975–85; Senate 1985– ; chair Senate Agriculture, Nutrition, and Forestry Jan. 3, 2001–Jan. 20, 2001, June 6, 2001–03.

Harlan, Aaron (cousin of Andrew Jackson Harlan) (W Ohio) Sept. 8, 1802–Jan. 8, 1868; House 1853–59.

Harlan, Andrew Jackson (cousin of Aaron Harlan) (D Ind.) March 29, 1815–May 19, 1907; House 1849–51, 1853–55.

Harlan, Byron Berry (D Ohio) Oct. 22, 1886–Nov. 11, 1949; House 1931–39.

Harlan, James (W Ky.) June 22, 1800–Feb. 18, 1863; House 1835–39.

Harlan, James (R Iowa) Aug. 26, 1820–Oct. 5, 1899; Senate Dec. 31, 1855–Jan. 12, 1857 (Free-Soiler), Jan. 29, 1857–May 15, 1865, 1867–73; secretary of the interior May 15, 1865–Aug. 31, 1866.

Harless, Richard Fielding (D Ariz.) Aug. 6, 1905–Nov. 24, 1970; House 1943–49.

Harman, Jane (D Calif.) June 28, 1945– ; House 1993–99, 2001– .

Harmanson, John Henry (D La.) Jan. 15, 1803–Oct. 24, 1850; House 1845–Oct. 24, 1850.

Harmer, Alfred Crout (R Pa.) Aug. 8, 1825–March 6, 1900; House 1871–75, 1877–March 6, 1900.

Harmon, Randall S. (D Ind.) July 19, 1903–Aug. 18, 1982; House 1959–61.

Harness, Forest Arthur (R Ind.) June 24, 1895–July 29, 1974; House 1939–49.

Harper, Alexander (W Ohio) Feb. 5, 1786–Dec. 1, 1860; House 1837–39, 1843–47, 1851–53.

Harper, Francis Jacob (D Pa.) March 5, 1800–March 18, 1837; House March 4–18, 1837.

Harper, James (W Pa.) March 28, 1780–March 31, 1873; House 1833–37 (1833–35 no party).

Harper, James Clarence (D N.C.) Dec. 6, 1819–Jan. 8, 1890; House 1871–73.

Harper, John Adams (R N.H.) Nov. 2, 1779–June 18, 1816; House 1811–13.

Harper, Joseph Morrill (J N.H.) June 21, 1787–Jan. 15, 1865; House 1831–35; Gov. Feb. 28–June 2, 1831.

Harper, Robert Goodloe (– Md.) Jan. 1765–Jan. 14, 1825; House Feb. 1795–March 1801 (S.C.); Senate Jan.–Dec. 1816.

Harper, William (J S.C.) Jan. 17, 1790–Oct. 10, 1847; Senate March 8–Nov. 29, 1826.

Harreld, John William (R Okla.) Jan. 24, 1872–Dec. 26, 1950; House Nov. 8, 1919–21; Senate 1921–27.

Harries, William Henry (D Minn.) Jan. 15, 1843–July 23, 1921; House 1891–93.

Harrington, Henry William (D Ind.) Sept. 12, 1825–March 20, 1882; House 1863–65.

Harrington, Michael Joseph (D Mass.) Sept. 2, 1936– ; House Sept. 30, 1969–79.

Harrington, Vincent Francis (D Iowa) May 16, 1903–Nov. 29, 1943; House 1937–Sept. 5, 1942.

Harris, Benjamin Gwinn (D Md.) Dec. 13, 1805–April 4, 1895; House 1863–67.

Harris, Benjamin Winslow (father of Robert Orr Harris) (R Mass.) Nov. 10, 1823–Feb. 7, 1907; House 1873–83.

Harris, Charles Murray (D Ill.) April 10, 1821–Sept. 20, 1896; House 1863–65.

Harris, Christopher Columbus (D Ala.) Jan. 28, 1842–Dec. 28, 1935; House May 11, 1914–15.

Harris, Claude Jr. (D Ala.) June 29, 1940–Oct. 2, 1994; House 1987–93.

Harris, Fred Roy (D Okla.) Nov. 13, 1930– ; Senate Nov. 4, 1964–Jan. 2, 1973; chair Dem. Nat. Comm. 1969–70.

Harris, George Emrick (R Miss.) Jan. 6, 1827–March 19, 1911; House Feb. 23, 1870–73.

Harris, Henry Richard (D Ga.) Feb. 2, 1828–Oct. 15, 1909; House 1873–79, 1885–87.

Harris, Henry Schenck (D N.J.) Dec. 27, 1850–May 2, 1902; House 1881–83.

Harris, Herbert Eugene II (D Va.) April 14, 1926– ; House 1975–81.

Harris, Ira (grandfather of Henry Riggs Rathbone) (R N.Y.) May 31, 1802–Dec. 2, 1875; Senate 1861–67.

Harris, Isham Green (D Tenn.) Feb. 10, 1818–July 8, 1897; House 1849–53; Senate 1877–July 8, 1897; elected pres. pro tempore March 22, 1893, Jan. 10, 1895; Gov. Nov. 3, 1857–March 12, 1862.

Harris, James Morrison (AP Md.) Nov. 20, 1817–July 16, 1898; House 1855–61.

Harris, John (cousin of Robert Harris) (R N.Y.) Sept. 26, 1760–Nov. 1824; House 1807–09.

Harris, John Spafford (R La.) Dec. 18, 1825–Jan. 25, 1906; Senate July 8, 1868–71.

Harris, John Thomas (cousin of John Hill of Virginia) (D Va.) May 8, 1823–Oct. 14, 1899; House 1859–61 (Independent Democrat), 1871–81.

Harris, Katherine (R Fla.) April 5, 1957– ; House 2003– .

Harris, Mark (– Maine) Jan. 27, 1779–March 2, 1843; House Dec. 2, 1822–23.

Harris, Oren (D Ark.) Dec. 20, 1903–Feb. 5, 1997; House 1941–Feb. 2, 1966; chair House Interstate and Foreign Commerce 1957–66.

Harris, Robert (cousin of John Harris) (– Pa.) Sept. 5, 1768–Sept. 3, 1851; House 1823–27.

Harris, Robert Orr (son of Benjamin Winslow Harris) (R Mass.) Nov. 8, 1854–June 13, 1926; House 1911–13.

Harris, Sampson Willis (D Ala.) Feb. 23, 1809–April 1, 1857; House 1847–57.

Harris, Stephen Ross (uncle of Ebenezer Byron Finley) (R Ohio) May 22, 1824–Jan. 15, 1905; House 1895–97.

Harris, Thomas K. (R Tenn.) ?–March 18, 1816; House 1813–15.

Harris, Thomas Langrell (D Ill.) Oct. 29, 1816–Nov. 24, 1858; House 1849–51, 1855–Nov. 24, 1858.

Harris, Wiley Pope (D Miss.) Nov. 9, 1818–Dec. 3, 1891; House 1853–55.

Harris, William Alexander (father of William Alexander Harris, below) (D Va.) Aug. 24, 1805–March 28, 1864; House 1841–43.

Harris, William Alexander (son of William Alexander Harris, above) (P Kan.) Oct. 29, 1841–Dec. 20, 1909; House 1893–95; Senate 1897–1903.

Harris, William Julius (great-grandson of Charles Hooks) (D Ga.) Feb. 3, 1868–April 18, 1932; Senate 1919–April 18, 1932.

Harris, Winder Russell (D Va.) Dec. 3, 1888–Feb. 24, 1973; House April 8, 1941–Sept. 15, 1944.

Harrison, Albert Galliton (D Mo.) June 26, 1800–Sept. 7, 1839; House 1835–39 (1835–37 Jacksonian).

Harrison, Benjamin (grandson of William Henry Harrison born in 1773, son of John Scott Harrison, grandfather of William Henry Harrison born in 1896) (R Ind.) Aug. 20, 1833–March 13, 1901; Senate 1881–87; president 1889–93.

Harrison, Burr Powell (son of Thomas Walter Harrison) (D Va.) July 2, 1904–Dec. 29, 1973; House Nov. 6, 1946–63.

Harrison, Byron Patton "Pat" (D Miss.) Aug. 29, 1881–June 22, 1941; House 1911–19; Senate 1919–June 22, 1941; elected pres. pro tempore Jan. 6, 1941.

Harrison, Carter Bassett (brother of William Henry Harrison born in 1773) (R Va.) ?–April 18, 1808; House 1793–99 (1793–95 no party).

Harrison, Carter Henry (D Ill.) Feb. 15, 1825–Oct. 28, 1893; House 1875–79.

Harrison, Francis Burton (D N.Y.) Dec. 18, 1873–Nov. 21, 1957; House 1903–05, 1907–Sept. 1, 1913.

Harrison, Frank Girard (D Pa.) Feb. 2, 1940– ; House 1983–85.

Harrison, George Paul (D Ala.) March 19, 1841–July 17, 1922; House Nov. 6, 1894–97.

Harrison, Horace Harrison (R Tenn.) Aug. 7, 1829–Dec. 20, 1885; House 1873–75.

Harrison, John Scott (son of William Henry Harrison born in 1773, father of Benjamin Harrison) (R Ohio) Oct. 4, 1804–May 25, 1878; House 1853–57 (1853–55 Whig).

Harrison, Richard Almgill (U Ohio) April 8, 1824–July 30, 1904; House July 4, 1861–63.

Harrison, Robert Dinsmore (R Neb.) Jan. 26, 1897–June 11, 1977; House Dec. 4, 1951–59.

Harrison, Samuel Smith (J Pa.) 1780–April 1853; House 1833–37.

Harrison, Thomas Walter (father of Burr Powell Harrison) (D Va.) Aug. 5, 1856–May 9, 1935; House Nov. 7, 1916–Dec. 15, 1922, 1923–29.

Harrison, William Henry (father of John Scott Harrison, brother of Carter Bassett Harrison, grandfather of Benjamin Harrison, great-great-grandfather of William Henry Harrison born in 1896) (– Ohio) Feb. 9, 1773–April 4, 1841; House (Terr. del.) 1799–May 14, 1800, (Rep.) Oct. 8, 1816–19; Senate 1825–May 20, 1828 (no party); Gov. (Ind. Terr.) 1801–13; president March 4–April 4, 1841.

Harrison, William Henry (great-great-grandson of William Henry Harrison, grandson of Benjamin Harrison and Alvin Saunders) (R Wyo.) Aug. 10, 1896–Oct. 8, 1990; House 1951–55, 1961–65, 1967–69.

Harsha, William Howard (R Ohio) Jan. 1, 1921– ; House 1961–81.

Hart, Alphonso (R Ohio) July 4, 1830–Dec. 23, 1910; House 1883–85.

Hart, Archibald Chapman (D N.J.) Feb. 27, 1873–July 24, 1935; House Nov. 5, 1912–March 3, 1913, July 22, 1913–17.

Hart, Edward Joseph (D N.J.) March 25, 1893–April 20, 1961; House 1935–55; chair House Merchant Marine and Fisheries 1950–53.

Hart, Elizur Kirke (D N.Y.) April 8, 1841–Feb. 18, 1893; House 1877–79.

Hart, Emanuel Bernard (D N.Y.) Oct. 27, 1809–Aug. 29, 1897; House 1851–53.

Hart, Gary Warren (D Colo.) Nov. 28, 1936– ; Senate 1975–87.

Hart, Joseph Johnson (D Pa.) April 18, 1859–July 13, 1926; House 1895–97.

Hart, Melissa A. (R Pa.) April 4, 1962– ; House 2001– .

Hart, Michael James (D Mich.) July 16, 1877–Feb. 14, 1951; House Nov. 3, 1931–35.

Hart, Philip Aloysius (D Mich.) Dec. 10, 1912–Dec. 26, 1976; Senate 1959–Dec. 26, 1976.

Hart, Roswell (R N.Y.) Aug. 4, 1824–April 20, 1883; House 1865–67.

Hart, Thomas Charles (R Conn.) June 12, 1877–July 4, 1971; Senate Feb. 15, 1945–Nov. 5, 1946.

Harter, Dow Watters (D Ohio) Jan. 2, 1885–Sept. 4, 1971; House 1933–43.

Harter, John Francis (R N.Y.) Sept. 1, 1897–Dec. 20, 1947; House 1939–41.

Harter, Michael Daniel (grandson of Robert Moore) (D Ohio) April 6, 1846–Feb. 22, 1896; House 1891–95.

Hartke, Rupert Vance (D Ind.) May 31, 1919–July 27, 2003; Senate 1959–77; chair Senate Veterans' Affairs 1971–77.

Hartley, Fred Allan Jr. (R N.J.) Feb. 22, 1902–May 11, 1969; House 1929–49; chair House Eduction and Labor 1947–49.

Hartley, Thomas (F Pa.) Sept. 7, 1748–Dec. 21, 1800; House 1789–Dec. 21, 1800 (1789–93 no party).

Hartman, Charles Sampson (Sil.R Mont.) March 1, 1861–Aug. 3, 1929; House 1893–99 (1893–97 Republican).

Hartman, Jesse Lee (R Pa.) June 18, 1853–Feb. 17, 1930; House 1911–13.

Hartnett, Thomas Forbes (R S.C.) Aug. 7, 1941– ; House 1981–87.

Hartridge, Julian (D Ga.) Sept. 9, 1829–Jan. 8, 1879; House 1875–Jan. 8, 1879.

Hartzell, William (D Ill.) Feb. 20, 1837–Aug. 14, 1903; House 1875–79.

Harvey, David Archibald (R Okla.) March 20, 1845–May 24, 1916; House (Terr. Del.) Nov. 4, 1890–93.

Harvey, James (R Mich.) July 4, 1922– ; House 1961–Jan. 31, 1974.

Harvey, James Madison (R Kan.) Sept. 21, 1833–April 15, 1894; Senate Feb. 2, 1874–77; Gov. Jan. 11, 1869–Jan. 13, 1873.

Harvey, Jonathan (brother of Matthew Harvey) (– N.H.) Feb. 25, 1780–Aug. 23, 1859; House 1825–31.

Harvey, Matthew (brother of Jonathan Harvey) (– N.H.) June 21, 1781–April 7, 1866; House 1821–25; Gov. June 3, 1830–Feb. 28, 1831 (Jacksonian).

Harvey, Ralph (R Ind.) Aug. 9, 1901–Nov. 7, 1991; House Nov. 4, 1947–59, 1961–67.

Hasbrouck, Abraham Bruyn (cousin of Abraham Joseph Hasbrouck) (– N.Y.) Nov. 29, 1791–Feb. 24, 1879; House 1825–27.

Hasbrouck, Abraham Joseph (cousin of Abraham Bruyn Hasbrouck) (R N.Y.) Oct. 16, 1773–Jan. 12, 1845; House 1813–15.

Hasbrouck, Josiah (R N.Y.) March 5, 1755–March 19, 1821; House April 28, 1803–05, 1817–19.

Hascall, Augustus Porter (W N.Y.) June 24, 1800–June 27, 1872; House 1851–53.

Haskell, Dudley Chase (grandfather of Otis Halbert Holmes) (R Kan.) March 23, 1842–Dec. 16, 1883; House 1877–Dec. 16, 1883.

Haskell, Floyd Kirk (D Colo.) Feb. 7, 1916–Aug. 25, 1998; Senate 1973–79.

Haskell, Harry Garner Jr. (R Del.) May 27, 1921– ; House 1957–59.

Haskell, Reuben Locke (R N.Y.) Oct. 5, 1878–Oct. 2, 1971; House 1915–Dec. 31, 1919.

Haskell, William T. (nephew of Charles Ready) (W Tenn.) July 21, 1818–March 12, 1859; House 1847–49.

Haskin, John Bussing (ALD N.Y.) Aug. 27, 1821–Sept. 18, 1895; House 1857–61 (1857–59 Democrat).

Haskins, Kittredge (R Vt.) April 8, 1836–Aug. 7, 1916; House 1901–09.

Hastert, John Dennis (R Ill.) Jan. 2, 1942– ; House 1987– ; Speaker 1999– .

Hastings, Alcee Lamar (D Fla.) Sept. 5, 1936– ; House 1993– .

Hastings, Daniel Oren (R Del.) March 5, 1874–May 9, 1966; Senate Dec. 10, 1928–Jan. 2, 1937.

Hastings, George (D N.Y.) March 13, 1807–Aug. 29, 1866; House 1853–55.

Hastings, James Fred (R N.Y.) April 10, 1926– ; House 1969–Jan. 20, 1976.

Hastings, John (D Ohio) 1778–Dec. 8, 1854; House 1839–43.

Hastings, Richard "Doc" (R Wash.) Feb. 7, 1941– ; House 1995– ; chair House Standards of Official Conduct 2005– .

Hastings, Serranus Clinton (D Iowa) Nov. 22, 1813–Feb. 18, 1893; House Dec. 28, 1846–47.

Hastings, Seth (father of William Soden Hastings) (F Mass.) April 8, 1762–Nov. 19, 1831; House Aug. 24, 1801–07.

Hastings, William Soden (son of Seth Hastings) (W Mass.) June 3, 1798–June 17, 1842; House 1837–June 17, 1842.

Hastings, William Wirt (D Okla.) Dec. 31, 1866–April 8, 1938; House 1915–21, 1923–35.

Hatch, Carl Atwood (D N.M.) Nov. 27, 1889–Sept. 15, 1963; Senate Oct. 10, 1933–Jan. 2, 1949.

Hatch, Herschel Harrison (R Mich.) Feb. 17, 1837–Nov. 30, 1920; House 1883–85.

Hatch, Israel Thompson (D N.Y.) June 30, 1808–Sept. 24, 1875; House 1857–59.

Hatch, Jethro Ayers (R Ind.) June 18, 1837–Aug. 3, 1912; House 1895–97.

Hatch, Orrin Grant (R Utah) March 22, 1934– ; Senate 1977– ; chair Senate Labor and Human Resources 1981–87; chair Senate Judiciary 1995–Jan. 3, 2001, Jan. 20, 2001–June 6, 2001, 2003–05.

Hatch, William Henry (D Mo.) Sept. 11, 1833–Dec. 23, 1896; House 1879–95.

Hatcher, Charles Floyd (D Ga.) July 1, 1939– ; House 1981–93.

Hatcher, Robert Anthony (D Mo.) Feb. 24, 1819–Dec. 4, 1886; House 1873–79.

Hatfield, Henry Drury (R W.Va.) Sept. 15, 1875–Oct. 23, 1962; Senate 1929–35; Gov. March 4, 1913–March 4, 1917.

Hatfield, Mark Odom (R Ore.) July 12, 1922– ; Senate Jan. 10, 1967–97; chair Senate Appropriations 1981–87; Gov. Jan. 12, 1959–Jan. 9, 1967; chair Senate Appropriations 1995–97.

Hatfield, Paul Gerhart (D Mont.) April 29, 1928–July 3, 2000; Senate Jan. 22–Dec. 14, 1978.

Hathaway, Samuel Gilbert (J N.Y.) July 18, 1780–May 2, 1867; House 1833–35.

Hathaway, William Dodd (D Maine) Feb. 21, 1924– ; House 1965–73; Senate 1973–79.

Hathorn, Henry Harrison (R N.Y.) Nov. 28, 1813–Feb. 20, 1887; House 1873–77.

Hathorn, John (R N.Y.) Jan. 9, 1749–Feb. 19, 1825; House 1789–91 (no party), 1795–97; Cont. Cong. (elected but did not attend) 1788.

Hatton, Robert Hopkins (O Tenn.) Nov. 2, 1826–May 31, 1862; House 1859–61.

Haugen, Gilbert Nelson (R Iowa) April 21, 1859–July 18, 1933; House 1899–1933.

Haugen, Nils Pederson (R Wis.) March 9, 1849–April 23, 1931; House 1887–95.

Haughey, Thomas (R Ala.) 1826–Aug. 5, 1869; House July 21, 1868–69.

Haun, Henry Peter (D Calif.) Jan. 18, 1815–June 6, 1860; Senate Nov. 3, 1859–March 4, 1860.

Haven, Nathaniel Appleton (F N.H.) July 19, 1762–March 13, 1831; House 1809–11.

Haven, Solomon George (W N.Y.) Nov. 27, 1810–Dec. 24, 1861; House 1851–57.

Havenner, Franck Roberts (D Calif.) Sept. 20, 1882–July 24, 1967; House 1937–41 (1937–39 Progressive), 1945–53.

Havens, Harrison Eugene (R Mo.) Dec. 15, 1837–Aug. 16, 1916; House 1871–75.

Havens, James Smith (D N.Y.) May 28, 1859–Feb. 27, 1927; House April 19, 1910–11.

Havens, Jonathan Nicoll (R N.Y.) June 18, 1757–Oct. 25, 1799; House 1795–Oct. 25, 1799.

Hawes, Albert Gallatin (brother of Richard Hawes, nephew of Aylett Hawes, great-uncle of Harry Bartow Hawes, cousin of Aylett Hawes Buckner) (J Ky.) April 1, 1804–March 14, 1849; House 1831–37.

Hawes, Aylett (uncle of Richard Hawes, Albert Gallatin Hawes and Aylett Hawes Buckner) (R Va.) April 21, 1768–Aug. 31, 1833; House 1811–17.

Hawes, Harry Bartow (great-nephew of Albert Gallatin Hawes) (D Mo.) Nov. 15, 1869–July 31, 1947; House 1921–Oct. 15, 1926; Senate Dec. 6, 1926–Feb. 3, 1933.

Hawes, Richard (brother of Albert Gallatin Hawes, nephew of Aylett Hawes, cousin of Aylett Hawes Buckner) (W Ky.) Feb. 6, 1797–May 25, 1877; House 1837–41.

Hawk, Robert Moffett Allison (R Ill.) April 23, 1839–June 29, 1882; House 1879–June 29, 1882.

Hawkes, Albert Wahl (R N.J.) Nov. 20, 1878–May 9, 1971; Senate 1943–49.

Hawkes, James (– N.Y.) Dec. 13, 1776–Oct. 2, 1865; House 1821–23.

Hawkins, Augustus Freeman (D Calif.) Aug. 31, 1907– ; House 1963–91; chair House Administration 1981–84; chair House Education and Labor 1984–91.

Hawkins, Benjamin (uncle of Micajah Thomas Hawkins) (– N.C.) Aug. 15, 1754–June 6, 1816; Senate Nov. 27, 1789–95; Cont. Cong. 1781–83, 1787.

Hawkins, George Sydney (D Fla.) 1808–March 15, 1878; House 1857–Jan. 21, 1861.

Hawkins, Isaac Roberts (R Tenn.) May 16, 1818–Aug. 12, 1880; House July 24, 1866–71 (July 24, 1866–67 Unionist).

Hawkins, Joseph (Ad.D N.Y.) Nov. 14, 1781–April 20, 1832; House 1829–31.

Hawkins, Joseph H. (R Ky.) ?–1823; House March 29, 1814–15.

Hawkins, Micajah Thomas (nephew of Benjamin Hawkins and Nathaniel Macon) (D N.C.) May 20, 1790–Dec. 22, 1858; House Dec. 15, 1831–41 (Dec. 15, 1831–37 Jacksonian).

Hawkins, Paula (R Fla.) Jan. 24, 1927– ; Senate Jan. 1, 1981–87.

Hawks, Charles Jr. (R Wis.) July 7, 1899–Jan. 6, 1960; House 1939–41.

Hawley, John Baldwin (R Ill.) Feb. 9, 1831–May 24, 1895; House 1869–75.

Hawley, Joseph Roswell (R Conn.) Oct. 31, 1826–March 17, 1905; House Dec. 2, 1872–75, 1879–81; Senate 1881–1905; Gov. May 2, 1866–May 1, 1867.

Hawley, Robert Bradley (R Texas) Oct. 25, 1849–Nov. 28, 1921; House 1897–1901.

Hawley, Willis Chatman (R Ore.) May 5, 1864–July 24, 1941; House 1907–33.

Haws, John Henry Hobart (W N.Y.) 1809–Jan. 27, 1858; House 1851–53.

Hay, Andrew Kessler (W N.J.) Jan. 19, 1809–Feb. 7, 1881; House 1849–51.

Hay, James (D Va.) Jan. 9, 1856–June 12, 1931; House 1897–Oct. 1, 1916.

Hay, John Breese (R Ill.) Jan. 8, 1834–June 16, 1916; House 1869–73.

Hayakawa, Samuel Ichiye (R Calif.) July 18, 1906–Feb. 27, 1992; Senate 1977–83.

Hayden, Carl Trumbull (D Ariz.) Oct. 2, 1877–Jan. 25, 1972; House Feb. 19, 1912–27; Senate 1927–69; chair Senate Rules and Administration 1949–53; chair Senate Appropriations 1955–69; elected pres. pro tempore Jan. 3, 1957.

Hayden, Edward Daniel (R Mass.) Dec. 27, 1833–Nov. 15, 1908; House 1885–89.

Hayden, Moses (– N.Y.) 1786–Feb. 13, 1830; House 1823–27.

Hayes, Charles Arthur (D Ill.) Feb. 17, 1918–April 8, 1997; House Aug. 23, 1983–93.

Hayes, Everis Anson (R Calif.) March 10, 1855–June 3, 1942; House 1905–19.

Hayes, James A. (R La.) Dec. 21, 1946– ; House 1987–97 (1987–Dec. 1, 1995 Democrat).

Hayes, Philip Cornelius (R Ill.) Feb. 3, 1833–July 13, 1916; House 1877–81.

Hayes, Philip Harold (D Ind.) Sept. 1, 1940– ; House 1975–77.

Hayes, Robert "Robin" (R N.C.) Aug. 14, 1945– ; House 1999– .

Hayes, Rutherford Birchard (R Ohio) Oct. 4, 1822–Jan. 17, 1893; House 1865–July 20, 1867; Gov. Jan. 13, 1868–Jan. 8, 1872, Jan. 10, 1876–March 2, 1877; president 1877–81.

Hayes, Walter Ingalls (D Iowa) Dec. 9, 1841–March 14, 1901; House 1887–95.

Haymond, Thomas Sherwood (W Va.) Jan. 15, 1794–April 5, 1869; House Nov. 8, 1849–51.

Haymond, William Summerville (D Ind.) Feb. 20, 1823–Dec. 24, 1885; House 1875–77.

Hayne, Arthur Peronneau (brother of Robert Young Hayne) (D S.C.) March 12, 1788 or 1790–Jan. 7, 1867; Senate May 11–Dec. 2, 1858.

Hayne, Robert Young (brother of Arthur Peronneau Hayne, son-in-law of Charles Pinckney) (J S.C.) Nov. 10, 1791–Sept. 24, 1839; Senate 1823–Dec. 13, 1832 (1823–29 no party); Gov. Dec. 13, 1832–Dec. 11, 1834 (State Rights Democrat).

Haynes, Charles Eaton (– Ga.) April 15, 1784–Aug. 29, 1841; House 1825–31, 1835–39.

Haynes, Martin Alonzo (R N.H.) July 30, 1842–Nov. 28, 1919; House 1883–87.

Haynes, William Elisha (cousin of George William Palmer) (D Ohio) Oct. 19, 1829–Dec. 5, 1914; House 1889–93.

Hays, Charles (R Ala.) Feb. 2, 1834–June 24, 1879; House 1869–77.

Hays, Edward Dixon (R Mo.) April 28, 1872–July 25, 1941; House 1919–23.

Hays, Edward Retilla (R Iowa) May 26, 1847–Feb. 28, 1896; House Nov. 4, 1890–91.

Hays, Lawrence Brooks (D Ark.) Aug. 9, 1898–Oct. 11, 1981; House 1943–59.

Hays, Samuel (D Pa.) Sept. 10, 1783–July 1, 1868; House 1843–45.

Hays, Samuel Lewis (D Va.) Oct. 20, 1794–March 17, 1871; House 1841–43.

Hays, Wayne Levere (D Ohio) May 13, 1911–Feb. 10, 1989; House 1949–Sept. 1, 1976; chair House Administration 1971–76.

Hayward, Monroe Leland (R Neb.) Dec. 22, 1840–Dec. 5, 1899; elected to the Senate March 8, 1899, to fill vacancy but died before qualifying.

Hayward, William Jr. (– Md.) 1787–Oct. 19, 1836; House 1823–25.

Haywood, William Henry Jr. (D N.C.) Oct. 23, 1801–Oct. 7, 1852; Senate 1843–July 25, 1846.

Hayworth, Donald (D Mich.) Jan. 13, 1898–Feb. 25, 1982; House 1955–57.

Hayworth, J. D. (R Ariz.) July 12, 1958– ; House 1995– .

Hazard, Nathaniel (– R.I.) 1776–Dec. 17, 1820; House 1819–Dec. 17, 1820.

Hazeltine, Abner (W N.Y.) June 10, 1793–Dec. 20, 1879; House 1833–37 (1833–35 Anti-Mason).

Hazeltine, Ira Sherwin (G Mo.) July 13, 1821–Jan. 13, 1899; House 1881–83.

Hazelton, George Cochrane (brother of Gerry Whiting Hazelton, nephew of Clark Betton Cochrane) (R Wis.) Jan. 3, 1832–Sept. 4, 1922; House 1877–83.

Hazelton, Gerry Whiting (brother of George Cochrane Hazelton, nephew of Clark Betton Cochrane) (R Wis.) Feb. 24, 1829–Sept. 29, 1920; House 1871–75.

Hazelton, John Wright (R N.J.) Dec. 10, 1814–Dec. 20, 1878; House 1871–75.

Hazlett, James Miller (R Pa.) Oct. 14, 1864–Nov. 8, 1941; House March 4–Oct. 20, 1927.

Heald, William Henry (R Del.) Aug. 27, 1864–June 3, 1939; House 1909–13.

Healey, Arthur Daniel (D Mass.) Dec. 29, 1889–Sept. 16, 1948; House 1933–Aug. 3, 1942.

Healey, James Christopher (D N.Y.) Dec. 24, 1909–Dec. 16, 1981; House Feb. 7, 1956–65.

Healy, Joseph (– N.H.) Aug. 21, 1776–Oct. 10, 1861; House 1825–29.

Healy, Ned Romeyn (D Calif.) Aug. 9, 1905–Sept. 10, 1977; House 1945–47.

Heard, John Thaddeus (D Mo.) Oct. 29, 1840–Jan. 27, 1927; House 1885–95.

Hearst, George (father of William Randolph Hearst) (D Calif.) Sept. 3, 1820–Feb. 28, 1891; Senate March 23–Aug. 4, 1886, 1887–Feb. 28, 1891.

Hearst, William Randolph (son of George Hearst) (D N.Y.) April 29, 1863–Aug. 14, 1951; House 1903–07.

Heath, James P. (J Md.) Dec. 21, 1777–June 12, 1854; House 1833–35.

Heath, John (R Va.) May 8, 1758–Oct. 13, 1810; House 1793–97.

Heaton, David (R N.C.) March 10, 1823–June 25, 1870; House July 15, 1868–June 25, 1870.

Heaton, Robert Douglas (R Pa.) July 1, 1873–June 11, 1933; House 1915–19.

Heatwole, Joel Prescott (R Minn.) Aug. 22, 1856–April 4, 1910; House 1895–1903.

Hebard, William (W Vt.) Nov. 29, 1800–Oct. 20, 1875; House 1849–53.

Hebert, Felix (R R.I.) Dec. 11, 1874–Dec. 14, 1969; Senate 1929–35.

Hebert, Felix Edward (D La.) Oct. 12, 1901–Dec. 29, 1979; House 1941–77; chair House Armed Services 1971–75.

Hechler, Ken (D W.Va.) Sept. 20, 1914– ; House 1959–77.

Hecht, Jacob Chic (R Nev.) Nov. 30, 1928– ; Senate 1983–89.

Heckler, Margaret Mary O'Shaughnessy (R Mass.) June 21, 1931– ; House 1967–83; secretary health and human services March 9, 1983–Dec. 13, 1985.

Hedge, Thomas (R Iowa) June 24, 1844–Nov. 28, 1920; House 1899–1907.

Hedrick, Erland Harold (D W.Va.) Aug. 9, 1894–Sept. 20, 1954; House 1945–53.

Heffernan, James Joseph (D N.Y.) Nov. 8, 1888–Jan. 27, 1967; House 1941–53.

Hefley, Joel M. (R Colo.) April 18, 1935– ; House 1987– ; chair House Standards of Official Conduct 2001–05.

Heflin, Howell Thomas (nephew of James Thomas Heflin) (D Ala.) June 19, 1921– ; Senate 1979–97; chair Senate Select Ethics 1987–91.

Heflin, James Thomas (uncle of Howell Thomas Heflin, nephew of Robert Stell Heflin) (D Ala.) April 9, 1869–April 22, 1951; House May 10, 1904–Nov. 1, 1920; Senate Nov. 3, 1920–31.

Heflin, Robert Stell (uncle of James Thomas Heflin) (R Ala.) April 15, 1815–Jan. 24, 1901; House 1869–71.

Hefner, Willie Gathrel "Bill" (D N.C.) April 11, 1930– ; House 1975–99.

Heftel, Cecil Landau (D Hawaii) Sept. 30, 1924– ; House 1977–July 11, 1986.

Heidinger, James Vandaveer (R Ill.) July 17, 1882–March 22, 1945; House 1941–March 22, 1945.

Heilman, William (great-grandfather of Charles Marion La Follette) (R Ind.) Oct. 11, 1824–Sept. 22, 1890; House 1879–83.

Heineman, Fred (R N.C.) Dec. 28, 1929– ; House 1995–97.

Heiner, Daniel Brodhead (R Pa.) Dec. 30, 1854–Feb. 14, 1944; House 1893–97.

Heinke, George Henry (R Neb.) July 22, 1882–Jan. 2, 1940; House 1939–Jan. 2, 1940.

Heintz, Victor (R Ohio) Nov. 20, 1876–Dec. 27, 1968; House 1917–19.

Heinz, Henry John III (R Pa.) Oct. 23, 1938–April 4, 1991; House Nov. 2, 1971–77; Senate 1977–April 4, 1991.

Heiskell, John Netherland (D Ark.) Nov. 2, 1872–Dec. 28, 1972; Senate Jan. 6–Jan. 29, 1913.

Heitfeld, Henry (P Idaho) Jan. 12, 1859–Oct. 21, 1938; Senate 1897–1903.

Helgesen, Henry Thomas (R N.D.) June 26, 1857–April 10, 1917; House 1911–April 10, 1917.

Heller, Louis Benjamin (D N.Y.) Feb. 10, 1905–Oct. 30, 1993; House Feb. 15, 1949–July 21, 1954.

Helm, Harvey (D Ky.) Dec. 2, 1865–March 3, 1919; House 1907–March 3, 1919.

Helmick, William (R Ohio) Sept. 6, 1817–March 31, 1888; House 1859–61.

Helms, Jesse Alexander (R N.C.) Oct. 18, 1921– ; Senate 1973–2003; chair Senate Agriculture, Nutrition, and Forestry 1981–87; chair Senate Foreign Relations 1995–Jan. 3, 2001, Jan. 20, 2001–June 6, 2001.

Helms, William (R N.J.) ?–1813; House 1801–11.

Helstoski, Henry (D N.J.) March 21, 1925–Dec. 16, 1999; House 1965–77.

Helvering, Guy Tresillian (D Kan.) Jan. 10, 1878–July 4, 1946; House 1913–19.

Hemenway, James Alexander (R Ind.) March 8, 1860–Feb. 10, 1923; House 1895–1905; Senate March 4, 1905–09.

Hemphill, John (uncle of John James Hemphill, great-great-uncle of Robert Witherspoon Hemphill) (SRD Texas) Dec. 18, 1803–Jan. 4, 1862; Senate 1859–July 1861.

Hemphill, John James (cousin of William Huggins Brawley, nephew of John Hemphill, great-uncle of Robert Witherspoon Hemphill) (D S.C.) Aug. 25, 1849–May 11, 1912; House 1883–93.

Hemphill, Joseph (J Pa.) Jan. 7, 1770–May 29, 1842; House 1801–03 (Federalist), 1819–26 (Federalist), 1829–31.

Hemphill, Robert Witherspoon (great-great-nephew of John Hemphill, great-nephew of John James Hemphill and William Huggins Brawley, great-great-grandson of Robert Witherspoon) (D S.C.) May 10, 1915–Dec. 25, 1983; House 1957–May 1, 1964.

Hempstead, Edward (– Mo.) June 3, 1780–Aug. 10, 1817; House (Terr. Del.) Nov. 9, 1812–Sept. 17, 1814.

Hendee, George Whitman (R Vt.) Nov. 30, 1832–Dec. 6, 1906; House 1873–79; Gov. Feb. 7–Oct. 6, 1870.

Henderson, Archibald (F N.C.) Aug. 7, 1768–Oct. 21, 1822; House 1799–1803.

Henderson, Bennett H. (R Tenn.) Sept. 5, 1784–?; House 1815–17.

Henderson, Charles Belknap (D Nev.) June 8, 1873–Nov. 8, 1954; Senate Jan. 12, 1918–21.

Henderson, David Bremner (R Iowa) March 14, 1840–Feb. 25, 1906; House 1883–1903; Speaker Dec. 4, 1899–1901, Dec. 2, 1901–03.

Henderson, David Newton (D N.C.) April 16, 1921–Jan. 13, 2004; House 1961–77; chair House Post Office and Civil Service 1975–77.

Henderson, James Henry Dickey (UR Ore.) July 23, 1810–Dec. 13, 1885; House 1865–67.

Henderson, James Pinckney (D Texas) March 31, 1808–June 4, 1858; Senate Nov. 9, 1857–June 4, 1858; Gov. Feb. 19, 1846–Dec. 21, 1847.

Henderson, John (W Miss.) Feb. 28, 1797–Sept. 15, 1857; Senate 1839–45.

Henderson, John Brooks (U Mo.) Nov. 16, 1826–April 12, 1913; Senate Jan. 17, 1862–69.

Henderson, John Earl (R Ohio) Jan. 4, 1917–Dec. 3, 1994; House 1955–61.

Henderson, John Steele (D N.C.) Jan. 6, 1846–Oct. 9, 1916; House 1885–95.

Henderson, Joseph (J Pa.) Aug. 2, 1791–Dec. 25, 1863; House 1833–37.

Henderson, Samuel (F Pa.) Nov. 27, 1764–Nov. 17, 1841; House Oct. 11, 1814–15.

Henderson, Thomas (F N.J.) Aug. 15, 1743–Dec. 15, 1824; House 1795–97; Cont. Cong. (elected but did not attend) 1779; Gov. March 30–June 3, 1793.

Henderson, Thomas Jefferson (R Ill.) Nov. 29, 1824–Feb. 6, 1911; House 1875–95.

Hendon, William Martin (R N.C.) Nov. 9, 1944– ; House 1981–83, 1985–87.

Hendrick, John Kerr (D Ky.) Oct. 10, 1849–June 20, 1921; House 1895–97.

Hendricks, Joseph Edward (D Fla.) Sept. 24, 1903–Oct. 20, 1974; House 1937–49.

Hendricks, Thomas Andrews (nephew of William Hendricks) (D Ind.) Sept. 7, 1819–Nov. 25, 1885; House 1851–55; Senate 1863–69; Gov. Jan. 13, 1873–Jan. 8, 1877; vice president Nov. 4–Nov. 25, 1885.

Hendricks, William (uncle of Thomas Andrews Hendricks) (– Ind.) Nov. 12, 1782–May 16, 1850; House Dec. 11, 1816–July 25, 1822; Senate 1825–37; Gov. Dec. 5, 1822–Feb. 12, 1825 (Democratic Republican).

Hendrickson, Robert Clymer (R N.J.) Aug. 12, 1898–Dec. 7, 1964; Senate 1949–55.

Hendrix, Joseph Clifford (D N.Y.) May 25, 1853–Nov. 9, 1904; House 1893–95.

Henkle, Eli Jones (D Md.) Nov. 24, 1828–Nov. 1, 1893; House 1875–81.

Henley, Barclay (son of Thomas Jefferson Henley) (D Calif.) March 17, 1843–Feb. 15, 1914; House 1883–87.

Henley, Thomas Jefferson (father of Barclay Henley) (D Ind.) April 2, 1810–Jan. 2, 1865; House 1843–49.

Henn, Bernhart (D Iowa) 1817–Aug. 30, 1865; House 1851–55.

Henney, Charles William Francis (D Wis.) Feb. 2, 1884–Nov. 16, 1969; House 1933–35.

Hennings, Thomas Carey Jr. (D Mo.) June 25, 1903–Sept. 13, 1960; House 1935–Dec. 31, 1940; Senate 1951–Sept. 13, 1960; chair Senate Rules and Administration 1957–60.

Henry, Charles Lewis (R Ind.) July 1, 1849–May 2, 1927; House 1895–99.

Henry, Daniel Maynadier (D Md.) Feb. 19, 1823–Aug. 31, 1899; House 1877–81.

Henry, Edward Stevens (R Conn.) Feb. 10, 1836–Oct. 10, 1921; House 1895–1913.

Henry, John (– Md.) Nov. 1750–Dec. 16, 1798; Senate 1789–Dec. 10, 1797; Gov. Nov. 17, 1797–Nov. 14, 1798; Cont. Cong. 1778–80, 1785–86.

Henry, John (W Ill.) Nov. 1, 1800–April 28, 1882; House Feb. 5–March 3, 1847.

Henry, John Flournoy (– Ky.) Jan. 17, 1793–Nov. 12, 1873; House Dec. 11, 1826–27.

Henry, Lewis (R N.Y.) June 8, 1885–July 23, 1941; House April 11, 1922–23.

Henry, Patrick (uncle of Patrick Henry, below) (D Miss.) Feb. 12, 1843–May 18, 1930; House 1897–1901.

Henry, Patrick (nephew of Patrick Henry, above) (D Miss.) Feb. 15, 1861–Dec. 28, 1933; House 1901–03.

Henry, Paul Brentwood (R Mich.) July 9, 1942–July 31, 1993; House 1985–July 31, 1993.

Henry, Robert Kirkland (R Wis.) Feb. 9, 1890–Nov. 20, 1946; House 1945–Nov. 20, 1946.

Henry, Robert Lee (D Texas) May 12, 1864–July 9, 1931; House 1897–1917.

Henry, Robert Pryor (– Ky.) Nov. 24, 1788–Aug. 25, 1826; House 1823–Aug. 25, 1826.

Henry, Thomas (W Pa.) 1779–July 20, 1849; House 1837–43 (1837–41 AMas.).

Henry, William (W Vt.) March 22, 1788–April 16, 1861; House 1847–51.

Henry, Winder Laird (great-grandson of Charles Goldsborough and Robert Henry Goldsborough) (D Md.) Dec. 20, 1864–July 5, 1940; House Nov. 6, 1894–95.

Hensarling, Jeb (R Texas) May 29, 1957– ; House 2003– .

Hensley, Walter Lewis (D Mo.) Sept. 3, 1871–July 18, 1946; House 1911–19.

Hepburn, William Peters (great-grandson of Matthew Lyon) (R Iowa) Nov. 4, 1833–Feb. 7, 1916; House 1881–87, 1893–1909.

Herbert, Hilary Abner (D Ala.) March 12, 1834–March 6, 1919; House 1877–93; secretary of the navy March 7, 1893–March 5, 1897.

Herbert, John Carlyle (F Md.) Aug. 16, 1775–Sept. 1, 1846; House 1815–19.

Herbert, Philemon Thomas (D Calif.) Nov. 1, 1825–July 23, 1864; House 1855–57.

Hereford, Frank (D W.Va.) July 4, 1825–Dec. 21, 1891; House 1871–Jan. 31, 1877; Senate Jan. 31, 1877–81.

Herger, Walter William "Wally" (R Calif.) May 20, 1945– ; House 1987– .

Herkimer, John (R N.Y.) 1773–June 8, 1848; House 1817–19, 1823–25.

Herlong, Albert Sydney Jr. (D Fla.) Feb. 14, 1909–Dec. 27, 1995; House 1949–69.

Hermann, Binger (R Ore.) Feb. 19, 1843–April 15, 1926; House 1885–97, June 1, 1903–07.

Hernandez, Benigno Cardenas (R N.M.) Feb. 13, 1862–Oct. 18, 1954; House 1915–17, 1919–21.

Hernandez, Joseph Marion (– Fla.) Aug. 4, 1793–June 8, 1857; House (Terr. Del.) Sept. 30, 1822–23.

Herndon, Thomas Hord (D Ala.) July 1, 1828–March 28, 1883; House 1879–March 28, 1883.

Herndon, William Smith (D Texas) Nov. 27, 1835–Oct. 11, 1903; House 1871–75.

Herod, William (W Ind.) March 31, 1801–Oct. 20, 1871; House Jan. 25, 1837–39.

Herrick, Anson (son of Ebenezer Herrick) (D N.Y.) Jan. 21, 1812–Feb. 6, 1868; House 1863–65.

Herrick, Ebenezer (father of Anson Herrick) (– Maine) Oct. 21, 1785–May 7, 1839; House 1821–27.

Herrick, Joshua (D Maine) March 18, 1793–Aug. 30, 1874; House 1843–45.

Herrick, Manuel (R Okla.) Sept. 20, 1876–Feb. 29, 1952; House 1921–23.

Herrick, Richard Platt (W N.Y.) March 23, 1791–June 20, 1846; House 1845–June 20, 1846.

Herrick, Samuel (R Ohio) April 14, 1779–June 4, 1852; House 1817–21.

Herring, Clyde LaVerne (D Iowa) May 3, 1879–Sept. 15, 1945; Senate Jan. 15, 1937–43; Gov. Jan. 12, 1933–Jan. 14, 1937.

Herseth, Stephanie (granddaughter of Gov. Ralph E. Herseth of S.D.) (D S.D.) Dec. 3, 1970– ; House June 3, 2004– .

Hersey, Ira Greenlief (R Maine) March 31, 1858–May 6, 1943; House 1917–29.

Hersey, Samuel Freeman (R Maine) April 12, 1812–Feb. 3, 1875; House 1873–Feb. 3, 1875.

Hersman, Hugh Steel (D Calif.) July 8, 1872–March 7, 1954; House 1919–21.

Hertel, Dennis Mark (D Mich.) Dec. 7, 1948– ; House 1981–93.

Herter, Christian Archibald (R Mass.) March 28, 1895–Dec. 30, 1966; House 1943–53; Gov. Jan. 8, 1953–Jan. 3, 1957; secretary of state April 22, 1959–Jan. 20, 1961.

Heselton, John Walter (R Mass.) March 17, 1900–Aug. 19, 1962; House 1945–59.

Hess, William Emil (R Ohio) Feb. 13, 1898–July 14, 1986; House 1929–37, 1939–49, 1951–61.

Hewitt, Abram Stevens (D N.Y.) July 31, 1822–Jan. 18, 1903; House 1875–79, 1881–Dec. 30, 1886; chair Dem. Nat. Comm. 1876–77.

Hewitt, Goldsmith Whitehouse (D Ala.) Feb. 14, 1834–May 27, 1895; House 1875–79, 1881–85.

Heyburn, Weldon Brinton (R Idaho) May 23, 1852–Oct. 17, 1912; Senate 1903–Oct. 17, 1912.

Hibbard, Ellery Albee (cousin of Harry Hibbard) (D N.H.) July 31, 1826–July 24, 1903; House 1871–73.

Hibbard, Harry (cousin of Ellery Albee Hibbard) (D N.H.) June 1, 1816–July 28, 1872; House 1849–55.

Hibshman, Jacob (– Pa.) Jan. 31, 1772–May 19, 1852; House 1819–21.

Hickenlooper, Bourke Blakemore (R Iowa) July 21, 1896–Sept. 4, 1971; Senate 1945–69; Gov. Jan. 14, 1943–Jan. 11, 1945.

Hickey, Andrew James (R Ind.) Aug. 27, 1872–Aug. 20, 1942; House 1919–31.

Hickey, John Joseph (D Wyo.) Aug. 22, 1911–Sept. 22, 1970; Senate 1961–Nov. 6, 1962; Gov. Jan. 5, 1959–Jan. 2, 1961.

Hickman, John (R Pa.) Sept. 11, 1810–March 23, 1875; House 1855–63 (1855–59 Democrat, 1859–61 Anti-Lecompton Democrat).

Hicks, Floyd Verne (D Wash.) May 29, 1915– ; House 1965–77.

Hicks, Frederick Cocks (original name Frederick Hicks Cocks, brother of William Willets Cocks) (R N.Y.) March 6, 1872–Dec. 14, 1925; House 1915–23.

Hicks, Josiah Duane (R Pa.) Aug. 1, 1844–May 9, 1923; House 1893–99.

Hicks, Louise Day (D Mass.) Oct. 16, 1923–Oct. 21, 2003; House 1971–73.

Hicks, Thomas Holliday (U Md.) Sept. 2, 1798–Feb. 14, 1865; Senate Dec. 29, 1862–Feb. 14, 1865; Gov. Jan. 13, 1858–Jan. 8, 1862 (American Party).

Hiestand, Edgar Willard (R Calif.) Dec. 3, 1888–Aug. 19, 1970; House 1953–63.

Hiestand, John Andrew (R Pa.) Oct. 2, 1824–Dec. 13, 1890; House 1885–89.

Hiester, Daniel (brother of John Hiester, cousin of Joseph Hiester, uncle of William Hiester and Daniel Hiester, below) (R Md.) June 25, 1747–March 7, 1804; House 1789–July 1, 1796 (no party Pa.), 1801–March 7, 1804.

Hiester, Daniel (son of John Hiester, nephew of Daniel Hiester, above) (– Pa.) 1774–March 8, 1834; House 1809–11.

Hiester, Isaac Ellmaker (son of William Hiester, cousin of Hiester Clymer) (W Pa.) May 29, 1824–Feb. 6, 1871; House 1853–55.

Hiester, John (father of Daniel Hiester born in 1774, brother of Daniel Hiester born in 1747, cousin of Joseph Hiester, uncle of William Hiester) (R Pa.) April 9, 1745–Oct. 15, 1821; House 1807–09.

Hiester, Joseph (cousin of John Hiester and Daniel Hiester born in 1747, grandfather of Henry Augustus Muhlenberg) (R Pa.) Nov. 18, 1752–June 10, 1832; House Dec. 1, 1797–1805, 1815–Dec.

1820; Gov. Dec. 19, 1820–Dec. 16, 1823 (Democratic Republican).

Hiester, William (father of Isaac Ellmaker Hiester, uncle of Hiester Clymer, nephew of John Hiester and Daniel Hiester born in 1747) (AMas. Pa.) Oct. 10, 1790–Oct. 13, 1853; House 1831–37.

Higby, William (R Calif.) Aug. 18, 1813–Nov. 27, 1887; House 1863–69.

Higgins, Anthony (R Del.) Oct. 1, 1840–June 26, 1912; Senate 1889–95.

Higgins, Brian M. (D N.Y.) Oct. 6, 1959– ; House 2005– .

Higgins, Edwin Werter (R Conn.) July 2, 1874–Sept. 24, 1954; House Oct. 2, 1905–13.

Higgins, John Patrick (D Mass.) Feb. 19, 1893–Aug. 2, 1955; House 1935–Sept. 30, 1937.

Higgins, William Lincoln (R Conn.) March 8, 1867–Nov. 19, 1951; House 1933–37.

Hightower, Jack English (D Texas) Sept. 6, 1926– ; House 1975–85.

Hilborn, Samuel Greeley (R Calif.) Dec. 9, 1834–April 19, 1899; House Dec. 5, 1892–April 4, 1894, 1895–99.

Hildebrandt, Fred Herman (D S.D.) Aug. 2, 1874–Jan. 26, 1956; House 1933–39.

Hildebrant, Charles Quinn (R Ohio) Oct. 17, 1864–March 31, 1953; House 1901–05.

Hiler, John Patrick (R Ind.) April 24, 1953– ; House 1981–91.

Hill, Baron (D Ind.) June 23, 1953– ; House 1999–2005.

Hill, Benjamin Harvey (cousin of Hugh Lawson White Hill) (D Ga.) Sept. 14, 1823–Aug. 16, 1882; House May 5, 1875–77; Senate 1877–Aug. 16, 1882.

Hill, Charles Augustus (R Ill.) Aug. 23, 1833–May 29, 1902; House 1889–91.

Hill, Clement Sidney (W Ky.) Feb. 13, 1813–Jan. 5, 1892; House 1853–55.

Hill, David Bennett (D N.Y.) Aug. 29, 1843–Oct. 20, 1910; Senate Jan. 7, 1892–97; Gov. Jan. 6, 1885–Jan. 1, 1892.

Hill, Ebenezer J. (R Conn.) Aug. 4, 1845–Sept. 27, 1917; House 1895–1913, 1915–Sept. 27, 1917.

Hill, Hugh Lawson White (cousin of Benjamin Harvey Hill) (D Tenn.) March 1, 1810–Jan. 18, 1892; House 1847–49.

Hill, Isaac (J N.H.) April 6, 1788–March 22, 1851; Senate 1831–May 30, 1836; Gov. June 2, 1836–June 5, 1839.

Hill, John (D N.C.) April 9, 1797–April 24, 1861; House 1839–41.

Hill, John (cousin of John Thomas Harris) (W Va.) July 18, 1800–April 19, 1880; House 1839–41.

Hill, John (R N.J.) June 10, 1821–July 24, 1884; House 1867–73, 1881–83.

Hill, John Boynton Philip Clayton (R Md.) May 2, 1879–May 23, 1941; House 1921–27.

Hill, Joseph Lister (D Ala.) Dec. 29, 1894–Dec. 21, 1984; House Aug. 14, 1923–Jan. 11, 1938; Senate Jan. 11, 1938–Jan. 2, 1969; chair Senate Labor and Public Welfare 1955–69.

Hill, Joshua (R Ga.) Jan. 10, 1812–March 6, 1891; House 1857–Jan. 23, 1861 (American Party); Senate Feb. 1, 1871–73.

Hill, Knute (D Wash.) July 31, 1876–Dec. 3, 1963; House 1933–43.

Hill, Mark Langdon (– Maine) June 30, 1772–Nov. 26, 1842; House 1819–21 (Mass.), 1821–23.

Hill, Nathaniel Peter (R Colo.) Feb. 18, 1832–May 22, 1900; Senate 1879–85.

Hill, Ralph (R Ind.) Oct. 12, 1827–Aug. 20, 1899; House 1865–67.

Hill, Rick (R Mont.) Dec. 30, 1946– ; House 1997–2001.

Hill, Robert Potter (D Okla.) April 18, 1874–Oct. 29, 1937; House 1913–15 (Ill.), Jan. 3–Oct. 29, 1937.

Hill, Samuel Billingsley (D Wash.) April 2, 1875–March 16, 1958; House Sept. 25, 1923–June 25, 1936.

Hill, William David (D Ohio) Oct. 1, 1833–Dec. 26, 1906; House 1879–81, 1883–87.

Hill, William Henry (F N.C.) May 1, 1767–1809; House 1799–1803.

Hill, William Henry (R N.Y.) March 23, 1877–July 24, 1972; House 1919–21.

Hill, William Luther (D Fla.) Oct. 17, 1873–Jan. 5, 1951; Senate July 1–Nov. 3, 1936.

Hill, William Silas (R Colo.) Jan. 20, 1886–Aug. 28, 1972; House 1941–59; chair House Select Small Business 1953–55.

Hill, Wilson Shedric (D Miss.) Jan. 19, 1863–Feb. 14, 1921; House 1903–09.

Hilleary, Van (R Tenn.) June 20, 1959– ; House 1995–2003.

Hillelson, Jeffrey Paul (R Mo.) March 9, 1919–May 28, 2003; House 1953–55.

Hillen, Solomon Jr. (D Md.) July 10, 1810–June 26, 1873; House 1839–41.

Hillhouse, James (– Conn.) Oct. 20, 1754–Dec. 29, 1832; House 1791–96; Senate Dec. 1796–June 10, 1810; elected pres. pro tempore Feb. 28, 1801; Cont. Cong. (elected but did not attend) 1786, 1788.

Hilliard, Benjamin Clark (D Colo.) Jan. 9, 1868–Aug. 7, 1951; House 1915–19.

Hilliard, Earl Frederick (D Ala.) April 9, 1942– ; House 1993–2003.

Hilliard, Henry Washington (W Ala.) Aug. 4, 1808–Dec. 17, 1892; House 1845–51.

Hillings, Patrick Jerome (R Calif.) Feb. 19, 1923–July 20, 1994; House 1951–59.

Hillis, Elwood Haynes (R Ind.) March 6, 1926– ; House 1971–87.

Hillyer, Junius (D Ga.) April 23, 1807–June 21, 1886; House 1851–55 (1851–53 Unionist).

Himes, Joseph Hendrix (R Ohio) Aug. 15, 1885–Sept. 9, 1960; House 1921–23.

Hinchey, Maurice D. (D N.Y.) Oct. 27, 1938– ; House 1993– .

Hindman, Thomas Carmichael (D Ark.) Jan. 28, 1828–Sept. 27, 1868; House 1859–61.

Hindman, William (F Md.) April 1, 1743–Jan. 19, 1822; House Jan. 30, 1793–99 (no party); Senate Dec. 12, 1800–Nov. 19, 1801; Cont. Cong. 1785–88.

Hinds, Asher Crosby (R Maine) Feb. 6, 1863–May 1, 1919; House 1911–17.

Hinds, James (R Ark.) Dec. 5, 1833–Oct. 22, 1868; House June 22–Oct. 22, 1868.

Hinds, Thomas (D Miss.) Jan. 9, 1780–Aug. 23, 1840; House Oct. 21, 1828–31.

Hinebaugh, William Henry (Prog. Ill.) Dec. 16, 1867–Sept. 22, 1943; House 1913–15.

Hines, Richard (– N.C.) ?–Nov. 20, 1851; House 1825–27.

Hines, William Henry (D Pa.) March 15, 1856–Jan. 17, 1914; House 1893–95.

Hinojosa, Ruben (D Texas) Aug. 20, 1940– ; House 1997– .

Hinrichsen, William Henry (D Ill.) May 27, 1850–Dec. 18, 1907; House 1897–99.

Hinshaw, Andrew Jackson (R Calif.) Aug. 4, 1923– ; House 1973–77.

Hinshaw, Edmund Howard (cousin of Edwin Bruce Brooks) (R Neb.) Dec. 8, 1860–June 15, 1932; House 1903–11.

Hinshaw, John Carl Williams (R Calif.) July 28, 1894–Aug. 5, 1956; House 1939–Aug. 5, 1956.

Hinson, Jon Clifton (R Miss.) March 16, 1942–July 21, 1995; House 1979–April 13, 1981.

Hires, George (R N.J.) Jan. 26, 1835–Feb. 16, 1911; House 1885–89.

Hiscock, Frank (R N.Y.) Sept. 6, 1834–June 18, 1914; House 1877–87; Senate 1887–93.

Hise, Elijah (D Ky.) July 4, 1802–May 8, 1867; House Dec. 3, 1866–May 8, 1867.

Hitchcock, Gilbert Monell (son of Phineas Warrener Hitchcock) (D Neb.) Sept. 18, 1859–Feb. 3, 1934; House 1903–05, 1907–11; Senate 1911–23.

Hitchcock, Herbert Emery (D S.D.) Aug. 22, 1867–Feb. 17, 1958; Senate Dec. 29, 1936–Nov. 8, 1938.

Hitchcock, Peter (– Ohio) Oct. 19, 1781–March 4, 1854; House 1817–19.

Hitchcock, Phineas Warrener (father of Gilbert Monell Hitchcock) (R Neb.) Nov. 30, 1831–July 10, 1881; House (Terr. Del.) 1865–March 1, 1867; Senate 1871–77.

Hitt, Robert Roberts (R Ill.) Jan. 16, 1834–Sept. 20, 1906; House Nov. 7, 1882–Sept. 20, 1906.

Hoag, Truman Harrison (D Ohio) April 9, 1816–Feb. 5, 1870; House 1869–Feb. 5, 1870.

Hoagland, Moses (D Ohio) June 19, 1812–April 16, 1865; House 1849–51.

Hoagland, Peter (D Neb.) Nov. 17, 1941– ; House 1989–95.

Hoar, Ebenezer Rockwood (son of Samuel Hoar, brother of George Frisbie Hoar, father of Sherman Hoar, uncle of Rockwood Hoar) (R Mass.) Feb. 21, 1816–Jan. 31, 1895; House 1873–75; attorney general March 5, 1869–June 23, 1870.

Hoar, George Frisbie (son of Samuel Hoar, brother of Ebenezer Rockwood Hoar, father of Rockwood Hoar, uncle of Sherman Hoar) (R Mass.) Aug. 29, 1826–Sept. 30, 1904; House 1869–77; Senate 1877–Sept. 30, 1904.

Hoar, Rockwood (son of George Frisbie Hoar, nephew of Ebenezer Rockwood Hoar, cousin of Sherman Hoar, grandson of Samuel Hoar) (R Mass.) Aug. 24, 1855–Nov. 1, 1906; House March 1, 1905–Nov. 1, 1906.

Hoar, Samuel (father of Ebenezer Rockwood Hoar and George Frisbie Hoar, grandfather of Sherman Hoar and Rockwood Hoar) (W Mass.) May 18, 1778–Nov. 2, 1856; House 1835–37.

Hoar, Sherman (son of Ebenezer Rockwood Hoar, nephew of George Frisbee Hoar, cousin of Rockwood Hoar, grandson of Samuel Hoar) (D Mass.) July 30, 1860–Oct. 7, 1898; House 1891–93.

Hoard, Charles Brooks (R N.Y.) June 5, 1805–Nov. 20, 1886; House 1857–61.

Hobart, Aaron (– Mass.) June 26, 1787–Sept. 19, 1858; House Nov. 24, 1820–27.

Hobart, John Sloss (F N.Y.) May 6, 1738–Feb. 4, 1805; Senate Jan. 11–April 16, 1798.

Hobbie, Selah Reeve (J N.Y.) March 10, 1797–March 23, 1854; House 1827–29.

Hobbs, Samuel Francis (D Ala.) Oct. 5, 1887–May 31, 1952; House 1935–51.

Hoblitzell, Fetter Schrier (D Md.) Oct. 7, 1838–May 2, 1900; House 1881–85.

Hoblitzell, John Dempsey Jr. (R W.Va.) Dec. 30, 1912–Jan. 6, 1962; Senate Jan. 25–Nov. 4, 1958.

Hobson, David Lee (R Ohio) Oct. 17, 1936– ; House 1991– .

Hobson, Richmond Pearson (D Ala.) Aug. 17, 1870–March 16, 1937; House 1907–15.

Hoch, Daniel Knabb (D Pa.) Jan. 31, 1866–Oct. 11, 1960; House 1943–47.

Hoch, Homer (R Kan.) July 4, 1879–Jan. 30, 1949; House 1919–33.

Hochbrueckner, George Joseph (D N.Y.) Sept. 20, 1938– ; House 1987–95.

Hodges, Asa (R Ark.) Jan. 22, 1822–June 6, 1900; House 1873–75.

Hodges, Charles Drury (D Ill.) Feb. 4, 1810–April 1, 1884; House Jan. 4–March 3, 1859.

Hodges, George Tisdale (R Vt.) July 4, 1789–Aug. 9, 1860; House Dec. 1, 1856–57.

Hodges, James Leonard (– Mass.) April 24, 1790–March 8, 1846; House 1827–33.

Hodges, Kaneaster Jr. (D Ark.) Aug. 20, 1928– ; Senate Dec. 10, 1977–79.

Hoeffel, Joseph M. III (D Pa.) Sept. 3, 1950– ; House 1999–2005.

Hoekstra, Peter (R Mich.) Oct. 30, 1953– ; House 1993– ; chair House Select Intelligence Aug. 25, 2004– .

Hoeppel, John Henry (D Calif.) Feb. 10, 1881–Sept. 21, 1976; House 1933–37.

Hoeven, Charles Bernard (R Iowa) March 30, 1895–Nov. 9, 1980; House 1943–65.

Hoey, Clyde Roark (D N.C.) Dec. 11, 1877–May 12, 1954; House Dec. 16, 1919–21; Senate 1945–May 12, 1954; Gov. Jan. 7, 1937–Jan. 9, 1941.

Hoffecker, John Henry (father of Walter Oakley Hoffecker) (R Del.) Sept. 12, 1827–June 16, 1900; House 1899–June 16, 1900.

Hoffecker, Walter Oakley (son of John Henry Hoffecker) (R Del.) Sept. 20, 1854–Jan. 23, 1934; House Nov. 6, 1900–01.

Hoffman, Carl Henry (R Pa.) Aug. 12, 1896–Nov. 30, 1980; House May 21, 1946–47.

Hoffman, Clare Eugene (R Mich.) Sept. 10, 1875–Nov. 3, 1967; House 1935–63; chair House Expenditures in the Executive Departments 1947–49; chair House Government Operations 1953–55.

Hoffman, Elmer Joseph (R Ill.) July 7, 1899–June 25, 1976; House 1959–65.

Hoffman, Harold Giles (R N.J.) Feb. 7, 1896–June 4, 1954; House 1927–31; Gov. Jan. 15, 1935–Jan. 18, 1938.

Hoffman, Henry William (AP Md.) Nov. 10, 1825–July 28, 1895; House 1855–57.

Hoffman, Josiah Ogden (W N.Y.) May 3, 1793–May 1, 1856; House 1837–41.

Hoffman, Michael (J N.Y.) Oct. 11, 1787–Sept. 27, 1848; House 1825–33 (1825–29 no party).

Hoffman, Richard William (R Ill.) Dec. 23, 1893–July 6, 1975; House 1949–57.

Hogan, Earl Lee (D Ind.) March 13, 1920– ; House 1959–61.

Hogan, John (D Mo.) Jan. 2, 1805–Feb. 5, 1892; House 1865–67.

Hogan, Lawrence Joseph (R Md.) Sept. 30, 1928– ; House 1969–75.

Hogan, Michael Joseph (R N.Y.) April 22, 1871–May 7, 1940; House 1921–23.

Hogan, William (J N.Y.) July 17, 1792–Nov. 25, 1874; House 1831–33.

Hoge, John (brother of William Hoge) (R Pa.) Sept. 10, 1760–Aug. 4, 1824; House Nov. 2, 1804–05.

Hoge, John Blair (D W.Va.) Feb. 2, 1825–March 1, 1896; House 1881–83.

Hoge, Joseph Pendleton (D Ill.) Dec. 15, 1810–Aug. 14, 1891; House 1843–47.

Hoge, Solomon Lafayette (R S.C.) July 11, 1836–Feb. 23, 1909; House April 8, 1869–71, 1875–77.

Hoge, William (brother of John Hoge) (R Pa.) 1762–Sept. 25, 1814; House 1801–Oct. 15, 1804, 1807–09.

Hogeboom, James Lawrence (– N.Y.) Aug. 25, 1766–Dec. 23, 1839; House 1823–25.

Hogg, Charles Edgar (father of Robert Lynn Hogg) (D W.Va.) Dec. 21, 1852–June 14, 1935; House 1887–89.

Hogg, David (R Ind.) Aug. 21, 1886–Oct. 23, 1973; House 1925–33.

Hogg, Herschel Millard (R Colo.) Nov. 21, 1853–Aug. 27, 1934; House 1903–07.

Hogg, Robert Lynn (son of Charles Edgar Hogg) (R W.Va.) Dec. 30, 1893–July 21, 1973; House Nov. 4, 1930–33.

Hogg, Samuel (R Tenn.) April 18, 1783–May 28, 1842; House 1817–19.

Hoidale, Einar (D Minn.) Aug. 17, 1870–Dec. 5, 1952; House 1933–35.

Hoke, Martin Rossiter (R Ohio) May 18, 1952– ; House 1993–97.

Holaday, William Perry (R Ill.) Dec. 14, 1882–Jan. 29, 1946; House 1923–33.

Holbrock, Greg John (D Ohio) June 21, 1906–Sept. 4, 1992; House 1941–43.

Holbrook, Edward Dexter (D Idaho) May 6, 1836–June 17, 1870; House (Terr. Del.) 1865–69.

Holcombe, George (– N.J.) March 1786–Jan. 14, 1828; House 1821–Jan. 14, 1828.

Holden, T. Timothy (D Pa.) March 5, 1957– ; House 1993– .

Holifield, Chester Earl (D Calif.) Dec. 3, 1903–Feb. 6, 1995; House 1943–Dec. 31, 1974; chair House Government Operations 1971–75.

Holladay, Alexander Richmond (D Va.) Sept. 18, 1811–Jan. 29, 1877; House 1849–53.

Holland, Cornelius (J Maine) July 9, 1783–June 2, 1870; House Dec. 6, 1830–33.

Holland, Edward Everett (D Va.) Feb. 26, 1861–Oct. 23, 1941; House 1911–21.

Holland, Elmer Joseph (D Pa.) Jan. 8, 1894–Aug. 9, 1968; House May 19, 1942–43, Jan. 24, 1956–Aug. 9, 1968.

Holland, James (R N.C.) 1754–May 19, 1823; House 1795–97, 1801–11.

Holland, Kenneth Lamar (D S.C.) Nov. 24, 1934– ; House 1975–83.

Holland, Spessard Lindsey (D Fla.) July 10, 1892–Nov. 6, 1971; Senate Sept. 25, 1946–71; Gov. Jan. 7, 1941–Jan. 2, 1945.

Holleman, Joel (D Va.) Oct. 1, 1799–Aug. 5, 1844; House 1839–40.

Hollenbeck, Harold Capistran (R N.J.) Dec. 29, 1938– ; House 1977–83.

Holley, John Milton (W N.Y.) Nov. 10, 1802–March 8, 1848; House 1847–March 8, 1848.

Holliday, Elias Selah (R Ind.) March 5, 1842–March 13, 1936; House 1901–09.

Hollings, Ernest Frederick (D S.C.) Jan. 1, 1922– ; Senate Nov. 9, 1966–2005; chair Senate Budget 1979–81; chair Senate Commerce, Science, and Transportation 1987–95, Jan. 3, 2001–Jan. 20, 2001, June 6, 2001–03; Gov. Jan. 20, 1959–Jan. 15, 1963.

Hollingsworth, David Adams (R Ohio) Nov. 21, 1844–Dec. 3, 1929; House 1909–11, 1915–19.

Hollis, Henry French (D N.H.) Aug. 30, 1869–July 7, 1949; Senate March 13, 1913–19.

Hollister, John Baker (R Ohio) Nov. 7, 1890–Jan. 4, 1979; House Nov. 3, 1931–37.

Holloway, Clyde Cecil (R La.) Nov. 28, 1943– ; House 1987–93.

Holloway, David Pierson (R Ind.) Dec. 7, 1809–Sept. 9, 1883; House 1855–57.

Holman, Rufus Cecil (R Ore.) Oct. 14, 1877–Nov. 27, 1959; Senate 1939–45.

Holman, William Steele (D Ind.) Sept. 6, 1822–April 22, 1897; House 1859–65, 1867–77, 1881–95, March 4–April 22, 1897.

Holmes, Adoniram Judson (R Iowa) March 2, 1842–Jan. 21, 1902; House 1883–89.

Holmes, Charles Horace (R N.Y.) Oct. 24, 1827–Oct. 2, 1874; House Dec. 6, 1870–71.

Holmes, David (R Miss.) March 10, 1770–Aug. 20, 1832; House 1797–1809 (no party Va.); Senate Aug. 30, 1820–Sept. 25, 1825; Gov. 1809–17 (Miss. Terr.), Dec. 10, 1817–Jan. 5, 1820, Jan. 7–July 25, 1826 (Democratic Republican).

Holmes, Elias Bellows (W N.Y.) May 22, 1807–July 31, 1866; House 1845–49.

Holmes, Gabriel (– N.C.) 1769–Sept. 26, 1829; House 1825–Sept. 26, 1829; Gov. Dec. 7, 1821–Dec. 7, 1824 (Democratic Republican).

Holmes, Isaac Edward (D S.C.) April 6, 1796–Feb. 24, 1867; House 1839–51.

Holmes, John (– Maine) March 14, 1773–July 7, 1843; House 1817–March 15, 1820 (Mass.); Senate June 13, 1820–27, Jan. 15, 1829–33.

Holmes, Otis Halbert (grandson of Dudley Chase Haskell) (R Wash.) Feb. 22, 1902–July 27, 1977; House 1943–59.

Holmes, Pehr Gustaf (R Mass.) April 9, 1881–Dec. 19, 1952; House 1931–47.

Holmes, Sidney Tracy (R N.Y.) Aug. 14, 1815–Jan. 16, 1890; House 1865–67.

Holmes, Uriel (F Conn.) Aug. 26, 1764–May 18, 1827; House 1817–18.

Holsey, Hopkins (D Ga.) Aug. 25, 1779–March 31, 1859; House Oct. 5, 1835–39 (Oct. 5, 1835–37 Jacksonian).

Holt, Hines (W Ga.) April 27, 1805–Nov. 4, 1865; House Feb. 1–March 3, 1841.

Holt, Joseph Franklin III (R Calif.) July 6, 1924–July 14, 1997; House 1953–61.

Holt, Marjorie Sewell (R Md.) Sept. 17, 1920– ; House 1973–87.

Holt, Orrin (D Conn.) March 13, 1792–June 20, 1855; House Dec. 5, 1836–39 (Dec. 5, 1836–37 Jacksonian).

Holt, Rush D. (son of Rush Dew Holt) (D N.J.) Oct. 15, 1948– ; House 1999– .

Holt, Rush Dew (father of Rush D. Holt) (D W.Va.) June 19, 1905–Feb. 8, 1955; Senate June 21, 1935–41.

Holten, Samuel (– Mass.) June 9, 1738–Jan. 2, 1816; House 1793–95; Cont. Cong. 1778–80, 1783–85, 1787.

Holton, Hart Benton (R Md.) Oct. 13, 1835–Jan. 4, 1907; House 1883–85.

Holtzman, Elizabeth (D N.Y.) Aug. 11, 1941– ; House 1973–81.

Holtzman, Lester (D N.Y.) June 1, 1913– ; House 1953–Dec. 31, 1961.

Honda, Michael M. (D Calif.) June 27, 1941– ; House 2001– .

Honeyman, Nan Wood (D Ore.) July 15, 1881–Dec. 10, 1970; House 1937–39.

Hood, George Ezekial (D N.C.) Jan. 25, 1875–March 8, 1960; House 1915–19.

Hook, Enos (D Pa.) Dec. 3, 1804–July 15, 1841; House 1839–April 18, 1841.

Hook, Frank Eugene (D Mich.) May 26, 1893–June 21, 1982; House 1935–43, 1945–47.

Hooker, Charles Edward (D Miss.) 1825–Jan. 8, 1914; House 1875–83, 1887–95, 1901–03.

Hooker, James Murray (D Va.) Oct. 29, 1873–Aug. 6, 1940; House Nov. 8, 1921–25.

Hooker, Warren Brewster (R N.Y.) Nov. 24, 1856–March 5, 1920; House 1891–Nov. 10, 1898.

Hooks, Charles (great-grandfather of William Julius Harris) (R N.C.) Feb. 20, 1768–Oct. 18, 1843; House Dec. 2, 1816–17, 1819–25.

Hooley, Darlene (D Ore.) April 4, 1939– ; House 1997– .

Hooper, Benjamin Stephen (Read. Va.) March 6, 1835–Jan. 17, 1898; House 1883–85.

Hooper, Joseph Lawrence (R Mich.) Dec. 22, 1877–Feb. 22, 1934; House Aug. 18, 1925–Feb. 22, 1934.

Hooper, Samuel (R Mass.) Feb. 3, 1808–Feb. 14, 1875; House Dec. 2, 1861–Feb. 14, 1875.

Hooper, William Henry (D Utah) Dec. 25, 1813–Dec. 30, 1882; House (Terr. Del.) 1859–61, 1865–73.

Hope, Clifford Ragsdale (R Kan.) June 9, 1893–May 16, 1970; House 1927–57; chair House Agriculture 1947–49, 1953–55.

Hopkins, Albert Cole (R Pa.) Sept. 15, 1837–June 9, 1911; House 1891–95.

Hopkins, Albert Jarvis (R Ill.) Aug. 15, 1846–Aug. 23, 1922; House Dec. 7, 1885–1903; Senate 1903–09.

Hopkins, Benjamin Franklin (R Wis.) April 22, 1829–Jan. 1, 1870; House 1867–Jan. 1, 1870.

Hopkins, David William (R Mo.) Oct. 31, 1897–Oct. 14, 1968; House Feb. 5, 1929–33.

Hopkins, Francis Alexander (D Ky.) May 27, 1853–June 5, 1918; House 1903–07.

Hopkins, George Washington (D Va.) Feb. 22, 1804–March 1, 1861; House 1835–47 (1835–37 Jacksonian, 1837–39 Democrat, 1839–41 Conservative), 1857–59.

Hopkins, James Herron (D Pa.) Nov. 3, 1832–June 17, 1904; House 1875–77, 1883–85.

Hopkins, Larry Jones (R Ky.) Oct. 25, 1933– ; House 1979–93.

Hopkins, Nathan Thomas (R Ky.) Oct. 27, 1852–Feb. 11, 1927; House Feb. 18–March 3, 1897.

Hopkins, Samuel (R Ky.) April 9, 1753–Sept. 16, 1819; House 1813–15.

Hopkins, Samuel Isaac (Lab. Va.) Dec. 12, 1843–Jan. 15, 1914; House 1887–89.

Hopkins, Samuel Miles (F N.Y.) May 9, 1772–March 9, 1837; House 1813–15.

Hopkins, Stephen Tyng (R N.Y.) March 25, 1849–March 3, 1892; House 1887–89.

Hopkinson, Joseph (F Pa.) Nov. 12, 1770–Jan. 15, 1842; House 1815–19.

Hopwood, Robert Freeman (R Pa.) July 24, 1856–March 1, 1940; House 1915–17.

Horan, Walter Franklin (R Wash.) Oct. 15, 1898–Dec. 19, 1966; House 1943–65.

Horn, Henry (J Pa.) 1786–Jan. 12, 1862; House 1831–33.

Horn, Joan Kelly (D Mo.) Oct. 18, 1936– ; House 1991–93.

Horn, Steve (R Calif.) May 31, 1931– ; House 1993–2003.

Hornbeck, John Westbrook (W Pa.) Jan. 24, 1804–Jan. 16, 1848; House 1847–Jan. 16, 1848.

Hornor, Lynn Sedwick (D W.Va.) Nov. 3, 1874–Sept. 23, 1933; House 1931–Sept. 23, 1933.

Horr, Ralph Ashley (R Wash.) Aug. 12, 1884–Jan. 26, 1960; House 1931–33.

Horr, Roswell Gilbert (R Mich.) Nov. 26, 1830–Dec. 19, 1896; House 1879–85.

Horsey, Outerbridge (F Del.) March 5, 1777–June 9, 1842; Senate Jan. 12, 1810–21.

Horsford, Jerediah (W N.Y.) March 8, 1791–Jan. 14, 1875; House 1851–53.

Horton, Frank Jefferson (R N.Y.) Dec. 12, 1919–Aug. 30, 2004; House 1963–93.

Horton, Frank Ogilvie (R Wyo.) Oct. 18, 1882–Aug. 17, 1948; House 1939–41.

Horton, Thomas Raymond (W N.Y.) April 1822–July 26, 1894; House 1855–57.

Horton, Valentine Baxter (R Ohio) Jan. 29, 1802–Jan. 14, 1888; House 1855–59, 1861–63.

Hoskins, George Gilbert (R N.Y.) Dec. 24, 1824–June 12, 1893; House 1873–77.

Hosmer, Craig (R Calif.) May 6, 1915–Oct. 11, 1982; House 1953–Dec. 31, 1974.

Hosmer, Hezekiah Lord (F N.Y.) June 7, 1765–June 9, 1814; House 1797–99.

Hostetler, Abraham Jonathan (D Ind.) Nov. 22, 1818–Nov. 24, 1899; House 1879–81.

Hostetter, Jacob (– Pa.) May 9, 1754–June 29, 1831; House Nov. 16, 1818–21.

Hostettler, John (R Ind.) July 19, 1961– ; House 1995– .

Hotchkiss, Giles Waldo (R N.Y.) Oct. 25, 1815–July 5, 1878; House 1863–67, 1869–71.

Hotchkiss, Julius (D Conn.) July 11, 1810–Dec. 23, 1878; House 1867–69.

Houck, Jacob Jr. (D N.Y.) Jan. 14, 1801–Oct. 2, 1857; House 1841–43.

Hough, David (F N.H.) March 13, 1753–April 18, 1831; House 1803–07.

Hough, William Jervis (D N.Y.) March 20, 1795–Oct. 4, 1869; House 1845–47.

Houghton, Alanson Bigelow (grandfather of Amory Houghton Jr.) (R N.Y.) Oct. 10, 1863–Sept. 15, 1941; House 1919–Feb. 28, 1922.

Houghton, Amory Jr. (grandson of Alanson Bigelow Houghton) (R N.Y.) Aug. 7, 1926– ; House 1987–2005.

Houghton, Sherman Otis (R Calif.) April 10, 1828–Aug. 31, 1914; House 1871–75.

Houk, George Washington (D Ohio) Sept. 25, 1825–Feb. 9, 1894; House 1891–Feb. 9, 1894.

Houk, John Chiles (son of Leonidas Campbell Houk) (R Tenn.) Feb. 26, 1860–June 3, 1923; House Dec. 7, 1891–95.

Houk, Leonidas Campbell (father of John Chiles Houk) (R Tenn.) June 8, 1836–May 25, 1891; House 1879–May 25, 1891.

House, John Ford (D Tenn.) Jan. 9, 1827–June 28, 1904; House 1875–83.

Houseman, Julius (D Mich.) Dec. 8, 1832–Feb. 8, 1891; House 1883–85.

Houston, Andrew Jackson (son of Samuel Houston) (D Texas) June 21, 1854–June 26, 1941; Senate April 21–June 26, 1941.

Houston, George Smith (D Ala.) Jan. 17, 1811–Dec. 31, 1879; House 1841–49, 1851–Jan. 21, 1861; Senate March 4–Dec. 31, 1879; Gov. Nov. 24, 1874–Nov. 28, 1878.

Houston, Henry Aydelotte (D Del.) July 10, 1847–April 5, 1925; House 1903–05.

Houston, John Mills (D Kan.) Sept. 15, 1890–April 29, 1975; House 1935–43.

Houston, John Wallace (uncle of Robert Griffith Houston) (W Del.) May 4, 1814–April 26, 1896; House 1845–51.

Houston, Robert Griffith (nephew of John Wallace Houston) (R Del.) Oct. 13, 1867–Jan. 29, 1946; House 1925–33.

Houston, Samuel (father of Andrew Jackson Houston, cousin of David Hubbard) (D Texas) March 2, 1793–July 26, 1863; House 1823–27 (no party Tenn.); Senate Feb. 21, 1846–59; Gov. Oct. 1, 1827–April 16, 1829 (Tenn.), Dec. 21, 1859–March 16, 1861.

Houston, Victor Stewart Kaleoaloha (R Hawaii) July 22, 1876–July 31, 1959; House (Terr. Del.) 1927–33.

Houston, William Cannon (D Tenn.) March 17, 1852–Aug. 30, 1931; House 1905–19.

Hovey, Alvin Peterson (R Ind.) Sept. 6, 1821–Nov. 23, 1891; House 1887–Jan. 17, 1889; Gov. Jan. 14, 1889–Nov. 21, 1891.

Howard, Benjamin (R Ky.) 1760–Sept. 18, 1814; House 1807–April 10, 1810; Gov. (La. Terr.) 1810–12.

Howard, Benjamin Chew (son of John Eager Howard) (D Md.) Nov. 5, 1791–March 6, 1872; House 1829–33 (Jacksonian), 1835–39 (1835–37 Jacksonian).

Howard, Edgar (D Neb.) Sept. 16, 1858–July 19, 1951; House 1923–35.

Howard, Everette Burgess (D Okla.) Sept. 19, 1873–April 3, 1950; House 1919–21, 1923–25, 1927–29.

Howard, Guy Victor (R Minn.) Nov. 28, 1879–Aug. 20, 1954; Senate Nov. 4, 1936–37.

Howard, Jacob Merritt (R Mich.) July 10, 1805–April 2, 1871; House 1841–43 (Whig); Senate Jan. 17, 1862–71.

Howard, James John (D N.J.) July 24, 1927–March 25, 1988; House 1965–March 25, 1988; chair House Public Works and Transportation 1981–88.

Howard, John Eager (father of Benjamin Chew Howard) (F Md.) June 4, 1752–Oct. 12, 1827; Senate Nov. 30, 1796–1803; elected pres. pro tempore Nov. 21, 1800; Gov. Nov. 24, 1788–Nov. 14, 1791; Cont. Cong. 1788.

Howard, Jonas George (D Ind.) May 22, 1825–Oct. 5, 1911; House 1885–89.

Howard, Milford Wriarson (P Ala.) Dec. 18, 1862–Dec. 28, 1937; House 1895–99.

Howard, Tilghman Ashurst (D Ind.) Nov. 14, 1797–Aug. 16, 1844; House Aug. 5, 1839–July 1, 1840.

Howard, Volney Erskine (D Texas) Oct. 22, 1809–May 14, 1889; House 1849–53.

Howard, William (D Ohio) Dec. 31, 1817–June 1, 1891; House 1859–61.

Howard, William Alanson (R Mich.) April 8, 1813–April 10, 1880; House 1855–59, May 15, 1860–61; Gov. (Dakota Terr.) 1878–80.

Howard, William Marcellus (D Ga.) Dec. 6, 1857–July 5, 1932; House 1897–1911.

Howard, William Schley (cousin of Augustus Octavius Bacon) (D Ga.) June 29, 1875–Aug. 1, 1953; House 1911–19.

Howe, Albert Richards (R Miss.) Jan. 1, 1840–June 1, 1884; House 1873–75.

Howe, Allan Turner (D Utah) Sept. 6, 1927– ; House 1975–77.

Howe, James Robinson (R N.Y.) Jan. 27, 1839–Sept. 21, 1914; House 1895–99.

Howe, John W. (W Pa.) 1801–Dec. 1, 1873; House 1849–53.

Howe, Thomas Marshall (father-in-law of James W. Brown) (W Pa.) April 20, 1808–July 20, 1877; House 1851–55.

Howe, Thomas Y. Jr. (D N.Y.) 1801–July 15, 1860; House 1851–53.

Howe, Timothy Otis (R Wis.) Feb. 24, 1816–March 25, 1883; Senate 1861–79; postmaster general Jan. 5, 1882–March 25, 1883.

Howell, Benjamin Franklin (R N.J.) Jan. 27, 1844–Feb. 1, 1933; House 1895–1911.

Howell, Charles Robert (D N.J.) April 23, 1904–July 5, 1973; House 1949–55.

Howell, Edward (J N.Y.) Oct. 16, 1792–Jan. 30, 1871; House 1833–35.

Howell, Elias (father of James Bruen Howell) (W Ohio) 1792–May 1844; House 1835–37.

Howell, George (D Pa.) June 28, 1859–Nov. 19, 1913; House 1903–Feb. 10, 1904.

Howell, George Evan (R Ill.) Sept. 21, 1905–Jan. 18, 1980; House 1941–Oct. 5, 1947.

Howell, James Bruen (son of Elias Howell) (R Iowa) July 4, 1816–June 17, 1880; Senate Jan. 18, 1870–71.

Howell, Jeremiah Brown (R R.I.) Aug. 28, 1771–Feb. 5, 1822; Senate 1811–17.

Howell, Joseph (R Utah) Feb. 17, 1857–July 18, 1918; House 1903–17.

Howell, Nathaniel Woodhull (F N.Y.) Jan. 1, 1770–Oct. 15, 1851; House 1813–15.

Howell, Robert Beecher (R Neb.) Jan. 21, 1864–March 11, 1933; Senate 1923–March 11, 1933.

Howey, Benjamin Franklin (nephew of Charles Creighton Stratton) (R N.J.) March 17, 1828–Feb. 6, 1895; House 1883–85.

Howland, Benjamin (R R.I.) July 27, 1755–May 1, 1821; Senate Oct. 29, 1804–09.

Howland, Leonard Paul (R Ohio) Dec. 5, 1865–Dec. 23, 1942; House 1907–13.

Hoxworth, Stephen Arnold (D Ill.) May 1, 1860–Jan. 25, 1930; House 1913–15.

Hoyer, Steny Hamilton (D Md.) June 14, 1939– ; House June 3, 1981– .

Hruska, Roman Lee (R Neb.) Aug. 16, 1904–April 25, 1999; House 1953–Nov. 8, 1954; Senate Nov. 8, 1954–Dec. 27, 1976.

Hubard, Edmund Wilcox (D Va.) Feb. 20, 1806–Dec. 9, 1878; House 1841–47.

Hubbard, Asahel Wheeler (father of Elbert Hamilton Hubbard) (R Iowa) Jan. 19, 1819–Sept. 22, 1879; House 1863–69.

Hubbard, Carroll Jr. (D Ky.) July 7, 1937– ; House 1975–93.

Hubbard, Chester Dorman (father of William Pallister Hubbard) (R W.Va.) Nov. 25, 1814–Aug. 23, 1891; House 1865–69 (1865–67 Unconditional Unionist).

Hubbard, David (cousin of Samuel Houston) (D Ala.) 1792–Jan. 20, 1874; House 1839–41, 1849–51.

Hubbard, Demas Jr. (R N.Y.) Jan. 17, 1806–Sept. 2, 1873; House 1865–67.

Hubbard, Elbert Hamilton (son of Asahel Wheeler Hubbard) (R Iowa) Aug. 19, 1849–June 4, 1912; House 1905–June 4, 1912.

Hubbard, Henry (J N.H.) May 3, 1784–June 5, 1857; House 1829–35; Senate 1835–41; Gov. June 2, 1842–June 6, 1844 (Democrat).

Hubbard, Joel Douglas (R Mo.) Nov. 6, 1860–May 26, 1919; House 1895–97.

Hubbard, John Henry (R Conn.) March 24, 1804–July 30, 1872; House 1863–67.

Hubbard, Jonathan Hatch (F Vt.) May 7, 1768–Sept. 20, 1849; House 1809–11.

Hubbard, Levi (R Mass.) Dec. 19, 1762–Feb. 18, 1836; House 1813–15.

Hubbard, Richard Dudley (D Conn.) Sept. 7, 1818–Feb. 28, 1884; House 1867–69; Gov. Jan. 3, 1877–Jan. 9, 1879.

Hubbard, Samuel Dickinson (W Conn.) Aug. 10, 1799–Oct. 8, 1855; House 1845–49; postmaster general Sept. 14, 1852–March 7, 1853.

Hubbard, Thomas Hill (R N.Y.) Dec. 5, 1781–May 21, 1857; House 1817–19, 1821–23.

Hubbard, William Pallister (son of Chester Dorman Hubbard) (R W.Va.) Dec. 24, 1843–Dec. 5, 1921; House 1907–11.

Hubbell, Edwin Nelson (D N.Y.) Aug. 13, 1815–?; House 1865–67.

Hubbell, James Randolph (R Ohio) July 13, 1824–Nov. 26, 1890; House 1865–67.

Hubbell, Jay Abel (R Mich.) Sept. 15, 1829–Oct. 13, 1900; House 1873–83.

Hubbell, William Spring (D N.Y.) Jan. 17, 1801–Nov. 16, 1873; House 1843–45.

Hubbs, Orlando (R N.C.) Feb. 18, 1840–Dec. 5, 1930; House 1881–83.

Huber, Robert James (R Mich.) Aug. 29, 1922–April 23, 2001; House 1973–75.

Huber, Walter B. (D Ohio) June 29, 1903–Aug. 8, 1982; House 1945–51.

Hubley, Edward Burd (D Pa.) 1792–Feb. 23, 1856; House 1835–39 (1835–37 Jacksonian).

Huck, Winnifred Sprague Mason (daughter of William Ernest Mason) (R Ill.) Sept. 14, 1882–Aug. 24, 1936; House Nov. 7, 1922–23.

Huckaby, Thomas Jerald (D La.) July 19, 1941– ; House 1977–93.

Hudd, Thomas Richard (D Wis.) Oct. 2, 1835–June 22, 1896; House March 8, 1886–89.

Huddleston, George (father of George Huddleston Jr.) (D Ala.) Nov. 11, 1869–Feb. 29, 1960; House 1915–37.

Huddleston, George Jr. (son of George Huddleston) (D Ala.) March 19, 1920–Sept. 14, 1971; House 1955–65.

Huddleston, Walter Darlington (D Ky.) April 15, 1926– ; Senate 1973–85.

Hudnut, William Herbert III (R Ind.) Oct. 17, 1932– ; House 1973–75.

Hudson, Charles (W Mass.) Nov. 14, 1795–May 4, 1881; House May 3, 1841–49.

Hudson, Grant Martin (R Mich.) July 23, 1868–Oct. 26, 1955; House 1923–31.

Hudson, Thomas Jefferson (P Kan.) Oct. 30, 1839–Jan. 4, 1923; House 1893–95.

Hudspeth, Claude Benton (D Texas) May 12, 1877–March 19, 1941; House 1919–31.

Huff, George Franklin (R Pa.) July 16, 1842–April 18, 1912; House 1891–93, 1895–97, 1903–11.

Huffington, Michael (R Calif.) Sept. 3, 1947– ; House 1993–95.

Huffman, James Wylie (D Ohio) Sept. 13, 1894–May 20, 1980; Senate Oct. 8, 1945–Nov. 5, 1946.

Hufty, Jacob (F N.J.) ?–May 20, 1814; House 1809–May 20, 1814 (1809–13 Republican).

Huger, Benjamin (F S.C.) 1768–July 7, 1823; House 1799–1805, 1815–17.

Huger, Daniel (father of Daniel Elliott Huger) (– S.C.) Feb. 20, 1742–July 6, 1799; House 1789–93; Cont. Cong. 1786–88.

Huger, Daniel Elliott (son of Daniel Huger) (SRD S.C.) June 28, 1779–Aug. 21, 1854; Senate 1843–45.

Hughes, Charles (D N.Y.) Feb. 27, 1822–Aug. 10, 1887; House 1853–55.

Hughes, Charles James Jr. (D Colo.) Feb. 16, 1853–Jan. 11, 1911; Senate 1909–Jan. 11, 1911.

Hughes, Dudley Mays (D Ga.) Oct. 10, 1848–Jan. 20, 1927; House 1909–17.

Hughes, George Wurtz (D Md.) Sept. 30, 1806–Sept. 3, 1870; House 1859–61.

Hughes, Harold Everett (D Iowa) Feb. 10, 1922–Oct. 23, 1996; Senate 1969–75; Gov. Jan. 17, 1963–Jan. 1, 1969.

Hughes, James (D Ind.) Nov. 24, 1823–Oct. 21, 1873; House 1857–59.

Hughes, James Anthony (R W.Va.) Feb. 27, 1861–March 2, 1930; House 1901–15, 1927–March 2, 1930.

Hughes, James Frederic (D Wis.) Aug. 7, 1883–Aug. 9, 1940; House 1933–35.

Hughes, James Hurd (D Del.) Jan. 14, 1867–Aug. 29, 1953; Senate 1937–43.

Hughes, James Madison (D Mo.) April 7, 1809–Feb. 26, 1861; House 1843–45.

Hughes, Thomas Hurst (– N.J.) Jan. 10, 1769–Nov. 10, 1839; House 1829–33.

Hughes, William (D N.J.) April 3, 1872–Jan. 30, 1918; House 1903–05, 1907–Sept. 27, 1912; Senate 1913–Jan. 30, 1918.

Hughes, William John (D N.J.) Oct. 17, 1932– ; House 1975–95.

Hughston, Jonas Abbott (W N.Y.) 1808–Nov. 10, 1862; House 1855–57.

Hugunin, Daniel Jr. (– N.Y.) Feb. 6, 1790–June 21, 1850; House Dec. 15, 1825–27.

Hukriede, Theodore Waldemar (R Mo.) Nov. 9, 1878–April 14, 1945; House 1921–23.

Hulbert, George Murray (D N.Y.) May 14, 1881–April 26, 1950; House 1915–Jan. 1, 1918.

Hulbert, John Whitefield (F Mass.) June 1, 1770–Oct. 19, 1831; House Sept. 26, 1814–17.

Hulburd, Calvin Tilden (R N.Y.) June 5, 1809–Oct. 25, 1897; House 1863–69.

Hulick, George Washington (R Ohio) June 29, 1833–Aug. 13, 1907; House 1893–97.

Huling, James Hall (R W.Va.) March 24, 1844–April 23, 1918; House 1895–97.

Hulings, Willis James (R Pa.) July 1, 1850–Aug. 8, 1924; House 1913–15 (Progressive), 1919–21.

Hull, Cordell (D Tenn.) Oct. 2, 1871–July 23, 1955; House 1907–21, 1923–31; Senate 1931–March 3, 1933; chair Dem. Nat. Comm. 1921–24; secretary of state March 4, 1933–Nov. 30, 1944.

Hull, Harry Edward (R Iowa) March 12, 1864–Jan. 16, 1938; House 1915–25.

Hull, John Albert Tiffin (R Iowa) May 1, 1841–Sept. 26, 1928; House 1891–1911.

Hull, Merlin (R Wis.) Dec. 18, 1870–May 17, 1953; House 1929–31 (Republican), 1935–May 17, 1953 (1935–47 Progressive).

Hull, Morton Denison (R Ill.) Jan. 13, 1867–Aug. 20, 1937; House April 3, 1923–33.

Hull, Noble Andrew (D Fla.) March 11, 1827–Jan. 28, 1907; House 1879–Jan. 22, 1881.

Hull, William Edgar (R Ill.) Jan. 13, 1866–May 30, 1942; House 1923–33.

Hull, William Raleigh Jr. (D Mo.) April 17, 1906–Aug. 15, 1977; House 1955–73.

Hulshof, Kenny (R Mo.) May 22, 1958– ; House 1997– .

Humphrey, Augustin Reed (R Neb.) Feb. 18, 1859–Dec. 10, 1937; House Nov. 7, 1922–23.

Humphrey, Charles (– N.Y.) Feb. 14, 1792–April 17, 1850; House 1825–27.

Humphrey, Gordon John (R N.H.) Oct. 9, 1940– ; Senate 1979–91.

Humphrey, Herman Leon (R Wis.) March 14, 1830–June 10, 1902; House 1877–83.

Humphrey, Hubert Horatio Jr. (husband of Muriel Buck Humphrey) (D Minn.) May 27, 1911–Jan. 13, 1978; Senate 1949–Dec. 29, 1964, 1971–Jan. 13, 1978; vice president 1965–69.

Humphrey, James (R N.Y.) Oct. 9, 1811–June 16, 1866; House 1859–61, 1865–June 16, 1866.

Humphrey, James Morgan (D N.Y.) Sept. 21, 1819–Feb. 9, 1899; House 1865–69.

Humphrey, Muriel Buck (widow of Hubert Horatio Humphrey Jr.) (D Minn.) Feb. 20, 1912–Sept. 20, 1998; Senate Jan. 25–Nov. 7, 1978.

Humphrey, Reuben (R N.Y.) Sept. 2, 1757–Aug. 12, 1831; House 1807–09.

Humphrey, William Ewart (R Wash.) March 31, 1862–Feb. 14, 1934; House 1903–17.

Humphreys, Andrew (D Ind.) March 30, 1821–June 14, 1904; House Dec. 5, 1876–77.

Humphreys, Benjamin Grubb (father of William Yerger Humphreys) (D Miss.) Aug. 17, 1865–Oct. 16, 1923; House 1903–Oct. 16, 1923.

Humphreys, Parry Wayne (R Tenn.) 1778–Feb. 12, 1839; House 1813–15.

Humphreys, Robert (D Ky.) Aug. 20, 1893–Dec. 31, 1977; Senate June 21–Nov. 6, 1956.

Humphreys, William Yerger (son of Benjamin Grubb Humphreys) (D Miss.) Sept. 9, 1890–Feb. 26, 1933; House Nov. 27, 1923–25.

Hungate, William Leonard (D Mo.) Dec. 24, 1922– ; House Nov. 3, 1964–77.

Hungerford, John Newton (R N.Y.) Dec. 31, 1825–April 2, 1883; House 1877–79.

Hungerford, John Pratt (R Va.) Jan. 2, 1761–Dec. 21, 1833; House March 4–Nov. 29, 1811, 1813–17.

Hungerford, Orville (D N.Y.) Oct. 29, 1790–April 6, 1851; House 1843–47.

Hunt, Carleton (nephew of Theodore Gaillard Hunt) (D La.) Jan. 1, 1836–Aug. 14, 1921; House 1883–85.

Hunt, Hiram Paine (W N.Y.) May 23, 1796–Aug. 14, 1865; House 1835–37, 1839–43.

Hunt, James Bennett (D Mich.) Aug. 13, 1799–Aug. 15, 1857; House 1843–47.

Hunt, John Edmund (R N.J.) Nov. 25, 1908–Sept. 22, 1989; House 1967–75.

Hunt, John Thomas (D Mo.) Feb. 2, 1860–Nov. 30, 1916; House 1903–07.

Hunt, Jonathan (– Vt.) Aug. 12, 1787–May 15, 1832; House 1827–May 15, 1832.

Hunt, Lester Callaway (D Wyo.) July 8, 1892–June 19, 1954; Senate 1949–June 19, 1954; Gov. Jan. 4, 1943–Jan. 3, 1949.

Hunt, Samuel (F N.H.) July 8, 1765–July 7, 1807; House Dec. 6, 1802–05.

Hunt, Theodore Gaillard (nephew of John Gaillard, uncle of Carleton Hunt) (W La.) Oct. 23, 1805–Nov. 15, 1893; House 1853–55.

Hunt, Washington (W N.Y.) Aug. 5, 1811–Feb. 2, 1867; House 1843–49; Gov. Jan. 1, 1851–Jan. 1, 1853.

Hunter, Allan Oakley (R Calif.) June 15, 1916–May 15, 1995; House 1951–55.

Hunter, Andrew Jackson (D Ill.) Dec. 17, 1831–Jan. 12, 1913; House 1893–95, 1897–99.

Hunter, Duncan Lee (R Calif.) May 31, 1948– ; House 1981– ; chair House Armed Services 2003– .

Hunter, John (R S.C.) 1732–1802; House 1793–95 (no party); Senate Dec. 8, 1796–Nov. 26, 1798.

Hunter, John Feeney (D Ohio) Oct. 19, 1896–Dec. 19, 1957; House 1937–43.

Hunter, John Ward (– N.Y.) Oct. 15, 1807–April 16, 1900; House Dec. 4, 1866–67.

Hunter, Morton Craig (R Ind.) Feb. 5, 1825–Oct. 25, 1896; House 1867–69, 1873–79.

Hunter, Narsworthy (– Miss.) ?–March 11, 1802; House (Terr. Del.) 1801–March 11, 1802.

Hunter, Richard Charles (D Neb.) Dec. 3, 1884–Jan. 23, 1941; Senate Nov. 7, 1934–35.

Hunter, Robert Mercer Taliaferro (– Va.) April 21, 1809–July 18, 1887; House 1837–43 (State Rights Whig), 1845–47; Senate 1847–March 28, 1861; Speaker Dec. 16, 1839–41.

Hunter, Whiteside Godfrey (R Ky.) Dec. 25, 1841–Nov. 2, 1917; House 1887–89, 1895–97, Nov. 10, 1903–05.

Hunter, William (R Vt.) Jan. 3, 1754–Nov. 30, 1827; House 1817–19.

Hunter, William (F R.I.) Nov. 26, 1774–Dec. 3, 1849; Senate Oct. 28, 1811–21.

Hunter, William Forrest (W Ohio) Dec. 10, 1808–March 30, 1874; House 1849–53.

Hunter, William H. (D Ohio) ?–1842; House 1837–39.

Huntington, Abel (J N.Y.) Feb. 21, 1777–May 18, 1858; House 1833–37.

Huntington, Benjamin (– Conn.) April 19, 1736–Oct. 16, 1800; House 1789–91; Cont. Cong. 1780, 1782–83, 1788.

Huntington, Ebenezer (F Conn.) Dec. 26, 1754–June 17, 1834; House Oct. 11, 1810–11, 1817–19.

Huntington, Jabez Williams (W Conn.) Nov. 8, 1788–Nov. 1, 1847; House 1829–Aug. 16, 1834 (no party); Senate May 4, 1840–Nov. 1, 1847.

Hunton, Eppa (D Va.) Sept. 22, 1822–Oct. 11, 1908; House 1873–81; Senate May 28, 1892–95.

Huntsman, Adam (J Tenn.) Feb. 11, 1786–Aug. 23, 1849; House 1835–37.

Huot, Joseph Oliva (D N.H.) Aug. 11, 1917–Aug. 5, 1983; House 1965–67.

Hurd, Frank Hunt (D Ohio) Dec. 25, 1840–July 10, 1896; House 1875–77, 1879–81, 1883–85.

Hurlbut, Stephen Augustus (R Ill.) Nov. 29, 1815–March 27, 1882; House 1873–77.

Hurley, Denis Michael (R N.Y.) March 14, 1843–Feb. 26, 1899; House 1895–Feb. 26, 1899.

Husted, James William (R N.Y.) March 16, 1870–Jan. 2, 1925; House 1915–23.

Husting, Paul Oscar (D Wis.) April 25, 1866–Oct. 21, 1917; Senate 1915–Oct. 21, 1917.

Hutcheson, Joseph Chappell (D Texas) May 18, 1842–May 25, 1924; House 1893–97.

Hutchins, John (cousin of Wells Andrews Hutchins) (R Ohio) July 25, 1812–Nov. 20, 1891; House 1859–63.

Hutchins, Waldo (D N.Y.) Sept. 30, 1822–Feb. 8, 1891; House Nov. 4, 1879–85.

Hutchins, Wells Andrews (cousin of John Hutchins) (D Ohio) Oct. 8, 1818–Jan. 25, 1895; House 1863–65.

Hutchinson, Asa (brother of Young Timothy Hutchinson) (R Ark.) Dec. 3, 1950– ; House 1997–Aug. 6, 2001.

Hutchinson, Elijah Cubberley (R N.J.) Aug. 7, 1855–June 25, 1932; House 1915–23.

Hutchinson, J. Edward (R Mich.) Oct. 13, 1914–July 22, 1985; House 1963–77.

Hutchinson, John Guiher (D W.Va.) Feb. 4, 1935– ; House June 3, 1980–81.

Hutchinson, Young Timothy "Tim" (brother of Asa Hutchinson) (R Ark.) Aug. 11, 1949– ; House 1993–97; Senate 1997–2003.

Hutchison, Katherine Ann Bailey "Kay" (R Texas) July 22, 1943– ; Senate June 14, 1993– .

Hutto, Earl Dewitt (D Fla.) May 12, 1926– ; House 1979–95.

Hutton, John Edward (D Mo.) March 28, 1828–Dec. 28, 1893; House 1885–89.

Huyler, John (D N.J.) April 9, 1808–Jan. 9, 1870; House 1857–59.

Hyde, DeWitt Stephen (R Md.) March 21, 1909–April 25, 1986; House 1953–59.

Hyde, Henry John (R Ill.) April 18, 1924– ; House 1975– ; chair House Judiciary 1995–2001; chair House International Relations 2001– .

Hyde, Ira Barnes (R Mo.) Jan. 18, 1838–Dec. 6, 1926; House 1873–75.

Hyde, Samuel Clarence (R Wash.) April 22, 1842–March 7, 1922; House 1895–97.

Hyman, John Adams (R N.C.) July 23, 1840–Sept. 14, 1891; House 1875–77.

Hyneman, John M. (R Pa.) April 25, 1771–April 16, 1816; House 1811–Aug. 2, 1813.

Hynes, William Joseph (LR Ark.) March 31, 1843–April 2, 1915; House 1873–75.

Ichord, Richard Howard II (D Mo.) June 27, 1926–Dec. 25, 1992; House 1961–81; chair House Internal Security 1969–74.

Iglesias, Santiago (formerly Santiago Iglesias Pantin) (Coal. P.R.) Feb. 22, 1872–Dec. 5, 1939; House (Res. Comm.) 1933–Dec. 5, 1939.

Igoe, James Thomas (D Ill.) Oct. 23, 1883–Dec. 2, 1971; House 1927–33.

Igoe, Michael Lambert (D Ill.) April 16, 1885–Aug. 21, 1967; House Jan. 3–June 2, 1935.

Igoe, William Leo (D Mo.) Oct. 19, 1879–April 20, 1953; House 1913–21.

Ihrie, Peter Jr. (– Pa.) Feb. 3, 1796–March 29, 1871; House Oct. 13, 1829–33.

Ikard, Frank Neville (D Texas) Jan. 30, 1913–May 1, 1991; House Sept. 8, 1951–Dec. 15, 1961.

Ikirt, George Pierce (D Ohio) Nov. 3, 1852–Feb. 12, 1927; House 1893–95.

Ilsley, Daniel (R Mass.) May 30, 1740–May 10, 1813; House 1807–09.

Imhoff, Lawrence E. (D Ohio) Dec. 28, 1895–April 18, 1988; House 1933–39, 1941–43.

Imlay, James Henderson (F N.J.) Nov. 26, 1764–March 6, 1823; House 1797–1801.

Ingalls, John James (R Kan.) Dec. 29, 1833–Aug. 16, 1900; Senate 1873–91; elected pres. pro tempore Feb. 25, 1887, March 7, 1889, April 2, 1889, Feb. 28, 1890, April 3, 1890.

Inge, Samuel Williams (nephew of William Marshall Inge) (D Ala.) Feb. 22, 1817–June 10, 1868; House 1847–51.

Inge, William Marshall (uncle of Samuel Williams Inge) (J Tenn.) 1802–46; House 1833–35.

Ingersoll, Charles Jared (brother of Joseph Reed Ingersoll) (D Pa.) Oct. 3, 1782–May 14, 1862; House 1813–15 (Republican), 1841–49.

Ingersoll, Colin Macrae (son of Ralph Isaacs Ingersoll) (D Conn.) March 11, 1819–Sept. 13, 1903; House 1851–55.

Ingersoll, Ebon Clark (R Ill.) Dec. 12, 1831–May 31, 1879; House May 20, 1864–71.

Ingersoll, Joseph Reed (brother of Charles Jared Ingersoll) (W Pa.) June 14, 1786–Feb. 20, 1868; House 1835–37, Oct. 12, 1841–49.

Ingersoll, Ralph Isaacs (father of Colin Macrae Ingersoll) (– Conn.) Feb. 8, 1789–Aug. 26, 1872; House 1825–33.

Ingham, Samuel (D Conn.) Sept. 5, 1793–Nov. 10, 1881; House 1835–39 (1835–37 Jacksonian).

Ingham, Samuel Delucenna (R Pa.) Sept. 16, 1779–June 5, 1860; House 1813–July 6, 1818, Oct. 8, 1822–29; secretary of the Treasury March 6, 1829–June 20, 1831.

Inglis, Robert Durden (R S.C.) Oct. 11, 1959– ; House 1993–99, 2005– .

Inhofe, James Mountain (R Okla.) Nov. 17, 1934– ; House 1987–Nov. 15, 1994; Senate Nov. 17, 1994– ; chair Senate Environment and Public Works 2003– .

Inouye, Daniel Ken (D Hawaii) Sept. 7, 1924– ; House Aug. 21, 1959–63; Senate 1963– ; chair Senate Select Intelligence Activities 1976–78; chair Senate Indian Affairs 1993–95, 2001–03.

Inslee, Jay Robert (D Wash.) Feb. 9, 1951– ; House 1993–95, 1999– .

Irby, John Laurens Manning (great-grandson of Elias Earle) (D S.C.) Sept. 10, 1854–Dec. 9, 1900; Senate 1891–97.

Iredell, James (J N.C.) Nov. 2, 1788–April 13, 1853; Senate Dec. 15, 1828–31; Gov. Dec. 8, 1827–Dec. 12, 1828 (Democratic Republican).

Ireland, Andrew Poysell "Andy" (R Fla.) Aug. 23, 1930– ; House 1977–93 (1977–July 5, 1984, Democrat).

Ireland, Clifford Cady (R Ill.) Feb. 14, 1878–May 24, 1930; House 1917–23.

Irion, Alfred Briggs (D La.) Feb. 18, 1833–May 21, 1903; House 1885–87.

Irvin, Alexander (W Pa.) Jan. 18, 1800–March 20, 1874; House 1847–49.

Irvin, James (W Pa.) Feb. 18, 1800–Nov. 28, 1862; House 1841–45.

Irvin, William W. (J Ohio) 1778–March 28, 1842; House 1829–33.

Irvine, William (– Pa.) Nov. 3, 1741–July 29, 1804; House 1793–95; Cont. Cong. 1786–88.

Irvine, William (R N.Y.) Feb. 14, 1820–Nov. 12, 1882; House 1859–61.

Irving, Theodore Leonard (D Mo.) March 24, 1898–March 8, 1962; House 1949–53.

Irving, William (R N.Y.) Aug. 15, 1766–Nov. 9, 1821; House Jan. 22, 1814–19.

Irwin, Donald Jay (D Conn.) Sept. 7, 1926– ; House 1959–61, 1965–69.

Irwin, Edward Michael (R Ill.) April 14, 1869–Jan. 30, 1933; House 1925–31.

Irwin, Harvey Samuel (R Ky.) Dec. 10, 1844–Sept. 3, 1916; House 1901–03.

Irwin, Jared (R Pa.) Jan. 19, 1768–Sept. 20, 1818; House 1813–17.

Irwin, Thomas (J Pa.) Feb. 22, 1785–May 14, 1870; House 1829–31.

Irwin, William Wallace (W Pa.) 1803–Sept. 15, 1856; House 1841–43.

Isacks, Jacob C. (J Tenn.) ?–?; House 1823–33 (1823–29 no party).

Isacson, Leo (AL N.Y.) April 20, 1910–Sept. 21, 1996; House Feb. 17, 1948–49.

Isakson, Johnny (R Ga.) Dec. 27, 1944– ; House Feb. 25, 1999–2005; Senate 2005– .

Israel, Steve (D N.Y.) May 30, 1958– ; House 2001– .

Issa, Darrell (R Calif.) Nov. 1, 1953– ; House 2001– .

Istook, Ernest James Jr. (R Okla.) Feb. 11, 1950– ; House 1993– .

Ittner, Anthony Friday (R Mo.) Oct. 8, 1837–Feb. 22, 1931; House 1877–79.

Iverson, Alfred Sr. (D Ga.) Dec. 3, 1798–March 4, 1873; House 1847–49; Senate 1855–Jan. 28, 1861.

Ives, Irving McNeil (R N.Y.) Jan. 24, 1896–Feb. 24, 1962; Senate 1947–59.

Ives, Willard (D N.Y.) July 7, 1806–April 19, 1896; House 1851–53.

Izac, Edouard Victor Michel (D Calif.) Dec. 18, 1891–Jan. 18, 1990; House 1937–47.

Izard, Ralph (– S.C.) Jan. 23, 1741 or 1742–May 30, 1804; Senate 1789–95; elected pres. pro tempore May 31, 1794; Cont. Cong. 1782–83.

Izlar, James Ferdinand (D S.C.) Nov. 25, 1832–May 26, 1912; House April 12, 1894–95.

Jack, Summers Melville (R Pa.) July 18, 1852–Sept. 16, 1945; House 1899–1903.

Jack, William (D Pa.) July 29, 1788–Feb. 28, 1852; House 1841–43.

Jackson, Alfred Metcalf (D Kan.) July 14, 1860–June 11, 1924; House 1901–03.

Jackson, Amos Henry (R Ohio) May 10, 1846–Aug. 30, 1924; House 1903–05.

Jackson, Andrew (R Tenn.) March 15, 1767–June 8, 1845; House Dec. 5, 1796–Sept. 1797 (no party); Senate Sept. 26, 1797–April 1798, 1823–Oct. 14, 1825; Gov. (Fla. Terr.) March 10–July 18, 1821; president 1829–37 (Democrat).

Jackson, David Sherwood (D N.Y.) 1813–Jan. 20, 1872; House 1847–April 19, 1848.

Jackson, Donald Lester (R Calif.) Jan. 23, 1910–May 27, 1981; House 1947–61.

Jackson, Ebenezer Jr. (– Conn.) Jan. 31, 1796–Aug. 17, 1874; House Dec. 1, 1834–35.

Jackson, Edward Brake (son of George Jackson, brother of John George Jackson) (– Va.) Jan. 25, 1793–Sept. 8, 1826; House Oct. 23, 1820–23.

Jackson, Fred Schuyler (R Kan.) April 19, 1868–Nov. 21, 1931; House 1911–13.

Jackson, George (father of John George Jackson and Edward Brake Jackson) (R Va.) Jan. 9, 1757–May 17, 1831; House 1795–97, 1799–1803.

Jackson, Henry Martin (D Wash.) May 31, 1912–Sept. 1, 1983; House 1941–53; Senate 1953–Sept. 1, 1983; chair Senate Interior and Insular Affairs 1963–77; chair Senate Energy and Natural Resources 1977–81; chair Dem. Nat. Comm. 1960–61.

Jackson, Howell Edmunds (D Tenn.) April 8, 1832–Aug. 8, 1895; Senate 1881–April 14, 1886; assoc. justice March 4, 1893–Aug. 8, 1895.

Jackson, Jabez Young (son of James Jackson born in 1757, uncle of James Jackson born in 1819) (D Ga.) July 1790–?; House Oct. 5, 1835–39 (1835–37 Jacksonian).

Jackson, James (father of Jabez Young Jackson, grandfather of James Jackson, below) (R Ga.) Sept. 21, 1757–March 19, 1806; House 1789–91 (no party); Senate 1793–95 (no party), 1801–March 19, 1806; Gov. Jan. 12, 1798–March 3, 1801 (Democratic Republican).

Jackson, James (grandson of James Jackson, above, nephew of Jabez Young Jackson) (D Ga.) Oct. 18, 1819–Jan. 13, 1887; House 1857–Jan. 23, 1861.

Jackson, James Monroe (cousin of William Thomas Bland) (D W.Va.) Dec. 3, 1825–Feb. 14, 1901; House 1889–Feb. 3, 1890.

Jackson, James Streshley (U Ky.) Sept. 27, 1823–Oct. 8, 1862; House March 4–Dec. 13, 1861.

Jackson, Jesse Jr. (D Ill.) March 11, 1965– ; House Dec. 14, 1995– .

Jackson, John George (son of George Jackson, brother of Edward Brake Jackson, grandfather of William Thomas Bland) (R Va.) Sept. 22, 1777–March 28, 1825; House 1803–Sept. 28, 1810, 1813–17.

Jackson, Joseph Webber (SR Ga.) Dec. 6, 1796–Sept. 29, 1854; House March 4, 1850–53 (March 4, 1850–51 Democrat).

Jackson, Oscar Lawrence (R Pa.) Sept. 2, 1840–Feb. 16, 1920; House 1885–89.

Jackson, Richard Jr. (F R.I.) July 3, 1764–April 18, 1838; House Nov. 11, 1808–15.

Jackson, Samuel Dillon (D Ind.) May 28, 1895–March 8, 1951; Senate Jan. 28–Nov. 13, 1944.

Jackson, Thomas Birdsall (D N.Y.) March 24, 1797–April 23, 1881; House 1837–41.

Jackson, William (W Mass.) Sept. 2, 1783–Feb. 27, 1855; House 1833–37 (1833–35 Anti-Mason).

Jackson, William Humphreys (father of William Purnell Jackson) (R Md.) Oct. 15, 1839–April 3, 1915; House 1901–05, 1907–09.

Jackson, William Purnell (son of William Humphreys Jackson) (R Md.) Jan. 11, 1868–March 7, 1939; Senate Nov. 29, 1912–Jan. 28, 1914.

Jackson, William Terry (W N.Y.) Dec. 29, 1794–Sept. 15, 1882; House 1849–51.

Jackson-Lee, Sheila (D Texas) Jan. 12, 1950– ; House 1995– .

Jacobs, Andrew (father of Andrew Jacobs Jr., father-in-law of Martha Elizabeth Keys) (D Ind.) Feb. 22, 1906–Nov. 12, 1992; House 1949–51.

Jacobs, Andrew Jr. (son of Andrew Jacobs, husband of Martha Elizabeth Keys) (D Ind.) Feb. 24, 1932– ; House 1965–73, 1975–97.

Jacobs, Ferris Jr. (R N.Y.) March 20, 1836–Aug. 30, 1886; House 1881–83.

Jacobs, Israel (– Pa.) June 9, 1726–about Dec. 10, 1796; House 1791–93.

Jacobs, Orange (R Wash.) May 2, 1827–May 21, 1914; House (Terr. Del.) 1875–79.

Jacobsen, Bernhard Martin (father of William Sebastian Jacobsen) (D Iowa) March 26, 1862–June 30, 1936; House 1931–June 30, 1936.

Jacobsen, William Sebastian (son of Bernhard Martin Jacobsen) (D Iowa) Jan. 15, 1887–April 10, 1955; House 1937–43.

Jacobstein, Meyer (D N.Y.) Jan. 25, 1880–April 18, 1963; House 1923–29.

Jacoway, Henderson Madison (D Ark.) Nov. 7, 1870–Aug. 4, 1947; House 1911–23.

Jadwin, Cornelius Comegys (R Pa.) March 27, 1835–Aug. 17, 1913; House 1881–83.

James, Addison Davis (grandfather of John Albert Whitaker) (R Ky.) Feb. 27, 1850–June 10, 1947; House 1907–09.

James, Amaziah Bailey (R N.Y.) July 1, 1812–July 6, 1883; House 1877–81.

James, Benjamin Franklin (R Pa.) Aug. 1, 1885–Jan. 26, 1961; House 1949–59.

James, Charles Tillinghast (D R.I.) Sept. 15, 1805–Oct. 17, 1862; Senate 1851–57.

James, Craig T. (R Fla.) May 5, 1941– ; House 1989–93.

James, Darwin Rush (R N.Y.) May 14, 1834–Nov. 19, 1908; House 1883–87.

James, Francis (W Pa.) April 4, 1799–Jan. 4, 1886; House 1839–43 (1839–41 Anti-Mason).

James, Hinton (D N.C.) April 24, 1884–Nov. 3, 1948; House Nov. 4, 1930–31.

James, Ollie Murray (D Ky.) July 27, 1871–Aug. 28, 1918; House 1903–13; Senate 1913–Aug. 28, 1918.

James, Rorer Abraham (D Va.) March 1, 1859–Aug. 6, 1921; House June 15, 1920–Aug. 6, 1921.

James, William Francis (R Mich.) May 23, 1873–Nov. 17, 1945; House 1915–35.

Jameson, John (D Mo.) March 6, 1802–Jan. 24, 1857; House Dec. 12, 1839–41, 1843–45, 1847–49.

Jamieson, William Darius (D Iowa) Nov. 9, 1873–Nov. 18, 1949; House 1909–11.

Janes, Henry Fisk (AMas. Vt.) Oct. 10, 1792–June 6, 1879; House Dec. 2, 1834–37.

Janklow, William John (R S.D.) Sept. 13, 1939– ; House 2003–Jan. 20, 2004; Gov. Jan. 1, 1979–Jan. 6, 1987, Jan. 4, 1995–Jan. 11, 2003.

Jarman, John (R Okla.) July 17, 1915–Jan. 15, 1982; House 1951–77 (1951–Jan. 24, 1975, Democrat).

Jarman, Pete (D Ala.) Oct. 31, 1892–Feb. 17, 1955; House 1937–49.

Jarnagin, Spencer (W Tenn.) 1792–June 25, 1853; Senate Oct. 17, 1843–47.

Jarrett, Benjamin (R Pa.) July 18, 1881–July 20, 1944; House 1937–43.

Jarrett, William Paul (D Hawaii) Aug. 22, 1877–Nov. 10, 1929; House (Terr. Del.) 1923–27.

Jarvis, Leonard (J Maine) Oct. 19, 1781–Oct. 18, 1854; House 1829–37.

Jarvis, Thomas Jordan (D N.C.) Jan. 18, 1836–June 17, 1915; Senate April 19, 1894–Jan. 23, 1895; Gov. Feb. 5, 1879–Jan. 21, 1885.

Javits, Jacob Koppel (R N.Y.) May 18, 1904–March 7, 1986; House 1947–Dec. 31, 1954; Senate Jan. 9, 1957–81.

Jayne, William (– Dakota) Oct. 8, 1826–March 20, 1916; House (Terr. Del.) 1863–June 17, 1864; Gov. (Terr.) 1861–63.

Jefferis, Albert Webb (R Neb.) Dec. 7, 1868–Sept. 14, 1942; House 1919–23.

Jeffers, Lamar (D Ala.) April 16, 1888–June 1, 1983; House June 7, 1921–35.

Jefferson, William J. (D La.) March 14, 1947– ; House 1991– .

Jeffords, Elza (R Miss.) May 23, 1826–March 19, 1885; House 1883–85.

Jeffords, James Merrill (I Vt.) May 11, 1934– ; House 1975–89 (Republican); Senate 1989– (1989–June 5, 2001 Republican); chair Senate Labor and Human Resources 1997–99; chair Senate Health, Education, Labor and Pensions 1999–Jan. 3, 2001, Jan. 20, 2001–June 6, 2001; chair Senate Environment and Public Works June 6, 2001–03.

Jeffrey, Harry Palmer (R Ohio) Dec. 26, 1901–Jan. 4, 1997; House 1943–45.

Jeffries, James Edmund (R Kan.) June 1, 1925– ; House 1979–83.

Jeffries, Walter Sooy (R N.J.) Oct. 16, 1893–Oct. 11, 1954; House 1939–41.

Jenckes, Thomas Allen (R R.I.) Nov. 2, 1818–Nov. 4, 1875; House 1863–71.

Jenckes, Virginia Ellis (D Ind.) Nov. 6, 1877–Jan. 9, 1975; House 1933–39.

Jenifer, Daniel (W Md.) April 15, 1791–Dec. 18, 1855; House 1831–33 (Anti-Jacksonian), 1835–41 (1835–37 Anti-Jacksonian).

Jenison, Edward Halsey (R Ill.) July 27, 1907–June 24, 1996; House 1947–53.

Jenkins, Albert Gallatin (D Va.) Nov. 10, 1830–May 21, 1864; House 1857–61.

Jenkins, Edgar Lanier (D Ga.) Jan. 4, 1933– ; House 1977–93.

Jenkins, John James (R Wis.) Aug. 24, 1843–June 8, 1911; House 1895–1909.

Jenkins, Lemuel (– N.Y.) Oct. 20, 1789–Aug. 18, 1862; House 1823–25.

Jenkins, Mitchell (R Pa.) Jan. 24, 1896–Sept. 15, 1977; House 1947–49.

Jenkins, Robert (R Pa.) July 10, 1769–April 18, 1848; House 1807–11.

Jenkins, Thomas Albert (R Ohio) Oct. 28, 1880–Dec. 21, 1959; House 1925–59.

Jenkins, Timothy (D N.Y.) Jan. 29, 1799–Dec. 24, 1859; House 1845–49, 1851–53.

Jenkins, William L. (R Tenn.) Nov. 29, 1936– ; House 1997– .

Jenks, Arthur Byron (R N.H.) Oct. 15, 1866–Dec. 14, 1947; House 1937–June 9, 1938, 1939–43.

Jenks, George Augustus (D Pa.) March 26, 1836–Feb. 10, 1908; House 1875–77.

Jenks, Michael Hutchinson (W Pa.) May 21, 1795–Oct. 16, 1867; House 1843–45.

Jenner, William Ezra (R Ind.) July 21, 1908–March 9, 1985; Senate Nov. 14, 1944–45, 1947–59; chair Senate Rules and Administration 1953–55.

Jenness, Benning Wentworth (– N.H.) July 14, 1806–Nov. 16, 1879; Senate Dec. 1, 1845–June 13, 1846.

Jennings, David (– Ohio) 1787–1834; House 1825–May 25, 1826.

Jennings, John Jr. (R Tenn.) June 6, 1880–Feb. 27, 1956; House Dec. 30, 1939–51.

Jennings, Jonathan (– Ind.) 1784–July 26, 1834; House Dec. 2, 1822–31; Gov. Nov. 7, 1816–Sept. 12, 1822 (Democratic Republican).

Jennings, William Pat (D Va.) Aug. 20, 1919–Aug. 2, 1994; House 1955–67.

Jenrette, John Wilson Jr. (D S.C.) May 19, 1936– ; House Nov. 5, 1975–Dec. 10, 1980.

Jensen, Benton Franklin (R Iowa) Dec. 16, 1892–Feb. 5, 1970; House 1939–65.

Jepsen, Roger William (R Iowa) Dec. 23, 1928– ; Senate 1979–85.

Jett, Thomas Marion (D Ill.) May 1, 1862–Jan. 10, 1939; House 1897–1903.

Jewett, Daniel Tarbox (R Mo.) Sept. 14, 1807–Oct. 7, 1906; Senate Dec. 19, 1870–Jan. 20, 1871.

Jewett, Freeborn Garrettson (J N.Y.) Aug. 4, 1791–Jan. 27, 1858; House 1831–33.

Jewett, Hugh Judge (brother of Joshua Husband Jewett) (D Ohio) July 1, 1817–March 6, 1898; House 1873–June 23, 1874.

Jewett, Joshua Husband (brother of Hugh Judge Jewett) (D Ky.) Sept. 30, 1815–July 14, 1861; House 1855–59.

Jewett, Luther (F Vt.) Dec. 24, 1772–March 8, 1860; House 1815–17.

Jindal, Robert "Bobby" (R La.) June 10, 1971– ; House 2005– .

Joelson, Charles Samuel (D N.J.) Jan. 27, 1916–Aug. 17, 1999; House 1961–Sept. 4, 1969.

Johansen, August Edgar (R Mich.) July 21, 1905–April 16, 1995; House 1955–65.

John, Chris (D La.) Jan. 5, 1960– ; House 1997–2005.

Johns, Joshua Leroy (R Wis.) Feb. 27, 1881–March 16, 1947; House 1939–43.

Johns, Kensey Jr. (– Del.) Dec. 10, 1791–March 28, 1857; House Oct. 2, 1827–31.

Johnson, Adna Romulus (R Ohio) Dec. 14, 1860–June 11, 1938; House 1909–11.

Johnson, Albert (R Wash.) March 5, 1869–Jan. 17, 1957; House 1913–33.

Johnson, Albert Walter (R Pa.) April 17, 1906–Sept. 1, 1998; House Nov. 5, 1963–77.

Johnson, Andrew (father-in-law of David Trotter Patterson) (R Tenn.) Dec. 29, 1808–July 31, 1875; House 1843–53 (Democrat); Senate Oct. 8, 1857–March 4, 1862 (Democrat), March 4–July 31, 1875; Gov. Oct. 17, 1853–Nov. 3, 1857 (Democrat), March 12,

1862–March 4, 1865 (Military); vice president March 4–April 15, 1865; president April 15, 1865–69.

Johnson, Anton Joseph (R Ill.) Oct. 20, 1878–April 16, 1958; House 1939–49.

Johnson, Ben (D Ky.) May 20, 1858–June 4, 1950; House 1907–27.

Johnson, Byron Lindberg (D Colo.) Oct. 12, 1917–Jan. 6, 2000; House 1959–61.

Johnson, Calvin Dean (R Ill.) Nov. 22, 1898–Oct. 13, 1985; House 1943–45.

Johnson, Cave (D Tenn.) Jan. 11, 1793–Nov. 23, 1866; House 1829–37 (Jacksonian), 1839–45; postmaster general March 7, 1845–March 5, 1849.

Johnson, Charles (R N.Y.) ?–July 23, 1802; House 1801–July 23, 1802.

Johnson, Charles Fletcher (D Maine) Feb. 14, 1859–Feb. 15, 1930; Senate 1911–17.

Johnson, Clete Donald "Don" (D Ga.) Jan. 30, 1948– ; House 1993–95.

Johnson, Dewey William (FL Minn.) March 14, 1899–Sept. 18, 1941; House 1937–39.

Johnson, Eddie Bernice (D Texas) Dec. 3, 1935– ; House 1993– .

Johnson, Edwin Carl (D Colo.) Jan. 1, 1884–May 30, 1970; Senate 1937–55; chair Senate Interstate and Foreign Commerce 1949–53; Gov. Jan. 10, 1933–Jan. 2, 1937, Jan. 11, 1955–Jan. 8, 1957.

Johnson, Edwin Stockton (D S.D.) Feb. 26, 1857–July 19, 1933; Senate 1915–21.

Johnson, Francis (– Ky.) June 19, 1776–May 16, 1842; House Nov. 13, 1820–27.

Johnson, Fred Gustus (R Neb.) Oct. 16, 1876–April 30, 1951; House 1929–31.

Johnson, Frederick Avery (– N.Y.) Jan. 2, 1833–July 17, 1893; House 1883–87.

Johnson, George William (D W.Va.) Nov. 10, 1869–Feb. 24, 1944; House 1923–25, 1933–43.

Johnson, Glen Dale (D Okla.) Sept. 11, 1911–Feb. 10, 1983; House 1947–49.

Johnson, Grove Lawrence (father of Hiram Warren Johnson) (R Calif.) March 27, 1841–Feb. 1, 1926; House 1895–97.

Johnson, Harold Terry (D Calif.) Dec. 2, 1907–March 16, 1988; House 1959–81; chair House Public Works and Transportation 1977–81.

Johnson, Harvey Hull (D Ohio) Sept. 7, 1808–Feb. 4, 1896; House 1853–55.

Johnson, Henry (W La.) Sept. 14, 1783–Sept. 4, 1864; Senate Jan. 12, 1818–May 27, 1824 (Republican), Feb. 12, 1844–49; House Sept. 25, 1834–39; Gov. Dec. 13, 1824–Dec. 15, 1828 (Democratic Republican).

Johnson, Henry Underwood (R Ind.) Oct. 28, 1850–June 4, 1939; House 1891–99.

Johnson, Herschel Vespasian (D Ga.) Sept. 18, 1812–Aug. 16, 1880; Senate Feb. 4, 1848–49; Gov. Nov. 9, 1853–Nov. 6, 1857.

Johnson, Hiram Warren (son of Grove Lawrence Johnson) (R Calif.) Sept. 2, 1866–Aug. 6, 1945; Senate March 16, 1917–Aug. 6, 1945; Gov. Jan. 3, 1911–March 15, 1917.

Johnson, Jacob (R Utah) Nov. 1, 1847–Aug. 15, 1925; House 1913–15.

Johnson, James (R Va.) ?–Dec. 7, 1825; House 1813–Feb. 1, 1820.

Johnson, James (brother of Richard Mentor Johnson and John Telemachus Johnson, uncle of Robert Ward Johnson) (– Ky.) Jan. 1, 1774–Aug. 13, 1826; House 1825–Aug. 13, 1826.

Johnson, James (U Ga.) Feb. 12, 1811–Nov. 20, 1891; House 1851–53; Provisional Gov. June 17–Dec. 14, 1865 (Democrat).

Johnson, James Augustus (D Calif.) May 16, 1829–May 11, 1896; House 1867–71.

Johnson, James Hutchins (D N.H.) June 3, 1802–Sept. 2, 1887; House 1845–49.

Johnson, James Leeper (W Ky.) Oct. 30, 1818–Feb. 12, 1877; House 1849–51.

Johnson, James Paul (R Colo.) June 2, 1930– ; House 1973–81.

Johnson, Jay (D Wis.) Sept. 30, 1943– ; House 1997–99.

Johnson, Jed Joseph (father of Jed Joseph Johnson Jr.) (D Okla.) July 31, 1888–May 8, 1963; House 1927–47.

Johnson, Jed Joseph Jr. (son of Jed Joseph Johnson) (D Okla.) Dec. 17, 1939–Dec. 16, 1993; House 1965–67.

Johnson, Jeromus (– N.Y.) Nov. 2, 1775–Sept. 7, 1846; House 1825–29.

Johnson, John (ID Ohio) 1805–Feb. 5, 1867; House 1851–53.

Johnson, John Telemachus (brother of James Johnson born in 1774 and Richard Mentor Johnson, uncle of Robert Ward Johnson) (– Ky.) Oct. 5, 1788–Dec. 17, 1856; House 1821–25.

Johnson, Joseph (uncle of Waldo Porter Johnson) (D Va.) Dec. 19, 1785–Feb. 27, 1877; House 1823–27 (no party), Jan. 21–March 3, 1833 (no party), 1835–41 (1835–37 Jacksonian), 1845–47; Gov. Jan. 16, 1852–Dec. 31, 1856.

Johnson, Joseph Travis (D S.C.) Feb. 28, 1858–May 8, 1919; House 1901–April 19, 1915.

Johnson, Justin Leroy (R Calif.) April 8, 1888–March 26, 1961; House 1943–57.

Johnson, Lester Roland (D Wis.) June 16, 1901–July 24, 1975; House Oct. 13, 1953–65.

Johnson, Luther Alexander (D Texas) Oct. 29, 1875–June 6, 1965; House 1923–July 17, 1946.

Johnson, Lyndon Baines (D Texas) Aug. 27, 1908–Jan. 22, 1973; House April 10, 1937–49; Senate 1949–Jan. 3, 1961; Senate minority leader 1953–55; Senate majority leader 1955–61; chair Senate Aeronautical and Space Sciences 1958–61; vice president 1961–Nov. 22, 1963; president Nov. 22, 1963–69.

Johnson, Magnus (FL Minn.) Sept. 19, 1871–Sept. 13, 1936; Senate July 16, 1923–25; House 1933–35.

Johnson, Martin Nelson (R N.D.) March 3, 1850–Oct. 21, 1909; House 1891–99; Senate March 4–Oct. 21, 1909.

Johnson, Nancy Lee (R Conn.) Jan. 5, 1935– ; House 1983– ; chair House Standards of Official Conduct 1995–97.

Johnson, Noadiah (J N.Y.) 1795–April 4, 1839; House 1833–35.

Johnson, Noble Jacob (R Ind.) Aug. 23, 1887–March 17, 1968; House 1925–31, 1939–July 1, 1948.

Johnson, Paul Burney (D Miss.) March 23, 1880–Dec. 26, 1943; House 1919–23; Gov. Jan. 16, 1940–Dec. 26, 1943.

Johnson, Perley Brown (W Ohio) Sept. 8, 1798–Feb. 9, 1870; House 1843–45.

Johnson, Philip (D Pa.) Jan. 17, 1818–Jan. 29, 1867; House 1861–Jan. 29, 1867.

Johnson, Reverdy (brother-in-law of Thomas Fielder Bowie) (D Md.) May 21, 1796–Feb. 10, 1876; Senate 1845–March 7, 1849 (Whig), 1863–July 10, 1868; attorney general March 8, 1849–July 20, 1850.

Johnson, Richard Mentor (brother of James Johnson born in 1774 and John Telemachus Johnson, uncle of Robert Ward Johnson) (R Ky.) Oct. 17, 1780–Nov. 19, 1850; House 1807–19, 1829–37; Senate Dec. 10, 1819–29; vice president 1837–41 (Democrat).

Johnson, Robert Davis (D Mo.) Aug. 12, 1883–Oct. 23, 1961; House Sept. 29, 1931–33.

Johnson, Robert Ward (nephew of James Johnson born in 1774, John Telemachus Johnson and Richard Mentor Johnson) (D Ark.) July 22, 1814–July 26, 1879; House 1847–53; Senate July 6, 1853–61.

Johnson, Royal Cleaves (R S.D.) Oct. 3, 1882–Aug. 2, 1939; House 1915–33.

Johnson, Samuel Robert (R Texas) Oct. 11, 1930– ; House May 22, 1991– .

Johnson, Thomas Francis (D Md.) June 26, 1909–Feb. 1, 1988; House 1959–63.

Johnson, Timothy Peter (D S.D.) Dec. 28, 1946– ; House 1987–97; Senate 1997– .

Johnson, Timothy V. (R Ill.) July 23, 1946– ; House 2001– .

Johnson, Tom Loftin (D Ohio) July 18, 1854–April 10, 1911; House 1891–95.

Johnson, Waldo Porter (nephew of Joseph Johnson) (D Mo.) Sept. 16, 1817–Aug. 14, 1885; Senate March 17, 1861–Jan. 10, 1862.

Johnson, William Cost (W Md.) Jan. 14, 1806–April 14, 1860; House 1833–35 (Anti-Jacksonian), 1837–43.

Johnson, William Richard (R Ill.) May 15, 1875–Jan. 2, 1938; House 1925–33.

Johnson, William Samuel (– Conn.) Oct. 7, 1727–Nov. 14, 1819; Senate 1789–March 4, 1791; Cont. Cong. 1785–87.

Johnson, William Ward (R Calif.) March 9, 1892–June 8, 1963; House 1941–45.

Johnston, Charles (W N.Y.) Feb. 14, 1793–Sept. 1, 1845; House 1839–41.

Johnston, Charles Clement (brother of Joseph Eggleston Johnston, uncle of John Warfield Johnston) (J Va.) April 30, 1795–June 17, 1832; House 1831–June 17, 1832.

Johnston, David Emmons (D W.Va.) April 10, 1845–July 7, 1917; House 1899–1901.

Johnston, Harry Allison II (D Fla.) Dec. 2, 1931– ; House 1989–97.

Johnston, James Thomas (R Ind.) Jan. 19, 1839–July 19, 1904; House 1885–89.

Johnston, John Bennett Jr. (father-in-law of Timothy J. Roemer) (D La.) June 10, 1932– ; Senate Nov. 14, 1972–97; chair Senate Energy and Natural Resources 1987–95.

Johnston, John Brown (D N.Y.) July 10, 1882–Jan. 11, 1960; House 1919–21.

Johnston, John Warfield (uncle of Henry Bowen, nephew of Charles Clement Johnston and Joseph Eggleston Johnston) (D Va.) Sept. 9, 1818–Feb. 27, 1889; Senate Jan. 26, 1870–March 3, 1871, March 15, 1871–83.

Johnston, Joseph Eggleston (brother of Charles Clement Johnston, uncle of John Warfield Johnston) (D Va.) Feb. 3, 1807–March 21, 1891; House 1879–81.

Johnston, Joseph Forney (D Ala.) March 23, 1843–Aug. 8, 1913; Senate Aug. 6, 1907–Aug. 8, 1913; Gov. Dec. 1, 1896–Dec. 1, 1900.

Johnston, Josiah Stoddard (– La.) Nov. 24, 1784–May 19, 1833; House 1821–23; Senate Jan. 15, 1824–May 19, 1833.

Johnston, Olin DeWitt Talmadge (father of Elizabeth Johnston Patterson) (D S.C.) Nov. 18, 1896–April 18, 1965; Senate 1945–April 18, 1965; chair Senate Post Office and Civil Service 1949–53, 1955–65; Gov. Jan. 15, 1935–Jan. 17, 1939, Jan. 19, 1943–Jan. 2, 1945.

Johnston, Rienzi Melville (cousin of Benjamin Edward Russell) (D Texas) Sept. 9, 1849–Feb. 28, 1926; Senate Jan. 4–29, 1913.

Johnston, Rowland Louis (R Mo.) April 23, 1872–Sept. 22, 1939; House 1929–31.

Johnston, Samuel (– N.C.) Dec. 15, 1733–Aug. 17, 1816; Senate Nov. 27, 1789–93; Cont. Cong. 1780–81; Gov. Dec. 20, 1787–Dec. 17, 1789 (Federalist).

Johnston, Thomas Dillard (D N.C.) April 1, 1840–June 22, 1902; House 1885–89.

Johnston, Walter Eugene III (R N.C.) March 3, 1936– ; House 1981–83.

Johnston, William (D Ohio) 1819–May 1, 1866; House 1863–65.

Johnstone, George (D S.C.) April 18, 1846–March 8, 1921; House 1891–93.

Jolley, John Lawlor (R S.D.) July 14, 1840–Dec. 14, 1926; House Dec. 7, 1891–93.

Jonas, Benjamin Franklin (D La.) July 19, 1834–Dec. 21, 1911; Senate 1879–85.

Jonas, Charles Andrew (father of Charles Raper Jonas) (R N.C.) Aug. 14, 1876–May 25, 1955; House 1929–31.

Jonas, Charles Raper (son of Charles Andrew Jonas) (R N.C.) Dec. 9, 1904–Sept. 28, 1988; House 1953–73.

Jonas, Edgar Allan (R Ill.) Oct. 14, 1885–Nov. 14, 1965; House 1949–55.

Jones, Alexander Hamilton (R N.C.) July 21, 1822–Jan. 29, 1901; House July 6, 1868–71.

Jones, Andrieus Aristieus (D N.M.) May 16, 1862–Dec. 20, 1927; Senate 1917–Dec. 20, 1927.

Jones, Ben (D Ga.) Aug. 30, 1941– ; House 1989–93.

Jones, Benjamin (J Ohio) April 13, 1787–April 24, 1861; House 1833–37.

Jones, Burr W. (D Wis.) March 9, 1846–Jan. 7, 1935; House 1883–85.

Jones, Charles William (D Fla.) Dec. 24, 1834–Oct. 11, 1897; Senate 1875–87.

Jones, Daniel Terryll (D N.Y.) Aug. 17, 1800–March 29, 1861; House 1851–55.

Jones, Ed (D Tenn.) April 20, 1912–Dec. 11, 1999; House March 25, 1969–89.

Jones, Evan John (R Pa.) Oct. 23, 1872–Jan. 9, 1952; House 1919–23.

Jones, Francis (R Tenn.) ?–?; House 1817–23.

Jones, Frank (D N.H.) Sept. 15, 1832–Oct. 2, 1902; House 1875–79.

Jones, George (– Ga.) Feb. 25, 1766–Nov. 13, 1838; Senate Aug. 27–Nov. 7, 1807.

Jones, George Wallace (D Iowa) April 12, 1804–July 22, 1896; House (Terr. Del.) 1835–April 1836 (no party Mich.), 1837–Jan. 14, 1839 (no party Wis.); Senate Dec. 7, 1848–59.

Jones, George Washington (D Tenn.) March 15, 1806–Nov. 14, 1884; House 1843–59.

Jones, George Washington (G Texas) Sept. 5, 1828–July 11, 1903; House 1879–83.

Jones, Hamilton Chamberlain (D N.C.) Sept. 26, 1884–Aug. 10, 1957; House 1947–53.

Jones, Homer Raymond (R Wash.) Sept. 3, 1893–Nov. 26, 1970; House 1947–49.

Jones, Isaac Dashiell (W Md.) Nov. 1, 1806–July 5, 1893; House 1841–43.

Jones, James (F Ga.) ?–Jan. 11, 1801; House 1799–Jan. 11, 1801.

Jones, James (– Va.) Dec. 11, 1772–April 25, 1848; House 1819–23.

Jones, James Chamberlain (W Tenn.) April 20, 1809–Oct. 29, 1859; Senate 1851–57; Gov. Oct. 15, 1841–Oct. 14, 1845.

Jones, James Henry (D Texas) Sept. 13, 1830–March 22, 1904; House 1883–87.

Jones, James Kimbrough (D Ark.) Sept. 29, 1839–June 1, 1908; House 1881–Feb. 19, 1885; Senate March 4, 1885–1903; chair Dem. Nat. Comm. 1896–1904.

Jones, James Robert (D Okla.) May 5, 1939– ; House 1973–87; chair House Budget 1981–85.

Jones, James Taylor (D Ala.) July 20, 1832–Feb. 15, 1895; House 1877–79, Dec. 3, 1883–89.

Jones, Jehu Glancy (D Pa.) Oct. 7, 1811–March 24, 1878; House 1851–53, Feb. 4, 1854–Oct. 30, 1858.

Jones, John James (D Ga.) Nov. 13, 1824–Oct. 19, 1898; House 1859–Jan. 23, 1861.

Jones, John Marvin (D Texas) Feb. 26, 1886–March 4, 1976; House 1917–Nov. 20, 1940.

Jones, John Percival (R Nev.) Jan. 27, 1829–Nov. 27, 1912; Senate 1873–1903.

Jones, John Sills (R Ohio) Feb. 12, 1836–April 11, 1903; House 1877–79.

Jones, John William (W Ga.) April 14, 1806–April 27, 1871; House 1847–49.

Jones, John Winston (D Va.) Nov. 22, 1791–Jan. 29, 1848; House 1835–45 (1835–37 Jacksonian); Speaker Dec. 4, 1843–45.

Jones, Morgan (D N.Y.) Feb. 26, 1830–July 13, 1894; House 1865–67.

Jones, Nathaniel (D N.Y.) Feb. 17, 1788–July 20, 1866; House 1837–41.

Jones, Owen (D Pa.) Dec. 29, 1819–Dec. 25, 1878; House 1857–59.

Jones, Paul Caruthers (D Mo.) March 12, 1901–Feb. 10, 1981; House Nov. 2, 1948–69.

Jones, Phineas (R N.J.) April 18, 1819–April 19, 1884; House 1881–83.

Jones, Robert Emmett Jr. (D Ala.) June 12, 1912–June 4, 1997; House Jan. 28, 1947–77; chair House Public Works and Transportation 1975–77.

Jones, Robert Franklin (R Ohio) June 25, 1907–June 22, 1968; House 1939–Sept. 2, 1947.

Jones, Roland (D La.) Nov. 18, 1813–Feb. 5, 1869; House 1853–55.

Jones, Seaborn (D Ga.) Feb. 1, 1788–March 18, 1864; House 1833–35 (Jacksonian), 1845–47.

Jones, Stephanie Tubbs (D Ohio) Sept. 10, 1949– ; House 1999– .

Jones, Thomas Laurens (D Ky.) Jan. 22, 1819–June 20, 1887; House 1867–71, 1875–77.

Jones, Walter (R Va.) Dec. 18, 1745–Dec. 31, 1815; House 1797–99, 1803–11.

Jones, Walter Beaman (father of Walter B. Jones Jr.) (D N.C.) Aug. 19, 1913–Sept. 15, 1992; House Feb. 5, 1966–Sept. 15, 1992; chair House Merchant Marine and Fisheries 1981–92.

Jones, Walter B. Jr. (son of Walter Beaman Jones) (R N.C.) Feb. 10, 1943– ; House 1995– .

Jones, Wesley Livsey (R Wash.) Oct. 9, 1863–Nov. 19, 1932; House 1899–1909; Senate 1909–Nov. 19, 1932.

Jones, William (R Pa.) 1760–Sept. 6, 1831; House 1801–03; secretary of the navy Jan. 19, 1813–Dec. 1, 1814.

Jones, William Atkinson (D Va.) March 21, 1849–April 17, 1918; House 1891–April 17, 1918.

Jones, William Carey (Sil.R Wash.) April 5, 1855–June 14, 1927; House 1897–99.

Jones, William Theopilus (R Wyo.) Feb. 20, 1842–Oct. 9, 1882; House (Terr. Del.) 1871–73.

Jones, Woodrow Wilson (D N.C.) Jan. 26, 1914– ; House Nov. 7, 1950–57.

Jonkman, Bartel John (R Mich.) April 28, 1884–June 13, 1955; House Feb. 19, 1940–49.

Jontz, James Prather (D Ind.) Dec. 18, 1951– ; House 1987–93.

Jordan, Barbara Charline (D Texas) Feb. 21, 1936–Jan. 17, 1996; House 1973–79.

Jordan, Benjamin Everett (D N.C.) Sept. 8, 1896–March 15, 1974; Senate April 19, 1958–73; chair Senate Rules and Administration 1963–72.

Jordan, Isaac M. (D Ohio) May 5, 1835–Dec. 3, 1890; House 1883–85.

Jordan, Leonard Beck (R Idaho) May 15, 1899–June 30, 1983; Senate Aug. 6, 1962–Jan. 2, 1973; Gov. Jan. 1, 1951–Jan. 3, 1955.

Jorden, Edwin James (R Pa.) Aug. 30, 1863–Sept. 7, 1903; House Feb. 23–March 4, 1895.

Jorgensen, Joseph (R Va.) Feb. 11, 1844–Jan. 21, 1888; House 1877–83.

Joseph, Antonio (D N.M.) Aug. 25, 1846–April 19, 1910; House (Terr. Del.) 1885–95.

Jost, Henry Lee (D Mo.) Dec. 6, 1873–July 13, 1950; House 1923–25.

Joy, Charles Frederick (R Mo.) Dec. 11, 1849–April 13, 1921; House 1893–April 3, 1894, 1895–1903.

Joyce, Charles Herbert (R Vt.) Jan. 30, 1830–Nov. 22, 1916; House 1875–83.

Joyce, James (R Ohio) July 2, 1870–March 25, 1931; House 1909–11.

Judd, Norman Buel (grandfather of Norman Judd Gould) (R Ill.) Jan. 10, 1815–Nov. 11, 1878; House 1867–71.

Judd, Walter Henry (R Minn.) Sept. 25, 1898–Feb. 13, 1994; House 1943–63.

Judson, Andrew Thompson (J Conn.) Nov. 29, 1784–March 17, 1853; House 1835–July 4, 1836.

Julian, George Washington (R Ind.) May 5, 1817–July 7, 1899; House 1849–51 (Free-Soiler), 1861–71.

Junkin, Benjamin Franklin (R Pa.) Nov. 12, 1822–Oct. 9, 1908; House 1859–61.

Juul, Niels (R Ill.) April 27, 1859–Dec. 4, 1929; House 1917–21.

Kading, Charles August (R Wis.) Jan. 14, 1874–June 19, 1956; House 1927–33.

Kahn, Florence Prag (widow of Julius Kahn) (R Calif.) Nov. 9, 1866–Nov. 16, 1948; House 1925–37.

Kahn, Julius (husband of Florence Prag Kahn) (R Calif.) Feb. 28, 1861–Dec. 18, 1924; House 1899–1903, 1905–Dec. 18, 1924.

Kalanianaole, Jonah Kuhio (R Hawaii) March 26, 1871–Jan. 7, 1922; House (Terr. Del.) 1903–Jan. 7, 1922.

Kalbfleisch, Martin (D N.Y.) Feb. 8, 1804–Feb. 12, 1873; House 1863–65.

Kane, Elias Kent (– Ill.) June 7, 1794–Dec. 12, 1835; Senate 1825–Dec. 12, 1835.

Kane, Nicholas Thomas (D N.Y.) Sept. 12, 1846–Sept. 14, 1887; House March 4–Sept. 14, 1887.

Kanjorski, Paul E. (D Pa.) April 2, 1937– ; House 1985– .

Kaptur, Marcia Carolyn "Marcy" (D Ohio) June 17, 1946– ; House 1983– .

Karch, Charles Adam (D Ill.) March 17, 1875–Nov. 6, 1932; House 1931–Nov. 6, 1932.

Karnes, David Kemp (R Neb.) Dec. 12, 1948– ; Senate March 13, 1987–89.

Karst, Raymond Willard (D Mo.) Dec. 31, 1902–Oct. 4, 1987; House 1949–51.

Karsten, Frank Melvin (D Mo.) Jan. 7, 1913–May 14, 1992; House 1947–69.

Karth, Joseph Edward (D Minn.) Aug. 26, 1922– ; House 1959–77.

Kasem, George Albert (D Calif.) April 6, 1919–Feb. 11, 2002; House 1959–61.

Kasich, John Richard (R Ohio) May 13, 1952– ; House 1983–2001; chair House Budget 1995–2001.

Kassebaum, Nancy Landon (later Nancy Kassebaum Baker) (R Kan.) July 29, 1932– ; Senate Dec. 23, 1978–97; chair Senate Labor and Human Resources 1995–97.

Kasson, John Adam (R Iowa) Jan. 11, 1822–May 19, 1910; House 1863–67, 1873–77, 1881–July 13, 1884.

Kasten, Robert Walter Jr. (R Wis.) June 19, 1942– ; House 1975–79; Senate 1981–93.

Kastenmeier, Robert William (D Wis.) Jan. 24, 1924– ; House 1959–91.

Kaufman, David Spangler (D Texas) Dec. 18, 1813–Jan. 31, 1851; House March 30, 1846–Jan. 31, 1851.

Kavanagh, Edward (J Maine) April 27, 1795–Jan. 22, 1844; House 1831–35; Gov. March 7, 1843–Jan. 1, 1844 (Democrat).

Kavanaugh, William Marmaduke (D Ark.) March 3, 1866–Feb. 21, 1915; Senate Jan. 29–March 3, 1913.

Kaynor, William Kirk (R Mass.) Nov. 29, 1884–Dec. 20, 1929; House March 4–Dec. 20, 1929.

Kazen, Abraham Jr. (D Texas) Jan. 17, 1919–Nov. 29, 1987; House 1967–85.

Kean, Hamilton Fish (father of Robert Winthrop Kean, brother of John Kean) (R N.J.) Feb. 27, 1862–Dec. 27, 1941; Senate 1929–35.

Kean, John (brother of Hamilton Fish Kean, uncle of Robert Winthrop Kean) (R N.J.) Dec. 4, 1852–Nov. 4, 1914; House 1883–85, 1887–89; Senate 1899–1911.

Kean, Robert Winthrop (son of Hamilton Fish Kean, nephew of John Kean) (R N.J.) Sept. 28, 1893–Sept. 21, 1980; House 1939–59.

Kearney, Bernard William (R N.Y.) May 23, 1889–June 3, 1976; House 1943–59.

Kearns, Carroll Dudley (R Pa.) May 7, 1900–June 11, 1976; House 1947–63.

Kearns, Charles Cyrus (R Ohio) Feb. 11, 1869–Dec. 17, 1931; House 1915–31.

Kearns, Thomas (R Utah) April 11, 1862–Oct. 18, 1918; Senate Jan. 23, 1901–05.

Keating, Edward (D Colo.) July 9, 1875–March 18, 1965; House 1913–19.

Keating, Kenneth Barnard (R N.Y.) May 18, 1900–May 5, 1975; House 1947–59; Senate 1959–65.

Keating, William John (R Ohio) March 30, 1927– ; House 1971–Jan. 3, 1974.

Kee, James (son of John Kee and Maude Elizabeth Kee) (D W.Va.) April 15, 1917–March 11, 1989; House 1965–73.

Kee, John (husband of Maude Elizabeth Kee, father of James Kee) (D W.Va.) Aug. 22, 1874–May 8, 1951; House 1933–May 8, 1951; chair House Foreign Affairs 1949–51.

Kee, Maude Elizabeth (widow of John Kee, mother of James Kee) (D W.Va.) ?–Feb. 16, 1975; House July 17, 1951–65.

Keefe, Frank Bateman (R Wis.) Sept. 23, 1887–Feb. 5, 1952; House 1939–51.

Keeney, Russell Watson (R Ill.) Dec. 29, 1897–Jan. 11, 1958; House 1957–Jan. 11, 1958.

Keese, Richard (– N.Y.) Nov. 23, 1794–Feb. 7, 1883; House 1827–29.

Kefauver, Carey Estes (D Tenn.) July 26, 1903–Aug. 10, 1963; House Sept. 13, 1939–49; Senate 1949–Aug. 10, 1963.

Kehoe, James Nicholas (D Ky.) July 15, 1862–June 16, 1945; House 1901–05.

Kehoe, James Walter (D Fla.) April 25, 1870–Aug. 20, 1938; House 1917–19.

Kehr, Edward Charles (D Mo.) Nov. 5, 1837–April 20, 1918; House 1875–77.

Keifer, Joseph Warren (R Ohio) Jan. 30, 1836–April 22, 1932; House 1877–85, 1905–11; Speaker Dec. 5, 1881–83.

Keightley, Edwin William (R Mich.) Aug. 7, 1843–May 4, 1926; House 1877–79.

Keim, George May (uncle of William High Keim) (D Pa.) March 23, 1805–June 10, 1861; House March 17, 1838–43.

Keim, William High (nephew of George May Keim) (R Pa.) June 13, 1813–May 18, 1862; House Dec. 7, 1858–59.

Keister, Abraham Lincoln (R Pa.) Sept. 10, 1852–May 26, 1917; House 1913–17.

Keith, Hastings (R Mass.) Nov. 22, 1915– ; House 1959–73.

Keitt, Laurence Massillon (D S.C.) Oct. 4, 1824–June 4, 1864; House 1853–July 16, 1856, Aug. 6, 1856–Dec. 1860.

Keliher, John Austin (D Mass.) Nov. 6, 1866–Sept. 20, 1938; House 1903–11.

Keller, Kent Ellsworth (D Ill.) June 4, 1867–Sept. 3, 1954; House 1931–41.

Keller, Oscar Edward (IR Minn.) July 30, 1878–Nov. 21, 1927; House July 1, 1919–27.

Keller, Ric (R Fla.) Sept. 5, 1964– ; House 2001– .

Kelley, Augustine Bernard (D Pa.) July 9, 1883–Nov. 20, 1957; House 1941–Nov. 20, 1957.

Kelley, Harrison (R Kan.) May 12, 1836–July 24, 1897; House Dec. 2, 1889–91.

Kelley, John Edward (P S.D.) March 27, 1853–Aug. 5, 1941; House 1897–99.

Kelley, Patrick Henry (R Mich.) Oct. 7, 1867–Sept. 11, 1925; House 1913–23.

Kelley, William Darrah (R Pa.) April 12, 1814–Jan. 9, 1890; House 1861–Jan. 9, 1890.

Kellogg, Charles (– N.Y.) Oct. 3, 1773–May 11, 1842; House 1825–27.

Kellogg, Francis William (R Ala.) May 30, 1810–Jan. 13, 1879; House 1859–65 (Mich.), July 22, 1868–69.

Kellogg, Frank Billings (R Minn.) Dec. 22, 1856–Dec. 21, 1937; Senate 1917–23; secretary of state March 5, 1925–March 28, 1929.

Kellogg, Orlando (W N.Y.) June 18, 1809–Aug. 24, 1865; House 1847–49, 1863–Aug. 24, 1865.

Kellogg, Stephen Wright (R Conn.) April 5, 1822–Jan. 27, 1904; House 1869–73.

Kellogg, William (R Ill.) July 8, 1814–Dec. 20, 1872; House 1857–63.

Kellogg, William Pitt (R La.) Dec. 8, 1830–Aug. 10, 1918; Senate July 9, 1868–Nov. 1, 1872, 1877–83; House 1883–85; Gov. Jan. 13, 1873–Jan. 8, 1877.

Kelly, Edna Flannery (D N.Y.) Aug. 20, 1906–Dec. 14, 1997; House Nov. 8, 1949–69.

Kelly, Edward Austin (D Ill.) April 3, 1892–Aug. 30, 1969; House 1931–43, 1945–47.

Kelly, George Bradshaw (D N.Y.) Dec. 12, 1900–June 26, 1971; House 1937–39.

Kelly, James (F Pa.) July 17, 1760–Feb. 4, 1819; House 1805–09.

Kelly, James Kerr (D Ore.) Feb. 16, 1819–Sept. 15, 1903; Senate 1871–77.

Kelly, John (D N.Y.) April 20, 1822–June 1, 1886; House 1855–Dec. 25, 1858.

Kelly, Melville Clyde (R Pa.) Aug. 4, 1883–April 29, 1935; House 1913–15, 1917–35.

Kelly, Richard (R Fla.) July 31, 1924– ; House 1975–81.

Kelly, Sue W. (R N.Y.) Sept. 26, 1936– ; House 1995– .

Kelly, William (– Ala.) Sept. 22, 1786–Aug. 24, 1834; Senate Dec. 12, 1822–25.

Kelsey, William Henry (R N.Y.) Oct. 2, 1812–April 20, 1879; House 1855–59 (1855–57 Whig), 1867–71.

Kelso, John Russell (IRad. Mo.) March 23, 1831–Jan. 26, 1891; House 1865–67.

Kem, James Preston (R Mo.) April 2, 1890–Feb. 24, 1965; Senate 1947–53.

Kem, Omar Madison (P Neb.) Nov. 13, 1855–Feb. 13, 1942; House 1891–97.

Kemble, Gouverneur (D N.Y.) Jan. 25, 1786–Sept. 16, 1875; House 1837–41.

Kemp, Bolivar Edwards (D La.) Dec. 28, 1871–June 19, 1933; House 1925–June 19, 1933.

Kemp, Jack French (R N.Y.) July 13, 1935– ; House 1971–89; secretary of housing and urban development Feb. 13, 1989–Jan. 20, 1993.

Kempshall, Thomas (W N.Y.) about 1796–Jan. 14, 1865; House 1839–41.

Kempthorne, Dirk (R Idaho) Oct. 29, 1951– ; Senate 1993–99; Gov. Jan. 8, 1999– .

Kenan, Thomas (R N.C.) Feb. 26, 1771–Oct. 22, 1843; House 1805–11.

Kendall, Charles West (D Nev.) April 22, 1828–June 25, 1914; House 1871–75.

Kendall, Elva Roscoe (R Ky.) Feb. 14, 1893–Jan. 29, 1968; House 1929–31.

Kendall, John Wilkerson (father of Joseph Morgan Kendall) (D Ky.) June 26, 1834–March 7, 1892; House 1891–March 7, 1892.

Kendall, Jonas (father of Joseph Gowing Kendall) (– Mass.) Oct. 27, 1757–Oct. 22, 1844; House 1819–21.

Kendall, Joseph Gowing (son of Jonas Kendall) (– Mass.) Oct. 27, 1788–Oct. 2, 1847; House 1829–33.

Kendall, Joseph Morgan (son of John Wilkerson Kendall) (D Ky.) May 12, 1863–Nov. 5, 1933; House April 21, 1892–93, 1895–Feb. 18, 1897.

Kendall, Nathan Edward (R Iowa) March 17, 1868–Nov. 5, 1936; House 1909–13; Gov. Jan. 13, 1921–Jan. 15, 1925.

Kendall, Samuel Austin (R Pa.) Nov. 1, 1859–Jan. 8, 1933; House 1919–Jan. 8, 1933.

Kendrick, John Benjamin (D Wyo.) Sept. 6, 1857–Nov. 3, 1933; Senate 1917–Nov. 3, 1933; Gov. Jan. 4, 1915–Feb. 26, 1917.

Kenna, John Edward (D W.Va.) April 10, 1848–Jan. 11, 1893; House 1877–83; Senate 1883–Jan. 11, 1893.

Kennedy, Ambrose (R R.I.) Dec. 1, 1875–March 10, 1967; House 1913–23.

Kennedy, Ambrose Jerome (D Md.) Jan. 6, 1893–Aug. 29, 1950; House Nov. 8, 1932–41.

Kennedy, Andrew (cousin of Case Broderick) (D Ind.) July 24, 1810–Dec. 31, 1847; House 1841–47.

Kennedy, Anthony (brother of John Pendleton Kennedy) (AP Md.) Dec. 21, 1810–July 31, 1892; Senate 1857–63.

Kennedy, Charles Augustus (R Iowa) March 24, 1869–Jan. 10, 1951; House 1907–21.

Kennedy, Edward Moore (father of Patrick J. Kennedy, brother of John Fitzgerald Kennedy and Robert Francis Kennedy, grandson of John Francis Fitzgerald, uncle of Joseph Patrick Kennedy II) (D Mass.) Feb. 22, 1932– ; Senate Nov. 7, 1962– ; chair Senate Judiciary 1979–81; chair Senate Labor and Human Resources 1987–95; chair Senate Health, Education, Labor, and Pensions Jan. 3, 2001–Jan. 20, 2001, June 6, 2001–03.

Kennedy, James (R Ohio) Sept. 3, 1853–Nov. 9, 1928; House 1903–11.

Kennedy, John Fitzgerald (brother of Edward Moore Kennedy and Robert Francis Kennedy, grandson of John Francis Fitzgerald, uncle of Joseph Patrick Kennedy II and Patrick J. Kennedy) (D Mass.) May 29, 1917–Nov. 22, 1963; House 1947–53; Senate 1953–Dec. 22, 1960; president 1961–Nov. 22, 1963.

Kennedy, John Lauderdale (R Neb.) Oct. 27, 1854–Aug. 30, 1946; House 1905–07.

Kennedy, John Pendleton (brother of Anthony Kennedy) (W Md.) Oct. 25, 1795–Aug. 18, 1870; House April 25, 1838–39, 1841–45; secretary of the navy July 26, 1852–March 7, 1853.

Kennedy, Joseph Patrick II (son of Robert Francis Kennedy, cousin of Patrick J. Kennedy, nephew of Edward Moore Kennedy and John Fitzgerald Kennedy, great-grandson of John Francis Fitzgerald) (D Mass.) Sept. 24, 1952– ; House 1987–99.

Kennedy, Mark (R Minn.) April 11, 1957– ; House 2001– .

Kennedy, Martin John (D N.Y.) Aug. 29, 1892–Oct. 27, 1955; House March 11, 1930–45.

Kennedy, Michael Joseph (D N.Y.) Oct. 25, 1897–Nov. 1, 1949; House 1939–43.

Kennedy, Patrick J. (son of Edward Moore Kennedy, cousin of Joseph Patrick Kennedy II, nephew of John Fitzgerald Kennedy and Robert Francis Kennedy, great-grandson of John Francis Fitzgerald) (D R.I.) July 14, 1967– ; House 1995– .

Kennedy, Robert Francis (father of Joseph Patrick Kennedy II, brother of Edward Moore Kennedy and John Fitzgerald Kennedy, uncle of Patrick J. Kennedy, grandson of John Francis Fitzgerald) (D N.Y.) Nov. 20, 1925–June 6, 1968; Senate 1965–June 6, 1968; attorney general Jan. 21, 1961–Sept. 3, 1964.

Kennedy, Robert Patterson (R Ohio) Jan. 23, 1840–May 6, 1918; House 1887–91.

Kennedy, William (R N.C.) July 31, 1768–Oct. 11, 1834; House 1803–05, 1809–11, Jan. 30, 1813–15.

Kennedy, William (D Conn.) Dec. 19, 1854–June 19, 1918; House 1913–15.

Kennelly, Barbara Bailey (D Conn.) July 10, 1936– ; House Jan. 25, 1982–99.

Kennett, Luther Martin (W Mo.) March 15, 1807–April 12, 1873; House 1855–57.

Kenney, Edward Aloysius (D N.J.) Aug. 11, 1884–Jan. 27, 1938; House 1933–Jan. 27, 1938.

Kenney, Richard Rolland (D Del.) Sept. 9, 1856–Aug. 14, 1931; Senate 1897–1901.

Kennon, William Sr. (cousin of William Kennon Jr.) (J Ohio) May 14, 1793–Nov. 2, 1881; House 1829–33, 1835–37.

Kennon, William Jr. (cousin of William Kennon Sr.) (D Ohio) June 12, 1802–Oct. 19, 1867; House 1847–49.

Kent, Everett (D Pa.) Nov. 15, 1888–Oct. 13, 1963; House 1923–25, 1927–29.

Kent, Joseph (R Md.) Jan. 14, 1779–Nov. 24, 1837; House 1811–15, 1819–Jan. 6, 1826; Senate 1833–Nov. 24, 1837; Gov. Jan. 9, 1826–Jan. 15, 1829 (Democratic Republican).

Kent, Moss (F N.Y.) April 3, 1766–May 30, 1838; House 1813–17.

Kent, William (I Calif.) March 29, 1864–March 13, 1928; House 1911–17 (1911–13 Progressive Republican).

Kenyon, William Scheuneman (R N.Y.) Dec. 13, 1820–Feb. 10, 1896; House 1859–61.

Kenyon, William Squire (R Iowa) June 10, 1869–Sept. 9, 1933; Senate April 12, 1911–Feb. 24, 1922.

Keogh, Eugene James (D N.Y.) Aug. 30, 1907–May 26, 1989; House 1937–67.

Kern, Frederick John (D Ill.) Sept. 6, 1864–Nov. 9, 1931; House 1901–03.

Kern, John Worth (D Ind.) Dec. 20, 1849–Aug. 17, 1917; Senate 1911–17; Senate majority leader 1913–17.

Kernan, Francis (D N.Y.) Jan. 14, 1816–Sept. 7, 1892; House 1863–65; Senate 1875–81.

Kerns, Brian D. (R Ind.) May 22, 1957– ; House 2001–03.

Kerr, Daniel (R Iowa) June 18, 1836–Oct. 8, 1916; House 1887–91.

Kerr, James (D Pa.) Oct. 2, 1851–Oct. 31, 1908; House 1889–91.

Kerr, John (father of John Kerr Jr., cousin of Bartlett Yancey, great-uncle of John Hosea Kerr) (R Va.) Aug. 4, 1782–Sept. 29, 1842; House 1813–15, Oct. 30, 1815–17.

Kerr, John Jr. (son of John Kerr) (W N.C.) Feb. 10, 1811–Sept. 5, 1879; House 1853–55.

Kerr, John Bozman (son of John Leeds Kerr) (W Md.) March 5, 1809–Jan. 27, 1878; House 1849–51.

Kerr, John Hosea (great-nephew of John Kerr) (D N.C.) Dec. 31, 1873–June 21, 1958; House Nov. 6, 1923–53.

Kerr, John Leeds (father of John Bozman Kerr) (W Md.) Jan. 15, 1780–Feb. 21, 1844; House 1825–29 (no party), 1831–33 (no party); Senate Jan. 5, 1841–43.

Kerr, Joseph (– Ohio) 1765–Aug. 22, 1837; Senate Dec. 10, 1814–15.

Kerr, Josiah Leeds (R Md.) Jan. 10, 1861–Sept. 27, 1920; House Nov. 6, 1900–01.

Kerr, Michael Crawford (D Ind.) March 15, 1827–Aug. 19, 1876; House 1865–73, 1875–Aug. 19, 1876; Speaker Dec. 6, 1875–Aug. 19, 1876.

Kerr, Robert Samuel (D Okla.) Sept. 11, 1896–Jan. 1, 1963; Senate 1949–Jan. 1, 1963; chair Senate Aeronautical and Space Sciences 1961–63; Gov. Jan. 11, 1943–Jan. 13, 1947.

Kerr, Winfield Scott (R Ohio) June 23, 1852–Sept. 11, 1917; House 1895–1901.

Kerrey, Robert "Bob" (D Neb.) Aug. 27, 1943– ; Senate 1989–2001; Gov. Jan. 6, 1983–Jan. 9, 1987.

Kerrigan, James (ID N.Y.) Dec. 25, 1828–Nov. 1, 1899; House 1861–63.

Kerry, John Forbes (D Mass.) Dec. 22, 1943– ; Senate 1985– ; chair Senate Small Business Jan. 3, 2001–Jan. 20, 2001, June 6, 2001–03.

Kershaw, John (R S.C.) Sept. 12, 1765–Aug. 4, 1829; House 1813–15.

Kersten, Charles Joseph (R Wis.) May 26, 1902–Oct. 31, 1972; House 1947–49, 1951–55.

Ketcham, John Clark (R Mich.) Jan. 1, 1873–Dec. 4, 1941; House 1921–33.

Ketcham, John Henry (R N.Y.) Dec. 21, 1832–Nov. 4, 1906; House 1865–73, 1877–93, 1897–Nov. 4, 1906.

Ketchum, William Matthew (R Calif.) Sept. 2, 1921–June 24, 1978; House 1973–June 24, 1978.

Ketchum, Winthrop Welles (R Pa.) June 29, 1820–Dec. 6, 1879; House 1875–July 19, 1876.

Kettner, William (D Calif.) Nov. 20, 1864–Nov. 11, 1930; House 1913–21.

Key, David McKendree (D Tenn.) Jan. 27, 1824–Feb. 3, 1900; Senate Aug. 18, 1875–Jan. 19, 1877; postmaster general March 13, 1877–Aug. 24, 1880.

Key, John Alexander (D Ohio) Dec. 30, 1871–March 4, 1954; House 1913–19.

Key, Philip (cousin of Philip Barton Key, great-grandfather of Barnes Compton) (– Md.) 1750–Jan. 4, 1820; House 1791–93.

Key, Philip Barton (cousin of Philip Key) (F Md.) April 12, 1757–July 28, 1815; House 1807–13.

Keyes, Elias (– Vt.) April 14, 1758–July 9, 1844; House 1821–23.

Keyes, Henry Wilder (R N.H.) May 23, 1863–June 19, 1938; Senate 1919–37; Gov. Jan. 3, 1917–Jan. 2, 1919.

Keys, Martha Elizabeth (wife of Andrew Jacobs Jr., daughter-in-law of Andrew Jacobs Sr.) (D Kan.) Aug. 10, 1930– ; House 1975–79.

Kidder, David (W Maine) Dec. 8, 1787–Nov. 1, 1860; House 1823–27.

Kidder, Jefferson Parish (R Dakota) June 4, 1815–Oct. 2, 1883; House (Terr. Del.) 1875–79.

Kidwell, Zedekiah (D Va.) Jan. 4, 1814–April 27, 1872; House 1853–57.

Kiefer, Andrew Robert (R Minn.) May 25, 1832–May 1, 1904; House 1893–97.

Kiefner, Charles Edward (R Mo.) Nov. 25, 1869–Dec. 13, 1942; House 1925–27, 1929–31.

Kiess, Edgar Raymond (R Pa.) Aug. 26, 1875–July 20, 1930; House 1913–July 20, 1930.

Kilbourne, James (R Ohio) Oct. 19, 1770–April 9, 1850; House 1813–17.

Kilburn, Clarence Evans (R N.Y.) April 13, 1893–May 20, 1975; House Feb. 13, 1940–65.

Kilday, Paul Joseph (D Texas) March 29, 1900–Oct. 12, 1968; House 1939–Sept. 24, 1961.

Kildee, Dale Edward (D Mich.) Sept. 16, 1929– ; House 1977– .

Kilgore, Constantine Buckley (D Texas) Feb. 20, 1835–Sept. 23, 1897; House 1887–95.

Kilgore, Daniel (D Ohio) 1793–Dec. 12, 1851; House Dec. 1, 1834–July 4, 1838 (Dec. 1, 1834–37 Jacksonian).

Kilgore, David (R Ind.) April 3, 1804–Jan. 22, 1879; House 1857–61.

Kilgore, Harley Martin (D W.Va.) Jan. 11, 1893–Feb. 28, 1956; Senate 1941–Feb. 28, 1956; chair Senate Judiciary 1955–56.

Kilgore, Joe Madison (D Texas) Dec. 10, 1918–Feb. 10, 1999; House 1955–65.

Kille, Joseph (D N.J.) April 12, 1790–March 1, 1865; House 1839–41.

Killinger, John Weinland (R Pa.) Sept. 18, 1824–June 30, 1896; House 1859–63, 1871–75, 1877–81.

Kilpatrick, Carolyn Cheeks (D Mich.) June 25, 1945– ; House 1997– .

Kim, Jay C. (R Calif.) March 27, 1939– ; House 1993–99.

Kimball, Alanson Mellen (R Wis.) March 12, 1827–May 26, 1913; House 1875–77.

Kimball, Henry Mahlon (R Mich.) Aug. 27, 1878–Oct. 19, 1935; House Jan. 3–Oct. 19, 1935.

Kimball, William Preston (D Ky.) Nov. 4, 1857–Feb. 24, 1926; House 1907–09.

Kimmel, William (D Md.) Aug. 15, 1812–Dec. 28, 1886; House 1877–81.

Kincaid, John (J Ky.) Feb. 15, 1791–Feb. 7, 1873; House 1829–31.

Kincheloe, David Hayes (D Ky.) April 9, 1877–April 16, 1950; House 1915–Oct. 5, 1930.

Kind, Ron (D Wis.) March 16, 1963– ; House 1997– .

Kindel, George John (D Colo.) March 2, 1855–Feb. 28, 1930; House 1913–15.

Kindness, Thomas Norman (R Ohio) Aug. 26, 1929–Jan. 8, 2004; House 1975–87.

Kindred, John Joseph (D N.Y.) July 15, 1864–Oct. 23, 1937; House 1911–13, 1921–29.

King, Adam (J Pa.) 1790–May 6, 1835; House 1827–33.

King, Andrew (D Mo.) March 20, 1812–Nov. 18, 1895; House 1871–73.

King, Austin Augustus (U Mo.) Sept. 21, 1802–April 22, 1870; House 1863–65; Gov. Nov. 27, 1848–Jan. 3, 1853 (Democrat).

King, Carleton James (R N.Y.) June 15, 1904–Nov. 19, 1977; House 1961–Dec. 31, 1974.

King, Cecil Rhodes (D Calif.) Jan. 13, 1898–March 17, 1974; House Aug. 25, 1942–69.

King, Cyrus (half-brother of Rufus King) (F Mass.) Sept. 6, 1772–April 25, 1817; House 1813–17.

King, Daniel Putnam (W Mass.) Jan. 8, 1801–July 25, 1850; House 1843–July 25, 1850.

King, David Sjodahl (son of William Henry King) (D Utah) June 20, 1917– ; House 1959–63, 1965–67.

King, Edward John (R Ill.) July 1, 1867–Feb. 17, 1929; House 1915–Feb. 17, 1929.

King, George Gordon (W R.I.) June 9, 1807–July 17, 1870; House 1849–53.

King, Henry (brother of Thomas Butler King, uncle of John Floyd King) (J Pa.) July 6, 1790–July 13, 1861; House 1831–35.

King, James Gore (son of Rufus King, brother of John Alsop King) (W N.J.) May 8, 1791–Oct. 3, 1853; House 1849–51.

King, John (J N.Y.) 1775–Sept. 1, 1836; House 1831–33.

King, John Alsop (son of Rufus King, brother of James Gore King) (W N.Y.) Jan. 3, 1788–July 7, 1867; House 1849–51; Gov. Jan. 1, 1857–Jan. 1, 1859 (Republican).

King, John Floyd (son of Thomas Butler King, nephew of Henry King) (D La.) April 20, 1842–May 8, 1915; House 1879–87.

King, John Pendleton (J Ga.) April 3, 1799–March 19, 1888; Senate Nov. 21, 1833–Nov. 1, 1837.

King, Karl Clarence (R Pa.) Jan. 26, 1897–April 16, 1974; House Nov. 6, 1951–57.

King, Perkins (J N.Y.) Jan. 12, 1784–Nov. 29, 1875; House 1829–31.

King, Peter Thomas (R N.Y.) April 5, 1944– ; House 1993– .

King, Preston (R N.Y.) Oct. 14, 1806–Nov. 12, 1865; House 1843–47 (Democrat), 1849–53 (Free-Soiler); Senate 1857–63.

King, Rufus (half-brother of Cyrus King, father of John Alsop King and James Gore King) (F N.Y.) March 24, 1755–April 29, 1827; Senate July 16, 1789–May 20, 1796 (no party), 1813–25; Cont. Cong. 1784–87 (Mass.).

King, Rufus H. (W N.Y.) Jan. 20, 1820–Sept. 13, 1890; House 1855–57.

King, Samuel Wilder (R Hawaii) Dec. 17, 1886–March 24, 1959; House (Terr. Del.) 1935–43; Gov. (Hawaii Terr.) Feb. 28, 1953–July 31, 1957.

King, Steve A. (D Iowa) May 28, 1949– ; House 2003– .

King, Thomas Butler (brother of Henry King, father of John Floyd King) (W Ga.) Aug. 27, 1800–May 10, 1864; House 1839–43, 1845–50.

King, William Henry (father of David Sjodahl King) (D Utah) June 3, 1863–Nov. 27, 1949; House 1897–99, April 2, 1900–01; Senate 1917–41; elected pres. pro tempore Nov. 19, 1940.

King, William Rufus deVane (D Ala.) April 7, 1786–April 18, 1853; House 1811–Nov. 4, 1816 (no party N.C.); Senate Dec. 14, 1819–April 15, 1844 (Dec. 14, 1819–21 Republican, 1821–April 15, 1844 Republican/Jacksonian), July 1, 1848–Dec. 20, 1852; elected pres. pro tempore July 1, 1836, Jan. 28, 1837, March 7, 1837, Oct. 13, 1837, July 2, 1838, Feb. 25, 1839, July 3, 1840, March 3, 1841, March 4, 1841, May 6, 1850, July 11, 1850; vice president March 24–April 18, 1853.

King, William Smith (R Minn.) Dec. 16, 1828–Feb. 24, 1900; House 1875–77.

Kingsbury, William Wallace (D Minn.) June 4, 1828–April 17, 1892; House (Terr. Del.) 1857–May 11, 1858.

Kingston, John Heddens "Jack" (R Ga.) April 24, 1955– ; House 1993– .

Kinkaid, Moses Pierce (R Neb.) Jan. 24, 1856–July 6, 1922; House 1903–July 6, 1922.

Kinkead, Eugene Francis (D N.J.) March 27, 1876–Sept. 6, 1960; House 1909–Feb. 4, 1915.

Kinnard, George L. (J Ind.) 1803–Nov. 26, 1836; House 1833–Nov. 26, 1836.

Kinney, John Fitch (D Utah) April 2, 1816–Aug. 16, 1902; House (Terr. Del.) 1863–65.

Kinsella, Thomas (D N.Y.) Dec. 31, 1832–Feb. 11, 1884; House 1871–73.

Kinsey, Charles (R N.J.) 1773–June 25, 1849; House 1817–19, Feb. 2, 1820–21.

Kinsey, William Medcalf (R Mo.) Oct. 28, 1846–June 20, 1931; House 1889–91.

Kinsley, Martin (– Mass.) June 2, 1754–June 20, 1835; House 1819–21.

Kinzer, John Roland (R Pa.) March 28, 1874–July 25, 1955; House Jan. 28, 1930–47.

Kipp, George Washington (D Pa.) March 28, 1847–July 24, 1911; House 1907–09, March 4–July 24, 1911.

Kirby, William Fosgate (D Ark.) Nov. 16, 1867–July 26, 1934; Senate Nov. 8, 1916–21.

Kirk, Andrew Jackson (R Ky.) March 19, 1866–May 25, 1933; House Feb. 13, 1926–27.

Kirk, Mark Steven (R Ill.) Sept. 15, 1959– ; House 2001– .

Kirkland, Joseph (– N.Y.) Jan. 18, 1770–Jan. 26, 1844; House 1821–23.

Kirkpatrick, Littleton (D N.J.) Oct. 19, 1797–Aug. 15, 1859; House 1843–45.

Kirkpatrick, Sanford (D Iowa) Feb. 11, 1842–Feb. 13, 1932; House 1913–15.

Kirkpatrick, Snyder Solomon (R Kan.) Feb. 21, 1848–April 5, 1909; House 1895–97.

Kirkpatrick, William (R N.Y.) Nov. 7, 1769–Sept. 2, 1832; House 1807–09.

Kirkpatrick, William Huntington (son of William Sebring Kirkpatrick) (R Pa.) Oct. 2, 1885–Nov. 28, 1970; House 1921–23.

Kirkpatrick, William Sebring (father of William Huntington Kirkpatrick) (R Pa.) April 21, 1844–Nov. 3, 1932; House 1897–99.

Kirkwood, Samuel Jordan (R Iowa) Dec. 20, 1813–Sept. 1, 1894; Senate Jan. 13, 1866–67, 1877–March 7, 1881; Gov. Jan. 11, 1860–Jan. 14, 1864, Jan. 13, 1876–Feb. 1, 1877; secretary of the interior March 8, 1881–April 17, 1882.

Kirtland, Dorrance (R N.Y.) July 28, 1770–May 23, 1840; House 1817–19.

Kirwan, Michael Joseph (D Ohio) Dec. 2, 1886–July 27, 1970; House 1937–July 27, 1970.

Kissel, John (R N.Y.) July 31, 1864–Oct. 3, 1938; House 1921–23.

Kitchell, Aaron (R N.J.) July 10, 1744–June 25, 1820; House 1791–93, Jan. 29, 1795–97, 1799–1801; Senate 1805–March 12, 1809.

Kitchen, Bethuel Middleton (R W.Va.) March 21, 1812–Dec. 15, 1895; House 1867–69.

Kitchens, Wade Hampton (D Ark.) Dec. 26, 1878–Aug. 22, 1966; House 1937–41.

Kitchin, Alvin Paul (nephew of Claude Kitchin and William Walton Kitchin, grandson of William Hodges Kitchin) (D N.C.) Sept. 13, 1908–Oct. 22, 1983; House 1957–63.

Kitchin, Claude (son of William Hodges Kitchin, brother of William Walton Kitchin, uncle of Alvin Paul Kitchin) (D N.C.) March 24, 1869–May 31, 1923; House 1901–May 31, 1923; House majority leader 1915–19; House minority leader 1921–23.

Kitchin, William Hodges (father of Claude Kitchin and William Walton Kitchin, grandfather of Alvin Paul Kitchin) (D N.C.) Dec. 22, 1837–Feb. 2, 1901; House 1879–81.

Kitchin, William Walton (son of William Hodges Kitchin, brother of Claude Kitchin, uncle of Alvin Paul Kitchin) (D N.C.) Oct. 9, 1866–Nov. 9, 1924; House 1897–Jan. 11, 1909; Gov. Jan. 12, 1909–Jan. 15, 1913.

Kittera, John Wilkes (father of Thomas Kittera) (F Pa.) Nov. 1752–June 6, 1801; House 1791–1801 (1791–95 no party).

Kittera, Thomas (son of John Wilkes Kittera) (– Pa.) March 21, 1789–June 16, 1839; House Oct. 10, 1826–27.

Kittredge, Alfred Beard (R S.D.) March 28, 1861–May 4, 1911; Senate July 11, 1901–09.

Kittredge, George Washington (D N.H.) Jan. 31, 1805–March 6, 1881; House 1853–55.

Kleberg, Richard Mifflin Sr. (nephew of Rudolph Kleberg, cousin of Robert Christian Eckhardt) (D Texas) Nov. 18, 1887–May 8, 1955; House Nov. 24, 1931–45.

Kleberg, Rudolph (great-uncle of Robert Christian Eckhardt, uncle of Richard Mifflin Kleberg Sr.) (D Texas) June 26, 1847–Dec. 28, 1924; House April 7, 1896–1903.

Kleczka, Gerald Daniel (D Wis.) Nov. 26, 1943– ; House April 10, 1984–2005.

Kleczka, John Casimir (R Wis.) May 6, 1885–April 21, 1959; House 1919–23.

Klein, Arthur George (D N.Y.) Aug. 8, 1904–Feb. 20, 1968; House July 29, 1941–45, Feb. 19, 1946–Dec. 31, 1956.

Klein, Herbert Charles (D N.J.) June 24, 1930– ; House 1993–95.

Kleiner, John Jay (D Ind.) Feb. 8, 1845–April 8, 1911; House 1883–87.

Kleppe, Thomas Savig (R N.D.) July 1, 1919– ; House 1967–71; secretary of the interior Oct. 17, 1975–Jan. 20, 1977.

Klepper, Frank B. (R Mo.) June 22, 1864–Aug. 4, 1933; House 1905–07.

Kline, Ardolph Loges (R N.Y.) Feb. 21, 1858–Oct. 13, 1930; House 1921–23.

Kline, Isaac Clinton (R Pa.) Aug. 18, 1858–Dec. 2, 1947; House 1921–23.

Kline, John P. (R Minn.) Sept. 6, 1947– ; House 2003– .

Kline, Marcus Charles Lawrence (D Pa.) March 26, 1855–March 10, 1911; House 1903–07.

Klingensmith, John Jr. (D Pa.) 1785–?; House 1835–39 (1835–37 Jacksonian).

Klink, Ron (D Pa.) Sept. 23, 1951– ; House 1993–2001.

Kloeb, Frank Le Blond (grandson of Francis Celeste Le Blond) (D Ohio) June 16, 1890–March 11, 1976; House 1933–Aug. 19, 1937.

Klotz, Robert (D Pa.) Oct. 27, 1819–May 1, 1895; House 1879–83.

Kluczynski, John Carl (D Ill.) Feb. 15, 1896–Jan. 26, 1975; House 1951–Jan. 26, 1975.

Klug, Scott L. (R Wis.) Jan. 16, 1953– ; House 1991–99.

Kluttz, Theodore Franklin (D N.C.) Oct. 4, 1848–Nov. 18, 1918; House 1899–1905.

Knapp, Anthony Lausett (brother of Robert McCarty Knapp) (D Ill.) June 14, 1828–May 24, 1881; House Dec. 12, 1861–65.

Knapp, Charles (father of Charles Junius Knapp) (R N.Y.) Oct. 8, 1797–May 14, 1880; House 1869–71.

Knapp, Charles Junius (son of Charles Knapp) (R N.Y.) June 30, 1845–June 1, 1916; House 1889–91.

Knapp, Charles Luman (R N.Y.) July 4, 1847–Jan. 3, 1929; House Nov. 5, 1901–11.

Knapp, Chauncey Langdon (R Mass.) Feb. 26, 1809–May 31, 1898; House 1855–59 (1855–57 American Party).

Knapp, Robert McCarty (brother of Anthony Lausett Knapp) (D Ill.) April 21, 1831–June 24, 1889; House 1873–75, 1877–79.

Knickerbocker, Herman (F N.Y.) July 27, 1779–Jan. 30, 1855; House 1809–11.

Kniffin, Frank Charles (D Ohio) April 26, 1894–April 30, 1968; House 1931–39.

Knight, Charles Landon (R Ohio) June 18, 1867–Sept. 26, 1933; House 1921–23.

Knight, Jonathan (W Pa.) Nov. 22, 1787–Nov. 22, 1858; House 1855–57.

Knight, Nehemiah (father of Nehemiah Rice Knight) (R R.I.) March 23, 1746–June 13, 1808; House 1803–June 13, 1808.

Knight, Nehemiah Rice (son of Nehemiah Knight) (W R.I.) Dec. 31, 1780–April 18, 1854; Senate Jan. 9, 1821–41 (Jan. 9, 1821–35 Republican); Gov. May 7, 1817–Jan. 9, 1821 (Democratic Republican).

Knollenberg, Joseph (R Mich.) Nov. 28, 1933– ; House 1993– .

Knopf, Philip (R Ill.) Nov. 18, 1847–Aug. 14, 1920; House 1903–09.

Knott, James Proctor (D Ky.) Aug. 29, 1830–June 18, 1911; House 1867–71, 1875–83; Gov. Sept. 4, 1883–Aug. 30, 1887.

Knowland, Joseph Russell (father of William Fife Knowland) (R Calif.) Aug. 5, 1873–Feb. 1, 1966; House Nov. 8, 1904–15.

Knowland, William Fife (son of Joseph Russell Knowland) (R Calif.) June 26, 1908–Feb. 23, 1974; Senate Aug. 26, 1945–59; Senate majority leader Aug. 4, 1953–55; Senate minority leader 1955–59.

Knowles, Freeman Tulley (P S.D.) Oct. 10, 1846–June 1, 1910; House 1897–99.

Knowlton, Ebenezer (R Maine) Dec. 6, 1815–Sept. 10, 1874; House 1855–57.

Knox, James (R Ill.) July 4, 1807–Oct. 8, 1876; House 1853–57 (1853–55 Whig).

Knox, Philander Chase (R Pa.) May 6, 1853–Oct. 12, 1921; Senate June 10, 1904–March 4, 1909, 1917–Oct. 12, 1921; attorney general April 5, 1901–June 30, 1904; secretary of state March 6, 1909–March 5, 1913.

Knox, Samuel (UU Mo.) March 21, 1815–March 7, 1905; House June 10, 1864–65.

Knox, Victor Alfred (R Mich.) Jan. 13, 1899–Dec. 13, 1976; House 1953–65.

Knox, William Shadrach (R Mass.) Sept. 10, 1843–Sept. 21, 1914; House 1895–1903.

Knutson, Coya Gjesdal (DFL Minn.) Aug. 22, 1912–Oct. 10, 1996; House 1955–59.

Knutson, Harold (R Minn.) Oct. 20, 1880–Aug. 21, 1953; House 1917–49; chair House Ways and Means 1947–49.

Koch, Edward Irving (D/L N.Y.) Dec. 12, 1924– ; House 1969–Dec. 31, 1977.

Kocialkowski, Leo Paul (D Ill.) Aug. 16, 1882–Sept. 27, 1958; House 1933–43.

Kogovsek, Raymond Peter (D Colo.) Aug. 19, 1941– ; House 1979–85.

Kohl, Herbert (D Wis.) Feb. 7, 1935– ; Senate 1989– .

Kolbe, James Thomas (R Ariz.) June 28, 1942– ; House 1985– .

Kolter, Joseph Paul (D Pa.) Sept. 3, 1926– ; House 1983–93.

Konig, George (D Md.) Jan. 26, 1865–May 31, 1913; House 1911–May 31, 1913.

Konnyu, Ernest Leslie (R Calif.) May 17, 1937– ; House 1987–89.

Konop, Thomas Frank (D Wis.) Aug. 17, 1879–Oct. 17, 1964; House 1911–17.

Koontz, William Henry (R Pa.) July 15, 1830–July 4, 1911; House July 18, 1866–69.

Kopetski, Michael (D Ore.) Oct. 27, 1949– ; House 1991–95.

Kopp, Arthur William (R Wis.) Feb. 28, 1874–June 2, 1967; House 1909–13.

Kopp, William Frederick (R Iowa) June 20, 1869–Aug. 24, 1938; House 1921–33.

Kopplemann, Herman Paul (D Conn.) May 1, 1880–Aug. 11, 1957; House 1933–39, 1941–43, 1945–47.

Korbly, Charles Alexander (D Ind.) March 24, 1871–July 26, 1937; House 1909–15.

Korell, Franklin Frederick (R Ore.) July 23, 1889–June 7, 1965; House Oct. 18, 1927–31.

Kornegay, Horace Robinson (D N.C.) March 12, 1924– ; House 1961–69.

Kostmayer, Peter Houston (D Pa.) Sept. 27, 1946– ; House 1977–81, 1983–93.

Kowalski, Frank (D Conn.) Oct. 18, 1907–Oct. 11, 1974; House 1959–63.

Kramer, Charles (D Calif.) April 18, 1879–Jan. 20, 1943; House 1933–43.

Kramer, Kenneth Bentley (R Colo.) Feb. 19, 1942– ; House 1979–87.

Kraus, Milton (R Ind.) June 26, 1866–Nov. 18, 1942; House 1917–23.

Krebs, Jacob (– Pa.) March 13, 1782–Sept. 26, 1847; House Dec. 4, 1826–27.

Krebs, John Hans (D Calif.) Dec. 17, 1926– ; House 1975–79.

Krebs, Paul Joseph (D N.J.) May 26, 1912–Sept. 17, 1996; House 1965–67.

Kreider, Aaron Shenk (R Pa.) June 26, 1863–May 19, 1929; House 1913–23.

Kreidler, Myron Bradley "Mike" (D Wash.) Sept. 28, 1943– ; House 1993–95.

Kremer, George (– Pa.) Nov. 21, 1775–Sept. 11, 1854; House 1823–29.

Kribbs, George Frederic (D Pa.) Nov. 8, 1846–Sept. 8, 1938; House 1891–95.

Kronmiller, John (R Md.) Dec. 6, 1858–June 19, 1928; House 1909–11.

Krueger, Otto (R N.D.) Sept. 7, 1890–June 6, 1963; House 1953–59.

Krueger, Robert Charles (D Texas) Sept. 19, 1935– ; House 1975–79; Senate Jan. 5, 1993–June 5, 1993.

Kruse, Edward H. (D Ind.) Oct. 22, 1918–Jan. 4, 2000; House 1949–51.

Kuchel, Thomas Henry (R Calif.) Aug. 15, 1910–Nov. 21, 1994; Senate Jan. 2, 1953–69.

Kucinich, Dennis J. (D Ohio) Oct. 8, 1946– ; House 1997– .

Kuhl, John "Randy" Jr. (R N.Y.) April 19, 1943– ; House 2005– .

Kuhns, Joseph Henry (W Pa.) Sept. 1800–Nov. 16, 1883; House 1851–53.

Kulp, Monroe Henry (R Pa.) Oct. 23, 1858–Oct. 19, 1911; House 1895–99.

Kunkel, Jacob Michael (D Md.) July 13, 1822–April 7, 1870; House 1857–61.

Kunkel, John Christian (grandfather of John Crain Kunkel) (R Pa.) Sept. 18, 1816–Oct. 14, 1870; House 1855–59 (1855–57 Whig).

Kunkel, John Crain (grandson of John Christian Kunkel, great-grandson of John Sergeant, great-great-grandson of Robert Whitehill) (R Pa.) July 21, 1898–July 27, 1970; House 1939–51, May 16, 1961–67.

Kunz, Stanley Henry (D Ill.) Sept. 26, 1864–April 23, 1946; House 1921–31, April 5, 1932–33.

Kupferman, Theodore Roosevelt (R N.Y.) May 12, 1920–Sept. 20, 2003; House Feb. 8, 1966–69.

Kurtz, Jacob Banks (R Pa.) Oct. 31, 1867–Sept. 18, 1960; House 1923–35.

Kurtz, William Henry (D Pa.) Jan. 31, 1804–June 24, 1868; House 1851–55.

Kustermann, Gustav (R Wis.) May 24, 1850–Dec. 25, 1919; House 1907–11.

Kuykendall, Andrew Jackson (R Ill.) March 3, 1815–May 11, 1891; House 1865–67.

Kuykendall, Dan Heflin (R Tenn.) July 9, 1924– ; House 1967–75.

Kuykendall, Steven (R Calif.) Jan. 27, 1947– ; House 1999–2001.

Kvale, Ole Juulson (father of Paul John Kvale) (FL Minn.) Feb. 6, 1869–Sept. 11, 1929; House 1923–Sept. 11, 1929.

Kvale, Paul John (son of Ole Juulson Kvale) (FL Minn.) March 27, 1896–June 14, 1960; House Oct. 16, 1929–39.

Kyl, John Henry (father of Jon Llewellyn Kyl) (R Iowa) May 9, 1919–Dec. 23, 2002; House Dec. 15, 1959–65, 1967–73.

Kyl, Jon Llewellyn (son of John Henry Kyl) (R Ariz.) April 25, 1942– ; House 1987–95; Senate 1995– .

Kyle, James Henderson (I S.D.) Feb. 24, 1854–July 1, 1901; Senate 1891–July 1, 1901.

Kyle, John Curtis (D Miss.) July 17, 1851–July 6, 1913; House 1891–97.

Kyle, Thomas Barton (R Ohio) March 10, 1856–Aug. 13, 1915; House 1901–05.

Kyros, Peter N. (D Maine) July 11, 1925– ; House 1967–75.

La Branche, Alcee Louis (D La.) 1806–Aug. 17, 1861; House 1843–45.

Lacey, Edward Samuel (R Mich.) Nov. 26, 1835–Oct. 2, 1916; House 1881–85.

Lacey, John Fletcher (R Iowa) May 30, 1841–Sept. 29, 1913; House 1889–91, 1893–1907.

Lacock, Abner (R Pa.) July 9, 1770–April 12, 1837; House 1811–13; Senate 1813–19.

Ladd, Edwin Freemont (R N.D.) Dec. 13, 1859–June 22, 1925; Senate 1921–June 22, 1925.

Ladd, George Washington (G Maine) Sept. 28, 1818–Jan. 30, 1892; House 1879–83.

La Dow, George Augustus (D Ore.) March 18, 1826–May 1, 1875; House March 4–May 1, 1875.

LaFalce, John Joseph (D N.Y.) Oct. 6, 1939– ; House 1975–2003; chair House Small Business 1987–95.

Lafean, Daniel Franklin (R Pa.) Feb. 7, 1861–April 18, 1922; House 1903–13, 1915–17.

Lafferty, Abraham Walter (R Ore.) June 10, 1875–Jan. 15, 1964; House 1911–15.

Laffoon, Polk (D Ky.) Oct. 24, 1844–Oct. 22, 1906; House 1885–89.

Laflin, Addison Henry (R N.Y.) Oct. 24, 1823–Sept. 24, 1878; House 1865–71.

La Follette, Charles Marion (great-grandson of William Heilman) (R Ind.) Feb. 27, 1898–June 27, 1974; House 1943–47.

La Follette, Robert Marion (father of Robert Marion La Follette Jr.) (R Wis.) June 14, 1855–June 18, 1925; House 1885–91; Senate Jan. 2, 1906–June 18, 1925; Gov. Jan. 7, 1901–Jan. 1, 1906.

La Follette, Robert Marion Jr. (son of Robert Marion La Follette) (Prog. Wis.) Feb. 6, 1895–Feb. 24, 1953; Senate Sept. 30, 1925–47 (Sept. 30, 1925–35 Republican).

La Follette, William Leroy (R Wash.) Nov. 30, 1860–Dec. 20, 1934; House 1911–19.

Lafore, John Armand Jr. (R Pa.) May 25, 1905–Jan. 24, 1993; House Nov. 5, 1957–61.

Lagan, Matthew Diamond (D La.) June 20, 1829–April 8, 1901; House 1887–89, 1891–93.

Lagomarsino, Robert John (R Calif.) Sept. 4, 1926– ; House March 5, 1974–93.

LaGuardia, Fiorello Henry (R N.Y.) Dec. 11, 1882–Sept. 20, 1947; House 1917–Dec. 31, 1919 (Republican), 1923–33 (1923–25 Republican, 1925–27 American Laborite).

Lahm, Samuel (D Ohio) April 22, 1812–June 16, 1876; House 1847–49.

LaHood, Ray (R Ill.) Dec. 6, 1945– ; House 1995– .

Laidlaw, William Grant (R N.Y.) Jan. 1, 1840–Aug. 19, 1908; House 1887–91.

Laird, James (R Neb.) June 20, 1849–Aug. 17, 1889; House 1883–Aug. 17, 1889.

Laird, Melvin Robert (R Wis.) Sept. 1, 1922– ; House 1953–Jan. 21, 1969; secretary of defense Jan. 22, 1969–Jan. 29, 1973.

Laird, William Ramsey III (D W.Va.) June 2, 1916–Jan. 7, 1974; Senate March 13–Nov. 6, 1956.

Lake, William Augustus (AP Miss.) Jan. 6, 1808–Oct. 15, 1861; House 1855–57.

Lamar, Henry Graybill (J Ga.) July 10, 1798–Sept. 10, 1861; House Dec. 7, 1829–33.

Lamar, James Robert (D Mo.) March 28, 1866–Aug. 11, 1923; House 1903–05, 1907–09.

Lamar, John Basil (D Ga.) Nov. 5, 1812–Sept. 15, 1862; House March 4–July 29, 1843.

Lamar, Lucius Quintus Cincinnatus (uncle of William Bailey Lamar, cousin of Absalom Harris Chappell) (D Miss.) Sept. 17, 1825–Jan. 23, 1893; House 1857–Dec. 1860, 1873–77; Senate 1877–March 6, 1885; secretary of the interior March 6, 1885–Jan. 10, 1888; assoc. justice Jan. 18, 1888–Jan. 23, 1893.

Lamar, William Bailey (nephew of Lucius Quintus Cincinnatus Lamar) (D Fla.) June 12, 1853–Sept. 26, 1928; House 1903–09.

Lamb, Alfred William (D Mo.) March 18, 1824–April 29, 1888; House 1853–55.

Lamb, John (D Va.) June 12, 1840–Nov. 21, 1924; House 1897–1913.

Lamb, John Edward (D Ind.) Dec. 26, 1852–Aug. 23, 1914; House 1883–85.

Lambert, John (R N.J.) Feb. 24, 1746–Feb. 4, 1823; House 1805–09; Senate 1809–15; Gov. Nov. 15, 1802–Oct. 29, 1803 (Democratic Republican).

Lambertson, William Purnell (R Kan.) March 23, 1880–Oct. 26, 1957; House 1929–45.

Lambeth, John Walter (D N.C.) Jan. 10, 1896–Jan. 12, 1961; House 1931–39.

Lamison, Charles Nelson (D Ohio) 1826–April 24, 1896; House 1871–75.

Lamneck, Arthur Philip (D Ohio) March 12, 1880–April 23, 1944; House 1931–39.

Lampert, Florian (R Wis.) July 8, 1863–July 18, 1930; House Nov. 5, 1918–July 18, 1930.

Lamport, William Henry (R N.Y.) May 27, 1811–July 21, 1891; House 1871–75.

Lampson, Nick (D Texas) Feb. 14, 1945– ; House 1997–2005.

Lancaster, Columbia (D Wash.) Aug. 26, 1803–Sept. 15, 1893; House (Terr. Del.) April 12, 1854–55.

Lancaster, Harold Martin (D N.C.) March 24, 1943– ; House 1987–95.

Landers, Franklin (D Ind.) March 22, 1825–Sept. 10, 1901; House 1875–77.

Landers, George Marcellus (D Conn.) Feb. 22, 1813–March 27, 1895; House 1875–79.

Landes, Silas Zephaniah (D Ill.) May 15, 1842–May 23, 1910; House 1885–89.

Landgrebe, Earl Frederick (R Ind.) Jan. 21, 1916–June 29, 1986; House 1969–75.

Landis, Charles Beary (brother of Frederick Landis) (R Ind.) July 9, 1858–April 24, 1922; House 1897–1909.

Landis, Frederick (brother of Charles Beary Landis) (R Ind.) Aug. 18, 1872–Nov. 15, 1934; House 1903–07.

Landis, Gerald Wayne (R Ind.) Feb. 23, 1895–Sept. 6, 1971; House 1939–49.

Landrieu, Mary L. (D La.) Nov. 23, 1955– ; Senate 1997– .

Landrum, John Morgan (D La.) July 3, 1815–Oct. 18, 1861; House 1859–61.

Landrum, Phillip Mitchell (D Ga.) Sept. 10, 1907–Nov. 19, 1990; House 1953–77.

Landry, Joseph Aristide (W La.) July 10, 1817–March 9, 1881; House 1851–53.

Landy, James (D Pa.) Oct. 13, 1813–July 25, 1875; House 1857–59.

Lane, Amos (father of James Henry Lane) (J Ind.) March 1, 1778–Sept. 2, 1849; House 1833–37.

Lane, Edward (D Ill.) March 27, 1842–Oct. 30, 1912; House 1887–95.

Lane, Harry (grandson of Joseph Lane, nephew of LaFayette Lane) (D Ore.) Aug. 28, 1855–May 23, 1917; Senate 1913–May 23, 1917.

Lane, Henry Smith (R Ind.) Feb. 24, 1811–June 18, 1881; House Aug. 3, 1840–43 (Whig); Senate 1861–67; Gov. Jan. 14–16, 1861.

Lane, James Henry (son of Amos Lane) (R Kan.) June 22, 1814–July 11, 1866; House 1853–55 (Democrat Ind.); Senate April 4, 1861–July 11, 1866.

Lane, Joseph (father of LaFayette Lane, grandfather of Harry Lane) (D Ore.) Dec. 14, 1801–April 19, 1881; House (Terr. Del.) June 2, 1851–Feb. 14, 1859 (no party); Senate Feb. 14, 1859–61; Gov. (Ore. Terr.) 1849–50, May 16–May 19, 1853.

Lane, Joseph Reed (R Iowa) May 6, 1858–May 1, 1931; House 1899–1901.

Lane, LaFayette (son of Joseph Lane, uncle of Harry Lane) (D Ore.) Nov. 12, 1842–Nov. 23, 1896; House Oct. 25, 1875–77.

Lane, Thomas Joseph (D Mass.) July 6, 1898–June 14, 1994; House Dec. 30, 1941–63.

Langdon, Chauncey (F Vt.) Nov. 8, 1763–July 23, 1830; House 1815–17.

Langdon, John (– N.H.) June 26, 1741–Sept. 18, 1819; Senate 1789–1801; elected pres. pro tempore April 6, 1789, Nov. 5, 1792, March 1, 1793; Cont. Cong. 1775–76, 1787; Gov. June 6, 1805–June 8, 1809, June 7, 1810–June 5, 1812 (Democratic Republican).

Langen, Odin Elsford Stanley (R Minn.) Jan. 5, 1913–July 6, 1976; House 1959–71.

Langer, William (R N.D.) Sept. 30, 1886–Nov. 8, 1959; Senate 1941–Nov. 8, 1959; chair Senate Post Office and Civil Service 1947–49; chair Senate Judiciary 1953–55; Gov. Dec. 31,

1932–July 17, 1934 (Independent), Jan. 6, 1937–Jan. 5, 1939 (Independent).

Langevin, James R. "Jim" (D R.I.) April 22, 1964– ; House 2001– .

Langham, Jonathan Nicholas (R Pa.) Aug. 4, 1861–May 21, 1945; House 1909–15.

Langley, John Wesley (husband of Katherine Gudger Langley, son-in-law of James Madison Gudger Jr.) (R Ky.) Jan. 14, 1868–Jan. 17, 1932; House 1907–Jan. 11, 1926.

Langley, Katherine Gudger (wife of John Wesley Langley, daughter of James Madison Gudger Jr.) (R Ky.) Feb. 14, 1888–Aug. 15, 1948; House 1927–31.

Langston, John Mercer (R Va.) Dec. 14, 1829–Nov. 15, 1897; House Sept. 23, 1890–91.

Lanham, Fritz Garland (son of Samuel Willis Tucker Lanham) (D Texas) Jan. 3, 1880–July 31, 1965; House April 19, 1919–47.

Lanham, Henderson Lovelace (D Ga.) Sept. 14, 1888–Nov. 10, 1957; House 1947–Nov. 10, 1957.

Lanham, Samuel Willis Tucker (father of Fritz Garland Lanham) (D Texas) July 4, 1846–July 29, 1908; House 1883–93, 1897–Jan. 15, 1903; Gov. Jan. 20, 1903–Jan. 15, 1907.

Laning, Jay Ford (R Ohio) May 15, 1853–Sept. 1, 1941; House 1907–09.

Lankford, Menalcus (R Va.) March 14, 1883–Dec. 27, 1937; House 1929–33.

Lankford, Richard Estep (D Md.) July 22, 1914–Sept. 22, 2003; House 1955–65.

Lankford, William Chester (D Ga.) Dec. 7, 1877–Dec. 10, 1964; House 1919–33.

Lanman, James (R Conn.) June 14, 1767–Aug. 7, 1841; Senate 1819–25.

Lanning, William Mershon (R N.J.) Jan. 1, 1849–Feb. 16, 1912; House 1903–June 6, 1904.

Lansing, Frederick (R N.Y.) Feb. 16, 1838–Jan. 31, 1894; House 1889–91.

Lansing, Gerrit Yates (J N.Y.) Aug. 4, 1783–Jan. 3, 1862; House 1831–37.

Lansing, William Esselstyne (R N.Y.) Dec. 29, 1821–July 29, 1883; House 1861–63, 1871–75.

Lantaff, William Courtland (D Fla.) July 31, 1913–Jan. 28, 1970; House 1951–55.

Lantos, Thomas Peter (father-in-law of Richard Swett) (D Calif.) Feb. 1, 1928– ; House 1981– .

Lanzetta, James Joseph (D N.Y.) Dec. 21, 1894–Oct. 27, 1956; House 1933–35, 1937–39.

Lapham, Elbridge Gerry (R N.Y.) Oct. 18, 1814–Jan. 8, 1890; House 1875–July 29, 1881; Senate Aug. 2, 1881–85.

Lapham, Oscar (D R.I.) June 29, 1837–March 29, 1926; House 1891–95.

Laporte, John (J Pa.) Nov. 4, 1798–Aug. 22, 1862; House 1833–37.

Larcade, Henry Dominique Jr. (D La.) July 12, 1890–March 15, 1966; House 1943–53.

Largent, Steve (R Okla.) Sept. 28, 1955– ; House Nov. 29, 1994–Feb. 15, 2002.

Larned, Simon (R Mass.) Aug. 3, 1753–Nov. 16, 1817; House Nov. 5, 1804–05.

LaRocco, Larry (D Idaho) Aug. 25, 1946– ; House 1991–95.

Larrabee, Charles Hathaway (D Wis.) Nov. 9, 1820–Jan. 20, 1883; House 1859–61.

Larrabee, William Henry (D Ind.) Feb. 21, 1870–Nov. 16, 1960; House 1931–43.

Larrazolo, Octaviano Ambrosio (R N.M.) Dec. 7, 1859–April 7, 1930; Senate Dec. 7, 1928–29; Gov. Jan. 1, 1919–Jan. 1, 1921.

Larrinaga, Tulio (U P.R.) Jan. 15, 1847–April 28, 1917; House (Res. Comm.) 1905–11.

Larsen, Richard Ray "Rick" (D Wash.) June 15, 1965– ; House 2001– .

Larsen, William Washington (D Ga.) Aug. 12, 1871–Jan. 5, 1938; House 1917–33.

Larson, John B. (D Conn.) July 22, 1948– ; House 1999– .

Larson, Oscar John (R Minn.) May 20, 1871–Aug. 1, 1957; House 1921–25.

La Sere, Emile (D La.) 1802–Aug. 14, 1882; House Jan. 29, 1846–51.

Lash, Israel George (R N.C.) Aug. 18, 1810–April 1, 1878; House July 20, 1868–71.

Lassiter, Francis Rives (great-nephew of Francis Everod Rives) (D Va.) Feb. 18, 1866–Oct. 31, 1909; House April 19, 1900–03, 1907–Oct. 31, 1909.

Latham, George Robert (UU W.Va.) March 9, 1832–Dec. 16, 1917; House 1865–67.

Latham, Henry Jepson (R N.Y.) Dec. 10, 1908–June 26, 2002; House 1945–Dec. 31, 1958.

Latham, Louis Charles (D N.C.) Sept. 11, 1840–Oct. 16, 1895; House 1881–83, 1887–89.

Latham, Milton Slocum (D Calif.) May 23, 1827–March 4, 1882; House 1853–55; Senate March 5, 1860–63; Gov. Jan. 9–Jan. 14, 1860.

Latham, Tom (R Iowa) July 14, 1948– ; House 1995– .

Lathrop, Samuel (– Mass.) May 1, 1772–July 11, 1846; House 1819–27.

Lathrop, William (R Ill.) April 17, 1825–Nov. 19, 1907; House 1877–79.

Latimer, Asbury Churchwell (D S.C.) July 31, 1851–Feb. 20, 1908; House 1893–1903; Senate 1903–Feb. 20, 1908.

Latimer, Henry (F Del.) April 24, 1752–Dec. 19, 1819; House Feb. 14, 1794–Feb. 7, 1795 (no party); Senate Feb. 7, 1795–Feb. 28, 1801.

LaTourette, Steven C. (R Ohio) July 22, 1954– ; House 1995– .

Latta, Delbert Leroy (R Ohio) March 5, 1920– ; House 1959–89.

Latta, James Polk (D Neb.) Oct. 31, 1844–Sept. 11, 1911; House 1909–Sept. 11, 1911.

Lattimore, William (– Miss.) Feb. 9, 1774–April 3, 1843; House (Terr. Del.) 1803–07, 1813–17.

Laughlin, Greg H. (R Texas) Jan. 21, 1942– ; House 1989–97 (1989–June 26, 1995 Democrat).

Laurance, John (– N.Y.) 1750–Nov. 11, 1810; House 1789–93; Senate Nov. 9, 1796–Aug. 1800; elected pres. pro tempore Dec. 6, 1798; Cont. Cong. 1785–87.

Lausche, Frank John (D Ohio) Nov. 14, 1895–April 21, 1990; Senate 1957–69; Gov. Jan. 8, 1945–Jan. 13, 1947, Jan. 10, 1949–Jan. 3, 1957.

Lautenberg, Frank Raleigh (D N.J.) Jan. 23, 1924– ; Senate Dec. 27, 1982–2001, 2003– .

Law, Charles Blakeslee (R N.Y.) Feb. 5, 1872–Sept. 15, 1929; House 1905–11.

Law, John (son of Lyman Law, grandson of Amasa Learned) (D Ind.) Oct. 28, 1796–Oct. 7, 1873; House 1861–65.

Law, Lyman (father of John Law) (F Conn.) Aug. 19, 1770–Feb. 3, 1842; House 1811–17.

Lawler, Frank (D Ill.) June 25, 1842–Jan. 17, 1896; House 1885–91.

Lawler, Joab (J Ala.) June 12, 1796–May 8, 1838; House 1835–May 8, 1838.

Lawrence, Abbott (W Mass.) Dec. 16, 1792–Aug. 18, 1855; House 1835–37, 1839–Sept. 18, 1840.

Lawrence, Cornelius Van Wyck (cousin of Effingham Lawrence) (J N.Y.) Feb. 28, 1791–Feb. 20, 1861; House 1833–May 14, 1834.

Lawrence, Effingham (cousin of Cornelius Van Wyck Lawrence) (D La.) March 2, 1820–Dec. 9, 1878; House March 3, 1875.

Lawrence, George Pelton (R Mass.) May 19, 1859–Nov. 21, 1917; House Nov. 2, 1897–1913.

Lawrence, George Van Eman (son of Joseph Lawrence) (R Pa.) Nov. 13, 1818–Oct. 2, 1904; House 1865–69, 1883–85.

Lawrence, Henry Franklin (R Mo.) Jan. 31, 1868–Jan. 12, 1950; House 1921–23.

Lawrence, John Watson (D N.Y.) Aug. 1800–Dec. 20, 1888; House 1845–47.

Lawrence, Joseph (father of George Van Eman Lawrence) (W Pa.) 1786–April 17, 1842; House 1825–29 (no party), 1841–April 17, 1842.

Lawrence, Samuel (brother of William Thomas Lawrence) (– N.Y.) May 23, 1773–Oct. 20, 1837; House 1823–25.

Lawrence, Sidney (D N.Y.) Dec. 31, 1801–May 9, 1892; House 1847–49.

Lawrence, William (D Ohio) Sept. 2, 1814–Sept. 8, 1895; House 1857–59.

Lawrence, William (R Ohio) June 26, 1819–May 8, 1899; House 1865–71, 1873–77.

Lawrence, William Thomas (brother of Samuel Lawrence) (– N.Y.) May 7, 1788–Oct. 25, 1859; House 1847–49.

Laws, Gilbert Lafayette (R Neb.) March 11, 1838–April 25, 1907; House Dec. 2, 1889–91.

Lawson, John Daniel (R N.Y.) Feb. 18, 1816–Jan. 24, 1896; House 1873–75.

Lawson, John William (D Va.) Sept. 13, 1837–Feb. 21, 1905; House 1891–93.

Lawson, Thomas Graves (D Ga.) May 2, 1835–April 16, 1912; House 1891–97.

Lawyer, Thomas (R N.Y.) Oct. 14, 1785–May 21, 1868; House 1817–19.

Laxalt, Paul Dominique (R Nev.) Aug. 2, 1922– ; Senate Dec. 18, 1974–87; Gov. Jan. 2, 1967–Jan. 4, 1971; general chair Rep. Nat. Comm. 1983–86.

Lay, Alfred Morrison (D Mo.) May 20, 1836–Dec. 8, 1879; House March 4–Dec. 8, 1879.

Lay, George Washington (W N.Y.) July 26, 1798–Oct. 21, 1860; House 1833–37 (1833–35 Anti-Mason).

Layton, Caleb Rodney (R Del.) Sept. 8, 1851–Nov. 11, 1930; House 1919–23.

Layton, Fernando Coello (D Ohio) April 11, 1847–June 22, 1926; House 1891–97.

Lazaro, Ladislas (D La.) June 5, 1872–March 30, 1927; House 1913–March 30, 1927.

Lazear, Jesse (D Pa.) Dec. 12, 1804–Sept. 2, 1877; House 1861–65.

Lazio, Enrico A. "Rick" (R N.Y.) March 13, 1958– ; House 1993–2001.

Lea, Clarence Frederick (D Calif.) July 11, 1874–June 20, 1964; House 1917–49.

Lea, Luke (brother of Pryor Lea, great-grandfather of Luke Lea, below) (White supporter Tenn.) Jan. 21, 1783–June 17, 1851; House 1833–37 (1833–35 Jacksonian).

Lea, Luke (great-grandson of Luke Lea, above, great-nephew of Pryor Lee) (D Tenn.) April 12, 1879–Nov. 18, 1945; Senate 1911–17.

Lea, Pryor (brother of Luke Lea born 1783, great-uncle of Luke Lea born 1879) (J Tenn.) Aug. 31, 1794–Sept. 14, 1879; House 1827–31.

Leach, Anthony Claude "Buddy" Jr. (D La.) March 30, 1934– ; House 1979–81.

Leach, DeWitt Clinton (R Mich.) Nov. 23, 1822–Dec. 21, 1909; House 1857–61.

Leach, James Albert Smith (R Iowa) Oct. 15, 1942– ; House 1977– ; chair House Banking and Financial Services 1995–2001.

Leach, James Madison (D N.C.) Jan. 17, 1815–June 1, 1891; House 1859–61 (Opposition Party), 1871–75.

Leach, Robert Milton (R Mass.) April 2, 1879–Feb. 18, 1952; House Nov. 4, 1924–25.

Leadbetter, Daniel Parkhurst (D Ohio) Sept. 10, 1797–Feb. 26, 1870; House 1837–41.

Leahy, Edward Laurence (D R.I.) Feb. 9, 1886–July 22, 1953; Senate Aug. 24, 1949–Dec. 18, 1950.

Leahy, Patrick Joseph (D Vt.) March 31, 1940– ; Senate 1975– ; chair Senate Agriculture, Nutrition, and Forestry 1987–95; chair Senate Judiciary Jan. 3, 2001–Jan. 20, 2001, June 6, 2001–03.

Leake, Eugene Walter (D N.J.) July 13, 1877–Aug. 23, 1959; House 1907–09.

Leake, Shelton Farrar (ID Va.) Nov. 30, 1812–March 4, 1884; House 1845–47 (Democrat), 1859–61.

Leake, Walter (R Miss.) May 25, 1762–Nov. 17, 1825; Senate Dec. 10, 1817–May 15, 1820; Gov. Jan. 7, 1822–Nov. 17, 1825.

Learned, Amasa (grandfather of John Law) (– Conn.) Nov. 15, 1750–May 4, 1825; House 1791–95.

Leary, Cornelius Lawrence Ludlow (U Md.) Oct. 22, 1813–March 21, 1893; House 1861–63.

Leath, James Marvin (D Texas) May 6, 1931–Dec. 8, 2000; House 1979–91.

Leatherwood, Elmer O. (R Utah) Sept. 4, 1872–Dec. 24, 1929; House 1921–Dec. 24, 1929.

Leavenworth, Elias Warner (R N.Y.) Dec. 20, 1803–Nov. 25, 1887; House 1875–77.

Leavitt, Humphrey Howe (J Ohio) June 18, 1796–March 15, 1873; House Dec. 6, 1830–July 10, 1834.

Leavitt, Scott (R Mont.) June 16, 1879–Oct. 19, 1966; House 1923–33.

Leavy, Charles Henry (D Wash.) Feb. 16, 1884–Sept. 25, 1952; House 1937–Aug. 1, 1942.

Le Blond, Francis Celeste (grandfather of Frank Le Blond Kloeb) (D Ohio) Feb. 14, 1821–Nov. 9, 1902; House 1863–67.

LeBoutillier, John (R N.Y.) May 26, 1953– ; House 1981–83.

Lecompte, Joseph (J Ky.) Dec. 15, 1797–April 25, 1851; House 1825–33 (1825–31 no party).

Le Compte, Karl Miles (R Iowa) May 25, 1887–Sept. 30, 1972; House 1939–59; chair House Administration 1947–49, 1953–55.

Lederer, Raymond Francis (D Pa.) May 19, 1938– ; House 1977–April 29, 1981.

Lee, Barbara (D Calif.) July 16, 1946– ; House April 21, 1998– .

Lee, Blair (great-grandson of Richard Henry Lee) (D Md.) Aug. 9, 1857–Dec. 25, 1944; Senate Jan. 28, 1914–17.

Lee, Frank Hood (D Mo.) March 29, 1873–Nov. 20, 1952; House 1933–35.

Lee, Gary Alcide (R N.Y.) Aug. 18, 1933– ; House 1979–83.

Lee, Gideon (J N.Y.) April 27, 1778–Aug. 21, 1841; House Nov. 4, 1835–37.

Lee, Gordon (D Ga.) May 29, 1859–Nov. 7, 1927; House 1905–27.

Lee, Henry (brother of Richard Bland Lee, grandfather of William Henry Fitzhugh Lee) (F Va.) Jan. 29, 1756–March 25, 1818; House 1799–1801; Cont. Cong. 1786–88; Gov. Dec. 1, 1791–Dec. 1, 1794.

Lee, John (– Md.) Jan. 30, 1788–May 17, 1871; House 1823–25.

Lee, Joshua (J N.Y.) 1783–Dec. 19, 1842; House 1835–37.

Lee, Joshua Bryan (D Okla.) Jan. 23, 1892–Aug. 10, 1967; House 1935–37; Senate 1937–43.

Lee, Moses Lindley (R N.Y.) May 29, 1805–May 19, 1876; House 1859–61.

Lee, Richard Bland (brother of Henry Lee, great-uncle of William Henry Fitzhugh Lee) (– Va.) Jan. 20, 1761–March 12, 1827; House 1789–95.

Lee, Richard Henry (great-grandfather of Blair Lee) (– Va.) Jan. 20, 1732–June 19, 1794; Senate 1789–Oct. 8, 1792; elected pres. pro tempore April 18, 1792; Cont. Cong. 1774–79, 1784–85, 1787.

Lee, Robert Emmett (D Pa.) Oct. 12, 1868–Nov. 19, 1916; House 1911–15.

Lee, Robert Quincy (D Texas) Jan. 12, 1869–April 18, 1930; House 1929–April 18, 1930.

Lee, Silas (F Mass.) July 3, 1760–March 1, 1814; House 1799–Aug. 20, 1801.

Lee, Thomas (J N.J.) Nov. 28, 1780–Nov. 2, 1856; House 1833–37.

Lee, Warren Isbell (R N.Y.) Feb. 5, 1876–Dec. 25, 1955; House 1921–23.

Lee, William Henry Fitzhugh (grandson of Henry Lee, great-nephew of Richard Bland Lee) (D Va.) May 31, 1837–Oct. 15, 1891; House 1887–Oct. 15, 1891.

Leech, James Russell (R Pa.) Nov. 19, 1888–Feb. 5, 1952; House 1927–Jan. 29, 1932.

Leedom, John Peter (D Ohio) Dec. 20, 1847–March 18, 1895; House 1881–83.

Leet, Isaac (D Pa.) 1801–June 10, 1844; House 1839–41.

LeFante, Joseph Anthony (D N.J.) Sept. 8, 1928–Feb. 26, 1997; House 1977–Dec. 14, 1978.

Le Fever, Jacob (father of Frank Jacob Le Fevre) (R N.Y.) April 20, 1830–Feb. 4, 1905; House 1893–97.

Le Fever, Joseph (R Pa.) April 3, 1760–Oct. 17, 1826; House 1811–13.

Le Fevre, Benjamin (D Ohio) Oct. 8, 1838–March 7, 1922; House 1879–87.

Le Fevre, Frank Jacob (son of Jacob Le Fever) (R N.Y.) Nov. 30, 1874–April 29, 1941; House 1905–07.

Le Fevre, Jay (R N.Y.) Sept. 6, 1893–April 26, 1970; House 1943–51.

Lefferts, John (R N.Y.) Dec. 17, 1785–Sept. 18, 1829; House 1813–15.

Leffler, Isaac (brother of Shepherd Leffler) (– Va.) Nov. 7, 1788–March 8, 1866; House 1827–29.

Leffler, Shepherd (brother of Isaac Leffler) (D Iowa) April 24, 1811–Sept. 7, 1879; House Dec. 28, 1846–51.

Leftwich, Jabez (– Va.) Sept. 22, 1765–June 22, 1855; House 1821–25.

Leftwich, John William (D Tenn.) Sept. 7, 1826–March 6, 1870; House July 24, 1866–67.

Legarda Y Tuason, Benito (– P.I.) Sept. 27, 1853–Aug. 27, 1915; House (Res. Comm.) Nov. 22, 1907–13.

Legare, George Swinton (D S.C.) Nov. 11, 1869–Jan. 31, 1913; House 1903–Jan. 31, 1913.

Legare, Hugh Swinton (D S.C.) Jan. 2, 1797–June 20, 1843; House 1837–39; attorney general Sept. 13, 1841–June 20, 1843.

Leggett, Robert Louis (D Calif.) July 26, 1926–Aug. 13, 1997; House 1963–79.

Lehlbach, Frederick Reimold (nephew of Herman Lehlbach) (R N.J.) Jan. 31, 1876–Aug. 4, 1937; House 1915–37.

Lehlbach, Herman (uncle of Frederick Reimold Lehlbach) (R N.J.) July 3, 1845–Jan. 11, 1904; House 1885–91.

Lehman, Herbert Henry (D N.Y.) March 28, 1878–Dec. 5, 1963; Senate Nov. 9, 1949–57; Gov. Jan. 1, 1933–Dec. 3, 1942.

Lehman, Richard Henry (D Calif.) July 20, 1948– ; House 1983–95.

Lehman, William (D Fla.) Oct. 4, 1913–March 16, 2005; House 1973–93.

Lehman, William Eckart (D Pa.) Aug. 21, 1821–July 19, 1895; House 1861–63.

Lehr, John Camillus (D Mich.) Nov. 18, 1878–Feb. 17, 1958; House 1933–35.

Leib, Michael (R Pa.) Jan. 8, 1760–Dec. 8, 1822; House 1799–Feb. 14, 1806 (no party); Senate Jan. 9, 1809–Feb. 14, 1814.

Leib, Owen D. (D Pa.) ?–June 17, 1848; House 1845–47.

Leidy, Paul (D Pa.) Nov. 13, 1813–Sept. 11, 1877; House Dec. 7, 1857–59.

Leigh, Benjamin Watkins (W Va.) June 18, 1781–Feb. 2, 1849; Senate Feb. 26, 1834–July 4, 1836.

Leighty, Jacob D. (R Ind.) Nov. 15, 1839–Oct. 18, 1912; House 1895–97.

Leiper, George Gray (J Pa.) Feb. 3, 1786–Nov. 18, 1868; House 1829–31.

Leisenring, John (R Pa.) June 3, 1853–Jan. 19, 1901; House 1895–97.

Leiter, Benjamin Franklin (R Ohio) Oct. 13, 1813–June 17, 1866; House 1855–59.

Leland, George Thomas "Mickey" (D Texas) Nov. 27, 1944–Aug. 7, 1989; House 1979–Aug. 7, 1989.

Lemke, William (R N.D.) Aug. 13, 1878–May 30, 1950; House 1933–41 (Nonpartisan Republican), 1943–May 30, 1950.

Le Moyne, John Valcoulon (D Ill.) Nov. 17, 1828–July 27, 1918; House May 6, 1876–77.

Lenahan, John Thomas (D Pa.) Nov. 15, 1852–April 28, 1920; House 1907–09.

L'Engle, Claude (D Fla.) Oct. 19, 1868–Nov. 6, 1919; House 1913–15.

Lennon, Alton Asa (D N.C.) Aug. 17, 1906–Dec. 28, 1986; Senate July 10, 1953–Nov. 28, 1954; House 1957–73.

Lenroot, Irvine Luther (R Wis.) Jan. 31, 1869–Jan. 26, 1949; House 1909–April 17, 1918; Senate April 18, 1918–27.

Lent, James (J N.Y.) 1782–Feb. 22, 1833; House 1829–Feb. 22, 1833.

Lent, Norman Frederick (R/C N.Y.) March 23, 1931– ; House 1971–93.

Lentz, John Jacob (D Ohio) Jan. 27, 1856–July 27, 1931; House 1897–1901.

Leonard, Fred Churchill (R Pa.) Feb. 16, 1856–Dec. 5, 1921; House 1895–97.

Leonard, George (F Mass.) July 4, 1729–July 26, 1819; House 1789–91 (no party), 1795–97.

Leonard, John Edwards (great-nephew of John Edwards of Pa.) (R La.) Sept. 22, 1845–March 15, 1878; House 1877–March 15, 1878.

Leonard, Moses Gage (D N.Y.) July 10, 1809–March 20, 1899; House 1843–45.

Leonard, Stephen Banks (D N.Y.) April 15, 1793–May 8, 1876; House 1835–37 (Jacksonian), 1839–41.

Lesher, John Vandling (D Pa.) July 27, 1866–May 3, 1932; House 1913–21.

Lesinski, John (father of John Lesinski Jr.) (D Mich.) Jan. 3, 1885–May 27, 1950; House 1933–May 27, 1950.

Lesinski, John Jr. (son of John Lesinski) (D Mich.) Dec. 28, 1914– ; House 1951–65; chair House Education and Labor 1949–50.

Lessler, Montague (R N.Y.) Jan. 1, 1869–Feb. 17, 1938; House Jan. 7, 1902–03.

Lester, Posey Green (D Va.) March 12, 1850–Feb. 9, 1929; House 1889–93.

Lester, Rufus Ezekiel (D Ga.) Dec. 12, 1837–June 16, 1906; House 1889–June 16, 1906.

Letcher, John (D Va.) March 29, 1813–Jan. 26, 1884; House 1851–59; Gov. Jan. 1, 1860–Dec. 31, 1863.

Letcher, Robert Perkins (– Ky.) Feb. 10, 1788–Jan. 24, 1861; House 1823–33, Aug. 6, 1834–35; Gov. June 1, 1840–June 1, 1844.

Letts, Fred Dickinson (cousin of Lester Jesse Dickinson) (R Iowa) April 26, 1875–Jan. 19, 1965; House 1925–31.

Lever, Asbury Francis (D S.C.) Jan. 5, 1875–April 28, 1940; House Nov. 5, 1901–Aug. 1, 1919.

Levering, Robert Woodrow (son-in-law of Usher L. Burdick, brother-in-law of Quentin N. Burdick, brother-in-law of Jocelyn Birch Burdick) (D Ohio) Oct. 3, 1914–Aug. 11, 1983; House 1959–61.

Levin, Carl Milton (brother of Sander Martin Levin) (D Mich.) June 28, 1934– ; Senate 1979– ; chair Senate Armed Services Jan. 3, 2001–Jan. 20, 2001, June 6, 2001–03.

Levin, Lewis Charles (AP Pa.) Nov. 10, 1808–March 14, 1860; House 1845–51.

Levin, Sander Martin (brother of Carl Milton Levin) (D Mich.) Sept. 6, 1931– ; House 1983– .

Levine, Meldon Edises "Mel" (D Calif.) June 7, 1943– ; House 1983–93.

Levitas, Elliott Harris (D Ga.) Dec. 26, 1930– ; House 1975–85.

Levy, David. (See Yulee, David Levy.)

Levy, David A. (R N.Y.) Dec. 18, 1953– ; House 1993–95.

Levy, Jefferson Monroe (D N.Y.) April 16, 1852–March 6, 1924; House 1899–1901, 1911–15.

Levy, William Mallory (D La.) Oct. 31, 1827–Aug. 14, 1882; House 1875–77.

Lewis, Abner (W N.Y.) ?–?; House 1845–47.

Lewis, Barbour (R Tenn.) Jan. 5, 1818–July 15, 1893; House 1873–75.

Lewis, Burwell Boykin (D Ala.) July 7, 1838–Oct. 11, 1885; House 1875–77, 1879–Oct. 1, 1880.

Lewis, Charles Jeremy "Jerry" (R Calif.) Oct. 21, 1934– ; House 1979– ; chair House Appropriations 2005– .

Lewis, Charles Swearinger (D Va.) Feb. 26, 1821–Jan. 22, 1878; House Dec. 4, 1854–55.

Lewis, Clarke (D Miss.) Nov. 8, 1840–March 13, 1896; House 1889–93.

Lewis, David John (D Md.) May 1, 1869–Aug. 12, 1952; House 1911–17, 1931–39.

Lewis, Dixon Hall (D Ala.) Aug. 10, 1802–Oct. 25, 1848; House 1829–April 22, 1844 (State Rights Democrat); Senate April 22, 1844–Oct. 25, 1848.

Lewis, Earl Ramage (R Ohio) Feb. 22, 1887–Feb. 1, 1956; House 1939–41, 1943–49.

Lewis, Edward Taylor (D La.) Oct. 26, 1834–April 26, 1927; House 1883–85.

Lewis, Elijah Banks (D Ga.) March 27, 1854–Dec. 10, 1920; House 1897–1909.

Lewis, Fred Ewing (R Pa.) Feb. 8, 1865–June 27, 1949; House 1913–15.

Lewis, James Hamilton (D Ill.) May 18, 1863–April 9, 1939; House 1897–99 (Wash.); Senate March 26, 1913–19, 1931–April 9, 1939.

Lewis, John Francis (R Va.) March 1, 1818–Sept. 2, 1895; Senate Jan. 26, 1870–75.

Lewis, John Henry (R Ill.) July 21, 1830–Jan. 6, 1929; House 1881–83.

Lewis, John R. (D Ga.) Feb. 21, 1940– ; House 1987– .

Lewis, John William (R Ky.) Oct. 14, 1841–Dec. 20, 1913; House 1895–97.

Lewis, Joseph Jr. (F Va.) 1772–March 30, 1834; House 1803–17.

Lewis, Joseph Horace (D Ky.) Oct. 29, 1824–July 6, 1904; House May 10, 1870–73.

Lewis, Lawrence (D Colo.) June 22, 1879–Dec. 9, 1943; House 1933–Dec. 9, 1943.

Lewis, Robert Jacob (R Pa.) Dec. 30, 1864–July 24, 1933; House 1901–03.

Lewis, Ron (R Ky.) Sept. 14, 1946– ; House May 26, 1994– .

Lewis, Thomas (F Va.) ?–?; House 1803–March 5, 1804.

Lewis, Thomas Francis (R Fla.) Oct. 26, 1924–Aug. 2, 2003; House 1983–95.

Lewis, William (R Ky.) Sept. 22, 1868–Aug. 8, 1959; House April 24, 1948–49.

Lewis, William J. (D Va.) July 4, 1766–Nov. 1, 1828; House 1817–19.

Libbey, Harry (R Va.) Nov. 22, 1843–Sept. 30, 1913; House 1883–87 (1883–85 Readjuster).

Libonati, Roland Victor (D Ill.) Dec. 29, 1900–May 30, 1991; House Dec. 31, 1957–65.

Lichtenwalner, Norton Lewis (D Pa.) June 1, 1889–May 3, 1960; House 1931–33.

Lichtenwalter, Franklin Herbert (R Pa.) March 28, 1910–March 4, 1973; House Sept. 9, 1947–51.

Lieb, Charles (D Ind.) May 20, 1852–Sept. 1, 1928; House 1913–17.

Liebel, Michael Jr. (D Pa.) Dec. 12, 1870–Aug. 8, 1927; House 1915–17.

Lieberman, Joseph I. (D Conn.) Feb. 24, 1942– ; Senate 1989– ; chair Senate Governmental Affairs Jan. 3, 2001–Jan. 20, 2001, June 6, 2001–03.

Lightfoot, Jim Ross (R Iowa) Sept. 27, 1938– ; House 1985–97.

Ligon, Robert Fulwood (D Ala.) Dec. 16, 1823–Oct. 11, 1901; House 1877–79.

Ligon, Thomas Watkins (D Md.) May 10, 1810–Jan. 12, 1881; House 1845–49; Gov. Jan. 11, 1854–Jan. 13, 1858.

Lilley, George Leavens (R Conn.) Aug. 3, 1859–April 21, 1909; House 1903–Jan. 5, 1909; Gov. Jan. 6–April 21, 1909.

Lilley, Mial Eben (R Pa.) May 30, 1850–Feb. 28, 1915; House 1905–07.

Lilly, Samuel (D N.J.) Oct. 28, 1815–April 3, 1880; House 1853–55.

Lilly, Thomas Jefferson (D W.Va.) June 3, 1878–April 2, 1956; House 1923–25.

Lilly, William (R Pa.) June 3, 1821–Dec. 1, 1893; House March 4–Dec. 1, 1893.

Lincoln, Abraham (R Ill.) Feb. 12, 1809–April 15, 1865; House 1847–49 (Whig); president 1861–April 15, 1865.

Lincoln, Blanche Lambert (D Ark.) Sept. 30, 1960– ; House 1993–97; Senate 1999– .

Lincoln, Enoch (son of Levi Lincoln, brother of Levi Lincoln Jr.) (R Maine) Dec. 28, 1788–Oct. 8, 1829; House Nov. 4, 1818–21 (Mass.), 1821–26; Gov. Jan. 3, 1827–Oct. 8, 1829.

Lincoln, Levi (father of Enoch Lincoln and Levi Lincoln Jr.) (R Mass.) May 15, 1749–April 14, 1820; House Dec. 15, 1800–March 5, 1801; Cont. Cong. (elected but did not attend) 1781; attorney general March 5, 1801–March 3, 1805; Gov. Dec. 10, 1808–May 1, 1809 (Democratic Republican).

Lincoln, Levi Jr. (son of Levi Lincoln, brother of Enoch Lincoln) (W Mass.) Oct. 25, 1782–May 29, 1868; House Feb. 17, 1834–March 16, 1841 (Feb. 17, 1834–35 Anti-Jacksonian); Gov. May 26, 1825–Jan. 9, 1834 (May 26, 1825–29 Anti-Democrat, 1829–Jan. 9, 1834 National Republican).

Lincoln, William Slosson (R N.Y.) Aug. 13, 1813–April 21, 1893; House 1867–69.

Lind, James Francis (D Pa.) Oct. 17, 1900–April 11, 1975; House 1949–53.

Lind, John (D Minn.) March 25, 1854–Sept. 18, 1930; House 1887–93 (Republican), 1903–05; Gov. Jan. 2, 1899–Jan. 7, 1901.

Lindbergh, Charles Augustus (R Minn.) Jan. 20, 1859–May 24, 1924; House 1907–17.

Linder, John Elmer (R Ga.) Sept. 9, 1942– ; House 1993– .

Lindley, James Johnson (W Mo.) Jan. 1, 1822–April 18, 1891; House 1853–57.

Lindquist, Francis Oscar (R Mich.) Sept. 27, 1869–Sept. 25, 1924; House 1913–15.

Lindsay, George Henry (father of George Washington Lindsay) (D N.Y.) Jan. 7, 1837–May 25, 1916; House 1901–13.

Lindsay, George Washington (son of George Henry Lindsay) (D N.Y.) March 28, 1865–March 15, 1938; House 1923–35.

Lindsay, John Vliet (R N.Y.) Nov. 24, 1921–Dec. 19, 2000; House 1959–Dec. 31, 1965.

Lindsay, William (D Ky.) Sept. 4, 1835–Oct. 15, 1909; Senate Feb. 15, 1893–1901.

Lindsey, Stephen Decatur (R Maine) March 3, 1828–April 26, 1884; House 1877–83.

Lindsley, James Girard (R N.Y.) March 19, 1819–Dec. 4, 1898; House 1885–87.

Lindsley, William Dell (D Ohio) Dec. 25, 1812–March 11, 1890; House 1853–55.

Lineberger, Walter Franklin (R Calif.) July 20, 1883–Oct. 9, 1943; House 1921–27.

Linehan, Neil Joseph (D Ill.) Sept. 23, 1895–Aug. 23, 1967; House 1949–51.

Link, Arthur Albert (D N.D.) May 24, 1914– ; House 1971–73; Gov. Jan. 2, 1973–Jan. 7, 1981.

Link, William Walter (D Ill.) Feb. 12, 1884–Sept. 23, 1950; House 1945–47.

Linn, Archibald Ladley (W N.Y.) Oct. 15, 1802–Oct. 10, 1857; House 1841–43.

Linn, James (R N.J.) 1749–Jan. 5, 1821; House 1799–1801.

Linn, John (R N.J.) Dec. 3, 1763–Jan. 5, 1821; House 1817–Jan. 5, 1821.

Linn, Lewis Fields (J Mo.) Nov. 5, 1796–Oct. 3, 1843; Senate Oct. 25, 1833–Oct. 3, 1843.

Linney, Romulus Zachariah (R N.C.) Dec. 26, 1841–April 15, 1910; House 1895–1901.

Linthicum, John Charles (D Md.) Nov. 26, 1867–Oct. 5, 1932; House 1911–Oct. 5, 1932.

Linton, William Seelye (R Mich.) Feb. 4, 1856–Nov. 22, 1927; House 1893–97.

Lipinski, Daniel (son of William Oliver Lipinski) (D Ill.) July 15, 1966– ; House 2005– .

Lipinski, William Oliver (father of Daniel Lipinski) (D Ill.) Dec. 22, 1937– ; House 1983–2005.

Lippitt, Henry Frederick (R R.I.) Oct. 12, 1856–Dec. 28, 1933; Senate 1911–17.

Lipscomb, Glenard Paul (R Calif.) Aug. 19, 1915–Feb. 1, 1970; House Nov. 10, 1953–Feb. 1, 1970.

Lisle, Marcus Claiborne (D Ky.) Sept. 23, 1862–July 7, 1894; House 1893–July 7, 1894.

Litchfield, Elisha (– N.Y.) July 12, 1785–Aug. 4, 1859; House 1821–25.

Littauer, Lucius Nathan (R N.Y.) Jan. 20, 1859–March 2, 1944; House 1897–1907.

Little, Chauncey Bundy (D Kan.) Feb. 10, 1877–Sept. 29, 1952; House 1925–27.

Little, Edward Campbell (R Kan.) Dec. 14, 1858–June 27, 1924; House 1917–June 27, 1924.

Little, Edward Preble (D Mass.) Nov. 7, 1791–Feb. 6, 1875; House Dec. 13, 1852–53.

Little, John (R Ohio) April 25, 1837–Oct. 18, 1900; House 1885–87.

Little, John Sebastian (D Ark.) March 15, 1853–Oct. 29, 1916; House Dec. 3, 1894–Jan. 1907; Gov. Jan. 8–Feb. 11, 1907.

Little, Joseph James (D N.Y.) June 5, 1841–Feb. 11, 1913; House Nov. 3, 1891–93.

Little, Peter (R Md.) Dec. 11, 1775–Feb. 5, 1830; House 1811–13, Sept. 2, 1816–29.

Littlefield, Charles Edgar (R Maine) June 21, 1851–May 2, 1915; House June 19, 1899–Sept. 30, 1908.

Littlefield, Nathaniel Swett (D Maine) Sept. 20, 1804–Aug. 15, 1882; House 1841–43, 1849–51.

Littlejohn, De Witt Clinton (R N.Y.) Feb. 7, 1818–Oct. 27, 1892; House 1863–65.

Littlepage, Adam Brown (D W.Va.) April 14, 1859–June 29, 1921; House 1911–13, 1915–19.

Littleton, Martin Wiley (D N.Y.) Jan. 12, 1872–Dec. 19, 1934; House 1911–13.

Litton, Jerry Lon (D Mo.) May 12, 1937–Aug. 3, 1976; House 1973–Aug. 3, 1976.

Lively, Robert Maclin (D Texas) Jan. 6, 1855–Jan. 15, 1929; House July 23, 1910–11.

Livermore, Arthur (son of Samuel Livermore, brother of Edward St. Loe Livermore) (R N.H.) July 29, 1766–July 1, 1853; House 1817–21, 1823–25.

Livermore, Edward St. Loe (son of Samuel Livermore, brother of Arthur Livermore) (F Mass.) April 5, 1762–Sept. 15, 1832; House 1807–11.

Livermore, Samuel (father of Arthur Livermore and Edward St. Loe Livermore) (R N.H.) May 14, 1732–May 18, 1803; House 1789–93 (no party); Senate 1793–June 12, 1801; elected pres. pro tempore May 6, 1796, Dec. 2, 1799; Cont. Cong. 1780–82, 1785–86.

Livernash, Edward James (subsequently Edward James de Nivernais) (D/UL Calif.) Feb. 14, 1866–June 1, 1938; House 1903–05.

Livingston, Edward (cousin of Gov. William Livingston of N.J.) (– La.) May 28, 1764–May 23, 1836; House 1795–1801 (N.Y.), 1823–29; Senate 1829–May 24, 1831; secretary of state May 24, 1831–May 29, 1833.

Livingston, Henry Walter (F N.Y.) 1768–Dec. 22, 1810; House 1803–07.

Livingston, Leonidas Felix (D Ga.) April 3, 1832–Feb. 11, 1912; House 1891–1911.

Livingston, Robert Le Roy (F N.Y.) 1778–1836; House 1809–May 6, 1812.

Livingston, Robert Linligthgow Jr. (R La.) April 30, 1943– ; House Sept. 7, 1977–Feb. 28, 1999; chair House Appropriations 1995–99.

Lloyd, Edward (R Md.) July 22, 1779–June 2, 1834; House Dec. 3, 1806–09 (no party); Senate 1819–Jan. 14, 1826; Gov. June 9, 1809–Nov. 16, 1811 (Democratic Republican).

Lloyd, James (F Md.) 1745–1820; Senate Dec. 11, 1797–Dec. 1, 1800.

Lloyd, James (F Mass.) Dec. 1769–April 5, 1831; Senate June 9, 1808–May 1, 1813, June 5, 1822–May 23, 1826.

Lloyd, James Frederick (D Calif.) Sept. 27, 1922– ; House 1975–81.

Lloyd, James Tilghman (D Mo.) Aug. 28, 1857–April 3, 1944; House June 1, 1897–1917.

Lloyd, Marilyn Laird (also known as Marilyn Laird Lloyd Bouquard) (D Tenn.) Jan. 3, 1929– ; House 1975–95.

Lloyd, Sherman Parkinson (R Utah) Jan. 11, 1914–Dec. 15, 1979; House 1963–65, 1967–73.

Lloyd, Wesley (D Wash.) July 24, 1883–Jan. 10, 1936; House 1933–Jan. 10, 1936.

Loan, Benjamin Franklin (R Mo.) Oct. 4, 1819–March 30, 1881; House 1863–69 (1863–65 Unconditional Unionist).

Lobeck, Charles Otto (D Neb.) April 6, 1852–Jan. 30, 1920; House 1911–19.

LoBiondo, Frank A. (R N.J.) May 12, 1946– ; House 1995– .

Locher, Cyrus (D Ohio) March 8, 1878–Aug. 17, 1929; Senate April 5–Dec. 14, 1928.

Locke, Francis (nephew of Matthew Locke) (– N.C.) Oct. 31, 1776–Jan. 8, 1823; elected to the Senate but resigned Dec. 5, 1815, without having qualified.

Locke, John (– Mass.) Feb. 14, 1764–March 29, 1855; House 1823–29.

Locke, Matthew (uncle of Francis Locke, great-great-great-grandfather of Effiegene Locke Wingo) (R N.C.) 1730–Sept. 7, 1801; House 1793–99 (1793–95 no party).

Lockhart, James (D Ind.) Feb. 13, 1806–Sept. 7, 1857; House 1851–53, March 4–Sept. 7, 1857.

Lockhart, James Alexander (D N.C.) June 2, 1850–Dec. 24, 1905; House 1895–June 5, 1896.

Lockwood, Daniel Newton (D N.Y.) June 1, 1844–June 1, 1906; House 1877–79, 1891–95.

Lodge, Henry Cabot (grandfather of Henry Cabot Lodge Jr. and John Davis Lodge, great-grandson of George Cabot) (R Mass.) May 12, 1850–Nov. 9, 1924; House 1887–93; Senate 1893–Nov. 9, 1924; Senate minority leader Aug. 24, 1918–19; Senate majority leader 1919–Nov. 9, 1924; elected pres. pro tempore March 25, 1912 (to serve March 25–March 26, 1912).

Lodge, Henry Cabot Jr. (grandson of Henry Cabot Lodge, brother of John Davis Lodge, nephew of Augustus Peabody Gardner, great-great-grandson of George Cabot) (R Mass.) July 5, 1902–Feb. 27, 1985; Senate 1937–Feb. 3, 1944, 1947–53.

Lodge, John Davis (grandson of Henry Cabot Lodge, brother of Henry Cabot Lodge Jr., nephew of Augustus Peabody Gardner, great-great-great-grandson of George Cabot) (R Conn.) Oct. 20, 1903–Oct. 29, 1985; House 1947–51; Gov. Jan. 3, 1951–Jan. 5, 1955.

Loeffler, Thomas Gilbert (R Texas) Aug. 1, 1946– ; House 1979–87.

Lofgren, Zoe (D Calif.) Dec. 21, 1947– ; House 1995– .

Lofland, James Rush (R Del.) Nov. 2, 1823–Feb. 10, 1894; House 1873–75.

Loft, George William (D N.Y.) Feb. 6, 1865–Nov. 6, 1943; House Nov. 4, 1913–17.

Loftin, Scott Marion (D Fla.) Sept. 14, 1878–Sept. 22, 1953; Senate May 26–Nov. 3, 1936.

Logan, George (R Pa.) Sept. 9, 1753–April 9, 1821; Senate July 13, 1801–07.

Logan, Henry (D Pa.) April 14, 1784–Dec. 26, 1866; House 1835–39 (1835–37 Jacksonian).

Logan, John Alexander (R Ill.) Feb. 9, 1826–Dec. 26, 1886; House 1859–April 2, 1862 (Democrat), 1867–71; Senate 1871–77, 1879–Dec. 26, 1886.

Logan, Marvel Mills (D Ky.) Jan. 7, 1874–Oct. 3, 1939; Senate 1931–Oct. 3, 1939.

Logan, William (R Ky.) Dec. 8, 1776–Aug. 8, 1822; Senate 1819–May 28, 1820.

Logan, William Turner (D S.C.) June 21, 1874–Sept. 15, 1941; House 1921–25.

Logue, James Washington (D Pa.) Feb. 22, 1863–Aug. 27, 1925; House 1913–15.

London, Meyer (Soc. N.Y.) Dec. 29, 1871–June 6, 1926; House 1915–19, 1921–23.

Lonergan, Augustine (D Conn.) May 20, 1874–Oct. 18, 1947; House 1913–15, 1917–21, 1931–33; Senate 1933–39.

Long, Alexander (D Ohio) Dec. 24, 1816–Nov. 28, 1886; House 1863–65.

Long, Cathy (widow of Gillis William Long) (D La.) Feb. 7, 1924– ; House April 4, 1985–87.

Long, Chester Isaiah (R Kan.) Oct. 12, 1860–July 1, 1934; House 1895–97, 1899–March 4, 1903; Senate 1903–09.

Long, Clarence Dickinson (D Md.) Dec. 11, 1908–Sept. 18, 1994; House 1963–85.

Long, Edward Henry Carroll (W Md.) Sept. 28, 1808–Oct. 16, 1865; House 1845–47.

Long, Edward Vaughn (D Mo.) July 18, 1908–Nov. 6, 1972; Senate Sept. 23, 1960–Dec. 27, 1968.

Long, George Shannon (brother of Huey Pierce "the Kingfish" Long and Earl Kemp Long, brother-in-law of Rose McConnell Long, uncle of Russell Billiu Long, cousin of Gillis William Long) (D La.) Sept. 11, 1883–March 22, 1958; House 1953–March 22, 1958.

Long, Gillis William (husband of Catherine Long, cousin of Huey Pierce "the Kingfish" Long and Earl Kemp Long, Rose McConnell Long, Russell Billiu Long and George Shannon Long) (D La.) May 4, 1923–Jan. 20, 1985; House 1963–65, 1973–Jan. 20, 1985.

Long, Huey Pierce "the Kingfish" (husband of Rose McConnell Long, father of Russell Billiu Long, brother of George Shannon Long and Earl Kemp Long, cousin of Gillis William Long) (D La.) Aug. 30, 1893–Sept. 10, 1935; Senate Jan. 25, 1932–Sept. 10, 1935; Gov. May 21, 1928–Jan. 25, 1932.

Long, Jefferson Franklin (R Ga.) March 3, 1836–Feb. 4, 1901; House Dec. 22, 1870–71.

Long, Jill (D Ind.) July 15, 1952– ; House April 5, 1989–95.

Long, John (– N.C.) Feb. 26, 1785–Aug. 11, 1857; House 1821–29.

Long, John Benjamin (D Texas) Sept. 8, 1843–April 27, 1924; House 1891–93.

Long, John Davis (R Mass.) Oct. 27, 1838–Aug. 28, 1915; House 1883–89; Gov. Jan. 8, 1880–Jan. 4, 1883; secretary of the navy March 6, 1897–April 30, 1902.

Long, Lewis Marshall (D Ill.) June 22, 1883–Sept. 9, 1957; House 1937–39.

Long, Oren Ethelbirt (D Hawaii) March 4, 1889–May 6, 1965; Senate (Terr. Sen.) 1956–59, (Sen.) Aug. 21, 1959–63; Gov. (Hawaii Terr.) 1951–53.

Long, Rose McConnell (widow of Huey Pierce "the Kingfish" Long, mother of Russell Billiu Long, daughter-in-law of George Shannon Long) (D La.) April 8, 1892–May 27, 1970; Senate Jan. 31, 1936–Jan. 2, 1937.

Long, Russell Billiu (son of Huey Pierce "the Kingfish" Long and Rose McConnell Long, nephew of George Shannon Long) (D La.) Nov. 3, 1918–May 9, 2003; Senate Dec. 31, 1948–87; chair Senate Finance 1965–81.

Long, Speedy Oteria (D La.) June 16, 1928– ; House 1965–73.

Longfellow, Stephen (– Maine) June 23, 1775–Aug. 2, 1849; House 1823–25.

Longley, James B. Jr. (R Maine) July 7, 1951– ; House 1995–97.

Longnecker, Henry Clay (R Pa.) April 17, 1820–Sept. 16, 1871; House 1859–61.

Longworth, Nicholas (nephew of Bellamy Storer) (R Ohio) Nov. 5, 1869–April 9, 1931; House 1903–13, 1915–April 9, 1931; House

majority leader 1923–25; Speaker Dec. 7, 1925–27, Dec. 5, 1927–29, April 15, 1929–31.

Longyear, John Wesley (R Mich.) Oct. 22, 1820–March 11, 1875; House 1863–67.

Loofbourow, Frederick Charles (R Utah) Feb. 8, 1874–July 8, 1949; House Nov. 4, 1930–33.

Loomis, Andrew Williams (W Ohio) June 27, 1797–Aug. 24, 1873; House March 4–Oct. 20, 1837.

Loomis, Arphaxed (D N.Y.) April 9, 1798–Sept. 15, 1885; House 1837–39.

Loomis, Dwight (R Conn.) July 27, 1821–Sept. 17, 1903; House 1859–63.

Lord, Bert (R N.Y.) Dec. 4, 1869–May 24, 1939; House 1935–May 24, 1939.

Lord, Frederick William (D N.Y.) Dec. 11, 1800–May 24, 1860; House 1847–49.

Lord, Henry William (R Mich.) March 8, 1821–Jan. 25, 1891; House 1881–83.

Lord, Scott (D N.Y.) Dec. 11, 1820–Sept. 10, 1885; House 1875–77.

Lore, Charles Brown (D Del.) March 16, 1831–March 6, 1911; House 1883–87.

Lorimer, William (R Ill.) April 27, 1861–Sept. 13, 1934; House 1895–1901, 1903–June 17, 1909; Senate June 18, 1909–July 13, 1912.

Loring, George Bailey (R Mass.) Nov. 8, 1817–Sept. 14, 1891; House 1877–81.

Loser, Joseph Carlton (D Tenn.) Oct. 1, 1892–July 31, 1984; House 1957–63.

Lott, Chester Trent (R Miss.) Oct. 9, 1941– ; House 1973–89; Senate 1989– ; Senate majority leader June 12, 1996–Jan. 3, 2001, Jan. 20, 2001–June 6, 2001; Senate minority leader Jan. 3–Jan. 20, 2001, June 6, 2001–03; chair Senate Rules and Administration 2003– .

Loud, Eugene Francis (R Calif.) March 12, 1847–Dec. 19, 1908; House 1891–1903.

Loud, George Alvin (R Mich.) June 18, 1852–Nov. 13, 1925; House 1903–13, 1915–17.

Loudenslager, Henry Clay (R N.J.) May 22, 1852–Aug. 12, 1911; House 1893–Aug. 12, 1911.

Loughridge, William (R Iowa) July 11, 1827–Sept. 26, 1889; House 1867–71, 1873–75.

Lounsbery, William (D N.Y.) Dec. 25, 1831–Nov. 8, 1905; House 1879–81.

Louttit, James Alexander (R Calif.) Oct. 16, 1848–July 26, 1906; House 1885–87.

Love, Francis Johnson (R W.Va.) Jan. 23, 1901–Oct. 1989; House 1947–49.

Love, James (AJ Ky.) May 12, 1795–June 12, 1874; House 1833–35.

Love, John (R Va.) ?–Aug. 17, 1822; House 1807–11.

Love, Peter Early (D Ga.) July 7, 1818–Nov. 8, 1866; House 1859–Jan. 23, 1861.

Love, Rodney Marvin (D Ohio) July 18, 1908–May 5, 1996; House 1965–67.

Love, Thomas Cutting (W N.Y.) Nov. 30, 1789–Sept. 17, 1853; House 1835–37.

Love, William Carter (R N.C.) 1784–1835; House 1815–17.

Love, William Franklin (D Miss.) March 29, 1850–Oct. 16, 1898; House 1897–Oct. 16, 1898.

Lovejoy, Owen (cousin of Nathan Allen Farwell) (R Ill.) Jan. 6, 1811–March 25, 1864; House 1857–March 25, 1864.

Lovering, Henry Bacon (D Mass.) April 8, 1841–April 5, 1911; House 1883–87.

Lovering, William Croad (R Mass.) Feb. 25, 1835–Feb. 4, 1910; House 1897–Feb. 4, 1910.

Lovett, John (F N.Y.) Feb. 20, 1761–Aug. 12, 1818; House 1813–17.

Lovette, Oscar Byrd (R Tenn.) Dec. 20, 1871–July 6, 1934; House 1931–33.

Lovre, Harold Orrin (R S.D.) Jan. 30, 1904–Jan. 17, 1972; House 1949–57.

Low, Frederick Ferdinand (R Calif.) June 30, 1828–July 21, 1894; House June 3, 1862–63; Gov. Dec. 10, 1863–Dec. 5, 1867 (Union Republican).

Low, Philip Burrill (R N.Y.) May 6, 1836–Aug. 23, 1912; House 1895–99.

Lowden, Frank Orren (R Ill.) Jan. 26, 1861–March 20, 1943; House Nov. 6, 1906–11; Gov. Jan. 8, 1917–Jan. 10, 1921.

Lowe, David Perley (R Kan.) Aug. 22, 1823–April 10, 1882; House 1871–75.

Lowe, William Manning (G Ala.) June 12, 1842–Oct. 12, 1882; House 1879–81, June 3–Oct. 12, 1882.

Lowell, Joshua Adams (D Maine) March 20, 1801–March 13, 1874; House 1839–43.

Lowenstein, Allard Kenneth (D N.Y.) Jan. 16, 1929–March 14, 1980; House 1969–71.

Lower, Christian (R Pa.) Jan. 7, 1740–Dec. 19, 1806; House 1805–Dec. 19, 1806.

Lowery, William David (R Calif.) May 2, 1947– ; House 1981–93.

Lowey, Nita Melnikoff (D N.Y.) July 5, 1937– ; House 1989– .

Lowndes, Lloyd Jr. (great-nephew of Edward Lloyd) (R Md.) Feb. 21, 1845–Jan. 8, 1905; House 1873–75; Gov. Jan. 8, 1896–Jan. 10, 1900.

Lowndes, Thomas (brother of William Lowndes) (F S.C.) Jan. 22, 1766–July 8, 1843; House 1801–05.

Lowndes, William (brother of Thomas Lowndes) (R S.C.) Feb. 11, 1782–Oct. 27, 1822; House 1811–May 8, 1822.

Lowrey, Bill Green (D Miss.) May 25, 1862–Sept. 2, 1947; House 1921–29.

Lowrie, Walter (D Pa.) Dec. 10, 1784–Dec. 14, 1868; Senate 1819–25.

Lowry, Michael Edward (D Wash.) March 8, 1939– ; House 1979–89; Gov. Jan. 13, 1993–Jan. 15, 1997.

Lowry, Robert (D Ind.) April 2, 1824–Jan. 27, 1904; House 1883–87.

Loyall, George (J Va.) May 29, 1789–Feb. 24, 1868; House March 9, 1830–31 (no party), 1833–37.

Lozier, Ralph Fulton (D Mo.) Jan. 28, 1866–May 28, 1945; House 1923–35.

Lucas, Edward (brother of William Lucas) (J Va.) Oct. 20, 1780–March 4, 1858; House 1833–37.

Lucas, Frank Dean (R Okla.) Jan. 6, 1960– ; House May 17, 1994– .

Lucas, John Baptiste Charles (R Pa.) Aug. 14, 1758–Aug. 17, 1842; House 1803–05.

Lucas, Ken (D Ky.) Aug. 22, 1933– ; House 1999–2005.

Lucas, Scott Wike (D Ill.) Feb. 19, 1892–Feb. 22, 1968; House 1935–39; Senate 1939–51; Senate majority leader 1949–51.

Lucas, William (brother of Edward Lucas) (D Va.) Nov. 30, 1800–Aug. 29, 1877; House 1839–41, 1843–45.

Lucas, William Vincent (R S.D.) July 3, 1835–Nov. 10, 1921; House 1893–95.

Lucas, Wingate Hezekiah (D Texas) May 1, 1908–May 26, 1989; House 1947–55.

Luce, Clare Boothe (stepdaughter of Albert Elmer Austin) (R Conn.) April 10, 1903–Oct. 9, 1987; House 1943–47.

Luce, Robert (R Mass.) Dec. 2, 1862–April 17, 1946; House 1919–35, 1937–41.

Luckey, Henry Carl (D Neb.) Nov. 22, 1868–Dec. 31, 1956; House 1935–39.

Lucking, Alfred (D Mich.) Dec. 18, 1856–Dec. 1, 1929; House 1903–05.

Ludlow, Louis Leon (D Ind.) June 24, 1873–Nov. 28, 1950; House 1929–49.

Luecke, John Frederick (D Mich.) July 4, 1889–March 21, 1952; House 1937–39.

Lufkin, Willfred Weymouth (R Mass.) March 10, 1879–March 28, 1934; House Nov. 6, 1917–June 30, 1921.

Lugar, Richard Green (R Ind.) April 4, 1932– ; Senate 1977– ; chair Senate Foreign Relations 1985–87, 2003– ; chair Senate Agriculture, Nutrition, and Forestry 1995–Jan. 3, 2001, Jan. 20, 2001–June 6, 2001.

Luhring, Oscar Raymond (R Ind.) Feb. 11, 1879–Aug. 20, 1944; House 1919–23.

Lujan, Manuel Jr. (R N.M.) May 12, 1928– ; House 1969–89; secretary of the interior Feb. 8, 1989–Jan. 20, 1993.

Luken, Charles (son of Thomas Andrew Luken) (D Ohio) July 18, 1951– ; House 1991–93.

Luken, Thomas Andrew (father of Charles Luken) (D Ohio) July 9, 1925– ; House March 5, 1974–75, 1977–91.

Lukens, Donald Edgar "Buz" (R Ohio) Feb. 11, 1931– ; House 1967–71, 1987–Oct. 24, 1990.

Lumpkin, Alva Moore (D S.C.) Nov. 13, 1886–Aug. 1, 1941; Senate July 22–Aug. 1, 1941.

Lumpkin, John Henry (nephew of Wilson Lumpkin) (D Ga.) June 13, 1812–July 10, 1860; House 1843–49, 1855–57.

Lumpkin, Wilson (uncle of John Henry Lumpkin, grandfather of Middleton Pope Barrow) (– Ga.) Jan. 14, 1783–Dec. 28, 1870; House 1815–17, 1827–31; Senate Nov. 22, 1837–41; Gov. Nov. 9, 1831–Nov. 4, 1835 (Union Democrat).

Luna, Tranquilino (R N.M.) Feb. 25, 1849–Nov. 20, 1892; House (Terr. Del.) 1881–March 5, 1884.

Lundeen, Ernest (FL Minn.) Aug. 4, 1878–Aug. 31, 1940; House 1917–19 (Republican), 1933–37; Senate 1937–Aug. 31, 1940.

Lundin, Frederick (R Ill.) May 18, 1868–Aug. 20, 1947; House 1909–11.

Lundine, Stanley Nelson (D N.Y.) Feb. 4, 1939– ; House March 2, 1976–87.

Lungren, Daniel Edward (R Calif.) Sept. 22, 1946– ; House 1979–89, 2005– .

Lunn, George Richard (D N.Y.) June 23, 1873–Nov. 27, 1948; House 1917–19.

Lusk, Georgia Lee (D N.M.) May 12, 1893–Jan. 5, 1971; House 1947–49.

Lusk, Hall Stoner (D Ore.) Sept. 21, 1883–May 15, 1983; Senate March 16–Nov. 8, 1960.

Luther, William Paul "Bill" (D Minn.) June 27, 1945– ; House 1995–2003.

Luttrell, John King (D Calif.) June 27, 1831–Oct. 4, 1893; House 1873–79.

Lybrand, Archibald (R Ohio) May 23, 1840–Feb. 7, 1910; House 1897–1901.

Lyle, Aaron (R Pa.) Nov. 17, 1759–Sept. 24, 1825; House 1809–17.

Lyle, John Emmett Jr. (D Texas) Sept. 4, 1910–Nov. 11, 2003; House 1945–55.

Lyman, Joseph (R Iowa) Sept. 13, 1840–July 9, 1890; House 1885–89.

Lyman, Joseph Stebbins (– N.Y.) Feb. 14, 1785–March 21, 1821; House 1819–21.

Lyman, Samuel (F Mass.) Jan. 25, 1749–June 5, 1802; House 1795–Nov. 6, 1800.

Lyman, Theodore (IR Mass.) Aug. 23, 1833–Sept. 9, 1897; House 1883–85.

Lyman, William (R Mass.) Dec. 7, 1755–Sept. 2, 1811; House 1793–97 (1793–95 no party).

Lynch, John (R Maine) Feb. 18, 1825–July 21, 1892; House 1865–73.

Lynch, John (D Pa.) Nov. 1, 1843–Aug. 17, 1910; House 1887–89.

Lynch, John Roy (R Miss.) Sept. 10, 1847–Nov. 2, 1939; House 1873–77, April 29, 1882–83.

Lynch, Stephen F. (D Mass.) March 31, 1955– ; House Oct. 16, 2001– .

Lynch, Thomas (D Wis.) Nov. 21, 1844–May 4, 1898; House 1891–95.

Lynch, Walter Aloysius (D N.Y.) July 7, 1894–Sept. 10, 1957; House Feb. 20, 1940–51.

Lynde, William Pitt (D Wis.) Dec. 16, 1817–Dec. 18, 1885; House June 5, 1848–49, 1875–79.

Lyon, Asa (F Vt.) Dec. 31, 1763–April 4, 1841; House 1815–17.

Lyon, Caleb (I N.Y.) Dec. 7, 1822–Sept. 8, 1875; House 1853–55; Gov. (Idaho Terr.) 1864–66.

Lyon, Chittenden (son of Matthew Lyon) (J Ky.) Feb. 22, 1787–Nov. 23, 1842; House 1827–35 (1827–29 no party).

Lyon, Francis Strother (W Ala.) Feb. 25, 1800–Dec. 31, 1882; House 1835–39 (1835–37 Anti-Jacksonian).

Lyon, Homer Le Grand (D N.C.) March 1, 1879–May 31, 1956; House 1921–29.

Lyon, Lucius (D Mich.) Feb. 26, 1800–Sept. 24, 1851; House (Terr. Del.) 1833–35, (Rep.) 1843–45; Senate Jan. 26, 1837–39.

Lyon, Matthew (father of Chittenden Lyon, great-grandfather of William Peters Hepburn) (R Ky.) July 14, 1746–Aug. 1, 1822; House 1797–1801 (Vt.), 1803–11.

Lytle, Robert Todd (nephew of John Rowan) (J Ohio) May 19, 1804–Dec. 22, 1839; House 1833–March 10, 1834, Dec. 27, 1834–35.

Maas, Melvin Joseph (R Minn.) May 14, 1898–April 13, 1964; House 1927–33, 1935–45.

MacCrate, John (R N.Y.) March 29, 1885–June 9, 1976; House 1919–Dec. 30, 1920.

MacDonald, John Lewis (D Minn.) Feb. 22, 1838–July 13, 1903; House 1887–89.

Macdonald, Moses (D Maine) April 8, 1815–Oct. 18, 1869; House 1851–55.

Macdonald, Torbert Hart (D Mass.) June 6, 1917–May 21, 1976; House 1955–May 21, 1976.

MacDonald, William Josiah (Prog. Mich.) Nov. 17, 1873–March 29, 1946; House Aug. 26, 1913–15.

MacDougall, Clinton Dugald (R N.Y.) June 14, 1839–May 24, 1914; House 1873–77.

Mace, Daniel (R Ind.) Sept. 5, 1811–July 26, 1867; House 1851–57 (1851–55 Democrat).

MacGregor, Clarence (R N.Y.) Sept. 16, 1872–Feb. 18, 1952; House 1919–Dec. 31, 1928.

MacGregor, Clark (R Minn.) July 12, 1922–Feb. 10, 2003; House 1961–71.

Machen, Hervey Gilbert (D Md.) Oct. 14, 1916–Nov. 29, 1994; House 1965–69.

Machen, Willis Benson (D Ky.) April 10, 1810–Sept. 29, 1893; Senate Sept. 27, 1872–73.

Machir, James (F Va.) ?–June 25, 1827; House 1797–99.

Machrowicz, Thaddeus Michael (D Mich.) Aug. 21, 1899–Feb. 17, 1970; House 1951–Sept. 18, 1961.

Machtley, Ronald K. (R R.I.) July 13, 1948– ; House 1989–95.

Maciejewski, Anton Frank (D Ill.) Jan. 3, 1893–Sept. 25, 1949; House 1939–Dec. 8, 1942.

Macintyre, Archibald Thompson (D Ga.) Oct. 27, 1822–Jan. 1, 1900; House 1871–73.

Maciora, Lucien John (D Conn.) Aug. 17, 1902–Oct. 19, 1993; House 1941–43.

Mack, Connie III (father of Connie Mack, step-grandson of Tom Connally, grandson of Morris Sheppard, great-grandson of John Levi Sheppard) (R Fla.) Oct. 29, 1940– ; House 1983–89; Senate 1989–2001.

Mack, Connie (son of Connie Mack III, step-great-grandson of Tom Connally, great-grandson of Morris Sheppard) (R Fla.) Aug. 12, 1967– ; House 2005– .

Mack, Peter Francis Jr. (D Ill.) Nov. 1, 1916–July 4, 1986; House 1949–63.

Mack, Russell Vernon (R Wash.) June 13, 1891–March 28, 1960; House June 7, 1947–March 28, 1960.

MacKay, James Armstrong (D Ga.) June 25, 1919–July 2, 2004; House 1965–67.

MacKay, Kenneth Hood "Buddy" Jr. (D Fla.) March 22, 1933– ; House 1983–89; Gov. Dec. 13, 1998–Jan. 5, 1999.

Mackey, Edmund William McGregor (R S.C.) March 8, 1846–Jan. 27, 1884; House 1875–July 19, 1876 (Independent Republican), May 31, 1882–Jan. 27, 1884.

Mackey, Levi Augustus (D Pa.) Nov. 25, 1819–Feb. 8, 1889; House 1875–79.

Mackie, John C. (D Mich.) June 1, 1920– ; House 1965–67.

MacKinnon, George Edward (R Minn.) April 22, 1906–May 1, 1995; House 1947–49.

MacLafferty, James Henry (R Calif.) Feb. 27, 1871–June 9, 1937; House Nov. 7, 1922–25.

Maclay, Samuel (brother of William Maclay, father of William Plunkett Maclay) (R Pa.) June 17, 1741–Oct. 5, 1811; House 1795–97 (no party); Senate 1803–Jan. 4, 1809.

Maclay, William (brother of Samuel Maclay, uncle of William Plunkett Maclay) (– Pa.) July 20, 1737–April 16, 1804; Senate 1789–91.

Maclay, William (R Pa.) March 22, 1765–Jan. 4, 1825; House 1815–19.

Maclay, William Brown (D N.Y.) March 20, 1812–Feb. 19, 1882; House 1843–49, 1857–61.

Maclay, William Plunkett (son of Samuel Maclay, nephew of William Maclay) (R Pa.) Aug. 23, 1774–Sept. 2, 1842; House Oct. 8, 1816–21.

Macon, Nathaniel (uncle of Willis Alston and Micajah Thomas Hawkins, great-grandfather of Charles Henry Martin of North Carolina) (R N.C.) Dec. 17, 1757–June 29, 1837; House 1791–Dec. 13, 1815 (no party); Senate Dec. 13, 1815–Nov. 14, 1828; Speaker Dec. 7, 1801–03, Oct. 17, 1803–05, Dec. 2, 1805–07; elected pres. pro tempore May 20, 1826, Jan. 2, 1827, March 2, 1827; Cont. Cong. (elected but did not attend) 1785.

Macon, Robert Bruce (D Ark.) July 6, 1859–Oct. 9, 1925; House 1903–13.

Macy, John B. (D Wis.) March 26, 1799–Sept. 24, 1856; House 1853–55.

Macy, William Kingsland (R N.Y.) Nov. 21, 1889–July 15, 1961; House 1947–51.

Madden, Martin Barnaby (R Ill.) March 21, 1855–April 27, 1928; House 1905–April 27, 1928.

Madden, Ray John (D Ind.) Feb. 25, 1892–Sept. 28, 1987; House 1943–77; chair House Rules 1973–77.

Maddox, John W. (D Ga.) June 3, 1848–Sept. 27, 1922; House 1893–1905.

Madigan, Edward Rell (R Ill.) Jan. 13, 1936–Dec. 7, 1994; House 1973–March 8, 1991; secretary of agriculture March 12, 1991–Jan. 20, 1993.

Madison, Edmond Haggard (R Kan.) Dec. 18, 1865–Sept. 18, 1911; House 1907–Sept. 18, 1911.

Madison, James (R Va.) March 16, 1751–June 28, 1836; House 1789–97 (1789–95 no party); Cont. Cong. 1780–83, 1787–88; secretary of state May 2, 1801–March 3, 1809; president 1809–17 (Democratic Republican).

Maffett, James Thompson (R Pa.) Feb. 2, 1837–Dec. 19, 1912; House 1887–89.

Magee, Clare (D Mo.) March 31, 1899–Aug. 7, 1969; House 1949–53.

Magee, James McDevitt (R Pa.) April 5, 1877–April 16, 1949; House 1923–27.

Magee, John (J N.Y.) Sept. 3, 1794–April 5, 1868; House 1827–31 (1827–29 no party).

Magee, John Alexander (D Pa.) Oct. 14, 1827–Nov. 18, 1903; House 1873–75.

Magee, Walter Warren (R N.Y.) May 23, 1861–May 25, 1927; House 1915–May 25, 1927.

Maginnis, Martin (D Mont.) Oct. 27, 1841–March 27, 1919; House (Terr. Del.) 1873–85.

Magner, Thomas Francis (uncle of John Francis Carew) (D N.Y.) March 8, 1860–Dec. 22, 1945; House 1889–95.

Magnuson, Donald Hammer (D Wash.) March 7, 1911–Oct. 5, 1979; House 1953–63.

Magnuson, Warren Grant (D Wash.) April 12, 1905–May 20, 1989; House 1937–Dec. 13, 1944; Senate Dec. 14, 1944–81; chair Senate Interstate and Foreign Commerce 1955–61; chair Senate Commerce 1961–77; chair Senate Commerce, Science, and Transportation 1977–78; chair Senate Appropriations 1978–81; elected pres. pro tempore Jan. 15, 1979.

Magoon, Henry Sterling (R Wis.) Jan. 31, 1832–March 3, 1889; House 1875–77.

Magrady, Frederick William (R Pa.) Nov. 24, 1863–Aug. 27, 1954; House 1925–33.

Magruder, Allan Bowie (D La.) 1775–April 15, 1822; Senate Sept. 3, 1812–13.

Magruder, Patrick (R Md.) 1768–Dec. 24, 1819; House 1805–07.

Maguire, Gene Andrew (D N.J.) March 11, 1939– ; House 1975–81.

Maguire, James George (D Calif.) Feb. 22, 1853–June 20, 1920; House 1893–99.

Maguire, John Arthur (D Neb.) Nov. 29, 1870–July 1, 1939; House 1909–15.

Mahan, Bryan Francis (D Conn.) May 1, 1856–Nov. 16, 1923; House 1913–15.

Mahany, Rowland Blennerhassett (R N.Y.) Sept. 28, 1864–May 2, 1937; House 1895–99.

Maher, James Paul (D N.Y.) Nov. 3, 1865–July 31, 1946; House 1911–21.

Mahon, Gabriel Heyward Jr. (D S.C.) Nov. 11, 1889–June 11, 1962; House Nov. 3, 1936–39.

Mahon, George Herman (D Texas) Sept. 22, 1900–Nov. 19, 1985; House 1935–79; chair House Appropriations 1964–77.

Mahon, Thaddeus Maclay (R Pa.) May 21, 1840–May 31, 1916; House 1893–1907.

Mahone, William (Read. Va.) Dec. 1, 1826–Oct. 8, 1895; Senate 1881–87.

Mahoney, Peter Paul (D N.Y.) June 25, 1848–March 27, 1889; House 1885–89.

Mahoney, William Frank (D Ill.) Feb. 22, 1856–Dec. 27, 1904; House 1901–Dec. 27, 1904.

Mailliard, William Somers (R Calif.) June 10, 1917–June 10, 1992; House 1953–March 5, 1974.

Main, Verner Wright (R Mich.) Dec. 16, 1885–July 6, 1965; House Dec. 17, 1935–37.

Maish, Levi (D Pa.) Nov. 22, 1837–Feb. 26, 1899; House 1875–79, 1887–91.

Majette, Denise L. (D Ga.) May 18, 1955– ; House 2003–05.

Major, James Earl (D Ill.) Jan. 5, 1887–Jan. 4, 1972; House 1923–25, 1927–29, 1931–Oct. 6, 1933.

Major, Samuel Collier (D Mo.) July 2, 1869–July 28, 1931; House 1919–21, 1923–29, March 4–July 28, 1931.

Majors, Thomas Jefferson (R Neb.) June 25, 1841–July 11, 1932; House Nov. 5, 1878–79.

Malbone, Francis (F R.I.) March 20, 1759–June 4, 1809; House 1793–97 (no party); Senate March 4–June 4, 1809.

Malby, George Roland (R N.Y.) Sept. 16, 1857–July 5, 1912; House 1907–July 5, 1912.

Mallary, Richard Walker (R Vt.) Feb. 21, 1929– ; House Jan. 7, 1972–75.

Mallary, Rollin Carolas (– Vt.) May 27, 1784–April 15, 1831; House Jan. 13, 1820–April 15, 1831.

Mallory, Francis (W Va.) Dec. 12, 1807–March 26, 1860; House 1837–39, Dec. 28, 1840–43.

Mallory, Meredith (D N.Y.) ?–?; House 1839–41.

Mallory, Robert (U Ky.) Nov. 15, 1815–Aug. 11, 1885; House 1859–65 (1859–61 Opposition Party).

Mallory, Rufus (R Ore.) Jan. 10, 1831–April 30, 1914; House 1867–69.

Mallory, Stephen Russell (father of Stephen Russell Mallory, below) (D Fla.) 1813–Nov. 9, 1873; Senate 1851–Jan. 21, 1861.

Mallory, Stephen Russell (son of Stephen Russell Mallory, above) (D Fla.) Nov. 2, 1848–Dec. 23, 1907; House 1891–95; Senate May 15, 1897–Dec. 23, 1907.

Malone, George Wilson (R Nev.) Aug. 7, 1890–May 19, 1961; Senate 1947–59.

Maloney, Carolyn Bosher (D N.Y.) Feb. 19, 1948– ; House 1993– .

Maloney, Francis Thomas (D Conn.) March 31, 1894–Jan. 16, 1945; House 1933–35; Senate 1935–Jan. 16, 1945.

Maloney, Franklin John (R Pa.) March 29, 1899–Sept. 15, 1958; House 1947–49.

Maloney, James H. (D Conn.) Sept. 17, 1948– ; House 1997–2003.

Maloney, Paul Herbert (D La.) Feb. 14, 1876–March 26, 1967; House 1931–Dec. 15, 1940, 1943–47.

Maloney, Robert Sarsfield (R Mass.) Feb. 3, 1881–Nov. 8, 1934; House 1921–23.

Manahan, James (R Minn.) March 12, 1866–Jan. 8, 1932; House 1913–15.

Manasco, Carter (D Ala.) Jan. 3, 1902–Feb. 5, 1992; House June 24, 1941–49.

Manderson, Charles Frederick (R Neb.) Feb. 9, 1837–Sept. 28, 1911; Senate 1883–95; elected pres. pro tempore March 2, 1891.

Mangum, Willie Person (W N.C.) May 10, 1792–Sept. 7, 1861; House 1823–March 18, 1826 (no party); Senate 1831–Nov. 26, 1836 (Jacksonian), Nov. 25, 1840–53; elected pres. pro tempore May 31, 1842.

Mankin, Helen Douglas (D Ga.) Sept. 11, 1896–July 25, 1956; House Feb. 12, 1946–47.

Manlove, Joe Jonathan (R Mo.) Oct. 1, 1876–Jan. 31, 1956; House 1923–33.

Mann, Abijah Jr. (J N.Y.) Sept. 24, 1793–Sept. 6, 1868; House 1833–37.

Mann, David (D Ohio) Sept. 25, 1939– ; House 1993–95.

Mann, Edward Coke (D S.C.) Nov. 21, 1880–Nov. 11, 1931; House Oct. 7, 1919–21.

Mann, Horace (FS Mass.) May 4, 1796–Aug. 2, 1859; House April 3, 1848–53 (1848–51 Whig).

Mann, James (D La.) June 22, 1822–Aug. 26, 1868; House July 18–Aug. 26, 1868.

Mann, James Robert (R Ill.) Oct. 20, 1856–Nov. 30, 1922; House 1897–Nov. 30, 1922; House minority leader 1911–19.

Mann, James Robert (D S.C.) April 27, 1920– ; House 1969–79.

Mann, Job (D Pa.) March 31, 1795–Oct. 8, 1873; House 1835–37 (Jacksonian), 1847–51.

Mann, Joel Keith (J Pa.) Aug. 1, 1780–Aug. 28, 1857; House 1831–35.

Manning, John Jr. (D N.C.) July 30, 1830–Feb. 12, 1899; House Dec. 7, 1870–71.

Manning, Richard Irvine (cousin of John Peter Richardson II) (J S.C.) May 1, 1789–May 1, 1836; House Dec. 8, 1834–May 1, 1836; Gov. Dec. 3, 1824–Dec. 9, 1826 (Democratic Republican).

Manning, Vannoy Hartrog (D Miss.) July 26, 1839–Nov. 3, 1892; House 1877–83.

Mansfield, Joseph Jefferson (D Texas) Feb. 9, 1861–July 12, 1947; House 1917–July 12, 1947.

Mansfield, Michael Joseph "Mike" (D Mont.) March 16, 1903–Oct. 5, 2001; House 1943–53; Senate 1953–77; chair Senate Rules and Administration 1961–63; Senate majority leader 1961–77.

Manson, Mahlon Dickerson (D Ind.) Feb. 20, 1820–Feb. 4, 1895; House 1871–73.

Mansur, Charles Harley (D Mo.) March 6, 1835–April 16, 1895; House 1887–93.

Mantle, Lee (R Mont.) Dec. 13, 1851–Nov. 18, 1934; Senate Jan. 16, 1895–99.

Manton, Thomas J. (D N.Y.) Nov. 3, 1932– ; House 1985–99.

Manzanares, Francisco Antonio (D N.M.) Jan. 25, 1843–Sept. 17, 1904; House (Terr. Del.) March 5, 1884–85.

Manzullo, Donald (R Ill.) March 24, 1944– ; House 1993– ; chair House Small Business 2001– .

Mapes, Carl Edgar (R Mich.) Dec. 26, 1874–Dec. 12, 1939; House 1913–Dec. 12, 1939.

Marable, John Hartwell (– Tenn.) Nov. 18, 1786–April 11, 1844; House 1825–29.

Maraziti, Joseph James (R N.J.) June 15, 1912–May 20, 1991; House 1973–75.

Marcantonio, Vito Anthony (AL N.Y.) Dec. 10, 1902–Aug. 9, 1954; House 1935–37 (Republican), 1939–51.

Marchand, Albert Gallatin (son of David Marchand) (D Pa.) Feb. 27, 1811–Feb. 5, 1848; House 1839–43.

Marchand, David (father of Albert Gallatin Marchand) (R Pa.) Dec. 10, 1776–March 11, 1832; House 1817–21.

Marchant, Kenneth "Kenny" (R Texas) Feb. 23, 1951– ; House 2005– .

Marcy, Daniel (D N.H.) Nov. 7, 1809–Nov. 3, 1893; House 1863–65.

Marcy, William Learned (J N.Y.) Dec. 12, 1786–July 4, 1857; Senate 1831–Jan. 1, 1833; Gov. Jan. 1, 1833–Jan. 1, 1839; secretary of war March 6, 1845–March 4, 1849; secretary of state March 8, 1853–March 6, 1857.

Mardis, Samuel Wright (J Ala.) June 12, 1800–Nov. 14, 1836; House 1831–35.

Margolies-Mezvinsky, Marjorie (wife of Edward Maurice Mezvinsky) (D Pa.) June 21, 1942– ; House 1993–95.

Marion, Robert (R S.C.) 1766–March 22, 1811; House 1805–Dec. 4, 1810.

Markell, Henry (son of Jacob Markell) (– N.Y.) Feb. 7, 1792–Aug. 30, 1831; House 1825–29.

Markell, Jacob (father of Henry Markell) (F N.Y.) May 8, 1770–Nov. 26, 1852; House 1813–15.

Markey, Edward John (D Mass.) July 11, 1946– ; House Nov. 2, 1976– .

Markham, Henry Harrison (R Calif.) Nov. 16, 1840–Oct. 9, 1923; House 1885–87; Gov. Jan. 8, 1891–Jan. 11, 1895.

Markley, Philip Swenk (– Pa.) July 2, 1789–Sept. 12, 1834; House 1823–27.

Marks, Marc Lincoln (R Pa.) Feb. 12, 1927– ; House 1977–83.

Marks, William (– Pa.) Oct. 13, 1778–April 10, 1858; Senate 1825–31.

Marland, Ernest Whitworth (D Okla.) May 8, 1874–Oct. 3, 1941; House 1933–35; Gov. Jan. 14, 1935–Jan. 9, 1939.

Marlenee, Ronald Charles (R Mont.) Aug. 8, 1935– ; House 1977–93.

Marquette, Turner Mastin (R Neb.) July 19, 1831–Dec. 22, 1894; House March 2, 1867–March 3, 1867.

Marr, Alem (J Pa.) June 18, 1787–March 29, 1843; House 1829–31.

Marr, George Washington Lent (R Tenn.) May 25, 1779–Sept. 5, 1856; House 1817–19.

Marriott, David Daniel (R Utah) Nov. 2, 1939– ; House 1977–85.

Marsalis, John Henry (D Colo.) May 9, 1904–June 26, 1971; House 1949–51.

Marsh, Benjamin Franklin (R Ill.) 1839–June 2, 1905; House 1877–83, 1893–1901, 1903–June 2, 1905.

Marsh, Charles (father of George Perkins Marsh) (F Vt.) July 10, 1765–Jan. 11, 1849; House 1815–17.

Marsh, George Perkins (son of Charles Marsh) (W Vt.) March 15, 1801–July 23, 1882; House 1843–May 1849.

Marsh, John Otho Jr. (D Va.) Aug. 7, 1926– ; House 1963–71.

Marshall, Alexander Keith (AP Ky.) Feb. 11, 1808–April 28, 1884; House 1855–57.

Marshall, Alfred (D Maine) about 1797–Oct. 2, 1868; House 1841–43.

Marshall, Edward Colston (D Calif.) June 29, 1821–July 9, 1893; House 1851–53.

Marshall, Fred (D Minn.) March 13, 1906–June 5, 1985; House 1949–63.

Marshall, George Alexander (D Ohio) Sept. 14, 1851–April 21, 1899; House 1897–99.

Marshall, Humphrey (grandfather of Humphrey Marshall, below, father of Thomas Alexander Marshall, cousin of John Marshall) (F Ky.) 1760–July 1, 1841; Senate 1795–1801.

Marshall, Humphrey (grandson of Humphrey Marshall, above) (AP Ky.) Jan. 13, 1812–March 28, 1872; House 1849–Aug. 4, 1852 (Whig), 1855–59.

Marshall, James William (D Va.) March 31, 1844–Nov. 27, 1911; House 1893–95.

Marshall, Jim (D Ga.) March 31, 1948– ; House 2003– .

Marshall, John (uncle of Thomas Francis Marshall, cousin of Humphrey Marshall born in 1760) (F Va.) Sept. 24, 1755–July 6, 1835; House 1799–June 7, 1800; secretary of state June 6, 1800–Feb. 4, 1801; chief justice Feb. 4, 1801–July 6, 1835.

Marshall, Leroy Tate (R Ohio) Nov. 8, 1883–Nov. 22, 1950; House 1933–37.

Marshall, Lycurgus Luther (R Ohio) July 9, 1888–Jan. 12, 1958; House 1939–41.

Marshall, Samuel Scott (D Ill.) March 12, 1821–July 26, 1890; House 1855–59, 1865–75.

Marshall, Thomas Alexander (son of Humphrey Marshall born in 1760) (AJ Ky.) Jan. 15, 1794–April 17, 1871; House 1831–35.

Marshall, Thomas Francis (nephew of John Marshall) (W Ky.) June 7, 1801–Sept. 22, 1864; House 1841–43.

Marshall, Thomas Frank (R N.D.) March 7, 1854–Aug. 20, 1921; House 1901–09.

Marston, Gilman (R N.H.) Aug. 20, 1811–July 3, 1890; House 1859–63, 1865–67; Senate March 4–June 18, 1889.

Martin, Alexander (– N.C.) 1740–Nov. 2, 1807; Senate 1793–99; Gov. Dec. 17, 1789–Dec. 14, 1792 (Federalist); Cont. Cong. (elected but did not attend) 1786.

Martin, Augustus Newton (D Ind.) March 23, 1847–July 11, 1901; House 1889–95.

Martin, Barclay (uncle of Lewis Tillman) (D Tenn.) Dec. 17, 1802–Nov. 8, 1890; House 1845–47.

Martin, Benjamin Franklin (D W.Va.) Oct. 2, 1828–Jan. 20, 1895; House 1877–81.

Martin, Charles (D Ill.) May 20, 1856–Oct. 28, 1917; House March 4–Oct. 28, 1917.

Martin, Charles Drake (D Ohio) Aug. 5, 1829–Aug. 27, 1911; House 1859–61.

Martin, Charles Henry (great-grandson of Nathaniel Macon) (P N.C.) Aug. 28, 1848–April 19, 1931; House June 5, 1896–99.

Martin, Charles Henry (D Ore.) Oct. 1, 1863–Sept. 22, 1946; House 1931–35; Gov. Jan. 14, 1935–Jan. 9, 1939.

Martin, David O'Brien (R N.Y.) April 26, 1944– ; House 1981–93.

Martin, David Thomas (R Neb.) July 9, 1907–May 15, 1997; House 1961–Dec. 31, 1974.

Martin, Eben Wever (R S.D.) April 12, 1855–May 22, 1932; House 1901–07, Nov. 3, 1908–15.

Martin, Edward (R Pa.) Sept. 18, 1879–March 19, 1967; Senate 1947–59; chair Senate Public Works 1953–55; Gov. Jan. 19, 1943–Jan. 2, 1947.

Martin, Edward Livingston (D Del.) March 29, 1837–Jan. 22, 1897; House 1879–83.

Martin, Elbert Sevier (brother of John Preston Martin) (ID Va.) about 1829–Sept. 3, 1876; House 1859–61.

Martin, Frederick Stanley (W N.Y.) April 25, 1794–June 28, 1865; House 1851–53.

Martin, George Brown (grandson of John Preston Martin) (D Ky.) Aug. 18, 1876–Nov. 12, 1945; Senate Sept. 7, 1918–19.

Martin, James Douglas (R Ala.) Sept. 1, 1918– ; House 1965–67.

Martin, James Grubbs (R N.C.) Dec. 11, 1935– ; House 1973–85; Gov. Jan. 5, 1985–Jan. 9, 1993.

Martin, James Stewart (R Ill.) Aug. 19, 1826–Nov. 20, 1907; House 1873–75.

Martin, John (D Kan.) Nov. 12, 1833–Sept. 3, 1913; Senate 1893–95.

Martin, John Andrew (D Colo.) April 10, 1868–Dec. 23, 1939; House 1909–13, 1933–Dec. 23, 1939.

Martin, John Cunningham (D Ill.) April 29, 1880–Jan. 27, 1952; House 1939–41.

Martin, John Mason (son of Joshua Lanier Martin) (D Ala.) Jan. 20, 1837–June 16, 1898; House 1885–87.

Martin, John Preston (brother of Elbert Sevier Martin, grandfather of George Brown Martin) (D Ky.) Oct. 11, 1811–Dec. 23, 1862; House 1845–47.

Martin, Joseph John (R N.C.) Nov. 21, 1833–Dec. 18, 1900; House 1879–Jan. 29, 1881.

Martin, Joseph William Jr. (R Mass.) Nov. 3, 1884–March 6, 1968; House 1925–67; House minority leader 1939–47, 1949–53, 1955–59; Speaker 1947–49, 1953–55; chair Rep. Nat. Comm. 1940–42.

Martin, Joshua Lanier (father of John Mason Martin) (D Ala.) Dec. 5, 1799–Nov. 2, 1856; House 1835–39 (1835–37 Jacksonian); Gov. Dec. 10, 1845–Dec. 16, 1847 (Independent).

Martin, Lewis J. (D N.J.) Feb. 22, 1844–May 5, 1913; House March 4–May 5, 1913.

Martin, Lynn Morley (R Ill.) Dec. 26, 1939– ; House 1981–91; secretary of labor Feb. 22, 1991–Jan. 20, 1993.

Martin, Morgan Lewis (cousin of James Duane Doty) (D Wis.) March 31, 1805–Dec. 10, 1887; House (Terr. Del.) 1845–47.

Martin, Patrick Minor (R Calif.) Nov. 25, 1924–July 18, 1968; House 1963–65.

Martin, Robert Nicols (– Md.) Jan. 14, 1798–July 20, 1870; House 1825–27.

Martin, Thomas Ellsworth (R Iowa) Jan. 18, 1893–June 27, 1971; House 1939–55; Senate 1955–61.

Martin, Thomas Staples (D Va.) July 29, 1847–Nov. 12, 1919; Senate 1895–Nov. 12, 1919; Senate minority leader 1911–13, March 4–Nov. 12, 1919; Senate majority leader 1917–19.

Martin, Whitmell Pugh (D La.) Aug. 12, 1867–April 6, 1929; House 1915–April 6, 1929 (1915–19 Progressive).

Martin, William Dickinson (J S.C.) Oct. 20, 1789–Nov. 17, 1833; House 1827–31.

Martin, William Harrison (D Texas) May 23, 1823–Feb. 3, 1898; House Nov. 4, 1887–91.

Martindale, Henry Clinton (AMas. N.Y.) May 6, 1780–April 22, 1860; House 1823–31 (no party), 1833–35.

Martine, James Edgar (D N.J.) Aug. 25, 1850–Feb. 26, 1925; Senate 1911–17.

Martinez, Matthew Gilbert (R Calif.) Feb. 14, 1929– ; House July 15, 1982–2001 (Democrat 1982–July 27, 2000).

Martinez, Melquiades Rafael "Mel" (R Fla.) Oct. 23, 1946– ; Senate 2005– ; secretary of housing and urban development Jan. 24, 2001–Dec. 9, 2003.

Martini, Bill (R N.J.) Feb. 10, 1947– ; House 1995–97.

Marvin, Dudley (W N.Y.) May 9, 1786–June 25, 1856; House 1823–29, 1847–49.

Marvin, Francis (R N.Y.) March 8, 1828–Aug. 14, 1905; House 1893–95.

Marvin, James Madison (R N.Y.) Feb. 27, 1809–April 25, 1901; House 1863–69.

Marvin, Richard Pratt (W N.Y.) Dec. 23, 1803–Jan. 11, 1892; House 1837–41.

Mascara, Frank R. (D Pa.) Jan. 19, 1930– ; House 1995–2003.

Mason, Armistead Thomson (son of Stevens Thomson Mason) (R Va.) Aug. 4, 1787–Feb. 6, 1819; Senate Jan. 3, 1816–17.

Mason, Harry Howland (D Ill.) Dec. 16, 1873–March 10, 1946; House 1935–37.

Mason, James Brown (F R.I.) Jan. 1775–Aug. 31, 1819; House 1815–19.

Mason, James Murray (D Va.) Nov. 3, 1798–April 28, 1871; House 1837–39 (Jacksonian); Senate Jan. 21, 1847–March 28, 1861; elected pres. pro tempore Jan. 6, 1857, March 4, 1857.

Mason, Jeremiah (F N.H.) April 27, 1768–Oct. 14, 1848; Senate June 10, 1813–June 16, 1817.

Mason, John Calvin (D Ky.) Aug. 4, 1802–Aug. 1865; House 1849–53, 1857–59.

Mason, John Thomson (D Md.) May 9, 1815–March 28, 1873; House 1841–43.

Mason, John Young (J Va.) April 18, 1799–Oct. 3, 1859; House 1831–Jan. 11, 1837; secretary of the navy March 26, 1844–March 10, 1845, Sept. 10, 1846–March 7, 1849; attorney general March 11, 1845–Sept. 9, 1846.

Mason, Jonathan (F Mass.) Sept. 12, 1756–Nov. 1, 1831; Senate Nov. 14, 1800–03; House 1817–May 15, 1820.

Mason, Joseph (R N.Y.) March 30, 1828–May 31, 1914; House 1879–83.

Mason, Moses Jr. (J Maine) June 2, 1789–June 25, 1866; House 1833–37.

Mason, Noah Morgan (R Ill.) July 19, 1882–March 29, 1965; House 1937–63.

Mason, Samson (W Ohio) July 24, 1793–Feb. 1, 1869; House 1835–43.

Mason, Stevens Thomson (father of Armistead Thomson Mason) (R Va.) Dec. 29, 1760–May 10, 1803; Senate Nov. 18, 1794–May 10, 1803 (Nov. 18, 1794–1803 no party).

Mason, William (J N.Y.) Sept. 10, 1786–Jan. 13, 1860; House 1835–37.

Mason, William Ernest (father of Winnifred Sprague Mason Huck) (R Ill.) July 7, 1850–June 16, 1921; House 1887–91, 1917–June 16, 1921; Senate 1897–1903.

Massey, William Alexander (R Nev.) Oct. 7, 1856–March 5, 1914; Senate July 1, 1912–Jan. 29, 1913.

Massey, Zachary David (R Tenn.) Nov. 14, 1864–July 13, 1923; House Nov. 8, 1910–11.

Massingale, Samuel Chapman (D Okla.) Aug. 2, 1870–Jan. 17, 1941; House 1935–Jan. 17, 1941.

Masters, Josiah (R N.Y.) Nov. 22, 1763–June 30, 1822; House 1805–09.

Matheson, James David (son of Gov. Scott Milne Matheson of Utah) (D Utah) March 21, 1960– ; House 2001– .

Mathews, Frank Asbury Jr. (R N.J.) Aug. 3, 1890–Feb. 5, 1964; House Nov. 6, 1945–49.

Mathews, George (– Ga.) Aug. 30, 1739–Aug. 30, 1812; House 1789–91; Gov. Nov. 7, 1793–Jan. 15, 1796 (Democratic Republican).

Mathews, George Arthur (R Dakota) June 4, 1852–April 19, 1941; House (Terr. Del.) March 4–Nov. 2, 1889.

Mathews, Harlan (D Tenn.) Jan. 17, 1927– ; Senate Jan. 5, 1993–Dec. 1, 1994.

Mathews, James (D Ohio) June 4, 1805–March 30, 1887; House 1841–45.

Mathews, Vincent (F N.Y.) June 29, 1766–Aug. 23, 1846; House 1809–11.

Mathewson, Elisha (R R.I.) April 18, 1767–Oct. 14, 1853; Senate Oct. 26, 1807–11.

Mathias, Charles McCurdy Jr. (R Md.) July 24, 1922– ; House 1961–69; Senate 1969–87; chair Senate Rules and Administration 1981–87.

Mathias, Robert Bruce (R Calif.) Nov. 17, 1930– ; House 1967–75.

Mathiot, Joshua (W Ohio) April 4, 1800–July 30, 1849; House 1841–43.

Mathis, Marvin Dawson (D Ga.) Nov. 30, 1940– ; House 1971–81.

Matlack, James (– N.J.) Jan. 11, 1775–Jan. 16, 1840; House 1821–25.

Matson, Aaron (– N.H.) 1770–July 18, 1855; House 1821–25.

Matson, Courtland Cushing (D Ind.) April 25, 1841–Sept. 4, 1915; House 1881–89.

Matsui, Doris (D Calif.) September 25, 1944– ; House March 2005– .

Matsui, Robert Takeo (D Calif.) Sept. 17, 1941–Jan. 1, 2005; House 1979–Jan. 1, 2005.

Matsunaga, Spark Masayuki (D Hawaii) Oct. 8, 1916–April 15, 1990; House 1963–77; Senate 1977–April 15, 1990.

Matteson, Orsamus Benajah (R N.Y.) Aug. 28, 1805–Dec. 22, 1889; House 1849–51 (Whig), 1853–Feb. 27, 1857 (Whig), March 4, 1857–59.

Matthews, Charles (R Pa.) Oct. 15, 1856–Dec. 12, 1932; House 1911–13.

Matthews, Donald Ray "Billy" (D Fla.) Oct. 3, 1907–Oct. 26, 1997; House 1953–67.

Matthews, Nelson Edwin (R Ohio) April 14, 1852–Oct. 13, 1917; House 1915–17.

Matthews, Stanley (uncle of Henry Watterson) (R Ohio) July 21, 1824–March 22, 1889; Senate March 21, 1877–79; assoc. justice May 17, 1881–March 22, 1889.

Matthews, William (F Md.) April 26, 1755–?; House 1797–99.

Mattingly, Mack Francis (R Ga.) Jan. 7, 1931– ; Senate 1981–87.

Mattocks, John (W Vt.) March 4, 1777–Aug. 14, 1847; House 1821–23 (no party), 1825–27 (no party), 1841–43; Gov. Oct. 13, 1843–Oct. 11, 1844.

Mattoon, Ebenezer (F Mass.) Aug. 19, 1755–Sept. 11, 1843; House Feb. 2, 1801–03.

Mattox, James Albon (D Texas) Aug. 29, 1943– ; House 1977–83.

Maurice, James (D N.Y.) Nov. 7, 1814–Aug. 4, 1884; House 1853–55.

Maury, Abram Poindexter (cousin of Fontaine Maury Maverick) (W Tenn.) Dec. 26, 1801–July 22, 1848; House 1835–39 (1835–37 White supporter).

Maverick, Fontaine Maury (cousin of Abram Poindexter Maury, nephew of James Luther Slayden, cousin of John Wood Fishburne) (D Texas) Oct. 23, 1895–June 7, 1954; House 1935–39.

Mavroules, Nicholas (D Mass.) Nov. 1, 1929–Dec. 25, 2003; House 1979–93.

Maxey, Samuel Bell (D Texas) March 30, 1825–Aug. 16, 1895; Senate 1875–87.

Maxwell, Augustus Emmett (grandfather of Emmett Wilson) (D Fla.) Sept. 21, 1820–May 5, 1903; House 1853–57.

Maxwell, George Clifford (father of John Patterson Bryan Maxwell, cousin of George Maxwell Robeson) (R N.J.) May 31, 1771–March 16, 1816; House 1811–13.

Maxwell, John Patterson Bryan (son of George Clifford Maxwell, uncle of George Maxwell Robeson) (W N.J.) Sept. 3, 1804–Nov. 14, 1845; House 1837–39, 1841–43.

Maxwell, Lewis (AJ Va.) April 17, 1790–Feb. 13, 1862; House 1827–33 (1827–31 no party).

Maxwell, Samuel (P Neb.) May 20, 1825–Feb. 11, 1901; House 1897–99.

Maxwell, Thomas (J N.Y.) Feb. 16, 1792–Nov. 4, 1864; House 1829–31.

May, Andrew Jackson (– Ky.) June 24, 1875–Sept. 6, 1959; House 1931–47.

May, Catherine Dean Barnes (later Catherine May Bedell) (R Wash.) May 18, 1914–May 28, 2004; House 1959–71.

May, Edwin Hyland Jr. (R Conn.) May 28, 1924–Feb. 20, 2002; House 1957–59.

May, Henry (D Md.) Feb. 13, 1816–Sept. 25, 1866; House 1853–55, 1861–63.

May, Mitchell (D N.Y.) July 10, 1870–March 24, 1961; House 1899–1901.

May, William L. (D Ill.) about 1793–Sept. 29, 1849; House Dec. 1, 1834–39 (Dec. 1, 1834–37 Jacksonian).

Mayall, Samuel (D Maine) June 21, 1816–Sept. 17, 1892; House 1853–55.

Maybank, Burnet Rhett (D S.C.) March 7, 1899–Sept. 1, 1954; Senate Nov. 5, 1941–Sept. 1, 1954; chair Senate Banking and Currency 1949–53; Gov. Jan. 17, 1939–Nov. 4, 1941.

Maybury, William Cotter (D Mich.) Nov. 20, 1848–May 6, 1909; House 1883–87.

Mayfield, Earle Bradford (D Texas) April 12, 1881–June 23, 1964; Senate 1923–29.

Mayham, Stephen Lorenzo (D N.Y.) Oct. 8, 1826–March 3, 1908; House 1869–71, 1877–79.

Maynard, Harry Lee (D Va.) June 8, 1861–Oct. 23, 1922; House 1901–11.

Maynard, Horace (R Tenn.) Aug. 30, 1814–May 3, 1882; House 1857–63 (1857–59 American Party, 1859–61 Opposition Party, 1861–63 Unionist), July 24, 1866–75 (1866–67 Unconditional Unionist); postmaster general Aug. 25, 1880–March 7, 1881.

Maynard, John (W N.Y.) ?–March 24, 1850; House 1827–29 (no party), 1841–43.

Mayne, Wiley (R Iowa) Jan. 19, 1917– ; House 1967–75.

Mayo, Robert Murphy (Read. Va.) April 28, 1836–March 29, 1896; House 1883–March 20, 1884.

Mayrant, William (R S.C.) ?–?; House 1815–Oct. 21, 1816.

Mays, Dannite Hill (D Fla.) April 28, 1852–May 9, 1930; House 1909–13.

Mays, James Henry (D Utah) June 29, 1868–April 19, 1926; House 1915–21.

Mazzoli, Romano Louis (D Ky.) Nov. 2, 1932– ; House 1971–95.

McAdoo, William (D N.J.) Oct. 25, 1853–June 7, 1930; House 1883–91.

McAdoo, William Gibbs (D Calif.) Oct. 31, 1863–Feb. 1, 1941; Senate 1933–Nov. 8, 1938; secretary of the Treasury March 6, 1913–Dec. 15, 1918.

McAleer, William (D Pa.) Jan. 6, 1838–April 19, 1912; House 1891–95 (1891–93 Democrat, 1893–95 Independent Democrat), 1897–1901.

McAllister, Archibald (grandson of John Andre Hanna) (D Pa.) Oct. 12, 1813–July 18, 1883; House 1863–65.

McAndrews, James (D Ill.) Oct. 22, 1862–Aug. 31, 1942; House 1901–05, 1913–21, 1935–41.

McArdle, Joseph A. (D Pa.) June 29, 1903–Dec. 27, 1967; House 1939–Jan. 5, 1942.

McArthur, Clifton Nesmith (grandson of James Willis Nesmith) (R Ore.) June 10, 1879–Dec. 9, 1923; House 1915–23.

McArthur, Duncan (– Ohio) Jan. 14, 1772–April 29, 1839; House (elected but never qualified and resigned April 5, 1813), 1823–25; Gov. Dec. 18, 1830–Dec. 7, 1832 (National Republican).

McBride, George Wycliffe (brother of John Rogers McBride) (R Ore.) March 13, 1854–June 18, 1911; Senate 1895–1901.

McBride, John Rogers (brother of George Wycliffe McBride) (R Ore.) Aug. 22, 1832–July 20, 1904; House 1863–65.

McBryde, Archibald (F N.C.) Sept. 28, 1766–Feb. 15, 1816; House 1809–13.

McCain, John Sidney III (R Ariz.) Aug. 29, 1936– ; House 1983–87; Senate 1987– ; chair Senate Indian Affairs 1995–97, 2005– ; chair Senate Commerce, Science, and Transportation 1997–Jan. 3, 2001, Jan. 20, 2001–June 6, 2001, 2003–05.

McCall, John Ethridge (R Tenn.) Aug. 14, 1859–Aug. 8, 1920; House 1895–97.

McCall, Samuel Walker (R Mass.) Feb. 28, 1851–Nov. 4, 1923; House 1893–1913; Gov. Jan. 6, 1916–Jan. 2, 1919.

McCandless, Alfred A. (R Calif.) July 23, 1927– ; House 1983–95.

McCandless, Lincoln Loy (D Hawaii) Sept. 18, 1859–Oct. 5, 1940; House (Terr. Del.) 1933–35.

McCarran, Patrick Anthony "Pat" (D Nev.) Aug. 8, 1876–Sept. 28, 1954; Senate 1933–Sept. 28, 1954; chair Senate Judiciary 1949–53.

McCarthy, Carolyn (D N.Y.) Jan. 5, 1944– ; House 1997– .

McCarthy, Dennis (R N.Y.) March 19, 1814–Feb. 14, 1886; House 1867–71.

McCarthy, Eugene Joseph (D Minn.) March 29, 1916– ; House 1949–59; Senate 1959–71.

McCarthy, John Henry (D N.Y.) Nov. 16, 1850–Feb. 5, 1908; House 1889–Jan. 14, 1891.

McCarthy, John Jay (R Neb.) July 19, 1857–March 30, 1943; House 1903–07.

McCarthy, Joseph Raymond (R Wis.) Nov. 14, 1908–May 2, 1957; Senate 1947–May 2, 1957; chair Senate Government Operations 1953–55.

McCarthy, Karen (D Mo.) March 18, 1947– ; House 1995–2005.

McCarthy, Kathryn O'Loughlin. (See O'Loughlin, Kathryn Ellen.)

McCarthy, Richard Dean (D N.Y.) Sept. 24, 1927–May 5, 1995; House 1965–71.

McCarty, Andrew Zimmerman (W N.Y.) July 14, 1808–April 23, 1879; House 1855–57.

McCarty, Johnathan (AJ Ind.) Aug. 3, 1795–March 30, 1852; House 1831–37 (1831–35 Jacksonian).

McCarty, Richard (– N.Y.) Feb. 19, 1780–May 18, 1844; House 1821–23.

McCarty, William Mason (W Va.) about 1789–Dec. 20, 1863; House Jan. 25, 1840–41; Gov. (Fla. Terr.) 1827.

McCaul, Michael T. (R Texas) Jan. 14, 1962– ; House 2005– .

McCauslen, William Cochran (D Ohio) 1796–March 13, 1863; House 1843–45.

McClammy, Charles Washington (D N.C.) May 29, 1839–Feb. 26, 1896; House 1887–91.

McClean, Moses (D Pa.) June 17, 1804–Sept. 30, 1870; House 1845–47.

McCleary, James Thompson (R Minn.) Feb. 5, 1853–Dec. 17, 1924; House 1893–1907.

McCleery, James (R La.) Dec. 2, 1837–Nov. 5, 1871; House March 4–Nov. 5, 1871.

McClellan, Abraham (D Tenn.) Oct. 4, 1789–May 3, 1866; House 1837–43.

McClellan, Charles A. O. (D Ind.) May 25, 1835–Jan. 31, 1898; House 1889–93.

McClellan, George (D N.Y.) Oct. 10, 1856–Feb. 20, 1927; House 1913–15.

McClellan, George Brinton (D N.Y.) Nov. 23, 1865–Nov. 30, 1940; House 1895–Dec. 21, 1903.

McClellan, John Little (D Ark.) Feb. 25, 1896–Nov. 28, 1977; House 1935–39; Senate 1943–Nov. 28, 1977; chair Senate Expenditures in the Exec. Depts. 1949–52; chair Senate Government Operations 1952–53, 1955–72; chair Senate Appropriations 1972–77.

McClellan, Robert (D N.Y.) Oct. 2, 1806–June 28, 1860; House 1837–39, 1841–43.

McClelland, Robert (D Mich.) Aug. 1, 1807–Aug. 30, 1880; House 1843–49; Gov. Jan. 1, 1851–March 7, 1853; secretary of the interior March 8, 1853–March 9, 1857.

McClelland, William (D Pa.) March 2, 1842–Feb. 7, 1892; House 1871–73.

McClenachan, Blair (R Pa.) ?–May 8, 1812; House 1797–99.

McClernand, John Alexander (D Ill.) May 30, 1812–Sept. 20, 1900; House 1843–51, Nov. 8, 1859–Oct. 28, 1861.

McClintic, James Vernon (D Okla.) Sept. 8, 1878–April 22, 1948; House 1915–35.

McClintock, Charles Blaine (R Ohio) May 25, 1886–Feb. 1, 1965; House 1929–33.

McClory, Robert (R Ill.) Jan. 31, 1908–July 24, 1988; House 1963–83.

McCloskey, Augustus (D Texas) Sept. 23, 1878–July 21, 1950; House 1929–Feb. 10, 1930.

McCloskey, Francis Xavier (D Ind.) June 12, 1939–Nov. 2, 2003; House 1983–85, May 1, 1985–95.

McCloskey, Paul Norton "Pete" Jr. (R Calif.) Sept. 29, 1927– ; House Dec. 12, 1967–83.

McClure, Addison S. (R Ohio) Oct. 10, 1839–April 17, 1903; House 1881–83, 1895–97.

McClure, Charles (D Pa.) 1804–Jan. 10, 1846; House 1837–39, Dec. 7, 1840–41.

McClure, James Albertus (R Idaho) Dec. 27, 1924– ; House 1967–73; Senate 1973–91; chair Senate Energy and Natural Resources 1981–87.

McClurg, Joseph Washington (R Mo.) Feb. 22, 1818–Dec. 2, 1900; House 1863–68 (1863–65 Unconditional Unionist); Gov. Jan. 12, 1869–Jan. 9, 1871.

McCoid, Moses Ayres (R Iowa) Nov. 5, 1840–May 19, 1904; House 1879–85.

McCollister, John Yetter (R Neb.) June 10, 1921– ; House 1971–77.

McCollum, Betty (D Minn.) July 12, 1954– ; House 2001– .

McCollum, Ira William "Bill" Jr. (R Fla.) July 12, 1944– ; House 1981–2001.

McComas, Louis Emory (grandfather of Katherine Edgar Byron, great-grandfather of Goodloe Edgar Byron) (R Md.) Oct. 28, 1846–Nov. 10, 1907; House 1883–91; Senate 1899–1905.

McComas, William (W Va.) 1795–June 3, 1865; House 1833–37 (1833–35 Jacksonian).

McConnell, Addison Mitchell "Mitch" Jr. (husband of secretary of labor Elaine Chao) (R Ky.) Feb. 20, 1942– ; Senate 1985– ; chair Senate Select Ethics 1995–97; chair Senate Rules and Administration 1999–Jan. 3, 2001, Jan. 20, 2001–June 6, 2001.

McConnell, Felix Grundy (D Ala.) April 1, 1809–Sept. 10, 1846; House 1843–Sept. 10, 1846.

McConnell, Samuel Kerns Jr. (R Pa.) April 6, 1901–April 11, 1985; House Jan. 18, 1944–Sept. 1, 1957; chair House Education and Labor 1953–55.

McConnell, William John (R Idaho) Sept. 18, 1839–March 30, 1925; Senate Dec. 18, 1890–91; Gov. Jan. 2, 1893–Jan. 4, 1897.

McCook, Anson George (R N.Y.) Oct. 10, 1835–Dec. 30, 1917; House 1877–83.

McCord, Andrew (R N.Y.) about 1754–1808; House 1803–05.

McCord, James Nance (D Tenn.) March 17, 1879–Sept. 2, 1968; House 1943–45; Gov. Jan. 16, 1945–Jan. 17, 1949.

McCord, Myron Hawley (R Wis.) Nov. 26, 1840–April 27, 1908; House 1889–91; Gov. (Ariz. Terr.) 1897–98.

McCorkle, Joseph Walker (D Calif.) June 24, 1819–March 18, 1884; House 1851–53.

McCorkle, Paul Grier (D S.C.) Dec. 19, 1863–June 2, 1934; House Feb. 24–March 3, 1917.

McCormack, John William (D Mass.) Dec. 21, 1891–Nov. 22, 1980; House Nov. 6, 1928–71; House majority leader Sept. 26, 1940–47, 1949–53, 1955–Jan. 10, 1962; Speaker Jan. 9, 1963–65, Jan. 4, 1965–67, Jan. 10, 1967–71.

McCormack, Mike (D Wash.) Dec. 14, 1921– ; House 1971–81.

McCormick, Henry Clay (R Pa.) June 30, 1844–May 26, 1902; House 1887–91.

McCormick, James Robinson (D Mo.) Aug. 1, 1824–May 19, 1897; House Dec. 17, 1867–73.

McCormick, John Watts (R Ohio) Dec. 20, 1831–June 25, 1917; House 1883–85.

McCormick, Joseph Medill (husband of Ruth Hanna McCormick) (R Ill.) May 16, 1877–Feb. 25, 1925; House 1917–19; Senate 1919–Feb. 25, 1925.

McCormick, Nelson B. (P Kan.) Nov. 20, 1847–April 10, 1914; House 1897–99.

McCormick, Richard Cunningham (R N.Y.) May 23, 1832–June 2, 1901; House (Unionist Terr. Del. Ariz.) 1869–75, (Rep.) 1895–97; Gov. (Unionist Ariz. Terr.) 1866.

McCormick, Ruth Hanna (daughter of Marcus Alonzo Hanna, wife of Joseph Medill McCormick and of Albert Gallatin Simms) (R Ill.) March 27, 1880–Dec. 31, 1944; House 1929–31.

McCormick, Washington Jay (R Mont.) Jan. 4, 1884–March 7, 1949; House 1921–23.

McCotter, Thaddeus "Thad" (R Mich.) Aug. 22, 1965– ; House 2003– .

McCowen, Edward Oscar (R Ohio) June 29, 1877–Nov. 4, 1953; House 1943–49.

McCoy, Robert (– Pa.) ?–June 7, 1849; House Nov. 22, 1831–33.

McCoy, Walter Irving (D N.J.) Dec. 8, 1859–July 17, 1933; House 1911–Oct. 3, 1914.

McCoy, William (J Va.) ?–1864; House 1811–33 (1811–29 Republican).

McCracken, Robert McDowell (R Idaho) March 15, 1874–May 16, 1934; House 1915–17.

McCrary, George Washington (R Iowa) Aug. 29, 1835–June 23, 1890; House 1869–77; secretary of war March 12, 1877–Dec. 10, 1879.

McCrate, John Dennis (D Maine) Oct. 1, 1802–Sept. 11, 1879; House 1845–47.

McCreary, George Deardorff (R Pa.) Sept. 28, 1846–July 26, 1915; House 1903–13.

McCreary, James Bennett (D Ky.) July 8, 1838–Oct. 8, 1918; House 1885–97; Senate 1903–09; Gov. Aug. 31, 1875–Aug. 31, 1879, Dec. 12, 1911–Dec. 7, 1915.

McCreary, John (– S.C.) 1761–Nov. 4, 1833; House 1819–21.

McCredie, William Wallace (R Wash.) April 27, 1862–May 10, 1935; House Nov. 2, 1909–11.

McCreery, Thomas Clay (D Ky.) Dec. 12, 1816–July 10, 1890; Senate Feb. 19, 1868–71, 1873–79.

McCreery, William (R Md.) 1750–March 8, 1814; House 1803–09.

McCreery, William (J Pa.) May 17, 1786–Sept. 27, 1841; House 1829–31.

McCrery, James O. III (R La.) Sept. 18, 1949– ; House April 26, 1988– .

McCulloch, George (D Pa.) Feb. 22, 1792–April 6, 1861; House Nov. 20, 1839–41.

McCulloch, John (W Pa.) Nov. 15, 1806–May 15, 1879; House 1853–55.

McCulloch, Philip Doddridge Jr. (D Ark.) June 23, 1851–Nov. 26, 1928; House 1893–1903.

McCulloch, Roscoe Conkling (R Ohio) Nov. 27, 1880–March 17, 1958; House 1915–21; Senate Nov. 5, 1929–Nov. 30, 1930.

McCulloch, William Moore (R Ohio) Nov. 24, 1901–Feb. 22, 1980; House Nov. 4, 1947–73.

McCullogh, Welty (R Pa.) Oct. 10, 1847–Aug. 31, 1889; House 1887–89.

McCullough, Hiram (D Md.) Sept. 26, 1813–March 4, 1885; House 1865–69.

McCullough, Thomas Grubb (– Pa.) April 20, 1785–Sept. 10, 1848; House Oct. 17, 1820–21.

McCumber, Porter James (R N.D.) Feb. 3, 1858–May 18, 1933; Senate 1899–1923.

McCurdy, David Keith (D Okla.) March 30, 1950– ; House 1981–95; chair House Select Intelligence 1991–93.

McDade, Joseph Michael (R Pa.) Sept. 29, 1931– ; House 1963–99.

McDaniel, William (D Mo.) ?–Dec. 14, 1866; House Dec. 7, 1846–47.

McDannold, John James (D Ill.) Aug. 29, 1851–Feb. 3, 1904; House 1893–95.

McDearmon, James Calvin (D Tenn.) June 13, 1844–July 19, 1902; House 1893–97.

McDermott, Allan Langdon (D N.J.) March 30, 1854–Oct. 26, 1908; House Dec. 3, 1900–07.

McDermott, James (D Wash.) Dec. 28, 1936– ; House 1989– ; chair House Standards of Official Conduct 1993–95.

McDermott, James Thomas (D Ill.) Feb. 13, 1872–Feb. 7, 1938; House 1907–July 21, 1914, 1915–17.

McDill, Alexander Stuart (R Wis.) March 18, 1822–Nov. 12, 1875; House 1873–75.

McDill, James Wilson (R Iowa) March 4, 1834–Feb. 28, 1894; House 1873–77; Senate March 8, 1881–83.

McDonald, Alexander (R Ark.) April 10, 1832–Dec. 13, 1903; Senate June 22, 1868–71.

McDonald, Edward Francis (D N.J.) Sept. 21, 1844–Nov. 5, 1892; House 1891–Nov. 5, 1892.

McDonald, Jack H. (R Mich.) June 28, 1932– ; House 1967–73.

McDonald, John (R Md.) May 24, 1837–Jan. 30, 1917; House 1897–99.

McDonald, Joseph Ewing (D Ind.) Aug. 29, 1819–June 21, 1891; House 1849–51; Senate 1875–81.

McDonald, Lawrence Patton (D Ga.) April 1, 1935–Sept. 1, 1983; House 1975–Sept. 1, 1983.

McDonough, Gordon Leo (R Calif.) Jan. 2, 1895–June 25, 1968; House 1945–63.

McDougall, James Alexander (D Calif.) Nov. 19, 1817–Sept. 3, 1867; House 1853–55; Senate 1861–67.

McDowell, Alexander (R Pa.) March 4, 1845–Sept. 30, 1913; House 1893–95.

McDowell, Harris Brown Jr. (D Del.) Feb. 10, 1906– ; House 1955–57, 1959–67.

McDowell, James (D Va.) Oct. 13, 1795–Aug. 24, 1851; House March 6, 1846–51; Gov. Jan. 1, 1843–Jan. 1, 1846.

McDowell, James Foster (D Ind.) Dec. 3, 1825–April 18, 1887; House 1863–65.

McDowell, John Anderson (D Ohio) Sept. 25, 1853–Oct. 2, 1927; House 1897–1901.

McDowell, John Ralph (R Pa.) Nov. 6, 1902–Dec. 11, 1957; House 1939–41, 1947–49.

McDowell, Joseph (father of Joseph Jefferson McDowell, cousin of Joseph McDowell, below) (R N.C.) Feb. 15, 1756–Feb. 5, 1801; House 1797–99; Cont. Cong. (elected but did not attend) 1787.

McDowell, Joseph (cousin of Joseph McDowell, above) (– N.C.) Feb. 25, 1758–March 7, 1799; House 1793–95.

McDowell, Joseph Jefferson (son of Joseph McDowell born 1756) (D Ohio) Nov. 13, 1800–Jan. 17, 1877; House 1843–47.

McDuffie, George (father-in-law of Wade Hampton) (D S.C.) Aug. 10, 1790–March 11, 1851; House 1821–34 (no party); Senate Dec. 23, 1842–Aug. 17, 1846; Gov. Dec. 11, 1834–Dec. 10, 1836 (State Rights Democrat).

McDuffie, John (D Ala.) Sept. 25, 1883–Nov. 1, 1950; House 1919–March 2, 1935.

McDuffie, John Van (R Ala.) May 16, 1841–Nov. 18, 1896; House June 4, 1890–91.

McEnery, Samuel Douglas (D La.) May 28, 1837–June 28, 1910; Senate 1897–June 28, 1910; Gov. Oct. 16, 1881–May 20, 1888.

McEttrick, Michael Joseph (ID Mass.) June 22, 1848–Dec. 31, 1921; House 1893–95.

McEwan, Thomas Jr. (R N.J.) Feb. 26, 1854–Sept. 11, 1926; House 1895–99.

McEwen, Robert Cameron (R N.Y.) Jan. 5, 1920–June 15, 1997; House 1965–81.

McEwen, Robert D. (R Ohio) Jan. 12, 1950– ; House 1981–93.

McFadden, Louis Thomas (R Pa.) July 25, 1876–Oct. 1, 1936; House 1915–35.

McFadden, Obadiah Benton (D Wash.) Nov. 18, 1815–June 25, 1875; House (Terr. Del.) 1873–75.

McFall, John Joseph (D Calif.) Feb. 20, 1918– ; House 1957–Dec. 31, 1978.

McFarlan, Duncan (R N.C.) ?–Sept. 7, 1816; House 1805–07.

McFarland, Ernest William (D Ariz.) Oct. 9, 1894–June 8, 1984; Senate 1941–53; Senate majority leader 1951–53; Gov. Jan. 3, 1955–Jan. 5, 1959.

McFarland, William (D Tenn.) Sept. 15, 1821–April 12, 1900; House 1875–77.

McFarlane, William Doddridge (D Texas) July 17, 1894–Feb. 18, 1980; House 1933–39.

McGann, Lawrence Edward (D Ill.) Feb. 2, 1852–July 22, 1928; House 1891–Dec. 27, 1895.

McGarvey, Robert Neill (R Pa.) Aug. 14, 1888–June 28, 1952; House 1947–49.

McGaughey, Edward Wilson (W Ind.) Jan. 16, 1817–Aug. 6, 1852; House 1845–47, 1849–51.

McGavin, Charles (R Ill.) Jan. 10, 1874–Dec. 17, 1940; House 1905–09.

McGee, Gale William (D Wyo.) March 17, 1915–April 9, 1992; Senate 1959–77; chair Senate Post Office and Civil Service 1969–77.

McGehee, Daniel Rayford (D Miss.) Sept. 10, 1883–Feb. 9, 1962; House 1935–47.

McGill, George (D Kan.) Feb. 12, 1879–May 14, 1963; Senate Dec. 1, 1930–39.

McGillicuddy, Daniel John (D Maine) Aug. 27, 1859–July 30, 1936; House 1911–17.

McGinley, Donald Francis (D Neb.) June 30, 1920– ; House 1959–61.

McGlennon, Cornelius Augustine (D N.J.) Dec. 10, 1878–June 13, 1931; House 1919–21.

McGlinchey, Herbert Joseph (D Pa.) Nov. 7, 1904–June 25, 1992; House 1945–47.

McGovern, George Stanley (D S.D.) July 19, 1922– ; House 1957–61; Senate 1963–81.

McGovern, James P. (D Mass.) Nov. 20, 1959– ; House 1997– .

McGowan, Jonas Hartzell (R Mich.) April 2, 1837–July 5, 1909; House 1877–81.

McGranery, James Patrick (D Pa.) July 8, 1895–Dec. 23, 1962; House 1937–Nov. 17, 1943; attorney general May 27, 1952–Jan. 20, 1953.

McGrath, Christopher Columbus (D N.Y.) May 15, 1902–July 7, 1986; House 1949–53.

McGrath, James Howard (D R.I.) Nov. 28, 1903–Sept. 2, 1966; Senate 1947–Aug. 23, 1949; chair Senate District of Columbia 1949–51; Gov. Jan. 7, 1941–Oct. 6, 1945; chair Dem. Nat. Comm. 1947–49; attorney general Aug. 24, 1949–April 7, 1952.

McGrath, John Joseph (D Calif.) July 23, 1872–Aug. 25, 1951; House 1933–39.

McGrath, Raymond Joseph (R N.Y.) March 27, 1942– ; House 1981–93.

McGrath, Thomas Charles Jr. (D N.J.) April 22, 1927–Jan. 15, 1994; House 1965–67.

McGregor, J. Harry (R Ohio) Sept. 30, 1896–Oct. 7, 1958; House Feb. 27, 1940–Oct. 7, 1958.

McGrew, James Clark (R W.Va.) Sept. 14, 1813–Sept. 18, 1910; House 1869–73.

McGroarty, John Steven (D Calif.) Aug. 20, 1862–Aug. 7, 1944; House 1935–39.

McGugin, Harold Clement (R Kan.) Nov. 22, 1893–March 7, 1946; House 1931–35.

McGuire, Bird Segle (cousin of William Neville) (R Okla.) Oct. 13, 1865–Nov. 9, 1930; House (Terr. Del.) 1903–07, (Rep.) Nov. 16, 1907–15.

McGuire, John Andrew (D Conn.) Feb. 28, 1906–May 28, 1976; House 1949–53.

McHale, Paul (D Pa.) July 26, 1950– ; House 1993–99.

McHatton, Robert Lytle (– Ky.) Nov. 17, 1788–May 20, 1835; House Dec. 7, 1826–29.

McHenry, Henry Davis (son of John Hardin McHenry) (D Ky.) Feb. 27, 1826–Dec. 17, 1890; House 1871–73.

McHenry, John Geiser (D Pa.) April 26, 1868–Dec. 27, 1912; House 1907–Dec. 27, 1912.

McHenry, John Hardin (father of Henry Davis McHenry) (W Ky.) Oct. 13, 1797–Nov. 1, 1871; House 1845–47.

McHenry, Patrick T. (R N.C.) Oct. 22, 1975– ; House 2005– .

McHugh, John Michael (R N.Y.) Sept. 29, 1948– ; House 1993– .

McHugh, Matthew Francis (D N.Y.) Dec. 6, 1938– ; House 1975–93.

McIlvaine, Abraham Robinson (W Pa.) Aug. 14, 1804–Aug. 22, 1863; House 1843–49.

McIlvaine, Joseph (– N.J.) Oct. 2, 1769–Aug. 19, 1826; Senate Nov. 12, 1823–Aug. 19, 1826.

McIndoe, Walter Duncan (R Wis.) March 30, 1819–Aug. 22, 1872; House Jan. 26, 1863–67.

McInnis, Scott (R Colo.) May 9, 1953– ; House 1993–2005.

McIntire, Clifford Guy (R Maine) May 4, 1908–Oct. 1, 1974; House Oct. 22, 1951–65.

McIntire, Rufus (J Maine) Dec. 19, 1784–April 28, 1866; House Sept. 10, 1827–35 (Sept. 10, 1827–29 no party).

McIntire, William Watson (R Md.) June 30, 1850–March 30, 1912; House 1897–99.

McIntosh, David M. (R Ind.) June 8, 1958– ; House 1995–2001.

McIntosh, Robert John (R Mich.) Sept. 16, 1922– ; House 1957–59.

McIntyre, John Joseph (D Wyo.) Dec. 17, 1904–Nov. 30, 1974; House 1941–43.

McIntyre, Mike (D N.C.) Aug. 6, 1956– ; House 1997– .

McIntyre, Thomas James (D N.H.) Feb. 20, 1915–Aug. 8, 1992; Senate Nov. 7, 1962–79.

McJunkin, Ebenezer (R Pa.) March 28, 1819–Nov. 10, 1907; House 1871–Jan. 1, 1875.

McKaig, William McMahon (D Md.) July 29, 1845–June 6, 1907; House 1891–95.

McKay, James Iver (D N.C.) 1793–Sept. 4, 1853; House 1831–49 (1831–37 Jacksonian).

McKay, Koln Gunn (D Utah) Feb. 23, 1925–Oct. 6, 2000; House 1971–81.

McKean, James Bedell (nephew of Samuel McKean) (R N.Y.) Aug. 5, 1821–Jan. 5, 1879; House 1859–63.

McKean, Samuel (uncle of James Bedell McKean) (J Pa.) April 7, 1787–Dec. 14, 1841; House 1823–29 (no party); Senate 1833–39.

McKee, George Colin (R Miss.) Oct. 2, 1837–Nov. 17, 1890; House 1869–75.

McKee, John (– Ala.) 1771–Aug. 12, 1832; House 1823–29.

McKee, Samuel (R Ky.) Oct. 13, 1774–Oct. 16, 1826; House 1809–17.

McKee, Samuel (R Ky.) Nov. 5, 1833–Dec. 11, 1898; House 1865–67 (Unconditional Unionist), June 22, 1868–69.

McKeighan, William Arthur (P Neb.) Jan. 19, 1842–Dec. 15, 1895; House 1891–95.

McKellar, Kenneth Douglas (D Tenn.) Jan. 29, 1869–Oct. 25, 1957; House Nov. 9, 1911–17; Senate 1917–53; elected pres. pro tempore Jan. 6, 1945, Jan. 3, 1949; chair Senate Appropriations 1949–53.

McKenna, Joseph (R Calif.) Aug. 10, 1843–Nov. 21, 1926; House 1885–March 28, 1892; attorney general March 5, 1897–Jan. 25, 1898; assoc. justice Jan. 26, 1898–Jan. 5, 1925.

McKennan, Thomas McKean Thompson (W Pa.) March 31, 1794–July 9, 1852; House 1831–39 (Anti-Mason), May 30, 1842–43; secretary of the interior Aug. 15–Aug. 26, 1850.

McKenney, William Robertson (D Va.) Dec. 2, 1851–Jan. 3, 1916; House 1895–May 2, 1896.

McKenty, Jacob Kerlin (D Pa.) Jan. 19, 1827–Jan. 3, 1866; House Dec. 3, 1860–61.

McKenzie, Charles Edgar (D La.) Oct. 3, 1896–June 7, 1956; House 1943–47.

McKenzie, James Andrew (uncle of John McKenzie Moss) (D Ky.) Aug. 1, 1840–June 25, 1904; House 1877–83.

McKenzie, John Charles (R Ill.) Feb. 18, 1860–Sept. 17, 1941; House 1911–25.

McKenzie, Lewis (C Va.) Oct. 7, 1810–June 28, 1895; House Feb. 16–March 3, 1863 (Unionist), Jan. 31, 1870–71.

McKeon, Howard Philip "Buck" (R Calif.) Sept. 9, 1939– ; House 1993– .

McKeon, John (D N.Y.) March 29, 1808–Nov. 22, 1883; House 1835–37 (Jacksonian), 1841–43.

McKeough, Raymond Stephen (D Ill.) April 29, 1888–Dec. 16, 1979; House 1935–43.

McKeown, Thomas Deitz (D Okla.) June 4, 1878–Oct. 22, 1951; House 1917–21, 1923–35.

McKernan, John Rettie Jr. (R Maine) May 20, 1948– ; House 1983–87; Gov. Jan. 7, 1987–Jan. 5, 1995.

McKevitt, James Douglas "Mike" (R Colo.) Oct. 26, 1928–Sept. 28, 2000; House 1971–73.

McKibbin, Joseph Chambers (D Calif.) May 14, 1824–July 1, 1896; House 1857–59.

McKim, Alexander (uncle of Isaac McKim) (R Md.) Jan. 10, 1748–Jan. 18, 1832; House 1809–15.

McKim, Isaac (nephew of Alexander McKim) (D Md.) July 21, 1775–April 1, 1838; House Jan. 4, 1823–25 (no party), 1833–April 1, 1838 (1833–37 Jacksonian).

McKiniry, Richard Francis (D N.Y.) March 23, 1878–May 30, 1950; House 1919–21.

McKinlay, Duncan E. (R Calif.) Oct. 6, 1862–Dec. 30, 1914; House 1905–11.

McKinley, John (J Ala.) May 1, 1780–July 19, 1852; Senate Nov. 27, 1826–31 (no party), March 4–April 22, 1837; House 1833–35; assoc. justice Jan. 9, 1838–July 19, 1852.

McKinley, William (R Va.) ?–?; House Dec. 21, 1810–11.

McKinley, William Brown (R Ill.) Sept. 5, 1856–Dec. 7, 1926; House 1905–13, 1915–21; Senate 1921–Dec. 7, 1926.

McKinley, William Jr. (R Ohio) Jan. 29, 1843–Sept. 14, 1901; House 1877–May 27, 1884, 1885–91; Gov. Jan. 11, 1892–Jan. 13, 1896; president 1897–Sept. 14, 1901.

McKinney, Cynthia A. (D Ga.) March 17, 1955– ; House 1993–2003, 2005– .

McKinney, James (R Ill.) April 14, 1852–Sept. 29, 1934; House Nov. 7, 1905–13.

McKinney, John Franklin (D Ohio) April 12, 1827–June 13, 1903; House 1863–65, 1871–73.

McKinney, Luther Franklin (D N.H.) April 25, 1841–July 30, 1922; House 1887–89, 1891–93.

McKinney, Stewart Brett (R Conn.) Jan. 30, 1931–May 7, 1987; House 1971–May 7, 1987.

McKinnon, Clinton Dotson (D Calif.) Feb. 5, 1906–Dec. 29, 2001; House 1949–53.

McKissock, Thomas (W N.Y.) April 17, 1790–June 26, 1866; House 1849–51.

McKneally, Martin Boswell (R N.Y.) Dec. 31, 1914–June 14, 1992; House 1969–71.

McKnight, Robert (R Pa.) Jan. 20, 1820–Oct. 25, 1885; House 1859–63.

McLachlan, James (R Calif.) Aug. 1, 1852–Nov. 21, 1940; House 1895–97, 1901–11.

McLain, Frank Alexander (D Miss.) Jan. 29, 1852–Oct. 10, 1920; House Dec. 12, 1898–1909.

McLanahan, James Xavier (grandson of Andrew Gregg) (D Pa.) 1809–Dec. 16, 1861; House 1849–53.

McLane, Louis (father of Robert Milligan McLane) (– Del.) May 28, 1786–Oct. 7, 1857; House 1817–27; Senate 1827–April 16, 1829; secretary of the Treasury Aug. 8, 1831–May 28, 1833; secretary of state May 29, 1833–June 30, 1834.

McLane, Patrick (D Pa.) March 14, 1875–Nov. 13, 1946; House 1919–Feb. 25, 1921.

McLane, Robert Milligan (son of Louis McLane) (D Md.) June 23, 1815–April 16, 1898; House 1847–51, 1879–83; Gov. Jan. 9, 1884–March 27, 1885; chair Dem. Nat. Comm. 1852–54.

McLaughlin, Charles Francis (D Neb.) June 19, 1887–Feb. 5, 1976; House 1935–43.

McLaughlin, James Campbell (R Mich.) Jan. 26, 1858–Nov. 29, 1932; House 1907–Nov. 29, 1932.

McLaughlin, Joseph (R Pa.) June 9, 1867–Nov. 21, 1926; House 1917–19, 1921–23.

McLaughlin, Melvin Orlando (R Neb.) Aug. 8, 1876–June 18, 1928; House 1919–27.

McLaurin, Anselm Joseph (D Miss.) March 26, 1848–Dec. 22, 1909; Senate Feb. 7, 1894–95, 1901–Dec. 22, 1909; Gov. Jan. 20, 1896–Jan. 16, 1900.

McLaurin, John Lowndes (D S.C.) May 9, 1860–July 29, 1934; House Dec. 5, 1892–May 31, 1897; Senate June 1, 1897–1903.

McLean, Alney (R Ky.) June 10, 1779–Dec. 30, 1841; House 1815–17, 1819–21.

McLean, Donald Holman (R N.J.) March 18, 1884–Aug. 19, 1975; House 1933–45.

McLean, Finis Ewing (brother of John McLean of Ill., uncle of James David Walker) (W Ky.) Feb. 19, 1806–April 12, 1881; House 1849–51.

McLean, George Payne (R Conn.) Oct. 7, 1857–June 6, 1932; Senate 1911–29; Gov. Jan. 9, 1901–Jan. 7, 1903.

McLean, James Henry (R Mo.) Aug. 13, 1829–Aug. 12, 1886; House Dec. 15, 1882–83.

McLean, John (brother of William McLean) (R Ohio) March 11, 1785–April 4, 1861; House 1813–16; postmaster general July 1, 1823–March 9, 1829; assoc. justice Jan. 11, 1830–April 4, 1861.

McLean, John (brother of Finis Ewing McLean, uncle of James David Walker) (– Ill.) Feb. 4, 1791–Oct. 14, 1830; House Dec. 3, 1818–19; Senate Nov. 23, 1824–25, 1829–Oct. 14, 1830.

McLean, Samuel (D Mont.) Aug. 7, 1826–July 16, 1877; House (Terr. Del.) Jan. 6, 1865–67.

McLean, William (brother of John McLean of Ohio) (– Ohio) Aug. 10, 1794–Oct. 12, 1839; House 1823–29.

McLean, William Pinkney (D Texas) Aug. 9, 1836–March 13, 1925; House 1873–75.

McLemore, Atkins Jefferson "Jeff" (D Texas) March 13, 1857–March 4, 1929; House 1915–19.

McLene, Jeremiah (J Ohio) 1767–March 19, 1837; House 1833–37.

McLeod, Clarence John (R Mich.) July 3, 1895–May 15, 1959; House Nov. 2, 1920–21, 1923–37, 1939–41.

McLoskey, Robert Thaddeus (R Ill.) June 26, 1907–Nov. 2, 1990; House 1963–65.

McMahon, Gregory (R N.Y.) March 19, 1915–June 27, 1989; House 1947–49.

McMahon, James O'Brien (born James O'Brien) (D Conn.) Oct. 6, 1903–July 28, 1952; Senate 1945–July 28, 1952.

McMahon, John A. (nephew of Clement Laird Vallandigham) (D Ohio) Feb. 19, 1833–March 8, 1923; House 1875–81.

McManus, William (– N.Y.) 1780–Jan. 18, 1835; House 1825–27.

McMaster, William Henry (R S.D.) May 10, 1877–Sept. 14, 1968; Senate 1925–31; Gov. Jan. 4, 1921–Jan. 6, 1925.

McMillan, Alexander (– N.C.) ?–1817; House 1817.

McMillan, J. Alex (R N.C.) May 9, 1932– ; House 1985–95.

McMillan, Clara Gooding (widow of Thomas Sanders McMillan) (D S.C.) Aug. 17, 1894–Nov. 8, 1976; House Nov. 7, 1939–41.

McMillan, James (R Mich.) May 12, 1838–Aug. 10, 1902; Senate 1889–Aug. 10, 1902.

McMillan, John Lanneau (D S.C.) April 12, 1898–Sept. 3, 1979; House 1939–73; chair House District of Columbia 1949–53, 1955–73.

McMillan, Samuel (R N.Y.) Aug. 6, 1850–May 6, 1924; House 1907–09.

McMillan, Samuel James Renwick (R Minn.) Feb. 22, 1826–Oct. 3, 1897; Senate 1875–87.

McMillan, Thomas Sanders (husband of Clara Gooding McMillan) (D S.C.) Nov. 27, 1888–Sept. 29, 1939; House 1925–Sept. 29, 1939.

McMillan, William (– N.W. Terr.) March 2, 1764–May 1804; House (Terr. Del.) Nov. 24, 1800–01.

McMillen, Charles Thomas (D Md.) May 26, 1952– ; House 1987–93.

McMillen, Rolla Coral (R Ill.) Oct. 5, 1880–May 6, 1961; House June 13, 1944–51.

McMillin, Benton (D Tenn.) Sept. 11, 1845–Jan. 8, 1933; House 1879–Jan. 6, 1899; Gov. Jan. 16, 1899–Jan. 19, 1903.

McMorran, Henry Gordon (R Mich.) June 11, 1844–July 19, 1929; House 1903–13.

McMorris, Catherine (R Wash.) May 22, 1969– ; House 2005– .

McMullen, Chester Bartow (D Fla.) Dec. 6, 1902–Nov. 3, 1953; House 1951–53.

McMullen, Fayette (D Va.) May 18, 1805–Nov. 8, 1880; House 1849–57; Gov. (Wash. Terr.) 1857–61.

McMurray, Howard Johnstone (D Wis.) March 3, 1901–Aug. 14, 1961; House 1943–45.

McNagny, William Forgy (D Ind.) April 19, 1850–Aug. 24, 1923; House 1893–95.

McNair, John (D Pa.) June 8, 1800–Aug. 12, 1861; House 1851–55.

McNamara, Patrick Vincent (D Mich.) Oct. 4, 1894–April 30, 1966; Senate 1955–April 30, 1966; chair Senate Public Works 1963–66.

McNary, Charles Linza (R Ore.) June 12, 1874–Feb. 25, 1944; Senate May 29, 1917–Nov. 5, 1918, Dec. 18, 1918–Feb. 25, 1944; Senate minority leader 1933–44.

McNary, William Sarsfield (D Mass.) March 29, 1863–June 26, 1930; House 1903–07.

McNeely, Thompson Ware (D Ill.) Oct. 5, 1835–July 23, 1921; House 1869–73.

McNeill, Archibald (– N.C.) ?–1849; House 1821–23, 1825–27.

McNulta, John (R Ill.) Nov. 9, 1837–Feb. 22, 1900; House 1873–75.

McNulty, Frank Joseph (D N.J.) Aug. 10, 1872–May 26, 1926; House 1923–25.

McNulty, James Francis Jr. (D Ariz.) Oct. 18, 1925– ; House 1983–85.

McNulty, Michael R. (D N.Y.) Sept. 16, 1947– ; House 1989– .

McPherson, Edward (R Pa.) July 31, 1830–Dec. 14, 1895; House 1859–63.

McPherson, Isaac Vanbert (R Mo.) March 8, 1868–Oct. 31, 1931; House 1919–23.

McPherson, John Rhoderic (D N.J.) May 9, 1833–Oct. 8, 1897; Senate 1877–95.

McPherson, Smith (R Iowa) Feb. 14, 1848–Jan. 17, 1915; House 1899–June 6, 1900.

McQueen, John (D S.C.) Feb. 9, 1804–Aug. 30, 1867; House Feb. 12, 1849–Dec. 21, 1860.

McRae, John Jones (D Miss.) Jan. 10, 1815–May 31, 1868; Senate Dec. 1, 1851–March 17, 1852; House Dec. 7, 1858–Jan. 12, 1861; Gov. Jan. 10, 1854–Nov. 16, 1857.

McRae, Thomas Chipman (cousin of Thomas Banks Cabaniss) (D Ark.) Dec. 21, 1851–June 2, 1929; House Dec. 7, 1885–1903; Gov. Jan. 11, 1921–Jan. 13, 1925.

McReynolds, Samuel Davis (D Tenn.) April 16, 1872–July 11, 1939; House 1923–July 11, 1939.

McRoberts, Samuel (D Ill.) April 12, 1799–March 27, 1843; Senate 1841–March 27, 1843.

McRuer, Donald Campbell (R Calif.) March 10, 1826–Jan. 29, 1898; House 1865–67.

McShane, John Albert (D Neb.) Aug. 25, 1850–Nov. 10, 1923; House 1887–89.

McSherry, James (– Pa.) July 29, 1776–Feb. 3, 1849; House 1821–23.

McSpadden, Clem Rogers (D Okla.) Nov. 9, 1925– ; House 1973–75.

McSwain, John Jackson (D S.C.) May 1, 1875–Aug. 6, 1936; House 1921–Aug. 6, 1936.

McSween, Harold Barnett (D La.) July 19, 1926–Jan. 12, 2002; House 1959–63.

McSweeney, John (D Ohio) Dec. 19, 1890–Dec. 13, 1969; House 1923–29, 1937–39, 1949–51.

McVean, Charles (J N.Y.) 1802–Dec. 22, 1848; House 1833–35.

McVey, Walter Lewis Jr. (R Kan.) Feb. 19, 1922– ; House 1961–63.

McVey, William Estus (R Ill.) Dec. 13, 1885–Aug. 10, 1958; House 1951–Aug. 10, 1958.

McVicker, Roy Harrison (D Colo.) Feb. 20, 1924–Sept. 15, 1973; House 1965–67.

McWilliams, John Dacher (R Conn.) July 23, 1891–March 30, 1975; House 1943–45.

McWillie, William (D Miss.) Nov. 17, 1795–March 3, 1869; House 1849–51; Gov. Nov. 16, 1857–Nov. 21, 1859.

Meacham, James (W Vt.) Aug. 16, 1810–Aug. 23, 1856; House Dec. 3, 1849–Aug. 23, 1856.

Mead, Cowles (– Ga.) Oct. 18, 1776–May 17, 1844; House March 4–Dec. 24, 1805.

Mead, James Michael (D N.Y.) Dec. 27, 1885–March 15, 1964; House 1919–Dec. 2, 1938; Senate Dec. 3, 1938–47.

Meade, Edwin Ruthven (D N.Y.) July 6, 1836–Nov. 28, 1889; House 1875–77.

Meade, Hugh Allen (D Md.) April 4, 1907–July 8, 1949; House 1947–49.

Meade, Richard Kidder (D Va.) July 29, 1803–April 20, 1862; House Aug. 5, 1847–53.

Meade, Wendell Howes (R Ky.) Jan. 18, 1912–June 2, 1986; House 1947–49.

Meader, George (R Mich.) Sept. 13, 1907–Oct. 15, 1994; House 1951–65.

Means, Rice William (R Colo.) Nov. 16, 1877–Jan. 30, 1949; Senate Dec. 1, 1924–27.

Mebane, Alexander (– N.C.) Nov. 26, 1744–July 5, 1795; House 1793–95.

Mechem, Edwin Leard (R N.M.) July 2, 1912–Nov. 27, 2002; Senate Nov. 30, 1962–Nov. 3, 1964; Gov. Jan. 1, 1951–Jan. 1, 1955, Jan. 1, 1957–Jan. 1, 1959, Jan. 1, 1961–Nov. 30, 1962.

Medill, William (D Ohio) Feb. 1802–Sept. 2, 1865; House 1839–43; Gov. July 13, 1853–Jan. 14, 1856.

Meech, Ezra (D Vt.) July 26, 1773–Sept. 23, 1856; House 1810–21, 1825–27.

Meeds, Lloyd (D Wash.) Dec. 11, 1927– ; House 1965–79.

Meehan, Martin Timothy (D Mass.) Dec. 30, 1956– ; House 1993– .

Meek, Carrie P. (D Fla.) (mother of Kendrick Meek) April 29, 1926– ; House 1993–2003.

Meek, Kendrick B. (D Fla.) (son of Carrie P. Meek) Sept. 6, 1966– ; House 2003– .

Meeker, Jacob Edwin (R Mo.) Oct. 7, 1878–Oct. 16, 1918; House 1915–Oct. 16, 1918.

Meekison, David (D Ohio) Nov. 14, 1849–Feb. 12, 1915; House 1897–1901.

Meeks, Gregory W. (D N.Y.) Sept. 25, 1953– ; House Feb. 5, 1998– .

Meeks, James Andrew (D Ill.) March 7, 1864–Nov. 10, 1946; House 1933–39.

Meigs, Henry (– N.Y.) Oct. 28, 1782–May 20, 1861; House 1819–21.

Meigs, Return Jonathan Jr. (R Ohio) Nov. 17, 1764–March 29, 1825; Senate Dec. 12, 1808–May 1, 1810; Gov. Dec. 8, 1810–March 24, 1814 (Democratic Republican); postmaster general April 11, 1814–June 30, 1823.

Meiklejohn, George de Rue (R Neb.) Aug. 26, 1857–April 19, 1929; House 1893–97.

Melancon, Charles J. (R La.) Oct. 3, 1947– ; House 2005– .

Melcher, John (D Mont.) Sept. 6, 1924– ; House June 24, 1969–77; Senate 1977–89; chair Senate Indian Affairs 1979–80.

Mellen, Prentiss (– Mass.) Oct. 11, 1764–Dec. 31, 1840; Senate June 5, 1818–May 15, 1820.

Mellish, David Batcheller (R N.Y.) Jan. 2, 1831–May 23, 1874; House 1873–May 23, 1874.

Menefee, Richard Hickman (W Ky.) Dec. 4, 1809–Feb. 21, 1841; House 1837–39.

Menendez, Robert (D N.J.) Jan. 1, 1954– ; House 1993– .

Menges, Franklin (R Pa.) Oct. 26, 1858–May 12, 1956; House 1925–31.

Menzies, John William (U Ky.) April 12, 1819–Oct. 3, 1897; House 1861–63.

Mercer, Charles Fenton (cousin of Robert Selden Garnett) (W Va.) June 16, 1778–May 4, 1858; House 1817–Dec. 26, 1839 (1817–31 Federalist, 1831–35 Anti-Jacksonian).

Mercer, David Henry (R Neb.) July 9, 1857–Jan. 10, 1919; House 1893–1903.

Mercer, John Francis (– Md.) May 17, 1759–Aug. 30, 1821; House Feb. 5, 1792–April 13, 1794; Cont. Cong. 1783–84 (Va.); Gov. Nov. 10, 1801–Nov. 15, 1803 (Democratic Republican).

Mercur, Ulysses (R Pa.) Aug. 12, 1818–June 6, 1887; House 1865–Dec. 2, 1872.

Meredith, Elisha Edward (D Va.) Dec. 26, 1848–July 29, 1900; House Dec. 9, 1891–97.

Meriwether, David (father of James Meriwether, grandfather of James A. Meriwether) (R Ga.) April 10, 1755–Nov. 16, 1822; House Dec. 6, 1802–07.

Meriwether, David (D Ky.) Oct. 30, 1800–April 4, 1893; Senate July 6–Aug. 31, 1852; Gov. (N.M. Terr.) 1853–55.

Meriwether, James (son of David Meriwether born in 1755, uncle of James A. Meriwether) (– Ga.) 1789–1854; House 1825–27.

Meriwether, James A. (nephew of James Meriwether, grandson of David Meriwether born in 1755) (W Ga.) Sept. 20, 1806–April 18, 1852; House 1841–43.

Merriam, Clinton Levi (R N.Y.) March 25, 1824–Feb. 18, 1900; House 1871–75.

Merrick, William Duhurst (father of William Matthew Merrick) (W Md.) Oct. 25, 1793–Feb. 5, 1857; Senate Jan. 4, 1838–45.

Merrick, William Matthew (son of William Duhurst Merrick) (D Md.) Sept. 1, 1818–Feb. 4, 1889; House 1871–73.

Merrill, D. Bailey (R Ind.) Nov. 22, 1912–Oct. 14, 1993; House 1953–55.

Merrill, Orsamus Cook (R Vt.) June 18, 1775–April 12, 1865; House 1817–Jan. 12, 1820.

Merriman, Truman Adams (D N.Y.) Sept. 5, 1839–April 16, 1892; House 1885–89 (1885–87 Independent Democrat).

Merrimon, Augustus Summerfield (D N.C.) Sept. 15, 1830–Nov. 14, 1892; Senate 1873–79.

Merritt, Edwin Albert (R N.Y.) July 25, 1860–Dec. 4, 1914; House Nov. 5, 1912–Dec. 4, 1914.

Merritt, Matthew Joseph (D N.Y.) April 2, 1895–Sept. 29, 1946; House 1935–45.

Merritt, Samuel Augustus (D Idaho) Aug. 15, 1827–Sept. 8, 1910; House (Terr. Del.) 1871–73.

Merritt, Schuyler (R Conn.) Dec. 16, 1853–April 1, 1953; House Nov. 6, 1917–31, 1933–37.

Merrow, Chester Earl (R N.H.) Nov. 15, 1906–Feb. 10, 1974; House 1943–63.

Merwin, Orange (– Conn.) April 7, 1777–Sept. 4, 1853; House 1825–29.

Mesick, William Smith (R Mich.) Aug. 26, 1856–Dec. 1, 1942; House 1897–1901.

Meskill, Thomas Joseph (R Conn.) Jan. 30, 1928– ; House 1967–71; Gov. Jan. 6, 1971–Jan. 8, 1975.

Metcalf, Arunah (R N.Y.) Aug. 15, 1771–Aug. 15, 1848; House 1811–13.

Metcalf, Jack (R Wash.) Nov. 30, 1927– ; House 1995–2001.

Metcalf, Jesse Houghton (R R.I.) Nov. 16, 1860–Oct. 9, 1942; Senate Nov. 5, 1924–37.

Metcalf, Lee Warren (D Mont.) Jan. 28, 1911–Jan. 12, 1978; House 1953–61; Senate 1961–Jan. 12, 1978.

Metcalf, Victor Howard (R Calif.) Oct. 10, 1853–Feb. 20, 1936; House 1899–July 1, 1904; secretary of commerce and labor July 1, 1904–Dec. 16, 1906; secretary of the navy Dec. 17, 1906–Nov. 30, 1908.

Metcalfe, Henry Bleecker (D N.Y.) Jan. 20, 1805–Feb. 7, 1881; House 1875–77.

Metcalfe, Lyne Shackelford (R Mo.) April 21, 1822–Jan. 31, 1906; House 1877–79.

Metcalfe, Ralph Harold (D Ill.) May 29, 1910–Oct. 10, 1978; House 1971–Oct. 10, 1978.

Metcalfe, Thomas (W Ky.) March 20, 1780–Aug. 18, 1855; House 1819–June 1, 1828 (no party); Senate June 23, 1848–49; Gov. June 1, 1828–June 1, 1832 (National Republican).

Metz, Herman August (D N.Y.) Oct. 19, 1867–May 17, 1934; House 1913–15.

Metzenbaum, Howard Morton (D Ohio) June 4, 1917– ; Senate Jan. 4–Dec. 23, 1974, Dec. 29, 1976–95.

Meyer, Adolph (D La.) Oct. 19, 1842–March 8, 1908; House 1891–March 8, 1908.

Meyer, Herbert Alton (R Kan.) Aug. 30, 1886–Oct. 2, 1950; House 1947–Oct. 2, 1950.

Meyer, John Ambrose (D Md.) May 15, 1899–Oct. 2, 1969; House 1941–43.

Meyer, William Henry (D Vt.) Dec. 29, 1914–Dec. 16, 1983; House 1959–61.

Meyers, Benjamin Franklin (D Pa.) July 6, 1833–Aug. 11, 1918; House 1871–73.

Meyers, Jan (R Kan.) July 20, 1928– ; House 1985–97; chair House Small Business 1995–97.

Meyner, Helen Stevenson (D N.J.) March 5, 1929–Nov. 2, 1997; House 1975–79.

Mezvinsky, Edward Maurice (D Iowa) Jan. 17, 1937– ; House 1973–77.

Mfume, Kweisi (D Md.) Oct. 24, 1948– ; House 1987–Feb. 18, 1996.

Mica, Daniel Andrew (D Fla.) Feb. 4, 1944– ; House 1979–89.

Mica, John L. (R Fla.) Jan. 27, 1943– ; House 1993– .

Michaelson, Magne Alfred (R Ill.) Sept. 7, 1878–Oct. 26, 1949; House 1921–31.

Michalek, Anthony (R Ill.) Jan. 16, 1878–Dec. 21, 1916; House 1905–07.

Michaud, Michael H. (D Maine) Jan. 18, 1955– ; House 2003– .

Michel, Robert Henry (R Ill.) March 2, 1923– ; House 1957–95; House minority leader 1981–95.

Michener, Earl Cory (R Mich.) Nov. 30, 1876–July 4, 1957; House 1919–33, 1935–51; chair House Judiciary 1947–49.

Mickey, J. Ross (D Ill.) Jan. 5, 1856–March 20, 1928; House 1901–03.

Middlesworth, Ner (W Pa.) Dec. 12, 1783–June 2, 1865; House 1853–55.

Middleton, George (D N.J.) Oct. 14, 1800–Dec. 31, 1888; House 1863–65.

Middleton, Henry (R S.C.) Sept. 28, 1770–June 14, 1846; House 1815–19; Gov. Dec. 10, 1810–Dec. 10, 1812.

Miers, Robert Walter (D Ind.) Jan. 27, 1848–Feb. 20, 1930; House 1897–1905.

Mikulski, Barbara Ann (D Md.) July 20, 1936– ; House 1977–87; Senate 1987– .

Mikva, Abner Joseph (D Ill.) Jan. 21, 1926– ; House 1969–73, 1975–Sept. 26, 1979.

Miles, Frederick (R Conn.) Dec. 19, 1815–Nov. 20, 1896; House 1879–83, 1889–91.

Miles, John Esten (D N.M.) July 28, 1884–Oct. 7, 1971; House 1949–51; Gov. Jan. 1, 1939–Jan. 1, 1943.

Miles, Joshua Weldon (D Md.) Dec. 9, 1858–March 4, 1929; House 1895–97.

Miles, William Porcher (D S.C.) July 4, 1822–May 11, 1899; House 1857–Dec. 1860.

Milford, Dale (D Texas) Feb. 18, 1926–Dec. 26, 1997; House 1973–79.

Millard, Charles Dunsmore (R N.Y.) Dec. 1, 1873–Dec. 11, 1944; House 1931–Sept. 29, 1937.

Millard, Joseph Hopkins (R Neb.) April 20, 1836–Jan. 13, 1922; Senate March 28, 1901–07.

Millard, Stephen Columbus (R N.Y.) Jan. 14, 1841–June 21, 1914; House 1883–87.

Milledge, John (R Ga.) 1757–Feb. 9, 1818; House Nov. 22, 1792–93 (no party), 1795–99 (no party), 1801–May 1802; Senate June 19, 1806–Nov. 14, 1809; elected pres. pro tempore Jan. 30, 1809; Gov. Nov. 4, 1802–Sept. 23, 1806 (Democratic Republican).

Millen, John (D Ga.) 1804–Oct. 15, 1843; House March 4–Oct. 15, 1843.

Millender-McDonald, Juanita (D Calif.) Sept. 7, 1938– ; House April 16, 1996– .

Miller, Arthur Lewis (R Neb.) May 24, 1892–March 16, 1967; House 1943–59; chair House Interior and Insular Affairs 1953–55.

Miller, Bert Henry (D Idaho) Dec. 15, 1879–Oct. 8, 1949; Senate Jan. 3–Oct. 8, 1949.

Miller, Brad (D N.C.) May 19, 1953– ; House 2003– .

Miller, Candice S. (R Mich.) May 7, 1954– ; House 2003– .

Miller, Clarence Benjamin (R Minn.) March 13, 1872–Jan. 10, 1922; House 1909–19.

Miller, Clarence E. (R Ohio) Nov. 1, 1917– ; House 1967–93.

Miller, Clement Woodnutt (nephew of Thomas Woodnutt Miller) (D Calif.) Oct. 28, 1916–Oct. 7, 1962; House 1959–Oct. 7, 1962.

Miller, Daniel Fry (W Iowa) Oct. 4, 1814–Dec. 9, 1895; House Dec. 20, 1850–51.

Miller, Daniel H. (J Pa.) ?–1846; House 1823–31 (1823–27 no party).

Miller, Edward Edwin (R Ill.) July 22, 1880–Aug. 1, 1946; House 1923–25.

Miller, Edward Tylor (R Md.) Feb. 1, 1895–Jan. 20, 1968; House 1947–59.

Miller, Frederick Daniel "Dan" (R Fla.) May 30, 1942– ; House 1993–2003.

Miller, Gary G. (R Calif.) Oct. 16, 1948– ; House 1999– .

Miller, George (D Calif.) May 17, 1945– ; House 1975– ; chair House Select Children, Youth, and Families 1983–91; chair House Interior and Insular Affairs 1991–93; chair House Natural Resources 1993–95.

Miller, George Funston (R Pa.) Sept. 5, 1809–Oct. 21, 1885; House 1865–69.

Miller, George Paul (D Calif.) Jan. 15, 1891–Dec. 29, 1982; House 1945–73; chair House Science and Astronautics 1961–73.

Miller, Homer Virgil Milton (D Ga.) April 29, 1814–May 31, 1896; Senate Feb. 24–March 3, 1871.

Miller, Howard Shultz (D Kan.) Feb. 27, 1879–Jan. 2, 1970; House 1953–55.

Miller, Jack Richard (R Iowa) June 6, 1916–Aug. 29, 1994; Senate 1961–73.

Miller, Jacob Welsh (W N.J.) Aug. 29, 1800–Sept. 30, 1862; Senate 1841–53.

Miller, James Francis (D Texas) Aug. 1, 1830–July 3, 1902; House 1883–87.

Miller, James Monroe (R Kan.) May 6, 1852–Jan. 20, 1926; House 1899–1911.

Miller, Jefferson B. "Jeff" (R Fla.) June 27, 1959– ; House Oct. 16, 2001– .

Miller, Jesse (father of William Henry Miller) (J Pa.) 1800–Aug. 20, 1850; House 1833–Oct. 30, 1836.

Miller, John (– N.Y.) Nov. 10, 1774–March 31, 1862; House 1825–27.

Miller, John (D Mo.) Nov. 25, 1781–March 18, 1846; House 1837–43; Gov. Jan. 20, 1826–Nov. 14, 1832 (Jacksonian).

Miller, John Elvis (D Ark.) May 15, 1888–Jan. 30, 1981; House 1931–Nov. 14, 1937; Senate Nov. 15, 1937–March 31, 1941.

Miller, John Franklin (uncle of John Franklin Miller, below) (R Calif.) Nov. 21, 1831–March 8, 1886; Senate 1881–March 8, 1886.

Miller, John Franklin (nephew of John Franklin Miller, above) (R Wash.) June 9, 1862–May 28, 1936; House 1917–31.

Miller, John Gaines (W Mo.) Nov. 29, 1812–May 11, 1856; House 1851–May 11, 1856.

Miller, John Krepps (D Ohio) May 25, 1819–Aug. 11, 1863; House 1847–51.

Miller, John Ripin (R Wash.) May 23, 1938– ; House 1985–93.

Miller, Joseph (D Ohio) Sept. 9, 1819–May 27, 1862; House 1857–59.

Miller, Killian (W N.Y.) July 30, 1785–Jan. 9, 1859; House 1855–57.

Miller, Louis Ebenezer (R Mo.) April 30, 1899–Nov. 1, 1952; House 1943–45.

Miller, Lucas Miltiades (D Wis.) Sept. 15, 1824–Dec. 4, 1902; House 1891–93.

Miller, Morris Smith (father of Rutger Bleecker Miller) (F N.Y.) July 31, 1779–Nov. 16, 1824; House 1813–15.

Miller, Orrin Larrabee (R Kan.) Jan. 11, 1856–Sept. 11, 1926; House 1895–97.

Miller, Pleasant Moorman (R Tenn.) ?–1849; House 1809–11.

Miller, Rutger Bleecker (son of Morris Smith Miller) (J N.Y.) July 28, 1805–Nov. 12, 1877; House Nov. 9, 1836–37.

Miller, Samuel Franklin (R N.Y.) May 27, 1827–March 16, 1892; House 1863–65, 1875–77.

Miller, Samuel Henry (R Pa.) April 19, 1840–Sept. 4, 1918; House 1881–85, 1915–17.

Miller, Smith (D Ind.) May 30, 1804–March 21, 1872; House 1853–57.

Miller, Stephen Decatur (N S.C.) May 8, 1787–March 8, 1838; House Jan. 2, 1817–19 (no party); Senate 1831–March 2, 1833; Gov. Dec. 10, 1828–Dec. 9, 1830 (Democrat).

Miller, Thomas Byron (R Pa.) Aug. 11, 1896–March 20, 1976; House May 9, 1942–45.

Miller, Thomas Ezekiel (R S.C.) June 17, 1849–April 8, 1938; House Sept. 24, 1890–91.

Miller, Thomas Woodnutt (uncle of Clement Woodnutt Miller) (R Del.) June 26, 1886–May 5, 1973; House 1915–17.

Miller, Ward MacLaughlin (R Ohio) Nov. 29, 1902–March 11, 1984; House Nov. 8, 1960–61.

Miller, Warner (R N.Y.) Aug. 12, 1838–March 21, 1918; House 1879–July 26, 1881; Senate July 27, 1881–87.

Miller, Warren (R W.Va.) April 2, 1847–Dec. 29, 1920; House 1895–99.

Miller, William Edward (R N.Y.) March 22, 1914–June 24, 1983; House 1951–65; chair Rep. Nat. Comm. June 1961–July 1964.

Miller, William Henry (son of Jesse Miller) (D Pa.) Feb. 28, 1829–Sept. 12, 1870; House 1863–65.

Miller, William Jennings (R Conn.) March 12, 1899–Nov. 22, 1950; House 1939–41, 1943–45, 1947–49.

Miller, William Starr (AP N.Y.) Aug. 22, 1793–Nov. 9, 1854; House 1845–47.

Miller, Zell (D Ga.) Feb. 24, 1932– ; Senate July 27, 2000–05; Gov. Jan. 14, 1991–Jan. 11, 1999.

Milligan, Jacob Le Roy (D Mo.) March 9, 1889–March 9, 1951; House Feb. 14, 1920–21, 1923–35.

Milligan, John Jones (W Del.) Dec. 10, 1795–April 20, 1875; House 1831–39 (1831–33 Anti-Jacksonian).

Milliken, Charles William (D Ky.) Aug. 15, 1827–Oct. 16, 1915; House 1873–77.

Milliken, Seth Llewellyn (R Maine) Dec. 12, 1831–April 18, 1897; House 1883–April 18, 1897.

Milliken, William H. Jr. (R Pa.) Aug. 19, 1897–July 4, 1969; House 1959–65.

Millikin, Eugene Donald (R Colo.) Feb. 12, 1891–July 26, 1958; Senate Dec. 20, 1941–57; chair Senate Finance 1947–49, 1953–55.

Millington, Charles Stephen (R N.Y.) March 13, 1855–Oct. 25, 1913; House 1909–11.

Mills, Daniel Webster (R Ill.) Feb. 25, 1838–Dec. 16, 1904; House 1897–99.

Mills, Elijah Hunt (F Mass.) Dec. 1, 1776–May 5, 1829; House 1815–19; Senate June 12, 1820–27.

Mills, Newt Virgus (D La.) Sept. 27, 1899–May 15, 1996; House 1937–43.

Mills, Ogden Livingston (R N.Y.) Aug. 23, 1884–Oct. 11, 1937; House 1921–27; secretary of the Treasury Feb. 13, 1932–March 4, 1933.

Mills, Roger Quarles (D Texas) March 30, 1832–Sept. 2, 1911; House 1873–March 28, 1892; Senate March 29, 1892–99.

Mills, Wilbur Daigh (D Ark.) May 24, 1909–May 2, 1992; House 1939–77; chair House Ways and Means 1958–75.

Mills, William Oswald (R Md.) Aug. 12, 1924–May 24, 1973; House May 27, 1971–May 24, 1973.

Millson, John Singleton (D Va.) Oct. 1, 1808–March 1, 1874; House 1849–61.

Millspaugh, Frank Crenshaw (R Mo.) Jan. 14, 1872–July 8, 1947; House 1921–Dec. 5, 1922.

Millward, William (R Pa.) June 30, 1822–Nov. 28, 1871; House 1855–57 (Whig), 1859–61.

Milnes, Alfred (R Mich.) May 28, 1844–Jan. 15, 1916; House Dec. 2, 1895–97.

Milnes, William Jr. (C Va.) Dec. 8, 1827–Aug. 14, 1889; House Jan. 27, 1870–71.

Milnor, James (F Pa.) June 20, 1773–April 8, 1844; House 1811–13.

Milnor, William (F Pa.) June 26, 1769–Dec. 13, 1848; House 1807–11, 1815–17, 1821–May 8, 1822.

Milton, John Gerald (D N.J.) Jan. 21, 1881–April 14, 1977; Senate Jan. 18–Nov. 8, 1938.

Milton, William Hall (D Fla.) March 2, 1864–Jan. 4, 1942; Senate March 27, 1908–09.

Minahan, Daniel Francis (D N.J.) Aug. 8, 1877–April 29, 1947; House 1919–21, 1923–25.

Miner, Ahiman Louis (W Vt.) Sept. 23, 1804–July 19, 1886; House 1851–53.

Miner, Charles (F Pa.) Feb. 1, 1780–Oct. 26, 1865; House 1825–29.

Miner, Henry Clay (D N.Y.) March 23, 1842–Feb. 22, 1900; House 1895–97.

Miner, Phineas (– Conn.) Nov. 27, 1777–Sept. 15, 1839; House Dec. 1, 1834–35.

Mineta, Norman Yoshio (D Calif.) Nov. 12, 1931– ; House 1975–Oct. 10, 1995; chair House Public Works and Transportation 1993–95; secretary of commerce July 21, 2000–Jan. 19, 2001; secretary of transportation Jan. 25, 2001– .

Minge, David (D Minn.) March 19, 1942– ; House 1993–2001.

Minish, Joseph George (D N.J.) Sept. 1, 1916– ; House 1963–85.

Mink, Patsy Takemoto (D Hawaii) Dec. 6, 1927–Sept. 28, 2002; House 1965–77, Sept. 27, 1990–Sept. 28, 2002.

Minor, Edward Sloman (R Wis.) Dec. 13, 1840–July 26, 1924; House 1895–1907.

Minshall, William Edwin Jr. (R Ohio) Oct. 24, 1911–Oct. 15, 1990; House 1955–Dec. 31, 1974.

Minton, Sherman (D Ind.) Oct. 20, 1890–April 9, 1965; Senate 1935–41; assoc. justice Oct. 12, 1949–Oct. 15, 1956.

Mitchel, Charles Burton (D Ark.) Sept. 19, 1815–Sept. 20, 1864; Senate March 4–July 11, 1861.

Mitchell, Alexander (father of John Lendrum Mitchell) (D Wis.) Oct. 18, 1817–April 19, 1887; House 1871–75.

Mitchell, Alexander Clark (R Kan.) Oct. 11, 1860–July 7, 1911; House March 4–July 7, 1911.

Mitchell, Anderson (W N.C.) June 13, 1800–Dec. 24, 1876; House April 27, 1842–43.

Mitchell, Arthur Wergs (D Ill.) Dec. 22, 1883–May 9, 1968; House 1935–43.

Mitchell, Charles F. (W N.Y.) about 1808–?; House 1837–41.

Mitchell, Charles Le Moyne (D Conn.) Aug. 6, 1844–March 1, 1890; House 1883–87.

Mitchell, Donald Jerome (R N.Y.) May 8, 1923–Sept. 27, 2003; House 1973–83.

Mitchell, Edward Archibald (R Ind.) Dec. 2, 1910–Dec. 11, 1979; House 1947–49.

Mitchell, George Edward (J Md.) March 3, 1781–June 28, 1832; House 1823–27 (no party), Dec. 7, 1829–June 28, 1832.

Mitchell, George John (D Maine) Aug. 20, 1933– ; Senate May 19, 1980–95; Senate majority leader 1989–95.

Mitchell, Harlan Erwin (D Ga.) Aug. 17, 1924– ; House Jan. 8, 1958–61.

Mitchell, Henry (J N.Y.) 1784–Jan. 12, 1856; House 1833–35.

Mitchell, Hugh Burnton (D Wash.) March 22, 1907–June 10, 1996; Senate Jan. 10, 1945–Dec. 25, 1946; House 1949–53.

Mitchell, James Coffield (– Tenn.) March 1786–Aug. 7, 1843; House 1825–29.

Mitchell, James S. (– Pa.) 1784–1844; House 1821–27.

Mitchell, John (– Pa.) March 8, 1781–Aug. 3, 1849; House 1825–29.

Mitchell, John Hipple (R Ore.) June 22, 1835–Dec. 8, 1905; Senate 1873–79, Nov. 18, 1885–97, 1901–Dec. 8, 1905.

Mitchell, John Inscho (R Pa.) July 28, 1838–Aug. 20, 1907; House 1877–81; Senate 1881–87.

Mitchell, John Joseph (D Mass.) May 9, 1873–Sept. 13, 1925; House Nov. 8, 1910–11, April 15, 1913–15.

Mitchell, John Lendrum (son of Alexander Mitchell) (D Wis.) Oct. 19, 1842–June 29, 1904; House 1891–93; Senate 1893–99.

Mitchell, John Murry (R N.Y.) March 18, 1858–May 31, 1905; House June 2, 1896–99.

Mitchell, John Ridley (D Tenn.) Sept. 26, 1877–Feb. 26, 1962; House 1931–39.

Mitchell, Nahum (F Mass.) Feb. 12, 1769–Aug. 1, 1853; House 1803–05.

Mitchell, Parren James (D Md.) April 29, 1922– ; House 1971–87; chair House Small Business 1981–87.

Mitchell, Robert (J Ohio) 1778–Nov. 13, 1848; House 1833–35.

Mitchell, Stephen Mix (– Conn.) Dec. 9, 1743–Sept. 30, 1835; Senate Dec. 2, 1793–95; Cont. Cong. 1785–88.

Mitchell, Thomas Rothmaler (J S.C.) May 1783–Nov. 2, 1837; House 1821–23 (no party), 1825–29 (no party), 1831–33.

Mitchell, William (R Ind.) Jan. 19, 1807–Sept. 11, 1865; House 1861–63.

Mitchill, Samuel Latham (R N.Y.) Aug. 20, 1764–Sept. 7, 1831; House 1801–Nov. 22, 1804, Dec. 4, 1810–13; Senate Nov. 23, 1804–09.

Mize, Chester Louis (R Kan.) Dec. 25, 1917–Jan. 11, 1994; House 1965–71.

Mizell, Wilmer David (R N.C.) Aug. 13, 1930–Feb. 21, 1999; House 1969–75.

Moakley, John Joseph (D Mass.) April 27, 1927–May 28, 2001; House 1973–May 28, 2001 (elected as Independent Democrat, changed to Democrat Jan. 2, 1973); chair House Rules 1989–95.

Mobley, William Carlton (D Ga.) Dec. 7, 1906–Oct. 14, 1981; House March 2, 1932–33.

Moeller, Walter Henry (D Ohio) March 15, 1910–April 6, 1999; House 1959–63, 1965–67.

Moffatt, Seth Crittenden (R Mich.) Aug. 10, 1841–Dec. 22, 1887; House 1885–Dec. 22, 1887.

Moffet, John (D Pa.) April 5, 1831–June 19, 1884; House March 4–April 9, 1869.

Moffett, Anthony John "Toby" Jr. (D Conn.) Aug. 18, 1944– ; House 1975–83.

Moffitt, Hosea (F N.Y.) Nov. 17, 1757–Aug. 31, 1825; House 1813–17.

Moffitt, John Henry (R N.Y.) Jan. 8, 1843–Aug. 14, 1926; House 1887–91.

Molinari, Guy Victor (father of Susan Molinari, father-in-law of L. William Paxon) (R N.Y.) Nov. 23, 1928– ; House 1981–Jan. 1, 1990.

Molinari, Susan (wife of L. William Paxon, daughter of Guy Victor Molinari) (R N.Y.) March 27, 1958– ; House March 27, 1990–Aug. 1, 1997.

Mollohan, Alan Bowlby (son of Robert Homer Mollohan) (D W.Va.) May 14, 1943– ; House 1983– .

Mollohan, Robert Homer (father of Alan Bowlby Mollohan) (D W.Va.) Sept. 18, 1909–Aug. 3, 1999; House 1953–57, 1969–83.

Molony, Richard Sheppard (D Ill.) June 28, 1811–Dec. 14, 1891; House 1851–53.

Monagan, John Stephen (D Conn.) Dec. 23, 1911– ; House 1959–73.

Monaghan, Joseph Patrick (D Mont.) March 26, 1906–July 4, 1985; House 1933–37.

Monahan, James Gideon (R Wis.) Jan. 12, 1855–Dec. 5, 1923; House 1919–21.

Monast, Louis (R R.I.) July 1, 1863–April 16, 1936; House 1927–29.

Mondale, Walter Frederick "Fritz" (D Minn.) Jan. 5, 1928– ; Senate Dec. 30, 1964–Dec. 30, 1976; vice president 1977–81.

Mondell, Franklin Wheeler (R Wyo.) Nov. 6, 1860–Aug. 6, 1939; House 1895–97, 1899–1923; House majority leader 1919–23.

Monell, Robert (J N.Y.) 1786–Nov. 29, 1860; House 1819–21 (no party), 1829–Feb. 21, 1831.

Money, Hernando De Soto (D Miss.) Aug. 26, 1839–Sept. 18, 1912; House 1875–85, 1893–97; Senate Oct. 8, 1897–1911.

Monkiewicz, Boleslaus Joseph (R Conn.) Aug. 8, 1898–July 2, 1971; House 1939–41, 1943–45.

Monroe, James (uncle of James Monroe, below) (– Va.) April 28, 1758–July 4, 1831; Senate Nov. 9, 1790–May 27, 1794; Cont. Cong. 1783–86; Gov. Dec. 1, 1799–Dec. 1, 1802 (Democratic Republican), Jan. 16–April 3, 1811 (Democratic Republican); secretary of state April 6, 1811–Sept. 30, 1814, Feb. 28, 1815–March 3, 1817; secretary of war Oct. 1, 1814–Feb. 28, 1815; president 1817–25 (Democratic Republican).

Monroe, James (nephew of James Monroe, above) (W N.Y.) Sept. 10, 1799–Sept. 7, 1870; House 1839–41.

Monroe, James (R Ohio) July 18, 1821–July 6, 1898; House 1871–81.

Monroney, Almer Stillwell Mike (D Okla.) March 2, 1902–Feb. 13, 1980; House 1939–51; Senate 1951–69; chair Senate Post Office and Civil Service 1965–69.

Monson, David Smith (R Utah) June 20, 1945– ; House 1985–87.

Montague, Andrew Jackson (D Va.) Oct. 3, 1862–Jan. 24, 1937; House 1913–Jan. 24, 1937; Gov. Jan. 1, 1902–Feb. 1, 1906.

Montet, Numa Francois (D La.) Sept. 17, 1892–Oct. 12, 1985; House Aug. 6, 1929–37.

Montgomery, Alexander Brooks (D Ky.) Dec. 11, 1837–Dec. 27, 1910; House 1887–95.

Montgomery, Daniel Jr. (R Pa.) Oct. 30, 1765–Dec. 30, 1831; House 1807–09.

Montgomery, Gillespie V. "Sonny" (D Miss.) Aug. 5, 1920– ; House 1967–97; chair House Veterans' Affairs 1981–95.

Montgomery, John (R Md.) 1764–July 17, 1828; House 1807–April 29, 1811.

Montgomery, John Gallagher (D Pa.) June 27, 1805–April 24, 1857; House March 4–April 24, 1857.

Montgomery, Samuel James (R Okla.) Dec. 1, 1896–June 4, 1957; House 1925–27.

Montgomery, Thomas (R Ky.) 1779–April 2, 1828; House 1813–15, Aug. 1, 1820–23.

Montgomery, William (– Pa.) Aug. 3, 1736–May 1, 1816; House 1793–95; Cont. Cong. (elected but did not attend) 1784.

Montgomery, William (D N.C.) Dec. 29, 1789–Nov. 27, 1844; House 1835–41 (1835–37 Jacksonian).

Montgomery, William (D Pa.) April 11, 1818–April 28, 1870; House 1857–61.

Montoya, Joseph Manuel (D N.M.) Sept. 24, 1915–June 5, 1978; House April 9, 1957–Nov. 3, 1964; Senate Nov. 4, 1964–77.

Montoya, Nestor (R N.M.) April 14, 1862–Jan. 13, 1923; House 1921–Jan. 13, 1923.

Moody, Arthur Edson Blair (D Mich.) Feb. 13, 1902–July 20, 1954; Senate April 23, 1951–Nov. 4, 1952.

Moody, Gideon Curtis (R S.D.) Oct. 16, 1832–March 17, 1904; Senate Nov. 2, 1889–91.

Moody, James Montraville (R N.C.) Feb. 12, 1858–Feb. 5, 1903; House 1901–Feb. 5, 1903.

Moody, Jim (D Wis.) Sept. 2, 1935– ; House 1983–93.

Moody, Malcolm Adelbert (R Ore.) Nov. 30, 1854–March 19, 1925; House 1899–1903.

Moody, William Henry (R Mass.) Dec. 23, 1853–July 2, 1917; House Nov. 5, 1895–May 1, 1902; secretary of the navy May 1, 1902–June 30, 1904; attorney general July 1, 1904–Dec. 17, 1906; assoc. justice Dec. 17, 1906–Nov. 20, 1910.

Moon, John Austin (D Tenn.) April 22, 1855–June 26, 1921; House 1897–1921.

Moon, John Wesley (R Mich.) Jan. 18, 1836–April 5, 1898; House 1893–95.

Moon, Reuben Osborne (R Pa.) July 22, 1847–Oct. 25, 1919; House Nov. 2, 1903–13.

Mooney, Charles Anthony (D Ohio) Jan. 5, 1879–May 29, 1931; House 1919–21, 1923–May 29, 1931.

Mooney, William Crittenden (R Ohio) June 15, 1855–July 24, 1918; House 1915–17.

Moor, Wyman Bradbury Seavy (D Maine) Nov. 11, 1811–March 10, 1869; Senate Jan. 5–June 7, 1848.

Moore, Allen Francis (R Ill.) Sept. 30, 1869–Aug. 18, 1945; House 1921–25.

Moore, Andrew (father of Samuel McDowell Moore) (– Va.) 1752–April 14, 1821; House 1789–97, March 5–Aug. 11, 1804; Senate Aug. 11, 1804–09.

Moore, Arch Alfred Jr. (R W.Va.) April 16, 1923– ; House 1957–69; Gov. Jan. 13, 1969–Jan. 17, 1977, Jan. 14, 1985–Jan. 16, 1989.

Moore, Arthur Harry (D N.J.) July 3, 1879–Nov. 18, 1952; Senate 1935–Jan. 17, 1938; Gov. Jan. 19, 1926–Jan. 15, 1929, Jan. 19, 1932–Jan. 3, 1935, Jan. 18, 1938–Jan. 21, 1941.

Moore, Charles Ellis (R Ohio) Jan. 3, 1884–April 2, 1941; House 1919–33.

Moore, Dennis (D Kan.) Nov. 8, 1945– ; House 1999– .

Moore, Edward Hall (R Okla.) Nov. 19, 1871–Sept. 2, 1950; Senate 1943–49.

Moore, Eliakim Hastings (R Ohio) June 19, 1812–April 4, 1900; House 1869–71.

Moore, Ely (D N.Y.) July 4, 1798–Jan. 27, 1860; House 1835–39 (1835–37 Jacksonian).

Moore, Gabriel (– Ala.) about 1785–1845; House 1821–29; Senate 1831–37; Gov. Nov. 25, 1829–March 3, 1831.

Moore, Gwendolynne S. "Gwen" (D Wis.) April 18, 1951– ; House 2005– .

Moore, Heman Allen (D Ohio) Aug. 27, 1809–April 3, 1844; House 1843–April 3, 1844.

Moore, Henry Dunning (W Pa.) April 13, 1817–Aug. 11, 1887; House 1849–53.

Moore, Horace Ladd (D Kan.) Feb. 25, 1837–May 1, 1914; House Aug. 2, 1894–95.

Moore, Jesse Hale (R Ill.) April 22, 1817–July 11, 1883; House 1869–73.

Moore, John (W La.) 1788–June 17, 1867; House Dec. 17, 1840–43, 1851–53.

Moore, John Matthew (D Texas) Nov. 18, 1862–Feb. 3, 1940; House June 6, 1905–13.

Moore, John William (D Ky.) June 9, 1877–Dec. 11, 1941; House Nov. 3, 1925–29, June 1, 1929–33.

Moore, Joseph Hampton (R Pa.) March 8, 1864–May 2, 1950; House Nov. 6, 1906–Jan. 4, 1920.

Moore, Laban Theodore (O Ky.) Jan. 13, 1829–Nov. 9, 1892; House 1859–61.

Moore, Littleton Wilde (D Texas) March 25, 1835–Oct. 29, 1911; House 1887–93.

Moore, Nicholas Ruxton (R Md.) July 21, 1756–Oct. 7, 1816; House 1803–11, 1813–15.

Moore, Orren Cheney (R N.H.) Aug. 10, 1839–May 12, 1893; House 1889–91.

Moore, Oscar Fitzallen (R Ohio) Jan. 27, 1817–June 24, 1885; House 1855–57.

Moore, Paul John (D N.J.) Aug. 5, 1868–Jan. 10, 1938; House 1927–29.

Moore, Robert (grandfather of Michael Daniel Harter) (R Pa.) March 30, 1778–Jan. 14, 1831; House 1817–21.

Moore, Robert Lee (D Ga.) Nov. 27, 1867–Jan. 14, 1940; House 1923–25.

Moore, Robert Walton (D Va.) Feb. 6, 1859–Feb. 8, 1941; House May 27, 1919–31.

Moore, Samuel (R Pa.) Feb. 8, 1774–Feb. 18, 1861; House Oct. 13, 1818–May 20, 1822.

Moore, Samuel McDowell (son of Andrew Moore) (AJ Va.) Feb. 9, 1796–Sept. 17, 1875; House 1833–35.

Moore, Sydenham (D Ala.) May 25, 1817–May 31, 1862; House 1857–Jan. 21, 1861.

Moore, Thomas (R S.C.) 1759–July 11, 1822; House 1801–13, 1815–17.

Moore, Thomas Love (– Va.) ?–1862; House Nov. 13, 1820–23.

Moore, Thomas Patrick (– Ky.) 1797–July 21, 1853; House 1823–29.

Moore, William (R N.J.) Dec. 25, 1810–April 26, 1878; House 1867–71.

Moore, William Henson III (R La.) Oct. 4, 1939– ; House Jan. 7, 1975–87.

Moore, William Robert (R Tenn.) March 28, 1830–June 12, 1909; House 1881–83.

Moore, William Sutton (R Pa.) Nov. 18, 1822–Dec. 30, 1877; House 1873–75.

Moorehead, Tom Van Horn (R Ohio) April 12, 1898–Oct. 21, 1979; House 1961–63.

Moores, Merrill (R Ind.) April 21, 1856–Oct. 21, 1929; House 1915–25.

Moorhead, Carlos John (R Calif.) May 6, 1922– ; House 1973–97; chair House Judiciary 1995–96.

Moorhead, James Kennedy (R Pa.) Sept. 7, 1806–March 6, 1884; House 1859–69.

Moorhead, William Singer (D Pa.) April 8, 1923–Aug. 3, 1987; House 1959–81.

Moorman, Henry DeHaven (D Ky.) June 9, 1880–Feb. 3, 1939; House 1927–29.

Moran, Edward Carleton Jr. (D Maine) Dec. 29, 1894–July 12, 1967; House 1933–37.

Moran, James Patrick Jr. (D Va.) May 16, 1945– ; House 1991– .

Moran, Jerry (R Kan.) May 29, 1954– ; House 1997– .

Morano, Albert Paul (R Conn.) Jan. 18, 1908–Dec. 16, 1987; House 1951–59.

Morehead, Charles Slaughter (W Ky.) July 7, 1802–Dec. 21, 1868; House 1847–51; Gov. Sept. 1, 1855–Aug. 30, 1859 (American Party).

Morehead, James Turner (W Ky.) May 24, 1797–Dec. 28, 1854; Senate 1841–47; Gov. Feb. 22, 1834–June 1, 1836 (Democrat).

Morehead, James Turner (W N.C.) Jan. 11, 1799–May 5, 1875; House 1851–53.

Morehead, John Henry (D Neb.) Dec. 3, 1861–May 31, 1942; House 1923–35; Gov. Jan. 9, 1913–Jan. 4, 1917.

Morehead, John Motley (R N.C.) July 20, 1866–Dec. 13, 1923; House 1909–11.

Morella, Constance Albanese (R Md.) Feb. 12, 1931– ; House 1987–2003.

Morey, Frank (R La.) July 11, 1840–Sept. 22, 1889; House 1869–June 8, 1876.

Morey, Henry Lee (R Ohio) April 8, 1841–Dec. 29, 1902; House 1881–June 20, 1884, 1889–91.

Morgan, Charles Henry (R Mo.) July 5, 1842–Jan. 4, 1912; House 1875–79 (Democrat), 1883–85 (Democrat), 1893–95 (Democrat), 1909–11.

Morgan, Christopher (brother of Edwin Barbour Morgan, nephew of Noyes Barber) (W N.Y.) June 4, 1808–April 3, 1877; House 1839–43.

Morgan, Daniel (F Va.) 1736–July 6, 1802; House 1797–99.

Morgan, Dick Thompson (R Okla.) Dec. 6, 1853–July 4, 1920; House 1909–July 4, 1920.

Morgan, Edwin Barber (brother of Christopher Morgan, nephew of Noyes Barber) (R N.Y.) May 2, 1806–Oct. 13, 1881; House 1853–59 (1853–57 Whig).

Morgan, Edwin Dennison (cousin of Morgan Gardner Bulkeley) (R N.Y.) Feb. 8, 1811–Feb. 14, 1883; Senate 1863–69; chair Rep. Nat. Comm. 1856–64, 1872–76; Gov. Jan. 1, 1859–Jan. 1, 1863.

Morgan, George Washington (D Ohio) Sept. 20, 1820–July 26, 1893; House 1867–June 3, 1868, 1869–73.

Morgan, James (R N.J.) Dec. 29, 1756–Nov. 11, 1822; House 1811–13.

Morgan, James Bright (D Miss.) March 14, 1833–June 18, 1892; House 1885–91.

Morgan, John Jordan (father-in-law of John Adams Dix) (J N.Y.) 1770–July 29, 1849; House 1821–25 (no party), Dec. 1, 1834–35.

Morgan, John Tyler (D Ala.) June 20, 1824–June 11, 1907; Senate 1877–June 11, 1907.

Morgan, Lewis Lovering (D La.) March 2, 1876–June 10, 1950; House Nov. 5, 1912–17.

Morgan, Robert Burren (D N.C.) Oct. 5, 1925– ; Senate 1975–81.

Morgan, Stephen (R Ohio) Jan. 25, 1854–Feb. 9, 1928; House 1899–1905.

Morgan, Thomas Ellsworth (D Pa.) Oct. 13, 1906–July 31, 1995; House 1945–77; chair House Foreign Affairs 1959–75; chair House International Relations 1975–77.

Morgan, William Mitchell (R Ohio) Aug. 1, 1870–Sept. 17, 1935; House 1921–31.

Morgan, William Stephen (D Va.) Sept. 7, 1801–Sept. 3, 1878; House 1835–39 (1835–37 Jacksonian).

Morin, John Mary (R Pa.) April 18, 1868–March 3, 1942; House 1913–29.

Moritz, Theodore Leo (D Pa.) Feb. 10, 1892–March 13, 1982; House 1935–37.

Morphis, Joseph Lewis (R Miss.) April 17, 1831–July 29, 1913; House Feb. 23, 1870–73.

Morrell, Daniel Johnson (R Pa.) Aug. 8, 1821–Aug. 20, 1885; House 1867–71.

Morrell, Edward de Veaux (R Pa.) Aug. 7, 1863–Sept. 1, 1917; House Nov. 6, 1900–07.

Morril, David Lawrence (R N.H.) June 10, 1772–Jan. 28, 1849; Senate 1817–23; Gov. June 3, 1824–June 7, 1827.

Morrill, Anson Peaslee (brother of Lot Myrick Morrill) (R Maine) June 10, 1803–July 4, 1887; House 1861–63; Gov. Jan. 3, 1855–Jan. 2, 1856.

Morrill, Edmund Needham (R Kan.) Feb. 12, 1834–March 14, 1909; House 1883–91; Gov. Jan. 14, 1895–Jan. 11, 1897.

Morrill, Justin Smith (R Vt.) April 14, 1810–Dec. 28, 1898; House 1855–67 (1855–57 Whig, 1857–67 Republican); Senate 1867–Dec. 28, 1898 (1867–73 Union Republican).

Morrill, Lot Myrick (brother of Anson Peaslee Morrill) (R Maine) May 3, 1813–Jan. 10, 1883; Senate Jan. 17, 1861–69, Oct. 30, 1869–July 7, 1876; Gov. Jan. 8, 1858–Jan. 2, 1861; secretary of the Treasury July 7, 1876–March 9, 1877.

Morrill, Samuel Plummer (R Maine) Feb. 11, 1816–Aug. 4, 1892; House 1869–71.

Morris, Calvary (W Ohio) Jan. 15, 1798–Oct. 13, 1871; House 1837–43.

Morris, Daniel (R N.Y.) Jan. 4, 1812–April 22, 1889; House 1863–67.

Morris, Edward Joy (R Pa.) July 16, 1815–Dec. 31, 1881; House 1843–45 (Whig), 1857–June 8, 1861.

Morris, Gouverneur (half-brother of Lewis Robert Morris, uncle of Lewis Robert Morris) (F N.Y.) Jan. 31, 1752–Nov. 6, 1816; Senate April 3, 1800–03; Cont. Cong. 1778–79.

Morris, Isaac Newton (son of Thomas Morris of Ohio, brother of Jonathan David Morris) (D Ill.) Jan. 22, 1812–Oct. 29, 1879; House 1857–61.

Morris, James Remley (son of Joseph Morris) (D Ohio) Jan. 10, 1819–Dec. 24, 1899; House 1861–65.

Morris, Jonathan David (son of Thomas Morris of Ohio, brother of Isaac Newton Morris) (D Ohio) Oct. 8, 1804–May 16, 1875; House 1847–51.

Morris, Joseph (father of James Remley Morris) (D Ohio) Oct. 16, 1795–Oct. 23, 1854; House 1843–47.

Morris, Joseph Watkins (D Ky.) Feb. 26, 1879–Dec. 21, 1937; House Nov. 30, 1923–25.

Morris, Lewis Robert (nephew of Gouverneur Morris) (F Vt.) Nov. 2, 1760–Dec. 29, 1825; House 1797–1803.

Morris, Mathias (W Pa.) Sept. 12, 1787–Nov. 9, 1839; House 1835–39.

Morris, Robert (father of Thomas Morris of N.Y.) (– Pa.) Jan. 20, 1734–May 8, 1806; Senate 1789–95; Cont. Cong. 1775–78.

Morris, Robert Page Walter (R Minn.) June 30, 1853–Dec. 16, 1924; House 1897–1903.

Morris, Samuel Wells (D Pa.) Sept. 1, 1786–May 25, 1847; House 1837–41.

Morris, Thomas (son of Robert Morris) (F N.Y.) Feb. 26, 1771–March 12, 1849; House 1801–03.

Morris, Thomas (father of Isaac Newton Morris and Jonathan David Morris) (J Ohio) Jan. 3, 1776–Dec. 7, 1844; Senate 1833–39.

Morris, Thomas Gayle (D N.M.) Aug. 20, 1919– ; House 1959–69.

Morris, Toby (D Okla.) Feb. 28, 1899–Sept. 1, 1973; House 1947–53, 1957–61.

Morrison, Bruce Andrew (D Conn.) Oct. 8, 1944– ; House 1983–91.

Morrison, Cameron A. (D N.C.) Oct. 5, 1869–Aug. 20, 1953; Senate Dec. 13, 1930–Dec. 4, 1932; House 1943–45; Gov. Jan. 12, 1921–Jan. 14, 1925.

Morrison, George Washington (D N.H.) Oct. 16, 1809–Dec. 21, 1888; House Oct. 8, 1850–51, 1853–55.

Morrison, James Hobson (D La.) Dec. 8, 1908–July 20, 2000; House 1943–67.

Morrison, James Lowery Donaldson (D Ill.) April 12, 1816–Aug. 14, 1888; House Nov. 4, 1856–57.

Morrison, John Alexander (D Pa.) Jan. 31, 1814–July 25, 1904; House 1851–53.

Morrison, Martin Andrew (D Ind.) April 15, 1862–July 9, 1944; House 1909–17.

Morrison, Sidney Wallace (R Wash.) May 13, 1933– ; House 1981–93.

Morrison, William Ralls (D Ill.) Sept. 14, 1824–Sept. 29, 1909; House 1863–65, 1873–87.

Morrissey, John (D N.Y.) Feb. 12, 1831–May 1, 1878; House 1867–71.

Morrow, Dwight Whitney (R N.J.) Jan. 11, 1873–Oct. 5, 1931; Senate Dec. 3, 1930–Oct. 5, 1931.

Morrow, Jeremiah (W Ohio) Oct. 6, 1771–March 22, 1852; House Oct. 17, 1803–13 (Republican), Oct. 13, 1840–43; Senate 1813–19 (Republican); Gov. Dec. 28, 1822–Dec. 19, 1826 (Jacksonian).

Morrow, John (R Va.) ?–?; House 1805–09.

Morrow, John (D N.M.) April 19, 1865–Feb. 25, 1935; House 1923–29.

Morrow, William W. (R Calif.) July 15, 1843–July 24, 1929; House 1885–91.

Morse, Elijah Adams (R Mass.) May 25, 1841–June 5, 1898; House 1889–97.

Morse, Elmer Addison (R Wis.) May 11, 1870–Oct. 4, 1945; House 1907–13.

Morse, Frank Bradford (R Mass.) Aug. 7, 1921–Dec. 18, 1994; House 1961–May 1, 1972.

Morse, Freeman Harlow (R Maine) Feb. 19, 1807–Feb. 5, 1891; House 1843–45 (Whig), 1857–61.

Morse, Isaac Edward (D La.) May 22, 1809–Feb. 11, 1866; House Dec. 2, 1844–51.

Morse, Leopold (– Mass.) Aug. 15, 1831–Dec. 15, 1892; House 1877–85, 1887–89.

Morse, Oliver Andrew (R N.Y.) March 26, 1815–April 20, 1870; House 1857–59.

Morse, Wayne Lyman (D Ore.) Oct. 20, 1900–July 22, 1974; Senate 1945–69 (1945–57 Republican).

Morton, Jackson (brother of Jeremiah Morton) (W Fla.) Aug. 10, 1794–Nov. 20, 1874; Senate 1849–55.

Morton, Jeremiah (brother of Jackson Morton) (W Va.) Sept. 3, 1799–Nov. 28, 1878; House 1849–51.

Morton, Levi Parsons (R N.Y.) May 16, 1824–May 16, 1920; House 1879–March 21, 1881; vice president 1889–93; Gov. Jan. 1, 1895–Jan. 1, 1897.

Morton, Marcus (R Mass.) Dec. 19, 1784–Feb. 6, 1864; House 1817–21; Gov. Feb. 6–May 26, 1825, Jan. 18, 1840–Jan. 7, 1841, Jan. 17, 1843–Jan. 3, 1844.

Morton, Oliver Hazard Perry Throck (R Ind.) Aug. 4, 1823–Nov. 1, 1877; Senate 1867–Nov. 1, 1877; Gov. Jan. 16, 1861–Jan. 23, 1867.

Morton, Rogers Clark Ballard (brother of Thruston Ballard Morton) (R Md.) Sept. 19, 1914–April 19, 1979; House 1963–Jan. 29, 1971; chair Rep. Nat. Comm. April 1969–Jan. 1971; secretary of the interior Jan. 29, 1971–April 30, 1975; secretary of commerce May 1, 1975–Feb. 2, 1976.

Morton, Thruston Ballard (brother of Rogers Clark Ballard Morton) (R Ky.) Aug. 19, 1907–Aug. 14, 1982; House 1947–53; Senate 1957–69; chair Rep. Nat. Comm. April 1959–June 1961.

Moseley, Jonathan Ogden (F Conn.) April 9, 1762–Sept. 9, 1838; House 1805–21.

Moseley, William Abbott (W N.Y.) Oct. 20, 1798–Nov. 19, 1873; House 1843–47.

Moseley-Braun, Carol (D Ill.) Aug. 16, 1947– ; Senate 1993–99.

Moser, Guy Louis (D Pa.) Jan. 23, 1866–May 9, 1961; House 1937–43.

Moses, Charles Leavell (D Ga.) May 2, 1856–Oct. 10, 1910; House 1891–97.

Moses, George Higgins (R N.H.) Feb. 9, 1869–Dec. 20, 1944; Senate Nov. 6, 1918–33; elected pres. pro tempore March 6, 1925, Dec. 15, 1927.

Moses, John (D N.D.) June 12, 1885–March 3, 1945; Senate Jan. 3–March 3, 1945; Gov. Jan. 5, 1939–Jan. 4, 1945.

Mosgrove, James (G Pa.) June 14, 1821–Nov. 27, 1900; House 1881–83.

Mosher, Charles Adams (R Ohio) May 7, 1906–Nov. 16, 1984; House 1961–77.

Mosier, Harold Gerard (D Ohio) July 24, 1889–Aug. 7, 1971; House 1937–39.

Moss, Frank Edward "Ted" (D Utah) Sept. 23, 1911–Jan. 29, 2003; Senate 1959–77; chair Senate Aeronautical and Space Sciences 1973–77.

Moss, Hunter Holmes Jr. (R W.Va.) May 26, 1874–July 15, 1916; House 1913–July 15, 1916.

Moss, John Emerson (D Calif.) April 13, 1915–Dec. 5, 1997; House 1953–Dec. 31, 1978.

Moss, John McKenzie (nephew of James Andrew McKenzie) (R Ky.) Jan. 3, 1868–June 11, 1929; House March 25, 1902–03.

Moss, Ralph Wilbur (D Ind.) April 21, 1862–April 26, 1919; House 1909–17.

Mott, Gordon Newell (R Nev.) Oct. 21, 1812–April 27, 1887; House (Terr. Del.) 1863–Oct. 31, 1864.

Mott, James (R N.J.) Jan. 18, 1739–Oct. 18, 1823; House 1801–05.

Mott, James Wheaton (R Ore.) Nov. 12, 1883–Nov. 12, 1945; House 1933–Nov. 12, 1945.

Mott, Luther Wright (R N.Y.) Nov. 30, 1874–July 10, 1923; House 1911–July 10, 1923.

Mott, Richard (R Ohio) July 21, 1804–Jan. 22, 1888; House 1855–59.

Mottl, Ronald Milton (D Ohio) Feb. 6, 1934– ; House 1975–83.

Moulder, Morgan Moore (D Mo.) Aug. 31, 1904–Nov. 12, 1976; House 1949–63.

Moulton, Mace (D N.H.) May 2, 1796–May 5, 1867; House 1845–47.

Moulton, Samuel Wheeler (D Ill.) Jan. 20, 1821–June 3, 1905; House 1865–67 (Republican), 1881–85.

Mouser, Grant Earl (father of Grant Earl Mouser Jr.) (R Ohio) Sept. 11, 1868–May 6, 1949; House 1905–09.

Mouser, Grant Earl Jr. (son of Grant Earl Mouser) (R Ohio) Feb. 20, 1895–Dec. 21, 1943; House 1929–33.

Mouton, Alexander (D La.) Nov. 19, 1804–Feb. 12, 1885; Senate Jan. 12, 1837–March 1, 1842; Gov. Jan. 30, 1843–Feb. 12, 1846.

Mouton, Robert Louis (D La.) Oct. 20, 1892–Nov. 26, 1956; House 1937–41.

Moxley, William James (R Ill.) May 22, 1851–Aug. 4, 1938; House Nov. 23, 1909–11.

Moynihan, Daniel Patrick (D N.Y.) March 16, 1927–March 26, 2003; Senate 1977–2001; chair Senate Environment and Public Works 1992; chair Senate Finance 1993–95.

Moynihan, Patrick Henry (R Ill.) Sept. 25, 1869–May 20, 1946; House 1933–35.

Mozley, Norman Adolphus (R Mo.) Dec. 11, 1865–May 9, 1922; House 1895–97.

Mrazek, Robert Jan (D N.Y.) Nov. 6, 1945– ; House 1983–93.

Mruk, Joseph (R N.Y.) Nov. 6, 1903–Jan. 21, 1995; House 1943–45.

Mudd, Sydney Emanuel (father of Sydney Emanuel Mudd, below) (R Md.) Feb. 12, 1858–Oct. 21, 1911; House March 20, 1890–91, 1897–1911.

Mudd, Sydney Emanuel (son of Sydney Emanuel Mudd, above) (R Md.) June 20, 1885–Oct. 11, 1924; House 1915–Oct. 11, 1924.

Muhlenberg, Francis Swaine (son of John Peter Gabriel Muhlenberg, nephew of Frederick Augustus Conrad Muhlenberg) (NR Ohio) April 22, 1795–Dec. 17, 1831; House Dec. 19, 1828–29.

Muhlenberg, Frederick Augustus (great-great-grandson of Frederick Augustus Conrad Muhlenberg, great-great-great-nephew of John Peter Gabriel Muhlenberg) (R Pa.) Sept. 25, 1887–Jan. 19, 1980; House 1947–49.

Muhlenberg, Frederick Augustus Conrad (brother of John Peter Gabriel Muhlenberg, uncle of Francis Swaine Muhlenberg and Henry Augustus Philip Muhlenberg, great-great-grandfather of Frederick Augustus Muhlenberg) (– Pa.) Jan. 1, 1750–June 4, 1801; House 1789–97; Speaker April 1, 1789–91, Dec. 2, 1793–95; Cont. Cong. 1779–80.

Muhlenberg, Henry Augustus (son of Henry Augustus Philip Muhlenberg, grandson of Joseph Hiester) (D Pa.) July 21, 1823–Jan. 9, 1854; House 1853–Jan. 9, 1854.

Muhlenberg, Henry Augustus Philip (father of Henry Augustus Muhlenberg, nephew of John Peter Gabriel Muhlenberg and Frederick Augustus Conrad Muhlenberg) (D Pa.) May 13, 1782–Aug. 11, 1844; House 1829–Feb. 9, 1838 (1829–37 Jacksonian).

Muhlenberg, John Peter Gabriel (father of Francis Swaine Muhlenberg, brother of Frederick Augustus Conrad Muhlenberg, uncle of

Henry Augustus Philip Muhlenberg, great-great-great-uncle of Frederick Augustus Muhlenberg) (– Pa.) Oct. 1, 1746–Oct. 1, 1807; House 1789–91, 1793–95, 1799–1801; Senate March 4–June 30, 1801.

Muldowney, Michael Joseph (R Pa.) Aug. 10, 1889–March 30, 1947; House 1933–35.

Muldrow, Henry Lowndes (D Miss.) Feb. 8, 1837–March 1, 1905; House 1877–85.

Mulkey, Frederick William (nephew of Joseph Norton Dolph) (R Ore.) Jan. 6, 1874–May 5, 1924; Senate Jan. 23–March 3, 1907, Nov. 6–Dec. 17, 1918.

Mulkey, William Oscar (D Ala.) July 27, 1871–June 30, 1943; House June 29, 1914–15.

Muller, Nicholas (D N.Y.) Nov. 15, 1836–Dec. 12, 1917; House 1877–81, 1883–87, 1899–Dec. 1, 1902.

Mullin, Joseph (W N.Y.) Aug. 6, 1811–May 17, 1882; House 1847–49.

Mullins, James (R Tenn.) Sept. 15, 1807–June 26, 1873; House 1867–69.

Multer, Abraham Jacob (D N.Y.) Dec. 24, 1900–Nov. 4, 1986; House Nov. 4, 1947–Dec. 31, 1967.

Mumford, George (R N.C.) ?–Dec. 31, 1818; House 1817–Dec. 31, 1818.

Mumford, Gurdon Saltonstall (R N.Y.) Jan. 29, 1764–April 30, 1831; House 1805–11.

Mumma, Walter Mann (R Pa.) Nov. 20, 1890–Feb. 25, 1961; House 1951–Feb. 25, 1961.

Mundt, Karl Earl (R S.D.) June 3, 1900–Aug. 16, 1974; House 1939–Dec. 30, 1948; Senate Dec. 31, 1948–73.

Mungen, William (D Ohio) May 12, 1821–Sept. 9, 1887; House 1867–71.

Murch, Thompson Henry (G Maine) March 29, 1838–Dec. 15, 1886; House 1879–83.

Murdock, John Robert (D Ariz.) April 20, 1885–Feb. 14, 1972; House 1937–53; chair House Interior and Insular Affairs 1951–53.

Murdock, Orrice Abram Jr. "Abe" (D Utah) July 18, 1893–Sept. 15, 1979; House 1933–41; Senate 1941–47.

Murdock, Victor (R Kan.) March 18, 1871–July 8, 1945; House May 26, 1903–15.

Murfree, William Hardy (uncle of David W. Dickinson) (R N.C.) Oct. 2, 1781–Jan. 19, 1827; House 1813–17.

Murkowski, Frank Hughes (father of Lisa A. Murkowski) (R Alaska) March 28, 1933– ; Senate 1981–Dec. 2, 2002; chair Senate Veterans' Affairs 1985–87; chair Senate Energy and Natural Resources 1995–Jan. 3, 2001, Jan. 20, 2001–June 6, 2001; Gov. Dec. 2, 2002– .

Murkowski, Lisa A. (daughter of Frank H. Murkowski) (R Alaska) May 22, 1957– ; Senate Dec. 20, 2002– .

Murphey, Charles (U Ga.) May 9, 1799–Jan. 16, 1861; House 1851–53.

Murphy, Arthur Phillips (R Mo.) Dec. 10, 1870–Feb. 1, 1914; House 1905–07, 1909–11.

Murphy, Austin John (D Pa.) June 17, 1927– ; House 1977–95.

Murphy, Benjamin Franklin (R Ohio) Dec. 24, 1867–March 6, 1938; House 1919–33.

Murphy, Edward Jr. (D N.Y.) Dec. 15, 1836–Aug. 3, 1911; Senate 1893–99.

Murphy, Everett Jerome (R Ill.) July 24, 1852–April 10, 1922; House 1895–97.

Murphy, George Lloyd (R Calif.) July 4, 1902–May 3, 1992; Senate Jan. 1, 1965–Jan. 2, 1971.

Murphy, Henry Cruse (D N.Y.) July 5, 1810–Dec. 1, 1882; House 1843–45, 1847–49.

Murphy, James Joseph (D N.Y.) Nov. 3, 1898–Oct. 19, 1962; House 1949–53.

Murphy, James William (D Wis.) April 17, 1858–July 11, 1927; House 1907–09.

Murphy, Jeremiah Henry (D Iowa) Feb. 19, 1835–Dec. 11, 1893; House 1883–87.

Murphy, John (J Ala.) 1785–Sept. 21, 1841; House 1833–35; Gov. Nov. 25, 1825–Nov. 25, 1829.

Murphy, John Michael (D N.Y.) Aug. 3, 1926– ; House 1963–81; chair House Merchant Marine and Fisheries 1977–81.

Murphy, John William (D Pa.) April 26, 1902–March 28, 1962; House 1943–July 17, 1946.

Murphy, Maurice J. Jr. (R N.H.) Oct. 3, 1927–Oct. 27, 2002; Senate Dec. 7, 1961–Nov. 6, 1962.

Murphy, Morgan Francis (D Ill.) April 16, 1932– ; House 1971–81.

Murphy, Nathan Oakes (R Ariz.) Oct. 14, 1849–Aug. 22, 1908; House (Terr. Del.) 1895–97; Gov. (Ariz. Terr.) 1892–94, 1898–1902.

Murphy, Richard Louis (D Iowa) Nov. 6, 1875–July 16, 1936; Senate 1933–July 16, 1936.

Murphy, Timothy (R Pa.) Sept. 11, 1952– ; House 2003– .

Murphy, William Thomas (D Ill.) Aug. 7, 1899–Jan. 29, 1978; House 1959–71.

Murray, Ambrose Spencer (brother of William Murray) (R N.Y.) Nov. 27, 1807–Nov. 8, 1885; House 1855–59 (1855–57 Whig).

Murray, George Washington (R S.C.) Sept. 22, 1853–April 21, 1926; House 1893–95, June 4, 1896–97.

Murray, James Cunningham (D Ill.) May 16, 1917–Oct. 19, 1999; House 1955–57.

Murray, James Edward (D Mont.) May 3, 1876–March 23, 1961; Senate Nov. 7, 1934–61; chair Senate Labor and Public Welfare 1951–53; chair Senate Interior and Insular Affairs 1955–61.

Murray, John (cousin of Thomas Murray Jr.) (R Pa.) 1768–March 7, 1834; House Oct. 14, 1817–21.

Murray, John L. (D Ky.) Jan. 25, 1806–Jan. 31, 1842; House 1837–39.

Murray, Patty (D Wash.) Oct. 11, 1950– ; Senate 1993– .

Murray, Reid Fred (R Wis.) Oct. 16, 1887–April 29, 1952; House 1939–April 29, 1952.

Murray, Robert Maynard (D Ohio) Nov. 28, 1841–Aug. 2, 1913; House 1883–85.

Murray, Thomas Jefferson (D Tenn.) Aug. 1, 1894–Nov. 28, 1971; House 1943–67; chair House Post Office and Civil Service 1949–53, 1955–67.

Murray, Thomas Jr. (cousin of John Murray) (– Pa.) 1770–Aug. 26, 1823; House Oct. 9, 1821–23.

Murray, William (brother of Ambrose Spencer Murray) (D N.Y.) Oct. 1, 1803–Aug. 25, 1875; House 1851–55.

Murray, William Francis (D Mass.) Sept. 7, 1881–Sept. 21, 1918; House 1911–Sept. 28, 1914.

Murray, William Henry David (D Okla.) Nov. 21, 1869–Oct. 15, 1956; House 1913–17; Gov. Jan. 12, 1931–Jan. 14, 1935.

Murray, William Vans (F Md.) Feb. 9, 1760–Dec. 11, 1803; House 1791–97 (1791–95 no party).

Murtha, John Patrick Jr. (D Pa.) Jan. 17, 1932– ; House Feb. 5, 1974– .

Musgrave, Marilyn N. (R Colo.) Jan. 27, 1949– ; House 2003– .

Muskie, Edmund Sixtus (D Maine) March 28, 1914–March 26, 1996; Senate 1959–May 7, 1980; chair Senate Budget 1975–79; Gov. Jan. 5, 1955–Jan. 3, 1959; secretary of state May 8, 1980–Jan. 18, 1981.

Musselwhite, Harry Webster (D Mich.) May 23, 1868–Dec. 14, 1955; House 1933–35.

Musto, Raphael John (D Pa.) March 30, 1929– ; House April 15, 1980–81.

Mutchler, Howard (son of William Mutchler) (D Pa.) Feb. 12, 1859–Jan. 4, 1916; House Aug. 7, 1893–95, 1901–03.

Mutchler, William (father of Howard Mutchler) (D Pa.) Dec. 21, 1831–June 23, 1893; House 1875–77, 1881–85, 1889–June 23, 1893.

Myers, Amos (R Pa.) April 23, 1824–Oct. 18, 1893; House 1863–65.

Myers, Francis John (D Pa.) Dec. 18, 1901–July 5, 1956; House 1939–45; Senate 1945–51.

Myers, Gary Arthur (R Pa.) Aug. 16, 1937– ; House 1975–79.

Myers, Henry Lee (D Mont.) Oct. 9, 1862–Nov. 11, 1943; Senate 1911–23.

Myers, John Thomas (R Ind.) Feb. 8, 1927– ; House 1967–97.

Myers, Leonard (R Pa.) Nov. 13, 1827–Feb. 11, 1905; House 1863–69, April 9, 1869–75.

Myers, Michael Joseph "Ozzie" (D Pa.) May 4, 1943– ; House Nov. 2, 1976–Oct. 2, 1980.

Myers, William Ralph (D Ind.) June 12, 1836–April 18, 1907; House 1879–81.

Myrick, Sue (R N.C.) Aug. 1, 1941– ; House 1995– .

Nabers, Benjamin Duke (U Miss.) Nov. 7, 1812–Sept. 6, 1878; House 1851–53.

Nadler, Jerrold Lewis (D N.Y.) June 13, 1947– ; House Nov. 4, 1992– .

Nagle, David Ray (D Iowa) April 15, 1943– ; House 1987–93.

Naphen, Henry Francis (D Mass.) Aug. 14, 1852–June 8, 1905; House 1899–1903.

Napier, John Light (R S.C.) May 16, 1947– ; House 1981–83.

Napolitano, Grace (D Calif.) Dec. 4, 1936– ; House 1999– .

Narey, Harry Elsworth (R Iowa) May 15, 1885–Aug. 18, 1962; House Nov. 3, 1942–43.

Nash, Charles Edmund (R La.) May 23, 1844–June 21, 1913; House 1875–77.

Natcher, William Huston (D Ky.) Sept. 11, 1909–March 29, 1994; House Aug. 1, 1953–March 29, 1994; chair House Appropriations 1993–94.

Naudain, Arnold (– Del.) Jan. 6, 1790–Jan. 4, 1872; Senate Jan. 13, 1830–June 16, 1836.

Naylor, Charles (W Pa.) Oct. 6, 1806–Dec. 24, 1872; House June 29, 1837–41.

Neal, Henry Safford (R Ohio) Aug. 25, 1828–July 13, 1906; House 1877–83.

Neal, John Randolph (D Tenn.) Nov. 26, 1836–March 26, 1889; House 1885–89.

Neal, Lawrence Talbot (D Ohio) Sept. 22, 1844–Nov. 2, 1905; House 1873–77.

Neal, Richard E. (D Mass.) Feb. 14, 1949– ; House 1989– .

Neal, Stephen Lybrook (D N.C.) Nov. 7, 1934– ; House 1975–95.

Neal, William Elmer (R W.Va.) Oct. 14, 1875–Nov. 12, 1959; House 1953–55, 1957–59.

Neale, Raphael (– Md.) ?–Oct. 19, 1833; House 1819–25.

Nedzi, Lucien Norbert (D Mich.) May 28, 1925– ; House Nov. 7, 1961–81; chair House Select Intelligence 1975.

Neece, William Henry (D Ill.) Feb. 26, 1831–Jan. 3, 1909; House 1883–87.

Needham, James Carson (R Calif.) Sept. 17, 1864–July 11, 1942; House 1899–1913.

Neeley, George Arthur (D Kan.) Aug. 1, 1879–Jan. 1, 1919; House Nov. 11, 1912–15.

Neely, Matthew Mansfield (D W.Va.) Nov. 9, 1874–Jan. 18, 1958; House Oct. 14, 1913–21, 1945–47; Senate 1923–29, 1931–Jan. 12, 1941, 1949–Jan. 18, 1958; chair Senate District of Columbia 1951–53, 1955–59; Gov. Jan. 13, 1941–Jan. 15, 1945.

Negley, James Scott (R Pa.) Dec. 22, 1826–Aug. 7, 1901; House 1869–75, 1885–87.

Neill, Robert (D Ark.) Nov. 12, 1838–Feb. 16, 1907; House 1893–97.

Nelligan, James Leo (R Pa.) Feb. 14, 1929– ; House 1981–83.

Nelsen, Ancher (R Minn.) Oct. 11, 1904–Nov. 30, 1992; House 1959–Dec. 31, 1974.

Nelson, Adolphus Peter (R Wis.) March 28, 1872–Aug. 21, 1927; House Nov. 5, 1918–23.

Nelson, Arthur Emanuel (R Minn.) May 10, 1892–April 11, 1955; Senate Nov. 18, 1942–43.

Nelson, Charles Pembroke (son of John Edward Nelson) (R Maine) July 2, 1907–June 8, 1962; House 1949–57.

Nelson, Clarence William "Bill" (D Fla.) Sept. 29, 1942– ; House 1979–91; Senate 2001– .

Nelson, Earl Benjamin "Ben" (D Neb.) May 17, 1941– ; Senate 2001– ; Gov. Jan. 9, 1991–Jan. 7, 1999.

Nelson, Gaylord Anton (D Wis.) June 4, 1916– ; Senate Jan. 8, 1963–81; chair Senate Select Small Business 1975–81; Gov. Jan. 5, 1959–Jan. 7, 1963.

Nelson, Homer Augustus (D N.Y.) Aug. 31, 1829–April 25, 1891; House 1863–65.

Nelson, Hugh (R Va.) Sept. 30, 1768–March 18, 1836; House 1811–Jan. 14, 1823.

Nelson, Jeremiah (AJ Mass.) Sept. 14, 1769–Oct. 2, 1838; House 1805–07 (Federalist), 1815–25 (Federalist), 1831–33.

Nelson, John (son of Roger Nelson) (– Md.) June 1, 1794–Jan. 18, 1860; House 1821–23; attorney general July 1, 1843–March 3, 1845.

Nelson, John Edward (father of Charles Pembroke Nelson) (R Maine) July 12, 1874–April 11, 1955; House March 27, 1922–33.

Nelson, John Mandt (R Wis.) Oct. 10, 1870–Jan. 29, 1955; House Sept. 4, 1906–19, 1921–33.

Nelson, Knute (R Minn.) Feb. 2, 1843–April 28, 1923; House 1883–89; Senate 1895–April 28, 1923; Gov. Jan. 4, 1893–Jan. 31, 1895.

Nelson, Roger (father of John Nelson) (R Md.) 1759–June 7, 1815; House Nov. 6, 1804–May 14, 1810.

Nelson, Thomas Amos Rogers (O Tenn.) March 19, 1812–Aug. 24, 1873; House 1859–61.

Nelson, Thomas Maduit (R Va.) Sept. 27, 1782–Nov. 10, 1853; House Dec. 4, 1816–19.

Nelson, William (W N.Y.) June 29, 1784–Oct. 3, 1869; House 1847–51.

Nelson, William Lester (D Mo.) Aug. 4, 1875–Dec. 31, 1946; House 1919–21, 1925–33, 1935–43.

Nes, Henry (W Pa.) May 20, 1799–Sept. 10, 1850; House 1843–45 (Independent Democrat), 1847–Sept. 10, 1850.

Nesbit, Walter (D Ill.) May 1, 1878–Dec. 6, 1938; House 1933–35.

Nesbitt, Wilson (R S.C.) ?–May 13, 1861; House 1817–19.

Nesmith, James Willis (cousin of Joseph Gardner Wilson, grandfather of Clifton Nesmith McArthur) (D Ore.) July 23, 1820–June 17, 1885; Senate 1861–67; House Dec. 1, 1873–75.

Nethercutt, George (R Wash.) Oct. 7, 1944– ; House 1995–2005.

Neuberger, Maurine Brown (widow of Richard Lewis Neuberger) (D Ore.) Jan. 9, 1907–Feb. 22, 2000; Senate Nov. 9, 1960–67.

Neuberger, Richard Lewis (husband of Maurine Brown Neuberger) (D Ore.) Dec. 26, 1912–March 9, 1960; Senate 1955–March 9, 1960.

Neugebauer, Randy (R Texas) Dec. 24, 1949– ; House June 3, 2003– .

Neumann, Mark W. (R Wis.) Feb. 27, 1954– ; House 1995–99.

Neville, Joseph (– Va.) 1730–March 4, 1819; House 1793–95.

Neville, William (cousin of Bird Segle McGuire) (P Neb.) Dec. 29, 1843–April 5, 1909; House Dec. 4, 1899–1903.

Nevin, Robert Murphy (R Ohio) May 5, 1850–Dec. 17, 1912; House 1901–07.

New, Anthony (R Ky.) 1747–March 2, 1833; House 1793–1805 (1793–95 no party Va.), 1811–13, 1817–19, 1821–23.

New, Harry Stewart (R Ind.) Dec. 31, 1858–May 9, 1937; Senate 1917–23; chair Rep. Nat. Comm. 1907–08; postmaster general March 4, 1923–March 5, 1929.

New, Jeptha Dudley (D Ind.) Nov. 28, 1830–July 9, 1892; House 1875–77, 1879–81.

Newberry, John Stoughton (father of Truman Handy Newberry) (R Mich.) Nov. 18, 1826–Jan. 2, 1887; House 1879–81.

Newberry, Truman Handy (son of John Stoughton Newberry) (R Mich.) Nov. 5, 1864–Oct. 3, 1945; Senate 1919–Nov. 18, 1922; secretary of the navy Dec. 1, 1908–March 5, 1909.

Newberry, Walter Cass (D Ill.) Dec. 23, 1835–July 20, 1912; House 1891–93.

Newbold, Thomas (R N.J.) Aug. 2, 1760–Dec. 18, 1823; House 1807–13.

Newcomb, Carman Adam (R Mo.) July 1, 1830–April 6, 1902; House 1867–69.

Newell, William Augustus (R N.J.) Sept. 5, 1817–Aug. 8, 1901; House 1847–51 (Whig), 1865–67; Gov. Jan. 20, 1857–Jan. 17, 1860, (Wash. Terr.) 1880–84.

Newhall, Judson Lincoln (R Ky.) March 26, 1870–July 23, 1952; House 1929–31.

Newhard, Peter (D Pa.) July 26, 1783–Feb. 19, 1860; House 1839–43.

Newlands, Francis Griffith (D Nev.) Aug. 28, 1848–Dec. 24, 1917; House 1893–1903; Senate 1903–Dec. 24, 1917.

Newman, Alexander (D Va.) Oct. 5, 1804–Sept. 8, 1849; House March 4–Sept. 8, 1849.

Newnan, Daniel (– Ga.) about 1780–Jan. 16, 1851; House 1831–33.

Newsham, Joseph Parkinson (R La.) May 24, 1837–Oct. 22, 1919; House July 18, 1868–69, May 23, 1870–71.

Newsome, John Parks (D Ala.) Feb. 13, 1893–Nov. 10, 1961; House 1943–45.

Newton, Cherubusco (D La.) May 15, 1848–May 26, 1910; House 1887–89.

Newton, Cleveland Alexander (R Mo.) Sept. 3, 1873–Sept. 17, 1945; House 1919–27.

Newton, Eben (W Ohio) Oct. 16, 1795–Nov. 6, 1885; House 1851–53.

Newton, Thomas Jr. (R Va.) Nov. 21, 1768–Aug. 5, 1847; House 1801–29, March 4, 1829–March 9, 1830, 1831–33.

Newton, Thomas Willoughby (W Ark.) Jan. 18, 1804–Sept. 22, 1853; House Feb. 6–March 3, 1847.

Newton, Walter Hughes (R Minn.) Oct. 10, 1880–Aug. 10, 1941; House 1919–June 30, 1929.

Newton, Willoughby (W Va.) Dec. 2, 1802–May 23, 1874; House 1843–45.

Ney, Robert William W. "Bob" (R Ohio) July 5, 1954– ; House 1995– ; chair House Administration 2001– .

Niblack, Silas Leslie (cousin of William Ellis Niblack) (D Fla.) March 17, 1825–Feb. 13, 1883; House Jan. 29–March 3, 1873.

Niblack, William Ellis (cousin of Silas Leslie Niblack) (D Ind.) May 19, 1822–May 7, 1893; House Dec. 7, 1857–61, 1865–75.

Nicholas, John (brother of Wilson Cary Nicholas, uncle of Robert Carter Nicholas) (R Va.) about 1757–Dec. 31, 1819; House 1793–1801 (1793–95 no party).

Nicholas, Robert Carter (nephew of John Nicholas and Wilson Cary Nicholas) (D La.) 1793–Dec. 24, 1857; Senate Jan. 13, 1836–41.

Nicholas, Wilson Cary (brother of John Nicholas, uncle of Robert Carter Nicholas) (R Va.) Jan. 31, 1761–Oct. 10, 1820; Senate Dec. 5, 1799–May 22, 1804; House 1807–Nov. 27, 1809; Gov. Dec. 1, 1814–Dec. 1, 1816.

Nicholls, John Calhoun (D Ga.) April 25, 1834–Dec. 25, 1893; House 1879–81, 1883–85.

Nicholls, Samuel Jones (D S.C.) May 7, 1885–Nov. 23, 1937; House Sept. 14, 1915–21.

Nicholls, Thomas David (ID Pa.) Sept. 16, 1870–Jan. 19, 1931; House 1907–11.

Nichols, Charles Archibald (R Mich.) Aug. 25, 1876–April 25, 1920; House 1915–April 25, 1920.

Nichols, John (I N.C.) Nov. 14, 1834–Sept. 22, 1917; House 1887–89.

Nichols, John Conover (D Okla.) Aug. 31, 1896–Nov. 7, 1945; House 1935–July 3, 1943.

Nichols, Matthias H. (R Ohio) Oct. 3, 1824–Sept. 15, 1862; House 1853–59 (1853–55 Democrat).

Nichols, Richard (R Kan.) April 29, 1926– ; House 1991–93.

Nichols, William Flynt (D Ala.) Oct. 16, 1918–Dec. 13, 1988; House 1967–Dec. 13, 1988.

Nicholson, Alfred Osborn Pope (D Tenn.) Aug. 31, 1808–March 23, 1876; Senate Dec. 25, 1840–Feb. 7, 1842, 1859–61.

Nicholson, Donald William (R Mass.) Aug. 11, 1888–Feb. 16, 1968; House Nov. 18, 1947–59.

Nicholson, John (R N.Y.) 1765–Jan. 20, 1820; House 1809–11.

Nicholson, John Anthony (D Del.) Nov. 17, 1827–Nov. 4, 1906; House 1865–69.

Nicholson, Joseph Hopper (R Md.) May 15, 1770–March 4, 1817; House 1799–March 1, 1806.

Nicholson, Samuel Danford (R Colo.) Feb. 22, 1859–March 24, 1923; Senate 1921–March 24, 1923.

Nickles, Donald Lee "Don" (R Okla.) Dec. 6, 1948– ; Senate 1981–2005; chair Senate Budget 2003–05.

Nicoll, Henry (D N.Y.) Oct. 23, 1812–Nov. 28, 1879; House 1847–49.

Niedringhaus, Frederick Gottlieb (uncle of Henry Frederick Niedringhaus) (R Mo.) Oct. 21, 1837–Nov. 25, 1922; House 1889–91.

Niedringhaus, Henry Frederick (nephew of Frederick Gottlieb Niedringhaus) (R Mo.) Dec. 15, 1864–Aug. 3, 1941; House 1927–33.

Nielson, Howard Curtis (R Utah) Sept. 12, 1924– ; House 1983–91.

Niles, Jason (R Miss.) Dec. 19, 1814–July 7, 1894; House 1873–75.

Niles, John Milton (D Conn.) Aug. 20, 1787–May 31, 1856; Senate Dec. 21, 1835–39, 1843–49; postmaster general May 26, 1840–March 3, 1841.

Niles, Nathaniel (– Vt.) April 3, 1741–Oct. 31, 1828; House Oct. 17, 1791–95.

Nimtz, F. Jay (R Ind.) Dec. 1, 1915–Dec. 6, 1990; House 1957–59.

Nisbet, Eugenius Aristides (cousin of Mark Anthony Cooper) (W Ga.) Dec. 7, 1803–March 18, 1871; House 1839–Oct. 12, 1841.

Niven, Archibald Campbell (D N.Y.) Dec. 8, 1803–Feb. 21, 1882; House 1845–47.

Nix, Robert Nelson Cornelius Sr. (D Pa.) Aug. 9, 1905–June 22, 1987; House May 20, 1958–79; chair House Post Office and Civil Service 1977–79.

Nixon, George Stuart (R Nev.) April 2, 1860–June 5, 1912; Senate 1905–June 5, 1912.

Nixon, John Thompson (R N.J.) Aug. 31, 1820–Sept. 28, 1889; House 1859–63.

Nixon, Richard Milhous (R Calif.) Jan. 9, 1913–April 22, 1994; House 1947–Nov. 30, 1950; Senate Dec. 1, 1950–Jan. 1, 1953; vice president 1953–61; president 1969–Aug. 9, 1974.

Noble, David Addison (D Mich.) Nov. 9, 1802–Oct. 13, 1876; House 1853–55.

Noble, James (R Ind.) Dec. 16, 1785–Feb. 26, 1831; Senate Dec. 11, 1816–Feb. 26, 1831.

Noble, Warren Perry (D Ohio) June 14, 1820–July 9, 1903; House 1861–65.

Noble, William Henry (D N.Y.) Sept. 22, 1788–Feb. 5, 1850; House 1837–39.

Nodar, Robert Joseph Jr. (R N.Y.) March 23, 1916–Sept. 11, 1974; House 1947–49.

Noell, John William (father of Thomas Estes Noell) (UU Mo.) Feb. 22, 1816–March 14, 1863; House 1859–March 14, 1863 (1859–63 Democrat).

Noell, Thomas Estes (son of John William Noell) (D Mo.) April 3, 1839–Oct. 3, 1867; House 1865–Oct. 3, 1867 (1865–67 Republican).

Nolan, John Ignatius (husband of Mae Ella Nolan) (R Calif.) Jan. 14, 1874–Nov. 18, 1922; House 1913–Nov. 18, 1922.

Nolan, Mae Ella (widow of John Ignatius Nolan) (R Calif.) Sept. 20, 1886–July 9, 1973; House Jan. 23, 1923–25.

Nolan, Michael Nicholas (D N.Y.) May 4, 1833–May 31, 1905; House 1881–83.

Nolan, Richard Michael (D Minn.) Dec. 17, 1943– ; House 1975–81.

Nolan, William Ignatius (R Minn.) May 14, 1874–Aug. 3, 1943; House June 17, 1929–33.

Noland, James Ellsworth (D Ind.) April 22, 1920–Aug. 12, 1992; House 1949–51.

Noonan, Edward Thomas (D Ill.) Oct. 23, 1861–Dec. 19, 1923; House 1899–1901.

Noonan, George Henry (R Texas) Aug. 20, 1828–Aug. 17, 1907; House 1895–97.

Norbeck, Peter (R S.D.) Aug. 27, 1870–Dec. 20, 1936; Senate 1921–Dec. 20, 1936; Gov. Jan. 2, 1917–Jan. 4, 1921.

Norblad, Albin Walter Jr. (R Ore.) Sept. 12, 1908–Sept. 20, 1964; House Jan. 11, 1946–Sept. 20, 1964.

Norcross, Amasa (R Mass.) Jan. 26, 1824–April 2, 1898; House 1877–83.

Norman, Fred Barthold (R Wash.) March 21, 1882–April 18, 1947; House 1943–45, Jan. 3–April 18, 1947.

Norrell, Catherine Dorris (widow of William Frank Norrell) (D Ark.) March 30, 1901–Aug. 26, 1981; House April 18, 1961–63.

Norrell, William Frank (husband of Catherine Dorris Norrell) (D Ark.) Aug. 29, 1896–Feb. 15, 1961; House 1939–Feb. 15, 1961.

Norris, Benjamin White (R Ala.) Jan. 22, 1819–Jan. 26, 1873; House July 21, 1868–69.

Norris, George William (IR Neb.) July 11, 1861–Sept. 2, 1944; House 1903–13 (Republican); Senate 1913–43 (1913–37 Republican).

Norris, Moses Jr. (D N.H.) Nov. 8, 1799–Jan. 11, 1855; House 1843–47; Senate 1849–Jan. 11, 1855.

North, Solomon Taylor (R Pa.) May 24, 1853–Oct. 19, 1917; House 1915–17.

North, William (F N.Y.) 1755–Jan. 3, 1836; Senate May 5–Aug. 17, 1798.

Northup, Anne M. (R Ky.) Jan. 22, 1948– ; House 1997– .

Northway, Stephen Asa (R Ohio) June 19, 1833–Sept. 8, 1898; House 1893–Sept. 8, 1898.

Norton, Daniel Sheldon (U Minn.) April 12, 1829–July 13, 1870; Senate 1865–July 13, 1870.

Norton, Ebenezer Foote (J N.Y.) Nov. 7, 1774–May 11, 1851; House 1829–31.

Norton, Eleanor Holmes (D D.C.) June 13, 1937– ; House (Del.) 1991– .

Norton, Elijah Hise (D Mo.) Nov. 24, 1821–Aug. 6, 1914; House 1861–63.

Norton, James (D S.C.) Oct. 8, 1843–Oct. 14, 1920; House Dec. 6, 1897–1901.

Norton, James Albert (D Ohio) Nov. 11, 1843–July 24, 1912; House 1897–1903.

Norton, Jesse Olds (R Ill.) Dec. 25, 1812–Aug. 3, 1875; House 1853–57 (1853–55 Whig), 1863–65.

Norton, John Nathaniel (D Neb.) May 12, 1878–Oct. 5, 1960; House 1927–29, 1931–33.

Norton, Mary Teresa (D N.J.) March 7, 1875–Aug. 2, 1959; House 1925–51; chair House Administration 1949–51.

Norton, Miner Gibbs (R Ohio) May 11, 1857–Sept. 7, 1926; House 1921–23.

Norton, Nelson Ira (R N.Y.) March 30, 1820–Oct. 28, 1887; House Dec. 6, 1875–77.

Norton, Patrick Daniel (R N.D.) May 17, 1876–Oct. 14, 1953; House 1913–19.

Norton, Richard Henry (D Mo.) Nov. 6, 1849–March 15, 1918; House 1889–93.

Norvell, John (D Mich.) Dec. 21, 1789–April 24, 1850; Senate Jan. 26, 1837–41.

Norwood, Charlie (R Ga.) July 27, 1941– ; House 1995– .

Norwood, Thomas Manson (D Ga.) April 26, 1830–June 19, 1913; Senate Nov. 14, 1871–77; House 1885–89.

Nott, Abraham (F S.C.) Feb. 5, 1768–June 19, 1830; House 1799–1801.

Nourse, Amos (– Maine) Dec. 17, 1794–April 7, 1877; Senate Jan. 16–March 3, 1857.

Nowak, Henry James (D N.Y.) Feb. 21, 1935– ; House 1975–93.

Noyes, John (F Vt.) April 2, 1764–Oct. 26, 1841; House 1815–17.

Noyes, Joseph Cobham (W Maine) Sept. 22, 1798–July 28, 1868; House 1837–39.

Nuckolls, Stephen Friel (D Wyo.) Aug. 16, 1825–Feb. 14, 1879; House (Terr. Del.) Dec. 6, 1869–71.

Nuckolls, William Thompson (J S.C.) Feb. 23, 1801–Sept. 27, 1855; House 1827–33.

Nugen, Robert Hunter (D Ohio) July 16, 1809–Feb. 28, 1872; House 1861–63.

Nugent, John Frost (D Idaho) June 28, 1868–Sept. 18, 1931; Senate Jan. 22, 1918–Jan. 14, 1921.

Nunes, Devin (R Calif.) Oct. 1, 1973– ; House 2003– .

Nunn, David Alexander (R Tenn.) July 26, 1833–Sept. 11, 1918; House 1867–69, 1873–75.

Nunn, Samuel Augustus (great-nephew of Carl Vinson) (D Ga.) Sept. 8, 1938– ; Senate Nov. 8, 1972–97; chair Senate Armed Services 1987–95.

Nussle, James (R Iowa) June 27, 1960– ; House 1991– ; chair House Budget 2001– .

Nute, Alonzo (R N.H.) Feb. 12, 1826–Dec. 24, 1892; House 1889–91.

Nutting, Newton Wright (R N.Y.) Oct. 22, 1840–Oct. 15, 1889; House 1883–85, 1887–Oct. 15, 1889.

Nye, Frank Mellen (R Minn.) March 7, 1852–Nov. 29, 1935; House 1907–13.

Nye, Gerald Prentice (R N.D.) Dec. 19, 1892–July 17, 1971; Senate Nov. 14, 1925–45.

Nye, James Warren (R Nev.) June 10, 1815–Dec. 25, 1876; Senate Dec. 16, 1864–73; Gov. (Nev. Terr.) 1861–64.

Nygaard, Hjalmar Carl (R N.D.) March 24, 1906–July 18, 1963; House 1961–July 18, 1963.

Oakar, Mary Rose (D Ohio) March 5, 1940– ; House 1977–93.

Oakey, Peter Davis (R Conn.) Feb. 25, 1861–Nov. 18, 1920; House 1915–17.

Oakley, Thomas Jackson (F N.Y.) Nov. 10, 1783–May 11, 1857; House 1813–15, 1827–May 9, 1828.

Oakman, Charles Gibb (R Mich.) Sept. 4, 1903–Oct. 28, 1973; House 1953–55.

Oates, William Calvin (D Ala.) Nov. 30, 1835–Sept. 9, 1910; House 1881–Nov. 5, 1894; Gov. Dec. 1, 1894–Dec. 1, 1896.

Obama, Barack (D Ill.) Aug. 4, 1961– ; Senate 2005– .

Oberstar, James Louis (D Minn.) Sept. 10, 1934– ; House 1975– .

Obey, David Ross (D Wis.) Oct. 3, 1938– ; House April 1, 1969– ; chair House Appropriations 1994–95.

O'Brien, Charles Francis Xavier (D N.J.) March 7, 1879–Nov. 14, 1940; House 1921–25.

O'Brien, George Donoghue (D Mich.) Jan. 1, 1900–Oct. 25, 1957; House 1937–39, 1941–47, 1949–55.

O'Brien, George Miller (R Ill.) June 17, 1917–July 17, 1986; House 1973–July 17, 1986.

O'Brien, James (ID N.Y.) March 13, 1841–March 5, 1907; House 1879–81.

O'Brien, James Henry (D N.Y.) July 15, 1860–Sept. 2, 1924; House 1913–15.

O'Brien, Jeremiah (– Maine) Jan. 21, 1778–May 30, 1858; House 1823–29.

O'Brien, Joseph John (R N.Y.) Oct. 9, 1897–Jan. 23, 1953; House 1939–45.

O'Brien, Leo William (D N.Y.) Sept. 21, 1900–May 4, 1982; House April 1, 1952–67.

O'Brien, Thomas Joseph (D Ill.) April 30, 1878–April 14, 1964; House 1933–39, 1943–April 14, 1964.

O'Brien, William James (D Md.) May 28, 1836–Nov. 13, 1905; House 1873–77.

O'Brien, William Smith (D W.Va.) Jan. 8, 1862–Aug. 10, 1948; House 1927–29.

Ocampo, Pablo (– P.I.) Jan. 25, 1853–Feb. 5, 1925; House (Res. Comm.) Nov. 22, 1907–Nov. 22, 1909.

Ochiltree, Thomas Peck (I Texas) Oct. 26, 1837–Nov. 25, 1902; House 1883–85.

O'Connell, David Joseph (D N.Y.) Dec. 25, 1868–Dec. 29, 1930; House 1919–21, 1923–Dec. 29, 1930.

O'Connell, Jeremiah Edward (D R.I.) July 8, 1883–Sept. 18, 1964; House 1923–27, 1929–May 9, 1930.

O'Connell, Jerry Joseph (D Mont.) June 14, 1909–Jan. 16, 1956; House 1937–39.

O'Connell, John Matthew (D R.I.) Aug. 10, 1872–Dec. 6, 1941; House 1933–39.

O'Connell, Joseph Francis (D Mass.) Dec. 7, 1872–Dec. 10, 1942; House 1907–11.

O'Connor, Charles (R Okla.) Oct. 26, 1878–Nov. 15, 1940; House 1929–31.

O'Connor, James (D La.) April 4, 1870–Jan. 7, 1941; House June 5, 1919–31.

O'Connor, James Francis (D Mont.) May 7, 1878–Jan. 15, 1945; House 1937–Jan. 15, 1945.

O'Connor, John Joseph (D N.Y.) Nov. 23, 1885–Jan. 26, 1960; House Nov. 6, 1923–39.

O'Connor, Michael Patrick (D S.C.) Sept. 29, 1831–April 26, 1881; House 1879–81 (received credentials for the term beginning 1881 but died pending contest).

O'Conor, Herbert Romulus (D Md.) Nov. 17, 1896–March 4, 1960; Senate 1947–53; Gov. Jan. 11, 1939–Jan. 3, 1947.

O'Daniel, Wilbert Lee "Pappy" (D Texas) March 11, 1890–May 11, 1969; Senate Aug. 4, 1941–49; Gov. Jan. 17, 1939–Aug. 4, 1941.

O'Day, Caroline Love Goodwin (D N.Y.) June 22, 1875–Jan. 4, 1943; House 1935–43.

Oddie, Tasker Lowndes (R Nev.) Oct. 20, 1870–Feb. 17, 1950; Senate 1921–33; Gov. Jan. 2, 1911–Jan. 4, 1915.

Odell, Benjamin Baker Jr. (R N.Y.) Jan. 14, 1854–May 9, 1926; House 1895–99; Gov. Jan. 1, 1901–Jan. 1, 1905.

Odell, Moses Fowler (D N.Y.) Feb. 24, 1818–June 13, 1866; House 1861–65.

Odell, Nathaniel Holmes (D N.Y.) Oct. 10, 1828–Oct. 30, 1904; House 1875–77.

O'Donnell, James (R Mich.) March 25, 1840–March 17, 1915; House 1885–93.

O'Ferrall, Charles Triplett (D Va.) Oct. 21, 1840–Sept. 22, 1905; House May 5, 1884–Dec. 28, 1893; Gov. Jan. 1, 1894–Jan. 1, 1898.

Ogden, Aaron (F N.J.) Dec. 3, 1756–April 19, 1839; Senate Feb. 28, 1801–03; Gov. Oct. 29, 1812–Oct. 29, 1813.

Ogden, Charles Franklin (R Ky.) ?–April 10, 1933; House 1919–23.

Ogden, David A. (F N.Y.) Jan. 10, 1770–June 9, 1829; House 1817–19.

Ogden, Henry Warren (D La.) Oct. 21, 1842–July 23, 1905; House May 12, 1894–99.

Ogle, Alexander (father of Charles Ogle, grandfather of Andrew Jackson Ogle) (R Pa.) Aug. 10, 1766–Oct. 14, 1832; House 1817–19.

Ogle, Andrew Jackson (grandson of Alexander Ogle, nephew of Charles Ogle) (W Pa.) March 25, 1822–Oct. 14, 1852; House 1849–51.

Ogle, Charles (son of Alexander Ogle, uncle of Andrew Jackson Ogle) (W Pa.) 1798–May 10, 1841; House 1837–May 10, 1841 (1837–41 Anti-Mason).

Oglesby, Richard James (cousin of Woodson Ratcliffe Oglesby) (R Ill.) July 25, 1824–April 24, 1899; Senate 1873–79; Gov. Jan. 16, 1865–Jan. 11, 1869, Jan. 13–Jan. 23, 1873, Jan. 30, 1885–Jan. 14, 1889.

Oglesby, Woodson Ratcliffe (cousin of Richard James Oglesby) (D N.Y.) Feb. 9, 1867–April 30, 1955; House 1913–17.

O'Gorman, James Aloysius (D N.Y.) May 5, 1860–May 17, 1943; Senate 1911–17.

O'Grady, James Mary Early (R N.Y.) March 31, 1863–Nov. 3, 1928; House 1899–1901.

O'Hair, Frank Trimble (D Ill.) March 12, 1870–Aug. 3, 1932; House 1913–15.

O'Hara, Barratt (D Ill.) April 28, 1882–Aug. 11, 1969; House 1949–51, 1953–69.

O'Hara, James Edward (R N.C.) Feb. 26, 1844–Sept. 15, 1905; House 1883–87.

O'Hara, James Grant (D Mich.) Nov. 8, 1925–March 13, 1989; House 1959–77.

O'Hara, Joseph Patrick (R Minn.) Jan. 23, 1895–March 4, 1975; House 1941–59.

Ohliger, Lewis Philip (D Ohio) Jan. 3, 1843–Jan. 9, 1923; House Dec. 5, 1892–93.

O'Konski, Alvin Edward (R Wis.) May 26, 1904–July 8, 1987; House 1943–73.

Olcott, Jacob Van Vechten (R N.Y.) May 17, 1856–June 1, 1940; House 1905–11.

Olcott, Simeon (F N.H.) Oct. 1, 1735–Feb. 22, 1815; Senate June 17, 1801–05.

Oldfield, Pearl Peden (widow of William Allan Oldfield) (D Ark.) Dec. 2, 1876–April 12, 1962; House Jan. 9, 1929–31.

Oldfield, William Allan (husband of Pearl Peden Oldfield) (D Ark.) Feb. 4, 1874–Nov. 19, 1928; House 1909–Nov. 19, 1928.

Olds, Edson Baldwin (D Ohio) June 3, 1802–Jan. 24, 1869; House 1849–55.

O'Leary, Denis (D N.Y.) Jan. 22, 1863–Sept. 27, 1943; House 1913–Dec. 31, 1914.

O'Leary, James Aloysius (D N.Y.) April 23, 1889–March 16, 1944; House 1935–March 16, 1944.

Olin, Abram Baldwin (son of Gideon Olin, cousin of Henry Olin) (R N.Y.) Sept. 21, 1808–July 7, 1879; House 1857–63.

Olin, Gideon (father of Abram Baldwin Olin, uncle of Henry Olin) (R Vt.) Nov. 2, 1743–Jan. 21, 1823; House 1803–07.

Olin, Henry (nephew of Gideon Olin, cousin of Abram Baldwin Olin) (– Vt.) May 7, 1768–Aug. 16, 1837; House Dec. 13, 1824–25.

Olin, James R. (D Va.) Feb. 28, 1920– ; House 1983–93.

Oliver, Andrew (D N.Y.) Jan. 16, 1815–March 6, 1889; House 1853–57.

Oliver, Daniel Charles (D N.Y.) Oct. 6, 1865–March 26, 1924; House 1917–19.

Oliver, Frank (D N.Y.) Oct. 2, 1883–Jan. 1, 1968; House 1923–June 18, 1934.

Oliver, George Tener (R Pa.) Jan. 26, 1848–Jan. 22, 1919; Senate March 17, 1909–17.

Oliver, James Churchill (D Maine) Aug. 6, 1895–Dec. 25, 1986; House 1937–43 (Republican), 1959–61.

Oliver, John (D Mass.) Aug. 6, 1895–Dec. 25, 1986; House 1937–43 (Republican), 1959–61.

Oliver, Mordecai (W Mo.) Oct. 22, 1819–April 25, 1898; House 1853–57.

Oliver, Samuel Addison (R Iowa) July 21, 1833–July 7, 1912; House 1875–79.

Oliver, William Bacon (cousin of Sydney Parham Epes) (D Ala.) May 23, 1867–May 27, 1948; House 1915–37.

Oliver, William Morrison (D N.Y.) Oct. 15, 1792–July 21, 1863; House 1841–43.

Olmsted, Marlin Edgar (R Pa.) May 21, 1847–July 19, 1913; House 1897–1913.

Olney, Richard (D Mass.) Jan. 5, 1871–Jan. 15, 1939; House 1915–21.

O'Loughlin, Kathryn Ellen (later married and served as Kathryn O'Loughlin McCarthy) (D Kan.) April 24, 1894–Jan. 16, 1952; House 1933–35.

Olpp, Archibald Ernest (R N.J.) May 12, 1882–July 26, 1949; House 1921–23.

Olsen, Arnold (D Mont.) Dec. 17, 1916–Oct. 9, 1990; House 1961–71.

Olson, Alec Gehard (DFL Minn.) Sept. 11, 1930– ; House 1963–67.

Olver, John Walker (D Mass.) Sept. 3, 1936– ; House June 18, 1991– .

O'Mahoney, Joseph Christopher (D Wyo.) Nov. 5, 1884–Dec. 1, 1962; Senate Jan. 1, 1934–53, Nov. 29, 1954–61; chair Senate Interior and Insular Affairs 1949–53.

O'Malley, Matthew Vincent (D N.Y.) June 26, 1878–May 26, 1931; House March 4–May 26, 1931.

O'Malley, Thomas David Patrick (D Wis.) March 24, 1903–Dec. 19, 1979; House 1933–39.

O'Neal, Emmet (D Ky.) April 14, 1887–July 18, 1967; House 1935–47.

O'Neal, Maston Emmett Jr. (D Ga.) July 19, 1907–Jan. 9, 1990; House 1965–71.

O'Neall, John Henry (D Ind.) Oct. 30, 1838–July 15, 1907; House 1887–91.

O'Neil, Joseph Henry (D Mass.) March 23, 1853–Feb. 19, 1935; House 1889–95.

O'Neill, Charles (R Pa.) March 21, 1821–Nov. 25, 1893; House 1863–71, 1873–Nov. 25, 1893.

O'Neill, Edward Leo (D N.J.) July 10, 1903–Dec. 12, 1948; House 1937–39.

O'Neill, Harry Patrick (D Pa.) Feb. 10, 1889–June 24, 1953; House 1949–53.

O'Neill, John (D Ohio) Dec. 17, 1822–May 25, 1905; House 1863–65.

O'Neill, John Joseph (D Mo.) June 25, 1846–Feb. 19, 1898; House 1883–89, 1891–93, April 3, 1894–95.

O'Neill, Thomas Phillip "Tip" Jr. (D Mass.) Dec. 9, 1912–Jan. 5, 1994; House 1953–87; House majority leader 1973–77; Speaker Jan. 4, 1977–79, Jan. 15, 1979–81, Jan. 5, 1981–87.

O'Reilly, Daniel (ID N.Y.) June 3, 1838–Sept. 23, 1911; House 1879–81.

Ormsby, Stephen (R Ky.) 1759–1844; House 1811–13, April 20, 1813–17.

Orr, Alexander Dalrymple (nephew of William Grayson, cousin of William John Grayson) (R Ky.) Nov. 6, 1761–June 21, 1835; House Nov. 8, 1792–97 (Nov. 8, 1792–95 no party).

Orr, Benjamin (F Mass.) Dec. 1, 1772–Sept. 3, 1828; House 1817–19.

Orr, Jackson (R Iowa) Sept. 21, 1832–March 15, 1926; House 1871–75.

Orr, James Lawrence (D S.C.) May 12, 1822–May 5, 1873; House 1849–59; Speaker Dec. 7, 1857–59; Gov. Nov. 29, 1865–July 6, 1868 (Republican).

Orr, Robert Jr. (– Pa.) March 5, 1786–May 22, 1876; House Oct. 11, 1825–29.

Orth, Godlove Stein (R Ind.) April 22, 1817–Dec. 16, 1882; House 1863–71, 1873–75, 1879–Dec. 16, 1882.

Ortiz, Solomon Porfirio (D Texas) June 3, 1938– ; House 1983– .

Orton, William (D Utah) Sept. 22, 1949– ; House 1991–97.

Osborn, Thomas Ward (R Fla.) March 9, 1836–Dec. 18, 1898; Senate June 25, 1868–73.

Osborne, Edwin Sylvanus (R Pa.) Aug. 7, 1839–Jan. 1, 1900; House 1885–91.

Osborne, Henry Zenas (R Calif.) Oct. 4, 1848–Feb. 8, 1923; House 1917–Feb. 8, 1923.

Osborne, John Eugene (D Wyo.) June 19, 1858–April 24, 1943; House 1897–99; Gov. Jan. 2, 1893–Jan. 7, 1895.

Osborne, Thomas Burr (W Conn.) July 8, 1798–Sept. 2, 1869; House 1839–43.

Osborne, Thomas "Tom" (R Neb.) Feb. 23, 1937– ; House 2001– .

Ose, Doug (R Calif.) June 27, 1955– ; House 1999–2005.

Osgood, Gayton Pickman (J Mass.) July 4, 1797–June 26, 1861; House 1833–35.

O'Shaunessy, George Francis (D R.I.) May 1, 1868–Nov. 28, 1934; House 1911–19.

Osias, Camilo (Nat. P.I.) March 23, 1889–May 20, 1976; House (Res. Comm.) 1929–35.

Osmer, James H. (R Pa.) Jan. 23, 1832–Oct. 3, 1912; House 1879–81.

Osmers, Frank Charles Jr. (R N.J.) Dec. 30, 1907–May 21, 1977; House 1939–43, Nov. 6, 1951–65.

Ostertag, Harold Charles (R N.Y.) June 22, 1896–May 2, 1985; House 1951–65.

O'Sullivan, Eugene Daniel (D Neb.) May 31, 1883–Feb. 7, 1968; House 1949–51.

O'Sullivan, Patrick Brett (D Conn.) Aug. 11, 1887–Nov. 10, 1978; House 1923–25.

Otero, Mariano Sabino (nephew of Miguel Antonio Otero) (R N.M.) Aug. 29, 1844–Feb. 1, 1904; House (Terr. Del.) 1879–81.

Otero, Miguel Antonio (uncle of Mariano Sabino Otero) (D N.M.) June 21, 1829–May 30, 1882; House (Terr. Del.) July 23, 1856–61.

Otey, Peter Johnston (D Va.) Dec. 22, 1840–May 4, 1902; House 1895–May 4, 1902.

Otis, Harrison Gray (F Mass.) Oct. 8, 1765–Oct. 28, 1848; House 1797–1801; Senate 1817–May 30, 1822.

Otis, John (W Maine) Aug. 3, 1801–Oct. 17, 1856; House 1849–51.

Otis, John Grant (P Kan.) Feb. 10, 1838–Feb. 22, 1916; House 1891–93.

Otis, Norton Prentiss (R N.Y.) March 18, 1840–Feb. 20, 1905; House 1903–Feb. 20, 1905.

Otjen, Theobald (R Wis.) Oct. 27, 1851–April 11, 1924; House 1895–1907.

O'Toole, Donald Lawrence (D N.Y.) Aug. 1, 1902–Sept. 12, 1964; House 1937–53.

Otter, C. L. "Butch" (R Idaho) May 3, 1942– ; House 2001– .

Ottinger, Richard Lawrence (D N.Y.) Jan. 27, 1929– ; House 1965–71, 1975–85.

Oury, Granville Henderson (D Ariz.) March 12, 1825–Jan. 11, 1891; House (Terr. Del.) 1881–85.

Outhwaite, Joseph Hodson (D Ohio) Dec. 5, 1841–Dec. 9, 1907; House 1885–95.

Outland, George Elmer (D Calif.) Oct. 8, 1906–March 2, 1981; House 1943–47.

Outlaw, David (cousin of George Outlaw) (W N.C.) Sept. 14, 1806–Oct. 22, 1868; House 1847–53.

Outlaw, George (cousin of David Outlaw) (– N.C.) ?–Aug. 15, 1825; House Jan. 19–March 3, 1825.

Overman, Lee Slater (D N.C.) Jan. 3, 1854–Dec. 12, 1930; Senate 1903–Dec. 12, 1930.

Overmyer, Arthur Warren (D Ohio) May 31, 1879–March 8, 1952; House 1915–19.

Overstreet, James (– S.C.) Feb. 11, 1773–May 24, 1822; House 1819–May 24, 1822.

Overstreet, James Whetstone (D Ga.) Aug. 28, 1866–Dec. 4, 1938; House Oct. 3, 1906–07, 1917–23.

Overstreet, Jesse (R Ind.) Dec. 14, 1859–May 27, 1910; House 1895–1909.

Overton, Edward Jr. (R Pa.) Feb. 4, 1836–Sept. 18, 1903; House 1877–81.

Overton, John Holmes (uncle of Overton Brooks) (D La.) Sept. 17, 1875–May 14, 1948; House May 12, 1931–33; Senate 1933–May 14, 1948.

Overton, Walter Hampden (J La.) 1788–Dec. 24, 1845; House 1829–31.

Owen, Allen Ferdinand (W Ga.) Oct. 9, 1816–April 7, 1865; House 1849–51.

Owen, Emmett Marshall (D Ga.) Oct. 19, 1877–June 21, 1939; House 1933–June 21, 1939.

Owen, George Washington (– Ala.) Oct. 20, 1796–Aug. 18, 1837; House 1823–29.

Owen, James (R N.C.) Dec. 7, 1784–Sept. 4, 1865; House 1817–19.

Owen, Robert Dale (D Ind.) Nov. 7, 1801–June 24, 1877; House 1843–47.

Owen, Robert Latham (D Okla.) Feb. 3, 1856–July 19, 1947; Senate Dec. 11, 1907–25.

Owen, Ruth Bryan (later Mrs. Borge Rohde, daughter of William Jennings Bryan) (D Fla.) Oct. 2, 1885–July 26, 1954; House 1929–33.

Owen, William Dale (R Ind.) Sept. 6, 1846–1906; House 1885–91.

Owens, Douglas Wayne (D Utah) May 2, 1937–Dec. 18, 2002; House 1973–75, 1987–93.

Owens, George Welshman (D Ga.) Aug. 29, 1786–March 2, 1856; House 1835–39 (1835–37 Jacksonian).

Owens, James W. (D Ohio) Oct. 24, 1837–March 30, 1900; House 1889–93.

Owens, Major Robert Odell (D N.Y.) June 28, 1936– ; House 1983– .

Owens, Thomas Leonard (R Ill.) Dec. 21, 1897–June 7, 1948; House 1947–June 7, 1948.

Owens, William Claiborne (D Ky.) Oct. 17, 1849–Nov. 18, 1925; House 1895–97.

Owsley, Bryan Young (W Ky.) Aug. 19, 1798–Oct. 27, 1849; House 1841–43.

Oxley, Michael Garver (R Ohio) Feb. 11, 1944– ; House June 25, 1981– ; chair House Financial Services 2001– .

Pace, Stephen (D Ga.) March 9, 1891–April 5, 1970; House 1937–51.

Pacheco, Romualdo (R Calif.) Oct. 31, 1831–Jan. 23, 1899; House 1877–Feb. 7, 1878, 1879–83; Gov. Feb. 27–Dec. 9, 1875.

Packard, Jasper (R Ind.) Feb. 1, 1832–Dec. 13, 1899; House 1869–75.

Packard, Ronald C. (R Calif.) Jan. 19, 1931– ; House 1983–2001.

Packer, Asa (D Pa.) Dec. 29, 1805–May 17, 1879; House 1853–57.

Packer, Horace Billings (R Pa.) Oct. 11, 1851–April 13, 1940; House 1897–1901.

Packer, John Black (R Pa.) March 21, 1824–July 7, 1891; House 1869–77.

Packwood, Robert William (R Ore.) Sept. 11, 1932– ; Senate 1969–Oct. 1, 1995; chair Senate Commerce, Science, and Transportation 1981–85; chair Senate Finance 1985–87, 1995.

Paddock, Algernon Sidney (R Neb.) Nov. 9, 1830–Oct. 17, 1897; Senate 1875–81, 1887–93.

Paddock, George Arthur (R Ill.) March 24, 1885–Dec. 29, 1964; House 1941–43.

Padgett, Lemuel Phillips (D Tenn.) Nov. 28, 1855–Aug. 2, 1922; House 1901–Aug. 2, 1922.

Pagan, Bolivar (Coal. P.R.) May 16, 1897–Feb. 9, 1961; House (Res. Comm.) Dec. 26, 1939–45.

Page, Carroll Smalley (R Vt.) Jan. 10, 1843–Dec. 3, 1925; Senate Oct. 21, 1908–23; Gov. Oct. 2, 1890–Oct. 6, 1892.

Page, Charles Harrison (D R.I.) July 19, 1843–July 21, 1912; House Feb. 21–March 3, 1887, 1891–93, April 5, 1893–95.

Page, Henry (D Md.) June 28, 1841–Jan. 7, 1913; House 1891–Sept. 3, 1892.

Page, Horace Francis (R Calif.) Oct. 20, 1833–Aug. 23, 1890; House 1873–83.

Page, John (R Va.) April 17, 1743–Oct. 11, 1808; House 1789–97 (1789–95 no party); Gov. Dec. 1, 1802–Dec. 1, 1805 (Democratic Republican).

Page, John (W N.H.) May 21, 1787–Sept. 8, 1865; Senate June 8, 1836–37; Gov. June 5, 1839–June 2, 1842 (Democrat).

Page, Robert (F Va.) Feb. 4, 1765–Dec. 8, 1840; House 1799–1801.

Page, Robert Newton (D N.C.) Oct. 26, 1859–Oct. 3, 1933; House 1903–17.

Page, Sherman (J N.Y.) May 9, 1779–Sept. 27, 1853; House 1833–37.

Paige, Calvin DeWitt (R Mass.) May 20, 1848–April 24, 1930; House Nov. 26, 1913–25.

Paige, David Raymond (D Ohio) April 8, 1844–June 30, 1901; House 1883–85.

Paine, Elijah (F Vt.) Jan. 21, 1757–April 28, 1842; Senate 1795–Sept. 1, 1801 (1795–1801 no party).

Paine, Halbert Eleazer (R Wis.) Feb. 4, 1826–April 14, 1905; House 1865–71.

Paine, Robert Treat (AP N.C.) Feb. 18, 1812–Feb. 8, 1872; House 1855–57.

Paine, William Wiseham (D Ga.) Oct. 10, 1817–Aug. 5, 1882; House Dec. 22, 1870–71.

Palen, Rufus (W N.Y.) Feb. 25, 1807–April 26, 1844; House 1839–41.

Palfrey, John Gorham (W Mass.) May 2, 1796–April 26, 1881; House 1847–49.

Pallone, Frank Jr. (D N.J.) Oct. 30, 1951– ; House Nov. 8, 1988– .

Palmer, Alexander Mitchell (D Pa.) May 4, 1872–May 11, 1936; House 1909–15; attorney general March 5, 1919–March 5, 1921.

Palmer, Beriah (R N.Y.) 1740–May 20, 1812; House 1803–05.

Palmer, Cyrus Maffet (R Pa.) Feb. 12, 1887–Aug. 16, 1959; House 1927–29.

Palmer, Francis Wayland "Frank" (R Iowa) Oct. 11, 1827–Dec. 3, 1907; House 1869–73.

Palmer, George William (nephew of John Palmer, cousin of William Elisha Haynes) (R N.Y.) Jan. 13, 1818–March 2, 1916; House 1857–61.

Palmer, Henry Wilber (R Pa.) July 10, 1839–Feb. 15, 1913; House 1901–07, 1909–11.

Palmer, John (uncle of George William Palmer) (D N.Y.) Jan. 29, 1785–Dec. 8, 1840; House 1817–19 (Republican), 1837–39.

Palmer, John McAuley (D Ill.) Sept. 13, 1817–Sept. 25, 1900; Senate 1891–97; Gov. Jan. 11, 1869–Jan. 13, 1873 (Republican).

Palmer, John William (R Mo.) Aug. 20, 1866–Nov. 3, 1958; House 1929–31.

Palmer, Thomas Witherell (R Mich.) Jan. 25, 1830–June 1, 1913; Senate 1883–89.

Palmer, William Adams (R Vt.) Sept. 12, 1781–Dec. 3, 1860; Senate Oct. 20, 1818–25; Gov. Oct. 18, 1831–Nov. 2, 1835 (Anti-Mason Democrat).

Palmisano, Vincent Luke (D Md.) Aug. 5, 1882–Jan. 12, 1953; House 1927–39.

Panetta, Leon Edward (D Calif.) June 28, 1938– ; House 1977–Jan. 21, 1993; chair House Budget 1989–93.

Pantin, Santiago Iglesias. (See Iglesias, Santiago.)

Pappas, Michael (R N.J.) Dec. 29, 1960– ; House 1997–99.

Paredes, Quintin (Nat. P.I.) Sept. 9, 1884–Jan. 30, 1973; House (Res. Comm.) Feb. 14, 1936–Sept. 29, 1938.

Park, Frank (D Ga.) March 3, 1864–Nov. 20, 1925; House Nov. 5, 1913–25.

Parke, Benjamin (– Ind.) Sept. 22, 1777–July 12, 1835; House (Terr. Del.) Dec. 12, 1805–March 1, 1808.

Parker, Abraham X. (R N.Y.) Nov. 14, 1831–Aug. 9, 1909; House 1881–89.

Parker, Amasa Junius (D N.Y.) June 2, 1807–May 13, 1890; House 1837–39.

Parker, Andrew (D Pa.) May 21, 1805–Jan. 15, 1864; House 1851–53.

Parker, Homer Cling (D Ga.) Sept. 25, 1885–June 22, 1946; House Sept. 10, 1931–35.

Parker, Hosea Washington (D N.H.) May 30, 1833–Aug. 21, 1922; House 1871–75.

Parker, Isaac (F Mass.) June 17, 1768–July 25, 1830; House 1797–99.

Parker, Isaac Charles (R Mo.) Oct. 15, 1838–Nov. 17, 1896; House 1871–75.

Parker, James (R Mass.) 1768–Nov. 9, 1837; House 1813–15, 1819–21.

Parker, James (grandfather of Richard Wayne Parker) (J N.J.) March 3, 1776–April 1, 1868; House 1833–37.

Parker, James Southworth (R N.Y.) June 3, 1867–Dec. 19, 1933; House 1913–Dec. 19, 1933.

Parker, John Mason (R N.Y.) June 14, 1805–Dec. 16, 1873; House 1855–59 (1855–57 Whig).

Parker, Josiah (F Va.) May 11, 1751–March 11, 1810; House 1789–1801 (1789–95 no party).

Parker, Nahum (R N.H.) March 4, 1760–Nov. 12, 1839; Senate 1807–June 1, 1810.

Parker, Paul Michael "Mike" (R Miss.) Oct. 31, 1949– ; House 1989–99 (1993–Nov. 10, 1995, Democrat).

Parker, Richard (D Va.) Dec. 22, 1810–Nov. 10, 1893; House 1849–51.

Parker, Richard Elliott (J Va.) Dec. 27, 1783–Sept. 10, 1840; Senate Dec. 12, 1836–March 13, 1837.

Parker, Richard Wayne (grandson of James Parker) (R N.J.) Aug. 6, 1848–Nov. 28, 1923; House 1895–1911, Dec. 1, 1914–19, 1921–23.

Parker, Samuel Wilson (W Ind.) Sept. 9, 1805–Feb. 1, 1859; House 1851–55.

Parker, Severn Eyre (– Va.) July 19, 1787–Oct. 21, 1836; House 1819–21.

Parker, William Henry (– S.D.) May 5, 1847–June 26, 1908; House 1907–June 26, 1908.

Parks, Gorham (J Maine) May 27, 1794–Nov. 23, 1877; House 1833–37.

Parks, Tilman Bacon (D Ark.) May 14, 1872–Feb. 12, 1950; House 1921–37.

Parmenter, William (D Mass.) March 30, 1789–Feb. 25, 1866; House 1837–45.

Parran, Thomas (R Md.) Feb. 12, 1860–March 29, 1955; House 1911–13.

Parrett, William Fletcher (D Ind.) Aug. 10, 1825–June 30, 1895; House 1889–93.

Parris, Albion Keith (cousin of Virgil Delphini Parris) (R Maine) Jan. 19, 1788–Feb. 11, 1857; House 1815–Feb. 3, 1818 (Mass.); Senate 1827–Aug. 26, 1828; Gov. Jan. 5, 1822–Jan. 3, 1827 (Democratic Republican).

Parris, Stanford E. (R Va.) Sept. 9, 1929– ; House 1973–75, 1981–91.

Parris, Virgil Delphini (cousin of Albion Keith Parris) (SRD Maine) Feb. 18, 1807–June 13, 1874; House May 29, 1838–41.

Parrish, Isaac (D Ohio) March 1804–Aug. 9, 1860; House 1839–41, 1845–47.

Parrish, Lucian Walton (D Texas) Jan. 10, 1878–March 27, 1922; House 1919–March 27, 1922.

Parrott, John Fabyan (– N.H.) Aug. 8, 1767–July 9, 1836; House 1817–19; Senate 1819–25.

Parrott, Marcus Junius (R Kan.) Oct. 27, 1828–Oct. 4, 1879; House (Terr. Del.) 1857–Jan. 29, 1861.

Parsons, Claude VanCleve (D Ill.) Oct. 7, 1895–May 23, 1941; House Nov. 4, 1930–41.

Parsons, Edward Young (D Ky.) Dec. 12, 1841–July 8, 1876; House 1875–July 8, 1876.

Parsons, Herbert (R N.Y.) Oct. 28, 1869–Sept. 16, 1925; House 1905–11.

Parsons, Richard Chappel (R Ohio) Oct. 10, 1826–Jan. 9, 1899; House 1873–75.

Partridge, Donald Barrows (R Maine) June 7, 1891–June 5, 1946; House 1931–33.

Partridge, Frank Charles (R Vt.) May 7, 1861–March 2, 1943; Senate Dec. 23, 1930–March 31, 1931.

Partridge, George (– Mass.) Feb. 8, 1740–July 7, 1828; House 1789–Aug. 14, 1790; Cont. Cong. 1779–85.

Partridge, Samuel (D N.Y.) Nov. 29, 1790–March 30, 1883; House 1841–43.

Paschal, Thomas Moore (D Texas) Dec. 15, 1845–Jan. 28, 1919; House 1893–95.

Pasco, Samuel (D Fla.) June 28, 1834–March 13, 1917; Senate May 19, 1887–April 18, 1899.

Pascrell, Bill Jr. (D N.J.) Jan. 25, 1937– ; House 1997– .

Pashayan, Charles "Chip" Jr. (R Calif.) March 27, 1941– ; House 1979–91.

Passman, Otto Ernest (D La.) June 27, 1900–Aug. 13, 1988; House 1947–77.

Pastor, Edward Lopez (D Ariz.) June 28, 1943– ; House Oct. 3, 1991– .

Pastore, John Orlando (D R.I.) March 17, 1907–July 15, 2000; Senate Dec. 19, 1950–Dec. 28, 1976; Gov. Oct. 6, 1945–Dec. 19, 1950.

Paterson, John (R N.Y.) 1744–July 19, 1808; House 1803–05.

Paterson, William (– N.J.) Dec. 24, 1745–Sept. 9, 1806; Senate 1789–Nov. 13, 1790; Cont. Cong. (elected but did not attend) 1780, 1787; Gov. Oct. 30, 1790–March 4, 1793 (Federalist); assoc. justice March 11, 1793–Sept. 9, 1806.

Patman, John William Wright (father of William Neff Patman) (D Texas) Aug. 6, 1893–March 7, 1976; House 1929–March 7, 1976; chair House Select Small Business 1949–53, 1955–63; chair House Banking and Currency 1963–75.

Patman, William Neff (son of John William Wright Patman) (D Texas) March 26, 1927– ; House 1981–85.

Patrick, Luther (D Ala.) Jan. 23, 1894–May 26, 1957; House 1937–43, 1945–47.

Patten, Edward James (D N.J.) Aug. 22, 1905–Sept. 17, 1994; House 1963–81.

Patten, Harold Ambrose (D Ariz.) Oct. 6, 1907–Sept. 6, 1969; House 1949–55.

Patten, John (R Del.) April 26, 1746–Dec. 26, 1800; House 1793–Feb. 14, 1794 (no party), 1795–97; Cont. Cong. 1786.

Patten, Thomas Gedney (D N.Y.) Sept. 12, 1861–Feb. 23, 1939; House 1911–17.

Patterson, David Trotter (D Tenn.) Feb. 28, 1818–Nov. 3, 1891; Senate May 4, 1865–69.

Patterson, Edward White (D Kan.) Oct. 4, 1895–March 6, 1940; House 1935–39.

Patterson, Elizabeth Johnston (daughter of Olin DeWitt Talmadge Johnston) (D S.C.) Nov. 18, 1939– ; House 1987–93.

Patterson, Ellis Ellwood (D Calif.) Nov. 28, 1897–Aug. 25, 1985; House 1945–47.

Patterson, Francis Ford Jr. (R N.J.) July 30, 1867–Nov. 30, 1935; House Nov. 2, 1920–27.

Patterson, George Robert (R Pa.) Nov. 9, 1863–March 21, 1906; House 1901–March 21, 1906.

Patterson, George Washington (brother of William Patterson, uncle of Augustus Frank) (R N.Y.) Nov. 11, 1799–Oct. 15, 1879; House 1877–79.

Patterson, Gilbert Brown (D N.C.) May 29, 1863–Jan. 26, 1922; House 1903–07.

Patterson, James O'Hanlon (D S.C.) June 25, 1857–Oct. 25, 1911; House 1905–11.

Patterson, James Thomas (R Conn.) Oct. 20, 1908–Feb. 7, 1989; House 1947–59.

Patterson, James Willis (R N.H.) July 2, 1823–May 4, 1893; House 1863–67; Senate 1867–73.

Patterson, Jerry Mumford (D Calif.) Oct. 25, 1934– ; House 1975–85.

Patterson, John (half-brother of Thomas Patterson) (– Ohio) Feb. 10, 1771–Feb. 7, 1848; House 1823–25.

Patterson, John James (R S.C.) Aug. 8, 1830–Sept. 28, 1912; Senate 1873–79.

Patterson, Josiah (father of Malcolm Rice Patterson) (D Tenn.) April 14, 1837–Feb. 10, 1904; House 1891–97.

Patterson, Lafayette Lee (D Ala.) Aug. 23, 1888–March 3, 1987; House Nov. 6, 1928–33.

Patterson, Malcolm Rice (son of Josiah Patterson) (D Tenn.) June 7, 1861–March 8, 1935; House 1901–Nov. 5, 1906; Gov. Jan. 17, 1907–Jan. 26, 1911.

Patterson, Roscoe Conkling (R Mo.) Sept. 15, 1876–Oct. 22, 1954; House 1921–23; Senate 1929–35.

Patterson, Thomas (half-brother of John Patterson) (R Pa.) Oct. 1, 1764–Nov. 16, 1841; House 1817–25.

Patterson, Thomas J. (W N.Y.) about 1808–?; House 1843–45.

Patterson, Thomas MacDonald (D Colo.) Nov. 4, 1839–July 23, 1916; House (Terr. Del.) 1875–Aug. 1, 1876; (Rep.) Dec. 13, 1877–79; Senate 1901–07.

Patterson, Walter (– N.Y.) ?–?; House 1821–23.

Patterson, William (brother of George Washington Patterson, uncle of Augustus Frank) (W N.Y.) June 4, 1789–Aug. 14, 1838; House 1837–Aug. 14, 1838.

Patterson, William (J Ohio) 1790–Aug. 17, 1868; House 1833–37.

Pattison, Edward Worthington (D N.Y.) April 29, 1932–Aug. 22, 1990; House 1975–79.

Pattison, John M. (D Ohio) June 13, 1847–June 18, 1906; House 1891–93; Gov. Jan. 8–June 18, 1906.

Patton, Charles Emory (son of John Patton, brother of John Patton Jr., cousin of William Irvin Swoope) (– Pa.) July 5, 1859–Dec. 15, 1937; House 1911–15.

Patton, David Henry (D Ind.) Nov. 26, 1837–Jan. 17, 1914; House 1891–93.

Patton, John (father of Charles Emory Patton and John Patton Jr., uncle of William Irvin Swoope) (R Pa.) Jan. 6, 1823–Dec. 23, 1897; House 1861–63, 1887–89.

Patton, John Jr. (son of John Patton, brother of Charles Emory Patton, cousin of William Irvin Swoope) (R Mich.) Oct. 30, 1850–May 24, 1907; Senate May 5, 1894–Jan. 14, 1895.

Patton, John Denniston (D Pa.) Nov. 28, 1829–Feb. 22, 1904; House 1883–85.

Patton, John Mercer (D Va.) Aug. 10, 1797–Oct. 29, 1858; House Nov. 25, 1830–April 7, 1838 (Nov. 25, 1830–37 Jacksonian); Gov. March 18–March 31, 1841 (State Rights Whig).

Patton, Nat (D Texas) Feb. 26, 1884–July 27, 1957; House 1935–45.

Paul, John (father of John Paul, below) (Read. Va.) June 30, 1839–Nov. 1, 1901; House 1881–Sept. 5, 1883.

Paul, John (son of John Paul, above) (R Va.) Dec. 9, 1883–Feb. 13, 1964; House Dec. 15, 1922–23.

Paul, Ronald Ernest (R Texas) Aug. 20, 1935– ; House April 3, 1976–77, 1979–85, 1997– .

Paulding, William Jr. (R N.Y.) March 7, 1770–Feb. 11, 1854; House 1811–13.

Pawling, Levi (F Pa.) July 25, 1773–Sept. 7, 1845; House 1817–19.

Paxon, L. William (husband of Susan Molinari, son-in-law of Guy Molinari) (R N.Y.) April 29, 1954– ; House 1989–99.

Payne, Donald Milford (D N.J.) July 16, 1934– ; House 1989– .

Payne, Frederick George (R Maine) July 24, 1904–June 15, 1978; Senate 1953–59; Gov. Jan. 5, 1949–Dec. 25, 1952.

Payne, Henry B. (grandfather of Frances Payne Bolton, great-grandfather of Oliver Payne Bolton) (D Ohio) Nov. 30, 1810–Sept. 9, 1896; House 1875–77; Senate 1885–91.

Payne, Lewis Franklin Jr. (D Va.) July 9, 1945– ; House June 21, 1988–97.

Payne, Sereno Elisha (R N.Y.) June 26, 1843–Dec. 10, 1914; House 1883–87, 1889–Dec. 10, 1914; House majority leader 1899–1911.

Payne, William Winter (D Ala.) Jan. 2, 1807–Sept. 2, 1874; House 1841–47.

Paynter, Lemuel (D Pa.) 1788–Aug. 1, 1863; House 1837–41.

Paynter, Thomas Hanson (D Ky.) Dec. 9, 1851–March 8, 1921; House 1889–Jan. 5, 1895; Senate 1907–13.

Payson, Lewis Edwin (R Ill.) Sept. 17, 1840–Oct. 4, 1909; House 1881–91.

Peace, Roger Craft (D S.C.) May 19, 1899–Aug. 20, 1968; Senate Aug. 5–Nov. 4, 1941.

Pearce, Charles Edward (R Mo.) May 29, 1842–Jan. 30, 1902; House 1897–1901.

Pearce, Dutee Jerauld (AMas. R.I.) April 3, 1789–May 9, 1849; House 1825–37 (1825–33 no party).

Pearce, James Alfred (D Md.) Dec. 8, 1805–Dec. 20, 1862; House 1835–39 (Whig), 1841–43 (Whig); Senate 1843–Dec. 20, 1862 (1843–61 Whig).

Pearce, John Jamison (R Pa.) Feb. 28, 1826–May 26, 1912; House 1855–57.

Pearce, Steve (R N.M.) Aug. 23, 1947– ; House 2003– .

Pearre, George Alexander (R Md.) July 16, 1860–Sept. 19, 1923; House 1899–1911.

Pearson, Albert Jackson (D Ohio) May 20, 1846–May 15, 1905; House 1891–95.

Pearson, Herron Carney (D Tenn.) July 31, 1890–April 24, 1953; House 1935–43.

Pearson, James Blackwood (R Kan.) May 7, 1920– ; Senate Jan. 31, 1962–Dec. 23, 1978.

Pearson, John James (W Pa.) Oct. 25, 1800–May 30, 1888; House Dec. 5, 1836–37.

Pearson, Joseph (F N.C.) 1776–Oct. 27, 1834; House 1809–15.

Pearson, Richmond (R N.C.) Jan. 26, 1852–Sept. 12, 1923; House 1895–99, May 10, 1900–01.

Pease, Donald James (D Ohio) Sept. 26, 1931–July 28, 2002; House 1977–93.

Pease, Edward A. (R Ind.) May 22, 1951– ; House 1997–2001.

Pease, Henry Roberts (R Miss.) Feb. 19, 1835–Jan. 2, 1907; Senate Feb. 3, 1874–75.

Peaslee, Charles Hazen (D N.H.) Feb. 6, 1804–Sept. 18, 1866; House 1847–53.

Peavey, Hubert Haskell (R Wis.) Jan. 12, 1881–Nov. 21, 1937; House 1923–35.

Peck, Erasmus Darwin (R Ohio) Sept. 16, 1808–Dec. 25, 1876; House April 23, 1870–73.

Peck, George Washington (D Mich.) June 4, 1818–June 30, 1905; House 1855–57.

Peck, Jared Valentine (D N.Y.) Sept. 21, 1816–Dec. 25, 1891; House 1853–55.

Peck, Lucius Benedict (D Vt.) Nov. 17, 1802–Dec. 28, 1866; House 1847–51.

Peck, Luther Christopher (W N.Y.) Jan. 1800–Feb. 5, 1876; House 1837–41.

Peckham, Rufus Wheeler (D N.Y.) Dec. 20, 1809–Nov. 22, 1873; House 1853–55.

Peddie, Thomas Baldwin (R N.J.) Feb. 11, 1808–Feb. 16, 1889; House 1877–79.

Peden, Preston Elmer (D Okla.) June 28, 1914–June 27, 1985; House 1947–49.

Peek, Harmanus (– N.Y.) June 24, 1782–Sept. 27, 1838; House 1819–21.

Peel, Samuel West (D Ark.) Sept. 13, 1831–Dec. 18, 1924; House 1883–93.

Peelle, Stanton Judkins (R Ind.) Feb. 11, 1843–Sept. 4, 1928; House 1881–May 22, 1884.

Peery, George Campbell (D Va.) Oct. 28, 1873–Oct. 14, 1952; House 1923–29; Gov. Jan. 17, 1934–Jan. 19, 1938.

Peffer, William Alfred (P Kan.) Sept. 10, 1831–Oct. 7, 1912; Senate 1891–97.

Pegram, John (R Va.) Nov. 16, 1773–April 8, 1831; House April 21, 1818–19.

Peirce, Joseph (F N.H.) June 25, 1748–Sept. 12, 1812; House 1801–02.

Peirce, Robert Bruce Fraser (R Ind.) Feb. 17, 1843–Dec. 5, 1898; House 1881–83.

Pelham, Charles (R Ala.) March 12, 1835–Jan. 18, 1908; House 1873–75.

Pell, Claiborne de Borda (son of Herbert Claiborne Pell Jr., great-great-grandson of John Francis Hamtramck Claiborne, great-great-great-nephew of George Mifflin Dallas, great-great-great-nephew of William Charles Cole Claiborne and Nathaniel Herbert Claiborne) (D R.I.) Nov. 22, 1918– ; Senate 1961–97; chair Senate Rules and Administration 1978–81; chair Senate Foreign Relations 1987–95.

Pell, Herbert Claiborne Jr. (great-grandson of John Francis Hamtramck Claiborne, great-great-great-nephew of William Charles Cole Claiborne and Nathaniel Herbert Claiborne, father of Claiborne de Borda Pell) (D N.Y.) Feb. 16, 1884–July 17, 1961; House 1919–21.

Pelly, Thomas Minor (R Wash.) Aug. 22, 1902–Nov. 21, 1973; House 1953–73.

Pelosi, Nancy (daughter of Thomas D'Alesandro Jr.) (D Calif.) March 26, 1940– ; House June 9, 1987– ; House minority leader 2003– .

Pelton, Guy Ray (W N.Y.) Aug. 3, 1824–July 24, 1890; House 1855–57.

Pence, Lafayette (P Colo.) Dec. 23, 1857–Oct. 22, 1923; House 1893–95.

Pence, Mike (R Ind.) June 7, 1959– ; House 2001– .

Pendleton, Edmund Henry (AJ N.Y.) 1788–Feb. 25, 1862; House 1831–33.

Pendleton, George Cassety (D Texas) April 23, 1845–Jan. 19, 1913; House 1893–97.

Pendleton, George Hunt (son of Nathanael Greene Pendleton) (D Ohio) July 19, 1825–Nov. 24, 1889; House 1857–65; Senate 1879–85.

Pendleton, James Monroe (R R.I.) Jan. 10, 1822–Feb. 16, 1889; House 1871–75.

Pendleton, John Overton (D W.Va.) July 4, 1851–Dec. 24, 1916; House 1889–Feb. 26, 1890, 1891–95.

Pendleton, John Strother (W Va.) March 1, 1802–Nov. 19, 1868; House 1845–49.

Pendleton, Nathanael Green (father of George Hunt Pendleton) (W Ohio) Aug. 25, 1793–June 16, 1861; House 1841–43.

Penington, John Brown (D Del.) Dec. 20, 1825–June 1, 1902; House 1887–91.

Penn, Alexander Gordon (D La.) May 10, 1799–May 7, 1866; House Dec. 30, 1850–53.

Penniman, Ebenezer Jenckes (W Mich.) Jan. 11, 1804–April 12, 1890; House 1851–53.

Pennington, Alexander Cumming McWhorter (cousin of William Pennington) (W N.J.) July 2, 1810–Jan. 25, 1867; House 1853–57.

Pennington, William (cousin of Alexander Cumming McWhorter Pennington) (R N.J.) May 4, 1796–Feb. 16, 1862; House 1859–61; Speaker Feb. 1, 1860–61; Gov. Oct. 27, 1837–Oct. 27, 1843 (Democratic Republican).

Penny, Timothy Joseph (DFL Minn.) Nov. 19, 1951– ; House 1983–95.

Pennybacker, Isaac Samuels (cousin of Green Berry Samuels) (D Va.) Sept. 3, 1805–Jan. 12, 1847; House 1837–39; Senate Dec. 3, 1845–Jan. 12, 1847.

Penrose, Boies (R Pa.) Nov. 1, 1860–Dec. 31, 1921; Senate 1897–Dec. 31, 1921.

Pepper, Claude Denson (D Fla.) Sept. 8, 1900–May 30, 1989; Senate Nov. 4, 1936–51; House 1963–May 30, 1989; chair House Rules 1983–89.

Pepper, George Wharton (R Pa.) March 16, 1867–May 24, 1961; Senate Jan. 9, 1922–27.

Pepper, Irvin St. Clair (D Iowa) June 10, 1876–Dec. 22, 1913; House 1911–Dec. 22, 1913.

Perce, Legrand Winfield (R Miss.) June 19, 1836–March 16, 1911; House Feb. 23, 1870–73.

Percy, Charles Harting (father-in-law of John Davison "Jay" Rockefeller IV) (R Ill.) Sept. 27, 1919– ; Senate 1967–85; chair Senate Foreign Relations 1981–85.

Percy, Le Roy (D Miss.) Nov. 9, 1860–Dec. 24, 1929; Senate Feb. 23, 1910–13.

Perea, Francisco (cousin of Pedro Perea) (R N.M.) Jan. 9, 1830–May 21, 1913; House (Terr. Del.) 1863–65.

Perea, Pedro (cousin of Francisco Perea) (R N.M.) April 22, 1852–Jan. 11, 1906; House (Terr. Del.) 1899–1901.

Perham, Sidney (R Maine) March 27, 1819–April 10, 1907; House 1863–69; Gov. Jan. 4, 1871–Jan. 7, 1874.

Perkins, Bishop (D N.Y.) Sept. 5, 1787–Nov. 20, 1866; House 1853–55.

Perkins, Bishop Walden (R Kan.) Oct. 18, 1841–June 20, 1894; House 1883–91; Senate Jan. 1, 1892–93.

Perkins, Carl Christopher "Chris" (son of Carl Dewey Perkins) (D Ky.) Aug. 6, 1954– ; House Nov. 6, 1984–93.

Perkins, Carl Dewey (father of Carl Christopher "Chris" Perkins) (D Ky.) Oct. 15, 1912–Aug. 3, 1984; House 1949–Aug. 3, 1984; chair House Education and Labor 1967–84.

Perkins, Elias (F Conn.) April 5, 1767–Sept. 27, 1845; House 1801–03.

Perkins, George Clement (R Calif.) Aug. 23, 1839–Feb. 26, 1923; Senate July 26, 1893–1915; Gov. Jan. 8, 1880–Jan. 10, 1883.

Perkins, George Douglas (R Iowa) Feb. 29, 1840–Feb. 3, 1914; House 1891–99.

Perkins, James Breck (R N.Y.) Nov. 4, 1847–March 11, 1910; House 1901–March 11, 1910.

Perkins, Jared (W N.H.) Jan. 5, 1793–Oct. 15, 1854; House 1851–53.

Perkins, John Jr. (D La.) July 1, 1819–Nov. 28, 1885; House 1853–55.

Perkins, Randolph (R N.J.) Nov. 30, 1871–May 25, 1936; House 1921–May 25, 1936.

Perky, Kirtland Irving (D Idaho) Feb. 8, 1867–Jan. 9, 1939; Senate Nov. 18, 1912–Feb. 5, 1913.

Perlman, Nathan David (R N.Y.) Aug. 2, 1887–June 29, 1952; House Nov. 2, 1920–27.

Perrill, Augustus Leonard (D Ohio) Jan. 20, 1807–June 2, 1882; House 1845–47.

Perry, Aaron Fyfe (R Ohio) Jan. 1, 1815–March 11, 1893; House 1871–72.

Perry, Eli (D N.Y.) Dec. 25, 1799–May 17, 1881; House 1871–75.

Perry, John Jasiel (R Maine) Aug. 2, 1811–May 2, 1897; House 1855–57, 1859–61.

Perry, Nehemiah (D N.J.) March 30, 1816–Nov. 1, 1881; House 1861–65.

Perry, Thomas Johns (D Md.) Feb. 17, 1807–June 27, 1871; House 1845–47.

Perry, William Hayne (D S.C.) June 9, 1839–July 7, 1902; House 1885–91.

Person, Seymour Howe (R Mich.) Feb. 2, 1879–April 7, 1957; House 1931–33.

Persons, Henry (ID Ga.) Jan. 30, 1834–June 17, 1910; House 1879–81.

Pesquera, José Lorenzo (Nonpart. P.R.) Aug. 10, 1882–July 25, 1950; House (Res. Comm.) April 15, 1932–33.

Peter, George (F Md.) Sept. 28, 1779–June 22, 1861; House Oct. 7, 1816–19, 1825–27.

Peters, Andrew James (D Mass.) April 3, 1872–June 26, 1938; House 1907–Aug. 15, 1914.

Peters, John Andrew (uncle of John Andrew Peters, below) (R Maine) Oct. 9, 1822–April 2, 1904; House 1867–73.

Peters, John Andrew (nephew of John Andrew Peters, above) (R Maine) Aug. 13, 1864–Aug. 22, 1953; House Sept. 8, 1913–Jan. 2, 1922.

Peters, Mason Summers (P Kan.) Sept. 3, 1844–Feb. 14, 1914; House 1897–99.

Peters, Samuel Ritter (R Kan.) Aug. 16, 1842–April 21, 1910; House 1883–91.

Petersen, Andrew Nicholas (R N.Y.) March 10, 1870–Sept. 28, 1952; House 1921–23.

Peterson, Collin Clark (D Minn.) June 29, 1944– ; House 1991– .

Peterson, Douglas Brian "Pete" (D Fla.) June 26, 1935– ; House 1991–97.

Peterson, Hugh (D Ga.) Aug. 21, 1898–Oct. 3, 1961; House 1935–47.

Peterson, James Hardin (D Fla.) Feb. 11, 1894–March 28, 1978; House 1933–51; chair House Public Lands 1949–51.

Peterson, John Barney (cousin of Horatio Clifford Claypool and Harold Kile Claypool) (D Ind.) July 4, 1850–July 16, 1944; House 1913–15.

Peterson, John E. (R Pa.) Dec. 25, 1938– ; House 1997– .

Peterson, Morris Blaine (D Utah) March 26, 1906–July 15, 1985; House 1961–63.

Petri, Thomas Evert (R Wis.) May 28, 1940– ; House April 3, 1979– .

Petrie, George (ID N.Y.) Sept. 8, 1793–May 8, 1879; House 1847–49.

Petrikin, David (D Pa.) Dec. 1, 1788–March 1, 1847; House 1837–41.

Pettengill, Samuel Barrett (nephew of William Horace Clagett) (D Ind.) Jan. 19, 1886–March 20, 1974; House 1931–39.

Pettibone, Augustus Herman (R Tenn.) Jan. 21, 1835–Nov. 26, 1918; House 1881–87.

Pettigrew, Ebenezer (W N.C.) March 10, 1783–July 8, 1848; House 1835–37.

Pettigrew, Richard Franklin (R S.D.) July 23, 1848–Oct. 5, 1926; House (Terr. Del.) 1881–83; Senate Nov. 2, 1889–1901.

Pettis, Jerry Lyle (husband of Shirley Neal Pettis) (R Calif.) July 18, 1916–Feb. 14, 1975; House 1967–Feb. 14, 1975.

Pettis, Shirley Neal (widow of Jerry Lyle Pettis) (R Calif.) July 12, 1924– ; House April 29, 1975–79.

Pettis, Solomon Newton (R Pa.) Oct. 10, 1827–Sept. 18, 1900; House Dec. 7, 1868–69.

Pettis, Spencer Darwin (J Mo.) 1802–Aug. 28, 1831; House 1829–Aug. 28, 1831.

Pettit, John (D Ind.) June 24, 1807–Jan. 17, 1877; House 1843–49; Senate Jan. 11, 1853–55.

Pettit, John Upfold (R Ind.) Sept. 11, 1820–March 21, 1881; House 1855–61.

Pettus, Edmund Winston (D Ala.) July 6, 1821–July 27, 1907; Senate 1897–July 27, 1907.

Peyser, Peter A. (D N.Y.) Sept. 7, 1921– ; House 1971–77 (Republican), 1979–83.

Peyser, Theodore Albert (D N.Y.) Feb. 18, 1873–Aug. 8, 1937; House 1933–Aug. 8, 1937.

Peyton, Balie (brother of Joseph Hopkins Peyton) (White supporter Tenn.) Nov. 26, 1803–Aug. 18, 1878; House 1833–37 (1833–35 Jacksonian).

Peyton, Joseph Hopkins (brother of Balie Peyton) (W Tenn.) May 20, 1808–Nov. 11, 1845; House 1843–Nov. 11, 1845.

Peyton, Samuel Oldham (D Ky.) Jan. 8, 1804–Jan. 4, 1870; House 1847–49, 1857–61.

Pfeifer, Joseph Lawrence (D N.Y.) Feb. 6, 1892–April 19, 1974; House 1935–51.

Pfeiffer, William Louis (R N.Y.) May 29, 1907–July 22, 1985; House 1949–51.

Pfost, Gracie Bowers (D Idaho) March 12, 1906–Aug. 11, 1965; House 1953–63.

Pheiffer, William Townsend (R N.Y.) July 15, 1898–Aug. 16, 1986; House 1941–43.

Phelan, James (D Tenn.) Dec. 7, 1856–Jan. 30, 1891; House 1887–Jan. 30, 1891.

Phelan, James Duval (D Calif.) April 20, 1861–Aug. 7, 1930; Senate 1915–21.

Phelan, Michael Francis (D Mass.) Oct. 22, 1875–Oct. 12, 1941; House 1913–21.

Phelps, Charles Edward (C Md.) May 1, 1833–Dec. 27, 1908; House 1865–69 (1865–67 Unconditional Unionist).

Phelps, Darwin (R Pa.) April 17, 1807–Dec. 14, 1879; House 1869–71.

Phelps, David (D Ill.) Oct. 26, 1947– ; House 1999–2003.

Phelps, Elisha (father of John Smith Phelps) (– Conn.) Nov. 16, 1779–April 6, 1847; House 1819–21, 1825–29.

Phelps, James (son of Lancelot Phelps) (D Conn.) Jan. 12, 1822–Jan. 15, 1900; House 1875–83.

Phelps, John Smith (son of Elisha Phelps) (D Mo.) Dec. 22, 1814–Nov. 20, 1886; House 1845–63; Gov. Jan. 8, 1877–Jan. 10, 1881.

Phelps, Lancelot (father of James Phelps) (D Conn.) Nov. 9, 1784–Sept. 1, 1866; House 1835–39 (1835–37 Jacksonian).

Phelps, Oliver (R N.Y.) Oct. 21, 1749–Feb. 21, 1809; House 1803–05.

Phelps, Samuel Shethar (W Vt.) May 13, 1793–March 25, 1855; Senate 1839–51, Jan. 17, 1853–March 16, 1854.

Phelps, Timothy Guy (R Calif.) Dec. 20, 1824–June 11, 1899; House 1861–63.

Phelps, William Wallace (D Minn.) June 1, 1826–Aug. 3, 1873; House May 11, 1858–59.

Phelps, William Walter (R N.J.) Aug. 24, 1839–June 17, 1894; House 1873–75 (no party), 1883–89.

Philbin, Philip Joseph (D Mass.) May 29, 1898–June 14, 1972; House 1943–71.

Philips, John Finis (D Mo.) Dec. 31, 1834–March 13, 1919; House 1875–77, Jan. 10, 1880–81.

Phillips, Alfred Noroton (D Conn.) April 23, 1894–Jan. 18, 1970; House 1937–39.

Phillips, Dayton Edward (R Tenn.) March 29, 1910–Oct. 23, 1980; House 1947–51.

Phillips, Fremont Orestes (R Ohio) March 16, 1856–Feb. 21, 1936; House 1899–1901.

Phillips, Henry Myer (D Pa.) June 30, 1811–Aug. 28, 1884; House 1857–59.

Phillips, John (F Pa.) ?–?; House 1821–23.

Phillips, John (R Calif.) Sept. 11, 1887–Dec. 18, 1983; House 1943–57.

Phillips, Philip (D Ala.) Dec. 13, 1807–Jan. 14, 1884; House 1853–55.

Phillips, Stephen Clarendon (W Mass.) Nov. 4, 1801–June 26, 1857; House Dec. 1, 1834–Sept. 28, 1838.

Phillips, Thomas Wharton (father of Thomas Wharton Phillips Jr.) (R Pa.) Feb. 23, 1835–July 21, 1912; House 1893–97.

Phillips, Thomas Wharton Jr. (son of Thomas Wharton Phillips) (R Pa.) Nov. 21, 1874–Jan. 2, 1956; House 1923–27.

Phillips, William Addison (R Kan.) Jan. 14, 1824–Nov. 30, 1893; House 1873–79.

Philson, Robert (– Pa.) 1759–July 25, 1831; House 1819–21.

Phipps, Lawrence Cowle (R Colo.) Aug. 30, 1862–March 1, 1958; Senate 1919–31.

Phister, Elijah Conner (D Ky.) Oct. 8, 1822–May 16, 1887; House 1879–83.

Phoenix, Jonas Phillips (W N.Y.) Jan. 14, 1788–May 4, 1859; House 1843–45, 1849–51.

Pickens, Andrew (grandfather of Francis Wilkinson Pickens) (– S.C.) Sept. 13, 1739–Aug. 11, 1817; House 1793–95.

Pickens, Francis Wilkinson (grandson of Andrew Pickens) (D S.C.) April 7, 1805–Jan. 25, 1869; House Dec. 8, 1834–43 (Dec. 8, 1834–39 Nullifier); Gov. Dec. 14, 1860–Dec. 17, 1862 (State Rights Democrat).

Pickens, Israel (R Ala.) Jan. 30, 1780–April 24, 1827; House 1811–17 (N.C.); Senate Feb. 17–Nov. 27, 1826; Gov. Nov. 9, 1821–Nov. 25, 1825 (Democratic Republican).

Pickering, Charles W. "Chip" Jr. (R Miss.) Aug. 10, 1963– ; House 1997– .

Pickering, Timothy (F Mass.) July 17, 1745–Jan. 29, 1829; Senate 1803–11; House 1813–17; postmaster general Aug. 19, 1791–Jan. 2, 1795; secretary of war Jan. 2–Dec. 10, 1795; secretary of state Dec. 10, 1795–May 12, 1800.

Pickett, Charles Edgar (R Iowa) Jan. 14, 1866–July 20, 1930; House 1909–13.

Pickett, Owen Bradford (D Va.) Aug. 31, 1930– ; House 1987–2001.

Pickett, Thomas Augustus (D Texas) Aug. 14, 1906–June 7, 1980; House 1945–June 30, 1952.

Pickle, James Jarrell "Jake" (D Texas) Oct. 11, 1913– ; House Dec. 21, 1963–95.

Pickler, John Alfred (R S.D.) Jan. 24, 1844–June 13, 1910; House Nov. 2, 1889–97.

Pickman, Benjamin Jr. (F Mass.) Sept. 30, 1763–Aug. 16, 1843; House 1809–11.

Pidcock, James Nelson (cousin of Alvah Augustus Clark) (D N.J.) Feb. 8, 1836–Dec. 17, 1899; House 1885–89.

Pierce, Charles Wilson (R Ala.) Oct. 7, 1823–Feb. 18, 1907; House July 21, 1868–69.

Pierce, Franklin (D N.H.) Nov. 23, 1804–Oct. 8, 1869; House 1833–37; Senate 1837–Feb. 28, 1842; president 1853–57.

Pierce, Gilbert Ashville (R N.D.) Jan. 11, 1839–Feb. 15, 1901; Senate Nov. 21, 1889–91; Gov. (Dakota Terr.) 1884–86.

Pierce, Henry Lillie (R Mass.) Aug. 23, 1825–Dec. 17, 1896; House Dec. 1, 1873–77.

Pierce, Ray Vaughn (R N.Y.) Aug. 6, 1840–Feb. 4, 1914; House 1879–Sept. 18, 1880.

Pierce, Rice Alexander (D Tenn.) July 3, 1848–July 12, 1936; House 1883–85, 1889–93, 1897–1905.

Pierce, Wallace Edgar (R N.Y.) Dec. 9, 1881–Jan. 3, 1940; House 1939–Jan. 3, 1940.

Pierce, Walter Marcus (D Ore.) May 30, 1861–March 27, 1954; House 1933–43; Gov. Jan. 8, 1923–Jan. 10, 1927.

Pierson, Isaac (– N.J.) Aug. 15, 1770–Sept. 22, 1833; House 1827–31.

Pierson, Jeremiah Halsey (– N.Y.) Sept. 13, 1766–Dec. 12, 1855; House 1821–23.

Pierson, Job (J N.Y.) Sept. 23, 1791–April 9, 1860; House 1831–35.

Pigott, James Protus (D Conn.) Sept. 11, 1852–July 1, 1919; House 1893–95.

Pike, Austin Franklin (R N.H.) Oct. 16, 1819–Oct. 8, 1886; House 1873–75; Senate 1883–Oct. 8, 1886.

Pike, Frederick Augustus (R Maine) Dec. 9, 1816–Dec. 2, 1886; House 1861–69.

Pike, James (R N.H.) Nov. 10, 1818–July 26, 1895; House 1855–59 (1855–57 American Party).

Pike, Otis Grey (D N.Y.) Aug. 31, 1921– ; House 1961–79; chair House Select Intelligence 1975–76.

Pilcher, John Leonard (D Ga.) Aug. 27, 1898–Aug. 20, 1981; House Feb. 4, 1953–65.

Pile, William Anderson (R Mo.) Feb. 11, 1829–July 7, 1889; House 1867–69; Gov. (N.M. Terr.) 1869, 1870.

Piles, Samuel Henry (R Wash.) Dec. 28, 1858–March 11, 1940; Senate 1905–11.

Pillion, John Raymond (R N.Y.) Aug. 10, 1904–Dec. 31, 1978; House 1953–65.

Pilsbury, Timothy (D Texas) April 12, 1789–Nov. 23, 1858; House March 30, 1846–49.

Pinckney, Charles Cotesworth (father of Henry Laurens Pinckney, father-in-law of Robert Young Hayne) (R S.C.) Oct. 26, 1757–Oct. 29, 1824; Senate Dec. 6, 1798–1801; House 1819–21; Cont.

Cong. 1785–87; Gov. Jan. 26, 1789–Dec. 5, 1792, Dec. 8, 1796–Dec. 6, 1798, Dec. 9, 1806–Dec. 10, 1808.

Pinckney, Henry Laurens (son of Charles Pinckney) (N S.C.) Sept. 24, 1794–Feb. 3, 1863; House 1833–37.

Pinckney, John McPherson (D Texas) May 4, 1845–April 24, 1905; House Nov. 17, 1903–April 24, 1905.

Pinckney, Thomas (F S.C.) Oct. 23, 1750–Nov. 2, 1828; House Nov. 23, 1797–1801; Gov. Feb. 20, 1787–Jan. 26, 1789.

Pindall, James (F Va.) about 1783–Nov. 22, 1825; House 1817–July 26, 1820.

Pindar, John Sigsbee (D N.Y.) Nov. 18, 1835–June 30, 1907; House 1885–87, Nov. 4, 1890–91.

Pine, William Bliss (R Okla.) Dec. 30, 1877–Aug. 25, 1942; Senate 1925–31.

Pinero, Jesus T. (PD P.R.) April 16, 1897–Nov. 19, 1952; House (Res. Comm.) 1945–Sept. 2, 1946; Gov. 1946–48.

Pinkney, William (R Md.) March 17, 1764–Feb. 25, 1822; House March 4–Nov. 1791 (no party), 1815–April 18, 1816 (no party); Senate Dec. 21, 1819–Feb. 25, 1822; attorney general Dec. 11, 1811–Feb. 10, 1814.

Piper, William (R Pa.) Jan. 1, 1774–1852; House 1811–17.

Piper, William Adam (D Calif.) May 21, 1826–Aug. 5, 1899; House 1875–77.

Pirce, William Almy (R R.I.) Feb. 29, 1824–March 5, 1891; House 1885–Jan. 25, 1887.

Pirnie, Alexander (R N.Y.) April 16, 1903–June 12, 1982; House 1959–73.

Pitcher, Nathaniel (J N.Y.) 1777–May 25, 1836; House 1819–23 (no party), 1831–33; Gov. (Acting) Feb. 11–Dec. 31, 1828..

Pitkin, Timothy (F Conn.) Jan. 21, 1766–Dec. 18, 1847; House Sept. 16, 1805–19.

Pitman, Charles Wesley (W Pa.) ?–June 8, 1871; House 1849–51.

Pitney, Mahlon (R N.J.) Feb. 5, 1858–Dec. 9, 1924; House 1895–Jan. 10, 1899; assoc. justice March 18, 1912–Dec. 31, 1922.

Pittenger, William Alvin (R Minn.) Dec. 29, 1885–Nov. 26, 1951; House 1929–33, 1935–37, 1939–47.

Pittman, Key (D Nev.) Sept. 19, 1872–Nov. 10, 1940; Senate Jan. 29, 1913–Nov. 10, 1940; elected pres. pro tempore March 9, 1933, Jan. 7, 1935.

Pitts, Joseph R. (R Pa.) Oct. 10, 1939– ; House 1997– .

Plaisted, Harris Merrill (R Maine) Nov. 2, 1828–Jan. 31, 1898; House Sept. 13, 1875–77; Gov. Jan. 13, 1881–Jan. 3, 1883 (Democrat).

Plant, David (– Conn.) March 29, 1783–Oct. 18, 1851; House 1827–29.

Plants, Tobias Avery (R Ohio) March 17, 1811–June 19, 1887; House 1865–69.

Plater, Thomas (F Md.) May 9, 1769–May 1, 1830; House 1801–05.

Platt, Edmund (R N.Y.) Feb. 2, 1865–Aug. 7, 1939; House 1913–June 7, 1920.

Platt, James Henry Jr. (R Va.) July 13, 1837–Aug. 13, 1894; House Jan. 26, 1870–75.

Platt, Jonas (F N.Y.) June 30, 1769–Feb. 22, 1834; House 1799–1801.

Platt, Orville Hitchcock (R Conn.) July 19, 1827–April 21, 1905; Senate 1879–April 21, 1905.

Platt, Thomas Collier (R N.Y.) July 15, 1833–March 6, 1910; House 1873–77; Senate March 4–May 16, 1881, 1897–1909.

Platts, Todd R. (R Pa.) March 5, 1962– ; House 2001– .

Plauche, Vance Gabriel (D La.) Aug. 25, 1897–April 2, 1976; House 1941–43.

Pleasants, James (R Va.) Oct. 24, 1769–Nov. 9, 1836; House 1811–Dec. 14, 1819; Senate Dec. 14, 1819–Dec. 15, 1822; Gov. Dec. 1, 1822–Dec. 10, 1825.

Ploeser, Walter Christian (R Mo.) Jan. 7, 1907–Nov. 17, 1993; House 1941–49; chair House Select Small Business 1947–49.

Plowman, Thomas Scales (D Ala.) June 8, 1843–July 26, 1919; House 1897–Feb. 9, 1898.

Plumb, Preston B. (R Kan.) Oct. 12, 1837–Dec. 20, 1891; Senate 1877–Dec. 20, 1891.

Plumb, Ralph (R Ill.) March 29, 1816–April 8, 1903; House 1885–89.

Plumer, Arnold (D Pa.) June 6, 1801–April 28, 1869; House 1837–39, 1841–43.

Plumer, George (– Pa.) Dec. 5, 1762–June 8, 1843; House 1821–27.

Plumer, William (father of William Plumer Jr.) (F N.H.) June 25, 1759–Dec. 22, 1850; Senate June 17, 1802–07; Gov. June 5, 1812–June 3, 1813, June 6, 1816–June 3, 1819 (Democratic Republican).

Plumer, William Jr. (son of William Plumer) (– N.H.) Feb. 9, 1789–Sept. 18, 1854; House 1819–25.

Plumley, Charles Albert (son of Frank Plumley) (R Vt.) April 14, 1875–Oct. 31, 1964; House Jan. 16, 1934–51.

Plumley, Frank (father of Charles Albert Plumley) (R Vt.) Dec. 17, 1844–April 30, 1924; House 1909–15.

Plummer, Franklin E. (J Miss.) ?–Sept. 24, 1847; House 1831–35.

Poage, William Robert (D Texas) Dec. 28, 1899–Jan. 3, 1987; House 1937–Dec. 31, 1978; chair House Agriculture 1967–75.

Podell, Bertram L. (D N.Y.) Dec. 27, 1925– ; House Feb. 20, 1968–75.

Poe, Ted (R Texas) Sept. 10, 1948– ; House 2005– .

Poehler, Henry (D Minn.) Aug. 22, 1833–July 18, 1912; House 1879–81.

Poff, Richard Harding (R Va.) Oct. 19, 1923– ; House 1953–Aug. 29, 1972.

Poindexter, George (– Miss.) 1779–Sept. 5, 1853; House (Terr. Del.) 1807–13; (Rep.) Dec. 10, 1817–19; Senate Oct. 15, 1830–35; elected pres. pro tempore June 28, 1834; Gov. Jan. 5, 1820–Jan. 7, 1822 (Democratic Republican).

Poindexter, Miles (R Wash.) April 22, 1868–Sept. 21, 1946; House 1909–11; Senate 1911–23.

Poinsett, Joel Roberts (D S.C.) March 2, 1779–Dec. 12, 1851; House 1821–March 7, 1825; secretary of war March 7, 1837–March 5, 1841.

Polanco-Abreu, Santiago (PD P.R.) Oct. 30, 1920–Jan. 18, 1988; House (Res. Comm.) 1965–69.

Poland, Luke Potter (R Vt.) Nov. 1, 1815–July 2, 1887; Senate Nov. 21, 1865–67; House 1867–75, 1883–85.

Polk, Albert Fawcett (D Del.) Oct. 11, 1869–Feb. 14, 1955; House 1917–19.

Polk, James Gould (D Ohio) Oct. 6, 1896–April 28, 1959; House 1931–41, 1949–April 28, 1959.

Polk, James Knox (brother of William Hawkins Polk) (D Tenn.) Nov. 2, 1795–June 15, 1849; House 1825–39 (1825–27 no party, 1827–37 Jacksonian); Speaker Dec. 7, 1835–37, Sept. 4, 1837–39; Gov. Oct. 14, 1839–Oct. 15, 1841; president 1845–49.

Polk, Rufus King (D Pa.) Aug. 23, 1866–March 5, 1902; House 1899–March 5, 1902.

Polk, Trusten (D Mo.) May 29, 1811–April 16, 1876; Senate 1857–Jan. 10, 1862; Gov. Jan. 5–Feb. 27, 1857.

Polk, William Hawkins (brother of James Knox Polk) (ID Tenn.) May 24, 1815–Dec. 16, 1862; House 1851–53.

Pollard, Ernest Mark (R Neb.) April 15, 1869–Sept. 24, 1939; House July 18, 1905–09.

Pollard, Henry Moses (R Mo.) June 14, 1836–Feb. 24, 1904; House 1877–79.

Pollock, Howard Wallace (R Alaska) April 11, 1920– ; House 1967–71.

Pollock, James (W Pa.) Sept. 11, 1810–April 19, 1890; House April 5, 1844–49; Gov. Jan. 16, 1855–Jan. 19, 1858.

Pollock, William Pegues (D S.C.) Dec. 9, 1870–June 2, 1922; Senate Nov. 6, 1918–19.

Polsley, Daniel Haymond (R W.Va.) Nov. 28, 1803–Oct. 14, 1877; House 1867–69.

Pombo, Richard William (R Calif.) Jan. 8, 1961– ; House 1993– ; chair House Resources 2003– .

Pomerene, Atlee (D Ohio) Dec. 6, 1863–Nov. 12, 1937; Senate 1911–23.

Pomeroy, Charles (R Iowa) Sept. 3, 1825–Feb. 11, 1891; House 1869–71.

Pomeroy, Earl Ralph (D N.D.) Sept. 2, 1952– ; House 1993– .

Pomeroy, Samuel Clarke (R Kan.) Jan. 3, 1816–Aug. 27, 1891; Senate April 4, 1861–73.

Pomeroy, Theodore Medad (R N.Y.) Dec. 31, 1824–March 23, 1905; House 1861–69; Speaker March 3, 1869.

Pond, Benjamin (R N.Y.) 1768–Oct. 6, 1814; House 1811–13.

Pool, Joe Richard (D Texas) Feb. 18, 1911–July 14, 1968; House 1963–July 14, 1968.

Pool, John (uncle of Walter Freshwater Pool) (R N.C.) June 16, 1826–Aug. 16, 1884; Senate July 4, 1868–73.

Pool, Walter Freshwater (nephew of John Pool) (R N.C.) Oct. 10, 1850–Aug. 25, 1883; House March 4–Aug. 25, 1883.

Poole, Theodore Lewis (R N.Y.) April 10, 1840–Dec. 23, 1900; House 1895–97.

Pope, James Pinckney (D Idaho) March 31, 1884–Jan. 23, 1966; Senate 1933–39.

Pope, John (W Ky.) 1770–July 12, 1845; Senate 1807–13; House 1837–43; elected pres. pro tempore Feb. 23, 1811; Gov. (Ark. Terr.) 1829–35.

Pope, Nathaniel (– Ill.) Jan. 5, 1784–Jan. 22, 1850; House (Terr. Del.) Sept. 5, 1816–Sept. 5, 1818.

Pope, Patrick Hamilton (J Ky.) March 17, 1806–May 4, 1841; House 1833–35.

Poppleton, Earley Franklin (D Ohio) Sept. 29, 1834–May 6, 1899; House 1875–77.

Porter, Albert Gallatin (R Ind.) April 20, 1824–May 3, 1897; House 1859–63; Gov. Jan. 10, 1881–Jan. 12, 1885.

Porter, Alexander (W La.) June 24, 1785–Jan. 13, 1844; Senate Dec. 19, 1833–Jan. 5, 1837.

Porter, Augustus Seymour (nephew of Peter Buell Porter) (W Mich.) Jan. 18, 1798–Sept. 18, 1872; Senate Jan. 20, 1840–45.

Porter, Charles Howell (R Va.) June 21, 1833–July 9, 1897; House Jan. 26, 1870–73.

Porter, Charles Orlando (D Ore.) April 4, 1919– ; House 1957–61.

Porter, Gilchrist (W Mo.) Nov. 1, 1817–Nov. 1, 1894; House 1851–53, 1855–57.

Porter, Henry Kirke (IR Pa.) Nov. 24, 1840–April 10, 1921; House 1903–05.

Porter, James (R N.Y.) April 18, 1787–Feb. 7, 1839; House 1817–19.

Porter, John (– Pa.) ?–?; House Dec. 8, 1806–11.

Porter, John Edward (R Ill.) June 1, 1935– ; House Jan. 22, 1980–2001.

Porter, Jon (R Nev.) May 16, 1955– ; House 2003– .

Porter, Peter Augustus (grandson of Peter Buell Porter) (IR N.Y.) Oct. 10, 1853–Dec. 15, 1925; House 1907–09.

Porter, Peter Buell (grandfather of Peter Augustus Porter, uncle of Augustus Seymour Porter) (R N.Y.) Aug. 14, 1773–March 20, 1844; House 1809–13, 1815–Jan. 23, 1816; secretary of war May 26, 1828–March 9, 1829.

Porter, Stephen Geyer (R Pa.) May 18, 1869–June 27, 1930; House 1911–June 27, 1930.

Porter, Timothy H. (– N.Y.) ?–about 1840; House 1825–27.

Portman, Robert Jones (R Ohio) Dec. 19, 1955– ; House May 5, 1993– .

Posey, Francis Blackburn (R Ind.) April 28, 1848–Oct. 31, 1915; House Jan. 29–March 3, 1889.

Posey, Thomas (– La.) July 9, 1750–March 19, 1818; Senate Oct. 8, 1812–Feb. 4, 1813; Gov. (Ind. Terr.) 1813–16.

Poshard, Glenn (D Ill.) Oct. 30, 1945– ; House 1989–99.

Post, George Adams (D Pa.) Sept. 1, 1854–Oct. 31, 1925; House 1883–85.

Post, James Douglass (D Ohio) Nov. 25, 1863–April 1, 1921; House 1911–15.

Post, Jotham Jr. (F N.Y.) April 4, 1771–May 15, 1817; House 1813–15.

Post, Morton Everel (D Wyo.) Dec. 25, 1840–March 19, 1933; House (Terr. Del.) 1881–85.

Post, Philip Sidney (R Ill.) March 19, 1833–Jan. 6, 1895; House 1887–Jan. 6, 1895.

Poston, Charles Debrille (R Ariz.) April 20, 1825–June 24, 1902; House (Terr. Del.) Dec. 5, 1864–65.

Potter, Allen (D Mich.) Oct. 2, 1818–May 8, 1885; House 1875–77.

Potter, Charles Edward (R Mich.) Oct. 30, 1916–Nov. 23, 1979; House Aug. 26, 1947–Nov. 4, 1952; Senate Nov. 5, 1952–59.

Potter, Clarkson Nott (D N.Y.) April 25, 1825–Jan. 23, 1882; House 1869–75, 1877–79.

Potter, Elisha Reynolds (father of Elisha Reynolds Potter, below) (F R.I.) Nov. 5, 1764–Sept. 26, 1835; House Nov. 15, 1796–97, 1809–15.

Potter, Elisha Reynolds (son of Elisha Reynolds Potter, above) (L&O R.I.) June 20, 1811–April 10, 1882; House 1843–45.

Potter, Emery Davis (D Ohio) Oct. 7, 1804–Feb. 12, 1896; House 1843–45, 1849–51.

Potter, John Fox (R Wis.) May 11, 1817–May 18, 1899; House 1857–63.

Potter, Orlando Brunson (D N.Y.) March 10, 1823–Jan. 2, 1894; House 1883–85.

Potter, Robert (J N.C.) about 1800–March 2, 1842; House 1829–Nov. 1831.

Potter, Samuel John (R R.I.) June 29, 1753–Oct. 14, 1804; Senate 1803–Oct. 14, 1804.

Potter, William Wilson (D Pa.) Dec. 18, 1792–Oct. 28, 1839; House 1837–Oct. 28, 1839.

Pottle, Emory Bemsley (R N.Y.) July 4, 1815–April 18, 1891; House 1857–61.

Potts, David Jr. (AMas. Pa.) Nov. 27, 1794–June 1, 1863; House 1831–39.

Potts, David Matthew (R N.Y.) March 12, 1906–Sept. 11, 1976; House 1947–49.

Potts, Richard (– Md.) July 19, 1753–Nov. 26, 1808; Senate Jan. 10, 1793–Oct. 24, 1796; Cont. Cong. 1781.

Pou, Edward William (cousin of James Paul Buchanan) (D N.C.) Sept. 9, 1863–April 1, 1934; House 1901–April 1, 1934.

Poulson, C. Norris (R Calif.) July 23, 1895–Sept. 25, 1982; House 1943–45, 1947–June 11, 1953.

Pound, Thaddeus Coleman (R Wis.) Dec. 6, 1833–Nov. 21, 1914; House 1877–83.

Powell, Adam Clayton Jr. (D N.Y.) Nov. 29, 1908–April 4, 1972; House 1945–Feb. 28, 1967, 1969–71; chair House Education and Labor 1961–67.

Powell, Alfred H. (– Va.) March 6, 1781–1831; House 1825–27.

Powell, Cuthbert (son of Levin Powell) (W Va.) March 4, 1775–May 8, 1849; House 1841–43.

Powell, Joseph (D Pa.) June 23, 1828–April 24, 1904; House 1875–77.

Powell, Lazarus Whitehead (D Ky.) Oct. 6, 1812–July 3, 1867; Senate 1859–65; Gov. Sept. 2, 1851–Sept. 1, 1855.

Powell, Levin (father of Cuthbert Powell) (F Va.) 1737–Aug. 23, 1810; House 1799–1801.

Powell, Paulus (D Va.) 1809–June 10, 1874; House 1849–59.

Powell, Samuel (R Tenn.) July 10, 1776–Aug. 2, 1841; House 1815–17.

Powell, Walter Eugene (R Ohio) April 25, 1931– ; House 1971–75.

Power, Thomas Charles (R Mont.) May 22, 1839–Feb. 16, 1923; Senate Jan. 2, 1890–95.

Powers, Caleb (R Ky.) Feb. 1, 1869–July 25, 1932; House 1911–19.

Powers, David Lane (R N.J.) July 29, 1896–March 28, 1968; House 1933–Aug. 30, 1945.

Powers, Gershom (J N.Y.) July 11, 1789–June 25, 1831; House 1829–31.

Powers, Horace Henry (R Vt.) May 29, 1835–Dec. 8, 1913; House 1891–1901.

Powers, Llewellyn (R Maine) Oct. 14, 1836–July 28, 1908; House 1877–79, April 8, 1901–July 28, 1908; Gov. Jan. 6, 1897–Jan. 2, 1901.

Powers, Samuel Leland (R Mass.) Oct. 26, 1848–Nov. 30, 1929; House 1901–05.

Poydras, Julien de Lallande (– Orleans) April 3, 1740–June 14, 1824; House (Terr. Del.) 1809–11.

Pracht, Charles Frederick (R Pa.) Oct. 20, 1880–Dec. 22, 1950; House 1943–45.

Prall, Anning Smith (D N.Y.) Sept. 17, 1870–July 23, 1937; House Nov. 6, 1923–35.

Pratt, Charles Clarence (R Pa.) April 23, 1854–Jan. 27, 1916; House 1909–11.

Pratt, Daniel Darwin (R Ind.) Oct. 26, 1813–June 17, 1877; Senate 1869–75.

Pratt, Eliza Jane (D N.C.) March 5, 1902–May 13, 1981; House May 25, 1946–47.

Pratt, Harcourt Joseph (R N.Y.) Oct. 23, 1866–May 21, 1934; House 1925–33.

Pratt, Harry Hayt (R N.Y.) Nov. 11, 1864–Nov. 13, 1932; House 1915–19.

Pratt, Henry Otis (R Iowa) Feb. 11, 1838–May 22, 1931; House 1873–77.

Pratt, James Timothy (D Conn.) Dec. 14, 1802–April 11, 1887; House 1853–55.

Pratt, Joseph Marmaduke (R Pa.) Sept. 4, 1891–July 19, 1946; House Jan. 18, 1944–45.

Pratt, Le Gage (D N.J.) Dec. 14, 1852–March 9, 1911; House 1907–09.

Pratt, Ruth Sears Baker (R N.Y.) Aug. 24, 1877–Aug. 23, 1965; House 1929–33.

Pratt, Thomas George (W Md.) Feb. 18, 1804–Nov. 9, 1869; Senate Jan. 12, 1850–57; Gov. Jan. 6, 1845–Jan. 3, 1848.

Pratt, Zadock (D N.Y.) Oct. 30, 1790–April 6, 1871; House 1837–39, 1843–45.

Pray, Charles Nelson (R Mont.) April 6, 1868–Sept. 12, 1963; House 1907–13.

Prentiss, John Holmes (brother of Samuel Prentiss) (D N.Y.) April 17, 1784–June 26, 1861; House 1837–41.

Prentiss, Samuel (brother of John Holmes Prentiss) (W Vt.) March 31, 1782–Jan. 15, 1857; Senate 1831–April 11, 1842.

Prentiss, Seargeant Smith (– Miss.) Sept. 30, 1808–July 1, 1850; House May 30, 1838–39.

Prescott, Cyrus Dan (R N.Y.) Aug. 15, 1836–Oct. 23, 1902; House 1879–83.

Pressler, Larry Lee (R S.D.) March 29, 1942– ; House 1975–79; Senate 1979–97; chair Senate Commerce, Science, and Transportation 1995–97.

Preston, Francis (father of William Campbell Preston, uncle of William Ballard Preston and William Preston, cousin of James Breckinridge, John Breckinridge, James Brown, and John Brown of Virginia and Kentucky) (R Va.) Aug. 2, 1765–May 26, 1836; House 1793–97 (1793–95 no party).

Preston, Jacob Alexander (W Md.) March 12, 1796–Aug. 2, 1868; House 1843–45.

Preston, Prince Hulon Jr. (D Ga.) July 5, 1908–Feb. 8, 1961; House 1947–61.

Preston, William (nephew of Francis Preston, cousin of William Ballard Preston and William Campbell Preston) (W Ky.) Oct. 16, 1816–Sept. 21, 1887; House Dec. 6, 1852–55.

Preston, William Ballard (nephew of Francis Preston, cousin of William Preston and William Campbell Preston) (W Va.) Nov. 25, 1805–Nov. 16, 1862; House 1847–49; secretary of the navy March 8, 1849–July 22, 1850.

Preston, William Campbell (son of Francis Preston, cousin of William Preston and William Ballard Preston) (W S.C.) Dec. 27, 1794–May 22, 1860; Senate Nov. 26, 1833–Nov. 29, 1842 (Nov. 26, 1833–37 Nullifier).

Preyer, Lunsford Richardson (D N.C.) Jan. 11, 1919– ; House 1969–81.

Price, Andrew (D La.) April 2, 1854–Feb. 5, 1909; House Dec. 2, 1889–97.

Price, Charles Melvin (D Ill.) Jan. 1, 1905–April 22, 1988; House 1945–April 22, 1988; chair House Standards of Official Conduct 1969–75; chair House Armed Services 1975–85.

Price, David Eugene (D N.C.) Aug. 17, 1940– ; House 1987–95, 1997– .

Price, Emory Hilliard (D Fla.) Dec. 3, 1899–Feb. 11, 1976; House 1943–49.

Price, Hiram (R Iowa) Jan. 10, 1814–May 30, 1901; House 1863–69, 1877–81.

Price, Hugh Hiram (son of William Thompson Price) (R Wis.) Dec. 2, 1859–Dec. 25, 1904; House Jan. 18–March 3, 1887.

Price, Jesse Dashiell (D Md.) Aug. 15, 1863–May 14, 1939; House Nov. 3, 1914–19.

Price, Robert Dale (R Texas) Sept. 7, 1927– ; House 1967–75.

Price, Rodman McCamley (D N.J.) May 5, 1816–June 7, 1894; House 1851–53; Gov. Jan. 17, 1854–Jan. 20, 1857.

Price, Samuel (O W.Va.) July 28, 1805–Feb. 25, 1884; Senate Aug. 26, 1876–Jan. 26, 1877.

Price, Sterling (D Mo.) Sept. 20, 1809–Sept. 29, 1867; House 1845–Aug. 12, 1846; Gov. Jan. 3, 1853–Jan. 5, 1857.

Price, Thomas (R Ga.) Oct. 8, 1954– ; House 2005– .

Price, Thomas Lawson (D Mo.) Jan. 19, 1809–July 15, 1870; House Jan. 21, 1862–63.

Price, William Pierce (D Ga.) Jan. 29, 1835–Nov. 4, 1908; House Dec. 22, 1870–73.

Price, William Thompson (father of Hugh Hiram Price) (R Wis.) June 17, 1824–Dec. 6, 1886; House 1883–Dec. 6, 1886.

Pridemore, Auburn Lorenzo (D Va.) June 27, 1837–May 17, 1900; House 1877–79.

Priest, James Percy (D Tenn.) April 1, 1900–Oct. 12, 1956; House 1941–Oct. 12, 1956 (1941–43 Independent Democrat); chair House Interstate and Foreign Commerce 1955–57.

Prince, Charles Henry (R Ga.) May 9, 1837–April 3, 1912; House July 25, 1868–69.

Prince, George Washington (R Ill.) March 4, 1854–Sept. 26, 1939; House Dec. 2, 1895–1913.

Prince, Oliver Hillhouse (– Ga.) 1787–Oct. 9, 1837; Senate Nov. 7, 1828–29.

Prince, William (– Ind.) 1772–Sept. 8, 1824; House 1823–Sept. 8, 1824.

Prindle, Elizur H. (R N.Y.) May 6, 1829–Oct. 7, 1890; House 1871–73.

Pringey, Joseph Colburn (R Okla.) May 22, 1858–Feb. 11, 1935; House 1921–23.

Pringle, Benjamin (W N.Y.) Nov. 9, 1807–June 7, 1887; House 1853–57.

Pritchard, George Moore (son of Jeter Connelly Pritchard) (R N.C.) Jan. 4, 1886–April 24, 1955; House 1929–31.

Pritchard, Jeter Connelly (father of George Moore Pritchard) (R N.C.) July 12, 1857–April 10, 1921; Senate Jan. 23, 1895–1903.

Pritchard, Joel McFee (R Wash.) May 5, 1925–Oct. 9, 1997; House 1973–85.

Proctor, Redfield (R Vt.) June 1, 1831–March 4, 1908; Senate Nov. 2, 1891–March 4, 1908; Gov. Oct. 3, 1878–Oct. 7, 1880; secretary of war March 5, 1889–Nov. 5, 1891.

Proffit, George H. (W Ind.) Sept. 7, 1807–Sept. 7, 1847; House 1839–43.

Prokop, Stanley A. (D Pa.) July 29, 1909–Nov. 11, 1977; House 1959–61.

Prosser, William Farrand (R Tenn.) March 16, 1834–Sept. 23, 1911; House 1869–71.

Prouty, Solomon Francis (R Iowa) Jan. 17, 1854–July 16, 1927; House 1911–15.

Prouty, Winston Lewis (R Vt.) Sept. 1, 1906–Sept. 10, 1971; House 1951–59; Senate 1959–Sept. 10, 1971.

Proxmire, William (D Wis.) Nov. 11, 1915– ; Senate Aug. 28, 1957–89; chair Senate Banking, Housing, and Urban Affairs 1975–81, 1987–89.

Pruyn, John Van Schaick Lansing (D N.Y.) June 22, 1811–Nov. 21, 1877; House Dec. 7, 1863–65, 1867–69.

Pryce, Deborah (R Ohio) July 29, 1951– ; House 1993– .

Pryor, David Hampton (father of Mark Pryor) (D Ark.) Aug. 29, 1934– ; House Nov. 8, 1966–73; Senate 1979–97; Gov. Jan. 14, 1975–Jan. 3, 1979.

Pryor, Luke (D Ala.) July 5, 1820–Aug. 5, 1900; Senate Jan. 7–Nov. 23, 1880 (no party); House 1883–85.

Pryor, Mark (son of David Hampton Pryor) (D Ark.) Jan. 10, 1963– ; Senate 2003– .

Pryor, Roger Atkinson (D Va.) July 19, 1828–March 14, 1919; House Dec. 7, 1859–61.

Pucinski, Roman Conrad (D Ill.) May 13, 1919– ; House 1959–73.

Pugh, George Ellis (D Ohio) Nov. 28, 1822–July 19, 1876; Senate 1855–61.

Pugh, James Lawrence (D Ala.) Dec. 12, 1820–March 9, 1907; House 1859–Jan. 21, 1861 (no party); Senate Nov. 24, 1880–97.

Pugh, John (R Pa.) June 2, 1761–July 13, 1842; House 1805–09.

Pugh, John Howard (R N.J.) June 23, 1827–April 30, 1905; House 1877–79.

Pugh, Samuel Johnson (R Ky.) Jan. 28, 1850–April 17, 1922; House 1895–1901.

Pugsley, Cornelius Amory (D N.Y.) July 17, 1850–Sept. 10, 1936; House 1901–03.

Pugsley, Jacob Joseph (R Ohio) Jan. 25, 1838–Feb. 5, 1920; House 1887–91.

Pujo, Arsène Paulin (D La.) Dec. 16, 1861–Dec. 31, 1939; House 1903–13.

Pulitzer, Joseph (D N.Y.) April 10, 1847–Oct. 29, 1911; House 1885–April 10, 1886.

Purcell, Graham Boynton Jr. (D Texas) May 5, 1919– ; House Jan. 27, 1962–73.

Purcell, William Edward (D N.D.) Aug. 3, 1856–Nov. 23, 1928; Senate Feb. 1, 1910–Feb. 1, 1911.

Purdy, Smith Meade (D N.Y.) July 31, 1796–March 30, 1870; House 1843–45.

Purman, William James (R Fla.) April 11, 1840–Aug. 14, 1928; House 1873–Jan. 25, 1875, 1875–77.

Purnell, Fred Sampson (R Ind.) Oct. 25, 1882–Oct. 21, 1939; House 1917–33.

Pursell, Carl Duane (R Mich.) Dec. 19, 1932– ; House 1977–93.

Purtell, William Arthur (R Conn.) May 6, 1897–May 31, 1978; Senate Aug. 29–Nov. 4, 1952, 1953–59.

Purviance, Samuel Anderson (R Pa.) Jan. 10, 1809–Feb. 14, 1882; House 1855–59 (1855–57 Whig).

Purviance, Samuel Dinsmore (F N.C.) Jan. 7, 1774–about 1806; House 1803–05.

Puryear, Richard Clauselle (AP N.C.) Feb. 9, 1801–July 30, 1867; House 1853–57 (1853–55 Whig).

Pusey, William Henry Mills (D Iowa) July 29, 1826–Nov. 15, 1900; House 1883–85.

Putnam, Adam H. (R Fla.) July 31, 1974– ; House 2001– .

Putnam, Harvey (W N.Y.) Jan. 5, 1793–Sept. 20, 1855; House Nov. 7, 1838–39, 1847–51.

Pyle, Gladys (R S.D.) Oct. 4, 1890–March 14, 1989; Senate Nov. 9, 1938–39.

Quackenbush, John Adam (R N.Y.) Oct. 15, 1828–May 11, 1908; House 1889–93.

Quarles, James Minor (O Tenn.) Feb. 8, 1823–March 3, 1901; House 1859–61.

Quarles, Joseph Very (R Wis.) Dec. 16, 1843–Oct. 7, 1911; Senate 1899–1905.

Quarles, Julian Minor (D Va.) Sept. 25, 1848–Nov. 18, 1929; House 1899–1901.

Quarles, Tunstall (R Ky.) about 1770–Jan. 7, 1855; House 1817–June 15, 1820.

Quay, Matthew Stanley (R Pa.) Sept. 30, 1833–May 28, 1904; Senate 1887–99, Jan. 16, 1901–May 28, 1904; chair Rep. Nat. Comm. 1888–91.

Quayle, James Danforth "Dan" (R Ind.) Feb. 4, 1947– ; House 1977–81; Senate 1981–Jan. 3, 1989; vice president 1989–93.

Quayle, John Francis (D N.Y.) Dec. 1, 1868–Nov. 27, 1930; House 1923–Nov. 27, 1930.

Quezon, Manuel Luis (Nat. P.I.) Aug. 19, 1878–Aug. 1, 1944; House (Res. Comm.) Nov. 23, 1909–Oct. 15, 1916; Pres. (P.I.) 1935–44.

Quie, Albert Harold (R Minn.) Sept. 18, 1923– ; House Feb. 18, 1958–79; Gov. Jan. 1, 1979–Jan. 3, 1983.

Quigg, Lemuel Ely (R N.Y.) Feb. 12, 1863–July 1, 1919; House Jan. 30, 1894–99.

Quigley, James Michael (D Pa.) March 30, 1918– ; House 1955–57, 1959–61.

Quillen, James Henry (R Tenn.) Jan. 11, 1916–Nov. 2, 2003; House 1963–97.

Quin, Percy Edwards (D Miss.) Oct. 30, 1872–Feb. 4, 1932; House 1913–Feb. 4, 1932.

Quincy, Josiah (F Mass.) Feb. 4, 1772–July 1, 1864; House 1805–13.

Quinn, James Leland (D Pa.) Sept. 8, 1875–Nov. 12, 1960; House 1935–39.

Quinn, John (D N.Y.) Aug. 9, 1839–Feb. 23, 1903; House 1889–91.

Quinn, John Francis "Jack" (R N.Y.) April 13, 1951– ; House 1993–2005.

Quinn, Peter Anthony (D N.Y.) May 10, 1904–Dec. 23, 1974; House 1945–47.

Quinn, Terence John (D N.Y.) Oct. 16, 1836–June 18, 1878; House 1877–June 18, 1878.

Quinn, Thomas Vincent (D N.Y.) March 16, 1903–March 1, 1982; House 1949–Dec. 30, 1951.

Quitman, John Anthony (D Miss.) Sept. 1, 1799–July 17, 1858; House 1855–July 17, 1858; Gov. Dec. 3, 1835–Jan. 7, 1836, Jan. 10, 1850–Feb. 3, 1851.

Rabaut, Louis Charles (D Mich.) Dec. 5, 1886–Nov. 12, 1961; House 1935–47, 1949–Nov. 12, 1961.

Rabin, Benjamin J. (D N.Y.) June 3, 1896–Feb. 22, 1969; House 1945–Dec. 31, 1947.

Race, John Abner (D Wis.) May 12, 1914–Nov. 10, 1983; House 1965–67.

Radanovich, George P. (R Calif.) June 20, 1955– ; House 1995– .

Radcliffe, Amos Henry (R N.J.) Jan. 16, 1870–Dec. 29, 1950; House 1919–23.

Radcliffe, George Lovic Pierce (D Md.) Aug. 22, 1877–July 29, 1974; Senate 1935–47.

Radford, William (D N.Y.) June 24, 1814–Jan. 18, 1870; House 1863–67.

Radwan, Edmund Patrick (R N.Y.) Sept. 22, 1911–Sept. 7, 1959; House 1951–59.

Ragon, Heartsill (D Ark.) March 20, 1885–Sept. 15, 1940; House 1923–June 16, 1933.

Ragsdale, James Willard (D S.C.) Dec. 14, 1872–July 23, 1919; House 1913–July 23, 1919.

Rahall, Nick Joe II (D W.Va.) May 20, 1949– ; House 1977– .

Railsback, Thomas Fisher (R Ill.) Jan. 22, 1932– ; House 1967–83.

Raines, John (R N.Y.) May 6, 1840–Dec. 16, 1909; House 1889–93.

Rainey, Henry Thomas (D Ill.) Aug. 20, 1860–Aug. 19, 1934; House 1903–21, 1923–Aug. 19, 1934; House majority leader 1931–33; Speaker March 9, 1933–Aug. 19, 1934.

Rainey, John William (D Ill.) Dec. 21, 1880–May 4, 1923; House April 2, 1918–May 4, 1923.

Rainey, Joseph Hayne (R S.C.) June 21, 1832–Aug. 2, 1887; House Dec. 12, 1870–79.

Rainey, Lilius Bratton (D Ala.) July 27, 1876–Sept. 27, 1959; House Sept. 30, 1919–23.

Rains, Albert M. (D Ala.) March 11, 1902–March 22, 1991; House 1945–65.

Raker, John Edward (D Calif.) Feb. 22, 1863–Jan. 22, 1926; House 1911–Jan. 22, 1926.

Ralston, Samuel Moffett (D Ind.) Dec. 1, 1857–Oct. 14, 1925; Senate 1923–Oct. 14, 1925; Gov. Jan. 13, 1913–Jan. 8, 1917.

Ramey, Frank Marion (R Ill.) Sept. 23, 1881–March 27, 1942; House 1929–31.

Ramey, Homer Alonzo (R Ohio) March 2, 1891–April 13, 1960; House 1943–49.

Ramsay, Robert Lincoln (D W.Va.) March 24, 1877–Nov. 14, 1956; House 1933–39, 1941–43, 1949–53.

Ramsey, Alexander (R Minn.) Sept. 8, 1815–April 22, 1903; House 1843–47 (Whig Pa.); Senate 1863–75; Gov. April 2, 1849–53 (Minn. Terr.), Jan. 2, 1860–July 10, 1863; secretary of war Dec. 10, 1879–March 5, 1881.

Ramsey, John Rathbone (R N.J.) April 25, 1862–April 10, 1933; House 1917–21.

Ramsey, Robert (W Pa.) Feb. 15, 1780–Dec. 12, 1849; House 1833–35, 1841–43.

Ramsey, William (D Pa.) Sept. 7, 1779–Sept. 29, 1831; House 1827–Sept. 29, 1831 (1827–29 no party).

Ramsey, William Sterrett (D Pa.) June 12, 1810–Oct. 17, 1840; House 1839–Oct. 17, 1840.

Ramseyer, Christian William (R Iowa) March 13, 1875–Nov. 1, 1943; House 1915–33.

Ramspeck, Robert C. Word (D Ga.) Sept. 5, 1890–Sept. 10, 1972; House Oct. 2, 1929–Dec. 31, 1945.

Ramstad, James (R Minn.) May 6, 1946– ; House 1991– .

Randall, Alexander (W Md.) Jan. 3, 1803–Nov. 21, 1881; House 1841–43.

Randall, Benjamin (W Maine) Nov. 14, 1789–Oct. 11, 1859; House 1839–43.

Randall, Charles Hiram (Prohib. Calif.) July 23, 1865–Feb. 18, 1951; House 1915–21.

Randall, Charles Sturtevant (R Mass.) Feb. 20, 1824–Aug. 17, 1904; House 1889–95.

Randall, Clifford Ellsworth (R Wis.) Dec. 25, 1876–Oct. 16, 1934; House 1919–21.

Randall, Samuel Jackson (D Pa.) Oct. 10, 1828–April 13, 1890; House 1863–April 13, 1890; Speaker Dec. 4, 1876–77, Oct. 15, 1877–79, March 18, 1879–81.

Randall, William Harrison (UU Ky.) July 15, 1812–Aug. 1, 1881; House 1863–67.

Randall, William Joseph (D Mo.) July 16, 1909– ; House March 3, 1959–77.

Randell, Choice Boswell (nephew of Lucius Jeremiah Gartrell) (D Texas) Jan. 1, 1857–Oct. 19, 1945; House 1901–13.

Randolph, James Fitz (father of Theodore Fitz Randolph) (– N.J.) June 26, 1791–Jan. 25, 1872; House Dec. 1, 1827–33.

Randolph, James Henry (R Tenn.) Oct. 18, 1825–Aug. 22, 1900; House 1877–79.

Randolph, Jennings (D W.Va.) March 8, 1902–May 8, 1998; House 1933–47; Senate Nov. 5, 1958–85; chair Senate Public Works 1966–77; chair Senate Environment and Public Works 1977–81.

Randolph, John (– Va.) June 2, 1773–May 24, 1833; House 1799–1813, 1815–17, 1819–Dec. 26, 1825, 1827–29, March 4–May 24, 1833; Senate Dec. 26, 1825–27.

Randolph, Joseph Fitz (W N.J.) March 14, 1803–March 20, 1873; House 1837–43.

Randolph, Theodore Fitz (son of James Fitz Randolph) (D N.J.) June 24, 1826–Nov. 7, 1883; Senate 1875–81; Gov. Jan. 19, 1869–Jan. 16, 1872.

Randolph, Thomas Mann (son-in-law of Pres. Thomas Jefferson) (R Va.) Oct. 1, 1768–June 20, 1828; House 1803–07; Gov. Dec. 1, 1819–Dec. 1, 1822.

Raney, John Henry (R Mo.) Sept. 28, 1849–Jan. 23, 1928; House 1895–97.

Rangel, Charles Bernard (D N.Y.) June 1, 1930– ; House 1971– .

Rankin, Christopher (– Miss.) 1788–March 14, 1826; House 1819–March 14, 1826.

Rankin, Jeannette (R Mont.) June 11, 1880–May 18, 1973; House 1917–19, 1941–43.

Rankin, John Elliott (D Miss.) March 29, 1882–Nov. 26, 1960; House 1921–53; chair House Veterans' Affairs 1949–53.

Rankin, Joseph (D Wis.) Sept. 25, 1833–Jan. 24, 1886; House 1883–Jan. 24, 1886.

Ranney, Ambrose Arnold (R Mass.) April 17, 1821–March 5, 1899; House 1881–87.

Ransdell, Joseph Eugene (D La.) Oct. 7, 1858–July 27, 1954; House Aug. 29, 1899–1913; Senate 1913–31.

Ransier, Alonzo Jacob (R S.C.) Jan. 3, 1834–Aug. 17, 1882; House 1873–75.

Ransley, Harry Clay (R Pa.) Feb. 5, 1863–Nov. 7, 1941; House Nov. 2, 1920–37.

Ransom, Matt Whitaker (cousin of Wharton Jackson Green) (D N.C.) Oct. 8, 1826–Oct. 8, 1904; Senate Jan. 30, 1872–95; elected pres. pro tempore Jan. 7, 1895.

Rantoul, Robert Jr. (D Mass.) Aug. 13, 1805–Aug. 7, 1852; Senate Feb. 1–March 3, 1851; House March 4, 1851–Aug. 7, 1852.

Rapier, James Thomas (R Ala.) Nov. 13, 1837–May 31, 1883; House 1873–75.

Rarick, John Richard (D La.) Jan. 29, 1924– ; House 1967–75.

Rariden, James (W Ind.) Feb. 14, 1795–Oct. 20, 1856; House 1837–41.

Ratchford, William Richard (D Conn.) May 24, 1934– ; House 1979–85.

Rathbone, Henry Riggs (grandson of Ira Harris) (R Ill.) Feb. 12, 1870–July 15, 1928; House 1923–July 15, 1928.

Rathbun, George Oscar (D N.Y.) 1803–Jan. 5, 1870; House 1843–47.

Rauch, George Washington (D Ind.) Feb. 22, 1876–Nov. 4, 1940; House 1907–17.

Raum, Green Berry (R Ill.) Dec. 3, 1829–Dec. 18, 1909; House 1867–69.

Ravenel, Arthur Jr. (R S.C.) March 29, 1927– ; House 1987–95.

Rawlins, Joseph Lafayette (D Utah) March 28, 1850–May 24, 1926; House (Terr. Del.) 1893–95; Senate 1897–1903.

Rawls, Morgan (D Ga.) June 29, 1829–Oct. 18, 1906; House 1873–March 24, 1874.

Rawson, Charles Augustus (R Iowa) May 29, 1867–Sept. 2, 1936; Senate Feb. 24–Dec. 1, 1922.

Ray, George Washington (R N.Y.) Feb. 3, 1844–Jan. 10, 1925; House 1883–85, 1891–Sept. 11, 1902.

Ray, John Henry (R N.Y.) Sept. 27, 1886–May 21, 1975; House 1953–63.

Ray, Joseph Warren (R Pa.) May 25, 1849–Sept. 15, 1928; House 1889–91.

Ray, Ossian (R N.H.) Dec. 13, 1835–Jan. 28, 1892; House Jan. 8, 1881–85.

Ray, Richard Belmont (D Ga.) Feb. 2, 1927–May 29, 1999; House 1983–93.

Ray, William Henry (R Ill.) Dec. 14, 1812–Jan. 25, 1881; House 1873–75.

Rayburn, Samuel Taliaferro (D Texas) Jan. 6, 1882–Nov. 16, 1961; House 1913–Nov. 16, 1961; House majority leader 1937–Sept. 16, 1940; House minority leader 1947–49, 1953–55; Speaker Sept.

16, 1940–43, Jan. 6, 1943–47, 1949–53, Jan. 5, 1955–59, Jan. 7, 1959–Nov. 16, 1961.

Rayfiel, Leo Frederick (D N.Y.) March 22, 1888–Nov. 18, 1978; House 1945–Sept. 13, 1947.

Raymond, Henry Jarvis (R N.Y.) Jan. 24, 1820–June 18, 1869; House 1865–67; chair Rep. Nat. Comm. 1864–66.

Raymond, John Baldwin (R Dakota) Dec. 5, 1844–Jan. 3, 1886; House (Terr. Del.) 1883–85.

Rayner, Isidor (D Md.) April 11, 1850–Nov. 25, 1912; House 1887–89, 1891–95; Senate 1905–Nov. 25, 1912.

Rayner, Kenneth (W N.C.) June 20, 1808–March 4, 1884; House 1839–45.

Rea, David (D Mo.) Jan. 19, 1831–June 13, 1901; House 1875–79.

Rea, John (R Pa.) Jan. 27, 1755–Feb. 26, 1829; House 1803–11, May 11, 1813–15.

Read, Almon Heath (D Pa.) June 12, 1790–June 3, 1844; House March 18, 1842–June 3, 1844.

Read, George (– Del.) Sept. 18, 1733–Sept. 21, 1798; Senate 1789–Sept. 18, 1793; Cont. Cong. 1774–77.

Read, Jacob (F S.C.) 1752–July 17, 1816; Senate 1795–1801; elected pres. pro tempore Nov. 22, 1797; Cont. Cong. 1783–85.

Read, Nathan (F Mass.) July 2, 1759–Jan. 20, 1849; House Nov. 25, 1800–03.

Read, William Brown (D Ky.) Dec. 14, 1817–Aug. 5, 1880; House 1871–75.

Reade, Edwin Godwin (AP N.C.) Nov. 13, 1812–Oct. 18, 1894; House 1855–57.

Reading, John Roberts (D Pa.) Nov. 1, 1826–Feb. 14, 1886; House 1869–April 13, 1870.

Ready, Charles (uncle of William T. Haskell) (W Tenn.) Dec. 22, 1802–June 4, 1878; House 1853–59.

Reagan, John Henninger (D Texas) Oct. 8, 1818–March 6, 1905; House 1857–61, 1875–87; Senate 1887–June 10, 1891.

Reames, Alfred Evan (D Ore.) Feb. 5, 1870–March 4, 1943; Senate Feb. 1–Nov. 8, 1938.

Reams, Henry Frazier (I Ohio) Jan. 15, 1897–Sept. 15, 1971; House 1951–55.

Reavis, Charles Frank (R Neb.) Sept. 5, 1870–May 26, 1932; House 1915–June 3, 1922.

Reber, John (R Pa.) Feb. 1, 1858–Sept. 26, 1931; House 1919–23.

Redden, Monroe Minor (D N.C.) Sept. 24, 1901–Dec. 16, 1987; House 1947–53.

Redfield, William Cox (D N.Y.) June 18, 1858–June 13, 1932; House 1911–13; secretary of commerce March 5, 1913–Oct. 31, 1919.

Reding, John Randall (D N.H.) Oct. 18, 1805–Oct. 8, 1892; House 1841–45.

Redlin, Rolland W. (D N.D.) Feb. 29, 1920– ; House 1965–67.

Redmond, Bill (R N.M.) Jan. 28, 1955– ; House May 20, 1997–99.

Reece, Brazilla Carroll (husband of Louise Goff Reece, son-in-law of Guy Despard Goff) (R Tenn.) Dec. 22, 1889–March 19, 1961; House 1921–31, 1933–47, 1951–March 19, 1961; chair Rep. Nat. Comm. 1946–48.

Reece, Louise Goff (widow of Brazilla Carroll Reece, daughter of Guy Despard Goff, granddaughter of Nathan Goff) (R Tenn.) Nov. 6, 1898–May 14, 1970; House May 16, 1961–63.

Reed, Charles Manning (W Pa.) April 3, 1803–Dec. 16, 1871; House 1843–45.

Reed, Chauncey William (R Ill.) June 2, 1890–Feb. 9, 1956; House 1935–Feb. 9, 1956; chair House Judiciary 1953–55.

Reed, Clyde Martin (R Kan.) Oct. 19, 1871–Nov. 8, 1949; Senate 1939–Nov. 8, 1949; Gov. Jan. 14, 1929–Jan. 12, 1931.

Reed, Daniel Alden (R N.Y.) Sept. 15, 1875–Feb. 19, 1959; House 1919–Feb. 19, 1959; chair House Ways and Means 1953–55.

Reed, David Aiken (R Pa.) Dec. 21, 1880–Feb. 10, 1953; Senate Aug. 8, 1922–35.

Reed, Edward Cambridge (J N.Y.) March 8, 1793–May 1, 1883; House 1831–33.

Reed, Eugene Elliott (D N.H.) April 23, 1866–Dec. 15, 1940; House 1913–15.

Reed, Isaac (W Maine) Aug. 22, 1809–Sept. 19, 1887; House June 25, 1852–53.

Reed, James Alexander (D Mo.) Nov. 9, 1861–Sept. 8, 1944; Senate 1911–29.

Reed, James Byron (D Ark.) Jan. 2, 1881–April 27, 1935; House Oct. 20, 1923–29.

Reed, John (father of John Reed, below) (F Mass.) Nov. 11, 1751–Feb. 17, 1831; House 1795–1801.

Reed, John (son of John Reed, above) (W Mass.) Sept. 2, 1781–Nov. 25, 1860; House 1813–17 (Federalist), 1821–41 (1821–35 Federalist, 1835–37 Anti-Mason).

Reed, John Francis "Jack" (D R.I.) Nov. 12, 1949– ; House 1991–97; Senate 1997– .

Reed, Joseph Rea (R Iowa) March 12, 1835–April 2, 1925; House 1889–91.

Reed, Philip (R Md.) 1760–Nov. 2, 1829; Senate Nov. 25, 1806–13; House 1817–19, March 19, 1822–23.

Reed, Robert Rentoul (W Pa.) March 12, 1807–Dec. 14, 1864; House 1849–51.

Reed, Stuart Felix (R W.Va.) Jan. 8, 1866–July 4, 1935; House 1917–25.

Reed, Thomas Brackett (R Maine) Oct. 18, 1839–Dec. 7, 1902; House 1877–Sept. 4, 1899; Speaker Dec. 2, 1889–91, Dec. 2, 1895–97, March 15, 1897–99.

Reed, Thomas Buck (– Miss.) May 7, 1787–Nov. 26, 1829; Senate Jan. 28, 1826–27, March 4–Nov. 26, 1829.

Reed, William (F Mass.) June 6, 1776–Feb. 18, 1837; House 1811–15.

Reeder, William Augustus (R Kan.) Aug. 28, 1849–Nov. 7, 1929; House 1899–1911.

Rees, Edward Herbert (R Kan.) June 3, 1886–Oct. 25, 1969; House 1937–61; chair House Post Office and Civil Service 1947–49, 1953–55.

Rees, Rollin Raymond (R Kan.) Jan. 10, 1865–May 30, 1935; House 1911–13.

Rees, Thomas Mankell (D Calif.) March 26, 1925–Dec. 9, 2003; House Dec. 15, 1965–77.

Reese, David Addison (W Ga.) March 3, 1794–Dec. 16, 1871; House 1853–55.

Reese, Seaborn (D Ga.) Nov. 28, 1846–March 1, 1907; House Dec. 4, 1882–87.

Reeves, Albert Lee Jr. (R Mo.) May 31, 1906–April 15, 1987; House 1947–49.

Reeves, Henry Augustus (D N.Y.) Dec. 7, 1832–March 4, 1916; House 1869–71.

Reeves, Walter (R Ill.) Sept. 25, 1848–April 9, 1909; House 1895–1903.

Regan, Kenneth Mills (D Texas) March 6, 1893–Aug. 15, 1959; House Aug. 23, 1947–55.

Regula, Ralph Straus (R Ohio) Dec. 3, 1924– ; House 1973– .

Rehberg, Dennis "Denny" (R Mont.) Oct. 5, 1955– ; House 2001– .

Reichert, David G. (R Wash.) Aug. 29, 1950– ; House 2005– .

Reid, Charles Chester (D Ark.) June 15, 1868–May 20, 1922; House 1901–11.

Reid, Charlotte Thompson (R Ill.) Sept. 27, 1913– ; House 1963–Oct. 7, 1971.

Reid, David Settle (nephew of Thomas Settle) (D N.C.) April 19, 1813–June 19, 1891; House 1843–47; Senate Dec. 6, 1854–59; Gov. Jan. 1, 1851–Dec. 6, 1854.

Reid, Frank R. (R Ill.) April 18, 1879–Jan. 25, 1945; House 1923–35.

Reid, Harry (D Nev.) Dec. 2, 1939– ; House 1983–87; Senate 1987– ; chair Senate Select Ethics Jan. 3, 2001–Jan. 20, 2001, June 6, 2001–03; Senate majority leader 2005– .

Reid, James Wesley (D N.C.) June 11, 1849–Jan. 1, 1902; House Jan. 28, 1885–Dec. 31, 1886.

Reid, John William (D Mo.) June 14, 1821–Nov. 22, 1881; House March 4–Dec. 2, 1861.

Reid, Ogden Rogers (D N.Y.) June 24, 1925– ; House 1963–75 (1963–March 22, 1972, Republican).

Reid, Robert Raymond (R Ga.) Sept. 8, 1789–July 1, 1841; House Feb. 18, 1819–23; Gov. (Fla. Terr.) 1839–41.

Reifel, Benjamin (R S.D.) Sept. 19, 1906–Jan. 2, 1990; House 1961–71.

Reilly, James Bernard (D Pa.) Aug. 12, 1845–May 14, 1924; House 1875–79, 1889–95.

Reilly, John (D Pa.) Feb. 22, 1836–April 19, 1904; House 1875–77.

Reilly, Michael Kieran (D Wis.) July 15, 1869–Oct. 14, 1944; House 1913–17, Nov. 4, 1930–39.

Reilly, Thomas Lawrence (D Conn.) Sept. 20, 1858–July 6, 1924; House 1911–15.

Reilly, Wilson (– Pa.) Aug. 8, 1811–Aug. 26, 1885; House 1857–59.

Reily, Luther (D Pa.) Oct. 17, 1794–Feb. 20, 1854; House 1837–39.

Reinecke, Edwin (R Calif.) Jan. 7, 1924– ; House 1965–Jan. 21, 1969.

Relfe, James Hugh (D Mo.) Oct. 17, 1791–Sept. 14, 1863; House 1843–47.

Remann, Frederick (R Ill.) May 10, 1847–July 14, 1895; House March 4–July 14, 1895.

Rencher, Abraham (W N.C.) Aug. 12, 1798–July 6, 1883; House 1829–39 (1829–33 Jacksonian, 1833–37 Anti-Jacksonian), 1841–43; Gov. (N.M. Terr.) 1857–61.

Renzi, Rick (R Ariz.) June 11, 1958– ; House 2003– .

Resa, Alexander John (D Ill.) Aug. 4, 1887–July 4, 1964; House 1945–47.

Resnick, Joseph Yale (D N.Y.) July 13, 1924–Oct. 6, 1969; House 1965–69.

Reuss, Henry Schoellkopf (D Wis.) Feb. 22, 1912– ; House 1955–83; chair House Banking, Currency, and Housing 1975–77; chair House Banking, Finance, and Urban Affairs 1977–81.

Revels, Hiram Rhodes (R Miss.) Sept. 27, 1827–Jan. 16, 1901; Senate Feb. 23, 1870–71.

Revercomb, William Chapman (R W.Va.) July 20, 1895–Oct. 6, 1979; Senate 1943–49, Nov. 7, 1956–59; chair Senate Public Works 1947–49.

Reyburn, John Edgar (father of William Stuart Reyburn) (R Pa.) Feb. 7, 1845–Jan. 4, 1914; House Feb. 18, 1890–97, Nov. 6, 1906–March 31, 1907.

Reyburn, William Stuart (son of John Edgar Reyburn) (R Pa.) Dec. 17, 1882–July 25, 1946; House May 23, 1911–13.

Reyes, Silvestre (D Texas) Nov. 10, 1944– ; House 1997– .

Reynolds, Edwin Ruthvin (R N.Y.) Feb. 16, 1816–July 4, 1908; House Dec. 5, 1860–61.

Reynolds, Gideon (W N.Y.) Aug. 9, 1813–July 13, 1896; House 1847–51.

Reynolds, James B. (R Tenn.) 1779–June 10, 1851; House 1815–17, 1823–25.

Reynolds, John (D Ill.) Feb. 26, 1788–May 8, 1865; House Dec. 1, 1834–37 (Jacksonian), 1839–43 (Democrat); Gov. Dec. 6, 1830–Nov. 17, 1834.

Reynolds, John Hazard (ALD N.Y.) June 21, 1819–Sept. 24, 1875; House 1859–61.

Reynolds, John Merriman (R Pa.) March 5, 1848–Sept. 14, 1933; House 1905–Jan. 17, 1911.

Reynolds, Joseph (J N.Y.) Sept. 14, 1785–Sept. 24, 1864; House 1835–37.

Reynolds, Melvin Jay (D Ill.) Jan. 8, 1952– ; House 1993–Oct. 1, 1995.

Reynolds, Robert Rice (D N.C.) June 18, 1884–Feb. 13, 1963; Senate Dec. 5, 1932–45.

Reynolds, Samuel Williams (R Neb.) Aug. 11, 1890–March 20, 1988; Senate July 3–Nov. 7, 1954.

Reynolds, Thomas M. (R N.Y.) Sept. 3, 1950– ; House 1999– .

Rhea, John (R Tenn.) 1753–May 27, 1832; House 1803–15, 1817–23.

Rhea, John Stockdale (D Ky.) March 9, 1855–July 29, 1924; House 1897–March 25, 1902, 1903–05.

Rhea, William Francis (D Va.) April 20, 1858–March 23, 1931; House 1899–1903.

Rhett, Robert Barnwell (formerly Robert Barnwell Smith) (D S.C.) Dec. 24, 1800–Sept. 14, 1876; House 1837–49; Senate Dec. 18, 1850–May 7, 1852.

Rhinock, Joseph Lafayette (D Ky.) Jan. 4, 1863–Sept. 20, 1926; House 1905–11.

Rhodes, George Milton (D Pa.) Feb. 24, 1898–Oct. 23, 1978; House 1949–69.

Rhodes, John Jacob (father of John Jacob Rhodes III) (R Ariz.) Sept. 18, 1916–Aug. 24, 2003; House 1953–83; House minority leader Dec. 7, 1974–81.

Rhodes, John Jacob III (son of John Jacob Rhodes) (R Ariz.) Sept. 8, 1943– ; House 1987–93.

Rhodes, Marion Edwards (R Mo.) Jan. 4, 1868–Dec. 25, 1928; House 1905–07, 1919–23.

Ribicoff, Abraham Alexander (D Conn.) April 9, 1910–Feb. 22, 1998; House 1949–53; Senate 1963–81; chair Senate Government Operations 1975–77; chair Senate Governmental Affairs 1977–81; Gov. Jan. 5, 1955–Jan. 21, 1961; secretary of health, education and welfare Jan. 21, 1961–July 13, 1962.

Ricaud, James Barroll (AP Md.) Feb. 11, 1808–Jan. 24, 1866; House 1855–59.

Rice, Alexander Hamilton (R Mass.) Aug. 30, 1818–July 22, 1895; House 1859–67; Gov. Jan. 5, 1876–Jan. 1, 1879.

Rice, Americus Vespucius (D Ohio) Nov. 18, 1835–April 4, 1904; House 1875–79.

Rice, Benjamin Franklin (R Ark.) May 26, 1828–Jan. 19, 1905; Senate June 23, 1868–73.

Rice, Edmund (brother of Henry Mower Rice) (D Minn.) Feb. 14, 1819–July 11, 1889; House 1887–89.

Rice, Edward Young (D Ill.) Feb. 8, 1820–April 16, 1883; House 1871–73.

Rice, Henry Mower (brother of Edmund Rice) (D Minn.) Nov. 29, 1817–Jan. 15, 1894; House (Terr. Del.) 1853–57; Senate May 11, 1858–63.

Rice, John Birchard (R Ohio) June 23, 1832–Jan. 14, 1893; House 1881–83.

Rice, John Blake (R Ill.) May 28, 1809–Dec. 17, 1874; House 1873–Dec. 17, 1874.

Rice, John Hovey (R Maine) Feb. 5, 1816–March 14, 1911; House 1861–67.

Rice, John McConnell (D Ky.) Feb. 19, 1831–Sept. 18, 1895; House 1869–73.

Rice, Theron Moses (G Mo.) Sept. 21, 1829–Nov. 7, 1895; House 1881–83.

Rice, Thomas (F Mass.) March 30, 1768–Aug. 25, 1854; House 1815–19.

Rice, William Whitney (R Mass.) March 7, 1826–March 1, 1896; House 1877–87.

Rich, Carl West (R Ohio) Sept. 12, 1898–June 26, 1972; House 1963–65.

Rich, Charles (R Vt.) Sept. 13, 1771–Oct. 15, 1824; House 1813–15.

Rich, John Tyler (R Mich.) April 23, 1841–March 28, 1926; House April 5, 1881–83; Gov. Jan. 1, 1893–Jan. 1, 1897.

Rich, Robert Fleming (R Pa.) June 23, 1883–April 28, 1968; House Nov. 4, 1930–43, 1945–51.

Richard, Gabriel (– Mich.) Oct. 15, 1767–Sept. 13, 1832; House (Terr. Del.) 1823–25.

Richards, Charles Lenmore (D Nev.) Oct. 3, 1877–Dec. 22, 1953; House 1923–25.

Richards, Jacob (R Pa.) 1773–July 20, 1816; House 1803–09.

Richards, James Alexander Dudley (D Ohio) March 22, 1845–Dec. 4, 1911; House 1893–95.

Richards, James Prioleau (D S.C.) Aug. 31, 1894–Feb. 21, 1979; House 1933–57; chair House Foreign Affairs 1951–53, 1955–57.

Richards, John (brother of Matthias Richards) (R Pa.) April 18, 1753–Nov. 13, 1822; House 1795–97.

Richards, John (– N.Y.) April 13, 1765–April 18, 1850; House 1823–25.

Richards, Mark (R Vt.) July 15, 1760–Aug. 10, 1844; House 1817–21.

Richards, Matthias (brother of John Richards) (R Pa.) Feb. 26, 1758–Aug. 4, 1830; House 1807–11.

Richardson, David Plunket (R N.Y.) May 28, 1833–June 21, 1904; House 1879–83.

Richardson, George Frederick (D Mich.) July 1, 1850–March 1, 1923; House 1893–95.

Richardson, Harry Alden (R Del.) Jan. 1, 1853–June 16, 1928; Senate 1907–13.

Richardson, James Daniel (D Tenn.) March 10, 1843–July 24, 1914; House 1885–1905; House minority leader 1899–1903.

Richardson, James Montgomery (D Ky.) July 1, 1858–Feb. 9, 1925; House 1905–07.

Richardson, John Peter (J S.C.) April 14, 1801–Jan. 24, 1864; House Dec. 19, 1836–39; Gov. Dec. 10, 1840–Dec. 8, 1842.

Richardson, John Smythe (D S.C.) Feb. 29, 1828–Feb. 24, 1894; House 1879–83.

Richardson, Joseph (– Mass.) Feb. 1, 1778–Sept. 25, 1871; House 1827–31.

Richardson, William (D Ala.) May 8, 1839–March 31, 1914; House Aug. 6, 1900–March 31, 1914.

Richardson, William Alexander (D Ill.) Jan. 16, 1811–Dec. 27, 1875; House Dec. 6, 1847–Aug. 25, 1856, 1861–Jan. 29, 1863; Senate Jan. 30, 1863–65.

Richardson, William Blaine "Bill" (D N.M.) Nov. 15, 1947– ; House 1983–Feb. 13, 1997; secretary of energy Aug. 18, 1998–Jan. 20, 2001; Gov. Jan. 1, 2003– .

Richardson, William Emanuel (D Pa.) Sept. 3, 1886–Nov. 3, 1948; House 1933–37.

Richardson, William Merchant (R Mass.) Jan. 4, 1774–March 15, 1838; House Nov. 4, 1811–April 18, 1814.

Richmond, Frederick William (D N.Y.) Nov. 15, 1923– ; House 1975–Aug. 25, 1982.

Richmond, Hiram Lawton (R Pa.) May 17, 1810–Feb. 19, 1885; House 1873–75.

Richmond, James Buchanan (D Va.) Feb. 27, 1842–April 30, 1910; House 1879–81.

Richmond, Jonathan (– N.Y.) July 31, 1774–July 28, 1853; House 1819–21.

Ricketts, Edwin Darlington (R Ohio) Aug. 3, 1867–July 3, 1937; House 1915–17, 1919–23.

Riddick, Carl Wood (R Mont.) Feb. 25, 1872–July 9, 1960; House 1919–23.

Riddle, Albert Gallatin (R Ohio) May 28, 1816–May 16, 1902; House 1861–63.

Riddle, George Read (D Del.) 1817–March 29, 1867; House 1851–55; Senate Feb. 2, 1864–March 29, 1867.

Riddle, Haywood Yancey (D Tenn.) June 20, 1834–March 28, 1879; House Dec. 14, 1875–79.

Riddleberger, Harrison Holt (Read. Va.) Oct. 4, 1844–Jan. 24, 1890; Senate 1883–89.

Rider, Ira Edgar (D N.Y.) Nov. 17, 1868–May 29, 1906; House 1903–05.

Ridge, Thomas Joseph (R Pa.) Aug. 26, 1945– ; House 1983–95; Gov. Jan. 17, 1995–Oct. 5, 2001; secretary of homeland security Jan. 24, 2003–Feb. 1, 2005.

Ridgely, Edwin Reed (P Kan.) May 9, 1844–April 23, 1927; House 1897–1901.

Ridgely, Henry Moore (F Del.) Aug. 6, 1779–Aug. 6, 1847; House 1811–15; Senate Jan. 12, 1827–29.

Ridgway, Joseph (W Ohio) May 6, 1783–Feb. 1, 1861; House 1837–43.

Ridgway, Robert (C Va.) April 21, 1823–Oct. 16, 1870; House Jan. 27–Oct. 16, 1870.

Riegle, Donald Wayne Jr. (D Mich.) Feb. 4, 1938– ; House 1967–Dec. 30, 1976 (1967–73 Republican); Senate Dec. 30, 1976–95; chair Senate Banking, Housing, and Urban Affairs 1989–95.

Riehlman, Roy Walter (R N.Y.) Aug. 26, 1899–July 16, 1978; House 1947–65.

Rife, John Winebrenner (R Pa.) Aug. 14, 1846–April 17, 1908; House 1889–93.

Riggs, Frank (R Calif.) Sept. 5, 1950– ; House 1991–93, 1995–99.

Riggs, James Milton (D Ill.) April 17, 1839–Nov. 18, 1933; House 1883–87.

Riggs, Jetur Rose (ALD N.J.) June 20, 1809–Nov. 5, 1869; House 1859–61.

Riggs, Lewis (D N.Y.) Jan. 16, 1789–Nov. 6, 1870; House 1841–43.

Rigney, Hugh McPheeters (D Ill.) July 31, 1873–Oct. 12, 1950; House 1937–39.

Riker, Samuel (R N.Y.) April 8, 1743–May 19, 1823; House Nov. 5, 1804–05, 1807–09.

Riley, Robert "Bob" (R Ala.) Oct. 3, 1944– ; House 1997–2003.

Riley, Corinne Boyd (widow of John Jacob Riley) (D S.C.) July 4, 1893–April 12, 1979; House April 10, 1962–63.

Riley, John Jacob (husband of Corinne Boyd Riley) (D S.C.) Feb. 1, 1895–Jan. 1, 1962; House 1945–49, 1951–Jan. 1, 1962.

Rinaker, John Irving (R Ill.) Nov. 1, 1830–Jan. 15, 1915; House June 5, 1896–97.

Rinaldo, Matthew John (R N.J.) Sept. 1, 1931– ; House 1973–93.

Ringgold, Samuel (R Md.) Jan. 15, 1770–Oct. 18, 1829; House Oct. 15, 1810–15, 1817–21.

Riordan, Daniel Joseph (D N.Y.) July 7, 1870–April 28, 1923; House 1899–1901, Nov. 6, 1906–April 28, 1923.

Ripley, Eleazar Wheelock (brother of James Wheelock Ripley) (D La.) April 15, 1782–March 2, 1839; House 1835–March 2, 1839 (1835–37 Jacksonian).

Ripley, James Wheelock (brother of Eleazar Wheelock Ripley) (J Maine) March 12, 1786–June 17, 1835; House Sept. 11, 1826–March 12, 1830 (Sept. 11, 1826–29 no party).

Ripley, Thomas C. (W N.Y.) ?–?; House Dec. 7, 1846–47.

Risenhoover, Theodore Marshall (D Okla.) Nov. 3, 1934– ; House 1975–79.

Risk, Charles Francis (R R.I.) Aug. 19, 1897–Dec. 26, 1943; House Aug. 6, 1935–37, 1939–41.

Risley, Elijah (W N.Y.) May 7, 1787–Jan. 9, 1870; House 1849–51.

Ritchey, Thomas (D Ohio) Jan. 19, 1801–March 9, 1863; House 1847–49, 1853–55.

Ritchie, Byron Foster (son of James Monroe Ritchie) (D Ohio) Jan. 29, 1853–Aug. 22, 1928; House 1893–95.

Ritchie, David (R Pa.) Aug. 19, 1812–Jan. 24, 1867; House 1853–59 (1853–57 Whig).

Ritchie, James Monroe (father of Byron Foster Ritchie) (R Ohio) July 28, 1829–Aug. 17, 1918; House 1881–83.

Ritchie, John (D Md.) Aug. 12, 1831–Oct. 27, 1887; House 1871–73.

Ritter, Burwell Clark (uncle of Walter Evans) (D Ky.) Jan. 6, 1810–Oct. 1, 1880; House 1865–67.

Ritter, Donald Lawrence (R Pa.) Oct. 21, 1940– ; House 1979–93.

Ritter, John (D Pa.) Feb. 6, 1779–Nov. 24, 1851; House 1843–47.

Rivera, Luis Muñoz (U P.R.) July 17, 1859–Nov. 15, 1916; House (Res. Comm.) 1911–Nov. 15, 1916.

Rivers, Lucius Mendel (D S.C.) Sept. 28, 1905–Dec. 28, 1970; House 1941–Dec. 28, 1970; chair House Armed Services 1965–71.

Rivers, Lynn (D Mich.) Dec. 19, 1956– ; House 1995–2003.

Rivers, Ralph Julian (D Alaska) May 23, 1903–Aug. 14, 1976; House 1959–67.

Rivers, Thomas (AP Tenn.) Sept. 18, 1819–March 18, 1863; House 1855–57.

Rives, Francis Everod (great-uncle of Francis Rives Lassiter) (D Va.) Jan. 14, 1792–Dec. 26, 1861; House 1837–41.

Rives, William Cabell (W Va.) May 4, 1793–April 25, 1868; House 1823–29 (no party); Senate Dec. 10, 1832–Feb. 22, 1834 (Jacksonian), 1836–39 (Jacksonian), Jan. 18, 1841–45.

Rives, Zeno John (R Ill.) Feb. 22, 1874–Sept. 2, 1939; House 1905–07.

Rixey, John Franklin (D Va.) Aug. 1, 1854–Feb. 8, 1907; House 1897–Feb. 8, 1907.

Rizley, Ross (R Okla.) July 5, 1892–March 4, 1969; House 1941–49.

Roach, Sidney Crain (R Mo.) July 25, 1876–June 29, 1934; House 1921–25.

Roach, William Nathaniel (D N.D.) Sept. 25, 1840–Sept. 7, 1902; Senate 1893–99.

Roane, John (father of John Jones Roane) (J Va.) Feb. 9, 1766–Nov. 15, 1838; House 1809–15 (Republican), 1827–31, 1835–37.

Roane, John Jones (son of John Roane) (J Va.) Oct. 31, 1794–Dec. 18, 1869; House 1831–33.

Roane, William Henry (D Va.) Sept. 17, 1787–May 11, 1845; House 1815–17 (Republican); Senate March 14, 1837–41.

Roark, Charles Wickliffe (R Ky.) Jan. 22, 1887–April 5, 1929; House March 4–April 5, 1929.

Robb, Edward (D Mo.) March 19, 1857–March 13, 1934; House 1897–1905.

Robb, Charles Spittal (son-in-law of Lyndon Baines Johnson) (D Va.) June 26, 1939– ; Senate 1989–2001; Gov. Jan. 16, 1982–Jan. 18, 1986.

Robbins, Asher (W R.I.) Oct. 26, 1757–Feb. 25, 1845; Senate Oct. 31, 1825–39.

Robbins, Edward Everett (R Pa.) Sept. 27, 1860–Jan. 25, 1919; House 1897–99, 1917–Jan. 25, 1919.

Robbins, Gaston Ahi (D Ala.) Sept. 26, 1858–Feb. 22, 1902; House 1893–March 13, 1896, 1899–March 8, 1900.

Robbins, George Robbins (R N.J.) Sept. 24, 1808–Feb. 22, 1875; House 1855–59 (1855–57 Whig).

Robbins, John (D Pa.) 1808–April 27, 1880; House 1849–55, 1875–77.

Robbins, William McKendree (D N.C.) Oct. 26, 1828–May 5, 1905; House 1873–79.

Roberts, Anthony Ellmaker (grandfather of Robert Grey Bushong) (R Pa.) Oct. 29, 1803–Jan. 25, 1885; House 1855–59 (1855–57 Independent Whig).

Roberts, Brigham Henry (D Utah) March 13, 1857–Sept. 27, 1933; House 1899–Jan. 25, 1900.

Roberts, Charles Boyle (D Md.) April 19, 1842–Sept. 10, 1899; House 1875–79.

Roberts, Charles Patrick "Pat" (R Kan.) April 20, 1936– ; House 1981–97; Senate 1997– ; chair House Agriculture 1995–97; chair Senate Select Intelligence Activities 2003– .

Roberts, Clint Ronald (R S.D.) Jan. 30, 1935– ; House 1981–83.

Roberts, Edwin Ewing (R Nev.) Dec. 12, 1870–Dec. 11, 1933; House 1911–19.

Roberts, Ellis Henry (R N.Y.) Sept. 30, 1827–Jan. 8, 1918; House 1871–75.

Roberts, Ernest William (R Mass.) Nov. 22, 1858–Feb. 27, 1924; House 1899–1917.

Roberts, Herbert Ray (D Texas) March 28, 1913–April 13, 1992; House Jan. 30, 1962–81; chair House Veterans' Affairs 1975–81.

Roberts, Jonathan (R Pa.) Aug. 16, 1771–July 24, 1854; House 1811–Feb. 24, 1814; Senate Feb. 24, 1814–21.

Roberts, Kenneth Allison (D Ala.) Nov. 1, 1912–May 9, 1989; House 1951–65.

Roberts, Robert Whyte (D Miss.) Nov. 28, 1784–Jan. 4, 1865; House 1843–47.

Roberts, William Randall (D N.Y.) Feb. 6, 1830–Aug. 9, 1897; House 1871–75.

Robertson, Absalom Willis (D Va.) May 27, 1887–Nov. 1, 1971; House 1933–Nov. 5, 1946; Senate Nov. 6, 1946–Dec. 30, 1966; chair Senate Banking and Currency 1959–67.

Robertson, Alice Mary (R Okla.) Jan. 2, 1854–July 1, 1931; House 1921–23.

Robertson, Charles Raymond (R N.D.) Sept. 5, 1889–Feb. 18, 1951; House 1941–43, 1945–49.

Robertson, Edward Vivian (R Wyo.) May 27, 1881–April 15, 1963; Senate 1943–49.

Robertson, Edward White (father of Samuel Matthews Robertson) (D La.) June 13, 1823–Aug. 2, 1887; House 1877–83, March 4–Aug. 2, 1887.

Robertson, George (R Ky.) Nov. 18, 1790–May 16, 1874; House 1817–21.

Robertson, John (brother of Thomas Bolling Robertson) (W Va.) April 13, 1787–July 5, 1873; House Dec. 8, 1834–39 (Dec. 8, 1834–35 no party).

Robertson, Samuel Matthews (son of Edward White Robertson) (D La.) Jan. 1, 1852–Dec. 24, 1911; House Dec. 5, 1887–1907.

Robertson, Thomas Austin (D Ky.) Sept. 9, 1848–July 18, 1892; House 1883–87.

Robertson, Thomas Bolling (brother of John Robertson) (R La.) Feb. 27, 1779–Oct. 5, 1828; House April 30, 1812–April 20, 1818; Gov. Dec. 18, 1820–Nov. 15, 1822 (Democratic Republican).

Robertson, Thomas James (R S.C.) Aug. 3, 1823–Oct. 13, 1897; Senate July 15, 1868–77.

Robertson, William Henry (R N.Y.) Oct. 10, 1823–Dec. 6, 1898; House 1867–69.

Robeson, Edward John Jr. (D Va.) Aug. 9, 1890–March 10, 1966; House May 2, 1950–59.

Robeson, George Maxwell (nephew of George Clifford Maxwell) (R N.J.) March 16, 1829–Sept. 27, 1897; House 1879–83; secretary of the navy June 26, 1869–March 12, 1877.

Robie, Reuben (D N.Y.) July 15, 1799–Jan. 21, 1872; House 1851–53.

Robinson, Arthur Raymond (R Ind.) March 12, 1881–March 17, 1961; Senate Oct. 20, 1925–35.

Robinson, Christopher (R R.I.) May 15, 1806–Oct. 3, 1889; House 1859–61.

Robinson, Edward (W Maine) Nov. 25, 1796–Feb. 19, 1857; House April 28, 1838–39.

Robinson, George Dexter (R Mass.) Jan. 20, 1834–Feb. 22, 1896; House 1877–Jan. 7, 1884; Gov. Jan. 3, 1884–Jan. 5, 1887.

Robinson, James Carroll (D Ill.) Aug. 19, 1823–Nov. 3, 1886; House 1859–65, 1871–75.

Robinson, James Kenneth (R Va.) May 14, 1916–April 8, 1990; House 1971–85.

Robinson, James McClellan (D Ind.) May 31, 1861–Jan. 16, 1942; House 1897–1905.

Robinson, James Sidney (R Ohio) Oct. 14, 1827–Jan. 14, 1892; House 1881–Jan. 12, 1885.

Robinson, James Wallace (R Ohio) Nov. 26, 1826–June 28, 1898; House 1873–75.

Robinson, James William (D Utah) Jan. 19, 1878–Dec. 2, 1964; House 1933–47.

Robinson, John Buchanan (R Pa.) May 23, 1846–Jan. 28, 1933; House 1891–97.

Robinson, John Larne (D Ind.) May 3, 1813–March 21, 1860; House 1847–53.

Robinson, John McCracken (J Ill.) April 10, 1794–April 25, 1843; Senate Dec. 11, 1830–41.

Robinson, John Seaton (D Neb.) May 4, 1856–May 25, 1903; House 1899–1903.

Robinson, Jonathan (brother of Moses Robinson) (R Vt.) Aug. 11, 1756–Nov. 3, 1819; Senate Oct. 10, 1807–15.

Robinson, Joseph Taylor (D Ark.) Aug. 26, 1872–July 14, 1937; House 1903–Jan. 14, 1913; Senate 1913–July 14, 1937; Senate minority leader 1923–33; Senate majority leader 1933–July 14, 1937; Gov. Jan. 15–March 10, 1913.

Robinson, Leonidas Dunlap (D N.C.) April 22, 1867–Nov. 7, 1941; House 1917–21.

Robinson, Milton Stapp (R Ind.) April 20, 1832–July 28, 1892; House 1875–79.

Robinson, Moses (brother of Jonathan Robinson) (– Vt.) March 20, 1741–May 26, 1813; Senate Oct. 17, 1791–Oct. 15, 1796; Gov. (Va. Terr.) 1789–90.

Robinson, Orville (D N.Y.) Oct. 28, 1801–Dec. 1, 1882; House 1843–45.

Robinson, Thomas Jr. (D Del.) 1800–Oct. 28, 1843; House 1839–41.

Robinson, Thomas John Bright (R Iowa) Aug. 12, 1868–Jan. 27, 1958; House 1923–33.

Robinson, Tommy Franklin (R Ark.) March 7, 1942– ; House 1985–91 (1985–July 28, 1989 Democrat).

Robinson, William Erigena (D N.Y.) May 6, 1814–Jan. 23, 1892; House 1867–69, 1881–85.

Robison, David Fullerton (nephew of David Fullerton) (W Pa.) May 28, 1816–June 24, 1859; House 1855–57.

Robison, Howard Winfield (R N.Y.) Oct. 30, 1915–Sept. 26, 1987; House Jan. 14, 1958–75.

Robsion, John Marshall (father of John Marshall Robsion Jr.) (R Ky.) Jan. 2, 1873–Feb. 17, 1948; House 1919–Jan. 10, 1930, 1935–Feb. 17, 1948; Senate Jan. 11–Nov. 30, 1930.

Robsion, John Marshall Jr. (son of John Marshall Robsion) (R Ky.) Aug. 28, 1904–Feb. 14, 1990; House 1953–59.

Rochester, William Beatty (D N.Y.) Jan. 29, 1789–June 14, 1838; House 1821–April 1823.

Rockefeller, John Davison "Jay" IV (great-grandson of Nelson Wilmarth Aldrich, great-nephew of Richard Steere Aldrich, nephew of Vice Pres. Nelson Aldrich Rockefeller and Gov. Winthrop Rockefeller of Ark., son-in-law of Charles Harting Percy) (D W.Va.) June 18, 1937– ; Senate Jan. 15, 1985– ; chair Senate Veterans' Affairs 1993–95, Jan. 3, 2001–Jan. 20, 2001, June 6, 2001–03; Gov. Jan. 17, 1977–Jan. 14, 1985.

Rockefeller, Lewis Kirby (R N.Y.) Nov. 25, 1875–Sept. 18, 1948; House Nov. 2, 1937–43.

Rockhill, William (D Ind.) Feb. 10, 1793–Jan. 15, 1865; House 1847–49.

Rockwell, Francis Williams (son of Julius Rockwell) (R Mass.) May 26, 1844–June 26, 1929; House Jan. 17, 1884–91.

Rockwell, Hosea Hunt (D N.Y.) May 31, 1840–Dec. 18, 1918; House 1891–93.

Rockwell, John Arnold (W Conn.) Aug. 27, 1803–Feb. 10, 1861; House 1845–49.

Rockwell, Julius (father of Francis Williams Rockwell) (W Mass.) April 26, 1805–May 19, 1888; House 1843–51; Senate June 3, 1854–Jan. 31, 1855.

Rockwell, Robert Fay (R Colo.) Feb. 11, 1886–Sept. 29, 1950; House Dec. 9, 1941–49.

Roddenbery, Seaborn Anderson (D Ga.) Jan. 12, 1870–Sept. 25, 1913; House Feb. 16, 1910–Sept. 25, 1913.

Rodenberg, William August (R Ill.) Oct. 30, 1865–Sept. 10, 1937; House 1899–1901, 1903–13, 1915–23.

Rodey, Bernard Shandon (R N.M.) March 1, 1856–March 10, 1927; House (Terr. Del.) 1901–05.

Rodgers, Robert Lewis (R Pa.) June 2, 1875–May 9, 1960; House 1939–47.

Rodino, Peter Wallace Jr. (D N.J.) June 7, 1909– ; House 1949–89; chair House Judiciary 1973–89.

Rodman, William (R Pa.) Oct. 7, 1757–July 27, 1824; House 1811–13.

Rodney, Caesar Augustus (cousin of George Brydges Rodney) (R Del.) Jan. 4, 1772–June 10, 1824; House 1803–05, 1821–Jan. 24, 1822; Senate Jan. 24, 1822–Jan. 29, 1823; attorney general Jan. 20, 1807–Dec. 11, 1811.

Rodney, Daniel (– Del.) Sept. 10, 1764–Sept. 2, 1846; House Oct. 1, 1822–23; Senate Nov. 8, 1826–Jan. 12, 1827; Gov. Jan. 18, 1814–Jan. 21, 1817 (Federalist).

Rodney, George Brydges (cousin of Caesar Augustus Rodney) (W Del.) April 2, 1803–June 18, 1883; House 1841–45.

Rodriguez, Ciro D. (D Texas) Dec. 9, 1946– ; House April 17, 1997–2005.

Roe, Dudley George (D Md.) March 23, 1881–Jan. 4, 1970; House 1945–47.

Roe, James A. (D N.Y.) July 9, 1896–April 22, 1967; House 1945–47.

Roe, Robert A. (D N.J.) Feb. 28, 1924– ; House Nov. 4, 1969–93; chair House Science, Space, and Technology 1987–91; chair House Public Works and Transportation 1991–93.

Roemer, Charles Elson III "Buddy" (D La.) Oct. 4, 1943– ; House 1981–March 14, 1988; Gov. March 14, 1988–Jan. 13, 1992 (March 11, 1991–Jan. 13, 1992 Republican).

Roemer, Timothy John (son-in-law of John Bennett Johnston Jr.) (D Ind.) Oct. 30, 1956– ; House 1991–2003.

Rogan, James E. (R Calif.) Aug. 21, 1957– ; House 1997–2001.

Rogers, Andrew Jackson (D N.J.) July 1, 1828–May 22, 1900; House 1863–67.

Rogers, Anthony Astley Cooper (D Ark.) Feb. 14, 1821–July 27, 1899; House 1869–71.

Rogers, Byron Giles (D Colo.) Aug. 1, 1900–Dec. 31, 1983; House 1951–71.

Rogers, Charles (W N.Y.) April 30, 1800–Jan. 13, 1874; House 1843–45.

Rogers, Dwight Laing (father of Paul Grant Rogers) (D Fla.) Aug. 17, 1886–Dec. 1, 1954; House 1945–Dec. 1, 1954.

Rogers, Edith Nourse (widow of John Jacob Rogers) (R Mass.) 1881–Sept. 10, 1960; House June 30, 1925–Sept. 10, 1960; chair House Veterans' Affairs 1947–49, 1953–55.

Rogers, Edward (D N.Y.) May 30, 1787–May 29, 1857; House 1839–41.

Rogers, George Frederick (D N.Y.) March 19, 1887–Nov. 20, 1948; House 1945–47.

Rogers, Harold Dallas (R Ky.) Dec. 31, 1937– ; House 1981– .

Rogers, James (D S.C.) Oct. 24, 1795–Dec. 21, 1873; House 1835–37 (Jacksonian), 1839–43.

Rogers, John (D N.Y.) May 9, 1813–May 11, 1879; House 1871–73.

Rogers, John Henry (D Ark.) Oct. 9, 1845–April 16, 1911; House 1883–91.

Rogers, John Jacob (husband of Edith Nourse Rogers) (R Mass.) Aug. 18, 1881–March 28, 1925; House 1913–March 28, 1925.

Rogers, Paul Grant (son of Dwight Laing Rogers) (D Fla.) June 4, 1921– ; House Jan. 11, 1955–79.

Rogers, Michael "Mike" (R Mich.) June 2, 1963– ; House 2001– .

Rogers, Mike Dennis (R Ala.) July 16, 1958– ; House 2003– .

Rogers, Sion Hart (D N.C.) Sept. 30, 1825–Aug. 14, 1874; House 1853–55 (Whig), 1871–73.

Rogers, Thomas Jones (father of William Findlay Rogers) (R Pa.) 1781–Dec. 7, 1832; House March 3, 1818–April 20, 1824.

Rogers, Walter Edward (D Texas) July 19, 1908– ; House 1951–67.

Rogers, Will (D Okla.) Dec. 12, 1898–Aug. 3, 1983; House 1933–43.

Rogers, William Findlay (son of Thomas Jones Rogers) (D N.Y.) March 1, 1820–Dec. 16, 1899; House 1883–85.

Rogers, William Nathaniel (D N.H.) Jan. 10, 1892–Sept. 25, 1945; House 1923–25, Jan. 5, 1932–37.

Rogers, William Vann Jr. (D Calif.) Oct. 20, 1911–July 9, 1993; House 1943–May 23, 1944.

Rohrabacher, Dana (R Calif.) June 21, 1947– ; House 1989– .

Rohrbough, Edward Gay (R W.Va.) 1874–Dec. 12, 1956; House 1943–45, 1947–49.

Rollins, Edward Henry (R N.H.) Oct. 3, 1824–July 31, 1889; House 1861–67; Senate 1877–83.

Rollins, James Sidney (U Mo.) April 19, 1812–Jan. 9, 1888; House 1861–65 (1861–63 Constitutional Unionist).

Rolph, Thomas (R Calif.) Jan. 17, 1885–May 10, 1956; House 1941–45.

Roman, James Dixon (W Md.) Aug. 11, 1809–Jan. 19, 1867; House 1847–49.

Romeis, Jacob (R Ohio) Dec. 1, 1835–March 8, 1904; House 1885–89.

Romero, Trinidad (R N.M.) June 15, 1835–Aug. 28, 1918; House (Terr. Del.) 1877–79.

Romero-Barceló, Carlos Antonio (D P.R.) Sept. 4, 1932– ; House (Res. Comm.) 1993–2001.

Romjue, Milton Andrew (D Mo.) Dec. 5, 1874–Jan. 23, 1968; House 1917–21, 1923–43.

Romulo, Carlos Peña (– P.I.) Jan. 14, 1899–Dec. 15, 1985; House (Res. Comm.) Aug. 10, 1944–July 4, 1946.

Ronan, Daniel John (D Ill.) July 13, 1914–Aug. 13, 1969; House 1965–Aug. 13, 1969.

Roncalio, Teno (D Wyo.) March 23, 1916–March 30, 2003; House 1965–67, 1971–Dec. 30, 1978.

Roncallo, Angelo Dominick (R N.Y.) May 28, 1927– ; House 1973–75.

Rooney, Frederick Bernard (D Pa.) Nov. 6, 1925– ; House July 30, 1963–79.

Rooney, John James (D N.Y.) Nov. 29, 1903–Oct. 26, 1975; House June 6, 1944–Dec. 31, 1974.

Roosevelt, Franklin Delano Jr. (son of Pres. Franklin Delano Roosevelt, brother of James Roosevelt) (D N.Y.) Aug. 17, 1914–Aug. 17, 1988; House May 17, 1949–55 (1949–51 Liberal).

Roosevelt, James (son of Pres. Franklin Delano Roosevelt, brother of Franklin Delano Roosevelt Jr.) (D Calif.) Dec. 23, 1907–Aug. 13, 1991; House 1955–Sept. 30, 1965.

Roosevelt, James I. (uncle of Robert Barnwell Roosevelt) (D N.Y.) Dec. 14, 1795–April 5, 1875; House 1841–43.

Roosevelt, Robert Barnwell (nephew of James I. Roosevelt, uncle of Theodore Roosevelt) (D N.Y.) Aug. 7, 1829–June 14, 1906; House 1871–73.

Root, Elihu (R N.Y.) Feb. 15, 1845–Feb. 7, 1937; Senate 1909–15; secretary of war Aug. 1, 1899–Jan. 31, 1904; secretary of state July 19, 1905–Jan. 27, 1909.

Root, Erastus (J N.Y.) March 16, 1773–Dec. 24, 1846; House 1803–05 (Republican), 1809–11 (Republican), Dec. 26, 1815–17 (Republican), 1831–33.

Root, Joseph Mosley (FS Ohio) Oct. 7, 1807–April 7, 1879; House 1845–51 (1845–49 Whig).

Roots, Logan Holt (R Ark.) March 26, 1841–May 30, 1893; House June 22, 1868–71.

Rose, Charles Grandison III (D N.C.) Aug. 10, 1939– ; House 1973–97; chair House Administration 1991–95.

Rose, John Marshall (R Pa.) May 18, 1856–April 22, 1923; House 1917–23.

Rose, Robert Lawson (son of Robert Selden Rose, son-in-law of Nathaniel Allen) (W N.Y.) Oct. 12, 1804–March 14, 1877; House 1847–51.

Rose, Robert Selden (father of Robert Lawson Rose) (AMas. N.Y.) Feb. 24, 1774–Nov. 24, 1835; House 1823–27 (no party), 1829–31.

Rosecrans, William Starke (D Calif.) Sept. 6, 1819–March 11, 1898; House 1881–85.

Rosenbloom, Benjamin Louis (R W.Va.) June 3, 1880–March 22, 1965; House 1921–25.

Rosenthal, Benjamin Stanley (D N.Y.) June 8, 1923–Jan. 4, 1983; House Feb. 20, 1962–Jan. 4, 1983.

Rosier, Joseph (D W.Va.) Jan. 24, 1870–Oct. 7, 1951; Senate Jan. 3, 1941–Nov. 17, 1942.

Ros-Lehtinen, Ileana (R Fla.) July 15, 1952– ; House Sept. 6, 1989– .

Ross, Edmund Gibson (R Kan.) Dec. 7, 1826–May 8, 1907; Senate July 19, 1866–71; Gov. (N.M. Terr.) 1885–89 (Democrat).

Ross, Henry Howard (– N.Y.) May 9, 1790–Sept. 14, 1862; House 1825–27.

Ross, James (F Pa.) July 12, 1762–Nov. 27, 1847; Senate April 24, 1794–1803; elected pres. pro tempore March 1, 1799.

Ross, John (father of Thomas Ross) (R Pa.) Feb. 24, 1770–Jan. 31, 1834; House 1809–11, 1815–Feb. 24, 1818.

Ross, Jonathan (R Vt.) April 30, 1826–Feb. 23, 1905; Senate Jan. 11, 1899–Oct. 18, 1900.

Ross, Lewis Winans (D Ill.) Dec. 8, 1812–Oct. 20, 1895; House 1863–69.

Ross, Michael Avery (D Ark.) Sept. 1, 1961– ; House 2001– .

Ross, Miles (D N.J.) April 30, 1827–Feb. 22, 1903; House 1875–83.

Ross, Robert Tripp (R N.Y.) June 4, 1903–Oct. 1, 1981; House 1947–49, Feb. 19, 1952–53.

Ross, Sobieski (R Pa.) May 16, 1828–Oct. 24, 1877; House 1873–77.

Ross, Thomas (son of John Ross) (D Pa.) Dec. 1, 1806–July 7, 1865; House 1849–53.

Ross, Thomas Randolph (D Ohio) Oct. 26, 1788–June 28, 1869; House 1819–25.

Rossdale, Albert Berger (R N.Y.) Oct. 23, 1878–April 17, 1968; House 1921–23.

Rostenkowski, Daniel David "Dan" (D Ill.) Jan. 2, 1928– ; House 1959–95; chair House Ways and Means 1981–94.

Roth, Tobias Anton "Toby" (R Wis.) Oct. 10, 1938– ; House 1979–97.

Roth, William Victor Jr. (R Del.) July 22, 1921–Dec. 13, 2003; House 1967–Dec. 31, 1970; Senate Jan. 1, 1971– ; chair Senate Governmental Affairs 1981–87, 1995–96; chair Senate Finance 1995–2001.

Rothermel, John Hoover (D Pa.) March 7, 1856–Aug. 1922; House 1907–15.

Rothman, Steven R. (D N.J.) Oct. 14, 1952– ; House 1997– .

Rothwell, Gideon Frank (D Mo.) April 24, 1836–Jan. 18, 1894; House 1879–81.

Roudebush, Richard Lowell (R Ind.) Jan. 18, 1918–Jan. 28, 1995; House 1961–71.

Roukema, Margaret Scafati "Marge" (R N.J.) Sept. 19, 1929– ; House 1981–2003.

Rouse, Arthur Blythe (D Ky.) June 20, 1874–Jan. 25, 1956; House 1911–27.

Roush, John Edward (D Ind.) Sept. 12, 1920–March 26, 2004; House 1959–69, 1971–77.

Rousseau, Lovell Harrison (UU Ky.) Aug. 4, 1818–Jan. 7, 1869; House 1865–July 21, 1866, Dec. 3, 1866–67.

Rousselot, John Harbin (R Calif.) Nov. 1, 1927–May 11, 2003; House 1961–63, June 30, 1970–83.

Routzohn, Harry Nelson (R Ohio) Nov. 4, 1881–April 14, 1953; House 1939–41.

Rowan, John (uncle of Robert Todd Lytle) (R Ky.) July 12, 1773–July 13, 1843; House 1807–09; Senate 1825–31.

Rowan, Joseph (D N.Y.) Sept. 8, 1870–Aug. 3, 1930; House 1919–21.

Rowan, William A. (D Ill.) Nov. 24, 1882–May 31, 1961; House 1943–47.

Rowbottom, Harry Emerson (R Ind.) Nov. 3, 1884–March 22, 1934; House 1925–31.

Rowe, Edmund (R Ohio) Dec. 21, 1892–Oct. 4, 1972; House 1943–45.

Rowe, Frederick William (R N.Y.) March 19, 1863–June 20, 1946; House 1915–21.

Rowe, Peter (D N.Y.) March 10, 1807–April 17, 1876; House 1853–55.

Rowell, Jonathan Harvey (R Ill.) Feb. 10, 1833–May 15, 1908; House 1883–91.

Rowland, Alfred (D N.C.) Feb. 9, 1844–Aug. 2, 1898; House 1887–91.

Rowland, Charles Hedding (R Pa.) Dec. 20, 1860–Nov. 24, 1921; House 1915–19.

Rowland, James Roy Jr. (D Ga.) Feb. 3, 1926– ; House 1983–95.

Rowland, John G. (R Conn.) May 24, 1957– ; House 1985–91; Gov. Jan. 4, 1995–July 1, 2004.

Roy, Alphonse (D N.H.) Oct. 26, 1897–Oct. 5, 1967; House June 9, 1938–39.

Roy, William Robert (D Kan.) Feb. 23, 1926– ; House 1971–75.

Roybal, Edward Ross (father of Lucille Roybal-Allard) (D Calif.) Feb. 10, 1916– ; House 1963–93.

Roybal-Allard, Lucille (daughter of Edward Ross Roybal) (D Calif.) June 12, 1941– ; House 1993– .

Royce, Edward Randall (R Calif.) Oct. 12, 1951– ; House 1993– .

Royce, Homer Elihu (R Vt.) June 14, 1819–April 24, 1891; House 1857–61.

Royer, William Howard (R Calif.) April 11, 1920– ; House April 3, 1979–81.

Royse, Lemuel Willard (R Ind.) Jan. 19, 1847–Dec. 18, 1946; House 1895–99.

Rubey, Thomas Lewis (D Mo.) Sept. 27, 1862–Nov. 2, 1928; House 1911–21, 1923–Nov. 2, 1928.

Rucker, Atterson Walden (D Colo.) April 3, 1847–July 19, 1924; House 1909–13.

Rucker, Tinsley White (D Ga.) March 24, 1848–Nov. 18, 1926; House Jan. 11–March 3, 1917.

Rucker, William Waller (D Mo.) Feb. 1, 1855–May 30, 1936; House 1899–1923.

Rudd, Eldon Dean (R Ariz.) July 15, 1920– ; House 1977–87.

Rudd, Stephen Andrew (D N.Y.) Dec. 11, 1874–March 31, 1936; House 1931–March 31, 1936.

Rudman, Warren Bruce (R N.H.) May 13, 1930– ; Senate Dec. 29, 1980–93; chair Senate Select Ethics 1985–87.

Ruffin, James Edward (D Mo.) July 24, 1893–April 9, 1977; House 1933–35.

Ruffin, Thomas (D N.C.) Sept. 9, 1820–Oct. 13, 1863; House 1853–61.

Ruggles, Benjamin (R Ohio) Feb. 21, 1783–Sept. 2, 1857; Senate 1815–33.

Ruggles, Charles Herman (– N.Y.) Feb. 10, 1789–June 16, 1865; House 1821–23.

Ruggles, John (J Maine) Oct. 8, 1789–June 20, 1874; Senate Jan. 20, 1835–41.

Ruggles, Nathaniel (F Mass.) Nov. 11, 1761–Dec. 19, 1819; House 1813–19.

Rumple, John Nicholas William (R Iowa) March 4, 1841–Jan. 31, 1903; House 1901–Jan. 31, 1903.

Rumsey, David (W N.Y.) Dec. 25, 1810–March 12, 1883; House 1847–51.

Rumsey, Edward (W Ky.) Nov. 5, 1796–April 6, 1868; House 1837–39.

Rumsfeld, Donald Henry (R Ill.) July 9, 1932– ; House 1963–May 25, 1969; secretary of defense Nov. 20, 1975–Jan. 20, 1977, Jan. 20, 2001– .

Runk, John (W N.J.) July 3, 1791–Sept. 22, 1872; House 1845–47.

Runnels, Harold Lowell (D N.M.) March 17, 1924–Aug. 5, 1980; House 1971–Aug. 5, 1980.

Rupley, Arthur Ringwalt (R Pa.) Nov. 13, 1868–Nov. 11, 1920; House 1913–15.

Ruppe, Philip Edward (R Mich.) Sept. 29, 1926– ; House 1967–79.

Ruppersberger, C. A. "Dutch" (D Md.) Jan. 31, 1946– ; House 2003– .

Ruppert, Jacob Jr. (D N.Y.) Aug. 5, 1867–Jan. 13, 1939; House 1899–1907.

Rush, Bobby Lee (D Ill.) Nov. 23, 1946– ; House 1993– .

Rusk, Harry Welles (D Md.) Oct. 17, 1852–Jan. 28, 1926; House Nov. 2, 1886–97.

Rusk, Jeremiah McLain (R Wis.) June 17, 1830–Nov. 21, 1893; House 1871–77; Gov. Jan. 2, 1882–Jan. 7, 1889; secretary of agriculture March 6, 1889–March 6, 1893.

Rusk, Thomas Jefferson (D Texas) Dec. 5, 1803–July 29, 1857; Senate Feb. 21, 1846–July 29, 1857; elected pres. pro tempore March 14, 1857.

Russ, John (– Conn.) Oct. 29, 1767–June 22, 1833; House 1819–23.

Russell, Benjamin Edward (cousin of Rienzi Melville Johnston) (D Ga.) Oct. 5, 1845–Dec. 4, 1909; House 1893–97.

Russell, Charles Addison (R Conn.) March 2, 1852–Oct. 23, 1902; House 1887–Oct. 23, 1902.

Russell, Charles Hinton (R Nev.) Dec. 27, 1903–Sept. 13, 1989; House 1947–49; Gov. Jan. 1, 1951–Jan. 5, 1959.

Russell, Daniel Lindsay (G N.C.) Aug. 7, 1845–May 14, 1908; House 1879–81; Gov. Jan. 12, 1897–Jan. 15, 1901.

Russell, David Abel (W N.Y.) 1780–Nov. 24, 1861; House 1835–41.

Russell, Donald Stuart (D S.C.) Feb. 22, 1906–Feb. 22, 1998; Senate April 22, 1965–Nov. 8, 1966; Gov. Jan. 15, 1963–April 22, 1965.

Russell, Gordon James (D Texas) Dec. 22, 1859–Sept. 14, 1919; House Nov. 4, 1902–June 14, 1910.

Russell, James McPherson (father of Samuel Lyon Russell) (W Pa.) Nov. 10, 1786–Nov. 14, 1870; House Dec. 21, 1841–43.

Russell, Jeremiah (D N.Y.) Jan. 26, 1786–Sept. 30, 1867; House 1843–45.

Russell, John (R N.Y.) Sept. 7, 1772–Aug. 2, 1842; House 1805–09.

Russell, John Edwards (D Mass.) Jan. 20, 1834–Oct. 28, 1903; House 1887–89.

Russell, Jonathan (– Mass.) Feb. 27, 1771–Feb. 17, 1832; House 1821–23.

Russell, Joseph (D N.Y.) ?–?; House 1845–47, 1851–53.

Russell, Joseph James (D Mo.) Aug. 23, 1854–Oct. 22, 1922; House 1907–09, 1911–19.

Russell, Joshua Edward (R Ohio) Aug. 9, 1867–June 21, 1953; House 1915–17.

Russell, Leslie W. (– N.Y.) April 15, 1840–Feb. 3, 1903; House March 4–Sept. 11, 1891.

Russell, Richard Brevard Jr. (D Ga.) Nov. 2, 1897–Jan. 21, 1971; Senate Jan. 12, 1933–Jan. 21, 1971; elected pres. pro tempore Jan. 3, 1969; chair Senate Armed Services 1951–53, 1955–69; chair Senate Appropriations 1969–71; Gov. June 27, 1931–Jan. 10, 1933.

Russell, Richard Manning (D Mass.) March 3, 1891–Feb. 27, 1977; House 1935–37.

Russell, Sam Morris (D Texas) Aug. 9, 1889–Oct. 19, 1971; House 1941–47.

Russell, Samuel Lyon (son of James McPherson Russell) (W Pa.) July 30, 1816–Sept. 27, 1891; House 1853–55.

Russell, William (W Ohio) 1782–Sept. 28, 1845; House 1827–33 (Jacksonian), 1841–43.

Russell, William Augustus (R Mass.) April 22, 1831–Jan. 10, 1899; House 1879–85.

Russell, William Fiero (D N.Y.) Jan. 14, 1812–April 29, 1896; House 1857–59.

Russo, Martin Anthony (D Ill.) Jan. 23, 1944– ; House 1975–93.

Rust, Albert (D Ark.) ?–April 3, 1870; House 1855–57, 1859–61.

Ruth, Earl Baker (R N.C.) Feb. 7, 1916–Aug. 15, 1989; House 1969–75.

Rutherford, Albert Greig (R Pa.) Jan. 3, 1879–Aug. 10, 1941; House 1937–Aug. 10, 1941.

Rutherford, J. T. (D Texas) May 30, 1921– ; House 1955–63.

Rutherford, Robert (R Va.) Oct. 20, 1728–Oct. 1803; House 1793–97 (1793–95 no party).

Rutherford, Samuel (D Ga.) March 15, 1870–Feb. 4, 1932; House 1925–Feb. 4, 1932.

Rutherfurd, John (– N.J.) Sept. 20, 1760–Feb. 23, 1840; Senate 1791–Dec. 5, 1798.

Rutledge, John Jr. (F S.C.) 1766–Sept. 1, 1819; House 1797–1803.

Ryall, Daniel Bailey (D N.J.) Jan. 30, 1798–Dec. 17, 1864; House 1839–41.

Ryan, Elmer James (D Minn.) May 26, 1907–Feb. 1, 1958; House 1935–41.

Ryan, Harold Martin (D Mich.) Feb. 6, 1911– ; House Feb. 13, 1962–65.

Ryan, James Wilfrid (D Pa.) Oct. 16, 1858–Feb. 26, 1907; House 1899–1901.

Ryan, Leo Joseph (D Calif.) May 5, 1925–Nov. 18, 1978; House 1973–Nov. 18, 1978.

Ryan, Paul D. (R Wis.) Jan. 29, 1970– ; House 1999– .

Ryan, Thomas (R Kan.) Nov. 25, 1837–April 5, 1914; House 1877–April 4, 1889.

Ryan, Thomas Jefferson (R N.Y.) June 17, 1890–Nov. 10, 1968; House 1921–23.

Ryan, Timothy J. (R Ohio) July 16, 1973– ; House 2003– .

Ryan, William (D N.Y.) March 8, 1840–Feb. 18, 1925; House 1893–95.

Ryan, William Fitts (D N.Y.) June 28, 1922–Sept. 17, 1972; House 1961–Sept. 17, 1972.

Ryan, William Henry (D N.Y.) May 10, 1860–Nov. 18, 1939; House 1899–1909.

Ryon, John Walker (D Pa.) March 4, 1825–March 12, 1901; House 1879–81.

Ryter, John Francis (D Conn.) Feb. 4, 1914–Feb. 5, 1978; House 1945–47.

Ryun, Jim (R Kan.) April 29, 1947– ; House Nov. 27, 1996– .

Sabath, Adolph Joachim (D Ill.) April 4, 1866–Nov. 6, 1952; House 1907–Nov. 6, 1952; chair House Rules 1949–53.

Sabin, Alvah (W Vt.) Oct. 23, 1793–Jan. 22, 1885; House 1853–57.

Sabin, Dwight May (R Minn.) April 25, 1843–Dec. 22, 1902; Senate 1883–89; chair Rep. Nat. Comm. 1883–84.

Sabine, Lorenzo (W Mass.) Feb. 28, 1803–April 14, 1877; House Dec. 13, 1852–53.

Sabo, Martin Olav (D Minn.) Feb. 28, 1938– ; House 1979– ; chair House Budget 1993–95.

Sackett, Frederick Mosley (R Ky.) Dec. 17, 1868–May 18, 1941; Senate 1925–Jan. 9, 1930.

Sackett, William Augustus (W N.Y.) Nov. 18, 1811–Sept. 6, 1895; House 1849–53.

Sacks, Leon (D Pa.) Oct. 7, 1902–March 11, 1972; House 1937–43.

Sadlak, Antoni Nicholas (R Conn.) June 13, 1908–Oct. 18, 1969; House 1947–59.

Sadler, Thomas William (D Ala.) April 17, 1831–Oct. 29, 1896; House 1885–87.

Sadowski, George Gregory (D Mich.) March 12, 1903–Oct. 9, 1961; House 1933–39, 1943–51.

Sage, Ebenezer (R N.Y.) Aug. 16, 1755–Jan. 20, 1834; House 1809–15.

Sage, Russell (W N.Y.) Aug. 4, 1816–July 22, 1906; House 1853–57.

Saiki, Patricia Fukuda (R Hawaii) May 28, 1930– ; House 1987–91.

Sailly, Peter (R N.Y.) April 20, 1754–March 16, 1826; House 1805–07.

St. George, Katharine Price Collier (R N.Y.) July 12, 1896–May 2, 1983; House 1947–65.

St Germain, Fernand Joseph (D R.I.) Jan. 9, 1928– ; House 1961–89; chair House Banking, Finance, and Urban Affairs 1981–89.

St. John, Charles (R N.Y.) Oct. 8, 1818–July 6, 1891; House 1871–75.

St. John, Daniel Bennett (W N.Y.) Oct. 8, 1808–Feb. 18, 1890; House 1847–49.

St. John, Henry (D Ohio) July 16, 1783–May 1869; House 1843–47.

St. Martin, Louis (D La.) May 17, 1820–Feb. 9, 1893; House 1851–53, 1885–87.

St. Onge, William Leon (D Conn.) Oct. 9, 1914–May 1, 1970; House 1963–May 1, 1970.

Salazar, John Tony (brother of Kenneth Lee Salazar) (D Colo.) July 21, 1953– ; House 2005– .

Salazar, Kenneth Lee (brother of John Tony Salazar) (D Colo.) March 2, 1955– ; Senate 2005– .

Salinger, Pierre Emil George (D Calif.) June 14, 1925–Oct. 16, 2004; Senate Aug. 4–Dec. 31, 1964.

Salmon, Joshua S. (D N.J.) Feb. 2, 1846–May 6, 1902; House 1899–May 6, 1902.

Salmon, Matt (R Ariz.) Jan. 21, 1958– ; House 1995–2001.

Salmon, William Charles (D Tenn.) April 3, 1868–May 13, 1925; House 1923–25.

Saltonstall, Leverett (great-grandfather of Leverett Saltonstall, below) (W Mass.) June 13, 1783–May 8, 1845; House Dec. 5, 1838–43.

Saltonstall, Leverett (great-grandson of Leverett Saltonstall, above) (R Mass.) Sept. 1, 1892–June 17, 1979; Senate Jan. 4, 1945–67; chair Senate Armed Services 1953–55; Gov. Jan. 5, 1939–Jan. 3, 1945.

Samford, William James (D Ala.) Sept. 16, 1844–June 11, 1901; House 1879–81; Gov. Dec. 26, 1900–June 11, 1901.

Sammons, Thomas (grandfather of John Henry Starin) (R N.Y.) Oct. 1, 1762–Nov. 20, 1838; House 1803–07, 1809–13.

Sample, Samuel Caldwell (W Ind.) Aug. 15, 1796–Dec. 2, 1855; House 1843–45.

Sampson, Ezekiel Silas (R Iowa) Dec. 6, 1831–Oct. 7, 1892; House 1875–79.

Sampson, Zabdiel (R Mass.) Aug. 22, 1781–July 19, 1828; House 1817–July 26, 1820.

Samuel, Edmund William (R Pa.) Nov. 27, 1857–March 7, 1930; House 1905–07.

Samuels, Green Berry (cousin of Isaac Samuels Pennybacker) (D Va.) Feb. 1, 1806–Jan. 5, 1859; House 1839–41.

Sanborn, John Carfield (R Idaho) Sept. 28, 1885–May 16, 1968; House 1947–51.

Sanchez, Linda T. (sister of Loretta Sanchez) (D Calif.) Jan. 28, 1969– ; House 2003– .

Sanchez, Loretta (sister of Linda T. Sanchez) (D Calif.) Jan. 7, 1960– ; House 1997– .

Sandager, Harry (R R.I.) April 12, 1887–Dec. 24, 1955; House 1939–41.

Sanders, Archie Dovell (R N.Y.) June 17, 1857–July 15, 1941; House 1917–33.

Sanders, Bernard (I Vt.) Sept. 8, 1941– ; House 1991– .

Sanders, Everett (R Ind.) March 8, 1882–May 12, 1950; House 1917–25; chair Rep. Nat. Comm. 1932–34.

Sanders, Jared Young (father of Jared Young Sanders Jr., cousin of Murphy James Foster) (D La.) Jan. 29, 1867–March 23, 1944; House 1917–21; Gov. May 18, 1908–May 14, 1912.

Sanders, Jared Young Jr. (son of Jared Young Sanders) (D La.) April 20, 1892–Nov. 29, 1960; House May 1, 1934–37, 1941–43.

Sanders, Morgan Gurley (D Texas) July 14, 1878–Jan. 7, 1956; House 1921–39.

Sanders, Newell (R Tenn.) July 12, 1850–Jan. 26, 1939; Senate April 11, 1912–Jan. 24, 1913.

Sanders, Wilbur Fiske (R Mont.) May 2, 1834–July 7, 1905; Senate Jan. 1, 1890–93.

Sandford, James T. (– Tenn.) ?–?; House 1823–25.

Sandford, Thomas (R Ky.) 1762–Dec. 10, 1808; House 1803–07.

Sandidge, John Milton (D La.) Jan. 7, 1817–March 30, 1890; House 1855–59.

Sandlin, John Nicholas (D La.) Feb. 24, 1872–Dec. 25, 1957; House 1921–37.

Sandlin, Max (D Texas) Sept. 29, 1952– ; House 1997–2005.

Sandman, Charles William Jr. (R N.J.) Oct. 23, 1921–Aug. 26, 1985; House 1967–75.

Sands, Joshua (F N.Y.) Oct. 12, 1757–Sept. 13, 1835; House 1803–05, 1825–27.

Sanford, John (father of Stephen Sanford, grandfather of John Sanford, below) (D N.Y.) June 3, 1803–Oct. 4, 1857; House 1841–43.

Sanford, John (son of Stephen Sanford, grandson of John Sanford, above) (R N.Y.) Jan. 18, 1851–Sept. 26, 1939; House 1889–93.

Sanford, John W. A. (D Ga.) Aug. 28, 1798–Sept. 12, 1870; House March 4–July 25, 1835.

Sanford, Jonah (great-grandfather of Rollin Brewster Sanford) (J N.Y.) Nov. 30, 1790–Dec. 25, 1867; House Nov. 3, 1830–31.

Sanford, Marshall Clement Jr. "Mark" (R S.C.) May 28, 1960– ; House 1995–2001; Gov. Jan. 15, 2003– .

Sanford, Nathan (D N.Y.) Nov. 5, 1777–Oct. 17, 1838; Senate 1815–21, Jan. 14, 1826–31.

Sanford, Rollin Brewster (great-grandson of Jonah Sanford) (R N.Y.) May 18, 1874–May 16, 1957; House 1915–21.

Sanford, Stephen (son of John Sanford born in 1803, father of John Sanford born in 1851) (R N.Y.) May 26, 1826–Feb. 13, 1913; House 1869–71.

Sanford, Terry (D N.C.) Aug. 20, 1917–April 18, 1998; Senate Nov. 4, 1986–93; Gov. Jan. 5, 1961–Jan. 8, 1965; chair Senate Select Ethics 1991–93.

Sangmeister, George E. (D Ill.) Feb. 16, 1931– ; House 1989–95.

Santangelo, Alfred Edward (D N.Y.) June 4, 1912–March 30, 1978; House 1957–63.

Santini, James David (D Nev.) Aug. 13, 1937– ; House 1975–83.

Santorum, Rick (R Pa.) May 10, 1958– ; House 1991–95; Senate 1995– .

Sapp, William Fletcher (nephew of William Robinson Sapp) (R Iowa) Nov. 20, 1824–Nov. 22, 1890; House 1877–81.

Sapp, William Robinson (uncle of William Fletcher Sapp) (R Ohio) March 4, 1804–Jan. 3, 1875; House 1853–57 (1853–55 Whig).

Sarasin, Ronald Arthur (R Conn.) Dec. 31, 1934– ; House 1973–79.

Sarbacher, George William Jr. (R Pa.) Sept. 30, 1919–March 4, 1973; House 1947–49.

Sarbanes, Paul Spyros (D Md.) Feb. 3, 1933– ; House 1971–77; Senate 1977– ; chair Senate Banking, Housing, and Urban Affairs Jan. 3, 2001–Jan. 20, 2001, June 6, 2001–03.

Sargent, Aaron Augustus (R Calif.) Sept. 28, 1827–Aug. 14, 1887; House 1861–63, 1869–73; Senate 1873–79.

Sarpalius, William "Bill" (D Texas) Jan. 10, 1948– ; House 1989–95.

Sasscer, Lansdale Ghiselin (D Md.) Sept. 30, 1893–Nov. 5, 1964; House Feb. 3, 1939–53.

Sasser, James Ralph (D Tenn.) Sept. 30, 1936– ; Senate 1977–95; chair Senate Budget 1989–95.

Satterfield, Dave Edward Jr. (father of David Edward Satterfield III) (D Va.) Sept. 11, 1894–Dec. 27, 1946; House Nov. 2, 1937–Feb. 15, 1945.

Satterfield, David Edward III (son of Dave Edward Satterfield Jr.) (D Va.) Dec. 2, 1920–Sept. 30, 1988; House 1965–81.

Sauerhering, Edward (R Wis.) June 24, 1864–March 1, 1924; House 1895–99.

Saulsbury, Eli (brother of Willard Saulsbury, uncle of Willard Saulsbury Jr.) (D Del.) Dec. 29, 1817–March 22, 1893; Senate 1871–89.

Saulsbury, Willard Sr. (brother of Eli Saulsbury, father of Willard Saulsbury Jr., below) (D Del.) June 2, 1820–April 6, 1892; Senate 1859–71.

Saulsbury, Willard Jr. (son of Willard Saulsbury Sr., above, nephew of Eli Saulsbury) (D Del.) April 17, 1861–Feb. 20, 1927; Senate 1913–19; elected pres. pro tempore Dec. 14, 1916.

Saund, Daliph Singh (D Calif.) Sept. 20, 1899–April 22, 1973; House 1957–63.

Saunders, Alvin (grandfather of William Henry Harrison of Wyo.) (R Neb.) July 12, 1817–Nov. 1, 1899; Senate March 5, 1877–83; Gov. (Neb. Terr.) 1861–67.

Saunders, Edward Watts (D Va.) Oct. 20, 1860–Dec. 16, 1921; House Nov. 6, 1906–Feb. 29, 1920.

Saunders, Romulus Mitchell (D N.C.) March 3, 1791–April 21, 1867; House 1821–27 (Republican), 1841–45.

Sauthoff, Harry (Prog. Wis.) June 3, 1879–June 16, 1966; House 1935–39, 1941–45.

Savage, Charles Raymon (D Wash.) April 12, 1906–Jan. 14, 1976; House 1945–47.

Savage, Gus (D Ill.) Oct. 30, 1925– ; House 1981–93.

Savage, John (R N.Y.) Feb. 22, 1779–Oct. 19, 1863; House 1815–19.

Savage, John Houston (D Tenn.) Oct. 9, 1815–April 5, 1904; House 1849–53, 1855–59.

Savage, John Simpson (D Ohio) Oct. 30, 1841–Nov. 24, 1884; House 1875–77.

Sawtelle, Cullen (D Maine) Sept. 25, 1805–Nov. 10, 1887; House 1845–47, 1849–51.

Sawyer, Frederick Adolphus (R S.C.) Dec. 12, 1822–July 31, 1891; Senate July 16, 1868–73.

Sawyer, Harold Samuel (R Mich.) March 21, 1920–April 3, 2003; House 1977–85.

Sawyer, John Gilbert (R N.Y.) June 5, 1825–Sept. 5, 1898; House 1885–91.

Sawyer, Lemuel (R N.C.) 1777–Jan. 9, 1852; House 1807–13, 1817–23, 1825–29.

Sawyer, Lewis Ernest (D Ark.) June 24, 1867–May 5, 1923; House March 4–May 5, 1923.

Sawyer, Philetus (R Wis.) Sept. 22, 1816–March 29, 1900; House 1865–75; Senate 1881–93.

Sawyer, Samuel Locke (ID Mo.) Nov. 27, 1813–March 29, 1890; House 1879–81.

Sawyer, Samuel Tredwell (W N.C.) 1800–Nov. 29, 1865; House 1837–39.

Sawyer, Thomas Charles (D Ohio) Aug. 15, 1945– ; House 1987–2003.

Sawyer, William (D Ohio) Aug. 5, 1803–Sept. 18, 1877; House 1845–49.

Saxbe, William Bart (R Ohio) June 24, 1916– ; Senate 1969–Jan. 3, 1974; attorney general Jan. 4, 1974–Feb. 3, 1975.

Saxton, Hugh James (R N.J.) Jan. 22, 1943– ; House Nov. 6, 1984– .

Say, Benjamin (R Pa.) Aug. 28, 1755–April 23, 1813; House Nov. 16, 1808–June 1809.

Sayers, Joseph Draper (D Texas) Sept. 23, 1841–May 15, 1929; House 1885–Jan. 16, 1899; Gov. Jan. 17, 1899–Jan. 20, 1903.

Sayler, Henry Benton (cousin of Milton Sayler) (R Ind.) March 31, 1836–June 18, 1900; House 1873–75.

Sayler, Milton (cousin of Henry Benton Sayler) (D Ohio) Nov. 4, 1831–Nov. 17, 1892; House 1873–79.

Saylor, John Phillips (R Pa.) July 23, 1908–Oct. 28, 1973; House Sept. 13, 1949–Oct. 28, 1973.

Scales, Alfred Moore (D N.C.) Nov. 26, 1827–Feb. 9, 1892; House 1857–59, 1875–Dec. 30, 1884; Gov. Jan. 21, 1885–Jan. 17, 1889.

Scamman, John Fairfield (D Maine) Oct. 24, 1786–May 22, 1858; House 1845–47.

Scanlon, Thomas Edward (D Pa.) Sept. 18, 1896–Aug. 9, 1955; House 1941–45.

Scarborough, Charles Joseph (R Fla.) April 9, 1963– ; House 1995–Sept. 6, 2001.

Scarborough, Robert Bethea (D S.C.) Oct. 29, 1861–Nov. 23, 1927; House 1901–05.

Schadeberg, Henry Carl (R Wis.) Oct. 12, 1913–Dec. 11, 1985; House 1961–65, 1967–71.

Schaefer, Daniel (R Colo.) Jan. 25, 1936– ; House March 29, 1983–99.

Schaefer, Edwin Martin (D Ill.) May 14, 1887–Nov. 8, 1950; House 1933–43.

Schafer, John Charles (R Wis.) May 7, 1893–June 9, 1962; House 1923–33, 1939–41.

Schaffer, Robert W. (R Colo.) July 24, 1962– ; House 1997–2003.

Schakowsky, Janice D. (D Ill.) May 26, 1944– ; House 1999– .

Schall, Thomas David (R Minn.) June 4, 1878–Dec. 22, 1935; House 1915–25; Senate 1925–Dec. 22, 1935.

Schell, Richard (D N.Y.) May 15, 1810–Nov. 10, 1879; House Dec. 7, 1874–75.

Schenck, Abraham Henry (uncle of Isaac Teller) (R N.Y.) Jan. 22, 1775–June 1, 1831; House 1815–17.

Schenck, Ferdinand Schureman (J N.J.) Feb. 11, 1790–May 16, 1860; House 1833–37.

Schenck, Paul Fornshell (R Ohio) April 19, 1899–Nov. 30, 1968; House Nov. 6, 1951–65.

Schenck, Robert Cumming (R Ohio) Oct. 4, 1809–March 23, 1890; House 1843–51 (Whig), 1863–Jan. 5, 1871.

Schenk, Lynn (D Calif.) Jan. 5, 1945– ; House 1993–95.

Scherer, Gordon Harry (R Ohio) Dec. 26, 1906–Aug. 13, 1988; House 1953–63.

Scherle, William Joseph (R Iowa) March 14, 1923–Aug. 27, 2003; House 1967–75.

Schermerhorn, Abraham Maus (W N.Y.) Dec. 11, 1791–Aug. 22, 1855; House 1849–53.

Schermerhorn, Simon Jacob (D N.Y.) Sept. 25, 1827–July 21, 1901; House 1893–95.

Scheuer, James Haas (D/L N.Y.) Feb. 6, 1920– ; House 1965–73, 1975–93.

Schiff, Adam B. (D Calif.) June 22, 1960– ; House 2001– .

Schiff, Steven Harvey (R N.M.) March 18, 1947–March 25, 1998; House 1989–March 25, 1998.

Schiffler, Andrew Charles (R W.Va.) Aug. 10, 1889–March 27, 1970; House 1939–41, 1943–45.

Schirm, Charles Reginald (R Md.) Aug. 12, 1864–Nov. 2, 1918; House 1901–03.

Schisler, Darwin Gale (D Ill.) March 2, 1933– ; House 1965–67.

Schleicher, Gustave (D Texas) Nov. 19, 1823–Jan. 10, 1879; House 1875–Jan. 10, 1879.

Schley, William (J Ga.) Dec. 15, 1786–Nov. 20, 1858; House 1833–July 1, 1835; Gov. Nov. 4, 1835–Nov. 8, 1837 (Unionist).

Schmidhauser, John Richard (D Iowa) Jan. 3, 1922– ; House 1965–67.

Schmitt, Harrison Hagan (R N.M.) July 3, 1935– ; Senate 1977–83.

Schmitz, John George (R Calif.) Aug. 12, 1930– ; House June 30, 1970–73.

Schneebeli, Gustav Adolphus (R Pa.) May 23, 1853–Feb. 6, 1923; House 1905–07.

Schneebeli, Herman Theodore (R Pa.) July 7, 1907–May 6, 1982; House April 26, 1960–77.

Schneider, Claudine (R R.I.) March 25, 1947– ; House 1981–91.

Schneider, George John (Prog. Wis.) Oct. 30, 1877–March 12, 1939; House 1923–33 (Republican), 1935–39.

Schoeppel, Andrew Frank (R Kan.) Nov. 23, 1894–Jan. 21, 1962; Senate 1949–Jan. 21, 1962; Gov. Jan. 11, 1943–Jan. 13, 1947.

Schoolcraft, John Lawrence (W N.Y.) 1804–July 7, 1860; House 1849–53.

Schoonmaker, Cornelius Corneliusen (grandfather of Marius Schoonmaker) (– N.Y.) June 1745–96; House 1791–93.

Schoonmaker, Marius (grandson of Cornelius Corneliusen Schoonmaker) (W N.Y.) April 24, 1811–Jan. 5, 1894; House 1851–53.

Schrock, Edward (R Va.) April 6, 1941– ; House 2001–05.

Schroeder, Patricia Scott (D Colo.) July 30, 1940– ; House 1973–97.

Schuette, William Duncan (R Mich.) Oct. 13, 1953– ; House 1985–91.

Schuetz, Leonard William (D Ill.) Nov. 16, 1887–Feb. 13, 1944; House 1931–Feb. 13, 1944.

Schulte, William Theodore (D Ind.) Aug. 19, 1890–Dec. 7, 1966; House 1933–43.

Schulze, Richard Taylor (R Pa.) Aug. 7, 1929– ; House 1975–93.

Schumaker, John Godfrey (D N.Y.) June 27, 1826–Nov. 23, 1905; House 1869–71, 1873–77.

Schumer, Charles Ellis (D N.Y.) Nov. 23, 1950– ; House 1981–99; Senate 1999– .

Schuneman, Martin Gerretsen (R N.Y.) Feb. 10, 1764–Feb. 21, 1827; House 1805–07.

Schureman, James (F N.J.) Feb. 12, 1756–Jan. 22, 1824; House 1789–91 (no party), 1797–99 (no party), 1813–15; Senate 1799–Feb. 16, 1801; Cont. Cong. 1786–87.

Schurz, Carl (R Mo.) March 2, 1829–May 14, 1906; Senate 1869–75; secretary of the interior March 12, 1877–March 7, 1881.

Schuyler, Karl Cortlandt (R Colo.) April 3, 1877–July 31, 1933; Senate Dec. 7, 1932–33.

Schuyler, Philip Jeremiah (son of Philip John Schuyler) (F N.Y.) Jan. 21, 1768–Feb. 21, 1835; House 1817–19.

Schuyler, Philip John (father of Philip Jeremiah Schuyler) (– N.Y.) Nov. 20, 1733–Nov. 18, 1804; Senate 1789–91, 1797–Jan. 3, 1798; Cont. Cong. 1775, 1777, 1779–80.

Schwabe, George Blaine (brother of Max Schwabe) (R Okla.) July 26, 1886–April 2, 1952; House 1945–49, 1951–April 2, 1952.

Schwabe, Max (brother of George Blaine Schwabe) (R Mo.) Dec. 6, 1905–July 31, 1983; House 1943–49.

Schwartz, Allyson Y. (D Pa.) Oct. 3, 1948– ; House 2005– .

Schwartz, Henry Herman "Harry" (D Wyo.) May 18, 1869–April 24, 1955; Senate 1937–43.

Schwartz, John (ALD Pa.) Oct. 27, 1793–June 20, 1860; House 1859–June 20, 1860.

Schwarz, John J. H. "Joe" (R Mich.) Nov. 15, 1937– ; House 2005– .

Schweiker, Richard Schultz (R Pa.) June 1, 1926– ; House 1961–69; Senate 1969–81; secretary of health and human services Jan. 22, 1981–Feb. 3, 1983.

Schwellenbach, Lewis Baxter (D Wash.) Sept. 20, 1894–June 10, 1948; Senate 1935–Dec. 16, 1940; secretary of labor July 1, 1945–June 10, 1948.

Schwengel, Frederick Delbert (R Iowa) May 28, 1906–April 1, 1993; House 1955–65, 1967–73.

Schwert, Pius Louis (D N.Y.) Nov. 22, 1892–March 11, 1941; House 1939–March 11, 1941.

Scoblick, James Paul (R Pa.) May 10, 1909–Dec. 4, 1981; House Nov. 5, 1946–49.

Scofield, Glenni William (R Pa.) March 11, 1817–Aug. 30, 1891; House 1863–75.

Scott, Byron Nicholson (D Calif.) March 21, 1903–Dec. 21, 1991; House 1935–39.

Scott, Charles Frederick (R Kan.) Sept. 7, 1860–Sept. 18, 1938; House 1901–11.

Scott, Charles Lewis (D Calif.) Jan. 23, 1827–April 30, 1899; House 1857–61.

Scott, David (– Pa.) ?–?; elected to the House for term beginning 1817 but resigned before Congress assembled.

Scott, David (D Ga.) June 27, 1946– ; House 2003– .

Scott, Frank Douglas (R Mich.) Aug. 25, 1878–Feb. 12, 1951; House 1915–27.

Scott, George Cromwell (R Iowa) Aug. 8, 1864–Oct. 6, 1948; House Nov. 5, 1912–15, 1917–19.

Scott, Hardie (son of John Roger Kirkpatrick Scott) (R Pa.) June 7, 1907–Nov. 2, 1999; House 1947–53.

Scott, Harvey David (R Ind.) Oct. 18, 1818–July 11, 1891; House 1855–57.

Scott, Hugh Doggett Jr. (R Pa.) Nov. 11, 1900–July 21, 1994; House 1941–45, 1947–59; Senate 1959–77; Senate minority leader Sept. 24, 1969–77; chair Rep. Nat. Comm. 1948–49.

Scott, John (– Mo.) May 18, 1785–Oct. 1, 1861; House (Terr. Del.) Aug. 6, 1816–Jan. 13, 1817, Aug. 4, 1817–March 3, 1821, (Rep.) Aug. 10, 1821–27.

Scott, John (father of John Scott, below) (J Pa.) Dec. 25, 1784–Sept. 22, 1850; House 1829–31.

Scott, John (son of John Scott, above) (R Pa.) July 24, 1824–Nov. 29, 1896; Senate 1869–75.

Scott, John Guier (D Mo.) Dec. 26, 1819–May 16, 1892; House Dec. 7, 1863–65.

Scott, John Roger Kirkpatrick (father of Hardie Scott) (R Pa.) July 6, 1873–Dec. 9, 1945; House 1915–Jan. 5, 1919.

Scott, Lon Allen (R Tenn.) Sept. 25, 1888–Feb. 11, 1931; House 1921–23.

Scott, Nathan Bay (R W.Va.) Dec. 18, 1842–Jan. 2, 1924; Senate 1899–1911.

Scott, Owen (D Ill.) July 6, 1848–Dec. 21, 1928; House 1891–93.

Scott, Ralph James (D N.C.) Oct. 15, 1905–Aug. 5, 1983; House 1957–67.

Scott, Robert Cortez (D Va.) April 30, 1947– ; House 1993– .

Scott, Thomas (– Pa.) 1739–March 2, 1796; House 1789–91, 1793–95.

Scott, William Kerr (D N.C.) April 17, 1896–April 16, 1958; Senate Nov. 29, 1954–April 16, 1958; Gov. Jan. 6, 1949–Jan. 8, 1953.

Scott, William Lawrence (D Pa.) July 2, 1828–Sept. 19, 1891; House 1885–89.

Scott, William Lloyd (R Va.) July 1, 1915–Feb. 14, 1997; House 1967–73; Senate 1973–Jan. 1, 1979.

Scoville, Jonathan (D N.Y.) July 14, 1830–March 4, 1891; House Nov. 12, 1880–83.

Scranton, George Whitfield (second cousin of Joseph Augustine Scranton) (R Pa.) May 11, 1811–March 24, 1861; House 1859–March 24, 1861.

Scranton, Joseph Augustine (great-grandfather of William Warren Scranton, second cousin of George Whitfield Scranton) (R Pa.) July 26, 1838–Oct. 12, 1908; House 1881–83, 1885–87, 1889–91, 1893–97.

Scranton, William Warren (great-grandson of Joseph Augustine Scranton) (R Pa.) July 19, 1917– ; House 1961–63; Gov. Jan. 15, 1963–Jan. 17, 1967.

Scrivner, Errett Power (R Kan.) March 20, 1898–May 5, 1978; House Sept. 14, 1943–59.

Scroggy, Thomas Edmund (R Ohio) March 18, 1843–March 6, 1915; House 1905–07.

Scrugham, James Graves (D Nev.) Jan. 19, 1880–June 23, 1945; House 1933–Dec. 7, 1942; Senate Dec. 7, 1942–June 23, 1945; Gov. Jan. 1, 1923–Jan. 3, 1927.

Scudder, Henry Joel (uncle of Townsend Scudder) (R N.Y.) Sept. 18, 1825–Feb. 10, 1886; House 1873–75.

Scudder, Hubert Baxter (R Calif.) Nov. 5, 1888–July 4, 1968; House 1949–59.

Scudder, Isaac Williamson (R N.J.) 1816–Sept. 10, 1881; House 1873–75.

Scudder, John Anderson (R N.J.) March 22, 1759–Nov. 6, 1836; House Oct. 31, 1810–11.

Scudder, Townsend (nephew of Henry Joel Scudder) (D N.Y.) July 26, 1865–Feb. 22, 1960; House 1899–1901, 1903–05.

Scudder, Tredwell (– N.Y.) Jan. 1, 1778–Oct. 31, 1834; House 1817–19.

Scudder, Zeno (W Mass.) Aug. 18, 1807–June 26, 1857; House 1851–March 4, 1854.

Scull, Edward (R Pa.) Feb. 5, 1818–July 10, 1900; House 1887–93.

Scully, Thomas Joseph (D N.J.) Sept. 19, 1868–Dec. 14, 1921; House 1911–21.

Scurry, Richardson (D Texas) Nov. 11, 1811–April 9, 1862; House 1851–53.

Seaman, Henry John (AP N.Y.) April 16, 1805–May 3, 1861; House 1845–47.

Searing, John Alexander (D N.Y.) May 14, 1805–May 6, 1876; House 1857–59.

Sears, William Joseph (D Fla.) Dec. 4, 1874–March 30, 1944; House 1915–29, 1933–37.

Sears, Willis Gratz (R Neb.) Aug. 16, 1860–June 1, 1949; House 1923–31.

Seastrand, Andrea (R Calif.) Aug. 5, 1941– ; House 1995–97.

Seaton, Frederick Andrew (R Neb.) Dec. 11, 1909–Jan. 16, 1974; Senate Dec. 10, 1951–Nov. 4, 1952; secretary of the interior June 8, 1956–Jan. 20, 1961.

Seaver, Ebenezer (R Mass.) July 5, 1763–March 1, 1844; House 1803–13.

Sebastian, William King (D Ark.) 1812–May 20, 1865; Senate May 12, 1848–July 11, 1861.

Sebelius, Keith George (R Kan.) Sept. 10, 1916–Aug. 5, 1982; House 1969–81.

Seccombe, James (R Ohio) Feb. 12, 1893–Aug. 23, 1970; House 1939–41.

Secrest, Robert Thompson (D Ohio) Jan. 22, 1904–May 15, 1994; House 1933–Aug. 3, 1942, 1949–Sept. 26, 1954, 1963–67.

Seddon, James Alexander (D Va.) July 13, 1815–Aug. 19, 1880; House 1845–47, 1849–51.

Sedgwick, Charles Baldwin (R N.Y.) March 15, 1815–Feb. 3, 1883; House 1859–63.

Sedgwick, Theodore (F Mass.) May 9, 1746–Jan. 24, 1813; House 1789–June 1796 (no party), 1799–1801; Speaker Dec. 2, 1799–1801; Senate June 11, 1796–99; elected pres. pro tempore June 27, 1798; Cont. Cong. 1785–86, 1788.

Seeley, John Edward (R N.Y.) Aug. 1, 1810–March 30, 1875; House 1871–73.

Seely-Brown, Horace Jr. (R Conn.) May 12, 1908–April 9, 1982; House 1947–49, 1951–59, 1961–63.

Seelye, Julius Hawley (I Mass.) Sept. 14, 1824–May 12, 1895; House 1875–77.

Seerley, John Joseph (D Iowa) March 13, 1852–Feb. 23, 1931; House 1891–93.

Segar, Joseph Eggleston (U Va.) June 1, 1804–April 30, 1880; House March 15, 1862–63.

Seger, George Nicholas (R N.J.) Jan. 4, 1866–Aug. 26, 1940; House 1923–Aug. 26, 1940.

Seiberling, Francis (cousin of John Frederick Seiberling) (R Ohio) Sept. 20, 1870–Feb. 1, 1945; House 1929–33.

Seiberling, John Frederick (cousin of Francis Seiberling) (D Ohio) Sept. 8, 1918– ; House 1971–87.

Selby, Thomas Jefferson (D Ill.) Dec. 4, 1840–March 10, 1917; House 1901–03.

Selden, Armistead Inge Jr. (D Ala.) Feb. 20, 1921–Nov. 14, 1985; House 1953–69.

Selden, Dudley (J N.Y.) ?–Nov. 7, 1855; House 1833–July 1, 1834.

Seldomridge, Harry Hunter (D Colo.) Oct. 1, 1864–Nov. 2, 1927; House 1913–15.

Sells, Sam Riley (R Tenn.) Aug. 2, 1871–Nov. 2, 1935; House 1911–21.

Selvig, Conrad George (R Minn.) Oct. 11, 1877–Aug. 2, 1953; House 1927–33.

Selye, Lewis (IR N.Y.) July 11, 1803–Jan. 27, 1883; House 1867–69.

Semmes, Benedict Joseph (– Md.) Nov. 1, 1789–Feb. 10, 1863; House 1829–33.

Semple, James (D Ill.) Jan. 5, 1798–Dec. 20, 1866; Senate Dec. 4, 1843–47.

Sener, James Beverley (R Va.) May 18, 1837–Nov. 18, 1903; House 1873–75.

Seney, George Ebbert (D Ohio) May 29, 1832–June 11, 1905; House 1883–91.

Seney, Joshua (– Md.) March 4, 1756–Oct. 20, 1798; House 1789–May 1, 1792; Cont. Cong. 1788.

Senner, George Frederick Jr. (D Ariz.) Nov. 24, 1921– ; House 1963–67.

Sensenbrenner, Frank James Jr. (R Wis.) June 14, 1943– ; House 1979– ; chair House Science 1997–2001; chair House Judiciary 2001– .

Senter, William Tandy (W Tenn.) May 12, 1801–Aug. 28, 1848; House 1843–45.

Sergeant, John (grandfather of John Sergeant Wise and Richard Alsop Wise, great-grandfather of John Crain Kunkel, father-in-law of Henry Alexander Wise) (W Pa.) Dec. 5, 1779–Nov. 23, 1852; House Oct. 10, 1815–23 (Federalist), 1827–29 (Federalist), 1837–Sept. 15, 1841.

Serrano, José Enrique (D N.Y.) Oct. 24, 1943– ; House March 28, 1990– .

Sessinghaus, Gustavus (R Mo.) Nov. 8, 1838–Nov. 16, 1887; House March 2, 1883–March 3, 1883.

Sessions, Jefferson Beauregard III "Jeff" (R Ala.) Dec. 24, 1946– ; Senate 1997– .

Sessions, Pete (R Texas) March 22, 1955– ; House 1997– .

Sessions, Walter Loomis (R N.Y.) Oct. 4, 1820–May 27, 1896; House 1871–75, 1885–87.

Settle, Evan Evans (D Ky.) Dec. 1, 1848–Nov. 16, 1899; House 1897–Nov. 16, 1899.

Settle, Thomas (uncle of David Settle Reid, grandfather of Thomas Settle, below) (R N.C.) March 9, 1789–Aug. 5, 1857; House 1817–21.

Settle, Thomas (grandson of Thomas Settle, above) (R N.C.) March 10, 1865–Jan. 20, 1919; House 1893–97.

Severance, Luther (W Maine) Oct. 26, 1797–Jan. 25, 1855; House 1843–47.

Sevier, Ambrose Hundley (cousin of Henry Wharton Conway) (D Ark.) Nov. 4, 1801–Dec. 31, 1848; House (Terr. Del.) Feb. 13, 1828–June 15, 1836; Senate Sept. 18, 1836–March 15, 1848; elected pres. pro tempore Dec. 27, 1845.

Sevier, John (R Tenn.) Sept. 23, 1745–Sept. 24, 1815; House June 16, 1790–91 (no party N.C.), 1811–Sept. 24, 1815; Gov. March 30, 1796–Sept. 23, 1801 (Democratic Republican), Sept. 23, 1803–Sept. 19, 1809 (Democratic Republican).

Sewall, Charles S. (D Md.) 1779–Nov. 3, 1848; House Oct. 1, 1832–33 (Jacksonian), Jan. 2–March 3, 1843.

Sewall, Samuel (F Mass.) Dec. 11, 1757–June 8, 1814; House Dec. 7, 1796–Jan. 10, 1800.

Seward, James Lindsay (D Ga.) Oct. 30, 1813–Nov. 21, 1886; House 1853–59.

Seward, William Henry (R N.Y.) May 16, 1801–Oct. 10, 1872; Senate 1849–61 (1849–55 Whig); secretary of state March 6, 1861–March 4, 1869; Gov. Jan. 1, 1839–Jan. 1, 1843 (Whig).

Sewell, William Joyce (R N.J.) Dec. 6, 1835–Dec. 27, 1901; Senate 1881–87, 1895–Dec. 27, 1901.

Sexton, Leonidas (R Ind.) May 19, 1827–July 4, 1880; House 1877–79.

Seybert, Adam (R Pa.) May 16, 1773–May 2, 1825; House Oct. 10, 1809–15, 1817–19.

Seymour, David Lowrey (D N.Y.) Dec. 2, 1803–Oct. 11, 1867; House 1843–45, 1851–53.

Seymour, Edward Woodruff (son of Origen Storrs Seymour) (D Conn.) Aug. 30, 1832–Oct. 16, 1892; House 1883–87.

Seymour, Henry William (R Mich.) July 21, 1834–April 7, 1906; House Feb. 14, 1888–89.

Seymour, Horatio (uncle of Origen Storrs Seymour) (– Vt.) May 31, 1778–Nov. 21, 1857; Senate 1821–33.

Seymour, John (R Calif.) Dec. 3, 1937– ; Senate Jan. 10, 1991–Nov. 3, 1992.

Seymour, Origen Storrs (father of Edward Woodruff Seymour, nephew of Horatio Seymour) (D Conn.) Feb. 9, 1804–Aug. 12, 1881; House 1851–55.

Seymour, Thomas Hart (D Conn.) Sept. 29, 1807–Sept. 3, 1868; House 1843–45; Gov. May 4, 1850–Oct. 13, 1853.

Seymour, William (J N.Y.) about 1780–Dec. 28, 1848; House 1835–37.

Shackelford, John Williams (D N.C.) Nov. 16, 1844–Jan. 18, 1883; House 1881–Jan. 18, 1883.

Shackleford, Dorsey William (D Mo.) Aug. 27, 1853–July 15, 1936; House Aug. 29, 1899–1919.

Shadegg, John (R Ariz.) Oct. 22, 1949– ; House 1995– .

Shafer, Jacob K. (D Idaho) Dec. 26, 1823–Nov. 22, 1876; House (Terr. Del.) 1869–71.

Shafer, Paul Werntz (R Mich.) April 27, 1893–Aug. 17, 1954; House 1937–Aug. 17, 1954.

Shaffer, Joseph Crockett (R Va.) Jan. 19, 1880–Oct. 19, 1958; House 1929–31.

Shafroth, John Franklin (D Colo.) June 9, 1854–Feb. 20, 1922; House 1895–Feb. 15, 1904 (1895–97 Republican, 1897–1903 Silver Republican); Senate 1913–19; Gov. Jan. 12, 1909–Jan. 14, 1913.

Shallenberger, Ashton Cokayne (D Neb.) Dec. 23, 1862–Feb. 22, 1938; House 1901–03, 1915–19, 1923–29, 1931–35; Gov. Jan. 7, 1909–Jan. 5, 1911.

Shallenberger, William Shadrack (R Pa.) Nov. 24, 1839–April 15, 1914; House 1877–83.

Shamansky, Robert Norton (D Ohio) April 18, 1927– ; House 1981–83.

Shanklin, George Sea (D Ky.) Dec. 23, 1807–April 1, 1883; House 1865–67.

Shanks, John Peter Cleaver (R Ind.) June 17, 1826–Jan. 23, 1901; House 1861–63, 1867–75.

Shanley, James Andrew (D Conn.) April 1, 1896–April 4, 1965; House 1935–43.

Shannon, James Michael (D Mass.) April 4, 1952– ; House 1979–85.

Shannon, Joseph Bernard (D Mo.) March 17, 1867–March 28, 1943; House 1931–43.

Shannon, Richard Cutts (R N.Y.) Feb. 12, 1839–Oct. 5, 1920; House 1895–99.

Shannon, Thomas (brother of Wilson Shannon) (– Ohio) Nov. 15, 1786–March 16, 1843; House Dec. 4, 1826–27.

Shannon, Thomas Bowles (R Calif.) Sept. 21, 1827–Feb. 21, 1897; House 1863–65.

Shannon, Wilson (brother of Thomas Shannon) (D Ohio) Feb. 24, 1802–Aug. 30, 1877; House 1853–55; Gov. Dec. 13, 1838–Dec. 16, 1840, Dec. 14, 1842–April 15, 1844, Aug. 10, 1855–Aug. 18, 1856 (Kansas Terr.).

Sharon, William (R Neb.) Jan. 9, 1821–Nov. 13, 1885; Senate 1875–81.

Sharp, Edgar Allan (R N.Y.) June 3, 1876–Nov. 27, 1948; House 1945–47.

Sharp, Philip Riley (D Ind.) July 15, 1942– ; House 1975–95.

Sharp, Solomon P. (R Ky.) 1780–Nov. 7, 1825; House 1813–17.

Sharp, William Graves (D Ohio) March 14, 1859–Nov. 17, 1922; House 1909–July 23, 1914.

Sharpe, Peter (– N.Y.) ?–?; House 1823–25.

Shartel, Cassius McLean (R Mo.) April 27, 1860–Sept. 27, 1943; House 1905–07.

Shattuc, William Bunn (R Ohio) June 11, 1841–July 13, 1911; House 1897–1903.

Shaw, Aaron (D Ill.) Dec. 19, 1811–Jan. 7, 1887; House 1857–59, 1883–85.

Shaw, Albert Duane (R N.Y.) Dec. 21, 1841–Feb. 10, 1901; House Nov. 6, 1900–Feb. 10, 1901.

Shaw, Eugene Clay Jr. (R Fla.) April 19, 1939– ; House 1981– .

Shaw, Frank Thomas (D Md.) Oct. 7, 1841–Feb. 24, 1923; House 1885–89.

Shaw, George Bullen (R Wis.) March 12, 1854–Aug. 27, 1894; House 1893–Aug. 27, 1894.

Shaw, Guy Loren (R Ill.) May 16, 1881–May 19, 1950; House 1921–23.

Shaw, Henry (son of Samuel Shaw) (R Mass.) 1788–Oct. 17, 1857; House 1817–21.

Shaw, Henry Marchmore (D N.C.) Nov. 20, 1819–Nov. 1, 1864; House 1853–55, 1857–59.

Shaw, John Gilbert (D N.C.) Jan. 16, 1859–July 21, 1932; House 1895–97.

Shaw, Samuel (father of Henry Shaw) (R Vt.) Dec. 1768–Oct. 23, 1827; House Sept. 6, 1808–13.

Shaw, Tristram (D N.H.) May 23, 1786–March 14, 1843; House 1839–43.

Shays, Christopher (R Conn.) Oct. 18, 1945– ; House Sept. 9, 1987– .

Sheafe, James (F N.H.) Nov. 16, 1755–Dec. 5, 1829; House 1799–1801; Senate 1801–June 14, 1802.

Sheakley, James (D Pa.) April 24, 1829–Dec. 10, 1917; House 1875–77; Gov. (Alaska Terr.) 1893–97.

Sheats, Charles Christopher (R Ala.) April 10, 1839–May 27, 1904; House 1873–75.

Sheehan, Timothy Patrick (R Ill.) Feb. 21, 1909–Oct. 8, 2000; House 1951–59.

Sheffer, Daniel (D Pa.) May 24, 1783–Feb. 16, 1880; House 1837–39.

Sheffey, Daniel (F Va.) 1770–Dec. 3, 1830; House 1809–17.

Sheffield, William Paine (father of William Paine Sheffield, below) (R R.I.) Aug. 30, 1820–June 2, 1907; House 1861–63; Senate Nov. 19, 1884–Jan. 20, 1885.

Sheffield, William Paine (son of William Paine Sheffield, above) (R R.I.) June 1, 1857–Oct. 19, 1919; House 1909–11.

Shelby, Richard Craig (R Ala.) May 6, 1934– ; House 1979–87 (Democrat); Senate 1987– (1979–Nov. 9, 1994 Democrat); chair Senate Select Intelligence Activities 1997–Jan. 3, 2001, Jan. 20, 2001–June 6, 2001; chair Senate Banking, Housing and Urban Affairs 2003– .

Shelden, Carlos Douglas (R Mich.) June 10, 1840–June 24, 1904; House 1897–1903.

Sheldon, Lionel Allen (R La.) Aug. 30, 1828–Jan. 17, 1917; House 1869–75; Gov. (N.M. Terr.) 1881–85.

Sheldon, Porter (R N.Y.) Sept. 29, 1831–Aug. 15, 1908; House 1869–71.

Shell, George Washington (D S.C.) Nov. 13, 1831–Dec. 15, 1899; House 1891–95.

Shellabarger, Samuel (R Ohio) Dec. 10, 1817–Aug. 7, 1896; House 1861–63, 1865–69, 1871–73.

Shelley, Charles Miller (D Ala.) Dec. 28, 1833–Jan. 20, 1907; House 1877–81, Nov. 7, 1882–Jan. 9, 1885.

Shelley, John Francis (D Calif.) Sept. 3, 1905–Sept. 1, 1974; House Nov. 8, 1949–Jan. 7, 1964.

Shelton, Samuel Azariah (R Mo.) Sept. 3, 1858–Sept. 13, 1948; House 1921–23.

Shepard, Charles Biddle (D N.C.) Dec. 5, 1808–Oct. 25, 1843; House 1837–41 (1837–39 Whig).

Shepard, William (F Mass.) Dec. 1, 1737–Nov. 16, 1817; House 1797–1803.

Shepard, William Biddle (W N.C.) May 14, 1799–June 20, 1852; House 1829–37 (no party).

Shepherd, Karen (D Utah) July 5, 1940– ; House 1993–95.

Shepler, Matthias (D Ohio) Nov. 11, 1790–April 7, 1863; House 1837–39.

Shepley, Ether (J Maine) Nov. 2, 1789–Jan. 15, 1877; Senate 1833–March 3, 1836.

Sheppard, Harry Richard (D Calif.) Jan. 10, 1885–April 28, 1969; House 1937–65.

Sheppard, John Levi (father of Morris Sheppard, great-grandfather of Connie Mack III) (D Texas) April 13, 1852–Oct. 11, 1902; House 1899–Oct. 11, 1902.

Sheppard, Morris (son of John Levi Sheppard) (D Texas) May 28, 1875–April 9, 1941; House Nov. 15, 1902–Feb. 3, 1913; Senate Feb. 3, 1913–April 9, 1941.

Shepperd, Augustine Henry (W N.C.) Feb. 24, 1792–July 11, 1864; House 1827–39, 1841–43, 1847–51.

Sherburne, John Samuel (R N.H.) 1757–Aug. 2, 1830; House 1793–97.

Sheredine, Upton (– Md.) 1740–Jan. 14, 1800; House 1791–93.

Sheridan, George Augustus (LR La.) Feb. 22, 1840–Oct. 7, 1896; House 1873–75.

Sheridan, John Edward (D Pa.) Sept. 15, 1902–Nov. 12, 1987; House Nov. 7, 1939–47.

Sherley, Joseph Swagar (D Ky.) Nov. 28, 1871–Feb. 13, 1941; House 1903–19.

Sherman, Brad (D Calif.) Oct. 24, 1954– ; House 1997– .

Sherman, James Schoolcraft (R N.Y.) Oct. 24, 1855–Oct. 30, 1912; House 1887–91, 1893–1909; vice president 1909–Oct. 30, 1912.

Sherman, John (R Ohio) May 10, 1823–Oct. 22, 1900; House 1855–March 21, 1861; Senate March 21, 1861–March 8, 1877, 1881–March 4, 1897; elected pres. pro tempore Dec. 7, 1885; secretary of the Treasury March 10, 1877–March 3, 1881; secretary of state March 6, 1897–April 27, 1898.

Sherman, Judson W. (R N.Y.) 1808–Nov. 12, 1881; House 1857–59.

Sherman, Lawrence Yates (R Ill.) Nov. 8, 1858–Sept. 15, 1939; Senate March 26, 1913–21.

Sherman, Roger (grandfather of William Maxwell Evarts) (– Conn.) April 19, 1721–July 23, 1793; House 1789–91; Senate June 13, 1791–July 23, 1793; Cont. Cong. 1774–81, 1784.

Sherman, Socrates Norton (R N.Y.) July 22, 1801–Feb. 1, 1873; House 1861–63.

Sherrill, Eliakim (W N.Y.) Feb. 16, 1813–July 4, 1863; House 1847–49.

Sherrod, William Crawford (D Ala.) Aug. 17, 1835–March 24, 1919; House 1869–71.

Sherwin, John Crocker (R Ill.) Feb. 8, 1838–Jan. 1, 1904; House 1879–83.

Sherwood, Donald L. (R Pa.) March 5, 1941– ; House 1999– .

Sherwood, Henry (D Pa.) Oct. 9, 1813–Nov. 10, 1896; House 1871–73.

Sherwood, Isaac R. (D Ohio) Aug. 13, 1835–Oct. 15, 1925; House 1873–75 (Republican), 1907–21, 1923–25.

Sherwood, Samuel (F N.Y.) April 24, 1779–Oct. 31, 1862; House 1813–15.

Sherwood, Samuel Burr (F Conn.) Nov. 26, 1767–April 27, 1833; House 1817–19.

Shiel, George Knox (D Ore.) 1825–Dec. 12, 1893; House July 30, 1861–63.

Shields, Benjamin Glover (D Ala.) 1808–?; House 1841–43.

Shields, Ebenezer J. (W Tenn.) Dec. 22, 1778–April 21, 1846; House 1835–39 (1835–37 White supporter).

Shields, James (uncle of James Shields, below) (J Ohio) April 13, 1762–Aug. 13, 1831; House 1829–31.

Shields, James (nephew of James Shields, above) (D Mo.) May 10, 1810–June 1, 1879; Senate March 6–15, 1849 (Ill.), Oct. 27, 1849–55 (Ill.), May 11, 1858–59 (Minn.), Jan. 27–March 3, 1879.

Shields, John Knight (D Tenn.) Aug. 15, 1858–Sept. 30, 1934; Senate 1913–25.

Shimkus, John (R Ill.) Feb. 21, 1958– ; House 1997– .

Shinn, William Norton (J N.J.) Oct. 24, 1782–Aug. 18, 1871; House 1833–37.

Shipherd, Zebulon Rudd (F N.Y.) Nov. 15, 1768–Nov. 1, 1841; House 1813–15.

Shipley, George Edward (D Ill.) April 21, 1927–June 28, 2003; House 1959–79.

Shipstead, Henrik (R Minn.) Jan. 8, 1881–June 26, 1960; Senate 1923–47 (1923–41 Farmer Laborite).

Shiras, George III (IR Pa.) Jan. 1, 1859–March 24, 1942; House 1903–05.

Shively, Benjamin Franklin (D Ind.) March 20, 1857–March 14, 1916; House Dec. 1, 1884–85 (National Anti-Monopolist), 1887–93; Senate 1909–March 14, 1916.

Shober, Francis Edwin (father of Francis Emanuel Shober) (D N.C.) March 12, 1831–May 29, 1896; House 1869–73.

Shober, Francis Emanuel (son of Francis Edwin Shober) (D N.Y.) Oct. 24, 1860–Oct. 7, 1919; House 1903–05.

Shoemaker, Francis Henry (FL Minn.) April 25, 1889–July 24, 1958; House 1933–35.

Shoemaker, Lazarus Denison (R Pa.) Nov. 5, 1819–Sept. 9, 1893; House 1871–75.

Shonk, George Washington (R Pa.) April 26, 1850–Aug. 14, 1900; House 1891–93.

Short, Dewey Jackson (R Mo.) April 7, 1898–Nov. 19, 1979; House 1929–31, 1935–57; chair House Armed Services 1953–55.

Short, Don Levingston (R N.D.) June 22, 1903–May 10, 1982; House 1959–65.

Shorter, Eli Sims (D Ala.) March 15, 1823–April 29, 1879; House 1855–59.

Shortridge, Samuel Morgan (R Calif.) Aug. 3, 1861–Jan. 15, 1952; Senate 1921–33.

Shott, Hugh Ike (R W.Va.) Sept. 3, 1866–Oct. 12, 1953; House 1929–33; Senate Nov. 18, 1942–43.

Shoup, George Laird (great-grandfather of Richard Gardner Shoup) (R Idaho) June 15, 1836–Dec. 21, 1904; Senate Dec. 18, 1890–1901; Gov. April 1889–90 (Idaho Terr.), Oct. 1–Dec. 1890.

Shoup, Richard Gardner (great-grandson of George Laird Shoup) (R Mont.) Nov. 29, 1923–Nov. 25, 1995; House 1971–75.

Shouse, Jouett (D Kan.) Dec. 10, 1879–June 2, 1968; House 1915–19.

Showalter, Joseph Baltzell (R Pa.) Feb. 11, 1851–Dec. 3, 1932; House April 20, 1897–1903.

Shower, Jacob (D Md.) Feb. 22, 1803–May 25, 1879; House 1853–55.

Shows, C. Ronald "Ronnie" (D Miss) Jan. 26, 1947– ; House 1999–2003.

Shreve, Milton William (R Pa.) May 3, 1858–Dec. 23, 1939; House 1913–15, 1919–33.

Shriver, Garner E. (R Kan.) July 6, 1912–March 1, 1998; House 1961–77.

Shuford, Alonzo Craig (P N.C.) March 1, 1858–Feb. 8, 1933; House 1895–99.

Shuford, George Adams (D N.C.) Sept. 5, 1895–Dec. 8, 1962; House 1953–59.

Shull, Joseph Horace (D Pa.) Aug. 17, 1848–Aug. 9, 1944; House 1903–05.

Shultz, Emanuel (R Ohio) July 25, 1819–Nov. 5, 1912; House 1881–83.

Shumway, Norman David (R Calif.) July 28, 1934– ; House 1979–91.

Shuster, E. G. "Bud" (father of William "Bill" Shuster) (R Pa.) Jan. 23, 1932– ; House 1973–Feb. 3, 2001; chair House Transportation and Infrastructure 1995–2001.

Shuster, William "Bill" (son of E. G. "Bud" Shuster) (R Pa.) Jan. 10, 1961– ; House May 15, 2001– .

Sibal, Abner Woodruff (R Conn.) April 11, 1921–Jan. 27, 2000; House 1961–65.

Sibley, Henry Hastings (son of Solomon Sibley) (– Minn.) Feb. 20, 1811–Feb. 18, 1891; House (Terr. Del.) Oct. 30, 1848–49 (Wis.), July 7, 1849–53; Gov. May 24, 1858–Jan. 2, 1860.

Sibley, Jonas (– Mass.) March 7, 1762–Feb. 5, 1834; House 1823–25.

Sibley, Joseph Crocker (R Pa.) Feb. 18, 1850–May 19, 1926; House 1893–95 (Democrat), 1899–1907 (1899–1901 Democrat).

Sibley, Mark Hopkins (W N.Y.) 1796–Sept. 8, 1852; House 1837–39.

Sibley, Solomon (father of Henry Hastings Sibley) (– Mich.) Oct. 7, 1769–April 4, 1846; House (Terr. Del.) Nov. 20, 1820–23.

Sickles, Carlton Ralph (D Md.) June 15, 1921–Jan. 17, 2004; House 1963–67.

Sickles, Daniel Edgar (D N.Y.) Oct. 20, 1819–May 3, 1914; House 1857–61, 1893–95.

Sickles, Nicholas (J N.Y.) Sept. 11, 1801–May 13, 1845; House 1835–37.

Siegel, Isaac (R N.Y.) April 12, 1880–June 29, 1947; House 1915–23.

Sieminski, Alfred Dennis (D N.J.) Aug. 23, 1911–Dec. 13, 1990; House 1951–59.

Sikes, Robert Lee Fulton (D Fla.) June 3, 1906–Sept. 28, 1994; House 1941–Oct. 19, 1944, 1945–79.

Sikorski, Gerald Edward "Gerry" (DFL Minn.) April 26, 1948– ; House 1983–93.

Siler, Eugene (R Ky.) June 26, 1900–Dec. 5, 1987; House 1955–65.

Siljander, Mark Deli (R Mich.) June 11, 1951– ; House April 21, 1981–87.

Sill, Thomas Hale (– Pa.) Oct. 11, 1783–Feb. 7, 1856; House March 14, 1826–27, 1829–31.

Silsbee, Nathaniel (D Mass.) Jan. 14, 1773–July 14, 1850; House 1817–21; Senate May 31, 1826–35.

Silvester, Peter (grandfather of Peter Henry Silvester) (– N.Y.) 1734–Oct. 15, 1808; House 1789–93.

Silvester, Peter Henry (grandson of Peter Silvester) (W N.Y.) Feb. 17, 1807–Nov. 29, 1882; House 1847–51.

Simkins, Eldred (R S.C.) Aug. 30, 1779–Nov. 17, 1831; House Jan. 24, 1818–21.

Simmons, Furnifold McLendel (D N.C.) Jan. 20, 1854–April 30, 1940; House 1887–89; Senate 1901–31.

Simmons, George Abel (W N.Y.) Sept. 8, 1791–Oct. 27, 1857; House 1853–57.

Simmons, James Fowler (W R.I.) Sept. 10, 1795–July 10, 1864; Senate 1841–47, 1857–Aug. 15, 1862.

Simmons, James Samuel (nephew of Milton George Urner) (R N.Y.) Nov. 25, 1861–Nov. 28, 1935; House 1909–13.

Simmons, Robert Glenmore (R Neb.) Dec. 25, 1891–Dec. 27, 1969; House 1923–33.

Simmons, Robert "Rob" (R Conn.) Feb. 11, 1943– ; House 2001– .

Simms, Albert Gallatin (husband of Ruth Hanna McCormick) (R N.M.) Oct. 8, 1882–Dec. 29, 1964; House 1929–31.

Simms, William Emmett (D Ky.) Jan. 2, 1822–June 25, 1898; House 1859–61.

Simon, Joseph (R Ore.) Feb. 7, 1851–Feb. 14, 1935; Senate Oct. 8, 1898–1903.

Simon, Paul Martin (D Ill.) Nov. 29, 1928–Dec. 9, 2003; House 1975–85; Senate 1985–97.

Simonds, William Edgar (R Conn.) Nov. 24, 1842–March 14, 1903; House 1889–91.

Simons, Samuel (D Conn.) 1792–Jan. 13, 1847; House 1843–45.

Simonton, Charles Bryson (D Tenn.) Sept. 8, 1838–June 10, 1911; House 1879–83.

Simonton, William (W Pa.) Feb. 12, 1788–May 17, 1846; House 1839–43.

Simpkins, John (R Mass.) June 27, 1862–March 27, 1898; House 1895–March 27, 1898.

Simpson, Alan Kooi (son of Milward Lee Simpson) (R Wyo.) Sept. 2, 1931– ; Senate Jan. 1, 1979–97; chair Senate Veterans' Affairs 1981–85, 1995–97.

Simpson, Edna Oakes (widow of Sidney Elmer "Sid" Simpson) (R Ill.) Oct. 28, 1891–May 15, 1984; House 1959–61.

Simpson, James Jr. (R Ill.) Jan. 7, 1905–Feb. 29, 1960; House 1933–35.

Simpson, Jeremiah "Jerry" (P Kan.) March 31, 1842–Oct. 23, 1905; House 1891–95, 1897–99.

Simpson, Kenneth Farrand (R N.Y.) May 4, 1895–Jan. 25, 1941; House Jan. 3–Jan. 25, 1941.

Simpson, Michael (R Idaho) Sept. 8, 1950– ; House 1999– .

Simpson, Milward Lee (father of Alan Kooi Simpson) (R Wyo.) Nov. 12, 1897–June 10, 1993; Senate Nov. 6, 1962–67; Gov. Jan. 3, 1955–Jan. 5, 1959.

Simpson, Richard Franklin (D S.C.) March 24, 1798–Oct. 28, 1882; House 1843–49.

Simpson, Richard Murray (R Pa.) Aug. 30, 1900–Jan. 7, 1960; House May 11, 1937–Jan. 7, 1960.

Simpson, Sidney Elmer "Sid" (husband of Edna Oakes Simpson) (R Ill.) Sept. 20, 1894–Oct. 26, 1958; House 1943–Oct. 26, 1958; chair House District of Columbia 1953–55.

Sims, Alexander Dromgoole (nephew of George Coke Dromgoole) (D S.C.) June 12, 1803–Nov. 22, 1848; House 1845–Nov. 22, 1848.

Sims, Hugo Sheridan Jr. (D S.C.) Oct. 14, 1921– ; House 1949–51.

Sims, Leonard Henly (D Mo.) Feb. 6, 1807–Feb. 28, 1886; House 1845–47.

Sims, Thetus Willrette (D Tenn.) April 25, 1852–Dec. 17, 1939; House 1897–1921.

Sinclair, James Herbert (R N.D.) Oct. 9, 1871–Sept. 5, 1943; House 1919–35.

Singiser, Theodore Frelinghuysen (R Idaho) March 15, 1845–Jan. 23, 1907; House (Terr. Del.) 1883–85.

Singleton, James Washington (D Ill.) Nov. 23, 1811–April 4, 1892; House 1879–83.

Singleton, Otho Robards (D Miss.) Oct. 14, 1814–Jan. 11, 1889; House 1853–55, 1857–Jan. 12, 1861, 1875–87.

Singleton, Thomas Day (N S.C.) ?–Nov. 25, 1833; House March 3–Nov. 25, 1833 (served without having qualified).

Sinnickson, Clement Hall (great-nephew of Thomas Sinnickson) (R N.J.) Sept. 16, 1834–July 24, 1919; House 1875–79.

Sinnickson, Thomas (great-uncle of Clement Hall Sinnickson, uncle of Thomas Sinnickson, below) (F N.J.) Dec. 21, 1744–May 15, 1817; House 1789–91 (no party), 1797–99.

Sinnickson, Thomas (nephew of Thomas Sinnickson, above) (– N.J.) Dec. 13, 1786–Feb. 17, 1873; House Dec. 1, 1828–29.

Sinnott, Nicholas John (R Ore.) Dec. 6, 1870–July 20, 1929; House 1913–May 31, 1928.

Sipe, William Allen (D Pa.) July 1, 1844–Sept. 10, 1935; House Dec. 5, 1892–95.

Sirovich, William Irving (D N.Y.) March 18, 1882–Dec. 17, 1939; House 1927–Dec. 17, 1939.

Sisisky, Norman (D Va.) June 9, 1927–March 29, 2001; House 1983–March 29, 2001.

Sisk, Bernice Frederic (D Calif.) Dec. 14, 1910–Oct. 25, 1995; House 1955–79.

Sisson, Frederick James (D N.Y.) March 31, 1879–Oct. 20, 1949; House 1933–37.

Sisson, Thomas Upton (D Miss.) Sept. 22, 1869–Sept. 26, 1923; House 1909–23.

Sites, Frank Crawford (D Pa.) Dec. 24, 1864–May 23, 1935; House 1923–25.

Sitgreaves, Charles (D N.J.) April 22, 1803–March 17, 1878; House 1865–69.

Sitgreaves, Samuel (F Pa.) March 16, 1764–April 4, 1827; House 1795–98.

Sittler, Edward Lewis Jr. (R Pa.) April 21, 1908–Dec. 26, 1978; House 1951–53.

Skaggs, David Evans (D Colo.) Feb. 22, 1943– ; House 1987–99.

Skeen, Joseph Richard (R N.M.) June 30, 1927–Dec. 7, 2003; House 1981–Dec. 7, 2003.

Skelton, Charles (D N.J.) April 19, 1806–May 20, 1879; House 1851–55.

Skelton, Isaac Newton "Ike" IV (D Mo.) Dec. 20, 1931– ; House 1977– .

Skiles, William Woodburn (R Ohio) Dec. 11, 1849–Jan. 9, 1904; House 1901–Jan. 9, 1904.

Skinner, Charles Rufus (R N.Y.) Aug. 4, 1844–June 30, 1928; House Nov. 8, 1881–85.

Skinner, Harry (brother of Thomas Gregory Skinner) (P N.C.) May 25, 1855–May 19, 1929; House 1895–99.

Skinner, Richard (R Vt.) May 30, 1778–May 23, 1833; House 1813–15; Gov. Oct. 13, 1820–Oct. 10, 1823 (Democratic Republican).

Skinner, Thomas Gregory (brother of Harry Skinner) (D N.C.) Jan. 22, 1842–Dec. 22, 1907; House Nov. 20, 1883–87, 1889–91.

Skinner, Thomson Joseph (R Mass.) May 24, 1752–Jan. 20, 1809; House Jan. 27, 1797–99, 1803–Aug. 10, 1804.

Skubitz, Joe (R Kan.) May 6, 1906–Sept. 11, 2000; House 1963–Dec. 31, 1978.

Slack, John Mark Jr. (D W.Va.) March 18, 1915–March 17, 1980; House 1959–March 17, 1980.

Slade, Charles (J Ill.) ?–July 26, 1834; House 1833–July 26, 1834.

Slade, William (W Vt.) May 9, 1786–Jan. 18, 1859; House Nov. 1, 1831–43 (Nov. 1, 1831–37 Anti-Mason); Gov. Oct. 11, 1844–Oct. 9, 1846.

Slater, James Harvey (D Ore.) Dec. 28, 1826–Jan. 28, 1899; House 1871–73; Senate 1879–85.

Slattery, James Charles (D Kan.) Aug. 4, 1948– ; House 1983–95.

Slattery, James Michael (D Ill.) July 29, 1878–Aug. 28, 1948; Senate April 14, 1939–Nov. 21, 1940.

Slaughter, Daniel French Jr. (R Va.) May 20, 1925–Oct. 2, 1998; House 1985–Nov. 5, 1991.

Slaughter, Louise M. (D N.Y.) Aug. 14, 1929– ; House 1987– .

Slaughter, Roger Caldwell (D Mo.) July 17, 1905–June 2, 1974; House 1943–47.

Slayden, James Luther (uncle of Fontaine Maury Maverick) (D Texas) June 1, 1853–Feb. 24, 1924; House 1897–1919.

Slaymaker, Amos (F Pa.) March 11, 1755–June 12, 1837; House Oct. 11, 1814–15.

Slemons, William Ferguson (D Ark.) March 15, 1830–Dec. 10, 1918; House 1875–81.

Slemp, Campbell (father of Campbell Bascom Slemp) (R Va.) Dec. 2, 1839–Oct. 13, 1907; House 1903–Oct. 13, 1907.

Slemp, Campbell Bascom (son of Campbell Slemp) (R Va.) Sept. 4, 1870–Aug. 7, 1943; House Dec. 17, 1907–23.

Slidell, John (D La.) 1793–July 26, 1871; House 1843–Nov. 10, 1845; Senate Dec. 5, 1853–Feb. 4, 1861.

Slingerland, John I. (W N.Y.) March 1, 1804–Oct. 26, 1861; House 1847–49.

Sloan, Andrew (R Ga.) June 10, 1845–Sept. 22, 1883; House March 24, 1874–75.

Sloan, Andrew Scott (brother of Ithamar Conkey Sloan) (R Wis.) June 12, 1820–April 8, 1895; House 1861–63.

Sloan, Charles Henry (R Neb.) May 2, 1863–June 2, 1946; House 1911–19, 1929–31.

Sloan, Ithamar Conkey (brother of Andrew Scott Sloan) (R Wis.) May 9, 1822–Dec. 24, 1898; House 1863–67.

Sloan, James (R N.J.) ?–Nov. 1811; House 1803–09.

Sloane, John (– Ohio) 1779–May 15, 1856; House 1819–29.

Sloane, Jonathan (W Ohio) Nov. 1785–April 25, 1854; House 1833–37 (1833–35 Anti-Mason).

Slocum, Henry Warner (D N.Y.) Sept. 24, 1827–April 14, 1894; House 1869–73, 1883–85.

Slocumb, Jesse (F N.C.) 1780–Dec. 20, 1820; House 1817–Dec. 20, 1820.

Sloss, Joseph Humphrey (D Ala.) Oct. 12, 1826–Jan. 27, 1911; House 1871–75.

Small, Frank Jr. (R Md.) July 15, 1896–Oct. 24, 1973; House 1953–55.

Small, John Humphrey (D N.C.) Aug. 29, 1858–July 13, 1946; House 1899–1921.

Small, William Bradbury (R N.H.) May 17, 1817–April 7, 1878; House 1873–75.

Smalls, Robert (R S.C.) April 5, 1839–Feb. 22, 1915; House 1875–79, July 19, 1882–83, March 18, 1884–87.

Smart, Ephraim Knight (D Maine) Sept. 3, 1813–Sept. 29, 1872; House 1847–49, 1851–53.

Smart, James Stevenson (R N.Y.) June 14, 1842–Sept. 17, 1903; House 1873–75.

Smathers, George Armistead (nephew of William Howell Smathers) (D Fla.) Nov. 14, 1913– ; House 1947–51; Senate 1951–69; chair Senate Select Small Business 1967–69.

Smathers, William Howell (uncle of George Armistead Smathers) (D N.J.) Jan. 7, 1891–Sept. 24, 1955; Senate April 15, 1937–43.

Smelt, Dennis (R Ga.) about 1750–?; House Sept. 1, 1806–11.

Smilie, John (R Pa.) 1741–Dec. 30, 1812; House 1793–95 (no party), 1799–Dec. 30, 1812.

Smith, Abraham Herr (R Pa.) March 7, 1815–Feb. 16, 1894; House 1873–85.

Smith, Adam (D Wash.) June 15, 1965– ; House 1997– .

Smith, Addison Taylor (R Idaho) Sept. 5, 1862–July 5, 1956; House 1913–33.

Smith, Albert (D Maine) Jan. 3, 1793–May 29, 1867; House 1839–41.

Smith, Albert (W N.Y.) June 22, 1805–Aug. 27, 1870; House 1843–47.

Smith, Albert Lee Jr. (R Ala.) Aug. 31, 1931–Aug. 12, 1997; House 1981–83.

Smith, Arthur (– Va.) Nov. 15, 1785–March 30, 1853; House 1821–25.

Smith, Ballard (R Va.) ?–?; House 1815–21.

Smith, Benjamin A. II (D Mass.) March 26, 1916–Sept. 26, 1991; Senate Dec. 27, 1960–Nov. 6, 1962.

Smith, Bernard (– N.J.) July 5, 1776–July 16, 1835; House 1819–21.

Smith, Caleb Blood (W Ind.) April 16, 1808–Jan. 7, 1864; House 1843–49; secretary of the interior March 5, 1861–Dec. 31, 1862.

Smith, Charles Bennett (D N.Y.) Sept. 14, 1870–May 21, 1939; House 1911–19.

Smith, Charles Brooks (R W.Va.) Feb. 24, 1844–Dec. 7, 1899; House Feb. 3, 1890–91.

Smith, Christopher Henry (R N.J.) March 4, 1953– ; House 1981– ; chair House Veterans' Affairs 2001–05.

Smith, Clyde Harold (husband of Margaret Chase Smith) (R Maine) June 9, 1876–April 8, 1940; House 1937–April 8, 1940.

Smith, Daniel (R Tenn.) Oct. 28, 1748–June 6, 1818; Senate Oct. 6, 1798–99, 1805–March 31, 1809.

Smith, David Highbaugh (D Ky.) Dec. 19, 1854–Dec. 17, 1928; House 1897–1907.

Smith, Delazon (D Ore.) Oct. 5, 1816–Nov. 19, 1860; Senate Feb. 14–March 3, 1859.

Smith, Dennis Alan "Denny" (cousin of Steven Douglas Symms) (R Ore.) Jan. 19, 1938– ; House 1981–91.

Smith, Dietrich Conrad (R Ill.) April 4, 1840–April 18, 1914; House 1881–83.

Smith, Edward Henry (D N.Y.) May 5, 1809–Aug. 7, 1885; House 1861–63.

Smith, Ellison DuRant (D S.C.) Aug. 1, 1866–Nov. 17, 1944; Senate 1909–Nov. 17, 1944.

Smith, Francis Ormand Jonathan (D Maine) Nov. 23, 1806–Oct. 14, 1876; House 1833–39 (1833–37 Jacksonian).

Smith, Francis Raphael (D Pa.) Sept. 25, 1911–Dec. 9, 1982; House 1941–43.

Smith, Frank Ellis (D Miss.) Feb. 21, 1918–Aug. 2, 1997; House 1951–Nov. 14, 1962.

Smith, Frank Leslie (R Ill.) Nov. 24, 1867–Aug. 30, 1950; House 1919–21; elected to the Senate for the term beginning 1927 but was not permitted to qualify and resigned Feb. 9, 1928.

Smith, Frank Owens (D Md.) Aug. 27, 1859–Jan. 29, 1924; House 1913–15.

Smith, Frederick Cleveland (R Ohio) July 29, 1884–July 16, 1956; House 1939–51.

Smith, George (R Pa.) ?–?; House 1809–13.

Smith, George Joseph (R N.Y.) Nov. 7, 1859–Dec. 24, 1913; House 1903–05.

Smith, George Luke (R La.) Dec. 11, 1837–July 9, 1884; House Nov. 24, 1873–75.

Smith, George Ross (R Minn.) May 28, 1864–Nov. 7, 1952; House 1913–17.

Smith, George Washington (R Ill.) Aug. 18, 1846–Nov. 30, 1907; House 1889–Nov. 30, 1907.

Smith, Gerrit (FS N.Y.) March 6, 1797–Dec. 28, 1874; House 1853–Aug. 7, 1854.

Smith, Gomer Griffith (D Okla.) July 11, 1896–May 26, 1953; House Dec. 10, 1937–39.

Smith, Gordon H. (R Ore.) May 25, 1952– ; Senate 1997– .

Smith, Green Clay (son of John Speed Smith) (UU Ky.) July 4, 1826–June 29, 1895; House 1863–66; Gov. (Mont. Terr.) 1866–69.

Smith, H. Allen (R Calif.) Oct. 8, 1909–June 4, 1998; House 1957–73.

Smith, Henry (Lab. Wis.) July 22, 1838–Sept. 16, 1916; House 1887–89.

Smith, Henry Cassorte (R Mich.) June 2, 1856–Dec. 7, 1911; House 1899–1903.

Smith, Henry P. III (R N.Y.) Sept. 29, 1911–Oct. 1, 1995; House 1965–75.

Smith, Hezekiah Bradley (D N.J.) July 24, 1816–Nov. 3, 1887; House 1879–81.

Smith, Hiram Ypsilanti (R Iowa) March 22, 1843–Nov. 4, 1894; House Dec. 2, 1884–85.

Smith, Hoke (D Ga.) Sept. 2, 1855–Nov. 27, 1931; Senate Nov. 16, 1911–21; secretary of the interior March 6, 1893–Sept. 1, 1896; Gov. June 29, 1907–June 26, 1909, July 1–Nov. 16, 1911.

Smith, Horace Boardman (R N.Y.) Aug. 18, 1826–Dec. 26, 1888; House 1871–75.

Smith, Howard Alexander (uncle of Peter H. Dominick) (R N.J.) Jan. 30, 1880–Oct. 27, 1966; Senate Dec. 7, 1944–59; chair Senate Labor and Public Welfare 1953–55.

Smith, Howard Worth (D Va.) Feb. 2, 1883–Oct. 3, 1976; House 1931–67; chair House Rules 1955–67.

Smith, Isaac (F N.J.) 1740–Aug. 29, 1807; House 1795–97.

Smith, Isaac (R Pa.) Jan. 4, 1761–April 4, 1834; House 1813–15.

Smith, Israel (R Vt.) April 4, 1759–Dec. 2, 1810; House Oct. 17, 1791–97 (no party), 1801–03 (no party); Senate 1803–Oct. 1, 1807; Gov. Oct. 9, 1807–Oct. 14, 1808 (Democratic Republican).

Smith, James Jr. (D N.J.) June 12, 1851–April 1, 1927; Senate 1893–99.

Smith, James Strudwick (R N.C.) Oct. 15, 1790–Aug. 1859; House 1817–21.

Smith, James Vernon (R Okla.) July 23, 1926–June 23, 1973; House 1967–69.

Smith, Jedediah Kilburn (R N.H.) Nov. 7, 1770–Dec. 17, 1828; House 1807–09.

Smith, Jeremiah (brother of Samuel Smith of N.H., uncle of Robert Smith) (F N.H.) Nov. 29, 1759–Sept. 21, 1842; House 1791–July 26, 1797 (1791–95 no party); Gov. June 8, 1809–June 7, 1810.

Smith, John (R Ohio) about 1735–July 30, 1824; Senate April 1, 1803–April 25, 1808.

Smith, John (R Va.) May 7, 1750–March 5, 1836; House 1801–15.

Smith, John (R N.Y.) Feb. 12, 1752–Aug. 12, 1816; House Feb. 6, 1800–Feb. 23, 1804 (no party); Senate Feb. 23, 1804–13.

Smith, John (father of Worthington Curtis Smith) (D Vt.) Aug. 12, 1789–Nov. 26, 1858; House 1839–41.

Smith, John Ambler (R Va.) Sept. 23, 1847–Jan. 6, 1892; House 1873–75.

Smith, John Armstrong (R Ohio) Sept. 23, 1814–March 7, 1892; House 1869–73.

Smith, John Cotton (F Conn.) Feb. 12, 1765–Dec. 7, 1845; House Nov. 17, 1800–Aug. 1806; Gov. Oct. 25, 1812–May 8, 1817.

Smith, John Hyatt (I N.Y.) April 10, 1824–Dec. 7, 1886; House 1881–83.

Smith, John Joseph (D Conn.) Jan. 25, 1904–Feb. 16, 1980; House 1935–Nov. 4, 1941.

Smith, John M. C. (R Mich.) Feb. 6, 1853–March 30, 1923; House 1911–21, June 28, 1921–March 30, 1923.

Smith, John Quincy (R Ohio) Nov. 5, 1824–Dec. 30, 1901; House 1873–75.

Smith, John Speed (father of Green Clay Smith) (– Ky.) July 1, 1792–June 6, 1854; House Aug. 6, 1821–23.

Smith, John T. (D Pa.) ?–?; House 1843–45.

Smith, John Walter (D Md.) Feb. 5, 1845–April 19, 1925; House 1899–Jan. 12, 1900; Senate March 25, 1908–21; Gov. Jan. 10, 1900–Jan. 13, 1904.

Smith, Joseph Francis (D Pa.) Jan. 24, 1920–May 14, 1999; House July 28, 1981–83.

Smith, Joseph Luther (D W.Va.) May 22, 1880–Aug. 23, 1962; House 1929–45.

Smith, Joseph Showalter (D Ore.) June 20, 1824–July 13, 1884; House 1869–71.

Smith, Josiah (R Mass.) Feb. 26, 1738–April 4, 1803; House 1801–03.

Smith, Lamar Seeligson (R Texas) Nov. 19, 1947– ; House 1987– ; chair House Standards of Official Conduct 1999–2001.

Smith, Larkin (R Miss.) June 26, 1944–Aug. 13, 1989; House Jan. 3–Aug. 13, 1989.

Smith, Lawrence Henry (R Wis.) Sept. 15, 1892–Jan. 22, 1958; House Aug. 29, 1941–Jan. 22, 1958.

Smith, Lawrence Jack (D Fla.) April 25, 1941– ; House 1983–93.

Smith, Linda (R Wash.) July 16, 1950– ; House 1995–99.

Smith, Madison Roswell (D Mo.) July 9, 1850–June 18, 1919; House 1907–09.

Smith, Marcus Aurelius (D Ariz.) Jan. 24, 1851–April 7, 1924; House (Terr. Del.) 1887–95, 1897–99, 1901–03, 1905–09; Senate March 27, 1912–21.

Smith, Margaret Chase (widow of Clyde Harold Smith) (R Maine) Dec. 14, 1897–May 29, 1995; House June 3, 1940–49; Senate 1949–73.

Smith, Martin Fernand (D Wash.) May 28, 1891–Oct. 25, 1954; House 1933–43.

Smith, Nathan (brother of Nathaniel Smith, uncle of Truman Smith) (W Conn.) Jan. 8, 1770–Dec. 6, 1835; Senate 1833–Dec. 6, 1835.

Smith, Nathaniel (brother of Nathan Smith, uncle of Truman Smith) (F Conn.) Jan. 6, 1762–March 9, 1822; House 1795–99.

Smith, Neal Edward (D Iowa) March 23, 1920– ; House 1959–95; chair House Small Business 1977–81.

Smith, Nicholas Hart (R Mich.) Nov. 5, 1934– ; House 1993–2005.

Smith, O'Brien (R S.C.) about 1756–April 27, 1811; House 1805–07.

Smith, Oliver Hampton (W Ind.) Oct. 23, 1794–March 19, 1859; House 1827–29 (no party); Senate 1837–43.

Smith, Perry (D Conn.) May 12, 1783–June 8, 1852; Senate 1837–43.

Smith, Peter (R Vt.) Oct. 31, 1945– ; House 1989–91.

Smith, Ralph Tyler (R Ill.) Oct. 6, 1915–Aug. 13, 1972; Senate Sept. 17, 1969–Nov. 3, 1970.

Smith, Robert (nephew of Jeremiah Smith and Samuel Smith of N.H.) (D Ill.) June 12, 1802–Dec. 21, 1867; House 1843–49 (1843–47 Democrat, 1847–49 Independent Democrat), 1857–59.

Smith, Robert Barnwell. (See Rhett, Robert Barnwell.)

Smith, Robert Clinton (R N.H.) March 30, 1941– ; House 1985–91; Senate 1991–2003 (July 13, 1999–Nov. 1, 1999 Independent); chair Senate Select Ethics 1997–2001; Senate chair Senate Environment and Public Works Jan. 20, 2001–June 6, 2001.

Smith, Robert Freeman (R Ore.) June 16, 1931– ; House 1983–95, 1997–99; chair House Agriculture 1997–99.

Smith, Samuel (R Md.) July 27, 1752–April 22, 1839; House 1793–1803 (no party), Jan. 31, 1816–Dec. 17, 1822; Senate 1803–15, Dec. 17, 1822–33; elected pres. pro tempore Dec. 2, 1805, March 18, 1806, March 2, 1807, April 16, 1808, May 15, 1828, March 13, 1829, May 29, 1830, March 1, 1831.

Smith, Samuel (R Pa.) ?–?; House Nov. 7, 1805–11.

Smith, Samuel (brother of Jeremiah Smith, uncle of Robert Smith) (F N.H.) Nov. 11, 1765–April 25, 1842; House 1813–15.

Smith, Samuel A. (J Pa.) 1795–May 15, 1861; House Oct. 13, 1829–33.

Smith, Samuel Axley (D Tenn.) June 26, 1822–Nov. 25, 1863; House 1853–59.

Smith, Samuel William (R Mich.) Aug. 23, 1852–June 19, 1931; House 1897–1915.

Smith, Sylvester Clark (R Calif.) Aug. 26, 1858–Jan. 26, 1913; House 1905–Jan. 26, 1913.

Smith, Thomas (F Pa.) ?–Jan. 29, 1846; House 1815–17.

Smith, Thomas (D Ind.) May 1, 1799–April 12, 1876; House 1839–41, 1843–47.

Smith, Thomas Alexander (D Md.) Sept. 3, 1850–May 1, 1932; House 1905–07.

Smith, Thomas Francis (D N.Y.) July 24, 1865–April 11, 1923; House April 12, 1917–21.

Smith, Thomas Vernor (D Ill.) April 26, 1890–May 24, 1964; House 1939–41.

Smith, Truman (nephew of Nathan Smith and Nathaniel Smith) (W Conn.) Nov. 27, 1791–May 3, 1884; House 1839–43, 1845–49; Senate 1849–May 24, 1854.

Smith, Virginia Dodd (R Neb.) June 30, 1911– ; House 1975–91.

Smith, Walter Inglewood (R Iowa) July 10, 1862–Jan. 27, 1922; House Dec. 3, 1900–March 15, 1911.

Smith, William (– Md.) April 12, 1728–March 27, 1814; House 1789–91; Cont. Cong. 1777.

Smith, William (R S.C.) about 1762–June 26, 1840; Senate Dec. 4, 1816–23, Nov. 29, 1826–31.

Smith, William (R S.C.) Sept. 20, 1751–June 22, 1837; House 1797–99.

Smith, William (– Va.) ?–?; House 1821–27.

Smith, William (D Va.) Sept. 6, 1797–May 18, 1887; House 1841–43, 1853–61; Gov. Jan. 1, 1846–Jan. 1, 1849 (Democrat), Jan. 1, 1864–April 1, 1865 (Confederate Democrat).

Smith, William Alden (R Mich.) May 12, 1859–Oct. 11, 1932; House 1895–Feb. 9, 1907; Senate Feb. 9, 1907–19.

Smith, William Alexander (R N.C.) Jan. 9, 1828–May 16, 1888; House 1873–75.

Smith, William Ephraim (D Ga.) March 14, 1829–March 11, 1890; House 1875–81.

Smith, William Jay (R Tenn.) Sept. 24, 1823–Nov. 29, 1913; House 1869–71.

Smith, William Loughton (F S.C.) 1758–Dec. 19, 1812; House 1789–July 10, 1797.

Smith, William Nathan Harrell (O N.C.) Sept. 24, 1812–Nov. 14, 1889; House 1859–61.

Smith, William Orlando (R Pa.) June 13, 1859–May 12, 1932; House 1903–07.

Smith, William Robert (D Texas) Aug. 18, 1863–Aug. 16, 1924; House 1903–17.

Smith, William Russell (AP Ala.) March 27, 1815–Feb. 26, 1896; House 1851–57 (1851–53 Unionist, 1853–55 Democrat).

Smith, William Stephens (F N.Y.) Nov. 8, 1755–June 10, 1816; House 1813–15.

Smith, Willis (D N.C.) Dec. 19, 1887–June 26, 1953; Senate Nov. 27, 1950–June 26, 1953.

Smith, Wint (R Kan.) Oct. 7, 1892–April 27, 1976; House 1947–61.

Smith, Worthington Curtis (son of John Smith of Vt.) (R Vt.) April 23, 1823–Jan. 2, 1894; House 1867–73.

Smithers, Nathaniel Barratt (UU Del.) Oct. 8, 1818–Jan. 16, 1896; House Dec. 7, 1863–65.

Smithwick, John Harris (D Fla.) July 17, 1872–Dec. 2, 1948; House 1919–27.

Smoot, Reed (R Utah) Jan. 10, 1862–Feb. 9, 1941; Senate 1903–33.

Smyser, Martin Luther (R Ohio) April 3, 1851–May 6, 1908; House 1889–91, 1905–07.

Smyth, Alexander (R Va.) 1765–April 17, 1830; House 1817–25, 1827–April 17, 1830.

Smyth, George Washington (D Texas) May 16, 1803–Feb. 21, 1866; House 1853–55.

Smyth, William (R Iowa) Jan. 3, 1824–Sept. 30, 1870; House 1869–Sept. 30, 1870.

Snapp, Henry (father of Howard Malcolm Snapp) (R Ill.) June 30, 1822–Nov. 26, 1895; House Dec. 4, 1871–73.

Snapp, Howard Malcolm (son of Henry Snapp) (R Ill.) Sept. 27, 1855–Aug. 14, 1938; House 1903–11.

Sneed, William Henry (AP Tenn.) Aug. 27, 1812–Sept. 18, 1869; House 1855–57.

Snell, Bertrand Hollis (R N.Y.) Dec. 9, 1870–Feb. 2, 1958; House Nov. 2, 1915–39; House minority leader 1931–39.

Snider, Samuel Prather (R Minn.) Oct. 9, 1845–Sept. 24, 1928; House 1889–91.

Snodgrass, Charles Edward (nephew of Henry Clay Snodgrass) (D Tenn.) Dec. 28, 1866–Aug. 3, 1936; House 1899–1903.

Snodgrass, Henry Clay (uncle of Charles Edward Snodgrass) (D Tenn.) March 29, 1848–April 22, 1931; House 1891–95.

Snodgrass, John Fryall (D Va.) March 2, 1804–June 5, 1854; House 1853–June 5, 1854.

Snook, John Stout (D Ohio) Dec. 18, 1862–Sept. 19, 1952; House 1901–05, 1917–19.

Snover, Horace Greeley (R Mich.) Sept. 21, 1847–July 21, 1924; House 1895–99.

Snow, Donald Francis (R Maine) Sept. 6, 1877–Feb. 12, 1958; House 1929–33.

Snow, Herman Wilber (D Ill.) July 3, 1836–Aug. 25, 1914; House 1891–93.

Snow, William W. (D N.Y.) April 27, 1812–Sept. 3, 1886; House 1851–53.

Snowbarger, Vincent (R Kan.) Sept. 16, 1949– ; House 1997–99.

Snowe, Olympia Jean Bouchles (wife of Gov. John Rettie McKernan Jr. of Maine) (R Maine) Feb. 21, 1947– ; House 1979–95; Senate 1995– ; chair Senate Small Business and Entrepreneurship 2003– .

Snyder, Adam Wilson (D Ill.) Oct. 6, 1799–May 14, 1842; House 1837–39.

Snyder, Charles Philip (D W.Va.) June 9, 1847–Aug. 21, 1915; House May 15, 1883–89.

Snyder, Homer Peter (R N.Y.) Dec. 6, 1863–Dec. 30, 1937; House 1915–25.

Snyder, John (– Pa.) Jan. 29, 1793–Aug. 15, 1850; House 1841–43.

Snyder, John Buell (D Pa.) July 30, 1877–Feb. 24, 1946; House 1933–Feb. 24, 1946.

Snyder, Marion Gene (R Ky.) Jan. 26, 1928– ; House 1963–65, 1967–87.

Snyder, Melvin Claude (R W.Va.) Oct. 29, 1898–Aug. 5, 1972; House 1947–49.

Snyder, Oliver P. (R Ark.) Nov. 13, 1833–Nov. 22, 1882; House 1871–75.

Snyder, Victor F. (D Ark.) Sept. 27, 1947– ; House 1997– .

Sodrel, Michael E. (R Ind.) Dec. 17, 1945– ; House 2005– .

Solarz, Stephen Joshua (D N.Y.) Sept. 12, 1940– ; House 1975–93.

Solis, Hilda L. (D Calif.) Oct. 20, 1957– ; House 2001– .

Sollers, Augustus Rhodes (W Md.) May 1, 1814–Nov. 26, 1862; House 1841–43, 1853–55.

Solomon, Gerald Brooks Hunt (R N.Y.) Aug. 14, 1930–Oct. 26, 2001; House 1979–99; chair House Rules 1995–99.

Somers, Andrew Lawrence (D N.Y.) March 21, 1895–April 6, 1949; House 1925–April 6, 1949; chair House Public Lands 1949.

Somers, Peter J. (D Wis.) April 12, 1850–Feb. 15, 1924; House Aug. 27, 1893–95.

Somes, Daniel Eton (R Maine) May 20, 1815–Feb. 13, 1888; House 1859–61.

Sorg, Paul John (D Ohio) Sept. 23, 1840–May 28, 1902; House May 21, 1894–97.

Sosnowski, John Bartholomew (R Mich.) Dec. 8, 1883–July 16, 1968; House 1925–27.

Souder, Mark (R Ind.) July 18, 1950– ; House 1995– .

Soule, Nathan (J N.Y.) ?–?; House 1831–33.

Soule, Pierre (D La.) Aug. 31, 1801–March 26, 1870; Senate Jan. 21–March 3, 1847, 1849–April 11, 1853.

South, Charles Lacy (D Texas) July 22, 1892–Dec. 20, 1965; House 1935–43.

Southall, Robert Goode (D Va.) Dec. 26, 1852–May 25, 1924; House 1903–07.

Southard, Henry (father of Isaac Southard and Samuel Lewis Southard) (R N.J.) Oct. 7, 1747–May 22, 1842; House 1801–11, 1815–21.

Southard, Isaac (son of Henry Southard, brother of Samuel Lewis Southard) (AJ N.J.) Aug. 30, 1783–Sept. 18, 1850; House 1831–33.

Southard, James Harding (R Ohio) Jan. 20, 1851–Feb. 20, 1919; House 1895–1907.

Southard, Milton Isaiah (D Ohio) Oct. 20, 1836–May 4, 1905; House 1873–79.

Southard, Samuel Lewis (son of Henry Southard, brother of Isaac Southard) (W N.J.) June 9, 1787–June 26, 1842; Senate Jan. 26, 1821–23 (Republican), 1833–June 26, 1842; elected pres. pro tempore March 11, 1841; secretary of the navy Sept. 16, 1823–March 3, 1829; Gov. Oct. 26, 1832–Feb. 27, 1833 (Republican).

Southgate, William Wright (W Ky.) Nov. 27, 1800–Dec. 26, 1849; House 1837–39.

Southwick, George Newell (R N.Y.) March 7, 1863–Oct. 17, 1912; House 1895–99, 1901–11.

Sowden, William Henry (D Pa.) June 6, 1840–March 3, 1907; House 1885–89.

Spaight, Richard Dobbs (grandfather of Richard Spaight Donnell, father of Richard Dobbs Spaight Jr.) (R N.C.) March 25, 1758–Sept. 6, 1802; House Dec. 10, 1798–1801; Cont. Cong. 1783–85; Gov. Dec. 14, 1792–Nov. 19, 1795 (Anti–Federalist).

Spaight, Richard Dobbs Jr. (son of Richard Dobbs Spaight, uncle of Richard Spaight Donnell) (– N.C.) 1796–May 2, 1850; House 1823–25; Gov. Dec. 10, 1835–Dec. 31, 1836 (Democrat).

Spalding, Burleigh Folsom (R N.D.) Dec. 3, 1853–March 17, 1934; House 1899–1901, 1903–05.

Spalding, George (R Mich.) Nov. 12, 1836–Sept. 13, 1915; House 1895–99.

Spalding, Rufus Paine (R Ohio) May 3, 1798–Aug. 29, 1886; House 1863–69.

Spalding, Thomas (R Ga.) March 26, 1774–Jan. 5, 1851; House Dec. 24, 1805–06.

Spangler, David (W Ohio) Dec. 2, 1796–Oct. 18, 1856; House 1833–37 (1833–35 Anti–Jacksonian).

Spangler, Jacob (R Pa.) Nov. 28, 1767–June 17, 1843; House 1817–April 20, 1818.

Sparkman, John Jackson (D Ala.) Dec. 20, 1899–Nov. 16, 1985; House 1937–Nov. 5, 1946; Senate Nov. 6, 1946–79; chair Senate Select Small Business 1950–53, 1955–67; chair Senate Banking and Currency 1967–71; chair Senate Banking, Housing, and Urban Affairs 1971–75; chair Senate Foreign Relations 1975–78.

Sparkman, Stephen Milancthon (D Fla.) July 29, 1849–Sept. 26, 1929; House 1895–1917.

Sparks, Charles Isaac (R Kan.) Dec. 20, 1872–April 30, 1937; House 1929–33.

Sparks, William Andrew Jackson (D Ill.) Nov. 19, 1828–May 7, 1904; House 1875–83.

Spaulding, Elbridge Gerry (R N.Y.) Feb. 24, 1809–May 5, 1897; House 1849–51 (Whig), 1859–63.

Spaulding, Oliver Lyman (R Mich.) Aug. 2, 1833–July 30, 1922; House 1881–83.

Speaks, John Charles (R Ohio) Feb. 11, 1859–Nov. 6, 1945; House 1921–31.

Spearing, James Zacharie (D La.) April 23, 1864–Nov. 2, 1942; House April 22, 1924–31.

Specter, Arlen (R Pa.) Feb. 12, 1930– ; Senate 1981– ; chair Senate Select Intelligence Activities 1995–97; chair Senate Veterans' Affairs 1997–Jan. 3, 2001, Jan. 20, 2001–June 6, 2001, 2003–05; chair Senate Judiciary 2005– .

Speed, Thomas (R Ky.) Oct. 25, 1768–Feb. 20, 1842; House 1817–19.

Speer, Emory (ID Ga.) Sept. 3, 1848–Dec. 13, 1918; House 1879–83.

Speer, Peter Moore (R Pa.) Dec. 29, 1862–Aug. 3, 1933; House 1911–13.

Speer, Robert Milton (D Pa.) Sept. 8, 1838–Jan. 17, 1890; House 1871–75.

Speer, Thomas Jefferson (R Ga.) Aug. 31, 1837–Aug. 18, 1872; House 1871–Aug. 18, 1872.

Speight, Jesse (D Miss.) Sept. 22, 1795–May 1, 1847; House 1829–37 (no party N.C.); Senate 1845–May 1, 1847.

Spellman, Gladys Noon (D Md.) March 1, 1918–June 19, 1988; House 1975–Feb. 24, 1981.

Spence, Brent (D Ky.) Dec. 24, 1874–Sept. 18, 1967; House 1931–63; chair House Banking and Currency 1949–53, 1955–63.

Spence, Floyd Davidson (R S.C.) April 9, 1928–Aug. 16, 2001; House 1971–Aug. 16, 2001; chair House National Security 1995–98; chair House Armed Services 1999–2000.

Spence, John Selby (uncle of Thomas Ara Spence) (W Md.) Feb. 29, 1788–Oct. 24, 1840; House 1823–25 (no party), 1831–33; Senate Dec. 31, 1836–Oct. 24, 1840.

Spence, Thomas Ara (nephew of John Selby Spence) (W Md.) Feb. 20, 1810–Nov. 10, 1877; House 1843–45.

Spencer, Ambrose (father of John Canfield Spencer) (– N.Y.) Dec. 13, 1765–March 13, 1848; House 1829–31.

Spencer, Elijah (– N.Y.) 1775–Dec. 15, 1852; House 1821–23.

Spencer, George Eliphaz (R Ala.) Nov. 1, 1836–Feb. 19, 1893; Senate July 13, 1868–79.

Spencer, George Lloyd (D Ark.) March 27, 1893–Jan. 14, 1981; Senate April 1, 1941–43.

Spencer, James Bradley (D N.Y.) April 26, 1781–March 26, 1848; House 1837–39.

Spencer, James Grafton (D Miss.) Sept. 13, 1844–Feb. 22, 1926; House 1895–97.

Spencer, John Canfield (son of Ambrose Spencer) (R N.Y.) Jan. 8, 1788–May 18, 1855; House 1817–19; secretary of war Oct. 12, 1841–March 3, 1843; secretary of the Treasury March 8, 1843–May 2, 1844.

Spencer, Richard (J Md.) Oct. 29, 1796–Sept. 3, 1868; House 1829–31.

Spencer, Selden Palmer (R Mo.) Sept. 16, 1862–May 16, 1925; Senate Nov. 6, 1918–May 16, 1925.

Spencer, William Brainerd (D La.) Feb. 5, 1835–Feb. 12, 1882; House June 8, 1876–Jan. 8, 1877.

Sperry, Lewis (D Conn.) Jan. 23, 1848–June 22, 1922; House 1891–95.

Sperry, Nehemiah Day (R Conn.) July 10, 1827–Nov. 13, 1911; House 1895–1911.

Spight, Thomas (D Miss.) Oct. 25, 1841–Jan. 5, 1924; House July 5, 1898–1911.

Spink, Cyrus (R Ohio) March 24, 1793–May 31, 1859; House March 4–May 31, 1859.

Spink, Solomon Lewis (R Dakota) March 20, 1831–Sept. 22, 1881; House (Terr. Del.) 1869–71.

Spinner, Francis Elias (R N.Y.) Jan. 21, 1802–Dec. 31, 1890; House 1855–61 (1855–57 Democrat).

Spinola, Francis Barretto (D N.Y.) March 19, 1821–April 14, 1891; House 1887–April 14, 1891.

Spong, William Belser Jr. (D Va.) Sept. 29, 1920–Oct. 8, 1997; Senate Dec. 31, 1966–73.

Spooner, Henry Joshua (R R.I.) Aug. 6, 1839–Feb. 9, 1918; House Dec. 5, 1881–91.

Spooner, John Coit (R Wis.) Jan. 6, 1843–June 11, 1919; Senate 1885–91, 1897–April 30, 1907.

Sprague, Charles Franklin (grandson of Peleg Sprague of Maine) (R Mass.) June 10, 1857–Jan. 30, 1902; House 1897–1901.

Sprague, Peleg (F N.H.) Dec. 10, 1756–April 20, 1800; House Dec. 15, 1797–99.

Sprague, Peleg (grandfather of Charles Franklin Sprague) (– Maine) April 27, 1793–Oct. 13, 1880; House 1825–29; Senate 1829–Jan. 1, 1835.

Sprague, William (W Mich.) Feb. 23, 1809–Sept. 19, 1868; House 1849–51.

Sprague, William (uncle of William Sprague, below) (W R.I.) Nov. 3, 1799–Oct. 19, 1856; House 1835–37; Senate Feb. 18, 1842–Jan. 17, 1844; Gov. May 2, 1838–May 1, 1839.

Sprague, William (nephew of William Sprague, above) (R R.I.) Sept. 12, 1830–Sept. 11, 1915; Senate 1863–75; Gov. May 29, 1860–March 3, 1863 (Unionist).

Sprague, William Peter (R Ohio) May 21, 1827–March 3, 1899; House 1871–75.

Spratt, John McKee Jr. (D S.C.) Nov. 1, 1942– ; House 1983– .

Sprigg, James Cresap (brother of Michael Cresap Sprigg) (W Ky.) 1802–Oct. 3, 1852; House 1841–43.

Sprigg, Michael Cresap (brother of James Cresap Sprigg) (J Md.) July 1, 1791–Dec. 18, 1845; House 1827–31.

Sprigg, Richard Jr. (nephew of Thomas Sprigg) (R Md.) ?–?; House May 5, 1796–99, 1801–Feb. 11, 1802.

Sprigg, Thomas (uncle of Richard Sprigg Jr.) (R Md.) 1747–Dec. 13, 1809; House 1793–97.

Spriggs, John Thomas (D N.Y.) April 5, 1825–Dec. 23, 1888; House 1883–87.

Springer, Raymond Smiley (R Ind.) April 26, 1882–Aug. 28, 1947; House 1939–Aug. 28, 1947.

Springer, William Lee (R Ill.) April 12, 1909–Sept. 20, 1992; House 1951–73.

Springer, William McKendree (D Ill.) May 30, 1836–Dec. 4, 1903; House 1875–95.

Sproul, Elliott Wilford (R Ill.) Dec. 28, 1856–June 22, 1935; House 1921–31.

Sproul, William Henry (R Kan.) Oct. 14, 1867–Dec. 27, 1932; House 1923–31.

Spruance, Presley (W Del.) Sept. 11, 1785–Feb. 13, 1863; Senate 1847–53.

Squire, Watson Carvosso (R Wash.) May 18, 1838–June 7, 1926; Senate Nov. 20, 1889–97; Gov. (Wash. Terr.) 1884–87.

Stabenow, Deborah (D Mich.) April 29, 1950– ; House 1997–2001; Senate 2001– .

Stack, Edmund John (D Ill.) Jan. 31, 1874–April 12, 1957; House 1911–13.

Stack, Edward John (D Fla.) April 29, 1910–Nov. 3, 1989; House 1979–81.

Stack, Michael Joseph (D Pa.) Sept. 29, 1888–Dec. 14, 1960; House 1935–39.

Stackhouse, Eli Thomas (D S.C.) March 27, 1824–June 14, 1892; House 1891–June 14, 1892.

Staebler, Neil Oliver (D Mich.) July 11, 1905–Dec. 8, 2000; House 1963–65.

Stafford, Robert Theodore (R Vt.) Aug. 8, 1913– ; House 1961–Sept. 16, 1971; Senate Sept. 16, 1971–89; chair Senate Environment and Public Works 1981–87; Gov. Jan. 8, 1959–Jan. 5, 1961.

Stafford, William Henry (R Wis.) Oct. 12, 1869–April 22, 1957; House 1903–11, 1913–19, 1921–23, 1929–33.

Staggers, Harley Orrin (father of Harley Orrin Staggers Jr.) (D W.Va.) Aug. 3, 1907–Aug. 20, 1991; House 1949–81; chair House Interstate and Foreign Commerce 1966–81.

Staggers, Harley Orrin Jr. (son of Harley Orrin Staggers) (D W.Va.) Feb. 22, 1951– ; House 1983–93.

Stahle, James Alonzo (R Pa.) Jan. 11, 1829–Dec. 21, 1912; House 1895–97.

Stahlnecker, William Griggs (D N.Y.) June 20, 1849–March 26, 1902; House 1885–93.

Stalbaum, Lynn Ellsworth (D Wis.) May 15, 1920–June 17, 1999; House 1965–67.

Stalker, Gale Hamilton (R N.Y.) Nov. 7, 1889–Nov. 4, 1985; House 1923–35.

Stallings, Jesse Francis (D Ala.) April 4, 1856–March 18, 1928; House 1893–1901.

Stallings, Richard Howard (D Idaho) Oct. 10, 1940– ; House 1985–93.

Stallworth, James Adams (D Ala.) April 7, 1822–Aug. 31, 1861; House 1857–Jan. 21, 1861.

Stanard, Edwin Obed (R Mo.) Jan. 5, 1832–March 12, 1914; House 1873–75.

Stanbery, William (AJ Ohio) Aug. 10, 1788–Jan. 23, 1873; House Oct. 9, 1827–33 (Oct. 9, 1827–29 no party, 1829–31 Jacksonian).

Standifer, James (W Tenn.) ?–Aug. 20, 1837; House 1823–25 (no party), 1829–Aug. 20, 1837 (1829–35 Jacksonian, 1835–37 White supporter).

Standiford, Elisha David (D Ky.) Dec. 28, 1831–July 26, 1887; House 1873–75.

Stanfield, Robert Nelson (R Ore.) July 9, 1877–April 13, 1945; Senate 1921–27.

Stanfill, William Abner (R Ky.) Jan. 16, 1892–June 12, 1971; Senate Nov. 19, 1945–Nov. 5, 1946.

Stanford, Leland (R Calif.) March 9, 1824–June 21, 1893; Senate 1885–June 21, 1893; Gov. Jan. 10, 1862–Dec. 10, 1863.

Stanford, Richard (grandfather of William Robert Webb) (R N.C.) March 2, 1767–April 9, 1816; House 1797–April 9, 1816.

Stangeland, Arlan Ingehart (R Minn.) Feb. 8, 1930– ; House March 1, 1977–91.

Stanley, Augustus Owsley (D Ky.) May 21, 1867–Aug. 12, 1958; House 1903–15; Senate May 19, 1919–25; Gov. Dec. 7, 1915–May 19, 1919.

Stanley, Thomas Bahnson (D Va.) July 16, 1890–July 10, 1970; House Nov. 5, 1946–Feb. 3, 1953; chair House Administration 1951–53; Gov. Jan. 20, 1954–Jan. 11, 1958.

Stanley, Winifred Claire (R N.Y.) Aug. 14, 1909–Feb. 29, 1996; House 1943–45.

Stanly, Edward (son of John Stanly) (W N.C.) Jan. 10, 1810–July 12, 1872; House 1837–43, 1849–53.

Stanly, John (father of Edward Stanly) (F N.C.) April 9, 1774–Aug. 2, 1834; House 1801–03, 1809–11.

Stanton, Benjamin (R Ohio) June 4, 1809–June 2, 1872; House 1851–53 (Whig), 1855–61.

Stanton, Frederick Perry (D Tenn.) Dec. 22, 1814–June 4, 1894; House 1845–55; Gov. (Kan. Terr.) 1858–61.

Stanton, James Vincent (D Ohio) Feb. 27, 1932– ; House 1971–77.

Stanton, John William (R Ohio) Feb. 20, 1924–April 11, 2002; House 1965–83.

Stanton, Joseph Jr. (R R.I.) July 19, 1739–1807; Senate June 7, 1790–93 (no party); House 1801–07.

Stanton, Richard Henry (D Ky.) Sept. 9, 1812–March 20, 1891; House 1849–55.

Stanton, William Henry (D Pa.) July 28, 1843–March 28, 1900; House Nov. 7, 1876–77.

Starin, John Henry (grandson of Thomas Sammons) (R N.Y.) Aug. 27, 1825–March 21, 1909; House 1877–81.

Stark, Benjamin (D Ore.) June 26, 1820–Oct. 10, 1898; Senate Oct. 29, 1861–Sept. 12, 1862.

Stark, Fortney Hillman "Pete" Jr. (D Calif.) Nov. 11, 1931– ; House 1973– ; chair House District of Columbia 1993–95.

Stark, William Ledyard (P Neb.) July 29, 1853–Nov. 11, 1922; House 1897–1903.

Starkey, Frank Thomas (D Minn.) Feb. 18, 1892–May 14, 1968; House 1945–47.

Starkweather, David Austin (D Ohio) Jan. 21, 1802–July 12, 1876; House 1839–41, 1845–47.

Starkweather, George Anson (D N.Y.) May 19, 1794–Oct. 15, 1879; House 1847–49.

Starkweather, Henry Howard (R Conn.) April 29, 1826–Jan. 28, 1876; House 1867–Jan. 28, 1876.

Starnes, Joe (D Ala.) March 31, 1895–Jan. 9, 1962; House 1935–45.

Starr, John Farson (R N.J.) March 25, 1818–Aug. 9, 1904; House 1863–67.

Staton, David Michael (R W.Va.) Feb. 11, 1940– ; House 1981–83.

Stauffer, Simon Walter (R Pa.) Aug. 13, 1888–Sept. 26, 1975; House 1953–55, 1957–59.

Steagall, Henry Bascom (D Ala.) May 19, 1873–Nov. 22, 1943; House 1915–Nov. 22, 1943.

Stearns, Asahel (F Mass.) June 17, 1774–Feb. 5, 1839; House 1815–17.

Stearns, Clifford Bundy "Cliff" (R Fla.) April 16, 1941– ; House 1989– .

Stearns, Foster Waterman (R N.H.) July 29, 1881–June 4, 1956; House 1939–45.

Stearns, Ozora Pierson (R Minn.) Jan. 15, 1831–June 2, 1896; Senate Jan. 23–March 3, 1871.

Stebbins, Henry George (D N.Y.) Sept. 15, 1811–Dec. 9, 1881; House 1863–Oct. 24, 1864.

Steck, Daniel Frederic (D Iowa) Dec. 16, 1881–Dec. 31, 1950; Senate April 12, 1926–31.

Stedman, Charles Manly (D N.C.) Jan. 29, 1841–Sept. 23, 1930; House 1911–Sept. 23, 1930.

Stedman, William (F Mass.) Jan. 21, 1765–Aug. 31, 1831; House 1803–July 16, 1810.

Steed, Thomas Jefferson (D Okla.) March 2, 1904–June 8, 1983; House 1949–81.

Steele, George Washington (R Ind.) Dec. 13, 1839–July 12, 1922; House 1881–89, 1895–1903; Gov. (Okla. Terr.) 1890–91.

Steele, Henry Joseph (D Pa.) May 10, 1860–March 19, 1933; House 1915–21.

Steele, John (– N.C.) Nov. 1, 1764–Aug. 14, 1815; House April 19, 1790–93.

Steele, John Benedict (D N.Y.) March 28, 1814–Sept. 24, 1866; House 1861–65.

Steele, John Nevett (AJ Md.) Feb. 22, 1796–Aug. 13, 1853; House May 29, 1834–37.

Steele, Leslie Jasper (D Ga.) Nov. 21, 1868–July 24, 1929; House 1927–July 24, 1929.

Steele, Robert Hampton (R Conn.) Nov. 3, 1938– ; House Nov. 3, 1970–75.

Steele, Thomas Jefferson (D Iowa) March 19, 1853–March 20, 1920; House 1915–17.

Steele, Walter Leak (D N.C.) April 18, 1823–Oct. 16, 1891; House 1877–81.

Steele, William Gaston (D N.J.) Dec. 17, 1820–April 22, 1892; House 1861–65.

Steele, William Randolph (D Wyo) July 24, 1842–Nov. 30, 1901; House (Terr. Del.) 1873–77.

Steelman, Alan Watson (R Texas) March 15, 1942– ; House 1973–77.

Steenerson, Halvor (R Minn.) June 30, 1852–Nov. 22, 1926; House 1903–23.

Steenrod, Lewis (D Va.) May 27, 1810–Oct. 3, 1862; House 1839–45.

Steers, Newton Ivan Jr. (R Md.) Jan. 13, 1917–Feb. 11, 1993; House 1977–79.

Stefan, Karl (R Neb.) March 1, 1884–Oct. 2, 1951; House 1935–Oct. 2, 1951.

Steiger, Sam (R Ariz.) March 10, 1929– ; House 1967–77.

Steiger, William Albert (R Wis.) May 15, 1938–Dec. 4, 1978; House 1967–Dec. 4, 1978.

Steiwer, Frederick (R Ore.) Oct. 13, 1883–Feb. 3, 1939; Senate 1927–Jan. 31, 1938.

Stenger, William Shearer (D Pa.) Feb. 13, 1840–March 29, 1918; House 1875–79.

Stengle, Charles Irwin (D N.Y.) Dec. 5, 1869–Nov. 23, 1953; House 1923–25.

Stenholm, Charles Walter (D Texas) Oct. 26, 1938– ; House 1979–2005.

Stennis, John Cornelius (D Miss.) Aug. 3, 1901–April 23, 1995; Senate Nov. 5, 1947–89; chair Senate Select Standards and Conduct 1966–75; chair Senate Armed Services 1969–81; elected pres. pro tempore Jan. 6, 1987; chair Senate Appropriations 1987–89.

Stephens, Abraham P. (D N.Y.) Feb. 18, 1796–Nov. 25, 1859; House 1851–53.

Stephens, Alexander Hamilton (great–great–uncle of Robert Grier Stephens Jr.) (D Ga.) Feb. 11, 1812–March 4, 1883; House Oct. 2, 1843–59 (Oct. 2, 1843–51 Whig, 1853–55 Whig, 1851–53 Unionist), Dec. 1, 1873–Nov. 4, 1882; Gov. Nov. 4, 1882–March 4, 1883.

Stephens, Ambrose Everett Burnside (R Ohio) June 3, 1862–Feb. 12, 1927; House 1919–Feb. 12, 1927.

Stephens, Dan Voorhees (D Neb.) Nov. 4, 1868–Jan. 13, 1939; House Nov. 7, 1911–19.

Stephens, Hubert Durrett (D Miss.) July 2, 1875–March 14, 1946; House 1911–21; Senate 1923–35.

Stephens, John Hall (D Texas) Nov. 22, 1847–Nov. 18, 1924; House 1897–1917.

Stephens, Philander (J Pa.) 1788–July 8, 1842; House 1829–33.

Stephens, Robert Grier Jr. (great–great–nephew of Alexander Hamilton Stephens) (D Ga.) Aug. 14, 1913–Feb. 20, 2003; House 1961–77.

Stephens, William Dennison (P Calif.) Dec. 26, 1859–April 25, 1944; House 1911–July 22, 1916 (1911–15 Republican); Gov. March 15, 1917–Jan. 9, 1923 (Republican).

Stephenson, Benjamin (D Ill.) ?–Oct. 10, 1822; House (Terr. Del.) Sept. 3, 1814–17.

Stephenson, Isaac (brother of Samuel Merritt Stephenson) (R Wis.) June 18, 1829–March 15, 1918; House 1883–89; Senate May 17, 1907–15.

Stephenson, James (F Va.) March 20, 1764–Aug. 7, 1833; House 1803–05, 1809–11, Oct. 28, 1822–25.

Stephenson, Samuel Merritt (brother of Isaac Stephenson) (R Mich.) Dec. 23, 1831–July 31, 1907; House 1889–97.

Sterett, Samuel (– Md.) 1758–July 12, 1833; House 1791–93.

Sterigere, John Benton (J Pa.) July 31, 1793–Oct. 13, 1852; House 1827–31 (1827–29 no party).

Sterling, Ansel (brother of Micah Sterling) (– Conn.) Feb. 3, 1782–Nov. 6, 1853; House 1821–25.

Sterling, Bruce Foster (D Pa.) Sept. 28, 1870–April 26, 1945; House 1917–19.

Sterling, John Allen (brother of Thomas Sterling) (R Ill.) Feb. 1, 1857–Oct. 17, 1918; House 1903–13, 1915–Oct. 17, 1918.

Sterling, Micah (brother of Ansel Sterling) (– N.Y.) Nov. 5, 1784–April 11, 1844; House 1821–23.

Sterling, Thomas (brother of John Allen Sterling) (R S.D.) Feb. 21, 1851–Aug. 26, 1930; Senate 1913–25.

Stetson, Charles (D Maine) Nov. 2, 1801–March 27, 1863; House 1849–51.

Stetson, Lemuel (D N.Y.) March 13, 1804–May 17, 1868; House 1843–45.

Stevens, Aaron Fletcher (R N.H.) Aug. 9, 1819–May 10, 1887; House 1867–71.

Stevens, Bradford Newcomb (D Ill.) Jan. 3, 1813–Nov. 10, 1885; House 1871–73.

Stevens, Charles Abbot (brother of Moses Tyler Stevens, cousin of Isaac Ingalls Stevens) (R Mass.) Aug. 9, 1816–April 7, 1892; House Jan. 27–March 3, 1875.

Stevens, Frederick Clement (R Minn.) Jan. 1, 1861–July 1, 1923; House 1897–1915.

Stevens, Hestor Lockhart (D Mich.) Oct. 1, 1803–May 7, 1864; House 1853–55.

Stevens, Hiram Sanford (D Ariz.) March 20, 1832–March 22, 1893; House (Terr. Del.) 1875–79.

Stevens, Isaac Ingalls (cousin of Charles Abbot Stevens and Moses Tyler Stevens) (D Wash.) March 25, 1818–Sept. 1, 1862; House (Terr. Del.) 1857–61; Gov. (Wash. Terr.) 1853–57.

Stevens, James (– Conn.) July 4, 1768–April 4, 1835; House 1819–21.

Stevens, Moses Tyler (brother of Charles Abbot Stevens, cousin of Isaac Ingalls Stevens) (D Mass.) Oct. 10, 1825–March 25, 1907; House 1891–95.

Stevens, Raymond Bartlett (D N.H.) June 18, 1874–May 18, 1942; House 1913–15.

Stevens, Robert Smith (D N.Y.) March 27, 1824–Feb. 23, 1893; House 1883–85.

Stevens, Thaddeus (R Pa.) April 4, 1792–Aug. 11, 1868; House 1849–53 (Whig), 1859–Aug. 11, 1868.

Stevens, Theodore F. "Ted" (R Alaska) Nov. 18, 1923– ; Senate Dec. 24, 1968– ; chair Senate Select Ethics 1983–85; chair Senate Rules and Administration 1995; chair Senate Governmental Affairs 1996–97; chair Senate Appropriations 1997–Jan. 3, 2001, Jan. 20, 2001–June 6, 2001, 2003–05; chair Senate Commerce, Science, and Transportation 2005– .

Stevenson, Adlai Ewing (great–grandfather of Adlai Ewing Stevenson III, grandfather of Gov. Adlai Ewing Stevenson II of Ill.) (D Ill.) Oct. 23, 1835–June 14, 1914; House 1875–77, 1879–81; vice president 1893–97.

Stevenson, Adlai Ewing III (great–grandson of Adlai Ewing Stevenson, son of Adlai Ewing Stevenson II of Ill.) (D Ill.) Oct.

10, 1930– ; Senate Nov. 17, 1970–81; chair Senate Select Ethics 1977–81.

Stevenson, Andrew (father of John White Stevenson) (J Va.) Jan. 21, 1784–Jan. 25, 1857; House 1821–June 2, 1834 (1821–29 no party); Speaker Dec. 3, 1827–29, Dec. 7, 1829–31, Dec. 5, 1831–33, Dec. 2, 1833–June 2, 1834.

Stevenson, James S. (– Pa.) 1780–Oct. 16, 1831; House 1825–29.

Stevenson, Job Evans (R Ohio) Feb. 10, 1832–July 24, 1922; House 1869–73.

Stevenson, John White (son of Andrew Stevenson) (D Ky.) May 4, 1812–Aug. 10, 1886; House 1857–61; Senate 1871–77; Gov. Sept. 8, 1867–Feb. 13, 1871.

Stevenson, William Francis (D S.C.) Nov. 23, 1861–Feb. 12, 1942; House 1917–33.

Stevenson, William Henry (R Wis.) Sept. 23, 1891–March 19, 1978; House 1941–49.

Steward, Lewis (D Ill.) Nov. 21, 1824–Aug. 27, 1896; House 1891–93.

Stewart, Alexander (R Wis.) Sept. 12, 1829–May 24, 1912; House 1895–1901.

Stewart, Andrew (father of Andrew Stewart, below) (W Pa.) June 11, 1791–July 16, 1872; House 1821–29 (no party), 1831–35 (Anti–Mason), 1843–49.

Stewart, Andrew (son of Andrew Stewart, above) (R Pa.) April 6, 1836–Nov. 9, 1903; House 1891–Feb. 26, 1892.

Stewart, Arthur Thomas "Tom" (D Tenn.) Jan. 11, 1892–Oct. 10, 1972; Senate Jan. 16, 1939–49.

Stewart, Bennett McVey (D Ill.) Aug. 6, 1912–April 26, 1988; House 1979–81.

Stewart, Charles (D Texas) May 30, 1836–Sept. 21, 1895; House 1883–93.

Stewart, David (W Md.) Sept. 13, 1800–Jan. 5, 1858; Senate Dec. 6, 1849–Jan. 12, 1850.

Stewart, David Wallace (R Iowa) Jan. 22, 1887–Feb. 10, 1974; Senate Aug. 7, 1926–27.

Stewart, Donald Wilbur (D Ala.) Feb. 8, 1940– ; Senate Nov. 7, 1978–81.

Stewart, Jacob Henry (R Minn.) Jan. 15, 1829–Aug. 25, 1884; House 1877–79.

Stewart, James (F N.C.) Nov. 11, 1775–Dec. 29, 1821; House Jan. 5, 1818–19.

Stewart, James Augustus (D Md.) Nov. 24, 1808–April 3, 1879; House 1855–61.

Stewart, James Fleming (R N.J.) June 15, 1851–Jan. 21, 1904; House 1895–1903.

Stewart, John (R Pa.) ?–1820; House Jan. 15, 1801–05.

Stewart, John (D Conn.) Feb. 10, 1795–Sept. 16, 1860; House 1843–45.

Stewart, John David (D Ga.) Aug. 2, 1833–Jan. 28, 1894; House 1887–91.

Stewart, John George (R Del.) June 2, 1890–May 24, 1970; House 1935–37.

Stewart, John Knox (R N.Y.) Oct. 20, 1853–June 27, 1919; House 1899–1903.

Stewart, John Wolcott (R Vt.) Nov. 24, 1825–Oct. 29, 1915; House 1883–91; Senate March 24–Oct. 21, 1908; Gov. Oct. 6, 1870–Oct. 3, 1872.

Stewart, Paul (D Okla.) Feb. 27, 1892–Nov. 13, 1950; House 1943–47.

Stewart, Percy Hamilton (D N.J.) Jan. 10, 1867–June 30, 1951; House Dec. 1, 1931–33.

Stewart, Thomas Elliott (CR N.Y.) Sept. 22, 1824–Jan. 9, 1904; House 1867–69.

Stewart, William (R Pa.) Sept. 10, 1810–Oct. 17, 1876; House 1857–61.

Stewart, William Morris (Sil.R Nev.) Aug. 9, 1827–April 23, 1909; Senate Dec. 15, 1864–75 (Republican), 1887–1905 (1887–93 Republican).

Stigler, William Grady (D Okla.) July 7, 1891–Aug. 21, 1952; House March 28, 1944–Aug. 21, 1952.

Stiles, John Dodson (D Pa.) Jan. 15, 1822–Oct. 29, 1896; House June 3, 1862–65, 1869–71.

Stiles, William Henry (grandson of Joseph Clay) (D Ga.) Jan. 1, 1808–Dec. 20, 1865; House 1843–45.

Stillwell, Thomas Neel (R Ind.) Aug. 29, 1830–Jan. 14, 1874; House 1865–67.

Stiness, Walter Russell (R R.I.) March 13, 1854–March 17, 1924; House 1915–23.

Stinson, K. William (R Wash.) April 20, 1930– ; House 1963–65.

Stivers, Moses Dunning (R N.Y.) Dec. 30, 1828–Feb. 2, 1895; House 1889–91.

Stobbs, George Russell (R Mass.) Feb. 7, 1877–Dec. 23, 1966; House 1925–31.

Stockbridge, Francis Brown (R Mich.) April 9, 1826–April 30, 1894; Senate 1887–April 30, 1894.

Stockbridge, Henry Jr. (R Md.) Sept. 18, 1856–March 22, 1924; House 1889–91.

Stockdale, Thomas Ringland (D Miss.) March 28, 1828–Jan. 8, 1899; House 1887–95.

Stockman, David Alan (R Mich.) Nov. 10, 1946– ; House 1977–Jan. 27, 1981.

Stockman, Lowell (R Ore.) April 12, 1901–Aug. 9, 1962; House 1943–53.

Stockman, Steve (R Texas) Nov. 14, 1956– ; House 1995–97.

Stockslager, Strother Madison (D Ind.) May 7, 1842–June 1, 1930; House 1881–85.

Stockton, John Potter (son of Robert Field Stockton, grandson of Richard Stockton) (D N.J.) Aug. 2, 1826–Jan. 22, 1900; Senate March 15, 1865–March 27, 1866, 1869–75.

Stockton, Richard (father of Robert Field Stockton, grandfather of John Potter Stockton) (F N.J.) April 17, 1764–March 7, 1828; Senate Nov. 12, 1796–99; House 1813–15.

Stockton, Robert Field (son of Richard Stockton, father of John Potter Stockton) (D N.J.) Aug. 20, 1795–Oct. 7, 1866; Senate 1851–Jan. 10, 1853.

Stoddard, Ebenezer (– Conn.) May 6, 1785–Aug. 19, 1847; House 1821–25.

Stoddert, John Truman (J Md.) Oct. 1, 1790–July 19, 1870; House 1833–35.

Stokely, Samuel (W Ohio) Jan. 25, 1796–May 23, 1861; House 1841–43.

Stokes, Edward Lowber (R Pa.) Sept. 29, 1880–Nov. 8, 1964; House Nov. 3, 1931–35.

Stokes, James William (D S.C.) Dec. 12, 1853–July 6, 1901; House 1895–June 1, 1896, Nov. 3, 1896–July 6, 1901.

Stokes, Louis (D Ohio) Feb. 23, 1925– ; House 1969–99; chair House Standards of Official Conduct 1981–85, 1991–93; chair House Select Intelligence 1987–89.

Stokes, Montfort (– N.C.) March 12, 1762–Nov. 4, 1842; Senate Dec. 4, 1816–23; Gov. Dec. 18, 1830–Dec. 6, 1832.

Stokes, William Brickly (R Tenn.) Sept. 9, 1814–March 14, 1897; House 1859–61 (Opposition Party), July 24, 1866–71 (July 24, 1866–67 Unconditional Unionist).

Stoll, Philip Henry (D S.C.) Nov. 5, 1874–Oct. 29, 1958; House Oct. 7, 1919–23.

Stone, Alfred Parish (D Ohio) June 28, 1813–Aug. 2, 1865; House Oct. 8, 1844–45.

Stone, Charles Warren (R Pa.) June 29, 1843–Aug. 15, 1912; House Nov. 4, 1890–99.

Stone, Claudius Ulysses (D Ill.) May 11, 1879–Nov. 13, 1957; House 1911–17.

Stone, David (R N.C.) Feb. 17, 1770–Oct. 7, 1818; House 1799–1801 (no party); Senate 1801–Feb. 17, 1807, 1813–Dec. 24, 1814; Gov. Dec. 12, 1808–Dec. 5, 1810 (Democratic Republican).

Stone, Eben Francis (R Mass.) Aug. 3, 1822–Jan. 22, 1895; House 1881–87.

Stone, Frederick (grandson of Michael Jenifer Stone) (D Md.) Feb. 7, 1820–Oct. 17, 1899; House 1867–71.

Stone, James W. (D Ky.) 1813–Oct. 13, 1854; House 1843–45, 1851–53.

Stone, John Wesley (R Mich.) July 18, 1838–March 24, 1922; House 1877–81.

Stone, Joseph Champlin (R Iowa) July 30, 1829–Dec. 3, 1902; House 1877–79.

Stone, Michael Jenifer (grandfather of Frederick Stone) (– Md.) 1747–1812; House 1789–91.

Stone, Richard Bernard (D Fla.) Sept. 22, 1928– ; Senate Jan. 1, 1975–Dec. 31, 1980.

Stone, Ulysses Stevens (R Okla.) Dec. 17, 1878–Dec. 8, 1962; House 1929–31.

Stone, William (– Tenn.) Jan. 26, 1791–Feb. 18, 1853; House Sept. 14, 1837–39.

Stone, William Alexis (R Pa.) April 18, 1846–March 1, 1920; House 1891–Nov. 9, 1898; Gov. Jan. 17, 1899–Jan. 20, 1903.

Stone, William Henry (D Mo.) Nov. 7, 1828–July 9, 1901; House 1873–77.

Stone, William Joel (D Mo.) May 7, 1848–April 14, 1918; House 1885–91; Senate 1903–April 14, 1918; Gov. Jan. 9, 1893–Jan. 11, 1897.

Stone, William Johnson (D Ky.) June 26, 1841–March 12, 1923; House 1885–95.

Storer, Bellamy (father of Bellamy Storer, below) (W Ohio) March 26, 1796–June 1, 1875; House 1835–37.

Storer, Bellamy (son of Bellamy Storer, above, uncle of Nicholas Longworth) (R Ohio) Aug. 28, 1847–Nov. 12, 1922; House 1891–95.

Storer, Clement (R N.H.) Sept. 20, 1760–Nov. 21, 1830; House 1807–09; Senate June 27, 1817–19.

Storke, Thomas More (D Calif.) Nov. 23, 1876–Oct. 12, 1971; Senate Nov. 9, 1938–39.

Storm, Frederic (R N.Y.) July 2, 1844–June 9, 1935; House 1901–03.

Storm, John Brutzman (D Pa.) Sept. 19, 1838–Aug. 13, 1901; House 1871–75, 1883–87.

Storrs, Henry Randolph (brother of William Lucius Storrs) (F N.Y.) Sept. 3, 1787–July 29, 1837; House 1817–21, 1823–31.

Storrs, William Lucius (brother of Henry Randolph Storrs) (W Conn.) March 25, 1795–June 25, 1861; House 1829–33 (no party), 1839–June 1840.

Story, Joseph (R Mass.) Sept. 18, 1779–Sept. 10, 1845; House May 23, 1808–09; assoc. justice Feb. 3, 1812–Sept. 10, 1845.

Stoughton, William Lewis (R Mich.) March 20, 1827–June 6, 1888; House 1869–73.

Stout, Byron Gray (D Mich.) Jan. 12, 1829–June 19, 1896; House 1891–93.

Stout, Lansing (D Ore.) March 27, 1828–March 4, 1871; House 1859–61.

Stout, Tom (D Mont.) May 20, 1879–Dec. 26, 1965; House 1913–17.

Stover, John Hubler (R Mo.) April 24, 1833–Oct. 27, 1889; House Dec. 7, 1868–69.

Stow, Silas (R N.Y.) Dec. 21, 1773–Jan. 19, 1827; House 1811–13.

Stowell, William Henry Harrison (R Va.) July 26, 1840–April 27, 1922; House 1871–77.

Stower, John G. (J N.Y.) ?–?; House 1827–29.

Strader, Peter Wilson (D Ohio) Nov. 6, 1818–Feb. 25, 1881; House 1869–71.

Strait, Horace Burton (R Minn.) Jan. 26, 1835–Feb. 25, 1894; House 1873–79, 1881–87.

Strait, Thomas Jefferson (D S.C.) Dec. 25, 1846–April 18, 1924; House 1893–99.

Stranahan, James Samuel Thomas (W N.Y.) April 25, 1808–Sept. 3, 1898; House 1855–57.

Strang, Michael Lathrop (R Col.) June 17, 1929– ; House 1985–87.

Strange, Robert (D N.C.) Sept. 20, 1796–Feb. 19, 1854; Senate Dec. 5, 1836–Nov. 16, 1840.

Stratton, Charles Creighton (uncle of Benjamin Franklin Howey) (W N.J.) March 6, 1796–March 30, 1859; House 1837–39, 1841–43; Gov. Jan. 21, 1845–Jan. 18, 1848.

Stratton, John (F Va.) Aug. 19, 1769–May 10, 1804; House 1801–03.

Stratton, John Leake Newbold (R N.J.) Nov. 27, 1817–May 17, 1899; House 1859–63.

Stratton, Nathan Taylor (D N.J.) March 17, 1813–March 9, 1887; House 1851–55.

Stratton, Samuel Studdiford (D N.Y.) Sept. 27, 1916–Sept. 13, 1990; House 1959–89.

Stratton, William Grant (R Ill.) Feb. 26, 1914–March 2, 2001; House 1941–43, 1947–49; Gov. Jan. 12, 1953–Jan. 9, 1961.

Straub, Christian Markle (D Pa.) 1804–?; House 1853–55.

Straus, Isidor (D N.Y.) Feb. 6, 1845–April 15, 1912; House Jan. 30, 1894–95.

Strawbridge, James Dale (R Pa.) April 7, 1824–July 19, 1890; House 1873–75.

Street, Randall S. (– N.Y.) 1780–Nov. 21, 1841; House 1819–21.

Strickland, Randolph (R Mich.) Feb. 4, 1823–May 5, 1880; House 1869–71.

Strickland, Ted (D Ohio) Aug. 4, 1941– ; House 1993–95, 1997– .

Stringer, Lawrence Beaumont (D Ill.) Feb. 24, 1866–Dec. 5, 1942; House 1913–15.

Stringfellow, Douglas R. (R Utah) Sept. 24, 1922–Oct. 19, 1966; House 1953–55.

Strode, Jesse Burr (R Neb.) Feb. 18, 1845–Nov. 10, 1924; House 1895–99.

Strohm, John (W Pa.) Oct. 16, 1793–Sept. 12, 1884; House 1845–49.

Strong, Caleb (– Mass.) Jan. 9, 1745–Nov. 7, 1819; Senate 1789–June 1, 1796; Gov. May 30, 1800–May 29, 1807, June 5, 1812–May 30, 1816; Cont. Cong. (elected but did not attend) 1780.

Strong, James (– N.Y.) 1783–Aug. 8, 1847; House 1819–21, 1823–31.

Strong, James George (R Kan.) April 23, 1870–Jan. 11, 1938; House 1919–33.

Strong, Julius Levi (R Conn.) Nov. 8, 1828–Sept. 7, 1872; House 1869–Sept. 7, 1872.

Strong, Luther Martin (R Ohio) June 23, 1838–April 26, 1903; House 1893–97.

Strong, Nathan Leroy (R Pa.) Nov. 12, 1859–Dec. 14, 1939; House 1917–35.

Strong, Selah Brewster (D N.Y.) May 1, 1792–Nov. 29, 1872; House 1843–45.

Strong, Solomon (F Mass.) March 2, 1780–Sept. 16, 1850; House 1815–19.

Strong, Stephen (D N.Y.) Oct. 11, 1791–April 15, 1866; House 1845–47.

Strong, Sterling Price (D Texas) Aug. 17, 1862–March 28, 1936; House 1933–35.

Strong, Theron Rudd (cousin of William Strong of Pa.) (D N.Y.) Nov. 7, 1802–May 14, 1873; House 1839–41.

Strong, William (R Vt.) 1763–Jan. 28, 1840; House 1811–15, 1819–21.

Strong, William (cousin of Theron Rudd Strong) (D Pa.) May 6, 1808–Aug. 19, 1895; House 1847–51; assoc. justice March 14, 1870–Dec. 14, 1880.

Strother, George French (father of James French Strother of Va., great–grandfather of James French Strother of W.Va.) (R Va.) 1783–Nov. 28, 1840; House 1817–Feb. 10, 1820.

Strother, James French (son of George French Strother, grandfather of James French Strother, below) (W Va.) Sept. 4, 1811–Sept. 20, 1860; House 1851–53.

Strother, James French (grandson of James French Strother, above, great–grandson of George French Strother) (R W.Va.) June 29, 1868–April 10, 1930; House 1925–29.

Strouse, Myer (D Pa.) Dec. 16, 1825–Feb. 11, 1878; House 1863–67.

Strowd, William Franklin (P N.C.) Dec. 7, 1832–Dec. 12, 1911; House 1895–99.

Struble, Isaac S. (R Iowa) Nov. 3, 1843–Feb. 17, 1913; House 1883–91.

Strudwick, William Francis (F N.C.) ?–1812; House Nov. 28, 1796–97.

Stuart, Alexander Hugh Holmes (cousin of Archibald Stuart) (W Va.) April 2, 1807–Feb. 13, 1891; House 1841–43; secretary of the interior Sept. 12, 1850–March 7, 1853.

Stuart, Andrew (D Ohio) Aug. 3, 1823–April 30, 1872; House 1853–55.

Stuart, Archibald (cousin of Alexander Hugh Holmes Stuart) (D Va.) Dec. 2, 1795–Sept. 20, 1855; House 1837–39.

Stuart, Charles Edward (D Mich.) Nov. 25, 1810–May 19, 1887; House Dec. 6, 1847–49, 1851–53; Senate 1853–59; elected pres. pro tempore June 9, 1856.

Stuart, David (D Mich.) March 12, 1816–Sept. 12, 1868; House 1853–55.

Stuart, John Todd (D Ill.) Nov. 10, 1807–Nov. 23, 1885; House 1839–43 (Whig), 1863–65.

Stuart, Philip (F Md.) 1760–Aug. 14, 1830; House 1811–19.

Stubblefield, Frank Albert (D Ky.) April 5, 1907–Oct. 14, 1977; House 1959–Dec. 31, 1974.

Stubbs, Henry Elbert (D Calif.) March 4, 1881–Feb. 28, 1937; House 1933–Feb. 28, 1937.

Stuckey, Williamson Sylvester Jr. (D Ga.) May 25, 1935– ; House 1967–77.

Studds, Gerry Eastman (D Mass.) May 12, 1937– ; House 1973–97; chair House Merchant Marine and Fisheries 1992–95.

Studley, Elmer Ebenezer (D N.Y.) Sept. 24, 1869–Sept. 6, 1942; House 1933–35.

Stull, Howard William (R Pa.) April 11, 1876–April 22, 1949; House April 26, 1932–33.

Stump, Herman (D Md.) Aug. 8, 1837–Jan. 9, 1917; House 1889–93.

Stump, Robert Lee "Bob" (R Ariz.) April 4, 1927–June 20, 2003; House 1977–2003 (1977–83 Democrat); chair House Veterans' Affairs 1995–2001; chair House Armed Services, 2001–2003.

Stupak, Bart (D Mich.) Feb. 29, 1952– ; House 1993– .

Sturgeon, Daniel (D Pa.) Oct. 27, 1789–July 3, 1878; Senate Jan. 14, 1840–51.

Sturges, Jonathan (father of Lewis Burr Sturges) (– Conn.) Aug. 23, 1740–Oct. 4, 1819; House 1789–93; Cont. Cong. 1786.

Sturges, Lewis Burr (son of Jonathan Sturges) (F Conn.) March 15, 1763–March 30, 1844; House Sept. 16, 1805–17.

Sturgiss, George Cookman (R W.Va.) Aug. 16, 1842–Feb. 26, 1925; House 1907–11.

Sturtevant, John Cirby (R Pa.) Feb. 20, 1835–Dec. 20, 1912; House 1897–99.

Sullivan, Christopher Daniel (D N.Y.) July 14, 1870–Aug. 3, 1942; House 1917–41.

Sullivan, George (F N.H.) Aug. 29, 1771–April 14, 1838; House 1811–13.

Sullivan, John (R Okla.) Jan. 1, 1965– ; House Feb. 15, 2002– .

Sullivan, John Andrew (D Mass.) May 10, 1868–May 31, 1927; House 1903–07.

Sullivan, John Berchmans (husband of Leonor Kretzer Sullivan) (D Mo.) Oct. 10, 1897–Jan. 29, 1951; House 1941–43, 1945–47, 1949–Jan. 29, 1951.

Sullivan, Leonor Kretzer (wife of John Berchmans Sullivan) (D Mo.) Aug. 21, 1902–Sept. 1, 1988; House 1953–77; chair House Merchant Marine and Fisheries 1973–77.

Sullivan, Maurice Joseph (D Nev.) Dec. 7, 1884–Aug. 9, 1953; House 1943–45.

Sullivan, Patrick Joseph (R Wyo.) March 17, 1865–April 8, 1935; Senate Dec. 5, 1929–Nov. 20, 1930.

Sullivan, Patrick Joseph (R Pa.) Oct. 12, 1877–Dec. 31, 1946; House 1929–33.

Sullivan, Timothy Daniel (D N.Y.) July 23, 1862–Aug. 31, 1913; House 1903–July 27, 1906 (also elected to the term beginning 1913 but never took his seat).

Sullivan, William Van Amberg (D Miss.) Dec. 18, 1857–March 21, 1918; House 1897–May 31, 1898; Senate May 31, 1898–1901.

Sulloway, Cyrus Adams (R N.H.) June 8, 1839–March 11, 1917; House 1895–1913, 1915–March 11, 1917.

Sulzer, Charles August (brother of William Sulzer) (D Alaska) Feb. 24, 1879–April 28, 1919; House (Terr Del.) 1917–Jan. 7, 1919, March 4–April 28, 1919.

Sulzer, William (brother of Charles August Sulzer) (D N.Y.) March 18, 1863–Nov. 6, 1941; House 1895–Dec. 31, 1912; Gov. Jan. 1–Oct. 17, 1913.

Summers, George William (W Va.) March 4, 1804–Sept. 19, 1868; House 1841–45.

Summers, John William (R Wash.) April 29, 1870–Sept. 25, 1937; House 1919–33.

Sumner, Charles (R Mass.) Jan. 6, 1811–March 11, 1874; Senate April 24, 1851–March 11, 1874 (1851–57 Free-Soiler).

Sumner, Charles Allen (D Calif.) Aug. 2, 1835–Jan. 31, 1903; House 1883–85.

Sumner, Daniel Hadley (D Wis.) Sept. 15, 1837–May 29, 1903; House 1883–85.

Sumner, Jessie (R Ill.) July 17, 1898–Aug. 10, 1994; House 1939–47.

Sumners, Hatton William (D Texas) May 30, 1875–April 19, 1962; House 1913–47.

Sumter, Thomas (grandfather of Thomas De Lage Sumter) (R S.C.) Aug. 14, 1734–June 1, 1832; House 1789–93 (no party), 1797–Dec. 15, 1801; Senate Dec. 15, 1801–Dec. 16, 1810; Cont. Cong. (elected but did not attend) 1783.

Sumter, Thomas De Lage (grandson of Thomas Sumter) (D S.C.) Nov. 14, 1809–July 2, 1874; House 1839–43.

Sundquist, Donald Kenneth (R Tenn.) March 15, 1936– ; House 1983–95; Gov. Jan. 21, 1995–Jan. 18, 2003.

Sundstrom, Frank Leander (R N.J.) Jan. 5, 1901–May 23, 1980; House 1943–49.

Sunia, Fofo Iosefa Fiti (D Am. Samoa) March 13, 1937– ; House (Del.) 1981–89.

Sununu, John E. (son of Gov. John Henry Sununu of N.H.) (R N.H.) Sept. 10, 1964– ; House 1997–2003; Senate 2003– .

Sutherland, Daniel Alexander (R Alaska) April 17, 1869–March 24, 1955; House (Terr. Del.) 1921–31.

Sutherland, George (R Utah) March 25, 1862–July 18, 1942; House 1901–03; Senate 1905–17; assoc. justice Oct. 2, 1922–Jan. 17, 1938.

Sutherland, Howard (R W.Va.) Sept. 8, 1865–March 12, 1950; House 1913–17; Senate 1917–23.

Sutherland, Jabez Gridley (D Mich.) Oct. 6, 1825–Nov. 20, 1902; House 1871–73.

Sutherland, Joel Barlow (J Pa.) Feb. 26, 1792–Nov. 15, 1861; House 1827–37.

Sutherland, Josiah (D N.Y.) June 12, 1804–May 25, 1887; House 1851–53.

Sutherland, Roderick Dhu (P Neb.) April 27, 1862–Oct. 18, 1915; House 1897–1901.

Sutphin, William Halstead (D N.J.) Aug. 30, 1887–Oct. 14, 1972; House 1931–43.

Sutton, James Patrick "Pat" (D Tenn.) Oct. 31, 1915– ; House 1949–55.

Swan, Samuel (– N.J.) 1771–Aug. 24, 1844; House 1821–31.

Swank, Fletcher B. (D Okla.) April 24, 1875–March 16, 1950; House 1921–29, 1931–35.

Swann, Edward (D N.Y.) March 10, 1862–Sept. 19, 1945; House Nov. 4, 1902–03.

Swann, Thomas (D Md.) Feb. 3, 1809–July 24, 1883; House 1869–79; Gov. Jan. 10, 1866–Jan. 13, 1869 (Union Democrat).

Swanson, Charles Edward (R Iowa) Jan. 3, 1879–Aug. 22, 1970; House 1929–33.

Swanson, Claude Augustus (D Va.) March 31, 1862–July 7, 1939; House 1893–Jan. 30, 1906; Senate Aug. 1, 1910–33; Gov. Feb. 1, 1906–Feb. 1, 1910; secretary of the navy March 4, 1933–July 7, 1939.

Swanwick, John (R Pa.) 1740–Aug. 1, 1798; House 1795–Aug. 1, 1798.

Swart, Peter (R N.Y.) July 5, 1752–Nov. 3, 1829; House 1807–09.

Swartz, Joshua William (R Pa.) June 9, 1867–May 27, 1959; House 1925–27.

Swasey, John Philip (R Maine) Sept. 4, 1839–May 27, 1928; House Nov. 3, 1908–11.

Swearingen, Henry (D Ohio) about 1792–?; House Dec. 3, 1838–41.

Sweat, Lorenzo De Medici (D Maine) May 26, 1818–July 26, 1898; House 1863–65.

Sweeney, David McCann "Mac" (R Texas) Sept. 15, 1955– ; House 1985–89.

Sweeney, John E. (R N.Y.) Aug. 9, 1955– ; House 1999– .

Sweeney, Martin Leonard (father of Robert E. Sweeney) (D Ohio) April 15, 1885–May 1, 1960; House Nov. 3, 1931–43.

Sweeney, Robert E. (son of Martin Leonard Sweeney) (D Ohio) Nov. 4, 1924– ; House 1965–67.

Sweeney, William Northcut (D Ky.) May 5, 1832–April 21, 1895; House 1869–71.

Sweeny, George (D Ohio) Feb. 22, 1796–Oct. 10, 1877; House 1839–43.

Sweet, Burton Erwin (R Iowa) Dec. 10, 1867–Jan. 3, 1957; House 1915–23.

Sweet, Edwin Forrest (D Mich.) Nov. 21, 1847–April 2, 1935; House 1911–13.

Sweet, John Hyde (R Neb.) Sept. 1, 1880–April 4, 1964; House April 9, 1940–41.

Sweet, Thaddeus C. (R N.Y.) Nov. 16, 1872–May 1, 1928; House Nov. 6, 1923–May 1, 1928.

Sweet, Willis (R Idaho) Jan. 1, 1856–July 9, 1925; House Oct. 1, 1890–95.

Sweetser, Charles (D Ohio) Jan. 22, 1808–April 14, 1864; House 1849–53.

Sweney, Joseph Henry (R Iowa) Oct. 2, 1845–Nov. 11, 1918; House 1889–91.

Swett, Richard (son-in-law of Thomas Peter Lantos) (D N.H.) May 1, 1957– ; House 1991–95.

Swick, Jesse Howard (R Pa.) Aug. 6, 1879–Nov. 17, 1952; House 1927–35.

Swift, Allan Byron (D Wash.) Sept. 12, 1935– ; House 1979–95.

Swift, Benjamin (W Vt.) April 3, 1781–Nov. 11, 1847; House 1827–31 (no party); Senate 1833–39.

Swift, George Robinson (D Ala.) Dec. 19, 1887–Sept. 10, 1972; Senate June 15–Nov. 5, 1946.

Swift, Oscar William (R N.Y.) April 11, 1869–June 30, 1940; House 1915–19.

Swift, Zephaniah (F Conn.) Feb. 27, 1759–Sept. 27, 1823; House 1793–97 (1793–95 no party).

Swigert, John Leonard (R Colo.) Aug. 30, 1931–Dec. 27, 1982; elected to the House for the term beginning 1983 but did not serve.

Swinburne, John (R N.Y.) May 30, 1820–March 28, 1889; House 1885–87.

Swindall, Charles (R Okla.) Feb. 13, 1876–June 19, 1939; House Nov. 2, 1920–21.

Swindall, Patrick Lynn (R Ga.) Oct. 18, 1950– ; House 1985–89.

Swing, Philip David (R Calif.) Nov. 30, 1884–Aug. 8, 1963; House 1921–33.

Switzer, Robert Mauck (R Ohio) March 6, 1863–Oct. 28, 1952; House 1911–19.

Swoope, Jacob (F Va.) ?–1832; House 1809–11.

Swoope, William Irvin (nephew of John Patton) (R Pa.) Oct. 3, 1862–Oct. 9, 1930; House 1923–27.

Swope, Guy Jacob (D Pa.) Dec. 26, 1892–July 25, 1969; House 1937–39; Gov. (P.R.) Feb. 3–Aug. 6, 1941.

Swope, John Augustus (D Pa.) Dec. 25, 1827–Dec. 6, 1910; House Dec. 23, 1884–85, Nov. 3, 1885–87.

Swope, King (R Ky.) Aug. 10, 1893–April 23, 1961; House Aug. 2, 1919–21.

Swope, Samuel Franklin (AP Ky.) March 1, 1809–April 19, 1865; House 1855–57 (affiliated with the Republican Party in 1856).

Sykes, George (D N.J.) Sept. 20, 1802–Feb. 25, 1880; House 1843–45, Nov. 4, 1845–47.

Symes, George Gifford (R Colo.) April 28, 1840–Nov. 3, 1893; House 1885–89.

Symington, James Wadsworth (son of Stuart Symington, grandson of James Wolcott Wadsworth Jr., great-grandson of James Wolcott Wadsworth) (D Mo.) Sept. 28, 1927– ; House 1969–77.

Symington, William Stuart (father of James Wadsworth Symington, son-in-law of James Wolcott Wadsworth Jr.) (D Mo.) June 26, 1901–Dec. 14, 1988; Senate 1953–Dec. 27, 1976.

Symms, Steven Douglas (R Idaho) April 23, 1938– ; House 1973–81; Senate 1981–93.

Synar, Michael Lynn (D Okla.) Oct. 17, 1950–Jan. 9, 1996; House 1979–95.

Sypher, Jacob Hale (R La.) June 22, 1837–May 9, 1905; House July 18, 1868–69, Nov. 7, 1870–75.

Taber, John (R N.Y.) May 5, 1880–Nov. 22, 1965; House 1923–63; chair House Appropriations 1947–49, 1953–55.

Taber, Stephen (son of Thomas Taber II) (D N.Y.) March 7, 1821–April 23, 1886; House 1865–69.

Taber, Thomas II (father of Stephen Taber) (J N.Y.) May 19, 1785–March 21, 1862; House Nov. 5, 1828–29.

Tabor, Horace Austin Warner (R Colo.) Nov. 26, 1830–April 10, 1899; Senate Jan. 27–March 3, 1883.

Tackett, Boyd Anderson (D Ark.) May 9, 1911–Feb. 23, 1985; House 1949–53.

Taffe, John (R Neb.) Jan. 30, 1827–March 14, 1884; House 1867–73.

Taft, Charles Phelps (brother of Pres. William Howard Taft, uncle of Robert Alphonso Taft, great-uncle of Robert Taft Jr.) (R Ohio) Dec. 21, 1843–Dec. 31, 1929; House 1895–97.

Taft, Kingsley Arter (R Ohio) July 19, 1903–March 28, 1970; Senate Nov. 5, 1946–47.

Taft, Robert Alphonso (son of Pres. William Howard Taft, father of Robert Taft Jr., grandfather of Gov. Robert A. Taft II of Ohio, nephew of Charles Phelps Taft) (R Ohio) Sept. 8, 1889–July 31, 1953; Senate 1939–July 31, 1953; chair Senate Labor and Public Welfare 1947–49; Senate majority leader Jan. 3–July 31, 1953.

Taft, Robert Jr. (son of Robert Alphonso Taft, grandson of Pres. William Howard Taft, great-nephew of Charles Phelps Taft, father of Gov. Robert A. Taft II of Ohio) (R Ohio) Feb. 26, 1917–Dec. 7, 1993; House 1963–65, 1967–71; Senate 1971–Dec. 28, 1976.

Taggart, Joseph (D Kan.) June 15, 1867–Dec. 3, 1938; House Nov. 7, 1911–17.

Taggart, Samuel (F Mass.) March 24, 1754–April 25, 1825; House 1803–17.

Taggart, Thomas (D Ind.) Nov. 17, 1856–March 6, 1929; Senate March 20–Nov. 7, 1916; chair Dem. Nat. Comm. 1904–08.

Tague, Peter Francis (D Mass.) June 4, 1871–Sept. 17, 1941; House 1915–19, Oct. 23, 1919–25.

Tait, Charles (R Ga.) Feb. 1, 1768–Oct. 7, 1835; Senate Nov. 27, 1809–19.

Talbert, William Jasper (D S.C.) Oct. 6, 1846–Feb. 5, 1931; House 1893–1903.

Talbot, Isham (R Ky.) 1773–Sept. 25, 1837; Senate Jan. 3, 1815–19, Oct. 19, 1820–25.

Talbot, Joseph Edward (R Conn.) March 18, 1901–April 30, 1966; House Jan. 20, 1942–47.

Talbot, Silas (F N.Y.) Jan. 11, 1751–June 30, 1813; House 1793–95.

Talbott, Albert Gallatin (uncle of William Clayton Anderson) (D Ky.) April 4, 1808–Sept. 9, 1887; House 1855–59.

Talbott, Joshua Frederick Cockey (D Md.) July 29, 1843–Oct. 5, 1918; House 1879–85, 1893–95, 1903–Oct. 5, 1918.

Talcott, Burt Lacklen (R Calif.) Feb. 22, 1920– ; House 1963–77.

Talcott, Charles Andrew (D N.Y.) June 10, 1857–Feb. 27, 1920; House 1911–15.

Talent, James Michael (R Mo.) Oct. 18, 1956– ; House 1993–2000; chair House Small Business 1997–2001; Senate Nov. 25, 2002– .

Taliaferro, Benjamin (F Ga.) 1750–Sept. 3, 1821; House 1799–1802.

Taliaferro, James Piper (D Fla.) Sept. 30, 1847–Oct. 6, 1934; Senate April 20, 1899–1911.

Taliaferro, John (W Va.) 1768–Aug. 12, 1852; House 1801–03 (Republican), Nov. 29, 1811–13 (Republican), March 24, 1824–31 (Republican), 1835–43.

Talle, Henry Oscar (R Iowa) Jan. 12, 1892–March 14, 1969; House 1939–59.

Tallmadge, Benjamin (father of Frederick Augustus Tallmadge) (F Conn.) Feb. 25, 1754–March 7, 1835; House 1801–17.

Tallmadge, Frederick Augustus (son of Benjamin Tallmadge) (W N.Y.) Aug. 29, 1792–Sept. 17, 1869; House 1847–49.

Tallmadge, James Jr. (R N.Y.) Jan. 20, 1778–Sept. 29, 1853; House June 6, 1817–19.

Tallmadge, Nathaniel Pitcher (D N.Y.) Feb. 8, 1795–Nov. 2, 1864; Senate 1833–June 17, 1844 (1833–39 Jacksonian); Gov. (Wis. Terr.) 1844–45.

Tallman, Peleg (R Mass.) July 24, 1764–March 12, 1840; House 1811–13.

Tallon, Robert Mooneyhan Jr. "Robin" (D S.C.) Aug. 8, 1946– ; House 1983–93.

Talmadge, Herman Eugene (D Ga.) Aug. 9, 1913–March 21, 2002; Senate 1957–81; chair Senate Agriculture and Forestry 1971–77; chair Senate Agriculture, Nutrition, and Forestry 1977–81; Gov. Jan. 14–March 18, 1947, Nov. 17, 1948–Jan. 11, 1955.

Tancredo, Thomas G. (R Colo.) Dec. 20, 1945– ; House 1999– .

Tannehill, Adamson (R Pa.) May 23, 1750–Dec. 23, 1820; House 1813–15.

Tanner, Adolphus Hitchcock (R N.Y.) May 23, 1833–Jan. 14, 1882; House 1869–71.

Tanner, John S. (D Tenn.) Sept. 22, 1944– ; House 1989– .

Tappan, Benjamin (D Ohio) May 25, 1773–April 20, 1857; Senate 1839–45.

Tappan, Mason Weare (R N.H.) Oct. 20, 1817–Oct. 25, 1886; House 1855–61 (1855–57 American Party).

Tarbox, John Kemble (D Mass.) May 6, 1838–May 28, 1887; House 1875–77.

Tarr, Christian (R Pa.) May 25, 1765–Feb. 24, 1833; House 1817–21.

Tarsney, John Charles (D Mo.) Nov. 7, 1845–Sept. 4, 1920; House 1889–Feb. 17, 1896.

Tarsney, Timothy Edward (D Mich.) Feb. 4, 1849–June 8, 1909; House 1885–89.

Tarver, Malcolm Connor (D Ga.) Sept. 25, 1885–March 5, 1960; House 1927–47.

Tate, Farish Carter (D Ga.) Nov. 20, 1856–Feb. 7, 1922; House 1893–1905.

Tate, Magnus (F Va.) 1760–March 30, 1823; House 1815–17.

Tate, Randy (R Wash.) Nov. 23, 1965– ; House 1995–97.

Tatgenhorst, Charles Jr. (R Ohio) Aug. 19, 1883–Jan. 13, 1961; House Nov. 8, 1927–29.

Tatom, Absalom (R N.C.) 1742–Dec. 20, 1802; House 1795–June 1, 1796.

Tattnall, Edward Fenwick (– Ga.) 1788–Nov. 21, 1832; House 1821–27.

Tattnall, Josiah (R Ga.) 1762–June 6, 1803; Senate Feb. 20, 1796–99; Gov. Nov. 7, 1801–Nov. 4, 1802 (Democratic Republican).

Tauke, Thomas Joseph (R Iowa) Oct. 11, 1950– ; House 1979–91.

Taul, Micah (grandfather of Taul Bradford) (R Ky.) May 14, 1785–May 27, 1850; House 1815–17.

Taulbee, William Preston (D Ky.) Oct. 22, 1851–March 11, 1890; House 1885–89.

Tauriello, Anthony Francis (D N.Y.) Aug. 14, 1899–Dec. 21, 1983; House 1949–51.

Tauscher, Ellen O. (D Calif.) Nov. 15, 1951– ; House 1997– .

Tauzin, Wilbert Joseph "Billy" (R La.) June 14, 1943– ; House May 17, 1980–2005 (1980–Aug. 6, 1995 Democrat); chair House Energy and Commerce 2001–Feb. 16, 2004.

Tavenner, Clyde Howard (D Ill.) Feb. 4, 1882–Feb. 6, 1942; House 1913–17.

Tawney, James Albertus (R Minn.) Jan. 3, 1855–June 12, 1919; House 1893–1911.

Tayler, Robert Walker (R Ohio) Nov. 26, 1852–Nov. 25, 1910; House 1895–1903.

Taylor, Abner (R Ill.) 1829–April 13, 1903; House 1889–93.

Taylor, Alexander Wilson (R Pa.) March 22, 1815–May 7, 1893; House 1873–75.

Taylor, Alfred Alexander (son of Nathaniel Green Taylor, brother of Robert Love Taylor) (R Tenn.) Aug. 6, 1848–Nov. 25, 1931; House 1889–95; Gov. Jan. 15, 1921–Jan. 16, 1923.

Taylor, Arthur Herbert (D Ind.) Feb. 29, 1852–Feb. 20, 1922; House 1893–95.

Taylor, Benjamin Irving (D N.Y.) Dec. 21, 1877–Sept. 5, 1946; House 1913–15.

Taylor, Caleb Newbold (R Pa.) July 27, 1813–Nov. 15, 1887; House 1867–69, April 13, 1870–71.

Taylor, Charles Hart (R N.C.) Jan. 23, 1941– ; House 1991– .

Taylor, Chester William (son of Samuel Mitchell Taylor) (D Ark.) July 16, 1883–July 17, 1931; House Oct. 31, 1921–23.

Taylor, Dean Park (R N.Y.) Jan. 1, 1902–Oct. 16, 1977; House 1943–61.

Taylor, Edward Livingston Jr. (R Ohio) Aug. 10, 1869–March 10, 1938; House 1905–13.

Taylor, Edward Thomas (D Colo.) June 19, 1858–Sept. 3, 1941; House 1909–Sept. 3, 1941.

Taylor, Ezra Booth (R Ohio) July 9, 1823–Jan. 29, 1912; House Dec. 13, 1880–93.

Taylor, Gary Eugene "Gene" (D Miss.) Sept. 17, 1953– ; House Oct. 24, 1989– .

Taylor, Gene (R Mo.) Feb. 10, 1928–Oct. 27, 1998; House 1973–89.

Taylor, George (D N.Y.) Oct. 19, 1820–Jan. 18, 1894; House 1857–59.

Taylor, George Washington (D Ala.) Jan. 16, 1849–Dec. 21, 1932; House 1897–1915.

Taylor, Glen Hearst (D Idaho) April 12, 1904–April 28, 1984; Senate 1945–51.

Taylor, Herbert Worthington (R N.J.) Feb. 19, 1869–Oct. 15, 1931; House 1921–23, 1925–27.

Taylor, Isaac Hamilton (R Ohio) April 18, 1840–Dec. 18, 1936; House 1885–87.

Taylor, James Alfred (D W.Va.) Sept. 25, 1878–June 9, 1956; House 1923–27.

Taylor, James Willis (R Tenn.) Aug. 28, 1880–Nov. 14, 1939; House 1919–Nov. 14, 1939.

Taylor, John (R Va.) Dec. 19, 1753–Aug. 20, 1824; Senate Oct. 18, 1792–May 11, 1794 (no party), June 4–Dec. 7, 1803, Dec. 18, 1822–Aug. 21, 1824.

Taylor, John (R S.C.) May 4, 1770–April 16, 1832; House 1807–Dec. 30, 1810; Senate Dec. 31, 1810–Nov. 1816; Gov. Dec. 9, 1826–Dec. 10, 1828 (Democratic Republican).

Taylor, John (R S.C.) ?–?; House 1815–17.

Taylor, John Clarence (D S.C.) March 2, 1890–March 25, 1983; House 1933–39.

Taylor, John James (D N.Y.) April 27, 1808–July 1, 1892; House 1853–55.

Taylor, John Lampkin (W Ohio) March 7, 1805–Sept. 6, 1870; House 1847–55.

Taylor, John May (D Tenn.) May 18, 1838–Feb. 17, 1911; House 1883–87.

Taylor, John W. (R N.Y.) March 26, 1784–Sept. 18, 1854; House 1813–33; Speaker Nov. 15, 1820–21, Dec. 5, 1825–27.

Taylor, Jonathan (D Ohio) 1796–April 1848; House 1839–41.

Taylor, Joseph Danner (R Ohio) Nov. 7, 1830–Sept. 19, 1899; House Jan. 2, 1883–85, 1887–93.

Taylor, Miles (D La.) July 16, 1805–Sept. 23, 1873; House 1855–Feb. 5, 1861.

Taylor, Nathaniel Green (father of Alfred Alexander Taylor and Robert Love Taylor) (U Tenn.) Dec. 29, 1819–April 1, 1887; House March 30, 1854–55 (Whig), July 24, 1866–67.

Taylor, Nelson (D N.Y.) June 8, 1821–Jan. 16, 1894; House 1865–67.

Taylor, Robert (– Va.) April 29, 1763–July 3, 1845; House 1825–27.

Taylor, Robert Love (son of Nathaniel Green Taylor, brother of Alfred Alexander Taylor) (D Tenn.) July 31, 1850–March 31, 1912; House 1879–81; Senate 1907–March 31, 1912; Gov. Jan. 17, 1887–Jan. 19, 1891, Jan. 21, 1897–Jan. 16, 1899.

Taylor, Roy Arthur (D N.C.) Jan. 31, 1910–Feb. 28, 1995; House June 25, 1960–77.

Taylor, Samuel Mitchell (father of Chester William Taylor) (D Ark.) May 25, 1852–Sept. 13, 1921; House Jan. 15, 1913–Sept. 13, 1921.

Taylor, Vincent Albert (R Ohio) Dec. 6, 1845–Dec. 2, 1922; House 1891–93.

Taylor, Waller (R Ind.) before 1786–Aug. 26, 1826; Senate Dec. 11, 1816–25.

Taylor, William (D N.Y.) Oct. 12, 1791–Sept. 16, 1865; House 1833–39.

Taylor, William (D Va.) April 5, 1788–Jan. 17, 1846; House 1843–Jan. 17, 1846.

Taylor, William Penn (AJ Va.) ?–?; House 1833–35.

Taylor, Zachary (R Tenn.) May 9, 1849–Feb. 19, 1921; House 1885–87.

Tazewell, Henry (father of Littleton Waller Tazewell) (– Va.) Nov. 27, 1753–Jan. 24, 1799; Senate Dec. 29, 1794–Jan. 24, 1799; elected pres. pro tempore Feb. 20, 1795, Dec. 7, 1795.

Tazewell, Littleton Waller (son of Henry Tazewell) (– Va.) Dec. 17, 1774–May 6, 1860; House Nov. 26, 1800–01; Senate Dec. 7, 1824–July 16, 1832; elected pres. pro tempore July 9, 1832; Gov. March 31, 1834–April 30, 1836 (Democrat).

Teague, Charles McKevett (R Calif.) Sept. 18, 1909–Jan. 1, 1974; House 1955–Jan. 1, 1974.

Teague, Olin Earl (D Texas) April 6, 1910–Jan. 23, 1981; House Aug. 24, 1946–Dec. 31, 1978; chair House Veterans' Affairs 1955–73; chair House Science and Astronautics 1973–75; chair House Science and Technology 1975–79.

Teese, Frederick Halstead (D N.J.) Oct. 21, 1823–Jan. 7, 1894; House 1875–77.

Teigan, Henry George (FL Minn.) Aug. 7, 1881–March 12, 1941; House 1937–39.

Tejeda, Frank Mariano (D Texas) Oct. 2, 1945–Jan. 30, 1997; House 1993–Jan. 30, 1997.

Telfair, Thomas (R Ga.) March 2, 1780–Feb. 18, 1818; House 1813–17.

Teller, Henry Moore (D Colo.) May 23, 1830–Feb. 23, 1914; Senate Nov. 15, 1876–April 17, 1882 (Republican), 1885–1909 (1885–97 Republican, 1897–1903 Silver Republican); secretary of the interior April 18, 1882–March 3, 1885.

Teller, Isaac (nephew of Abraham Henry Schenck) (W N.Y.) Feb. 7, 1799–April 30, 1868; House Nov. 7, 1854–55.

Teller, Ludwig (D N.Y.) June 22, 1911–Oct. 4, 1965; House 1957–61.

Temple, Henry Wilson (R Pa.) March 31, 1864–Jan. 11, 1955; House 1913–15 (Progressive), Nov. 2, 1915–33.

Temple, William (D Del.) Feb. 28, 1814–May 28, 1863; House March 4–May 28, 1863.

Templeton, Thomas Weir (R Pa.) Nov. 8, 1867–Sept. 5, 1935; House 1917–19.

Tener, John Kinley (R Pa.) July 25, 1863–May 19, 1946; House 1909–Jan. 16, 1911; Gov. Jan. 17, 1911–Jan. 19, 1915.

Tenerowicz, Rudolph Gabriel (D Mich.) June 14, 1890–Aug. 31, 1963; House 1939–43.

Ten Eyck, Egbert (– N.Y.) April 18, 1779–April 11, 1844; House 1823–Dec. 15, 1825.

Ten Eyck, John Conover (R N.J.) March 12, 1814–Aug. 24, 1879; Senate 1859–65.

Ten Eyck, Peter Gansevoort (D N.Y.) Nov. 7, 1873–Sept. 2, 1944; House 1913–15, 1921–23.

Tenney, Samuel (F N.H.) Nov. 27, 1748–Feb. 6, 1816; House Dec. 8, 1800–07.

Tenzer, Herbert (D N.Y.) Nov. 1, 1905–March 24, 1993; House 1965–69.

Terrell, George Butler (D Texas) Dec. 5, 1862–April 18, 1947; House 1933–35.

Terrell, James C. (U Ga.) Nov. 7, 1806–Dec. 1, 1835; House March 4–July 8, 1835.

Terrell, Joseph Meriwether (D Ga.) June 6, 1861–Nov. 17, 1912; Senate Nov. 17, 1910–July 14, 1911; Gov. Oct. 25, 1902–June 29, 1907.

Terrell, William (R Ga.) 1778–July 4, 1855; House 1817–21.

Terry, David Dickson (son of William Leake Terry) (D Ark.) Jan. 31, 1881–Oct. 7, 1963; House Dec. 19, 1933–Jan. 2, 1943.

Terry, John Hart (R N.Y.) Nov. 14, 1924– ; House 1971–73.

Terry, Lee (R Neb.) Jan. 29, 1962– ; House 1999– .

Terry, Nathaniel (F Conn.) Jan. 30, 1768–June 14, 1844; House 1817–19.

Terry, William (D Va.) Aug. 14, 1824–Sept. 5, 1888; House 1871–73, 1875–77.

Terry, William Leake (father of David Dickson Terry) (D Ark.) Sept. 27, 1850–Nov. 4, 1917; House 1891–1901.

Test, John (– Ind.) Nov. 12, 1771–Oct. 9, 1849; House 1823–27, 1829–31.

Tewes, Donald Edgar (R Wis.) Aug. 4, 1916– ; House 1957–59.

Thacher, Thomas Chandler (D Mass.) July 20, 1858–April 11, 1945; House 1913–15.

Thatcher, George (F Mass.) April 12, 1754–April 6, 1824; House 1789–1801 (1789–95 no party); Cont. Cong. 1787–89.

Thatcher, Maurice Hudson (R Ky.) Aug. 15, 1870–Jan. 6, 1973; House 1923–33.

Thatcher, Samuel (F Mass.) July 1, 1776–July 18, 1872; House Dec. 6, 1802–05.

Thayer, Andrew Jackson (D Ore.) Nov. 27, 1818–April 28, 1873; House March 4–July 30, 1861.

Thayer, Eli (father of John Alden Thayer) (R Mass.) June 11, 1819–April 15, 1899; House 1857–61.

Thayer, Harry Irving (R Mass.) Sept. 10, 1869–March 10, 1926; House 1925–March 10, 1926.

Thayer, John Alden (son of Eli Thayer) (D Mass.) Dec. 22, 1857–July 31, 1917; House 1911–13.

Thayer, John Milton (uncle of Arthur Laban Bates) (R Neb.) Jan. 24, 1820–March 19, 1906; Senate March 1, 1867–71; Gov. 1875–79 (Wyo. Terr.), Jan. 6, 1887–Jan. 15, 1891, May 5, 1891–Feb. 8, 1892.

Thayer, John Randolph (D Mass.) March 9, 1845–Dec. 19, 1916; House 1899–1905.

Thayer, Martin Russell (R Pa.) Jan. 27, 1819–Oct. 14, 1906; House 1863–67.

Theaker, Thomas Clarke (R Ohio) Feb. 1, 1812–July 16, 1883; House 1859–61.

Thibodeaux, Bannon Goforth (– La.) Dec. 22, 1812–March 5, 1866; House 1845–49.

Thill, Lewis Dominic (R Wis.) Oct. 18, 1903–May 6, 1975; House 1939–43.

Thistlewood, Napoleon Bonaparte (R Ill.) March 30, 1837–Sept. 15, 1915; House Feb. 15, 1908–13.

Thom, William Richard (D Ohio) July 7, 1885–Aug. 28, 1960; House 1933–39, 1941–43, 1945–47.

Thomas, Albert (husband of Lera Millard Thomas) (D Texas) April 12, 1898–Feb. 15, 1966; House 1937–Feb. 15, 1966.

Thomas, Benjamin Franklin (U Mass.) Feb. 12, 1813–Sept. 27, 1878; House June 11, 1861–63.

Thomas, Charles Randolph (father of Charles Randolph Thomas, below) (R N.C.) Feb. 7, 1827–Feb. 18, 1891; House 1871–75.

Thomas, Charles Randolph (son of Charles Randolph Thomas, above) (D N.C.) Aug. 21, 1861–March 8, 1931; House 1899–1911.

Thomas, Charles Spalding (D Colo.) Dec. 6, 1849–June 24, 1934; Senate Jan. 15, 1913–21; Gov. Jan. 10, 1899–Jan. 8, 1901.

Thomas, Christopher Yancy (R Va.) March 24, 1818–Feb. 11, 1879; House March 5, 1874–75.

Thomas, Craig (R Wyo.) Feb. 17, 1933– ; House May 2, 1989–95; Senate 1995– .

Thomas, David (R N.Y.) June 11, 1762–Nov. 27, 1831; House 1801–May 1, 1808.

Thomas, Elbert Duncan (D Utah) June 17, 1883–Feb. 11, 1953; Senate 1933–51; chair Senate Labor and Public Welfare 1949–51.

Thomas, Francis (R Md.) Feb. 3, 1799–Jan. 22, 1876; House 1831–41 (1831–37 Jacksonian), 1861–69 (1861–63 Unionist, 1863–67 Unconditional Unionist); Gov. Jan. 3, 1841–Jan. 6, 1845 (Democrat).

Thomas, George Morgan (R Ky.) Nov. 23, 1828–Jan. 7, 1914; House 1887–89.

Thomas, Henry Franklin (R Mich.) Dec. 17, 1843–April 16, 1912; House 1893–97.

Thomas, Isaac (R Tenn.) Nov. 4, 1784–Feb. 2, 1859; House 1815–17.

Thomas, James Houston (D Tenn.) Sept. 22, 1808–Aug. 4, 1876; House 1847–51, 1859–61.

Thomas, Jesse Burgess (R Ill.) 1777–May 3, 1853; House (Terr. Del.) Oct. 22, 1808–09 (no party Ind.); Senate Dec. 3, 1818–29.

Thomas, John (R Idaho) Jan. 4, 1874–Nov. 10, 1945; Senate June 30, 1928–33, Jan. 27, 1940–Nov. 10, 1945.

Thomas, John Chew (F Md.) Oct. 15, 1764–May 10, 1836; House 1799–1801.

Thomas, John Lewis Jr. (UU Md.) May 20, 1835–Oct. 15, 1893; House Dec. 4, 1865–67.

Thomas, John Parnell (R N.J.) Jan. 16, 1895–Nov. 19, 1970; House 1937–Jan. 2, 1950; chair House Un–American Activities 1947–49.

Thomas, John Robert (R Ill.) Oct. 11, 1846–Jan. 19, 1914; House 1879–89.

Thomas, John William Elmer (D Okla.) Sept. 8, 1876–Sept. 19, 1965; House 1923–27; Senate 1927–51; chair Senate Agriculture and Forestry 1949–51.

Thomas, Lera Millard (widow of Albert Thomas) (D Texas) Aug. 3, 1900–July 23, 1993; House March 26, 1966–67.

Thomas, Lot (R Iowa) Oct. 17, 1843–March 17, 1905; House 1899–1905.

Thomas, Ormsby Brunson (R Wis.) Aug. 21, 1832–Oct. 24, 1904; House 1885–91.

Thomas, Philemon (– La.) Feb. 9, 1763–Nov. 18, 1847; House 1831–35.

Thomas, Phillip Francis (D Md.) Sept. 12, 1810–Oct. 2, 1890; House 1839–41, 1875–77; Gov. Jan. 3, 1848–Jan. 6, 1851; secretary of the Treasury Dec. 12, 1860–Jan. 14, 1861.

Thomas, Richard (F Pa.) Dec. 30, 1744–Jan. 19, 1832; House 1795–1801.

Thomas, Robert Lindsay (D Ga.) Nov. 20, 1943– ; House 1983–93.

Thomas, Robert Young Jr. (D Ky.) July 13, 1855–Sept. 3, 1925; House 1909–Sept. 3, 1925.

Thomas, William Aubrey (R Ohio) June 7, 1866–Sept. 8, 1951; House Nov. 8, 1904–11.

Thomas, William David (R N.Y.) March 22, 1880–May 17, 1936; House Jan. 30, 1934–May 17, 1936.

Thomas, William Marshall (R Calif.) Dec. 6, 1941– ; House 1979– ; chair House Oversight 1995–99; chair House Administration 1999–2001; chair House Ways and Means 2001– .

Thomason, Robert Ewing (D Texas) May 30, 1879–Nov. 8, 1973; House 1931–July 31, 1947.

Thomasson, William Poindexter (W Ky.) Oct. 8, 1797–Dec. 29, 1882; House 1843–47.

Thompson, Albert Clifton (R Ohio) Jan. 23, 1842–Jan. 26, 1910; House 1885–91.

Thompson, Benjamin (W Mass.) Aug. 5, 1798–Sept. 24, 1852; House 1845–47, 1851–Sept. 24, 1852.

Thompson, Bennie G. (D Miss.) Jan. 28, 1948– ; House April 20, 1993– .

Thompson, Charles James (R Ohio) Jan. 24, 1862–March 27, 1932; House 1919–31.

Thompson, Charles Perkins (D Mass.) July 30, 1827–Jan. 19, 1894; House 1875–77.

Thompson, Charles Winston (D Ala.) Dec. 30, 1860–March 20, 1904; House 1901–March 20, 1904.

Thompson, Chester Charles (D Ill.) Sept. 19, 1893–Jan. 30, 1971; House 1933–39.

Thompson, Clark Wallace (D Texas) Aug. 6, 1896–Dec. 16, 1981; House June 24, 1933–35, Aug. 23, 1947–67.

Thompson, Fountain Land (D N.D.) Nov. 18, 1854–Feb. 4, 1942; Senate Nov. 10, 1909–Jan. 31, 1910.

Thompson, Frank Jr. (D N.J.) July 26, 1918–July 22, 1989; House 1955–Dec. 29, 1980; chair House Administration 1976–80.

Thompson, Fred (R Tenn.) Aug. 19, 1942– ; Senate Dec. 9, 1994–2003; chair Senate Governmental Affairs 1997–Jan. 3, 2001, Jan. 20, 2001–June 6, 2001.

Thompson, George Western (D Va.) May 14, 1806–Feb. 24, 1888; House 1851–July 30, 1852.

Thompson, Hedge (– N.J.) Jan. 28, 1780–July 23, 1828; House 1827–July 23, 1828.

Thompson, Jacob (D Miss.) May 15, 1810–March 24, 1885; House 1839–51; secretary of the interior March 10, 1857–Jan. 8, 1861.

Thompson, James (D Pa.) Oct. 1, 1806–Jan. 28, 1874; House 1845–51.

Thompson, Joel (F N.Y.) Oct. 3, 1760–Feb. 8, 1843; House 1813–15.

Thompson, John (R N.Y.) March 20, 1749–1823; House 1799–1801, 1807–11.

Thompson, John (R N.Y.) July 4, 1809–June 1, 1890; House 1857–59.

Thompson, John Burton (AP Ky.) Dec. 14, 1810–Jan. 7, 1874; House Dec. 7, 1840–43 (Whig), 1847–51 (Whig); Senate 1853–59.

Thompson, John McCandless (brother of William George Thompson) (R Pa.) Jan. 4, 1829–Sept. 3, 1903; House Dec. 22, 1874–75, 1877–79.

Thompson, Joseph Bryan (D Okla.) April 29, 1871–Sept. 18, 1919; House 1913–Sept. 18, 1919.

Thompson, Michael (D Calif.) Jan. 24, 1951– ; House 1999– .

Thompson, Philip (– Ky.) Aug. 20, 1789–Nov. 25, 1836; House 1823–25.

Thompson, Philip Burton Jr. (D Ky.) Oct. 15, 1845–Dec. 15, 1909; House 1879–85.

Thompson, Philip Rootes (R Va.) March 26, 1766–July 27, 1837; House 1801–07.

Thompson, Richard Wigginton (W Ind.) June 9, 1809–Feb. 9, 1900; House 1841–43, 1847–49; secretary of the navy March 13, 1877–Dec. 20, 1880.

Thompson, Robert Augustine (father of Thomas Larkin Thompson) (D Va.) Feb. 14, 1805–Aug. 31, 1876; House 1847–49.

Thompson, Ruth (R Mich.) Sept. 15, 1887–April 5, 1970; House 1951–57.

Thompson, Standish Fletcher (R Ga.) Feb. 5, 1925– ; House 1967–73.

Thompson, Theo Ashton (D La.) March 31, 1916–July 1, 1965; House 1953–July 1, 1965.

Thompson, Thomas Larkin (son of Robert Augustine Thompson) (D Calif.) May 31, 1838–Feb. 1, 1898; House 1887–89.

Thompson, Thomas Weston (F N.H.) March 15, 1766–Oct. 1, 1821; House 1805–07; Senate June 24, 1814–17.

Thompson, Waddy Jr. (W S.C.) Jan. 8, 1798–Nov. 23, 1868; House Sept. 10, 1835–41 (Sept. 10, 1835–37 Anti–Jacksonian).

Thompson, Wiley (J Ga.) Sept. 23, 1781–Dec. 28, 1835; House 1821–33.

Thompson, William (D Iowa) Nov. 10, 1813–Oct. 6, 1897; House 1847–June 29, 1850.

Thompson, William George (brother of John McCandless Thompson) (R Iowa) Jan. 17, 1830–April 2, 1911; House Oct. 14, 1879–83.

Thompson, William Henry (D Neb.) Dec. 14, 1853–June 6, 1937; Senate May 24, 1933–Nov. 6, 1934.

Thompson, William Howard (D Kan.) Oct. 14, 1871–Feb. 9, 1928; Senate 1913–19.

Thomson, Alexander (– Pa.) Jan. 12, 1788–Aug. 2, 1848; House Dec. 6, 1824–May 1, 1826.

Thomson, Charles Marsh (Prog. Ill.) Feb. 13, 1877–Dec. 30, 1943; House 1913–15.

Thomson, Edwin Keith (R Wyo) Feb. 8, 1919–Dec. 9, 1960; House 1955–Dec. 9, 1960; did not seek nomination but was elected to the Senate for the term beginning 1961, did not serve.

Thomson, John (J Ohio) Nov. 20, 1780–Dec. 2, 1852; House 1825–27 (no party), 1829–37.

Thomson, John Renshaw (D N.J.) Sept. 25, 1800–Sept. 12, 1862; Senate 1853–Sept. 12, 1862.

Thomson, Mark (F N.J.) 1739–Dec. 14, 1803; House 1795–99.

Thomson, Vernon Wallace (R Wis.) Nov. 5, 1905–April 12, 1988; House 1961–Dec. 31, 1974; Gov. Jan. 7, 1957–Jan. 5, 1959.

Thone, Charles (R Neb.) Jan. 4, 1924– ; House 1971–79; Gov. Jan. 4, 1979–Jan. 6, 1983.

Thorington, James (W Iowa) May 7, 1816–June 13, 1887; House 1855–57.

Thorkelson, Jacob (R Mont.) Sept. 24, 1876–Nov. 20, 1945; House 1939–41.

Thornberry, William Homer (D Texas) Jan. 9, 1909–Dec. 12, 1995; House 1949–Dec. 20, 1963.

Thornberry, William M. "Mac" (R Texas) July 15, 1958– ; House 1995– .

Thornburgh, Jacob Montgomery (R Tenn.) July 3, 1837–Sept. 19, 1890; House 1873–79.

Thornton, Anthony (D Ill.) Nov. 9, 1814–Sept. 10, 1904; House 1865–67.

Thornton, John Randolph (D La.) Aug. 25, 1846–Dec. 28, 1917; Senate Dec. 7, 1910–15.

Thornton, Raymond Hoyt Jr. (R Ark.) July 16, 1928– ; House 1973–79 (Democrat), 1991–97.

Thorp, Robert Taylor (R Va.) March 12, 1850–Nov. 26, 1938; House May 2, 1896–97, March 23, 1898–99.

Thorpe, Roy Henry (R Neb.) Dec. 13, 1874–Sept. 19, 1951; House Nov. 7, 1922–23.

Throckmorton, James Webb (D Texas) Feb. 1, 1825–April 21, 1894; House 1875–79, 1883–87; Gov. Aug. 9, 1866–Aug. 8, 1867.

Throop, Enos Thompson (R N.Y.) Aug. 21, 1784–Nov. 1, 1874; House 1815–June 4, 1816; Gov. March 12, 1829–Jan. 1, 1833 (Jacksonian).

Thropp, Joseph Earlston (R Pa.) Oct. 4, 1847–July 27, 1927; House 1899–1901.

Thruston, Buckner (R Ky.) Feb. 9, 1763–Aug. 30, 1845; Senate 1805–Dec. 18, 1809.

Thune, John (R S.D.) Jan. 7, 1961– ; House 1997–2003; Senate 2005– .

Thurman, Allen Granberry (D Ohio) Nov. 13, 1813–Dec. 12, 1895; House 1845–47; Senate 1869–81; elected pres. pro tempore April 15, 1879, April 7, 1880, May 6, 1880.

Thurman, John Richardson (W N.Y.) Oct. 6, 1814–July 24, 1854; House 1849–51.

Thurman, Karen Loveland (D Fla.) Jan. 12, 1951– ; House 1993–2003.

Thurmond, James Strom (R S.C.) Dec. 5, 1902–June 26, 2003; Senate Dec. 24, 1954–April 4, 1956 (Democrat), Nov. 7, 1956–2003 (Nov. 7, 1956–Sept. 16, 1964 Democrat); elected pres. pro tempore 1981–87, 1995–June 6, 2001; Gov. Jan. 21, 1947–Jan. 16, 1951 (Democrat); chair Senate Judiciary 1981–87; chair Senate Armed Services 1995–99.

Thurston, Benjamin Babcock (AP R.I.) June 29, 1804–May 17, 1886; House 1847–49 (Democrat), 1851–57 (1851–55 Democrat).

Thurston, John Mellen (R Neb.) Aug. 21, 1847–Aug. 9, 1916; Senate 1895–1901.

Thurston, Lloyd (R Iowa) March 27, 1880–May 7, 1970; House 1925–39.

Thurston, Samuel Royal (D Ore.) April 15, 1816–April 9, 1851; House (Terr. Del.) 1849–51.

Thye, Edward John (R Minn.) April 26, 1896–Aug. 28, 1969; Senate 1947–59; chair Senate Select Small Business 1953–55; Gov. April 27, 1943–Jan. 8, 1947.

Tiahrt, Todd (R Kan.) June 15, 1951– ; House 1995– .

Tibbatts, John Wooleston (D Ky.) June 12, 1802–July 5, 1852; House 1843–47.

Tibbits, George (F N.Y.) Jan. 14, 1763–July 19, 1849; House 1803–05.

Tibbott, Harve (R Pa.) May 27, 1885–Dec. 31, 1969; House 1939–49.

Tiberi, Patrick J. "Pat" (R Ohio) Oct. 21, 1962– ; House 2001– .

Tichenor, Isaac (F Vt.) Feb. 8, 1754–Dec. 11, 1838; Senate Oct. 18, 1796–Oct. 1797, 1815–21; Gov. Oct. 1797–Oct. 9, 1807, Oct. 17, 1808–Oct. 14, 1809.

Tiernan, Robert Owens (D R.I.) Feb. 24, 1929– ; House March 28, 1967–75.

Tierney, John F. (D Mass.) Sept. 18, 1951– ; House 1997– .

Tierney, William Laurence (D Conn.) Aug. 6, 1876–April 13, 1958; House 1931–33.

Tiffin, Edward (R Ohio) June 19, 1766–Aug. 9, 1829; Senate 1807–09; Gov. March 3, 1803–March 4, 1807 (Democratic Republican).

Tift, Nelson (D Ga.) July 23, 1810–Nov. 21, 1891; House July 25, 1868–69.

Tilden, Daniel Rose (W Ohio) Nov. 5, 1804–March 4, 1890; House 1843–47.

Tillinghast, Joseph Leonard (cousin of Thomas Tillinghast) (W R.I.) 1791–Dec. 30, 1844; House 1837–43.

Tillinghast, Thomas (cousin of Joseph Leonard Tillinghast) (R R.I.) Aug. 21, 1742–Aug. 26, 1821; House Nov. 13, 1797–99 (Federalist), 1801–03.

Tillman, Benjamin Ryan (brother of George Dionysius Tillman) (D S.C.) Aug. 11, 1847–July 3, 1918; Senate 1895–July 3, 1918; Gov. Dec. 4, 1890–Dec. 4, 1894.

Tillman, George Dionysius (brother of Benjamin Ryan Tillman) (D S.C.) Aug. 21, 1826–Feb. 2, 1902; House 1879–June 19, 1882, 1883–93.

Tillman, John Newton (D Ark.) Dec. 13, 1859–March 9, 1929; House 1915–29.

Tillman, Lewis (nephew of Barclay Martin) (R Tenn.) Aug. 18, 1816–May 3, 1886; House 1869–71.

Tillotson, Thomas (– N.Y.) 1750–May 5, 1832; elected to the House for the term beginning 1801 but did not qualify or take his seat, resigned Aug. 10, 1801.

Tilson, John Quillin (R Conn.) April 5, 1866–Aug. 14, 1958; House 1909–13, 1915–Dec. 3, 1932; House majority leader 1925–31.

Timberlake, Charles Bateman (R Colo.) Sept. 25, 1854–May 31, 1941; House 1915–33.

Tincher, Jasper Napoleon (R Kan.) Nov. 2, 1878–Nov. 6, 1951; House 1919–27.

Tinkham, George Holden (R Mass.) Oct. 29, 1870–Aug. 28, 1956; House 1915–43.

Tipton, John (D Ind.) Aug. 14, 1786–April 5, 1839; Senate Jan. 3, 1832–39.

Tipton, Thomas Foster (R Ill.) Aug. 29, 1833–Feb. 7, 1904; House 1877–79.

Tipton, Thomas Weston (R Neb.) Aug. 5, 1817–Nov. 26, 1899; Senate March 1, 1867–75.

Tirrell, Charles Quincy (R Mass.) Dec. 10, 1844–July 31, 1910; House 1901–July 31, 1910.

Titus, Obadiah (D N.Y.) Jan. 20, 1789–Sept. 2, 1854; House 1837–39.

Tobey, Charles William (R N.H.) July 22, 1880–July 24, 1953; House 1933–39; Senate 1939–July 24, 1953; chair Senate Banking and Currency 1947–49; chair Senate Interstate and Foreign Commerce 1953; Gov. Jan. 3, 1929–Jan. 1, 1931.

Tod, John (D Pa.) 1779–March 27, 1830; House 1821–24.

Todd, Albert May (D Mich.) June 3, 1850–Oct. 6, 1931; House 1897–99.

Todd, John Blair Smith (D Dakota) April 4, 1814–Jan. 5, 1872; House (Terr. Del.) Dec. 9, 1861–63, June 17, 1864–65.

Todd, Lemuel (R Pa.) July 29, 1817–May 12, 1891; House 1855–57, 1873–75.

Todd, Paul Harold Jr. (D Mich.) Sept. 22, 1921– ; House 1965–67.

Tolan, John Harvey (D Calif.) Jan. 15, 1877–June 30, 1947; House 1935–47.

Toland, George Washington (W Pa.) Feb. 8, 1796–Jan. 30, 1869; House 1837–43.

Toll, Herman (D Pa.) March 15, 1907–July 26, 1967; House 1959–67.

Tollefson, Thor Carl (R Wash.) May 2, 1901–Dec. 30, 1982; House 1947–65.

Tolley, Harold Sumner (R N.Y.) Jan. 16, 1894–May 20, 1956; House 1925–27.

Tomlinson, Gideon (– Conn.) Dec. 31, 1780–Oct. 8, 1854; House 1819–27; Senate 1831–37; Gov. May 2, 1827–March 2, 1831 (Democratic Republican).

Tomlinson, Thomas Ash (W N.Y.) March 1802–June 18, 1872; House 1841–43.

Tompkins, Arthur Sidney (R N.Y.) Aug. 26, 1865–Jan. 20, 1938; House 1899–1903.

Tompkins, Caleb (brother of Daniel D. Tompkins) (R N.Y.) Dec. 22, 1759–Jan. 1, 1846; House 1817–21.

Tompkins, Christopher (AJ Ky.) March 24, 1780–Aug. 9, 1858; House 1831–35.

Tompkins, Cydnor Bailey (father of Emmett Tompkins) (R Ohio) Nov. 8, 1810–July 23, 1862; House 1857–61.

Tompkins, Daniel D. (brother of Caleb Tompkins) (– N.Y.) June 21, 1774–June 11, 1825; elected to the House for the term beginning 1805 but resigned before taking seat; Gov. July 1, 1807–Feb. 24, 1817; vice president 1817–25.

Tompkins, Emmett (son of Cydnor Bailey Tompkins) (R Ohio) Sept. 1, 1853–Dec. 18, 1917; House 1901–03.

Tompkins, Patrick Watson (W Miss.) 1804–May 8, 1953; House 1847–49.

Tongue, Thomas H. (R Ore.) June 23, 1844–Jan. 11, 1903; House 1897–Jan. 11, 1903.

Tonry, Richard Alvin (D La.) June 25, 1935– ; House Jan. 3–May 4, 1977.

Tonry, Richard Joseph (D N.Y.) Sept. 30, 1893–Jan. 17, 1971; House 1935–37.

Toole, Joseph Kemp (D Mont.) May 12, 1851–March 11, 1929; House (Terr. Del.) 1885–89; Gov. Nov. 8, 1889–Jan. 2, 1893, Jan. 7, 1901–April 1, 1908.

Toombs, Robert (D Ga.) July 2, 1810–Dec. 15, 1885; House 1845–53 (Whig); Senate 1853–Feb. 4, 1861.

Toomey, Patrick J. (R Pa.) Nov. 17, 1961– ; House 1999–2005.

Torkildsen, Peter Gerard (R Mass.) Jan. 28, 1958– ; House 1993–97.

Torrens, James H. (D N.Y.) Sept. 12, 1874–April 5, 1952; House Feb. 29, 1944–47.

Torres, Estaban Edward (D Calif.) Jan. 27, 1930– ; House 1983–99.

Torricelli, Robert Guy (D N.J.) Aug. 26, 1951– ; House 1983–97; Senate 1997–2003.

Toucey, Isaac (D Conn.) Nov. 15, 1792–July 30, 1869; House 1835–39; Senate May 12, 1852–57; Gov. May 6, 1846–May 5, 1847; attorney general June 21, 1848–March 3, 1849; secretary of the navy March 7, 1857–March 6, 1861.

Tou Velle, William Ellsworth (D Ohio) Nov. 23, 1862–Aug. 14, 1951; House 1907–11.

Towe, Harry Lancaster (R N.J.) Nov. 3, 1898–Feb. 8, 1991; House 1943–Sept. 7, 1951.

Towell, David Gilmer (R Nev.) June 9, 1937–June 11, 2003; House 1973–75.

Tower, John Goodwin (R Texas) Sept. 29, 1925–April 5, 1991; Senate June 15, 1961–85; chair Senate Armed Services 1981–85.

Towey, Frank William Jr. (D N.J.) Nov. 5, 1895–Sept. 4, 1979; House 1937–39.

Towne, Charles Arnette (D N.Y.) Nov. 21, 1858–Oct. 22, 1928; House 1895–97 (Republican Minn.), 1905–07; Senate Dec. 5, 1900–Jan. 28, 1901 (Minn.).

Towner, Horace Mann (R Iowa) Oct. 23, 1855–Nov. 23, 1937; House 1911–April 1, 1923; Gov. (P.R.) 1923–29.

Towns, Edolphus "Ed" (D N.Y.) July 21, 1934– ; House 1983– .

Towns, George Washington Bonaparte (D Ga.) May 4, 1801–July 15, 1854; House 1835–Sept. 1, 1836 (Jacksonian), 1837–39, Jan. 5, 1846–47; Gov. Nov. 3, 1847–Nov. 5, 1851.

Townsend, Amos (R Ohio) 1821–March 17, 1895; House 1877–83.

Townsend, Charles Champlain (R Pa.) Nov. 24, 1841–July 10, 1910; House 1889–91.

Townsend, Charles Elroy (R Mich.) Aug. 15, 1856–Aug. 3, 1924; House 1903–11; Senate 1911–23.

Townsend, Dwight (D N.Y.) Sept. 26, 1826–Oct. 29, 1899; House Dec. 5, 1864–65, 1871–73.

Townsend, Edward Waterman (D N.J.) Feb. 10, 1855–March 15, 1942; House 1911–15.

Townsend, George (R N.Y.) 1769–Aug. 17, 1844; House 1815–19.

Townsend, Hosea (R Colo.) June 16, 1840–March 4, 1909; House 1889–93.

Townsend, John Gillis Jr. (R Del.) May 31, 1871–April 10, 1964; Senate 1929–41; Gov. Jan. 17, 1917–Jan. 18, 1921.

Townsend, Martin Ingham (R N.Y.) Feb. 6, 1810–March 8, 1903; House 1875–79.

Townsend, Washington (R Pa.) Jan. 20, 1813–March 18, 1894; House 1869–77.

Townshend, Norton Strange (D Ohio) Dec. 25, 1815–July 13, 1895; House 1851–53.

Townshend, Richard Wellington (D Ill.) April 30, 1840–March 9, 1889; House 1877–March 9, 1889.

Tracewell, Robert John (R Ind.) May 7, 1852–July 28, 1922; House 1895–97.

Tracey, Charles (D N.Y.) May 27, 1847–March 24, 1905; House Nov. 8, 1887–95.

Tracey, John Plank (R Mo.) Sept. 18, 1836–July 24, 1910; House 1895–97.

Tracy, Albert Haller (brother of Phineas Lyman Tracy) (– N.Y.) June 17, 1793–Sept. 19, 1859; House 1819–25.

Tracy, Andrew (W Vt.) Dec. 15, 1797–Oct. 28, 1868; House 1853–55.

Tracy, Henry Wells (IR Pa.) Sept. 24, 1807–April 11, 1886; House 1863–65.

Tracy, Phineas Lyman (brother of Albert Haller Tracy) (AMas. N.Y.) Dec. 25, 1786–Dec. 22, 1876; House Nov. 5, 1827–33 (Nov. 5, 1827–29 no party).

Tracy, Uri (R N.Y.) Feb. 8, 1764–July 21, 1838; House 1805–07, 1809–13.

Tracy, Uriah (F Conn.) Feb. 2, 1755–July 19, 1807; House 1793–Oct. 13, 1796 (no party); Senate Oct. 13, 1796–July 19, 1807; elected pres. pro tempore May 14, 1800.

Traeger, William Isham (R Calif.) Feb. 26, 1880–Jan. 20, 1935; House 1933–35.

Traficant, James Anthony Jr. (D Ohio) May 8, 1941– ; House 1985–July 24, 2002.

Trafton, Mark (AP Mass.) Aug. 1, 1810–March 8, 1901; House 1855–57.

Train, Charles Russell (R Mass.) Oct. 18, 1817–July 28, 1885; House 1859–63.

Trammell, Park (D Fla.) April 9, 1876–May 8, 1936; Senate 1917–May 8, 1936; Gov. Jan. 7, 1913–Jan. 2, 1917.

Transue, Andrew Jackson (D Mich.) Jan. 12, 1903–June 24, 1995; House 1937–39.

Traxler, Jerome Bob (D Mich.) July 21, 1931– ; House April 16, 1974–93.

Traynor, Philip Andrew (D Del.) May 31, 1874–Dec. 5, 1962; House 1941–43, 1945–47.

Treadway, Allen Towner (R Mass.) Sept. 16, 1867–Feb. 16, 1947; House 1913–45.

Treadway, William Marshall (D Va.) Aug. 24, 1807–May 1, 1891; House 1845–47.

Tredwell, Thomas (grandfather of Thomas Treadwell Davis) (– N.Y.) Feb. 6, 1743–Dec. 30, 1831; House May 1791–95.

Treen, David Conner (R La.) July 16, 1928– ; House 1973–March 10, 1980; Gov. March 10, 1980–March 12, 1984.

Treloar, William Mitchellson (R Mo.) Sept. 21, 1850–July 3, 1935; House 1895–97.

Tremain, Lyman (R N.Y.) June 14, 1819–Nov. 30, 1878; House 1873–75.

Trezvant, James (J Va.) ?–Sept. 2, 1841; House 1825–31.

Tribble, Samuel Joelah (D Ga.) Nov. 15, 1869–Dec. 8, 1916; House 1911–Dec. 8, 1916.

Trible, Paul Seward Jr. (R Va.) Dec. 29, 1946– ; House 1977–83; Senate 1983–89.

Trigg, Abram (brother of John Johns Trigg) (R Va.) 1750–?; House 1797–1809.

Trigg, Connally Findlay (D Va.) Sept. 18, 1847–April 23, 1907; House 1885–87.

Trigg, John Johns (brother of Abram Trigg) (R Va.) 1748–May 17, 1804; House 1797–May 17, 1804.

Trimble, Carey Allen (R Ohio) Sept. 13, 1813–May 4, 1887; House 1859–63.

Trimble, David (R Ky.) June 1782–Oct. 20, 1842; House 1817–27.

Trimble, James William (D Ark.) Feb. 3, 1894–March 10, 1972; House 1945–67.

Trimble, John (R Tenn.) Feb. 7, 1812–Feb. 23, 1884; House 1867–69.

Trimble, Lawrence Strother (D Ky.) Aug. 26, 1825–Aug. 9, 1904; House 1865–71.

Trimble, South (D Ky.) April 13, 1864–Nov. 23, 1946; House 1901–07.

Trimble, William Allen (– Ohio) April 4, 1786–Dec. 13, 1821; Senate 1819–Dec. 13, 1821.

Triplett, Philip (W Ky.) Dec. 24, 1799–March 30, 1852; House 1839–43.

Trippe, Robert Pleasant (AP Ga.) Dec. 21, 1819–July 22, 1900; House 1855–59.

Trotter, James Fisher (D Miss.) Nov. 5, 1802–March 9, 1866; Senate Jan. 22–July 10, 1838.

Trotti, Samuel Wilds (D S.C.) July 18, 1810–June 24, 1856; House Dec. 17, 1842–43.

Troup, George Michael (R Ga.) Sept. 8, 1780–April 26, 1856; House 1807–15; Senate Nov. 13, 1816–Sept. 23, 1818, 1829–Nov. 8, 1833; Gov. Nov. 7, 1823–Nov. 7, 1827 (Democratic Republican).

Trout, Michael Carver (D Pa.) Sept. 30, 1810–June 25, 1873; House 1853–55.

Troutman, William Irvin (R Pa.) Jan. 13, 1905–Jan. 27, 1971; House 1943–Jan. 2, 1945.

Trowbridge, Rowland Ebenezer (R Mich.) June 18, 1821–April 20, 1881; House 1861–63, 1865–69.

Truax, Charles Vilas (D Ohio) Feb. 1, 1887–Aug. 9, 1935; House 1933–Aug. 9, 1935.

Truman, Harry S. (D Mo.) May 8, 1884–Dec. 26, 1972; Senate 1935–Jan. 17, 1945; vice president Jan. 20–April 12, 1945; president April 12, 1945–53.

Trumbo, Andrew (W Ky.) Sept. 15, 1797–Aug. 21, 1871; House 1845–47.

Trumbull, Jonathan Jr. (– Conn.) March 26, 1740–Aug. 7, 1809; House 1789–95; Speaker Oct. 24, 1791–93; Senate 1795–June 10, 1796; Gov. Dec. 1, 1797–Aug. 7, 1809.

Trumbull, Joseph (W Conn.) Dec. 7, 1782–Aug. 4, 1861; House Dec. 1, 1834–35 (no party), 1839–43; Gov. May 2, 1849–May 4, 1850.

Trumbull, Lyman (– Ill.) Oct. 12, 1813–June 25, 1896; Senate 1855–73.

Tsongas, Paul Efthemios (D Mass.) Feb. 14, 1941–Jan. 18, 1997; House 1975–79; Senate 1979–85.

Tuck, Amos (W N.H.) Aug. 2, 1810–Dec. 11, 1879; House 1847–53 (1847–49 Independent, 1849–51 Free–Soiler).

Tuck, William Munford (D Va.) Sept. 28, 1896–June 9, 1983; House April 14, 1953–69; Gov. June 16, 1946–Jan. 18, 1950.

Tucker, Ebenezer (– N.J.) Nov. 15, 1758–Sept. 5, 1845; House 1825–29.

Tucker, George (cousin of Henry St. George Tucker) (– Va.) Aug. 20, 1775–April 10, 1861; House 1819–25.

Tucker, Henry St. George (father of John Randolph Tucker, grandfather of Henry St. George Tucker, below, cousin of George Tucker, nephew of Thomas Tudor Tucker) (R Va.) Dec. 29, 1780–Aug. 28, 1848; House 1815–19.

Tucker, Henry St. George (son of John Randolph Tucker, grandson of Henry St. George Tucker, above) (D Va.) April 5, 1853–July 23, 1932; House 1889–97, March 21, 1922–July 23, 1932.

Tucker, James Guy Jr. (D Ark.) June 13, 1943– ; House 1977–79; Gov. Dec. 12, 1992–July 15, 1996.

Tucker, John Randolph (son of Henry St. George Tucker born in 1780, father of Henry St. George Tucker born in 1853) (D Va.) Dec. 24, 1823–Feb. 13, 1897; House 1875–87.

Tucker, Starling (J S.C.) 1770–Jan. 3, 1834; House 1817–31 (1817–27 Republican).

Tucker, Thomas Tudor (uncle of Henry St. George Tucker born in 1780) (– S.C.) June 25, 1745–May 2, 1828; House 1789–93; Cont. Cong. 1787–88.

Tucker, Tilghman Mayfield (D Miss.) Feb. 5, 1802–April 3, 1859; House 1843–45; Gov. Jan. 10, 1842–Jan. 10, 1844.

Tucker, Walter Rayford III (D Calif.) May 28, 1957– ; House 1993–Dec. 15, 1995.

Tufts, John Quincy (R Iowa) July 12, 1840–Aug. 10, 1908; House 1875–77.

Tully, Pleasant Britton (D Calif.) March 21, 1829–March 24, 1897; House 1883–85.

Tumulty, Thomas James (D N.J.) March 2, 1913–Nov. 23, 1981; House 1955–57.

Tunnell, James Miller (D Del.) Aug. 2, 1879–Nov. 14, 1957; Senate 1941–47.

Tunney, John Varick (D Calif.) June 26, 1934– ; House 1965–Jan. 2, 1971; Senate Jan. 2, 1971–Jan. 1, 1977.

Tupper, Stanley Roger (R Maine) Jan. 25, 1921– ; House 1961–67.

Turley, Thomas Battle (D Tenn.) April 5, 1845–July 1, 1910; Senate July 20, 1897–1901.

Turnbull, Robert (D Va.) Jan. 11, 1850–Jan. 22, 1920; House March 8, 1910–13.

Turner, Benjamin Sterling (R Ala.) March 17, 1825–March 21, 1894; House 1871–73.

Turner, Charles Henry (D N.Y.) May 26, 1861–Aug. 31, 1913; House Dec. 9, 1889–91.

Turner, Charles Jr. (R Mass.) June 20, 1760–May 16, 1839; House June 28, 1809–13.

Turner, Clarence Wyly (D Tenn.) Oct. 22, 1866–March 23, 1939; House Nov. 7, 1922–23, 1933–March 23, 1939.

Turner, Daniel (son of James Turner of N.C.) (– N.C.) Sept. 21, 1796–July 21, 1860; House 1827–29.

Turner, Erastus Johnson (R Kan.) Dec. 26, 1846–Feb. 10, 1933; House 1887–91.

Turner, George (Fus./Sil.R/D/P Wash.) Feb. 25, 1850–Jan. 26, 1932; Senate 1897–1903.

Turner, Henry Gray (D Ga.) March 20, 1839–June 9, 1904; House 1881–97.

Turner, James (father of Daniel Turner) (R N.C.) Dec. 20, 1766–Jan. 15, 1824; Senate 1805–Nov. 21, 1816; Gov. Dec. 6, 1802–Dec. 10, 1805.

Turner, James (J Md.) Nov. 7, 1783–March 28, 1861; House 1833–37.

Turner, Jim (D Texas) Feb. 6, 1946– ; House 1997–2005.

Turner, Michael R. (R Ohio) Jan. 11, 1960– ; House 2003– .

Turner, Oscar (father of Oscar Turner, below) (ID Ky.) Feb. 3, 1825–Jan. 22, 1896; House 1879–85 (1879–81 Independent Democrat, 1881–83 Democrat).

Turner, Oscar (son of Oscar Turner, above) (D Ky.) Oct. 19, 1867–July 17, 1902; House 1899–1901.

Turner, Smith Spangler (D Va.) Nov. 21, 1842–April 8, 1898; House Jan. 30, 1894–97.

Turner, Thomas (D Ky.) Sept. 10, 1821–Sept. 11, 1900; House 1877–81.

Turner, Thomas Johnston (D Ill.) April 5, 1815–April 4, 1874; House 1847–49.

Turney, Hopkins Lacy (D Tenn.) Oct. 3, 1797–Aug. 1, 1857; House 1837–43; Senate 1845–51.

Turney, Jacob (D Pa.) Feb. 18, 1825–Oct. 4, 1891; House 1875–79.

Turpie, David (D Ind.) July 8, 1828–April 21, 1909; Senate Jan. 14–March 3, 1863, 1887–99.

Turpin, Charles Murray (R Pa.) March 4, 1878–June 4, 1946; House June 4, 1929–37.

Turpin, Louis Washington (D Ala.) Feb. 22, 1849–Feb. 3, 1903; House 1889–June 4, 1890, 1891–95.

Turrill, Joel (J N.Y.) Feb. 22, 1794–Dec. 28, 1859; House 1833–37.

Tuten, James Russell (D Ga.) July 23, 1911–Aug. 16, 1968; House 1963–67.

Tuthill, Joseph Hasbrouck (nephew of Selah Tuthill) (D N.Y.) Feb. 25, 1811–July 27, 1877; House 1871–73.

Tuthill, Selah (uncle of Joseph Hasbrouck Tuthill) (– N.Y.) Oct. 26, 1771–Sept. 7, 1821; House March 4–Sept. 7, 1821.

Tuttle, William Edgar Jr. (D N.J.) Dec. 10, 1870–Feb. 11, 1923; House 1911–15.

Tweed, William Marcy (D N.Y.) April 3, 1823–April 12, 1878; House 1853–55.

Tweedy, John Hubbard (W Wis.) Nov. 9, 1814–Nov. 12, 1891; House (Terr. Del.) 1847–May 29, 1848.

Tweedy, Samuel (AJ Conn.) March 8, 1776–July 1, 1868; House 1833–35.

Twichell, Ginery (R Mass.) Aug. 26, 1811–July 23, 1883; House 1867–73.

Twyman, Robert Joseph (R Ill.) June 18, 1897–June 28, 1976; House 1947–49.

Tydings, Joseph Davies (adoptive son of Millard Evelyn Tydings) (D Md.) May 4, 1928– ; Senate 1965–71; chair Senate District of Columbia 1969–71.

Tydings, Millard Evelyn (adoptive father of Joseph Davies Tydings) (D Md.) April 6, 1890–Feb. 9, 1961; House 1923–27; Senate 1927–51; chair Senate Armed Services 1949–51.

Tyler, Asher (W N.Y.) May 10, 1798–Aug. 1, 1875; House 1843–45.

Tyler, David Gardiner (son of John Tyler, grandson of Gov. John Tyler of Va.) (D Va.) July 12, 1846–Sept. 5, 1927; House 1893–97.

Tyler, James Manning (R Vt.) April 27, 1835–Oct. 13, 1926; House 1879–83.

Tyler, John (father of David Gardiner Tyler, son of Gov. John Tyler of Va.) (R Va.) March 29, 1790–Jan. 18, 1862; House Dec. 16, 1817–21; Senate 1827–Feb. 29, 1836; elected pres. pro tempore March 3, 1835; Gov. Dec. 10, 1825–March 4, 1827 (Democratic Republican); vice president March 4–April 6, 1841 (Whig); president April 6, 1841–45 (Whig).

Tyndall, William Thomas (R Mo.) Jan. 16, 1862–Nov. 26, 1928; House 1905–07.

Tyner, James Noble (R Ind.) Jan. 17, 1826–Dec. 5, 1904; House 1869–75; postmaster general July 13, 1876–March 12, 1877.

Tyson, Jacob (– N.Y.) Oct. 8, 1773–July 16, 1848; House 1823–25.

Tyson, Joe Roberts (W Pa.) Feb. 8, 1803–June 27, 1858; House 1855–57.

Tyson, John Russell (D Ala.) Nov. 28, 1856–March 27, 1923; House 1921–March 27, 1923.

Tyson, Lawrence Davis (D Tenn.) July 4, 1861–Aug. 24, 1929; Senate 1925–Aug. 24, 1929.

Udall, Mark Emery (son of Morris King Udall, nephew of Stewart Lee Udall, cousin of Thomas S. Udall) (D Colo.) July 18, 1950– ; House 1999– .

Udall, Morris King (father of Mark Emery Udall, brother of Stewart Lee Udall, uncle of Thomas S. Udall) (D Ariz.) June 15, 1922–Nov. 12, 1998; House May 2, 1961–May 4, 1991; chair House Interior and Insular Affairs 1977–91.

Udall, Stewart Lee (father of Thomas S. Udall, brother of Morris King Udall, uncle of Mark Emery Udall) (D Ariz.) Jan. 31, 1920– ; House 1955–Jan. 18, 1961; secretary of the interior Jan. 21, 1961–Jan. 20, 1969.

Udall, Thomas S. (son of Stewart Lee Udall, nephew of Morris King Udall, cousin of Mark Emery Udall) (D N.M.) May 18, 1948– ; House 1999– .

Udree, Daniel (R Pa.) Aug. 5, 1751–July 15, 1828; House Oct. 12, 1813–15, Dec. 26, 1820–21, Dec. 10, 1822–25.

Ullman, Albert Conrad (D Ore.) March 9, 1914–Oct. 11, 1986; House 1957–81; chair House Ways and Means 1975–81.

Umstead, William Bradley (D N.C.) May 13, 1895–Nov. 7, 1954; House 1933–39; Senate Dec. 18, 1946–Dec. 30, 1948; Gov. Jan. 8, 1953–Nov. 7, 1954.

Underhill, Charles Lee (R Mass.) July 20, 1867–Jan. 28, 1946; House 1921–33.

Underhill, Edwin Stewart (D N.Y.) Oct. 7, 1861–Feb. 7, 1929; House 1911–15.

Underhill, John Quincy (D N.Y.) Feb. 19, 1848–May 21, 1907; House 1899–1901.

Underhill, Walter (W N.Y.) Sept. 12, 1795–Aug. 17, 1866; House 1849–51.

Underwood, John William Henderson (D Ga.) Nov. 20, 1816–July 18, 1888; House 1859–Jan. 23, 1861.

Underwood, Joseph Rogers (brother of Warner Lewis Underwood, grandfather of Oscar Wilder Underwood) (W Ky.) Oct. 24, 1791–Aug. 23, 1876; House 1835–43; Senate 1847–53.

Underwood, Mell Gilbert (D Ohio) Jan. 30, 1892–March 8, 1972; House 1923–April 10, 1936.

Underwood, Oscar Wilder (grandson of Joseph Rogers Underwood, great–nephew of Warner Lewis Underwood) (D Ala.) May 6, 1862–Jan. 25, 1929; House 1895–June 9, 1896, 1897–1915; House majority leader 1911–15; Senate 1915–27; Senate minority leader April 27, 1920–23.

Underwood, Robert A. (D Guam) July 13, 1948– ; House (Del.) 1993–2003.

Underwood, Thomas Rust (D Ky.) March 3, 1898–June 29, 1956; House 1949–March 17, 1951; Senate March 19, 1951–Nov. 4, 1952.

Underwood, Warner Lewis (brother of Joseph Rogers Underwood, great–uncle of Oscar Wilder Underwood) (AP Ky.) Aug. 7, 1808–March 12, 1872; House 1855–59.

Unsoeld, Jolene (D Wash.) Dec. 3, 1931– ; House 1989–95.

Updegraff, Jonathan Taylor (R Ohio) May 13, 1822–Nov. 30, 1882; House 1879–Nov. 30, 1882.

Updegraff, Thomas (R Iowa) April 3, 1834–Oct. 4, 1910; House 1879–83, 1893–99.

Updike, Ralph Eugene (R Ind.) May 27, 1894–Sept. 16, 1953; House 1925–29.

Upham, Charles Wentworth (cousin of George Baxter Upham and Jabez Upham) (W Mass.) May 4, 1802–June 15, 1875; House 1853–55.

Upham, George Baxter (brother of Jabez Upham, cousin of Charles Wentworth Upham) (F N.H.) Dec. 27, 1768–Feb. 10, 1848; House 1801–03.

Upham, Jabez (brother of George Baxter Upham, cousin of Charles Wentworth Upham) (F Mass.) Aug. 23, 1764–Nov. 8, 1811; House 1807–10.

Upham, Nathaniel (R N.H.) June 9, 1774–July 10, 1829; House 1817–23.

Upham, William (W Vt.) Aug. 5, 1792–Jan. 14, 1853; Senate 1843–Jan. 14, 1853.

Upshaw, William David (D Ga.) Oct. 15, 1866–Nov. 21, 1952; House 1919–27.

Upson, Charles (R Mich.) March 19, 1821–Sept. 5, 1885; House 1863–69.

Upson, Christopher Columbus (D Texas) Oct. 17, 1829–Feb. 8, 1902; House April 15, 1879–83.

Upson, William Hanford (R Ohio) Jan. 11, 1823–April 13, 1910; House 1869–73.

Upton, Charles Horace (U Va.) Aug. 23, 1812–June 17, 1877; House May 23, 1861–Feb. 27, 1862.

Upton, Frederick Stephen (R Mich.) April 23, 1953– ; House 1987– .

Upton, Robert William (R N.H.) Feb. 3, 1884–April 28, 1972; Senate Aug. 14, 1953–Nov. 7, 1954.

Urner, Milton George (uncle of James Samuel Simmons) (R Md.) July 29, 1839–Feb. 9, 1926; House 1879–83.

Utt, James Boyd (R Calif.) March 11, 1899–March 1, 1970; House 1953–March 1, 1970.

Utter, George Herbert (R R.I.) July 24, 1854–Nov. 3, 1912; House 1911–Nov. 3, 1912; Gov. Jan. 3, 1905–Jan. 1, 1907.

Utterback, Hubert (cousin of John Gregg Utterback) (D Iowa) June 28, 1880–May 12, 1942; House 1935–37.

Utterback, John Gregg (cousin of Hubert Utterback) (D Maine) July 12, 1872–July 11, 1955; House 1933–35.

Vail, George (D N.J.) July 21, 1809–May 23, 1875; House 1853–57.

Vail, Henry (D N.Y.) 1782–June 25, 1853; House 1837–39.

Vail, Richard Bernard (R Ill.) Aug. 31, 1895–July 29, 1955; House 1947–49, 1951–53.

Vaile, William Newell (R Colo.) June 22, 1876–July 2, 1927; House 1919–July 2, 1927.

Valentine, Edward Kimble (R Neb.) June 1, 1843–April 11, 1916; House 1879–85.

Valentine, Itimous Thaddeus Jr. "Tim" (D N.C.) March 15, 1926– ; House 1983–95.

Valk, William Weightman (AP N.Y.) Oct. 12, 1806–Sept. 20, 1879; House 1855–57.

Vallandigham, Clement Laird (uncle of John A. McMahon) (D Ohio) July 29, 1820–June 17, 1871; House May 25, 1858–63.

Van Aernam, Henry (R N.Y.) March 11, 1819–June 1, 1894; House 1865–69, 1879–83.

Van Alen, James Isaac (half–brother of Martin Van Buren) (R N.Y.) 1776–Dec. 23, 1870; House 1807–09.

Van Alen, John Evert (F N.Y.) 1749–March 1807; House 1793–99 (1793–95 no party).

Van Alstyne, Thomas Jefferson (D N.Y.) July 25, 1827–Oct. 26, 1903; House 1883–85.

Van Auken, Daniel Myers (D Pa.) Jan. 15, 1826–Nov. 7, 1908; House 1867–71.

Van Buren, John (D N.Y.) May 13, 1799–Jan. 16, 1855; House 1841–43.

Van Buren, Martin (half–brother of James Isaac Van Alen) (– N.Y.) Dec. 5, 1782–July 24, 1862; Senate 1821–Dec. 20, 1828; Gov. Jan. 1–March 12, 1829 (Jeffersonian Republican); secretary of state March 28, 1829–March 23, 1831; vice president 1833–37 (Democrat); president 1837–41 (Democrat).

Vance, John Luther (D Ohio) July 19, 1839–June 10, 1921; House 1875–77.

Vance, Joseph (W Ohio) March 21, 1786–Aug. 24, 1852; House 1821–35 (1821–33 no party, 1833–35 Anti–Jacksonian), 1843–47; Gov. Dec. 12, 1836–Dec. 13, 1838.

Vance, Robert Brank (uncle of Zebulon Baird Vance and Robert Brank Vance, below) (– N.C.) 1793–1827; House 1823–25.

Vance, Robert Brank (nephew of Robert Brank Vance, above, brother of Zebulon Baird Vance) (D N.C.) April 24, 1828–Nov. 28, 1899; House 1873–85.

Vance, Robert Johnstone (D Conn.) March 15, 1854–June 15, 1902; House 1887–89.

Vance, Zebulon Baird (brother of Robert Brank Vance born in 1828, nephew of Robert Brank Vance born in 1793) (D N.C.) May 13, 1830–April 14, 1894; House Dec. 7, 1858–61; Senate 1879–April 14, 1894; Gov. Sept. 8, 1862–May 29, 1865, Jan. 1, 1877–Feb. 5, 1879.

Van Cortlandt, Philip (brother of Pierre Van Cortlandt Jr.) (R N.Y.) Aug. 21, 1749–Nov. 1, 1831; House 1793–1809 (1793–95 no party).

Van Cortlandt, Pierre Jr. (brother of Philip Van Cortlandt) (R N.Y.) Aug. 29, 1762–July 13, 1848; House 1811–13.

Van Deerlin, Lionel (D Calif.) July 25, 1914– ; House 1963–81.

Vandenberg, Arthur Hendrick (R Mich.) March 22, 1884–April 18, 1951; Senate March 31, 1928–April 18, 1951; elected pres. pro tempore Jan. 4, 1947; chair Senate Foreign Relations 1947–49.

Vandergriff, Tommy Joe "Tom" (D Texas) Jan. 29, 1926– ; House 1983–85.

Vander Jagt, Guy Adrian (R Mich.) Aug. 26, 1931– ; House Nov. 8, 1966–93.

Vanderpoel, Aaron (D N.Y.) Feb. 5, 1799–July 18, 1870; House 1833–37 (Jacksonian), 1839–41.

Vander Veen, Richard Franklin (D Mich.) Nov. 26, 1922– ; House Feb. 18, 1974–77.

Vanderveer, Abraham (D N.Y.) 1781–July 21, 1839; House 1837–39.

Vandever, William (R Calif.) March 31, 1817–July 23, 1893; House 1859–Sept. 24, 1861 (Iowa), 1887–91.

Vandiver, Willard Duncan (D Mo.) March 30, 1854–May 30, 1932; House 1897–1905.

Van Duzer, Clarence Dunn (D Nev.) May 4, 1866–Sept. 28, 1947; House 1903–07.

Van Dyke, Carl Chester (D Minn.) Feb. 18, 1881–May 20, 1919; House 1915–May 20, 1919.

Van Dyke, John (W N.J.) April 3, 1807–Dec. 24, 1878; House 1847–51.

Van Dyke, Nicholas (F Del.) Dec. 20, 1770–May 21, 1826; House Oct. 6, 1807–11; Senate 1817–May 21, 1826.

Van Eaton, Henry Smith (D Miss.) Sept. 14, 1826–May 30, 1898; House 1883–87.

Van Gaasbeck, Peter (– N.Y.) Sept. 27, 1754–1797; House 1793–95.

Van Hollen, Christopher (D Md.) Jan. 10, 1959– ; House 2003– .

Van Horn, Burt (R N.Y.) Oct. 28, 1823–April 1, 1896; House 1861–63, 1865–69.

Van Horn, George (D N.Y.) Feb. 5, 1850–May 3, 1904; House 1891–93.

Van Horn, Robert Thompson (R Mo.) May 19, 1824–Jan. 3, 1916; House 1865–71, 1881–83, Feb. 27, 1896–97.

Van Horne, Archibald (R Md.) ?–1817; House 1807–11.

Van Horne, Espy (– Pa.) 1795–Aug. 25, 1829; House 1825–29.

Van Horne, Isaac (R Pa.) Jan. 13, 1754–Feb. 2, 1834; House 1801–05.

Van Houten, Isaac B. (J N.Y.) June 4, 1776–Aug. 16, 1850; House 1833–35.

Vanik, Charles Albert (D Ohio) April 7, 1913– ; House 1955–81.

Vanmeter, John Inskeep (W Ohio) Feb. 1798–Aug. 3, 1875; House 1843–45.

Van Ness, John Peter (R N.Y.) 1770–March 7, 1846; House Oct. 6, 1801–Jan. 17, 1803.

Van Nuys, Frederick (D Ind.) April 16, 1874–Jan. 25, 1944; Senate 1933–Jan. 25, 1944.

Van Pelt, William Kaiser (R Wis.) March 10, 1905–June 2, 1996; House 1951–65.

Van Rensselaer, Henry Bell (son of Stephen Van Rensselaer) (W N.Y.) May 14, 1810–March 23, 1864; House 1841–43.

Van Rensselaer, Jeremiah (father of Solomon Van Vechten Van Rensselaer, cousin of Killian Killian Van Rensselaer) (– N.Y.) Aug. 27, 1738–Feb. 19, 1810; House 1789–91.

Van Rensselaer, Killian Killian (cousin of Jeremiah Van Rensselaer, uncle of Solomon Van Vechten Van Renssealer) (F N.Y.) June 9, 1763–June 18, 1845; House 1801–11.

Van Rensselaer, Solomon Van Vechten (son of Jeremiah Van Rensselaer, nephew of Killian Killian Van Rensselaer) (F N.Y.) Aug. 6, 1774–April 23, 1852; House 1819–Jan. 14, 1822.

Van Rensselaer, Stephen (father of Henry Bell Van Rensselaer) (– N.Y.) Nov. 1, 1764–Jan. 26, 1839; House Feb. 27, 1822–29.

Van Sant, Joshua (D Md.) Dec. 31, 1803–April 8, 1884; House 1853–55.

Van Schaick, Isaac Whitbeck (uncle of Aaron Van Schaick Cochrane) (R Wis.) Dec. 7, 1817–Aug. 22, 1901; House 1885–87, 1889–91.

Van Swearingen, Thomas (– Va.) May 5, 1784–Aug. 19, 1822; House 1819–Aug. 19, 1822.

Van Trump, Philadelph (D Ohio) Nov. 15, 1810–July 31, 1874; House 1867–73.

Van Valkenburgh, Robert Bruce (R N.Y.) Sept. 4, 1821–Aug. 1, 1888; House 1861–65.

Van Voorhis, Henry Clay (R Ohio) May 11, 1852–Dec. 12, 1927; House 1893–1905.

Van Voorhis, John (R N.Y.) Oct. 22, 1826–Oct. 20, 1905; House 1879–83, 1893–95.

Van Vorhes, Nelson Holmes (R Ohio) Jan. 23, 1822–Dec. 4, 1882; House 1875–79.

Van Winkle, Marshall (great–nephew of Peter Godwin Van Winkle) (R N.J.) Sept. 28, 1869–May 10, 1957; House 1905–07.

Van Winkle, Peter Godwin (great–uncle of Marshall Van Winkle) (U W.Va.) Sept. 7, 1808–April 15, 1872; Senate Aug. 4, 1863–69.

Van Wyck, Charles Henry (R Neb.) May 10, 1824–Oct. 24, 1895; House 1859–63, 1867–69, Feb. 17, 1870–71 (N.Y.); Senate 1881–87.

Van Wyck, William William (– N.Y.) Aug. 9, 1777–Aug. 27, 1840; House 1821–25.

Van Zandt, James Edward (R Pa.) Dec. 18, 1898–Jan. 6, 1986; House 1939–Sept. 24, 1943, 1947–63.

Vardaman, James Kimble (D Miss.) July 26, 1861–June 25, 1930; Senate 1913–19; Gov. Jan. 19, 1904–Jan. 21, 1908.

Vare, William Scott (R Pa.) Dec. 24, 1867–Aug. 7, 1934; House April 24, 1912–Jan. 2, 1923, 1923–27; elected to the Senate for the term beginning 1927 but was not permitted to qualify.

Varnum, John (F Mass.) June 25, 1778–July 23, 1836; House 1825–31.

Varnum, Joseph Bradley (R Mass.) Jan. 29, 1750 or 1751–Sept. 21, 1821; House 1795–June 29, 1811 (no party); Speaker Oct. 26, 1807–09, May 22, 1809–11; Senate June 29, 1811–17; elected pres. pro tempore Dec. 6, 1813.

Vaughan, Horace Worth (D Texas) Dec. 2, 1867–Nov. 10, 1922; House 1913–15.

Vaughan, William Wirt (D Tenn.) July 2, 1831–Aug. 19, 1878; House 1871–73.

Vaughn, Albert Clinton Sr. (R Pa.) Oct. 9, 1894–Sept. 1, 1951; House Jan. 3–Sept. 1, 1951.

Vaux, Richard (D Pa.) Dec. 19, 1816–March 22, 1895; House May 20, 1890–91.

Veeder, William Davis (D N.Y.) May 19, 1835–Dec. 2, 1910; House 1877–79.

Vehslage, John Herman George (D N.Y.) Dec. 20, 1842–July 21, 1904; House 1897–99.

Velázquez, Nydia Margarita (D N.Y.) March 22, 1953– ; House 1993– .

Velde, Harold Himmel (R Ill.) April 1, 1910–Sept. 1, 1985; House 1949–57; chair House Un–American Activities 1953–55.

Venable, Abraham Bedford, (uncle of Abraham Watkins Venable) (– Va.) Nov. 20, 1758–Dec. 26, 1811; House 1791–1799; Senate Dec. 7, 1803–June 7, 1804.

Venable, Abraham Watkins (nephew of Abraham Bedford Venable) (D N.C.) Oct. 17, 1799–Feb. 24, 1876; House 1847–53.

Venable, Edward Carrington (D Va.) Jan. 31, 1853–Dec. 8, 1908; House 1889–Sept. 23, 1890.

Venable, William Webb (D Miss.) Sept. 25, 1880–Aug. 2, 1948; House Jan. 4, 1916–21.

Vento, Bruce Frank (DFL Minn.) Oct. 7, 1940–Oct. 10, 2000; House 1977–Oct. 10, 2000.

Verplanck, Daniel Crommelin (father of Gulian Crommelin Verplanck) (R N.Y.) March 19, 1762–March 29, 1834; House Oct. 17, 1803–09.

Verplanck, Gulian Crommelin (son of Daniel Crommelin Verplanck) (J N.Y.) Aug. 6, 1786–March 18, 1870; House 1825–33 (1825–29 no party).

Verree, John Paul (R Pa.) March 9, 1817–June 27, 1889; House 1859–63.

Vest, George Graham (D Mo.) Dec. 6, 1830–Aug. 9, 1904; Senate 1879–1903.

Vestal, Albert Henry (R Ind.) Jan. 18, 1875–April 1, 1932; House 1917–April 1, 1932.

Veysey, Victor Vincent (R Calif.) April 14, 1915–Feb. 13, 2001; House 1971–75.

Vibbard, Chauncey (D N.Y.) Nov. 11, 1811–June 5, 1891; House 1861–63.

Vickers, George (D Md.) Nov. 19, 1801–Oct. 8, 1879; Senate March 7, 1868–73.

Vidal, Michel (R La.) Oct. 1, 1824–?; House July 18, 1868–69.

Viele, Egbert Ludoricus (D N.Y.) June 17, 1825–April 22, 1902; House 1885–87.

Vigorito, Joseph Phillip (D Pa.) Nov. 10, 1918–Feb. 5, 2003; House 1965–77.

Vilas, William Freeman (D Wis.) July 9, 1840–Aug. 27, 1908; Senate 1891–97; postmaster general March 7, 1885–Jan. 16, 1888; secretary of the interior Jan. 16, 1888–March 6, 1889.

Vincent, Beverly Mills (D Ky.) March 28, 1890–Aug. 15, 1980; House 1937–45.

Vincent, Bird J. (R Mich.) March 6, 1880–July 18, 1931; House 1923–July 18, 1931.

Vincent, Earl W. (R Iowa) March 27, 1886–May 22, 1953; House June 4, 1928–29.

Vincent, William Davis (P Kan.) Oct. 11, 1852–Feb. 28, 1922; House 1897–99.

Vining, John (– Del.) Dec. 23, 1758–Feb. 1802; House 1789–93; Senate 1793–Jan. 19, 1798; Cont. Cong. 1784–85.

Vinson, Carl (great–uncle of Samuel Augustus Nunn) (D Ga.) Nov. 18, 1883–June 1, 1981; House Nov. 3, 1914–65; chair House Armed Services 1949–53, 1955–65.

Vinson, Frederick Moore (D Ky.) Jan. 22, 1890–Sept. 8, 1953; House Jan. 12, 1924–29, 1931–May 12, 1938; secretary of the Treasury July 23, 1945–June 23, 1946; chief justice June 24, 1946–Sept. 8, 1953.

Vinton, Samuel Finley (W Ohio) Sept. 25, 1792–May 11, 1862; House 1823–37 (1823–33 no party, 1833–35 Anti–Jacksonian), 1843–51.

Visclosky, Peter (D Ind.) Aug. 13, 1949– ; House 1985– .

Vitter, David (R La.) May 16, 1961– ; House June 8, 1999–2005; Senate 2005– .

Vivian, Weston Edward (D Mich.) Oct. 25, 1924– ; House 1965–67.

Voigt, Edward (R Wis.) Dec. 1, 1873–Aug. 26, 1934; House 1917–27.

Voinovich, George V. (R Ohio) July 15, 1936– ; Senate 1999– ; chair Senate Select Ethics 2003– ; Gov. Jan. 14, 1991–Jan. 1, 1999.

Volk, Lester David (R N.Y.) Sept. 17, 1884–April 30, 1962; House Nov. 2, 1920–23.

Volkmer, Harold Lee (D Mo.) April 4, 1931– ; House 1977–97.

Vollmer, Henry (D Iowa) July 28, 1867–Aug. 25, 1930; House Feb. 10, 1914–15.

Volstead, Andrew John (R Minn.) Oct. 31, 1860–Jan. 20, 1947; House 1903–23.

Voorhees, Charles Stewart (son of Daniel Wolsey Voorhees) (D Wash.) June 4, 1853–Dec. 26, 1909; House (Terr. Del.) 1885–89.

Voorhees, Daniel Wolsey (father of Charles Stewart Voorhees) (D Ind.) Sept. 26, 1827–April 10, 1897; House 1861–Feb. 23, 1866, 1869–73; Senate Nov. 6, 1877–97.

Voorhis, Charles Henry (R N.J.) March 13, 1833–April 15, 1896; House 1879–81.

Voorhis, Horace Jeremiah "Jerry" (D Calif.) April 6, 1901–Sept. 11, 1984; House 1937–47.

Vorys, John Martin (R Ohio) June 16, 1896–Aug. 25, 1968; House 1939–59.

Vose, Roger (F N.H.) Feb. 24, 1763–Oct. 26, 1841; House 1813–17.

Vreeland, Albert Lincoln (R N.J.) July 2, 1901–May 3, 1975; House 1939–43.

Vreeland, Edward Butterfield (R N.Y.) Dec. 7, 1856–May 8, 1936; House Nov. 7, 1899–1913.

Vroom, Peter Dumont (D N.J.) Dec. 12, 1791–Nov. 18, 1873; House 1839–41; Gov. Nov. 6, 1829–Oct. 26, 1832, Oct. 25, 1833–Oct. 28, 1836.

Vucanovich, Barbara Farrell (R Nev.) June 22, 1921– ; House 1983–97.

Vursell, Charles Wesley (cousin of Carl Bert Albert) (R Ill.) Feb. 8, 1881–Sept. 21, 1974; House 1943–59.

Wachter, Frank Charles (R Md.) Sept. 16, 1861–July 1, 1910; House 1899–1907.

Waddell, Alfred Moore (D N.C.) Sept. 16, 1834–March 17, 1912; House 1871–79.

Waddill, Edmund Jr. (R Va.) May 22, 1855–April 9, 1931; House April 12, 1890–91.

Waddill, James Richard (D Mo.) Nov. 22, 1842–June 14, 1917; House 1879–81.

Wade, Benjamin Franklin (brother of Edward Wade) (R Ohio) Oct. 27, 1800–March 2, 1878; Senate March 15, 1851–69 (1851–57 Whig); elected pres. pro tempore March 2, 1867.

Wade, Edward (brother of Benjamin Franklin Wade) (R Ohio) Nov. 22, 1802–Aug. 13, 1866; House 1853–61 (1853–55 Free-Soiler).

Wade, Martin Joseph (D Iowa) Oct. 20, 1861–April 16, 1931; House 1903–05.

Wade, William Henry (R Mo.) Nov. 3, 1835–Jan. 13, 1911; House 1885–91.

Wadleigh, Bainbridge (R N.H.) Jan. 4, 1831–Jan. 24, 1891; Senate 1873–79.

Wadsworth, James Wolcott (father of James Wolcott Wadsworth Jr., great-grandfather of James Wadsworth Symington) (R N.Y.) Oct. 12, 1846–Dec. 24, 1926; House Nov. 8, 1881–85, 1891–1907.

Wadsworth, James Wolcott Jr. (son of James Wolcott Wadsworth, grandfather of James Wadsworth Symington, father-in-law of Stuart Symington) (R N.Y.) Aug. 12, 1877–June 21, 1952; Senate 1915–27; House 1933–51.

Wadsworth, Jeremiah (– Conn.) July 12, 1743–April 30, 1804; House 1789–95; Cont. Cong. 1788.

Wadsworth, Peleg (F Mass.) May 6, 1748–Nov. 12, 1829; House 1793–1807.

Wadsworth, William Henry (R Ky.) July 4, 1821–April 2, 1893; House 1861–65 (Unionist), 1885–87.

Wagener, David Douglas (D Pa.) Oct. 11, 1792–Oct. 1, 1860; House 1833–41 (1833–37 Jacksonian).

Waggaman, George Augustus (– La.) 1782–March 31, 1843; Senate Nov. 15, 1831–35.

Waggonner, Joseph David Jr. (D La.) Sept. 7, 1918– ; House Dec. 19, 1961–79.

Wagner, Earl Thomas (D Ohio) April 27, 1908–March 6, 1990; House 1949–51.

Wagner, Peter Joseph (W N.Y.) Aug. 14, 1795–Sept. 13, 1884; House 1839–41.

Wagner, Robert Ferdinand (D N.Y.) June 8, 1877–May 4, 1953; Senate 1927–June 28, 1949.

Wagoner, George Chester Robinson (R Mo.) Sept. 3, 1863–April 27, 1946; House Feb. 26, 1901–03.

Wainwright, Jonathan Mayhew (R N.Y.) Dec. 10, 1864–June 3, 1945; House 1923–31.

Wainwright, Stuyvesant II (R N.Y.) March 16, 1921– ; House 1953–61.

Wait, John Turner (R Conn.) Aug. 27, 1811–April 21, 1899; House April 12, 1876–87.

Wakefield, James Beach (R Minn.) March 21, 1825–Aug. 25, 1910; House 1883–87.

Wakeman, Abram (W N.Y.) May 31, 1824–June 29, 1889; House 1855–57.

Wakeman, Seth (R N.Y.) Jan. 15, 1811–Jan. 4, 1880; House 1871–73.

Walbridge, David Safford (R Mich.) July 30, 1802–June 15, 1868; House 1855–59.

Walbridge, Henry Sanford (cousin of Hiram Walbridge) (W N.Y.) April 8, 1801–Jan. 27, 1869; House 1851–53.

Walbridge, Hiram (cousin of Henry Sanford Walbridge) (D N.Y.) Feb. 2, 1821–Dec. 6, 1870; House 1853–55.

Walcott, Frederic Collin (R Conn.) Feb. 19, 1869–April 27, 1949; Senate 1929–35.

Walden, Greg (R Ore.) Jan. 10, 1957– ; House 1999– .

Walden, Hiram (D N.Y.) Aug. 21, 1800–July 21, 1880; House 1849–51.

Walden, Madison Miner (R Iowa) Oct. 6, 1836–July 24, 1891; House 1871–73.

Waldholtz, Enid Greene (later Enid Greene) (R Utah) Oct. 5, 1958– ; House 1995–97.

Waldie, Jerome Russell (D Calif.) Feb. 15, 1925– ; House June 7, 1966–75.

Waldo, George Ernest (R N.Y.) Jan. 11, 1851–June 16, 1942; House 1905–09.

Waldo, Loren Pinckney (D Conn.) Feb. 2, 1802–Sept. 8, 1881; House 1849–51.

Waldon, Alton R. Jr. (D N.Y.) Dec. 21, 1936– ; House July 29, 1986–87.

Waldow, William Frederick (R N.Y.) Aug. 26, 1882–April 16, 1930; House 1917–19.

Waldron, Alfred Marpole (R Pa.) Sept. 21, 1865–June 28, 1952; House 1933–35.

Waldron, Henry (R Mich.) Oct. 11, 1819–Sept. 13, 1880; House 1855–61, 1871–77.

Wales, George Edward (– Vt.) May 13, 1792–Jan. 8, 1860; House 1825–29.

Wales, John (W Del.) July 31, 1783–Dec. 3, 1863; Senate Feb. 3, 1849–51.

Walgren, Douglas (D Pa.) Dec. 28, 1940– ; House 1977–91.

Walker, Amasa (R Mass.) May 4, 1799–Oct. 29, 1875; House Dec. 1, 1862–63.

Walker, Benjamin (F N.Y.) 1753–Jan. 13, 1818; House 1801–03.

Walker, Charles Christopher Brainerd (D N.Y.) June 27, 1824–Jan. 26, 1888; House 1875–77.

Walker, David (brother of George Walker, grandfather of James David Walker) (R Ky.) ?–March 1, 1820; House 1817–March 1, 1820.

Walker, E. S. Johnny (D N.M.) June 18, 1911–Oct. 8, 2000; House 1965–69.

Walker, Felix (R N.C.) July 19, 1753–1828; House 1817–23.

Walker, Francis (brother of John Walker) (– Va.) June 22, 1764–March 1806; House 1793–95.

Walker, Freeman (– Ga.) Oct. 25, 1780–Sept. 23, 1827; Senate Nov. 6, 1819–Aug. 6, 1821.

Walker, George (brother of David Walker, great-uncle of James David Walker) (– Ky.) 1763–1819; Senate Aug. 30–Dec. 16, 1814.

Walker, Gilbert Carlton (D Va.) Aug. 1, 1833–May 11, 1885; House 1875–79; Gov. (Provisional) Sept. 21, 1869–Jan. 1, 1870, Jan. 1, 1870–Jan. 1, 1874 (Conservative).

Walker, Isaac Pigeon (D Wis.) Nov. 2, 1815–March 29, 1872; Senate June 8, 1848–55.

Walker, James Alexander (R Va.) Aug. 27, 1832–Oct. 21, 1901; House 1895–99.

Walker, James David (grandson of David Walker, nephew of Finis Ewing McLean and John McLean born in 1791, cousin of Wilkinson Call, great-nephew of George Walker) (D Ark.) Dec. 13, 1830–Oct. 17, 1906; Senate 1879–85.

Walker, James Peter (D Mo.) March 14, 1851–July 19, 1890; House 1887–July 19, 1890.

Walker, John (brother of Francis Walker) (– Va.) Feb. 13, 1744–Dec. 2, 1809; Senate March 31–Nov. 9, 1790; Cont. Cong. 1780.

Walker, John Randall (D Ga.) Feb. 23, 1874–?; House 1913–19.

Walker, John Williams (father of Percy Walker, great-great-grandfather of Richard Walker Bolling) (D Ala.) Aug. 12, 1783–April 23, 1823; Senate Dec. 14, 1819–Dec. 12, 1822.

Walker, Joseph Henry (R Mass.) Dec. 21, 1829–April 3, 1907; House 1889–99.

Walker, Lewis Leavell (R Ky.) Feb. 15, 1873–June 30, 1944; House 1929–31.

Walker, Percy (son of John Williams Walker, great-great-uncle of Richard Walker Bolling) (AP Ala.) Dec. 1812–Dec. 31, 1880; House 1855–57.

Walker, Prentiss Lafayette (R Miss.) Aug. 23, 1917–June 5, 1998; House 1965–67.

Walker, Robert Jarvis Cochran (R Pa.) Oct. 20, 1838–Dec. 19, 1903; House 1881–83.

Walker, Robert John (D Miss.) July 19, 1801–Nov. 11, 1869; Senate 1835–March 5, 1845; secretary of the Treasury March 8, 1845–March 5, 1849; Gov. (Kan. Terr.) April–Dec. 1857.

Walker, Robert Smith (R Pa.) Dec. 23, 1942– ; House 1977–97; chair House Science 1995–97.

Walker, Walter (D Colo.) April 3, 1883–Oct. 8, 1956; Senate Sept. 26–Dec. 6, 1932.

Walker, William Adams (D N.Y.) June 5, 1805–Dec. 18, 1861; House 1853–55.

Wall, Garret Dorset (father of James Walter Wall) (J N.J.) March 10, 1783–Nov. 22, 1850; Senate 1835–41.

Wall, James Walter (son of Garret Dorset Wall) (D N.J.) May 26, 1820–June 9, 1872; Senate Jan. 14–March 3, 1863.

Wall, William (R N.Y.) March 20, 1800–April 20, 1872; House 1861–63.

Wallace, Alexander Stuart (R S.C.) Dec. 30, 1810–June 27, 1893; House May 27, 1870–77.

Wallace, Daniel (D S.C.) May 9, 1801–May 13, 1859; House June 12, 1848–53.

Wallace, David (W Ind.) April 24, 1799–Sept. 4, 1859; House 1841–43; Gov. Dec. 6, 1837–Dec. 9, 1840.

Wallace, James M. (R Pa.) 1750–Dec. 17, 1823; House Oct. 10, 1815–21.

Wallace, John Winfield (R Pa.) Dec. 20, 1818–June 24, 1889; House 1861–63, 1875–77.

Wallace, Jonathan Hasson (D Ohio) Oct. 31, 1824–Oct. 28, 1892; House May 27, 1884–85.

Wallace, Nathaniel Dick (D La.) Oct. 27, 1845–July 16, 1894; House Dec. 9, 1886–87.

Wallace, Robert Minor (D Ark.) Aug. 6, 1856–Nov. 9, 1942; House 1903–11.

Wallace, Rodney (R Mass.) Dec. 21, 1823–Feb. 27, 1903; House 1889–91.

Wallace, William Andrew (D Pa.) Nov. 28, 1827–May 22, 1896; Senate 1875–81.

Wallace, William Copeland (R N.Y.) May 21, 1856–Sept. 4, 1901; House 1889–91.

Wallace, William Henson (R Idaho) July 19, 1811–Feb. 7, 1879; House (Terr. Del. Wash.) 1861–63, (Terr. Del. Idaho) Feb. 1, 1864–65; Gov. (Idaho Terr.) 1863.

Walley, Samuel Hurd (W Mass.) Aug. 31, 1805–Aug. 27, 1877; House 1853–55.

Wallgren, Monrad Charles (D Wash.) April 17, 1891–Sept. 18, 1961; House 1933–Dec. 19, 1940; Senate Dec. 19, 1940–Jan. 9, 1945; Gov. Jan. 8, 1945–Jan. 10, 1949.

Wallhauser, George Marvin (R N.J.) Feb. 10, 1900–Aug. 4, 1993; House 1959–65.

Wallin, Samuel (R N.Y.) July 31, 1856–Dec. 1, 1917; House 1913–15.

Walling, Ansel Tracy (D Ohio) Jan. 10, 1824–June 22, 1896; House 1875–77.

Wallop, Malcolm (R Wyo.) Feb. 27, 1933– ; Senate 1977–95; chair Senate Select Ethics 1981–83.

Walls, Josiah Thomas (R Fla.) Dec. 30, 1842–May 5, 1905; House 1871–Jan. 29, 1873 (no party), 1873–April 19, 1876.

Waln, Robert (F Pa.) Feb. 22, 1765–Jan. 24, 1836; House Dec. 3, 1798–1801.

Walsh, Allan Bartholomew (D N.J.) Aug. 29, 1874–Aug. 5, 1953; House 1913–15.

Walsh, Arthur (D N.J.) Feb. 26, 1896–Dec. 13, 1947; Senate Nov. 26, 1943–Dec. 7, 1944.

Walsh, David Ignatius (D Mass.) Nov. 11, 1872–June 11, 1947; Senate 1919–25, Dec. 6, 1926–47; Gov. Jan. 8, 1914–Jan. 6, 1916.

Walsh, James Joseph (D N.Y.) May 22, 1858–May 8, 1909; House 1895–June 2, 1896.

Walsh, James T. (son of William Francis Walsh) (R N.Y.) June 19, 1947– ; House 1989– .

Walsh, John Richard (D Ind.) May 22, 1913–Jan. 23, 1975; House 1949–51.

Walsh, Joseph (R Mass.) Dec. 16, 1875–Jan. 13, 1946; House 1915–Aug. 2, 1922.

Walsh, Michael (D N.Y.) March 8, 1810–March 17, 1859; House 1853–55.

Walsh, Patrick (D Ga.) Jan. 1, 1840–March 19, 1899; Senate April 2, 1894–95.

Walsh, Thomas James (D Mont.) June 12, 1859–March 2, 1933; Senate 1913–March 2, 1933.

Walsh, Thomas Yates (W Md.) 1809–Jan. 20, 1865; House 1851–53.

Walsh, William (D Md.) May 11, 1828–May 17, 1892; House 1875–79.

Walsh, William Francis (father of James T. Walsh) (R/C N.Y.) July 11, 1912– ; House 1973–79.

Walter, Francis Eugene (D Pa.) May 26, 1894–May 31, 1963; House 1933–May 31, 1963; chair House Un-American Activities 1955–63.

Walters, Anderson Howell (R Pa.) May 18, 1862–Dec. 7, 1927; House 1913–15, 1919–23, 1925–27.

Walters, Herbert Sanford (D Tenn.) Nov. 17, 1891–Aug. 17, 1973; Senate Aug. 20, 1963–Nov. 3, 1964.

Walthall, Edward Cary (D Miss.) April 4, 1831–April 21, 1898; Senate March 9, 1885–Jan. 24, 1894, 1895–April 21, 1898.

Walton, Charles Wesley (R Maine) Dec. 9, 1819–Jan. 24, 1900; House 1861–May 26, 1862.

Walton, Eliakim Persons (R Vt.) Feb. 17, 1812–Dec. 19, 1890; House 1857–63.

Walton, George (cousin of Matthew Walton) (– Ga.) 1749–Feb. 2, 1804; Senate Nov. 16, 1795–Feb. 20, 1796; Cont. Cong. 1776–77, 1780–81; Gov. Jan. 7–Nov. 9, 1789 (Democratic Republican).

Walton, Matthew (cousin of George Walton) (R Ky.) ?–Jan. 18, 1819; House 1803–07.

Walton, William Bell (D N.M.) Jan. 23, 1871–April 14, 1939; House 1917–19.

Walworth, Reuben Hyde (– N.Y.) Oct. 26, 1788–Nov. 27, 1867; House 1821–23.

Wamp, Zach (R Tenn.) Oct. 28, 1957– ; House 1995– .

Wampler, Fred (D Ind.) Oct. 15, 1909–June 8, 1999; House 1959–61.

Wampler, William Creed (R Va.) April 21, 1926– ; House 1953–55, 1967–83.

Wanger, Irving Price (R Pa.) March 5, 1852–Jan. 14, 1940; House 1893–1911.

Warburton, Herbert Birchby (R Del.) Sept. 21, 1916–July 30, 1983; House 1953–55.

Warburton, Stanton (R Wash.) April 13, 1865–Dec. 24, 1926; House 1911–13.

Ward, Aaron (uncle of Elijah Ward) (D N.Y.) July 5, 1790–March 2, 1867; House 1825–29 (no party), 1831–37 (Jacksonian), 1841–43.

Ward, Andrew Harrison (D Ky.) Jan. 3, 1815–April 16, 1904; House Dec. 3, 1866–67.

Ward, Artemas (father of Artemas Ward Jr.) (– Mass.) Nov. 26, 1727–Oct. 28, 1800; House 1791–95; Cont. Cong. 1780–81.

Ward, Artemas Jr. (son of Artemas Ward) (F Mass.) Jan. 9, 1762–Oct. 7, 1847; House 1813–17.

Ward, Charles Bonnell (R N.Y.) April 27, 1879–May 27, 1946; House 1915–25.

Ward, David Jenkins (D Md.) Sept. 17, 1871–Feb. 18, 1961; House June 6, 1939–45.

Ward, Elijah (nephew of Aaron Ward) (D N.Y.) Sept. 16, 1816–Feb. 7, 1882; House 1857–59, 1861–65, 1875–77.

Ward, Hallett Sydney (D N.C.) Aug. 31, 1870–March 31, 1956; House 1921–25.

Ward, Hamilton (R N.Y.) July 3, 1829–Dec. 28, 1898; House 1865–71.

Ward, James Hugh (D Ill.) Nov. 30, 1853–Aug. 15, 1916; House 1885–87.

Ward, Jasper Delos (R Ill.) Feb. 1, 1829–Aug. 6, 1902; House 1873–75.

Ward, Jonathan (R N.Y.) Sept. 21, 1768–Sept. 28, 1842; House 1815–17.

Ward, Marcus Lawrence (R N.J.) Nov. 9, 1812–April 25, 1884; House 1873–75; Gov. Jan. 16, 1866–Jan. 19, 1869; chair Rep. Nat. Comm. 1866–68.

Ward, Matthias (D Texas) Oct. 13, 1805–Oct. 5, 1861; Senate Sept. 27, 1858–Dec. 5, 1859.

Ward, Mike (D Ky.) Jan. 7, 1951– ; House 1995–97.

Ward, Thomas (R N.J.) about 1759–March 4, 1842; House 1813–17.

Ward, Thomas Bayless (D Ind.) April 27, 1835–Jan. 1, 1892; House 1883–87.

Ward, William (R Pa.) Jan. 1, 1837–Feb. 27, 1895; House 1877–83.

Ward, William Lukens (R N.Y.) Sept. 2, 1856–July 16, 1933; House 1897–99.

Ward, William Thomas (W Ky.) Aug. 9, 1808–Oct. 12, 1878; House 1851–53.

Wardwell, Daniel (J N.Y.) May 28, 1791–March 27, 1878; House 1831–37.

Ware, John Haines III (R Pa.) Aug. 29, 1908–July 29, 1997; House Nov. 3, 1970–75.

Ware, Nicholas (R Ga.) 1769–Sept. 7, 1824; Senate Nov. 10, 1821–Sept. 7, 1824.

Ware, Orie Solomon (D Ky.) May 11, 1882–Dec. 16, 1974; House 1927–29.

Warfield, Henry Ridgely (– Md.) Sept. 14, 1774–March 18, 1839; House 1819–25.

Warner, Adoniram Judson (D Ohio) Jan. 13, 1834–Aug. 12, 1910; House 1879–81, 1883–87.

Warner, Hiram (D Ga.) Oct. 29, 1802–June 30, 1881; House 1855–57.

Warner, John De Witt (D N.Y.) Oct. 30, 1851–May 27, 1925; House 1891–95.

Warner, John William (R Va.) Feb. 18, 1927– ; Senate Jan. 2, 1979– ; chair Senate Rules and Administration 1995–99; chair Senate Armed Services 1999–Jan. 3, 2001, Jan. 20, 2001–June 6, 2001, 2003– .

Warner, Levi (brother of Samuel Larkin Warner) (D Conn.) Oct. 10, 1831–April 12, 1911; House Dec. 4, 1876–79.

Warner, Richard (D Tenn.) Sept. 19, 1835–March 4, 1915; House 1881–85.

Warner, Samuel Larkin (brother of Levi Warner) (R Conn.) June 14, 1828–Feb. 6, 1893; House 1865–67.

Warner, Vespasian (R Ill.) April 23, 1842–March 31, 1925; House 1895–1905.

Warner, Willard (R Ala.) Sept. 4, 1826–Nov. 23, 1906; Senate July 13, 1868–71.

Warner, William (R Mo.) June 11, 1840–Oct. 4, 1916; House 1885–89; Senate March 18, 1905–11.

Warnock, William Robert (R Ohio) Aug. 29, 1838–July 30, 1918; House 1901–05.

Warren, Cornelius (W N.Y.) March 15, 1790–July 28, 1849; House 1847–49.

Warren, Edward Allen (D Ark.) May 2, 1818–July 2, 1875; House 1853–55, 1857–59.

Warren, Francis Emroy (R Wyo.) June 20, 1844–Nov. 24, 1929; Senate Nov. 18, 1890–93, 1895–Nov. 24, 1929; Gov. Feb. 1885–86 (Wyo. Terr.), March 1889–Sept. 1890 (Wyo. Terr.), Sept. 11–Nov. 24, 1890.

Warren, Joseph Mabbett (D N.Y.) Jan. 28, 1813–Sept. 9, 1896; House 1871–73.

Warren, Lindsay Carter (D N.C.) Dec. 16, 1889–Dec. 28, 1976; House 1925–Oct. 31, 1940.

Warren, Lott (W Ga.) Oct. 30, 1797–June 17, 1861; House 1839–43.

Warren, William Wirt (D Mass.) Feb. 27, 1834–May 2, 1880; House 1875–77.

Warwick, John George (D Ohio) Dec. 23, 1830–Aug. 14, 1892; House 1891–Aug. 14, 1892.

Washburn, Cadwallader Colden (brother of Israel Washburn Jr., Elihu Benjamin Washburne and William Drew Washburn) (R Wis.) April 22, 1818–May 15, 1882; House 1855–61, 1867–71; Gov. Jan. 1, 1872–Jan. 5, 1874.

Washburn, Charles Grenfill (R Mass.) Jan. 28, 1857–May 25, 1928; House Dec. 18, 1906–11.

Washburn, Henry Dana (R Ind.) March 28, 1832–Jan. 26, 1871; House Feb. 23, 1866–69.

Washburn, Israel Jr. (brother of Elihu Benjamin Washburne, Cadwallader Colden Washburn and William Drew Washburn) (R Maine) June 6, 1813–May 12, 1883; House 1851–Jan. 1, 1861 (1851–55 Whig); Gov. Jan. 2, 1861–Jan. 7, 1863.

Washburn, William Barrett (R Mass.) Jan. 31, 1820–Oct. 5, 1887; House 1863–Dec. 5, 1871; Senate April 29, 1874–75; Gov. Jan. 3, 1872–April 17, 1874.

Washburn, William Drew (brother of Israel Washburn Jr., Elihu Benjamin Washburne, and Cadwallader Colden Washburn) (R Minn.) Jan. 14, 1831–July 29, 1912; House 1879–85; Senate 1889–95.

Washburne, Elihu Benjamin (brother of Israel Washburn Jr., Cadwallader Colden Washburn and William Drew Washburn) (R Ill.) Sept. 23, 1816–Oct. 23, 1887; House 1853–March 6, 1869 (1853–55 Whig); secretary of state March 5–March 16, 1869.

Washington, Craig (D Texas) Oct. 12, 1941– ; House Jan. 23, 1990–95.

Washington, George Corbin (great-nephew of Pres. George Washington) (AJ Md.) Aug. 20, 1789–July 17, 1854; House 1827–33 (no party), 1835–37.

Washington, Harold (D Ill.) April 15, 1922–Nov. 25, 1987; House 1981–April 30, 1983.

Washington, Joseph Edwin (D Tenn.) Nov. 10, 1851–Aug. 28, 1915; House 1887–97.

Washington, William Henry (W N.C.) Feb. 7, 1813–Aug. 12, 1860; House 1841–43.

Wasielewski, Thaddeus Francis Boleslaw (D Wis.) Dec. 2, 1904–April 25, 1976; House 1941–47.

Waskey, Frank Hinman (D Alaska) April 20, 1875–Jan. 18, 1964; House (Terr. Del.) Aug. 14, 1906–07.

Wason, Edward Hills (R N.H.) Sept. 2, 1865–Feb. 6, 1941; House 1915–33.

Wasserman Schultz, Debbie (D Fla.) Sept. 27, 1966– ; House 2005– .

Waterman, Charles Winfield (R Colo.) Nov. 2, 1861–Aug. 27, 1932; Senate 1927–Aug. 27, 1932.

Waters, Maxine (D Calif.) Aug. 31, 1938– ; House 1991– .

Waters, Russell Judson (R Calif.) June 6, 1843–Sept. 25, 1911; House 1899–1901.

Watkins, Albert Galiton (D Tenn.) May 5, 1818–Nov. 9, 1895; House 1849–53 (Whig), 1855–59.

Watkins, Arthur Vivian (R Utah) Dec. 18, 1886–Sept. 1, 1973; Senate 1947–59.

Watkins, Elton (D Ore.) July 6, 1881–June 24, 1956; House 1923–25.

Watkins, George Robert (R Pa.) May 21, 1902–Aug. 7, 1970; House 1965–Aug. 7, 1970.

Watkins, John Thomas (D La.) Jan. 15, 1854–April 25, 1925; House 1905–21.

Watkins, Wesley Wade (R Okla.) Dec. 15, 1938– ; House 1977–91 (Democrat), 1997–2003.

Watmough, John Goddard (AJ Pa.) Dec. 6, 1793–Nov. 27, 1861; House 1831–35.

Watres, Laurence Hawley (R Pa.) July 18, 1882–Feb. 6, 1964; House 1923–31.

Watson, Albert William (R S.C.) Aug. 30, 1922–Sept. 25, 1994; House 1963–Feb. 1, 1965 (Democrat), June 15, 1965–71.

Watson, Clarence Wayland (D W.Va.) May 8, 1864–May 24, 1940; Senate Feb. 1, 1911–13.

Watson, Cooper Kinderdine (R Ohio) June 18, 1810–May 20, 1880; House 1855–57.

Watson, David Kemper (R Ohio) June 8, 1849–Sept. 28, 1918; House 1895–97.

Watson, Diane E. (D Calif.) Nov. 12, 1933– ; House June 5, 2001– .

Watson, Henry Winfield (R Pa.) June 24, 1856–Aug. 27, 1933; House 1915–Aug. 27, 1933.

Watson, James (F N.Y.) April 6, 1750–May 15, 1806; Senate Aug. 17, 1798–March 19, 1800.

Watson, James Eli (R Ind.) Nov. 2, 1864–July 29, 1948; House 1895–97, 1899–1909; Senate Nov. 8, 1916–33; Senate majority leader 1929–33.

Watson, Lewis Findlay (R Pa.) April 14, 1819–Aug. 25, 1890; House 1877–79, 1881–83, 1889–Aug. 25, 1890.

Watson, Thomas Edward (D Ga.) Sept. 5, 1856–Sept. 26, 1922; House 1891–93 (Populist); Senate 1921–Sept. 26, 1922.

Watson, Walter Allen (D Va.) Nov. 25, 1867–Dec. 24, 1919; House 1913–Dec. 24, 1919.

Watt, Melvin L. (D N.C.) Aug. 26, 1945– ; House 1993– .

Watterson, Harvey Magee (father of Henry Watterson) (D Tenn.) Nov. 23, 1811–Oct. 1, 1891; House 1839–43.

Watterson, Henry (son of Harvey Magee Watterson, nephew of Stanley Matthews) (D Ky.) Feb. 16, 1840–Dec. 22, 1921; House Aug. 12, 1876–77.

Watts, J. C. (R Okla.) Nov. 18, 195– ; House 1995–2003.

Watts, John (– N.Y.) Aug. 27, 1749–Sept. 3, 1836; House 1793–95.

Watts, John Clarence (D Ky.) July 9, 1902–Sept. 24, 1971; House April 14, 1951–Sept. 24, 1971.

Watts, John Sebrie (R N.M.) Jan. 19, 1816–June 11, 1876; House (Terr. Del.) 1861–63.

Waugh, Daniel Webster (R Ind.) March 7, 1842–March 14, 1921; House 1891–95.

Waxman, Henry Arnold (D Calif.) Sept. 12, 1939– ; House 1975– .

Wayne, Anthony (father of Isaac Wayne) (– Ga.) Jan. 1, 1745–Dec. 15, 1796; House 1791–March 21, 1792.

Wayne, Isaac (son of Anthony Wayne) (– Pa.) 1772–Oct. 25, 1852; House 1823–25.

Wayne, James Moore (J Ga.) 1790–July 5, 1867; House 1829–Jan. 13, 1835; assoc. justice Jan. 14, 1835–July 5, 1867.

Weadock, Thomas Addis Emmet (D Mich.) Jan. 1, 1850–Nov. 18, 1938; House 1891–95.

Weakley, Robert (R Tenn.) July 20, 1764–Feb. 4, 1845; House 1809–11.

Wearin, Otha Donner (D Iowa) Jan. 10, 1903–April 3, 1990; House 1933–39.

Weatherford, Zadoc Lorenzo (D Ala.) Feb. 4, 1888–May 21, 1983; House Nov. 5, 1940–41.

Weaver, Archibald Jerard (grandfather of Phillip Hart Weaver) (R Neb.) April 15, 1843–April 18, 1887; House 1883–87.

Weaver, Claude (D Okla.) March 19, 1867–May 19, 1954; House 1913–15.

Weaver, James Baird (G Iowa) June 12, 1833–Feb. 6, 1912; House 1879–81, 1885–89.

Weaver, James Dorman (R Pa.) Sept. 27, 1920–Nov. 15, 2003; House 1963–65.

Weaver, James Howard (D Ore.) Aug. 8, 1927– ; House 1975–87.

Weaver, Phillip Hart (grandson of Archibald Jerard Weaver) (R Neb.) April 9, 1919–April 16, 1989; House 1955–63.

Weaver, Walter Lowrie (R Ohio) April 1, 1851–May 26, 1909; House 1897–1901.

Weaver, Zebulon (D N.C.) May 12, 1872–Oct. 29, 1948; House 1917–March 1, 1919, March 4, 1919–29, 1931–47.

Webb, Edwin Yates (D N.C.) May 23, 1872–Feb. 7, 1955; House 1903–Nov. 10, 1919.

Webb, William Robert (grandson of Richard Stanford) (D Tenn.) Nov. 11, 1842–Dec. 19, 1926; Senate Jan. 24–March 3, 1913.

Webber, Amos Richard (R Ohio) Jan. 21, 1852–Feb. 25, 1948; House Nov. 8, 1904–07.

Webber, George Washington (R Mich.) Nov. 25, 1825–Jan. 15, 1900; House 1881–83.

Weber, Edward Ford (R Ohio) July 26, 1931– ; House 1981–83.

Weber, John Baptiste (R N.Y.) Sept. 21, 1842–Dec. 18, 1926; House 1885–89.

Weber, John Vincent (R Minn.) July 24, 1952– ; House 1981–93.

Webster, Daniel (W Mass.) Jan. 18, 1782–Oct. 24, 1852; House 1813–17 (Federalist N.H.), 1823–May 30, 1827 (Federalist); Senate May 30, 1827–Feb. 22, 1841 (1827–33 Federalist), 1845–July 22, 1850; secretary of state March 6, 1841–May 8, 1843, July 23, 1850–Oct. 24, 1852.

Webster, Edwin Hanson (UU Md.) March 31, 1829–April 24, 1893; House 1859–July 1865 (1859–61 American Party, 1861–63 Unionist).

Webster, John Stanley (R Wash.) Feb. 22, 1877–Dec. 24, 1962; House 1919–May 8, 1923.

Webster, Taylor (D Ohio) Oct. 1, 1800–April 27, 1876; House 1833–39 (1833–37 Jacksonian).

Wedemeyer, William Walter (R Mich.) March 22, 1873–Jan. 2, 1913; House 1911–Jan. 2, 1913.

Weeks, Charles Sinclair (son of John Wingate Weeks of Mass.) (R Mass.) June 15, 1893–Feb. 7, 1972; Senate Feb. 8–Dec. 19, 1944; secretary of commerce Jan. 21, 1953–Nov. 10, 1958.

Weeks, Edgar (cousin of John Wingate Weeks of Mass.) (R Mich.) Aug. 3, 1839–Dec. 17, 1904; House 1899–1903.

Weeks, John Eliakim (R Vt.) June 14, 1853–Sept. 10, 1949; House 1931–33; Gov. Jan. 6, 1927–Jan. 8, 1931.

Weeks, John Wingate (great-uncle of John Wingate Weeks, below) (J N.H.) March 31, 1781–April 3, 1853; House 1829–33.

Weeks, John Wingate (father of Sinclair Weeks, cousin of Edgar Weeks, great-nephew of John Wingate Weeks, above) (R Mass.) April 11, 1860–July 12, 1926; House 1905–March 4, 1913; Senate 1913–19; secretary of war March 5, 1921–Oct. 13, 1925.

Weeks, Joseph (grandfather of Joseph Weeks Babcock) (D N.H.) Feb. 13, 1773–Aug. 4, 1845; House 1835–39 (1835–37 Jacksonian).

Weems, Capell Lane (R Ohio) July 7, 1860–Jan. 5, 1913; House Nov. 3, 1903–09.

Weems, John Crompton (– Md.) 1778–Jan. 20, 1862; House Feb. 1, 1826–29.

Wefald, Knud (FL Minn.) Nov. 3, 1869–Oct. 25, 1936; House 1923–27.

Weichel, Alvin F. (R Ohio) Sept. 11, 1891–Nov. 27, 1956; House 1943–55; chair House Merchant Marine and Fisheries 1947–49, 1953–55.

Weicker, Lowell Palmer Jr. (R Conn.) May 16, 1931– ; House 1969–71; Senate 1971–89; chair Senate Small Business 1981–87; Gov. Jan. 9, 1991–Jan. 4, 1995.

Weideman, Carl May (D Mich.) March 5, 1898–March 5, 1972; House 1933–35.

Weightman, Richard Hanson (D N.M.) Dec. 28, 1816–Aug. 10, 1861; House (Terr. Del.) 1851–53.

Weiner, Anthony D. (D N.Y.) Sept. 4, 1964– ; House 1999– .

Weis, Jessica McCullough (R N.Y.) July 8, 1901–May 1, 1963; House 1959–63.

Weiss, Samuel Arthur (D Pa.) April 15, 1902–Feb. 1, 1977; House 1941–Jan. 7, 1946.

Weiss, Theodore S. (D N.Y.) Sept. 17, 1927–Sept. 14, 1992; House 1977–Sept. 14, 1992.

Weisse, Charles Herman (D Wis.) Oct. 24, 1866–Oct. 8, 1919; House 1903–11.

Welborn, John (R Mo.) Nov. 20, 1857–Oct. 27, 1907; House 1905–07.

Welch, Adonijah Strong (R Fla.) April 12, 1821–March 14, 1889; Senate June 25, 1868–69.

Welch, Frank (R Neb.) Feb. 10, 1835–Sept. 4, 1878; House 1877–Sept. 4, 1878.

Welch, John (W Ohio) Oct. 28, 1805–Aug. 5, 1891; House 1851–53.

Welch, Philip James (D Mo.) April 4, 1895–April 26, 1963; House 1949–53.

Welch, Richard Joseph (R Calif.) Feb. 13, 1869–Sept. 10, 1949; House Aug. 31, 1926–Sept. 10, 1949; chair House Public Lands 1947–49.

Welch, William Wickham (AP Conn.) Dec. 10, 1818–July 30, 1892; House 1855–57.

Weldon, Dave (R Fla.) Aug. 31, 1953– ; House 1995– .

Weldon, Wayne Curtis "Curt" (R Pa.) July 22, 1947– ; House 1987– .

Welker, Herman (R Idaho) Dec. 11, 1906–Oct. 30, 1957; Senate 1951–57.

Welker, Martin (R Ohio) April 25, 1819–March 15, 1902; House 1865–71.

Wellborn, Marshall Johnson (D Ga.) May 29, 1808–Oct. 16, 1874; House 1849–51.

Wellborn, Olin (D Texas) June 18, 1843–Dec. 6, 1921; House 1879–87.

Weller, Jerry (R Ill.) July 7, 1957– ; House 1995– .

Weller, John B. (D Calif.) Feb. 22, 1812–Aug. 17, 1875; House 1839–45 (Democrat Ohio); Senate Jan. 30, 1852–57; Gov. Jan. 8, 1858–Jan. 9, 1860.

Weller, Luman Hamlin (G Iowa) Aug. 24, 1833–March 2, 1914; House 1883–85.

Weller, Ovington Eugene (R Md.) Jan. 23, 1862–Jan. 5, 1947; Senate 1921–27.

Weller, Royal Hurlburt (D N.Y.) July 2, 1881–March 1, 1929; House 1923–March 1, 1929.

Welling, Milton Holmes (D Utah) Jan. 25, 1876–May 28, 1947; House 1917–21.

Wellington, George Louis (R Md.) Jan. 28, 1852–March 20, 1927; House 1895–97; Senate 1897–1903.

Wells, Alfred (R N.Y.) May 27, 1814–July 18, 1867; House 1859–61.

Wells, Daniel Jr. (D Wis.) July 16, 1808–March 18, 1902; House 1853–57.

Wells, Erastus (D Mo.) Dec. 2, 1823–Oct. 2, 1893; House 1869–77, 1879–81.

Wells, Guilford Wiley (IR Miss.) Feb. 14, 1840–March 21, 1909; House 1875–77.

Wells, John (W N.Y.) July 1, 1817–May 30, 1877; House 1851–53.

Wells, John Sullivan (– N.H.) Oct. 18, 1803–Aug. 1, 1860; Senate Jan. 16–March 3, 1855.

Wells, Owen Augustine (D Wis.) Feb. 4, 1844–Jan. 29, 1935; House 1893–95.

Wells, William Hill (F Del.) Jan. 7, 1769–March 11, 1829; Senate Jan. 17, 1799–Nov. 6, 1804, May 28, 1813–17.

Wellstone, Paul (D Minn.) July 21, 1944–Oct. 25, 2002; Senate 1991– Oct. 25, 2002.

Welsh, George Austin (R Pa.) Aug. 9, 1878–Oct. 22, 1970; House 1923–May 31, 1932.

Weltner, Charles Longstreet (D Ga.) Dec. 17, 1927–Aug. 31, 1992; House 1963–67.

Welty, Benjamin Franklin (D Ohio) Aug. 9, 1870–Oct. 23, 1962; House 1917–21.

Wemple, Edward (D N.Y.) Oct. 23, 1843–Dec. 18, 1920; House 1883–85.

Wendover, Peter Hercules (R N.Y.) Aug. 1, 1768–Sept. 24, 1834; House 1815–21.

Wene, Elmer H. (D N.J.) May 1, 1892–Jan. 25, 1957; House 1937–39, 1941–45.

Wentworth, John (R Ill.) March 5, 1815–Oct. 16, 1888; House 1843–51 (Democrat), 1853–55 (Democrat), 1865–67.

Wentworth, Tappan (W Mass.) Feb. 24, 1802–June 12, 1875; House 1853–55.

Werdel, Thomas Harold (R Calif.) Sept. 13, 1905–Sept. 30, 1966; House 1949–53.

Werner, Theodore B. (D S.D.) June 2, 1892–Jan. 24, 1989; House 1933–37.

Wertz, George M. (R Pa.) July 19, 1856–Nov. 19, 1928; House 1923–25.

West, Charles Franklin (D Ohio) Jan. 12, 1895–Dec. 27, 1955; House 1931–35.

West, George (R N.Y.) Feb. 17, 1823–Sept. 20, 1901; House 1881–83, 1885–89.

West, Joseph Rodman (R La.) Sept. 19, 1822–Oct. 31, 1898; Senate 1871–77.

West, Milton Horace (D Texas) June 30, 1888–Oct. 28, 1948; House April 22, 1933–Oct. 28, 1948.

West, William Stanley (– Ga.) Aug. 23, 1849–Dec. 22, 1914; Senate March 2–Nov. 3, 1914.

Westbrook, John (D Pa.) Jan. 9, 1789–Oct. 8, 1852; House 1841–43.

Westbrook, Theodoric Romeyn (D N.Y.) Nov. 20, 1821–Oct. 6, 1885; House 1853–55.

Westcott, James Diament Jr. (D Fla.) May 10, 1802–Jan. 19, 1880; Senate July 1, 1845–49.

Westerlo, Rensselaer (F N.Y.) April 29, 1776–April 18, 1851; House 1817–19.

Westland, Aldred John (R Wash.) Dec. 14, 1904–Nov. 3, 1982; House 1953–65.

Westmoreland, Lynn A. (R Ga.) April 2, 1950– ; House 2005– .

Wethered, John (W Md.) May 8, 1809–Feb. 15, 1888; House 1843–45.

Wetmore, George Peabody (R R.I.) Aug. 2, 1846–Sept. 11, 1921; Senate 1895–1907, Jan. 22, 1908–13; Gov. May 26, 1885–May 31, 1887.

Wever, John Madison (R N.Y.) Feb. 24, 1847–Sept. 27, 1914; House 1891–95.

Wexler, Robert (D Fla.) Jan. 2, 1961– ; House 1997– .

Weygand, Robert A. (D R.I.) May 10, 1948– ; House 1997–2001.

Weymouth, George Warren (R Mass.) Aug. 25, 1850–Sept. 7, 1910; House 1897–1901.

Whalen, Charles William Jr. (R Ohio) July 31, 1920– ; House 1967–79.

Whaley, Kellian Van Rensalear (UU W.Va.) May 6, 1821–May 20, 1876; House 1861–63 (Unionist Va.), Dec. 7, 1863–67.

Whaley, Richard Smith (D S.C.) July 15, 1874–Nov. 8, 1951; House April 29, 1913–21.

Whalley, John Irving (R Pa.) Sept. 14, 1902–March 8, 1980; House Nov. 8, 1960–73.

Whallon, Reuben (J N.Y.) Dec. 7, 1776–April 15, 1843; House 1833–35.

Wharton, Charles Stuart (R Ill.) April 22, 1875–Sept. 4, 1939; House 1905–07.

Wharton, James Ernest (R N.Y.) Oct. 4, 1899–Jan. 12, 1990; House 1951–65.

Wharton, Jesse (grandfather of Wharton Jackson Green) (R Tenn.) July 29, 1782–July 22, 1833; House 1807–09; Senate March 17, 1814–Oct. 10, 1815.

Wheat, Alan Dupree (D Mo.) Oct. 16, 1951– ; House 1983–95.

Wheat, William Howard (R Ill.) Feb. 19, 1879–Jan. 16, 1944; House 1939–Jan. 16, 1944.

Wheaton, Horace (D N.Y.) Feb. 24, 1803–June 23, 1882; House 1843–47.

Wheaton, Laban (F Mass.) March 13, 1754–March 23, 1846; House 1809–17.

Wheeler, Burton Kendall (D Mont.) Feb. 27, 1882–Jan. 6, 1975; Senate 1923–47.

Wheeler, Charles Kennedy (D Ky.) April 18, 1863–June 15, 1933; House 1897–1903.

Wheeler, Ezra (D Wis.) Dec. 23, 1820–Sept. 19, 1871; House 1863–65.

Wheeler, Frank Willis (R Mich.) March 2, 1853–Aug. 9, 1921; House 1889–91.

Wheeler, Grattan Henry (AMas. N.Y.) Aug. 25, 1783–March 11, 1852; House 1831–33.

Wheeler, Hamilton Kinkaid (R Ill.) Aug. 5, 1848–July 19, 1918; House 1893–95.

Wheeler, Harrison H. (D Mich.) March 22, 1839–July 28, 1896; House 1891–93.

Wheeler, John (D N.Y.) Feb. 11, 1823–April 1, 1906; House 1853–57.

Wheeler, Joseph (D Ala.) Sept. 10, 1836–Jan. 25, 1906; House 1881–June 3, 1882, Jan. 15–March 3, 1883, 1885–April 20, 1900.

Wheeler, Loren Edgar (R Ill.) Oct. 7, 1862–Jan. 8, 1932; House 1915–23, 1925–27.

Wheeler, Nelson Platt (R Pa.) Nov. 4, 1841–March 3, 1920; House 1907–11.

Wheeler, William Almon (R N.Y.) June 30, 1819–June 4, 1887; House 1861–63, 1869–77; vice president 1877–81.

Wheeler, William McDonald (D Ga.) July 11, 1915–May 5, 1989; House 1947–55.

Whelchel, Benjamin Frank (D Ga.) Dec. 16, 1895–May 11, 1954; House 1935–45.

Wherry, Kenneth Spicer (R Neb.) Feb. 28, 1892–Nov. 29, 1951; Senate 1943–Nov. 29, 1951; Senate minority leader 1949–Nov. 29, 1951.

Whipple, Thomas Jr. (– N.H.) 1787–Jan. 23, 1835; House 1821–29.

Whitacre, John Jefferson (D Ohio) Dec. 28, 1860–Dec. 2, 1938; House 1911–15.

Whitaker, John Albert (grandson of Addison Davis James) (D Ky.) Oct. 31, 1901–Dec. 15, 1951; House April 17, 1948–Dec. 15, 1951.

Whitcomb, James (D Ind.) Dec. 1, 1795–Oct. 4, 1852; Senate 1849–Oct. 4, 1852; Gov. Dec. 6, 1843–Dec. 27, 1849.

White, Addison (cousin of John White) (W Ky.) May 1, 1824–Feb. 4, 1909; House 1851–53.

White, Albert Smith (R Ind.) Oct. 24, 1803–Sept. 24, 1864; House 1837–39 (Whig), 1861–63; Senate 1839–45 (Whig).

White, Alexander (– Va.) 1738–Sept. 19, 1804; House 1789–93.

White, Alexander (R Ala.) Oct. 16, 1816–Dec. 13, 1893; House 1851–53 (Whig), 1873–75.

White, Alexander Colwell (R Pa.) Dec. 12, 1833–June 11, 1906; House 1885–87.

White, Allison (D Pa.) Dec. 21, 1816–April 5, 1886; House 1857–59.

White, Bartow (– N.Y.) Nov. 7, 1776–Dec. 12, 1862; House 1825–27.

White, Benjamin (D Maine) May 13, 1790–June 7, 1860; House 1843–45.

White, Campbell Patrick (J N.Y.) Nov. 30, 1787–Feb. 12, 1859; House 1829–35.

White, Cecil Fielding (D Calif.) Dec. 12, 1900–March 29, 1992; House 1949–51.

White, Chilton Allen (D Ohio) Feb. 6, 1826–Dec. 7, 1900; House 1861–65.

White, Compton Ignatius (father of Compton Ignatius White Jr.) (D Idaho) July 31, 1877–March 31, 1956; House 1933–47, 1949–51.

White, Compton Ignatius Jr. (son of Compton Ignatius White) (D Idaho) Dec. 19, 1920–Oct. 19, 1998; House 1963–67.

White, David (– Ky.) 1785–Oct. 19, 1834; House 1823–25.

White, Dudley Allen (R Ohio) Jan. 3, 1901–Oct. 14, 1957; House 1937–41.

White, Edward Douglass Sr. (son of James White, father of Edward Douglass White) (W La.) March 1795–April 18, 1847; House 1829–Nov. 15, 1834 (no party), 1839–43; Gov. Feb. 2, 1835–Feb. 4, 1839.

White, Edward Douglass (grandson of James White, son of Edward Douglas White Sr.) (D La.) Nov. 3, 1845–May 19, 1921; Senate 1891–March 12, 1894; assoc. justice March 12, 1894–Dec. 18, 1910; chief justice Dec. 19, 1910–May 19, 1921.

White, Francis (F Va.) ?–Nov. 1826; House 1813–15.

White, Francis Shelley "Frank" (D Ala.) March 13, 1847–Aug. 1, 1922; Senate May 11, 1914–15.

White, Frederick Edward (D Iowa) Jan. 19, 1844–Jan. 14, 1920; House 1891–93.

White, George (D Ohio) Aug. 21, 1872–Dec. 15, 1953; House 1911–15, 1917–19; chair Dem. Nat. Comm. 1920–21; Gov. Jan. 12, 1931–Jan. 14, 1935.

White, George Elon (R Ill.) March 7, 1848–May 17, 1935; House 1895–99.

White, George Henry (R N.C.) Dec. 18, 1852–Dec. 28, 1918; House 1897–1901.

White, Harry (R Pa.) Jan. 12, 1834–June 23, 1920; House 1877–81.

White, Hays Baxter (R Kan.) Sept. 21, 1855–Sept. 29, 1930; House 1919–29.

White, Hugh (W N.Y.) Dec. 25, 1798–Oct. 6, 1870; House 1845–51.

White, Hugh Lawson (J Tenn.) Oct. 30, 1773–April 10, 1840; Senate Oct. 28, 1825–Jan. 13, 1840 (Oct. 28, 1825–29 no party); elected pres. pro tempore Dec. 3, 1832.

White, James (father of Edward Douglass White Sr., grandfather of Edward Douglass White) (– Tenn.) June 16, 1749–Oct. 1809; House (Terr. Del.) Sept. 3, 1794–June 1, 1796; Cont. Cong. 1786–88 (N.C.).

White, James Bain (R Ind.) June 26, 1835–Oct. 9, 1897; House 1887–89.

White, James Bamford (D Ky.) June 6, 1842–March 25, 1931; House 1901–03.

White, John (cousin of Addison White, uncle of John Daugherty White) (W Ky.) Feb. 14, 1802–Sept. 22, 1845; House 1835–45; Speaker May 31, 1841–43.

White, John Daugherty (nephew of John White) (R Ky.) Jan. 16, 1849–Jan. 5, 1920; House 1875–77, 1881–85.

White, Joseph Livingston (W Ind.) ?–Jan. 12, 1861; House 1841–43.

White, Joseph M. (– Fla.) May 10, 1781–Oct. 19, 1839; House (Terr. Del.) 1825–37.

White, Joseph Worthington (D Ohio) Oct. 2, 1822–Aug. 6, 1892; House 1863–65.

White, Leonard (F Mass.) May 3, 1767–Oct. 10, 1849; House 1811–13.

White, Michael Doherty (R Ind.) Sept. 8, 1827–Feb. 6, 1917; House 1877–79.

White, Milo (R Minn.) Aug. 17, 1830–May 18, 1913; House 1883–87.

White, Phineas (– Vt.) Oct. 30, 1770–July 6, 1847; House 1821–23.

White, Richard Crawford (D Texas) April 29, 1923–Feb. 18, 1998; House 1965–83.

White, Rick (R Wash.) Nov. 6, 1953– ; House 1995–99.

White, Samuel (F Del.) Dec. 1770–Nov. 4, 1809; Senate Feb. 28, 1801–Nov. 4, 1809.

White, Sebastian Harrison (D Colo.) Dec. 24, 1864–Dec. 21, 1945; House Nov. 15, 1927–29.

White, Stephen Mallory (D Calif.) Jan. 19, 1853–Feb. 21, 1901; Senate 1893–99.

White, Stephen Van Culen (R N.Y.) Aug. 1, 1831–Jan. 18, 1913; House 1887–89.

White, Wallace Humphrey Jr. (grandson of William Pierce Frye) (R Maine) Aug. 6, 1877–March 31, 1952; House 1917–31; Senate 1931–49; Senate minority leader 1945–47; Senate majority leader 1947–49; chair Senate Interstate and Foreign Commerce 1947–49.

White, Wilbur McKee (R Ohio) Feb. 22, 1890–Dec. 31, 1973; House 1931–33.

White, William John (R Ohio) Oct. 7, 1850–Feb. 16, 1923; House 1893–95.

Whiteaker, John (D Ore.) May 4, 1820–Oct. 2, 1902; House 1879–81; Gov. March 3, 1859–Sept. 10, 1862.

Whitehead, Joseph (D Va.) Oct. 31, 1867–July 8, 1938; House 1925–31.

Whitehead, Thomas (D Va.) Dec. 27, 1825–July 1, 1901; House 1873–75.

Whitehill, James (son of John Whitehill, nephew of Robert Whitehill) (R Pa.) Jan. 31, 1762–Feb. 26, 1822; House 1813–Sept. 1, 1814.

Whitehill, John (father of James Whitehill, brother of Robert Whitehill) (R Pa.) Dec. 11, 1729–Sept. 16, 1815; House 1803–07.

Whitehill, Robert (brother of John Whitehill, uncle of James Whitehill, great-great-grandfather of John Crain Kunkel) (R Pa.) July 21, 1738–April 8, 1813; House Nov. 7, 1805–April 8, 1813.

Whitehouse, John Osborne (D N.Y.) July 19, 1817–Aug. 24, 1881; House 1873–77.

Whitehurst, George William (R Va.) March 12, 1925– ; House 1969–87.

Whitelaw, Robert Henry (D Mo.) Jan. 30, 1854–July 27, 1937; House Nov. 4, 1890–91.

Whiteley, Richard Henry (R Ga.) Dec. 22, 1830–Sept. 26, 1890; House Dec. 22, 1870–75.

Whiteley, William Gustavus (D Del.) Aug. 7, 1819–April 23, 1886; House 1857–61.

Whitener, Basil Lee (D N.C.) May 14, 1915–March 20, 1989; House 1957–69.

Whiteside, Jenkin (R Tenn.) 1772–Sept. 25, 1822; Senate April 11, 1809–Oct. 8, 1811.

Whiteside, John (R Pa.) 1773–July 28, 1830; House 1815–19.

Whitfield, John Wilkins (D Kan.) March 11, 1818–Oct. 27, 1879; House (Terr. Del.) Dec. 20, 1854–Aug. 1, 1856, Dec. 9, 1856–57.

Whitfield, Wayne Edward (R Ky.) May 25, 1943– ; House 1995– .

Whiting, Justin Rice (D Mich.) Feb. 18, 1847–Jan. 31, 1903; House 1887–95.

Whiting, Richard Henry (uncle of Ira Clifton Copley) (R Ill.) Jan. 17, 1826–May 24, 1888; House 1875–77.

Whiting, William (R Mass.) March 3, 1813–June 29, 1873; House March 4–June 29, 1873.

Whiting, William (R Mass.) May 24, 1841–Jan. 9, 1911; House 1883–89.

Whitley, Charles Orville (D N.C.) Jan. 3, 1927–Oct. 27, 2002; House 1977–Dec. 31, 1986.

Whitley, James Lucius (R N.Y.) May 24, 1872–May 17, 1959; House 1929–35.

Whitman, Ezekiel (F Maine) March 9, 1776–Aug. 1, 1866; House 1809–11 (Mass.), 1817–21 (Mass.), 1821–June 1, 1822.

Whitman, Lemuel (– Conn.) June 8, 1780–Nov. 13, 1841; House 1823–25.

Whitmore, Elias (– N.Y.) March 2, 1772–Dec. 26, 1853; House 1825–27.

Whitmore, George Washington (R Texas) Aug. 26, 1824–Oct. 14, 1876; House March 30, 1870–71.

Whitney, Thomas Richard (AP N.Y.) May 2, 1807–April 12, 1858; House 1855–57.

Whittaker, Robert Russell (R Kan.) Sept. 18, 1939– ; House 1979–91.

Whittemore, Benjamin Franklin (R S.C.) May 18, 1824–Jan. 25, 1894; House July 18, 1868–Feb. 24, 1870.

Whitten, Jamie Lloyd (D Miss.) April 18, 1910–Sept. 9, 1995; House Nov. 4, 1941–95; chair House Appropriations 1978–93.

Whitthorne, Washington Curran (D Tenn.) April 19, 1825–Sept. 21, 1891; House 1871–83, 1887–91; Senate April 16, 1886–87.

Whittington, William Madison (D Miss.) May 4, 1878–Aug. 20, 1962; House 1925–51; chair House Public Works 1949–51.

Whittlesey, Elisha (uncle of William Augustus Whittlesey, cousin of Frederick Whittlesey and Thomas Tucker Whittlesey) (W Ohio) Oct. 19, 1783–Jan. 7, 1863; House 1823–July 9, 1838 (1823–33 no party, 1833–35 Anti-Mason).

Whittlesey, Frederick (cousin of Elisha Whittlesey and Thomas Tucker Whittlesey) (AMas. N.Y.) June 12, 1799–Sept. 19, 1851; House 1831–35.

Whittlesey, Thomas Tucker (cousin of Elisha Whittlesey and Frederick Whittlesey) (D Conn.) Dec. 8, 1798–Aug. 20, 1868; House April 29, 1836–39 (April 29, 1836–37 Jacksonian).

Whittlesey, William Augustus (nephew of Elisha Whittlesey) (D Ohio) July 14, 1796–Nov. 6, 1866; House 1849–51.

Whyte, William Pinkney (D Md.) Aug. 9, 1824–March 17, 1908; Senate July 13, 1868–69, 1875–81, June 8, 1906–March 17, 1908; Gov. Jan. 10, 1872–March 4, 1874.

Wick, William Watson (D Ind.) Feb. 23, 1796–May 19, 1868; House 1839–41, 1845–49.

Wicker, Roger F. (R Miss.) July 5, 1951– ; House 1995– .

Wickersham, James (R Alaska) Aug. 24, 1857–Oct. 24, 1939; House (Terr. Del.) 1909–17, Jan. 7–March 3, 1919, March 1, 1921–March 3, 1921, 1931–33.

Wickersham, Victor Eugene (D Okla.) Feb. 9, 1906–March 15, 1988; House April 1, 1941–47, 1949–57, 1961–65.

Wickes, Eliphalet (R N.Y.) April 1, 1769–June 7, 1850; House 1805–07.

Wickham, Charles Preston (R Ohio) Sept. 15, 1836–March 18, 1925; House 1887–91.

Wickliffe, Charles Anderson (grandfather of Robert Charles Wickliffe and John Crepps Wickliffe Beckham) (U Ky.) June 8, 1788–Oct. 31, 1869; House 1823–33 (1823–27 no party, 1827–33 Jacksonian), 1861–63; Gov. Oct. 5, 1839–June 1, 1840 (Whig); postmaster general Oct. 13, 1841–March 6, 1845.

Wickliffe, Robert Charles (grandson of Charles Anderson Wickliffe, cousin of John Crepps Wickliffe Beckham) (D La.) May 1, 1874–June 11, 1912; House 1909–June 11, 1912.

Widgery, William (R Mass.) about 1753–July 31, 1822; House 1811–13.

Widnall, William Beck (R N.J.) March 17, 1906–Dec. 28, 1983; House Feb. 6, 1950–Dec. 31, 1974.

Wier, Roy William (D Minn.) Feb. 25, 1888–June 27, 1963; House 1949–61.

Wigfall, Louis Tresvant (D Texas) April 21, 1816–Feb. 18, 1874; Senate Dec. 5, 1859–March 23, 1861.

Wiggins, Charles Edward (R Calif.) Dec. 3, 1927–March 2, 2000; House 1967–79.

Wigginton, Peter Dinwiddie (D Calif.) Sept. 6, 1839–July 7, 1890; House 1875–77, Feb. 7, 1878–79.

Wigglesworth, Richard Bowditch (R Mass.) April 25, 1891–Oct. 22, 1960; House Nov. 6, 1928–Nov. 13, 1958.

Wike, Scott (D Ill.) April 6, 1834–Jan. 15, 1901; House 1875–77, 1889–93.

Wilber, David (father of David Forrest Wilber) (R N.Y.) Oct. 5, 1820–April 1, 1890; House 1873–75, 1879–81, 1887–April 1, 1890.

Wilber, David Forrest (son of David Wilber) (R N.Y.) Dec. 7, 1859–Aug. 14, 1928; House 1895–99.

Wilbour, Isaac (R R.I.) April 25, 1763–Oct. 4, 1837; House 1807–09; Gov. May 7, 1806–May 6, 1807 (Democratic Republican).

Wilcox, James Mark (D Fla.) May 21, 1890–Feb. 3, 1956; House 1933–39.

Wilcox, Jeduthun (father of Leonard Wilcox) (F N.H.) Nov. 18, 1768–July 18, 1838; House 1813–17.

Wilcox, John A. (U Miss.) April 18, 1819–Feb. 7, 1864; House 1851–53.

Wilcox, Leonard (son of Jeduthun Wilcox) (D N.H.) Jan. 29, 1799–June 18, 1850; Senate March 1, 1842–43.

Wilcox, Robert William (– Hawaii) Feb. 15, 1855–Oct. 23, 1903; House (Terr. Del.) Nov. 6, 1900–03.

Wilde, Richard Henry (R Ga.) Sept. 24, 1789–Sept. 10, 1847; House 1815–17, Feb. 7–March 3, 1825, Nov. 17, 1827–35.

Wilder, Abel Carter (R Kan.) March 18, 1828–Dec. 22, 1875; House 1863–65.

Wilder, William Henry (R Mass.) May 14, 1855–Sept. 11, 1913; House 1911–Sept. 11, 1913.

Wildman, Zalmon (J Conn.) Feb. 16, 1775–Dec. 10, 1835; House March 4–Dec. 10, 1835.

Wildrick, Isaac (D N.J.) March 3, 1803–March 22, 1892; House 1849–53.

Wiley, Alexander (R Wis.) May 26, 1884–May 26, 1967; Senate 1939–63; chair Senate Judiciary 1947–49; chair Senate Foreign Relations 1953–55.

Wiley, Ariosto Appling (brother of Oliver Cicero Wiley) (D Ala.) Nov. 6, 1848–June 17, 1908; House 1901–June 17, 1908.

Wiley, James Sullivan (D Maine) Jan. 22, 1808–Dec. 21, 1891; House 1847–49.

Wiley, John McClure (D N.Y.) Aug. 11, 1846–Aug. 13, 1912; House 1889–91.

Wiley, Oliver Cicero (brother of Ariosto Appling Wiley) (D Ala.) Jan. 30, 1851–Oct. 18, 1917; House Nov. 3, 1908–09.

Wiley, William Halsted (R N.J.) July 10, 1842–May 2, 1925; House 1903–07, 1909–11.

Wilfley, Xenophon Pierce (D Mo.) March 18, 1871–May 4, 1931; Senate April 30–Nov. 5, 1918.

Wilkin, James Whitney (father of Samuel Jones Wilkin) (R N.Y.) 1762–Feb. 23, 1845; House June 7, 1815–19.

Wilkin, Samuel Jones (son of James Whitney Wilkin) (AJ N.Y.) Dec. 17, 1793–March 11, 1866; House 1831–33.

Wilkins, Beriah (D Ohio) July 10, 1846–June 7, 1905; House 1883–89.

Wilkins, William (D Pa.) Dec. 20, 1779–June 23, 1865; Senate 1831–June 30, 1834 (Jacksonian); House 1843–Feb. 14, 1844; secretary of war Feb. 15, 1844–March 4, 1845.

Wilkinson, Morton Smith (R Minn.) Jan. 22, 1819–Feb. 4, 1894; Senate 1859–65; House 1869–71.

Wilkinson, Theodore Stark (D La.) Dec. 18, 1847–Feb. 1, 1921; House 1887–91.

Willard, Charles Wesley (R Vt.) June 18, 1827–June 8, 1880; House 1869–75.

Willard, George (R Mich.) March 20, 1824–March 26, 1901; House 1873–77.

Willcox, Washington Frederick (D Conn.) Aug. 22, 1834–March 8, 1909; House 1889–93.

Willett, William Forte Jr. (D N.Y.) Nov. 27, 1869–Feb. 12, 1938; House 1907–11.

Willey, Calvin (– Conn.) Sept. 15, 1776–Aug. 23, 1858; Senate May 4, 1825–31.

Willey, Earle Dukes (R Del.) July 21, 1889–March 17, 1950; House 1943–45.

Willey, Waitman Thomas (R W.Va.) Oct. 18, 1811–May 2, 1900; Senate July 9, 1861–63 (Va.), Aug. 4, 1863–71 (Aug. 4, 1863–65 Unionist).

Willford, Albert Clinton (D Iowa) Sept. 21, 1877–March 10, 1937; House 1933–35.

Williams, Abram Pease (R Calif.) Feb. 3, 1832–Oct. 17, 1911; Senate Aug. 4, 1886–87.

Williams, Alpheus Starkey (D Mich.) Sept. 20, 1810–Dec. 21, 1878; House 1875–Dec. 21, 1878.

Williams, Andrew (R N.Y.) Aug. 27, 1828–Oct. 6, 1907; House 1875–79.

Williams, Archibald Hunter Arrington (nephew of Archibald Hunter Arrington) (D N.C.) Oct. 22, 1842–Sept. 5, 1895; House 1891–93.

Williams, Arthur Bruce (R Mich.) Jan. 27, 1872–May 1, 1925; House June 19, 1923–May 1, 1925.

Williams, Benjamin (– N.C.) Jan. 1, 1751–July 20, 1814; House 1793–95; Gov. Nov. 23, 1799–Dec. 6, 1802, Dec. 1, 1807–Dec. 12, 1808 (Democratic Republican).

Williams, Charles Grandison (R Wis.) Oct. 18, 1829–March 30, 1892; House 1873–83.

Williams, Christopher Harris (grandfather of John Sharp Williams) (W Tenn.) Dec. 18, 1798–Nov. 27, 1857; House 1837–43, 1849–53.

Williams, Clyde (D Mo.) Oct. 13, 1873–Nov. 12, 1954; House 1927–29, 1931–43.

Williams, David Rogerson (R S.C.) March 8, 1776–Nov. 17, 1830; House 1805–09, 1811–13; Gov. Dec. 10, 1814–Dec. 5, 1816 (Democrat Republican).

Williams, Elihu Stephen (R Ohio) Jan. 24, 1835–Dec. 1, 1903; House 1887–91.

Williams, George Fred (D Mass.) July 10, 1852–July 11, 1932; House 1891–93.

Williams, George Henry (R Ore.) March 26, 1823–April 4, 1910; Senate 1865–71; attorney general Jan. 10, 1872–May 15, 1875.

Williams, George Howard (R Mo.) Dec. 1, 1871–Nov. 25, 1963; Senate May 25, 1925–Dec. 5, 1926.

Williams, George Short (R Del.) Oct. 21, 1877–Nov. 22, 1961; House 1939–41.

Williams, Guinn (D Texas) April 22, 1871–Jan. 9, 1948; House May 13, 1922–33.

Williams, Harrison Arlington Jr. (D N.J.) Dec. 10, 1919–Nov. 17, 2001; House Nov. 3, 1953–57; Senate 1959–March 11, 1982; chair Senate Labor and Public Welfare 1971–77; chair Senate Human Resources 1977–79; chair Senate Labor and Human Resources 1979–81.

Williams, Henry (D Mass.) Nov. 30, 1805–May 8, 1887; House 1839–41, 1843–45.

Williams, Hezekiah (D Maine) July 28, 1798–Oct. 23, 1856; House 1845–49.

Williams, Isaac Jr. (R N.Y.) April 5, 1777–Nov. 9, 1860; House Dec. 20, 1813–15, 1817–19, 1823–25.

Williams, James (D Del.) Aug. 4, 1825–April 12, 1899; House 1875–79.

Williams, James Douglas (D Ind.) Jan. 16, 1808–Nov. 20, 1880; House 1875–Dec. 1, 1876; Gov. Jan. 8, 1877–Nov. 20, 1880.

Williams, James Robert (D Ill.) Dec. 27, 1850–Nov. 8, 1923; House Dec. 2, 1889–95, 1899–1905.

Williams, James Wray (D Md.) Oct. 8, 1792–Dec. 2, 1842; House 1841–Dec. 2, 1842.

Williams, Jared (– Va.) March 4, 1766–Jan. 2, 1831; House 1819–25.

Williams, Jared Warner (D N.H.) Dec. 22, 1796–Sept. 29, 1864; House 1837–41; Senate Nov. 29, 1853–July 15, 1854; Gov. June 3, 1847–June 7, 1849.

Williams, Jeremiah Norman (D Ala.) May 29, 1829–May 8, 1915; House 1875–79.

Williams, John (F N.Y.) Sept. 1752–July 22, 1806; House 1795–99.

Williams, John (brother of Lewis Williams and Robert Williams, father of Joseph Lanier Williams, cousin of Marmaduke Williams) (R Tenn.) Jan. 29, 1778–Aug. 10, 1837; Senate Oct. 10, 1815–23.

Williams, John (D N.Y.) Jan. 7, 1807–March 26, 1875; House 1855–57.

Williams, John Bell (D Miss.) Dec. 4, 1918–March 25, 1983; House 1947–Jan. 16, 1968; Gov. Jan. 16, 1968–Jan. 18, 1972.

Williams, John James (R Del.) May 17, 1904–Jan. 11, 1988; Senate 1947–Dec. 31, 1970.

Williams, John McKeown Snow (R Mass.) Aug. 13, 1818–March 19, 1886; House 1873–75.

Williams, John Patrick (D Mont.) Oct. 30, 1937– ; House 1979–97.

Williams, John Sharp (grandson of Christopher Harris Williams) (D Miss.) July 30, 1854–Sept. 27, 1932; House 1893–1909; House minority leader 1903–08; Senate 1911–23.

Williams, John Stuart (D Ky.) July 10, 1818–July 17, 1898; Senate 1879–85.

Williams, Jonathan (– Pa.) May 20, 1750–May 16, 1815; House March 4–May 16, 1815.

Williams, Joseph Lanier (son of John Williams of Tenn., nephew of Lewis Williams and Robert Williams) (W Tenn.) Oct. 23, 1810–Dec. 14, 1865; House 1837–43.

Williams, Lawrence Gordon (R Pa.) Sept. 15, 1913–July 13, 1975; House 1967–75.

Williams, Lemuel (F Mass.) June 18, 1747–Nov. 8, 1828; House 1799–1805.

Williams, Lewis (brother of John Williams of Tenn. and Robert Williams, cousin of Marmaduke Williams, uncle of Joseph Lanier Williams) (W N.C.) Feb. 1, 1782–Feb. 23, 1842; House 1815–Feb. 23, 1842 (1815–35 Republican).

Williams, Lyle (R Ohio) Aug. 23, 1942– ; House 1979–85.

Williams, Marmaduke (cousin of John Williams of Tenn., Lewis Williams and Robert Williams) (R N.C.) April 6, 1774–Oct. 29, 1850; House 1803–09.

Williams, Morgan B. (R Pa.) Sept. 17, 1831–Oct. 13, 1903; House 1897–99.

Williams, Nathan (R N.Y.) Dec. 19, 1773–Sept. 25, 1835; House 1805–07.

Williams, Reuel (D Maine) June 2, 1783–July 25, 1862; Senate 1837–Feb. 15, 1843.

Williams, Richard (R Ore.) Nov. 15, 1836–June 19, 1914; House 1877–79.

Williams, Robert (brother of John Williams of Tenn. and Lewis Williams, cousin of Marmaduke Williams, uncle of Joseph Lanier Williams) (R N.C.) July 12, 1773–Jan. 25, 1836; House 1797–1803; Gov. (Miss. Terr.) 1805–09.

Williams, Seward Henry (R Ohio) Nov. 7, 1870–Sept. 2, 1922; House 1915–17.

Williams, Sherrod (W Ky.) 1804–?; House 1835–41.

Williams, Thomas (R Pa.) Aug. 28, 1806–June 16, 1872; House 1863–69.

Williams, Thomas (D Ala.) Aug. 11, 1825–April 13, 1903; House 1879–85.

Williams, Thomas Hickman (D Miss.) Jan. 20, 1801–May 3, 1851; Senate Nov. 12, 1838–39.

Williams, Thomas Hill (R Miss.) 1780–1840; Senate Dec. 10, 1817–29.

Williams, Thomas Scott (F Conn.) June 26, 1777–Dec. 15, 1861; House 1817–19.

Williams, Thomas Sutler (R Ill.) Feb. 14, 1872–April 5, 1940; House 1915–Nov. 11, 1929.

Williams, Thomas Wheeler (W Conn.) Sept. 28, 1789–Dec. 31, 1874; House 1839–43.

Williams, William (D N.Y.) Sept. 6, 1815–Sept. 10, 1876; House 1871–73.

Williams, William (R Ind.) May 11, 1821–April 22, 1896; House 1867–75.

Williams, William Brewster (R Mich.) July 28, 1826–March 4, 1905; House Dec. 1, 1873–77.

Williams, William Elza (D Ill.) May 5, 1857–Sept. 13, 1921; House 1899–1901, 1913–17.

Williams, William Robert (R N.Y.) Aug. 11, 1884–May 9, 1972; House 1951–59.

Williamson, Ben Mitchell (D Ky.) Oct. 16, 1864–June 23, 1941; Senate Dec. 1, 1930–31.

Williamson, Hugh (F N.C.) Dec. 5, 1735–May 22, 1819; House March 19, 1790–93; Cont. Cong. 1782–85, 1788.

Williamson, John Newton (R Ore.) Nov. 8, 1855–Aug. 29, 1943; House 1903–07.

Williamson, William (R S.D.) Oct. 7, 1875–July 15, 1972; House 1921–33.

Williamson, William Durkee (– Maine) July 31, 1779–May 27, 1846; House 1821–23; Gov. May 29–Dec. 25, 1821.

Willie, Asa Hoxie (D Texas) Oct. 11, 1829–March 16, 1899; House 1873–75.

Willis, Albert Shelby (D Ky.) Jan. 22, 1843–Jan. 6, 1897; House 1877–87.

Willis, Benjamin Albertson (D N.Y.) March 24, 1840–Oct. 14, 1886; House 1875–79.

Willis, Edwin Edward (D La.) Oct. 2, 1904–Oct. 24, 1972; House 1949–69; chair House Un-American Activities 1963–69.

Willis, Francis (– Ga.) Jan. 5, 1745–Jan. 25, 1829; House 1791–93.

Willis, Frank Bartlett (R Ohio) Dec. 28, 1871–March 30, 1928; House 1911–Jan. 9, 1915; Senate Jan. 14, 1921–March 30, 1928; Gov. Jan. 11, 1915–Jan. 8, 1917.

Willis, Jonathan Spencer (R Del.) April 5, 1830–Nov. 24, 1903; House 1895–97.

Willis, Raymond Eugene (R Ind.) Aug. 11, 1875–March 21, 1956; Senate 1941–47.

Willits, Edwin (R Mich.) April 24, 1830–Oct. 22, 1896; House 1877–83.

Willoughby, Westel Jr. (R N.Y.) Nov. 20, 1769–Oct. 3, 1844; House Dec. 13, 1815–17.

Wilmot, David (R Pa.) Jan. 20, 1814–March 16, 1868; House 1845–51 (Democrat); Senate March 14, 1861–63.

Wilshire, William Wallace (D Ark.) Sept. 8, 1830–Aug. 19, 1888; House 1873–June 16, 1874 (Republican), 1875–77.

Wilson, Alexander (R Va.) ?–?; House Dec. 4, 1804–09.

Wilson, Benjamin (D W.Va.) April 30, 1825–April 26, 1901; House 1875–83.

Wilson, Charles (D Texas) June 1, 1933– ; House 1973–Oct. 8, 1996.

Wilson, Charles Herbert (D Calif.) Feb. 15, 1917–July 21, 1984; House 1963–81.

Wilson, Earl (R Ind.) April 18, 1906–April 27, 1990; House 1941–59, 1961–65.

Wilson, Edgar (Sil.R Idaho) Feb. 25, 1861–Jan. 3, 1915; House 1895–97 (Republican), 1899–1901.

Wilson, Edgar Campbell (son of Thomas Wilson of Va., father of Eugene McLanahan Wilson) (AJ Va.) Oct. 18, 1800–April 24, 1860; House 1833–35.

Wilson, Emmett (grandson of Augustus Emmett Maxwell) (D Fla.) Sept. 17, 1882–May 29, 1918; House 1913–17.

Wilson, Ephraim King (father of Ephraim King Wilson, below) (J Md.) Sept. 15, 1771–Jan. 2, 1834; House 1827–31 (1827–29 no party).

Wilson, Ephraim King (son of Ephraim King Wilson, above) (D Md.) Dec. 22, 1821–Feb. 24, 1891; House 1873–75; Senate 1885–Feb. 24, 1891.

Wilson, Eugene McLanahan (son of Edgar Campbell Wilson, grandson of Thomas Wilson of Va., great-grandson of Isaac Griffin) (D Minn.) Dec. 25, 1833–April 10, 1890; House 1869–71.

Wilson, Francis Henry (R N.Y.) Feb. 11, 1844–Sept. 25, 1910; House 1895–Sept. 30, 1897.

Wilson, Frank Eugene (D N.Y.) Dec. 22, 1857–July 12, 1935; House 1899–1905, 1911–15.

Wilson, George Allison (R Iowa) April 1, 1884–Sept. 8, 1953; Senate Jan. 14, 1943–49; Gov. Jan. 12, 1939–Jan. 14, 1943.

Wilson, George Howard (D Okla.) Aug. 21, 1905–July 16, 1985; House 1949–51.

Wilson, George Washington (R Ohio) Feb. 22, 1840–Nov. 27, 1909; House 1893–97.

Wilson, Heather A. (R N.M.) Dec. 30, 1960– ; House June 25, 1998– .

Wilson, Henry (– Pa.) 1778–Aug. 14, 1826; House 1823–Aug. 14, 1826.

Wilson, Henry (R Mass.) Feb. 16, 1812–Nov. 22, 1875; Senate Jan. 31, 1855–73 (1855–59 Free-Soiler/American Party/Democrat); vice president 1873–Nov. 22, 1875.

Wilson, Isaac (– N.Y.) June 25, 1780–Oct. 25, 1848; House 1823–Jan. 7, 1824.

Wilson, James (father of James Wilson, below) (F N.H.) Aug. 16, 1766–Jan. 4, 1839; House 1809–11.

Wilson, James (son of James Wilson, above) (W N.H.) March 18, 1797–May 29, 1881; House 1847–Sept. 9, 1850.

Wilson, James (– Pa.) April 28, 1779–July 19, 1868; House 1823–39.

Wilson, James (father of John Lockwood Wilson) (R Ind.) April 9, 1825–Aug. 8, 1867; House 1857–61.

Wilson, James (R Iowa) Aug. 16, 1835–Aug. 26, 1920; House 1873–77, 1883–85; secretary of agriculture March 6, 1897–March 5, 1913.

Wilson, James Clifton (D Texas) June 21, 1874–Aug. 3, 1951; House 1917–19.

Wilson, James Falconer (R Iowa) Oct. 19, 1828–April 22, 1895; House Oct. 8, 1861–69; Senate 1883–95.

Wilson, James Jefferson (R N.J.) 1775–July 28, 1834; Senate 1815–Jan. 8, 1821.

Wilson, Jeremiah Morrow (R Ind.) Nov. 25, 1828–Sept. 24, 1901; House 1871–75.

Wilson, John (– S.C.) Aug. 11, 1773–Aug. 13, 1828; House 1821–27.

Wilson, John (F Mass.) Jan. 10, 1777–Aug. 9, 1848; House 1813–15, 1817–19.

Wilson, John Frank (D Ariz.) May 7, 1846–April 7, 1911; House (Terr. Del.) 1899–1901, 1903–05.

Wilson, John Haden (D Pa.) Aug. 20, 1867–Jan. 28, 1946; House 1919–21.

Wilson, John Henry (R Ky.) Jan. 30, 1846–Jan. 14, 1923; House 1889–93.

Wilson, John Lockwood (son of James Wilson of Ind.) (R Wash.) Aug. 7, 1850–Nov. 6, 1912; House Nov. 20, 1889–Feb. 18, 1895; Senate Feb. 19, 1895–99.

Wilson, John Thomas (R Ohio) April 16, 1811–Oct. 6, 1891; House 1867–73.

Wilson, Addison Graves "Joe" (R S.C.) July 31, 1947– ; House Dec. 18, 2001– .

Wilson, Joseph Franklin (D Texas) March 18, 1901–Oct. 13, 1968; House 1947–55.

Wilson, Joseph Gardner (cousin of James Willis Nesmith) (R Ore.) Dec. 13, 1826–July 2, 1873; House March 4–July 2, 1873.

Wilson, Nathan (R N.Y.) Dec. 23, 1758–July 25, 1834; House June 3, 1808–09.

Wilson, Pete (R Calif.) Aug. 23, 1933– ; Senate 1983–Jan. 7, 1991; Gov. Jan. 7, 1991–Jan. 4, 1999.

Wilson, Riley Joseph (D La.) Nov. 12, 1871–Feb. 23, 1946; House 1915–37.

Wilson, Robert (U Mo.) Nov. 1803–May 10, 1870; Senate Jan. 17, 1862–Nov. 13, 1863.

Wilson, Robert Carlton (R Calif.) April 5, 1916–Aug. 12, 1999; House 1953–81.

Wilson, Robert Patterson Clark (D Mo.) Aug. 8, 1834–Dec. 21, 1916; House Dec. 2, 1889–93.

Wilson, Stanyarne (D S.C.) Jan. 10, 1860–Feb. 14, 1928; House 1895–1901.

Wilson, Stephen Fowler (R Pa.) Sept. 4, 1821–March 30, 1897; House 1865–69.

Wilson, Thomas (father of Edgar Campbell Wilson, grandfather of Eugene McLanahan Wilson) (F Va.) Sept. 11, 1765–Jan. 24, 1826; House 1811–13.

Wilson, Thomas (R Pa.) 1772–Oct. 4, 1824; House May 4, 1813–17.

Wilson, Thomas (D Minn.) May 16, 1827–April 3, 1910; House 1887–89.

Wilson, Thomas Webber (D Miss.) Jan. 24, 1893–Jan. 31, 1948; House 1923–29.

Wilson, William (R Pa.) ?–?; House 1815–19.

Wilson, William (– Ohio) March 19, 1773–June 6, 1827; House 1823–June 6, 1827.

Wilson, William Bauchop (D Pa.) April 2, 1862–May 25, 1934; House 1907–13; secretary of labor March 4, 1913–March 4, 1921.

Wilson, William Edward (D Ind.) March 9, 1870–Sept. 29, 1948; House 1923–25.

Wilson, William Henry (R Pa.) Dec. 6, 1877–Aug. 11, 1937; House 1935–37.

Wilson, William Lyne (D W.Va.) May 3, 1843–Oct. 17, 1900; House 1883–95; postmaster general April 4, 1895–March 5, 1897.

Wilson, William Warfield (R Ill.) March 2, 1868–July 22, 1942; House 1903–13, 1915–21.

Winans, Edwin Baruch (D Mich.) May 16, 1826–July 4, 1894; House 1883–87; Gov. Jan. 1, 1891–Jan. 1, 1893.

Winans, James January (R Ohio) June 7, 1818–April 28, 1879; House 1869–71.

Winans, John (D Wis.) Sept. 27, 1831–Jan. 17, 1907; House 1883–85.

Winchester, Boyd (D Ky.) Sept. 23, 1836–May 18, 1923; House 1869–73.

Windom, William (R Minn.) May 10, 1827–Jan. 29, 1891; House 1859–69; Senate July 15, 1870–Jan. 22, 1871, March 4, 1871–March 7, 1881, Nov. 15, 1881–83; secretary of the Treasury March 8–Nov. 13, 1881, March 7, 1889–Jan. 29, 1891.

Winfield, Charles Henry (D N.Y.) April 22, 1822–June 10, 1888; House 1863–67.

Wing, Austin Eli (– Mich.) Feb. 3, 1792–Aug. 27, 1849; House (Terr. Del.) 1825–29, 1831–33.

Wingate, Joseph Ferdinand (D Maine) June 29, 1786–?; House 1827–31.

Wingate, Paine (– N.H.) May 14, 1739–March 7, 1838; Senate 1789–93; House 1793–95; Cont. Cong. 1788.

Wingo, Effiegene Locke (widow of Otis Theodore Wingo, great-great-great-granddaughter of Matthew Locke) (D Ark.) April 13, 1883–Sept. 19, 1962; House Nov. 4, 1930–33.

Wingo, Otis Theodore (husband of Effiegene Locke Wingo) (D Ark.) June 18, 1877–Oct. 21, 1930; House 1913–Oct. 21, 1930.

Winn, Edward Lawrence "Larry" Jr. (R Kan.) Aug. 22, 1919– ; House 1967–85.

Winn, Richard (R S.C.) 1750–Dec. 19, 1818; House 1793–97 (1793–95 no party), Jan. 24, 1803–13.

Winn, Thomas Elisha (D Ga.) May 21, 1839–June 5, 1925; House 1891–93.

Winslow, Samuel Ellsworth (R Mass.) April 11, 1862–July 11, 1940; House 1913–25.

Winslow, Warren (D N.C.) Jan. 1, 1810–Aug. 16, 1862; House 1855–61; Gov. Dec. 6, 1854–Jan. 1, 1855.

Winstead, William Arthur (D Miss.) Jan. 6, 1904–March 4, 1995; House 1943–65.

Winston, Joseph (R N.C.) June 17, 1746–April 21, 1815; House 1793–95 (no party), 1803–07.

Winter, Charles Edwin (R Wyo.) Sept. 13, 1870–April 22, 1948; House 1923–29.

Winter, Elisha I. (F N.Y.) July 15, 1781–June 30, 1849; House 1813–15.

Winter, Thomas Daniel (R Kan.) July 7, 1896–Nov. 7, 1951; House 1939–47.

Winthrop, Robert Charles (W Mass.) May 12, 1809–Nov. 16, 1894; House Nov. 9, 1840–May 25, 1842, Nov. 29, 1842–July 30, 1850; Senate July 30, 1850–Feb. 1, 1851; Speaker Dec. 6, 1847–49.

Wirth, Timothy Endicott (D Colo.) Sept. 22, 1939– ; House 1975–87; Senate 1987–93.

Wise, George Douglas (cousin of John Sergeant Wise and Richard Alsop Wise, nephew of Henry Alexander Wise) (D Va.) June 4, 1831–Feb. 4, 1898; House 1881–April 10, 1890, 1891–95.

Wise, Henry Alexander (father of John Sergeant Wise and Richard Alsop Wise, uncle of George Douglas Wise, son-in-law of John Sergeant) (D Va.) Dec. 3, 1806–Sept. 12, 1876; House 1833–Feb. 12, 1844 (1833–37 Jacksonian, 1837–43 Whig); Gov. Jan. 1, 1856–Dec. 31, 1859.

Wise, James Walter (D Ga.) March 3, 1868–Sept. 8, 1925; House 1915–25.

Wise, John Sergeant (son of Henry Alexander Wise, grandson of John Sergeant, brother of Richard Alsop Wise, cousin of George Douglas Wise) (Read. Va.) Dec. 27, 1846–May 12, 1913; House 1883–85.

Wise, Morgan Ringland (D Pa.) June 7, 1825–April 13, 1903; House 1879–83.

Wise, Richard Alsop (son of Henry Alexander Wise, grandson of John Sergeant, brother of John Sergeant Wise, cousin of George Douglas Wise) (R Va.) Sept. 2, 1843–Dec. 21, 1900; House April 26, 1898–99, March 12–Dec. 21, 1900.

Wise, Robert Ellsworth Jr. "Bob" (D W.Va.) Jan. 6, 1948– ; House 1983–2001; Gov. Jan. 15, 2001–Jan. 17, 2005 .

Witcher, John Seashoal (R W.Va.) July 15, 1839–July 8, 1906; House 1869–71.

Witherell, James (R Vt.) June 16, 1759–Jan. 9, 1838; House 1807–May 1, 1808.

Withers, Garrett Lee (D Ky.) June 21, 1884–April 30, 1953; Senate Jan. 20, 1949–Nov. 26, 1950; House Aug. 2, 1952–April 30, 1953.

Withers, Robert Enoch (cousin of Thomas Withers Chinn) (D Va.) Sept. 18, 1821–Sept. 21, 1907; Senate 1875–81.

Witherspoon, Robert (great-great-grandfather of Robert Witherspoon Hemphill) (R S.C.) Jan. 29, 1767–Oct. 11, 1837; House 1809–11.

Witherspoon, Samuel Andrew (D Miss.) May 4, 1855–Nov. 24, 1915; House 1911–Nov. 24, 1915.

Withrow, Gardner Robert (R Wis.) Oct. 5, 1892–Sept. 23, 1964; House 1931–39 (1931–35 Republican, 1935–39 Progressive), 1949–61.

Witte, William Henry (D Pa.) Oct. 4, 1817–Nov. 24, 1876; House 1853–55.

Wofford, Harris Llewellyn (D Pa.) April 9, 1926– ; Senate May 9, 1991–95.

Wofford, Thomas Albert (D S.C.) Sept. 27, 1908–Feb. 25, 1978; Senate April 5–Nov. 6, 1956.

Wolcott, Edward Oliver (R Colo.) March 26, 1848–March 1, 1905; Senate 1889–1901.

Wolcott, Jesse Paine (R Mich.) March 3, 1893–Jan. 28, 1969; House 1931–57; chair House Banking and Currency 1947–49, 1953–55.

Wolcott, Josiah Oliver (D Del.) Oct. 31, 1877–Nov. 11, 1938; Senate 1917–July 2, 1921.

Wold, John Schiller (R Wyo.) Aug. 31, 1916– ; House 1969–71.

Wolf, Frank Rudolph (R Va.) Jan. 30, 1939– ; House 1981– .

Wolf, George (– Pa.) Aug. 12, 1777–March 11, 1840; House Dec. 9, 1824–29; Gov. Dec. 15, 1829–Dec. 15, 1835 (Jacksonian).

Wolf, Harry Benjamin (D Md.) June 16, 1880–Feb. 17, 1944; House 1907–09.

Wolf, Leonard George (D Iowa) Oct. 29, 1925–March 28, 1970; House 1959–61.

Wolf, William Penn (R Iowa) Dec. 1, 1833–Sept. 19, 1896; House Dec. 6, 1870–71.

Wolfe, Simeon Kalfius (D Ind.) Feb. 14, 1824–Nov. 18, 1888; House 1873–75.

Wolfenden, James (R Pa.) July 25, 1889–April 8, 1949; House Nov. 6, 1928–47.

Wolff, Joseph Scott (D Mo.) June 14, 1878–Feb. 27, 1958; House 1923–25.

Wolff, Lester Lionel (D N.Y.) Jan. 4, 1919– ; House 1965–81.

Wolford, Frank Lane (D Ky.) Sept. 2, 1817–Aug. 2, 1895; House 1883–87.

Wolpe, Howard Eliot III (D Mich.) Nov. 2, 1939– ; House 1979–93.

Wolverton, Charles Anderson (R N.J.) Oct. 24, 1880–May 16, 1969; House 1927–59; chair House Interstate and Foreign Commerce 1947–49, 1953–55.

Wolverton, John Marshall (R W.Va.) Jan. 31, 1872–Aug. 19, 1944; House 1925–27, 1929–31.

Wolverton, Simon Peter (D Pa.) Jan. 28, 1837–Oct. 25, 1910; House 1891–95.

Won Pat, Antonio Borja (D Guam) Dec. 10, 1908–May 1, 1987; House (Del.) 1973–85.

Wood, Abiel (R Mass.) July 22, 1772–Oct. 26, 1834; House 1813–15.

Wood, Alan Jr. (nephew of John Wood) (R Pa.) July 6, 1834–Oct. 31, 1902; House 1875–77.

Wood, Amos Eastman (D Ohio) Jan. 2, 1810–Nov. 19, 1850; House Dec. 3, 1849–Nov. 19, 1850.

Wood, Benjamin (brother of Fernando Wood) (D N.Y.) Oct. 13, 1820–Feb. 21, 1900; House 1861–65, 1881–83.

Wood, Benson (R Ill.) March 31, 1839–Aug. 27, 1915; House 1895–97.

Wood, Bradford Ripley (D N.Y.) Sept. 3, 1800–Sept. 26, 1889; House 1845–47.

Wood, Ernest Edward (D Mo.) Aug. 24, 1875–Jan. 10, 1952; House 1905–June 23, 1906.

Wood, Fernando (brother of Benjamin Wood) (D N.Y.) June 14, 1812–Feb. 14, 1881; House 1841–43, 1863–65, 1867–Feb. 14, 1881.

Wood, Ira Wells (R N.J.) June 19, 1856–Oct. 5, 1931; House Nov. 8, 1904–13.

Wood, John (uncle of Alan Wood Jr.) (R Pa.) Sept. 6, 1816–May 28, 1898; House 1859–61.

Wood, John Jacob (– N.Y.) Feb. 16, 1784–May 20, 1874; House 1827–29.

Wood, John M. (R Maine) Nov. 17, 1813–Dec. 24, 1864; House 1855–59.

Wood, John Stephens (D Ga.) Feb. 8, 1885–Sept. 12, 1968; House 1931–35, 1945–53; chair House Un-American Activities 1949–53.

Wood, John Travers (R Idaho) Nov. 25, 1878–Nov. 2, 1954; House 1951–53.

Wood, Reuben Terrell (D Mo.) Aug. 7, 1884–July 16, 1955; House 1933–41.

Wood, Silas (– N.Y.) Sept. 14, 1769–March 2, 1847; House 1819–29.

Wood, Thomas Jefferson (D Ind.) Sept. 30, 1844–Oct. 13, 1908; House 1883–85.

Wood, Walter Abbott (R N.Y.) Oct. 23, 1815–Jan. 15, 1892; House 1879–83.

Wood, William Robert (R Ind.) Jan. 5, 1861–March 7, 1933; House 1915–33.

Woodard, Frederick Augustus (D N.C.) Feb. 12, 1854–May 8, 1915; House 1893–97.

Woodbridge, Frederick Enoch (R Vt.) Aug. 29, 1818–April 25, 1888; House 1863–69.

Woodbridge, William (W Mich.) Aug. 20, 1780–Oct. 20, 1861; House (no party Terr. Del.) 1819–Aug. 9, 1820; Senate 1841–47; Gov. Jan. 7, 1840–Feb. 23, 1841.

Woodburn, William (R Nev.) April 14, 1838–Jan. 15, 1915; House 1875–77, 1885–89.

Woodbury, Levi (D N.H.) Dec. 22, 1789–Sept. 4, 1851; Senate March 16, 1825–31 (no party), 1841–Nov. 20, 1845; Gov. June 5, 1823–June 2, 1824 (Democratic Republican); secretary of the navy May 23, 1831–June 30, 1834; secretary of the Treasury July 1, 1834–March 2, 1841; assoc. justice Sept. 23, 1845–Sept. 4, 1851.

Woodcock, David (– N.Y.) 1785–Sept. 18, 1835; House 1821–23, 1827–29.

Woodford, Stewart Lyndon (R N.Y.) Sept. 3, 1835–Feb. 14, 1913; House 1873–July 1, 1874.

Woodhouse, Chase Going (D Conn.) 1890–Dec. 12, 1984; House 1945–47, 1949–51.

Woodman, Charles Walhart (R Ill.) March 11, 1844–March 18, 1898; House 1895–97.

Woodruff, George Catlin (D Conn.) Dec. 1, 1805–Nov. 21, 1885; House 1861–63.

Woodruff, John (R Conn.) Feb. 12, 1826–May 20, 1868; House 1855–57 (American Party), 1859–61.

Woodruff, Roy Orchard (R Mich.) March 14, 1876–Feb. 12, 1953; House 1913–15 (Progressive), 1921–53.

Woodruff, Thomas M. (AP N.Y.) May 3, 1804–March 28, 1855; House 1845–47.

Woodrum, Clifton Alexander (D Va.) April 27, 1887–Oct. 6, 1950; House 1923–Dec. 31, 1945.

Woods, Frank Plowman (R Iowa) Dec. 11, 1868–April 25, 1944; House 1909–19.

Woods, Henry (brother of John Woods born in 1761) (F Pa.) 1764–1826; House 1799–1803.

Woods, James Pleasant (D Va.) Feb. 4, 1868–July 7, 1948; House Feb. 25, 1919–23.

Woods, John (brother of Henry Woods) (F Pa.) 1761–Dec. 16, 1816; elected to the House for the term beginning 1815 but never attended or qualified.

Woods, John (– Ohio) Oct. 18, 1794–July 30, 1855; House 1825–29.

Woods, Samuel Davis (R Calif.) Sept. 19, 1845–Dec. 24, 1915; House Dec. 3, 1900–03.

Woods, William (– N.Y.) 1790–Aug. 7, 1837; House Nov. 3, 1823–25.

Woodson, Samuel Hughes (father of Samuel Hughes Woodson, below) (– Ky.) Sept. 15, 1777–July 28, 1827; House 1821–23.

Woodson, Samuel Hughes (son of Samuel Hughes Woodson, above) (AP Mo.) Oct. 24, 1815–June 23, 1881; House 1857–61.

Woodward, George Washington (D Pa.) March 26, 1809–May 10, 1875; House Nov. 21, 1867–71.

Woodward, Gilbert Motier (D Wis.) Dec. 25, 1835–March 13, 1913; House 1883–85.

Woodward, Joseph Addison (son of William Woodward) (D S.C.) April 11, 1806–Aug. 3, 1885; House 1843–53.

Woodward, William (father of Joseph Addison Woodward) (R S.C.) ?–?; House 1815–17.

Woodworth, James Hutchinson (R Ill.) Dec. 4, 1804–March 26, 1869; House 1855–57.

Woodworth, Laurin Dewey (R Ohio) Sept. 10, 1837–March 13, 1897; House 1873–77.

Woodworth, William W. (D N.Y.) March 16, 1807–Feb. 13, 1873; House 1845–47.

Woodyard, Harry Chapman (R W.Va.) Nov. 13, 1867–June 21, 1929; House 1903–11, Nov. 7, 1916–23, 1925–27.

Woolsey, Lynn (D Calif.) Nov. 3, 1937– ; House 1993– .

Woomer, Ephraim Milton (R Pa.) Jan. 14, 1844–Nov. 29, 1897; House 1893–97.

Wooten, Dudley Goodall (D Texas) June 19, 1860–Feb. 7, 1929; House July 13, 1901–03.

Worcester, Samuel Thomas (R Ohio) Aug. 30, 1804–Dec. 6, 1882; House July 4, 1861–63.

Word, Thomas Jefferson (W Miss.) ?–?; House May 30, 1838–39.

Works, John Downey (R Calif.) March 29, 1847–June 6, 1928; Senate 1911–17.

Worley, Francis Eugene (D Texas) Oct. 10, 1908–Dec. 17, 1974; House 1941–April 3, 1950.

Worman, Ludwig (F Pa.) 1761–Oct. 17, 1822; House 1821–Oct. 17, 1822.

Wortendyke, Jacob Reynier (D N.J.) Nov. 27, 1818–Nov. 7, 1868; House 1857–59.

Worthington, Henry Gaither (R Nev.) Feb. 9, 1828–July 29, 1909; House Oct. 31, 1864–65.

Worthington, John Tolley Hood (D Md.) Nov. 1, 1788–April 27, 1849; House 1831–33 (Jacksonian), 1837–41.

Worthington, Nicholas Ellsworth (D Ill.) March 30, 1836–March 4, 1916; House 1883–87.

Worthington, Thomas (R Ohio) July 16, 1773–June 20, 1827; Senate April 1, 1803–07, Dec. 15, 1810–Dec. 1, 1814; Gov. Dec. 8, 1814–Dec. 14, 1818 (Democratic Republican).

Worthington, Thomas Contee (nephew of Benjamin Contee) (– Md.) Nov. 25, 1782–April 12, 1847; House 1825–27.

Wortley, George Cornelius (R N.Y.) Dec. 8, 1926– ; House 1981–89.

Wren, Thomas (R Nev.) Jan. 2, 1826–Feb. 5, 1904; House 1877–79.

Wright, Ashley Bascom (R Mass.) May 25, 1841–Aug. 14, 1897; House 1893–Aug. 14, 1897.

Wright, Augustus Romaldus (D Ga.) June 16, 1813–March 31, 1891; House 1857–59.

Wright, Charles Frederick (brother of Myron Benjamin Wright) (R Pa.) May 3, 1856–Nov. 10, 1925; House 1899–1905.

Wright, Daniel Boone (D Miss.) Feb. 17, 1812–Dec. 27, 1887; House 1853–57.

Wright, Edwin Ruthvin Vincent (D N.J.) Jan. 2, 1812–Jan. 21, 1871; House 1865–67.

Wright, George Grover (brother of Joseph Albert Wright) (R Iowa) March 24, 1820–Jan. 11, 1896; Senate 1871–77.

Wright, George Washington (I Calif.) June 4, 1816–April 7, 1885; House Sept. 11, 1850–51.

Wright, Hendrick Bradley (G Pa.) April 24, 1808–Sept. 2, 1881; House 1853–55 (Democrat), July 4, 1861–63 (Democrat), 1877–81 (1877–79 Democrat).

Wright, James Assion (D Pa.) Aug. 11, 1902–Nov. 7, 1963; House 1941–45.

Wright, James Claude Jr. (D Texas) Dec. 22, 1922– ; House 1955–June 30, 1989; House majority leader 1977–87; Speaker Jan. 6, 1987–June 6, 1989.

Wright, John Crafts (– Ohio) Aug. 17, 1783–Feb. 13, 1861; House 1823–29.

Wright, John Vines (D Tenn.) June 28, 1828–June 11, 1908; House 1855–61.

Wright, Joseph Albert (brother of George Grover Wright) (U Ind.) April 17, 1810–May 11, 1867; House 1843–45 (Democrat); Senate Feb. 24, 1862–Jan. 14, 1863; Gov. Dec. 5, 1849–Jan. 12, 1857.

Wright, Myron Benjamin (brother of Charles Frederick Wright) (R Pa.) June 12, 1847–Nov. 13, 1894; House 1889–Nov. 13, 1894.

Wright, Robert (R Md.) Nov. 20, 1752–Sept. 7, 1826; Senate Nov. 19, 1801–Nov. 12, 1806; House Nov. 29, 1810–17, 1821–23; Gov. Nov. 12, 1806–May 6, 1809 (Democratic Republican).

Wright, Samuel Gardiner (W N.J.) Nov. 18, 1781–July 30, 1845; House March 4–July 30, 1845.

Wright, Silas Jr. (J N.Y.) May 24, 1795–Aug. 27, 1847; House 1827–Feb. 16, 1829 (no party); Senate Jan. 4, 1833–Nov. 26, 1844; Gov. Jan. 1, 1845–Jan. 1, 1847.

Wright, William (D N.J.) Nov. 13, 1794–Nov. 1, 1866; House 1843–47 (Whig); Senate 1853–59, 1863–Nov. 1, 1866.

Wright, William Carter (D Ga.) Jan. 6, 1866–June 11, 1933; House Jan. 24, 1918–33.

Wu, David (D Ore.) April 8, 1955– ; House 1999– .

Wurts, John (– Pa.) Aug. 13, 1792–April 23, 1861; House 1825–27.

Wurzbach, Harry McLeary (uncle of Robert Christian Eckhardt) (R Texas) May 19, 1874–Nov. 6, 1931; House 1921–29, Feb. 10, 1930–Nov. 6, 1931.

Wyant, Adam Martin (R Pa.) Sept. 15, 1869–Jan. 5, 1935; House 1921–33.

Wyatt, Joseph Peyton Jr. (D Texas) Oct. 12, 1941– ; House 1979–81.

Wyatt, Wendell (R Ore.) June 15, 1917– ; House Nov. 3, 1964–75.

Wyden, Ronald Lee (D Ore.) May 3, 1949– ; House 1981–Feb. 5, 1996; Senate Feb. 6, 1996– .

Wydler, John Waldemar (R N.Y.) June 9, 1924–Aug. 4, 1987; House 1963–81.

Wylie, Chalmers Pangburn (R Ohio) Nov. 23, 1920–Aug. 14, 1998; House 1967–93.

Wyman, Louis Crosby (R N.H.) March 16, 1917–May 5, 2002; House 1963–65, 1967–Dec. 31, 1974; Senate Dec. 31, 1974–75.

Wynkoop, Henry (– Pa.) March 2, 1737–March 25, 1816; House 1789–91; Cont. Cong. 1779–82.

Wynn, Albert Russell (D Md.) Sept. 10, 1951– ; House 1993– .

Wynn, William Joseph (D Calif.) June 12, 1860–Jan. 4, 1935; House 1903–05.

Wynns, Thomas (R N.C.) 1764–June 3, 1825; House Dec. 7, 1802–07.

Yancey, Bartlett (cousin of John Kerr) (R N.C.) Feb. 19, 1785–Aug. 30, 1828; House 1813–17.

Yancey, Joel (J Ky.) Oct. 21, 1773–April 1838; House 1827–31.

Yancey, William Lowndes (uncle of Joseph Haynsworth Earle) (D Ala.) Aug. 10, 1814–July 28, 1863; House Dec. 2, 1844–Sept. 1, 1846.

Yangco, Teodoro Rafael (Nat. P.I.) Nov. 9, 1861–April 20, 1939; House (Res. Comm.) 1917–March 3, 1920.

Yaple, George Lewis (D Mich.) Feb. 20, 1851–Dec. 16, 1939; House 1883–85.

Yarborough, Ralph Webster (D Texas) June 8, 1903–Jan. 27, 1996; Senate April 29, 1957–71; chair Senate Labor and Public Welfare 1969–71.

Yardley, Robert Morris (R Pa.) Oct. 9, 1850–Dec. 8, 1902; House 1887–91.

Yates, John Barentse (R N.Y.) Feb. 1, 1784–July 10, 1836; House 1815–17.

Yates, Richard (father of Richard Yates) (R Ill.) Jan. 18, 1818–Nov. 27, 1873; House 1851–55 (Whig); Senate 1865–71; Gov. Jan. 14, 1861–Jan. 16, 1865.

Yates, Richard (son of Richard Yates) (R Ill.) Dec. 12, 1860–April 11, 1936; House 1919–33; Gov. Jan. 14, 1901–Jan. 9, 1905.

Yates, Sidney Richard (D Ill.) Aug. 27, 1909–Oct. 5, 2000; House 1949–63, 1965–99.

Yatron, Gus (D Pa.) Oct. 16, 1927–March 13, 2003; House 1969–93.

Yeaman, George Helm (U Ky.) Nov. 1, 1829–Feb. 23, 1908; House Dec. 1, 1862–65.

Yeates, Jesse Johnson (D N.C.) May 29, 1829–Sept. 5, 1892; House 1875–79, Jan. 29–March 3, 1881.

Yell, Archibald (D Ark.) 1797–Feb. 22, 1847; House Aug. 1, 1836–39 (Aug. 1, 1836–37 Jacksonian), 1845–July 1, 1846; Gov. Nov. 4, 1840–April 29, 1844.

Yoakum, Charles Henderson (D Texas) July 10, 1849–Jan. 1, 1909; House 1895–97.

Yocum, Seth Hartman (G Pa.) Aug. 2, 1834–April 19, 1895; House 1879–81.

Yoder, Samuel S. (D Ohio) Aug. 16, 1841–May 11, 1921; House 1887–91.

Yon, Thomas Alva (D Fla.) March 14, 1882–Feb. 16, 1971; House 1927–33.

York, Tyre (ID N.C.) May 4, 1836–Jan. 28, 1916; House 1883–85.

Yorke, Thomas Jones (W N.J.) March 25, 1801–April 4, 1882; House 1837–39, 1841–43.

Yorty, Samuel William (D Calif.) Oct. 1, 1909–June 5, 1998; House 1951–55.

Yost, Jacob (R Va.) April 1, 1853–Jan. 25, 1933; House 1887–89, 1897–99.

Yost, Jacob Senewell (D Pa.) July 29, 1801–March 7, 1872; House 1843–47.

Youmans, Henry Melville (D Mich.) May 15, 1832–July 8, 1920; House 1891–93.

Young, Andrew Jackson Jr. (D Ga.) March 12, 1932– ; House 1973–Jan. 29, 1977.

Young, Augustus (W Vt.) March 20, 1784–June 17, 1857; House 1841–43.

Young, Bryan Rust (brother of William Singleton Young, uncle of John Young Brown born in 1835) (W Ky.) Jan. 14, 1800–May 14, 1882; House 1845–47.

Young, Charles William "Bill" (R Fla.) Dec. 16, 1930– ; House 1971– ; chair House Appropriations 1999–2005.

Young, Clarence Clifton (R Nev.) Nov. 7, 1922– ; House 1953–57.

Young, Donald Edwin (R Alaska) June 9, 1933– ; House March 6, 1973– ; chair House Resources 1995–2001; chair House Transportation and Infrastructure 2001– .

Young, Ebenezer (– Conn.) Dec. 25, 1783–Aug. 18, 1851; House 1829–35.

Young, Edward Lunn (R S.C.) Sept. 7, 1920– ; House 1973–75.

Young, George Morley (R N.D.) Dec. 11, 1870–May 27, 1932; House 1913–Sept. 2, 1924.

Young, Hiram Casey (D Tenn.) Dec. 14, 1828–Aug. 17, 1899; House 1875–81, 1883–85.

Young, Horace Olin (R Mich.) Aug. 4, 1850–Aug. 5, 1917; House 1903–May 16, 1913.

Young, Isaac Daniel (R Kan.) March 29, 1849–Dec. 10, 1927; House 1911–13.

Young, James (D Texas) July 18, 1866–April 29, 1942; House 1911–21.

Young, James Rankin (R Pa.) March 10, 1847–Dec. 18, 1924; House 1897–1903.

Young, John (W N.Y.) June 12, 1802–April 23, 1852; House Nov. 9, 1836–37, 1841–43; Gov. Jan. 1, 1847–Jan. 1, 1849.

Young, John Andrew (D Texas) Nov. 10, 1916–Jan. 22, 2002; House 1957–79.

Young, John Duncan (D Ky.) Sept. 22, 1823–Dec. 26, 1910; House 1873–75.

Young, John Smith (D La.) Nov. 4, 1834–Oct. 11, 1916; House Nov. 5, 1878–79.

Young, Lafayette (R Iowa) May 10, 1848–Nov. 15, 1926; Senate Nov. 12, 1910–April 11, 1911.

Young, Milton Ruben (R N.D.) Dec. 6, 1897–May 31, 1983; Senate March 12, 1945–81; elected pres. pro tempore Dec. 4, 1980 (to serve Dec. 5, 1980).

Young, Pierce Manning Butler (D Ga.) Nov. 15, 1836–July 6, 1896; House July 25, 1868–69, Dec. 22, 1870–75.

Young, Richard (R N.Y.) Aug. 6, 1846–June 9, 1935; House 1909–11.

Young, Richard Montgomery (D Ill.) Feb. 20, 1798–Nov. 28, 1861; Senate 1837–43.

Young, Robert Anton III (D Mo.) Nov. 27, 1923– ; House 1977–87.

Young, Samuel Hollingsworth (R Ill.) Dec. 26, 1922– ; House 1973–75.

Young, Stephen Marvin (D Ohio) May 4, 1889–Dec. 1, 1984; House 1933–37, 1941–43, 1949–51; Senate 1959–71.

Young, Thomas Lowry (R Ohio) Dec. 14, 1832–July 20, 1888; House 1879–83; Gov. March 2, 1877–Jan. 14, 1878.

Young, Timothy Roberts (D Ill.) Nov. 19, 1811–May 12, 1898; House 1849–51.

Young, William Albin (– Va.) May 17, 1860–March 12, 1928; House 1897–April 26, 1898, 1899–March 12, 1900.

Young, William Singleton (brother of Bryan Rust Young, uncle of John Young Brown born in 1835) (– Ky.) April 10, 1790–Sept. 20, 1827; House 1825–Sept. 20, 1827.

Youngblood, Harold Francis (R Mich.) Aug. 7, 1907–May 10, 1983; House 1947–49.

Youngdahl, Oscar Ferdinand (R Minn.) Oct. 13, 1893–Feb. 3, 1946; House 1939–43.

Younger, Jesse Arthur (R Calif.) April 11, 1893–June 20, 1967; House 1953–June 20, 1967.

Yulee, David Levy (formerly David Levy) (D Fla.) June 12, 1810–Oct. 10, 1886; House (Terr. Del.) 1841–45 (Whig Democrat); Senate July 1, 1845–51, 1855–Jan. 21, 1861.

Zablocki, Clement John (D Wis.) Nov. 18, 1912–Dec. 3, 1983; House 1949–Dec. 3, 1983; chair House International Relations 1977–79; chair House Foreign Affairs 1979–83.

Zeferetti, Leo C. (D N.Y.) July 15, 1927– ; House 1975–83.

Zelenko, Herbert (D N.Y.) March 16, 1906–Feb. 23, 1979; House 1955–63.

Zeliff, William (R N.H.) June 12, 1936– ; House 1991–97.

Zenor, William Taylor (D Ind.) April 30, 1846–June 2, 1916; House 1897–1907.

Ziegler, Edward Danner (D Pa.) March 3, 1844–Dec. 21, 1931; House 1899–1901.

Zihlman, Frederick Nicholas (R Md.) Oct. 2, 1879–April 22, 1935; House 1917–31.

Zimmer, Richard (R N.J.) Aug. 16, 1944– ; House 1991–97.

Zimmerman, Orville (D Mo.) Dec. 31, 1880–April 7, 1948; House 1935–April 7, 1948.

Zion, Roger Herschel (R Ind.) Sept. 17, 1921– ; House 1967–75.

Zioncheck, Marion Anthony (D Wash.) Dec. 5, 1901–Aug. 7, 1936; House 1933–Aug. 7, 1936.

Zollicoffer, Felix Kirk (AP Tenn.) May 19, 1812–Jan. 19, 1862; House 1853–59 (1853–55 Whig).

Zorinsky, Edward (D Neb.) Nov. 11, 1928–March 6, 1987; Senate Dec. 28, 1976–March 6, 1987.

Zschau, Edwin Van Wyck (R Calif.) Jan. 6, 1940– ; House 1983–87.

Zwach, John Matthew (R Minn.) Feb. 8, 1907–Nov. 11, 1990; House 1967–75.

Governors

The newly freed states looked with suspicion on the office of governor. In the colonial era, the British-appointed governors were the symbols of the mother country's control and, the revolutionaries argued, of tyranny. Colonial assemblies, however, were able to gain control over appropriations and thus became the champions of colonial rights against the governors. After the Revolutionary War, when drawing up their constitutions, states gave most of the power to the legislative bodies and imposed restrictions on governors, including the length of the term of office and the method of election.

Length of Terms

As of 1789 the four New England states—Connecticut, Massachusetts, New Hampshire, and Rhode Island—held gubernatorial elections every year. Some of the Middle Atlantic states favored somewhat longer terms; New York and Pennsylvania had three-year terms for their governors, although New Jersey instituted a one-year term. The border and southern states had a mix: Maryland and North Carolina governors served a one-year term; South Carolina had a two-year term; and Delaware, Virginia, and Georgia had three-year terms. No state had a four-year term.

Over the years states have changed the length of gubernatorial terms. With some occasional back and forth movement, the general trend has been toward lengthening terms. New York, for example, has changed the term of office of its governor four times. Beginning in 1777 with a three-year term, the state switched to a two-year term in 1820, back to a three-year term in 1876, back to a two-year term in 1894, and to a four-year term beginning in 1938.

Maryland is another state that has changed its gubernatorial term several times. Beginning with one year in 1776, the state extended the term to three years in 1838, then to four years in 1851. Regular gubernatorial elections were held every second odd year from then through 1923, when the state had one three-year term so that future elections would be held in even-numbered years, beginning in 1926. Thus, the state held gubernatorial elections in 1919, 1923, and 1926 and then every four years after that.

The trend toward longer gubernatorial terms shows up clearly by comparing the length of terms in 1900 and 2005. Of the forty-five states in the Union in 1900,

twenty-two, almost half, had two-year terms. One (New Jersey) had a three-year term, while Rhode Island and Massachusetts were the only states left with one-year terms. The remaining twenty states had four-year gubernatorial terms. *(See box, Length of Governor Terms, p. 273.)*

As of January 2005, forty-three of those same states had four-year terms, and the five states admitted to the Union after 1900—Oklahoma (1907), Arizona and New Mexico (1912), Alaska and Hawaii (1959)—had four-year gubernatorial terms. This left only two states with two-year terms: New Hampshire and Vermont.

Arkansas, one of the last holdouts, voted in 1984 to switch to a four-year term, effective in 1986. Rhode Island voters in 1992 approved a constitutional change to a four-year term beginning with the 1994 election. New Hampshire voters, on the other hand, in 1984 rejected a proposal for a four-year gubernatorial term.

Elections in Nonpresidential Years

Along with the change to longer terms for governors came another trend—away from holding gubernatorial elections in presidential election years. Except for North Dakota, every state that switched in the twentieth century to four-year gubernatorial terms scheduled its elections in nonpresidential years. Moreover, Florida, which held its quadrennial gubernatorial elections in presidential years, changed to nonpresidential years in 1966. To make the switch, the state shortened to two years the term of the governor elected in 1964, then resumed the four-year term in 1966. Thus, Florida held gubernatorial elections in 1960, 1964, 1966, 1970, and every four years since then. Louisiana switched its gubernatorial election to nonpresidential years in 1975. Illinois made a similar switch in 1976. All of these states held one election on a shorter than regular cycle and then resumed their regular four-year rotation. When Arkansas decided in 1984 to switch to a four-year term, it chose to select its governors in nonpresidential election years beginning in 1986. These changes left only nine states—Delaware, Indiana, Missouri, Montana, North Carolina, North Dakota, Utah, Washington, and West Virginia—holding quadrennial gubernatorial elections at the same time as the presidential election. New Hampshire and Vermont still had two-year terms, so every other gubernatorial election in these two states occurred in a presidential year. Four states—

Party Lineups

The figures below show the number of governorships held by the two parties after each even-numbered election since 1950. They do not reflect midterm changes or the results of elections in odd-numbered years. D stands for Democrat; R, Republican; and O, Other.

Year	D	R	O
1950	23	25	0
1952	18	30	0
1954	27	21	0
1956	29	19	0
1958	35	14	0
1960	34	16	0
1962	34	16	0
1964	33	17	0
1966	25	25	0
1968	19	31	0
1970	29	21	0
1972	31	19	0
1974	36	13	1
1976	37	12	1
1978	32	18	0
1980	26	24	0
1982	34	16	0
1984	34	16	0
1986	26	24	0
1988	28	22	0
1990	27	21	2
1992	30	18	2
1994	19	30	1
1996	18	31	1
1998	17	31	2
2000	19	29	2
2002	24	26	0
2004	22	28	0

Louisiana, Mississippi, New Jersey, and Virginia—elect governors in odd-numbered years.

Methods of Election

Yet another way in which Americans of the early federal period restricted their governors was by the method of election. In 1789 only in New York and the four New England states did the people directly choose their governors by popular vote. In the remaining eight states, governors were chosen by the state legislatures, thus enhancing the power of the legislatures in their dealing with the governors. But several factors—including the democratic trend to elect public officials directly, the increasing trust in the office of governor, and the need for a stronger and more independent chief executive—led to the gradual introduction of popular votes in all the states.

By the 1860s the remaining eight original states had switched to popular ballots. Pennsylvania was first, in 1790, and was followed by Delaware in 1792, Georgia in 1824, North Carolina in 1835, Maryland in 1838, New Jersey in 1844, Virginia in 1851, and South Carolina in 1865, after the Civil War.

All the states admitted to the Union after the original thirteen, with one exception, made provision from the very beginning for popular election of their governors. The exception was Louisiana, which from its admission in 1812 until a change in the state constitution in 1845 had a unique system of gubernatorial elections. The people participated by voting in a first-step popular election. In a second step, the Legislature was to select the governor from the two candidates receiving the highest popular vote.

Number of Terms

Another limitation placed on governors is a restriction on the number of terms they are allowed to serve. In the early years at least three states had such limitations: governors of Maryland were eligible to serve three consecutive one-year terms and then were required to retire for at least one year; Pennsylvania allowed its governors three consecutive three-year terms and then forced retirement for at least one term; and in New Jersey, according to the constitution of 1844, a governor could serve only one three-year term before retiring for at least one term.

In the last several decades of the twentieth century, increasing voter discontent with government performance and with politicians stoked a movement to limit the number of years a person could serve in public office. The movement was especially pronounced at the gubernatorial level. By the year 2005 only ten states did not impose some term limits on their governors: Connecticut, Illinois, Iowa, Minnesota, New Hampshire, New York, North Dakota, Texas, Vermont, and Wisconsin. Most of the other states placed a limit of two consecutive terms on a governor, which meant eight years continuously in office. A few states had variations on this theme. *(See box, Limitations on Governor Terms, p. 274.)*

Majority Vote Requirement

A peculiarity of gubernatorial voting that has almost disappeared from the American political scene is the requirement that the winning gubernatorial candidate receive a majority of the popular vote. Otherwise, the choice devolves to the state legislature or, in some cases, a runoff between the two highest candidates is required. Centered in New England, this practice was used mainly in the nineteenth century. All six present-day New England states and Georgia had such a provision in their state constitutions at one time. New Hampshire, Vermont, Massachusetts, and Connecticut already had the provision when they entered the Union between 1789 and 1791.

Length of Governor Terms

(In years)

State	1900	2005	Year of change	State	1900	2005	Year of change
Alabama	2	4	1901	Montana	4	4	–
Alaska[a]	–	4	–	Nebraska	2	4	1966
Arizona[a]	–	4	1970	Nevada	4	4	–
Arkansas	2	4	1986	New Hampshire	2	2	–
California	4	4	–	New Jersey	3	4	1949
Colorado	2	4	1958	New Mexico[a]	–	4	1970
Connecticut	2	4	1950	New York	2	4	1938
Delaware	4	4	–	North Carolina	4	4	–
Florida	4	4	–	North Dakota	2	4	1964
Georgia	2	4	1942	Ohio	2	4	1958
Hawaii[a]	–	4	–	Oklahoma[a]	–	4	–
Idaho	2	4	1946	Oregon	4	4	–
Illinois	4	4	–	Pennsylvania	4	4	–
Indiana	4	4	–	Rhode Island[c]	1	4	1912, 1994
Iowa	2	4	1974	South Carolina	2	4	1926
Kansas	2	4	1974	South Dakota	2	4	1974
Kentucky	4	4	–	Tennessee	2	4	1954
Louisiana	4	4	–	Texas	2	4	1974
Maine	2	4	1958	Utah	4	4	–
Maryland	4	4	–	Vermont	2	2	–
Massachusetts[b]	1	4	1920, 1966	Virginia	4	4	–
Michigan	2	4	1966	Washington	4	4	–
Minnesota	2	4	1962	West Virginia	4	4	–
Mississippi	4	4	–	Wisconsin	2	4	1970
Missouri	4	4	–	Wyoming	4	4	–

a. Oklahoma was admitted to the Union in 1907, Arizona and New Mexico in 1912, and Alaska and Hawaii in 1959. Oklahoma, Alaska, and Hawaii always have had four-year gubernatorial terms; Arizona began with a two-year term and switched to four years in 1970. New Mexico (1912) began with a four-year term, changed to two years in 1916, and went back to four years in 1970.

b. Massachusetts switched from a one- to a two-year term in 1920 and to a four-year term in 1966.

c. Rhode Island switched from a one- to a two-year term in 1912 and to a four-year term in 1994.

Source: *Book of the States, 2004* (Lexington, Ky.: Council of State Governments, 2004); David Hawkings and Brian Nutting, eds., *CQ's Politics in America 2004: The 108th Congress* (Washington, D.C.: Congressional Quarterly, 2003).

Rhode Island required a majority election but did not adopt a provision for legislative election until 1842; Maine adopted a majority provision when it split off from Massachusetts to form a separate state in 1820. Georgia put the majority provision in its constitution when it switched from legislative to popular election of governors in 1825. Arizona adopted a runoff in 1990.

The purpose of the majority provision appears to have been to safeguard against a candidate's winning with a small fraction of the popular vote in a multiple field. In most of New England, the provision was part of the early state constitutions, formed largely in the 1780s, before the development of the two-party system.

The prospect of multiple-candidate fields diminished with the coming of the two-party system. Nevertheless, each of these states had occasion to use the provision at least once. Sometimes, in an extremely close election, minor party candidates received enough of a vote to keep the winner from getting a majority of the total vote. At other times strong third-party movements or disintegration of the old party structure resulted in the election's being thrown into the state legislature.

Limitations on Governor Terms

(As of January 2004)

State	Term limit	State	Term limit
Alabama[a]	2	Montana[c]	2
Alaska[a]	2	Nebraska[a]	2
Arizona[a]	2	Nevada	2
Arkansas	2	New Hampshire	None
California	2	New Jersey[a]	2
Colorado	2	New Mexico[a]	2
Connecticut	None	New York	None
Delaware	2	North Carolina[a]	2
Florida	2	North Dakota	None
Georgia	2	Ohio	2
Hawaii[a]	2	Oklahoma	2
Idaho[b]	2	Oregon	2
Illinois	None	Pennsylvania[a]	2
Indiana	2	Rhode Island	2
Iowa	None	South Carolina[a]	2
Kansas	2	South Dakota[a]	2
Kentucky	2	Tennessee	2
Louisiana	2	Texas	None
Maine[a]	2	Utah[a]	3
Maryland	2	Vermont	None
Massachusetts	2	Virginia[d]	1
Michigan	2	Washington	2
Minnesota	None	West Virginia[a]	2
Mississippi	2	Wisconsin	None
Missouri	2	Wyoming[c]	2

a. Consecutive terms.
b. Two terms; can run again in eight years.
c. Eight years in a sixteen-year period.
d. Cannot serve consecutive terms.

Source: David Hawkings and Brian Nutting, eds., *CQ's Politics in America 2004: The 108th Congress* (Washington, D.C.: Congressional Quarterly, 2003); and Congressional Quarterly.

Vermont retains the majority vote provision, and its Legislature chose the governor in January 1987, the first time it did so since 1912. Georgia maintains the requirement for a majority vote for governor but, instead of legislative election, provides for a runoff between the top two contenders three weeks after the general election. Mississippi has a majority vote provision under the 1890 state constitution, but the provision was not used until 2000. The Democratic Party nominee always had received a majority through 1987 and the Republican Party won a majority in 1991 and 1995. However, in the fall 1999 elections neither major party candidate quite received a majority of the vote, throwing the election into the Democrat-controlled House of the Legislature. On Jan. 4, 2000, as expected, the House elected the Democratic candidate, Lt. Gov. Ronnie Musgrove.

Following are the states that had the majority vote provision for governor, the years in which the choice devolved on the legislature because of it, and the year, if any, in which the requirement was repealed or changed:

Arizona. Arizona adopted and used a runoff provision in 1990 following impeachment of a governor elected with less than a majority.

Connecticut. No gubernatorial candidate received a majority of the popular vote, thus throwing the election into the Legislature, in the following years: 1796, 1810, 1833, 1834, 1842, 1844, 1846, 1849, 1850, 1851, 1854,

1855, 1856, 1878, 1884, 1886, 1888, and 1890. A dispute arose after the 1890 election, when the Democrats claimed that their candidate had won a majority and the Republicans insisted that he had not and that the Legislature had to decide the election. When the divided Legislature could not agree on what to do, the outgoing governor, Morgan G. Bulkeley, R, continued to serve through the entire new term (1891–93).

The provision was repealed in 1901.

Georgia. Although the majority vote requirement was contained in the constitution as early as 1825, it was not used until the twentieth century. In 1966, with an emerging Republican Party, a controversial Democratic nominee, and an Independent Democrat all affecting the gubernatorial race, no candidate received a majority. The Legislature chose Democrat Lester Maddox. Controversy surrounding this experience led to the change from legislative choice to a runoff between the top two contenders. Earlier, in 1946, the Georgia Legislature also attempted to choose the governor, under unusual circumstances not covered by the majority vote requirement. The governor-elect, Eugene Talmadge, D, died before taking office. When it met, the Legislature chose Talmadge's son, Herman E. Talmadge, as the new governor. Herman Talmadge was eligible for consideration on the basis that he received enough write-in votes in the general election to make him the second-place candidate. But the state supreme court voided the Legislature's choice and declared that the lieutenant governor-elect, Melvin E. Thompson, D, should be governor.

Maine. Maine entered statehood in 1820 with a majority vote provision for governor but repealed it in 1880. During this sixty-year span, the Legislature was called on to choose the governor nine times, in 1840, 1846, 1848, 1852, 1853, 1854, 1855, 1878, and 1879.

Massachusetts. As with the other New England states, Massachusetts originally had a requirement for majority voting in gubernatorial elections. However, after the Legislature was forced to choose the governor for six straight elections from 1848 to 1853, Massachusetts repealed the provision in 1855. The years in which it was used were 1785, 1833, 1842, 1843, 1845, 1848, 1849, 1850, 1851, 1852, and 1853.

Mississippi. This state had a majority voting requirement since its 1890 constitution but the provision was never needed for more than a century. In 1999, for the first time, no candidate received a majority, throwing the election into the Mississippi House, which chose a Democrat.

New Hampshire. New Hampshire's mandated majority vote for governor was in force from 1784 through 1912, when it was repealed. The outcome of the following gubernatorial elections was determined by the Legislature: 1785, 1787, 1789, 1790, 1812, 1824, 1846, 1851, 1856, 1863, 1871, 1874, 1875, 1886, 1888, 1890, 1906, and 1912.

Rhode Island. Under the constitution of 1842, Rhode Island required a majority to win the gubernatorial election. Under this mandate, the Legislature chose the governor in the years 1846, 1875, 1876, 1880, 1889, 1890, and 1891. Because of a disagreement between the two houses of the state Legislature, the ballots for governor were not counted in 1893, and Gov. D. Russell Brown, R, continued in office for another term of one year. The provision for majority voting then was repealed.

Before 1842 there also was a requirement for a popular majority, but the Legislature was not allowed to choose a new governor if no candidate achieved a majority. Three times—in 1806, 1832, and 1839—there was a lack of a majority in a gubernatorial election, with a different outcome each time. In 1806 the lieutenant governor-elect served as acting governor for the term. In 1832 the Legislature mandated a new election, but still no majority choice was reached; three more elections were held, all without a majority being achieved, so the same state officers were continued until the next regular election. In 1839, when neither the gubernatorial nor lieutenant governor's race yielded a winner by majority, the senior state senator acted as governor for the term.

Vermont. Vermont's provision for majority gubernatorial election resulted in the Legislature's picking the governor twenty times: 1789, 1797, 1813, 1814, 1830, 1831, 1832, 1834, 1841, 1843, 1845, 1846, 1847, 1848, 1849, 1852, 1853, 1902, 1912, and 1987. On a twenty-first occasion, 1835, the Legislature failed to choose a new governor because of a deadlock and the lieutenant governor-elect served as governor for the term. The Vermont provision remains in force.

Governors: Biographies

This biographical summary lists, by state in chronological order of service, governors of the United States since 1789. For each governor, the material is organized as follows: name; relationship to other governors, presidents, or vice presidents; party (at time of service as governor); date of birth; date of death (if applicable); dates of service as governor and service in other public or party office. Dates of service and birth and death are given by day where available; otherwise the month only is used. Service in other than gubernatorial office and relationships to other individuals also are given where that information has been located. *(See Party abbreviations, p. 324.)*

For presidential, vice presidential, and congressional terms, only the years are given for beginning and ending dates if the standard terms were served. Presidential and vice presidential terms from 1789 to 1933 were from

March 4 to March 4; since 1934, the four-year term has been from Jan. 20 to Jan. 20. Terms of service for representatives and senators from 1789 to 1933 were from March 4 to March 4; since 1934, service has been from Jan. 3 to Jan. 3.

The major sources of information for this list were Joseph E. Kallenbach and Jessamine S. Kallenbach, *American State Governors, 1776–1976,* 3 vols. (Dobbs Ferry, N.Y.: Oceana Publishing, 1977); *Congressional Quarterly's Guide to U.S. Elections,* 4th ed. (Washington, D.C.: CQ Press, 2001).; David Hawkings and Brian Nutting, eds., *CQ's Politics in America 2004: The 108th Congress* (Washington, D.C.: Congressional Quarterly, 2003); *Book of the States, 2004* (Lexington, Ky.: Council of State Governments, 2004); *CQ Weekly*; and individual state offices and historical societies. *(See also box, State Sources for Governors, p. 321.)*

Alabama

(Became a state Dec. 14, 1819)

Bibb, William Wyatt (brother of Thomas Bibb, below, cousin of David Bibb Graves, below) (DR) Oct. 2, 1781–July 9, 1820; Nov. 9, 1819–July 10, 1820; House Jan. 26, 1807–Nov. 6, 1813 (Republican Ga.); Senate Nov. 6, 1813–Nov. 9, 1816 (Republican Ga.).

Bibb, Thomas (brother of William Wyatt Bibb, above, cousin of David Bibb Graves, below) (DR) 1783–Sept. 20, 1839; July 15, 1820–Nov. 9, 1821.

Pickens, Israel (DR) Jan. 30, 1780–April 24, 1827; Nov. 9, 1821–Nov. 25, 1825; House 1811–17 (Republican N.C.); Senate Feb. 17–Nov. 27, 1826 (Republican).

Murphy, John (J) 1785–Sept. 21, 1841; Nov. 25, 1825–Nov. 25, 1829; House 1833–35.

Moore, Gabriel (brother of Samuel B. Moore, below) (-) about 1785–1845; Nov. 25, 1829–March 3, 1831; House 1821–29; Senate 1831–37.

Moore, Samuel B. (brother of Gabriel Moore, above) (D) 1789–Nov. 7, 1846; March 3–Nov. 26, 1831.

Gayle, John (D) Sept. 11, 1792–July 21, 1859; Nov. 26, 1831–Nov. 21, 1835; House 1847–49 (Whig).

Clay, Clement Comer (D) Dec. 17, 1789–Sept. 7, 1866; Nov. 21, 1835–July 17, 1837; House 1829–35 (no party); Senate June 19, 1837–Nov. 15, 1841.

McVay, Hugh (D) 1788–May 9, 1851; July 17–Nov. 21, 1837.

Bagby, Arthur Pendleton (D) 1794–Sept. 21, 1858; Nov. 21, 1837–Nov. 22, 1841; Senate Nov. 24, 1841–June 16, 1848.

Fitzpatrick, Benjamin (D) June 30, 1802–Nov. 21, 1869; Nov. 22, 1841–Dec. 10, 1845; Senate Nov. 25, 1848–Nov. 30, 1849, Jan. 14, 1853–55, Nov. 26, 1855–Jan. 21, 1861; elected pres. pro tempore Dec. 7, 1857, March 29, 1858, June 14, 1858, Jan. 25, 1859, March 9, 1859, Dec. 19, 1859, Feb. 20, 1860, June 26, 1860.

Martin, Joshua Lanier (I) Dec. 5, 1799–Nov. 2, 1856; Dec. 10, 1845–Dec. 16, 1847; House 1835–39 (1835–37 Anti-Jacksonian, 1837–39 Democrat).

Chapman, Reuben (D) July 15, 1799–May 16, 1882; Dec. 16, 1847–Dec. 17, 1849; House 1835–47 (1835–37 Jacksonian).

Collier, Henry Watkins (D) Jan. 17, 1801–Aug. 28, 1855; Dec. 17, 1849–Dec. 20, 1853.

Winston, John Anthony (brother-in-law of Robert Burns Lindsay, below) (D) Sept. 4, 1812–Dec. 21, 1871; Dec. 20, 1853–Dec. 1, 1857.

Moore, Andrew Barry (W) March 7, 1807–April 5, 1873; Dec. 1, 1857–Dec. 2, 1861.

Shorter, John Gill (D) April 23, 1818–May 29, 1872; Dec. 2, 1861–Dec. 1, 1863.

Watts, Thomas Hill (W) Jan. 3, 1819–Sept. 16, 1892; Dec. 1, 1863–April 12, 1865.

Parsons, Lewis Eliphalet (W) April 28, 1817–June 8, 1895; (Provisional) June 21–Dec. 20, 1865.

Patton, Robert Miller (W) July 10, 1809–Feb. 28, 1885; Dec. 20, 1865–July 14, 1868.

Smith, William Hugh (D) April 26, 1826–Jan. 1, 1899; July 14, 1868–Nov. 26, 1870.

Lindsay, Robert Burns (brother-in-law of John Anthony Winston, above) (D) July 4, 1824–Feb. 13, 1902; Nov. 26, 1870–Nov. 17, 1872.

Lewis, David Peter (R) 1820–July 3, 1884; Nov. 25, 1872–Nov. 24, 1874.

Houston, George Smith (D) Jan. 17, 1811–Dec. 31, 1879; Nov. 24, 1874–Nov. 28, 1878; House 1841–49, 1851–Jan. 21, 1861; Senate March 4–Dec. 31, 1879.

Cobb, Rufus Wills (D) Feb. 25, 1829–Nov. 26, 1913; Nov. 28, 1878–Dec. 1, 1882.

O'Neal, Edward Asbury (father of Emmet O'Neal, below) (D) Sept. 20, 1818–Nov. 7, 1890; Dec. 1, 1882–Dec. 1, 1886.

Seay, Thomas (D) Nov. 20, 1846–March 30, 1896; Dec. 1, 1886–Dec. 1, 1890.

Jones, Thomas Goode (D) Nov. 26, 1844–April 28, 1914; Dec. 1, 1890–Dec. 1, 1894.

Oates, William Calvin (D) Nov. 30, 1835–Sept. 9, 1910; Dec. 1, 1894–Dec. 1, 1896; House 1881–Nov. 5, 1894.

Johnston, Joseph Forney (D) March 23, 1843–Aug. 8, 1913; Dec. 1, 1896–Dec. 1, 1900; Senate Aug. 6, 1907–Aug. 8, 1913.

Jelks, William Dorsey (D) Nov. 7, 1855–Dec. 13, 1931; Dec. 1–Dec. 26, 1900, June 11, 1901–April 25, 1904, March 5, 1905–Jan. 14, 1907.

Samford, William James (D) Sept. 16, 1844–June 11, 1901; Dec. 1, 1900–June 11, 1901; House 1879–81.

Jelks, William Dorsey (D) June 11, 1901–April 25, 1904 (for previous term see above).

Cunningham, Russell McWhortor (D) Aug. 25, 1855–June 6, 1921; April 25, 1904–March 5, 1905.

Jelks, William Dorsey (D) March 5, 1905–Jan. 14, 1907 (for previous terms see above).

Comer, Braxton Bragg (D) Nov. 7, 1848–Aug. 15, 1927; Jan. 14, 1907–Jan. 17, 1911; Senate March 5–Nov. 2, 1920.

O'Neal, Emmet (son of Edward Asbury O'Neal, above) (D) Sept. 23, 1853–Sept. 7, 1922; Jan. 17, 1911–Jan. 18, 1915.

Henderson, Charles (D) April 26, 1860–Jan. 7, 1937; Jan. 18, 1915–Jan. 20, 1919.

Kilby, Thomas Erby (D) July 9, 1865–Oct. 22, 1943; Jan. 20, 1919–Jan. 15, 1923.

Brandon, William Woodward (D) June 5, 1868–Dec. 7, 1934; Jan. 15, 1923–Jan. 17, 1927.

McDowell, Charles Samuel (D) Oct. 17, 1871–May 22, 1943; (Acting) July 10–July 11, 1924.

Graves, David Bibb (cousin of William Wyatt Bibb and Thomas Bibb, above) (D) April 1, 1873–March 14, 1942; Jan. 17, 1927–Jan. 19, 1931, Jan. 14, 1935–Jan. 17, 1939.

Miller, Benjamin Meek (D) March 13, 1864–Feb. 6, 1944; Jan. 19, 1931–Jan. 14, 1935.

Graves, David Bibb (D) Jan. 14, 1935–Jan. 17, 1939 (for previous term see above).

Dixon, Frank Murray (D) July 25, 1892–Oct. 11, 1965; Jan. 17, 1939–Jan. 19, 1943.

Sparks, George Chauncey (D) Oct. 8, 1884–Nov. 6, 1968; Jan. 19, 1943–Jan. 20, 1947.

Folsom, James Elisha "Big Jim" (father of James Elisha Folsom Jr., below) (D) Oct. 9, 1908–Nov. 21, 1987; Jan. 20, 1947–Jan. 15, 1951, Jan. 17, 1955–Jan. 19, 1959.

Persons, Seth Gordon (D) Feb. 5, 1902–May 29, 1965; Jan. 15, 1951–Jan. 17, 1955.

Folsom, James Elisha (D) Jan. 17, 1955–Jan. 19, 1959 (for previous term see above).

Patterson, John Malcolm (D) Sept. 27, 1921– ; Jan. 19, 1959–Jan. 14, 1963.

Wallace, George Corley (husband of Lurleen Burns Wallace, below) (D) Aug. 25, 1919–Sept. 13, 1998; Jan. 14, 1963–Jan. 16, 1967, Jan. 18, 1971–June 5, 1972, July 7, 1972–Jan. 15, 1979, Jan. 17, 1983–Jan. 19, 1987.

Wallace, Lurleen Burns (wife of George Corley Wallace, above) (D) Sept. 19, 1926–May 7, 1968; Jan. 16, 1967–May 7, 1968.

Brewer, Albert Preston (D) Oct. 26, 1928– ; May 7, 1968–Jan. 18, 1971.

Wallace, George Corley (D) Jan. 18, 1971–June 5, 1972 (for previous term see above).

Beasley, Jere Locke (D) Dec. 12, 1935– ; June 5–July 7, 1972.

Wallace, George Corley (D) July 7, 1972–Jan. 15, 1979 (for previous terms see above).

James, Forrest Hood "Fob" Jr. (D) Sept. 15, 1934– ; Jan. 15, 1979–Jan. 17, 1983, Jan. 16, 1995–Jan. 18, 1999.

Wallace, George Corley (D) Jan. 17, 1983–Jan. 19, 1987 (for previous terms see above).

Hunt, Harold Guy (R) June 17, 1933– ; Jan. 19, 1987–April 22, 1993.

Folsom, James Elisha Jr. (son of James Elisha "Big Jim" Folsom, above) (D) May 14, 1949– ; April 22, 1993–Jan. 16, 1995.

James, Forrest Hood "Fob" Jr. (R) Jan. 16, 1995–Jan. 18, 1999 (for previous term see above).

Siegelman, Don (D) Feb. 24, 1946– ; Jan. 18, 1999–Jan. 21, 2003.

Riley, Bob (R) Oct. 3, 1944– ; Jan. 21, 2003– .

Alaska
(Became a state Jan. 3, 1959)

Egan, William Allen (D) Oct. 8, 1914–May 6, 1984; Jan. 3, 1959–Dec. 5, 1966, Dec. 5, 1970–Dec. 2, 1974.

Hickel, Walter Joseph (I) Aug. 18, 1919– ; Dec. 5, 1966–Jan. 29, 1969 (Republican), Dec. 3, 1990–Dec. 5, 1994; secretary of the interior Jan. 24, 1969–Nov. 25, 1970.

Miller, Keith Harvey (R) March 1, 1925– ; Jan. 29, 1969–Dec. 5, 1970.

Egan, William Allen (D) Dec. 5, 1970–Dec. 2, 1974 (for previous term see above).

Hammond, Jay Sterner (R) July 21, 1922– ; Dec. 2, 1974–Dec. 6, 1982.

Sheffield, William Jennings (D) June 26, 1928– ; Dec. 6, 1982–Dec. 1, 1986.

Cowper, Steve Camberling (D) Aug. 21, 1938– ; Dec. 1, 1986–Dec. 3, 1990.

Hickel, Walter Joseph (I) Dec. 3, 1990–Dec. 5, 1994 (for previous term see above).

Knowles, Tony (D) Jan. 1, 1943– ; Dec. 5, 1994–Dec. 2, 2002.

Murkowski, Frank Hughes (R) March 28, 1933– ; Dec. 2, 2002– ; Senate 1981–Dec. 2, 2002.

Arizona
(Became a state Feb. 14, 1912)

Hunt, George Wylie Paul (D) Nov. 1, 1859–Dec. 24, 1934; Feb. 14, 1912–Jan. 1, 1917, Dec. 25, 1917–Jan. 6, 1919, Jan. 1, 1923–Jan. 7, 1929, Jan. 5, 1931–Jan. 2, 1933.

Campbell, Thomas Edward (R) Jan. 18, 1878–March 1, 1944; Jan. 1, 1917–Dec. 25, 1917, Jan. 6, 1919–Jan. 1, 1923.

Hunt, George Wylie Paul (D) Dec. 25, 1917–Jan. 6, 1919 (for previous term see above).

Campbell, Thomas Edward (R) Jan. 6, 1919–Jan. 1, 1923 (for previous term see above).

Hunt, George Wylie Paul (D) Jan. 1, 1923–Jan. 7, 1929 (for previous terms see above).

Phillips, John C. (R) Nov. 13, 1870–June 25, 1943; Jan. 7, 1929–Jan. 5, 1931.

Hunt, George Wylie Paul (D) Jan. 5, 1931–Jan. 2, 1933 (for previous terms see above).

Moeur, Benjamin Baker (D) Dec. 22, 1869–March 16, 1937; Jan. 2, 1933–Jan. 4, 1937.

Stanford, Rawghlie Clement (D) Aug. 2, 1879–Dec. 15, 1963; Jan. 4, 1937–Jan. 2, 1939.

Jones, Robert Taylor (D) Feb. 8, 1884–June 11, 1958; Jan. 2, 1939–Jan. 6, 1941.

Osborn, Sidney Preston (D) May 17, 1884–May 25, 1948; Jan. 6, 1941–May 25, 1948.

Garvey, Daniel E. (D) June 19, 1886–Feb. 5, 1974; May 25, 1948–Jan. 1, 1951.

Pyle, John Howard (R) March 25, 1906–Nov. 29, 1987; Jan. 1, 1951–Jan. 3, 1955.

McFarland, Ernest William (D) Oct. 9, 1894–June 8, 1984; Jan. 3, 1955–Jan. 5, 1959; Senate 1941–53; Senate majority leader 1951–53.

Fannin, Paul Jones (R) Jan. 29, 1907–Jan. 13, 2002; Jan. 5, 1959–Jan. 4, 1965; Senate 1965–77.

Goddard, Samuel Pearson Jr. (D) Aug. 8, 1919– ; Jan. 4, 1965–Jan. 2, 1967.

Williams, John Richard (R) Oct. 29, 1909–Aug. 24, 1998; Jan. 2, 1967–Jan. 6, 1975.

Castro, Raul Hector (D) June 12, 1916– ; Jan. 6, 1975–Oct. 20, 1977.

Bolin, Wesley H. (D) July 1, 1908–March 4, 1978; Oct. 20, 1977–March 4, 1978.

Babbitt, Bruce Edward (D) June 27, 1938– ; March 4, 1978–Jan. 5, 1987; secretary of the interior Jan. 22, 1993–Jan. 20, 2001.

Mecham, Evan (R) May 12, 1924– ; Jan. 5, 1987–April 4, 1988.

Mofford, Rose (D) June 10, 1922– ; April 5, 1988–March 6, 1991.

Symington, Fife (R) Aug. 12, 1945– ; March 6, 1991–Sept. 5, 1997.

Hull, Jane Dee (R) Aug. 8, 1935– ; Sept. 5, 1997–Jan. 6, 2003.

Napolitano, Janet (D) Nov. 29, 1957– ; Jan. 6, 2003– .

Arkansas

(Became a state June 15, 1836)

Conway, James Sevier (brother of Elias Nelson Conway, below) (D) Dec. 9, 1798–March 3, 1855; Sept. 13, 1836–Nov. 4, 1840.

Yell, Archibald (D) Aug. 1797–Feb. 22, 1847; Nov. 4, 1840–April 29, 1844; House Aug. 1, 1836–39 (Aug. 1, 1836–37 Jacksonian), 1845–46.

Adams, Samuel (D) June 5, 1805–Feb. 27, 1850; April 29–Nov. 5, 1844.

Drew, Thomas Stevenson (D) Aug. 25, 1802–1879; Nov. 5, 1844–Jan. 10, 1849.

Byrd, Richard C. (D) 1805–June 1, 1854; Jan. 11–April 19, 1849.

Roane, John Selden (D) Jan. 8, 1817–April 17, 1867; April 19, 1849–Nov. 15, 1852.

Conway, Elias Nelson (brother of James Sevier Conway, above) (D) May 17, 1812–Feb. 28, 1892; Nov. 15, 1852–Nov. 16, 1860.

Rector, Henry Massey (ID) May 1, 1816–Aug. 12, 1899; Nov. 16, 1860–Nov. 4, 1862.

Fletcher, Thomas (D) April 8, 1819–Feb. 21, 1900; Nov. 4–Nov. 15, 1862.

Flanagin, Harris (D) Nov. 3, 1817–Sept. 23, 1874; Nov. 15, 1862–April 18, 1864.

Murphy, Isaac (U) Oct. 16, 1802–Sept. 8, 1882; April 18, 1864–July 2, 1868.

Clayton, Powell (R) Aug. 7, 1833–Aug. 25, 1914; July 2, 1868–March 17, 1871; Senate 1871–77.

Hadley, Ozra A. (R) June 30, 1826–July 18, 1915; March 17, 1871–Jan. 6, 1873.

Baxter, Elisha (R) Sept. 1, 1827–May 31, 1899; Jan. 6, 1873–Nov. 12, 1874.

Garland, Augustus Hill (D) June 11, 1832–Jan. 26, 1899; Nov. 12, 1874–Jan. 11, 1877; Senate 1877–March 6, 1885; attorney general March 6, 1885–March 5, 1889.

Miller, William Read (D) Nov. 23, 1823–Nov. 29, 1887; Jan. 11, 1877–Jan. 13, 1881.

Churchill, Thomas James (D) March 10, 1824–March 10, 1905; Jan. 13, 1881–Jan. 13, 1883.

Berry, James Henderson (D) May 15, 1841–Jan. 30, 1913; Jan. 13, 1883–Jan. 17, 1885; Senate March 20, 1885–1907.

Hughes, Simon P. (D) April 14, 1830–June 29, 1906; Jan. 17, 1885–Jan. 17, 1889.

Eagle, James Philip (D) Aug. 10, 1837–Dec. 20, 1904; Jan. 17, 1889–Jan. 10, 1893.

Fishback, William Meade (D) Nov. 5, 1831–Feb. 9, 1903; Jan. 10, 1893–Jan. 18, 1895.

Clarke, James Paul (D) Aug. 18, 1854–Oct. 1, 1916; Jan. 18, 1895–Jan. 12, 1897; Senate 1903–Oct. 1, 1916; elected pres. pro tempore March 13, 1913, Dec. 6, 1915.

Jones, Daniel Webster (D) Dec. 15, 1839–Dec. 25, 1918; Jan. 12, 1897–Jan. 8, 1901.

Davis, Jeff (D) May 6, 1862–Jan. 3, 1913; Jan. 8, 1901–Jan. 8, 1907; Senate 1907–Jan. 3, 1913.

Little, John Sebastian (D) March 15, 1853–Oct. 29, 1916; Jan. 8–Feb. 11, 1907; House Dec. 3, 1894–Jan. 1907.

Moore, John I. (D) Feb. 7, 1856–March 18, 1937; Feb. 11–May 11, 1907.

Pindall, Xenophon Overton (D) Aug. 21, 1873–Jan. 2, 1935; May 15, 1907–Jan. 11, 1909.

Martin, Jesse M. (D) March 1, 1877–Jan. 22, 1915; Jan. 11–Jan. 14, 1909.

Donaghey, George W. (D) July 1, 1856–Dec. 15, 1937; Jan. 14, 1909–Jan. 15, 1913.

Robinson, Joseph Taylor (D) Aug. 26, 1872–July 14, 1937; Jan. 15–March 10, 1913; House 1903–Jan. 14, 1913; Senate 1913–July 14, 1937; Senate minority leader 1923–33; Senate majority leader 1933–July 14, 1937.

Oldham, William Kavanaugh (D) May 29, 1865–May 6, 1938; March 10–March 13, 1913.

Futrell, Junius Marion (D) Aug. 14, 1870–June 20, 1955; March 13–July 23, 1913, Jan. 10, 1933–Jan. 12, 1937.

Hays, George Washington (D) Sept. 23, 1863–Sept. 15, 1927; July 23, 1913–Jan. 9, 1917.

Brough, Charles Hillman (D) July 9, 1876–Dec. 26, 1935; Jan. 9, 1917–Jan. 11, 1921.

McRae, Thomas Chipman (D) Dec. 21, 1851–June 2, 1929; Jan. 11, 1921–Jan. 13, 1925; House Dec. 7, 1885–1903.

Terral, Thomas Jefferson (D) Dec. 21, 1882–March 9, 1946; Jan. 13, 1925–Jan. 11, 1927.

Martineau, John Ellis (D) Dec. 2, 1873–March 6, 1937; Jan. 11, 1927–March 4, 1928.

Parnell, Harvey (D) Feb. 28, 1880–Jan. 16, 1936; March 14, 1928–Jan. 10, 1933.

Futrell, Junius Marion (D) Jan. 10, 1933–Jan. 12, 1937 (for previous term see above).

Bailey, Carl Edward (D) Oct. 8, 1894–Oct. 23, 1948; Jan. 12, 1937–Jan. 14, 1941.

Adkins, Homer Martin (D) Oct. 15, 1890–Feb. 26, 1964; Jan. 14, 1941–Jan. 9, 1945.

Laney, Benjamin Travis (D) Nov. 25, 1896–Jan. 21, 1977; Jan. 9, 1945–Jan. 11, 1949.

McMath, Sidney Sanders (D) June 14, 1912–Oct. 4, 2003; Jan. 11, 1949–Jan. 13, 1953.

Cherry, Francis Adams (D) Sept. 5, 1908–July 15, 1965; Jan. 13, 1953–Jan. 11, 1955.

Faubus, Orval Eugene (D) Jan. 7, 1910–Dec. 14, 1994; Jan. 11, 1955–Jan. 10, 1967.

Rockefeller, Winthrop (brother of Vice Pres. Nelson Aldrich Rockefeller, uncle of John Davison "Jay" Rockefeller IV of W.Va., grandson of Sen. Nelson Wilmarth Aldrich of R.I., nephew of Rep. Richard Steere Aldrich of R.I.) (R) May 1, 1912–Feb. 22, 1973; Jan. 10, 1967–Jan. 12, 1971.

Bumpers, Dale Leon (D) Aug. 12, 1925– ; Jan. 12, 1971–Jan. 2, 1975; Senate 1975–99.

Riley, Robert Cowley (D) Sept. 18, 1924– ; Jan. 2–Jan. 14, 1975.

Pryor, David Hampton (D) Aug. 29, 1934– ; Jan. 14, 1975–Jan. 3, 1979; House Nov. 8, 1966–73; Senate 1979– .

Purcell, Joe (D) July 29, 1923–March 1987; Jan. 3–Jan. 9, 1979.

Clinton, William Jefferson "Bill" (D) Aug. 19, 1946– ; Jan. 9, 1979–Jan. 19, 1981, Jan. 11, 1983–Dec. 12, 1992.

White, Frank D. (R) June 4, 1933–May 21, 2003; Jan. 19, 1981–Jan. 11, 1983.

Clinton, William Jefferson "Bill" (D) Jan. 11, 1983–Dec. 12, 1992 (for previous term see above); president 1993–2001.

Tucker, James Guy Jr. (D) June 13, 1943– ; Dec. 12, 1992–July 15, 1996; House 1977–79.

Huckabee, Mike (R) Aug. 24, 1955– ; July 15, 1996– .

California

(Became a state Sept. 9, 1850)

Burnett, Peter Hardeman (ID) Nov. 15, 1807–May 17, 1895; Dec. 20, 1849–Jan. 9, 1851.

McDougal, John (ID) 1818–March 30, 1866; Jan. 9, 1851–Jan. 8, 1852.

Bigler, John (brother of William Bigler of Pa.) (D) Jan. 8, 1805–Nov. 29, 1871; Jan. 8, 1852–Jan. 9, 1856.

Johnson, James Neely (AP) Aug. 2, 1825–Aug. 31, 1872; Jan. 9, 1856–Jan. 8, 1858.

Weller, John B. (D) Feb. 22, 1812–Aug. 17, 1875; Jan. 8, 1858–Jan. 9, 1860; House 1839–45 (Ohio); Senate Jan. 30, 1852–57.

Latham, Milton Slocum (D) May 23, 1827–March 4, 1882; Jan. 9–Jan. 14, 1860; House 1853–55; Senate March 5, 1860–63.

Downey, John Gately (D) June 24, 1827–March 1, 1894; Jan. 14, 1860–Jan. 10, 1862.

Stanford, Leland (R) March 9, 1824–June 21, 1893; Jan. 10, 1862–Dec. 10, 1863; Senate 1885–June 21, 1893.

Low, Frederick Ferdinand (UR) June 30, 1828–July 21, 1894; Dec. 10, 1863–Dec. 5, 1867; House June 3, 1862–63 (Republican).

Haight, Henry Huntly (D) May 20, 1825–Sept. 2, 1878; Dec. 5, 1867–Dec. 8, 1871.

Booth, Newton (R) Dec. 30, 1825–July 14, 1892; Dec. 8, 1871–Feb. 27, 1875; Senate 1875–81 (Anti-Monopolist).

Pacheco, Romualdo (R) Oct. 31, 1831–Jan. 23, 1899; Feb. 27–Dec. 9, 1875; House 1877–Feb. 7, 1878, 1879–83.

Irwin, William (D) 1827–March 15, 1886; Dec. 9, 1875–Jan. 8, 1880.

Perkins, George Clement (R) Aug. 23, 1839–Feb. 26, 1923; Jan. 8, 1880–Jan. 10, 1883; Senate July 26, 1893–1915.

Stoneman, George (D) Aug. 8, 1822–Sept. 5, 1894; Jan. 10, 1883–Jan. 8, 1887.

Bartlett, Washington (D) Feb. 29, 1824–Sept. 12, 1887; Jan. 8–Sept. 12, 1887.

Waterman, Robert Whitney (R) Dec. 15, 1826–April 12, 1891; Sept. 13, 1887–Jan. 8, 1891.

Markham, Henry Harrison (R) Nov. 16, 1840–Oct. 9, 1923; Jan. 8, 1891–Jan. 11, 1895; House 1885–87.

Budd, James Herbert (D) May 18, 1851–July 30, 1908; Jan. 11, 1895–Jan. 3, 1899; House 1883–85.

Gage, Henry Tifft (R) Dec. 25, 1852–Aug. 28, 1924; Jan. 3, 1899–Jan. 6, 1903.

Pardee, George Cooper (R) July 25, 1857–Sept. 1, 1941; Jan. 6, 1903–Jan. 8, 1907.

Gillett, James Norris (R) Sept. 20, 1860–April 20, 1937; Jan. 8, 1907–Jan. 3, 1911; House 1903–Nov. 4, 1906.

Johnson, Hiram Warren (R, Prog.) Sept. 2, 1866–Aug. 6, 1945; Jan. 3, 1911–March 15, 1917; Senate March 16, 1917–Aug. 6, 1945.

Stephens, William Dennison (R) Dec. 26, 1859–April 25, 1944; March 15, 1917–Jan. 9, 1923; House 1911–July 22, 1916 (1911–15 Republican, 1915–July 22, 1916 Progressive).

Richardson, Friend William (R) Dec. 1865–Sept. 6, 1943; Jan. 9, 1923–Jan. 4, 1927.

Young, Clement Calhoun (R) April 28, 1869–Dec. 24, 1947; Jan. 4, 1927–Jan. 6, 1931.

Rolph, James Jr. (R) Aug. 23, 1869–June 2, 1934; Jan. 6, 1931–June 2, 1934.

Merriam, Frank Finley (R) Dec. 22, 1865–April 25, 1955; June 2, 1934–Jan. 2, 1939.

Olson, Culbert Levy (D) Nov. 7, 1876–April 13, 1962; Jan. 2, 1939–Jan. 4, 1943.

Warren, Earl (R) March 19, 1891–July 9, 1974; Jan. 4, 1943–Oct. 5, 1953; chief justice Oct. 5, 1953–June 23, 1969.

Knight, Goodwin Jess (R) Dec. 9, 1896–May 22, 1970; Oct. 5, 1953–Jan. 5, 1959.

Brown, Edmund Gerald "Pat" Sr. (father of Edmund Gerald "Jerry" Brown Jr., below) (D) April 21, 1905–Feb. 16, 1996; Jan. 5, 1959–Jan. 2, 1967.

Reagan, Ronald Wilson (R) Feb. 6, 1911– ; Jan. 5, 1967–Jan. 6, 1975; president 1981–89.

Brown, Edmund Gerald "Jerry" Jr. (son of Edmund Gerald "Pat" Brown Sr., above) (D) April 7, 1938– ; Jan. 6, 1975–Jan. 3, 1983.

Deukmejian, George (R) June 6, 1928– ; Jan. 3, 1983–Jan. 7, 1991.

Wilson, Peter Barton "Pete" (R) Aug. 23, 1933– ; Jan. 7, 1991–Jan. 4, 1999; Senate 1983–Jan. 7, 1991.

Davis, Gray (D) Dec. 26, 1942– ; Jan. 4, 1999–Nov. 17, 2003.

Schwarzenegger, Arnold (R) July 30, 1947– ; Nov. 17, 2003– .

Colorado

(Became a state Aug. 1, 1876)

Routt, John Long (R) April 25, 1826–Aug. 13, 1907; Nov. 3, 1876–Jan. 14, 1879, Jan. 13, 1891–Jan. 10, 1893.

Pitkin, Frederick Walker (R) Aug. 31, 1837–Dec. 18, 1886; Jan. 14, 1879–Jan. 9, 1883.

Grant, James Benton (D) Jan. 2, 1848–Nov. 1, 1911; Jan. 9, 1883–Jan. 13, 1885.

Eaton, Benjamin Harrison (R) Dec. 15, 1833–Oct. 29, 1904; Jan. 13, 1885–Jan. 11, 1887.

Adams, Alva (brother of William Herbert Adams, below) (D) May 14, 1850–Nov. 1, 1922; Jan. 11, 1887–Jan. 10, 1889, Jan. 12, 1897–Jan. 10, 1899, Jan. 10–March 17, 1905.

Cooper, Job Adams (R) Nov. 6, 1843–Jan. 20, 1899; Jan. 10, 1889–Jan. 13, 1891.

Routt, John Long (R) Jan. 13, 1891–Jan. 10, 1893 (for previous term see above).

Waite, Davis Hanson (P) April 9, 1825–Nov. 27, 1901; Jan. 10, 1893–Jan. 8, 1895.

McIntire, Albert Wills (R) Jan. 15, 1853–Jan. 30, 1935; Jan. 8, 1895–Jan. 12, 1897.

Adams, Alva (D) Jan. 12, 1897–Jan. 10, 1899 (for previous term see above).

Thomas, Charles Spalding (D) Dec. 6, 1849–June 24, 1934; Jan. 10, 1899–Jan. 8, 1901; Senate Jan. 15, 1913–21.

Orman, James B. (D) Nov. 4, 1849–July 21, 1919; Jan. 8, 1901–Jan. 13, 1903.

Peabody, James Hamilton (R) Aug. 21, 1852–Nov. 23, 1917; Jan. 13, 1903–Jan. 10, 1905, March 17, 1905.

Adams, Alva (D) Jan. 10–March 17, 1905 (for previous terms see above).

Peabody, James Hamilton (R) March 17, 1905 (for previous term see above).

McDonald, Jesse Fuller (R) June 30, 1858–Feb. 25, 1942; March 17, 1905–Jan. 8, 1907.

Buchtel, Henry Augustus (R) Sept. 30, 1847–Oct. 22, 1924; Jan. 8, 1907–Jan. 12, 1909.

Shafroth, John Franklin (D) June 9, 1854–Feb. 20, 1922; Jan. 12, 1909–Jan. 14, 1913; House 1895–Feb. 15, 1904 (1895–97 Republican, 1897–1903 Silver Republican); Senate 1913–19.

Ammons, Elias Milton (father of Teller Ammons, below) (D) July 28, 1860–May 20, 1925; Jan. 14, 1913–Jan. 12, 1915.

Carlson, George Alfred (R) Oct. 23, 1876–Dec. 6, 1926; Jan. 12, 1915–Jan. 9, 1917.

Gunter, Julius Caldeen (D) Oct. 31, 1858–Oct. 26, 1940; Jan. 9, 1917–Jan. 14, 1919.

Shoup, Oliver Henry Nelson (R) Dec. 13, 1869–Sept. 30, 1940; Jan. 14, 1919–Jan. 9, 1923.

Sweet, William Ellery (D) Jan. 27, 1869–May 9, 1942; Jan. 9, 1923–Jan. 13, 1925.

Morley, Clarence J. (R) Feb. 9, 1869–Nov. 15, 1948; Jan. 13, 1925–Jan. 11, 1927.

Adams, William Herbert (brother of Alva Adams, above) (D) Feb. 15, 1861–Feb. 4, 1954; Jan. 11, 1927–Jan. 10, 1933.

Johnson, Edwin Carl (D) Jan. 1, 1884–May 30, 1970; Jan. 10, 1933–Jan. 2, 1937, Jan. 11, 1955–Jan. 8, 1957; Senate 1937–55.

Talbot, Ray H. (D) Aug. 19, 1896–Jan. 31, 1955; Jan. 3–Jan. 12, 1937.

Ammons, Teller (son of Elias Milton Ammons, above) (D) Dec. 3, 1895–Jan. 16, 1972; Jan. 12, 1937–Jan. 10, 1939.

Carr, Ralph L. (R) Dec. 11, 1887–Sept. 22, 1950; Jan. 10, 1939–Jan. 12, 1943.

Vivian, John Charles (R) June 30, 1887–Feb. 10, 1964; Jan. 12, 1943–Jan. 14, 1947.

Knous, William Lee (D) Feb. 2, 1889–Dec. 13, 1959; Jan. 14, 1947–April 15, 1950.

Johnson, Walter Walfred (D) April 16, 1904–March 23, 1987; April 15, 1950–Jan. 9, 1951.

Thornton, Daniel Isaac J. (R) Jan. 31, 1911–Jan. 18, 1976; Jan. 9, 1951–Jan. 11, 1955.

Johnson, Edwin Carl (D) Jan. 11, 1955–Jan. 8, 1957 (for previous term see above).

McNichols, Stephen L. R. (D) March 17, 1914–Nov. 25, 1997; Jan. 8, 1957–Jan. 8, 1963.

Love, John A. (R) Nov. 29, 1916–Jan. 21, 2002; Jan. 8, 1963–July 16, 1973.

Vanderhoof, John David (R) May 27, 1922– ; July 16, 1973–Jan. 14, 1975.

Lamm, Richard David (D) Aug. 3, 1935– ; Jan. 14, 1975–Jan. 13, 1987.

Romer, Roy (D) Oct. 31, 1928– ; Jan. 13, 1987–Jan. 12, 1999; general chair Dem. Nat. Comm. 1997–99.

Owens, Bill (R) Oct. 22, 1950– ; Jan. 12, 1999– .

Connecticut

(Ratified the Constitution Jan. 9, 1788)

Huntington, Samuel (uncle of Samuel H. Huntington of Ohio) (F) July 3, 1731–Jan. 5, 1796; May 11, 1786–Jan. 5, 1796; Cont. Cong. 1776, 1778–81, 1783.

Wolcott, Oliver Sr. (father of Oliver Wolcott Jr., below, uncle of Roger Griswold, below) (F) Dec. 20, 1726–Dec. 1, 1797; Jan. 5, 1796–Dec. 1, 1797; Cont. Cong. 1776–78, 1780–83.

Trumbull, Jonathan Jr. (-) March 26, 1740–Aug. 7, 1809; Dec. 1, 1797–Aug. 7, 1809; House 1789–95; Speaker Oct. 24, 1791–93; Senate 1795–June 10, 1796.

Treadwell, John (F) Nov. 23, 1745–Aug. 18, 1823; Aug. 7, 1809–May 9, 1811; Cont. Cong. (elected but did not attend) 1784, 1785, 1787.

Griswold, Roger (nephew of Oliver Wolcott Sr., above, cousin of Oliver Wolcott Jr., below) (F) May 21, 1762–Oct. 25, 1812; May 9, 1811–Oct. 25, 1812; House 1795–1805.

Smith, John Cotton (F) Feb. 12, 1765–Dec. 7, 1845; Oct. 25, 1812–May 8, 1817; House Nov. 17, 1800–Aug. 1806.

Wolcott, Oliver Jr. (son of Oliver Wolcott Sr., above, cousin of Roger Griswold, above) (DR) Jan. 11, 1760–June 1, 1833; May 8, 1817–May 2, 1827; secretary of the Treasury Feb. 3, 1795–Dec. 31, 1800.

Tomlinson, Gideon (DR) Dec. 31, 1780–Oct. 8, 1854; May 2, 1827–March 2, 1831; House 1819–27 (no party); Senate 1831–37 (no party).

Peters, John Samuel (NR) Sept. 21, 1772–March 30, 1858; March 2, 1831–May 4, 1833.

Edwards, Henry Waggaman (D) Oct. 1779–July 22, 1847; May 4, 1833–May 7, 1834, May 6, 1835–May 2, 1838; House 1819–23; Senate Oct. 8, 1823–27.

Foot, Samuel Augustus (W) Nov. 8, 1780–Sept. 15, 1846; May 7, 1834–May 6, 1835; House 1819–21 (no party), 1823–25 (no party), 1833–May 9, 1834 (no party); Senate 1827–33 (no party).

Edwards, Henry Waggaman (D) May 6, 1835–May 2, 1838 (for previous term see above).

Ellsworth, William Wolcott (W) Nov. 10, 1791–Jan. 15, 1868; May 2, 1838–May 4, 1842; House 1829–July 8, 1834 (no party).

Cleveland, Chauncey Fitch (D) Feb. 16, 1799–June 6, 1887; May 4, 1842–May 1844; House 1849–53.

Baldwin, Roger Sherman (father of Simeon Eben Baldwin, below) (W) Jan. 4, 1793–Feb. 19, 1863; May 1844–May 6, 1846; Senate Nov. 11, 1847–51.

Toucey, Isaac (D) Nov. 15, 1792–July 30, 1869; May 6, 1846–May 5, 1847; House 1835–39; Senate May 12, 1852–57; attorney general June 21, 1848–March 3, 1849; secretary of the navy March 7, 1857–March 6, 1861.

Bissell, Clark (W) Sept. 7, 1782–Sept. 15, 1857; May 5, 1847–May 2, 1849.

Trumbull, Joseph (W) Dec. 7, 1782–Aug. 4, 1861; May 2, 1849–May 4, 1850; House Dec. 1, 1834–35 (no party), 1839–43.

Seymour, Thomas Hart (D) Sept. 29, 1807–Sept. 3, 1868; May 4, 1850–Oct. 13, 1853; House 1843–45 (Democrat).

Pond, Charles Hobby (D) April 26, 1781–April 28, 1861; Oct. 13, 1853–May 1854.

Dutton, Henry (W) Feb. 12, 1796–April 26, 1869; May 1854–May 1855.

Minor, William Thomas (AP) Oct. 3, 1815–Oct. 13, 1889; May 3, 1855–May 6, 1857.

Holley, Alexander Hamilton (R) Aug. 12, 1804–Oct. 2, 1887; May 6, 1857–May 5, 1858.

Buckingham, William Alfred (R) May 28, 1804–Feb. 5, 1875; May 5, 1858–May 2, 1866; Senate 1869–Feb. 5, 1875.

Hawley, Joseph Roswell (R) Oct. 31, 1826–March 17, 1905; May 2, 1866–May 1, 1867; House Dec. 2, 1872–75, 1879–81; Senate 1881–1905.

English, James Edward (D) March 13, 1812–March 2, 1890; May 1, 1867–May 5, 1869, May 4, 1870–May 16, 1871; House 1861–65; Senate Nov. 27, 1875–May 17, 1876.

Jewell, Marshall (R) Oct. 20, 1825–Feb. 10, 1883; May 5, 1869–May 4, 1870, May 16, 1871–May 7, 1873; postmaster general Sept. 1, 1874–July 12, 1876; chair Rep. Nat. Comm. 1880–83.

English, James Edward (D) May 4, 1870–May 16, 1871 (for previous term see above).

Jewell, Marshall (R) May 16, 1871–May 7, 1873 (for previous term see above).

Ingersoll, Charles Roberts (D) Sept. 16, 1821–Jan. 25, 1903; May 7, 1873–Jan. 3, 1877.

Hubbard, Richard Dudley (D) Sept. 7, 1818–Feb. 28, 1884; Jan. 3, 1877–Jan. 9, 1879; House 1867–69.

Andrews, Charles Bartlett (R) Nov. 4, 1836–Sept. 12, 1902; Jan. 9, 1879–Jan. 5, 1881.

Bigelow, Hobart B. (R) May 16, 1834–Oct. 12, 1891; Jan. 5, 1881–Jan. 3, 1883.

Waller, Thomas MacDonald (D) 1839–Jan. 24, 1924; Jan. 3, 1883–Jan. 8, 1885.

Harrison, Henry Baldwin (R) Sept. 11, 1821–Oct. 29, 1901; Jan. 8, 1885–Jan. 7, 1887.

Lounsbury, Phineas Chapman (brother of George Edward Lounsbury, below) (R) Jan. 10, 1841–June 22, 1925; Jan. 7, 1887–Jan. 10, 1889.

Bulkeley, Morgan Gardner (cousin of Edwin Denison Morgan of N.Y.) (R) Dec. 26, 1837–Nov. 6, 1922; Jan. 10, 1889–Jan. 4, 1893; Senate 1905–11.

Morris, Luzon Burritt (D) April 16, 1827–Aug. 22, 1895; Jan. 4, 1893–Jan. 9, 1895.

Coffin, Owen Vincent (R) June 20, 1836–Jan. 3, 1921; Jan. 9, 1895–Jan. 6, 1897.

Cooke, Lorrin Alamson (R) April 6, 1831–Aug. 12, 1902; Jan. 6, 1897–Jan. 4, 1899.

Lounsbury, George Edward (brother of Phineas Chapman Lounsbury, above) (R) May 7, 1838–Aug. 16, 1904; Jan. 4, 1899–Jan. 9, 1901.

McLean, George Payne (R) Oct. 7, 1857–June 6, 1932; Jan. 9, 1901–Jan. 7, 1903; Senate 1911–29.

Chamberlain, Abiram (R) Dec. 7, 1837–May 15, 1911; Jan. 7, 1903–Jan. 4, 1905.

Roberts, Henry (R) Jan. 22, 1853–May 1, 1929; Jan. 4, 1905–Jan. 9, 1907.

Woodruff, Rollin Simmons (R) July 14, 1854–June 30, 1925; Jan. 9, 1907–Jan. 6, 1909.

Lilley, George Leavens (R) Aug. 3, 1859–April 21, 1909; Jan. 6–April 21, 1909; House 1903–Jan. 5, 1909.

Weeks, Frank Bentley (R) Jan. 20, 1854–Oct. 2, 1935; April 21, 1909–Jan. 4, 1911.

Baldwin, Simeon Eben (son of Roger Sherman Baldwin, above) (D) Feb. 5, 1840–Jan. 30, 1927; Jan. 4, 1911–Jan. 6, 1915.

Holcomb, Marcus Hensey (R) Nov. 28, 1884–March 5, 1932; Jan. 6, 1915–Jan. 5, 1921.

Lake, Everett John (R) Feb. 8, 1871–Sept. 16, 1948; Jan. 5, 1921–Jan. 3, 1923.

Templeton, Charles Augustus (R) March 3, 1871–Aug. 15, 1955; Jan. 3, 1923–Jan. 7, 1925.

Bingham, Hiram (R) Nov. 19, 1875–June 6, 1956; Jan. 7–Jan. 8, 1925; Senate Dec. 17, 1924–33.

Trumbull, John Harper (R) March 4, 1873–May 21, 1961; Jan. 8, 1925–Jan. 7, 1931.

Cross, Wilbur Lucius (D) April 10, 1862–Oct. 5, 1948; Jan. 7, 1931–Jan. 4, 1939.

Baldwin, Raymond Earl (R) Aug. 31, 1893–Oct. 4, 1986; Jan. 4, 1939–Jan. 8, 1941, Jan. 6, 1943–Dec. 27, 1946; Senate Dec. 27, 1946–Dec. 16, 1949.

Hurley, Robert Augustine (D) Aug. 25, 1895–May 3, 1968; Jan. 8, 1941–Jan. 6, 1943.

Baldwin, Raymond Earl (R) Jan. 6, 1943–Dec. 27, 1946 (for previous term see above).

Snow, Charles Wilbert (D) April 6, 1884–Sept. 28, 1977; Dec. 27, 1946–Jan. 8, 1947.

McConaughy, James Lukens (R) Oct. 21, 1887–March 7, 1948; Jan. 8, 1947–March 7, 1948.

Shannon, James Coughlin (R) July 21, 1896–March 1980; March 7, 1948–Jan. 5, 1949.

Bowles, Chester Bliss (D) April 5, 1901–May 25, 1986; Jan. 5, 1949–Jan. 3, 1951; House 1959–61.

Lodge, John Davis (R) Oct. 20, 1903–Oct. 29, 1985; Jan. 3, 1951–Jan. 5, 1955; House 1947–51.

Ribicoff, Abraham Alexander (D) April 9, 1910–Feb. 22, 1998; Jan. 5, 1955–Jan. 21, 1961; House 1949–53; Senate 1963–81; secretary of health, education and welfare Jan. 21, 1961–July 13, 1962.

Dempsey, John Noel (D) Jan. 3, 1915–July 16, 1989; Jan. 21, 1961–Jan. 6, 1971.

Meskill, Thomas Joseph (R) Jan. 30, 1928– ; Jan. 6, 1971–Jan. 8, 1975; House 1967–71.

Grasso, Ella Tambussi (D) May 10, 1919–Feb. 5, 1981; Jan. 8, 1975–Dec. 31, 1980; House 1971–75.

O'Neill, William Atchinson (D) Aug. 11, 1930– ; Dec. 31, 1980–Jan. 9, 1991.

Weicker, Lowell Palmer Jr. (I) May 16, 1931– ; Jan. 9, 1991–Jan. 4, 1995; House 1969–71 (Republican); Senate 1971–89 (Republican).

Rowland, John G. (R) May 24, 1957– ; Jan. 4, 1995–July 1, 2004; House 1985–91.

Rell, M. Jodi (R) June 16, 1946– ; July 1, 2004– .

Delaware

(Ratified the Constitution Dec. 7, 1787)

Clayton, Joshua (son-in-law of Richard Bassett, below) (F) July 20, 1744–Aug. 11, 1798; June 2, 1789–Jan. 13, 1796; Senate Jan. 19–Aug. 11, 1798 (no party).

Bedford, Gunning Sr. (F) April 7, 1742–Sept. 28, 1797; Jan. 13, 1796–Sept. 28, 1797; Cont. Cong. (elected but did not attend) 1786.

Rogers, Daniel (F) Jan. 3, 1754–Feb. 2, 1806; Sept. 28, 1797–Jan. 9, 1799.

Bassett, Richard (father-in-law of Joshua Clayton, above) (F) April 2, 1745–Aug. 15, 1815; Jan. 9, 1799–March 3, 1801; Senate 1789–93.

Sykes, James (F) March 27, 1761–Oct. 18, 1822; March 3, 1801–Jan. 19, 1802.

Hall, David (DR) Jan. 4, 1752–Sept. 18, 1817; Jan. 19, 1802–Jan. 15, 1805.

Mitchell, Nathaniel (F) 1753–Feb. 21, 1814; Jan. 15, 1805–Jan. 19, 1808; Cont. Cong. 1787–88.

Truitt, George (F) 1756–Oct. 8, 1818; Jan. 19, 1808–Jan. 15, 1811.

Haslet, Joseph (DR) 1769–June 20, 1823; Jan. 15, 1811–Jan. 18, 1814, Jan. 21–June 20, 1823.

Rodney, Daniel (brother of Caleb Rodney, below) (F) Sept. 10, 1764–Sept. 2, 1846; Jan. 18, 1814–Jan. 21, 1817; House Oct. 1, 1822–23 (no party); Senate Nov. 8, 1826–Jan. 12, 1827 (no party).

Clark, John (F) Feb. 1, 1761–Aug. 14, 1821; Jan. 21, 1817–Jan. 15, 1820.

Stout, Jacob (F) 1764–Nov. 1855; Jan. 15, 1820–Jan. 16, 1821.

Collins, John (DR) 1775–April 15, 1822; Jan. 16, 1821–April 15, 1822.

Rodney, Caleb (brother of Daniel Rodney, above) (DR) April 29, 1767–April 29, 1840; April 15, 1822–Jan. 21, 1823.

Haslet, Joseph (DR) Jan. 21–June 20, 1823 (for previous term see above).

Thomas, Charles (DR) June 23, 1790–Feb. 8, 1848; June 20, 1823–Jan. 20, 1824.

Paynter, Samuel (F) 1768–Oct. 2, 1845; Jan. 20, 1824–Jan. 16, 1827.

Polk, Charles (F) Nov. 15, 1788–Oct. 27, 1857; Jan. 16, 1827–Jan. 19, 1830, May 9, 1836–Jan. 17, 1837.

Hazzard, David (D) May 18, 1781–July 8, 1864; Jan. 19, 1830–Jan. 15, 1833.

Bennett, Caleb Prew (D) Nov. 11, 1758–May 9, 1836; Jan. 15, 1833–May 9, 1836.

Polk, Charles (F) May 9, 1836–Jan. 17, 1837 (for previous term see above).

Comegys, Cornelius Parsons (W) Jan. 15, 1780–Jan. 27, 1851; Jan. 17, 1837–Jan. 19, 1841.

Cooper, William B. (W) Dec. 16, 1771–April 27, 1849; Jan. 19, 1841–Jan. 21, 1845.

Stockton, Thomas (W) April 1, 1781–March 2, 1846; Jan. 21, 1845–March 2, 1846.

Maull, Joseph (W) Sept. 6, 1781–May 1, 1846; March 2–May 1, 1846.

Temple, William (W) Feb. 28, 1814–May 28, 1863; May 1, 1846–Jan. 19, 1847.

Tharp, William (grandfather of William T. Watson, below) (D) Nov. 27, 1803–Jan. 1, 1865; Jan. 19, 1847–Jan. 21, 1851.

Ross, William Henry Harrison (D) June 2, 1814–June 29, 1887; Jan. 21, 1851–Jan. 16, 1855.

Causey, Peter Foster (uncle of Trusten Polk of Mo.) (AW) Jan. 11, 1801–Feb. 15, 1871; Jan. 16, 1855–Jan. 18, 1859.

Burton, William (D) Oct. 16, 1789–Aug. 5, 1866; Jan. 18, 1859–Jan. 20, 1863.

Cannon, William (U) March 15, 1809–March 1, 1865; Jan. 20, 1863–March 1, 1865.

Saulsbury, Gove (D) May 29, 1815–July 31, 1881; March 1, 1865–Jan. 17, 1871.

Ponder, James (D) Oct. 31, 1819–Nov. 5, 1897; Jan. 17, 1871–Jan. 19, 1875.

Cochran, John P. (D) Feb. 7, 1809–Dec. 27, 1898; Jan. 19, 1875–Jan. 21, 1879.

Hall, John Wood (D) Jan. 1, 1817–Jan. 23, 1892; Jan. 21, 1879–Jan. 16, 1883.

Stockley, Charles Clark (D) Nov. 6, 1819–April 20, 1901; Jan. 16, 1883–Jan. 18, 1887.

Biggs, Benjamin Thomas (D) Oct. 1, 1821–Dec. 25, 1893; Jan. 18, 1887–Jan. 20, 1891; House 1869–73.

Reynolds, Robert John (D) March 17, 1838–June 10, 1909; Jan. 20, 1891–Jan. 15, 1895.

Marviel, Joshua Hopkins (R) Sept. 3, 1825–April 8, 1895; Jan. 15–April 8, 1895.

Watson, William T. (grandson of William Tharp, above) (D) June 6, 1849–April 14, 1917; April 8, 1895–Jan. 19, 1897.

Tunnel, Ebe Walter (D) Dec. 31, 1844–Dec. 13, 1917; Jan. 19, 1897–Jan. 15, 1901.

Hunn, John (R) June 23, 1849–Sept. 1, 1926; Jan. 15, 1901–Jan. 17, 1905.

Lea, Preston (R) Nov. 12, 1841–Dec. 4, 1916; Jan. 17, 1905–Jan. 19, 1909.

Pennewill, Simeon Selby (R) July 23, 1867–Sept. 9, 1935; Jan. 19, 1909–Jan. 21, 1913.

Miller, Charles R. (R) Sept. 30, 1857–Sept. 18, 1927; Jan. 21, 1913–Jan. 17, 1917.

Townsend, John Gillis Jr. (R) May 31, 1871–April 10, 1964; Jan. 17, 1917–Jan. 18, 1921; Senate 1929–41.

Denney, William Du Hamel (R) March 31, 1873–Nov. 22, 1953; Jan. 18, 1921–Jan. 20, 1925.

Robinson, Robert P. (R) March 28, 1869–March 4, 1939; Jan. 20, 1925–Jan. 15, 1929.

Buck, Clayton Douglass (R) March 21, 1890–Jan. 27, 1965; Jan. 15, 1929–Jan. 19, 1937; Senate 1943–49.

McMullen, Richard Cann (D) Jan. 2, 1868–Feb. 18, 1944; Jan. 19, 1937–Jan. 21, 1941.

Bacon, Walter W. (R) Jan. 20, 1879–March 18, 1962; Jan. 21, 1941–Jan. 18, 1949.

Carvel, Elbert Nostrand (D) Feb. 9, 1910–Feb. 6, 2005; Jan. 18, 1949–Jan. 20, 1953, Jan. 17, 1961–Jan. 19, 1965.

Boggs, James Caleb (R) May 15, 1909–March 26, 1993; Jan. 20, 1953–Dec. 30, 1960; House 1947–53; Senate 1961–73.

Buckson, David Penrose (R) July 25, 1920– ; Dec. 30, 1960–Jan. 17, 1961.

Carvel, Elbert Nostrand (D) Jan. 17, 1961–Jan. 19, 1965 (for previous term see above).

Terry, Charles Laymen Jr. (D) Sept. 17, 1900–Feb. 6, 1970; Jan. 19, 1965–Jan. 21, 1969.

Peterson, Russell Wilbur (R) Oct. 3, 1916– ; Jan. 21, 1969–Jan. 16, 1973.

Tribbitt, Sherman Willard (D) Nov. 9, 1922–Jan. 16, 1973–Jan. 18, 1977.

du Pont, Pierre Samuel "Pete" IV (R) Jan. 22, 1935– ; Jan. 18, 1977–Jan. 15, 1985; House 1971–77.

Castle, Michael Newbold (R) July 2, 1939– ; Jan. 15, 1985–Dec. 31, 1992; House 1993– .

Wolf, Dale Edward (R) Sept. 6, 1924– ; Jan. 1–Jan. 19, 1993.

Carper, Thomas Richard (D) Jan. 23, 1947– ; Jan. 19, 1993–Jan. 3, 2001; House 1983–93; Senate 2001– .

Minner, Ruth Ann (D) Jan. 17, 1935– ; Jan. 3, 2001– .

Florida

(Became a state March 3, 1845)

Moseley, William Dunn (D) Feb. 1, 1795–Jan. 4, 1863; June 25, 1845–Oct. 1, 1849.

Brown, Thomas (W) Oct. 24, 1785–Aug. 24, 1867; Oct. 1, 1849–Oct. 3, 1853.

Broome, James E. (D) Dec. 15, 1808–Nov. 23, 1883; Oct. 3, 1853–Oct. 5, 1857.

Perry, Madison Stark (D) 1814–March 1865; Oct. 5, 1857–Oct. 7, 1861.

Milton, John (D) April 20, 1807–April 1, 1865; Oct. 7, 1861–April 1, 1865.

Marvin, William (D) April 14, 1808–July 9, 1902; July 13–Dec. 20, 1865.

Walker, David Shelby (C) May 2, 1815–July 20, 1891; Dec. 20, 1865–July 9, 1868.

Reed, Harrison (R) Aug. 26, 1813–March 25, 1899; July 9, 1868–Jan. 7, 1873.

Hart, Ossian Bingley (R) Jan. 17, 1821–March 18, 1874; Jan. 7, 1873–March 18, 1874.

Stearns, Marcellus Lovejoy (R) April 29, 1839–Dec. 8, 1891; March 18, 1874–Jan. 2, 1877.

Drew, George Franklin (D) Aug. 6, 1827–Sept. 26, 1900; Jan. 2, 1877–Jan. 4, 1881.

Bloxham, William Dunnington (D) July 9, 1835–March 15, 1911; Jan. 4, 1881–Jan. 6, 1885, Jan. 5, 1897–Jan. 8, 1901.

Perry, Edward Alysworth (D) March 15, 1831–Oct. 15, 1889; Jan. 6, 1885–Jan. 8, 1889.

Fleming, Francis Philip (D) Sept. 28, 1841–Dec. 20, 1908; Jan. 8, 1889–Jan. 3, 1893.

Mitchell, Henry Laurens (D) Sept. 3, 1831–Oct. 14, 1903; Jan. 3, 1893–Jan. 5, 1897.

Bloxham, William Dunnington (D) Jan. 5, 1897–Jan. 8, 1901 (for previous term see above).

Jennings, William Sherman (D) March 24, 1863–Feb. 28, 1920; Jan. 8, 1901–Jan. 3, 1905.

Broward, Napoleon Bonaparte (D) April 19, 1857–Oct. 1, 1910; Jan. 3, 1905–Jan. 5, 1909.

Gilchrist, Albert Waller (D) Jan. 15, 1858–May 15, 1926; Jan. 5, 1909–Jan. 7, 1913.

Trammell, Park (D) April 9, 1876–May 8, 1936; Jan. 7, 1913–Jan. 2, 1917; Senate 1917–May 8, 1936.

Catts, Sidney Johnston (Prohib.) July 31, 1863–March 9, 1936; Jan. 2, 1917–Jan. 4, 1921.

Hardee, Cary Augustus (D) Nov. 13, 1876–Nov. 21, 1957; Jan. 4, 1921–Jan. 6, 1925.

Martin, John Wellborn (D) June 21, 1884–Feb. 22, 1958; Jan. 6, 1925–Jan. 8, 1929.

Carlton, Doyle Elam (D) July 6, 1887–Oct. 25, 1972; Jan. 8, 1929–Jan. 3, 1933.

Sholtz, David (D) Oct. 6, 1891–March 21, 1953; Jan. 3, 1933–Jan. 5, 1937.

Cone, Frederick Preston (D) Sept. 28, 1871–July 28, 1948; Jan. 5, 1937–Jan. 7, 1941.

Holland, Spessard Lindsey (D) July 10, 1892–Nov. 6, 1971; Jan. 7, 1941–Jan. 2, 1945; Senate Sept. 25, 1946–71.

Caldwell, Millard Fillmore (D) Feb. 6, 1897–Oct. 23, 1984; Jan. 2, 1945–Jan. 4, 1949; House 1933–41.

Warren, Fuller (D) Oct. 3, 1905–Sept. 23, 1973; Jan. 4, 1949–Jan. 6, 1953.

McCarty, Daniel Thomas (D) Jan. 18, 1912–Sept. 28, 1953; Jan. 6–Sept. 28, 1953.

Johns, Charley Eugene (D) Feb. 27, 1905–Jan. 23, 1990; Sept. 28, 1953–Jan. 4, 1955.

Collins, Thomas LeRoy (D) March 19, 1909–March 12, 1991; Jan. 4, 1955–Jan. 3, 1961.

Bryant, Cecil Farris (D) July 26, 1914– ; Jan. 3, 1961–Jan. 5, 1965.

Burns, William Haydon (D) March 17, 1912–Nov. 11, 1989; Jan. 5, 1965–Jan. 3, 1967.

Kirk, Claude Roy Jr. (R) Jan. 7, 1926– ; Jan. 3, 1967–Jan. 5, 1971.

Askew, Reubin O'Donovan (D) Sept. 11, 1928– ; Jan. 5, 1971–Jan. 2, 1979.

Graham, Daniel Robert "Bob" (D) Nov. 9, 1936– ; Jan. 2, 1979–Jan. 3, 1987; Senate 1987–2005.

Mixon, John Wayne (D) June 16, 1922– ; Jan. 3–Jan. 6, 1987.

Martinez, Robert (R) Dec. 25, 1934– ; Jan. 6, 1987–Jan. 8, 1991.

Chiles, Lawton Mainor Jr. (D) April 3, 1930–Dec. 12, 1998; Jan. 8, 1991–Dec. 12, 1998; Senate 1971–89.

MacKay, Buddy (D) March 22, 1933– ; Dec. 13, 1998–Jan. 5, 1999; House 1983–89.

Bush, John Ellis "Jeb" (son of Pres. George Herbert Walker Bush, brother of Pres. George W. Bush) (R) Feb. 11, 1953– ; Jan. 5, 1999– .

Georgia

(Ratified the Constitution Jan. 2, 1788)

Handley, George (DR) Feb. 9, 1752–Sept. 17, 1793; Jan. 26, 1788–Jan. 7, 1789.

Walton, George (DR) 1749–Feb. 2, 1804; Jan. 7–Nov. 9, 1789; Cont. Cong. 1776–77, 1780–81; Senate Nov. 16, 1795–Feb. 20, 1796 (no party).

Telfair, Edward (DR) 1735–Sept. 17, 1807; Nov. 9, 1789–Nov. 7, 1793; Cont. Cong. 1778, 1780–82.

Mathews, George (DR) Aug. 30, 1739–Aug. 30, 1812; Nov. 7, 1793–Jan. 15, 1796; House 1789–91 (no party).

Irwin, Jared (DR) 1750–March 1, 1818; Jan. 15, 1796–Jan. 12, 1798, Sept. 23, 1806–Nov. 10, 1809.

Jackson, James (DR) Sept. 21, 1757–March 19, 1806; Jan. 12, 1798–March 3, 1801; House 1789–91 (no party); Senate 1793–95 (no party), 1801–March 19, 1806 (Republican).

Emanuel, David (DR) 1744–Feb. 19, 1808; March 31–Nov. 7, 1801.

Tattnall, Josiah (DR) 1764–June 6, 1803; Nov. 7, 1801–Nov. 4, 1802; Senate Feb. 20, 1796–99 (Republican).

Milledge, John (DR) 1757–Feb. 9, 1818; Nov. 4, 1802–Sept. 23, 1806; House Nov. 22, 1792–93 (no party), 1795–99 (no party), 1801–May 1802 (Republican); Senate June 19, 1806–Nov. 14, 1809 (Republican); elected pres. pro tempore Jan. 30, 1809.

Irwin, Jared (DR) Sept. 23, 1806–Nov. 10, 1809 (for previous term see above).

Mitchell, David Brydie (DR) Oct. 22, 1766–April 22, 1837; Nov. 10, 1809–Nov. 5, 1813, Nov. 10, 1815–March 4, 1817.

Early, Peter (DR) June 20, 1773–Aug. 15, 1817; Nov. 5, 1813–Nov. 10, 1815; House Jan. 10, 1803–07 (Republican).

Mitchell, David Brydie (DR) Nov. 10, 1815–March 4, 1817 (for previous term see above).

Rabun, William (DR) April 8, 1771–Oct. 25, 1819; March 4, 1817–Oct. 24, 1819.

Talbot, Matthew (DR) 1767–Sept. 17, 1827; Oct. 24–Nov. 5, 1819.

Clark, John (father of Edward Clark of Texas) (DR) Feb. 28, 1766–Oct. 2, 1832; Nov. 5, 1819–Nov. 7, 1823.

Troup, George Michael (DR) Sept. 8, 1780–April 26, 1856; Nov. 7, 1823–Nov. 7, 1827; House 1807–15 (Republican); Senate Nov. 13, 1816–Sept. 23, 1818 (Republican), 1829–Nov. 8, 1833 (Republican).

Forsyth, John (DR) Oct. 22, 1780–Oct. 21, 1841; Nov. 7, 1827–Nov. 4, 1829; House 1813–Nov. 23, 1818 (Republican), 1823–Nov. 7, 1827 (Republican); Senate Nov. 23, 1818–Feb. 17, 1819 (Republican), Nov. 9, 1829–June 27, 1834 (Jacksonian); secretary of state July 1, 1834–March 3, 1841.

Gilmer, George Rockingham (W) April 11, 1790–Nov. 16, 1859; Nov. 4, 1829–Nov. 9, 1831 (Jacksonian), Nov. 8, 1837–Nov. 6, 1839; House 1821–23 (no party), Oct. 1, 1827–29 (no party), 1833–35 (Jacksonian).

Lumpkin, Wilson (UD) Jan. 14, 1783–Dec. 28, 1870; Nov. 9, 1831–Nov. 4, 1835; House 1815–17 (no party), 1827–31 (no party); Senate Nov. 22, 1837–41 (no party).

Schley, William (U) Dec. 15, 1786–Nov. 20, 1858; Nov. 4, 1835–Nov. 8, 1837; House 1833–July 1, 1835 (Jacksonian).

Gilmer, George Rockingham (W) Nov. 8, 1837–Nov. 6, 1839 (for previous term see above).

McDonald, Charles James (D) July 9, 1793–Dec. 16, 1860; Nov. 6, 1839–Nov. 8, 1843.

Crawford, George W. (W) Dec. 22, 1798–July 27, 1872; Nov. 8, 1843–Nov. 3, 1847; House Jan. 7–March 3, 1843; secretary of war March 8, 1849–July 23, 1850.

Towns, George Washington Bonaparte (D) May 4, 1801–July 15, 1854; Nov. 3, 1847–Nov. 5, 1851; House 1835–Sept. 1, 1836 (Jacksonian), 1837–39, Jan. 5, 1846–47.

Cobb, Howell (UD) Sept. 7, 1815–Oct. 9, 1868; Nov. 5, 1851–Nov. 9, 1853; House 1843–51 (Democrat), 1855–57 (Democrat); Speaker Dec. 22, 1849–51; secretary of the Treasury March 7, 1857–Dec. 8, 1860.

Johnson, Herschel Vespasian (D) Sept. 18, 1812–Aug. 16, 1880; Nov. 9, 1853–Nov. 6, 1857; Senate Feb. 4, 1848–49.

Brown, Joseph Emerson (father of Joseph Mackey Brown, below) (D) April 15, 1821–Nov. 30, 1894; Nov. 6, 1857–June 17, 1865; Senate May 26, 1880–91.

Johnson, James (D) Feb. 12, 1811–Nov. 20, 1891; (Provisional) June 17–Dec. 14, 1865; House 1851–53 (Unionist).

Jenkins, Charles Jones (D) Jan. 6, 1805–June 14, 1883; Dec. 14, 1865–Jan. 13, 1868.

Ruger, Thomas Howard April 2, 1833–June 3, 1907; (Military) Jan. 13–July 4, 1868.

Bullock, Rufus Brown (R) March 28, 1834–April 27, 1907; July 4, 1868–Oct. 23, 1871.

Conley, Benjamin (R) March 1, 1815–Jan. 10, 1886; Oct. 30, 1871–Jan. 12, 1872.

Smith, James Milton (D) Oct. 24, 1823–Nov. 25, 1890; Jan. 12, 1872–Jan. 12, 1877.

Colquitt, Alfred Holt (D) April 20, 1824–March 26, 1894; Jan. 12, 1877–Nov. 4, 1882; House 1853–55 (no party); Senate 1883–March 26, 1894.

Stephens, Alexander Hamilton (D) Feb. 11, 1812–March 4, 1883; Nov. 4, 1882–March 4, 1883; House Oct. 2, 1843–59 (1843–51 Whig, 1851–53 Unionist, 1853–55 Whig), Dec. 1, 1873–Nov. 4, 1882.

Boynton, James Stoddard (D) May 7, 1833–Dec. 22, 1902; March 5–May 10, 1883.

McDaniel, Henry Dickerson (D) Sept. 4, 1836–July 25, 1926; May 10, 1883–Nov. 9, 1886.

Gordon, John Brown (D) Feb. 6, 1832–Jan. 9, 1904; Nov. 9, 1886–Nov. 8, 1890; Senate 1873–May 26, 1880, 1891–97.

Northen, William Jonathan (D) July 9, 1835–March 25, 1913; Nov. 8, 1890–Oct. 27, 1894.

Atkinson, William Yates (D) Nov. 11, 1854–Aug. 8, 1899; Oct. 27, 1894–Oct. 29, 1898.

Candler, Allen Daniel (D) Nov. 4, 1834–Oct. 26, 1910; Oct. 29, 1898–Oct. 25, 1902; House 1883–91.

Terrell, Joseph Meriwether (D) June 6, 1861–Nov. 17, 1912; Oct. 25, 1902–June 29, 1907; Senate Nov. 17, 1910–July 14, 1911.

Smith, Hoke (D) Sept. 2, 1855–Nov. 27, 1931; June 29, 1907–June 26, 1909, July 1–Nov. 16, 1911; Senate Nov. 16, 1911–21; secretary of the interior March 6, 1893–Sept. 1, 1896.

Brown, Joseph Mackey (son of Joseph Emerson Brown, above) (D) Dec. 28, 1851–March 3, 1932; June 26, 1909–July 1, 1911, Jan. 25, 1912–June 28, 1913.

Smith, Hoke (D) July 1–Nov. 16, 1911 (for previous term see above).

Slaton, John Marshall (D) Dec. 25, 1866–Jan. 11, 1955; Nov. 16, 1911–Jan. 25, 1912, June 28, 1913–June 26, 1915.

Brown, Joseph Mackey (D) Jan. 25, 1912–June 28, 1913 (for previous term see above).

Slaton, John Marshall (D) June 28, 1913–June 26, 1915 (for previous term see above).

Harris, Nathaniel Edwin (D) Jan. 21, 1846–Sept. 21, 1929; June 26, 1915–June 30, 1917.

Dorsey, Hugh Manson (D) July 10, 1871–June 11, 1948; June 30, 1917–June 25, 1921.

Hardwick, Thomas William (D) Dec. 9, 1872–Jan. 31, 1944; June 25, 1921–June 30, 1923; House 1903–Nov. 2, 1914; Senate Nov. 4, 1914–19.

Walker, Clifford Mitchell (D) July 4, 1877–Nov. 9, 1954; June 30, 1923–June 25, 1927.

Hardman, Lamartine Griffin (D) April 14, 1856–Feb. 18, 1937; June 25, 1927–June 27, 1931.

Russell, Richard Brevard Jr. (D) Nov. 2, 1897–Jan. 21, 1971; June 27, 1931–Jan. 10, 1933; Senate Jan. 12, 1933–Jan. 21, 1971; elected pres. pro tempore Jan. 3, 1969.

Talmadge, Eugene (father of Herman Eugene Talmadge, below) (D) Sept. 23, 1884–Dec. 21, 1946; Jan. 10, 1933–Jan. 12, 1937, Jan. 14, 1941–Jan. 12, 1943.

Rivers, Eurith Dickinson (D) Dec. 1, 1895–June 11, 1967; Jan. 12, 1937–Jan. 14, 1941.

Talmadge, Eugene (D) Jan. 14, 1941–Jan. 12, 1943 (for previous term see above).

Arnall, Ellis Gibbs (D) March 20, 1907–Dec. 13, 1992; Jan. 12, 1943–Jan. 14, 1947.

Talmadge, Herman Eugene (son of Eugene Talmadge, above) (D) Aug. 9, 1913–March 21, 2002; Jan. 14–March 18, 1947, Nov. 17, 1948–Jan. 11, 1955; Senate 1957–81.

Thompson, Melvin Ernest (D) May 1, 1903–Oct. 3, 1980; March 18, 1947–Nov. 17, 1948.

Talmadge, Herman Eugene (D) Nov. 17, 1948–Jan. 11, 1955 (for previous term see above).

Griffin, Samuel Marvin (D) Sept. 4, 1907–June 13, 1982; Jan. 11, 1955–Jan. 13, 1959.

Vandiver, Samuel Ernest Jr. (D) July 3, 1918–Feb. 21, 2005; Jan. 13, 1959–Jan. 15, 1963.

Sanders, Carl Edward (D) July 15, 1925– ; Jan. 15, 1963–Jan. 10, 1967.

Maddox, Lester Garfield (D) Sept. 30, 1915–June 25, 2003; Jan. 11, 1967–Jan. 12, 1971.

Carter, James Earl "Jimmy" Jr. (D) Oct. 1, 1924– ; Jan. 12, 1971–Jan. 14, 1975; president 1977–81.

Busbee, George Dekle (D) Aug. 7, 1927–July 16, 2004; Jan. 14, 1975–Jan. 11, 1983.

Harris, Joe Frank (D) Feb. 26, 1936– ; Jan. 11, 1983–Jan. 14, 1991.

Miller, Zell (D) Feb. 24, 1932– ; Jan. 14, 1991–Jan. 11, 1999; Senate July 27, 2000–05.

Barnes, Roy E. (D) March 11, 1948– ; Jan. 11, 1999–Jan. 13, 2003.

Perdue, Sonny (R) Dec. 20, 1946– ; Jan. 13, 2003– .

Hawaii

(Became a state Aug. 21, 1959)

Quinn, William Francis (R) July 31, 1919– ; Aug. 21, 1959–Dec. 3, 1962.

Burns, John Anthony (D) Nov. 30, 1909–April 5, 1975; Dec. 3, 1962–Dec. 2, 1974; House (Terr. Del.) 1957–Aug. 21, 1959.

Ariyoshi, George Ryoichi (D) March 12, 1926– ; Dec. 2, 1974–Dec. 1, 1986.

Waihee, John III (D) May 19, 1946– ; Dec. 1, 1986–Dec. 5, 1994.

Cayetano, Benjamin J. (D) Nov. 4, 1939– ; Dec. 5, 1994–Dec. 2, 2002.

Lingle, Linda (R) June 4, 1953– ; Dec. 2, 2002– .

Idaho

(Became a state July 3, 1890)

Shoup, George Laird (R) June 15, 1836–Dec. 21, 1904; April 1889–90 (Idaho Terr.), Oct. 1–Dec. 1890; Senate Dec. 18, 1890–1901.

Willey, Norman Bushnell (R) March 25, 1838–Oct. 20, 1921; Dec. 19, 1890–Jan. 1, 1893.

McConnell, William John (R) Sept. 18, 1839–March 30, 1925; Jan. 2, 1893–Jan. 4, 1897; Senate Dec. 18, 1890–91.

Steunenberg, Frank (D) Aug. 8, 1861–Dec. 30, 1905; Jan. 4, 1897–Jan. 7, 1901.

Hunt, Frank Williams (D) Dec. 16, 1871–Nov. 25, 1906; Jan. 7, 1901–Jan. 5, 1903.

Morrison, John Tracy (R) Dec. 25, 1860–Dec. 20, 1915; Jan. 5, 1903–Jan. 2, 1905.

Gooding, Frank Robert (R) Sept. 16, 1859–June 24, 1928; Jan. 2, 1905–Jan. 4, 1909; Senate Jan. 15, 1921–June 24, 1928.

Brady, James Henry (R) June 12, 1862–Jan. 13, 1918; Jan. 4, 1909–Jan. 2, 1911; Senate Feb. 6, 1913–Jan. 13, 1918.

Hawley, James Henry (D) Jan. 17, 1847–Aug. 3, 1929; Jan. 2, 1911–Jan. 6, 1913.

Haines, John Michiner (R) Jan. 1, 1863–June 4, 1917; Jan. 6, 1913–Jan. 4, 1915.

Alexander, Moses (D) Nov. 15, 1853–Jan. 4, 1932; Jan. 4, 1915–Jan. 6, 1919.

Davis, David William (R) April 23, 1873–Aug. 5, 1959; Jan. 6, 1919–Jan. 1, 1923.

Moore, Charles Calvin (R) Feb. 26, 1866–March 19, 1958; Jan. 1, 1923–Jan. 3, 1927.

Baldrige, H. Clarence (R) Nov. 24, 1868–June 8, 1947; Jan. 3, 1927–Jan. 5, 1931.

Ross, C. Ben (D) Dec. 27, 1876–March 31, 1946; Jan. 5, 1931–Jan. 4, 1937.

Clark, Barzilla Worth (brother of Chase Addison Clark, below) (D) Dec. 22, 1880–Sept. 21, 1943; Jan. 4, 1937–Jan. 2, 1939.

Bottolfsen, Clarence Alfred (R) Oct. 10, 1891–July 19, 1964; Jan. 2, 1939–Jan. 6, 1941, Jan. 4, 1943–Jan. 1, 1945.

Clark, Chase Addison (brother of Barzilla Worth Clark, above) (D) Aug. 20, 1883–Dec. 29, 1966; Jan. 6, 1941–Jan. 4, 1943.

Bottolfsen, Clarence Alfred (R) Jan. 4, 1943–Jan. 1, 1945 (for previous term see above).

Gossett, Charles Clinton (D) Sept. 2, 1888–Sept. 20, 1974; Jan. 1–Nov. 17, 1945; Senate Nov. 17, 1945–47.

Williams, Arnold (D) May 21, 1898–May 25, 1970; Nov. 17, 1945–Jan. 6, 1947.

Robins, Charles Armington (R) Dec. 8, 1894–Sept. 20, 1970; Jan. 6, 1947–Jan. 1, 1951.

Jordan, Leonard Beck (R) May 15, 1899–June 30, 1983; Jan. 1, 1951–Jan. 3, 1955; Senate Aug. 6, 1962–Jan. 2, 1973.

Smylie, Robert Eben (R) Oct. 31, 1914–July 17, 2004; Jan. 3, 1955–Jan. 2, 1967.

Samuelson, Don William (R) July 27, 1913– ; Jan. 2, 1967–Jan. 4, 1971.

Andrus, Cecil Dale (D) Aug. 25, 1931– ; Jan. 4, 1971–Jan. 24, 1977, Jan. 5, 1987–Jan. 2, 1995; secretary of the interior Jan. 23, 1977–Jan. 20, 1981.

Evans, John Victor (D) Jan. 18, 1925– ; Jan. 24, 1977–Jan. 5, 1987.

Andrus, Cecil Dale (D) Jan. 5, 1987–Jan. 2, 1995 (for previous term see above).

Bratt, Philip E. (R) March 4, 1927– ; Jan. 2, 1995–Jan. 8, 1999.

Kempthorne, Dirk (R) Oct. 29, 1951– ; Jan. 8, 1999– ; Senate 1993–99.

Illinois

(Became a state Dec. 3, 1818)

Bond, Shadrack (DR) Nov. 24, 1773–April 12, 1832; Oct. 6, 1818–Dec. 5, 1822; House (Terr. Del.) Dec. 3, 1812–Aug. 2, 1813 (no party).

Coles, Edward (brother-in-law of John Rutherford of Va.) (DR) Dec. 15, 1786–July 7, 1868; Dec. 5, 1822–Dec. 6, 1826.

Edwards, Ninian (R) March 17, 1775–July 20, 1833; 1809–18 (Ill. Terr.), Dec. 6, 1826–Dec. 6, 1830; Senate Dec. 3, 1818–24.

Reynolds, John (brother of Thomas Reynolds of Mo.) (D) Feb. 26, 1788–May 8, 1865; Dec. 6, 1830–Nov. 17, 1834; House 1834–Dec. 1, 1837 (Jacksonian), 1839–43.

Ewing, William Lee Davidson (-) Aug. 31, 1795–March 25, 1846; Nov. 17–Dec. 3, 1834; Senate Dec. 30, 1835–37.

Duncan, Joseph (W) Feb. 22, 1794–Jan. 15, 1844; Dec. 3, 1834–Dec. 7, 1838; House 1827–Sept. 21, 1834 (Jacksonian).

Carlin, Thomas (D) July 18, 1789–Feb. 14, 1852; Dec. 7, 1838–Dec. 8, 1842.

Ford, Thomas (D) Dec. 5, 1800–Nov. 3, 1850; Dec. 8, 1842–Dec. 9, 1846.

French, Augustus C. (D) Aug. 2, 1808–Sept. 4, 1864; Dec. 9, 1946–Jan. 10, 1853.

Matteson, Joel Aldrich (D) Aug. 2, 1808–Jan. 31, 1873; Jan. 10, 1853–Jan. 12, 1857.

Bissell, William Harrison (R) April 25, 1811–March 18, 1860; Jan. 12, 1857–March 18, 1860; House 1849–55 (1849–53 Democrat, 1853–55 Independent Democrat).

Wood, John (R) Dec. 20, 1798–June 11, 1880; March 21, 1860–Jan. 14, 1861.

Yates, Richard (father of Richard Yates, below) (R) Jan. 18, 1818–Nov. 27, 1873; Jan. 14, 1861–Jan. 16, 1865; House 1851–55 (Whig); Senate 1865–71 (Republican).

Oglesby, Richard James (R) July 25, 1824–April 24, 1899; Jan. 16, 1865–Jan. 11, 1869, Jan. 13–Jan. 23, 1873, Jan. 30, 1885–Jan. 14, 1889; Senate 1873–79.

Palmer, John McAuley (R) Sept. 13, 1817–Sept. 25, 1900; Jan. 11, 1869–Jan. 13, 1873; Senate 1891–97 (Democrat).

Oglesby, Richard James (R) Jan. 13–Jan. 23, 1873 (for previous term see above).

Beveridge, John Lourie (R) July 6, 1824–May 3, 1910; Jan. 23, 1873–Jan. 8, 1877; House Nov. 7, 1871–Jan. 4, 1873.

Cullom, Shelby Moore (R) Nov. 22, 1829–Jan. 28, 1914; Jan. 8, 1877–Feb. 8, 1883; House 1865–71; Senate 1883–1913; Senate majority leader 1911–13.

Hamilton, John Marshall (R) May 28, 1847–Sept. 22, 1905; Feb. 16, 1883–Jan. 30, 1885.

Oglesby, Richard James (R) Jan. 30, 1885–Jan. 14, 1889 (for previous terms see above).

Fifer, Joseph Wilson (R) Oct. 28, 1840–Aug. 6, 1938; Jan. 14, 1889–Jan. 10, 1893.

Altgeld, John Peter (D) Dec. 30, 1847–March 12, 1902; Jan. 10, 1893–Jan. 11, 1897.

Tanner, John Riley (R) April 4, 1844–May 23, 1901; Jan. 11, 1897–Jan. 14, 1901.

Yates, Richard (son of Richard Yates, above) (R) Dec. 12, 1860–April 11, 1936; Jan. 14, 1901–Jan. 9, 1905; House 1919–33.

Deneen, Charles Samuel (R) May 4, 1863–Feb. 5, 1940; Jan. 9, 1905–Feb. 3, 1913; Senate Feb. 26, 1925–31.

Dunne, Edward Fitzsimmons (D) Oct. 12, 1853–May 14, 1937; Feb. 3, 1913–Jan. 8, 1917.

Lowden, Frank Orren (R) Jan. 26, 1861–March 20, 1943; Jan. 8, 1917–Jan. 10, 1921; House Nov. 6, 1906–11.

Small, Lennington (R) June 16, 1862–May 17, 1936; Jan. 10, 1921–Jan. 14, 1929.

Emmerson, Louis Lincoln (R) Dec. 27, 1883–Feb. 4, 1941; Jan. 14, 1929–Jan. 9, 1933.

Horner, Henry (D) Nov. 30, 1879–Oct. 6, 1940; Jan. 9, 1933–Oct. 6, 1940.

Stelle, John Henry (D) Aug. 10, 1891–July 5, 1962; Oct. 6, 1940–Jan. 13, 1941.

Green, Dwight Herbert (R) Jan. 9, 1897–Feb. 20, 1958; Jan. 13, 1941–Jan. 10, 1949.

Stevenson, Adlai Ewing II (grandson of Vice Pres. Adlai Ewing Stevenson, father of Sen. Adlai Ewing Stevenson III) (D) Feb. 5, 1900–July 14, 1965; Jan. 10, 1949–Jan. 12, 1953.

Stratton, William Grant (R) Feb. 26, 1914–March 2, 2001; Jan. 12, 1953–Jan. 9, 1961; House 1941–43, 1947–49.

Kerner, Otto (D) Aug. 15, 1908–May 8, 1976; Jan. 9, 1961–May 22, 1968.

Shapiro, Samuel Harvey (D) April 25, 1907–March 16, 1987; May 22, 1968–Jan. 13, 1969.

Ogilvie, Richard Buell (R) Feb. 2, 1923–May 10, 1988; Jan. 13, 1969–Jan. 8, 1973.

Walker, Daniel (D) Aug. 6, 1922– ; Jan. 8, 1973–Jan. 10, 1977.

Thompson, James Robert (R) May 8, 1936– ; Jan. 10, 1977–Jan. 14, 1991.

Edgar, James (R) Jan. 22, 1946– ; Jan. 14, 1991–Jan. 11, 1999.

Ryan, George H. (R) Feb. 24, 1934– ; Jan. 11, 1999–Jan. 13, 2003.

Blagojevich, Rod R. (D) Dec. 10, 1956– ; Jan. 13, 2003– ; House 1997–2003.

Indiana

(Became a state Dec. 11, 1816)

Jennings, Jonathan (DR) 1784–July 26, 1834; Nov. 7, 1816–Sept. 12, 1822; House Dec. 2, 1822–31 (no party).

Boon, Ratliff (D) Jan. 18, 1781–Nov. 20, 1844; Sept. 12–Dec. 4, 1822; House 1825–27 (no party), 1829–39 (1829–37 Jacksonian).

Hendricks, William (uncle of Thomas Andrews Hendricks, below) (DR) Nov. 12, 1782–May 16, 1850; Dec. 5, 1822–Feb. 12, 1825; House Dec. 11, 1816–July 25, 1822 (no party); Senate 1825–37 (no party).

Ray, James Brown (AJ/I) Feb. 19, 1794–Aug. 4, 1848; Feb. 12, 1825–Dec. 7, 1831 (1828–31 Independent).

Noble, Noah (NR/W) Jan. 14, 1794–Feb. 8, 1844; Dec. 7, 1831–Dec. 6, 1837.

Wallace, David (W) April 24, 1799–Sept. 4, 1859; Dec. 6, 1837–Dec. 9, 1840; House 1841–43.

Bigger, Samuel (W) March 20, 1802–Sept. 9, 1846; Dec. 9, 1840–Dec. 6, 1843.

Whitcomb, James (father-in-law of Claude Matthews, below) (D) Dec. 1, 1795–Oct. 4, 1852; Dec. 6, 1843–Dec. 27, 1848; Senate 1849–Oct. 4, 1852.

Dunning, Paris Chipman (D) March 15, 1806–May 9, 1884; Dec. 27, 1848–Dec. 5, 1849.

Wright, Joseph Albert (U) April 17, 1810–May 11, 1867; Dec. 5, 1849–Jan. 12, 1857; House 1843–45 (Democrat); Senate Feb. 24, 1862–Jan. 14, 1863.

Willard, Ashbel Parsons (D) Oct. 31, 1820–Oct. 4, 1860; Jan. 12, 1857–Oct. 4, 1860.

Hammond, Abram Adams (D) March 21, 1814–Aug. 27, 1874; Oct. 4, 1860–Jan. 14, 1861.

Lane, Henry Smith (R) Feb. 24, 1811–June 18, 1881; Jan. 14–Jan. 16, 1861; House Aug. 3, 1840–43 (Whig); Senate 1861–67.

Morton, Oliver Hazard Perry Throck (R) Aug. 4, 1823–Nov. 1, 1877; Jan. 16, 1861–Jan. 23, 1867; Senate 1867–Nov. 1, 1877.

Baker, Conrad (R) Feb. 12, 1817–April 28, 1885; Jan. 24, 1867–Jan. 13, 1873.

Hendricks, Thomas Andrews (nephew of William Hendricks, above) (D) Sept. 7, 1819–Nov. 25, 1885; Jan. 13, 1873–Jan. 8, 1877; House 1851–55; Senate 1863–69; vice president Nov. 4–Nov. 25, 1885.

Williams, James Douglas (D) Jan. 16, 1808–Nov. 20, 1880; Jan. 8, 1877–Nov. 20, 1880; House 1875–Dec. 1, 1876.

Gray, Isaac Pusey (D) Oct. 18, 1828–Feb. 14, 1895; Nov. 20, 1880–Jan. 10, 1881, Jan. 12, 1885–Jan. 14, 1889.

Porter, Albert Gallatin (R) April 20, 1824–May 3, 1897; Jan. 10, 1881–Jan. 12, 1885; House 1859–63.

Gray, Isaac Pusey (D) Jan. 12, 1885–Jan. 14, 1889 (for previous term see above).

Hovey, Alvin Peterson (R) Sept. 6, 1821–Nov. 23, 1891; Jan. 1889–Nov. 21, 1891; House 1887–Jan. 17, 1889.

Chase, Ira Joy (R) Dec. 7, 1834–May 11, 1895; Nov. 21, 1891–Jan. 9, 1893.

Matthews, Claude (son-in-law of James Whitcomb, above) (D) Dec. 14, 1845–April 28, 1898; Jan. 9, 1893–Jan. 11, 1897.

Mount, James Atwell (R) March 24, 1843–Jan. 16, 1901; Jan. 11, 1897–Jan. 14, 1901.

Durbin, Winfield Taylor (R) May 4, 1847–Dec. 18, 1928; Jan. 14, 1901–Jan. 9, 1905.

Hanly, James Franklin (R) April 4, 1863–Aug. 1, 1920; Jan. 9, 1905–Jan. 11, 1909; House 1895–97.

Marshall, Thomas Riley (D) March 14, 1854–June 1, 1925; Jan. 11, 1909–Jan. 13, 1913; vice president 1913–21.

Ralston, Samuel Moffett (D) Dec. 1, 1857–Oct. 14, 1925; Jan. 13, 1913–Jan. 8, 1917; Senate 1923–Oct. 14, 1925.

Goodrich, James Putnam (R) Feb. 18, 1864–Aug. 15, 1940; Jan. 8, 1917–Jan. 10, 1921.

McCray, Warren Terry (R) Feb. 4, 1865–Dec. 19, 1938; Jan. 10, 1921–April 30, 1924.

Branch, Emmett Forest (R) May 16, 1874–Feb. 23, 1932; April 30, 1924–Jan. 12, 1925.

Jackson, Edward L. (R) Dec. 27, 1873–Nov. 18, 1954; Jan. 12, 1925–Jan. 14, 1929.

Leslie, Harry Guyer (R) Aug. 6, 1878–Dec. 10, 1937; Jan. 14, 1929–Jan. 9, 1933.

McNutt, Paul Vories (D) July 19, 1891–March 24, 1955; Jan. 9, 1933–Jan. 11, 1937.

Townsend, Maurice Clifford (D) Aug. 11, 1884–Nov. 11, 1954; Jan. 11, 1937–Jan. 13, 1941.

Schricker, Henry Frederick (D) Aug. 30, 1883–Dec. 28, 1966; Jan. 13, 1941–Jan. 8, 1945, Jan. 10, 1949–Jan. 12, 1953.

Gates, Ralph Fesler (R) Feb. 24, 1893–July 28, 1978; Jan. 8, 1945–Jan. 10, 1949.

Schricker, Henry Frederick (D) Jan. 10, 1949–Jan. 12, 1953 (for previous term see above).

Craig, George North (R) Aug. 6, 1909–Dec. 17, 1992; Jan. 12, 1953–Jan. 14, 1957.

Handley, Harold Willis (R) Nov. 27, 1909–Aug. 30, 1972; Jan. 14, 1957–Jan. 9, 1961.

Welsh, Matthew Empson (D) Sept. 15, 1912–May 28, 1995; Jan. 9, 1961–Jan. 11, 1965.

Branigin, Roger Douglas (D) July 26, 1902–Nov. 19, 1975; Jan. 11, 1965–Jan. 13, 1969.

Whitcomb, Edgar Doud (R) Nov. 6, 1917– ; Jan. 13, 1969–Jan. 8, 1973.

Bowen, Otis Ray (R) Feb. 26, 1918– ; Jan. 8, 1973–Jan. 12, 1981; secretary of health and human services Dec. 13, 1985–Jan. 20, 1989.

Orr, Robert Dunkerson (R) Nov. 17, 1917–March 10, 2004; Jan. 12, 1981–Jan. 9, 1989.

Bayh, Evan (D) Dec. 26, 1955– ; Jan. 9, 1989–Jan. 13, 1997; Senate 1999– .

O'Bannon, Frank L. (D) Jan. 30, 1930–Sept. 13, 2003; Jan. 13, 1997–Sept. 13, 2003.

Kernan, Joseph E. (D) April 8, 1946– ; Sept. 13, 2003–Jan. 10, 2005.

Daniels, Mitchell E. Jr. (R) April 7, 1949–; Jan. 10, 2005– .

Iowa

(Became a state Dec. 28, 1846)

Briggs, Ansel (D) Feb. 3, 1806–May 5, 1881; Dec. 3, 1846–Dec. 4, 1850.

Hempstead, Stephen P. (D) Oct. 1, 1812–Feb. 16, 1883; Dec. 4, 1850–Dec. 9, 1854.

Grimes, James Wilson (W) Oct. 20, 1816–Feb. 7, 1872; Dec. 9, 1854–Jan. 13, 1858; Senate 1859–Dec. 6, 1869 (Republican).

Lowe, Ralph Phillips (R) Nov. 27, 1805–Dec. 22, 1883; Jan. 13, 1858–Jan. 11, 1860.

Kirkwood, Samuel Jordan (R) Dec. 20, 1813–Sept. 1, 1894; Jan. 11, 1860–Jan. 14, 1864, Jan. 13, 1876–Feb. 1, 1877; Senate Jan. 13, 1866–67, 1877–March 7, 1881; secretary of the interior March 8, 1881–April 17, 1882.

Stone, William Milo (R) Oct. 14, 1827–July 8, 1893; Jan. 14, 1864–Jan. 16, 1868.

Merrill, Samuel (R) Aug. 7, 1822–Aug. 31, 1899; Jan. 16, 1868–Jan. 11, 1872.

Carpenter, Cyrus Clay (R) Nov. 24, 1829–May 29, 1898; Jan. 11, 1872–Jan. 13, 1876; House 1879–83.

Kirkwood, Samuel Jordan (R) Jan. 13, 1876–Feb. 1, 1877 (for previous term see above).

Newbold, Joshua G. (R) May 12, 1830–June 10, 1903; Feb. 1, 1877–Jan. 17, 1878.

Gear, John Henry (R) April 7, 1825–July 14, 1900; Jan. 17, 1878–Jan. 12, 1882; House 1887–91, 1893–95; Senate 1895–July 14, 1900.

Sherman, Buren Robinson (R) May 28, 1836–Nov. 4, 1904; Jan. 12, 1882–Jan. 14, 1886.

Larrabee, William (R) Jan. 20, 1832–Nov. 16, 1912; Jan. 14, 1886–Feb. 26, 1890.

Boies, Horace (D) Dec. 7, 1827–April 4, 1923; Feb. 27, 1890–Jan. 11, 1894.

Jackson, Frank Darr (R) Jan. 26, 1854–Nov. 16, 1938; Jan. 11, 1894–Jan. 16, 1896.

Drake, Francis Marion (R) Dec. 30, 1830–Nov. 20, 1903; Jan. 16, 1896–Jan. 13, 1898.

Shaw, Leslie Mortier (R) Nov. 2, 1848–March 28, 1932; Jan. 13, 1898–Jan. 16, 1902; secretary of the Treasury Feb. 1, 1902–March 3, 1907.

Cummins, Albert Baird (R) Feb. 15, 1850–July 30, 1926; Jan. 16, 1902–Nov. 24, 1908; Senate Nov. 24, 1908–July 30, 1926; elected pres. pro tempore May 19, 1919, March 7, 1921.

Garst, Warren (R) Dec. 4, 1850–Oct. 5, 1924; Nov. 24, 1908–Jan. 14, 1909.

Carroll, Beryl Franklin (R) March 15, 1860–Dec. 16, 1939; Jan. 14, 1909–Jan. 16, 1913.

Clarke, George W. (R) Oct. 24, 1852–Nov. 28, 1936; Jan. 16, 1913–Jan. 11, 1917.

Harding, William Lloyd (R) Oct. 3, 1877–Dec. 17, 1934; Jan. 11, 1917–Jan. 13, 1921.

Kendall, Nathan Edward (R) March 17, 1868–Nov. 5, 1936; Jan. 13, 1921–Jan. 15, 1925; House 1909–13.

Hammill, John (R) Oct. 14, 1875–April 6, 1936; Jan. 15, 1925–Jan. 15, 1931.

Turner, Daniel Webster (R) March 17, 1877–April 15, 1969; Jan. 15, 1931–Jan. 12, 1933.

Herring, Clyde LaVerne (D) May 3, 1879–Sept. 15, 1945; Jan. 12, 1933–Jan. 14, 1937; Senate Jan. 15, 1937–43.

Kraschel, Nelson George (D) Oct. 27, 1889–March 15, 1957; Jan. 14, 1937–Jan. 12, 1939.

Wilson, George Allison (R) April 1, 1884–Sept. 8, 1953; Jan. 12, 1939–Jan. 14, 1943; Senate Jan. 14, 1943–49.

Hickenlooper, Bourke Blakemore (R) July 21, 1896–Sept. 4, 1971; Jan. 14, 1943–Jan. 11, 1945; Senate 1945–69.

Blue, Robert Donald (R) Sept. 24, 1898–Dec. 14, 1989; Jan. 11, 1945–Jan. 13, 1949.

Beardsley, William S. (R) May 17, 1901–Nov. 21, 1954; Jan. 13, 1949–Nov. 21, 1954.

Elthon, Leo (R) June 9, 1898–April 16, 1967; Nov. 22, 1954–Jan. 13, 1955.

Hoegh, Leo Arthur (R) March 30, 1908– ; Jan. 13, 1955–Jan. 17, 1957.

Loveless, Herschel Celiel (D) May 5, 1911–May 4, 1989; Jan. 17, 1957–Jan. 12, 1961.

Erbe, Norman Arthur (R) Oct. 25, 1919–June 8, 2000; Jan. 12, 1961–Jan. 17, 1963.

Hughes, Harold Everett (D) Feb. 10, 1922–Oct. 24, 1996; Jan. 17, 1963–Jan. 1, 1969; Senate 1969–75.

Fulton, Robert David (D) May 13, 1929– ; Jan. 1–Jan. 16, 1969.

Ray, Robert D. (R) Sept. 26, 1928– ; Jan. 16, 1969–Jan. 14, 1983.

Branstad, Terry Edward (R) Nov. 17, 1946– ; Jan. 14, 1983–Jan. 15, 1999.

Vilsack, Thomas J. (D) Dec. 13, 1950– ; Jan. 15, 1999– .

Kansas

(Became a state Jan. 29, 1861)

Robinson, Charles Lawrence (R) July 21, 1818–Aug. 17, 1894; Feb. 9, 1861–Jan. 12, 1863.

Carney, Thomas (R) Aug. 20, 1824–July 28, 1888; Jan. 12, 1863–Jan. 9, 1865.

Crawford, Samuel Johnson (father-in-law of Arthur Capper, below) (R) April 10, 1835–Oct. 21, 1913; Jan. 9, 1865–Nov. 4, 1868.

Green, Nehemiah (R) March 8, 1837–Jan. 12, 1890; Nov. 4, 1868–Jan. 11, 1869.

Harvey, James Madison (R) Sept. 21, 1833–April 15, 1894; Jan. 11, 1869–Jan. 13, 1873; Senate Feb. 2, 1874–77.

Osborn, Thomas Andrew (R) Oct. 26, 1836–Feb. 4, 1898; Jan. 13, 1873–Jan. 18, 1877.

Anthony, George Tobey (R) June 9, 1824–Aug. 5, 1896; Jan. 18, 1877–Jan. 13, 1879.

St. John, John Pierce (R) Feb. 25, 1833–Aug. 31, 1916; Jan. 13, 1879–Jan. 8, 1883.

Glick, George Washington (D) July 4, 1827–April 13, 1911; Jan. 8, 1883–Jan. 13, 1885.

Martin, John Alexander (R) March 10, 1839–Oct. 2, 1889; Jan. 13, 1885–Jan. 14, 1889.

Humphrey, Lyman Underwood (R) July 25, 1844–Sept. 12, 1915; Jan. 14, 1889–Jan. 9, 1893.

Lewelling, Lorenzo Dow (P) Dec. 21, 1846–Sept. 3, 1900; Jan. 9, 1893–Jan. 14, 1895.

Morrill, Edmund Needham (R) Feb. 12, 1834–March 14, 1909; Jan. 14, 1895–Jan. 11, 1897; House 1883–91.

Leedy, John Whitnah (P) March 4, 1849–March 24, 1935; Jan. 11, 1897–Jan. 9, 1899.

Stanley, William Eugene (R) Dec. 28, 1844–Oct. 13, 1910; Jan. 9, 1899–Jan. 12, 1903.

Bailey, Willis Joshua (R) Oct. 12, 1854–May 19, 1932; Jan. 12, 1903–Jan. 9, 1905; House 1899–1901.

Hoch, Edward Wallis (R) March 17, 1849–June 1, 1925; Jan. 9, 1905–Jan. 11, 1909.

Stubbs, Walter Roscoe (R) Nov. 7, 1858–March 25, 1929; Jan. 11, 1909–Jan. 13, 1913.

Hodges, George Hartshorn (D) Feb. 6, 1866–Oct. 7, 1947; Jan. 13, 1913–Jan. 11, 1915.

Capper, Arthur (son-in-law of Samuel Johnson Crawford, above) (R) July 14, 1865–Dec. 19, 1951; Jan. 11, 1915–Jan. 13, 1919; Senate 1919–49.

Allen, Henry Justin (R) Sept. 11, 1868–Jan. 17, 1950; Jan. 13, 1919–Jan. 8, 1923; Senate April 1, 1929–Nov. 30, 1930.

Davis, Jonathan McMillan (D) April 27, 1871–June 27, 1943; Jan. 8, 1923–Jan. 12, 1925.

Paulen, Benjamin Sanford (R) July 14, 1869–July 11, 1961; Jan. 12, 1925–Jan. 14, 1929.

Reed, Clyde Martin (R) Oct. 19, 1871–Nov. 8, 1949; Jan. 14, 1929–Jan. 12, 1931; Senate 1939–Nov. 8, 1949.

Woodring, Harry Hines (D) May 31, 1890–Sept. 9, 1967; Jan. 12, 1931–Jan. 9, 1933; secretary of war Sept. 25, 1936–June 30, 1940.

Landon, Alfred Mossman (R) Sept. 9, 1887–Oct. 12, 1987; Jan. 9, 1933–Jan. 11, 1937.

Huxman, Walter Augustus (D) Feb. 16, 1887–June 26, 1972; Jan. 11, 1937–Jan. 9, 1939.

Ratner, Payne Harry (R) Oct. 3, 1896–Dec. 27, 1974; Jan. 9, 1939–Jan. 11, 1943.

Schoeppel, Andrew Frank (R) Nov. 23, 1894–Jan. 21, 1962; Jan. 11, 1943–Jan. 13, 1947; Senate 1949–Jan. 21, 1962.

Carlson, Frank (R) Jan. 23, 1893–May 30, 1987; Jan. 13, 1947–Nov. 28, 1950; House 1935–47; Senate Nov. 29, 1950–69.

Hagaman, Frank Leslie (R) June 1, 1894–June 23, 1966; Nov. 28, 1950–Jan. 8, 1951.

Arn, Edward Ferdinand (R) May 19, 1906–Jan. 22, 1998; Jan. 8, 1951–Jan. 10, 1955.

Hall, Frederick Lee (R) July 24, 1916–March 18, 1970; Jan. 10, 1955–Jan. 3, 1957.

McCuish, John Berridge (R) June 22, 1906–March 12, 1962; Jan. 3–Jan. 14, 1957.

Docking, George (father of Robert Blackwell Docking, below) (D) Feb. 23, 1904–Jan. 20, 1964; Jan. 14, 1957–Jan. 9, 1961.

Anderson, John Jr. (R) May 8, 1917– ; Jan. 9, 1961–Jan. 11, 1965.

Avery, William Henry (R) Aug. 11, 1911– ; Jan. 11, 1965–Jan. 9, 1967; House 1955–65.

Docking, Robert Blackwell (son of George Docking, above) (D) Oct. 9, 1925–Oct. 8, 1983; Jan. 9, 1967–Jan. 13, 1975.

Bennett, Robert Frederick (R) May 23, 1927–Oct. 9, 2000; Jan. 13, 1975–Jan. 8, 1979.

Carlin, John (D) Aug. 3, 1940– ; Jan. 8, 1979–Jan. 12, 1987.

Hayden, John Michael "Mike" (R) March 16, 1944– ; Jan. 12, 1987–Jan. 14, 1991.

Finney, Joan (D) Feb. 12, 1925–July 28, 2001; Jan. 14, 1991–Jan. 9, 1995.

Graves, Bill (R) Jan. 9, 1953– ; Jan. 9, 1995–Jan. 13, 2003.

Sebelius, Kathleen (D) May 15, 1948– ; Jan. 13, 2003– .

Kentucky

(Became a state June 1, 1792)

Shelby, Isaac (DR) Dec. 11, 1750–July 18, 1826; June 4, 1792–June 7, 1796, June 1, 1812–June 1, 1816.

Garrard, James (DR) Jan. 14, 1749–Jan. 19, 1822; June 7, 1796–June 1, 1804.

Greenup, Christopher (R) 1750–April 27, 1818; June 1, 1804–June 1, 1808; House Nov. 9, 1792–97 (Nov. 9, 1792–95 no party).

Scott, Charles (DR) 1739–Oct. 22, 1813; June 1, 1808–June 1, 1812.

Shelby, Isaac (DR) June 1, 1812–June 1, 1816 (for previous term see above).

Madison, George (DR) 1763–Oct. 14, 1816; June 1–Oct. 14, 1816.

Slaughter, Gabriel (DR) Dec. 12, 1767–Sept. 19, 1830; Oct. 21, 1816–June 1, 1820.

Adair, John (DR) Jan. 9, 1757–May 19, 1840; June 1, 1820–June 1, 1824; Senate Nov. 8, 1805–Nov. 18, 1806 (no party); House 1831–33 (Jacksonian).

Desha, Joseph (DR) Dec. 9, 1768–Oct. 11, 1842; June 1, 1824–June 1, 1828; House 1807–19 (Republican).

Metcalfe, Thomas (NR) March 20, 1780–Aug. 18, 1855; June 1, 1828–June 1, 1832; House 1819–June 1, 1828 (no party); Senate June 23, 1848–49 (Whig).

Breathitt, John (D) Sept. 9, 1786–Feb. 21, 1834; June 1, 1832–Feb. 21, 1834.

Morehead, James Turner (cousin of John Motley Morehead of N.C.) (D) May 24, 1797–Dec. 28, 1854; Feb. 22, 1834–June 1, 1836; Senate 1841–47 (Whig).

Clark, James (W) Jan. 16, 1770–Sept. 27, 1839; June 1, 1836–Sept. 27, 1839; House 1813–16 (Republican), Aug. 1, 1825–31 (Republican).

Wickliffe, Charles Anderson (father of Robert Charles Wickliffe of La., grandfather of John Cripps Wickliffe Beckham, below) (W) June 8, 1788–Oct. 31, 1869; Oct. 5, 1839–June 1, 1840; House 1823–33 (1823–27 no party, 1827–33 Jacksonian), 1861–63 (Unionist); postmaster general Oct. 13, 1841–March 6, 1845.

Letcher, Robert Perkins (-) Feb. 10, 1788–Jan. 24, 1861; June 1, 1840–June 1, 1844; House 1823–33, Aug. 6, 1834–35.

Owsley, William (W) March 24, 1782–Dec. 9, 1862; June 1, 1844–June 1, 1848.

Crittenden, John Jordan (uncle of Thomas Theodore Crittenden of Mo.) (W) Sept. 10, 1786–July 26, 1863; June 1, 1848–July 1850; Senate 1817–19 (no party), 1835–41, March 31, 1842–June 12, 1848, 1855–61; House 1861–63 (Unionist); attorney general March 5–Sept. 13, 1841, July 22, 1850–March 3, 1853.

Helm, John Larue (D) July 4, 1802–Sept. 8, 1867; July 31, 1850–Sept. 2, 1851 (Whig), Sept. 3–Sept. 8, 1867.

Powell, Lazarus Whitehead (D) Oct. 6, 1812–July 3, 1867; Sept. 2, 1851–Sept. 1, 1855; Senate 1859–65.

Morehead, Charles Slaughter (AP) July 7, 1802–Dec. 21, 1868; Sept. 1, 1855–Aug. 30, 1859; House 1847–51 (Whig).

Magoffin, Beriah (D) April 18, 1815–Feb. 28, 1885; Aug. 30, 1859–Aug. 16, 1862.

Robinson, James Fisher (D) Oct. 4, 1800–Oct. 31, 1882; Aug. 18, 1862–Sept. 1, 1863.

Bramlette, Thomas E. (UD) Jan. 3, 1817–Jan. 12, 1875; Sept. 1, 1863–Sept. 3, 1867.

Helm, John Larue (D) Sept. 3–Sept. 8, 1867 (for previous term see above).

Stevenson, John White (D) May 4, 1812–Aug. 10, 1886; Sept. 8, 1867–Feb. 13, 1871; House 1857–61; Senate 1871–77.

Leslie, Preston Hopkins (D) March 8, 1819–Feb. 7, 1907; Feb. 13, 1871–Aug. 31, 1875.

McCreary, James Bennett (D) July 8, 1838–Oct. 8, 1918; Aug. 31, 1875–Aug. 31, 1879, Dec. 12, 1911–Dec. 7, 1915; House 1885–97; Senate 1903–09.

Blackburn, Luke Pryor (D) June 16, 1816–Sept. 14, 1887; Sept. 2, 1879–Sept. 4, 1883.

Knott, James Proctor (D) Aug. 29, 1830–June 18, 1911; Sept. 4, 1883–Aug. 30, 1887; House 1867–71, 1875–83.

Buckner, Simon Bolivar (D) April 1, 1823–Jan. 8, 1914; Aug. 30, 1887–Sept. 1, 1891.

Brown, John Young (D) June 28, 1835–Jan. 11, 1904; Sept. 1, 1891–Dec. 10, 1895; House 1859–61, 1873–77.

Bradley, William O'Connell (uncle of Edwin Porch Morrow, below) (R) March 18, 1847–May 23, 1914; Dec. 10, 1895–Dec. 12, 1899; Senate 1909–May 23, 1814.

Taylor, William Sylvester (R) Oct. 10, 1853–Aug. 2, 1928; Dec. 12, 1899–Jan. 31, 1900.

Goebel, William (D) Jan. 4, 1856–Feb. 3, 1900; Jan. 31–Feb. 3, 1900.

Beckham, John Crepps Wickliffe (grandson of Charles Anderson Wickliffe, above, cousin of Robert Charles Wickliffe of La.) (D) Aug. 5, 1869–Jan. 9, 1940; Feb. 3, 1900–Dec. 10, 1907; Senate 1915–21.

Willson, Augustus Everett (R) Oct. 13, 1846–Aug. 24, 1931; Dec. 10, 1907–Dec. 12, 1911.

McCreary, James Bennett (D) Dec. 12, 1911–Dec. 7, 1915 (for previous term see above).

Stanley, Augustus Owsley (D) May 21, 1867–Aug. 12, 1958; Dec. 7, 1915–May 19, 1919; House 1903–15; Senate May 19, 1919–25.

Black, James Dixon (D) Sept. 24, 1849–Aug. 4, 1938; May 19–Dec. 9, 1919.

Morrow, Edwin Porch (nephew of William O'Connell Bradley, above) (R) Nov. 28, 1877–June 15, 1935; Dec. 9, 1919–Dec. 11, 1923.

Fields, William Jason (D) Dec. 29, 1874–Oct. 21, 1954; Dec. 11, 1923–Dec. 13, 1927; House 1911–Dec. 11, 1923.

Sampson, Flemon Davis (R) Jan. 25, 1875–May 25, 1967; Dec. 13, 1927–Dec. 8, 1931.

Lafoon, Ruby (D) Jan. 15, 1869–March 1, 1941; Dec. 8, 1931–Dec. 10, 1935.

Chandler, Albert Benjamin "Happy" (D) July 14, 1898–June 15, 1991; Dec. 10, 1935–Oct. 9, 1939, Dec. 13, 1955–Dec. 8, 1959; Senate Oct. 10, 1939–Nov. 1, 1945.

Johnson, Keen (D) Jan. 12, 1896–Feb. 7, 1970; Oct. 9, 1939–Dec. 7, 1943.

Willis, Simeon Slavens (R) Dec. 1, 1879–April 2, 1965; Dec. 7, 1943–Dec. 9, 1947.

Clements, Earle Chester (D) Oct. 22, 1896–March 12, 1985; Jan. 1948–Nov. 27, 1950; House 1945–Jan. 6, 1948; Senate Nov. 27, 1950–57.

Wetherby, Lawrence Winchester (D) Jan. 2, 1908–March 27, 1994; Nov. 27, 1950–Dec. 13, 1955.

Chandler, Albert Benjamin "Happy" (D) Dec. 13, 1955–Dec. 8, 1959 (for previous term see above).

Combs, Bertram Thomas (D) Aug. 13, 1911–Dec. 4, 1991; Dec. 8, 1959–Dec. 10, 1963.

Breathitt, Edward Thompson "Ned" (D) Nov. 26, 1926–Oct. 14, 2003; Dec. 10, 1963–Dec. 12, 1967.

Nunn, Louis Broady (R) March 8, 1924–Jan. 29, 2004; Dec. 12, 1967–Dec. 7, 1971.

Ford, Wendell Hampton (D) Sept. 8, 1924– ; Dec. 7, 1971–Dec. 28, 1974; Senate Dec. 28, 1974–99.

Carroll, Julian Morton (D) April 16, 1931– ; Dec. 28, 1974–Dec. 11, 1979.

Brown, John Young Jr. (D) Dec. 28, 1933– ; Dec. 11, 1979–Dec. 13, 1983.

Collins, Martha Layne (D) Dec. 7, 1936– ; Dec. 13, 1983–Dec. 8, 1987.

Wilkinson, Wallace G. (D) Dec. 12, 1941–July 5, 2002; Dec. 8, 1987–Dec. 10, 1991.

Jones, Brereton Chandler (D) June 27, 1939– ; Dec. 10, 1991–Dec. 12, 1995.

Patton, Paul E. (D) May 26, 1937– ; Dec. 12, 1995–Dec. 9, 2003.

Fletcher, Ernest L. "Ernie" (R) Nov. 12, 1952– ; Dec. 9, 2003– ; House 1999–Dec. 8, 2003.

Louisiana

(Became a state April 30, 1812)

Claiborne, William Charles Cole (DR) 1775–Nov. 23, 1817; 1801–03 (Miss. Terr.), 1804–12 (Orleans Terr.), July 30, 1812–Dec. 16, 1816; House 1797–1801 (Republican Tenn.); Senate March 4–Nov. 23, 1817 (Democrat).

Villere, Jacques Philippe (DR) April 28, 1760–March 7, 1830; Dec. 17, 1816–Dec. 18, 1820.

Robertson, Thomas Bolling (brother of Wyndham Robertson of Va.) (DR) Feb. 27, 1779–Oct. 5, 1828; Dec. 18, 1820–Nov. 15, 1822; House April 30, 1812–April 20, 1818 (Republican).

Thibodeaux, Henry Schuyler (DR) 1769–Oct. 24, 1827; Nov. 15–Dec. 13, 1824.

Johnson, Henry (DR) Sept. 14, 1783–Sept. 4, 1864; Dec. 13, 1824–Dec. 15, 1828; Senate Jan. 12, 1818–May 27, 1824 (Republican), Feb. 12, 1844–49 (Whig); House Sept. 25, 1834–39 (Whig).

Derbigny, Pierre Auguste Charles Bourguignon (NR) 1767–Oct. 6, 1829; Dec. 15, 1828–Oct. 6, 1829.

Beauvais, Armand (NR) Sept. 6, 1783–Nov. 18, 1843; Oct. 6, 1829–Jan. 14, 1830.

Dupre, Jacques (NR) Feb. 12, 1773–Sept. 14, 1846; Jan. 14, 1830–Jan. 31, 1831.

Roman, Andre Bienvenu (W) March 5, 1795–Jan. 26, 1866; Jan. 31, 1831–Feb. 4, 1835 (National Republican), Feb. 4, 1839–Jan. 30, 1843.

White, Edward Douglass Sr. (W) March 1795–April 18, 1847; Feb. 2, 1835–Feb. 4, 1839; House 1829–Nov. 15, 1834 (no party), 1839–43.

Roman, Andre Bienvenu (W) Feb. 4, 1839–Jan. 30, 1843 (for previous term see above).

Mouton, Alexander (D) Nov. 19, 1804–Feb. 12, 1885; Jan. 30, 1843–Feb. 12, 1846; Senate Jan. 12, 1837–March 1, 1842.

Johnson, Isaac (D) Nov. 1, 1803–March 15, 1853; Feb. 12, 1846–Jan. 27, 1850.

Walker, Joseph Marshall (D) July 1, 1784–Jan. 21, 1856; Jan. 28, 1850–Jan. 17, 1853.

Hebert, Paul Octave (D) Dec. 12, 1818–Aug. 29, 1880; Jan. 18, 1853–Jan. 28, 1856.

Wickliffe, Robert Charles (son of Charles Anderson Wickliffe of Ky., uncle of John Crepps Wickliffe Beckham of Ky.) (D) Jan. 6, 1819–April 18, 1895; Jan. 28, 1856–Jan. 22, 1860.

Moore, Thomas Overton (D) April 10, 1804–June 25, 1876; Jan. 23, 1860–Jan. 25, 1864.

Shepley, George Foster (-) Jan. 1, 1819–July 20, 1878; (Military) June 10, 1862–March 4, 1864.

Allen, Henry Watkins (D) April 29, 1820–April 22, 1866; Jan. 25, 1864–June 2, 1865.

Hahn, Michael (SRFT) Nov. 24, 1830–March 15, 1886; March 4, 1864–March 3, 1865; House Dec. 3, 1862–63 (Unionist), 1885– March 15, 1886 (Republican).

Wells, James Madison (ND) Jan. 8, 1808–Feb. 28, 1899; March 4, 1865–June 3, 1867.

Flanders, Benjamin Franklin (-) Jan. 26, 1816–March 13, 1896; (Military) June 6, 1867–Jan. 8, 1868; House Dec. 3, 1862–63 (Unionist).

Baker, Joshua (-) March 23, 1799–April 16, 1885; (Military) Jan. 2– June 27, 1868.

Warmoth, Henry Clay (R) May 9, 1842–Sept. 30, 1931; June 29, 1868–Dec. 9, 1872.

Pinchback, Pinckney Benton Stewart (R) May 10, 1837–Dec. 21, 1921; Dec. 9, 1872–Jan. 13, 1873.

Kellogg, William Pitt (R) Dec. 8, 1830–Aug. 10, 1918; Jan. 13, 1873–Jan. 8, 1877; Senate July 9, 1868–Nov. 1, 1872, 1877–83; House 1883–85.

Nicholls, Francis Redding Tillou (D) Aug. 20, 1834–Jan. 4, 1912; Jan. 8, 1877–Jan. 13, 1880, May 21, 1888–May 10, 1892.

Wiltz, Louis Alfred (D) Jan. 21, 1843–Oct. 16, 1881; Jan. 14, 1880–Oct. 16, 1881.

McEnery, Samuel Douglas (D) May 28, 1837–June 28, 1910; Oct. 16, 1881–May 20, 1888; Senate 1897–June 28, 1910.

Nicholls, Francis Redding Tillou (D) May 21, 1888–May 10, 1892 (for previous term see above).

Foster, Murphy James (cousin of Jared Young Sanders, below) (ALot.) Jan. 12, 1849–June 12, 1921; May 16, 1892–May 21, 1900; Senate 1901–13 (Democrat).

Heard, William Wright (D) April 28, 1853–June 1, 1926; May 21, 1900–May 10, 1904.

Blanchard, Newton Crain (D) Jan. 29, 1849–June 22, 1922; May 10, 1904–May 18, 1908; House 1881–March 12, 1894; Senate March 12, 1894–97.

Sanders, Jared Young (cousin of Murphy James Foster, above) (D) Jan. 29, 1867–March 23, 1944; May 18, 1908–May 14, 1912; House 1917–21.

Hall, Luther Egbert (D) Aug. 30, 1869–Nov. 6, 1921; May 20, 1912–May 15, 1916.

Pleasant, Ruffin Golson (D) June 2, 1871–Sept. 12, 1937; May 15, 1916–May 17, 1920.

Parker, John Milliken (D) March 16, 1863–May 20, 1939; May 17, 1920–May 19, 1924.

Fuqua, Henry Luce (D) Nov. 8, 1865–Oct. 11, 1926; May 19, 1924–Oct. 11, 1926.

Simpson, Oramel Hinckley (D) March 20, 1870–Nov. 17, 1932; Oct. 11, 1926–May 21, 1928.

Long, Huey Pierce "The Kingfish" (father of Sen. Russell B. Long, brother of Earl Kemp Long, below) (D) Aug. 30, 1893–Sept. 10, 1935; May 21, 1928–Jan. 25, 1932; Senate Sept. 25, 1932–Sept. 10, 1935.

King, Alvin Olin (D) June 21, 1890–Feb. 21, 1958; Jan. 25–May 16, 1932.

Allen, Oscar Kelly (D) Aug. 8, 1882–Jan. 28, 1936; May 16, 1932–Jan. 28, 1936.

Noe, James Albert (D) Dec. 21, 1893–April 2, 1976; Jan. 28–May 12, 1936.

Leche, Richard Webster (D) May 17, 1898–Feb. 22, 1965; May 12, 1936–June 26, 1939.

Long, Earl Kemp (brother of Huey Pierce "the Kingfish" Long, above, uncle of Sen. Russell B. Long) (D) Aug. 26, 1895–Sept. 5, 1960; June 26, 1939–May 14, 1940, May 11, 1948–May 13, 1952, May 15, 1956–May 10, 1960.

Jones, Sam Houston (D) July 15, 1897–Feb. 8, 1978; May 14, 1940– May 9, 1944.

Davis, James Houston (D) Sept. 11, 1902–Nov. 5, 2000; May 9, 1944–May 11, 1948, May 10, 1960–May 12, 1964.

Long, Earl Kemp (D) May 11, 1948–May 13, 1952 (for previous term see above).

Kennon, Robert Floyd (D) Aug. 21, 1902–Jan. 11, 1988; May 13, 1952–May 8, 1956.

Long, Earl Kemp (D) May 15, 1956–May 10, 1960 (for previous terms see above).

Davis, James Houston (D) May 10, 1960–May 12, 1964 (for previous term see above).

McKeithen, John Julian (D) May 28, 1918–June 4, 1999; May 12, 1964–May 9, 1972.

Edwards, Edwin Washington (D) Aug. 7, 1927– ; May 9, 1972– March 10, 1980, March 12, 1984–March 14, 1988, Jan. 8, 1992– Jan. 8, 1996; House Oct. 18, 1965–May 9, 1972.

Treen, David Conner (R) July 16, 1928– ; March 10, 1980–March 12, 1984; House 1973–March 10, 1980.

Edwards, Edwin Washington (D) March 12, 1984–March 14, 1988 (for previous terms see above).

Roemer, Charles Elson "Buddy" III (R) Oct. 4, 1943– ; March 14, 1988–Jan. 8, 1992 (March 14, 1988–March 11, 1991 Democrat); House 1981–March 14, 1988 (Democrat).

Edwards, Edwin Washington (D) Jan. 8, 1992–Jan. 8, 1996 (for previous term see above).

Foster, Mike Jr. (R) July 11, 1930– ; Jan. 8, 1996–Jan. 12, 2004.

Blanco, Kathleen Babineaux (D) Dec. 15, 1942– ; Jan. 12, 2004– .

Maine

(Became a state March 15, 1820)

King, William (DR) Feb. 9, 1768–June 17, 1852; May 31, 1820–May 28, 1821.

Williamson, William Durkee (-) July 31, 1779–May 27, 1846; May 29–Dec. 25, 1821; House 1821–23.

Ames, Benjamin (DR) Oct. 30, 1778–Sept. 28, 1835; Dec. 25, 1821– Jan. 2, 1822.

Rose, Daniel (DR) 1771–Oct. 25, 1833; Jan. 2–Jan. 5, 1822,

Parris, Albion Keith (DR) Jan. 19, 1788–Feb. 11, 1857; Jan. 5, 1822–Jan. 3, 1827; House 1815–Feb. 3, 1818 (Republican Mass.); Senate 1827–Aug. 26, 1828 (Republican).

Lincoln, Enoch (son of Levi Lincoln of Mass., brother of Levi Lincoln Jr. of Mass., great-uncle of Frederick Robie, below) (R) Dec. 28, 1788–Oct. 8, 1829; Jan. 3, 1827–Oct. 8, 1829; House Nov. 4, 1818–21 (Mass.), 1821–26.

Cutler, Nathan (D) May 29, 1775–June 8, 1861; Oct. 12, 1829–Feb. 5, 1830.

Hall, Joshua (D) Oct. 22, 1768–Dec. 25, 1862; Feb. 5–Feb. 10, 1830.

Hunton, Jonathan Glidden (NR) March 14, 1781–Oct. 12, 1851; Feb. 10, 1830–Jan. 5, 1831.

Smith, Samuel Emerson (J) March 12, 1788–March 3, 1860; Jan. 5, 1831–Jan. 1, 1834.

Dunlap, Robert Pinckney (D) Aug. 17, 1794–Oct. 20, 1859; Jan. 1, 1834–Jan. 3, 1838; House 1843–47.

Kent, Edward (W) Jan. 8, 1802–May 19, 1877; Jan. 3, 1838–Jan. 2, 1839, Jan. 13, 1841–Jan. 5, 1842.

Fairfield, John (D) Jan. 30, 1797–Dec. 24, 1847; Jan. 2, 1839–Jan. 6, 1841, Jan. 5, 1842–March 7, 1843; House 1835–Dec. 24, 1838; Senate 1843–Dec. 24, 1847.

Vose, Richard H. (-) Nov. 8, 1803–?; Jan. 12–Jan. 13, 1841.

Kent, Edward (W) Jan. 13, 1841–Jan. 5, 1842 (for previous term see above).

Fairfield, John (D) Jan. 5, 1842–March 7, 1843 (for previous term see above).

Kavanagh, Edward (D) April 27, 1795–Jan. 22, 1844; March 7, 1843–Jan. 1, 1844; House 1831–35 (Jacksonian).

Dunn, David (D) Jan. 17, 1811–Feb. 17, 1894; Jan. 1–Jan. 3, 1844.

Dana, John Winchester (D) June 21, 1808–Dec. 22, 1867; Jan. 3–Jan. 5, 1844, May 13, 1847–May 8, 1850.

Anderson, Hugh Johnston (D) May 10, 1801–May 31, 1881; Jan. 5, 1844–May 12, 1847; House 1837–41.

Dana, John Winchester (D) May 13, 1847–May 8, 1850 (for previous term see above).

Hubbard, John (D) March 22, 1794–Feb. 6, 1869; May 8, 1850–Jan. 5, 1853.

Crosby, William George (W) Sept. 10, 1805–March 21, 1881; Jan. 5, 1853–Jan. 3, 1855.

Morrill, Anson Peaslee (brother of Lot Myrick Morrill, below) (R) June 10, 1803–July 4, 1887; Jan. 3, 1855–Jan. 2, 1856; House 1861–63.

Wells, Samuel (D) Aug. 15, 1801–July 15, 1868; Jan. 2, 1856–Jan. 8, 1857.

Hamlin, Hannibal (R) Aug. 27, 1809–July 4, 1891; Jan. 8–Feb. 25, 1857; House 1843–47 (Democrat); Senate June 8, 1848–Jan. 7, 1857 (Democrat), 1857–Jan. 17, 1861, 1869–81; vice president 1861–65.

Williams, Joseph Hartwell (R) June 2, 1814–July 19, 1896; Feb. 26, 1857–Jan. 8, 1858.

Morrill, Lot Myrick (brother of Anson Peaslee Morrill, above) (R) May 3, 1813–Jan. 10, 1883; Jan. 8, 1858–Jan. 2, 1861; Senate Jan. 17, 1861–69, Oct. 30, 1869–July 7, 1876; secretary of the Treasury July 7, 1876–March 9, 1877.

Washburn, Israel Jr. (brother of Cadwallader Colden Washburn of Wis.) (R) June 6, 1813–May 12, 1883; Jan. 2, 1861–Jan. 7, 1863; House 1851–Jan. 1, 1861 (1851–55 Whig).

Coburn, Abner (R) March 22, 1803–Jan. 4, 1885; Jan. 7, 1863–Jan. 6, 1864.

Cony, Samuel (R) Feb. 27, 1811–Oct. 5, 1870; Jan. 6, 1864–Jan. 2, 1867.

Chamberlain, Joshua Lawrence (R) Sept. 8, 1828–March 2, 1908; Jan. 2, 1867–Jan. 4, 1871.

Perham, Sidney (R) March 27, 1819–April 10, 1907; Jan. 4, 1871–Jan. 7, 1874; House 1863–69 (Republican).

Dingley, Nelson Jr. (R) Feb. 15, 1832–Jan. 13, 1899; Jan. 7, 1874–Jan. 5, 1876; House Sept. 12, 1881–Jan. 13, 1899.

Connor, Seldon (R) Jan. 25, 1839–July 9, 1917; Jan. 5, 1876–Jan. 8, 1879.

Garcelon, Alonzo (D) May 6, 1813–Dec. 8, 1906; Jan. 8, 1879–Jan. 17, 1880.

Davis, Daniel Franklin (R) Sept. 12, 1848–Jan. 9, 1897; Jan. 17, 1880–Jan. 13, 1881.

Plaisted, Harris Merrill (father of Frederick William Plaisted, below) (D) Nov. 2, 1828–Jan. 31, 1898; Jan. 13, 1881–Jan. 3, 1883; House Sept. 13, 1875–77 (Republican).

Robie, Frederick (great-great-nephew of Levi Lincoln of Mass., great-nephew of Levi Lincoln Jr. of Mass. and Enoch Lincoln, above) (R) Aug. 12, 1822–Feb. 3, 1912; Jan. 3, 1883–Jan. 5, 1887.

Bodwell, Joseph Robinson (R) June 18, 1818–Dec. 15, 1887; Jan. 5–Dec. 15, 1887.

Marble, Sebastian Streeter (R) March 1, 1817–May 10, 1902; Dec. 16, 1887–Jan. 2, 1889.

Burleigh, Edwin Chick (R) Nov. 27, 1843–June 16, 1916; Jan. 2, 1889–Jan. 4, 1893; House June 21, 1897–1911; Senate 1913–June 16, 1916.

Cleaves, Henry B. (R) Feb. 6, 1840–June 22, 1912; Jan. 4, 1893–Jan. 6, 1897.

Powers, Llewellyn (R) Oct. 14, 1836–July 28, 1908; Jan. 6, 1897–Jan. 2, 1901; House 1877–79, April 8, 1901–July 28, 1908.

Hill, John Fremont (R) Oct. 29, 1855–March 16, 1912; Jan. 2, 1901–Jan. 4, 1905; chair Rep. Nat. Comm. 1910–12.

Cobb, William Titcomb (R) July 23, 1857–July 24, 1937; Jan. 4, 1905–Jan. 6, 1909.

Fernald, Bert Manfred (R) April 3, 1858–Aug. 23, 1926; Jan. 6, 1909–Jan. 4, 1911; Senate Sept. 12, 1916–Aug. 23, 1926.

Plaisted, Frederick William (son of Harris Merrill Plaisted, above) (D) July 26, 1865–March 4, 1943; Jan. 4, 1911–Jan. 1, 1913.

Haines, William Thomas (R) Aug. 7, 1854–June 4, 1919; Jan. 1, 1913–Jan. 6, 1915.

Curtis, Oakley Chester (D) March 29, 1865–Feb. 22, 1924; Jan. 6, 1915–Jan. 3, 1917.

Milliken, Carl Elias (R) July 13, 1877–May 1, 1961; Jan. 3, 1917–Jan. 5, 1921.

Parkhurst, Frederick Hale (R) Nov. 5, 1864–Jan. 31, 1921; Jan. 5–Jan. 31, 1921.

Baxter, Percival Proctor (R) Nov. 22, 1876–June 12, 1969; Jan. 31, 1921–Jan. 8, 1925.

Brewster, Ralph Owen (R) Feb. 22, 1888–Dec. 25, 1961; Jan. 8, 1925–Jan. 2, 1929; House 1935–41; Senate 1941–Dec. 31, 1952.

Gardiner, William Tudor (R) June 12, 1892–Aug. 3, 1953; Jan. 2, 1929–Jan. 4, 1933.

Brann, Louis Jefferson (D) July 6, 1876–Feb. 3, 1948; Jan. 4, 1933–Jan. 6, 1937.

Barrows, Lewis Orin (R) June 7, 1893–Jan. 30, 1967; Jan. 6, 1937–Jan. 1, 1941.

Sewall, Sumner (R) June 17, 1897–Jan. 25, 1965; Jan. 1, 1941–Jan. 3, 1945.

Hildreth, Horace Augustus (R) Dec. 2, 1901– ; Jan. 3, 1945–Jan. 5, 1949.

Payne, Frederick George (R) July 24, 1904–June 15, 1978; Jan. 5, 1949–Dec. 25, 1952; Senate 1953–59.

Cross, Burton Melvin (R) Nov. 15, 1902–Oct. 22, 1998; Dec. 26, 1952–Jan. 5, 1955.

Muskie, Edmund Sixtus (D) March 28, 1914–March 26, 1996; Jan. 5, 1955–Jan. 3, 1959; Senate 1959–May 7, 1980; secretary of state May 8, 1980–Jan. 18, 1981.

Haskell, Robert Nelson (R) Aug. 24, 1903–Dec. 1987; Jan. 3–Jan. 8, 1959.

Clauson, Clinton Amos (D) March 24, 1898–Dec. 30, 1959; Jan. 8–Dec. 30, 1959.

Reed, John Hathaway (R) Jan. 5, 1921– ; Dec. 30, 1959–Jan. 5, 1967.

Curtis, Kenneth M. (D) Feb. 8, 1931– ; Jan. 5, 1967–Jan. 1, 1975; chair Dem. Nat. Comm. 1977–78.

Longley, James Bernard (I) April 22, 1924–Aug. 16, 1980; Jan. 2, 1975–Jan. 3, 1979.

Brennan, Joseph Edward (D) Nov. 2, 1934– ; Jan. 3, 1979–Jan. 7, 1987; House 1987–91.

McKernan, John Rettie Jr. (husband of Sen. Olympia Jean Bouchles Snowe) (R) May 20, 1948– ; Jan. 7, 1987–Jan. 5, 1995; House 1983–87.

King, Angus S. Jr. (I) March 31, 1944– ; Jan. 5, 1995–Jan. 8, 2003.

Baldacci, John E. (D) Jan. 30, 1955– ; Jan. 8, 2003– ; House 1995–2003.

Maryland

(Ratified the Constitution April 28, 1788)

Howard, John Eager (father of George Howard, below) (F) June 4, 1752–Oct. 12, 1827; Nov. 24, 1788–Nov. 14, 1791; Cont. Cong. 1788; Senate Nov. 30, 1796–1803; elected pres. pro tempore Nov. 21, 1800.

Plater, George (F) Nov. 8, 1735–Feb. 10, 1792; Nov. 14, 1791–Feb. 10, 1792; Cont. Cong. 1778–80.

Brice, James (F) Aug. 26, 1746–July 11, 1801; Feb. 13–April 5, 1792.

Lee, Thomas Sim (great-great-grandfather of John Lee Carroll, below) (F) Oct. 29, 1745–Nov. 9, 1819; April 5, 1792–Nov. 14, 1794.

Stone, John Hoskins (F) 1745–Oct. 5, 1804; Nov. 14, 1794–Nov. 17, 1797.

Henry, John (great-grandfather of Henry Lloyd, below) (F) Nov. 1750–Dec. 16, 1798; Nov. 17, 1797–Nov. 14, 1798; Cont. Cong. 1778–80, 1785–86; Senate 1789–Dec. 10, 1797.

Ogle, Benjamin (F) Jan. 27, 1749–July 6, 1809; Nov. 14, 1798–Nov. 10, 1801.

Mercer, John Francis (DR) May 17, 1759–Aug. 30, 1821; Nov. 10, 1801–Nov. 15, 1803; Cont. Cong. (Va.) 1783–84; House Feb. 5, 1792–April 13, 1794 (Democrat).

Bowie, Robert (DR) March 1750–Jan. 8, 1818; Nov. 15, 1803–Nov. 10, 1806, Nov. 16, 1811–Nov. 25, 1812.

Wright, Robert (father-in-law of Philip Francis Thomas, below) (DR) Nov. 20, 1752–Sept. 7, 1826; Nov. 12, 1806–May 6, 1809; Senate Nov. 19, 1801–Nov. 12, 1806 (Republican); House Nov. 29, 1810–17 (Republican), 1821–23 (Republican).

Butcher, James (DR) ?–Jan. 12, 1824; May 6–June 9, 1809.

Lloyd, Edward (grandfather of Henry Lloyd, below) (DR) July 22, 1779–June 2, 1834; June 9, 1809–Nov. 16, 1811; House Dec. 3, 1806–09 (no party); Senate 1819–Jan. 14, 1826 (Republican).

Bowie, Robert (DR) Nov. 16, 1811–Nov. 25, 1812 (for previous term see above).

Winder, Levin (F) Sept. 4, 1757–July 1, 1819; Nov. 25, 1812–Jan. 2, 1816.

Ridgely, Charles Carnan (father-in-law of George Howard, below) (F) Dec. 6, 1762–July 17, 1829; Jan. 2, 1816–Jan. 8, 1819.

Goldsborough, Charles (F) July 15, 1765–Dec. 13, 1834; Jan. 8–Dec. 20, 1819; House 1805–17.

Sprigg, Samuel (DR) 1783–April 21, 1855; Dec. 20, 1819–Dec. 16, 1822.

Stevens, Samuel Jr. (DR) July 13, 1778–Feb. 7, 1860; Dec. 16, 1822–Jan. 9, 1826.

Kent, Joseph (DR) Jan. 14, 1779–Nov. 24, 1837; Jan. 9, 1826–Jan. 15, 1829; House 1811–15 (Republican), 1819–Jan. 6, 1826 (Republican); Senate 1833–Nov. 24, 1837 (Republican).

Martin, Daniel (AJ) 1780–July 11, 1831; Jan. 15, 1829–Jan. 15, 1830, Jan. 13–July 11, 1831.

Carroll, Thomas King (J) April 29, 1793–Oct. 3, 1873; Jan. 15, 1830–Jan. 13, 1831.

Martin, Daniel (AJ) Jan. 13–July 11, 1831 (for previous term see above).

Howard, George (son of John Eager Howard, above, son-in-law of Charles Carnan Ridgely, above) (AJ) Nov. 21, 1789–Aug. 2, 1846; July 22, 1831–Jan. 17, 1833.

Thomas, James (AJ) March 11, 1785–Dec. 25, 1845; Jan. 17, 1833–Jan. 14, 1836.

Veazey, Thomas Ward (W) Jan. 31, 1774–July 1, 1842; Jan. 14, 1836–Jan. 7, 1839.

Grason, William (D) March 11, 1788–July 2, 1868; Jan. 7, 1839–Jan. 3, 1842.

Thomas, Francis (son-in-law of James McDowell of Va.) (D) Feb. 3, 1799–Jan. 22, 1876; Jan. 3, 1842–Jan. 6, 1845; House 1831–41 (1831–37 Jacksonian, 1837–41 Republican), 1861–69 (1861–63 Unionist, 1863–67 Unconditional Unionist, 1867–69 Republican).

Pratt, Thomas George (W) Feb. 18, 1804–Nov. 9, 1869; Jan. 6, 1845–Jan. 3, 1848; Senate Jan. 12, 1850–57.

Thomas, Philip Francis (son-in-law of Robert Wright, above) (D) Sept. 12, 1810–Oct. 2, 1890; Jan. 3, 1848–Jan. 6, 1851; House 1839–41, 1875–77; secretary of the Treasury Dec. 12, 1860–Jan. 14, 1861.

Lowe, Enoch Louis (D) Aug. 10, 1820–Aug. 23, 1892; Jan. 6, 1851–Jan. 11, 1854.

Ligon, Thomas Watkins (D) May 10, 1810–Jan. 12, 1881; Jan. 11, 1854–Jan. 13, 1858; House 1845–49.

Hicks, Thomas Holliday (AP) Sept. 2, 1798–Feb. 14, 1865; Jan. 13, 1858–Jan. 8, 1862; Senate Dec. 29, 1862–Feb. 14, 1865 (Unionist).

Bradford, Augustus Williamson (UR) Jan. 9, 1806–March 1, 1881; Jan. 8, 1862–Jan. 10, 1866.

Swann, Thomas (UD) Feb. 3, 1809–July 24, 1883; Jan. 10, 1866–Jan. 13, 1869; House 1869–79 (Democrat).

Bowie, Oden (D) Nov. 10, 1826–Dec. 4, 1894; Jan. 13, 1869–Jan. 10, 1872.

Whyte, William Pinkney (D) Aug. 9, 1824–March 17, 1908; Jan. 10, 1872–March 4, 1874; Senate July 13, 1868–69, 1875–81, June 8, 1906–March 17, 1908.

Groome, James Black (D) April 4, 1838–Oct. 5, 1893; March 4, 1874–Jan. 12, 1876; Senate 1879–85.

Carroll, John Lee (great-great-grandson of Thomas Sim Lee, above) (D) Sept. 30, 1830–Feb. 27, 1911; Jan. 12, 1876–Jan. 14, 1880.

Hamilton, William Thomas (D) Sept. 8, 1820–Oct. 26, 1888; Jan. 14, 1880–Jan. 9, 1884; House 1849–55; Senate 1869–75.

McLane, Robert Milligan (D) June 23, 1815–April 16, 1898; Jan. 9, 1884–March 27, 1885; House 1847–51, 1879–83; chair Dem. Nat. Comm. 1852–54.

Lloyd, Henry (grandson of Edward Lloyd, above, great-grandson of John Henry, above) (D) Feb. 21, 1852–Dec. 30, 1920; March 27, 1885–Jan. 11, 1888.

Jackson, Elihu Emory (D) Nov. 3, 1836–Dec. 27, 1907; Jan. 11, 1888–Jan. 13, 1892.

Brown, Frank (D) Aug. 8, 1846–Feb. 3, 1920; Jan. 13, 1892–Jan. 8, 1896.

Lowndes, Lloyd Jr. (R) Feb. 21, 1845–Jan. 8, 1905; Jan. 8, 1896–Jan. 10, 1900; House 1873–75.

Smith, John Walter (D) Feb. 5, 1845–April 19, 1925; Jan. 10, 1900–Jan. 13, 1904; House 1899–Jan. 12, 1900; Senate March 25, 1908–21.

Warfield, Edwin (D) May 7, 1848–March 31, 1920; Jan. 13, 1904–Jan. 8, 1908.

Crothers, Austin Lane (D) May 17, 1860–May 25, 1912; Jan. 8, 1908–Jan. 10, 1912.

Goldsborough, Phillips Lee (R) Aug. 6, 1865–Oct. 22, 1946; Jan. 10, 1912–Jan. 12, 1916; Senate 1929–35.

Harrington, Emerson Columbus (D) March 26, 1864–Dec. 15, 1945; Jan. 12, 1916–Jan. 14, 1920.

Ritchie, Albert Cabell (D) Aug. 29, 1876–Feb. 24, 1936; Jan. 14, 1920–Jan. 9, 1935.

Nice, Harry Whinna (R) Dec. 5, 1877–Feb. 25, 1941; Jan. 9, 1935–Jan. 11, 1939.

O'Conor, Herbert Romulus (D) Nov. 17, 1896–March 4, 1960; Jan. 11, 1939–Jan. 3, 1947; Senate 1947–53.

Lane, William Preston Jr. (D) May 12, 1892–Feb. 7, 1967; Jan. 3, 1947–Jan. 10, 1951.

McKeldin, Theodore Roosevelt (R) Nov. 20, 1900–Aug. 10, 1974; Jan. 10, 1951–Jan. 14, 1959.

Tawes, John Millard (D) April 8, 1894–June 25, 1979; Jan. 14, 1959–Jan. 25, 1967.

Agnew, Spiro Theodore (R) Nov. 9, 1918–Sept. 17, 1996; Jan. 25, 1967–Jan. 7, 1969; vice president 1969–Oct. 10, 1973.

Mandel, Marvin (D) April 19, 1920– ; Jan. 7, 1969–June 1977, Jan. 15–Jan. 17, 1979.

Lee, Blair III (D) May 19, 1916–Oct. 25, 1985; June 1977–Jan. 15, 1979.

Mandel, Marvin (D) Jan. 15–Jan. 17, 1979 (for previous term see above).

Hughes, Harry R. (D) Nov. 13, 1926– ; Jan. 17, 1979–Jan. 20, 1987.

Schaefer, William Donald (D) Nov. 2, 1921– ; Jan. 21, 1987–Jan. 18, 1995.

Glendening, Parris N. (D) June 11, 1942– ; Jan. 18, 1995–Jan. 15, 2003.

Ehrlich, Robert L. Jr. (R) Nov. 25, 1957– ; Jan. 15, 2003– ; House 1995–2003.

Massachusetts

(Ratified the Constitution Feb. 6, 1788)

Hancock, John (-) Jan. 23, 1737–Oct. 8, 1793; Oct. 30, 1787–Oct. 8, 1793; Cont. Cong. 1775–78.

Adams, Samuel (DR) Sept. 27, 1722–Oct. 2, 1803; Oct. 8, 1793–June 2, 1797; Cont. Cong. 1774–81.

Sumner, Increase (F) Nov. 27, 1746–June 7, 1799; June 2, 1797–June 7, 1799.

Gill, Moses (F) Jan. 18, 1734–May 20, 1800; June 7, 1799–May 20, 1800.

Strong, Caleb (-) Jan. 9, 1745–Nov. 7, 1819; May 30, 1800–May 29, 1807, June 5, 1812–May 30, 1816; Senate 1789–June 1, 1796; Cont. Cong. (elected but did not attend) 1780.

Sullivan, James (brother of John Sullivan of N.H.) (DR) April 22, 1744–Dec. 10, 1808; May 29, 1807–Dec. 10, 1808; Cont. Cong. (elected but did not attend) 1782, 1783.

Lincoln, Levi (father of Levi Lincoln Jr., below, and Enoch Lincoln of Maine, great-great-uncle of Frederick Robie of Maine) (DR) May 15, 1749–April 14, 1820; Dec. 10, 1808–May 1, 1809; House Dec. 15, 1800–March 5, 1801 (Republican); Cont. Cong. (elected but did not attend) 1781; attorney general March 5, 1801–March 3, 1805.

Gore, Christopher (F) Sept. 21, 1758–March 1, 1827; May 1, 1809–June 2, 1810; Senate May 5, 1813–May 30, 1816.

Gerry, Elbridge (DR) July 17, 1744–Nov. 23, 1814; June 2, 1810–June 5, 1812; Cont. Cong. 1776–80, 1783–85; House 1789–93 (no party); vice president 1813–Nov. 23, 1814 (Democratic Republican).

Strong, Caleb (F) June 5, 1812–May 30, 1816 (for previous term see above).

Brooks, John (F) May 4, 1752–March 1, 1825; May 30, 1816–May 31, 1823.

Eustis, William (R) June 10, 1753–Feb. 6, 1825; May 31, 1823–Feb. 6, 1825; House 1801–05, Aug. 21, 1820–23; secretary of war March 7, 1809–Jan. 13, 1813.

Morton, Marcus (R) Dec. 19, 1784–Feb. 6, 1864; Feb. 6–May 26, 1825, Jan. 18, 1840–Jan. 7, 1841, Jan. 17, 1843–Jan. 3, 1844; House 1817–21 (Republican).

Lincoln, Levi Jr. (son of Levi Lincoln, above, brother of Enoch Lincoln of Maine, great-uncle of Frederick Robie of Maine) (NR) Oct. 25, 1782–May 29, 1868; May 26, 1825–Jan. 9, 1834 (1825–29 Anti-Democrat); House Feb. 17, 1834–March 16, 1841 (Feb. 17, 1834–35 Anti-Jacksonian, 1835–March 16, 1841 Whig).

Davis, John (W) Jan. 13, 1787–April 19, 1854; Jan. 9, 1834–March 1, 1835, Jan. 7, 1841–Jan. 17, 1843; House 1825–Jan. 14, 1834 (no party); Senate 1835–Jan. 5, 1941, March 24, 1845–53.

Armstrong, Samuel Turell (IW) April 29, 1784–March 26, 1850; March 1, 1835–Jan. 13, 1836.

Everett, Edward (W) April 11, 1794–Jan. 15, 1865; Jan. 13, 1836–Jan. 18, 1840; House 1825–35 (no party); Senate 1853–June 1, 1854; secretary of state Nov. 6, 1852–March 3, 1853.

Morton, Marcus (D) Jan. 18, 1840–Jan. 7, 1841 (for previous term see above).

Davis, John (W) Jan. 7, 1841–Jan. 17, 1843 (for previous term see above).

Morton, Marcus (D) Jan. 17, 1843–Jan. 3, 1844 (for previous terms see above).

Briggs, George Nixon (W) April 12, 1796–Sept. 11, 1861; Jan. 3, 1844–Jan. 11, 1851; House 1831–43 (1831–35 Anti-Jacksonian).

Boutwell, George Sewel (D) Jan. 28, 1818–Feb. 27, 1905; Jan. 11, 1851–Jan. 14, 1853; House 1863–March 12, 1869 (Republican); Senate March 17, 1873–77 (Republican); secretary of the Treasury March 12, 1869–March 16, 1873.

Clifford, John Henry (W) Jan. 16, 1809–Jan. 2, 1876; Jan. 14, 1853–Jan. 4, 1854.

Washburn, Emory (W) Feb. 14, 1800–March 18, 1877; Jan. 12, 1854–Jan. 4, 1855.

Gardner, Henry Joseph (AP) June 14, 1819–July 21, 1892; Jan. 4, 1855–Jan. 6, 1858.

Banks, Nathaniel Prentice (R) Jan. 30, 1816–Sept. 1, 1894; Jan. 6, 1858–Jan. 2, 1861; House 1853–Dec. 24, 1857, Dec. 4, 1865–73, 1875–79, 1889–91 (1853–55 Democrat, 1855–57 American Party, March 4–Dec. 24, 1857 Republican, Dec. 4, 1865–67 Union Republican, 1867–73 Republican, 1875–77 Independent); Speaker Feb. 2, 1856–57.

Andrew, John Albion (R) May 31, 1818–Oct. 30, 1867; Jan. 2, 1861–Jan. 4, 1866.

Bullock, Alexander Hamilton (R) March 2, 1816–Jan. 17, 1882; Jan. 4, 1866–Jan. 7, 1869.

Claflin, William (R) March 6, 1818–Jan. 5, 1905; Jan. 7, 1869–Jan. 4, 1872; House 1877–81; chair Rep. Nat. Comm. 1868–72.

Washburn, William Barrett (R) Jan. 31, 1820–Oct. 5, 1887; Jan. 3, 1872–April 17, 1874; House 1863–Dec. 5, 1871; Senate April 29, 1874–75.

Talbot, Thomas (R) Sept. 7, 1818–Oct. 6, 1886; April 29, 1874–Jan. 6, 1875, Jan. 1, 1879–Jan. 7, 1880.

Gaston, William (D) Oct. 3, 1820–Jan. 19, 1894; Jan. 6, 1875–Jan. 5, 1876.

Rice, Alexander Hamilton (R) Aug. 30, 1818–July 22, 1895; Jan. 5, 1876–Jan. 1, 1879; House 1859–67.

Talbot, Thomas (R) Jan. 1, 1879–Jan. 7, 1880 (for previous term see above).

Long, John Davis (R) Oct. 27, 1838–Aug. 28, 1915; Jan. 8, 1880–Jan. 4, 1883; House 1883–89; secretary of the navy March 6, 1897–April 30, 1902.

Butler, Benjamin Franklin (father-in-law of Adelbert Ames of Miss.) (D/G) Nov. 5, 1818–Jan. 11, 1893; Jan. 4, 1883–Jan. 3, 1884; House 1867–75 (Republican), 1877–79 (Republican).

Robinson, George Dexter (R) Jan. 20, 1834–Feb. 22, 1896; Jan. 3, 1884–Jan. 5, 1887; House 1877–Jan. 7, 1884.

Ames, Oliver (R) Feb. 4, 1831–Oct. 22, 1895; Jan. 5, 1887–Jan. 1, 1890.

Brackett, John Quincy Adams (R) June 8, 1842–April 6, 1918; Jan. 1, 1890–Jan. 7, 1891.

Russell, William Eustis (D) Jan. 6, 1857–July 14, 1896; Jan. 7, 1891–Jan. 3, 1894.

Greenhalge, Frederic Thomas (R) July 19, 1842–March 5, 1896; Jan. 3, 1894–March 5, 1896; House 1889–91.

Wolcott, Roger (R) July 13, 1847–Dec. 21, 1900; March 5, 1896–Jan. 4, 1900.

Crane, Winthrop Murray (R) April 23, 1853–Oct. 2, 1920; Jan. 4, 1900–Jan. 8, 1903; Senate Oct. 12, 1904–13.

Bates, John Lewis (R) Sept. 18, 1859–June 8, 1946; Jan. 8, 1903–Jan. 5, 1905.

Douglas, William Lewis (D) Aug. 22, 1845–Sept. 17, 1924; Jan. 5, 1905–Jan. 4, 1906.

Guild, Curtis Jr. (R) Feb., 2, 1860–April 6, 1915; Jan. 4, 1906–Jan. 7, 1909.

Draper, Eben Sumner (R) June 17, 1858–April 9, 1914; Jan. 7, 1909–Jan. 5, 1911.

Foss, Eugene Noble (D) Sept. 24, 1858–Sept. 13, 1939; Jan. 5, 1911–Jan. 8, 1914; House March 22, 1910–Jan. 4, 1911.

Walsh, David Ignatius (D) Nov. 11, 1872–June 11, 1947; Jan. 8, 1914–Jan. 6, 1916; Senate 1919–25, Dec. 6, 1926–47.

McCall, Samuel Walker (R) Feb. 28, 1851–Nov. 4, 1923; Jan. 6, 1916–Jan. 2, 1919; House 1893–1913.

Coolidge, John Calvin (cousin of William Wallace Stickney of Vt.) (R) July 4, 1872–Jan. 5, 1933; Jan. 2, 1919–Jan. 6, 1921; vice president 1921–Aug. 3, 1923; president Aug. 3, 1923–29.

Cox, Channing Harris (R) Oct. 28, 1879–Aug. 20, 1968; Jan. 6, 1921–Jan. 8, 1925.

Fuller, Alvan Tufts (R) Feb. 27, 1878–April 30, 1958; Jan. 8, 1925–Jan. 3, 1929; House 1917–Jan. 5, 1921 (1917–19 Independent Republican).

Allen, Frank G. (R) Oct. 6, 1874–Oct. 9, 1950; Jan. 3, 1929–Jan. 8, 1931.

Ely, Joseph Buell (D) Feb. 22, 1881–June 13, 1956; Jan. 8, 1931–Jan. 3, 1935.

Curley, James Michael (D) Nov. 20, 1874–Nov. 12, 1958; Jan. 3, 1935–Jan. 7, 1937; House 1911–Feb. 4, 1914, 1943–47.

Hurley, Charles Francis (D) Nov. 24, 1893–March 24, 1946; Jan. 7, 1937–Jan. 5, 1939.

Saltonstall, Leverett (R) Sept. 1, 1892–June 17, 1979; Jan. 5, 1939–Jan. 3, 1945; Senate Jan. 4, 1945–67.

Tobin, Maurice Joseph (D) May 22, 1901–July 19, 1953; Jan. 3, 1945–Jan. 2, 1947; secretary of labor Aug. 13, 1948–Jan. 20, 1953.

Bradford, Robert Fiske (R) Dec. 15, 1902–March 18, 1983; Jan. 2, 1947–Jan. 6, 1949.

Dever, Paul Andrew (D) Jan. 15, 1903–April 11, 1958; Jan. 6, 1949–Jan. 8, 1953.

Herter, Christian Archibald (R) March 28, 1895–Dec. 30, 1966; Jan. 8, 1953–Jan. 3, 1957; House 1943–53; secretary of state April 22, 1959–Jan. 20, 1961.

Furcolo, Foster (D) July 29, 1911–July 5, 1995; Jan. 3, 1957–Jan. 5, 1961; House 1949–Sept. 30, 1952.

Volpe, John Anthony (R) Dec. 8, 1908–Nov. 11, 1994; Jan. 5, 1961–Jan. 3, 1963, Jan. 7, 1965–Jan. 22, 1969; secretary of transportation Jan. 22, 1969–Feb. 1, 1973.

Peabody, Endicott "Chub" (D) Feb. 15, 1920–Dec. 2, 1997; Jan. 3, 1963–Jan. 7, 1965.

Volpe, John Anthony (R) Jan. 7, 1965–Jan. 22, 1969 (for previous term see above).

Sargent, Francis Williams (R) July 29, 1915–Oct. 22, 1998; Jan. 22, 1969–Jan. 2, 1975.

Dukakis, Michael Stanley (D) Nov. 3, 1933– ; Jan. 2, 1975–Jan. 4, 1979, Jan. 6, 1983–Jan. 3, 1991.

King, Edward J. (D) May 11, 1925– ; Jan. 4, 1979–Jan. 6, 1983.

Dukakis, Michael Stanley (D) Jan. 6, 1983–Jan. 3, 1991 (for previous term see above).

Weld, William Floyd (R) July 31, 1945– ; Jan. 3, 1991–July 29, 1997.

Cellucci, Argeo Paul (R) April 24, 1948– ; July 29, 1997–April 10, 2001.

Swift, Jane (R) Feb. 24, 1965– ; April 10, 2001–Jan. 2, 2003.

Romney, Mitt (R) March 12, 1947– ; Jan. 2, 2003– .

Michigan

(Became a state Jan. 26, 1837)

Mason, Stevens Thomson (D) Oct. 22, 1811–Jan. 4, 1843; Nov. 3, 1835–Jan. 1840.

Woodbridge, William (W) Aug. 20, 1780–Oct. 20, 1861; Jan. 7, 1840–Feb. 23, 1841; House (no party Terr. Del.) 1819–Aug. 9, 1820; Senate 1841–47.

Gordon, James Wright (W) 1809–Dec. 1853; Feb. 23, 1841–Jan. 3, 1842.

Barry, John Stewart (D) Jan. 29, 1802–Jan. 14, 1870; Jan. 3, 1842–Jan. 5, 1846, Jan. 7, 1850–Jan. 1, 1851.

Felch, Alpheus (D) Sept. 28, 1804–June 13, 1896; Jan. 5, 1846–March 3, 1847; Senate 1847–53.

Greenly, William L. (D) Sept. 18, 1813–Nov. 29, 1883; March 3, 1847–Jan. 3, 1848.

Ransom, Epaphroditus (D) Feb. 1787–Nov. 9, 1859; Jan. 3, 1848–Jan. 7, 1850.

Barry, John Stewart (D) Jan. 7, 1850–Jan. 1, 1851 (for previous term see above).

McClelland, Robert (D) Aug. 1, 1807–Aug. 30, 1880; Jan. 1, 1851–March 7, 1853; House 1843–49; secretary of the interior March 8, 1853–March 9, 1857.

Parsons, Andrew (D) July 22, 1817–June 6, 1855; March 7, 1853–Jan. 3, 1855.

Bingham, Kinsley Scott (R) Dec. 16, 1808–Oct. 5, 1861; Jan. 3, 1855–Jan. 5, 1859; House 1847–51 (Democrat); Senate 1859–Oct. 5, 1861.

Wisner, Moses (R) June 3, 1815–Jan. 5, 1863; Jan. 5, 1859–Jan. 2, 1861.

Blair, Austin (R) Feb. 8, 1818–Aug. 6, 1894; Jan. 2, 1861–Jan. 4, 1865; House 1867–73.

Crapo, Henry Howland (R) May 22, 1804–July 22, 1869; Jan. 4, 1865–Jan. 6, 1869.

Baldwin, Henry Porter (R) Feb. 22, 1814–Dec. 31, 1892; Jan. 6, 1869–Jan. 1, 1873; Senate Nov. 17, 1879–81.

Bagley, John Judson (R) July 24, 1832–Dec. 27, 1881; Jan. 1, 1873–Jan. 3, 1877.

Croswell, Charles Miller (R) Oct. 31, 1825–Dec. 13, 1886; Jan. 3, 1877–Jan. 1, 1881.

Jerome, David Howell (R) Nov. 17, 1869–April 23, 1896; Jan. 1, 1881–Jan. 1, 1883.

Begole, Josiah William (D) Jan. 20, 1815–June 5, 1896; Jan. 1, 1883–Jan. 1, 1885; House 1873–75.

Alger, Russell Alexander (R) Feb. 27, 1836–Jan. 24, 1907; Jan. 1, 1885–Jan. 1, 1887; Senate Sept. 27, 1902–Jan. 24, 1907; secretary of war March 5, 1897–Aug. 1, 1899.

Luce, Cyrus Gray (R) July 2, 1824–March 18, 1905; Jan. 1, 1887–Jan. 1, 1891.

Winans, Edwin Baruch (D) May 16, 1826–July 4, 1894; Jan. 1, 1891–Jan. 1, 1893; House 1883–87.

Rich, John Tyler (R) April 23, 1841–March 28, 1926; Jan. 1, 1893–Jan. 1, 1897; House April 5, 1881–83.

Pingree, Hazen Stuart (R) Aug. 30, 1840–June 18, 1901; Jan. 1, 1897–Jan. 1, 1901.

Bliss, Aaron Thomas (R) May 22, 1837–Sept. 16, 1906; Jan. 1, 1901–Jan. 1, 1905; House 1889–91.

Warner, Fred Maltby (R) July 21, 1865–April 17, 1823; Jan. 1, 1905–Jan. 1, 1911.

Osborn, Chase Salmon (R) June 22, 1860–April 11, 1949; Jan. 1, 1911–Jan. 1, 1913.

Ferris, Woodbridge Nathan (D) Jan. 6, 1853–March 23, 1928; Jan. 1, 1913–Jan. 1, 1917; Senate 1923–March 23, 1928.

Sleeper, Albert Edson (R) Dec. 31, 1862–May 13, 1934; Jan. 1, 1917–Jan. 1, 1921.

Groesbeck, Alexander Joseph (R) Nov. 7, 1873–March 10, 1953; Jan. 1, 1921–Jan. 1, 1927.

Green, Fred Warren (R) Oct. 20, 1871–Nov. 30, 1936; Jan. 1, 1927–Jan. 1, 1931.

Brucker, Wilber Marion (R) June 23, 1894–Oct. 28, 1968; Jan. 1, 1931–Jan. 1, 1933.

Comstock, William Alfred (D) July 2, 1877–June 16, 1949; Jan. 1, 1933–Jan. 1, 1935.

Fitzgerald, Frank Dwight (R) Jan. 27, 1885–March 16, 1939; Jan. 1, 1935–Jan. 1, 1937, Jan. 2–March 16, 1939.

Murphy, Francis William (D) April 13, 1890–July 19, 1949; Jan. 1, 1937–Jan. 1, 1939; attorney general Jan. 17, 1939–Jan. 18, 1940; assoc. justice Feb. 5, 1940–July 19, 1949.

Fitzgerald, Frank Dwight (R) Jan. 2–March 16, 1939 (for previous term see above).

Dickenson, Luren Dudley (R) April 15, 1859–April 22, 1943; March 16, 1939–Jan. 1, 1941.

Van Wagoner, Murray Delos (D) March 18, 1898–June 12, 1986; Jan. 1, 1941–Jan. 1, 1943.

Kelly, Harry Francis (R) April 19, 1895–Feb. 8, 1971; Jan. 1, 1943–Jan. 1, 1947.

Sigler, Kim (R) May 2, 1894–Nov. 30, 1953; Jan. 1, 1947–Jan. 1, 1949.

Williams, Gerhard Mennen (D) Feb. 23, 1911–Feb. 2, 1988; Jan. 1, 1949–Jan. 2, 1961.

Swainson, John Burley (D) July 30, 1925–May 13, 1994; Jan. 2, 1961–Jan. 1, 1963.

Romney, George Wilcken (R) July 8, 1907–July 26, 1995; Jan. 1, 1963–Jan. 22, 1969; secretary of housing and urban development Jan. 20, 1969–Feb. 2, 1973.

Milliken, William Grawn (R) March 26, 1922–July 27, 1995; Jan. 22, 1969–Jan. 1, 1983.

Blanchard, James Johnston (D) Aug. 8, 1942– ; Jan. 1, 1983–Jan. 1, 1991; House 1975–83.

Engler, John (R) Oct. 12, 1948– ; Jan. 1, 1991–Jan. 1, 2003.

Granholm, Jennifer (D) Feb. 5, 1959– ; Jan. 1, 2003– .

Minnesota

(Became a state May 11, 1858)

Sibley, Henry Hastings (D) Feb. 20, 1811–Feb. 18, 1891; May 24, 1858–Jan. 2, 1860; House (Terr. Del.) Oct. 30, 1848–49 (Wis.), July 7, 1849–53.

Ramsey, Alexander (R) Sept. 8, 1815–April 22, 1903; April 2, 1849–53 (Minn. Terr.), Jan. 2, 1860–July 10, 1863; House 1843–47 (Whig Pa.); Senate 1863–75; secretary of war Dec. 10, 1879–March 5, 1881.

Swift, Henry Adoniram (R) March 23, 1823–Feb. 25, 1869; July 10, 1863–Jan. 11, 1864.

Miller, Stephen (R) Jan. 17, 1816–Aug. 18, 1881; Jan. 11, 1864–Jan. 8, 1866.

Marshall, William Rogerson (R) Oct. 17, 1825–Jan. 8, 1896; Jan. 8, 1866–Jan. 9, 1870.

Austin, Horace (R) Oct. 15, 1831–Nov. 2, 1905; Jan. 9, 1870–Jan. 7, 1874.

Davis, Cushman Kellogg (R) June 16, 1838–Nov. 27, 1900; Jan. 7, 1874–Jan. 7, 1876; Senate 1887–Nov. 27, 1900.

Pillsbury, John Sargent (R) July 29, 1828–Oct. 10, 1901; Jan. 7, 1876–Jan. 10, 1882.

Hubbard, Lucius Frederick (R) Jan. 26, 1836–Feb. 5, 1913; Jan. 10, 1882–Jan. 5, 1887.

McGill, Andrew Ryan (R) Feb. 19, 1840–Oct. 31, 1905; Jan. 5, 1887–Jan. 9, 1889.

Merriam, William Rush (R) July 26, 1849–Feb. 18, 1931; Jan. 9, 1889–Jan. 4, 1893.

Nelson, Knute (R) Feb. 2, 1843–April 28, 1923; Jan. 4, 1893–Jan. 31, 1895; House 1883–89; Senate 1895–April 28, 1923.

Clough, David Marston (father-in-law of Roland Hill Hartley of Wash.) (R) Dec. 27, 1846–Aug. 28, 1924; Jan. 31, 1895–Jan. 2, 1899.

Lind, John (D) March 25, 1854–Sept. 18, 1930; Jan. 2, 1899–Jan. 7, 1901; House 1887–93 (Republican), 1903–05.

Van Sant, Samuel Rinnah (R) May 11, 1844–Oct. 3, 1936; Jan. 7, 1901–Jan. 4, 1905.

Johnson, John Albert (D) July 28, 1861–Sept. 21, 1909; Jan. 4, 1905–Sept. 21, 1909.

Eberhart, Adolph Olson (R) June 23, 1870–Dec. 6, 1944; Sept. 21, 1909–Jan. 5, 1915.

Hammond, Winfield Scott (D) Nov. 17, 1863–Dec. 30, 1915; Jan. 7–Dec. 30, 1915; House 1907–Jan. 6, 1915.

Burnquist, Joseph Alfred Arner (R) July 21, 1879–Jan. 12, 1961; Dec. 30, 1915–Jan. 5, 1921.

Preus, Jacob Aall Ottesen (R) Aug. 28, 1883–May 24, 1961; Jan. 5, 1921–Jan. 6, 1925.

Christianson, Theodore (R) Sept. 12, 1883–Dec. 9, 1948; Jan. 6, 1925–Jan. 6, 1931; House 1933–37.

Olson, Floyd Bjornstjerne (FL) Nov. 13, 1891–Aug. 22, 1936; Jan. 6, 1931–Aug. 22, 1936.

Petersen, Hjalmar (FL) Jan. 2, 1890–March 29, 1968; Aug. 22, 1936–Jan. 4, 1937.

Benson, Elmer Austin (FL) Sept. 22, 1895–March 13, 1985; Jan. 4, 1937–Jan. 2, 1939; Senate Dec. 27, 1935–Nov. 3, 1936.

Stassen, Harold Edward (R) April 13, 1907–March 4, 2001; Jan. 2, 1939–April 27, 1943.

Thye, Edward John (R) April 26, 1896–Aug. 28, 1969; April 27, 1943–Jan. 8, 1947; Senate 1947–59.

Youngdahl, Luther Wallace (R) May 29, 1896–June 21, 1978; Jan. 8, 1947–Sept. 27, 1951.

Anderson, Clyde Elmer (R) March 16, 1912–Jan. 12, 1998; Sept. 27, 1951–Jan. 5, 1955.

Freeman, Orville Lothrop (DFL) May 9, 1918–Feb. 20, 2003; Jan. 5, 1955–Jan. 2, 1961; secretary of agriculture Jan. 21, 1961–Jan. 20, 1969.

Andersen, Elmer Lee (R) June 17, 1909– ; Jan. 2, 1961–March 25, 1963.

Rolvaag, Karl Fritjof (DFL) July 18, 1913–Dec. 20, 1990; March 25, 1963–Jan. 2, 1967.

Levander, Harold (R) Oct. 10, 1910–March 30, 1992; Jan. 2, 1967–Jan. 4, 1971.

Anderson, Wendell Richard (DFL) Feb. 1, 1933– ; Jan. 4, 1971–Dec. 29, 1976; Senate Dec. 30, 1976–Dec. 29, 1978.

Perpich, Rudolph George "Rudy" (DFL) June 27, 1928–Sept. 21, 1995; Dec. 29, 1976–Jan. 1, 1979, Jan. 3, 1983–Jan. 7, 1991.

Quie, Albert Harold (IR) Sept. 18, 1923–Sept. 24, 1995; Jan. 1, 1979–Jan. 3, 1983; House 1958–79.

Perpich, Rudolph George "Rudy" (DFL) Jan. 3, 1983–Jan. 7, 1991 (for previous term see above).

Carlson, Arne H. (R) Sept. 24, 1934– ; Jan. 7, 1991–Jan. 5, 1999.

Ventura, Jesse (REF) July 15, 1951– ; Jan. 4, 1999–Jan. 6, 2003.

Pawlenty, Tim (R) Nov. 21, 1960– ; Jan. 6, 2003– .

Mississippi

(Became a state Dec. 10, 1817)

Holmes, David (DR) March 10, 1770–Aug. 20, 1832; 1809–17 (Miss. Terr.), Dec. 10, 1817–Jan. 5, 1820, Jan. 7–July 25, 1826; House 1797–1809 (no party Va.); Senate Aug. 30, 1820–Sept. 25, 1825 (Republican).

Poindexter, George (DR) 1779–Sept. 5, 1853; Jan. 5, 1820–Jan. 7, 1822; House (Terr. Del.) 1807–13 (no party), (Rep.) Dec. 10, 1817–19 (no party); Senate Oct. 15, 1830–35 (no party); elected pres. pro tempore June 28, 1834.

Leake, Walter (R) May 25, 1762–Nov. 17, 1825; Jan. 7, 1822–Nov. 17, 1825; Senate Dec. 10, 1817–May 15, 1820.

Brandon, Gerard Chittoque (J) Sept. 15, 1788–March 28, 1850; Nov. 17, 1825–Jan. 7, 1826 (Democratic Republican), July 25, 1826–Jan. 9, 1832.

Holmes, David (DR) Jan. 7–July 25, 1826 (for previous term see above).

Brandon, Gerard Chittoque (J) July 25, 1826–Jan. 9, 1832 (for previous term see above).

Scott, Abram Marshall (NR) 1785–July 12, 1833; Jan. 9, 1832–June 12, 1833.

Lynch, Charles (W) 1783–Feb. 9, 1853; June 12–Nov. 20, 1833, Jan. 7, 1836–Jan. 8, 1838.

Runnels, Hiram George (uncle of Hardin R. Runnels of Texas) (J) Dec. 15, 1796–Dec. 15, 1857; Nov. 20, 1833–Nov. 20, 1835.

Quitman, John Anthony (D) Sept. 1, 1799–July 17, 1858; Dec. 3, 1835–Jan. 7, 1836, Jan. 10, 1850–Feb. 3, 1851; House 1855–July 17, 1858.

Lynch, Charles (W) Jan. 7, 1836–Jan. 8, 1838 (for previous term see above).

McNutt, Alexander Gallatin (D) Jan. 3, 1802–Oct. 22, 1848; Jan. 8, 1838–Jan. 10, 1842.

Tucker, Tilghman Mayfield (D) Feb. 5, 1802–April 3, 1859; Jan. 10, 1842–Jan. 10, 1844; House 1843–45.

Brown, Albert Gallatin (D) May 31, 1813–June 12, 1880; Jan. 10, 1844–Jan. 10, 1848; House 1839–41, 1847–53; Senate Jan. 7, 1854–Jan. 12, 1861.

Matthews, Joseph W. (D) 1812–Aug. 27, 1862; Jan. 10, 1848–Jan. 10, 1850.

Quitman, John Anthony (D) Jan. 10, 1850–Feb. 3, 1851 (for previous term see above).

Guion, John Isaac (D) Nov. 18, 1802–June 26, 1855; Feb. 3–Nov. 4, 1851.

Whitfield, James (D) Dec. 15, 1791–June 25, 1875; Nov. 24, 1851–Jan. 10, 1852.

Foote, Henry Stuart (D) Feb. 28, 1804–May 19, 1880; Jan. 10, 1852–Jan. 5, 1854; Senate 1847–Jan. 8, 1852.

Pettus, John Jones (D) Oct. 9, 1813–Jan. 28, 1867; Jan. 5–Jan. 10, 1854, Nov. 21, 1859–Nov. 16, 1863.

McRae, John Jones (D) Jan. 10, 1815–May 31, 1868; Jan. 10, 1854–Nov. 16, 1857; Senate Dec. 1, 1851–March 17, 1852; House Dec. 7, 1858–Jan. 12, 1861.

McWillie, William (D) Nov. 17, 1795–March 3, 1869; Nov. 16, 1857–Nov. 21, 1859; House 1849–51.

Pettus, John Jones (D) Nov. 21, 1859–Nov. 16, 1863 (for previous term see above).

Clark, Charles (D) Feb. 19, 1810–Dec. 18, 1877; Nov. 16, 1863–May 22, 1865.

Sharkey, William Lewis July 12, 1798–April 29, 1873; (Provisional) June 13–Oct. 16, 1865.

Humphreys, Benjamin Grubb (D) Aug. 26, 1808–Dec. 20, 1822; Oct. 16, 1865–June 15, 1868.

Ames, Adelbert (son-in-law of Benjamin Franklin Butler of Mass.) Oct. 31, 1835–April 12, 1933; (Military) June 15, 1868–March 10, 1870, Jan. 4, 1874–March 20, 1876 (Republican); Senate Feb. 23, 1870–Jan. 10, 1874 (Republican).

Alcorn, James Lusk (R) Nov. 4, 1816–Dec. 19, 1894; March 10, 1870–Nov. 30, 1871; Senate Dec. 1, 1871–77.

Powers, Ridgely Ceylon (R) Dec. 24, 1836–Nov. 11, 1912; Nov. 30, 1871–Jan. 4, 1874.

Ames, Adelbert (R) Jan. 4, 1874–March 20, 1876 (for previous term see above).

Stone, John Marshall (D) April 30, 1830–March 2, 1900; March 29, 1876–Jan. 29, 1882, Jan. 13, 1890–Jan. 20, 1896.

Lowry, Robert (D) March 10, 1831–Jan. 18, 1910; Jan. 29, 1882–Jan. 13, 1890.

Stone, John Marshall (D) Jan. 13, 1890–Jan. 20, 1896 (for previous term see above).

McLaurin, Anselm Joseph (D) March 28, 1848–Dec. 22, 1909; Jan. 20, 1896–Jan. 16, 1900; Senate Feb. 7, 1894–95, 1901–Dec. 22, 1909.

Longino, Andrew Houston (D) May 16, 1855–Feb. 24, 1942; Jan. 16, 1900–Jan. 19, 1904.

Vardaman, James Kimble (D) July 26, 1861–June 25, 1930; Jan. 19, 1904–Jan. 21, 1908; Senate 1913–19.

Noel, Edmond Favor (D) March 4, 1856–July 30, 1927; Jan. 21, 1908–Jan. 16, 1912.

Brewer, Earl LeRoy (D) Aug. 11, 1869–March 10, 1942; Jan. 16, 1912–Jan. 18, 1916.

Bilbo, Theodore Gilmore (D) Oct. 13, 1877–Aug. 21, 1947; Jan. 18, 1916–Jan. 20, 1920, Jan. 17, 1928–Jan. 19, 1932; Senate 1935–Aug. 21, 1947.

Russell, Lee Maurice (D) Nov. 16, 1875–May 16, 1943; Jan. 20, 1920–Jan. 22, 1924.

Whitfield, Henry Lewis (D) June 20, 1868–March 18, 1927; Jan. 22, 1924–March 18, 1927.

Murphree, Herron Dennis (D) Jan. 6, 1886–Feb. 9, 1949; March 18, 1927–Jan. 17, 1928, Dec. 26, 1943–Jan. 18, 1944.

Bilbo, Theodore Gilmore (D) Jan. 17, 1928–Jan. 19, 1932 (for previous term see above).

Conner, Martin Sennett "Mike" (D) Aug. 31, 1891–Sept. 16, 1950; Jan. 19, 1932–Jan. 21, 1936.

White, Hugh Lawson (D) Aug. 19, 1881–Sept. 20, 1965; Jan. 21, 1936–Jan. 16, 1940, Jan. 22, 1952–Jan. 17, 1956.

Johnson, Paul Burney (father of Paul Burney Johnson Jr., below) (D) March 23, 1880–Dec. 26, 1943; Jan. 16, 1940–Dec. 26, 1943; House 1919–23.

Murphree, Herron Dennis (D) Dec. 26, 1943–Jan. 18, 1944 (for previous term see above).

Bailey, Thomas Lowry (D) Jan. 6, 1888–Nov. 2, 1946; Jan. 18, 1944–Nov. 2, 1946.

Wright, Fielding Lewis (D) May 16, 1895–May 4, 1956; Nov. 2, 1946–Jan. 22, 1952.

White, Hugh Lawson (D) Jan. 22, 1952–Jan. 17, 1956 (for previous term see above).

Coleman, James Plemon (D) Jan. 9, 1914–Sept. 28, 1991; Jan. 17, 1956–Jan. 19, 1960.

Barnett, Ross Robert (D) Jan. 22, 1898–Nov. 6, 1987; Jan. 19, 1960–Jan. 21, 1964.

Johnson, Paul Burney Jr. (son of Paul Burney Johnson, above) (D) Jan. 23, 1916–Oct. 14, 1985; Jan. 21, 1964–Jan. 16, 1968.

Williams, John Bell (D) Dec. 4, 1918–March 25, 1983; Jan. 16, 1968–Jan. 18, 1972; House 1947–Jan. 16, 1968.

Waller, William Lowe (D) Oct. 21, 1926– ; Jan. 18, 1972–Jan. 20, 1976.

Finch, Charles Clifton (D) April 4, 1927–April 22, 1986; Jan. 20, 1976–Jan. 22, 1980.

Winter, William Forrest (D) Feb. 21, 1923– ; Jan. 22, 1980–Jan. 10, 1984.

Allain, William A. (D) Feb. 14, 1928– ; Jan. 10, 1984–Jan. 12, 1988.

Mabus, Ray Jr. (D) Oct. 11, 1948– ; Jan. 12, 1988–Jan. 14, 1992.

Fordice, Kirk (R) Feb. 10, 1934–Sept. 7, 2004; Jan. 14, 1992–Jan. 11, 2000.

Musgrove, Ronnie (D) July 29, 1956– ; Jan. 11, 2000–Jan. 13, 2004.

Barbour, Haley (R) Oct. 22, 1947– ; Jan. 13, 2004– ; chair Rep. Nat. Comm. 1993–97.

Missouri

(Became a state Aug. 10, 1821)

McNair, Alexander (DR) May 5, 1775–March 18, 1826; Aug. 10, 1821–Nov. 15, 1824.

Bates, Frederick (AR) June 23, 1777–Aug. 4, 1825; Nov. 15, 1824–Aug. 4, 1825.

Williams, Abraham J. (DR) Feb. 26, 1781–Dec. 30, 1839; Aug. 4, 1825–Jan. 20, 1826.

Miller, John (J) Nov. 25, 1781–March 18, 1846; Jan. 20, 1826–Nov. 14, 1832; House 1837–43 (Democrat).

Dunklin, Daniel (D) Jan. 14, 1790–July 25, 1844; Nov. 14, 1832–Sept. 13, 1836.

Boggs, Lilburn W. (D) Dec. 14, 1792–March 14, 1860; Sept. 13, 1836–Nov. 16, 1840.

Reynolds, Thomas (brother of John Reynolds of Ill.) (D) March 12, 1796–Feb. 9, 1844; Nov. 16, 1840–Feb. 9, 1844.

Marmaduke, Meredith Miles (father of John Sappington Marmaduke, below, brother-in-law of Claiborne Fox Jackson, below) (D) Aug. 25, 1791–March 26, 1864; Feb. 9–Nov. 20, 1844.

Edwards, John Cummins (D) June 24, 1804–Sept. 14, 1888; Nov. 20, 1844–Nov. 27, 1848; House 1841–43.

King, Austin Augustus (D) Sept. 21, 1802–April 22, 1870; Nov. 27, 1848–Jan. 3, 1853; House 1863–65 (Unionist).

Price, Sterling (D) Sept. 20, 1809–Sept. 29, 1867; Jan. 3, 1853–Jan. 5, 1857; House 1845–Aug. 12, 1846.

Polk, Trusten (nephew of Peter Foster Causey of Del.) (D) May 29, 1811–April 16, 1876; Jan. 5–Feb. 27, 1857; Senate 1857–Jan. 10, 1882.

Jackson, Hancock Lee (D) May 12, 1796–March 19, 1876; Feb. 27–Oct. 22, 1857.

Stewart, Robert Marcellus (D) March 12, 1815–Sept. 21, 1871; Oct. 22, 1857–Jan. 3, 1861.

Jackson, Claiborne Fox (brother-in-law of Meredith Miles Marmaduke, above) (D) April 4, 1806–Dec. 6, 1862; Jan. 3–July 30, 1861.

Gamble, Hamilton Rowan (U) Nov. 29, 1798–Jan. 31, 1864; July 31, 1861–Jan. 31, 1864.

Hall, Willard Preble (U) May 9, 1820–Nov. 3, 1882; Jan. 31, 1864–Jan. 2, 1865; House 1847–53 (Democrat).

Fletcher, Thomas Clement (UR) Jan. 21, 1827–March 25, 1899; Jan. 2, 1865–Jan. 12, 1869.

McClurg, Joseph Washington (R) Feb. 22, 1818–Dec. 2, 1900; Jan. 12, 1869–Jan. 9, 1871; House 1863–68 (1863–65 Unconditional Unionist, 1865–68 Republican).

Brown, Benjamin Gratz (LR) May 28, 1826–Dec. 13, 1885; Jan. 9, 1871–Jan. 8, 1873; Senate Nov. 13, 1863–67 (Unconditional Unionist).

Woodson, Silas (D) May 18, 1819–Oct. 9, 1896; Jan. 8, 1873–Jan. 12, 1875.

Hardin, Charles Henry (D) July 15, 1820–July 29, 1892; Jan. 12, 1875–Jan. 8, 1877.

Phelps, John Smith (D) Dec. 22, 1814–Nov. 20, 1886; Jan. 8, 1877–Jan. 10, 1881; House 1845–63.

Crittenden, Thomas Theodore (nephew of John Jordan Crittenden of Ky.) (D) Jan. 1, 1832–May 29, 1909; Jan. 10, 1881–Jan. 12, 1885; House 1873–75, 1877–79.

Marmaduke, John Sappington (son of Meredith Miles Marmaduke, above, great-grandson of John Breathitt of Ky.) (D) March 14, 1833–Dec. 28, 1887; Jan. 12, 1885–Dec. 28, 1887.

Morehouse, Albert Pickett (D) July 11, 1835–Sept. 30, 1891; Dec. 28, 1887–Jan. 14, 1889.

Francis, David Rowland (D) Oct. 1, 1850–Jan. 15, 1927; Jan. 14, 1889–Jan. 9, 1893; secretary of the interior Sept. 3, 1896–March 5, 1897.

Stone, William Joel (D) May 7, 1848–April 14, 1918; Jan. 9, 1893–Jan. 11, 1897; House 1885–91; Senate 1903–April 14, 1918.

Stephens, Lawrence Vest "Lon" (D) Dec. 21, 1858–Jan. 10, 1923; Jan. 11, 1897–Jan. 14, 1901.

Dockery, Alexander Monroe (D) Feb. 11, 1845–Dec. 26, 1926; Jan. 14, 1901–Jan. 9, 1905; House 1883–99.

Folk, Joseph Wingate (D) Oct. 28, 1869–May 28, 1923; Jan. 9, 1905–Jan. 11, 1909.

Hadley, Herbert Spencer (R) Feb. 20, 1872–Dec. 1, 1927; Jan. 11, 1909–Jan. 13, 1913.

Major, Elliot Woolfolk (D) Oct. 20, 1864–July 9, 1949; Jan. 13, 1913–Jan. 8, 1917.

Gardner, Frederick D. (D) Nov. 6, 1869–Dec. 18, 1933; Jan. 8, 1917–Jan. 10, 1921.

Hyde, Arthur Mastick (R) July 12, 1877–Oct. 17, 1947; Jan. 10, 1921–Jan. 12, 1925; secretary of agriculture March 6, 1929–March 4, 1933.

Baker, Samuel Aaron (R) Nov. 7, 1874–Sept. 16, 1933; Jan. 12, 1925–Jan. 14, 1929.

Caulfield, Henry Stewart (R) Dec. 9, 1873–May 11, 1966; Jan. 14, 1929–Jan. 9, 1933; House 1907–09.

Park, Guy Brasfield (D) June 10, 1872–Oct. 1, 1946; Jan. 9, 1933–Jan. 11, 1937.

Stark, Lloyd Crow (D) Nov. 23, 1886–Sept. 17, 1972; Jan. 11, 1937–Jan. 13, 1941.

Donnell, Forrest C. (R) Aug. 20, 1884–March 3, 1980; Jan. 13, 1941–Jan. 8, 1945; Senate 1945–51.

Donnelly, Philip Matthew (D) March 6, 1891–Sept. 12, 1961; Jan. 8, 1945–Jan. 10, 1949, Jan. 12, 1953–Jan. 14, 1957.

Smith, Forrest (D) Feb. 14, 1886–March 8, 1962; Jan. 10, 1949–Jan. 12, 1953.

Donnelly, Philip Matthew (D) Jan. 12, 1953–Jan. 14, 1957 (for previous term see above).

Blair, James Thomas Jr. (D) March 15, 1902–July 12, 1962; Jan. 14, 1957–Jan. 9, 1961.

Dalton, John Montgomery (D) Nov. 9, 1900–July 7, 1972; Jan. 9, 1961–Jan. 11, 1965.

Hearnes, Warren E. (D) July 24, 1923– ; Jan. 11, 1965–Jan. 8, 1973.

Bond, Christopher S. "Kit" (R) March 6, 1939– ; Jan. 8, 1973–Jan. 10, 1977, Jan. 12, 1981–Jan. 14, 1985; Senate 1987– .

Teasdale, Joseph P. (D) March 29, 1936– ; Jan. 10, 1977–Jan. 12, 1981.

Bond, Christopher S. "Kit" (R) Jan. 12, 1981–Jan. 14, 1985 (for previous term see above).

Ashcroft, John (R) May 9, 1942– ; Jan. 14, 1985–Jan. 11, 1993; Senate 1995–2001; attorney general Feb. 1, 2001–Feb. 3, 2005.

Carnahan, Mel Eugene (D) Feb. 11, 1934–Oct. 16, 2000; Jan. 11, 1993–Oct. 16, 2000.

Wilson, Roger B. (D) Oct. 10, 1948– ; Oct. 18, 2000–Jan. 8, 2001.

Holden, Bob (D) Aug. 24, 1949– ; Jan. 8, 2001–Jan. 10, 2005.

Blunt, Matt (R) Nov. 20, 1970– ; Jan. 10, 2005– .

Montana

(Became a state Nov. 8, 1889)

Toole, Joseph Kemp (D) May 12, 1851–March 11, 1929; Nov. 8, 1889–Jan. 2, 1893, Jan. 7, 1901–April 1, 1908; House (Terr. Del.) 1885–89.

Rickards, John Ezra (R) July 23, 1848–Dec. 26, 1927; Jan. 2, 1893–Jan. 4, 1897.

Smith, Robert Burns (P, D) Dec. 29, 1854–Nov. 16, 1908; Jan. 4, 1897–Jan. 7, 1901.

Toole, Joseph Kemp (D) Jan. 7, 1901–April 1, 1908 (for previous term see above).

Norris, Edwin Lee (D) Aug. 16, 1865–April 25, 1924; April 1, 1908–Jan. 5, 1913.

Stewart, Samuel Vernon (D) Aug. 2, 1872–Sept. 15, 1939; Jan. 6, 1913–Jan. 2, 1921.

Dixon, Joseph Moore (R) July 31, 1867–May 22, 1934; Jan. 3, 1921–Jan. 4, 1925; House 1903–07; Senate 1907–13.

Erickson, John Edward (D) March 14, 1863–May 25, 1946; Jan. 5, 1925–March 13, 1933; Senate March 13, 1933–Nov. 6, 1934.

Cooney, Frank Henry (D) Dec. 31, 1872–Dec. 15, 1935; March 13, 1933–Dec. 15, 1935.

Holt, William Elmer (D) Oct. 14, 1884–March 1, 1945; Dec. 16, 1935–Jan. 4, 1937.

Ayers, Roy Elmer (D) Nov. 9, 1882–May 23, 1955; Jan. 4, 1937–Jan. 6, 1941; House 1933–37.

Ford, Samuel Clarence (R) Nov. 7, 1882–Nov. 25, 1961; Jan. 6, 1941–Jan. 3, 1949.

Bonner, John Woodrow (D) July 16, 1902–March 28, 1970; Jan. 3, 1949–Jan. 5, 1953.

Aronson, John Hugo (R) Sept. 1, 1891–Feb. 25, 1978; Jan. 5, 1953–Jan. 4, 1961.

Nutter, Donald Grant (R) Nov. 28, 1915–Jan. 25, 1962; Jan. 4, 1961–Jan. 25, 1962.

Babcock, Tim M. (R) Oct. 27, 1919– ; Jan. 26, 1962–Jan. 6, 1969.

Anderson, Forrest Howard (D) Jan. 30, 1913–July 20, 1989; Jan. 6, 1969–Jan. 1, 1973.

Judge, Thomas Lee (D) Oct. 12, 1934– ; Jan. 1, 1973–Jan. 5, 1981.

Schwinden, Ted (D) Aug. 31, 1925– ; Jan. 5, 1981–Jan. 2, 1989.

Stephens, Stan (R) Sept. 16, 1929– ; Jan. 2, 1989–Jan. 4, 1993.

Racicot, Marc Francis (R) July 24, 1948– ; Jan. 4, 1993–Jan. 2, 2001; chair Rep. Nat. Comm. 2002–03.

Martz, Judy (R) July 28, 1943– ; Jan. 2, 2001–Jan. 3, 2005.

Schweitzer, Brian (D) Sept. 4, 1955– ; Jan. 3, 2005– .

Nebraska

(Became a state March 1, 1867)

Butler, David C. (R) Dec. 15, 1829–May 25, 1891; March 27, 1867–June 2, 1871.

James, William Hartford (R) Oct. 16, 1831–Feb. 1, 1920; June 2, 1871–Jan. 13, 1873.

Furnas, Robert Wilkinson (R) May 5, 1824–June 1, 1905; Jan. 13, 1873–Jan. 12, 1875.

Garber, Silas (R) Sept. 21, 1833–Jan. 12, 1905; Jan. 12, 1875–Jan. 9, 1879.

Nance, Albinus (R) March 30, 1848–Dec. 7, 1911; Jan. 9, 1879–Jan. 4, 1883.

Dawes, James William (R) Jan. 8, 1844–Oct. 8, 1918; Jan. 4, 1883–Jan. 6, 1887.

Thayer, John Milton (R) Jan. 24, 1820–March 19, 1906; 1875–79 (Wyo. Terr.), Jan. 6, 1887–Jan. 15, 1891, May 5, 1891–Feb. 8, 1892; Senate March 1, 1867–71.

Boyd, James E. (D) Sept. 9, 1834–April 30, 1906; Jan. 15–May 5, 1891, Feb. 8, 1892–Jan. 13, 1893.

Thayer, John Milton (R) May 5, 1891–Feb. 8, 1892 (for previous term see above).

Boyd, James E. (D) Feb. 8, 1892–Jan. 13, 1893 (for previous term see above).

Crounse, Lorenzo (R) Jan. 27, 1834–May 13, 1909; Jan. 13, 1893–Jan. 3, 1895; House 1873–77.

Holcomb, Silas Alexander (P) Aug. 25, 1858–April 25, 1920; Jan. 3, 1895–Jan. 5, 1899.

Poynter, William Amos (Fus) May 29, 1848–April 5, 1909; Jan. 5, 1899–Jan. 3, 1901.

Dietrich, Charles Henry (R) Nov. 26, 1853–April 10, 1924; Jan. 3–May 1, 1901; Senate March 28, 1901–05.

Savage, Ezra Perin (R) April 3, 1842–Jan. 8, 1920; May 1, 1901–Jan. 8, 1903.

Mickey, John Hopwood (R) Sept. 30, 1845–June 2, 1910; Jan. 8, 1903–Jan. 3, 1907.

Sheldon, George Lawson (R) May 31, 1870–April 4, 1960; Jan. 3, 1907–Jan. 7, 1909.

Shallenberger, Ashton Cockayne (D) Dec. 23, 1862–Feb. 22, 1938; Jan. 7, 1909–Jan. 5, 1911; House 1901–03, 1915–19, 1923–29, 1931–35.

Aldrich, Chester Hardy (R) Nov. 10, 1862–March 10, 1924; Jan. 5, 1911–Jan. 9, 1913.

Morehead, John Henry (D) Dec. 3, 1861–May 31, 1942; Jan. 9, 1913–Jan. 4, 1917; House 1923–35.

Neville, M. Keith (D) Feb. 25, 1884–Dec. 4, 1959; Jan. 4, 1917–Jan. 9, 1919.

McKelvie, Samuel Roy (R) April 15, 1881–Jan. 6, 1956; Jan. 9, 1919–Jan. 3, 1923.

Bryan, Charles Wayland (D) Feb. 10, 1867–March 4, 1945; Jan. 4, 1923–Jan. 8, 1925, Jan. 8, 1931–Jan. 3, 1935.

McMullen, Adam (R) June 12, 1872–March 2, 1959; Jan. 8, 1925–Jan. 3, 1929.

Weaver, Arthur J. (R) Nov. 18, 1873–Oct. 17, 1945; Jan. 3, 1929–Jan. 8, 1931.

Bryan, Charles Wayland (D) Jan. 8, 1931–Jan. 3, 1935 (for previous term see above).

Cochran, Robert LeRoy (D) Jan. 28, 1886–Feb. 23, 1963; Jan. 3, 1935–Jan. 9, 1941.

Griswold, Dwight Palmer (R) Nov. 27, 1893–April 12, 1954; Jan. 9, 1941–Jan. 9, 1947; Senate Nov. 5, 1952–April 12, 1954.

Peterson, Val Frederick Demar Erastus (R) July 18, 1903–Oct. 17, 1983; Jan. 9, 1947–Jan. 8, 1953.

Crosby, Robert Berkey (R) March 26, 1911– ; Jan. 8, 1953–Jan. 6, 1955.

Anderson, Victor Emanuel (R) March 30, 1902–Aug. 15, 1962; Jan. 6, 1955–Jan. 8, 1959.

Brooks, Ralph Gilmour (D) July 6, 1898–Sept. 9, 1960; Jan. 8, 1959–Sept. 9, 1960.

Burney, Dwight Willard (R) Jan. 7, 1892–March 10, 1987; Sept. 9, 1960–Jan. 5, 1961.

Morrison, Frank Brenner (D) May 20, 1905–April 19, 2004; Jan. 5, 1961–Jan. 5, 1967.

Tiemann, Norbert Theodore (R) July 18, 1924– ; Jan. 5, 1967–Jan. 7, 1971.

Exon, John James (D) Aug. 9, 1921– ; Jan. 7, 1971–Jan. 3, 1979; Senate 1979–97.

Thone, Charles (R) Jan. 4, 1924– ; Jan. 4, 1979–Jan. 6, 1983; House 1971–79.

Kerrey, Robert "Bob" (D) Aug. 27, 1943– ; Jan. 6, 1983–Jan. 9, 1987; Senate 1989–2001.

Orr, Kay A. (R) Jan. 2, 1939– ; Jan. 9, 1987–Jan. 9, 1991.

Nelson, Earl Benjamin "Ben" (D) May 17, 1941– ; Jan. 9, 1991–Jan. 7, 1999. Senate 2001– .

Johanns, Mike (R) June 18, 1950– ; Jan. 7, 1999–Jan. 20, 2005; secretary of agriculture Jan. 21, 2005– .

Heineman, Dave (R) May 12, 1948– ; Jan. 21, 2005– .

Nevada

(Became a state Oct. 31, 1864)

Blasdel, Henry Goode (R) Jan. 20, 1825–July 26, 1900; Dec. 5, 1864–Jan. 2, 1871.

Bradley, Lewis Rice (D) Feb. 18, 1805–March 21, 1879; Jan. 3, 1871–Jan. 6, 1879.

Kinkead, John Henry (R) Dec. 10, 1826–Aug. 15, 1924; Jan. 7, 1879–Jan. 1, 1883.

Adams, Jewett William (D) Aug. 6, 1835–June 18, 1920; Jan. 2, 1883–Jan. 3, 1887.

Stevenson, Charles Clark (R) Feb. 20, 1826–Sept. 21, 1890; Jan. 4, 1887–Sept. 2, 1890.

Bell, Francis Jardine (R) Jan. 28, 1840–Feb. 13, 1927; Sept. 21, 1890–Jan. 5, 1891.

Colcord, Roswell Keyes (R) April 25, 1839–Oct. 30, 1939; Jan. 6, 1891–Jan. 7, 1895.

Jones, John Edward (Sil.D) Dec. 5, 1840–April 10, 1896; Jan. 8, 1895–April 10, 1896.

Sadler, Reinhold (Sil.R) Jan. 10, 1848–Jan. 30, 1906; April 10, 1896–Jan. 1, 1903.

Sparks, John (Sil.D) Aug. 30, 1843–May 22, 1908; Jan. 1, 1903–May 22, 1908.

Dickerson, Denver Sylvester (Sil.D) Jan. 24, 1872–Nov. 28, 1925; May 22, 1908–Jan. 2, 1911.

Oddie, Tasker Lowndes (R) Oct. 20, 1870–Feb. 17, 1950; Jan. 2, 1911–Jan. 4, 1915; Senate 1921–33.

Boyle, Emmet Derby (D) July 26, 1879–Jan. 3, 1926; Jan. 4, 1915–Jan. 1, 1923.

Scrugham, James Graves (D) Jan. 19, 1880–June 23, 1945; Jan. 1, 1923–Jan. 3, 1927; House 1933–Dec. 7, 1942; Senate Dec. 7, 1942–June 23, 1945.

Balzar, Frederick Bennett (R) June 15, 1880–March 21, 1934; Jan. 3, 1927–March 21, 1934.

Griswold, Morley Isaac (R) Oct. 10, 1890–Oct. 3, 1951; March 21, 1934–Jan. 7, 1935.

Kirman, Richard Sr. (D) Jan. 14, 1877–Jan. 19, 1959; Jan. 7, 1935–Jan. 2, 1939.

Carville, Edward Peter (D) May 14, 1885–June 27, 1956; Jan. 2, 1939–July 24, 1945; Senate July 25, 1945–47.

Pittman, Vail Montgomery (D) Sept. 17, 1883–Jan. 29, 1964; July 24, 1945–Jan. 1, 1951.

Russell, Charles Hinton (R) Dec. 27, 1903–Sept. 13, 1989; Jan. 1, 1951–Jan. 5, 1959; House 1947–49.

Sawyer, Grant "Frank" (D) Dec. 14, 1918–Feb. 19, 1996; Jan. 5, 1959–Jan. 2, 1967.

Laxalt, Paul Dominique (R) Aug. 2, 1922– ; Jan. 2, 1967–Jan. 4, 1971; Senate Dec. 18, 1974–87; general chair Rep. Nat. Comm. 1983–86.

O'Callaghan, Donald Neil "Mike" (D) Sept. 10, 1929–March 5, 2004; Jan. 4, 1971–Jan. 1, 1979.

List, Robert Frank (R) Sept. 1, 1936– ; Jan. 1, 1979–Jan. 3, 1983.

Bryan, Richard Hudson (D) July 16, 1937– ; Jan. 3, 1983–Jan. 3, 1989; Senate 1989– .

Miller, Robert Joseph "Bob" (D) March 30, 1945– ; Jan. 3, 1989–Jan. 4, 1999.

Guinn, Kenny C. (R) Aug. 24, 1936– ; Jan. 4, 1999– .

New Hampshire

(Ratified the Constitution June 21, 1788)

Sullivan, John (brother of James Sullivan of Mass.) (F) Feb. 17, 1740–Jan. 23, 1795; June 6, 1789–June 5, 1790; Cont. Cong. 1774–75, 1780–81.

Bartlett, Josiah (DR) Nov. 21, 1729–May 19, 1795; June 5, 1790–June 5, 1794.

Gilman, John Taylor (F) Dec. 19, 1753–Sept. 1, 1828; June 5, 1794–June 6, 1805, June 13, 1813–June 6, 1816; Cont. Cong. 1782–83.

Langdon, John (DR) June 26, 1741–Sept. 18, 1819; June 6, 1805–June 8, 1809, June 7, 1810–June 5, 1812; Senate 1789–1801 (no party); elected pres. pro tempore April 6, 1789, Nov. 5, 1792, March 1, 1793; Cont. Cong. 1775–76, 1787.

Smith, Jeremiah (F) Nov. 29, 1759–Sept. 21, 1842; June 8, 1809–June 7, 1810; House 1791–July 26, 1797 (1791–95 no party).

Langdon, John (DR) June 7, 1810–June 5, 1812 (for previous term see above).

Plumer, William (DR) June 25, 1759–Dec. 22, 1850; June 5, 1812–June 3, 1813, June 6, 1816–June 3, 1819; Senate June 17, 1802–07 (Federalist).

Gilman, John Taylor (F) June 13, 1813–June 6, 1816 (for previous term see above).

Plumer, William (DR) June 6, 1816–June 3, 1819 (for previous term see above).

Bell, Samuel (brother of John Bell, below, uncle of Charles Henry Bell, below) (DR) Feb. 9, 1770–Dec. 23, 1850; June 3, 1819–June 5, 1823; Senate 1823–35 (Whig).

Woodbury, Levi (DR) Dec. 22, 1789–Sept. 4, 1851; June 5, 1823–June 2, 1824; Senate March 16, 1825–31 (no party), 1841–Nov. 20, 1845 (Democrat); secretary of the navy May 23, 1831, June 30, 1834; secretary of the Treasury July 1, 1834–March 3, 1841; assoc. justice Sept. 23, 1845–Sept. 4, 1851.

Morrill, David Lawrence (R) June 10, 1772–Jan. 28, 1849; June 3, 1824–June 7, 1827; Senate 1817–23.

Pierce, Benjamin (J) (father of Pres. Franklin Pierce) Dec. 25, 1757–April 1, 1839; June 7, 1827–June 5, 1828 (Democratic Republican), June 4, 1829–June 3, 1830.

Bell, John (brother of Samuel Bell, above, father of Charles Henry Bell, below) (NR) July 20, 1765–March 22, 1836; June 5, 1828–June 4, 1829.

Pierce, Benjamin (J) June 4, 1829–June 3, 1830 (for previous term see above).

Harvey, Matthew (J) June 21, 1781–April 7, 1866; June 3, 1830–Feb. 28, 1831; House 1821–25 (no party).

Harper, Joseph Morrill (J) June 21, 1787–Jan. 15, 1865; Feb. 28–June 2, 1831; House 1831–35.

Dinsmoor, Samuel (father of Samuel Dinsmoor Jr., below) (J) July 1, 1766–March 15, 1835; June 2, 1831–June 5, 1834; House 1811–13 (Republican).

Badger, William (D) Jan. 13, 1779–Sept. 21, 1852; June 5, 1834–June 2, 1836.

Hill, Isaac (J) April 6, 1788–March 22, 1851; June 2, 1836–June 5, 1839; Senate 1831–May 30, 1836.

Page, John (D) May 21, 1787–Sept. 8, 1865; June 5, 1839–June 2, 1842; Senate June 8, 1836–37 (Whig).

Hubbard, Henry (D) May 3, 1784–June 5, 1857; June 2, 1842–June 6, 1844; House 1829–35 (Jacksonian) Senate 1835–41 (Jacksonian).

Steele, John Hardy (D) Jan. 4, 1789–July 3, 1865; June 6, 1844–June 4, 1846.

Colby, Anthony (W) Nov. 13, 1795–July 13, 1873; June 4, 1846–June 3, 1847.

Williams, Jared Warner (D) Dec. 22, 1796–Sept. 29, 1864; June 3, 1847–June 7, 1849; House 1837–41; Senate Nov. 29, 1853–July 15, 1854.

Dinsmoor, Samuel Jr. (son of Samuel Dinsmoor, above) (D) May 8, 1799–Feb. 24, 1869; June 7, 1849–June 3, 1852.

Martin, Noah (D) July 26, 1801–May 28, 1863; June 3, 1852–June 8, 1854.

Baker, Nathaniel Bradley (D) Sept. 29, 1818–Sept. 11, 1876; June 8, 1854–June 7, 1855.

Metcalf, Ralph (AP) Nov. 21, 1798–Aug. 26, 1858; June 7, 1855–June 4, 1857.

Haile, William (R) May 1807–July 22, 1876; June 4, 1857–June 2, 1859.

Goodwin, Ichabod (R) Oct. 10, 1796–July 4, 1882; June 2, 1859–June 6, 1861.

Berry, Nathaniel Springer (R) Sept. 1, 1796–April 27, 1894; June 6, 1861–June 3, 1863.

Gilmore, Joseph Albree (R) June 10, 1811–April 7, 1867; June 3, 1863–June 8, 1865.

Smyth, Frederick (U) March 9, 1819–April 22, 1899; June 8, 1865–June 6, 1867.

Harriman, Walter (R) April 8, 1817–July 25, 1884; June 6, 1867–June 2, 1869.

Stearns, Onslow (R) Aug. 30, 1810–Dec. 29, 1878; June 3, 1869–June 8, 1871.

Weston, James Adams (D) Aug. 27, 1827–May 8, 1895; June 14, 1871–June 6, 1872, June 3, 1874–June 10, 1875.

Straw, Ezekiel Albert (R) Dec. 30, 1819–Oct. 23, 1882; June 6, 1872–June 3, 1874.

Weston, James Adams (D) June 3, 1874–June 10, 1875 (for previous term see above).

Cheney, Person Colby (R) Feb. 25, 1828–June 19, 1901; June 10, 1875–June 6, 1877; Senate Nov. 24, 1886–June 14, 1887.

Prescott, Benjamin Franklin (R) Feb. 26, 1833–Feb. 21, 1895; June 7, 1877–June 5, 1879.

Head, Nathaniel (R) May 20, 1828–Nov. 12, 1883; June 5, 1879–June 2, 1881.

Bell, Charles Henry (son of John Bell, above, nephew of Samuel Bell, above) (R) Nov. 18, 1823–Nov. 11, 1893; June 2, 1881–June 7, 1883; Senate March 13–June 18, 1879.

Hale, Samuel Whitney (R) April 2, 1823–Oct. 16, 1891; June 7, 1883–June 4, 1885.

Currier, Moody (R) April 22, 1806–Aug. 23, 1898; June 4, 1885–June 2, 1887.

Sawyer, Charles Henry (R) March 30, 1840–Jan. 18, 1908; June 2, 1887–June 6, 1889.

Goodell, David Harvey (R) May 6, 1834–Jan. 22, 1915; June 6, 1889–Jan. 8, 1891.

Tuttle, Hiram Americus (R) Oct. 16, 1837–Feb. 10, 1911; Jan. 8, 1891–Jan. 5, 1893.

Smith, John Butler (R) April 12, 1838–Aug. 10, 1914; Jan. 5, 1893–Jan. 3, 1895.

Busiel, Charles Albert (R) Nov. 24, 1842–Aug. 29, 1901; Jan. 3, 1895–Jan. 7, 1897.

Ramsdell, George Allen (R) March 11, 1834–Nov. 16, 1900; Jan. 7, 1897–Jan. 5, 1899.

Rollins, Frank West (R) Feb. 24, 1860–Oct. 27, 1915; Jan. 5, 1899–Jan. 3, 1901.

Jordan, Chester Bradley (R) Oct. 15, 1839–Aug. 24, 1914; Jan. 3, 1901–Jan. 1, 1903.

Batchelder, Nahum Josiah (R) Sept. 3, 1859–April 22, 1934; Jan. 1, 1903–Jan. 5, 1905.

McLane, John (R) Feb. 27, 1852–April 13, 1911; Jan. 5, 1905–Jan. 3, 1907.

Floyd, Charles Miller (R) June 5, 1861–Feb. 3, 1923; Jan. 3, 1907–Jan. 7, 1909.

Quinby, Henry Brewer (R) June 10, 1846–Feb. 8, 1924; Jan. 7, 1909–Jan. 5, 1911.

Bass, Robert Perkins (R) Sept. 11, 1873–July 29, 1960; Jan. 5, 1911–Jan. 2, 1913.

Felker, Samuel Demeritt (D) April 16, 1859–Nov. 14, 1932; Jan. 2, 1913–Jan. 7, 1915.

Spaulding, Rolland Harty (brother of Huntley Nowel Spaulding, below) (R) March 15, 1873–March 14, 1942; Jan. 7, 1915–Jan. 3, 1917.

Keyes, Henry Wilder (R) May 23, 1863–June 19, 1938; Jan. 3, 1917–Jan. 2, 1919; Senate 1919–37.

Bartlett, John Henry (R) March 15, 1869–March 19, 1952; Jan. 2, 1919–Jan. 6, 1921.

Brown, Albert Oscar (R) July 18, 1853–March 28, 1937; Jan. 6, 1921–Jan. 4, 1923.

Brown, Fred Herbert (D) April 12, 1879–Feb. 3, 1955; Jan. 4, 1923–Jan. 1, 1925; Senate 1933–39.

Winant, John Gilbert (R) Feb. 23, 1889–Nov. 3, 1947; Jan. 1, 1925–Jan. 6, 1927, Jan. 1, 1931–Jan. 3, 1935.

Spaulding, Huntley Nowel (brother of Rolland Harty Spaulding, above) (R) Oct. 20, 1869–Nov. 14, 1955; Jan. 6, 1927–Jan. 3, 1929.

Tobey, Charles William (R) July 22, 1880–July 24, 1953; Jan. 3, 1929–Jan. 1, 1931; House 1933–39; Senate 1939–July 24, 1953.

Winant, John Gilbert (R) Jan. 1, 1931–Jan. 3, 1935 (for previous term see above).

Bridges, Henry Styles (R) Sept. 9, 1898–Nov. 26, 1961; Jan. 3, 1935–Jan. 7, 1937; Senate 1937–Nov. 26, 1861; Senate minority leader Jan. 8, 1952–53; elected pres. pro tempore Jan. 3, 1953.

Murphy, Francis Parnell (R) Aug. 16, 1877–Dec. 19, 1958; Jan. 7, 1937–Jan. 2, 1941.

Blood, Robert Oscar (R) Nov. 10, 1887–Aug. 3, 1975; Jan. 2, 1941–Jan. 4, 1945.

Dale, Charles Milby (R) March 8, 1893–Sept. 28, 1978; Jan. 4, 1945–Jan. 6, 1949.

Adams, Sherman (R) Jan. 8, 1899–Oct. 27, 1986; Jan. 6, 1949–Jan. 1, 1953; House 1945–47.

Gregg, Hugh (R) Nov. 22, 1917–Sept. 24, 2003; Jan. 1, 1953–Jan. 6, 1955.

Dwinell, Lane (R) Nov. 14, 1906–March 27, 1997; Jan. 6, 1955–Jan. 1, 1959.

Powell, Wesley (R) Oct. 13, 1915–Jan. 6, 1981; Jan. 1, 1959–Jan. 3, 1963.

King, John William (D) Oct. 10, 1918–Aug. 9, 1996; Jan. 3, 1963–Jan. 2, 1969.

Peterson, Walter Rutherford (R) Sept. 19, 1922– ; Jan. 2, 1969–Jan. 4, 1973.

Thomson, Meldrim Jr. (R) March 8, 1912–April 19, 2001; Jan. 4, 1973–Jan. 4, 1979.

Gallen, Hugh J. (D) July 30, 1924–Dec. 29, 1982; Jan. 4, 1979–Nov. 11, 1982.

Monier, Robert B. (D) March 5, 1922–Sept. 1986; Nov. 11–30, 1982.

Gardner, William Michael (D) Oct. 26, 1948– ; Nov. 30–Dec. 1, 1982.

Roy, Vesta M. (R) March 26, 1925–Feb. 8, 2002; Dec. 1, 1982–Jan. 6, 1983.

Sununu, John Henry (R) July 2, 1939– ; Jan. 6, 1983–Jan. 4, 1989.

Gregg, Judd Alan (R) Feb. 14, 1947–Sept. 24, 2003; Jan. 4, 1989–Jan. 7, 1993; House 1981–89; Senate 1993– .

Merrill, Stephen "Steve" (R) June 21, 1946– ; Jan. 7, 1993–Jan. 9, 1997.

Shaheen, Jeanne (D) Jan. 28, 1947– ; Jan. 9, 1997–Jan. 9, 2003.

Benson, Craig (R) Oct. 8, 1954– ; Jan. 9, 2003–Jan. 6, 2005.

Lynch, John (D) Nov. 25, 1952– ; Jan. 6, 2005– .

New Jersey

(Ratified the Constitution Dec. 18, 1787)

Livingston, William (father-in-law of John Jay of N.Y.) (F) Nov. 30, 1723–July 25, 1790; Aug. 27, 1776–July 25, 1790; Cont. Cong. 1774–76.

Lawrence, Elisha (F) 1746–July 23, 1799; July 25–Oct. 30, 1790.

Paterson, William (F) Dec. 24, 1745–Sept. 9, 1806; Oct. 30, 1790–March 4, 1793; Cont. Cong. (elected but did not attend) 1780, 1787; Senate 1789–Nov. 13, 1790 (no party); assoc. justice March 11, 1793–Sept. 9, 1806.

Henderson, Thomas (F) Aug. 15, 1743–Dec. 15, 1824; (Acting) March 30–June 3, 1793; House 1795–97.

Howell, Richard (F) Oct. 25, 1754–April 28, 1802; June 3, 1793–Oct. 31, 1801.

Bloomfield, Joseph (R) Oct. 18, 1753–Oct. 3, 1823; Oct. 31, 1801–Oct. 28, 1802, Oct. 29, 1803–Oct. 29, 1812; House 1817–21.

Lambert, John (DR) Feb. 24, 1746–Feb. 4, 1823; Nov. 15, 1802–Oct. 29, 1803; House 1805–09 (Republican); Senate 1809–15 (Republican).

Bloomfield, Joseph (DR) Oct. 29, 1803–Oct. 29, 1812 (for previous term see above).

Ogden, Aaron (great-uncle of Daniel Haines, below) (F) Dec. 3, 1756–April 19, 1839; Oct. 29, 1812–Oct. 29, 1813; Senate Feb. 28, 1801–03.

Pennington, William Sandford (father of William Pennington Jr., below) (DR) 1757–Sept. 18, 1826; Oct. 29, 1813–June 19, 1815.

Kennedy, William (DR) ?–Jan. 1, 1826; June 19–Oct. 25, 1815.

Dickerson, Mahlon (brother of Philemon Dickerson, below) (R) April 17, 1770–Oct. 5, 1853; Oct. 26, 1815–Feb. 1, 1817; Senate 1817–Jan. 30, 1829; secretary of the navy July 1, 1834–June 30, 1838.

Williamson, Isaac Halstead (F) Sept. 27, 1767–July 10, 1844; Feb. 6, 1817–Oct. 30, 1829.

Vroom, Peter Dumont (D) Dec. 12, 1791–Nov. 18, 1873; Nov. 6, 1829–Oct. 26, 1832, Oct. 25, 1833–Oct. 28, 1836; House 1839–41.

Southard, Samuel Lewis (R) June 9, 1787–June 26, 1842; Oct. 26, 1832–Feb. 27, 1833; Senate Jan. 26, 1821–23 (Republican), 1833–June 26, 1842 (Whig); elected pres. pro tempore March 11, 1841; secretary of the navy Sept. 16, 1823–March 3, 1829.

Seeley, Elias P. (W) Nov. 10, 1791–Aug. 23, 1846; Feb. 27–Oct. 23, 1833.

Vroom, Peter Dumont (D) Oct. 25, 1833–Oct. 28, 1836 (for previous term see above).

Dickerson, Philemon (brother of Mahlon Dickerson, above) (D) Jan. 11, 1788–Dec. 10, 1862; Nov. 3, 1836–Oct. 27, 1837; House 1833–Nov. 3, 1836 (Jacksonian), 1839–41 (Democrat).

Pennington, William (son of William Sandford Pennington, above) (DR) May 4, 1796–Feb. 16, 1862; Oct. 27, 1837–Oct. 27, 1843; House 1859–61 (Republican); Speaker Feb. 1, 1860–61.

Haines, Daniel (great-nephew of Aaron Ogden, above) (D) Jan. 6, 1801–Jan. 26, 1877; Oct. 27, 1843–Jan. 21, 1845, Jan. 18, 1848–Jan. 20, 1851.

Stratton, Charles Creighton (W) March 6, 1796–March 30, 1859; Jan. 21, 1845–Jan. 18, 1848; House 1837–39, 1841–43.

Haines, Daniel (D) Jan. 18, 1848–Jan. 20, 1851 (for previous term see above).

Fort, George Franklin (uncle of John Franklin Fort, below) (D) March 1809–April 22, 1872; Jan. 21, 1851–Jan. 17, 1854.

Price, Rodman McCamley (D) May 5, 1816–June 7, 1894; Jan. 17, 1854–Jan. 20, 1857; House 1851–53.

Newell, William Augustus (R) Sept. 5, 1817–Aug. 8, 1901; Jan. 20, 1857–Jan. 17, 1860, (Wash. Terr.) 1880–84; House 1847–51 (Whig), 1865–67 (Republican).

Olden, Charles Smith (R) Nov. 19, 1799–April 7, 1876; Jan. 17, 1860–Jan. 20, 1863.

Parker, Joel (D) Nov. 24, 1816–Jan. 2, 1888; Jan. 20, 1863–Jan. 16, 1866, Jan. 16, 1872–Jan. 19, 1875.

Ward, Marcus Lawrence (R) Nov. 9, 1812–April 25, 1884; Jan. 16, 1866–Jan. 19, 1869; House 1873–75; chair Rep. Nat. Comm. 1866–68.

Randolph, Theodore Fitz (D) June 24, 1826–Nov. 7, 1883; Jan. 19, 1869–Jan. 16, 1872; Senate 1875–81.

Parker, Joel (D) Jan. 16, 1872–Jan. 19, 1875 (for previous term see above).

Bedle, Joseph Dorsett (D) Jan. 5, 1821–Oct. 21, 1894; Jan. 19, 1875–Jan. 15, 1878.

McClellan, George Brinton (D) Dec. 3, 1826–Oct. 29, 1885; Jan. 15, 1878–Jan. 18, 1881.

Ludlow, George Craig (D) April 6, 1830–Dec. 18, 1900; Jan. 18, 1881–Jan. 15, 1884.

Abbett, Leon (D) Oct. 8, 1836–Dec. 4, 1894; Jan. 15, 1884–Jan. 18, 1887, Jan. 21, 1890–Jan. 17, 1893.

Green, Robert Stockton (D) March 25, 1831–May 7, 1895; Jan. 18, 1887–Jan. 21, 1890; House 1885–Jan. 17, 1887.

Abbett, Leon (D) Jan. 21, 1890–Jan. 17, 1893 (for previous term see above).

Werts, George Theodore (D) March 24, 1846–Jan. 17, 1910; Jan. 17, 1893–Jan. 21, 1896.

Griggs, John William (R) July 10, 1849–Nov. 28, 1927; Jan. 21, 1896–Jan. 31, 1898; attorney general June 25, 1898–March 29, 1901.

Voorhees, Foster MacGowan (R) Nov. 5, 1856–June 14, 1927; Feb. 1–Oct. 18, 1898, Jan. 17, 1899–Jan. 21, 1902.

Watkins, David Ogden (R) June 8, 1862–June 20, 1938; Oct. 18, 1898–Jan. 16, 1899.

Voorhees, Foster MacGowan (R) Jan. 17, 1899–Jan. 21, 1902 (for previous term see above).

Murphy, Franklin (R) Jan. 3, 1846–Feb. 24, 1920; Jan. 21, 1902–Jan. 17, 1905.

Stokes, Edward Casper (R) Dec. 22, 1860–Nov. 4, 1942; Jan. 17, 1905–Jan. 21, 1908.

Fort, John Franklin (nephew of George Franklin Fort, above) (R) March 20, 1852–Nov. 17, 1920; Jan. 21, 1908–Jan. 17, 1911.

Wilson, Thomas Woodrow (D) Dec. 28, 1856–Feb. 3, 1924; Jan. 17, 1911–March 1, 1913; president 1913–21.

Fielder, James Fairman (D) Feb. 26, 1867–Dec. 2, 1954; March 1–Oct. 28, 1913, Jan. 20, 1914–Jan. 15, 1917.

Taylor, Leon R. (D) Oct. 26, 1883–April 1, 1924; Oct. 28, 1913–Jan. 20, 1914.

Fielder, James Fairman (D) Jan. 20, 1914–Jan. 15, 1917 (for previous term see above).

Edge, Walter Evans (R) Nov. 20, 1873–Oct. 29, 1956; Jan. 15, 1917–May 16, 1919, Jan. 18, 1944–Jan. 21, 1947; Senate 1919–Nov. 21, 1929.

Runyon, William Nelson (R) March 5, 1871–Nov. 9, 1931; May 16, 1919–Jan. 13, 1920.

Case, Clarence Edwards (R) Sept. 24, 1877–Sept. 3, 1961; Jan. 13–Jan. 20, 1920.

Edwards, Edward Irving (D) Dec. 1, 1863–Jan. 26, 1931; Jan. 20, 1920–Jan. 15, 1923; Senate 1923–29.

Silzer, George Sebastian (D) April 14, 1870–Oct. 16, 1940; Jan. 15, 1923–Jan. 19, 1926.

Moore, Arthur Harry (D) July 3, 1879–Nov. 18, 1952; Jan. 19, 1926–Jan. 15, 1929, Jan. 19, 1932–Jan. 3, 1935, Jan. 18, 1938–Jan. 21, 1941; Senate 1935–Jan. 17, 1938.

Larson, Morgan Foster (R) June 15, 1882–March 21, 1961; Jan. 15, 1929–Jan. 19, 1932.

Moore, Arthur Harry (D) Jan. 19, 1932–Jan. 3, 1935 (for previous term see above).

Powell, Clifford R. (R) July 26, 1893–March 28, 1973; Jan. 3–Jan. 8, 1935.

Prall, Horace Griggs (R) March 6, 1881–April 23, 1951; Jan. 8–Jan. 15, 1935.

Hoffman, Harold Giles (R) Feb. 7, 1896–June 4, 1954; Jan. 15, 1935–Jan. 18, 1938; House 1927–31.

Moore, Arthur Harry (D) Jan. 18, 1938–Jan. 21, 1941 (for previous terms see above).

Edison, Charles (D) Aug. 3, 1890–July 31, 1969; Jan. 21, 1941–Jan. 18, 1944; secretary of the navy Jan. 2–June 24, 1940.

Edge, Walter Evans (R) Jan. 18, 1944–Jan. 21, 1947 (for previous term see above).

Driscoll, Alfred Eastlack (R) Oct. 25, 1902–March 9, 1975; Jan. 21, 1947–Jan. 19, 1954.

Meyner, Robert Baumle (D) July 3, 1908–May 27, 1990; Jan. 19, 1954–Jan. 16, 1962.

Hughes, Richard Joseph (D) Aug. 10, 1909–Dec. 7, 1992; Jan. 16, 1962–Jan. 20, 1970.

Cahill, William Thomas (R) June 25, 1912–July 1, 1996; Jan. 20, 1970–Jan. 15, 1974; House 1959–Jan. 19, 1970.

Byrne, Brendan Thomas (D) April 1, 1924– ; Jan. 15, 1974–Jan. 19, 1982.

Kean, Thomas H. (R) April 21, 1935– ; Jan. 19, 1982–Jan. 16, 1990.

Florio, James Joseph (D) Aug. 29, 1937– ; Jan. 16, 1990–Jan. 18, 1994; House 1975–Jan. 16, 1990.

Whitman, Christine Todd (R) Sept. 26, 1946– ; Jan. 18, 1994–Feb. 1, 2001.

DiFrancesco, Donald T. (R) Nov. 20, 1944– ; Feb. 1, 2001–Jan. 8, 2002.

Bennett, John O. III (R) Aug. 6, 1948; Jan. 8, 2002–Jan. 12, 2002.

Codey, Richard J. (D) Nov. 27, 1946– ; Jan. 12, 2002–Jan. 15, 2002, Nov. 15, 2004– .

McGreevey, James E. (D) Aug. 6, 1957– ; Jan. 15, 2002–Nov. 15, 2004.

Codey, Richard J. (D) Nov. 15, 2004– (for previous term see above).

New Mexico

(Became a state Jan. 6, 1912)

McDonald, William C. (D) July 25, 1858–April 11, 1918; Jan. 6, 1912–Jan. 1, 1917.

De Baca, Ezequiel Cabeza (D) Nov. 1, 1864–Feb. 18, 1917; Jan. 1–Feb. 18, 1917.

Lindsey, Washington Ellsworth (R) Dec. 20, 1862–April 5, 1926; Feb. 19, 1917–Jan. 1, 1919.

Larrazolo, Octaviano Amrosio (R) Dec. 7, 1859–April 7, 1930; Jan. 1, 1919–Jan. 1, 1921; Senate Dec. 7, 1928–29.

Mechem, Merrit Cramer (uncle of Edwin Leard Mechem, below) (R) Oct. 10, 1870–May 24, 1946; Jan. 1, 1921–Jan. 1, 1923.

Hinkle, James Fielding (D) Oct. 20, 1862–March 26, 1951; Jan. 1, 1923–Jan. 1, 1925.

Hannett, Arthur Thomas (D) Feb. 17, 1884–March 18, 1966; Jan. 1, 1925–Jan. 1, 1927.

Dillon, Richard Charles (R) June 24, 1877–Jan. 4, 1966; Jan. 1, 1927–Jan. 1, 1931.

Seligman, Arthur (D) June 14, 1871–Sept. 25, 1933; Jan. 1, 1931–Sept. 25, 1933.

Hockenhull, Andrew W. (D) Jan. 16, 1877–June 20, 1974; Sept. 25, 1933–Jan. 1, 1935.

Tingley, Clyde (D) Jan. 5, 1983–Dec. 24, 1960; Jan. 1, 1935–Jan. 1, 1939.

Miles, John Esten (D) July 28, 1984–Oct. 7, 1971; Jan. 1, 1939–Jan. 1, 1943; House 1949–51.

Dempsey, John Joseph (D) June 22, 1879–March 11, 1958; Jan. 1, 1943–Jan. 1, 1947; House 1935–41, 1951–March 11, 1958.

Mabry, Thomas Jewett (D) Oct. 17, 1884–Dec. 23, 1962; Jan. 1, 1947–Jan. 1, 1951.

Mechem, Edwin Leard (nephew of Merrit Cramer Mechem, above) (R) July 2, 1912–Nov. 27, 2002; Jan. 1, 1951–Jan. 1, 1955, Jan. 1, 1957–Jan. 1, 1959, Jan. 1, 1961–Nov. 30, 1962; Senate Nov. 30, 1962–Nov. 3, 1964.

Simms, John Field Jr. (D) Dec. 18, 1916–April 11, 1975; Jan. 1, 1955–Jan. 1, 1957.

Mechem, Edwin Leard (R) Jan. 1, 1957–Jan. 1, 1959 (for previous term see above).

Burroughs, John (D) April 7, 1907–May 21, 1978; Jan. 1, 1959–Jan. 1, 1961.

Mechem, Edwin Leard (R) Jan. 1, 1961–Nov. 30, 1962 (for previous terms see above).

Bolack, Thomas Felix (R) May 18, 1918–May 20, 1998; Nov. 30, 1962–Jan. 1, 1963.

Campbell, John M. "Jack" (D) Sept. 10, 1916–June 14, 1999; Jan. 1, 1963–Jan. 1, 1967.

Cargo, David Francis (R) Jan. 13, 1929– ; Jan. 1, 1967–Jan. 1, 1971.

King, Bruce (D) April 6, 1924– ; Jan. 1, 1971–Jan. 1, 1975, Jan. 1, 1979–Jan. 1, 1983, Jan. 1, 1991–Jan. 1, 1995.

Apodaca, Raymond S. "Jerry" (D) Oct. 3, 1934– ; Jan. 1, 1975–Jan. 1, 1979.

King, Bruce (D) Jan. 1, 1979–Jan. 1, 1983 (for previous term see above).

Anaya, Toney (D) April 29, 1941– ; Jan. 1, 1983–Jan. 1, 1987.

Carruthers, Garrey Edward (R) Aug. 29, 1939– ; Jan. 1, 1987–Jan. 1, 1991.

King, Bruce (D) Jan. 1, 1991–Jan. 1, 1995 (for previous terms see above).

Johnson, Gary E. (R) Jan. 1, 1953– ; Jan. 1, 1995–Jan. 1, 2003.

Richardson, William Blaine "Bill" (D) Nov. 15, 1947– ; Jan. 1, 2003– ; House 1983–Feb. 13, 1997; secretary of energy Aug. 18, 1998–Jan. 20, 2001.

New York

(Ratified the Constitution July 26, 1788)

Clinton, George (father of Rep. George Clinton, uncle of Rep. James Graham Clinton and De Witt Clinton, below) (DR) July 26, 1739–April 20, 1812; July 30, 1777–June 30, 1795, July 1, 1801–July 1, 1804; Cont. Cong. 1775–76; vice president 1805–April 20, 1812.

Jay, John (son-in-law of William Livingston of N.J.) (F) Dec. 12, 1745–May 17, 1829; July 1, 1795–June 30, 1801; Cont. Cong. 1774–76, 1778–79 (president); secretary of foreign affairs 1784–89; chief justice Oct. 19, 1789–June 29, 1795.

Clinton, George (DR) July 1, 1801–July 1, 1804 (for previous term see above).

Lewis, Morgan (F) Oct. 16, 1754–April 7, 1844; July 1, 1804–July 1, 1807.

Tompkins, Daniel D. (DR) June 21, 1774–June 11, 1825; July 1, 1807–Feb. 24, 1817; elected to the House for term beginning 1805 but resigned before taking seat; vice president 1817–26.

Tayler, John (DR) July 4, 1742–April 19, 1829; Feb. 24–July 1, 1817.

Clinton, De Witt (nephew of George Clinton, half-brother of James Graham Clinton, cousin of Rep. George Clinton) (R) March 2, 1769–Feb. 11, 1828; July 1, 1817–Jan. 1, 1823, Jan. 1, 1825–Feb. 11, 1828; Senate Feb. 9, 1802–Nov. 4, 1803.

Yates, Joseph Christopher (DR) Nov. 9, 1768–March 19, 1837; Jan. 1, 1823–Dec. 31, 1824.

Clinton, De Witt (Clinton R) Jan. 1, 1825–Feb. 11, 1828 (for previous term see above).

Pitcher, Nathaniel (DR) 1777–May 25, 1836; (Acting) Feb. 11–Dec. 31, 1828; House 1819–23 (no party), 1831–33 (Jacksonian).

Van Buren, Martin (half-brother of Rep. James Isaac Van Alen) (Jeff.R) Dec. 5, 1782–July 24, 1862; Jan. 1–March 12, 1829; Senate 1821–Dec. 20, 1828 (no party); secretary of state March 28, 1829–March 23, 1831; vice president 1833–37 (Democrat); president 1837–41 (Democrat).

Throop, Enos Thompson (J) Aug. 21, 1764–Nov. 1, 1874; March 12, 1829–Jan. 1, 1833; House 1815–June 4, 1816 (Republican).

Marcy, William Learned (J) Dec. 12, 1786–July 4, 1857; Jan. 1, 1833–Jan. 1, 1839; Senate 1831–Jan. 1, 1833; secretary of war March 6, 1845–March 4, 1849; secretary of state March 8, 1853–March 6, 1857.

Seward, William Henry (W) May 16, 1801–Oct. 10, 1872; Jan. 1, 1839–Jan. 1, 1843; Senate 1849–61 (1849–55 Whig, 1855–61 Republican); secretary of state March 6, 1861–March 4, 1869.

Bouck, William C. (D) Jan. 7, 1786–April 19, 1859; Jan. 1, 1843–Jan. 1, 1845.

Wright, Silas Jr. (J) May 24, 1795–Aug. 27, 1847; Jan. 1, 1845–Jan. 1, 1847; House 1827–Feb. 16, 1829 (no party); Senate Jan. 4, 1833–Nov. 26, 1844 (Jacksonian).

Young, John (W) June 12, 1802–April 23, 1852; Jan. 1, 1847–Jan. 1, 1849; House Nov. 9, 1836–37, 1841–43.

Fish, Hamilton (W) Aug. 3, 1808–Sept. 7, 1893; Jan. 1, 1849–Jan. 1, 1851; House 1843–45; Senate 1851–57; secretary of state March 17, 1869–March 12, 1877.

Hunt, Washington (W) Aug. 5, 1811–Feb. 2, 1867; Jan. 1, 1851–Jan. 1, 1853; House 1843–49.

Seymour, Horatio (D) May 31, 1810–Feb. 12, 1886; Jan. 1, 1853–Jan. 1, 1855, Jan. 1, 1863–Jan. 1, 1865.

Clark, Myron Holley (W/FS) Oct. 23, 1806–Aug. 23, 1892; Jan. 1, 1855–Jan. 1, 1857.

King, John Alsop (R) Jan. 3, 1788–July 7, 1867; Jan. 1, 1857–Jan. 1, 1859; House 1849–51 (Whig).

Morgan, Edwin Dennison (cousin of Morgan Gardner Bulkeley of Conn.) (R) Feb. 8, 1811–Feb. 14, 1883; Jan. 1, 1859–Jan. 1, 1863; Senate 1863–69; chair Rep. Nat. Comm. 1856–64, 1872–76.

Seymour, Horatio (D) Jan. 1, 1863–Jan. 1, 1865 (for previous term see above).

Fenton, Reuben Eaton (UR) July 4, 1819–Aug. 25, 1885; Jan. 1, 1865–Jan. 1, 1869; House 1853–55 (Democrat), 1857–Dec. 20, 1864 (Democrat); Senate 1869–75 (Republican).

Hoffman, John Thompson (D) Jan. 10, 1828–March 24, 1888; Jan. 1, 1869–Jan. 1, 1873.

Dix, John Adams (R) July 24, 1798–April 21, 1879; Jan. 1, 1873–Jan. 1, 1875; Senate Jan. 27, 1845–49 (Democrat); secretary of the Treasury Jan. 15–March 6, 1861.

Tilden, Samuel Jones (D) Feb. 9, 1814–Aug. 4, 1886; Jan. 1, 1875–Jan. 1, 1877.

Robinson, Lucius (D) Nov. 4, 1810–March 23, 1891; Jan. 1, 1877–Jan. 1, 1880.

Cornell, Alonzo B. (R) Jan. 22, 1832–Oct. 15, 1904; Jan. 1, 1880–Jan. 1, 1883.

Cleveland, Stephen Grover (D) March 18, 1837–June 24, 1908; Jan. 1, 1883–Jan. 6, 1885; president 1885–89, 1893–97.

Hill, David Bennett (D) Aug. 29, 1843–Oct. 20, 1910; Jan. 6, 1885–Jan. 1, 1892; Senate Jan. 7, 1892–97.

Flower, Roswell Pettibone (D) Aug. 7, 1835–May 12, 1899; Jan. 1, 1892–Jan. 1, 1895; House Nov. 8, 1881–83, 1889–Sept. 16, 1891.

Morton, Levi Parsons (R) May 16, 1824–May 16, 1920; Jan. 1, 1895–Jan. 1, 1897; House 1879–March 21, 1881; vice president 1889–93.

Black, Frank Swett (R) March 8, 1853–March 22, 1913; Jan. 1, 1897–Jan. 1, 1899; House 1895–Jan. 7, 1897.

Roosevelt, Theodore (R) Oct. 27, 1858–Jan. 6, 1919; Jan. 1, 1899–Jan. 1, 1901; vice president March 4–Sept. 14, 1901; president Sept. 14, 1901–09.

Odell, Benjamin Baker Jr. (R) Jan. 14, 1854–May 9, 1926; Jan. 1, 1901–Jan. 1, 1905; House 1895–99.

Higgins, Frank Wayland (R) Aug. 18, 1856–Feb. 12, 1907; Jan. 1, 1905–Jan. 1, 1907.

Hughes, Charles Evans (R) April 11, 1862–Aug. 27, 1948; Jan. 1, 1907–Oct. 6, 1910; assoc. justice Oct. 10, 1910–June 10, 1916;

secretary of state March 5, 1921–March 4, 1925; chief justice Feb. 24, 1930–July 1, 1941.

White, Horace (R) Oct. 7, 1865–Nov. 26, 1943; Oct. 6, 1910–Jan. 1, 1911.

Dix, John Alden (D) Dec. 25, 1860–April 9, 1928; Jan. 1, 1911–Jan. 1, 1913.

Sulzer, William (D) March 18, 1863–Nov. 6, 1941; Jan. 1–Oct. 17, 1913; House 1895–Dec. 31, 1912.

Glynn, Martin Henry (D) Sept. 27, 1871–Dec. 14, 1924; Oct. 17, 1913–Jan. 1, 1915; House 1899–1901.

Whitman, Charles Seymour (R) Aug. 28, 1868–March 29, 1947; Jan. 1, 1915–Jan. 1, 1919.

Smith, Alfred Emanuel (D) Dec. 30, 1873–Oct. 4, 1944; Jan. 1, 1919–Jan. 1, 1921, Jan. 1, 1923–Jan. 1, 1929.

Miller, Nathan Lewis (R) Oct. 10, 1868–June 26, 1953; Jan. 1, 1921–Jan. 1, 1923.

Smith, Alfred Emanuel (D) Jan. 1, 1923–Jan. 1, 1929 (for previous term see above).

Roosevelt, Franklin Delano (D) Jan. 30, 1882–April 12, 1945; Jan. 1, 1929–Jan. 1, 1933; president 1933–April 12, 1945.

Lehman, Herbert Henry (D) March 28, 1878–Dec. 5, 1963; Jan. 1, 1933–Dec. 3, 1942; Senate Nov. 9, 1949–57.

Poletti, Charles (D) July 2, 1903– ; Dec. 3, 1942–Jan. 1, 1943.

Dewey, Thomas Edmund (R) March 24, 1902–March 16, 1971; Jan. 1, 1943–Jan. 1, 1955.

Harriman, William Averell (D) Nov. 15, 1891–July 26, 1986; Jan. 1, 1955–Jan. 1, 1959; secretary of commerce Oct. 7, 1946–April 22, 1948.

Rockefeller, Nelson Aldrich (brother of Winthrop Rockefeller of Ark., uncle of Sen. John Davison "Jay" Rockefeller IV, nephew of Rep. Richard Steere Aldrich, grandson of Sen. Nelson Wilmarth Aldrich) (R) July 8, 1908–Jan. 26, 1979; Jan. 1, 1959–Dec. 18, 1973; vice president Dec. 19, 1974–77.

Wilson, Malcolm (R) Feb. 26, 1914–March 13, 2000; Dec. 18, 1973–Jan. 1, 1975.

Carey, Hugh Leo (D) April 11, 1919– ; Jan. 1, 1975–Jan. 1, 1983; House 1961–Dec. 31, 1974.

Cuomo, Mario Matthew (D) June 15, 1932– ; Jan. 1, 1983–Jan. 1, 1995.

Pataki, George E. (R) June 24, 1945– ; Jan. 1, 1995– .

North Carolina

(Ratified the Constitution Nov. 21, 1789)

Johnston, Samuel (F) Dec. 15, 1733–Aug. 17, 1816; Dec. 20, 1787–Dec. 17, 1789; Cont. Cong. 1780–81; Senate Nov. 27, 1789–93 (no party).

Martin, Alexander (F) 1740–Nov. 2, 1807; Dec. 17, 1789–Dec. 14, 1792; Senate 1793–99 (no party); Cont. Cong. (elected but did not attend) 1786.

Spaight, Richard Dobbs (father of Richard Dobbs Spaight Jr., below) (AF) March 25, 1758–Sept. 6, 1802; Dec. 14, 1792–Nov. 19, 1795; Cont. Cong. 1783–85; House Dec. 10, 1798–1801 (Republican).

Ashe, Samuel (AF) 1725–Feb. 3, 1813; Nov. 19, 1795–Dec. 7, 1798.

Davie, William Richardson (F) June 20, 1756–Nov. 18, 1820; Dec. 7, 1798–Nov. 23, 1799.

Williams, Benjamin (DR) Jan. 1, 1751–July 20, 1814; Nov. 23, 1799–Dec. 6, 1802, Dec. 1, 1807–Dec. 12, 1808; House 1793–95 (no party).

Turner, James (R) Dec. 20, 1766–Jan. 15, 1824; Dec. 6, 1802–05; Senate 1805–Nov. 21, 1816.

Alexander, Nathaniel (DR) March 5, 1756–March 7, 1808; Dec. 10, 1805–Dec. 1, 1807; House 1803–Nov. 18, 1805 (Republican).

Williams, Benjamin (DR) Dec. 1, 1807–Dec. 12, 1808 (for previous term see above).

Stone, David (DR) Feb. 17, 1770–Oct. 7, 1818; Dec. 12, 1808–Dec. 5, 1810; House 1799–1801 (no party); Senate 1801–Feb. 17, 1807 (Republican), 1813–Dec. 24, 1814 (Republican).

Smith, Benjamin (DR) Jan. 10, 1756–Jan. 27, 1826; Dec. 5, 1810–Dec. 9, 1811; Cont. Cong. (elected but did not attend) 1784.

Hawkins, William (DR) Oct. 10, 1777–May 17, 1819; Dec. 9, 1811–Dec. 7, 1814.

Miller, William (DR) 1770–1825; Dec. 7, 1814–Dec. 3, 1817.

Branch, John (DR) Nov. 4, 1782–Jan. 3, 1863; Dec. 6, 1817–Dec. 7, 1820; Senate 1823–March 9, 1829 (Democrat); House May 12, 1831–33 (Democrat); secretary of the navy March 9, 1829–May 12, 1831.

Franklin, Jesse (DR) March 24, 1760–Aug. 31, 1823; Dec. 7, 1820–Dec. 7, 1821; House 1795–97 (no party); Senate 1799–1805 (Republican), 1807–13 (Republican); elected pres. pro tempore March 10, 1804.

Holmes, Gabriel (DR) 1769–Sept. 26, 1829; Dec. 7, 1821–Dec. 7, 1824; House 1825–Sept. 26, 1829 (no party).

Burton, Hutchins Gordon (F) 1782–April 21, 1836; Dec. 7, 1824–Dec. 8, 1827; House Dec. 6, 1819–March 23, 1824 (no party).

Iredell, James (DR) Nov. 2, 1788–April 13, 1853; Dec. 8, 1827–Dec. 12, 1828; Senate Dec. 15, 1828–31 (Jacksonian).

Owen, John (DR) Aug. 1787–Oct. 9, 1841; Dec. 12, 1828–Dec. 18, 1830.

Stokes, Montfort (D) March 12, 1762–Nov. 4, 1842; Dec. 18, 1830–Dec. 6, 1832; Senate Dec. 4, 1816–23.

Swain, David Lowry (W) Jan. 4, 1801–Aug. 27, 1868; Dec. 6, 1832–Dec. 10, 1835.

Spaight, Richard Dobbs Jr. (son of Richard Dobbs Spaight, above) (D) 1796–Nov. 2, 1850; Dec. 10, 1835–Dec. 31, 1836; House 1823–25 (no party).

Dudley, Edward Bishop (W) Dec. 15, 1789–Oct. 30, 1855; Dec. 31, 1836–Jan. 1, 1841; House Nov. 10, 1829–31 (no party).

Morehead, John Motley (cousin of James Turner Morehead of Ky.) (W) July 4, 1796–Aug. 27, 1866; Jan. 1, 1841–Jan. 1, 1845.

Graham, William Alexander (W) Sept. 5, 1804–Aug. 11, 1875; Jan. 1, 1845–Jan. 1, 1849; Senate Nov. 25, 1840–43; secretary of the navy Aug. 2, 1850–July 25, 1852.

Manly, Charles (W) May 13, 1795–May 1, 1871; Jan. 1, 1849–Jan. 1, 1851.

Reid, David Settle (D) April 19, 1813–June 19, 1891; Jan. 1, 1851–Dec. 6, 1854; House 1843–47; Senate Dec. 6, 1854–59.

Winslow, Warren (D) Jan. 1, 1810–Aug. 16, 1862; (Acting) Dec. 6, 1854–Jan. 1, 1855; House 1855–61.

Bragg, Thomas (D) Nov. 9, 1810–Jan. 21, 1872; Jan. 1, 1855–Jan. 1, 1859; Senate 1859–March 6, 1861.

Ellis, John Willis (D) Nov. 23, 1820–July 7, 1861; Jan. 1, 1859–July 7, 1861.

Clark, Henry Toole (D) Feb. 7, 1808–April 14, 1874; July 7, 1861–Sept. 8, 1862.

Vance, Zebulon Baird (D) May 13, 1830–April 14, 1894; Sept. 8, 1862–May 29, 1865, Jan. 1, 1877–Feb. 5, 1879; House Dec. 7, 1858–61; Senate 1879–April 14, 1894.

Holden, William Woods (R) Nov. 24, 1818–March 1, 1892; May 29–Dec. 15, 1865, July 1, 1868–Dec. 15, 1870.

Worth, Jonathan (D) Nov. 18, 1802–Sept. 5, 1869; Dec. 15, 1865–July 1, 1868.

Holden, William Woods (R) July 1, 1868–Dec. 15, 1870 (for previous term see above).

Caldwell, Tod Robinson (R) Feb. 19, 1818–July 11, 1874; Dec. 15, 1870–July 11, 1874.

Brogden, Curtis Hooks (R) Nov. 6, 1816–Jan. 5, 1901; July 11, 1874–Jan. 1, 1877; House 1877–79.

Vance, Zebulon Baird (D) Jan. 1, 1877–Feb. 5, 1879 (for previous term see above).

Jarvis, Thomas Jordan (D) Jan. 18, 1836–June 17, 1915; Feb. 5, 1879–Jan. 21, 1885; Senate April 19, 1894–Jan. 23, 1895.

Scales, Alfred Moore (D) Nov. 26, 1827–Feb. 9, 1892; Jan. 21, 1885–Jan. 17, 1889; House 1857–59, 1875–Dec. 30, 1884.

Fowle, Daniel Gould (D) March 3, 1831–April 7, 1891; Jan. 17, 1889–April 7, 1891.

Holt, Thomas Michael (D) July 15, 1831–April 11, 1896; April 8, 1891–Jan. 18, 1893.

Carr, Elias (D) Feb. 25, 1839–July 22, 1900; Jan. 18, 1893–Jan. 12, 1897.

Russell, Daniel Lindsay (G) Aug. 7, 1945–May 14, 1908; Jan. 12, 1897–Jan. 15, 1901; House 1879–81.

Aycock, Charles Brantley (D) Nov. 1, 1859–April 4, 1912; Jan. 15, 1901–Jan. 11, 1905.

Glenn, Robert Brodnax (D) Aug. 11, 1854–May 16, 1920; Jan. 11, 1905–Jan. 12, 1909.

Kitchin, William Walton (D) Oct. 9, 1866–Nov. 9, 1924; Jan. 12, 1909–Jan. 15, 1913; House 1897–Jan. 11, 1909.

Craig, Locke (D) Aug. 16, 1860–June 9, 1924; Jan. 15, 1913–Jan. 11, 1917.

Bickett, Thomas Walter (D) Feb. 28, 1869–Dec. 28, 1921; Jan. 11, 1917–Jan. 12, 1921.

Morrison, Cameron A. (D) Oct. 5, 1869–Aug. 20, 1953; Jan. 12, 1921–Jan. 14, 1925; Senate Dec. 13, 1930–Dec. 4, 1932; House 1943–45.

McLean, Angus Wilton (D) April 20, 1870–June 21, 1935; Jan. 14, 1925–Jan. 11, 1929.

Gardner, Oliver Max (brother-in-law of Clyde Roark Hoey, below) (D) March 22, 1882–Feb. 6, 1947; Jan. 11, 1929–Jan. 5, 1933.

Ehringhaus, John Christoph Blucher (D) Feb. 5, 1882–July 31, 1949; Jan. 5, 1933–Jan. 7, 1937.

Hoey, Clyde Roark (brother-in-law of Oliver Max Gardner, above) (D) Dec. 11, 1877–May 12, 1954; Jan. 7, 1937–Jan. 9, 1941; House Dec. 16, 1919–21; Senate 1945–May 12, 1954.

Broughton, Joseph Melville (D) Nov. 17, 1888–March 6, 1949; Jan. 9, 1941–Jan. 4, 1945; Senate Dec. 31, 1948–March 6, 1949.

Cherry, Robert Gregg (D) Oct. 17, 1891–June 25, 1957; Jan. 4, 1945–Jan. 6, 1949.

Scott, William Kerr (father of Robert Walter Scott, below) (D) April 17, 1896–April 16, 1958; Jan. 6, 1949–Jan. 8, 1953; Senate Nov. 29, 1954–April 16, 1958.

Umstead, William Bradley (D) May 13, 1895–Nov. 7, 1954; Jan. 8, 1953–Nov. 7, 1954; House 1933–39; Senate Dec. 18, 1946–Dec. 30, 1948.

Hodges, Luther Hartwell (D) March 9, 1898–Oct. 6, 1974; Nov. 7, 1954–Jan. 5, 1961; secretary of commerce Jan. 21, 1961–Jan. 15, 1965.

Sanford, Terry (D) Aug. 20, 1917–April 18, 1998; Jan. 5, 1961–Jan. 8, 1965; Senate Nov. 4, 1986–93.

Moore, Daniel Killian (D) April 2, 1906–Sept. 7, 1986; Jan. 8, 1965–Jan. 3, 1969.

Scott, Robert Walter (son of William Kerr Scott, above) (D) June 13, 1929– ; Jan. 3, 1969–Jan. 5, 1973.

Holshouser, James Eubert Jr. (R) Oct. 8, 1934– ; Jan. 5, 1973–Jan. 8, 1977.

Hunt, James Baxter Jr. (D) May 18, 1937– ; Jan. 8, 1977–Jan. 5, 1985, Jan. 9, 1993–Jan. 6, 2001.

Martin, James Grubbs (R) Dec. 11, 1935– ; Jan. 5, 1985–Jan. 9, 1993; House 1973–85.

Hunt, James Baxter Jr. (D) Jan. 9, 1993–Jan. 6, 2001 (for previous term see above).

Easley, Michael F. (D) March 23, 1950– ; Jan. 6, 2001– .

North Dakota
(Became a state Nov. 2, 1889)

Miller, John (R) Oct. 6, 1843–Oct. 26, 1908; Nov. 4, 1889–Jan. 6, 1891.

Burke, Andrew Horace (R) May 15, 1850–Nov. 17, 1918; Jan. 7, 1891–Jan. 3, 1893.

Shortridge, Eli C. D. (I) March 29, 1830–Feb. 4, 1908; Jan. 4, 1893–Jan. 7, 1895.

Allin, Roger (R) Dec. 18, 1848–Jan. 1, 1936; Jan. 7, 1895–Jan. 5, 1897.

Briggs, Frank Arlington (R) Sept. 16, 1858–Aug. 9, 1898; Jan. 5, 1897–Aug. 9, 1898.

Devine, Joseph McMurray (R) March 15, 1861–Aug. 31, 1938; Aug. 9, 1898–Jan. 3, 1899.

Fancher, Frederick Bartlett (R) April 2, 1852–Jan. 10, 1944; Jan. 3, 1899–Jan. 10, 1901.

White, Frank (R) Dec. 12, 1856–March 23, 1940; Jan. 10, 1901–Jan. 4, 1905.

Sarles, Elmore Yocum (R) Jan. 15, 1859–Feb. 14, 1929; Jan. 5, 1905–Jan. 9, 1907.

Burke, John (D) Feb. 25, 1859–May 14, 1937; Jan. 9, 1907–Jan. 8, 1913.

Hanna, Louis Benjamin (R) Aug. 9, 1861–April 23, 1948; Jan. 8, 1913–Jan. 3, 1917; House 1909–Jan. 7, 1913.

Frazier, Lynn Joseph (R) Dec. 21, 1874–Jan. 11, 1947; Jan. 3, 1917–Nov. 23, 1921; Senate 1923–41.

Nestos, Ragnvald Anderson (R) April 12, 1877–July 15, 1942; Nov. 23, 1921–Jan. 7, 1925.

Sorlie, Arthur Gustav (R) April 26, 1874–Aug. 28, 1928; Jan. 7, 1925–Aug. 28, 1928.

Maddock, Walter Jeremiah (R) Sept. 13, 1880–Jan. 25, 1951; Aug. 28, 1928–Jan. 9, 1929.

Shafer, George F. (R) Nov. 23, 1888–Aug. 13, 1948; Jan. 9, 1929–Dec. 31, 1932.

Langer, William (I) Sept. 30, 1886–Nov. 8, 1959; Dec. 31, 1932–July 17, 1934, Jan. 6, 1937–Jan. 5, 1939; Senate 1941–Nov. 8, 1959 (Republican).

Olson, Ole H. (R) Sept. 19, 1872–Jan. 29, 1954; July 17, 1934–Jan. 7, 1935.

Moodie, Thomas Hilliard (D) May 26, 1878–March 3, 1948; Jan. 7–Feb. 2, 1935.

Welford, Walter (R) May 21, 1868–June 28, 1952; Feb. 2, 1935–Jan. 6, 1937.

Langer, William (I) Jan. 6, 1937–Jan. 5, 1939 (for previous term see above).

Moses, John (D) June 12, 1885–March 3, 1945; Jan. 5, 1939–Jan. 4, 1945; Senate Jan. 3–March 3, 1945.

Aandahl, Fred George (R) April 9, 1897–April 7, 1966; Jan. 4, 1945–Jan. 3, 1951; House 1951–53.

Brunsdale, Clarence Norman (R) July 9, 1891–Jan. 27, 1978; Jan. 3, 1951–Jan. 9, 1957; Senate Nov. 19, 1959–Aug. 7, 1960.

Davis, John Edward (R) April 18, 1913–May 20, 1990; Jan. 9, 1957–Jan. 4, 1961.

Guy, William Lewis (D) Sept. 30, 1919– ; Jan. 4, 1961–Jan. 2, 1973.

Link, Arthur Albert (D) May 24, 1914– ; Jan. 2, 1973–Jan. 7, 1981; House 1971–73.

Olson, Allen Ingvar (R) Nov. 5, 1938– ; Jan. 7, 1981–Jan. 8, 1985.

Sinner, George A. (D) May 29, 1928– ; Jan. 8, 1985–Jan. 5, 1993.

Schafer, Edward Thomas (R) Aug. 8, 1946– ; Jan. 5, 1993–Jan. 9, 2001.

Hoeven, John (R) March 13, 1957– ; Jan. 9, 2001– .

Ohio

(Became a state March 1, 1803)

Tiffin, Edward (brother-in-law of Thomas Worthington, below) (DR) June 19, 1766–Aug. 9, 1829; March 3, 1803–March 4, 1807; Senate 1807–09 (Republican).

Kirker, Thomas (DR) 1760–Feb. 20, 1837; March 4, 1807–Dec. 12, 1808.

Huntington, Samuel H. (nephew of Samuel Huntington of Conn.) (DR) Oct. 4, 1765–June 8, 1817; Dec. 12, 1808–Dec. 8, 1810.

Meigs, Return Jonathan Jr. (DR) Nov. 17, 1764–March 29, 1825; Dec. 8, 1810–March 24, 1814; Senate Dec. 12, 1808–May 1, 1810 (Republican); postmaster general April 11, 1814–June 30, 1823.

Looker, Othneil (DR) Oct. 4, 1757–July 23, 1845; March 24–Dec. 8, 1814.

Worthington, Thomas (brother-in-law of Edward Tiffin, above) (DR) July 16, 1773–June 20, 1827; Dec. 8, 1814–Dec. 14, 1818; Senate April 1, 1803–07 (Republican), Dec. 15, 1810–Dec. 1, 1814 (Republican).

Brown, Ethan Allen (DR) July 4, 1776–Feb. 24, 1852; Dec. 14, 1818–Jan. 4, 1822; Senate Jan. 3, 1822–25.

Trimble, Allen (NR) Nov. 24, 1783–Feb. 3, 1870; Jan. 4–Dec. 28, 1822 (Federalist), Dec. 19, 1826–Dec. 18, 1830.

Morrow, Jeremiah (J) Oct. 6, 1771–March 22, 1852; Dec. 28, 1822–Dec. 19, 1826; House Oct. 17, 1803–13 (Republican), Oct. 13, 1840–43 (Whig); Senate 1813–19 (Republican).

Trimble, Allen (NR) Dec. 19, 1826–Dec. 18, 1830 (for previous term see above).

McArthur, Duncan (NR) Jan. 14, 1772–April 29, 1839; Dec. 18, 1830–Dec. 7, 1832; House (elected but never qualified and resigned April 5, 1813); 1823–25 (no party).

Lucas, Robert (J) April 1, 1781–Feb. 7, 1853; Dec. 7, 1832–Dec. 12, 1836.

Vance, Joseph (W) March 21, 1786–Aug. 24, 1852; Dec. 12, 1836–Dec. 13, 1838; House 1821–35 (1821–33 no party, 1833–35 Anti-Jacksonian), 1843–47 (Whig).

Shannon, Wilson (D) Feb. 24, 1802–Aug. 30, 1877; Dec. 13, 1838–Dec. 16, 1840, Dec. 14, 1842–April 15, 1844; Aug. 10, 1855–Aug. 18, 1856 (Kansas Terr.); House 1853–55.

Corwin, Thomas (W) July 29, 1794–Dec. 18, 1865; Dec. 16, 1840–Dec. 14, 1842; House 1831–May 30, 1840 (Whig), 1859–March 12, 1861 (Republican); Senate 1845–July 20, 1850 (Whig); secretary of the Treasury July 23, 1850–March 6, 1853.

Shannon, Wilson (D) Dec. 14, 1842–April 15, 1844 (for previous term see above).

Bartley, Thomas Welles (son of Mordecai Bartley, below) (D) Feb. 11, 1812–June 20, 1885; April 15–Dec. 3, 1844.

Bartley, Mordecai (father of Thomas Welles Bartley, above) (W) Dec. 16, 1783–Oct. 10, 1870; Dec. 3, 1844–Dec. 12, 1846; House 1823–31 (no party).

Bebb, William (W) Dec. 2, 1801–Oct. 23, 1873; Dec. 12, 1846–Jan. 22, 1849.

Ford, Seabury (W) Oct. 15, 1801–May 8, 1855; Jan. 22, 1849–Dec. 12, 1850.

Wood, Reuben (D) 1792–Oct. 1, 1864; Dec. 12, 1850–July 13, 1853.

Medill, William (D) Feb. 1802–Sept. 2, 1865; July 13, 1853–Jan. 14, 1856; House 1839–43.

Chase, Salmon Portland (father-in-law of William Sprague of R.I.) (R) Jan. 13, 1808–May 7, 1873; Jan. 14, 1856–Jan. 9, 1860; Senate 1849–55 (Free-Soiler), March 4–March 6, 1861 (Republican); secretary of the Treasury March 7, 1861–June 30, 1864; chief justice Dec. 15, 1864–May 7, 1873.

Dennison, William Jr. (R) Nov. 23, 1815–June 15, 1882; Jan. 9, 1860–Jan. 13, 1862; postmaster general Oct. 1, 1864–July 16, 1866.

Tod, David (U) Feb. 21, 1805–Nov. 13, 1868; Jan. 13, 1862–Jan. 11, 1864.

Brough, John (U) Sept. 17, 1811–Aug. 29, 1865; Jan. 11, 1864–Aug. 29, 1865.

Anderson, Charles (U) June 1, 1814–Sept. 2, 1895; Aug. 29, 1865–Jan. 8, 1866.

Cox, Jacob Dolson (R) Oct. 27, 1828–Aug. 4, 1900; Jan. 8, 1866–Jan. 13, 1868; secretary of the interior March 5, 1869–Oct. 31, 1870; House 1877–79.

Hayes, Rutherford B. (R) Oct. 4, 1822–Jan. 17, 1893; Jan. 13, 1868–Jan. 8, 1872, Jan. 10, 1876–March 2, 1877; House 1865–July 20, 1867; president 1877–81.

Noyes, Edward Follansbee (R) Oct. 3, 1832–Sept. 4, 1890; Jan. 8, 1872–Jan. 12, 1874.

Allen, William (D) Dec. 18 or Dec. 27, 1803–July 11, 1879; Jan. 12, 1874–Jan. 10, 1876; House 1833–35 (Jacksonian); Senate 1837–49 (Democrat).

Hayes, Rutherford B. (R) Jan. 10, 1876–March 2, 1877 (for previous term see above).

Young, Thomas Lowry (R) Dec. 14, 1832–July 20, 1888; March 2, 1877–Jan. 14, 1878; House 1879–83.

Bishop, Richard Moore (D) Nov. 4, 1812–March 2, 1893; Jan. 14, 1878–Jan. 12, 1880.

Foster, Charles (R) April 12, 1828–Jan. 9, 1904; Jan. 12, 1880–Jan. 14, 1884; House 1871–79; secretary of the Treasury Feb. 25, 1891–March 6, 1893.

Hoadly, George (D) July 31, 1826–Aug. 26, 1902; Jan. 14, 1884–Jan. 11, 1886.

Foraker, Joseph Benson (R) July 5, 1846–May 10, 1917; Jan. 11, 1886–Jan. 13, 1890; Senate 1897–1909.

Campbell, James Edwin (D) July 7, 1843–Dec. 18, 1924; Jan. 13, 1890–Jan. 11, 1892; House Jan. 20, 1884–89.

McKinley, William Jr. (R) Jan. 29, 1843–Sept. 14, 1901; Jan. 11, 1892–Jan. 13, 1896; House 1877–May 27, 1884, 1885–91; president 1897–Sept. 14, 1901.

Bushnell, Asa Smith (R) Sept. 16, 1834–Jan. 15, 1904; Jan. 13, 1896–Jan. 8, 1900.

Nash, George Kilborn (R) Aug. 14, 1842–Oct. 28, 1904; Jan. 8, 1900–Jan. 11, 1904.

Herrick, Myron Timothy (R) Oct. 9, 1854–March 31, 1929; Jan. 11, 1904–Jan. 8, 1906.

Pattison, John M. (D) June 13, 1847–June 18, 1906; Jan. 8–June 18, 1906; House 1891–93.

Harris, Andrew Lintner (R) Nov. 17, 1835–Sept. 13, 1915; June 18, 1906–Jan. 11, 1909.

Harmon, Judson (D) Feb. 3, 1846–Feb. 22, 1927; Jan. 11, 1909–Jan. 13, 1913; attorney general June 8, 1895–March 5, 1897.

Cox, James Middleton (D) March 31, 1870–July 15, 1957; Jan. 13, 1913–Jan. 11, 1915, Jan. 8, 1917–Jan. 10, 1921; House 1909–Jan. 12, 1913.

Willis, Frank Bartlett (R) Dec. 28, 1871–March 30, 1928; Jan. 11, 1915–Jan. 8, 1917; House 1911–Jan. 9, 1915; Senate Jan. 14, 1921–March 30, 1928.

Cox, James Middleton (D) Jan. 8, 1917–Jan. 10, 1921 (for previous term see above).

Davis, Harry Lyman (R) Jan. 25, 1878–May 21, 1950; Jan. 10, 1921–Jan. 8, 1923.

Donahey, Alvin Victor (D) July 7, 1873–April 8, 1946; Jan. 8, 1923–Jan. 14, 1929; Senate 1935–41.

Cooper, Myers Young (R) Nov. 25, 1873–Dec. 7, 1958; Jan. 14, 1929–Jan. 12, 1931.

White, George (D) Aug. 21, 1872–Dec. 15, 1953; Jan. 12, 1931–Jan. 14, 1935; House 1911–15, 1917–19; chair Dem. Nat. Comm. 1920–21.

Davey, Martin Luther (D) July 25, 1884–March 31, 1946; Jan. 14, 1935–Jan. 9, 1939; House Nov. 5, 1918–21, 1923–29.

Bricker, John William (R) Sept. 6, 1893–March 22, 1986; Jan. 9, 1939–Jan. 8, 1945; Senate 1947–59.

Lausche, Frank John (D) Nov. 14, 1895–April 21, 1990; Jan. 8, 1945–Jan. 13, 1947, Jan. 10, 1949–Jan. 3, 1957; Senate 1957–69.

Herbert, Thomas James (R) Oct. 28, 1894–Oct. 26, 1974; Jan. 13, 1947–Jan. 10, 1949.

Lausche, Frank John (D) Jan. 10, 1949–Jan. 3, 1957 (for previous term see above).

Brown, John William (R) Dec. 28, 1913–Oct. 29, 1993; Jan. 3–Jan. 14, 1957.

O'Neill, C. William (R) Feb. 14, 1916–Aug. 20, 1978; Jan. 14, 1957–Jan. 12, 1959.

Di Salle, Michael Vincent (D) Jan. 6, 1908–Sept. 16, 1981; Jan. 12, 1959–Jan. 14, 1963.

Rhodes, James Allen (R) Sept. 13, 1909–March 4, 2001; Jan. 14, 1963–Jan. 11, 1971, Jan. 13, 1975–Jan. 10, 1983.

Gilligan, John Joyce (D) March 22, 1921– ; Jan. 11, 1971–Jan. 13, 1975; House 1965–67.

Rhodes, James Allen (R) Jan. 13, 1975–Jan. 10, 1983 (for previous term see above).

Celeste, Richard F. (D) Nov. 11, 1937– ; Jan. 10, 1983–Jan. 14, 1991.

Voinovich, George Victor (R) July 15, 1936– ; Jan. 14, 1991–Dec. 31, 1998; Senate 1999– .

Hollister, Nancy (R) 1949– ; Dec. 31, 1998–Jan. 11, 1999.

Taft, Robert A. II (R) (son of Sen. Robert A. Taft Jr., grandson of Sen. Robert A. Taft, great-grandson of Pres. William Howard Taft) Jan. 8, 1942– ; Jan. 11, 1999– .

Oklahoma

(Became a state Nov. 16, 1907)

Haskell, Charles Nathaniel (D) March 13, 1860–July 5, 1933; Nov. 16, 1907–Jan. 9, 1911.

Cruce, Lee (D) July 8, 1863–Jan. 16, 1933; Jan. 9, 1911–Jan. 11, 1915.

Williams, Robert Lee (D) Dec. 20, 1868–April 10, 1948; Jan. 11, 1915–Jan. 13, 1919.

Robertson, James Brooks Ayers (D) March 15, 1871–March 7, 1938; Jan. 13, 1919–Jan. 8, 1923.

Walton, John Calloway "Jack" (D) March 6, 1881–Nov. 25, 1949; Jan. 8–Nov. 19, 1923.

Trapp, Martin Edwin (D) April 19, 1877–July 27, 1951; Nov. 19, 1923–Jan. 10, 1927.

Johnston, Henry Simpson (D) Dec. 30, 1870–Jan. 7, 1965; Jan. 10, 1927–March 20, 1929.

Holloway, William Judson (D) Dec. 15, 1888–Jan. 28, 1970; March 20, 1929–Jan. 12, 1931.

Murray, William Henry David (father of Johnston Murray, below) (D) Nov. 21, 1869–Oct. 15, 1956; Jan. 12, 1931–Jan. 14, 1935; House 1913–17.

Marland, Ernest Whitworth (D) May 8, 1874–Oct. 3, 1941; Jan. 14, 1935–Jan. 9, 1939; House 1933–35.

Phillips, Leon Chase (D) Dec. 9, 1890–March 27, 1958; Jan. 9, 1939–Jan. 11, 1943.

Kerr, Robert Samuel (D) Sept. 11, 1896–Jan. 1, 1963; Jan. 11, 1943–Jan. 13, 1947; Senate 1949–Jan. 1, 1963.

Turner, Roy Joseph (D) Nov. 6, 1894–June 11, 1973; Jan. 13, 1947–Jan. 8, 1951.

Murray, Johnston (son of William Henry Murray, above) (D) July 21, 1902–April 16, 1974; Jan. 8, 1951–Jan. 10, 1955.

Gary, Raymond Dancel (D) Jan. 21, 1908–Dec. 11, 1993; Jan. 10, 1955–Jan. 19, 1959.

Edmondson, James Howard (D) Sept. 27, 1925–Nov. 17, 1971; Jan. 12, 1959–Jan. 6, 1963; Senate Jan. 7, 1963–Nov. 3, 1964.

Nigh, George Patterson (D) June 9, 1927– ; Jan. 6–Jan. 14, 1963, Jan. 3, 1979–Jan. 12, 1987.

Bellmon, Henry Louis (R) Sept. 3, 1921– ; Jan. 14, 1963–Jan. 9, 1967, Jan. 12, 1987–Jan. 14, 1991; Senate 1969–81.

Bartlett, Dewey Follett (R) March 28, 1919–March 1, 1979; Jan. 9, 1967–Jan. 11, 1971; Senate 1973–79.

Hall, David (D) Oct. 20, 1930– ; Jan. 11, 1971–Jan. 13, 1975.

Boren, David Lyle (D) April 21, 1941– ; Jan. 13, 1975–Jan. 3, 1979; Senate 1979–Nov. 15, 1994.

Nigh, George Patterson (D) Jan. 3, 1979–Jan. 12, 1987 (for previous term see above).

Bellmon, Henry Louis (R) Jan. 12, 1987–Jan. 14, 1991 (for previous term see above).

Walters, David (D) Nov. 20, 1951– ; Jan. 14, 1991–Jan. 9, 1995.

Keating, Frank (R) Feb. 10, 1944– ; Jan. 9, 1995–Jan. 13, 2003.

Henry, Brad (D) June 10, 1963– ; Jan. 13, 2003– .

Oregon

(Became a state Feb. 14, 1859)

Whiteaker, John (D) May 4, 1820–Oct. 2, 1902; March 3, 1859–Sept. 10, 1862; House 1879–81.

Gibbs, Addison Crandall (UR) July 9, 1825–Dec. 29, 1886; Sept. 10, 1862–Sept. 12, 1866.

Woods, George Lemuel (R) July 30, 1832–Jan. 7, 1890; Sept. 12, 1866–Sept. 14, 1870.

Grover, La Fayette (D) Nov. 29, 1823–May 10, 1911; Sept. 14, 1870–Feb. 1, 1877; House Feb. 15–March 13, 1859; Senate 1877–83.

Chadwick, Stephen Fowler (D) Dec. 25, 1825–Jan. 15, 1895; Feb. 1, 1877–Sept. 11, 1878.

Thayer, William Wallace (D) July 15, 1827–Oct. 15, 1899; Sept. 11, 1878–Sept. 13, 1882.

Moody, Zenas Ferry (R) May 27, 1832–March 14, 1917; Sept. 13, 1882–Jan. 12, 1887.

Pennoyer, Sylvester (PD) July 6, 1831–May 30, 1902; Jan. 12, 1887–Jan. 14, 1895.

Lord, William Paine (R) July 1, 1839–Feb. 17, 1911; Jan. 14, 1895–Jan. 9, 1899.

Geer, Theodore Thurston (R) March 12, 1851–Feb. 21, 1924; Jan. 9, 1899–Jan. 14, 1903.

Chamberlain, George Earle (D) Jan. 1, 1854–July 9, 1928; Jan. 14, 1903–Feb. 28, 1909; Senate 1909–21.

Benson, Frank Williamson (R) March 20, 1858–April 14, 1911; March 1, 1909–June 17, 1910.

Bowerman, Jay (R) Aug. 15, 1876–Oct. 25, 1957; June 17, 1910–Jan. 8, 1911.

West, Oswald (D) May 20, 1873–Aug. 22, 1960; Jan. 10, 1911–Jan. 12, 1915.

Withycombe, James (R) March 21, 1854–March 3, 1919; Jan. 12, 1915–March 3, 1919.

Olcott, Ben Wilson (R) Oct. 15, 1872–July 21, 1952; March 3, 1919–Jan. 8, 1923.

Pierce, Walter Marcus (D) May 30, 1861–March 27, 1954; Jan. 8, 1923–Jan. 10, 1927; House 1933–43.

Patterson, Isaac Lee (R) Sept. 17, 1859–Dec. 21, 1929; Jan. 10, 1927–Dec. 21, 1929.

Norblad, Albin Walter (R) March 19, 1881–April 17, 1960; Dec. 22, 1929–Jan. 12, 1931.

Meier, Julius L. (I) Dec. 31, 1874–July 14, 1937; Jan. 12, 1931–Jan. 14, 1935.

Martin, Charles Henry (D) Oct. 1, 1863–Sept. 22, 1946; Jan. 14, 1935–Jan. 9, 1939; House 1931–35.

Sprague, Charles Arthur (R) Nov. 12, 1887–March 13, 1969; Jan. 9, 1939–Jan. 11, 1943.

Snell, Earl Wilcox (R) July 11, 1895–Oct. 28, 1947; Jan. 11, 1943–Oct. 28, 1947.

Hall, John Hubert (R) Feb. 7, 1899–Nov. 14, 1970; Oct. 30, 1947–Jan. 10, 1949.

McKay, Douglas James (R) June 24, 1893–July 22, 1959; Jan. 10, 1949–Dec. 27, 1952; secretary of the interior Jan. 21, 1953–April 15, 1956.

Patterson, Paul Linton (R) July 18, 1900–Jan. 31, 1956; Dec. 27, 1952–Jan. 31, 1956.

Smith, Elmo Everett (R) Nov. 19, 1909–July 15, 1968; Feb. 1, 1956–Jan. 14, 1957.

Holmes, Robert Denison (D) May 11, 1909–June 6, 1976; Jan. 14, 1957–Jan. 12, 1959.

Hatfield, Mark Odom (R) July 12, 1922– ; Jan. 12, 1959–Jan. 9, 1967; Senate Jan. 10, 1967–97.

McCall, Thomas Lawson (R) March 22, 1913–Jan. 8, 1983; Jan. 9, 1967–Jan. 13, 1975.

Straub, Robert William (D) May 6, 1920–Nov. 27, 2002; Jan. 13, 1975–Jan. 8, 1979.

Atiyeh, Victor George (R) Feb. 20, 1923– ; Jan. 8, 1979–Jan. 12, 1987.

Goldschmidt, Neil (D) June 16, 1940– ; Jan. 12, 1987–Jan. 14, 1991; secretary of transportation July 27, 1979–Jan. 20, 1981.

Roberts, Barbara (D) Dec. 21, 1936– ; Jan. 14, 1991–Jan. 9, 1995.

Kitzhaber, John A. (D) March 5, 1947– ; Jan. 9, 1995–Jan. 13, 2003.

Kulongoski, Ted (D) Nov. 5, 1940– ; Jan. 13, 2003– .

Pennsylvania

(Ratified the Constitution Dec. 12, 1787)

Mifflin, Thomas (DR) Jan. 10, 1744–Jan. 20, 1800; Dec. 21, 1790–Dec. 17, 1799.

McKean, Thomas (DR) March 19, 1734–June 24, 1817; Dec. 17, 1799–Dec. 20, 1808.

Snyder, Simon (DR) Nov. 5, 1789–Nov. 9, 1819; Dec. 20, 1808–Dec. 16, 1817.

Findlay, William (father-in-law of Francis Rawn Shunk, below) (DR) June 20, 1768–Nov. 12, 1846; Dec. 16, 1817–Dec. 19, 1820; Senate Dec. 10, 1821–27 (Republican).

Hiester, Joseph (DR) Nov. 18, 1752–June 10, 1832; Dec. 19, 1820–Dec. 16, 1823; House Dec. 1, 1797–1805 (Republican), 1815–Dec. 18, 1820.

Shulze, John Andrew (J) July 19, 1775–Nov. 18, 1852; Dec. 16, 1823–Dec. 15, 1829.

Wolf, George (J) Aug. 12, 1777–March 11, 1840; Dec. 15, 1829–Dec. 15, 1835; House Dec. 9, 1824–29 (no party).

Ritner, Joseph (AMas.) March 25, 1780–Oct. 16, 1869; Dec. 15, 1835–Jan. 15, 1839.

Porter, David Rittenhouse (D) Oct. 31, 1788–Aug. 6, 1867; Jan. 15, 1839–Jan. 21, 1845.

Shunk, Francis Rawn (son-in-law of William Findlay, above) (D) Aug. 7, 1788–July 20, 1848; Jan. 21, 1845–July 9, 1848.

Johnston, William Freame (W) Nov. 29, 1808–Oct. 25, 1872; July 26, 1848–Jan. 20, 1852.

Bigler, William (brother of John Bigler of Calif.) (D) Jan. 1, 1814–Aug. 9, 1880; Jan. 20, 1852–Jan. 16, 1855; Senate Jan. 14, 1856–61.

Pollock, James (W) Sept. 11, 1810–April 19, 1890; Jan. 16, 1855–Jan. 19, 1858; House April 5, 1844–49.

Packer, William Fisher (D) April 2, 1807–Sept. 27, 1870; Jan. 19, 1858–Jan. 15, 1861.

Curtin, Andrew Gregg (R) April 22, 1815–Oct. 7, 1894; Jan. 15, 1861–Jan. 15, 1867; House 1881–87 (Democrat).

Geary, John White (R) Dec. 30, 1819–Feb. 8, 1873; Jan. 15, 1867–Jan. 21, 1873.

Hartranft, John Frederick (R) Dec. 16, 1830–Oct. 17, 1889; Jan. 21, 1873–Jan. 18, 1879.

Hoyt, Henry Martyn (R) June 8, 1830–Dec. 1, 1892; Jan. 21, 1879–Jan. 16, 1883.

Pattison, Robert Emory (D) Dec. 8, 1850–Aug. 1, 1904; Jan. 16, 1883–Jan. 18, 1887, Jan. 20, 1891–Jan. 15, 1895.

Beaver, James Addams (R) Oct. 21, 1837–Jan. 31, 1914; Jan. 18, 1887–Jan. 20, 1891.

Pattison, Robert Emory (D) Jan. 20, 1891–Jan. 15, 1895 (for previous term see above).

Hastings, Daniel Hartman (R) Feb. 26, 1849–Jan. 9, 1903; Jan. 15, 1895–Jan. 17, 1899.

Stone, William Alexis (R) April 18, 1846–March 1, 1920; Jan. 17, 1899–Jan. 20, 1903; House 1891–Nov. 9, 1898.

Pennypacker, Samuel Whitaker (R) April 9, 1843–Sept. 2, 1916; Jan. 20, 1903–Jan. 15, 1907.

Stuart, Edwin Sydney (R) Dec. 28, 1853–March 21, 1937; Jan. 15, 1907–Jan. 17, 1911.

Tener, John Kinley (R) July 25, 1863–May 19, 1946; Jan. 17, 1911–Jan. 19, 1915; House 1909–Jan. 16, 1911.

Brumbaugh, Martin Grove (R) April 14, 1862–March 14, 1930; Jan. 19, 1915–Jan. 21, 1919.

Sproul, William Cameron (R) Sept. 16, 1870–March 21, 1928; Jan. 21, 1919–Jan. 16, 1923.

Pinchot, Gifford (R) Aug. 11, 1865–Oct. 4, 1946; Jan. 16, 1923–Jan. 18, 1927, Jan. 20, 1931–Jan. 15, 1935.

Fisher, John Stuchell (R) May 25, 1867–June 25, 1940; Jan. 18, 1927–Jan. 20, 1931.

Pinchot, Gifford (R) Jan. 20, 1931–Jan. 15, 1935 (for previous term see above).

Earle, George Howard III (D) Dec. 5, 1890–Dec. 30, 1974; Jan. 15, 1935–Jan. 17, 1939.

James, Arthur Horace (R) July 14, 1883–April 27, 1973; Jan. 17, 1939–Jan. 19, 1943.

Martin, Edward (R) Sept. 18, 1879–March 19, 1967; Jan. 19, 1943–Jan. 2, 1947; Senate 1947–59.

Bell, John Cromwell Jr. (R) Oct. 25, 1892–March 18, 1974; Jan. 2–Jan. 21, 1947.

Duff, James Henderson (R) Jan. 21, 1883–Dec. 20, 1969; Jan. 21, 1947–Jan. 16, 1951; Senate Jan. 18, 1951–57.

Fine, John Sydney (R) April 10, 1893–May 21, 1978; Jan. 16, 1951–Jan. 18, 1955.

Leader, George Michael (D) Jan. 17, 1918– ; Jan. 18, 1955–Jan. 20, 1959.

Lawrence, David Leo (D) June 18, 1889–Nov. 21, 1966; Jan. 20, 1959–Jan. 15, 1963.

Scranton, William Warren (R) July 19, 1917– ; Jan. 15, 1963–Jan. 17, 1967; House 1961–63.

Shafer, Raymond Philip (R) March 5, 1917– ; Jan. 17, 1967–Jan. 19, 1971.

Shapp, Milton Jerrold (D) June 25, 1912–Nov. 24, 1994; Jan. 19, 1971–Jan. 16, 1979.

Thornburgh, Richard Lewis (R) July 16, 1932– ; Jan. 16, 1979–Jan. 20, 1987; attorney general Aug. 12, 1988–Aug. 9, 1991.

Casey, Robert Patrick (D) Jan. 9, 1932–May 30, 2000; Jan. 20, 1987–Jan. 17, 1995.

Ridge, Thomas Joseph (R) Aug. 26, 1945– ; Jan. 17, 1995–Oct. 5, 2001; secretary of homeland security Jan. 24, 2003–Feb. 1, 2005.

Schweiker, Mark S. (R) Jan. 31, 1953– ; Oct. 5, 2001–Jan. 21, 2003.

Rendell, Edward G. (D) Jan. 5, 1944– ; Jan. 21, 2003– ; general chair Dem. Nat. Comm. 1999–2001.

Rhode Island

(Ratified the Constitution May 29, 1790)

Fenner, Arthur (father of James Fenner, below) (AF) Dec. 10, 1745–Oct. 15, 1805; May 5, 1790–Oct. 15, 1805.

Smith, Henry (DR) Feb. 10, 1766–June 28, 1818; Oct. 15, 1805–May 7, 1806.

Wilbour, Isaac (DR) April 25, 1763–Oct. 4, 1837; May 7, 1806–May 6, 1807; House 1807–09 (Republican).

Fenner, James (son of Arthur Fenner, above) (L&OW) Jan. 22, 1771–April 17, 1846; May 6, 1807–May 1, 1811 (Democratic Republican), May 5, 1824–May 4, 1831 (Democratic Republican), May 2, 1843–May 6, 1845; Senate 1805–Sept. 1807 (Republican).

Jones, William (F) Oct. 8, 1753–April 9, 1822; May 1, 1811–May 7, 1817.

Knight, Nehemiah Rice (DR) Dec. 31, 1780–April 18, 1854; May 7, 1817–Jan. 9, 1821; Senate Jan. 9, 1821–41 (Jan. 9, 1821–35 Republican, 1835–41 Whig).

Wilcox, Edward (DR) July 5, 1783–Sept. 7, 1838; Jan. 9–May 2, 1821.

Gibbs, William Channing (DR) Feb. 10, 1789–Feb. 24, 1871; May 2, 1821–May 5, 1824.

Fenner, James (L&OW) May 5, 1824–May 4, 1831 (Democratic Republican) (for previous term see above).

Arnold, Lemuel Hastings (great-great-uncle of Theodore Francis Green, below) (DR) Jan. 29, 1792–June 27, 1852; May 4, 1831–May 1, 1833; House 1845–47 (Whig).

Francis, John Brown (D) May 31, 1791–Aug. 9, 1864; May 1, 1833–May 2, 1838; Senate Jan. 25, 1844–45 (Whig).

Sprague, William (uncle of William Sprague, below) (W) Nov. 3, 1799–Oct. 19, 1856; May 2, 1838–May 1, 1839; House 1835–37; Senate Feb. 18, 1842–Jan. 17, 1844.

King, Samuel Ward (W) May 22, 1786–Jan. 20, 1851; May 2, 1839–May 2, 1843.

Fenner, James (L&OW) May 2, 1843–May 6, 1845 (for previous terms see above).

Jackson, Charles (LW) March 3, 1797–Jan. 21, 1876; May 6, 1845–May 6, 1846.

Diman, Byron (L&OW) Aug. 5, 1795–Aug. 1, 1865; May 6, 1846–May 4, 1847.

Harris, Elisha (father-in-law of Henry Howard, below) (W) 1791–Feb. 1, 1861; May 4, 1847–May 1, 1849.

Anthony, Henry Bowen (W) April 1, 1815–Sept. 2, 1884; May 1, 1849–May 6, 1851; Senate 1859–Sept. 2, 1884 (Republican); elected pres. pro tempore March 23, 1869, April 9, 1869, May 28, 1870, July 1, 1870, July 14, 1870, March 10, 1871, April 17, 1871, May 23, 1871, Dec. 21, 1871, Feb. 23, 1872, June 8, 1872, Dec. 4, 1872, Dec. 13, 1872, Dec. 20, 1872, Jan. 24, 1873, Jan. 23, 1875, Feb. 15, 1875.

Allen, Philip (D) Sept. 1, 1785–Dec. 16, 1865; May 6, 1851–July 20, 1853; Senate July 20, 1853–59.

Dimond, Francis M. (D) 1796–April 23, 1859; July 20, 1853–May 2, 1854.

Hoppin, William Warner (AW) Sept. 1, 1807–April 19, 1890; May 2, 1854–May 26, 1857.

Dyer, Elisha II (father of Elisha Dyer III, below) (R) July 20, 1811–May 17, 1890; May 26, 1857–May 31, 1859.

Turner, Thomas Goodwin (R) Oct. 24, 1810–Jan. 3, 1875; May 31, 1859–May 29, 1860.

Sprague, William (nephew of William Sprague, above, son-in-law of Salmon Portland Chase of Ohio) (U) Sept. 12, 1830–Sept. 11, 1915; May 29, 1860–March 3, 1863; Senate 1863–75 (Republican).

Cozzens, William Cole (Fus) Aug. 26, 1811–Dec. 17, 1876; March 3–May 26, 1863.

Smith, James Youngs (UR) Sept. 15, 1809–March 26, 1876; May 26, 1863–May 29, 1866.

Burnside, Ambrose Everett (R) May 23, 1824–Sept. 13, 1881; May 29, 1866–May 25, 1869; Senate 1875–Sept. 13, 1881.

Padelford, Seth (R) Oct. 3, 1807–Aug. 26, 1878; May 25, 1869–May 27, 1873.

Howard, Henry (son-in-law of Elisha Harris, above) (R) April 2, 1826–Sept. 22, 1905; May 27, 1873–May 25, 1875.

Lippitt, Henry (father of Charles Warren Lippitt, below) (R) Oct. 9, 1818–June 5, 1891; May 25, 1875–May 29, 1877.

Van Zandt, Charles Collins (R/Prohib.) Aug. 10, 1830–June 4, 1894; May 29, 1877–May 25, 1880.

Littlefield, Alfred Henry (R) April 2, 1829–Dec. 21, 1893; May 25, 1880–May 29, 1883.

Bourn, Augustus Osborn (R) Oct. 1, 1834–Jan. 28, 1925; May 29, 1883–May 26, 1885.

Wetmore, George Peabody (R) Aug. 2, 1846–Sept. 11, 1921; May 26, 1885–May 31, 1887; Senate 1895–1907, Jan. 22, 1908–13.

Davis, John William (D) March 7, 1826–Jan. 26, 1907; May 31, 1887–May 29, 1888, May 27, 1890–May 26, 1891.

Taft, Royal Chapin (R) Feb. 14, 1823–June 4, 1912; May 29, 1888–May 28, 1889.

Ladd, Herbert Warren (R) Oct. 15, 1843–Nov. 29, 1913; May 28, 1889–May 27, 1890, May 26, 1891–May 31, 1892.

Davis, John William (D) May 27, 1890–May 26, 1891 (for previous term see above).

Ladd, Herbert Warren (R) May 26, 1891–May 31, 1892 (for previous term see above).

Brown, Daniel Russell (R) March 28, 1848–Feb. 28, 1919; May 31, 1892–May 29, 1895.

Lippitt, Charles Warren (son of Henry Lippitt, above) (R) Oct. 8, 1846–April 4, 1924; May 29, 1895–May 25, 1897.

Dyer, Elisha III (son of Elisha Dyer II, above) (R) Nov. 29, 1839–Nov. 29, 1906; May 25, 1897–May 29, 1900.

Gregory, William (R) Aug. 3, 1849–Dec. 16, 1901; May 29, 1900–Dec. 16, 1901.

Kimball, Charles Dean (R) Sept. 13, 1859–Dec. 8, 1930; Dec. 16, 1901–Jan. 6, 1903.

Garvin, Lucius Fayette Clark (D) Nov. 13, 1841–Oct. 22, 1922; Jan. 6, 1903–Jan. 3, 1905.

Utter, George Herbert (R) July 24, 1854–Nov. 3, 1912; Jan. 3, 1905–Jan. 1, 1907; House 1911–Nov. 3, 1912.

Higgins, James Henry (D) Jan. 22, 1876–Sept. 16, 1927; Jan. 1, 1907–Jan. 5, 1909.

Pothier, Aram J. (R) July 26, 1854–Feb. 3, 1928; Jan. 5, 1909–Jan. 5, 1915, Jan. 6, 1925–Feb. 4, 1928.

Beeckman, Robert Livingston (R) April 15, 1866–Jan. 21, 1935; Jan. 5, 1915–Jan. 4, 1921.

San Souci, Emery John (R) July 24, 1857–Aug. 10, 1936; Jan. 4, 1921–Jan. 2, 1923.

Flynn, William Smith (D) Aug. 14, 1885–April 6, 1966; Jan. 2, 1923–Jan. 6, 1925.

Pothier, Aram J. (R) Jan. 6, 1925–Feb. 4, 1928 (for previous term see above).

Case, Norman Stanley (R) Oct. 11, 1888–Oct. 9, 1967; Feb. 4, 1928–Jan. 3, 1933.

Green, Theodore Francis (great-great-nephew of Lemuel Hastings Arnold, above) (D) Oct. 2, 1867–May 19, 1966; Jan. 3, 1933–Jan. 5, 1937; Senate 1937–61.

Quinn, Robert Emmet (D) April 2, 1894–May 20, 1975; Jan. 5, 1937–Jan. 3, 1939.

Vanderbilt, William Henry (R) Nov. 24, 1901–April 14, 1981; Jan. 3, 1939–Jan. 7, 1941.

McGrath, James Howard (D) Nov. 28, 1903–Sept. 2, 1966; Jan. 7, 1941–Oct. 6, 1945; Senate 1947–Aug. 23, 1949; chair Dem. Nat. Comm. 1947–49; attorney general Aug. 24, 1949–April 7, 1952.

Pastore, John Orlando (D) March 17, 1907–July 15, 2000; Oct. 6, 1945–Dec. 19, 1950; Senate Dec. 19, 1950–Dec. 28, 1976.

McKiernan, John Sammon (D) Oct. 15, 1911– ; Dec. 19, 1950–Jan. 2, 1951.

Roberts, Dennis Joseph (D) April 8, 1903–June 30, 1994; Jan. 2, 1951–Jan. 6, 1959.

Del Sesto, Christopher (R) March 10, 1907–Dec. 23, 1973; Jan. 6, 1959–Jan. 3, 1961.

Notte, John Anthony Jr. (D) May 3, 1909–March 7, 1983; Jan. 3, 1961–Jan. 1, 1963.

Chafee, John Hubbard (R) Oct. 22, 1922–Oct. 24, 1999; Jan. 1, 1963–Jan. 7, 1969; Senate Dec. 29, 1976–Oct. 24, 1999.

Licht, Frank (D) March 13, 1916–May 30, 1987; Jan. 7, 1969–Jan. 2, 1973.

Noel, Philip William (D) June 6, 1931– ; Jan. 2, 1973–Jan. 4, 1977.

Garrahy, John Joseph (D) Nov. 26, 1930– ; Jan. 4, 1977–Jan. 1, 1985.

DiPrete, Edward Daniel (R) July 8, 1934– ; Jan. 1, 1985–Jan. 1, 1991.

Sundlun, Bruce (D) Jan. 15, 1920– ; Jan. 1, 1991–Jan. 3, 1995.

Almond, Lincoln C. (R) June 16, 1936– ; Jan. 3, 1995–Jan. 7, 2003.

Carcieri, Don (R) Dec. 16, 1942– ; Jan. 7, 2003– .

South Carolina

(Ratified the Constitution May 23, 1788)

Pinckney, Thomas (F) Oct. 23, 1750–Nov. 2, 1828; Feb. 20, 1787–Jan. 26, 1789; House Nov. 23, 1797–1801.

Pinckney, Charles (father-in-law of Robert Young Hayne, below) (R) Oct. 26, 1757–Oct. 29, 1824; Jan. 26, 1789–Dec. 5, 1792, Dec. 8, 1796–Dec. 6, 1798, Dec. 9, 1806–Dec. 10, 1808; Cont. Cong. 1785–87; Senate Dec. 6, 1798–1801; House 1819–21.

Moultrie, William (F) Nov. 23, 1730–Sept. 27, 1805; Dec. 5, 1792–Dec. 17, 1794; Cont. Cong. (elected but did not attend) 1784.

Van der Horst, Arnoldus (F) March 21, 1748–Jan. 29, 1815; Dec. 17, 1794–Dec. 8, 1796.

Pinckney, Charles (DR) Dec. 8, 1796–Dec. 6, 1798 (for previous term see above).

Rutledge, Edward (brother-in-law of Henry Middleton, below) (F) Nov. 23, 1749–Jan. 23, 1800; Dec. 18, 1798–Jan. 23, 1800; Cont. Cong. 1774–76.

Drayton, John (DR) June 22, 1767–Nov. 27, 1822; Jan. 23, 1800–Dec. 8, 1802, Dec. 10, 1808–Dec. 8, 1810.

Richardson, James Burchill (uncle of John Peter Richardson II and Richard Irvine Manning I, below, great-uncle of John Peter Richardson III and John Laurence Manning, below, great-great-uncle of Richard Irvine Manning III, below) (DR) Oct. 28, 1770–April 28, 1836; Dec. 8, 1802–Dec. 7, 1804.

Hamilton, Paul (DR) Oct. 16, 1762–June 30, 1816; Dec. 7, 1804–Dec. 9, 1806; secretary of the navy May 15, 1809–Dec. 31, 1812.

Pinckney, Charles (DR) Dec. 9, 1806–Dec. 10, 1808 (for previous terms see above).

Drayton, John (DR) Dec. 10, 1808–Dec. 8, 1810 (for previous term see above).

Middleton, Henry (brother-in-law of Edward Rutledge, above) (R) Sept. 28, 1770–June 14, 1846; Dec. 10, 1810–Dec. 10, 1812; House 1815–19.

Alston, Joseph (son-in-law of Vice Pres. Aaron Burr, brother-in-law of John Lyde Wilson, below) (DR) 1779–Sept. 10, 1816; Dec. 10, 1812–Dec. 10, 1814.

Williams, David Rogerson (DR) March 8, 1776–Nov. 17, 1830; Dec. 10, 1814–Dec. 5, 1816; House 1805–09 (Republican), 1811–13 (Republican).

Pickens, Andrew (father of Francis Wilkinson Pickens, below) (DR) Nov. 13, 1779–July 1, 1838; Dec. 5, 1816–Dec. 8, 1818.

Geddes, John (DR) Dec. 25, 1777–March 4, 1828; Dec. 8, 1818–Dec. 7, 1820.

Bennett, Thomas (DR) Aug. 14, 1781–Jan. 30, 1865; Dec. 20, 1820–Dec. 7, 1822.

Wilson, John Lyde (brother-in-law of Joseph Alston, above) (DR) May 24, 1784–Feb. 12, 1849; Dec. 7, 1822–Dec. 3, 1824.

Manning, Richard Irvine (father of John Laurence Manning, below, grandfather of Richard Irvine Manning III, below, nephew of James Burchill Richardson, above, cousin of John Peter Richardson II, below, second cousin of John Peter Richardson III, below) (DR) May 1, 1789–May 1, 1836; Dec. 3, 1824–Dec. 9, 1826; House Dec. 8, 1834–May 1, 1836 (Jacksonian).

Taylor, John (DR) May 4, 1770–April 16, 1832; Dec. 9, 1826–Dec. 10, 1828; House 1807–Dec. 30, 1810 (Republican); Senate Dec. 31, 1810–Nov. 1816 (Republican).

Miller, Stephen Decatur (D) May 8, 1787–March 8, 1838; Dec. 10, 1828–Dec. 9, 1830; House Jan. 2, 1817–19 (no party); Senate 1831–March 2, 1833 (Nullifier).

Hamilton, James Jr. (SRD) May 8, 1786–Nov. 15, 1857; Dec. 9, 1830–Dec. 13, 1832; House Dec. 13, 1822–29 (no party).

Hayne, Robert Young (son-in-law of Charles Pinckney, above) (SRD) Nov. 10, 1791–Sept. 24, 1839; Dec. 13, 1832–Dec. 11, 1834; Senate 1823–Dec. 13, 1832 (1823–29 no party, 1829–Dec. 13, 1832 Jacksonian).

McDuffie, George (father-in-law of Wade Hampton, below) (SRD) Aug. 10, 1790–March 11, 1851; Dec. 11, 1834–Dec. 10, 1836; House 1821–34 (no party); Senate Dec. 23, 1842–Aug. 17, 1846 (Democrat).

Butler, Pierce Mason (SRD) April 11, 1798–Aug. 20, 1847; Dec. 10, 1836–Dec. 10, 1838.

Noble, Patrick (SRD) 1787–April 7, 1840; Dec. 10, 1838–April 7, 1840.

Henagan, Barnabas Kelet (D) June 7, 1798–Jan. 10, 1855; April 7–Dec. 10, 1840.

Richardson, John Peter II (father of John Peter Richardson III, below, nephew of James Burchill Richardson, above, cousin of Richard Irvine Manning I, above, second cousin of John Laurence Manning, above) (J) April 14, 1801–Jan. 24, 1864; Dec. 10, 1840–Dec. 8, 1842; House Dec. 19, 1836–39.

Hammond, James Henry (D) Nov. 15, 1807–Nov. 13, 1864; Dec. 8, 1842–Dec. 7, 1844; House 1835–Feb. 26, 1836 (Nullifier); Senate Dec. 7, 1857–Nov. 11, 1860 (Democrat).

Aiken, William (D) Jan. 28, 1806–Sept. 7, 1887; Dec. 7, 1844–Dec. 8, 1846; House 1851–57.

Johnson, David (D) Oct. 3, 1782–Jan. 7, 1855; Dec. 8, 1846–Dec. 12, 1848.

Seabrook, Whitemarsh Benjamin (D) June 30, 1792–April 16, 1855; Dec. 12, 1848–Dec. 13, 1850.

Means, John Hugh (SRD) Aug. 18, 1812–Aug. 29, 1862; Dec. 13, 1850–Dec. 9, 1852.

Manning, John Laurence (son of Richard Irvine Manning I, above, great-nephew of James Burchill Richardson, above, uncle of Richard Irvine Manning III, below, second cousin of John Peter Richardson II, above) (SRD) Jan. 29, 1816–Oct. 29, 1889; Dec. 9, 1852–Dec. 11, 1854.

Adams, James Hopkins (SRD) March 15, 1812–July 13, 1861; Dec. 11, 1854–Dec. 9, 1856.

Allston, Robert Francis Withers (D) April 21, 1801–April 7, 1864; Dec. 9, 1856–Dec. 10, 1858.

Gist, William Henry (SRD) Aug. 20, 1809–Sept. 30, 1874; Dec. 10, 1858–Dec. 17, 1860.

Pickens, Francis Wilkinson (son of Andrew Pickens, above) (SRD) April 7, 1805–Jan. 25, 1869; Dec. 14, 1860–Dec. 17, 1862; House Dec. 8, 1834–43 (Dec. 8, 1834–39 Nullifier, 1839–43 Democrat).

Bonham, Milledge Luke (Confed. D) Dec. 25, 1813–Aug. 27, 1890; Dec. 17, 1862–Dec. 20, 1864; House 1857–Dec. 21, 1860 (Democrat).

McGrath, Andrew Gordon (Confed. D) Feb. 8, 1813–April 9, 1893; Dec. 20, 1864–May 25, 1865.

Perry, Benjamin Franklin (UD) Nov. 20, 1805–Dec. 3, 1886; (Provisional) June 30–Nov. 29, 1865.

Orr, James Lawrence (R) May 12, 1822–May 5, 1873; Nov. 29, 1865–July 6, 1868; House 1849–59 (Democrat); Speaker Dec. 7, 1857–59.

Scott, Robert Kingston (R) July 3, 1826–Aug. 13, 1900; July 9, 1868–Dec. 7, 1872.

Moses, Franklin J. Jr. (R) 1838–Dec. 11, 1906; Dec. 7, 1872–Dec. 1, 1874.

Chamberlain, Daniel Henry (R) June 23, 1835–April 14, 1907; Dec. 1, 1874–April 10, 1877.

Hampton, Wade (son-in-law of George McDuffie, above) (D) March 28, 1818–April 11, 1902; Dec. 14, 1876–Feb. 26, 1879; Senate 1879–91.

Simpson, William Dunlap (D) Oct. 27, 1823–Dec. 26, 1890; Feb. 26, 1879–Sept. 1, 1880.

Jeter, Thomas Bothwell (D) Oct. 13, 1827–May 20, 1883; Sept. 1–Nov. 30, 1880.

Hagood, Johnson (D) Feb. 21, 1829–Jan. 4, 1898; Nov. 30, 1880–Dec. 5, 1882.

Thompson, Hugh Smith (D) Jan. 24, 1836–Nov. 20, 1904; Dec. 5, 1882–July 10, 1886.

Sheppard, John Calhoun (D) July 5, 1850–Oct. 17, 1931; July 10–Nov. 30, 1886.

Richardson, John Peter III (son of John Peter Richardson II, above, great-nephew of James Burchill Richardson, above, second cousin of Richard Irvine Manning I, above) (D) Sept. 25, 1831–July 6, 1899; Nov. 30, 1886–Dec. 4, 1890.

Tillman, Benjamin Ryan (D) Aug. 11, 1847–July 3, 1918; Dec. 4, 1890–Dec. 4, 1894; Senate 1895–July 3, 1918.

Evans, John Gary (D) Oct. 15, 1863–June 27, 1942; Dec. 4, 1894–Jan. 18, 1897.

Ellerbe, William Haselden (D) April 7, 1862–June 2, 1899; Jan. 18, 1897–June 2, 1899.

McSweeney, Miles Benjamin (D) April 18, 1855–Sept. 29, 1909; June 2, 1899–Jan. 20, 1903.

Heyward, Duncan Clinch (D) June 24, 1864–Jan. 23, 1943; Jan. 20, 1903–Jan. 15, 1907.

Ansel, Martin Frederick (D) Dec. 12, 1850–Aug. 24, 1945; Jan. 15, 1907–Jan. 17, 1911.

Blease, Coleman Livingston (D) Oct. 8, 1868–Jan. 19, 1942; Jan. 17, 1911–Jan. 14, 1915; Senate 1925–31.

Smith, Charles Aurelius (D) Jan. 22, 1861–April 1, 1916; Jan. 14–Jan. 19, 1915.

Manning, Richard Irvine III (grandson of Richard Irvine Manning I, above, nephew of John Laurence Manning, above, great-great-nephew of James Burchill Richardson, above) (D) Aug. 15, 1859–Sept. 11, 1931; Jan. 19, 1915–Jan. 21, 1919.

Cooper, Robert Archer (D) June 12, 1874–Aug. 7, 1953; Jan. 21, 1919–May 20, 1922.

Harvey, Wilson Godfrey (D) Sept. 8, 1866–Oct. 7, 1932; May 20, 1922–Jan. 16, 1923.

McLeod, Thomes Gordon (D) Dec. 17, 1868–Dec. 11, 1932; Jan. 16, 1923–Jan. 18, 1927.

Richards, John Gardiner (D) Sept. 11, 1864–Oct. 9, 1941; Jan. 18, 1927–Jan. 20, 1931.

Blackwood, Ibra Charles (D) Nov. 21, 1878–Feb. 12, 1936; Jan. 20, 1931–Jan. 15, 1935.

Johnston, Olin Dewitt Talmadge (D) Nov. 18, 1896–April 18, 1965; Jan. 15, 1935–Jan. 17, 1939, Jan. 19, 1943–Jan. 2, 1945; Senate 1945–April 18, 1965.

Maybank, Burnet Rhett (D) March 7, 1899–Sept. 1, 1954; Jan. 17, 1939–Nov. 4, 1941; Senate Nov. 5, 1941–Sept. 1, 1954.

Harley, Joseph Emile (D) Sept. 14, 1880–Feb. 27, 1942; Nov. 4, 1941–Feb. 27, 1942.

Jeffries, Richard Manning (D) Feb. 27, 1889–April 20, 1964; March 2, 1942–Jan. 19, 1943.

Johnston, Olin Dewitt Talmadge (D) Jan. 19, 1943–Jan. 2, 1945 (for previous term see above).

Williams, Ransome Judson (D) Jan. 4, 1892–Jan. 7, 1970; Jan. 2, 1945–Jan. 21, 1947.

Thurmond, James Strom (D) Dec. 5, 1902–June 26, 2003; Jan. 21, 1947–Jan. 16, 1951; Senate Dec. 24, 1954–April 4, 1956, Nov. 7, 1956–2003 (Sept. 16, 1964–2003 Republican); elected pres. pro tempore 1981–87, 1995–June 6, 2001.

Byrnes, James Francis (D) May 2, 1879–April 9, 1972; Jan. 16, 1951–Jan. 18, 1955; House 1911–25; Senate 1931–July 8, 1941; assoc. justice July 8, 1941–Oct. 3, 1942; secretary of state July 3, 1945–Jan. 21, 1947.

Timmerman, George Bell Jr. (D) Aug. 11, 1912–Nov. 29, 1994; Jan. 18, 1955–Jan. 20, 1959.

Hollings, Ernest Frederick (D) Jan. 1, 1922– ; Jan. 20, 1959–Jan. 15, 1963; Senate Nov. 9, 1966–2005.

Russell, Donald Stuart (D) Feb. 22, 1906–Feb. 22, 1998; Jan. 15, 1963–April 22, 1965; Senate April 22, 1965–Nov. 8, 1966.

McNair, Robert Evander (D) Dec. 14, 1923– ; April 22, 1965–Jan. 19, 1971.

West, John Carl (D) Aug. 27, 1922–March 21, 2004; Jan. 19, 1971–Jan. 21, 1975.

Edwards, James Burrows (R) June 24, 1927– ; Jan. 21, 1975–Jan. 10, 1979; secretary of energy Jan. 23, 1981–Nov. 5, 1982.

Riley, Richard Wilson (D) Jan. 2, 1933– ; Jan. 10, 1979–Jan. 14, 1987; secretary of education Jan. 22, 1993–Jan. 20, 2001.

Campbell, Carroll Ashmore Jr. (R) July 24, 1940–Jan. 11, 1995; Jan. 14, 1987–Jan. 11, 1995; House 1979–87.

Beasley, David (R) Feb. 26, 1957– ; Jan. 11, 1995–Jan. 13, 1999.

Hodges, Jim (D) Nov. 19, 1956– ; Jan. 13, 1999–Jan. 15, 2003.

Sanford, Marshall Clement Jr. "Mark" (R) May 28, 1960– ; Jan. 15, 2003– ; House 1995–2001.

South Dakota

(Became a state Nov. 2, 1889)

Melette, Arthur Calvin (R) June 23, 1842–May 25, 1896; Nov. 2, 1889–Jan. 3, 1893.

Sheldon, Charles Henry (R) Sept. 12, 1840–Oct. 20, 1898; Jan. 3, 1893–Jan. 5, 1897.

Lee, Andrew Erickson (uncle of Carl Gunderson, below) (P) March 18, 1847–March 19, 1934; Jan. 5, 1897–Jan. 8, 1901.

Herreid, Charles Nelson (R) Oct. 20, 1857–July 6, 1928; Jan. 8, 1901–Jan. 3, 1905.

Elrod, Samuel Harrison (R) May 1, 1856–July 13, 1935; Jan. 3, 1905–Jan. 8, 1907.

Crawford, Coe Isaac (R) Jan. 14, 1858–April 25, 1944; Jan. 8, 1907–Jan. 5, 1909; Senate 1909–15.

Vessey, Robert Scadden (R) May 16, 1858–Oct. 18, 1929; Jan. 5, 1909–Jan. 7, 1913.

Byrne, Frank Michael (R) Oct. 23, 1858–Dec. 24, 1927; Jan. 7, 1913–Jan. 2, 1917.

Norbeck, Peter (R) Aug. 27, 1870–Dec. 20, 1936; Jan. 2, 1917–Jan. 4, 1921; Senate 1921–Dec. 20, 1936.

McMaster, William Henry (R) May 10, 1877–Sept. 14, 1968; Jan. 4, 1921–Jan. 6, 1925; Senate 1925–31.

Gunderson, Carl (nephew of Andrew Erickson Lee, above) (R) June 20, 1864–Feb. 26, 1933; Jan. 6, 1925–Jan. 4, 1927.

Bulow, William John (D) Jan. 13, 1869–Feb. 26, 1960; Jan. 4, 1927–Jan. 6, 1931; Senate 1931–43.

Green, Warren Everett (R) March 10, 1870–April 27, 1945; Jan. 6, 1931–Jan. 3, 1933.

Berry, Thomas Matthew (D) April 23, 1879–Oct. 30, 1951; Jan. 3, 1933–Jan. 5, 1937.

Jensen, Leslie (R) Sept. 15, 1892–Dec. 14, 1964; Jan. 5, 1937–Jan. 3, 1939.

Bushfield, Harlan John (R) Aug. 6, 1882–Sept. 27, 1948; Jan. 3, 1939–Jan. 5, 1943; Senate 1943–Sept. 27, 1948.

Sharpe, Merrell Quentin (R) Jan. 11, 1888–Jan. 22, 1962; Jan. 5, 1943–Jan. 7, 1947.

Mickelson, George Theodore (father of George Speaker Mickelson, below) (R) July 23, 1903–Feb. 28, 1965; Jan. 7, 1947–Jan. 2, 1951.

Anderson, Sigurd (R) Jan. 22, 1904–Dec. 21, 1990; Jan. 2, 1951–Jan. 4, 1955.

Foss, Joseph Jacob (R) April 17, 1915–Dec. 2, 2003; Jan. 4, 1955–Jan. 6, 1959.

Herseth, Ralph E. (D) July 2, 1909–Jan. 24, 1969; Jan. 6, 1959–Jan. 3, 1961.

Gubbrud, Archie M. (R) Dec. 31, 1910–April 1982; Jan. 3, 1961–Jan. 5, 1965.

Boe, Nils Andreas (R) Sept. 10, 1913–July 30, 1992; Jan. 5, 1965–Jan. 7, 1969.

Farrar, Frank Leroy (R) April 2, 1929– ; Jan. 7, 1969–Jan. 5, 1971.

Kneip, Richard Francis (D) Jan. 7, 1933–March 9, 1987; Jan. 5, 1971–July 24, 1978.

Wollman, Harvey L. (D) May 14, 1935– ; July 24, 1978–Jan. 1, 1979.

Janklow, William John (R) Sept. 13, 1939– ; Jan. 1, 1979–Jan. 6, 1987, Jan. 4, 1995–Jan. 11, 2003; House 2003–Jan. 20, 2004.

Mickelson, George Speaker (son of George Theodore Mickelson, above) (R) Jan. 31, 1941–April 19, 1993; Jan. 6, 1987–April 19, 1993.

Miller, Walter Dale (R) Oct. 5, 1925– ; April 20, 1993–Jan. 4, 1995.

Janklow, William John (R) Jan. 4, 1995–Jan. 11, 2003 (for previous term see above).

Rounds, M. Michael "Mike" (R) Oct. 24, 1954– ; Jan. 11, 2003– .

Tennessee

(Became a state June 1, 1796)

Sevier, John (DR) Sept. 23, 1745–Sept. 24, 1815; March 30, 1796–Sept. 23, 1801, Sept. 23, 1803–Sept. 19, 1809; House June 16, 1790–91 (no party N.C.), 1811–Sept. 24, 1815 (Republican Tenn.).

Roane, Archibald (DR) 1760–Jan. 18, 1819; Sept. 23, 1801–Sept. 23, 1803.

Sevier, John (DR) Sept. 23, 1803–Sept. 19, 1809 (for previous term see above).

Blount, William (great-great-grandfather of Harry Hill McAlister, below) (DR) April 18, 1768–Sept. 10, 1835; Sept. 20, 1809–Sept. 27, 1815.

McMinn, Joseph (DR) June 27, 1758–Nov. 17, 1824; Sept. 27, 1815–Oct. 1, 1821.

Carroll, William (D) March 3, 1788–March 22, 1844; Oct. 1, 1821–Oct. 1, 1827 (Democratic Republican), Oct. 1, 1829–Oct. 12, 1835.

Houston, Samuel (father of Rep. Andrew Jackson Houston, cousin of Rep. David Hubbard) (D) March 2, 1793–July 26, 1863; Oct. 1, 1827–April 16, 1829, Dec. 21, 1859–March 16, 1861 (Texas); House 1823–27 (no party); Senate Feb. 21, 1846–59 (Democrat Texas).

Hall, William (DR) Feb. 11, 1775–Oct. 7, 1856; April 16–Oct. 1, 1829; House 1831–33 (Jacksonian).

Carroll, William (D) Oct. 1, 1829–Oct. 12, 1835 (for previous term see above).

Cannon, Newton (W) May 22, 1781–Sept. 16, 1841; Oct. 12, 1835–Oct. 14, 1839; House Sept. 16, 1814–17 (Republican), 1819–23 (Republican).

Polk, James Knox (brother of Rep. William Hawkins Polk) (D) Nov. 2, 1795–June 15, 1849; Oct. 14, 1839–Oct. 15, 1841; House 1825–39 (1825–27 no party, 1827–37 Jacksonian, 1837–39 Democrat); Speaker Dec. 7, 1835–37, Sept. 4, 1837–39; president 1845–49.

Jones, James Chamberlain (W) April 20, 1809–Oct. 29, 1859; Oct. 15, 1841–Oct. 14, 1845; Senate 1851–57.

Brown, Aaron Venable (D) Aug. 15, 1795–March 8, 1859; Oct. 14, 1845–Oct. 16, 1847; House 1839–45; postmaster general March 7, 1857–March 8, 1859.

Brown, Neill Smith (brother of John Calvin Brown, below) (W) April 18, 1810–Jan. 30, 1886; Oct. 17, 1847–Oct. 16, 1849.

Trousdale, William (D) Sept. 23, 1790–March 27, 1872; Oct. 16, 1849–Oct. 16, 1851.

Campbell, William Bowen (W) Feb. 1, 1807–Aug. 19, 1867; Oct. 16, 1851–Oct. 16, 1853; House 1837–43, July 24, 1866–67 (Unionist).

Johnson, Andrew (father-in-law of Sen. David Trotter Patterson) (D) Dec. 29, 1808–July 31, 1875; Oct. 17, 1853–Nov. 3, 1857, (Military) March 12, 1862–March 4, 1865; House 1843–53 (Democrat); Senate Oct. 8, 1857–March 4, 1862 (Democrat), March 4–July 31, 1875 (Republican); vice president March 4–April 15, 1865 (Republican); president April 15, 1865–69 (Republican).

Harris, Isham Green (D) Feb. 10, 1818–July 8, 1897; Nov. 3, 1857–March 12, 1862; House 1849–53; Senate 1877–July 8, 1897; elected pres. pro tempore March 22, 1893, Jan. 10, 1895.

Johnson, Andrew (R) (Military) March 12, 1862–March 4, 1865 (for previous term see above).

East, Edward Hazzard (Prohib.) Oct. 1, 1830–Nov. 12, 1904; March 4–April 5, 1865.

Brownlow, William Gannaway (R) Aug. 29, 1805–April 29, 1877; April 5, 1865–Feb. 25, 1869; Senate 1869–75.

Senter, Dewitt Clinton (CR) March 26, 1830–June 14, 1898; Feb. 25, 1869–Oct. 10, 1871.

Brown, John Calvin (brother of Neill Smith Brown, father-in-law of Benton McMillin) (D) Jan. 6, 1827–Aug. 17, 1889; Oct. 10, 1871–Jan. 18, 1875.

Porter, James Davis Jr. (D) Dec. 7, 1828–May 18, 1912; Jan. 18, 1875–Feb. 16, 1879.

Marks, Albert Smith (D) Oct. 16, 1836–Nov. 4, 1891; Feb. 16, 1879–Jan. 17, 1881.

Hawkins, Alvin (R) Dec. 2, 1821–April 27, 1905; Jan. 17, 1881–Jan. 15, 1883.

Bate, William Brimage (D) Oct. 7, 1826–March 9, 1905; Jan. 15, 1883–Jan. 17, 1887; Senate 1887–March 9, 1905.

Taylor, Robert Love (brother of Alfred Alexander Taylor, below) (D) July 31, 1850–March 31, 1912; Jan. 17, 1887–Jan. 19, 1891, Jan. 21, 1897–Jan. 16, 1899; House 1879–81; Senate 1907–March 31, 1912.

Buchanan, John Price (D) Oct. 24, 1837–May 14, 1930; Jan. 19, 1891–Jan. 16, 1893.

Turney, Peter (D) Sept. 27, 1827–Oct. 28, 1903; Jan. 16, 1893–Jan. 21, 1897.

Taylor, Robert Love (D) Jan. 21, 1897–Jan. 16, 1899 (for previous term see above).

McMillin, Benton (son-in-law of John Calvin Brown, above) (D) Sept. 11, 1845–Jan. 8, 1933; Jan. 16, 1899–Jan. 19, 1903; House 1879–Jan. 6, 1899.

Frazier, James Beriah (D) Oct. 18, 1856–March 28, 1937; Jan. 19, 1903–March 21, 1905; Senate March 21, 1905–11.

Cox, John Isaac (D) Nov. 23, 1855–Sept. 5, 1946; March 21, 1905–Jan. 17, 1907.

Patterson, Malcolm Rice (D) June 7, 1861–March 8, 1935; Jan. 17, 1907–Jan. 26, 1911; House 1901–Nov. 5, 1906.

Hooper, Ben Walker (R) Oct. 13, 1870–April 18, 1957; Jan. 26, 1911–Jan. 17, 1915.

Rye, Thomas Clarke (D) June 2, 1863–Sept. 12, 1953; Jan. 17, 1915–Jan. 15, 1919.

Roberts, Albert Houston (D) July 4, 1868–June 25, 1946; Jan. 15, 1919–Jan. 15, 1921.

Taylor, Alfred Alexander (brother of Robert Love Taylor, above) (R) Aug. 6, 1848–Nov. 25, 1931; Jan. 15, 1921–Jan. 16, 1923; House 1889–95.

Peay, Austin III (D) June 1, 1876–Oct. 2, 1927; Jan. 16, 1923–Oct. 2, 1927.

Horton, Henry Hollis (D) Feb. 17, 1866–July 2, 1934; Oct. 3, 1927–Jan. 17, 1933.

McAlister, Harry Hill (great-great-grandson of William Blount, above) (D) July 15, 1875–Oct. 30, 1959; Jan. 17, 1933–Jan. 15, 1937.

Browning, Gordon Weaver (D) Nov. 22, 1889–May 23, 1976; Jan. 15, 1937–Jan. 16, 1939, Jan. 17, 1949–Jan. 15, 1953; House 1923–35.

Cooper, William Prentice (D) Sept. 28, 1895–May 18, 1969; Jan. 16, 1939–Jan. 16, 1945.

McCord, James Nance (D) March 17, 1879–Sept. 2, 1968; Jan. 16, 1945–Jan. 17, 1949; House 1943–45.

Browning, Gordon Weaver (D) Jan. 17, 1949–Jan. 15, 1953 (for previous term see above).

Clement, Frank Goad (D) June 2, 1920–Nov. 4, 1969; Jan. 15, 1953–Jan. 16, 1959, Jan. 15, 1963–Jan. 16, 1967.

Ellington, Earl Buford (D) June 27, 1907–April 3, 1972; Jan. 19, 1959–Jan. 15, 1963, Jan. 16, 1967–Jan. 16, 1971.

Clement, Frank Goad (D) Jan. 15, 1963–Jan. 16, 1967 (for previous term see above).

Ellington, Earl Buford (D) Jan. 16, 1967–Jan. 16, 1971 (for previous term see above).

Dunn, Bryant Winfield Culberson (R) July 1, 1927– ; Jan. 16, 1971–Jan. 18, 1975.

Blanton, Leonard Ray (D) April 10, 1930–Nov. 22, 1996; Jan. 18, 1975–Jan. 17, 1979; House 1967–73.

Alexander, Lamar (R) July 3, 1940– ; Jan. 17, 1979–Jan. 17, 1987; secretary of education March 22, 1991–Jan. 20, 1993; Senate 2003–.

McWherter, Ned Ray (D) Oct. 15, 1930– ; Jan. 17, 1987–Jan. 21, 1995.

Sundquist, Donald Kenneth (R) March 15, 1936– ; Jan. 21, 1995–Jan. 18, 2003.

Bredesen, Phil (D) Nov. 21, 1943– ; Jan. 18, 2003– .

Texas

(Became a state Dec. 29, 1845)

Henderson, James Pinckney (D) March 31, 1808–June 4, 1858; Feb. 19, 1846–Dec. 21, 1847; Senate Nov. 9, 1857–June 4, 1858.

Wood, George Thomas (D) March 12, 1795–Sept. 3, 1858; Dec. 21, 1847–Dec. 21, 1849.

Bell, Peter Hansbrough (D) May 12, 1812–March 8, 1898; Dec. 21, 1849–Nov. 23, 1853; House 1853–57.

Henderson, James Wilson (D) Aug. 15, 1817–Aug. 30, 1880; Nov. 23–Dec. 21, 1853.

Pease, Elisha Marshall (D) Jan. 3, 1812–Aug. 26, 1883; Dec. 21, 1853–Dec. 21, 1857, Aug. 8, 1867–Sept. 30, 1869.

Runnels, Hardin Richard (nephew of Hiram George Runnels of Miss.) (D) Aug. 30, 1820–Dec. 25, 1873; Dec. 21, 1857–Dec. 21, 1859.

Houston, Samuel (father of Rep. Andrew Jackson Houston, cousin of Rep. David Hubbard) (D) March 2, 1793–July 26, 1863; Dec. 21, 1859–March 16, 1861, Oct. 1, 1827–April 16, 1829 (Tenn.); House 1823–27 (no party Tenn.); Senate Feb. 21, 1846–59 (Democrat).

Clark, Edward (son of John Clark of Ga.) (D) April 1, 1815–May 4, 1880; March 16–Nov. 7, 1861.

Lubbock, Francis Richard (D) Oct. 16, 1815–June 22, 1905; Nov. 7, 1861–Nov. 5, 1863.

Murrah, Pendleton (D) 1824–Aug. 4, 1865; Nov. 5, 1863–June 11, 1865.

Stockdale, Fletcher S. (D) 1823–1902; June 11–June 16, 1865.

Hamilton, Andrew Jackson (ID) Jan. 28, 1815–April 11, 1875; 1862–65 (Military), June 17, 1865–Aug. 9, 1866 (Provisional); House 1859–61.

Throckmorton, James Webb (C) Feb. 1, 1825–April 21, 1894; Aug. 9, 1866–Aug. 8, 1867; House 1875–79, 1883–87.

Pease, Elisha Marshall (D) Aug. 8, 1867–Sept. 30, 1869 (for previous term see above).

Davis, Edmund Jackson (R) Oct. 2, 1827–Feb. 7, 1883; Jan. 8, 1870–Jan. 15, 1874.

Coke, Richard (D) March 13, 1829–May 14, 1897; Jan. 15, 1874–Dec. 1, 1876; Senate 1877–95.

Hubbard, Richard Bennett (D) Nov. 1, 1832–July 12, 1901; Dec. 1, 1876–Jan. 21, 1879.

Roberts, Oran Milo (D) July 9, 1815–May 19, 1898; Jan. 21, 1879–Jan. 16, 1883.

Ireland, John (D) Jan. 21, 1827–March 5, 1896; Jan. 16, 1883–Jan. 18, 1887.

Ross, Lawrence Sullivan "Sul" (D) Sept. 27, 1838–Jan. 3, 1898; Jan. 18, 1887–Jan. 20, 1891.

Hogg, James Stephen (D) March 24, 1851–March 3, 1906; Jan. 20, 1891–Jan. 15, 1895.

Culberson, Charles Allen (D) June 10, 1855–March 19, 1925; Jan. 15, 1895–Jan. 17, 1899; Senate 1899–1923.

Sayers, Joseph Draper (D) Sept. 23, 1841–May 15, 1929; Jan. 17, 1899–Jan. 20, 1903; House 1885–Jan. 16, 1899.

Lanham, Samuel Willis Tucker (D) July 4, 1846–July 29, 1908; Jan. 20, 1903–Jan. 15, 1907; House 1883–93, 1897–Jan. 15, 1903.

Campbell, Thomas Mitchell (D) April 22, 1856–April 1, 1923; Jan. 15, 1907–Jan. 17, 1911.

Colquitt, Oscar Branch (D) Dec. 16, 1861–March 8, 1940; Jan. 17, 1911–Jan. 19, 1915.

Ferguson, James Edward "Pa" (husband of Miriam Amanda "Ma" Ferguson, below) (D) Aug. 31, 1871–Sept. 21, 1944; Jan. 19, 1915–Aug. 25, 1917.

Hobby, William Pettus (D) March 26, 1878–June 7, 1964; Aug. 25, 1917–Jan. 18, 1921.

Neff, Patrick Morris (D) Nov. 26, 1871–Jan. 20, 1952; Jan. 18, 1921–Jan. 20, 1925.

Ferguson, Miriam Amanda "Ma" (wife of James Edward "Pa" Ferguson, above) (D) June 13, 1875–June 25, 1961; Jan. 20, 1925–Jan. 18, 1927, Jan. 17, 1933–Jan. 15, 1935.

Moody, Daniel J. (D) June 1, 1893–May 22, 1966; Jan. 18, 1927–Jan. 20, 1931.

Sterling, Ross Shaw (D) Feb. 11, 1875–March 25, 1949; Jan. 20, 1931–Jan. 17, 1933.

Ferguson, Miriam Amanda "Ma" (D) Jan. 17, 1933–Jan. 15, 1935 (for previous term see above).

Allred, James V. (D) March 29, 1889–Sept. 24, 1959; Jan. 15, 1935–Jan. 17, 1939.

O'Daniel, Wilbert Lee "Pappy" (D) March 11, 1890–May 11, 1969; Jan. 17, 1939–Aug. 4, 1941; Senate Aug, 4, 1941–49.

Stevenson, Coke Robert (D) March 20, 1888–June 28, 1975; Aug. 4, 1941–Jan. 21, 1947.

Jester, Beauford Halbert (D) Jan. 12, 1893–July 11, 1949; Jan. 21, 1947–July 11, 1949.

Shivers, Allan (D) Oct. 5, 1907–Jan. 14, 1985; July 11, 1949–Jan. 15, 1957.

Daniel, Price Marion (D) Oct. 10, 1910–Aug. 25, 1988; Jan. 15, 1957–Jan. 15, 1963; Senate 1953–Jan. 14, 1957.

Connally, John Bowden (D) Feb. 27, 1917–June 15, 1993; Jan. 15, 1963–Jan. 21, 1969; secretary of the Treasury Feb. 11, 1971–June 12, 1972.

Smith, Preston Earnest (D) March 8, 1912–Oct. 18, 2003; Jan. 21, 1969–Jan. 16, 1973.

Briscoe, Dolph Jr. (D) April 23, 1923– ; Jan. 16, 1973–Jan. 16, 1979.

Clements, William Perry Jr. (R) April 13, 1917– ; Jan. 16, 1979–Jan. 18, 1983, Jan. 20, 1987–Jan. 15, 1991.

White, Mark (D) March 17, 1940– ; Jan. 18, 1983–Jan. 20, 1987.

Clements, William Perry Jr. (R) Jan. 20, 1987–Jan. 15, 1991 (for previous term see above).

Richards, Dorothy "Ann" Willis (D) Sept. 1, 1933– ; Jan. 15, 1991–Jan. 17, 1995.

Bush, George W. (son of Pres. George Herbert Walker Bush, brother of John Ellis "Jeb" Bush of Fla.) (R) July 6, 1946– ; Jan. 17, 1995–Dec. 20, 2000; president 2001– .

Perry, Rick (R) March 4, 1950– ; Dec. 21, 2000– .

Utah

(Became a state Jan. 4, 1896)

Wells, Heber Manning (R) Aug. 11, 1859–March 12, 1938; Jan. 6, 1896–Jan. 2, 1905.

Cutler, John Christopher (R) Feb. 5, 1846–July 30, 1928; Jan. 2, 1905–Jan. 4, 1909.

Spry, William (R) Jan. 11, 1864–April 21, 1929; Jan. 4, 1909–Jan. 1, 1917.

Bamberger, Simon (D) Feb. 27, 1846–Oct. 6, 1926; Jan. 1, 1917–Jan. 3, 1921.

Mabey, Charles Rendell (R) Oct. 4, 1877–April 26, 1959; Jan. 3, 1921–Jan. 5, 1925.

Dern, George Henry (D) Sept. 8, 1872–Aug. 27, 1936; Jan. 5, 1925–Jan. 2, 1933; secretary of war March 4, 1933–Aug. 27, 1936.

Blood, Henry Hooper (D) Oct. 1, 1872–June 19, 1942; Jan. 2, 1933–Jan. 6, 1941.

Maw, Herbert Brown (D) March 11, 1893–Nov. 17, 1990; Jan. 6, 1941–Jan. 3, 1949.

Lee, Joseph Bracken (R) Jan. 7, 1899–Oct. 20, 1996; Jan. 3, 1949–Jan. 7, 1957.

Clyde, George Dewey (R) July 21, 1898–April 2, 1972; Jan. 7, 1957–Jan. 4, 1965.

Rampton, Calvin Lewellyn (D) Nov. 6, 1913– ; Jan. 4, 1965–Jan. 3, 1977.

Matheson, Scott Milne (D) Jan. 8, 1929–Oct. 7, 1990; Jan. 3, 1977–Jan. 7, 1985.

Bangerter, Norman Howard (R) Jan. 4, 1933– ; Jan. 7, 1985–Jan. 3, 1993.

Leavitt, Michael Okerlund (R) Feb. 11, 1951– ; Jan. 3, 1993–Nov. 5, 2003; secretary of health and human services Jan. 26, 2005– .

Walker, Olene S. (R) Nov. 15, 1930– ; Nov. 5, 2003–Jan. 3, 2005.

Huntsman, Jon M. Jr. (R) March 26, 1960– ; Jan. 3, 2005– .

Vermont

(Became a state March 4, 1791)

Chittenden, Thomas (father of Martin Chittenden, below, father-in-law of Jonas Galusha, below) Jan. 6, 1730–Aug. 25, 1797; March 4, 1791–Aug. 25, 1797.

Brigham, Paul (DR) Jan. 6, 1746–June 15, 1824; Aug. 25–Oct. 16, 1797.

Tichenor, Isaac (F) Feb. 8, 1754–Dec. 11, 1838; Oct. 1797–Oct. 9, 1807, Oct. 17, 1808–Oct. 14, 1809; Senate Oct. 18, 1796–Oct. 1797, 1815–21.

Smith, Israel (DR) April 4, 1759–Dec. 2, 1810; Oct. 9, 1807–Oct. 14, 1808; House Oct. 17, 1791–97 (no party), 1801–03 (no party); Senate 1803–Oct. 1, 1807 (Republican).

Tichenor, Isaac (F) Oct. 17, 1808–Oct. 14, 1809 (for previous term see above).

Galusha, Jonas (son-in-law of Thomas Chittenden, above, brother-in-law of Martin Chittenden, below) (DR) Feb. 11, 1753–Sept. 24, 1834; Oct. 14, 1809–Oct. 23, 1813, Oct. 14, 1815–Oct. 13, 1820.

Chittenden, Martin (son of Thomas Chittenden, above, brother-in-law of Jonas Galusha, above) (F) March 12, 1763–Sept. 5, 1840; Oct. 23, 1813–Oct. 14, 1815; House 1803–13.

Galusha, Jonas (DR) Oct. 14, 1815–Oct. 13, 1820 (for previous term see above).

Skinner, Richard (DR) May 30, 1778–May 23, 1833; Oct. 13, 1820–Oct. 10, 1823; House 1813–15 (Republican).

Van Ness, Cornelius P. (DR) Jan. 26, 1782–Dec. 15, 1852; Oct. 10, 1823–Oct. 13, 1826.

Butler, Ezra (DR) Sept. 24, 1763–July 12, 1838; Oct. 13, 1826–Oct. 10, 1828; House 1813–15 (Republican).

Crafts, Samuel Chandler (NR) Oct. 6, 1768–Nov. 19, 1853; Oct. 10, 1828–Oct. 18, 1831; House 1817–25 (no party); Senate April 23, 1842–43 (no party).

Palmer, William Adams (AMas.D) Sept. 12, 1781–Dec. 3, 1860; Oct. 18, 1831–Nov. 2, 1835; Senate Oct. 20, 1818–25 (Republican).

Jenison, Silas Hemenway (W) May 17, 1791–Sept. 30, 1849; Nov. 2, 1835–Oct. 15, 1841.

Paine, Charles (W) April 15, 1799–July 6, 1853; Oct. 15, 1841–Oct. 13, 1843.

Mattocks, John (W) March 4, 1777–Aug. 14, 1847; Oct. 13, 1843–Oct. 11, 1844; House 1821–23 (no party), 1825–27 (no party), 1841–43 (Whig).

Slade, William (W) May 9, 1786–Jan. 18, 1859; Oct. 11, 1844–Oct. 9, 1846; House Nov. 1, 1831–43 (Nov. 1, 1831–37 Anti-Masonic, 1837–43 Whig).

Eaton, Horace (W) June 22, 1804–July 4, 1855; Oct. 9, 1846–Oct. 1848.

Coolidge, Carlos (W) June 25, 1792–Aug. 15, 1866; Oct. 1848–Oct. 11, 1850.

Williams, Charles Kilborn (W) Jan. 24, 1782–March 9, 1853; Oct. 11, 1850–Oct. 18, 1852.

Fairbanks, Erastus (father of Horace Fairbanks, below) (W) Oct. 28, 1792–Nov. 20, 1864; Oct. 18, 1852–Nov. 2, 1853, Oct. 12, 1860–Oct. 11, 1861.

Robinson, John Staniford (D) Nov. 10, 1804–April 25, 1860; Nov. 2, 1853–Oct. 13, 1854.

Royce, Stephen (W, R) Aug. 12, 1787–Nov. 11, 1868; Oct. 13, 1854–Oct. 10, 1856.

Fletcher, Ryland (R) Feb. 18, 1799–Dec. 19, 1885; Oct. 10, 1856–Oct. 10, 1858.

Hall, Hiland (R) July 20, 1795–Dec. 18, 1885; Oct. 10, 1858–Oct. 12, 1860; House Jan. 1, 1833–43 (Jan. 1–Jan. 3, 1833 no party, 1833–35 Anti-Jacksonian, 1835–43 Whig).

Fairbanks, Erastus (R) Oct. 12, 1860–Oct. 11, 1861 (for previous term see above).

Holbrook, Frederick (R) Feb. 15, 1813–April 28, 1909; Oct. 11, 1861–Oct. 9, 1863.

Smith, John Gregory (father of Edward Curtis Smith, below) (R) July 22, 1818–Nov. 6, 1891; Oct. 9, 1863–Oct. 13, 1865.

Dillingham, Paul Jr. (father of William Paul Dillingham, below) (R) Aug. 10, 1799–July 16, 1891; Oct. 13, 1865–Oct. 13, 1867; House 1843–47 (Democrat).

Page, John Boardman (R) Feb. 25, 1826–Oct. 24, 1885; Oct. 13, 1867–Oct. 15, 1869.

Washburn, Peter Thacher (R) Sept. 7, 1814–Feb. 7, 1870; Oct. 15, 1869–Feb. 7, 1870.

Hendee, George Whitman (R) Nov. 30, 1832–Dec. 6, 1906; Feb. 7–Oct. 6, 1870; House 1873–79.

Stewart, John Wolcott (R) Nov. 24, 1825–Oct. 29, 1915; Oct. 6, 1870–Oct. 3, 1872; House 1883–91; Senate March 24–Oct. 21, 1908.

Converse, Julius (R) Dec. 17, 1798–Aug. 16, 1885; Oct. 3, 1872–Oct. 8, 1874.

Peck, Asahel (R) Feb. 6, 1803–May 18, 1879; Oct. 8, 1874–Oct. 5, 1876.

Fairbanks, Horace (son of Erastus Fairbanks, above) (R) March 21, 1820–March 17, 1888; Oct. 5, 1876–Oct. 3, 1878.

Proctor, Redfield Sr. (father of Fletcher Dutton Proctor and Redfield Proctor Jr., below, grandfather of Mortimer Robinson Proctor, below) (R) June 1, 1831–March 4, 1908; Oct. 3, 1878–Oct. 7, 1880; Senate Nov. 2, 1891–March 4, 1908; secretary of war March 5, 1889–Nov. 5, 1891.

Farnham, Roswell (R) July 23, 1827–Jan. 5, 1903; Oct. 7, 1880–Oct. 5, 1882.

Barstow, John Lester (R) Feb. 21, 1832–June 28, 1913; Oct. 5, 1882–Oct. 2, 1884.

Pingree, Samuel Everett (R) Aug. 2, 1832–June 1, 1922; Oct. 2, 1884–Oct. 7, 1886.

Ormsbee, Ebenezer Jolls (R) June 8, 1834–April 3, 1924; Oct. 7, 1886–Oct. 4, 1888.

Dillingham, William Paul (son of Paul Dillingham Jr., above) (R) Dec. 12, 1843–July 12, 1923; Oct. 4, 1888–Oct. 2, 1890; Senate Oct. 18, 1900–July 12, 1923.

Page, Carroll Smalley (R) Jan. 10, 1843–Dec. 3, 1925; Oct. 2, 1890–Oct. 6, 1892; Senate Oct. 21, 1908–23.

Fuller, Levi Knight (R) Feb. 24, 1841–Oct. 10, 1896; Oct. 6, 1892–Oct. 4, 1894.

Woodbury, Urban Andrain (R) July 11, 1838–April 15, 1915; Oct. 4, 1894–Oct. 8, 1896.

Grout, Josiah (brother of William Wallace Grout, below) (R) May 28, 1841–July 19, 1925; Oct. 8, 1896–Oct. 6, 1898.

Smith, Edward Curtis (son of John Gregory Smith, above) (R) Jan. 5, 1854–April 6, 1925; Oct. 6, 1898–Oct. 4, 1900.

Stickney, William Wallace (cousin of Pres. John Calvin Coolidge) (R) March 21, 1853–Dec. 15, 1932; Oct. 4, 1900–Oct. 3, 1902.

McCullough, John Griffith (R) Sept. 16, 1835–May 29, 1915; Oct. 3, 1902–Oct. 6, 1904.

Bell, Charles James (R) March 10, 1845–Sept. 25, 1909; Oct. 6, 1904–Oct. 4, 1906.

Proctor, Fletcher Dutton (father of Mortimer Robinson Proctor, below, son of Redfield Proctor Sr., above, brother of Redfield Proctor Jr., below) (R) Nov. 7, 1860–Sept. 27, 1911; Oct. 4, 1906–Oct. 8, 1908.

Prouty, George Herbert (R) March 4, 1862–Aug. 19, 1918; Oct. 8, 1908–Oct. 5, 1910.

Mead, John Abner (R) April 20, 1841–Jan. 12, 1920; Oct. 5, 1910–Oct. 3, 1912.

Fletcher, Allen Miller (R) Sept. 25, 1853–May 11, 1922; Oct. 3, 1912–Jan. 7, 1915.

Gates, Charles Winslow (R) Jan. 12, 1856–July 1, 1927; Jan. 7, 1915–Jan. 4, 1917.

Graham, Horace French (R) Feb. 7, 1862–Nov. 23, 1941; Jan. 4, 1917–Jan. 9, 1919.

Clement, Percival Wood (R) July 7, 1846–Jan. 9, 1927; Jan. 9, 1919–Jan. 6, 1921.

Hartness, James (R) Sept. 3, 1861–Feb. 2, 1934; Jan. 6, 1921–Jan. 4, 1923.

Proctor, Redfield Jr. (son of Redfield Proctor Sr., above, brother of Fletcher Dutton Proctor, above, uncle of Mortimer Robinson Proctor, below) (R) April 13, 1879–Feb. 5, 1957; Jan. 4, 1923–Jan. 8, 1925.

Billings, Franklin Swift (R) May 11, 1862–Jan. 16, 1935; Jan. 8, 1925–Jan. 6, 1927.

Weeks, John Eliakim (R) June 14, 1853–Sept. 10, 1949; Jan. 6, 1927–Jan. 8, 1931; House 1931–33.

Wilson, Stanley Calef (R) Sept. 10, 1879–Oct. 5, 1967; Jan. 8, 1931–Jan. 10, 1935.

Smith, Charles Manley (R) Aug. 3, 1868–Aug. 12, 1937; Jan. 10, 1935–Jan. 7, 1937.

Aiken, George David (R) Aug. 20, 1892–Nov. 19, 1984; Jan. 7, 1937–Jan. 9, 1941; Senate Jan. 10, 1941–75.

Wills, William Henry (R) Oct. 26, 1882–March 6, 1946; Jan. 9, 1941–Jan. 4, 1945.

Proctor, Mortimer Robinson (son of Fletcher Dutton Proctor, above, grandson of Redfield Proctor Sr., above, nephew of Redfield Proctor Jr., above) (R) May 30, 1889–April 28, 1968; Jan. 4, 1945–Jan. 9, 1947.

Gibson, Ernest William Jr. (R) March 6, 1901–Nov. 4, 1969; Jan. 9, 1947–Jan. 16, 1950; Senate June 24, 1940–41.

Arthur, Harold John (R) Feb. 9, 1904–July 19, 1971; Jan. 16, 1950–Jan. 4, 1951.

Emerson, Lee Earl (R) Dec. 19, 1898–May 21, 1976; Jan. 4, 1951–Jan. 6, 1955.

Johnson, Joseph Blaine (R) Aug. 29, 1893–Oct. 25, 1986; Jan. 6, 1955–Jan. 8, 1959.

Stafford, Robert Theodore (R) Aug. 8, 1913– ; Jan. 8, 1959–Jan. 5, 1961; House 1961–Sept. 16, 1971; Senate Sept. 16, 1971–89.

Keyser, Frank Ray Jr. (R) Aug. 17, 1927– ; Jan. 5, 1961–Jan. 10, 1963.

Hoff, Philip Henderson (D) June 29, 1924– ; Jan. 10, 1963–Jan. 9, 1969.

Davis, Deane Chandler (R) Nov. 7, 1900–Dec. 8, 1990; Jan. 9, 1969–Jan. 4, 1973.

Salmon, Thomas Paul (D) Aug. 19, 1932– ; Jan. 4, 1973–Jan. 6, 1977.

Snelling, Richard Arkwright (R) Feb. 18, 1927–Aug. 14, 1991; Jan. 3, 1977–Jan. 10, 1985, Jan. 10–Aug. 14, 1991.

Kunin, Madeleine May (D) Sept. 28, 1933– ; Jan. 10, 1985–Jan. 10, 1991.

Snelling, Richard Arkwright (R) Jan. 10–Aug. 14, 1991 (for previous term see above).

Dean, Howard (D) Nov. 17, 1948– ; Aug. 14, 1991–Jan. 9, 2003; chair Dem. Nat. Comm. 2005– .

Douglas, James H. (R) June 21, 1951– ; Jan. 9, 2003– .

Virginia

(Ratified the Constitution June 25, 1788)

Randolph, Beverley (-) 1754–Feb. 1797; Dec. 3, 1788–Dec. 1, 1791.

Lee, Henry (F) Jan. 29, 1756–March 25, 1818; Dec. 1, 1791–Dec. 1, 1794; Cont. Cong. 1786–88; House 1799–1801.

Brooke, Robert (DR) 1751–Feb. 27, 1799; Dec. 1, 1794–Dec. 1, 1796.

Wood, James (F) 1747–June 16, 1813; Dec. 1, 1796–Dec. 1, 1799.

Monroe, James (uncle of Rep. James Monroe) (DR) April 28, 1758–July 4, 1831; Dec. 1, 1799–Dec. 1, 1802, Jan. 16–April 3, 1811; Cont. Cong. 1783–86; Senate Nov. 9, 1790–May 27, 1794 (no party); secretary of state April 6, 1811–Sept. 30, 1814, Feb. 28, 1815–March 3, 1817; president 1817–25 (Democratic Republican); secretary of war Oct. 1, 1814–Feb. 28, 1815.

Page, John (DR) April 17, 1743–Oct. 11, 1808; Dec. 1, 1802–Dec. 1, 1805; House 1789–97 (1789–95 no party, 1795–97 Republican).

Cabell, William Henry (DR) Dec. 16, 1772–Jan. 12, 1853; Dec. 7, 1805–Dec. 1, 1808.

Tyler, John (father of Pres. John Tyler, below, grandfather of Rep. David Gardiner Tyler) (DR) Feb. 28, 1747–Jan. 6, 1813; Dec. 1, 1808–Jan. 15, 1811.

Monroe, James (DR) Jan. 16–April 3, 1811 (for previous term see above).

Smith, George William (DR) 1762–Dec. 26, 1811; April 6–Dec. 26, 1811.

Randolph, Peyton (DR) 1779–Dec. 26, 1828; Dec. 27, 1811–Jan. 3, 1812.

Barbour, James (AD/SR) June 10, 1775–June 7, 1842; Jan. 3, 1812–Dec. 1, 1814; Senate Jan. 2, 1815–March 7, 1825; elected pres. pro tempore Feb. 15, 1819; secretary of war March 7, 1825–May 23, 1828.

Nicholas, Wilson Cary (R) Jan. 31, 1761–Oct. 10, 1820; Dec. 1, 1814–Dec. 1, 1816; Senate Dec. 5, 1799–May 22, 1804; House 1807–Nov. 27, 1809.

Preston, James Patton (brother-in-law of John Floyd, below, uncle of James McDowell and John Buchanan Floyd, below) (DR) June 21, 1774–May 4, 1853; Dec. 1, 1816–Dec. 1, 1819.

Randolph, Thomas Mann (son-in-law of Pres. Thomas Jefferson) (R) Oct. 1, 1768–June 20, 1828; Dec. 1, 1819–Dec. 1, 1822; House 1803–07.

Pleasants, James (R) Oct. 24, 1769–Nov. 9, 1836; Dec. 1, 1822–Dec. 10, 1825; House 1811–Dec. 14, 1819; Senate Dec. 14, 1819–Dec. 15, 1822.

Tyler, John (son of John Tyler, above, father of Rep. David Gardiner Tyler) (DR) March 29, 1790–Jan. 18, 1862; Dec. 10, 1825–March 4, 1827; House Dec. 16, 1817–21 (Republican); Senate 1827–Feb. 29, 1836 (Republican); elected pres. pro tempore March 3, 1835; vice president March 4–April 6, 1841 (Whig); president April 6, 1841–45 (Whig).

Giles, William Branch (R) Aug. 12, 1762–Dec. 4, 1830; March 4, 1827–March 4, 1830; House Dec. 7, 1790–Oct. 2, 1798 (no party), 1801–03 (Republican); Senate Aug. 11, 1804–15 (Republican).

Floyd, John (father of John Buchanan Floyd, below, uncle of James McDowell, below, brother-in-law of James Patton Preston, above) (D) April 24, 1783–Aug. 17, 1837; March 4, 1830–March 31, 1834; House 1817–29 (Republican).

Tazewell, Littleton Waller (D) Dec. 17, 1774–May 6, 1860; March 31, 1834–April 30, 1836; House Nov. 26, 1800–01 (no party); Senate Dec. 7, 1824–July 16, 1832 (no party); elected pres. pro tempore July 9, 1832.

Robertson, Wyndham (brother of Thomas Bolling Robertson of La.) (SRD) Jan. 26, 1803–Feb. 11, 1888; April 30, 1836–March 31, 1837.

Campbell, David (W) Aug. 2, 1779–March 19, 1859; March 31, 1837–March 31, 1840.

Gilmer, Thomas Walker (W) April 6, 1802–Feb. 28, 1844; March 31, 1840–March 1, 1841; House 1841–Feb. 16, 1844 (1841–43 Whig, 1843–Feb. 16, 1844 Democrat); secretary of the navy Feb. 19–Feb. 28, 1844.

Patton, John Mercer (SRW) Aug. 10, 1797–Oct. 29, 1858; March 18–March 31, 1841; House Nov. 25, 1830–April 7, 1838 (Nov. 25, 1830–37 Jacksonian, 1837–April 7, 1838 Democrat).

Rutherford, John (brother-in-law of Edward Coles of Ill.) (SRW) Dec. 6, 1792–Aug. 3, 1866; March 31, 1841–March 31, 1842.

Gregory, John Munford (SRW) July 8, 1804–April 9, 1884; March 31, 1842–Jan. 1, 1843.

McDowell, James (nephew of James Patton Preston and John Floyd, above, cousin of John Buchanan Floyd, below, father-in-law of Francis Thomas of Md.) (D) Oct. 13, 1795–Aug. 24, 1851; Jan. 1, 1843–Jan. 1, 1846; House March 6, 1846–51.

Smith, William (Confed. D) Sept. 6, 1797–May 18, 1887; Jan. 1, 1846–Jan. 1, 1849 (Democrat), Jan. 1, 1864–April 1865; House 1841–43 (Democrat), 1853–61 (Democrat).

Floyd, John Buchanan (son of John Floyd, above, nephew of James Patton Preston, above, cousin of James McDowell, above) (D) June 1, 1806–Aug. 26, 1863; Jan. 1, 1849–Jan. 16, 1852; secretary of war March 6, 1857–Dec. 29, 1860.

Johnson, Joseph (D) Dec. 19, 1785–Feb. 27, 1877; Jan. 16, 1852–Dec. 31, 1855; House 1823–27 (no party), Jan. 21–March 3, 1833 (no party), 1835–41 (1835–37 Jacksonian, 1837–41 Democrat), 1845–47 (Democrat).

Wise, Henry Alexander (D) Dec. 3, 1806–Sept. 12, 1876; Jan. 1, 1856–Dec. 31, 1859; House 1833–Feb. 12, 1844 (1833–37 Jacksonian, 1837–43 Whig, 1843–Feb. 12, 1844 Democrat).

Letcher, John (D) March 29, 1813–Jan. 26, 1884; Jan. 1, 1860–Dec. 31, 1863; House 1851–59.

Smith, William (Confed. D) Jan. 1, 1864–April 1865 (for previous term see above).

Pierpoint, Francis Harrison (U) Jan. 25, 1814–March 24, 1899; May 24, 1865–April 16, 1868.

Wells, Henry Horatio Sept. 17, 1823–Feb. 13, 1890; (Provisional) April 16, 1868–Sept. 21, 1869.

Walker, Gilbert Carlton (C) Aug. 1, 1833–May 11, 1885; (Provisional) Sept. 21, 1869–Jan. 1, 1870, Jan. 1, 1870–Jan. 1, 1874; House 1875–79 (Democrat).

Kemper, James Lawson (D) June 11, 1823–April 7, 1895; Jan. 1, 1874–Jan. 1, 1878.

Holliday, Frederick William Mackey (D) Feb. 22, 1828–May 29, 1899; Jan. 1, 1878–Jan. 1, 1882.

Cameron, William Ewan (Read) Nov. 29, 1842–Jan. 26, 1927; Jan. 1, 1882–Jan. 1, 1886.

Lee, Fitzhugh (D) Nov. 19, 1835–April 28, 1905; Jan. 1, 1886–Jan. 1, 1890.

McKinney, Philip Watkins (D) May 1, 1832–March 1, 1899; Jan. 1, 1890–Jan. 1, 1894.

O'Ferrall, Charles Triplett (D) Oct. 21, 1840–Sept. 22, 1905; Jan. 1, 1894–Jan. 1, 1898; House May 5, 1884–Dec. 28, 1893.

Tyler, James Hoge (D) Aug. 11, 1846–Jan. 3, 1925; Jan. 1, 1898–Jan. 1, 1902.

Montague, Andrew Jackson (D) Oct. 3, 1862–Jan. 24, 1937; Jan. 1, 1902–Feb. 1, 1906; House 1913–Jan. 24, 1937.

Swanson, Claude Augustus (D) March 31, 1862–July 7, 1939; Feb. 1, 1906–Feb. 1, 1910; House 1893–Jan. 30, 1906; Senate Aug. 1, 1910–33; secretary of the navy March 4, 1933–July 7, 1939.

Mann, William Hodges (D) July 30, 1843–Dec. 12, 1927; Feb. 1, 1910–Feb. 1, 1914.

Stuart, Henry Carter (D) Jan. 18, 1855–July 24, 1933; Feb. 1, 1914–Feb. 1, 1918.

Davis, Westmoreland (D) Aug. 21, 1859–Sept. 7, 1942; Feb. 1, 1918–Feb. 1, 1922.

Trinkle, Elbert Lee (D) March 12, 1876–Nov. 25, 1939; Feb. 1, 1922–Feb. 1, 1926.

Byrd, Harry Flood (D) June 10, 1887–Oct. 20, 1966; Feb. 1, 1926–Jan. 15, 1930; Senate 1933–Nov. 10, 1965,

Pollard, John Garland (D) Aug. 9, 1871–April 28, 1937; Jan. 15, 1930–Jan. 17, 1934.

Peery, George Campbell (D) Oct. 28, 1873–Oct. 14, 1952; Jan. 17, 1934–Jan. 19, 1938; House 1923–29.

Price, James Hubert (D) Sept. 7, 1878–Nov. 22, 1943; Jan. 19, 1938–Jan. 21, 1942.

Darden, Colgate Whitehead Jr. (D) Feb. 11, 1897–June 9, 1981; Jan. 21, 1942–Jan. 16, 1946; House 1933–37, 1939–March 1, 1941.

Tuck, William Munford (D) Sept. 28, 1896–June 9, 1983; Jan. 16, 1946–Jan. 18, 1950; House April 14, 1953–69.

Battle, John Stewart (D) July 11, 1890–April 9, 1972; Jan. 18, 1950–Jan. 20, 1954.

Stanley, Thomas Bahnson (D) July 16, 1890–July 10, 1970; Jan. 20, 1954–Jan. 11, 1958; House Nov. 5, 1946–Feb. 3, 1953.

Almond, James Lindsay Jr. (D) June 15, 1898–April 14, 1986; Jan. 11, 1958–Jan. 13, 1962; House Jan. 22, 1946–April 17, 1948.

Harrison, Albertis Sydney Jr. (D) Jan. 11, 1907–Jan. 24, 1995; Jan. 13, 1962–Jan. 15, 1966.

Godwin, Mills Edwin Jr. (R) Nov. 19, 1914–Jan. 30, 1999; Jan. 16, 1966–Jan. 17, 1970 (Democrat), Jan. 12, 1974–Jan. 14, 1978.

Holton, Abner Linwood Jr. (R) Sept. 21, 1923– ; Jan. 17, 1970–Jan. 12, 1974.

Godwin, Mills Edwin Jr. (R) Jan. 12, 1974–Jan. 14, 1978 (for previous term see above).

Dalton, John Nichols (R) July 11, 1931–July 30, 1986; Jan. 14, 1978–Jan. 16, 1982.

Robb, Charles Spittal (D) June 26, 1939– ; Jan. 16, 1982–Jan. 18, 1986; Senate 1989–2001.

Baliles, Gerald L. (D) July 8, 1940– ; Jan. 18, 1986–Jan. 14, 1990.

Wilder, Lawrence Douglas (D) Jan. 17, 1931– ; Jan. 14, 1990–Jan. 15, 1994.

Allen, George Felix (R) March 8, 1952– ; Jan. 15, 1994–Jan. 17, 1998; House 1991–93; Senate 2001– .

Gilmore, James S. III (R) Oct. 6, 1949– ; Jan. 17, 1998–Jan. 12, 2002; chair Rep. Nat. Comm. 2001–02.

Warner, Mark R. (D) Dec. 15, 1954– ; Jan. 12, 2002– .

Washington

(Became a state Nov. 11, 1889)

Ferry, Elisha Peyre (R) Aug. 9, 1825–Oct. 14, 1895; Nov. 11, 1889–Jan. 9, 1893.

McGraw, John Harte (R) Oct. 4, 1850–June 23, 1910; Jan. 9, 1893–Jan. 11, 1897.

Rogers, John Rankin (PD) Sept. 4, 1838–Dec. 26, 1901; Jan. 11, 1897–Dec. 26, 1901.

McBride, Henry (R) Feb. 7, 1856–Oct. 6, 1937; Dec. 26, 1901–Jan. 9, 1905.

Mead, Albert Edward (R) Dec. 14, 1861–March 19, 1913; Jan. 9, 1905–Jan. 27, 1909.

Cosgrove, Samuel Goodlove (R) April 10, 1847–March 28, 1909; Jan. 27–March 28, 1909.

Hay, Marion E. (R) Dec. 9, 1865–Nov. 21, 1933; March 29, 1909–Jan. 11, 1913.

Lister, Ernest (D) June 15, 1870–June 14, 1919; Jan. 11, 1913–June 14, 1919.

Hart, Louis Folwell (R) Jan. 4, 1862–Dec. 5, 1929; June 14, 1919–Jan. 12, 1925.

Hartley, Roland Hill (son-in-law of David Martson Clough of Minn.) (R) June 26, 1864–Sept. 21, 1952; Jan. 12, 1925–Jan. 9, 1933.

Martin, Clarence Daniel (D) June 29, 1887–Aug. 11, 1955; Jan. 9, 1933–Jan. 13, 1941.

Langlie, Arthur Bernard (R) July 25, 1900–July 24, 1966; Jan. 13, 1941–Jan. 8, 1945, Jan. 10, 1949–Jan. 14, 1957.

Wallgren, Monrad Charles (D) April 17, 1891–Sept. 18, 1961; Jan. 1945–Jan. 10, 1949; House 1933–Dec. 19, 1940; Senate Dec. 19, 1940–Jan. 9, 1945.

Langlie, Arthur Bernard (R) Jan. 10, 1949–Jan. 14, 1957 (for previous term see above).

Rosellini, Albert Dean (D) Jan. 21, 1910– ; Jan. 14, 1957–Jan. 11, 1965.

Evans, Daniel Jackson (R) Oct. 16, 1925– ; Jan. 11, 1965–Jan. 12, 1977; Senate Sept. 12, 1983–89.

Ray, Dixy Lee (D) Sept. 3, 1914–Jan. 2, 1994; Jan. 12, 1977–Jan. 14, 1981.

Spellman, John D. (R) Dec. 29, 1926– ; Jan. 14, 1981–Jan. 16, 1985.

Gardner, Booth (D) Aug. 21, 1936– ; Jan. 16, 1985–Jan. 13, 1993.

Lowry, Michael Edward (D) March 8, 1939– ; Jan. 13, 1993–Jan. 15, 1997; House 1979–89.

Locke, Gary (D) Jan. 26, 1950– ; Jan. 15, 1997–Jan. 12, 2005.

Gregoire, Christine (D) March 24, 1947– ; Jan. 12, 2005– .

West Virginia

(Became a state June 19, 1863)

Boreman, Arthur Inghram (R) July 24, 1823–April 19, 1896; June 20, 1863–Feb. 26, 1869; Senate 1869–75.

Farnsworth, Daniel Duane Tompkins (R) Dec. 28, 1819–Dec. 5, 1892; Feb. 27–March 4, 1869.

Stevenson, William Erskine (R) March 18, 1820–Nov. 29, 1883; March 4, 1869–March 4, 1871.

Jacob, John Jeremiah (D/I) Dec. 9, 1829–Nov. 24, 1893; March 4, 1871–March 4, 1877.

Mathews, Henry Mason (D) March 29, 1834–April 28, 1884; March 4, 1877–March 4, 1881.

Jackson, Jacob Beeson (D) April 6, 1829–Dec. 11, 1893; March 4, 1881–March 4, 1885.

Wilson, Emanuel Willis (D) Aug. 11, 1844–May 28, 1909; March 4, 1885–Feb. 5, 1890.

Fleming, Aretas Brooks (D) Oct. 15, 1839–Oct. 13, 1923; Feb. 5, 1890–March 4, 1893.

MacCorkle, William Alexander (D) May 7, 1857–Sept. 24, 1930; March 4, 1893–March 4, 1897.

Atkinson, George Wesley (R) June 29, 1845–April 4, 1925; March 4, 1897–March 4, 1901; House Feb. 26, 1890–91.

White, Albert Blakeslee (R) Sept. 22, 1856–July 3, 1941; March 4, 1901–March 4, 1905.

Dawson, William Mercer Owens (R) May 21, 1853–March 12, 1916; March 4, 1905–March 4, 1909.

Glasscock, William Ellsworth (R) Dec. 13, 1862–April 12, 1925; March 4, 1909–March 4, 1913.

Hatfield, Henry Drury (R) Sept. 15, 1875–Oct. 23, 1962; March 4, 1913–March 4, 1917; Senate 1929–35.

Cornwell, John Jacob (D) July 11, 1867–Sept. 8, 1953; March 4, 1917–March 4, 1921.

Morgan, Ephraim Franklin (R) Jan. 16, 1869–Jan. 15, 1950; March 4, 1921–March 4, 1925.

Gore, Howard Mason (R) Oct. 12, 1877–June 20, 1947; March 4, 1925–March 4, 1929; secretary of agriculture Nov. 22, 1924–March 4, 1925.

Conley, William Gustavus (R) Jan. 8, 1866–Oct. 21, 1940; March 4, 1929–March 4, 1933.

Kump, Herman Guy (D) Oct. 31, 1877–Feb. 14, 1962; March 4, 1933–Jan. 18, 1937.

Holt, Homer Adams (D) March 1, 1898–Jan. 16, 1975; Jan. 18, 1937–Jan. 12, 1941.

Neely, Matthew Mansfield (D) Nov. 9, 1874–Jan. 18, 1958; Jan. 13, 1941–Jan. 15, 1945; House Oct. 14, 1913–21, 1945–47; Senate 1923–29, 1931–Jan. 12, 1941, 1949–Jan. 18, 1958.

Meadows, Clarence Watson (D) Feb. 11, 1904–Sept. 12, 1961; Jan. 15, 1945–Jan. 17, 1949.

Patteson, Okey Leonidas (D) Sept. 14, 1898–July 3, 1989; Jan. 17, 1949–Jan. 19, 1953.

Marland, William Casey (D) March 26, 1918–Nov. 26, 1965; Jan. 19, 1953–Jan. 13, 1957.

Underwood, Cecil Harland (R) Nov. 5, 1922– ; Jan. 13, 1957–Jan. 16, 1961, Jan. 13, 1997–Jan. 15, 2001.

Barron, William Wallace (D) Dec. 8, 1911– ; Jan. 16, 1961–Jan. 18, 1965.

Smith, Hulett Carlson (D) Oct. 12, 1918– ; Jan. 18, 1965–Jan. 13, 1969.

Moore, Arch Alfred Jr. (R) April 16, 1923– ; Jan. 13, 1969–Jan. 17, 1977; House 1957–69.

Rockefeller, John Davidson "Jay" IV (nephew of Vice Pres. Nelson Aldrich Rockefeller and Winthrop Rockefeller of Ark., great-grandson of Sen. Nelson Wilmarth Aldrich, great-uncle of Rep. Richard Steere Aldrich) (D) June 18, 1937– ; Jan. 17, 1977–Jan. 14, 1985; Senate Jan. 15, 1985– .

Moore, Arch Alfred Jr. (R) Jan. 14, 1985–Jan. 16, 1989 (for previous term see above).

Caperton, Gaston (D) Feb. 21, 1940– ; Jan. 16, 1989–Jan. 13, 1997.

Underwood, Cecil Harland (R) Jan. 13, 1997–Jan. 15, 2001 (for previous term see above).

Wise, Robert Ellsworth Jr. "Bob" (D) Jan. 6, 1948– ; Jan. 15, 2001–Jan. 17, 2005; House 1983–2001.

Manchin, Joe III (D) Aug. 24, 1947– ; Jan. 17, 2005– .

Wisconsin

(Became a state May 29, 1848)

Dewey, Nelson (D) Dec. 19, 1813–July 21, 1889; June 7, 1848–Jan. 5, 1852.

Farwell, Leonard James (W) Jan. 5, 1819–April 11, 1889; Jan. 5, 1852–Jan. 2, 1854.

Barstow, William Augustus (D) Sept. 13, 1813–Dec. 13, 1865; Jan. 2, 1854–March 21, 1856.

MacArthur, Arthur (D) Jan. 26, 1815–Aug. 26, 1896; March 21–March 25, 1856.

Bashford, Coles (R) Jan. 24, 1816–April 25, 1878; March 25, 1856–Jan. 4, 1858; House (Terr. Del.) 1867–69 (Independent Ariz.).

Randall, Alexander Williams (R) Oct. 31, 1819–July 26, 1872; Jan. 4, 1858–Jan. 6, 1862; postmaster general July 25, 1866–March 4, 1869.

Harvey, Louis Powell (R) July 22, 1820–April 19, 1862; Jan. 6–April 19, 1862.

Salomon, Edward P. (R) Aug. 11, 1828–April 21, 1909; April 19, 1862–Jan. 4, 1864.

Lewis, James Taylor (R) Oct. 30, 1819–Aug. 4, 1904; Jan. 4, 1864–Jan. 1, 1866.

Fairchild, Lucius (R) Dec. 27, 1831–May 23, 1896; Jan. 1, 1866–Jan. 1, 1872.

Washburn, Cadwallader Colden (brother of Israel Washburn Jr. of Maine) (R) April 22, 1818–May 15, 1882; Jan. 1, 1872–Jan. 5, 1874; House 1855–61, 1867–71.

Taylor, William Robert (D) July 10, 1820–March 17, 1909; Jan. 5, 1874–Jan. 3, 1876.

Ludington, Harrison (R) July 30, 1812–June 17, 1891; Jan. 3, 1876–Jan. 7, 1878.

Smith, William E. (R) June 18, 1824–Feb. 13, 1883; Jan. 7, 1878–Jan. 2, 1882.

Rusk, Jeremiah McLain (R) June 17, 1830–Nov. 21, 1893; Jan. 2, 1882–Jan. 7, 1889; House 1871–77; secretary of agriculture March 6, 1889–March 6, 1893.

Hoard, William Dempster (R) Oct. 10, 1836–Nov. 22, 1918; Jan. 7, 1889–Jan. 5, 1891.

Peck, George Wilbur (D) Sept. 28, 1840–April 16, 1916; Jan. 5, 1891–Jan. 7, 1895.

Upham, William Henry (R) May 3, 1841–July 2, 1924; Jan. 7, 1895–Jan. 4, 1897.

Scofield, Edward (R) March 28, 1842–Feb. 3, 1925; Jan. 4, 1897–Jan. 7, 1901.

La Follette, Robert Marion (father of Philip Fox La Follette, below) (R) June 14, 1855–June 18, 1925; Jan. 7, 1901–Jan. 1, 1906; House 1885–91; Senate Jan. 2, 1906–June 18, 1925.

Davidson, James Ole (R) Feb. 10, 1854–Dec. 16, 1922; Jan. 1, 1906–Jan. 2, 1911.

McGovern, Francis Edward (R) Jan. 21, 1866–May 16, 1946; Jan. 2, 1911–Jan. 4, 1915.

Philipp, Emanuel Lorenz (R) March 25, 1861–June 15, 1925; Jan. 4, 1915–Jan. 3, 1921.

Blaine, John James (R) May 4, 1875–April 16, 1934; Jan. 3, 1921–Jan. 3, 1927; Senate 1927–33.

Zimmerman, Fred R. (R) Nov. 20, 1880–Dec. 14, 1954; Jan. 3, 1927–Jan. 7, 1929.

Kohler, Walter Jodok Sr. (father of Walter Jodok Kohler Jr., below) (R) March 3, 1875–April 21, 1940; Jan. 7, 1929–Jan. 5, 1931.

La Follette, Philip Fox (son of Robert Marion La Follette, above) (Prog.) May 8, 1897–Aug. 18, 1965; Jan. 5, 1931–Jan. 2, 1933 (Republican), Jan. 7, 1935–Jan. 2, 1939.

Schmedeman, Albert George (D) Nov. 25, 1864–Nov. 26, 1946; Jan. 2, 1933–Jan. 7, 1935.

La Follette, Philip Fox (Prog.) Jan. 7, 1935–Jan. 2, 1939 (for previous term see above).

Heil, Julius Peter (R) July 24, 1876–Nov. 30, 1949; Jan. 2, 1939–Jan. 4, 1943.

Goodland, Walter Samuel (R) Dec. 22, 1862–March 12, 1947; Jan. 4, 1943–March 12, 1947.

Rennebohm, Oscar (R) May 25, 1889–Oct. 15, 1968; March 12, 1947–Jan. 1, 1951.

Kohler, Walter Jodok Jr. (son of Walter Jodok Kohler Sr., above) (R) April 4, 1904–March 21, 1976; Jan. 1, 1951–Jan. 7, 1957.

Thomson, Vernon Wallace (R) Nov. 5, 1905–April 2, 1988; Jan. 7, 1957–Jan. 5, 1959; House 1961–Dec. 31, 1974.

Nelson, Gaylord Anton (D) June 4, 1916– ; Jan. 5, 1959–Jan. 7, 1963; Senate Jan. 8, 1963–81.

Reynolds, John Whitcome (D) April 4, 1921– ; Jan. 7, 1963–Jan. 4, 1965.

Knowles, Warren Perley (R) Aug. 19, 1908–May 1, 1993; Jan. 4, 1965–Jan. 4, 1971.

Lucey, Patrick Joseph (D) March 21, 1918– ; Jan. 4, 1971–July 7, 1977.

Schreiber, Martin James (D) April 8, 1939– ; July 7, 1977–Jan. 1, 1979.

Dreyfus, Lee Sherman (R) June 20, 1926– ; Jan. 1, 1979–Jan. 3, 1983.

Earl, Anthony Scully (D) April 12, 1936– ; Jan. 3, 1983–Jan. 5, 1987.

Thompson, Tommy George (R) Nov. 19, 1941– ; Jan. 5, 1987–Feb. 1, 2001; secretary of health and human services Feb. 2, 2001–Jan. 26, 2005.

McCallum, Scott (R) May 2, 1950– ; Feb. 1, 2001–Jan. 6, 2003.

Doyle, James (D) Nov. 23, 1945– ; Jan. 6, 2003– .

Wyoming

(Became a state July 10, 1890)

Warren, Francis Emroy (R) June 20, 1884–Nov. 24, 1929; Feb. 1885–Nov. 1886 (Wyo. Terr.), March 1889–Sept. 1890 (Wyo. Terr.), Sept. 11–Nov. 24, 1890; Senate Nov. 18, 1890–93, 1895–Nov. 24, 1929.

Barber, Amos Walker (R) July 25, 1861–May 18, 1915; Nov. 24, 1890–Jan. 2, 1893.

Osborne, John Eugene (D) June 19, 1858–April 24, 1943; Jan. 2, 1893–Jan. 7, 1895; Hotme 1897–99.

Richards, William Alford (R) March 9, 1849–July 25, 1912; Jan. 7, 1895–Jan. 2, 1899.

Richards, DeForest (R) Aug. 6, 1846–April 28, 1903; Jan. 2, 1899–April 28, 1903.

Chatterton, Fenimore (R) July 21, 1860–May 9, 1958; April 28, 1903–Jan. 2, 1905.

Brooks, Bryant Butler (R) Feb. 5, 1861–Dec. 7, 1944; Jan. 2, 1905–Jan. 2, 1911.

Carey, Joseph Maull (father of Robert Davis Carey, below) (R) Jan. 19, 1845–Feb. 5, 1924; Jan. 2, 1911–Jan. 4, 1915; House (Terr. Del.) 1885–July 10, 1890; Senate Nov. 15, 1890–95.

Kendrick, John Benjamin (D) Sept. 6, 1857–Nov. 3, 1933; Jan. 4, 1915–Feb. 26, 1917; Senate 1917–Nov. 3, 1933.

Houx, Frank L. (D) Dec. 12, 1860–April 3, 1941; Feb. 26, 1917–Jan. 6, 1919.

Carey, Robert Davis (son of Joseph Maull Carey, above) (R) Aug. 12, 1878–Jan. 17, 1937; Jan. 6, 1919–Jan. 1, 1923; Senate Dec. 1, 1930–37.

Ross, William Bradford (husband of Nellie Tayloe Ross, below) (D) Dec. 4, 1873–Oct. 2, 1924; Jan. 1, 1923–Oct. 2, 1924.

Lucas, Franklin Earl (R) Aug. 4, 1876–Nov. 26, 1948; Oct. 2, 1924–Jan. 5, 1925.

Ross, Nellie Tayloe (wife of William Bradford Ross, above) (D) Nov. 29, 1876–Dec. 19, 1977; Jan. 5, 1925–Jan. 3, 1927.

Emerson, Frank Collins (R) May 26, 1882–Feb. 18, 1931; Jan. 3, 1927–Feb. 18, 1931.

Clark, Alonzo Monroe (R) Aug. 13, 1868–Oct. 12, 1952; Feb. 18, 1931–Jan. 2, 1933.

Miller, Leslie Andrew (D) Jan. 29, 1886–Sept. 29, 1970; Jan. 2, 1933–Jan. 2, 1939.

Smith, Nels Hanson (R) Aug. 27, 1884–July 5, 1976; Jan. 2, 1939–Jan. 4, 1943.

Hunt, Lester Calloway (D) July 8, 1892–June 19, 1954; Jan. 4, 1943–Jan. 3, 1949; Senate 1949–June 19, 1954.

Crane, Arthur Griswold (R) Sept. 1, 1877–Aug. 12, 1955; Jan. 3, 1949–Jan. 1, 1951.

Barrett, Frank Aloysius (R) Nov. 10, 1892–May 30, 1962; Jan. 1, 1951–Jan. 3, 1953; House 1943–Dec. 31, 1950; Senate 1953–59.

Rogers, Clifford Joy "Doc" (R) Dec. 20, 1897–May 18, 1962; Jan. 3, 1953–Jan. 3, 1955.

Simpson, Milward Lee (R) Nov. 12, 1897–June 10, 1993; Jan. 3, 1955–Jan. 5, 1959; Senate Nov. 6, 1962–67.

Hickey, John Joseph (D) Aug. 22, 1911–Sept. 22, 1970; Jan. 5, 1959–Jan. 2, 1961; Senate 1961–Nov. 6, 1962.

Gage, Jack Robert (D) Jan. 13, 1899–March 14, 1970; Jan. 2, 1961–Jan. 6, 1963.

Hansen, Clifford Peter (R) Oct. 16, 1912– ; Jan. 6, 1963–Jan. 2, 1967; Senate 1967–Dec. 31, 1978.

Hathaway, Stanley Knapp (R) July 19, 1924– ; Jan. 2, 1967–Jan. 6, 1975; secretary of the interior June 12–Oct. 9, 1975.

Herschler, Edgar J. (D) Oct. 27, 1918–Feb. 5, 1990; Jan. 6, 1975–Jan. 5, 1987.

Sullivan, Michael John (D) Sept. 22, 1939– ; Jan. 5, 1987–Jan. 2, 1995.

Geringer, Jim (R) April 24, 1944– ; Jan. 2, 1995–Jan. 6, 2003.

Freudenthal, David (D) Oct. 12, 1950– ; Jan. 6, 2003– .

State Sources for Governors

The following individual state archives, historical societies, libraries, and secretary of state offices provided information used to compile the governors' biographies. *(For other sources, see p. 276.)*

Alabama: State of Alabama, Department of Archives and History; **Alaska:** State Archives of Alaska; **Arizona:** State of Arizona, Department of Library, Archives, and Public Records; **Arkansas:** Arkansas State Library, Office of State Library Services; **California:** California State Library; **Colorado:** State of Colorado, Division of Archives and Public Records; Colorado Historical Society; **Delaware:** State of Delaware, Bureau of Archives and Records Management; **Florida:** Historic Tallahassee Preservation Board. Florida; **Georgia:** State of Georgia, Department of Archives and History; **Hawaii:** Office of Janice C. Lipsen. Washington representative, State of Hawaii; **Idaho:** Idaho State Historical Society; **Indiana:** Indiana Historical Bureau: **Iowa:** Iowa State Historical Department, Division of Historical Museums and Archives; **Kansas:** Kansas State Historical Society; **Kentucky:** Kentucky Historical Society; **Louisiana:** Louisiana State Library; **Maine:** Maine State Archives; **Maryland:** Maryland State Law Library; Maryland State Archives: **Massachusetts:** Commonwealth of Massachusetts State Library, George Fingold Library; **Michigan:** Library of Michigan; **Minnesota:** Minnesota Historical Society; **Missouri:** State of Missouri, Office of the Secretary of State; **Montana:** Montana Historical Society Library; **Nebraska:** Nebraska Historical Society; **Nevada:** Nevada State Library and Archives, Division of Archives and Records; **New Jersey:** State of New Jersey, Division of Archives and Records Management; **New Mexico:** State of New Mexico, State Records Center and Archives; **New York:** New York State Library; **North Carolina:** North Carolina Department of Cultural Resources; **North Dakota:** State Historical Society of North Dakota; **Ohio:** Ohio Historical Society; **Oklahoma:** Oklahoma Historical Society, Library Resources Division; **Oregon:** Oregon Historical Society; **Pennsylvania:** Commonwealth of Pennsylvania Historical and Museum Commission; **Rhode Island:** Office of the Secretary of State, Rhode Island State Archives; **South Dakota:** South Dakota Historical Society; **Tennessee:** Tennessee State Library and Archives; **Texas:** Texas Historical Commission; **Utah:** Utah State Historical Society; **Vermont:** State of Vermont, Office of the Secretary of State; **Virginia:** Commonwealth of Virginia State Library; **West Virginia:** West Virginia Department of Culture and History; **Wisconsin:** The State Historical Society of Wisconsin; **Wyoming:** Wyoming State Archives Museums, and Historical Department.

Appendix

Party Abbreviations

AD	Anti-Democrat		L&O	Law & Order
Ad.D	Adams Democrat		LR	Liberal Republican
AF	Anti-Federalist		N	Nullifier
AJ	Anti-Jacksonian		Nat.	Nationalist
AL	American Laborite		New Prog.	New Progressive
ALD	Anti-Lecompton Democrat		Nonpart.	Nonpartisan
ALot.	Anti-Lottery Democrat		NR	National Republican
AM	Anti-Monopolist		O	Opposition Party
AMas.	Anti-Mason		P	Populist
AP	American Party		PD	Popular Democrat
C	Conservative		PP	People's Party
Coal.	Coalitionist		PR	Progressive Republican
Confed. D	Confederate Democrat		Prog.	Progressive
Const. U	Constitutional Unionist		Prohib.	Prohibitionist
CR	Conservative Republican		R	Republican
D	Democrat		Read	Readjuster
DFL	Democrat Farmer Labor		REF	Reform
DR	Democratic Republican		Sil.R	Silver Republican
F	Federalist		Soc.	Socialist
FL	Farmer Laborite		SR	State Rights Party
FS	Free-Soiler		SRD	State Rights Democrat
FSD	Free-Soil Democrat		SRFT	State Rights Free-Trader
FSil.	Free-Silver		U	Unionist
G	Greenbacker		UD	Union Democrat
I	Independent		UL	Union Laborite
ID	Independent Democrat		UR	Union Republican
IP	Independent Populist		UU	Unconditional Unionist
IR	Independent Republican		UW	Union Whig
IRad.	Independent Radical		W	Whig
IW	Independent Whig			
J	Jacksonian			
Jeff.R	Jeffersonian Republican			
L	Liberal			
Lab.	Laborite			

U.S. Presidents and Vice Presidents

President and political party	Born	Died	Age at inauguration	Native of	Elected from	Term of service	Vice president
George Washington (F)	1732	1799	57	Va.	Va.	April 30, 1789–March 4, 1793	John Adams
George Washington (F)			61			March 4, 1793–March 4, 1797	John Adams
John Adams (F)	1735	1826	61	Mass.	Mass.	March 4, 1797–March 4, 1801	Thomas Jefferson
Thomas Jefferson (DR)	1743	1826	57	Va.	Va.	March 4, 1801–March 4, 1805	Aaron Burr
Thomas Jefferson (DR)			61			March 4, 1805–March 4, 1809	George Clinton
James Madison (DR)	1751	1836	57	Va.	Va.	March 4, 1809–March 4, 1813	George Clinton
James Madison (DR)			61			March 4, 1813–March 4, 1817	Elbridge Gerry
James Monroe (DR)	1758	1831	58	Va.	Va.	March 4, 1817–March 4, 1821	Daniel D. Tompkins
James Monroe (DR)			62			March 4, 1821–March 4, 1825	Daniel D. Tompkins
John Q. Adams (DR)	1767	1848	57	Mass.	Mass.	March 4, 1825–March 4, 1829	John C. Calhoun
Andrew Jackson (D)	1767	1845	61	S.C.	Tenn.	March 4, 1829–March 4, 1833	John C. Calhoun
Andrew Jackson (D)			65			March 4, 1833–March 4, 1837	Martin Van Buren
Martin Van Buren (D)	1782	1862	54	N.Y.	N.Y.	March 4, 1837–March 4, 1841	Richard M. Johnson
W. H. Harrison (W)	1773	1841	68	Va.	Ohio	March 4, 1841–April 4, 1841	John Tyler
John Tyler (W)	1790	1862	51	Va.	Va.	April 6, 1841–March 4, 1845	
James K. Polk (D)	1795	1849	49	N.C.	Tenn.	March 4, 1845–March 4, 1849	George M. Dallas
Zachary Taylor (W)	1784	1850	64	Va.	La.	March 4, 1849–July 9, 1850	Millard Fillmore
Millard Fillmore (W)	1800	1874	50	N.Y.	N.Y.	July 10, 1850–March 4, 1853	
Franklin Pierce (D)	1804	1869	48	N.H.	N.H.	March 4, 1853–March 4, 1857	William R. King
James Buchanan (D)	1791	1868	65	Pa.	Pa.	March 4, 1857–March 4, 1861	John C. Breckinridge
Abraham Lincoln (R)	1809	1865	52	Ky.	Ill.	March 4, 1861–March 4, 1865	Hannibal Hamlin
Abraham Lincoln (R)			56			March 4, 1865–April 15, 1865	Andrew Johnson
Andrew Johnson (R)	1808	1875	56	N.C.	Tenn.	April 15, 1865–March 4, 1869	
Ulysses S. Grant (R)	1822	1885	46	Ohio	Ill.	March 4, 1869–March 4, 1873	Schuyler Colfax
Ulysses S. Grant (R)			50			March 4, 1873–March 4, 1877	Henry Wilson
Rutherford B. Hayes (R)	1822	1893	54	Ohio	Ohio	March 4, 1877–March 4, 1881	William A. Wheeler
James A. Garfield (R)	1831	1881	49	Ohio	Ohio	March 4, 1881–Sept. 19, 1881	Chester A. Arthur
Chester A. Arthur (R)	1830	1886	50	Vt.	N.Y.	Sept. 20, 1881–March 4, 1885	
Grover Cleveland (D)	1837	1908	47	N.J.	N.Y.	March 4, 1885–March 4, 1889	Thomas A. Hendricks
Benjamin Harrison (R)	1833	1901	55	Ohio	Ind.	March 4, 1889–March 4, 1893	Levi P. Morton
Grover Cleveland (D)	1837	1908	55	N.J.	N.Y.	March 4, 1893–March 4, 1897	Adlai E. Stevenson
William McKinley (R)	1843	1901	54	Ohio	Ohio	March 4, 1897–March 4, 1901	Garret A. Hobart
William McKinley (R)			58			March 4, 1901–Sept. 14, 1901	Theodore Roosevelt
Theodore Roosevelt (R)	1858	1919	42	N.Y.	N.Y.	Sept. 14, 1901–March 4, 1905	
Theodore Roosevelt (R)			46			March 4, 1905–March 4, 1909	Charles W. Fairbanks
William H. Taft (R)	1857	1930	51	Ohio	Ohio	March 4, 1909–March 4, 1913	James S. Sherman
Woodrow Wilson (D)	1856	1924	56	Va.	N.J.	March 4, 1913–March 4, 1917	Thomas R. Marshall
Woodrow Wilson (D)			60			March 4, 1917–March 4, 1921	Thomas R. Marshall
Warren G. Harding (R)	1865	1923	55	Ohio	Ohio	March 4, 1921–Aug. 2, 1923	Calvin Coolidge
Calvin Coolidge (R)	1872	1933	51	Vt.	Mass.	Aug. 3, 1923–March 4, 1925	
Calvin Coolidge (R)			52			March 4, 1925–March 4, 1929	Charles G. Dawes
Herbert Hoover (R)	1874	1964	54	Iowa	Calif.	March 4, 1929–March 4, 1933	Charles Curtis
Franklin D. Roosevelt (D)	1882	1945	51	N.Y.	N.Y.	March 4, 1933–Jan. 20, 1937	John N. Garner
Franklin D. Roosevelt (D)			55			Jan. 20, 1937–Jan. 20, 1941	John N. Garner
Franklin D. Roosevelt (D)			59			Jan. 20, 1941–Jan. 20, 1945	Henry A. Wallace
Franklin D. Roosevelt (D)			63			Jan. 20, 1945–April 12, 1945	Harry S. Truman
Harry S. Truman (D)	1884	1972	60	Mo.	Mo.	April 12, 1945–Jan. 20, 1949	
Harry S. Truman (D)			64			Jan. 20, 1949–Jan. 20, 1953	Alben W. Barkley
Dwight D. Eisenhower (R)	1890	1969	62	Texas	N.Y.	Jan. 20, 1953–Jan. 20, 1957	Richard Nixon
Dwight D. Eisenhower (R)			66		Pa.	Jan. 20, 1957–Jan. 20, 1961	Richard Nixon
John F. Kennedy (D)	1917	1963	43	Mass.	Mass.	Jan. 20, 1961–Nov. 22, 1963	Lyndon B. Johnson
Lyndon B. Johnson (D)	1908	1973	55	Texas	Texas	Nov. 22, 1963–Jan. 20, 1965	
Lyndon B. Johnson (D)			56			Jan. 20, 1965–Jan. 20, 1969	Hubert H. Humphrey
Richard Nixon (R)	1913	1994	56	Calif.	N.Y.	Jan. 20, 1969–Jan. 20, 1973	Spiro T. Agnew
Richard Nixon (R)			60		Calif.	Jan. 20, 1973–Aug. 9, 1974	Spiro T. Agnew Gerald R. Ford
Gerald R. Ford (R)	1913		61	Neb.	Mich.	Aug. 9, 1974–Jan. 20, 1977	Nelson A. Rockefeller
Jimmy Carter (D)	1924		52	Ga.	Ga.	Jan. 20, 1977–Jan. 20, 1981	Walter F. Mondale

U.S. Presidents and Vice Presidents *(cont.)*

President and political party	Born	Died	Age at inaugu- ration	Native of	Elected from	Term of service	Vice president
Ronald Reagan (R)	1911	2004	69	Ill.	Calif.	Jan. 20, 1981–Jan. 20, 1985	George Bush
Ronald Reagan (R)			73			Jan. 20, 1985–Jan. 20, 1989	George Bush
George Bush (R)	1924		64	Mass.	Texas	Jan. 20, 1989–Jan. 20, 1993	Dan Quayle
Bill Clinton (D)	1946		46	Ark.	Ark.	Jan. 20, 1993–Jan. 20, 1997	Albert Gore Jr.
Bill Clinton (D)			50			Jan. 20, 1997–Jan. 20, 2001	Albert Gore Jr.
George W. Bush (R)	1946		54	Texas	Texas	Jan. 20, 2001–Jan. 20, 2005	Richard B. Cheney
George W. Bush (R)			58			Jan. 20, 2005–	Richard B. Cheney

Note: D—Democrat; DR—Democratic—Republican; F—Federalist; R—Republican; W—Whig.

Sources: *Congressional Quarterly's Guide to U.S. Elections,* 4th ed. (Washington, D.C.: CQ Press, 2001); and *CQ Weekly, selected issues.*

Cabinet Members and Chief Justices, 1789–2005

Following is a list of cabinet members and chief justices by administration from George Washington to George W. Bush. Included are dates of service. The list does not include those who served in ad interim appointments.

George Washington, 1789–1797

Chief Justice
John Jay
Oct. 19, 1789–June 29, 1795
Oliver Ellsworth
March 8, 1796–Dec. 15, 1800

Vice President
John Adams
April 21, 1789–March 4, 1797

Secretary of State
Thomas Jefferson
March 22, 1790–Dec. 31, 1793
Edmund Randolph
Jan. 2, 1794–Aug. 20, 1795
Timothy Pickering
Dec. 10, 1795–May 12, 1800

Secretary of the Treasury
Alexander Hamilton
Sept. 11, 1789–Jan. 31, 1795
Oliver Wolcott Jr.
Feb. 3, 1795–Dec. 31, 1800

Secretary of War
Henry Knox
Sept. 12, 1789–Dec. 31, 1794
Timothy Pickering
Jan. 2–Dec. 10, 1795
James McHenry
Jan. 27, 1796–May 13, 1800

Attorney General
Edmund Randolph
Sept. 26, 1789–Jan. 2, 1794
William Bradford
Jan. 27, 1794–Aug. 23, 1795
Charles Lee
Dec. 10, 1795–Feb. 18, 1801

Postmaster General
Samuel Osgood
Sept. 26, 1789–Aug. 18, 1791
Timothy Pickering
Aug. 19, 1791–Jan. 2, 1795
Joseph Habersham
July 1, 1795–Nov. 2, 1801

John Adams, 1797–1801

Chief Justice
Oliver Ellsworth
March 8, 1796–Dec. 15, 1800
John Marshall
Feb. 4, 1801–July 6, 1835

Vice President
Thomas Jefferson
March 4, 1797–March 4, 1801

Secretary of State
Timothy Pickering
Dec. 10, 1795–May 12, 1800
John Marshall
June 6, 1800–Feb. 4, 1801

Secretary of the Treasury
Oliver Wolcott Jr.
Feb. 3, 1795–Dec. 31, 1800
Samuel Dexter
Jan. 1–May 13, 1801

Secretary of War
James McHenry
Jan. 27, 1796–May 13, 1800
Samuel Dexter
May 13–Dec. 31, 1800

Attorney General
Charles Lee
Dec. 10, 1795–Feb. 18, 1801

Postmaster General
Joseph Habersham
July 1, 1795–Nov. 2, 1801

Secretary of the Navy
Benjamin Stoddert
June 18, 1798–March 31, 1801

Thomas Jefferson, 1801–1809

Chief Justice
John Marshall
Feb. 4, 1801–July 6, 1835

Vice President
Aaron Burr
March 4, 1801–March 4, 1805
George Clinton
March 4, 1805–April 20, 1812

Secretary of State
James Madison
May 2, 1801–March 3, 1809

Secretary of the Treasury
Samuel Dexter
Jan. 1–May 13, 1801
Albert Gallatin
May 14, 1801–Feb. 8, 1814

Secretary of War
Henry Dearborn
March 5, 1801–March 7, 1809

Attorney General
Levi Lincoln
March 5, 1801–March 3, 1805
John C. Breckinridge
Aug. 7, 1805–Dec. 14, 1806
Caesar Augustus Rodney
Jan. 20, 1807–Dec. 11, 1811

Postmaster General
Joseph Habersham
July 1, 1795–Nov. 2, 1801
Gideon Granger
Nov. 28, 1801–Feb. 25, 1814

Secretary of the Navy
Benjamin Stoddert
June 18, 1798–March 31, 1801
Robert Smith
July 27, 1801–March 7, 1809

James Madison, 1809–1817

Chief Justice
John Marshall
Feb. 4, 1801–July 6, 1835

Vice President
George Clinton
March 4, 1805–April 20, 1812
Elbridge Gerry
March 4, 1813–Nov. 23, 1814

Secretary of State
Robert Smith
March 6, 1809–April 1, 1811
James Monroe
April 6, 1811–Sept. 30, 1814
Feb. 28, 1815–March 3, 1817

Secretary of the Treasury
Albert Gallatin
May 14, 1801–Feb. 8, 1814
George Washington Campbell
Feb. 9–Oct. 5, 1814
Alexander James Dallas
Oct. 6, 1814–Oct. 21, 1816
William Harris Crawford
Oct. 22, 1816–March 6, 1825

Secretary of War
William Eustis
March 7, 1809–Jan. 13, 1813
John Armstrong
Jan. 13, 1813–Sept. 27, 1814
James Monroe
Oct. 1, 1814–Feb. 28, 1815
William Harris Crawford
Aug. 1, 1815–Oct. 22, 1816

Attorney General
Caesar Augustus Rodney
Jan. 20, 1807–Dec. 11, 1811
William Pinkney
Dec. 11, 1811–Feb. 10, 1814

Richard Rush
Feb. 10, 1814–Nov. 13, 1817

Postmaster General
Gideon Granger
Nov. 28, 1801–Feb. 25, 1814
Return Jonathan Meigs Jr.
April 11, 1814–June 30, 1823

Secretary of the Navy
Robert Smith
July 27, 1801–March 7, 1809
Paul Hamilton
May 15, 1809–Dec. 31, 1812
William Jones
Jan. 19, 1813–Dec. 1, 1814
Benjamin Williams Crowninshield
Jan. 16, 1815–Sept. 30, 1818

James Monroe, 1817–1825

Chief Justice
John Marshall
Feb. 4, 1801–July 6, 1835

Vice President
Daniel D. Tompkins
March 4, 1817–March 4, 1825

Secretary of State
John Quincy Adams
Sept. 22, 1817–March 3, 1825

Secretary of the Treasury
William Harris Crawford
Oct. 22, 1816–March 6, 1825

Secretary of War
John C. Calhoun
Oct. 8, 1817–March 7, 1825

Attorney General
Richard Rush
Feb. 10, 1814–Nov. 13, 1817
William Wirt
Nov. 13, 1817–March 3, 1829

Postmaster General
Return Jonathan Meigs Jr.
April 11, 1814–June 30, 1823
John McLean
July 1, 1823–March 9, 1829

Secretary of the Navy
Benjamin Williams Crowninshield
Jan. 16, 1815–Sept. 30, 1818
Smith Thompson
Jan. 1, 1819–Aug. 31, 1823
Samuel Lewis Southard
Sept. 16, 1823–March 3, 1829

John Quincy Adams, 1825–1829

Chief Justice
John Marshall
Feb. 4, 1801–July 6, 1835

Vice President
John C. Calhoun
March 4, 1825–Dec. 28, 1832

Secretary of State
Henry Clay
March 7, 1825–March 3, 1829

Secretary of the Treasury
Richard Rush
March 7, 1825–March 5, 1829

Secretary of War
James Barbour
March 7, 1825–May 23, 1828
Peter Buell Porter
May 26, 1828–March 9, 1829

Attorney General
William Wirt
Nov. 13, 1817–March 3, 1829

Postmaster General
John McLean
July 1, 1823–March 9, 1829

Secretary of the Navy
Samuel Lewis Southard
Sept. 16, 1823–March 3, 1829

Andrew Jackson, 1829–1837

Chief Justice
John Marshall
Feb. 4, 1801–July 6, 1835
Roger B. Taney
March 28, 1836–Oct. 12, 1864

Vice President
John C. Calhoun
March 4, 1825–Dec. 28, 1832
Martin Van Buren
March 4, 1833–March 4, 1837

Secretary of State
Martin Van Buren
March 28, 1829–March 23, 1831
Edward Livingston
May 24, 1831–May 29, 1833
Louis McLane
May 29, 1833–June 30, 1834
John Forsyth
July 1, 1834–March 3, 1841

Secretary of the Treasury
Samuel Delucenna Ingham
March 6, 1829–June 20, 1831
Louis McLane
Aug. 8, 1831–May 28, 1833

William John Duane
May 29–Sept. 22, 1833
Roger B. Taney
Sept. 23, 1833–June 25, 1834
Levi Woodbury
July 1, 1834–March 3, 1841

Secretary of War
John Henry Eaton
March 9, 1829–June 18, 1831
Lewis Cass
Aug. 1, 1831–Oct. 5, 1836

Attorney General
John Macpherson Berrien
March 9, 1829–July 20, 1831
Roger B. Taney
July 20, 1831–Sept. 23, 1833
Benjamin Franklin Butler
Nov. 15, 1833–Sept. 1, 1838

Postmaster General
John McLean
July 1, 1823–March 9, 1829
William Taylor Barry
April 6, 1829–April 30, 1835
Amos Kendall
May 1, 1835–May 25, 1840

Secretary of the Navy
John Branch
March 9, 1829–May 12, 1831
Levi Woodbury
May 23, 1831–June 30, 1834
Mahlon Dickerson
July 1, 1834–June 30, 1838

Martin Van Buren, 1837–1841

Chief Justice
Roger B. Taney
March 28, 1836–Oct. 12, 1864

Vice President
Richard M. Johnson
March 4, 1837–March 4, 1841

Secretary of State
John Forsyth
July 1, 1834–March 3, 1841

Secretary of the Treasury
Levi Woodbury
July 1, 1834–March 3, 1841

Secretary of War
Joel Roberts Poinsett
March 7, 1837–March 5, 1841

Attorney General
Benjamin Franklin Butler
Nov. 15, 1833–Sept. 1, 1838
Felix Grundy
Sept. 1, 1838–Dec. 1, 1839

Henry Dilworth Gilpin
Jan. 11, 1840–March 4, 1841

Postmaster General
Amos Kendall
May 1, 1835–May 25, 1840
John Milton Niles
May 26, 1840–March 3, 1841

Secretary of the Navy
Mahlon Dickerson
July 1, 1834–June 30, 1838
James Kirke Paulding
July 1, 1838–March 3, 1841

William Henry Harrison, 1841

Chief Justice
Roger B. Taney
March 28, 1836–Oct. 12, 1864

Vice President
John Tyler
March 4, 1841–April 6, 1841

Secretary of State
Daniel Webster
March 6, 1841–May 8, 1843
July 23, 1850–Oct. 24, 1852

Secretary of the Treasury
Thomas Ewing
March 4–Sept. 11, 1841

Secretary of War
John Bell
March 5–Sept. 13, 1841

Attorney General
John Jordan Crittenden
March 5–Sept. 13, 1841
July 22, 1850–March 3, 1853

Postmaster General
Francis Granger
March 8–Sept. 13, 1841

Secretary of the Navy
George Edmund Badger
March 6–Sept. 11, 1841

John Tyler, 1841–1845

Chief Justice
Roger B. Taney
March 28, 1836–Oct. 12, 1864

Vice President
None

Secretary of State
Daniel Webster
March 6, 1841–May 8, 1843
July 23, 1850–Oct. 24, 1852
Abel Parker Upshur
July 24, 1843–Feb. 28, 1844

John C. Calhoun
April 1, 1844–March 10, 1845

Secretary of the Treasury
Thomas Ewing
March 4–Sept. 11, 1841
Walter Forward
Sept. 13, 1841–March 1, 1843
John Canfield Spencer
March 8, 1843–May 2, 1844
George Mortimer Bibb
July 4, 1844–March 7, 1845

Secretary of War
John Bell
March 5–Sept. 13, 1841
John Canfield Spencer
Oct. 12, 1841–March 3, 1843
James Madison Porter
March 8, 1843–Jan. 30, 1844
William Wilkins
Feb. 15, 1844–March 4, 1845

Attorney General
John Jordan Crittenden
March 5–Sept. 13, 1841
July 22, 1850–March 3, 1853
Hugh Swinton Legare
Sept. 13, 1841–June 20, 1843
John Nelson
July 1, 1843–March 3, 1845

Postmaster General
Francis Granger
March 8–Sept. 13, 1841
Charles Anderson Wickliffe
Oct. 13, 1841–March 6, 1845

Secretary of the Navy
George Edmund Badger
March 6–Sept. 11, 1841
Abel Parker Upshur
Oct. 11, 1841–July 23, 1843
David Henshaw
July 24, 1843–Feb. 18, 1844
Thomas Walker Gilmer
Feb. 19–Feb. 28, 1844
John Young Mason
March 26, 1844–March 10, 1845
Sept. 10, 1846–March 7, 1849

James K. Polk, 1845–1849

Chief Justice
Roger B. Taney
March 28, 1836–Oct. 12, 1864

Vice President
George M. Dallas
March 4, 1845–March 4, 1849

Secretary of State
John C. Calhoun
April 1, 1844–March 10, 1845

James Buchanan
March 10, 1845–March 7, 1849

Secretary of the Treasury
George Mortimer Bibb
July 4, 1844–March 7, 1845
Robert John Walker
March 8, 1845–March 5, 1849

Secretary of War
William Wilkins
Feb. 15, 1844–March 4, 1845
William Learned Marcy
March 6, 1845–March 4, 1849

Attorney General
John Nelson
July 1, 1843–March 3, 1845
John Young Mason
March 11, 1845–Sept. 9, 1846
Nathan Clifford
Oct. 17, 1846–March 17, 1848
Isaac Toucey
June 21, 1848–March 3, 1849

Postmaster General
Charles Anderson Wickliffe
Oct. 13, 1841–March 6, 1845
Cave Johnson
March 7, 1845–March 5, 1849

Secretary of the Navy
John Young Mason
March 26, 1844–March 10, 1845
Sept. 10, 1846–March 7, 1849
George Bancroft
March 11, 1845–Sept. 9, 1846

Zachary Taylor, 1849–1850

Chief Justice
Roger B. Taney
March 28, 1836–Oct. 12, 1864

Vice President
Millard Fillmore
March 4, 1849–July 10, 1850

Secretary of State
James Buchanan
March 10, 1845–March 7, 1849
John Middleton Clayton
March 8, 1849–July 22, 1850

Secretary of the Treasury
Robert John Walker
March 8, 1845–March 5, 1849
William Morris Meredith
March 8, 1849–July 22, 1850

Secretary of War
William Learned Marcy
March 6, 1845–March 4, 1849
George Washington Crawford
March 8, 1849–July 23, 1850

Attorney General
Isaac Toucey
June 21, 1848–March 3, 1849
Reverdy Johnson
March 8, 1849–July 20, 1850

Postmaster General
Cave Johnson
March 7, 1845–March 5, 1849
Jacob Collamer
March 8, 1849–July 22, 1850

Secretary of the Navy
John Young Mason
March 26, 1844–March 10, 1845
Sept. 10, 1846–March 7, 1849
William Ballard Preston
March 8, 1849–July 22, 1850

Secretary of the Interior
Thomas Ewing
March 8, 1849–July 22, 1850

Millard Fillmore, 1850–1853

Chief Justice
Roger B. Taney
March 28, 1836–Oct. 12, 1864

Vice President
None

Secretary of State
John Middleton Clayton
March 8, 1849–July 22, 1850
Daniel Webster
March 6, 1841–May 8, 1843
July 23, 1850–Oct. 24, 1852
Edward Everett
Nov. 6, 1852–March 3, 1853

Secretary of the Treasury
William Morris Meredith
March 8, 1849–July 22, 1850
Thomas Corwin
July 23, 1850–March 6, 1853

Secretary of War
George W. Crawford
March 8, 1849–July 23, 1850
Charles Magill Conrad
Aug. 15, 1850–March 7, 1853

Attorney General
Reverdy Johnson
March 8, 1849–July 20, 1850
John Jordan Crittenden
March 5–Sept. 13, 1841
July 22, 1850–March 3, 1853

Postmaster General
Jacob Collamer
March 8, 1849–July 22, 1850
Nathan Kelsey Hall
July 23, 1850–Sept. 13, 1852

Samuel Dickinson Hubbard
Sept. 14, 1852–March 7, 1853

Secretary of the Navy
William Ballard Preston
March 8, 1849–July 22, 1850
William Alexander Graham
Aug. 2, 1850–July 25, 1852
John Pendleton Kennedy
July 26, 1852–March 7, 1853

Secretary of the Interior
Thomas Ewing
March 8, 1849–July 22, 1850
Thomas McKean Thompson McKennan
Aug. 15–Aug. 26, 1850
Alexander Hugh Holmes Stuart
Sept. 12, 1850–March 7, 1853

Franklin Pierce, 1853–1857

Chief Justice
Roger B. Taney
March 28, 1836–Oct. 12, 1864

Vice President
William R. King
March 4, 1853–April 18, 1853

Secretary of State
William Learned Marcy
March 8, 1853–March 6, 1857

Secretary of the Treasury
Thomas Corwin
July 23, 1850–March 6, 1853
James Guthrie
March 7, 1853–March 6, 1857

Secretary of War
Charles Magill Conrad
Aug. 15, 1850–March 7, 1853
Jefferson Davis
March 7, 1853–March 6, 1857

Attorney General
John Jordan Crittenden
March 5–Sept. 13, 1841
July 22, 1850–March 3, 1853
Caleb Cushing
March 7, 1853–March 3, 1857

Postmaster General
Samuel Dickinson Hubbard
Sept. 14, 1852–March 7, 1853
James Campbell
March 8, 1853–March 6, 1857

Secretary of the Navy
John Pendleton Kennedy
July 26, 1852–March 7, 1853
James Cochran Dobbin
March 8, 1853–March 6, 1857

Secretary of the Interior
Alexander Hugh Holmes Stuart
Sept. 12, 1850–March 7, 1853
Robert McClelland
March 8, 1853–March 9, 1857

James Buchanan, 1857–1861

Chief Justice
Roger B. Taney
March 28, 1836–Oct. 12, 1864

Vice President
John C. Breckinridge
March 4, 1857–March 4, 1861

Secretary of State
William Learned Marcy
March 8, 1853–March 6, 1857
Lewis Cass
March 6, 1857–Dec. 14, 1860
Jeremiah Sullivan Black
Dec. 17, 1860–March 5, 1861

Secretary of the Treasury
James Guthrie
March 7, 1853–March 6, 1857
Howell Cobb
March 7, 1857–Dec. 8, 1860
Philip Francis Thomas
Dec. 12, 1860–Jan. 14, 1861
John Adams Dix
Jan. 15–March 6, 1861

Secretary of War
John Buchanan Floyd
March 6, 1857–Dec. 29, 1860
Joseph Holt
Jan. 18–March 5, 1861

Attorney General
Caleb Cushing
March 7, 1853–March 3, 1857
Jeremiah Sullivan Black
March 6, 1857–Dec. 17, 1860
Edwin Stanton
Dec. 20, 1860–March 3, 1861

Postmaster General
James Campbell
March 8, 1853–March 6, 1857
Aaron Venable Brown
March 7, 1857–March 8, 1859
Joseph Holt
March 14, 1859–Dec. 31, 1860
Horatio King
Feb. 12–March 9, 1861

Secretary of the Navy
James Cochran Dobbin
March 8, 1853–March 6, 1857
Isaac Toucey
March 7, 1857–March 6, 1861

Secretary of the Interior
Robert McClelland
March 8, 1853–March 9, 1857
Jacob Thompson
March 10, 1857–Jan. 8, 1861

Abraham Lincoln, 1861–1865

Chief Justice
Roger B. Taney
March 28, 1836–Oct. 12, 1864
Salmon P. Chase
Dec. 15, 1864–May 7, 1873

Vice President
Hannibal Hamlin
March 4, 1861–March 4, 1865
Andrew Johnson
March 4, 1865–April 15, 1865

Secretary of State
Jeremiah Sullivan Black
Dec. 17, 1860–March 5, 1861
William Henry Seward
March 6, 1861–March 4, 1869

Secretary of the Treasury
John Adams Dix
Jan. 15–March 6, 1861
Salmon P. Chase
March 7, 1861–June 30, 1864
William Pitt Fessenden
July 5, 1864–March 3, 1865
Hugh McCulloch
March 9, 1865–March 3, 1869
Oct. 31, 1884–March 7, 1885

Secretary of War
Joseph Holt
Jan. 18–March 5, 1861
Simon Cameron
March 5, 1861–Jan. 14, 1862
Edwin Stanton
Jan. 20, 1862–May 28, 1868

Attorney General
Edwin Stanton
Dec. 20, 1860–March 3, 1861
Edward Bates
March 5, 1861–Sept. 1864
James Speed
Dec. 2, 1864–July 17, 1866

Postmaster General
Horatio King
Feb. 12–March 9, 1861
Montgomery Blair
March 9, 1861–Sept. 30, 1864
William Dennison Jr.
Oct. 1, 1864–July 16, 1866

Secretary of the Navy
Isaac Toucey
March 7, 1857–March 6, 1861

Gideon Welles
March 7, 1861–March 3, 1869

Secretary of the Interior
Caleb Blood Smith
March 5, 1861–Dec. 31, 1862
John Palmer Usher
Jan. 1, 1863–May 15, 1865

Andrew Johnson, 1865–1869

Chief Justice
Salmon P. Chase
Dec. 15, 1864–May 7, 1873

Vice President
None

Secretary of State
William Henry Seward
March 6, 1861–March 4, 1869

Secretary of the Treasury
Hugh McCulloch
March 9, 1865–March 3, 1869
Oct. 31, 1884–March 7, 1885

Secretary of War
Edwin Stanton
Jan. 20, 1862–May 28, 1868
John McAllister Schofield
June 1, 1868–March 13, 1869

Attorney General
James Speed
Dec. 2, 1864–July 17, 1866
Henry Stanberry
July 23, 1866–March 12, 1868
William Maxwell Evarts
July 15, 1868–March 3, 1869

Postmaster General
William Dennison Jr.
Oct. 1, 1864–July 16, 1866
Alexander Williams Randall
July 25, 1866–March 4, 1869

Secretary of the Navy
Gideon Welles
March 7, 1861–March 3, 1869

Secretary of the Interior
John Palmer Usher
Jan. 1, 1863–May 15, 1865
James Harlan
May 15, 1865–Aug. 31, 1866
Orville Hickman Browning
Sept. 1, 1866–March 4, 1869

Ulysses S. Grant, 1869–1877

Chief Justice
Salmon P. Chase
Dec. 15, 1864–May 7, 1873

Morrison R. Waite
March 4, 1874–March 23, 1888

Vice President
Schuyler Colfax
March 4, 1869–March 4, 1873
Henry Wilson
March 4, 1873–Nov. 22, 1875

Secretary of State
William Henry Seward
March 6, 1861–March 4, 1869
Elihu Benjamin Washburne
March 5–March 16, 1869
Hamilton Fish
March 17, 1869–March 12, 1877

Secretary of the Treasury
Hugh McCulloch
March 9, 1865–March 3, 1869
Oct. 31, 1884–March 7, 1885
George Sewel Boutwell
March 12, 1869–March 16, 1873
William Adams Richardson
March 17, 1873–June 3, 1874
Benjamin Helm Bristow
June 4, 1874–June 20, 1876
Lot Myrick Morrill
July 7, 1876–March 9, 1877

Secretary of War
John McAllister Schofield
June 1, 1868–March 13, 1869
John Aaron Rawlins
March 13–Sept. 6, 1869
William Tecumseh Sherman
Sept. 11–Oct. 25, 1869
William Worth Belknap
Oct. 25, 1869–March 2, 1876
Alphonso Taft
March 8–May 22, 1876
James Donald Cameron
May 22, 1876–March 3, 1877

Attorney General
Ebenezer Rockwood Hoar
March 5, 1869–June 23, 1870
Amos Tappan Akerman
June 23, 1870–Jan. 10, 1872
George Henry Williams
Jan. 10, 1872–May 15, 1875
Edwards Pierrepont
May 15, 1875–May 22, 1876
Alphonso Taft
May 22, 1876–March 11, 1877

Postmaster General
John Angel James Creswell
March 6, 1869–July 6, 1874
James William Marshall
July 7–Aug. 31, 1874
Marshall Jewell
Sept. 1, 1874–July 12, 1876

James Noble Tyner
July 13, 1876–March 12, 1877

Secretary of the Navy
Adolph Edward Borie
March 9–June 25, 1869
George Maxwell Robeson
June 26, 1869–March 12, 1877

Secretary of the Interior
Jacob Dolson Cox
March 5, 1869–Oct. 31, 1870
Columbus Delano
Nov. 1, 1870–Sept. 30, 1875
Zachariah Chandler
Oct. 19, 1875–March 11, 1877

Rutherford B. Hayes, 1877–1881

Chief Justice
Morrison R. Waite
March 4, 1874–March 23, 1888

Vice President
William A. Wheeler
March 4, 1877–March 4, 1881

Secretary of State
Hamilton Fish
March 17, 1869–March 12, 1877
William Maxwell Evarts
March 12, 1877–March 7, 1881

Secretary of the Treasury
Lot Myrick Morrill
July 7, 1876–March 9, 1877
John Sherman
March 10, 1877–March 3, 1881

Secretary of War
James Donald Cameron
May 22, 1876–March 3, 1877
George Washington McCrary
March 12, 1877–Dec. 10, 1879
Alexander Ramsey
Dec. 10, 1879–March 5, 1881

Attorney General
Alphonso Taft
May 22, 1876–March 11, 1877
Charles Devens
March 12, 1877–March 6, 1881

Postmaster General
James Noble Tyner
July 13, 1876–March 12, 1877
David McKendree Key
March 13, 1877–Aug. 24, 1880
Horace Maynard
Aug. 25, 1880–March 7, 1881

Secretary of the Navy
George Maxwell Robeson
June 26, 1869–March 12, 1877

Richard Wigginton Thompson
March 13, 1877–Dec. 20, 1880
Nathan Goff Jr.
Jan. 7–March 6, 1881

Secretary of the Interior
Zachariah Chandler
Oct. 19, 1875–March 11, 1877
Carl Schurz
March 12, 1877–March 7, 1881

James A. Garfield, 1881

Chief Justice
Morrison R. Waite
March 4, 1874–March 23, 1888

Vice President
Chester A. Arthur
March 4, 1881–Sept. 20, 1881

Secretary of State
William Maxwell Evarts
March 12, 1877–March 7, 1881
James G. Blaine
March 7–Dec. 19, 1881
March 7, 1889–June 4, 1892

Secretary of the Treasury
William Windom
March 8–Nov. 13, 1881
March 7, 1889–Jan. 29, 1891

Secretary of War
Alexander Ramsey
Dec. 10, 1879–March 5, 1881
Robert Todd Lincoln
March 5, 1881–March 5, 1885

Attorney General
Charles Devens
March 12, 1877–March 6, 1881
Wayne MacVeagh
March 7–Oct. 24, 1881

Postmaster General
Horace Maynard
Aug. 25, 1880–March 7, 1881
Thomas Lemuel James
March 8, 1881–Jan. 4, 1882

Secretary of the Navy
Nathan Goff Jr.
Jan. 7–March 6, 1881
William Henry Hunt
March 7, 1881–April 16, 1882

Secretary of the Interior
Carl Schurz
March 12, 1877–March 7, 1881
Samuel Jordan Kirkwood
March 8, 1881–April 17, 1882

Chester A. Arthur, 1881–1885

Chief Justice
Morrison R. Waite
March 4, 1874–March 23, 1888

Vice President
None

Secretary of State
James G. Blaine
March 7–Dec. 19, 1881
March 7, 1889–June 4, 1892
Frederick Theodore Frelinghuysen
Dec. 19, 1881–March 6, 1885

Secretary of the Treasury
William Windom
March 8–Nov. 13, 1881
March 7, 1889–Jan. 29, 1891
Charles James Folger
Nov. 14, 1881–Sept. 4, 1884
Walter Quintin Gresham
Sept. 5–Oct. 30, 1884
Hugh McCulloch
March 9, 1865–March 3, 1869
Oct. 31, 1884–March 7, 1885

Secretary of War
Robert Todd Lincoln
March 5, 1881–March 5, 1885

Attorney General
Wayne Macffeagh
March 7–Oct. 24, 1881
Benjamin Harris Brewster
Jan. 2, 1882–March 5, 1885

Postmaster General
Thomas Lemuel James
March 8, 1881–Jan. 4, 1882
Timothy Otis Howe
Jan. 5, 1882–March 25, 1883
Walter Quintin Gresham
April 11, 1883–Sept. 24, 1884
Frank Hatton
Oct. 15, 1884–March 6, 1885

Secretary of the Navy
William Henry Hunt
March 7, 1881–April 16, 1882
William Eaton Chandler
April 16, 1882–March 6, 1885

Secretary of the Interior
Samuel Jordan Kirkwood
March 8, 1881–April 17, 1882
Henry Moore Teller
April 18, 1882–March 3, 1885

Grover Cleveland, 1885–1889

Chief Justice
Morrison R. Waite
March 4, 1874–March 23, 1888

Melville W. Fuller
Oct. 8, 1888–July 4, 1910

Vice President
Thomas A. Hendricks
March 4, 1885–Nov. 25, 1885

Secretary of State
Frederick Theodore Frelinghuysen
Dec. 19, 1881–March 6, 1885
Thomas Francis Bayard Sr.
March 7, 1885–March 6, 1889

Secretary of the Treasury
Hugh McCulloch
March 9, 1865–March 3, 1869
Oct. 31, 1884–March 7, 1885
Daniel Manning
March 8, 1885–March 31, 1887
Charles Stebbins Fairchild
April 1, 1887–March 6, 1889

Secretary of War
Robert Todd Lincoln
March 5, 1881–March 5, 1885
William Crowninshield Endicott
March 5, 1885–March 5, 1889

Attorney General
Benjamin Harris Brewster
Jan. 2, 1882–March 5, 1885
Augustus Hill Garland
March 6, 1885–March 5, 1889

Postmaster General
Frank Hatton
Oct. 15, 1884–March 6, 1885
William Freeman Vilas
March 7, 1885–Jan. 16, 1888
Donald McDonald Dickinson
Jan. 17, 1888–March 5, 1889

Secretary of the Navy
William Eaton Chandler
April 16, 1882–March 6, 1885
William Collins Whitney
March 7, 1885–March 5, 1889

Secretary of the Interior
Lucius Quintus Cincinnatus Lamar
March 6, 1885–Jan. 10, 1888
William Freeman Vilas
Jan. 16, 1888–March 6, 1889

Secretary of Agriculture
Norman Jay Colman
Feb. 15–March 6, 1889

Benjamin Harrison, 1889–1893

Chief Justice
Melville W. Fuller
Oct. 8, 1888–July 4, 1910

Vice President
Levi P. Morton
March 4, 1889–March 4, 1893

Secretary of State
Thomas Francis Bayard Sr.
March 7, 1885–March 6, 1889
James G. Blaine
March 7–Dec. 19, 1881, March 7, 1889–June 4, 1892
John Watson Foster
June 29, 1892–Feb. 23, 1893

Secretary of the Treasury
Charles Stebbins Fairchild
April 1, 1887–March 6, 1889
William Windom
March 8–Nov. 13, 1881
March 7, 1889–Jan. 29, 1891
Charles Foster
Feb. 25, 1891–March 6, 1893

Secretary of War
William Crowninshield Endicott
March 5, 1885–March 5, 1889
Redfield Proctor
March 5, 1889–Nov. 5, 1891
Stephen Benton Elkins
Dec. 17, 1891–March 5, 1893

Attorney General
Augustus Hill Garland
March 6, 1885–March 5, 1889
William Henry Harrison Miller
March 5, 1889–March 6, 1893

Postmaster General
Donald McDonald Dickinson
Jan. 17, 1888–March 5, 1889
John Wanamaker
March 6, 1889–March 7, 1893

Secretary of the Navy
William Collins Whitney
March 7, 1885–March 5, 1889
Benjamin Franklin Tracy
March 6, 1889–March 6, 1893

Secretary of the Interior
William Freeman Vilas
Jan. 16, 1888–March 6, 1889
John Willock Noble
March 7, 1889–March 6, 1893

Secretary of Agriculture
Norman Jay Colman
Feb. 15–March 6, 1889
Jeremiah McLain Rusk
March 6, 1889–March 6, 1893

Grover Cleveland, 1893–1897

Chief Justice
Melville W. Fuller
Oct. 8, 1888–July 4, 1910

Vice President
Adlai E. Stevenson
March 4, 1893–March 4, 1897

Secretary of State
Walter Quintin Gresham
March 7, 1893–May 28, 1895
Richard Olney
June 10, 1895–March 5, 1897

Secretary of the Treasury
Charles Foster
Feb. 25, 1891–March 6, 1893
John GriYn Carlisle
March 7, 1893–March 5, 1897

Secretary of War
Stephen Benton Elkins
Dec. 17, 1891–March 5, 1893
Daniel Scott Lamont
March 5, 1893–March 5, 1897

Attorney General
William Henry Harrison Miller
March 5, 1889–March 6, 1893
Richard Olney
March 6, 1893–June 7, 1895
Judson Harmon
June 8, 1895–March 5, 1897

Postmaster General
John Wanamaker
March 6, 1889–March 7, 1893
Wilson Shannon Bissel
March 8, 1893–April 3, 1895
William Lyne Wilson
April 4, 1895–March 5, 1897

Secretary of the Navy
Benjamin Franklin Tracy
March 6, 1889–March 6, 1893
Hilary Abner Herbert
March 7, 1893–March 5, 1897

Secretary of the Interior
John Willock Noble
March 7, 1889–March 6, 1893
Hoke Smith
March 6, 1893–Sept. 1, 1896
David Rowland Francis
Sept. 3, 1896–March 5, 1897

Secretary of Agriculture
Jeremiah McLain Rusk
March 6, 1889–March 6, 1893
Julius Sterling Morton
March 7, 1893–March 5, 1897

William McKinley, 1897–1901

Chief Justice
Melville W. Fuller
Oct. 8, 1888–July 4, 1910

Vice President
Garret A. Hobart
March 4, 1897–Nov. 21, 1899
Theodore Roosevelt
March 4, 1901–Sept. 14, 1901

Secretary of State
Richard Olney
June 10, 1895–March 5, 1897
John Sherman
March 6, 1897–April 27, 1898
William Rufus Day
April 28–Sept. 16, 1898
John Milton Hay
Sept. 30, 1898–July 1, 1905

Secretary of the Treasury
John Griffin Carlisle
March 7, 1893–March 5, 1897
Lyman Judson Gage
March 6, 1897–Jan. 31, 1902

Secretary of War
Daniel Scott Lamont
March 5, 1893–March 5, 1897
Russell Alexander Alger
March 5, 1897–Aug. 1, 1899
Elihu Root
Aug. 1, 1899–Jan. 31, 1904

Attorney General
Judson Harmon
June 8, 1895–March 5, 1897
Joseph McKenna
March 5, 1897–Jan. 25, 1898
John William Griggs
June 25, 1898–March 29, 1901
Philander Chase Knox
April 5, 1901–June 30, 1904

Postmaster General
William Lyne Wilson
April 4, 1895–March 5, 1897
James Albert Gary
March 6, 1897–April 22, 1898
Charles Emory Smith
April 23, 1898–Jan. 14, 1902

Secretary of the Navy
Hilary Abner Herbert
March 7, 1893–March 5, 1897
John Davis Long
March 6, 1897–April 30, 1902

Secretary of the Interior
David Rowland Francis
Sept. 3, 1896–March 5, 1897
Cornelius Newton Bliss
March 6, 1897–Feb. 19, 1899
Ethan Allen Hitchcock
Feb. 20, 1899–March 4, 1907

Secretary of Agriculture
Julius Sterling Morton
March 7, 1893–March 5, 1897

James Wilson
March 6, 1897–March 5, 1913

Theodore Roosevelt, 1901–1909

Chief Justice
Melville W. Fuller
Oct. 8, 1888–July 4, 1910

Vice President
Charles W. Fairbanks
March 4, 1905–March 4, 1909

Secretary of State
John Milton Hay
Sept. 30, 1898–July 1, 1905
Elihu Root
July 19, 1905–Jan. 27, 1909
Robert Bacon
Jan. 27–March 5, 1909

Secretary of the Treasury
Lyman Judson Gage
March 6, 1897–Jan. 31, 1902
Leslie Mortier Shaw
Feb. 1, 1902–March 3, 1907
George Bruce Cortelyou
March 4, 1907–March 7, 1909

Secretary of War
Elihu Root
Aug. 1, 1899–Jan. 31, 1904
William Howard Taft
Feb. 1, 1904–June 30, 1908
Luke Edward Wright
July 1, 1908–March 11, 1909

Attorney General
Philander Chase Knox
April 5, 1901–June 30, 1904
William Henry Moody
July 1, 1904–Dec. 17, 1906
Charles Joseph Bonaparte
Dec. 17, 1906–March 4, 1909

Postmaster General
Charles Emory Smith
April 23, 1898–Jan. 14, 1902
Henry Clay Payne
Jan. 15, 1902–Oct. 4, 1904
Robert John Wynne
Oct. 10, 1904–March 4, 1905
George Bruce Cortelyou
March 7, 1905–March 3, 1907
George von Lengerke Meyer
March 4, 1907–March 5, 1909

Secretary of the Navy
John Davis Long
March 6, 1897–April 30, 1902
William Henry Moody
May 1, 1902–June 30, 1904
Paul Morton
July 1, 1904–July 1, 1905

Charles Joseph Bonaparte
July 1, 1905–Dec. 16, 1906
Victor Howard Metcalf
Dec. 17, 1906–Nov. 30, 1908
Truman Handy Newberry
Dec. 1, 1908–March 5, 1909

Secretary of the Interior
Ethan Allen Hitchcock
Feb. 20, 1899–March 4, 1907
James Rudolph Garfield
March 5, 1907–March 5, 1909

Secretary of Agriculture
James Wilson
March 6, 1897–March 5, 1913

Secretary of Commerce and Labor
George Bruce Cortelyou
Feb. 18, 1903–June 30, 1904
Victor Howard Metcalf
July 1, 1904–Dec. 16, 1906
Oscar Solomon Straus
Dec. 17, 1906–March 5, 1909

William Howard Taft, 1909–1913

Chief Justice
Melville W. Fuller
Oct. 8, 1888–July 4, 1910
Edward D. White
Dec. 19, 1910–May 19, 1921

Vice President
James S. Sherman
March 4, 1909–Oct. 30, 1912

Secretary of State
Robert Bacon
Jan. 27–March 5, 1909
Philander Chase Knox
March 6, 1909–March 5, 1913

Secretary of the Treasury
George Bruce Cortelyou
March 4, 1907–March 7, 1909
Franklin MacVeagh
March 8, 1909–March 5, 1913

Secretary of War
Luke Edward Wright
July 1, 1908–March 11, 1909
Jacob McGavock Dickinson
March 12, 1909–May 21, 1911
Henry Lewis Stimson
May 22, 1911–March 4, 1913
July 10, 1940–Sept. 21, 1945

Attorney General
Charles Joseph Bonaparte
Dec. 17, 1906–March 4, 1909
George Woodward Wickersham
March 5, 1909–March 5, 1913

Postmaster General
George von Lengerke Meyer
March 4, 1907–March 5, 1909
Frank Harris Hitchcock
March 6, 1909–March 4, 1913

Secretary of the Navy
Truman Handy Newberry
Dec. 1, 1908–March 5, 1909
George von Lengerke Meyer
March 6, 1909–March 4, 1913

Secretary of the Interior
James Rudolph Garfield
March 5, 1907–March 5, 1909
Richard Achilles Ballinger
March 6, 1909–March 12, 1911
Walter Lowrie Fisher
March 13, 1911–March 5, 1913

Secretary of Agriculture
James Wilson
March 6, 1897–March 5, 1913

Secretary of Commerce and Labor
Oscar Solomon Straus
Dec. 17, 1906–March 5, 1909
Charles Nagel
March 6, 1909–March 4, 1913

Woodrow Wilson, 1913–1921

Chief Justice
Edward D. White
Dec. 19, 1910–May 19, 1921

Vice President
Thomas R. Marshall
March 4, 1913–March 4, 1921

Secretary of State
Philander Chase Knox
March 6, 1909–March 5, 1913
William Jennings Bryan
March 5, 1913–June 9, 1915
Robert Lansing
June 24, 1915–Feb. 13, 1920
Bainbridge Colby
March 23, 1920–March 4, 1921

Secretary of the Treasury
Franklin MacVeagh
March 8, 1909–March 5, 1913
William Gibbs McAdoo
March 6, 1913–Dec. 15, 1918
Carter Glass
Dec. 16, 1918–Feb. 1, 1920
David Franklin Houston
Feb. 2, 1920–March 3, 1921

Secretary of War
Henry Lewis Stimson
May 22, 1911–March 4, 1913
July 10, 1940–Sept. 21, 1945

Lindley Miller Garrison
March 5, 1913–Feb. 10, 1916
Newton Diehl Baker
March 9, 1916–March 4, 1921

Attorney General
George W. Wickersham
March 5, 1909–March 5, 1913
James Clark McReynolds
March 5, 1913–Aug. 29, 1914
Thomas Watt Gregory
Sept. 3, 1914–March 4, 1919
Alexander Mitchell Palmer
March 5, 1919–March 5, 1921

Postmaster General
Frank Harris Hitchcock
March 6, 1909–March 4, 1913
Albert Sidney Burleson
March 5, 1913–March 4, 1921

Secretary of the Navy
George von Lengerke Meyer
March 6, 1909–March 4, 1913
Josephus Daniels
March 5, 1913–March 5, 1921

Secretary of the Interior
Walter Lowrie Fisher
March 13, 1911–March 5, 1913
Franklin Knight Lane
March 6, 1913–Feb. 29, 1920
John Barton Payne
March 15, 1920–March 4, 1921

Secretary of Agriculture
James Wilson
March 6, 1897–March 5, 1913
David Franklin Houston
March 6, 1913–Feb. 2, 1920
Edwin Thomas Meredith
Feb. 2, 1920–March 4, 1921

Secretary of Commerce
Charles Nagel
March 6, 1909–March 4, 1913
William Cox Redfield
March 5, 1913–Oct. 31, 1919
Joshua Willis Alexander
Dec. 16, 1919–March 4, 1921

Secretary of Labor
William Bauchop Wilson
March 4, 1913–March 4, 1921

Warren G. Harding, 1921–1923

Chief Justice
Edward D. White
Dec. 19, 1910–May 19, 1921
William Howard Taft
July 11, 1921–Feb. 3, 1930

Vice President
Calvin Coolidge
March 4, 1921–Aug. 3, 1923

Secretary of State
Bainbridge Colby
March 23, 1920–March 4, 1921
Charles Evans Hughes
March 5, 1921–March 4, 1925

Secretary of the Treasury
David Houston
Feb. 2, 1920–March 3, 1921
Andrew William Mellon
March 4, 1921–Feb. 12, 1932

Secretary of War
Newton Diehl Baker
March 9, 1916–March 4, 1921
John Wingate Weeks
March 5, 1921–Oct. 13, 1925

Attorney General
Alexander Mitchell Palmer
March 5, 1919–March 5, 1921
Harry Micajah Daugherty
March 5, 1921–March 28, 1924

Postmaster General
Albert Sidney Burleson
March 5, 1913–March 4, 1921
William Harrison Hays
March 5, 1921–March 3, 1922
Hubert Work
March 4, 1922–March 4, 1923
Harry Stewart New
March 4, 1923–March 5, 1929

Secretary of the Navy
Josephus Daniels
March 5, 1913–March 5, 1921
Edwin Denby
March 6, 1921–March 10, 1924

Secretary of the Interior
John Barton Payne
March 15, 1920–March 4, 1921
Albert Bacon Fall
March 5, 1921–March 4, 1923
Hubert Work
March 5, 1923–July 24, 1928

Secretary of Agriculture
Edwin Thomas Meredith
Feb. 2, 1920–March 4, 1921
Henry Wallace
March 5, 1921–Oct. 25, 1924

Secretary of Commerce
Joshua Willis Alexander
Dec. 16, 1919–March 4, 1921
Herbert Clark Hoover
March 5, 1921–Aug. 21, 1928

Secretary of Labor
William Bauchop Wilson
March 4, 1913–March 4, 1921
James John Davis
March 5, 1921–Nov. 30, 1930

Calvin Coolidge, 1923–1929

Chief Justice
William Howard Taft
July 11, 1921–Feb. 3, 1930

Vice President
Charles G. Dawes
March 4, 1925–March 4, 1929

Secretary of State
Charles Evans Hughes
March 5, 1921–March 4, 1925
Frank Billings Kellogg
March 5, 1925–March 28, 1929

Secretary of the Treasury
Andrew William Mellon
March 4, 1921–Feb. 12, 1932

Secretary of War
John Wingate Weeks
March 5, 1921–Oct. 13, 1925
Dwight Filley Davis
Oct. 14, 1925–March 5, 1929

Attorney General
Harry Micajah Daugherty
March 5, 1921–March 28, 1924
Harlan Fiske Stone
April 7, 1924–March 2, 1925
John Garibaldi Sargent
March 17, 1925–March 5, 1929

Postmaster General
Harry Stewart New
March 4, 1923–March 5, 1929

Secretary of the Navy
Edwin Denby
March 6, 1921–March 10, 1924
Curtis Dwight Wilbur
March 19, 1924–March 4, 1929

Secretary of the Interior
Hubert Work
March 5, 1923–July 24, 1928
Roy Owen West
July 25, 1928–March 4, 1929

Secretary of Agriculture
Henry Wallace
March 5, 1921–Oct. 25, 1924
Howard Mason Gore
Nov. 22, 1924–March 4, 1925
William Marion Jardine
March 5, 1925–March 4, 1929

Secretary of Commerce
Herbert C. Hoover
March 5, 1921–Aug. 21, 1928
William Fairfield Whiting
Aug. 22, 1928–March 4, 1929

Secretary of Labor
James John Davis
March 5, 1921–Nov. 30, 1930

Herbert C. Hoover, 1929–1933

Chief Justice
William Howard Taft
July 11, 1921–Feb. 3, 1930
Charles Evans Hughes
Feb. 24, 1930–July 1, 1941

Vice President
Charles Curtis
March 4, 1929–March 4, 1933

Secretary of State
Frank Billings Kellogg
March 5, 1925–March 28, 1929
Henry Lewis Stimson
March 28, 1929–March 4, 1933

Secretary of the Treasury
Andrew William Mellon
March 4, 1921–Feb. 12, 1932
Ogden Livingston Mills
Feb. 13, 1932–March 4, 1933

Secretary of War
Dwight Filley Davis
Oct. 14, 1925–March 5, 1929
James William Good
March 6–Nov. 18, 1929
Patrick Jay Hurley
Dec. 9, 1929–March 3, 1933

Attorney General
John Garibaldi Sargent
March 17, 1925–March 5, 1929
William DeWitt Mitchell
March 5, 1929–March 3, 1933

Postmaster General
Harry Stewart New
March 4, 1923–March 5, 1929
Walter Folger Brown
March 5, 1929–March 5, 1933

Secretary of the Navy
Curtis Dwight Wilbur
March 19, 1924–March 4, 1929
Charles Francis Adams
March 5, 1929–March 4, 1933

Secretary of the Interior
Roy Owen West
July 25, 1928–March 4, 1929
Ray Lyman Wilbur
March 5, 1929–March 4, 1933

Secretary of Agriculture
William Marion Jardine
March 5, 1925–March 4, 1929
Arthur Mastick Hyde
March 6, 1929–March 4, 1933

Secretary of Commerce
William Fairfield Whiting
Aug. 22, 1928–March 4, 1929
Robert Patterson Lamont
March 5, 1929–Aug. 7, 1932
Roy Dikeman Chapin
Aug. 8, 1932–March 3, 1933

Secretary of Labor
James John Davis
March 5, 1921–Nov. 30, 1930
William Nuckles Doak
Dec. 9, 1930–March 4, 1933

Franklin D. Roosevelt, 1933–1945

Chief Justice
Charles Evans Hughes
Feb. 24, 1930–July 1, 1941
Harlan Fiske Stone
July 3, 1941–April 22, 1946

Vice President
John Nance Garner
March 4, 1933–Jan. 20, 1941
Henry A. Wallace
Jan. 20, 1941–Jan. 20, 1945
Harry S. Truman
Jan. 20, 1945–April 12, 1945

Secretary of State
Cordell Hull
March 4, 1933–Nov. 30, 1944
Edward Reilly Stettinius Jr.
Dec. 1, 1944–June 27, 1945

Secretary of the Treasury
William Hartman Woodin
March 5–Dec. 31, 1933
Henry Morgenthau Jr.
Jan. 1, 1934–July 22, 1945

Secretary of War
George Henry Dern
March 4, 1933–Aug. 27, 1936
Harry Hines Woodring
Sept. 25, 1936–June 20, 1940
Henry Lewis Stimson
May 22, 1911–March 4, 1913
July 10, 1940–Sept. 21, 1945

Attorney General
Homer Stille Cummings
March 4, 1933–Jan. 2, 1939
Francis William Murphy
Jan. 17, 1939–Jan. 18, 1940
Robert Houghwout Jackson
Jan. 18, 1940–July 10, 1941

Francis Beverley Biddle
Sept. 15, 1941–June 30, 1945

Postmaster General
James Aloysius Farley
March 6, 1933–Aug. 31, 1940
Frank Comerford Walker
Sept. 11, 1940–June 30, 1945

Secretary of the Navy
Claude Augustus Swanson
March 4, 1933–July 7, 1939
Charles Edison
Jan. 2–June 24, 1940
William Franklin "Frank" Knox
July 11, 1940–April 28, 1944
James V. Forrestal
May 19, 1944–Sept. 17, 1947

Secretary of the Interior
Harold Ickes Sr.
March 4, 1933–Feb. 15, 1946

Secretary of Agriculture
Henry A. Wallace
March 4, 1933–Sept. 4, 1940
Claude Raymond Wickard
Sept. 5, 1940–June 29, 1945

Secretary of Commerce
Daniel Calhoun Roper
March 4, 1933–Dec. 23, 1938
Harry Hopkins
Dec. 24, 1938–Sept. 18, 1940
Jesse Holman Jones
Sept. 19, 1940–March 1, 1945
Henry A. Wallace
March 2, 1945–Sept. 20, 1946

Secretary of Labor
Frances Perkins
March 4, 1933–June 30, 1945

Harry S. Truman, 1945–1953

Chief Justice
Harlan Fiske Stone
July 3, 1941–April 22, 1946
Frederick M. Vinson
June 24, 1946–Sept. 8, 1953

Vice President
Alben W. Barkley
Jan. 20, 1949–Jan. 20, 1953

Secretary of State
Edward Reilly Stettinius Jr.
Dec. 1, 1944–June 27, 1945
James Francis Byrnes
July 3, 1945–Jan. 21, 1947
George C. Marshall
Jan. 21, 1947–Jan. 20, 1949
Dean Acheson
Jan. 21, 1949–Jan. 20, 1953

Secretary of the Treasury
Henry Morgenthau Jr.
Jan. 1, 1934–July 22, 1945
Frederick Moore Vinson
July 23, 1945–June 23, 1946
John Wesley Snyder
June 25, 1946–Jan. 20, 1953

Secretary of War
Henry Lewis Stimson
May 22, 1911–March 4, 1913
July 10, 1940–Sept. 21, 1945
Robert Porter Patterson
Sept. 27, 1945–July 18, 1947
Kenneth Claiborne Royall
July 19–Sept. 17, 1947

Secretary of Defense
James Vincent Forrestal
Sept. 17, 1947–March 27, 1949
Louis Arthur Johnson
March 28, 1949–Sept. 19, 1950
George Catlett Marshall
Sept. 21, 1950–Sept. 12, 1951
Robert Abercrombie Lovett
Sept. 17, 1951–Jan. 20, 1953

Attorney General
Francis Beverley Biddle
Sept. 15, 1941–June 30, 1945
Thomas Campbell Clark
July 1, 1945–Aug. 24, 1949
James Howard McGrath
Aug. 24, 1949–April 7, 1952
James Patrick McGranery
May 27, 1952–Jan. 20, 1953

Postmaster General
Frank Comerford Walker
Sept. 11, 1940–June 30, 1945
Robert Emmet Hannegan
July 1, 1945–Dec. 15, 1947
Jesse Monroe Donaldson
Dec. 16, 1947–Jan. 20, 1953

Secretary of the Navy
James Vincent Forrestal
May 19, 1944–Sept. 17, 1947

Secretary of the Interior
Harold Ickes Sr.
March 4, 1933–Feb. 15, 1946
Julius Albert Krug
March 18, 1946–Dec. 1, 1949
Oscar Littleton Chapman
Dec. 1, 1949–Jan. 20, 1953

Secretary of Agriculture
Claude Raymond Wickard
Sept. 5, 1940–June 29, 1945
Clinton Presba Anderson
June 30, 1945–May 10, 1948
Charles Franklin Brannan
June 2, 1948–Jan. 20, 1953

Secretary of Commerce
Henry A. Wallace
March 2, 1945–Sept. 20, 1946
W. Averell Harriman
Oct. 7, 1946–April 22, 1948
Charles Sawyer
May 6, 1948–Jan. 20, 1953

Secretary of Labor
Frances Perkins
March 4, 1933–June 30, 1945
Lewis Baxter Schwellenbach
July 1, 1945–June 10, 1948
Maurice Joseph Tobin
Aug. 13, 1948–Jan. 20, 1953

Dwight D. Eisenhower, 1953–1961

Chief Justice
Frederick M. Vinson
June 24, 1946–Sept. 8, 1953
Earl Warren
Oct. 5, 1953–June 23, 1969

Vice President
Richard Nixon
Jan. 20, 1953–Jan. 20, 1961

Secretary of State
John Foster Dulles
Jan. 21, 1953–April 22, 1959
Christian Archibald Herter
April 22, 1959–Jan. 20, 1961

Secretary of the Treasury
George Magoffin Humphrey
Jan. 21, 1953–July 29, 1957
Robert Bernard Anderson
July 29, 1957–Jan. 20, 1961

Secretary of Defense
Charles Erwin Wilson
Jan. 28, 1953–Oct. 8, 1957
Neil Hosler McElroy
Oct. 9, 1957–Dec. 1, 1959
Thomas Sovereign Gates Jr.
Dec. 2, 1959–Jan. 20, 1961

Attorney General
Herbert Brownell Jr.
Jan. 21, 1953–Nov. 8, 1957
William Pierce Rogers
Nov. 8, 1957–Jan. 20, 1961

Postmaster General
Arthur Summerfield
Jan. 21, 1953–Jan. 20, 1961

Secretary of the Interior
Douglas McKay
Jan. 21, 1953–April 15, 1956
Fred Andrew Seaton
June 8, 1956–Jan. 20, 1961

Secretary of Agriculture
Ezra Taft Benson
Jan. 21, 1953–Jan. 20, 1961

Secretary of Commerce
Charles Sinclair Weeks
Jan. 21, 1953–Nov. 10, 1958
Frederick Henry Mueller
Aug. 10, 1959–Jan. 19, 1961

Secretary of Labor
Martin Patrick Durkin
Jan. 21–Sept. 10, 1953
James Paul Mitchell
Oct. 9, 1953–Jan. 20, 1961

Secretary of Health, Education and Welfare
Oveta Culp Hobby
April 11, 1953–July 31, 1955
Marion Bayard Folsom
Aug. 1, 1955–July 31, 1958
Arthur Sherwood Flemming
Aug. 1, 1958–Jan. 19, 1961

John F. Kennedy, 1961–1963

Chief Justice
Earl Warren
Oct. 5, 1953–June 23, 1969

Vice President
Lyndon B. Johnson
Jan. 20, 1961–Nov. 22, 1963

Secretary of State
David Dean Rusk
Jan. 21, 1961–Jan. 20, 1969

Secretary of the Treasury
C. Douglas Dillon
Jan. 21, 1961–April 1, 1965

Secretary of Defense
Robert S. McNamara
Jan. 21, 1961–Feb. 29, 1968

Attorney General
Robert F. Kennedy
Jan. 21, 1961–Sept. 3, 1964

Postmaster General
James Edward Day
Jan. 21, 1961–Aug. 9, 1963
John A. Gronouski Jr.
Sept. 30, 1963–Nov. 2, 1965

Secretary of the Interior
Stewart Lee Udall
Jan. 21, 1961–Jan. 20, 1969

Secretary of Agriculture
Orville Lothrop Freeman
Jan. 21, 1961–Jan. 20, 1969

Secretary of Commerce
Luther Hartwell Hodges
Jan. 21, 1961–Jan. 15, 1965

Secretary of Labor
Arthur Joseph Goldberg
Jan. 21, 1961–Sept. 20, 1962
William Willard Wirtz
Sept. 25, 1962–Jan. 20, 1969

Secretary of Health, Education and Welfare
Abraham Alexander Ribicoff
Jan. 21, 1961–July 13, 1962
Anthony Joseph Celebrezze
July 31, 1962–Aug. 17, 1965

Lyndon B. Johnson, 1963–1969

Chief Justice
Earl Warren
Oct. 5, 1953–June 23, 1969

Vice President
Hubert H. Humphrey
Jan. 20, 1965–Jan. 20, 1969

Secretary of State
David Dean Rusk
Jan. 21, 1961–Jan. 20, 1969

Secretary of the Treasury
C. Douglas Dillon
Jan. 21, 1961–April 1, 1965
Henry Hamill Fowler
April 1, 1965–Dec. 20, 1968
Joseph Walker Barr
Dec. 21, 1968–Jan. 20, 1969

Secretary of Defense
Robert S. McNamara
Jan. 21, 1961–Feb. 29, 1968
Clark McAdams Clifford
March 1, 1968–Jan. 20, 1969

Attorney General
Robert F. Kennedy
Jan. 21, 1961–Sept. 3, 1964
Nicholas de Belleville Katzenbach
Feb. 11, 1965–Oct. 2, 1966
William Ramsey Clark
March 2, 1967–Jan. 20, 1969

Postmaster General
John A. Gronouski Jr.
Sept. 30, 1963–Nov. 2, 1965
Lawrence Francis O'Brien
Nov. 3, 1965–April 26, 1968
William Marvin Watson
April 26, 1968–Jan. 20, 1969

Secretary of the Interior
Stewart Lee Udall
Jan. 21, 1961–Jan. 20, 1969

Secretary of Agriculture
Orville Lothrop Freeman
Jan. 21, 1961–Jan. 20, 1969

Secretary of Commerce
Luther Hartwell Hodges
Jan. 21, 1961–Jan. 15, 1965
John Thomas Connor
Jan. 18, 1965–Jan. 31, 1967
Alexander Buel Trowbridge
June 14, 1967–March 1, 1968
Cyrus Rowlett Smith
March 6, 1968–Jan. 19, 1969

Secretary of Labor
William Willard Wirtz
Sept. 25, 1962–Jan. 20, 1969

Secretary of Health, Education and Welfare
Anthony Joseph Celebrezze
July 31, 1962–Aug. 17, 1965
John William Gardner
Aug. 18, 1965–March 1, 1968
Wilbur Joseph Cohen
May 16, 1968–Jan. 20, 1969

Secretary of Housing and Urban Development
Robert Clifton Weaver
Jan. 18, 1966–Dec. 3, 1968

Secretary of Transportation
Alan Stephenson Boyd
Jan. 23, 1967–Jan. 20, 1969

Richard Nixon, 1969–1974

Chief Justice
Earl Warren
Oct. 5, 1953–June 23, 1969
Warren Earl Burger
June 23, 1969–Sept. 26, 1986

Vice President
Spiro T. Agnew
Jan. 20, 1969–Oct. 10, 1973
Gerald R. Ford
Dec. 6, 1973–Aug. 9, 1974

Secretary of State
William Pierce Rogers
Jan. 22, 1969–Sept. 3, 1973
Henry Alfred Kissinger
Sept. 22, 1973–Jan. 20, 1977

Secretary of the Treasury
David Matthew Kennedy
Jan. 22, 1969–Feb. 10, 1971
John Bowden Connally
Feb. 11, 1971–June 12, 1972
George Pratt Shultz
June 12, 1972–May 8, 1974
William Edward Simon
May 8, 1974–Jan. 20, 1977

Secretary of Defense
Melvin Robert Laird
Jan. 22, 1969–Jan. 29, 1973
Elliot Lee Richardson
Jan. 30–May 24, 1973
James Rodney Schlesinger
July 2, 1973–Nov. 19, 1975

Attorney General
John Newton Mitchell
Jan. 21, 1969–March 1, 1972
Richard Gordon Kleindienst
June 12, 1972–May 24, 1973
Elliot Lee Richardson
May 25–Oct. 20, 1973
William Bart Saxbe
Jan. 4, 1974–Feb. 3, 1975

Postmaster General
Winton Malcolm Blount
Jan. 22, 1969–Jan. 12, 1971

Secretary of the Interior
Walter Joseph Hickel
Jan. 24, 1969–Nov. 25, 1970
Rogers Clark Ballard Morton
Jan. 29, 1971–April 30, 1975

Secretary of Agriculture
Clifford Morris Hardin
Jan. 21, 1969–Nov. 17, 1971
Earl Lauer Butz
Dec. 2, 1971–Oct. 4, 1976

Secretary of Commerce
Maurice Hubert Stans
Jan. 21, 1969–Feb. 15, 1972
Peter George Peterson
Feb. 29, 1972–Feb. 1, 1973
Frederick Baily Dent
Feb. 2, 1973–March 26, 1975

Secretary of Labor
George Pratt Shultz
Jan. 22, 1969–July 1, 1970
James Day Hodgson
July 2, 1970–Feb. 1, 1973
Peter Joseph Brennan
Feb. 2, 1973–March 15, 1975

Secretary of Health, Education and Welfare
Robert Hutchinson Finch
Jan. 21, 1969–June 23, 1970
Elliot Lee Richardson
June 24, 1970–Jan. 29, 1973
Caspar Willard Weinberger
Feb. 12, 1973–Aug. 8, 1975

Secretary of Housing and Urban Development
George Wilcken Romney
Jan. 20, 1969–Feb. 2, 1973
James Thomas Lynn
Feb. 2, 1973–Feb. 10, 1975

Secretary of Transportation
John Anthony Volpe
Jan. 22, 1969–Feb. 1, 1973
Claude Stout Brinegar
Feb. 2, 1973–Feb. 1, 1975

Gerald R. Ford, 1974–1977

Chief Justice
Warren Earl Burger
June 23, 1969–Sept. 26, 1986

Vice President
Nelson A. Rockefeller
Dec. 19, 1974–Jan. 20, 1977

Secretary of State
Henry Alfred Kissinger
Sept. 22, 1973–Jan. 20, 1977

Secretary of the Treasury
William Edward Simon
May 8, 1974–Jan. 20, 1977

Secretary of Defense
James Rodney Schlesinger
July 2, 1973–Nov. 19, 1975
Donald Henry Rumsfeld
Nov. 20, 1975–Jan. 20, 1977

Attorney General
William Bart Saxbe
Jan. 4, 1974–Feb. 3, 1975
Edward Hirsh Levi
Feb. 6, 1975–Jan. 20, 1977

Secretary of the Interior
Rogers Clark Ballard Morton
Jan. 29, 1971–April 30, 1975
Stanley Knapp Hathaway
June 12–Oct. 9, 1975
Thomas Savig Kleppe
Oct. 17, 1975–Jan. 20, 1977

Secretary of Agriculture
Earl Lauer Butz
Dec. 2, 1971–Oct. 4, 1976
John Albert Knebel
Nov. 4, 1976–Jan. 20, 1977

Secretary of Commerce
Frederick Baily Dent
Feb. 2, 1973–March 26, 1975
Rogers Clark Ballard Morton
May 1, 1975–Feb. 2, 1976
Elliot Lee Richardson
Feb. 2, 1976–Jan. 20, 1977

Secretary of Labor
Peter Joseph Brennan
Feb. 2, 1973–March 15, 1975
John Thomas Dunlop
March 18, 1975–Jan. 31, 1976

William Julian Usery Jr.
Feb. 10, 1976–Jan. 20, 1977

Secretary of Health, Education and Welfare
Caspar Willard Weinberger
Feb. 12, 1973–Aug. 8, 1975
Forrest David Mathews
Aug. 8, 1975–Jan. 20, 1977

Secretary of Housing and Urban Development
James Thomas Lynn
Feb. 2, 1973–Feb. 10, 1975
Carla Anderson Hills
March 10, 1975–Jan. 20, 1977

Secretary of Transportation
Claude Stout Brinegar
Feb. 2, 1973–Feb. 1, 1975
William Thaddeus Coleman Jr.
March 7, 1975–Jan. 20, 1977

Jimmy Carter 1977–1981

Chief Justice
Warren Earl Burger
June 23, 1969–Sept. 26, 1986

Vice President
Walter F. Mondale
Jan. 20, 1977–Jan. 20, 1981

Secretary of State
Cyrus Roberts Vance
Jan. 23, 1977–April 28, 1980
Edmund Sixtus Muskie
May 8, 1980–Jan. 18, 1981

Secretary of the Treasury
Werner Michael Blumenthal
Jan. 23, 1977–Aug. 4, 1979
George William Miller
Aug. 7, 1979–Jan. 20, 1981

Secretary of Defense
Harold Brown
Jan. 21, 1977–Jan. 20, 1981

Attorney General
Griffin Boyette Bell
Jan. 26, 1977–Aug. 16, 1979
Benjamin Richard Civiletti
Aug. 16, 1979–Jan. 19, 1981

Secretary of the Interior
Cecil Dale Andrus
Jan. 23, 1977–Jan. 20, 1981

Secretary of Agriculture
Robert Selmer Bergland
Jan. 23, 1977–Jan. 20, 1981

Secretary of Commerce
Juanita Morris Kreps
Jan. 23, 1977–Oct. 31, 1979
Philip M. Klutznick
Jan. 9, 1980–Jan. 19, 1981

Secretary of Labor
Fred Ray Marshall
Jan. 27, 1977–Jan. 20, 1981

Secretary of Health, Education and Welfare
Joseph Anthony Califano Jr.
Jan. 25, 1977–Aug. 3, 1979
Patricia Roberts Harris
Aug. 3, 1979–May 4, 1980

Secretary of Health and Human Services
Patricia Roberts Harris
May 4, 1980–Jan. 20, 1981

Secretary of Housing and Urban Development
Patricia Roberts Harris
Jan. 23, 1977–Aug. 3, 1979
Maurice Edwin "Moon" Landrieu
Sept. 24, 1979–Jan. 20, 1981

Secretary of Transportation
Brockman "Brock" Adams
Jan. 23, 1977–July 22, 1979
Neil Goldschmidt
July 27, 1979–Jan. 20, 1981

Secretary of Energy
James Rodney Schlesinger
Aug. 6, 1977–Aug. 23, 1979
Charles William Duncan Jr.
Aug. 24, 1979–Jan. 20, 1981

Secretary of Education
Shirley Mount Hufstedler
Dec. 6, 1979–Jan. 19, 1981

Ronald Reagan, 1981–1989

Chief Justice
Warren Earl Burger
June 23, 1969–Sept. 26, 1986
William Rehnquist
Sept. 26, 1986–

Vice President
George Bush
Jan. 20, 1981–Jan. 20, 1989

Secretary of State
Alexander Meigs Haig Jr.
Jan. 22, 1981–July 5, 1982
George Pratt Shultz
July 16, 1982–Jan. 20, 1989

Secretary of the Treasury
Donald Thomas Regan
Jan. 22, 1981–Feb. 1, 1985
James Addison Baker III
Feb. 4, 1985–Aug. 17, 1988
Nicholas Frederick Brady
Sept. 16, 1988–Jan. 19, 1993

Secretary of Defense
Caspar Willard Weinberger
Jan. 21, 1981–Nov. 21, 1987

Frank Charles Carlucci
Nov. 23, 1987–Jan. 20, 1989

Attorney General
William French Smith
Jan. 23, 1981–Feb. 24, 1985
Edwin Meese III
Feb. 25, 1985–Aug. 12, 1988
Richard Lewis Thornburgh
Aug. 12, 1988–Aug. 9, 1991

Secretary of the Interior
James Gaius Watt
Jan. 23, 1981–Nov. 8, 1983
William Patrick Clark
Nov. 18, 1983–Feb. 7, 1985
Donald Paul Hodel
Feb. 8, 1985–Jan. 20, 1989

Secretary of Agriculture
John Rusling Block
Jan. 23, 1981–Feb. 14, 1986
Richard Edmund Lyng
March 7, 1986–Jan. 20, 1989

Secretary of Commerce
Malcolm Baldrige
Jan. 20, 1981–July 25, 1987
Calvin William Verity Jr.
Oct. 19, 1987–Jan. 20, 1989

Secretary of Labor
Raymond James Donovan
Feb. 4, 1981–March 15, 1985
William Emerson Brock III
April 29, 1985–Oct. 31, 1987
Ann Dore McLaughlin
Dec. 17, 1987–Jan. 20, 1989

Secretary of Health and Human Services
Richard Schultz Schweiker
Jan. 22, 1981–Feb. 3, 1983
Margaret Mary O'Shaughnessy Heckler
March 9, 1983–Dec. 13, 1985
Otis Ray Bowen
Dec. 13, 1985–Jan. 20, 1989

Secretary of Housing and Urban Development
Samuel Riley Pierce Jr.
Jan. 23, 1981–Jan. 20, 1989

Secretary of Transportation
Andrew Lindsay "Drew" Lewis Jr.
Jan. 23, 1981–Feb. 1, 1983
Elizabeth Hanford Dole
Feb. 7, 1983–Sept. 30, 1987
James Horace Burnley IV
Dec. 3, 1987–Jan. 30, 1989

Secretary of Energy
James Burrows Edwards
Jan. 23, 1981–Nov. 5, 1982
Donald Paul Hodel
Nov. 5, 1982–Feb. 7, 1985

John Stewart Herrington
Feb. 11, 1985–Jan. 20, 1989

Secretary of Education
Terrel Howard Bell
Jan. 23, 1981–Dec. 31, 1984
William John Bennett
Feb. 6, 1985–Sept. 20, 1988
Lauro Fred Cavazos
Sept. 20, 1988–Dec. 12, 1990

George Bush, 1989–1993

Chief Justice
William Rehnquist
Sept. 26, 1986–

Vice President
Dan Quayle
Jan. 20, 1989–Jan. 20, 1993

Secretary of State
James Addison Baker III
Jan. 27, 1989–Aug. 23, 1992
Lawrence Sidney Eagleburger
Dec. 8, 1992–Jan. 19, 1993

Secretary of the Treasury
Nicholas Frederick Brady
Sept. 16, 1988–Jan. 19, 1993

Secretary of Defense
Richard Bruce Cheney
March 21, 1989–Jan. 20, 1993

Attorney General
Richard Lewis Thornburgh
Aug. 12, 1988–Aug. 9, 1991
William Pelham Barr
Nov. 26, 1991–Jan. 15, 1993

Secretary of the Interior
Manuel Lujan Jr.
Feb. 8, 1989–Jan. 20, 1993

Secretary of Agriculture
Clayton Keith Yeutter
Feb. 16, 1989–March 1, 1991
Edward Rell Madigan
March 12, 1991–Jan. 20, 1993

Secretary of Commerce
Robert Adam Mosbacher
Feb. 3, 1989–Jan. 15, 1992
Barbara Hackman Franklin
Feb. 27, 1992–Jan. 20, 1993

Secretary of Labor
Elizabeth Hanford Dole
Jan. 30, 1989–Nov. 23, 1990
Lynn Morley Martin
Feb. 22, 1991–Jan. 20, 1993

Secretary of Health and Human Services
Louis Wade Sullivan
March 10, 1989–Jan. 20, 1993

Secretary of Housing and Urban Development
Jack French Kemp
Feb. 13, 1989–Jan. 20, 1993

Secretary of Transportation
Samuel Knox Skinner
Feb. 6, 1989–Dec. 16, 1991
Andrew Hill Card Jr.
Feb. 24, 1992–Jan. 20, 1993

Secretary of Energy
James David Watkins
March 9, 1989–Jan. 20, 1993

Secretary of Education
Lauro Fred Cavazos
Sept. 20, 1988–Dec. 12, 1990
Lamar Alexander
March 22, 1991–Jan. 20, 1993

Secretary of Veterans Affairs
Edward Joseph Derwinski
March 15, 1989–Sept. 26, 1992

Bill Clinton, 1993–2001

Chief Justice
William Rehnquist
Sept. 26, 1986–

Vice President
Albert Gore Jr.
Jan. 20, 1993–Jan. 20, 2001

Secretary of State
Warren Minor Christopher
Jan. 20, 1993–Jan. 20, 1997
Madeleine Korbel Albright
Jan. 23, 1997–Jan. 20, 2001

Secretary of the Treasury
Lloyd Millard Bentsen Jr.
Jan. 22, 1993–Dec. 22, 1994
Robert E. Rubin
Jan. 10, 1995–July 2, 1999
Lawrence H. Summers
July 2, 1999–Jan. 20, 2001

Secretary of Defense
Leslie Aspin
Jan. 22, 1993–Feb. 2, 1994
William James Perry
Feb. 3, 1994–Jan. 22, 1997
William S. Cohen
Jan. 24, 1997–Jan. 20, 2001

Attorney General
Janet Reno
March 12, 1993–Jan. 20, 2001

Secretary of the Interior
Bruce Edward Babbitt
Jan. 22, 1993–Jan. 2, 2001

Secretary of Agriculture
Albert Michael "Mike" Espy
Jan. 22, 1993–Dec. 31, 1994

Daniel Glickman
March 30, 1995–Jan. 19, 2001

Secretary of Commerce
Ronald Harmon Brown
Jan. 22, 1993–April 3, 1996
Michael "Mickey" Kantor
April 12, 1996–Jan. 21, 1997
William M. Daley
Jan. 30, 1997–July 19, 2000
Norman Y. Mineta
July 21, 2000–Jan. 19, 2001

Secretary of Labor
Robert Bernard Reich
Jan. 22, 1993–Jan. 10, 1997
Alexis M. Herman
May 1, 1997–Jan. 20, 2001

Secretary of Health and Human Services
Donna Edna Shalala
Jan. 22, 1993–Jan. 20, 2001

Secretary of Housing and Urban Development
Henry Gabriel Cisneros
Jan. 22, 1993–Jan. 17, 1997
Andrew Cuomo
Jan. 30, 1997–Jan. 20, 2001

Secretary of Transportation
Frederico F. Peña
Jan. 22, 1993–Feb. 14, 1997
Rodney Slater
Feb. 14, 1997–Jan. 20, 2001

Secretary of Energy
Hazel Rollins O'Leary
Jan. 22, 1993–Jan. 20, 1997
Frederico F. Peña
March 12, 1997–June 30, 1998
Bill Richardson
July 31, 1998–Jan. 20, 2001

Secretary of Education
Richard Wilson Riley
Jan. 22, 1993–Jan. 20, 2001

Secretary of Veterans Affairs
Jesse Brown
Jan. 22, 1993–July 1, 1997
Togo D. West Jr.
May 5, 1998–July 24, 2000

George W. Bush, 2001–

Chief Justice
William Rehnquist
Sept. 26, 1986–

Vice President
Richard B. Cheney
Jan. 20, 2001–

Secretary of State
Colin Powell
Jan. 20, 2001–Jan. 26, 2005

Condoleeza Rice
Jan. 26, 2005–

Secretary of the Treasury
Paul O'Neill
Jan. 20, 2001–Dec. 31, 2002
John W. Snow
Feb. 3, 2003–

Secretary of Defense
Donald H. Rumsfeld
Jan. 20, 2001–

Attorney General
John Ashcroft
Feb. 1, 2001–Feb. 3, 2005
Alberto R. Gonzales
Feb. 3, 2005–

Secretary of the Interior
Gale A. Norton
Jan. 31, 2001–

Secretary of Agriculture
Ann M. Veneman
Jan. 20, 2001–Jan. 20, 2005
Mike Johanns
Jan. 21, 2005–

Secretary of Commerce
Donald Evans
Jan. 20, 2001–Feb. 7, 2005
Carlos Gutierrez
Feb. 7, 2005–

Secretary of Labor
Elaine L. Chao
Jan. 31, 2001–

Secretary of Health and Human Services
Tommy Thompson
Feb. 2, 2001–Jan. 26, 2005

Michael O. Leavitt
Jan. 26, 2005–

Secretary of Housing and Urban Development
Melquiades R. "Mel" Martinez
Jan. 24, 2001–Dec. 9, 2003
Alphonso R. Jackson
April 1, 2004–

Secretary of Transportation
Norman Y. Mineta
Jan. 25, 2001–

Secretary of Energy
Spencer Abraham
Jan. 20, 2001–Feb. 1, 2005
Samuel Wright Bodman
Feb. 1, 2005–

Secretary of Education
Roderick Paige
Jan. 24, 2001–Jan. 20, 2005
Margaret Spellings
Jan. 20, 2005–

Secretary of Veterans Affairs
Anthony Principi
Jan. 24, 2001–Jan. 24, 2005
Jim Nicholson
Jan. 26, 2005–

Secretary of Homeland Security
Tom Ridge
Jan. 24, 2003–Feb. 1, 2005
Michael Chertoff
Feb. 16, 2005–

Political Party Affiliations in Congress and the Presidency, 1789–2005

		House		Senate		
Year	Congress	Majority party	Principal minority party	Majority party	Principal minority party	President
1789–1791	1st	AD-38	Op-26	AD-17	Op-9	F (Washington)
1791–1793	2nd	F-37	DR-33	F-16	DR-13	F (Washington)
1793–1795	3rd	DR-57	F-48	F-17	DR-13	F (Washington)
1795–1797	4th	F-54	DR-52	F-19	DR-13	F (Washington)
1797–1799	5th	F-58	DR-48	F-20	DR-12	F (John Adams)
1799–1801	6th	F-64	DR-42	F-19	DR-13	F (John Adams)
1801–1803	7th	DR-69	F-36	DR-18	F-13	DR (Jefferson)
1803–1805	8th	DR-102	F-39	DR-25	F-9	DR (Jefferson)
1805–1807	9th	DR-116	F-25	DR-27	F-7	DR (Jefferson)
1807–1809	10th	DR-118	F-24	DR-28	F-6	DR (Jefferson)
1809–1811	11th	DR-94	F-48	DR-28	F-6	DR (Madison)
1811–1813	12th	DR-108	F-36	DR-30	F-6	DR (Madison)
1813–1815	13th	DR-112	F-68	DR-27	F-9	DR (Madison)
1815–1817	14th	DR-117	F-65	DR-25	F-11	DR (Madison)
1817–1819	15th	DR-141	F-42	DR-34	F-10	DR (Monroe)
1819–1821	16th	DR-156	F-27	DR-35	F-7	DR (Monroe)
1821–1823	17th	DR-158	F-25	DR-44	F-4	DR (Monroe)
1823–1825	18th	DR-187	F-26	DR-44	F-4	DR (Monroe)
1825–1827	19th	AD-105	J-97	AD-26	J-20	DR (John Q. Adams)
1827–1829	20th	J-119	AD-94	J-28	AD-20	DR (John Q. Adams)
1829–1831	21st	D-139	NR-74	D-26	NR-22	DR (Jackson)
1831–1833	22nd	D-141	NR-58	D-25	NR-21	D (Jackson)
1833–1835	23rd	D-147	AM-53	D-20	NR-20	D (Jackson)
1835–1837	24th	D-145	W-98	D-27	W-25	D (Jackson)
1837–1839	25th	D-108	W-107	D-30	W-18	D (Van Buren)
1839–1841	26th	D-124	W-118	D-28	W-22	D (Van Buren)
1841–1843	27th	W-133	D-102	W-28	D-22	W (W. Harrison) / W (Tyler)
1843–1845	28th	D-142	W-79	W-28	D-25	W (Tyler)
1845–1847	29th	D-143	W-77	D-31	W-25	D (Polk)
1847–1849	30th	W-115	D-108	D-36	W-21	D (Polk)
1849–1851	31st	D-112	W-109	D-35	W-25	W (Taylor) / W (Fillmore)
1851–1853	32nd	D-140	W-88	D-35	W-24	W (Fillmore)
1853–1855	33rd	D-159	W-71	D-38	W-22	D (Pierce)
1855–1857	34th	R-108	D-83	D-40	R-15	D (Pierce)
1857–1859	35th	D-118	R-92	D-36	R-20	D (Buchanan)
1859–1861	36th	R-114	D-92	D-36	R-26	D (Buchanan)
1861–1863	37th	R-105	D-43	R-31	D-10	R (Lincoln)
1863–1865	38th	R-102	D-75	R-36	D-9	R (Lincoln)
1865–1867	39th	U-149	D-42	U-42	D-10	R (Lincoln) / R (A. Johnson)
1867–1869	40th	R-143	D-49	R-42	D-11	R (A. Johnson)
1869–1871	41st	R-149	D-63	R-56	D-11	R (Grant)
1871–1873	42nd	R-134	D-104	R-52	D-17	R (Grant)
1873–1875	43rd	R-194	D-92	R-49	D-19	R (Grant)
1875–1877	44th	D-169	R-109	R-45	D-29	R (Grant)
1877–1879	45th	D-153	R-140	R-39	D-36	R (Hayes)
1879–1881	46th	D-149	R-130	D-42	R-33	R (Hayes)
1881–1883	47th	R-147	D-135	R-37	D-37	R (Garfield) / R (Arthur)
1883–1885	48th	D-197	R-118	R-38	D-36	R (Arthur)
1885–1887	49th	D-183	R-140	R-43	D-34	D (Cleveland)
1887–1889	50th	D-169	R-152	R-39	D-37	D (Cleveland)
1889–1891	51st	R-166	D-159	R-39	D-37	R (B. Harrison)
1891–1893	52nd	D-235	R-88	R-47	D-39	R (B. Harrison)
1893–1895	53rd	D-218	R-127	D-44	R-38	D (Cleveland)
1895–1897	54th	R-244	D-105	R-43	D-39	D (Cleveland)
1897–1899	55th	R-204	D-113	R-47	D-34	R (McKinley)
1899–1901	56th	R-185	D-163	R-53	D-26	R (McKinley)
1901–1903	57th	R-197	D-151	R-55	D-31	R (McKinley) / R (T. Roosevelt)

Year	Congress	House Majority party	House Principal minority party	Senate Majority party	Senate Principal minority party	President
1903–1905	58th	R-208	D-178	R-57	D-33	R (T. Roosevelt)
1905–1907	59th	R-250	D-136	R-57	D-33	R (T. Roosevelt)
1907–1909	60th	R-222	D-164	R-61	D-31	R (T. Roosevelt)
1909–1911	61st	R-219	D-172	R-61	D-32	R (Taft)
1911–1913	62nd	D-228	R-161	R-51	D-41	R (Taft)
1913–1915	63rd	D-291	R-127	D-51	R-44	D (Wilson)
1915–1917	64th	D-230	R-196	D-56	R-40	D (Wilson)
1917–1919	65th	D-216	R-210	D-53	R-42	D (Wilson)
1919–1921	66th	D-240	R-190	R-49	D-47	D (Wilson)
1921–1923	67th	R-301	D-131	R-59	D-37	R (Harding)
1923–1925	68th	R-225	D-205	R-51	D-43	R (Coolidge)
1925–1927	69th	R-247	D-183	R-56	D-39	R (Coolidge)
1927–1929	70th	R-237	D-195	R-49	D-46	R (Coolidge)
1929–1931	71st	R-267	D-167	R-56	D-39	R (Hoover)
1931–1933	72nd	D-220	R-214	R-48	D-47	R (Hoover)
1933–1935	73rd	D-310	R-117	D-60	R-35	D (F. Roosevelt)
1935–1937	74th	D-319	R-103	D-69	R-25	D (F. Roosevelt)
1937–1939	75th	D-331	R-89	D-76	R-16	D (F. Roosevelt)
1939–1941	76th	D-261	R-164	D-69	R-23	D (F. Roosevelt)
1941–1943	77th	D-268	R-162	D-66	R-28	D (F. Roosevelt)
1943–1945	78th	D-218	R-208	D-58	R-37	D (F. Roosevelt)
1945–1947	79th	D-242	R-190	D-56	R-38	D (F. Roosevelt) D (Truman)
1947–1949	80th	R-245	D-188	R-51	D-45	D (Truman)
1949–1951	81st	D-263	R-171	D-54	R-42	D (Truman)
1951–1953	82nd	D-234	R-199	D-49	R-47	D (Truman)
1953–1955	83rd	R-221	D-211	R-48	D-47	R (Eisenhower)
1955–1957	84th	D-232	R-203	D-48	R-47	R (Eisenhower)
1957–1959	85th	D-233	R-200	D-49	R-47	R (Eisenhower)
1959–1961	86th	D-283	R-153	D-64	R-34	R (Eisenhower)
1961–1963	87th	D-263	R-174	D-65	R-35	D (Kennedy)
1963–1965	88th	D-258	R-177	D-67	R-33	D (Kennedy) D (L. Johnson)
1965–1967	89th	D-295	R-140	D-68	R-32	D (L. Johnson)
1967–1969	90th	D-247	R-187	D-64	R-36	D (L. Johnson)
1969–1971	91st	D-243	R-192	D-57	R-43	R (Nixon)
1971–1973	92nd	D-254	R-180	D-54	R-44	R (Nixon)
1973–1975	93rd	D-239	R-192	D-56	R-42	R (Nixon) R (Ford)
1975–1977	94th	D-291	R-144	D-60	R-37	R (Ford)
1977–1979	95th	D-292	R-143	D-61	R-38	D (Carter)
1979–1981	96th	D-276	R-157	D-58	R-41	D (Carter)
1981–1983	97th	D-243	R-192	R-53	D-46	R (Reagan)
1983–1985	98th	D-269	R-165	R-54	D-46	R (Reagan)
1985–1987	99th	D-252	R-182	R-53	D-47	R (Reagan)
1987–1989	100th	D-258	R-177	D-55	R-45	R (Reagan)
1989–1991	101st	D-259	R-174	D-55	R-45	R (Bush)
1991–1993	102nd	D-267	R-167	D-56	R-44	R (Bush)
1993–1995	103rd	D-258	R-176	D-57	R-43	D (Clinton)
1995–1997	104th	R-230	D-204	R-53	D-47	D (Clinton)
1997–1999	105th	R-227	D-207	R-55	D-45	D (Clinton)
1999–2001	106th	R-222	D-211	R-55	D-45	D (Clinton)
2001–2003	107th	R-221	D-212	R-50	D-50	R (G.W. Bush)
2003–2005	108th	R-229	D-205	R-51	D-48	R (G.W. Bush)
2005–2007	109th	R-232	D-202	R-55	D-44	R (G.W. Bush)

Note: Figures are for the beginning of the first session of each Congress. Key to abbreviations: AD—Administration; AM—Anti-Masonic; D—Democratic; DR—Democratic-Republican; F—Federalist; J—Jacksonian; NR—National Republican; Op—Opposition; R—Republican; U—Unionist; W—Whig.

Sources: U.S. Bureau of the Census, *Historical Statistics of the United States, Colonial Times to 1970* (Washington, D.C.: Government Printing Office, 1975); and U.S. Congress, Joint Committee on Printing, *Official Congressional Directory* (Washington, D.C.: Government Printing Office, 1967–); and *CQ Weekly,* selected issues.

Sessions of the U.S. Congress, 1789–2005

Congress	Session	Date of beginning[1]	Date of adjournment[2]	Length in days	President pro tempore of the Senate[3]	Speaker of the House of Representatives
1st	1	Mar. 4, 1789	Sept. 29, 1789	210	John Langdon of New Hampshire[4]	Frederick A. C. Muhlenberg of Pennsylvania
	2	Jan. 4, 1790	Aug. 12, 1790	221		
	3	Dec. 6, 1790	Mar. 3, 1791			
2nd	1	Oct. 24, 1791	May 8, 1792	197	Richard Henry Lee of Virginia	Jonathan Trumbull of Connecticut
	2	Nov. 5, 1792	Mar. 2, 1793	119	John Langdon of New Hampshire	
3rd	1	Dec. 2, 1793	June 9, 1794	190	Langdon Ralph Izard of South Carolina	Frederick A. C. Muhlenberg of Pennsylvania
	2	Nov. 3, 1794	Mar. 3, 1795	121	Henry Tazewell of Virginia	
4th	1	Dec. 7, 1795	June 1, 1796	177	Tazewell Samuel Livermore of New Hampshire	Jonathan Dayton of New Jersey
	2	Dec. 5, 1796	Mar. 3, 1797	89	William Bingham of Pennsylvania	
5th	1	May 15, 1797	July 10, 1797	57	William Bradford of Rhode Island	Dayton
	2	Nov. 13, 1797	July 16, 1798	246	Jacob Read of South Carolina Theodore Sedgwick of Massachusetts	George Dent of Maryland[5]
	3	Dec. 3, 1798	Mar. 3, 1799	91	John Laurence of New York James Ross of Pennsylvania	
6th	1	Dec. 2, 1799	May 14, 1800	164	Samuel Livermore of New Hampshire Uriah Tracy of Connecticut	Theodore Sedgwick of Massachusetts
	2	Nov. 17, 1800	Mar. 3, 1801	107	John E. Howard of Maryland James Hillhouse of Connecticut	
7th	1	Dec. 7, 1801	May 3, 1802	148	Abraham Baldwin of Georgia	Nathaniel Macon of North Carolina
	2	Dec. 6, 1802	Mar. 3, 1803	88	Stephen R. Bradley of Vermont	
8th	1	Oct. 17, 1803	Mar. 27, 1804	163	John Brown of Kentucky Jesse Franklin of North Carolina	Macon
	2	Nov. 5, 1804	Mar. 3, 1805	119	Joseph Anderson of Tennessee	
9th	1	Dec. 2, 1805	Apr. 21, 1806	141	Samuel Smith of Maryland	Macon
	2	Dec. 1, 1806	Mar. 3, 1807	93	Smith	
10th	1	Oct. 26, 1807	Apr. 25, 1808	182	Smith	Joseph B. Varnum of Massachusetts
	2	Nov. 7, 1808	Mar. 3, 1809	117	Stephen R. Bradley of Vermont John Milledge of Georgia	
11th	1	May 22, 1809	June 28, 1809	38	Andrew Gregg of Pennsylvania	Varnum
	2	Nov. 27, 1809	May 1, 1810	156	John Gaillard of South Carolina	
	3	Dec. 3, 1810	Mar. 3, 1811	91	John Pope of Kentucky	
12th	1	Nov. 4, 1811	July 6, 1812	245	William H. Crawford of Georgia	Henry Clay of Kentucky
	2	Nov. 2, 1812	Mar. 3, 1813	122	Crawford	
13th	1	May 24, 1813	Aug. 2, 1813	71	Crawford	Clay
	2	Dec. 6, 1813	Apr. 18, 1814	134	Joseph B. Varnum of Massachusetts	
	3	Sept. 19, 1814	Mar. 3, 1815	166	John Gaillard of South Carolina	Langdon Cheves of South Carolina[6]
14th	1	Dec. 4, 1815	Apr. 30, 1816	148	Gaillard	Henry Clay of Kentucky
	2	Dec. 2, 1816	Mar. 3, 1817	92	Gaillard	
15th	1	Dec. 1, 1817	Apr. 20, 1818	141	Gaillard	Clay
	2	Nov. 16, 1818	Mar. 3, 1819	108	James Barbour of Virginia	
16th	1	Dec. 6, 1819	May 15, 1820	162	John Gaillard of South Carolina	Clay

Congress	Session	Date of beginning[1]	Date of adjournment[2]	Length in days	President pro tempore of the Senate[3]	Speaker of the House of Representatives
	2	Nov. 13, 1820	Mar. 3, 1821	111	Gaillard	John W. Taylor of New York[7]
17th	1	Dec. 3, 1821	May 8, 1822	157	Gaillard	Philip P. Barbour of Virginia
	2	Dec. 2, 1822	Mar. 3, 1823	92	Gaillard	
18th	1	Dec. 1, 1823	May 27, 1824	178	Gaillard	Henry Clay of Kentucky
	2	Dec. 6, 1824	Mar. 3, 1825	88	Gaillard	
19th	1	Dec. 5, 1825	May 22, 1826	169	Nathaniel Macon of North Carolina	John W. Taylor of New York
	2	Dec. 4, 1826	Mar. 3, 1827	90	Macon	
20th	1	Dec. 3, 1827	May 26, 1828	175	Samuel Smith of Maryland	Andrew Stevenson of Virginia
	2	Dec. 1, 1828	Mar. 3, 1829	93	Smith	
21st	1	Dec. 7, 1829	May 31, 1830	176	Smith	Stevenson
	2	Dec. 6, 1830	Mar. 3, 1831	88	Littleton Waller Tazewell of Virginia	
22nd	1	Dec. 5, 1831	July 16, 1832	225	Tazewell	Stevenson
	2	Dec. 3, 1832	Mar. 2, 1833	91	Hugh Lawson White of Tennessee	
23rd	1	Dec. 2, 1833	June 30, 1834	211	George Poindexter of Mississippi	Stevenson
	2	Dec. 1, 1834	Mar. 3, 1835	93	John Tyler of Virginia	John Bell of Tennessee[8]
24th	1	Dec. 7, 1835	July 4, 1836	211	William R. King of Alabama	James K. Polk of Tennessee
	2	Dec. 5, 1836	Mar. 3, 1837	89	King	
25th	1	Sept. 4, 1837	Oct. 16, 1837	43	King	Polk
	2	Dec. 4, 1837	July 9, 1838	218	King	
	3	Dec. 3, 1838	Mar. 3, 1839	91	King	
26th	1	Dec. 2, 1839	July 21, 1840	233	King	Robert M. T. Hunter of Virginia
	2	Dec. 7, 1840	Mar. 3, 1841	87	King	
27th	1	May 31, 1841	Sept. 13, 1841	106	Samuel L. Southard of New Jersey	John White of Kentucky
	2	Dec. 6, 1841	Aug. 31, 1842	269	Willie P. Mangum of North Carolina	
	3	Dec. 5, 1842	Mar. 3, 1843	89	Mangum	
28th	1	Dec. 4, 1843	June 17, 1844	196	Mangum	John W. Jones of Virginia
	2	Dec. 2, 1844	Mar. 3, 1845	92	Mangum	
29th	1	Dec. 1, 1845	Aug. 10, 1846	253	David R. Atchison of Missouri	John W. Davis of Indiana
	2	Dec. 7, 1846	Mar. 3, 1847	87	Atchison	
30th	1	Dec. 6, 1847	Aug. 14, 1848	254	Atchison	Robert C. Winthrop of Massachusetts
	2	Dec. 4, 1848	Mar. 3, 1849	90	Atchison	
31st	1	Dec. 3, 1849	Sept. 30, 1850	302	William R. King of Alabama	Howell Cobb of Georgia
	2	Dec. 2, 1850	Mar. 3, 1851	92	King	
32nd	1	Dec. 1, 1851	Aug. 31, 1852	275	King	Linn Boyd of Kentucky
	2	Dec. 6, 1852	Mar. 3, 1853	88	David R. Atchison of Missouri	
33rd	1	Dec. 5, 1853	Aug. 7, 1854	246	Atchison	Boyd
	2	Dec. 4, 1854	Mar. 3, 1855	90	Jesse D. Bright of Indiana Lewis Cass of Michigan	
34th	1	Dec. 3, 1855	Aug. 18, 1856	260	Jesse D. Bright of Indiana	Nathaniel P. Banks of of Massachusetts
	2	Aug. 21, 1856	Aug. 30, 1856	10	Bright	
	3	Dec. 1, 1856	Mar. 3, 1857	93	James M. Mason of Virginia Thomas J. Rusk of Texas	

Sessions of the U.S. Congress *(cont.)*

Congress	Session	Date of beginning[1]	Date of adjournment[2]	Length in days	President pro tempore of the Senate[3]	Speaker of the House of Representatives
35th	1	Dec. 7, 1857	June 14, 1858	189	Benjamin Fitzpatrick of Alabama	James L. Orr of South Carolina
	2	Dec. 6, 1858	Mar. 3, 1859	88	Fitzpatrick	
36th	1	Dec. 5, 1859	June 25, 1860	202	Fitzpatrick Jesse D. Bright of Indiana	William Pennington of New Jersey
	2	Dec. 3, 1860	Mar. 3, 1861	93	Solomon Foot of Vermont	
37th	1	July 4, 1861	Aug. 6, 1861	34	Foot	Galusha A. Grow of Pennsylvania
	2	Dec. 2, 1861	July 17, 1862	228	Foot	
	3	Dec. 1, 1862	Mar. 3, 1863	93	Foot	
38th	1	Dec. 7, 1863	July 4, 1864	209	Foot Daniel Clark of New Hampshire	Schuyler Colfax of Indiana
	2	Dec. 5, 1864	Mar. 3, 1865	89	Clark	
39th	1	Dec. 4, 1865	July 28, 1866	237	Lafayette S. Foster of Connecticut	Colfax
	2	Dec. 3, 1866	Mar. 3, 1867	91	Benjamin F. Wade of Ohio	
40th	1	Mar. 4, 1867[9]	Dec. 2, 1867	274	Wade	Colfax
	2	Dec. 2, 1867[10]	Nov. 10, 1868	345	Wade	
	3	Dec. 7, 1868	Mar. 3, 1869	87	Wade	Theodore M. Pomeroy of New York[11]
41st	1	Mar. 4, 1869	Apr. 10, 1869	38	Henry B. Anthony of Rhode Island	James G. Blaine of Maine
	2	Dec. 6, 1869	July 15, 1870	222	Anthony	
	3	Dec. 5, 1870	Mar. 3, 1871	89	Anthony	
42nd	1	Mar. 4, 1871	Apr. 20, 1871	48	Anthony	Blaine
	2	Dec. 4, 1871	June 10, 1872	190	Anthony	
	3	Dec. 2, 1872	Mar. 3, 1873	92	Anthony	
43rd	1	Dec. 1, 1873	June 23, 1874	204	Matthew H. Carpenter of Wisconsin	Blaine
	2	Dec. 7, 1874	Mar. 3, 1875	87	Carpenter Henry B. Anthony of Rhode Island	
44th	1	Dec. 6, 1875	Aug. 15, 1876	254	Thomas W. Ferry of Michigan	Michael C. Kerr of Indiana[12] Samuel S. Cox of New York, pro tempore[13] Milton Sayler of Ohio, pro tempore[14]
	2	Dec. 4, 1876	Mar. 3, 1877	90	Ferry	Samuel J. Randall of Pennsylvania
45th	1	Oct. 15, 1877	Dec. 3, 1877	50	Ferry	Randall
	2	Dec. 3, 1877	June 20, 1878	200	Ferry	
	3	Dec. 2, 1878	Mar. 3, 1879	92	Ferry	
46th	1	Mar. 18, 1879	July 1, 1879	106	Allen G. Thurman of Ohio	Randall
	2	Dec. 1, 1879	June 16, 1880	199	Thurman	
	3	Dec. 6, 1880	Mar. 3, 1881	88	Thurman	
47th	1	Dec. 5, 1881	Aug. 8, 1882	247	Thomas F. Bayard of Delaware David Davis of Illinois	J. Warren Keifer of Ohio
	2	Dec. 4, 1882	Mar. 3, 1883	90	George F. Edmunds of Vermont	
48th	1	Dec. 3, 1883	July 7, 1884	218	Edmunds	John G. Carlisle of Kentucky
	2	Dec. 1, 1884	Mar. 3, 1885	93	Edmunds	

Congress	Session	Date of beginning[1]	Date of adjournment[2]	Length in days	President pro tempore of the Senate[3]	Speaker of the House of Representatives
49th	1	Dec. 7, 1885	Aug. 5, 1886	242	John Sherman of Ohio	Carlisle
	2	Dec. 6, 1886	Mar. 3, 1887	88	John J. Ingalls of Kansas	
50th	1	Dec. 5, 1887	Oct. 20, 1888	321	Ingalls	Carlisle
	2	Dec. 3, 1888	Mar. 3, 1889	91	Ingalls	
51st	1	Dec. 2, 1889	Oct. 1, 1890	304	Ingalls	Thomas B. Reed of Maine
	2	Dec. 1, 1890	Mar. 3, 1891	93	Charles F. Manderson of Nebraska	
52nd	1	Dec. 7, 1891	Aug. 5, 1892	251	Manderson	Charles F. Crisp of Georgia
	2	Dec. 5, 1892	Mar. 3, 1893	89	Isham G. Harris of Tennessee	
53rd	1	Aug. 7, 1893	Nov. 3, 1893	89	Harris	Crisp
	2	Dec. 4, 1893	Aug. 28, 1894	268	Harris	
	3	Dec. 3, 1894	Mar. 3, 1895	97	Matt W. Ransom of North Carolina Isham G. Harris of Tennessee	
54th	1	Dec. 2, 1895	June 11, 1896	193	William P. Frye of Maine	Thomas B. Reed of Maine
	2	Dec. 7, 1896	Mar. 3, 1897	87	Frye	
55th	1	Mar. 15, 1897	July 24, 1897	131	Frye	Reed
	2	Dec. 6, 1897	July 8, 1898	215	Frye	
	3	Dec. 5, 1898	Mar. 3, 1899	89	Frye	
56th	1	Dec. 4, 1899	June 7, 1900	186	Frye	David B. Henderson of Iowa
	2	Dec. 3, 1900	Mar. 3, 1901	91	Frye	
57th	1	Dec. 2, 1901	July 1, 1902	212	Frye	Henderson
	2	Dec. 1, 1902	Mar. 3, 1903	93	Frye	
58th	1	Nov. 9, 1903	Dec. 7, 1903	29	Frye	Joseph G. Cannon of Illinois
	2	Dec. 7, 1903	Apr. 28, 1904	144	Frye	
	3	Dec. 5, 1904	Mar. 3, 1905	89	Frye	
59th	1	Dec. 4, 1905	June 30, 1906	209	Frye	Cannon
	2	Dec. 3, 1906	Mar. 3, 1907	91	Frye	
60th	1	Dec. 2, 1907	May 30, 1908	181	Frye	Cannon
	2	Dec. 7, 1908	Mar. 3, 1909	87	Frye	
61st	1	Mar. 15, 1909	Aug. 5, 1909	144	Frye	Cannon
	2	Dec. 6, 1909	June 25, 1910	202	Frye	
	3	Dec. 5, 1910	Mar. 3, 1911	89	Frye	
62nd	1	Apr. 4, 1911	Aug. 22, 1911	141	Frye[15]	Champ Clark of Missouri
	2	Dec. 4, 1911	Aug. 26, 1912	267	Augustus O. Bacon of Georgia[16] Frank B. Brandegee of Connecticut[17] Charles Curtis of Kansas[18] Jacob H. Gallinger of New Hampshire[19] Henry Cabot Lodge of Massachusetts[20]	
	3	Dec. 2, 1912	Mar. 3, 1913	92	Bacon;[21] Gallinger[22]	
63rd	1	Apr. 7, 1913	Dec. 1, 1913	239	James P. Clarke of Arkansas	Clark
	2	Dec. 1, 1913	Oct. 24, 1914	328	Clarke	
	3	Dec. 7, 1914	Mar. 3, 1915	87	Clarke	
64th	1	Dec. 6, 1915	Sept. 8, 1916	278	Clarke[23]	Clark
	2	Dec. 4, 1916	Mar. 3, 1917	90	Willard Saulsbury of Delaware	
65th	1	Apr. 2, 1917	Oct. 6, 1917	188	Saulsbury	Clark
	2	Dec. 3, 1917	Nov. 21, 1918	354	Saulsbury	
	3	Dec. 2, 1918	Mar. 3, 1919	92	Saulsbury	

Sessions of the U.S. Congress *(cont.)*

Congress	Session	Date of beginning[1]	Date of adjournment[2]	Length in days	President pro tempore of the Senate[3]	Speaker of the House of Representatives
66th	1	May 19, 1919	Nov. 19, 1919	185	Albert B. Cummins of Iowa	Frederick H. Gillett of Massachusetts
	2	Dec. 1, 1919	June 5, 1920	188	Cummins	
	3	Dec. 6, 1920	Mar. 3, 1921	88	Cummins	
67th	1	Apr. 11, 1921	Nov. 23, 1921	227	Cummins	Gillett
	2	Dec. 5, 1921	Sept. 22, 1922	292	Cummins	
	3	Nov. 20, 1922	Dec. 4, 1922	15	Cummins	
	4	Dec. 4, 1922	Mar. 3, 1923	90	Cummins	
68th	1	Dec. 3, 1923	June 7, 1924	188	Cummins	Gillett
	2	Dec. 1, 1924	Mar. 3, 1925	93	Cummins	
69th	1	Dec. 7, 1925	July 3, 1926	209	George H. Moses of New Hampshire	Nicholas Longworth of Ohio
	2	Dec. 6, 1926	Mar. 3, 1927	88	Moses	
70th	1	Dec. 5, 1927	May 29, 1928	177	Moses	Longworth
	2	Dec. 3, 1928	Mar. 3, 1929	91	Moses	
71st	1	Apr. 15, 1929	Nov. 22, 1929	222	Moses	Longworth
	2	Dec. 2, 1929	July 3, 1930	214	Moses	
	3	Dec. 1, 1930	Mar. 3, 1931	93	Moses	
72nd	1	Dec. 7, 1931	July 16, 1932	223	Moses	John N. Garner of Texas
	2	Dec. 5, 1932	Mar. 3, 1933	89	Moses	
73rd	1	Mar. 9, 1933	June 15, 1933	99	Key Pittman of Nevada	Henry T. Rainey of Illinois[24]
	2	Jan. 3, 1934	June 18, 1934	167	Pittman	
74th	1	Jan. 3, 1935	Aug. 26, 1935	236	Pittman	Joseph W. Byrns of Tennessee[25]
	2	Jan. 3, 1936	June 20, 1936	170	Pittman	William B. Bankhead of Alabama[26]
75th	1	Jan. 5, 1937	Aug. 21, 1937	229	Pittman	Bankhead
	2	Nov. 15, 1937	Dec. 21, 1937	37	Pittman	
	3	Jan. 3, 1938	June 16, 1938	165	Pittman	
76th	1	Jan. 3, 1939	Aug. 5, 1939	215	Pittman	Bankhead[27]
	2	Sept. 21, 1939	Nov. 3, 1939	44	Pittman	
	3	Jan. 3, 1940	Jan. 3, 1941	367	Pittman[28] William H. King of Utah[30]	Sam Rayburn of Texas[29]
77th	1	Jan. 3, 1941	Jan. 2, 1942	365	Pat Harrison of Mississippi[31] Carter Glass of Virginia[32]	Rayburn
	2	Jan. 5, 1942	Dec. 16, 1942	346		
78th	1	Jan. 6, 1943[33]	Dec. 21, 1943	350	Glass	Rayburn
	2	Jan. 10, 1944[34]	Dec. 19, 1944	345	Glass	
79th	1	Jan. 3, 1945[35]	Dec. 21, 1945	353	Kenneth McKellar of Tennessee	Rayburn
	2	Jan. 14, 1946[36]	Aug. 2, 1946	201	McKellar	
80th	1	Jan. 3, 1947[37]	Dec. 19, 1947	351	Arthur H. Vandenberg of Michigan	Joseph W. Martin Jr. of Massachusetts
	2	Jan. 6, 1948[38]	Dec. 31, 1948	361	Vandenberg	
81st	1	Jan. 3, 1949	Oct. 19, 1949	290	Kenneth McKellar of Tennessee	Sam Rayburn of Texas
	2	Jan. 3, 1950[39]	Jan. 2, 1951	365	McKellar	
82nd	1	Jan. 3, 1951[40]	Oct. 20, 1951	291	McKellar	Rayburn
	2	Jan. 8, 1952[41]	July 7, 1952	182	McKellar	

Congress	Session	Date of beginning[1]	Date of adjournment[2]	Length in days	President pro tempore of the Senate[3]	Speaker of the House of Representatives
83rd	1	Jan. 3, 1953[42]	Aug. 3, 1953	213	Styles Bridges of New Hampshire	Joseph W. Martin Jr. of Massachusetts
	2	Jan. 6, 1954[43]	Dec. 2, 1954	331	Bridges	
84th	1	Jan. 5, 1955[44]	Aug. 2, 1955	210	Walter F. George of Georgia	Sam Rayburn of Texas
	2	Jan. 3, 1956[45]	July 27, 1956	207	George	
85th	1	Jan. 3, 1957[46]	Aug. 30, 1957	239	Carl Hayden of Arizona	Rayburn
	2	Jan. 7, 1958[47]	Aug. 24, 1958	230	Hayden	
86th	1	Jan. 7, 1959[48]	Sept. 15, 1959	252	Hayden	Rayburn
	2	Jan. 6, 1960[49]	Sept. 1, 1960	240	Hayden	
87th	1	Jan. 3, 1961[50]	Sept. 27, 1961	268	Hayden	Rayburn[51]
	2	Jan. 10, 1962[52]	Oct. 13, 1962	277	Hayden	John W. McCormack of Massachusetts[53]
88th	1	Jan. 9, 1963[54]	Dec. 30, 1963	356	Hayden	McCormack
	2	Jan. 7, 1964[55]	Oct. 3, 1964	270	Hayden	
89th	1	Jan. 4, 1965	Oct. 23, 1965	293	Hayden	McCormack
	2	Jan. 10, 1966[56]	Oct. 22, 1966	286	Hayden	
90th	1	Jan. 10, 1967[57]	Dec. 15, 1967	340	Hayden	McCormack
	2	Jan. 15, 1968[58]	Oct. 14, 1968	274	Hayden	
91st	1	Jan. 3, 1969[59]	Dec. 23, 1969	355	Richard B. Russell of Georgia	McCormack
	2	Jan. 19, 1970[60]	Jan. 2, 1971	349	Russell	
92nd	1	Jan. 21, 1971[61]	Dec. 17, 1971	331	Russell[62] Allen J. Ellender of Louisiana[63]	Carl Albert of Oklahoma
	2	Jan. 18, 1972[64]	Oct. 18, 1972	275	Ellender[65] James O. Eastland of Mississippi[66]	
93rd	1	Jan. 3, 1973[67]	Dec. 22, 1973	354	Eastland	Albert
	2	Jan. 21, 1974[68]	Dec. 20, 1974	334	Eastland	
94th	1	Jan. 14, 1975[69]	Dec. 19, 1975	340	Eastland	Albert
	2	Jan. 19, 1976[70]	Oct. 1, 1976	257	Eastland	
95th	1	Jan. 4, 1977[71]	Dec. 15, 1977	346	Eastland	Thomas P. O'Neill Jr. of Massachusetts
	2	Jan. 19, 1978[72]	Oct. 15, 1978	270	Eastland	
96th	1	Jan. 15, 1979[73]	Jan. 3, 1980	354	Warren G. Magnuson of Washington	O'Neill
	2	Jan. 3, 1980[74]	Dec. 16, 1980	349	Magnuson	
97th	1	Jan. 5, 1981[75]	Dec. 16, 1981	347	Strom Thurmond of South Carolina	O'Neill
	2	Jan. 25, 1982[76]	Dec. 23, 1982	333	Thurmond	
98th	1	Jan. 3, 1983[77]	Nov. 18, 1983	320	Thurmond	O'Neill
	2	Jan. 23, 1984[78]	Oct. 12, 1984	264	Thurmond	
99th	1	Jan. 3, 1985[79]	Dec. 20, 1985	352	Thurmond	O'Neill
	2	Jan. 21, 1986[80]	Oct. 18, 1986	278	Thurmond	
100th	1	Jan. 6, 1987[81]	Dec. 22, 1987	351	John C. Stennis of Mississippi	Jim Wright of Texas
	2	Jan. 25, 1988[82]	Oct. 22, 1988	272	Stennis	
101st	1	Jan. 3, 1989[83]	Nov. 22, 1989	324	Robert C. Byrd of West Virginia	Wright; Thomas S. Foley of Washington[84]
	2	Jan. 23, 1990[85]	Oct. 28, 1990	260	Byrd	Foley
102nd	1	Jan. 3, 1991[86]	Jan. 3, 1992	366	Byrd	Foley

Sessions of the U.S. Congress *(cont.)*

Congress	Session	Date of beginning[1]	Date of adjournment[2]	Length in days	President pro tempore of the Senate[3]	Speaker of the House of Representatives
	2	Jan. 3, 1992[87]	Oct. 9, 1992	281	Byrd	
103rd	1	Jan. 5, 1993[88]	Nov. 26, 1993	326	Byrd	Foley
	2	Jan. 25, 1994[89]	Dec. 1, 1994	311	Byrd	
104th	1	Jan. 4, 1995[90]	Jan. 3, 1996	365	Strom Thurmond of South Carolina	Newt Gingrich of Georgia
	2	Jan. 3, 1996[91]	Oct. 4, 1996	276	Thurmond	
105th	1	Jan. 7, 1997[92]	Nov. 13, 1997	311	Thurmond	Gingrich
	2	Jan. 27, 1998[93]	Dec. 19, 1998	327	Thurmond	
106th	1	Jan. 6, 1999[94]	Nov. 22, 1999	351	Thurmond	J. Dennis Hastert of Illinois
	2	Jan. 24, 2000	Dec. 15, 2000	326	Thurmond	Hastert
107th	1	Jan. 3, 2001[95]	Dec. 20, 2001	352	Robert C. Byrd[96] of West Virginia	Hastert
					Strom Thurmond of South Carolina	
					Byrd	
	2	Jan. 23, 2002[97]	Nov. 22, 2002	304	Byrd	Hastert
108th	1	Jan. 7, 2003[98]	Dec. 9, 2003	336	Ted Stevens of Alaska	Hastert
	2	Jan. 20, 2004[99]	Dec. 8, 2004	323	Stevens	Hastert
109th	1	Jan. 4, 2005[100]	—	—	Stevens	Hastert

Notes:

1. The Constitution (art. I, sec. 4) provided that "The Congress shall assemble at least once in every year . . . on the first Monday in December, unless they shall by law appoint a different day." Pursuant to a resolution of the Continental Congress, the first session of the First Congress convened March 4, 1789. Up to and including May 20, 1820, 18 acts were passed providing for the meeting of Congress on other days in the year. After 1820 Congress met regularly on the first Monday in December until 1934, when the Twentieth Amendment to the Constitution became effective changing the meeting date to Jan. 3. (Until then, brief special sessions of the Senate only were held at the beginning of each presidential term to confirm Cabinet and other nominations—and occasionally at other times for other purposes. The Senate last met in special session from March 4 to March 6, 1933.) The first and second sessions of the First Congress were held in New York City. Subsequently, including the first session of the Sixth Congress, Philadelphia was the meeting place; since then, Congress has convened in Washington.

2. Until adoption of the Twentieth Amendment, the deadline for adjournment of Congress in odd-numbered years was March 3. However, the expiring Congress often extended the "legislative day" of March 3 up to noon of March 4, when the new Congress came officially into being. After ratification of the Twentieth Amendment, the deadline for adjournment of Congress in odd-numbered years was noon on Jan. 3.

3. At one time, the appointment or election of a president pro tempore was considered by the Senate to be for the occasion only, so that more than one appear in several sessions, and in others none was chosen. Since March 12, 1890, they have served until "the Senate otherwise ordered."

4. Elected to count the vote for president and vice president, which was done April 6, 1789, because there was a quorum of the Senate for the first time. John Adams, vice president, appeared April 21, 1789, and took his seat as president of the Senate.

5. Elected Speaker pro tempore for April 20, 1798, and again for May 28, 1798.

6. Elected Speaker Jan. 19, 1814, to succeed Henry Clay, who resigned Jan. 19, 1814.

7. Elected Speaker Nov. 15, 1820, to succeed Henry Clay, who resigned Oct. 28, 1820.

8. Elected Speaker June 2, 1834, to succeed Andrew Stevenson of Virginia, who resigned.

9. There were recesses in this session from Saturday, Mar. 30, to Wednesday, July 1, and from Saturday, July 20, to Thursday, Nov. 21.

10. There were recesses in this session from Monday, July 27, to Monday, Sept. 21, to Friday, Oct. 16, and to Tuesday, Nov. 10. No business was transacted subsequent to July 27.

11. Elected Speaker Mar. 3, 1869, and served one day.

12. Died Aug. 19, 1876.

13. Appointed Speaker pro tempore Feb. 17, May 12, June 19.

14. Appointed Speaker pro tempore June 4.

15. Resigned as president pro tempore Apr. 27, 1911.

16. Elected to serve Jan. 11–17, Mar. 11–12, Apr. 8, May 10, May 30 to June 1 and 3, June 13 to July 5, Aug. 1–10, and Aug. 27 to Dec. 15, 1912.

17. Elected to serve May 25, 1912.

18. Elected to serve Dec. 4–12, 1911.

19. Elected to serve Feb. 12–14, Apr. 26–27, May 7, July 6–31, Aug. 12–26, 1912.

20. Elected to serve Mar. 25–26, 1912.

21. Elected to serve Aug. 27 to Dec. 15, 1912, Jan. 5–18, and Feb. 2–15, 1913.

22. Elected to serve Dec. 16, 1912, to Jan. 4, 1913, Jan. 19 to Feb. 1, and Feb. 16 to Mar. 3, 1913.

23. Died Oct. 1, 1916.

24. Died Aug. 19, 1934.

25. Died June 4, 1936.

26. Elected June 4, 1936.

27. Died Sept. 15, 1940.

28. Died Nov. 10, 1940.

29. Elected Sept. 16, 1940.

30. Elected Nov. 19, 1940.

31. Elected Jan. 6, 1941; died June 22, 1941.

32. Elected July 10, 1941.

33. There was a recess in this session from Thursday, July 8, to Tuesday, Sept. 14.

34. There were recesses in this session from Saturday, Apr. 1, to Wednesday, Apr. 12; from Friday, June 23, to Tuesday, Aug. 1; and from Thursday, Sept. 21, to Tuesday, Nov. 14.

35. The House was in recess in this session from Saturday, July 21, 1945, to Wednesday, Sept. 5, 1945, and the Senate from Wednesday, Aug. 1, 1945, to Wednesday, Sept. 5, 1945.

36. The House was in recess in this session from Thursday, Apr. 18, 1946, to Tuesday, Apr. 30, 1946.

37. There was a recess in this session from Sunday, July 27, 1947, to Monday, Nov. 17, 1947.

38. There were recesses in this session from Sunday, June 20, 1948, to Monday, July 26, 1948, and from Saturday, Aug. 7, 1948, to Friday, Dec. 31, 1948.

39. The House was in recess in this session from Thursday, Apr. 6, 1950, to Tuesday, Apr. 18, 1950, and both the Senate and the House were in recess from Saturday, Sept. 23, 1950, to Monday, Nov. 27, 1950.

40. The House was in recess in this session from Thursday, Mar. 22, 1951, to Monday, Apr. 2, 1951, and from Thursday, Aug. 23, 1951, to Wednesday, Sept. 12, 1951.

41. The House was in recess in this session from Thursday, Apr. 10, 1952, to Tuesday, Apr. 22, 1952.

42. The House was in recess in this session from Thursday, Apr. 2, 1953, to Monday, Apr. 13, 1953.

43. The House was in recess in this session from Thursday, Apr. 15, 1954, to Monday, Apr. 26, 1954, and adjourned sine die Aug. 20, 1954. The Senate was in recess in this session from Friday, Aug. 20, 1954, to Monday, Nov. 8, 1954; from Thursday, Nov. 18, 1954, to Monday, Nov. 29, 1954, and adjourned sine die Dec. 2, 1954.

44. There was a recess in this session from Monday, Apr. 4, 1955, to Wednesday, Apr. 13, 1955.

45. There was a recess in this session from Thursday, Mar. 29, 1956, to Monday, Apr. 9, 1956.

46. There was a recess in this session from Thursday, Apr. 18, 1957, to Monday, Apr. 29, 1957.

47. There was a recess in this session from Thursday, Apr. 3, 1958, to Monday, Apr. 14, 1958.

48. There was a recess in this session from Thursday, Mar. 26, 1959, to Tuesday, Apr. 7, 1959.

49. The Senate was in recess in this session from Thursday, Apr. 14, 1960, to Monday, Apr. 18, 1960; from Friday, May 27, 1960, to Tuesday, May 31, 1960, and from Sunday, July 3, 1960, to Monday, Aug. 8, 1960. The House was in recess in this session from Thursday, Apr. 14, 1960, to Monday, Apr. 18, 1960; from Friday, May 27, 1960, to Tuesday, May 31, 1960, and from Sunday, July 3, 1960, to Monday, Aug. 15, 1960.

50. The House was in recess in this session from Thursday, Mar. 30, 1961, to Monday, Apr. 10, 1961.

51. Died Nov. 16, 1961.

52. The House was in recess in this session from Thursday, Apr. 19, 1962, to Monday, Apr. 30, 1962.

53. Elected Jan. 10, 1962.

54. The House was in recess in this session from Thursday, Apr. 11, 1963, to Monday, Apr. 22, 1963.

55. The House was in recess in this session from Thursday, Mar. 26, 1964, to Monday, Apr. 6, 1964; from Thursday, July 2, 1964, to Monday, July 20, 1964; from Friday, Aug. 21, 1964, to Monday, Aug. 31, 1964. The Senate was in recess in this session from Friday, July 10, 1964, to Monday, July 20, 1964; from Friday, Aug. 21, 1964, to Monday, Aug. 31, 1964.

56. The House was in recess in this session from Thursday, Apr. 7, 1966, to Monday, Apr. 18, 1966; from Thursday, June 30, 1966, to Monday, July 11, 1966. The Senate was in recess in this session from Thursday, Apr. 7, 1966, to Wednesday, Apr. 13, 1966; from Thursday, June 30, 1966, to Monday, July 11, 1966.

57. There was a recess in this session from Thursday, Mar. 23, 1967, to Monday, Apr. 3, 1967; from Thursday, June 29, 1967, to Monday, July 10, 1967; from Thursday, Aug. 31, 1967, to Monday, Sept. 11, 1967; and from Wednesday, Nov. 22, 1967, to Monday, Nov. 27, 1967.

58. The House was in recess in this session from Thursday, Apr. 11, 1968, to Monday, Apr. 22, 1968; from Wednesday, May 29, 1968, to Monday, June 3, 1968; from Wednesday, July 3, 1968, to Monday, July 8, 1968; from Friday, Aug. 2, 1968, to Wednesday, Sept. 4, 1968. The Senate was in recess this session from Thursday, Apr. 11, 1968, to Wednesday, Apr. 17, 1968; from Wednesday, May 29, 1968, to Monday, June 3, 1968; from Wednesday, July 3, 1968, to Monday, July 8, 1968; from Friday, Aug. 2, 1968, to Wednesday, Sept. 4, 1968.

59. The House was in recess this session from Friday, Feb. 7, 1969, to Monday, Feb. 17, 1969; from Thursday, Apr. 3, 1969, to Monday, Apr. 14, 1969; from Wednesday, May 28, 1969, to Monday, June 2, 1969; from Wednesday, July 2, 1969, to Monday, July 7, 1969; from Wednesday, Aug. 13, 1969, to Wednesday, Sept. 3, 1969; from Thursday, Nov. 6, 1969, to Wednesday, Nov. 12, 1969; from Wednesday, Nov. 26, 1969, to Monday, Dec. 1, 1969. The Senate was in recess this session from Friday, Feb. 7, 1969, to Monday, Feb. 17, 1969; from Thursday, Apr. 3, 1969, to Monday, Apr. 14, 1969; from Wednesday, July 2, 1969, to Monday, July 7, 1969; from Wednesday, Aug. 13, 1969, to Wednesday, Sept. 3, 1969; from Wednesday, Nov. 26, 1969, to Monday, Dec. 1, 1969.

60. The House was in recess this session from Tuesday, Feb. 10, 1970, to Monday, Feb. 16, 1970; from Thursday, Mar. 26, 1970, to Tuesday, Mar. 31, 1970; from Wednesday, May 27, 1970, to Monday, June 1, 1970; from Wednesday, July 1, 1970, to Monday, July 6, 1970; from Friday, Aug. 14, 1970, to Wednesday, Sept. 9, 1970; from Wednesday, Oct. 14, 1970, to Monday, Nov. 16, 1970; from Wednesday, Nov. 25, 1970, to Monday, Nov. 30, 1970; from Tuesday, Dec. 22, 1970, to Tuesday, Dec. 29, 1970. The Senate was in recess this session from Tuesday, Feb. 10, 1970, to Monday, Feb. 16, 1970; from Thursday, Mar. 26, 1970, to Tuesday, Mar. 31, 1970; from Wednesday, Sept. 2, 1970, to Tuesday, Sept. 8, 1970; from Wednesday, Oct. 14, 1970, to Monday, Nov. 16, 1970; from Wednesday, Nov. 25, 1970, to Monday, Nov. 30, 1970; from Tuesday, Dec. 22, 1970, to Monday, Dec. 28, 1970.

61. The House was in recess this session from Wednesday, Feb. 10, 1971, to Wednesday, Feb. 17, 1971; from Wednesday, Apr. 7, 1971, to Monday, Apr. 19, 1971; from Thursday, May 27, 1971, to Tuesday, June 1, 1971; from Thursday, July 1, 1971, to Tuesday, July 6, 1971; from Friday, Aug. 6, 1971, to Wednesday, Sept. 8, 1971; from Thursday, Oct. 7, 1971, to Tuesday, Oct. 12, 1971; from Thursday, Oct. 21, 1971, to Tuesday, Oct. 26, 1971; from Friday, Nov. 19, 1971, to Monday, Nov. 29, 1971. The Senate was in recess this session from Thursday, Feb. 11, 1971, to Wednesday, Feb. 17, 1971; from Wednesday, Apr. 7, 1971, to Wednesday, Apr. 14, 1971; from Wednesday, May 26, 1971, to Tuesday, June 1, 1971; from Wednesday, June 30, 1971, to Tuesday, July 6, 1971; from Friday, Aug. 6, 1971, to Wednesday, Sept. 8, 1971; from Thursday, Oct. 21, 1971, to Tuesday, Oct. 26, 1971; from Wednesday, Nov. 24, 1971, to Monday, Nov. 29, 1971.

62. Died Jan. 21, 1971.

63. Elected Jan. 22, 1971.

64. The House was in recess this session from Wednesday, Feb. 9, 1972, to Wednesday, Feb. 16, 1972; from Wednesday, Mar. 29, 1972, to Monday, Apr. 10, 1972; from Wednesday, May 24, 1972, to Tuesday, May 30, 1972; from Friday, June 30, 1972, to Monday, July 17, 1972; from

Friday, Aug. 18, 1972, to Tuesday, Sept. 5, 1972. The Senate was in recess this session from Wednesday, Feb. 9, 1972, to Monday, Feb. 14, 1972; from Thursday, Mar. 30, 1972, to Tuesday, Apr. 4, 1972; from Thursday, May 25, 1972, to Tuesday, May 30, 1972; from Friday, June 30, 1972, to Monday, July 17, 1972; from Friday, Aug. 18, 1972, to Tuesday, Sept. 5, 1972.

65. Died July 27, 1972.

66. Elected July 28, 1972.

67. The House was in recess this session from Thursday, Feb. 8, 1973, to Monday, Feb. 19, 1973; from Thursday, Apr. 19, 1973, to Monday, Apr. 30, 1973; from Thursday, May 24, 1973, to Tuesday, May 29, 1973; from Saturday, June 30, 1973, to Tuesday, July 10, 1973; from Friday, Aug. 3, 1973, to Wednesday, Sept. 5, 1973; from Thursday, Oct. 4, 1973, to Tuesday, Oct. 9, 1973; from Thursday, Oct. 18, 1973, to Tuesday, Oct. 23, 1973; from Thursday, Nov. 15, 1973 to Monday, Nov. 26, 1973. The Senate was in recess this session from Thursday, Feb. 8, 1973, to Thursday, Feb. 15, 1973; from Wednesday, Apr. 18, 1973, to Monday, Apr. 30, 1973; from Wednesday, May 23, 1973, to Tuesday, May 29, 1973; from Saturday, June 30, 1973, to Monday, July 9, 1973; from Friday, Aug. 3, 1973, to Wednesday, Sept. 5, 1973; from Thursday, Oct. 18, 1973, to Tuesday, Oct. 23, 1973; from Wednesday, Nov. 21, 1973, to Monday, Nov. 26, 1973.

68. The House was in recess this session from Thursday, Feb. 7, 1974, to Wednesday, Feb. 13, 1974; from Thursday, Apr. 11, 1974, to Monday, Apr. 22, 1974; from Thursday, May 23, 1974, to Tuesday, May 28, 1974; from Thursday, Aug. 22, 1974, to Wednesday, Sept. 11, 1974; from Thursday, Oct. 17, 1974, to Monday, Nov. 18, 1974; from Tuesday, Nov. 26, 1974, to Tuesday, Dec. 3, 1974. The Senate was in recess this session from Friday, Feb. 8, 1974, to Monday, Feb. 18, 1974; from Wednesday, Mar. 13, 1974, to Tuesday, Mar. 19, 1974; from Thursday, Apr. 11, 1974, to Monday, Apr. 22, 1974; from Wednesday, May 23, 1974, to Tuesday, May 28, 1974; from Thursday, Aug. 22, 1974, to Wednesday, Sept. 4, 1974; from Thursday, Oct. 17, 1974, to Monday, Nov. 18, 1974; from Tuesday, Nov. 26, 1974, to Monday, Dec. 2, 1974.

69. The House was in recess this session from Wednesday, Mar. 26, 1975, to Monday, Apr. 7, 1975; from Thursday, May 22, 1975, to Monday, June 2, 1975; from Thursday, June 26, 1975, to Tuesday, July 8, 1975; from Friday, Aug. 1, 1975, to Wednesday, Sept. 3, 1975; from Thursday, Oct. 9, 1975, to Monday, Oct. 20, 1975; from Thursday, Oct. 23, 1975, to Tuesday, Oct. 28, 1975; from Thursday, Nov. 20, 1975, to Monday, Dec. 1, 1975. The Senate was in recess this session from Wednesday, Mar. 26, 1975, to Monday, Apr. 7, 1975; from Thursday, May 22, 1975, to Monday, June 2, 1975; from Friday, June 27, 1975, to Monday, July 7, 1975; from Friday, Aug. 1, 1975, to Wednesday, Sept. 3, 1975; from Thursday, Oct. 9, 1975, to Monday, Oct. 20, 1975; from Thursday, Oct. 23, 1975, to Tuesday, Oct. 28, 1975; from Thursday, Nov. 20, 1975, to Monday, Dec. 1, 1975.

70. The House was in recess this session from Wednesday, Feb. 11, 1976, to Monday, Feb. 16, 1976; from Wednesday, Apr. 14, 1976, to Monday, Apr. 26, 1976; from Thursday, May 27, 1976, to Tuesday, June 1, 1976; from Friday, July 2, 1976, to Monday, July 19, 1976; from Tuesday, Aug. 10, 1976, to Monday, Aug. 23, 1976; from Thursday, Sept. 2, 1976, to Wednesday, Sept. 8, 1976. The Senate was in recess this session from Friday, Feb. 6, 1976, to Monday, Feb. 16, 1976; from Wednesday, Apr. 14, 1976, to Monday, Apr. 26, 1976; from Friday, May 28, 1976, to Wednesday, June 2, 1976; from Friday, July 2, 1976, to Monday, July 19, 1976; from Tuesday, Aug. 10, 1976, to Monday, Aug. 23, 1976; from Wednesday, Sept. 1, 1976, to Tuesday, Sept. 7, 1976.

71. The House was in recess this session from Wednesday, Feb. 9, 1977, to Wednesday, Feb. 16, 1977; from Wednesday, Apr. 6, 1977, to Monday, Apr. 18, 1977; from Thursday, May 26, 1977, to Wednesday, June 1, 1977; from Thursday, June 30, 1977, to Monday, July 11, 1977; from Friday, Aug. 5, 1977, to Wednesday, Sept. 7, 1977; from Thursday, Oct. 6, 1977, to Tuesday, Oct. 11, 1977. The Senate was in recess this session from Friday, Feb. 11, 1977, to Monday, Feb. 21, 1977; from Thursday, Apr. 7, 1977, to Monday, Apr. 18, 1977; from Friday, May 27, 1977, to Monday, June 6, 1977; from Friday, July 1, 1977, to Monday, July 11, 1977; from Saturday, Aug. 6, 1977, to Wednesday, Sept. 7, 1977.

72. The House was in recess this session from Thursday, Feb. 9, 1978, to Tuesday, Feb. 14, 1978; from Wednesday, Mar. 22, 1978, to Monday, Apr. 3, 1978; from Thursday, May 25, 1978, to Wednesday, May 31, 1978; from Thursday, June 29, 1978, to Monday, July 10, 1978; from Thursday, Aug. 17, 1978, to Wednesday, Sept. 6, 1978. The Senate was in recess this session from Friday, Feb. 10, 1978, to Monday, Feb. 20, 1978; from Thursday, Mar. 23, 1978, to Monday, Apr. 3, 1978; from Friday, May 26, 1978, to Monday, June 5, 1978; from Thursday, June 29, 1978, to Monday, July 10, 1978; from Friday, Aug. 25, 1978, to Wednesday, Sept. 6, 1978.

73. The House was in recess this session from Thursday, Feb. 8, 1979, to Tuesday, Feb. 13, 1979; from Tuesday, Apr. 10, 1979, to Monday, Apr. 23, 1979; from Thursday, May 24, 1979, to Wednesday, May 30, 1979; from Friday, June 29, 1979, to Monday, July 9, 1979; from Thursday, Aug. 2, 1979, to Wednesday, Sept. 5, 1979; from Tuesday, Nov. 20, 1979, to Monday, Nov. 26, 1979. The Senate was in recess this session from Friday, Feb. 9, 1979, to Monday, Feb. 19, 1979; from Tuesday, Apr. 10, 1979, to Monday, Apr. 23, 1979; from Friday, May 25, 1979, to Monday, June 4, 1979; from Friday, Aug. 3, 1979, to Wednesday, Sept. 5, 1979; from Tuesday, Nov. 20, 1979, to Monday, Nov. 26, 1979.

74. The House was in recess this session from Wednesday, Feb. 13, 1980, to Tuesday, Feb. 19, 1980; from Wednesday, Apr. 2, 1980, to Tuesday, Apr. 15, 1980; from Thursday, May 22, 1980, to Wednesday, May 28, 1980; from Wednesday, July 2, 1980, to Monday, July 21, 1980; from Friday, Aug. 1, 1980, to Monday, Aug. 18, 1980; from Thursday, Aug. 28, 1980, to Wednesday, Sept. 13, 1980. The Senate was in recess this session from Monday, Feb. 11, 1980, to Thursday, Feb. 14, 1980; from Thursday, Apr. 3, 1980, to Tuesday, Apr. 15, 1980; from Thursday, May 22, 1980, to Wednesday, May 28, 1980; from Wednesday, July 2, 1980, to Monday, July 21, 1980; from Wednesday, Aug. 6, 1980, to Monday, Aug. 18, 1980; from Wednesday, Aug. 27, 1980, to Wednesday, Sept. 3, 1980; from Wednesday, Oct. 1, 1980, to Wednesday, Nov. 12, 1980; from Monday, Nov. 24, 1980, to Monday, Dec. 1, 1980.

75. The House was in recess this session from Friday, Feb. 6, 1981, to Tuesday, Feb. 17, 1981; from Friday, Apr. 10, 1981, to Monday, Apr. 27, 1981; from Friday, June 26, 1981, to Wednesday, July 8, 1981; from Tuesday, Aug. 4, 1981, to Wednesday, Sept. 9, 1981; from Wednesday, Oct. 7, 1981, to Tuesday, Oct. 13, 1981; from Monday, Nov. 23, 1981, to Monday, Nov. 30, 1981. The Senate was in recess this session from Friday, Feb. 6, 1981, to Monday, Feb. 16, 1981; from Friday, Apr. 10, 1981, to Monday, Apr. 27, 1981; from Thursday, June 25, 1981, to Wednesday, July 8, 1981; from Monday, Aug. 3, 1981, to Wednesday, Sept. 9, 1981; from Wednesday, Oct. 7, 1981, to Wednesday, Oct. 14, 1981; from Tuesday, Nov. 24, 1981, to Monday, Nov. 30, 1981.

76. The House was in recess this session from Wednesday, Feb. 10, 1982, to Monday, Feb. 22, 1982; from Tuesday, Apr. 6, 1982, to Tuesday, Apr. 20, 1982; from Thursday, May 27, 1982, to Wednesday, June 2, 1982; from Thursday, July 1, 1982, to Monday, July 12, 1982; from Friday, Aug. 20, 1982, to Wednesday, Sept. 8, 1982; from Friday, Oct. 1, 1982, to Monday, Nov. 29, 1982. The Senate was in recess this session from Thursday, Feb. 11, 1982, to Monday, Feb. 22, 1982; from Thursday, Apr. 1, 1982, to Tuesday, Apr. 13, 1982; from Thursday, May 27, 1982, to Tuesday, June 8, 1982; from Thursday, July 1, 1982, to Monday, July 12, 1982; from Friday, Aug. 20, 1982, to Wednesday, Sept. 8, 1982; from Friday, Oct. 1, 1982, to Monday, Nov. 29, 1982.

77. The House adjourned for recess this session Friday, Jan. 7, 1983, to Tuesday, Jan. 25, 1983; Thursday, Feb. 17, 1983, to Tuesday, Feb. 22, 1983; Thursday, March 24, 1983, to Tuesday, Apr. 5, 1983; Thursday, May 26, 1983, to Wednesday, June 1, 1983; Thursday, June 30, 1983, to Monday, July 11, 1983; Friday, Aug. 5, 1983, to Monday, Sept. 12, 1983; Friday, Oct. 7, 1983, to Monday, Oct. 17, 1983. The Senate adjourned for recess this session Monday, Jan. 3, 1983, to Tuesday, Jan. 25, 1983; Friday, Feb. 4, 1983, to Monday, Feb. 14, 1983; Friday, March 25, 1983, to Tuesday, Apr. 5, 1983; Friday, May 27, 1983, to Monday, June 6, 1983; Friday, July 1, 1983, to Monday, July 11, 1983; Friday, Aug. 5, 1983, to Monday, Sept. 12, 1983; Monday Oct. 10, 1983, to Monday, Oct. 17, 1983.

78. The House adjourned for recess this session Thursday, Feb. 9, 1984, to Tuesday, Feb. 21, 1984; Friday, Apr. 13, 1984, to Tuesday, Apr. 24, 1984; Friday, May 25, 1984, to Wednesday, May 30, 1984; Friday, June 29, 1984, to Monday, July 23, 1984; Friday, Aug. 10, 1984, to Wednesday,

Sept. 5, 1984. The Senate adjourned for recess this session Friday, Feb. 10, 1984, to Monday, Feb. 20, 1984; Friday, Apr. 13, 1984, to Tuesday, Apr. 24, 1984; from Friday, May 25, 1984, to Thursday, May 31, 1984; from Friday, June 29, 1984, to Monday, July 23, 1984; Friday, Aug. 10, 1984, to Wednesday, Sept. 5, 1984.

79. The House adjourned for recess this session Monday, Jan. 7, 1985, to Monday, Jan. 21, 1985; Thursday, Feb. 7, 1985, to Tuesday, Feb. 19, 1985; Thursday, March 7, 1985, to Tuesday, March 19, 1985; Thursday, Apr. 4, 1985, to Monday, Apr. 15, 1985; Thursday, May 23, 1985, to Monday, June 3, 1985; Thursday, June 27, 1985, to Monday, July 8, 1985; Thursday, Aug. 1, 1985, to Wednesday, Sept. 4, 1985; Thursday, Nov. 21, 1985, to Monday, Dec. 2, 1985. The Senate adjourned for recess this session Monday, Jan. 7, 1985, to Monday, Jan. 21, 1985; Thursday, Feb. 7, 1985, to Monday, Feb. 18, 1985; Tuesday, March 12, 1985, to Thursday, March 14, 1985; Thursday, Apr. 4, 1985, to Monday, Apr. 15, 1985; Friday, May 24, 1985, to Monday, June 3, 1985; Thursday, June 27, 1985, to Monday, July 8, 1985; Thursday, Aug. 1, 1985, to Monday, Sept. 9, 1985; Saturday, Nov. 23, 1985, to Monday, Dec. 2, 1985.

80. The House adjourned for recess this session Tuesday, Jan. 7, 1986, to Tuesday, Jan. 21, 1986; Friday, Feb. 7, 1986, to Tuesday, Feb. 18, 1986; Tuesday, March 25, 1986, to Tuesday, Apr. 8, 1986; Thursday, May 22, 1986, to Tuesday, June 3, 1986; Thursday, June 26, 1986, to Monday, July 14, 1986; Friday, Aug. 15, 1986, to Monday, Sept. 8, 1986. The Senate adjourned for recess this session Tuesday, Jan. 7, 1986, to Tuesday, Jan. 21, 1986; Friday, Feb. 7, 1986, to Monday, Feb. 17, 1986; Thursday, March 27, 1986, to Tuesday, Apr. 8, 1986; Wednesday, May 21, 1986, to Monday, June 2, 1986; Thursday, June 26, 1986, to Monday, July 14, 1986; Friday, Aug. 15, 1986, to Monday, Sept. 8, 1986.

81. The House adjourned for recess this session Thursday, Jan. 8, 1987, to Tuesday, Jan. 20, 1987; Wednesday, Feb. 11, 1987, to Wednesday, Feb. 18, 1987; Thursday, Apr. 9, 1987, to Tuesday, Apr. 21, 1987; Thursday, May 21, 1987, to Wednesday, May 27, 1987; Wednesday, July 1, 1987, to Tuesday, July 7, 1987; Wednesday, July 15, 1987, to Monday, July 20, 1987; Friday, Aug. 7, 1987, to Wednesday, Sept. 9, 1987; Tuesday, Nov. 10, 1987, to Monday, Nov. 16, 1987; Friday, Nov. 20, 1987, to Monday, Nov. 30, 1987. The Senate adjourned for recess this session Tuesday, Jan. 6, 1987, to Monday, Jan. 12, 1987; Thursday, Feb. 5, 1987, to Monday, Feb. 16, 1987; Friday, Apr. 10, 1987, to Tuesday, Apr. 21, 1987; Thursday, May 21, 1987, to Wednesday, May 27, 1987; Wednesday, July 1, 1987, to Tuesday, July 7, 1987; Friday, Aug. 7, 1987, to Wednesday, Sept. 9, 1987; Friday, Nov. 20, 1987, to Monday, Nov. 30, 1987.

82. The House adjourned for recess this session Tuesday, Feb. 9, 1988, to Tuesday, Feb. 16, 1988; Thursday, March 31, 1988, to Monday, Apr. 11, 1988; Thursday, May 26, 1988, to Wednesday, June 1, 1988; Thursday, June 30, 1988, to Thursday, July 7, 1988; Thursday, July 14, 1988, to Tuesday, July 26, 1988; Thursday, Aug. 11, 1988, to Wednesday, Sept. 7, 1988. The Senate adjourned for recess this session Thursday, Feb. 4, 1988, to Monday, Feb. 15, 1988; Friday, March 4, 1988, to Monday, March 14, 1988; Thursday, March 31, 1988, to Monday, Apr. 11, 1988; Friday, Apr. 29, 1988, to Monday, May 9, 1988; Friday, May 27, 1988, to Monday, June 6, 1988; Wednesday, June 29, 1988, to Wednesday, July 6, 1988; Thursday, July 14, 1988, to Monday, July 25, 1988; Thursday, Aug. 11, 1988, to Wednesday, Sept. 7, 1988.

83. The House adjourned for recess this session Wednesday, Jan. 4, 1989, to Thursday, Jan. 19, 1989; Thursday, Feb. 9, 1989, to Tuesday, Feb. 21, 1989; Thursday, March 23, 1989, to Monday, Apr. 3, 1989; Tuesday, Apr. 18, 1989, to Tuesday, Apr. 25, 1989; Thursday, May 25, 1989, to Wednesday, May 31, 1989; Thursday, June 29, 1989, to Monday, July 10, 1989; Saturday, Aug. 5, 1989, to Wednesday, Sept. 6, 1989. The Senate adjourned for recess this session Wednesday, Jan. 4, 1989, to Friday, Jan. 20, 1989; Friday, Jan. 20, 1989, to Wednesday, Jan. 25, 1989; Thursday, Feb. 9, 1989, to Tuesday, Feb. 21, 1989; Friday, March 17, 1989, to Tuesday, Apr. 4, 1989; Wednesday, Apr. 19, 1989, to Monday, May 1, 1989; Thursday, May 18, 1989, to Wednesday, May 31, 1989; Friday, June 23, 1989, to Tuesday, July 11, 1989; Friday, Aug. 4, 1989, to Wednesday, Sept. 6, 1989.

84. Elected Speaker June 6, 1989, to succeed Jim Wright, who resigned the Speakership that day.

85. The House adjourned for recess this session Wednesday, Feb. 7, 1990, to Tuesday, Feb. 20, 1990; Wednesday, Apr. 4, 1990, to Wednesday, Apr. 18, 1990; Friday, May 25, 1990, to Tuesday, June 5, 1990; Thursday, June 28, 1990, to Tuesday, July 10, 1990; Saturday, Aug. 4, 1990, to Wednesday, Sept. 5, 1990. The Senate adjourned for recess this session Thursday, Feb. 8, 1990, to Tuesday, Feb. 20, 1990; Friday, March 9, 1990, to Tuesday, March 20, 1990; Thursday, Apr. 5, 1990, to Wednesday, Apr. 18, 1990; Thursday, May 24, 1990, to Tuesday, June 5, 1990; Thursday, June 28, 1990, to Tuesday, July 10, 1990; Saturday, Aug. 4, 1990, to Monday, Sept. 10, 1990.

86. The House adjourned for recess this session Wednesday, Feb. 6, 1991, to Tuesday, Feb. 19, 1991; Friday, March 22, 1991, to Tuesday, Apr. 9, 1991; Thursday, June 27, 1991, to Tuesday, July 9, 1991; Friday, Aug. 2, 1991, to Wednesday, Sept. 11, 1991. The Senate adjourned for recess this session Wednesday, Feb. 6, 1991, to Tuesday, Feb. 19, 1991; Friday, March 22, 1991, to Tuesday, Apr. 9, 1991; Thursday, Apr. 25, 1991, to Monday, May 6, 1991; Friday, May 24, 1991, to Monday, June 3, 1991; Friday, June 28, 1991, to Monday, July 8, 1991; Friday, Aug. 2, 1991, to Tuesday, Sept. 10, 1991.

87. The House adjourned for recess this session Friday, Jan. 3, 1992, to Wednesday, Jan. 22, 1992; Friday, Apr. 10, 1992, to Tuesday, April 28, 1992; Thursday, July 2, 1992, to Tuesday, July 7, 1992; Friday, July 9, 1992, to Tuesday, July 21, 1992; Wednesday, Aug. 12, 1992, to Wednesday, Sept. 9, 1992. The Senate adjourned for recess this session Monday, Jan. 6, 1992, to Monday, Jan. 20, 1992; Monday, Feb. 10, 1992, to Monday, Feb. 17, 1992; Monday, Apr. 13, 1992, to Friday, Apr. 24, 1992; Monday, May 25, 1992, to Friday, May 29, 1992; Monday, July 6, 1992, to Friday, July 17, 1992; Thursday, Aug. 13, 1992, to Monday, Sept. 7, 1992.

88. The House adjourned for recess this session Thursday, Jan. 7, 1993, to Tuesday, Jan. 19, 1993; Friday, Feb. 5, 1993, to Monday, Feb. 15, 1993; Thursday, Apr. 8, 1993, to Sunday, Apr. 18, 1993; Friday, May 28, 1993, to Monday, June 7, 1993; Friday, July 2, 1993, to Monday, July 12, 1993; Saturday, Aug. 7, 1993, to Tuesday, Sept. 7, 1993. The Senate adjourned for recess this session Friday, Jan. 8, 1993, to Tuesday, Jan. 19, 1993; Friday, Feb. 5, 1993, to Monday, Feb. 15, 1993; Monday, Apr. 5, 1993, to Friday, Apr. 16, 1993; Monday, May 31, 1993, to Friday, June 4, 1993; Friday, July 2, 1993, to Friday, July 9, 1993; Monday, Aug. 9, 1993, to Monday, Sept. 6, 1993; Friday, Oct. 8, 1993, to Tuesday, Oct. 12, 1993; Friday, Nov. 12, 1993, to Monday Nov. 15, 1993.

89. The House adjourned for recess this session Thursday, Jan. 27, 1994, to Monday, Jan. 31, 1994; Saturday, Feb. 12, 1994, to Monday, Feb. 21, 1994; Friday, March 25, 1994, to Monday, Apr. 11, 1994; Friday, May 27, 1994, to Tuesday, June 7, 1994; Friday, July 1, 1994, to Monday, July 11, 1994; Saturday, Aug. 27, 1994, to Sunday, Sept. 11, 1994. The Senate adjourned for recess this session Monday, Feb. 14, 1994, to Monday, Feb. 21, 1994; Monday, March 28, 1994, to Friday, Apr. 8, 1994; Monday, May 30, 1994, to Monday, June 6, 1994; Monday, July 4, 1994, to Friday, July 8, 1994; Friday, Aug. 26, 1994, to Friday, Sept. 9, 1994.

90. The House adjourned for recess this session Saturday, Apr. 8, 1995, to Monday, May 1, 1995; Friday, May 26, 1995, to Monday, June 5, 1995; Saturday, July 1, 1995, to Monday, July 10, 1995; Saturday, Aug. 5, 1995, to Tuesday, Sept. 5, 1995; Saturday, Sept. 30, 1995, to Thursday, Oct. 5, 1995. The Senate adjourned for recess this session Friday, Feb. 17, 1995, to Tuesday, Feb. 21, 1995; Saturday, Apr. 8, 1995, to Monday, Apr. 24, 1995; Saturday, May 27, 1995, to Monday, June 4, 1995; Saturday, July 1, 1995, to Monday, July 10, 1995; Saturday, Aug. 12, 1995, to Monday, Sept. 4, 1995; Monday, Oct. 1, 1995, to Monday, Oct. 9, 1995; Saturday, Nov. 21, 1995, to Monday, Nov. 27, 1995.

91. The House adjourned for recess this session Wednesday, Jan. 10, 1996, to Monday, Jan. 22, 1996; Saturday, March 30, 1996, to Monday, Apr. 15, 1996; Saturday, June 29, 1996, to Monday, July 8, 1996; Saturday, Aug. 3, 1996, to Tuesday, Sept. 3, 1996. The Senate adjourned for recess this session Thursday, Jan. 11, 1996, to Monday, Jan. 22, 1996; Saturday, March 30, 1996, to Saturday, Apr. 14, 1996; Saturday, May 25, 1996, to Monday, June 3, 1996; Saturday, June 29, 1996, to Monday, July 8, 1996; Saturday, Aug. 3, 1996, to Monday, Sept. 2, 1996.

92. The House adjourned for recess this session Friday, Jan. 10, 1997, to Monday, Jan. 20, 1997; Wednesday, Jan. 22, 1997, to Monday, Feb. 3, 1997; Friday, Feb. 14, 1997, to Monday, Feb. 24, 1997; Saturday, March 22, 1997, to Monday, Apr. 7, 1997; Friday, June 27, 1997, to Monday,

July 7, 1997; Saturday, Aug. 2, 1997, to Tuesday, Sept. 2, 1997; Friday, Oct. 10, 1997, to Monday, Oct. 20, 1997. The Senate adjourned for recess this session Friday, Jan. 10, 1997, to Monday, Jan. 20, 1997; Friday, Feb. 14, 1997, to Monday, Feb. 24, 1997; Saturday, March 22, 1997, to Monday, Apr. 6, 1997; Saturday, May 24, 1997, to Monday, June 2, 1997; Saturday, June 28, 1997, to Monday, July 7, 1997; Saturday, Aug. 2, 1997, to Monday, Sept. 1, 1997; Friday, Oct. 10, 1997, to Monday, Oct. 20, 1997.

93. The House adjourned for recess this session Friday, Feb. 13, 1998, to Monday, Feb. 23, 1998; Thursday, Apr. 2, 1998, to Monday, Apr. 20, 1998; Saturday, May 23, 1998, to Tuesday, June 2, 1998; Friday, June 26, 1998, to Monday, July 13, 1998; Saturday, Aug. 8, 1998, to Tuesday, Sept. 8, 1998. The House adjourned Oct. 21, 1998, and was called back by the Speaker for a resumption of the second session Thursday, Dec. 17, 1998, to Saturday, Dec. 19, 1998. The Senate adjourned for recess this session Thursday, Jan. 1, 1998, to Monday, Jan. 26, 1998; Saturday, Feb. 14, 1998, to Monday, Feb. 23, 1998; Saturday, Apr. 4, 1998, to Monday, Apr. 20, 1998; Saturday, May 23, 1998, to Monday, June 1, 1998; Saturday, June 27, 1998, to Monday, July 5, 1998; Saturday, Aug. 1, 1998, to Monday, Aug. 31, 1998; Saturday, Sept. 5, 1998, to Monday, Sept. 7, 1998.

94. The House adjourned for recess this session Wednesday, Jan. 6, 1999, to Tuesday, Jan. 19, 1999; Tuesday, Jan. 19, 1999, to Tuesday, Feb. 2, 1999; Friday, Feb. 12, 1999, to Tuesday, Feb. 23, 1999; Thursday, Mar. 25, 1999, to Monday, Apr. 12, 1999; Thursday, May 27, 1999, to Monday, June 7, 1999; Saturday, July 3, 1999, to Monday, July 12, 1999; Saturday, Aug. 7, 1999, to Tuesday, Sept. 7, 1999. The Senate adjourned for recess this session Friday, Feb. 12, 1999, to Monday, Feb. 22, 1999; Thursday, Mar. 25, 1999, to Monday, Apr. 12, 1999; Thursday, May 27, 1999, to Monday, June 7, 1999; Saturday, July 3, 1999, to Monday, July 12, 1999; Saturday, Aug. 7, 1999, to Tuesday, Sept. 7, 1999; Saturday, Oct. 9, 1999, to Monday, Oct. 11, 1999. The Senate adjourned on Friday, Nov. 19, 1999, three days earlier than the House.

95. The House adjourned for recess this session Saturday, Jan. 6, 2001, to Saturday, Jan. 20, 2001; Saturday, Jan. 20, 2001, to Tuesday, Jan. 30, 2001; Wednesday, Jan. 31, 2001, to Tuesday, Feb. 6, 2001; Wednesday, Feb. 14, 2001, to Monday, Feb. 26, 2001; Wednesday, Apr. 4, 2001, to Tuesday, Apr. 24, 2001; Saturday, May 26, 2001, to Tuesday, June 5, 2001; Thursday, June 28, 2001, to Tuesday, July 10, 2001; Thursday, Aug. 2, 2001, to Wednesday, Sept. 5, 2001; Wednesday, Oct. 17, 2001, to Tuesday, Oct. 23, 2001; Monday, Nov. 19, 2001, to Tuesday, Nov. 27, 2001. The Senate adjourned for recession this session Monday, Jan. 8, 2001, to Saturday, Jan. 20, 2001; Thursday, Feb. 15, 2001, to Monday. Feb. 26, 2001; Friday, Apr. 6, 2001, to Monday, April 23, 2001; Saturday, May 26, 2001, to Tuesday, June 5, 2001; Friday, June 29, 2001, to Monday, July 9, 2001; Fri., Aug. 3, 2001, to Tuesday, Sept. 4, 2001; Thursday, Oct. 18, 2001, to Tuesday, Oct. 23, 2001; Friday, Nov. 16, 2001, to Tuesday, Nov. 27, 2001.

96. The 2000 election resulted in an even split in the Senate between Republicans and Democrats. From Jan. 3, 2001, when the 107th Congress convened, to Inauguration Day, Jan. 20, 2001, outgoing Vice President Al Gore gave the Democrats a majority, making Robert C. Byrd, D-W. Va., the pres. pro tempore. When Vice President Richard B. Cheney took office on Jan. 20, the Republicans came into majority and Strom Thurmond, R-S.C., was pres. pro tempore. On June 6, 2001, Sen. James Jeffords of Vermont switched from Republican to Independent giving the Democrats majority status and returning Byrd to the position of pres. pro tempore.

97. The House adjourned for recess this session Tuesday, Jan. 29, 2002, to Monday, Feb. 4, 2002; Thursday, Feb. 14, 2002, to Tuesday, Feb. 26, 2002; Wednesday, Mar. 20, 2002, to Tuesday, Apr. 9, 2002; Friday, May 24, 2002, to Tuesday, June 4, 2002; Friday, June 28, 2002, to Monday, July 8, 2002; Saturday, July 27, 2002, to Wednesday, Sept. 4, 2002. The Senate adjourned for recess this session Tuesday, Jan. 29, 2002, to Monday, Feb. 4, 2002; Friday, Feb. 15, 2002, to Monday, Feb. 25, 2002; Friday, Mar. 22, 2002, to Monday, Apr. 11, 2002; Thursday, May 23, 2002, to Monday, June 2, 2002; Friday, June 28, 2002, to Monday, July 8, 2002; Thursday, Aug. 1, 2002, to Tuesday, Sept. 3, 2002.

98. The House adjourned for recess this session Wednesday, Jan. 8, 2003, to Monday, Jan. 27, 2003; Thursday, Feb. 13, 2003, to Tuesday, Feb. 25, 2003; Saturday, Apr. 12, 2003, to Tuesday, Apr. 29, 2003; Friday, May 23, 2003, to Monday, June 2, 2003; Friday, June 27, 2003, to Monday, July 7, 2003; Saturday, July 26, 2003, to Tuesday, Sept. 2, 2003; Saturday, Nov. 22, 2003, to Sunday, Dec. 7, 2003. The Senate adjourned for recess this session Friday, Feb. 14, 2003, to Monday, Feb. 24, 2003; Friday, Apr. 11, 2003, to Monday, Apr. 28, 2003; Friday, May 23, 2003, to Monday, June 2, 2003; Friday, June 27, 2003, to Monday, July 7, 2003; Friday, Aug. 1, 2003, to Tuesday, Sept. 2, 2003; Tuesday, Nov. 25, 2003, to Tuesday, Dec. 9, 2003.

99. The House adjourned for recess this session; Thursday, Feb. 12, 2004, to Monday, Feb. 23, 2004; Saturday, Apr. 3, 2004, to Monday, Apr. 19, 2004; Friday, May 21, 2004, to Monday, May 31, 2004; Thursday, June 10, 2004, to Sunday, June 13, 2004; Saturday, June 26, 2004, to Monday, July 5, 2004; Friday, July 23, 2004, to Monday, Sept. 6, 2004; Saturday, Oct. 9, 2004, to Monday, Nov. 15, 2004; Saturday, Nov. 20, 2004, to Sunday, Dec. 5, 2004. The Senate adjourned for this recess Thursday, Feb. 12, 2004, to Monday, Feb. 23, 2004; Thursday, Apr. 8, 2004, to Monday, Apr. 19, 2004; Friday, May 21, 2004, to Tuesday, June 1, 2004; Thursday, July 22, 2004, to Tuesday, Sept. 7, 2004; Monday, Oct. 11, 2004, to Tuesday, Nov. 16, 2004; Wednesday, Nov. 24, 2004, to Tuesday, Dec. 7, 2004.

100. As of February 2005, the House adjourned for recess this session Friday, Jan. 7, 2005, to Wednesday, Jan. 19, 2005; Friday, Jan. 21, 2005, to Monday, Jan. 24, 2005; Thursday, Jan. 27, 2005, to Monday, Jan. 31, 2005; Thursday, Feb. 3, 2005, to Monday, Feb. 7, 2005. The Senate adjourned for recess this session Thursday, Jan. 7, 2005, to Wednesday, Jan. 19, 2005.

Sources: For 1789–1990: *Official Congressional Directory.* For 1991–2005: Calendars of the U.S. House of Representatives and the U.S. Senate.

Speakers of the House of Representatives, 1789–2005

Congress		Speaker	Congress		Speaker
1st	(1789–1791)	Frederick A. C. Muhlenberg, Pa.	55th	(1897–1899)	Reed
2nd	(1791–1793)	Jonathan Trumbull, F-Conn.	56th	(1899–1901)	David B. Henderson, R-Iowa
3rd	(1793–1795)	Muhlenberg	57th	(1901–1903)	Henderson
4th	(1795–1797)	Jonathan Dayton, F-N.J.	58th	(1903–1905)	Joseph G. Cannon, R-Ill.
5th	(1797–1799)	Dayton	59th	(1905–1907)	Cannon
6th	(1799–1801)	Theodore Sedgwick, F-Mass.	60th	(1907–1909)	Cannon
7th	(1801–1803)	Nathaniel Macon, D-N.C.	61st	(1909–1911)	Cannon
8th	(1803–1805)	Macon	62nd	(1911–1913)	James B. "Champ" Clark, D-Mo.
9th	(1805–1807)	Macon	63rd	(1913–1915)	Clark
10th	(1807–1809)	Joseph B. Varnum, Mass.	64th	(1915–1917)	Clark
11th	(1809–1811)	Varnum	65th	(1917–1919)	Clark
12th	(1811–1813)	Henry Clay, R-Ky.	66th	(1919–1921)	Frederick H. Gillett, R-Mass.
13th	(1813–1814)	Clay	67th	(1921–1923)	Gillett
	(1814–1815)	Langdon Cheves, D-S.C.	68th	(1923–1925)	Gillett
14th	(1815–1817)	Clay	69th	(1925–1927)	Nicholas Longworth, R-Ohio
15th	(1817–1819)	Clay	70th	(1927–1929)	Longworth
16th	(1819–1820)	Clay	71st	(1929–1931)	Longworth
	(1820–1821)	John W. Taylor, D-N.Y.	72nd	(1931–1933)	John Nance Garner, D-Texas
17th	(1821–1823)	Philip P. Barbour, D-Va.	73rd	(1933–1934)	Henry T. Rainey, D-Ill.a
18th	(1823–1825)	Clay	74th	(1935–1936)	Joseph W. Byrns, D-Tenn.
19th	(1825–1827)	Taylor		(1936–1937)	William B. Bankhead, D-Ala.
20th	(1827–1829)	Andrew Stevenson, D-Va.	75th	(1937–1939)	Bankhead
21st	(1829–1831)	Stevenson	76th	(1939–1940)	Bankhead
22nd	(1831–1833)	Stevenson		(1940–1941)	Sam Rayburn, D-Texas
23rd	(1833–1834)	Stevenson	77th	(1941–1943)	Rayburn
	(1834–1835)	John Bell, W-Tenn.	78th	(1943–1945)	Rayburn
24th	(1835–1837)	James K. Polk, D-Tenn.	79th	(1945–1947)	Rayburn
25th	(1837–1839)	Polk	80th	(1947–1949)	Joseph W. Martin Jr., R-Mass.
26th	(1839–1841)	Robert M. T. Hunter, D-Va.	81st	(1949–1951)	Rayburn
27th	(1841–1843)	John White, W-Ky.	82nd	(1951–1953)	Rayburn
28th	(1843–1845)	John W. Jones, D-Va.	83rd	(1953–1955)	Martin
29th	(1845–1847)	John W. Davis, D-Ind.	84th	(1955–1957)	Rayburn
30th	(1847–1849)	Robert C. Winthrop, W-Mass.	85th	(1957–1959)	Rayburn
31st	(1849–1851)	Howell Cobb, D-Ga.	86th	(1959–1961)	Rayburn
32nd	(1851–1853)	Linn Boyd, D-Ky.	87th	(1961)	Rayburn
33rd	(1853–1855)	Boyd		(1962–1963)	John W. McCormack, D-Mass.
34th	(1855–1857)	Nathaniel P. Banks, R-Mass.	88th	(1963–1965)	McCormack
35th	(1857–1859)	James L. Orr, D-S.C.	89th	(1965–1967)	McCormack
36th	(1859–1861)	William Pennington, R-N.J.	90th	(1967–1969)	McCormack
37th	(1861–1863)	Galusha A. Grow, R-Pa.	91st	(1969–1971)	McCormack
38th	(1863–1865)	Schuyler Colfax, R-Ind.	92nd	(1971–1973)	Carl Albert, D-Okla.
39th	(1865–1867)	Colfax	93rd	(1973–1975)	Albert
40th	(1867–1869)	Colfax	94th	(1975–1977)	Albert
	(1869)	Theodore M. Pomeroy, R-N.Y.	95th	(1977–1979)	Thomas P. O'Neill Jr., D-Mass.
41st	(1869–1871)	James G. Blaine, R-Maine	96th	(1979–1981)	O'Neill
42nd	(1871–1873)	Blaine	97th	(1981–1983)	O'Neill
43rd	(1873–1875)	Blaine	98th	(1983–1985)	O'Neill
44th	(1875–1876)	Michael C. Kerr, D-Ind.	99th	(1985–1987)	O'Neill
	(1876–1877)	Samuel J. Randall, D-Pa.	100th	(1987–1989)	Jim Wright, D-Texas
45th	(1877–1879)	Randall	101st	(1989)	Wrightb
46th	(1879–1881)	Randall		(1989–1991)	Thomas S. Foley, D-Wash.
47th	(1881–1883)	Joseph Warren Keifer, R-Ohio	102nd	(1991–1993)	Foley
48th	(1883–1885)	John G. Carlisle, D-Ky.	103rd	(1993–1995)	Foley
49th	(1885–1887)	Carlisle	104th	(1995–1997)	Newt Gingrich, R-Ga.
50th	(1887–1889)	Carlisle	105th	(1997–1999)	Gingrich
51st	(1889–1891)	Thomas Brackett Reed, R-Maine	106th	(1999–2001)	J. Dennis Hastert, R-Ill.
52nd	(1891–1893)	Charles F. Crisp, D-Ga.	107th	(2001–2003)	Hastert
53rd	(1893–1895)	Crisp	108th	(2003–2005)	Hastert
54th	(1895–1897)	Reed	109th	(2005–)	Hastert

Notes: Key to abbreviations: D—Democrat; F—Federalist; R—Republican; W—Whig.

    a. Rainey died in 1934, but was not replaced until the next Congress.
    b. Wright resigned and was succeeded by Foley on June 6, 1989.

Sources: *2003–2004 Congressional Directory, 108th Congress* (Washington, D.C.: Government Printing Office, 2003); and *CQ Weekly,* selected issues.

Leaders of the House since 1899

Congress	House Floor Leaders		House Whips	
	Majority	**Minority**	**Majority**	**Minority**
56th (1899–1901)	Sereno E. Payne (R N.Y.)	James D. Richardson (D Tenn.)	James A. Tawney (R Minn.)	Oscar W. Underwood (D Ala.)[a]
57th (1901–1903)	Payne	Richardson	Tawney	James T. Lloyd (D Mo.)
58th (1903–1905)	Payne	John Sharp Williams (D Miss.)	Tawney	Lloyd
59th (1905–1907)	Payne	Williams	James E. Watson (R Ind.)	Lloyd
60th (1907–1909)	Payne	Williams/Champ Clark (D Mo.)[b]	Watson	Lloyd[c]
61st (1909–1911)	Payne	Clark	John W. Dwight (R N.Y.)	None
62nd (1911–1913)	Oscar W. Underwood (D Ala.)	James R. Mann (R Ill.)	None	John W. Dwight (R N.Y.)
63rd (1913–1915)	Underwood	Mann	Thomas M. Bell (D Ga.)	Charles H. Burke (R S.D.)
64th (1915–1917)	Claude Kitchin (D N.C.)	Mann	None	Charles M. Hamilton (R N.Y.)
65th (1917–1919)	Kitchin	Mann	None	Hamilton
66th (1919–1921)	Franklin W. Mondell (R Wyo.)	Clark	Harold Knutson (R Minn.)	None
67th (1921–1923)	Mondell	Claude Kitchin (D N.C.)	Knutson	William A. Oldfield (D Ark.)
68th (1923–1925)	Nicholas Longworth (R Ohio)	Finis J. Garrett (D Tenn.)	Albert H. Vestal (R Ind.)	Oldfield
69th (1925–1927)	John Q. Tilson (R Conn.)	Garrett	Vestal	Oldfield
70th (1927–1929)	Tilson	Garrett	Vestal	Oldfield/John McDuffie (D Ala.)[d]
71st (1929–1931)	Tilson	John N. Garner (D Texas)	Vestal	McDuffie
72nd (1931–1933)	Henry T. Rainey (D Ill.)	Bertrand H. Snell (R N.Y.)	John McDuffie (D Ala.)	Carl G. Bachmann (R W.Va.)
73rd (1933–1935)	Joseph W. Byrns (D Tenn.)	Snell	Arthur H. Greenwood (D Ind.)	Harry L. Englebright (R Calif.)
74th (1935–1937)	William B. Bankhead (D Ala.)[e]	Snell	Patrick J. Boland (D Pa.)	Englebright
75th (1937–1939)	Sam Rayburn (D Texas)	Snell	Boland	Englebright
76th (1939–1941)	Rayburn/John W. McCormack (D Mass.)[f]	Joseph W. Martin Jr. (R Mass.)	Boland	Englebright
77th (1941–1943)	McCormack	Martin	Boland/Robert Ramspeck (D Ga.)[g]	Englebright
78th (1943–1945)	McCormack	Martin	Ramspeck	Leslie C. Arends (R Ill.)
79th (1945–1947)	McCormack	Martin	Ramspeck/John J. Sparkman (D Ala.)[h]	Arends
80th (1947–1949)	Charles A. Halleck (R Ind.)	Sam Rayburn (D Texas)	Leslie C. Arends (R Ill.)	John W. McCormack (D Mass.)
81st (1949–1951)	McCormack	Martin	J. Percy Priest (D Tenn.)	Arends
82nd (1951–1953)	McCormack	Martin	Priest	Arends
83rd (1953–1955)	Halleck	Rayburn	Arends	McCormack
84th (1955–1957)	McCormack	Martin	Carl Albert (D Okla.)	Arends
85th (1957–1959)	McCormack	Martin	Albert	Arends
86th (1959–1961)	McCormack	Charles A. Halleck (R Ind.)	Albert	Arends
87th (1961–1963)	McCormack/Carl Albert (D Okla.)[i]	Halleck	Albert/Hale Boggs (D La.)[j]	Arends
88th (1963–1965)	Albert	Halleck	Boggs	Arends
89th (1965–1967)	Albert	Gerald R. Ford (R Mich.)	Boggs	Arends
90th (1967–1969)	Albert	Ford	Boggs	Arends
91st (1969–1971)	Albert	Ford	Boggs	Arends
92nd (1971–1973)	Hale Boggs (D La.)	Ford	Thomas P. O'Neill Jr. (D Mass.)	Arends
93rd (1973–1975)	Thomas P. O'Neill Jr. (D Mass.)	Ford/John J. Rhodes (R Ariz.)[k]	John J. McFall (D Calif.)	Arends
94th (1975–1977)	O'Neill	Rhodes	McFall	Robert H. Michel (R Ill.)
95th (1977–1979)	Jim Wright (D Texas)	Rhodes	John Brademas (D Ind.)	Michel
96th (1979–1981)	Wright	Rhodes	Brademas	Michel
97th (1981–1983)	Wright	Robert H. Michel (R Ill.)	Thomas S. Foley (D Wash.)	Trent Lott (R Miss.)
98th (1983–1985)	Wright	Michel	Foley	Lott
99th (1985–1987)	Wright	Michel	Foley	Lott
100th (1987–1989)	Thomas S. Foley (D Wash.)	Michel	Tony Coelho (D Calif.)	Lott
101st (1989–1991)	Foley/Richard A. Gephardt (D Mo.)[l]	Michel	Coelho/William H. Gray III (D Pa.)[m]	Richard Cheney (R Wyo.)/Newt Gingrich (R Ga.)[n]
102nd (1991–1993)	Gephardt	Michel	Gray/David E. Bonior (D Mich.)[o]	Gingrich
103rd (1993–1995)	Gephardt	Michel	Bonior	Gingrich
104th (1995–1997)	Dick Armey (R Texas)	Richard A. Gephardt (D Mo.)	Tom DeLay (R Texas)	David E. Bonior (D Mich.)
105th (1997–1999)	Armey	Gephardt	DeLay	Bonoir
106th (1999–2001)	Armey	Gephardt	DeLay	Bonoir

Congress	House Floor Leaders		House Whips	
	Majority	Minority	Majority	Minority
107th (2001–2003)	Armey	Gephardt	DeLay	Bonoir/Nancy Pelosi (D Calif.)[p]
108th (2003–2005)	Tom DeLay (R Texas)	Nancy Pelosi (D Calif.)	Roy Blunt (R Mo.)	Steny Hoyer (D Md.)
109th[q] (2005–)	DeLay	Pelosi	Blunt	Hoyer

Notes:

a. Underwood did not become minority whip until 1901.

b. Clark became minority leader in 1908.

c. Lloyd resigned to become chairman of the Democratic Congressional Campaign Committee in 1908. The post of minority whip remained vacant until the beginning of the 62nd Congress.

d. McDuffie became minority whip after the death of Oldfield on Nov. 19, 1928.

e. Bankhead became Speaker of the House on June 4, 1936. The post of majority leader remained vacant until the next Congress.

f. McCormack became majority leader on Sept. 26, 1940, filling the vacancy caused by the elevation of Rayburn to the post of Speaker of the House on Sept. 16, 1940.

g. Ramspeck became majority whip on June 8, 1942, filling the vacancy caused by the death of Boland on May 18, 1942.

h. Sparkman became majority whip on Jan. 14, 1946, filling the vacancy caused by the resignation of Ramspeck on Dec. 31, 1945.

i. Albert became majority leader on Jan. 10, 1962, filling the vacancy caused by the elevation of McCormack to the post of Speaker of the House on Jan. 10, 1962.

j. Boggs became majority whip on Jan. 10, 1962, filling the vacancy caused by the elevation of Albert to the post of majority leader on Jan. 10, 1962.

k. Rhodes became minority leader on Dec. 7, 1973, filling the vacancy caused by the resignation of Ford on Dec. 6, 1973, to become vice president.

l. Gephardt became majority leader on June 14, 1989, filling the vacancy created when Foley succeeded Wright as Speaker of the House on June 6, 1989.

m. Gray became majority whip on June 14, 1989, filling the vacancy caused by Coehlo's resignation from Congress on June 15, 1989.

n. Gingrich became minority whip on March 23, 1989, filling the vacancy caused by the resignation of Cheney on March 17, 1989, to become secretary of defense.

o. Bonior became majority whip on Sept. 11, 1991, filling the vacancy caused by Gray's resignation from Congress on Sept. 11, 1991.

p. Pelosi became minority whip Jan. 15, 2002, when Bonior stepped down.

q. As of February 2005.

Sources: Randall B. Ripley, *Party Leaders in the House of Representatives* (Washington, D.C.: Brookings Institution, 1967); Congressional Directory (Washington, D.C.: Government Printing Office), various years; *Biographical Directory of the American Congress, 1774–1996 (Alexandria, Va.: CQ Staff Directories, 1997), and* CQ Weekly, *various issues.*

Leaders of the Senate since 1911

Congress	House Floor Leaders		House Whips	
	Majority	**Minority**	**Majority**	**Minority**
62nd (1911–1913)	Shelby M. Cullom (R Ill.)	Thomas S. Martin (D Va.)	None	None
63rd (1913–1915)	John W. Kern (D Ind.)	Jacob H. Gallinger (R N.H.)	J. Hamilton Lewis (D Ill.)	None
64th (1915–1917)	Kern	Gallinger	Lewis	James W. Wadsworth Jr. (R N.Y.)/Charles Curtis (R Kan[a])
65th (1917–1919)	Thomas S. Martin (D Va.)	Gallinger/Henry Cabot Lodge (R Mass.)[b]	Lewis	Curtis
66th (1919–1921)	Henry Cabot Lodge (R Mass.)	Martin/Oscar W. Underwood (D Ala.)[c]	Charles Curtis (R Kan.)	Peter G. Gerry (D R.I.)
67th (1921–1923)	Lodge	Underwood	Curtis	Gerry
68th (1923–1925)	Lodge/Charles Curtis (R Kan.)[d]	Joseph T. Robinson (D Ark.)	Curtis/Wesley L. Jones (R Wash.)[e]	Gerry
69th (1925–1927)	Curtis	Robinson	Jones	Gerry
70th (1927–1929)	Curtis	Robinson	Jones	Gerry
71st (1929–1931)	James E. Watson (R Ind.)	Robinson	Simeon D. Fess (R Ohio)	Morris Sheppard (D Texas)
72nd (1931–1933)	Watson	Robinson	Fess	Sheppard
73rd (1933–1935)	Joseph T. Robinson (D Ark.)	Charles L. McNary (R Ore.)	Lewis	Felix Hebert (R R.I.)
74th (1935–1937)	Robinson	McNary	Lewis	None
75th (1937–1939)	Robinson/Alben W. Barkley (D Ky.)[f]	McNary	Lewis	None
76th (1939–1941)	Barkley	McNary	Sherman Minton (D Ind.)	None
77th (1941–1943)	Barkley	McNary	Lister Hill (D Ala.)	None
78th (1943–1945)	Barkley	McNary	Hill	Kenneth Wherry (R Neb.)
79th (1945 –1947)	Barkley	Wallace H. White Jr. (R Maine)	Hill	Wherry
80th (1947–1949)	Wallace H. White Jr. (R Maine)	Alben W. Barkley (D Ky.)	Kenneth Wherry (R Neb.)	Scott Lucas (D Ill.)
81st (1949–1951)	Scott W. Lucas (D Ill.)	Kenneth S. Wherry (R Neb.)	Francis Myers (D Pa.)	Leverett Saltonstall (R Mass.)
82nd (1951–1953)	Ernest W. McFarland (D Ariz.)	Wherry/Styles Bridges (R N.H.)[g]	Lyndon B. Johnson (D Texas)	Saltonstall
83rd (1953–1955)	Robert A. Taft (R Ohio)/William F. Knowland (R Calif.)[h]	Lyndon B. Johnson (D Texas)	Leverett Saltonstall (R Mass.)	Earle Clements (D Ky.)
84th (1955–1957)	Lyndon B. Johnson (D Texas)	William F. Knowland (R Calif.)	Earle Clements (D Ky.)	Leverett Saltonstall (R Mass.)
85th (1957–1959)	Johnson	Knowland	Mike Mansfield (D Mont.)	Everett McKinley Dirksen (R Ill.)
86th (1959–1961)	Johnson	Everett McKinley Dirksen (R Ill.)	Mansfield	Thomas H. Kuchel (R Calif.)
87th (1961–1963)	Mike Mansfield (D Mont.)	Dirksen	Hubert H. Humphrey (D Minn.)	Kuchel
88th (1963–1965)	Mansfield	Dirksen	Humphrey	Kuchel
89th (1965–1967)	Mansfield	Dirksen	Russell Long (D La.)	Kuchel
90th (1967–1969)	Mansfield	Dirksen	Long	Kuchel
91st (1969–1971)	Mansfield	Dirksen/Hugh Scott (R Pa.)[i]	Edward M. Kennedy (D Mass.)	Hugh Scott (R Pa.)/Robert P. Griffin (R Mich.)[j]
92nd (1971–1973)	Mansfield	Scott	Robert C. Byrd (D W.Va.)	Griffin
93rd (1973–1975)	Mansfield	Scott	Byrd	Griffin
94th (1975–1977)	Mansfield	Scott	Byrd	Griffin
95th (1977–1979)	Robert C. Byrd (D W.Va.)	Howard H. Baker Jr. (R Tenn.)	Alan Cranston (D Calif.)	Ted Stevens (R Alaska)
96th (1979–1981)	Byrd	Baker	Cranston	Stevens
97th (1981–1983)	Howard H. Baker Jr. (R Tenn.)	Robert C. Byrd (D W.Va.)	Ted Stevens (R Alaska)	Alan Cranston (D Calif.)
98th (1983–1985)	Baker	Byrd	Stevens	Cranston
99th (1985–1987)	Bob Dole (R Kan.)	Byrd	Alan K. Simpson (R Wyo.)	Cranston
100th (1987–1989)	Byrd	Bob Dole (R Kan.)	Alan Cranston (D Calif.)	Alan K. Simpson (R Wyo.)
101st (1989–1991)	George J. Mitchell (D Maine)	Dole	Cranston	Simpson
102nd (1991–1993)	Mitchell	Dole	Wendell H. Ford (D Ky.)	Simpson
103rd (1993–1995)	Mitchell	Dole	Ford	Simpson
104th (1995–1997)	Bob Dole (R Kan.)/Trent Lott (R Miss.)[k]	Tom Daschle (D S.D.)	Trent Lott (R Miss.)/Don Nickles (R Okla.)[k]	Wendell H. Ford (D Ky.)
105th (1997–1999)	Lott	Daschle	Nickles	Ford
106th (1999–2001)	Lott	Daschle	Nickles	Harry Reid (D Nev.)
107th (2001–2003)	Tom Daschle (D S.D.)/Trent Lott (R Miss.)/Daschle[l]	Trent Lott (R Miss.)/Daschle (D S.D.)/Lott[l]	Harry Reid (D Nev.)/Tom Nickles (R Okla.)/Reid[l]	Don Nickles (R Okla.)

Congress	House Floor Leaders		House Whips	
	Majority	**Minority**	**Majority**	**Minority**
108th (2003–2005)	Bill Frist (R Tenn.)	Tom Daschle (D S.D.)	Mitch McConnell (R Ky.)	Reid
109th[m] (2005–2007)	Frist	Harry Reid (D Nev.)	McConnell	Richard J. Durbin (D Ill.)

Notes:

a. Wadsworth served as minority whip for only one week, from Dec. 6 to Dec. 13, 1915.

b. Lodge became minority leader on Aug. 24, 1918, filling the vacancy caused by the death of Gallinger on Aug. 17, 1918.

c. Underwood became minority leader on April 27, 1920, filling the vacancy caused by the death of Martin on Nov. 12, 1919. Gilbert M. Hitchcock (D Neb.) served as acting minority leader in the interim.

d. Curtis became majority leader on Nov. 28, 1924, filling the vacancy caused by the death of Lodge on Nov. 9, 1924.

e. Jones became majority whip filling the vacancy caused by the elevation of Curtis to the post of majority leader.

f. Barkley became majority leader on July 22, 1937, filling the vacancy caused by the death of Robinson on July 14, 1937.

g. Bridges became minority leader on Jan. 8, 1952, filling the vacancy caused by the death of Wherry on Nov. 29, 1951.

h. Knowland became majority leader on Aug. 4, 1953, filling the vacancy caused by the death of Taft on July 31, 1953. Taft's vacant seat was filled by a Democrat, Thomas Burke, on Nov. 10, 1953. The division of the Senate changed to 48 Democrats, 47 Republicans, and 1 Independent, thus giving control of the Senate to the Democrats. However, Knowland remained as majority leader until the end of the 83rd Congress.

i. Scott became minority leader on Sept. 24, 1969, filling the vacancy caused by the death of Dirksen on Sept. 7, 1969.

j. Griffin became minority whip on Sept. 24, 1969, filling the vacancy caused by the elevation of Scott to the post of minority leader.

k. Lott became majority leader on June 12, following the resignation of Dole on June 11. Don Nickles was subsequently elected majority whip.

l. The 2000 elections resulted in an even, fifty-fifty split in seats between Democrats and Republicans. From Jan. 3, 2001, when the 107th Congress convened, to Inauguration Day, Jan. 20, 2001, outgoing Vice President Al Gore, as president of the Senate, gave the Democrats a majority. When Vice President Richard B. Cheney took office on Jan. 20, the Republicans came into majority. During this time the two parties worked out a power-sharing arrangement on committees. On June 6, 2001, Sen. James Jeffords of Vermont switched from Republican to Independent giving the Democrats majority status for the remainder of the 107th Congress.

m. As of February 2005.

Sources: Walter J. Oleszek, "Party Whips in the United States Senate," *Journal of Politics* 33 (November 1971): 955–979; *Congressional Directory* (Washington, D.C.: Government Printing Office), various years; *Biographical Directory of the American Congress, 1774–1996* (Alexandria, Va.: CQ Staff Directories, 1997); *Majority and Minority Leaders of the Senate,* comp. Floyd M. Riddick, 94th Cong., 1st sess., 1975, S. Doc. 66; and *CQ Weekly,* various issues.

Congressional Committee Chairs since 1947

Following is a list of House and Senate standing committee chairs from January 1947 through February 2005. The years listed reflect the tenure of the committee chairs. Because committee names have changed through the years, the committees are listed by their names as of February 2005; former committee names are listed as well. This list also includes chairs of committees that were disbanded during the period.

House

Agriculture

Clifford R. Hope (R-Kan. 1947–1949)
Harold D. Cooley (D-N.C. 1949–1953)
Clifford R. Hope (R-Kan. 1953–1955)
Harold D. Cooley (D-N.C. 1955–1967)
W. R. Poage (D-Texas 1967–1975)
Thomas S. Foley (D-Wash. 1975–1981)
E. "Kika" de la Garza (D-Texas 1981–1995)
Pat Roberts (R-Kan. 1995–1997)
Bob Smith (R-Ore. 1997–1999)
Larry Combest (R-Texas 1999–2003)
Robert W. Goodlatte (R-Va. 2003–)

Appropriations

John Taber (R-N.Y. 1947–1949)
Clarence Cannon (D-Mo. 1949–1953)
John Taber (R-N.Y. 1953–1955)
Clarence Cannon (D-Mo. 1955–1964)
George H. Mahon (D-Texas 1964–1979)
Jamie L. Whitten (D-Miss. 1979–1993)
William H. Natcher (D-Ky. 1993–1994)
David Obey (D-Wis. 1994–1995)
Robert L. Livingston (R-La. 1995–1999)
C. W. "Bill" Young (R-Fla. 1999–2005)
Charles "Jerry" Lewis (R-Calif. 2005–)

Armed Services

(formerly Armed Services, 1947–1995; National Security, 1995–1998)

Walter G. Andrews (R-N.Y. 1947–1949)
Carl Vinson (D-Ga. 1949–1953)
Dewey Short (R-Mo. 1953–1955)
Carl Vinson (D-Ga. 1955–1965)
L. Mendel Rivers (D-S.C. 1965–1971)
F. Edward Hébert (D-La. 1971–1975)
Melvin Price (D-Ill. 1975–1985)
Les Aspin (D-Wis. 1985–1993)
Ronald V. Dellums (D-Calif. 1993–1995)
Floyd D. Spence (R-S.C. 1995–2001)
Bob Stump (R-Ariz. 2001–2003)
Duncan Hunter (R-Calif. 2003–)

Budget

Brock Adams (D-Wash. 1975–1977)
Robert N. Giaimo (D-Conn. 1977–1981)
James R. Jones (D-Okla. 1981–1985)
William H. Gray III (D-Pa. 1985–1989)

Leon E. Panetta (D-Calif. 1989–1993)
Martin Olav Sabo (D-Minn. 1993–1995)
John R. Kasich (R-Ohio 1995–2001)
Jim Nussle (R-Iowa 2001–)

District of Columbia

Everett McKinley Dirksen (R-Ill. 1947–1949)
John L. McMillan (D-S.C. 1949–1953)
Sidney Elmer Simpson (R-Ill. 1953–1955)
John L. McMillan (D-S.C. 1955–1973)
Charles C. Diggs Jr. (D-Mich. 1973–1979)
Ronald V. Dellums (D-Calif. 1979–1993)
Pete Stark (D-Calif. 1993–1995)
(Reorganized as a subcommittee of the Government Reform and Oversight in 1995.)

Education and the Workforce

(formerly Education and Labor, 1947–1995; Economic and Educational Opportunities, 1995–1997)

Fred A. Hartley Jr. (R-N.J. 1947–1949)
John Lesinski (D-Mich. 1949–1950)
Graham A. Barden (D-N.C. 1950–1953)
Samuel K. McConnell Jr. (R-Pa. 1953–1955)
Graham A. Barden (D-N.C. 1955–1961)
Adam Clayton Powell Jr. (D-N.Y. 1961–1967)
Carl D. Perkins (D-Ky. 1967–1984)
Augustus F. Hawkins (D-Calif. 1984–1991)
William D. Ford (D-Mich. 1991–1995)
Bill Goodling (R-Pa. 1995–2001)
John A. Boehner (R-Ohio 2001–)

Energy and Commerce

(formerly Interstate and Foreign Commerce, 1947–1981; Energy and Commerce, 1981–1995; Commerce 1995–2001)

Charles A. Wolverton (R-N.J. 1947–1949)
Robert Crosser (D-Ohio 1949–1953)
Charles A. Wolverton (R-N.J. 1953–1955)
J. Percy Priest (D-Tenn. 1955–1957)
Oren Harris (D-Ark. 1957–1966)
Harley O. Staggers (D-W.Va. 1966–1981)
John D. Dingell (D-Mich. 1981–1995)
Thomas J. Bliley Jr. (R-Va. 1995–2001)
W. J. "Billy" Tauzin (R-La. 2001–2004)
Joe L. Barton (R-Texas 2004–)

Financial Services

(formerly Banking and Currency, 1947–1975; Banking, Currency and Housing, 1975–1977; Banking, Finance and

Urban Affairs, 1977–1995; Banking and Financial Services 1995–2001)

Jesse P. Wolcott (R-Mich. 1947–1949)
Brent Spence (D-Ky. 1949–1953)
Jesse P. Wolcott (R-Mich. 1953–1955)
Brent Spence (D-Ky. 1955–1963)
Wright Patman (D-Texas 1963–1975)
Henry S. Reuss (D-Wis. 1975–1981)
Fernand J. St Germain (D-R.I. 1981–1989)
Henry B. Gonzalez (D-Texas 1989–1995)
Jim Leach (R-Iowa 1995–2001)
Michael G. Oxley (R-Ohio 2001–)

Government Reform

(formerly Expenditures in the Executive Departments, 1947–1952; Government Operations, 1952–1995; Government Reform and Oversight, 1995–1998)

Clare E. Hoffman (R-Mich. 1947–1949)
William L. Dawson (D-Ill. 1949–1953)
Clare E. Hoffman (R-Mich. 1953–1955)
William L. Dawson (D-Ill. 1955–1971)
Chet Holifield (D-Calif. 1971–1975)
Jack Brooks (D-Texas 1975–1989)
John Conyers (D-Mich. 1989–1995)
William F. Clinger (R-Pa. 1995–1997)
Dan Burton (R-Ind. 1997–2003)
Thomas M. Davis III (R-Va. 2003–)

Homeland Security, Select Committee on

Christopher Cox (R-Calif. 2003–)

House Administration

(formerly House Administration, 1947–1995; House Oversight, 1995–1998)

Karl M. LeCompte (R-Iowa 1947–1949)
Mary T. Norton (D-N.J. 1949–1951)
Thomas B. Stanley (D-Va. 1951–1953)
Karl M. LeCompte (R-Iowa 1953–1955)
Omar Burleson (D-Texas 1955–1968)
Samuel N. Friedel (D-Md. 1968–1971)
Wayne L. Hays (D-Ohio 1971–1976)
Frank Thompson Jr. (D-N.J. 1976–1980)
Augustus F. Hawkins (D-Calif. 1981–1984)
Frank Annunzio (D-Ill. 1985–1991)
Charlie Rose (D-N.C. 1991–1995)
William "Bill" Thomas (R-Calif. 1995–2001)
Bob Ney (R-Ohio 2001–)

Intelligence, Permanent Select Committee on

(formerly Select Committee on Intelligence, 1975–1976)

Lucien N. Nedzi (D-Mich. 1975)
Otis G. Pike (D-N.Y. 1975–1976)
Edward P. Boland (D-Mass. 1977–1985)
Lee H. Hamilton (D-Ind. 1985–1987)
Louis Stokes (D-Ohio 1987–1989)
Anthony C. Beilenson (D-Calif. 1989–1991)
Dave McCurdy (D-Okla. 1991–1993)
Dan Glickman (D-Kan. 1993–1995)

Larry Combest (R-Texas 1995–1997)
Porter J. Goss (R-Fla. 1997–2004)
Peter Hoekstra (R-Mich. 2004–)

Internal Security

(formerly Un-American Activities, 1947–1969)

J. Parnell Thomas (R-N.J. 1947–1949)
John S. Wood (D-Ga. 1949–1953)
Harold H. Velde (R-Ill. 1953–1955)
Francis E. Walter (D-Pa. 1955–1963)
Edwin E. Willis (D-La. 1963–1969)
Richard H. Ichord (D-Mo. 1969–1975)
(The panel was abolished in 1975.)

International Relations

(formerly Foreign Affairs, 1947–1975; International Relations, 1975–1979; Foreign Affairs, 1979–1995)

Charles A. Eaton (R-N.J. 1947–1949)
John Kee (D-W.Va. 1949–1951)
James P. Richards (D-S.C. 1951–1953)
Robert B. Chiperfield (R-Ill. 1953–1955)
James P. Richards (D-S.C. 1955–1957)
Thomas S. Gordon (D-Ill. 1957–1959)
Thomas E. Morgan (D-Pa. 1959–1977)
Clement J. Zablocki (D-Wis. 1977–1983)
Dante B. Fascell (D-Fla. 1984–1993)
Lee H. Hamilton (D-Ind. 1993–1995)
Benjamin A. Gilman (R-N.Y. 1995–2001)
Henry J. Hyde (R-Ill. 2001–)

Judiciary

Earl C. Michener (R-Mich. 1947–1949)
Emanuel Celler (D-N.Y. 1949–1953)
Chauncey W. Reed (R-Ill. 1953–1955)
Emanuel Celler (D-N.Y. 1955–1973)
Peter W. Rodino Jr. (D-N.J. 1973–1989)
Jack Brooks (D-Texas 1989–1995)
Henry J. Hyde (R-Ill. 1995–2001)
F. James Sensenbrenner Jr. (R-Wis. 2001–)

Merchant Marine and Fisheries

Fred Bradley (R-Mich. 1947)
Alvin F. Weichel (R-Ohio 1947–1949)
Schuyler Otis Bland (D-Va. 1949–1950)
Edward J. Hart (D-N.J. 1950–1953)
Alvin F. Weichel (R-Ohio 1953–1955)
Herbert C. Bonner (D-N.C. 1955–1965)
Edward A. Garmatz (D-Md. 1966–1973)
Leonor K. Sullivan (D-Mo. 1973–1977)
John M. Murphy (D-N.Y. 1977–1981)
Walter B. Jones (D-N.C. 1981–1992)
Gerry E. Studds (D-Mass. 1992–1995)
(Abolished in 1995 and matters under its jurisdiction split among other committees.)

Post Office and Civil Service

Edward H. Rees (R-Kan. 1947–1949)
Tom Murray (D-Tenn. 1949–1953)

Edward H. Rees (R-Kan. 1953–1955)
Tom Murray (D-Tenn. 1955–1967)
Thaddeus J. Dulski (D-N.Y. 1967–1975)
David N. Henderson (D-N.C. 1975–1977)
Robert N. C. Nix Sr. (D-Pa. 1977–1979)
James M. Hanley (D-N.Y. 1979–1981)
William D. Ford (D-Mich. 1981–1991)
William L. Clay (D-Mo. 1991–1995)
(Reorganized as a subcommittee of Government Reform and Oversight in 1995.)

Resources

(formerly Public Lands, 1947–1951; Interior and Insular Affairs, 1951–1992; Natural Resources, 1993–1995)

Richard J. Welch (R-Calif. 1947–1949)
Andrew L. Somers (D-N.Y. 1949)
J. Hardin Peterson (D-Fla. 1949–1951)
John R. Murdock (D-Ariz. 1951–1953)
A. L. Miller (R-Neb. 1953–1955)
Claire Engle (D-Calif. 1955–1959)
Wayne N. Aspinall (D-Colo. 1959–1973)
James A. Haley (D-Fla. 1973–1977)
Morris K. Udall (D-Ariz. 1977–1991)
George Miller (D-Calif. 1991–1995)
Don Young (R-Alaska 1995–2001)
James V. Hansen (R-Utah 2001–2003)
Richard W. Pombo (R-Calif. 2003–)

Rules

Leo E. Allen (R-Ill. 1947–1949)
Adolph J. Sabath (D-Ill. 1949–1953)
Leo E. Allen (R-Ill. 1953–1955)
Howard W. Smith (D-Va. 1955–1967)
William M. Colmer (D-Miss. 1967–1973)
Ray J. Madden (D-Ind. 1973–1977)
James J. Delaney (D-N.Y. 1977–1978)
Richard Bolling (D-Mo. 1979–1983)
Claude Pepper (D-Fla. 1983–1989)
Joe Moakley (D-Mass. 1989–1995)
Gerald B. H. Solomon (R-N.Y. 1995–1999)
David Dreier (R-Calif. 1999–)

Science

(formerly Science and Astronautics, 1959–1975; Science and Technology, 1975–1987; Science, Space and Technology, 1987–1995)

Overton Brooks (D-La. 1959–1961)
George P. Miller (D-Calif. 1961–1973)
Olin E. Teague (D-Texas 1973–1979)
Don Fuqua (D-Fla. 1979–1987)
Robert A. Roe (D-N.J. 1987–1991)
George E. Brown Jr. (D-Calif. 1991–1995)
Robert S. Walker (R-Pa. 1995–1997)
F. James Sensenbrenner Jr. (R-Wis. 1997–2001)
Sherwood L. Boehlert (R-N.Y. 2001–)

Small Business

(formerly Select Committee on Small Business, 1947–1975)

Walter C. Ploeser (R-Mo. 1947–1949)
Wright Patman (D-Texas 1949–1953)
William S. Hill (R-Colo. 1953–1955)
Wright Patman (D-Texas 1955–1963)
Joe L. Ervins (D-Tenn. 1963–1977)
Neal Smith (D-Iowa 1977–1981)
Parren J. Mitchell (D-Md. 1981–1987)
John J. LaFalce (D-N.Y. 1987–1995)
Jan Meyers (R-Kan. 1995–1997)
James M. Talent (R-Mo. 1997–2001)
Donald Manzullo (R-Ill. 2001–)

Standards of Official Conduct

Melvin Price (D-Ill. 1969–1975)
John J. Flynt Jr. (D-Ga. 1975–1977)
Charles E. Bennett (D-Fla. 1977–1981)
Louis Stokes (D-Ohio 1981–1985)
Julian C. Dixon (D-Calif. 1985–1991)
Louis Stokes (D-Ohio 1991–1993)
Jim McDermott (D-Wash. 1993–1995)
Nancy L. Johnson (R-Conn. 1995–1997)
James V. Hansen (R-Utah 1997–1999)
Lamar Smith (R-Texas 1999–2001)
Joel Hefley (R-Colo. 2001–2005)
Richard "Doc" Hastings (R-Wash. 2005–)

Transportation and Infrastructure

(formerly Public Works, 1947–1975; Public Works and Transportation, 1975–1995)

George A. Dondero (R-Mich. 1947–1949)
William M. Whittington (D-Miss. 1949–1951)
Charles A. Buckley (D-N.Y. 1951–1953)
George A. Dondero (R-Mich. 1953–1955)
Charles A. Buckley (D-N.Y. 1955–1965)
George H. Fallon (D-Md. 1965–1971)
John A. Blatnik (D-Minn. 1971–1975)
Robert E. Jones Jr. (D-Ala. 1975–1977)
Harold T. Johnson (D-Calif. 1977–1981)
James J. Howard (D-N.J. 1981–1988)
Glenn M. Anderson (D-Calif. 1988–1991)
Robert A. Roe (D-N.J. 1991–1993)
Norman Y. Mineta (D-Calif. 1993–1995)
Bud Shuster (R-Pa. 1995–2001)
Don Young (R-Alaska 2001–)

Veterans' Affairs

Edith Nourse Rogers (R-Mass. 1947–1949)
John E. Rankin (D-Miss. 1949–1953)
Edith Nourse Rogers (R-Mass. 1953–1955)
Olin E. Teague (D-Texas 1955–1973)
William Jennings Bryan Dorn (D-S.C. 1973–1975)
Ray Roberts (D-Texas 1975–1981)
G.V. "Sonny" Montgomery (D-Miss. 1981–1995)
Bob Stump (R-Ariz. 1995–2001)

Christopher H. Smith (R-N.J. 2001–2005)
Steve Buyer (R-Ind. 2005–)

Ways and Means

Harold Knutson (R-Minn. 1947–1949)
Robert L. Doughton (D-N.C. 1949–1953)
Daniel A. Reed (R-N.Y. 1953–1955)
Jere Cooper (D-Tenn. 1955–1957)
Wilbur D. Mills (D-Ark. 1958–1975)
Al Ullman (D-Ore. 1975–1981)
Dan Rostenkowski (D-Ill. 1981–1994)
Sam M. Gibbons (D-Fla. 1994–1995)
Bill Archer (R-Texas 1995–2001)
William "Bill" Thomas (R-Calif. 2001–)

Senate

Aeronautical and Space Sciences

Lyndon B. Johnson (D-Texas 1958–1961)
Robert S. Kerr (D-Okla. 1961–1963)
Clinton P. Anderson (D-N.M. 1963–1973)
Frank E. Moss (D-Utah 1973–1977)
(Abolished in 1977, when its jurisdiction was consolidated under Commerce.)

Agriculture, Nutrition and Forestry

(formerly Agriculture and Forestry, 1947–1977)

Arthur Capper (R-Kan. 1947–1949)
Elmer Thomas (D-Okla. 1949–1951)
Allen J. Ellender (D-La. 1951–1953)
George D. Aiken (R-Vt. 1953–1955)
Allen J. Ellender (D-La. 1955–1971)
Herman E. Talmadge (D-Ga. 1971–1981)
Jesse Helms (R-N.C. 1981–1987)
Patrick J. Leahy (D-Vt. 1987–1995)
Richard G. Lugar (R-Ind. 1995–2001)[a]
Tom Harkin (R-Iowa 2001–2003)[a]
Thad Cochran (R-Miss. 2003–2005)
Saxby Chambliss (R-Ga. 2005–)

Appropriations

Styles Bridges (R-N.H. 1947–1949)
Kenneth McKellar (D-Tenn. 1949–1953)
Styles Bridges (R-N.H. 1953–1955)
Carl Hayden (D-Ariz. 1955–1969)
Richard B. Russell (D-Ga. 1969–1971)
Allen J. Ellender (D-La. 1971–1972)
John L. McClellan (D-Ark. 1972–1977)
Warren G. Magnuson (D-Wash. 1978–1981)
Mark O. Hatfield (R-Ore. 1981–1987)
John C. Stennis (D-Miss. 1987–1989)
Robert C. Byrd (D-W.Va. 1989–1995)
Mark O. Hatfield (R-Ore. 1995–1997)
Ted Stevens (R-Alaska 1997–2001)[a]
Robert C. Byrd (D-W.Va. 2001–2003)[a]

Ted Stevens (R-Alaska 2003–2005)
Thad Cochran (R-Miss. 2005–)

Armed Services

Chan Gurney (R-S.D. 1947–1949)
Millard E. Tydings (D-Md. 1949–1951)
Richard B. Russell (D-Ga. 1951–1953)
Leverett Saltonstall (R-Mass. 1953–1955)
Richard B. Russell (D-Ga. 1955–1969)
John C. Stennis (D-Miss. 1969–1981)
John Tower (R-Texas 1981–1985)
Barry Goldwater (R-Ariz. 1985–1987)
Sam Nunn (D-Ga. 1987–1995)
Strom Thurmond (R-S.C. 1995–1999)
John W. Warner (R-Va. 1999–2001)[a]
Carl Levin (D-Mich. 2001–2003)[a]
John W. Warner (R-Va. 2003–)

Banking, Housing and Urban Affairs

(formerly Banking and Currency, 1947–1971)

Charles W. Tobey (R-N.H. 1947–1949)
Burnet R. Maybank (D-S.C. 1949–1953)
Homer E. Capehart (R-Ind. 1953–1955)
J. W. Fulbright (D-Ark. 1955–1959)
A. Willis Robertson (D-Va. 1959–1967)
John J. Sparkman (D-Ala. 1967–1975)
William Proxmire (D-Wis. 1975–1981)
Jake Garn (R-Utah 1981–1987)
William Proxmire (D-Wis. 1987–1989)
Donald W. Riegle Jr. (D-Mich. 1989–1995)
Alfonse M. D'Amato (R-N.Y. 1995–1999)
Phil Gramm (R-Texas 1999–2001)[a]
Paul S. Sarbanes (D-Md. 2001–2003)[a]
Richard C. Shelby (R-Ala. 2003–)

Budget

Edmund S. Muskie (D-Maine 1975–1979)
Ernest F. Hollings (D-S.C. 1979–1981)
Pete V. Domenici (R-N.M. 1981–1987)
Lawton Chiles Jr. (D-Fla. 1987–1989)
Jim Sasser (D-Tenn. 1989–1995)
Pete V. Domenici (R-N.M. 1995–2001)[a]
Kent Conrad (D-N.D. 2001–2003)[a]
Don Nickles (R-Okla. 2003–2005)
Judd Gregg (R-N.H. 2005–)

Commerce, Science and Transportation

(formerly Interstate and Foreign Commerce, 1947–1961; Commerce, 1961–1977)

Wallace H. White (R-Maine 1947–1949)
Edwin C. Johnson (D-Colo. 1949–1953)
Charles W. Tobey (R-N.H. 1953)
John W. Bricker (R-Ohio 1953–1955)
Warren G. Magnuson (D-Wash. 1955–1978)
Howard W. Cannon (D-Nev. 1978–1981)
Bob Packwood (R-Ore. 1981–1985)

John C. Danforth (R-Mo. 1985–1987)
Ernest F. Hollings (D-S.C. 1987–1995)
Larry Pressler (R-S.D. 1995–1997)
John McCain (R-Ariz. 1997–2001)[a]
Ernest F. Hollings (D-S.C. 2001–2003)[a]
John McCain (R-Ariz. 2003–2005)
Ted Stevens (R-Alaska 2005–)

District of Columbia

C. Douglass Buck (R-Del. 1947–1949)
J. Howard McGrath (D-R.I. 1949–1951)
Matthew M. Neely (D-W.Va. 1951–1953)
Francis Case (R-S.D. 1953–1955)
Matthew M. Neely (D-W.Va. 1955–1959)
Alan Bible (D-Nev. 1959–1969)
Joseph D. Tydings (D-Md. 1969–1971)
Thomas Eagleton (D-Mo. 1971–1977)
(Abolished in 1977 and its responsibilities transferred to the Governmental Affairs Committee.)

Energy and Natural Resources

Henry M. Jackson (D-Wash. 1977–1981)
James A. McClure (R-Idaho 1981–1987)
J. Bennett Johnston (D-La. 1987–1995)
Frank H. Murkowski (R-Alaska 1995–2001)[a]
Jeff Bingaman (D-N.M. 2001–2003)[a]
Pete V. Domenici (R-N.M. 2003–)

Environment and Public Works

(formerly Public Works, 1947–1977)

Chapman Revercomb (R-W.Va. 1947–1949)
Dennis Chavez (D-N.M. 1949–1953)
Edward Martin (R-Pa. 1953–1955)
Dennis Chavez (D-N.M. 1955–1962)
Pat McNamara (D-Mich. 1963–1966)
Jennings Randolph (D-W.Va. 1966–1981)
Robert T. Stafford (R-Vt. 1981–1987)
Quentin N. Burdick (D-N.D. 1987–1992)
Daniel Patrick Moynihan (D-N.Y. 1992)
Max Baucus (D-Mont. 1993–1995)
John H. Chafee (R-R.I. 1995–1999)
Robert C. Smith (R-N.H. 1999–2001)[a]
James M. Jeffords (I-Vt. 2001–2003)[a]
James M. Inhofe (R-Okla. 2003–)

Ethics, Select Committee on

(formerly the Select Committee on Standards and Conduct, 1966–1977)

John C. Stennis (D-Miss. 1966–1975)
Howard W. Cannon (D-Nev. 1975–1977)
Adlai Ewing Stevenson III (D-Ill. 1977–1981)
Malcolm Wallop (R-Wyo. 1981–1983)
Ted Stevens (R-Alaska 1983–1985)
Warren B. Rudman (R-N.H. 1985–1987)
Howell Heflin (D-Ala. 1987–1991)
Terry Sanford (D-N.C. 1991–1993)

Richard H. Bryan (D-Nev. 1993–1995)
Mitch McConnell (R-Ky. 1995–1997)
Robert C. Smith (R-N.H. 1997–2001)[a]
Harry Reid (D-Nev. 2001–2003)[a]
George V. Voinovich (R-Ohio 2003–)

Finance

Eugene D. Millikin (R-Colo. 1947–1949)
Walter F. George (D-Ga. 1949–1953)
Eugene D. Millikin (R-Colo. 1953–1955)
Harry Flood Byrd (D-Va. 1955–1965)
Russell B. Long (D-La. 1965–1981)
Robert Dole (R-Kan. 1981–1985)
Bob Packwood (R-Ore. 1985–1987)
Lloyd Bentsen (D-Texas 1987–1993)
Daniel Patrick Moynihan (D-N.Y. 1993–1995)
Bob Packwood (R-Ore. 1995)
William V. Roth Jr. (R-Del. 1995–2001)
Charles E. Grassley (R-Iowa 2001)[a]
Max Baucus (D-Mont. 2001–2003)[a]
Charles E. Grassley (R-Iowa 2003–)

Foreign Relations

Arthur H. Vandenberg (R-Mich. 1947–1949)
Tom Connally (D-Texas 1949–1953)
Alexander Wiley (R-Wis. 1953–1955)
Walter F. George (D-Ga. 1955–1957)
Theodore Francis Green (D-R.I. 1957–1959)
J. W. Fulbright (D-Ark. 1959–1975)
John J. Sparkman (D-Ala. 1975–1979)
Frank Church (D-Idaho 1979–1981)
Charles Percy (R-Ill. 1981–1985)
Richard G. Lugar (R-Ind. 1985–1987)
Claiborne Pell (D-R.I. 1987–1995)
Jesse Helms (R-N.C. 1995–2001)[a]
Joseph R. Biden Jr. (D-Del. 2001–2003)[a]
Richard G. Lugar (R-Ind. 2003–)

Health, Education, Labor and Pensions

(formerly Labor and Public Welfare, 1947–1977; Human Resources, 1977–1979; Labor and Human Resources, 1979–1999)

Robert A. Taft (R-Ohio 1947–1949)
Elbert D. Thomas (D-Utah 1949–1951)
James E. Murray (D-Mont. 1951–1953)
H. Alexander Smith (R-N.J. 1953–1955)
Lister Hill (D-Ala. 1955–1969)
Ralph W. Yarborough (D-Texas 1969–1971)
Harrison A. Williams Jr. (D-N.J. 1971–1981)
Orrin G. Hatch (R-Utah 1981–1987)
Edward M. Kennedy (D-Mass. 1987–1995)
Nancy Landon Kassebaum (R-Kan. 1995–1997)
James M. Jeffords (R-Vt. 1997–2001)[a]
Edward M. Kennedy (D-Mass. 2001–2003)[a]
Judd Gregg (R-N.H. 2003–2005)
Michael B. Enzi, (R-Wyo. 2005–)

Homeland Security and Governmental Affairs

(formerly Expenditures in Executive Departments, 1947–1952; Government Operations, 1952–1977; Governmental Affairs 1977–2004)

George D. Aiken (R-Vt. 1947–1949)
John L. McClellan (D-Ark. 1949–1953)
Joseph R. McCarthy (R-Wis. 1953–1955)
John L. McClellan (D-Ark. 1955–1972)
Sam J. Ervin Jr. (D-N.C. 1972–1974)
Abraham A. Ribicoff (D-Conn. 1975–1981)
William V. Roth Jr. (R-Del. 1981–1987)
John Glenn (D-Ohio 1987–1995)
William V. Roth Jr. (R-Del. 1995–1996)
Ted Stevens (R-Alaska 1996–1997)
Fred Thompson (R-Tenn. 1997–2001)[a]
Joseph I. Lieberman (D-Conn. 2001–2003)[a]
Susan Collins (R-Maine 2003–)

Indian Affairs

(formerly a temporary select committee; redesignated as a permanent committee in 1993)

Daniel Inouye (D-Hawaii 1993–1995)
John McCain (R-Ariz. 1995–1997)
Ben Nighthorse Campbell (R-Colo. 1997–2001)[a]
Daniel Inouye (D-Hawaii 2001–2003)[a]
Ben Nighthorse Campbell (R-Colo. 2003–2005)
John McCain (R-Ariz. 2005–)

Intelligence, Select Committee on

Daniel K. Inouye (D-Hawaii 1976–1978)
Birch Bayh (D-Ind. 1978–1981)
Barry Goldwater (R-Ariz. 1981–1985)
Dave Durenberger (R-Minn. 1985–1987)
David L. Boren (D-Okla. 1987–1993)
Dennis DeConcini (D-Ariz. 1993–1995)
Arlen Specter (R-Pa. 1995–1997)
Richard C. Shelby (R-Ala. 1997–2001)[a]
Bob Graham (D-Fla. 2001–2003)[a]
Pat Roberts (R-Kan. 2003–)

Interior and Insular Affairs

(formerly Public Lands, 1947–1948)

Hugh Butler (R-Neb. 1947–1949)
Joseph C. O'Mahoney (D-Wyo. 1949–1953)
Hugh Butler (R-Neb. 1953–1954)
Guy Gordon (R-Ore. 1954–1955)
James E. Murray (D-Mont. 1955–1961)
Clinton P. Anderson (D-N.M. 1961–1963)
Henry M. Jackson (D-Wash. 1963–1977)
(Most of its jurisdiction transferred to Energy and Natural Resources in 1977.)

Judiciary

Alexander Wiley (R-Wis. 1947–1949)
Pat McCarran (D-Nev. 1949–1953)
William Langer (R-N.D. 1953–1955)
Harley M. Kilgore (D-W.Va. 1955–1956)

James O. Eastland (D-Miss. 1956–1978)
Edward M. Kennedy (D-Mass. 1979–1981)
Strom Thurmond (R-S.C. 1981–1987)
Joseph R. Biden Jr. (D-Del. 1987–1995)
Orrin G. Hatch (R-Utah 1995–2001)[a]
Patrick J. Leahy (D-Vt. 2001–2003)[a]
Orrin G. Hatch (R-Utah 2003–2005)
Arlen Specter (R-Pa. 2005–)

Post Office and Civil Service

William Langer (R-N.D. 1947–1949)
Olin D. Johnston (D-S.C. 1949–1953)
Frank Carlson (R-Kan. 1953–1955)
Olin D. Johnston (D-S.C. 1955–1965)
A. S. Mike Monroney (D-Okla. 1965–1969)
Gale W. McGee (D-Wyo. 1969–1977)
(Abolished in 1977, when its jurisdiction was transferred to the Governmental Affairs Committee.)

Rules and Administration

C. Wayland Brooks (R-Ill. 1947–1949)
Carl Hayden (D-Ariz. 1949–1953)
William E. Jenner (R-Ind. 1953–1955)
Theodore Francis Green (D-R.I. 1955–1957)
Thomas C. Hennings Jr. (D-Mo. 1957–1960)
Mike Mansfield (D-Mont. 1961–1963)
B. Everett Jordan (D-N.C. 1963–1972)
Howard W. Cannon (D-Nev. 1973–1977)
Claiborne Pell (D-R.I. 1978–1981)
Charles McC. Mathias Jr. (R-Md. 1981–1987)
Wendell H. Ford (D-Ky. 1987–1995)
Ted Stevens (R-Alaska 1995–1996)
John Warner (R-Va. 1996–1999)
Mitch McConnell (R-Ky. 1999–2001)[a]
Christopher J. Dodd (D-Conn. 2001–2003)[a]
Trent Lott (R-Miss. 2003–)

Small Business and Entrepreneurship

(formerly the Select Committee on Small Business, 1950–1981; Small Business 1981–2001)

John J. Sparkman (D-Ala. 1950–1953)
Edward J. Thye (R-Minn. 1953–1955)
John J. Sparkman (D-Ala. 1955–1967)
George A. Smathers (D-Fla. 1967–1969)
Alan Bible (D-Nev. 1969–1975)
Gaylord Nelson (D-Wis. 1975–1981)[a]
Lowell P. Weicker Jr. (R-Conn. 1981–1987)
Dale Bumpers (D-Ark. 1987–1995)
Christopher S. Bond (R-Mo. 1995–2001)[a]
John Kerry (D-Mass. 2001–2003)[a]
Olympia Snowe (R-Maine 2003–)

Veterans' Affairs

Vance Hartke (D-Ind. 1971–1977)
Alan Cranston (D-Calif. 1977–1981)
Alan K. Simpson (R-Wyo. 1981–1985)
Frank H. Murkowski (R-Alaska 1985–1987)

Alan Cranston (D-Calif. 1987–1993)
John D. Rockefeller III (D-W.Va. 1993–1995)
Alan K. Simpson (R-Wyo. 1995–1997)
Arlen Specter (R-Pa. 1997–2001)[a]

John D. Rockefeller IV (D-W.Va. 2001–2003)[a]
Arlen Specter (R-Pa. 2003–2005)
Larry E. Craig (R-Idaho 2005–)

Notes:

a. The 2000 elections resulted in an even, fifty-fifty split in seats between Democrats and Republicans. From Jan. 3, 2001, when the 107th Congress convened, to Inauguration Day, Jan. 20, 2001, outgoing Vice President Al Gore, as president of the Senate, gave the Democrats a majority. During this short period the Democrats held committee chairs. When Vice President Richard B. Cheney took office on Jan. 20, the Republicans became the majority party and held committee chairs—although the two parties worked out a power-sharing arrangement on committees. On June 6, 2001, Sen. James Jeffords of Vermont switched from Republican to Independent giving the Democrats majority status for the remainder of the 107th Congress.

Women Members of Congress, 1917–2005

As of February 2005, a total of 223 women had been elected or appointed to Congress. Of the 220 women who actually served in Congress (two others were never sworn in and another resigned her seat the day after she was sworn in), 187 in the House only, twenty-six in the Senate only, and seven—Maine Republicans Margaret Chase Smith and Olympia Snowe, Maryland Democrat Barbara Mikulski, California Democrat Barbara Boxer, Arkansas Democrat Blanche Lambert Lincoln, Washington Democrat Maria Cantwell, and Michigan Democrat Debbie Stabenow—in both chambers. Following is a list of the women members, their political affiliations and states, and the years in which they served. In addition, Mary E. Farrington, R-Hawaii (1954–1957), Eleanor Holmes Norton, D-D.C. (1991–), Donna M. C. Christensen, D-V.I. (1997–), and Madeleine Z. Bordallo, D-Guam (2003–), served as delegates.

Senate

Rebecca L. Felton, Ind. D-Ga.[a]	1922
Hattie W. Caraway, D-Ark.	1931–1945
Rose McConnell Long, D-La.	1936–1937
Dixie Bibb Graves, D-Ala.	1937–1938
Gladys Pyle, R-S.D.[b]	1938–1939
Vera C. Bushfield, R-S.D.	1948
Margaret Chase Smith, R-Maine	1949–1973
Hazel H. Abel, R-Neb.	1954
Eva K. Bowring, R-Neb.	1954
Maurine B. Neuberger, D-Ore.	1960–1967
Elaine S. Edwards, D-La.	1972
Maryon Pittman Allen, D-Ala.	1978
Muriel Buck Humphrey, D-Minn.	1978
Nancy Landon Kassebaum, R-Kan.	1978–1997
Paula Hawkins, R-Fla.	1981–1987
Barbara Mikulski, D-Md.	1987–
Jocelyn B. Burdick, D-N.D.	1992
Dianne Feinstein, D-Calif.	1992–
Barbara Boxer, D-Calif.	1993–
Kay Bailey Hutchison, R-Texas	1993–
Carol Moseley-Braun, D-Ill.	1993–1999
Patty L. Murray, D-Wash.	1993–
Olympia J. Snowe, R-Maine	1995–
Sheila Frahm, R-Kan.	1996
Susan Collins, R-Maine	1997–
Mary L. Landrieu, D-La.	1997–
Blanche Lambert Lincoln, D-Ark.	1999–
Jean Carnahan, D-Mo.	2001–2003
Maria Cantwell, D-Wash.	2001–
Hillary Rodham Clinton, D-N.Y.	2001–
Debbie Stabenow, D-Mich.	2001–
Elizabeth Dole, R-N.C.	2003–
Lisa A. Murkowski, R-Alaska	2003–

House

Jeannette Rankin, R-Mont.	1917–1919; 1941–1943
Alice M. Robertson, R-Okla.	1921–1923
Winnifred S. M. Huck, R-Ill.	1922–1923
Mae E. Nolan, R-Calif.	1923–1925
Florence P. Kahn, R-Calif.	1925–1937
Mary T. Norton, D-N.J.	1925–1951
Edith N. Rogers, R-Mass.	1925–1960
Katherine G. Langley, R-Ky.	1927–1931
Ruth H. McCormick, R-Ill.	1929–1931
Pearl P. Oldfield, D-Ark.	1929–1931
Ruth B. Owen, D-Fla.	1929–1933
Ruth S. B. Pratt, R-N.Y.	1929–1933
Effiegene Locke Wingo, D-Ark.	1930–1933
Willa M. B. Eslick, D-Tenn.	1932–1933
Marian W. Clarke, R-N.Y.	1933–1935
Virginia E. Jenckes, D-Ind.	1933–1939
Kathryn O'Loughlin McCarthy, D-Kan.	1933–1935
Isabella S. Greenway, D-Ariz.	1933–1937
Caroline L. G. O'Day, D-N.Y.	1935–1943
Nan W. Honeyman, D-Ore.	1937–1939
Elizabeth H. Gasque, D-S.C.	1938–1939
Clara G. McMillan, D-S.C.	1939–1941
Jessie Sumner, R-Ill.	1939–1947
Frances P. Bolton, R-Ohio	1940–1969
Florence R. Gibbs, D-Ga.	1940–1941
Margaret Chase Smith, R-Maine	1940–1949
Katherine E. Byron, D-Md.	1941–1943
Veronica G. Boland, D-Pa.	1942–1943
Clare Boothe Luce, R-Conn.	1943–1947
Winifred C. Stanley, R-N.Y.	1943–1945
Willa L. Fulmer, D-S.C.	1944–1945
Emily Taft Douglas, D-Ill.	1945–1947
Helen G. Douglas, D-Calif.	1945–1951
Chase G. Woodhouse, D-Conn.	1945–1947; 1949–1951
Helen D. Mankin, D-Ga.	1946–1947
Eliza J. Pratt, D-N.C.	1946–1947
Georgia L. Lusk, D-N.M.	1947–1949
Katharine P. C. St. George, R-N.Y.	1947–1965
Reva Z. B. Bosone, D-Utah	1949–1953
Cecil M. Harden, R-Ind.	1949–1959
Edna F. Kelly, D-N.Y.	1949–1969
Vera D. Buchanan, D-Pa.	1951–1955
Marguerite S. Church, R-Ill.	1951–1963
Maude E. Kee, D-W.Va.	1951–1965
Ruth Thompson, R-Mich.	1951–1957
Gracie B. Pfost, D-Idaho	1953–1963
Leonor K. Sullivan, D-Mo.	1953–1977
Iris F. Blitch, D-Ga.	1955–1963
Edith Starrett Green, D-Ore.	1955–1975
Martha W. Griffiths, D-Mich.	1955–1974
Coya G. Knutson, DFL-Minn.	1955–1959
Kathryn E. Granahan, D-Pa.	1956–1963

Women Members of Congress *(cont.)*

Florence P. Dwyer, R-N.J.	1957–1973	Cathy Long, D-La.	1985–1987
Catherine D. May, R-Wash.	1959–1971	Constance A. Morella, R-Md.	1987–2003
Edna O. Simpson, R-Ill.	1959–1961	Elizabeth J. Patterson, D-S.C.	1987–1993
Jessica McCullough Weis, R-N.Y.	1959–1963	Patricia Saiki, R-Hawaii	1987–1991
Julia B. Hansen, D-Wash.	1960–1974	Louise M. Slaughter, D-N.Y.	1987–
Catherine D. Norrell, D-Ark.	1961–1963	Nancy Pelosi, D-Calif.	1987–
Louise G. Reece, R-Tenn.	1961–1963	Nita M. Lowey, D-N.Y.	1989–
Corinne B. Riley, D-S.C.	1962–1963	Jolene Unsoeld, D-Wash.	1989–1995
Charlotte T. Reid, R-Ill.	1963–1971	Jill L. Long, D-Ind.	1989–1995
Irene B. Baker, R-Tenn.	1964–1965	Ileana Ros-Lehtinen, R-Fla.	1989–
Patsy T. Mink, D-Hawaii	1965–1977;	Susan Molinari, R-N.Y.	1990–1997
	1990–2002	Barbara-Rose Collins, D-Mich.	1991–1997
Lera M. Thomas, D-Texas	1966–1967	Rosa DeLauro, D-Conn.	1991–
Margaret M. Heckler, R-Mass.	1967–1983	Joan Kelly Horn, D-Mo.	1991–1993
Shirley A. Chisholm, D-N.Y.	1969–1983	Maxine Waters, D-Calif.	1991–
Bella S. Abzug, D-N.Y.	1971–1977	Eva M. Clayton, D-N.C.	1992–2003
Ella T. Grasso, D-Conn.	1971–1975	Corrine Brown, D-Fla.	1993–
Louise Day Hicks, D-Mass.	1971–1973	Leslie L. Byrne, D-Va.	1993–1995
Elizabeth B. Andrews, D-Ala.	1972–1973	Maria E. Cantwell, D-Wash.	1993–1995
Yvonne B. Burke, D-Calif.	1973–1979	Pat Danner, D-Mo.	1993–2001
Marjorie Sewell Holt, R-Md.	1973–1987	Jennifer B. Dunn, R-Wash.	1993–2005
Elizabeth Holtzman, D-N.Y.	1973–1981	Karan English, D-Ariz.	1993–1995
Barbara C. Jordan, D-Texas	1973–1979	Anna G. Eshoo, D-Calif.	1993–
Patricia Schroeder, D-Colo.	1973–1997	Tillie Fowler, R-Fla.	1993–2001
Corinne "Lindy" Boggs, D-La.	1973–1991	Elizabeth Furse, D-Ore.	1993–1999
Cardiss R. Collins, D-Ill.	1973–1997	Jane F. Harman, D-Calif.	1993–1999;
Marilyn Lloyd, D-Tenn.	1975–1995		2001–
Millicent Fenwick, R-N.J.	1975–1983	Eddie Bernice Johnson, D-Texas	1993–
Martha E. Keys, D-Kan.	1975–1979	Blanche Lambert Lincoln, D-Ark.	1993–1997
Helen S. Meyner, D-N.J.	1975–1979	Carolyn B. Maloney, D-N.Y.	1993–
Virginia Smith, R-Neb.	1975–1991	Cynthia Ann McKinney, D-Ga.	1993–2003;
Gladys Noon Spellman, D-Md.	1975–1981		2005–
Shirley N. Pettis, R-Calif.	1975–1979	Carrie P. Meek, D-Fla.	1993–2003
Barbara A. Mikulski, D-Md.	1977–1987	Marjorie Margolies-Mezvinsky, D-Pa.	1993–1995
Mary Rose Oakar, D-Ohio	1977–1993	Deborah D. Pryce, R-Ohio	1993–
Beverly Byron, D-Md.	1979–1993	Lucille Roybal-Allard, D-Calif.	1993–
Geraldine Ferraro, D-N.Y.	1979–1985	Lynn Schenk, D-Calif.	1993–1995
Olympia J. Snowe, R-Maine	1979–1995	Karen Shepherd, D-Utah	1993–1995
Bobbi Fiedler, R-Calif.	1981–1987	Karen L. Thurman, D-Fla.	1993–2003
Lynn M. Martin, R-Ill.	1981–1991	Nydia M. Velazquez, D-N.Y.	1993–
Marge Roukema, R-N.J.	1981–2003	Lynn Woolsey, D-Calif.	1993–
Claudine Schneider, R-R.I.	1981–1991	Helen Chenoweth, R-Idaho	1995–2001
Jean Spencer Ashbrook, R-Ohio	1982–1983	Barbara Cubin, R-Wyo.	1995–
Barbara B. Kennelly, D-Conn.	1982–1999	Sheila Jackson-Lee, D-Texas	1995–
Katie Beatrice Hall, D-Ind.	1982–1985	Sue W. Kelly, R-N.Y.	1995–
Sala Burton, D-Calif.	1983–1987	Zoe Lofgren, D-Calif.	1995–
Barbara Boxer, D-Calif.	1983–1993	Karen McCarthy, D-Mo.	1995–2005
Nancy L. Johnson, R-Conn.	1983–	Sue Myrick, R-N.C.	1995–
Marcy Kaptur, D-Ohio	1983–	Lynn N. Rivers, D-Mich.	1995–2003
Barbara Farrell Vucanovich, R-Nev.	1983–1997	Andrea Seastrand, R-Calif.	1995–1997
Helen Delich Bentley, R-Md.	1985–1995	Linda Smith, R-Wash.	1995–1999
Jan Meyers, R-Kan.	1985–1997	Enid Greene Waldholtz, R-Utah	1995–1997

Juanita Millender-McDonald, D-Calif.	1996–	Jo Ann Davis, R-Va.	2001–
Jo Ann Emerson, R-Mo.	1996–	Susan A. Davis, D-Calif.	2001–
Julia Carson, D-Ind.	1997–	Melissa Hart, R-Pa.	2001–
Diana DeGette, D-Colo.	1997–	Betty McCollum, D-Minn.	2001–
Kay Granger, R-Texas	1997–	Hilda Solis, D-Calif.	2001–
Darlene Hooley, D-Ore.	1997–	Diane E. Watson, D-Calif.	2001–
Carolyn Cheeks Kilpatrick, D-Mich.	1997–	Candice S. Miller, R-Mich.	2002–
Carolyn McCarthy, D-N.Y.	1997–	Marsha Blackburn, R-Tenn.	2003–
Anne M. Northup, R-Ky.	1997–	Ginny Brown-Waite, R-Fla.	2003–
Loretta Sanchez, D-Calif.	1997–	Katherine Harris, R-Fla.	2003–
Deborah Ann Stabenow, D-Mich.	1997–2001	Denise L. Majette, D-Ga.	2003–2005
Ellen O. Tauscher, D-Calif.	1997–	Marilyn Musgrave, R-Colo.	2003–
Mary Bono, R-Calif.	1998–	Linda T. Sanchez, D-Calif.	2003–
Lois Capps, D-Calif.	1998–	Stephanie Herseth, D-S.D.	2004–
Barbara Lee, D-Calif.	1998–	Melissa Bean, D-Ill.	2005–
Heather Wilson, R-N.M.	1998–	Thelma Drake, R-Va.	2005–
Tammy Baldwin, D-Wis.	1999–	Virginia Foxx, R-N.C.	2005–
Shelley Berkley, D-Nev.	1999–	Doris Matsui, D-Calif.	2005–
Judy Biggert, R-Ill.	1999–	Cathy McMorris, R-Wash.	2005–
Stephanie Tubbs Jones, D-Ohio	1999–	Gwen Moore, D-Wisc.	2005–
Grace F. Napolitano, D-Calif.	1999–	Allyson Y. Schwartz, D-Pa.	2005–
Jan Schakowsky, D-Ill.	1999–	Debbie Wasserman-Schultz, D-Fla.	2005–
Shelley Moore Capito, R-W.Va.	2001–		

Notes:

a. Felton was sworn in Nov. 21, 1922, to fill the vacancy created by the death of Thomas E. Watson, D. The next day she gave up her seat to Walter F. George, D, the elected candidate for the vacancy.

b. Pyle was never sworn in because Congress was not in session between election and expiration of term.

Sources: Commission on the Bicentenary of the U.S. House of Representatives, *Women in Congress, 1917–1990*(Washington, D.C.: Government Printing Office, 1991); *Biographical Directory of the American Congress, 1774–1996*(Alexandria, Va.: CQ Staff Directories, 1997); and *CQ Weekly,*selected issues.

Black Members of Congress, 1870–2005

As of February 2005, 112 black Americans had served in Congress; five in the Senate and 107 in the House. Following is a list of the black members, their political affiliations and states, and the years in which they served. John W. Menard, R-La., won a disputed election in 1868 but was not permitted to take his seat in Congress. In addition to those listed below, Walter E. Fauntroy, D-D.C. (1971–1991), Eleanor Holmes Norton, D-D.C. (1991–), and Donna M. C. Christensen, D-V.I. (1997–), served as delegates.

Senate

Hiram R. Revels, R-Miss.	1870–1871
Blanche K. Bruce, R-Miss.	1875–1881
Edward W. Brooke III, R-Mass.	1967–1979
Carol Moseley-Braun, D-Ill.	1993–1999
Barack Obama, D-Ill.	2005–

House

Joseph H. Rainey, R-S.C.	1870–1879
Jefferson F. Long, R-Ga.	1870–1871
Robert C. De Large, R-S.C.	1871–1873
Robert B. Elliott, R-S.C.	1871–1874
Benjamin S. Turner, R-Ala.	1871–1873
Josiah T. Walls, R-Fla.	1871–1876
Richard H. Cain, R-S.C.	1873–1875; 1877–1879
John R. Lynch, R-Miss.	1873–1877; 1882–1883
Alonzo J. Ransier, R-S.C.	1873–1875
James T. Rapier, R-Ala.	1873–1875
Jeremiah Haralson, R-Ala.	1875–1877
John A. Hyman, R-N.C.	1875–1877
Charles E. Nash, R-La.	1875–1877
Robert Smalls, R-S.C.	1875–1879; 1882–1883; 1884–1887
James E. O'Hara, R-N.C.	1883–1887
Henry P. Cheatham, R-N.C.	1889–1893
John M. Langston, R-Va.	1890–1891
Thomas E. Miller, R-S.C.	1890–1891
George W. Murray, R-S.C.	1893–1895; 1896–1897
George H. White, R-N.C.	1897–1901
Oscar S. De Priest, R-Ill.	1929–1935
Arthur W. Mitchell, D-Ill.	1935–1943
William L. Dawson, D-Ill.	1943–1970
Adam Clayton Powell Jr., D-N.Y.	1945–1967; 1969–1971
Charles C. Diggs Jr., D-Mich.	1955–1980
Robert N. C. Nix, D-Pa.	1958–1979
Augustus F. Hawkins, D-Calif.	1963–1991
John Conyers Jr., D-Mich.	1965–
Shirley A. Chisholm, D-N.Y.	1969–1983
William L. Clay, D-Mo.	1969–2001
Louis Stokes, D-Ohio	1969–1999
George W. Collins, D-Ill.	1970–1972
Ronald V. Dellums, D-Calif.	1971–1998
Ralph H. Metcalfe, D-Ill.	1971–1978
Parren J. Mitchell, D-Md.	1971–1987
Charles B. Rangel, D-N.Y.	1971–
Yvonne B. Burke, D-Calif.	1973–1979
Cardiss Collins, D-Ill.	1973–1997
Barbara C. Jordan, D-Texas	1973–1979
Andrew J. Young Jr., D-Ga.	1973–1977
Harold E. Ford, D-Tenn.	1975–1997
Julian C. Dixon, D-Calif.	1979–2000
William H. Gray III, D-Pa.	1979–1991
George T. Leland, D-Texas	1979–1989
Bennett McVey Stewart, D-Ill.	1979–1981
George W. Crockett Jr., D-Mich.	1980–1991
Mervyn M. Dymally, D-Calif.	1981–1993
Gus Savage, D-Ill.	1981–1993
Harold Washington, D-Ill.	1981–1983
Katie B. Hall, D-Ind.	1982–1985
Charles A. Hayes, D-Ill.	1983–1993
Major R. Owens, D-N.Y.	1983–
Edolphus Towns, D-N.Y.	1983–
Alan D. Wheat, D-Mo.	1983–1995
Alton R. Waldon Jr., D-N.Y.	1986–1987
Mike Espy, D-Miss.	1987–1993
Floyd H. Flake, D-N.Y.	1987–1997
John Lewis, D-Ga.	1987–
Kweisi Mfume, D-Md.	1987–1996
Donald M. Payne, D-N.J.	1989–
Craig A. Washington, D-Texas	1990–1995
Barbara-Rose Collins, D-Mich.	1991–1997
Gary A. Franks, R.-Conn.	1991–1997
William J. Jefferson, D-La.	1991–
Maxine Waters, D-Calif.	1991–
Lucien E. Blackwell, D-Pa	1991–1995
Eva Clayton, D-N.C.	1992–2003
Sanford D. Bishop Jr., D-Ga.	1993–
Corrine Brown, D-Fla.	1993–
James E. Clyburn, D-S.C.	1993–
Cleo Fields, D-La.	1993–1997
Alcee L. Hastings, D-Fla.	1993–
Earl F. Hilliard, D-Ala.	1993–2003
Eddie Bernice Johnson, D-Texas	1993–
Cynthia McKinney, D-Ga.	1993–2003; 2005–
Carrie P. Meek, D-Fla.	1993–2003
Melvin J. Reynolds, D-Ill.	1993–1995
Bobby L. Rush, D-Ill.	1993–
Robert C. Scott, D-Va.	1993–

Bennie Thompson, D-Miss.	1993–	Barbara Lee, D-Calif.	1998–
Walter R. Tucker III, D-Calif.	1993–1995	Gregory W. Meeks, D-N.Y.	1998–
Melvin Watt, D-N.C.	1993–	Stephanie Tubbs Jones, D-Ohio	1999–
Albert R. Wynn, D-Md.	1993–	William Lacy Clay Jr., D-Mo.	2001–
Chaka Fattah, D-Pa.	1995–	Diane E. Watson, D-Calif.	2001–
Jesse Jackson Jr., D-Ill.	1995–	Frank W. Balance Jr., D-N.C.	2003–2004
Sheila Jackson-Lee, D-Texas	1995–	Artur Davis, D-Ala.	2003–
J. C. Watts Jr., R-Okla.	1995–2003	Kendrick B. Meek, D-Fla.	2003–
Elijah E. Cummings, D-Md.	1996–	Denise L. Majette, D-Ga.	2003–2005
Juanita Millender-McDonald, D-Calif.	1996–	David Scott, D-Ga.	2003–
Julia Carson, D-Ind.	1997–	G. K. Butterfield, D-N.C.	2005–
Danny K. Davis, D-Ill.	1997–	Emanuel Cleaver II, D-Mo.	2005–
Harold E. Ford Jr., D-Tenn.	1997–	Al Green, D-Texas	2005–
Carolyn Cheeks Kilpatrick, D-Mich.	1997–	Gwen Moore, D-Wisc.	2005–

Sources: Maurine Christopher, *America's Black Congressmen* (New York: Crowell, 1971); *Biographical Directory of the American Congress, 1774–1996* (Alexandria, Va.: CQ Staff Directories, 1997); and *CQ Weekly,* selected issues.

Hispanic Members of Congress, 1877–2005

As of February 2005, forty-eight Hispanics had served in Congress, two in both the Senate and the House, two in the Senate, and forty-four in the House only. Following is a list of the members who claimed Hispanic heritage, their political affiliations and states, and the years in which they served. Not included are Hispanics who served as territorial delegates.

Senate

Dennis Chavez, D-N.M.	1935–1962
Joseph M. Montoya, D-N.M.	1964–1977
Ken Salazar, D-Colo.	2005–
Mel Martinez, R-Fla.	2005–

House

Romualdo Pacheco, R-Calif.	1877–1878; 1879–1883
Ladislas Lazaro, D-La.	1913–1927
Benigno Cardenas Hernandez, R-N.M.	1915–1917; 1919–1921
Nestor Montoya, R-N.M.	1921–1923
Dennis Chavez, D-N.M.	1931–1935
Joachim Octave Fernandez, D-La.	1931–1941
Antonio Manuel Fernandez, D-N.M.	1943–1956
Joseph Manuel Montoya, D-N.M.	1957–1964
Henry B. Gonzalez, D-Texas	1961–1999
Edward R. Roybal, D-Calif.	1963–1993
E. "Kika" de la Garza II, D-Texas	1965–1997
Manuel Lujan Jr., R-N.M.	1969–1989
Herman Badillo, D-N.Y.	1971–1977
Robert Garcia, D-N.Y.	1978–1990
Anthony Lee Coelho, D-Calif.	1979–1989
Matthew G. Martinez, D-Calif.	1982–2001
Solomon P. Ortiz, D-Texas	1983–
William B. Richardson, D-N.M.	1983–1997
Esteban E. Torres, D-Calif.	1983–1999
Albert G. Bustamante, D-Texas	1985–1993
Ileana Ros-Lehtinen, R-Fla.	1989–
José E. Serrano, D-N.Y.	1990–
Ed Pastor, D-Ariz.	1991–
Xavier Becerra, D-Calif.	1993–
Henry Bonilla, R-Texas	1993–
Lincoln Diaz-Balart, R-Fla.	1993–
Luis V. Gutierrez, D-Ill.	1993–
Robert Menendez, D-N.J.	1993–
Lucille Roybal-Allard, D-Calif.	1993–
Frank Tejeda, D-Texas	1993–1997
Nydia M. Velázquez, D-N.Y.	1993–
Rubén Hinojosa, D-Texas	1997–
Silvestre Reyes, D-Texas	1997–
Ciro D. Rodriguez, D-Texas	1997–2005
Loretta Sanchez, D-Calif.	1997–
Charlie Gonzalez, D-Texas	1999–
Grace Napolitano, D-Calif.	1999–
Joe Baca, D-Calif.	1999–
Hilda L. Solis, D-Calif.	2001–
Mario Diaz-Balart, R-Fla.	2003–
Raúl M. Grijalva, D-Ariz.	2003–
Linda T. Sanchez, D-Calif.	2003–
John Salazar, D-Colo.	2005–
Henry Roberto Cuellar, D-Texas	2005–

Sources: *Biographical Directory of the American Congress, 1774–1996* (Alexandria, Va.: CQ Staff Directories, 1997); Congressional Hispanic Caucus; and *CQ Weekly,* selected issues.

Name Index

Ashley, Delos Rodeyn, 74
Ashley, Henry, 74
Ashley, James Mitchell, 74
Ashley, Thomas William Ludlow, 74
Ashley, William Henry, 74
Ashmore, John Durant, 74
Ashmore, Robert Thomas, 74
Ashmun, Eli Porter, 74
Ashmun, George, 74
Ashurst, Henry Fountain, 74
Askew, Reubin O'Donovan, 7, 283
Asper, Joel Funk, 74
Aspin, Leslie "Les," 29, 74
Aspinall, Wayne Norviel, 74
Aswell, James Benjamin, 74
Atchison, David Rice, 74
Atherton, Charles Gordon, 74
Atherton, Charles Humphrey, 74
Atherton, Gibson, 74
Atiyeh, Victor George, 308
Atkeson, William Oscar, 74
Atkins, Chester Greenough, 75
Atkins, John DeWitt Clinton, 75
Atkinson, Archibald, 75
Atkinson, Eugene Vincent, 75
Atkinson, George Wesley, 75, 318
Atkinson, Louis Evans, 75
Atkinson, Richard Merrill, 75
Atkinson, William Yates, 284
Atwater, John Wilbur, 75
Atwood, David, 75
Atwood, Harrison Henry, 75
Auchincloss, James Coats, 75
AuCoin, Les, 75
Auf der Heide, Oscar Louis, 75
Austin, Albert Elmer, 75
Austin, Archibald, 75
Austin, Horace, 295
Austin, Richard Wilson, 75
Austin, Warren Robinson, 75
Averett, Thomas Hamlet, 75
Averill, John Thomas, 75
Avery, Daniel, 75
Avery, John, 75
Avery, William Henry, 75, 288
Avery, William Tecumsah, 75
Avis, Samuel Brashear, 75
Axtell, Samuel Beach, 75
Aycock, Charles Brantley, 305
Aycrigg, John Bancker, 75
Ayer, Richard Small, 75
Ayers, Roy Elmer, 75, 298
Ayres, Steven Beckwith, 75
Ayres, William Augustus, 75
Ayres, William Hanes, 75

Babbitt, Bruce Edward, 7, 29, 278
Babbitt, Clinton, 75
Babbitt, Elijah, 75
Babcock, Alfred, 75
Babcock, Joseph Weeks, 75
Babcock, Leander, 75
Babcock, Tim M., 298
Babcock, William, 75
Babka, John Joseph, 75
Baca, Joseph, 75
Bacchus, James, 75
Bacharach, Isaac, 75

Bachman, Nathan Lynn, 75
Bachman, Reuben Knecht, 75
Bachmann, Carl George, 75
Bachus, Spencer, 75
Bacon, Augustus Octavius, 75
Bacon, Ezekiel, 75
Bacon, Henry, 75
Bacon, John, 75
Bacon, Mark Reeves, 75
Bacon, Robert, 29
Bacon, Robert Low, 75
Bacon, Walter W., 282
Bacon, William Johnson, 75
Badger, De Witt Clinton, 75
Badger, George Edmund, 29, 46, 75
Badger, Luther, 75
Badger, William, 300
Badham, Robert Edward, 75
Badillo, Herman, 75
Baer, George Jr., 75
Baer, John Miller, 75
Baesler, Scotty, 75
Bafalis, Louis Arthur, 75
Bagby, Arthur Pendleton, 75, 276
Bagby, John Courts, 76
Bagley, George Augustus, 76
Bagley, John Holroyd Jr., 76
Bagley, John Judson, 294
Bailey, Alexander Hamilton, 76
Bailey, Carl Edward, 278
Bailey, Cleveland Monroe, 76
Bailey, David Jackson, 76
Bailey, Donald Allen, 76
Bailey, Goldsmith Fox, 76
Bailey, James Edmund, 76
Bailey, Jeremiah, 76
Bailey, John, 76
Bailey, John Mosher, 76
Bailey, Joseph, 76
Bailey, Joseph Weldon, 76
Bailey, Joseph Weldon Jr., 76
Bailey, Josiah William, 76
Bailey, Ralph Emerson, 76
Bailey, Theodorus, 76
Bailey, Thomas Lowry, 296
Bailey, Warren Worth, 76
Bailey, Wendell, 76
Bailey, Willis Joshua, 76, 288
Baird, Brian, 76
Baird, David, 76
Baird, David Jr., 76
Baird, Joseph Edward, 76
Baird, Samuel Thomas, 76
Baker, Caleb, 76
Baker, Charles Simeon, 76
Baker, Conrad, 286
Baker, David Jewett, 76
Baker, Edward Dickinson, 76
Baker, Ezra, 76
Baker, Henry Moore, 76
Baker, Howard Henry, 76
Baker, Howard Henry Jr., 10, 64, 76
Baker, Irene Bailey, 76
Baker, Jacob Thompson, 76
Baker, James Addison III, 29
Baker, Jehu, 76
Baker, John, 76
Baker, John Harris, 76

Baker, Joshua, 290
Baker, LaMar, 76
Baker, Lucien, 76
Baker, Nathaniel Bradley, 300
Baker, Newton Diehl, 29
Baker, Osmyn, 76
Baker, Richard Hugh, 76
Baker, Robert, 76
Baker, Samuel Aaron, 297
Baker, Stephen, 76
Baker, William, 76
Baker, William Benjamin, 76
Baker, William Henry, 76
Baker, William P. "Bill," 76
Bakewell, Charles Montague, 76
Bakewell, Claude Ignatius, 76
Baldacci, John E., 76, 291
Baldrige, H. Clarence, 285
Baldrige, Howard Malcolm, 76
Baldrige, Malcolm, 29
Baldus, Alvin James, 76
Baldwin, Abraham, 76
Baldwin, Augustus Carpenter, 76
Baldwin, Harry Streett, 76
Baldwin, Henry Alexander, 76
Baldwin, Henry, 49 (box), 52, 76
Baldwin, Henry Porter, 76, 294
Baldwin, John, 76
Baldwin, John Denison, 76
Baldwin, John Finley Jr., 76
Baldwin, Joseph Clark, 77
Baldwin, Melvin Riley, 77
Baldwin, Raymond Earl, 77, 281
Baldwin, Roger Sherman, 77, 280
Baldwin, Simeon, 77
Baldwin, Simeon Eben, 281
Baldwin, Tammy, 77
Baliles, Gerald L., 317
Ball, Edward, 77
Ball, Joseph Hurst, 77
Ball, Lewis Heisler, 77
Ball, Thomas Henry, 77
Ball, Thomas Raymond, 77
Ball, William Lee, 77
Ballance, Frank W., 77
Ballenger, Cass, 77
Ballentine, John Goff, 77
Ballinger, Richard Achilles, 29
Ballou, Latimer Whipple, 77
Baltz, William Nicolas, 77
Balzar, Frederick Bennett, 299
Bamberger, Simon, 314
Bancroft, George, 29
Bandstra, Bert Andrew, 77
Bangerter, Norman Howard, 314
Bankhead, John Hollis, 77
Bankhead, John Hollis II, 77
Bankhead, Walter Will, 77
Bankhead, William Brockman, 77
Banks, John, 77
Banks, Linn, 77
Banks, Nathaniel Prentice, 77, 293
Banning, Henry Blackstone, 77
Bannon, Henry Towne, 77
Banta, Parke Monroe, 77
Barber, Amos Walker, 319
Barber, Hiram Jr., 77
Barber, Isaac Ambrose, 77

Bingham, Hiram, 83, 281
Bingham, John Armor, 83
Bingham, Jonathan Brewster, 83
Bingham, Kinsley Scott, 83, 294
Bingham, William, 83
Binney, Horace, 83
Birch, William Fred, 83
Bird, John, 83
Bird, John Taylor, 83
Bird, Richard Ely, 83
Birdsall, Ausburn, 83
Birdsall, Benjamin Pixley, 83
Birdsall, James, 83
Birdsall, Samuel, 83
Birdseye, Victory, 83
Bisbee, Horatio Jr., 83
Bishop, Cecil William "Runt," 83
Bishop, James, 83
Bishop, Phanuel, 83
Bishop, Richard Moore, 306
Bishop, Robert, 83
Bishop, Roswell Peter, 83
Bishop, Sanford D. Jr., 83
Bishop, Timothy H., 83
Bishop, William Darius, 83
Bissell, Clark, 280
Bissell, William Harrison, 83, 285
Bissell, Wilson Shannon, 30
Bixler, Harris Jacob, 83
Black, Edward Junius, 83
Black, Eugene, 83
Black, Frank Swett, 83, 303
Black, George Robison, 83
Black, Henry, 83
Black, Hugo Lafayette, 46, 48, 52, 83
Black, James, 83
Black, James Augustus, 83
Black, James Conquest Cross, 84
Black, James Dixon, 289
Black, Jeremiah Sullivan, 30, 49 (box)
Black, John, 84
Black, John Charles, 84
Black, Loring Milton Jr., 84
Blackburn, Benjamin Bentley, 84
Blackburn, Edmond Spencer, 84
Blackburn, Joseph Clay Stiles, 84
Blackburn, Luke Pryor, 289
Blackburn, Marsha, 84
Blackburn, Robert E. Lee, 84
Blackburn, William Jasper, 84
Blackledge, William, 84
Blackledge, William Salter, 84
Blackmar, Esbon, 84
Blackmon, Fred Leonard, 84
Blackmun, Harry Andrew, 43, 46 (box), 48, 52
Blackney, William Wallace, 84
Blackwell, Julius W., 84
Blackwell, Lucien E., 84
Blackwood, Ibra Charles, 311
Blagojevich, Rod R., 84, 286
Blaine, James Gillespie, 5, 30, 84
Blaine, John James, 84, 319
Blair, Austin, 84, 294
Blair, Bernard, 84
Blair, Francis Preston Jr., 84
Blair, Henry William, 84
Blair, Jacob Beeson, 84

Blair, James, 84
Blair, James Gorrall, 84
Blair, James Thomas Jr., 298
Blair, John, 84
Blair, John Jr., 41, 44, 45 (box), 52
Blair, Montgomery, 30
Blair, Samuel Steel, 84
Blaisdell, Daniel, 84
Blake, Harrison Gray Otis, 84
Blake, John Jr., 84
Blake, John Lauris, 84
Blake, Thomas Holdsworth, 84
Blakeney, Albert Alexander, 84
Blakley, William Arvis, 84
Blanchard, George Washington, 84
Blanchard, James Johnston, 84, 295
Blanchard, John, 84
Blanchard, Newton Crain, 84, 290
Blanco, Kathleen Babineaux, 290
Bland, Oscar Edward, 84
Bland, Richard Parks, 84
Bland, Schuyler Otis, 84
Bland, Theodorick, 84
Bland, William Thomas, 84
Blanton, Leonard Ray, 84, 313
Blanton, Thomas Lindsay, 84
Blasdel, Henry Goode, 299
Blatchford, Samuel, 45 (box), 52
Blatnik, John Anton, 84
Blaz, Ben Garrido, 84
Bleakley, Orrin Dubbs, 84
Blease, Coleman Livingston, 84, 311
Bledsoe, Jesse, 84
Bleecker, Harmanus, 84
Bliley, Thomas Jerome Jr., 84
Bliss, Aaron Thomas, 84, 295
Bliss, Archibald Meserole, 84
Bliss, Cornelius Newton, 30
Bliss, George, 84
Bliss, Philemon, 84
Blitch, Iris Faircloth, 84
Block, John Rusling, 30
Blodgett, Rufus, 84
Blood, Henry Hooper, 314
Blood, Robert Oscar, 301
Bloodworth, Timothy, 84
Bloom, Isaac, 85
Bloom, Sol, 85
Bloomfield, Joseph, 85, 301
Blouin, Michael Thomas, 85
Blount, James Henderson, 85
Blount, Thomas, 85
Blount, William, 85
Blount, William, 312
Blount, William Grainger, 85
Blount, Winton Malcolm, 30
Blow, Henry Taylor, 85
Bloxham, William Dunnington, 283
Blue, Richard Whiting, 85
Blue, Robert Donald, 287
Blumenauer, Earl, 85
Blumenthal, Werner Michael, 30
Blunt, Matt, 298
Blunt, Roy, 85
Blute, Peter I., 85
Boardman, Elijah, 85
Boardman, William Whiting, 85
Boarman, Alexander "Aleck," 85

Boatner, Charles Jahleal, 85
Bockee, Abraham, 85
Bocock, Thomas Stanley, 85
Boden, Andrew, 85
Bodine, Robert Nall, 85
Bodle, Charles, 85
Bodman, Samuel Wright, 30
Bodwell, Joseph Robinson, 291
Boe, Nils Andreas, 312
Boehlert, Sherwood Louis, 85
Boehne, John William, 85
Boehne, John William Jr., 85
Boehner, John A., 85
Boen, Haldor Erickson, 85
Boggs, Corinne Claiborne "Lindy," 85
Boggs, James Caleb, 85, 282
Boggs, Lilburn W., 297
Boggs, Thomas Hale Sr., 85
Bogy, Lewis Vital, 85
Bohn, Frank Probasco, 85
Boies, Horace, 287
Boies, William Dayton, 85
Boileau, Gerald John, 85
Bokee, David Alexander, 85
Bolack, Thomas Felix, 303
Boland, Edward Patrick, 85
Boland, Patrick Joseph, 85
Boland, Veronica Grace, 85
Boles, Thomas, 85
Bolin, Wesley H., 278
Bolles, Stephen, 85
Bolling, Richard Walker, 85
Bolton, Chester Castle, 85
Bolton, Frances Payne, 85
Bolton, Oliver Payne, 85
Bolton, William P., 85
Bonaparte, Charles Joseph, 30
Bond, Charles Grosvenor, 85
Bond, Christopher S. "Kit," 85, 298
Bond, Shadrack, 85, 285
Bond, William Key, 85
Bone, Homer Truett, 85
Boner, William Hill, 85
Bonham, Milledge Luke, 85, 311
Bonilla, Henry, 85
Bonin, Edward John, 85
Bonior, David Edward, 85
Bonker, Don Leroy, 85
Bonner, Herbert Covington, 85
Bonner, John Woodrow, 298
Bonner, Josiah Robbins Jr. "Jo," 86
Bono, Mary, 86
Bono, Sonny, 86
Bonynge, Robert William, 86
Boody, Azariah, 86
Boody, David Augustus, 86
Booher, Charles Ferris, 86
Booker, George William, 86
Boon, Ratliff, 86, 286
Boone, Andrew Rechmond, 86
Booth, Newton, 86, 279
Booth, Walter, 86
Boothman, Melvin Morella, 86
Booze, William Samuel, 86
Boozman, John, 86
Borah, William Edgar, 86
Borchers, Charles Martin, 86
Bordallo, Madeleine Z., 86

Dornan, Robert Kenneth, 121
Dorr, Charles Phillips, 121
Dorsey, Clement, 121
Dorsey, Frank Joseph Gerard, 121
Dorsey, George Washington Emery, 121
Dorsey, Hugh Manson, 284
Dorsey, John Lloyd Jr., 121
Dorsey, Stephen Wallace, 121
Dorsheimer, William, 121
Doty, James Duane, 121
Doubleday, Ulysses Freeman, 121
Dougherty, Charles, 121
Dougherty, Charles Francis, 121
Dougherty, John, 121
Doughton, Robert Lee, 121
Douglas, Albert, 121
Douglas, Beverly Browne, 121
Douglas, Charles Gwynn III "Chuck," 121
Douglas, Emily Taft, 64, 121
Douglas, Fred James, 121
Douglas, Helen Gahagan, 121
Douglas, James H., 316
Douglas, Lewis Williams, 121
Douglas, Paul Howard, 64, 121
Douglas, Stephen Arnold, 9, 49 (box), 121
Douglas, William Harris, 121
Douglas, William Lewis, 294
Douglas, William Orville, 48, 50, 53
Douglass, John Joseph, 121
Doutrich, Isaac Hoffer, 121
Dovener, Blackburn Barrett, 121
Dow, John Goodchild, 121
Dowd, Clement, 121
Dowdell, James Ferguson, 121
Dowdney, Abraham, 121
Dowdy, Charles Wayne, 121
Dowdy, John Vernard, 121
Dowell, Cassius Clay, 122
Downey, John Gately, 279
Downey, Sheridan, 122
Downey, Stephen Wheeler, 122
Downey, Thomas Joseph, 122
Downing, Charles, 122
Downing, Finis Ewing, 122
Downing, Thomas Nelms, 122
Downs, Le Roy Donnelly, 122
Downs, Solomon Weathersbee, 122
Dowse, Edward, 122
Dox, Peter Myndert, 122
Doxey, Charles Taylor, 122
Doxey, Wall, 122
Doyle, Clyde Gilman, 122
Doyle, James, 319
Doyle, Mike, 122
Doyle, Thomas Aloysius, 122
Drake, Charles Daniel, 122
Drake, Francis Marion, 287
Drake, John Reuben, 122
Drake, Thelma Sawyers, 122
Drane, Herbert Jackson, 122
Draper, Eben Sumner, 294
Draper, Joseph, 122
Draper, William Franklin, 122
Draper, William Henry, 122
Drayton, John, 310
Drayton, William, 122

Dreier, David Timothy, 122
Dresser, Solomon Robert, 122
Drew, George Franklin, 283
Drew, Ira Walton, 122
Drew, Irving Webster, 122
Drew, Thomas Stevenson, 278
Drewry, Patrick Henry, 122
Dreyfus, Lee Sherman, 319
Driggs, Edmund Hope, 122
Driggs, John Fletcher, 122
Drinan, Robert Frederick, 61, 122
Driscoll, Alfred Eastlack, 302
Driscoll, Daniel Angelus, 122
Driscoll, Denis Joseph, 122
Driscoll, Michael Edward, 122
Driver, William Joshua, 122
Dromgoole, George Coke, 122
Drukker, Dow Henry, 122
Drum, Augustus, 122
Dryden, John Fairfield, 122
Duane, William John, 32
Dubois, Fred Thomas, 122
Du Bose, Dudley McIver, 122
Dudley, Charles Edward, 122
Dudley, Edward Bishop, 122, 304
Duell, Rodolphus Holland, 122
Duer, William, 122
Duff, James Henderson, 122, 309
Duffey, Warren Joseph, 122
Duffy, Francis Ryan, 122
Duffy, James Patrick Bernard, 122
Dugro, Philip Henry, 122
Dukakis, Michael Stanley, 7, 10, 294
Duke, Richard Thomas Walker, 122
Dulles, John Foster, 32, 122
Dulski, Thaddeus Joseph, 122
Dumont, Ebenezer, 122
Dunbar, James Whitson, 122
Dunbar, William, 122
Duncan, Alexander, 122
Duncan, Charles William Jr., 32
Duncan, Daniel, 122
Duncan, James, 122
Duncan, James Henry, 122
Duncan, John J. "Jimmy" Jr., 123
Duncan, John James, 123
Duncan, Joseph, 123, 285
Duncan, Richard Meloan, 123
Duncan, Robert Blackford, 123
Duncan, William Addison, 123
Duncan, William Garnett, 123
Dungan, James Irvine, 123
Dunham, Cyrus Livingston, 123
Dunham, Ransom Williams, 123
Dunklin, Daniel, 297
Dunlap, George Washington, 123
Dunlap, Robert Pickney, 123, 290
Dunlap, William Claiborne, 123
Dunlop, John Thomas, 32
Dunn, Aubert Culberson, 123
Dunn, Bryant Winfield Culberson, 313
Dunn, David, 291
Dunn, George Grundy, 123
Dunn, George Hedford, 123
Dunn, James Whitney, 123
Dunn, Jennifer, 123
Dunn, John Thomas, 123
Dunn, Matthew Anthony, 123

Dunn, Poindexter, 123
Dunn, Thomas Byrne, 123
Dunn, William McKee, 123
Dunne, Edward Fitzsimmons, 285
Dunnell, Mark Hill, 123
Dunning, Paris Chipman, 286
Dunphy, Edward John, 123
Dunwell, Charles Tappan, 123
Du Pont, Henry Algernon, 123
Du Pont, Pierre Samuel "Pete" IV, 123, 282
Du Pont, Thomas Coleman, 123
Dupre, Henry Garland, 123
Dupre, Jacques, 289
Durand, George Harman, 123
Durbin, Richard Joseph, 123
Durbin, Winfield Taylor, 286
Durborow, Allan Cathcart Jr., 123
Durell, Daniel Meserve, 123
Durenberger, David Ferdinand, 123
Durey, Cyrus, 123
Durfee, Job, 123
Durfee, Nathaniel Briggs, 123
Durgan, George Richard, 123
Durham, Carl Thomas, 123
Durham, Milton Jameson, 123
Durkee, Charles, 123
Durkin, John Anthony, 123
Durkin, Martin Patrick, 32
Durno, Edwin Russell, 123
Dutton, Henry, 280
Duval, Isaac Harding, 123
Duval, William Pope, 123
Duvall, Gabriel, 45 (box), 48, 53, 123
Dwight, Henry Williams, 123
Dwight, Jeremiah Wilbur, 123
Dwight, John Wilbur, 123
Dwight, Theodore, 123
Dwight, Thomas, 123
Dwinell, Justin, 123
Dwinell, Lane, 301
Dworshak, Henry Clarence, 123
Dwyer, Bernard James, 123
Dwyer, Florence Price, 123
Dyal, Kenneth Warren, 123
Dyer, David Patterson, 123
Dyer, Elisha II, 309
Dyer, Elisha III, 310
Dyer, Leonidas Carstarphen, 123
Dymally, Mervyn Malcolm, 123
Dyson, Royden Patrick "Roy," 124

Eagan, John Joseph, 124
Eager, Samuel Watkins, 124
Eagle, James Philip, 278
Eagle, Joe Henry, 124
Eagleburger, Lawrence Sidney, 32
Eagleton, Thomas Francis, 124
Eames, Benjamin Tucker, 124
Earhart, Daniel Scofield, 124
Earl, Anthony Scully, 319
Earle, Elias, 124
Earle, George Howard III, 308
Earle, John Baylis, 124
Earle, Joseph Haynsworth, 124
Earle, Samuel, 124
Earll, Jonas Jr., 124
Earll, Nehemiah Hezekiah, 124

Hampton, James Giles, 147
Hampton, Moses, 147
Hampton, Wade, 147
Hampton, Wade, 147, 311
Hanback, Lewis, 147
Hanbury, Harry Alfred, 147
Hance, Kent Ronald, 147
Hanchett, Luther, 147
Hancock, Clarence Eugene, 147
Hancock, Franklin Wills Jr., 147
Hancock, George, 147
Hancock, John, 147, 293
Hancock, Milton D. "Mel," 147
Hancock, Winfield Scott, 7
Hand, Augustus Cincinnatus, 147
Hand, Thomas Millet, 147
Handley, George, 283
Handley, Harold Willis, 286
Handley, William Anderson, 147
Handy, Levin Irving, 147
Hanks, James Millander, 147
Hanley, James Michael, 147
Hanly, James Franklin, 147, 286
Hanna, John, 147
Hanna, John Andre, 147
Hanna, Louis Benjamin, 147, 305
Hanna, Marcus Alonzo, 147
Hanna, Richard Thomas, 147
Hanna, Robert, 147
Hannaford, Mark Warren, 147
Hannegan, Edward Allen, 147
Hannegan, Robert Emmet, 34
Hannett, Arthur Thomas, 302
Hanrahan, Robert Paul, 147
Hansbrough, Henry Clay, 147
Hansen, Clifford Peter, 147, 320
Hansen, George Vernon, 147
Hansen, James Vear, 147
Hansen, John Robert, 147
Hansen, Julia Butler, 147
Hansen, Orval Howard, 147
Hanson, Alexander Contee, 147
Haralson, Hugh Anderson, 147
Haralson, Jeremiah, 147
Hard, Gideon, 147
Hardee, Cary Augustus, 283
Hardeman, Thomas Jr., 147
Harden, Cecil Murray, 148
Hardenbergh, Augustus Albert, 148
Hardin, Benjamin, 148
Hardin, Charles Henry, 297
Hardin, Clifford Morris, 34
Hardin, John J., 148
Hardin, Martin Davis, 148
Harding, Aaron, 148
Harding, Abner Clark, 148
Harding, Benjamin Franklin, 148
Harding, Florence Kling DeWolfe, 9
  (box)
Harding, John Eugene, 148
Harding, Ralph R., 148
Harding, Warren Gamaliel, 9, 12, 13, 42,
  46 (box), 47, 58 (box), 148
Harding, William Lloyd, 287
Hardman, Lamartine Griffin, 284
Hardwick, Thomas William, 148, 284
Hardy, Alexander Merrill, 148
Hardy, Guy Urban, 148

Hardy, John, 148
Hardy, Porter Jr., 148
Hardy, Rufus, 148
Hare, Butler Black, 148
Hare, Darius Dodge, 148
Hare, James Butler, 148
Hare, Silas, 148
Hargis, Denver David, 148
Harkin, Thomas Richard, 10, 148
Harlan, Aaron, 148
Harlan, Andrew Jackson, 148
Harlan, Byron Berry, 148
Harlan, James, 34, 148
Harlan, James, 148
Harlan, John Marshall, 48, 53
Harlan, John Marshall, 53
Harless, Richard Fielding, 148
Harley, Joseph Emile, 311
Harman, Jane, 148
Harmanson, John Henry, 148
Harmer, Alfred Crout, 148
Harmon, Judson, 34, 306
Harmon, Randall S., 148
Harness, Forest Arthur, 148
Harper, Alexander, 148
Harper, Francis Jacob, 148
Harper, James, 148
Harper, James Clarence, 148
Harper, John Adams, 148
Harper, Joseph Morrill, 148, 300
Harper, Robert Goodloe, 148
Harper, William, 148
Harreld, John William, 148
Harries, William Henry, 148
Harriman, Walter, 300
Harriman, William Averell, 34, 304
Harrington, Emerson Columbus, 292
Harrington, Henry William, 148
Harrington, Michael Joseph, 148
Harrington, Vincent Francis, 148
Harris, Andrew Lintner, 306
Harris, Benjamin Gwinn, 148
Harris, Benjamin Winslow, 148
Harris, Charles Murray, 148
Harris, Christopher Columbus, 148
Harris, Claude Jr., 148
Harris, Elisha, 309
Harris, Fred Roy, 148
Harris, George Emrick, 148
Harris, Henry Richard, 148
Harris, Henry Schenck, 148
Harris, Herbert Eugene II, 148
Harris, Ira, 148
Harris, Isham Green, 148, 313
Harris, James Morrison, 148
Harris, Joe Frank, 284
Harris, John, 149
Harris, John Spafford, 149
Harris, John Thomas, 149
Harris, Katherine, 149
Harris, Mark, 149
Harris, Nathaniel Edwin, 284
Harris, Oren, 149
Harris, Patricia Roberts, 34
Harris, Robert, 149
Harris, Robert Orr, 149
Harris, Sampson Willis, 149
Harris, Stephen Ross, 149

Harris, Thomas K., 149
Harris, Thomas Langrell, 149
Harris, Wiley Pope, 149
Harris, William Alexander, 149
Harris, William Alexander, 149
Harris, William Julius, 149
Harris, Winder Russell, 149
Harrison, Albert Galliton, 149
Harrison, Albertis Sydney Jr., 317
Harrison, Anna Symmes, 9 (box), 11
  (box)
Harrison, Benjamin, 6, 11 (box), 13, 42,
  58 (box), 149
Harrison, Burr Powell, 149
Harrison, Byron Patton "Pat," 149
Harrison, Caroline Lavinia Scott, 9
  (box), 11 (box)
Harrison, Carter Bassett, 149
Harrison, Carter Henry, 149
Harrison, Francis Burton, 149
Harrison, Frank Girard, 149
Harrison, George Paul, 149
Harrison, Henry Baldwin, 281
Harrison, Horace Harrison, 149
Harrison, Jane Irwin, 11 (box)
Harrison, John Scott, 149
Harrison, Richard Almgill, 149
Harrison, Robert Dinsmore, 149
Harrison, Samuel Smith, 149
Harrison, Thomas Walter, 149
Harrison, William Henry, 4, 7, 11 (box),
  12, 13, 16, 17, 41, 49 (box), 58 (box),
  149
Harrison, William Henry, 149
Harsha, William Howard, 149
Hart, Alphonso, 149
Hart, Archibald Chapman, 149
Hart, Edward Joseph, 149
Hart, Elizur Kirke, 149
Hart, Emanuel Bernard, 149
Hart, Gary Warren, 10, 149
Hart, Joseph Johnson, 149
Hart, Louis Folwell, 317
Hart, Melissa A., 149
Hart, Michael James, 149
Hart, Ossian Bingley, 282
Hart, Philip Aloysius, 149
Hart, Roswell, 149
Hart, Thomas Charles, 149
Harter, Dow Watters, 149
Harter, John Francis, 149
Harter, Michael Daniel, 149
Hartke, Rupert Vance, 149
Hartley, Fred Allan Jr., 149
Hartley, Roland Hill, 317
Hartley, Thomas, 149
Hartman, Charles Sampson, 149
Hartman, Jesse Lee, 149
Hartness, James, 316
Hartnett, Thomas Forbes, 149
Hartranft, John Frederick, 308
Hartridge, Julian, 149
Hartzell, William, 149
Harvey, David Archibald, 150
Harvey, James, 150
Harvey, James Madison, 150, 287
Harvey, Jonathan, 150
Harvey, Louis Powell, 318

Hobson, David Lee, 155
Hobson, Richmond Pearson, 155
Hoch, Daniel Knabb, 155
Hoch, Edward Wallis, 288
Hoch, Homer, 155
Hochbrueckner, George Joseph, 155
Hockenhull, Andrew W., 302
Hodel, Donald Paul, 34
Hodges, Asa, 155
Hodges, Charles Drury, 156
Hodges, George Hartshorn, 288
Hodges, George Tisdale, 156
Hodges, James Leonard, 156
Hodges, Jim, 312
Hodges, Kaneaster Jr., 156
Hodges, Luther Hartwell, 34, 305
Hodgson, James Day, 34
Hoeffel, Joseph M. III, 156
Hoegh, Leo Arthur, 287
Hoekstra, Peter, 156
Hoeppel, John Henry, 156
Hoeven, Charles Bernard, 156
Hoeven, John, 306
Hoey, Clyde Roark, 156, 305
Hoff, Philip Henderson, 316
Hoffecker, John Henry, 156
Hoffecker, Walter Oakley, 156
Hoffman, Carl Henry, 156
Hoffman, Clare Eugene, 156
Hoffman, Elmer Joseph, 156
Hoffman, Harold Giles, 156, 302
Hoffman, Henry William, 156
Hoffman, John Thompson, 303
Hoffman, Josiah Ogden, 156
Hoffman, Michael, 156
Hoffman, Richard William, 156
Hogan, Earl Lee, 156
Hogan, John, 156
Hogan, Lawrence Joseph, 156
Hogan, Michael Joseph, 156
Hogan, William, 156
Hoge, John, 156
Hoge, John Blair, 156
Hoge, Joseph Pendleton, 156
Hoge, Solomon Lafayette, 156
Hoge, William, 156
Hogeboom, James Lawrence, 156
Hogg, Charles Edgar, 156
Hogg, David, 156
Hogg, Herschel Millard, 156
Hogg, James Stephen, 314
Hogg, Robert Lynn, 156
Hogg, Samuel, 156
Hoidale, Einar, 156
Hoke, Martin Rossiter, 156
Holaday, William Perry, 156
Holbrock, Greg John, 156
Holbrook, Edward Dexter, 156
Holbrook, Frederick, 315
Holcomb, Marcus Hensey, 281
Holcomb, Silas Alexander, 298
Holcombe, George, 156
Holden, Bob, 298
Holden, T. Timothy, 156
Holden, William Woods, 304, 305
Holifield, Chester Earl, 156
Holladay, Alexander Richmond, 156
Holland, Cornelius, 156

Holland, Edward Everett, 156
Holland, Elmer Joseph, 156
Holland, James, 156
Holland, Kenneth Lamar, 156
Holland, Spessard Lindsey, 156, 283
Holleman, Joel, 156
Hollenbeck, Harold Capistran, 156
Holley, Alexander Hamilton, 280
Holley, John Milton, 156
Holliday, Elias Selah, 156
Holliday, Frederick William Mackey, 317
Hollings, Ernest Frederick, 10, 156, 312
Hollingsworth, David Adams, 156
Hollis, Henry French, 156
Hollister, John Baker, 156
Hollister, Nancy, 307
Holloway, Clyde Cecil, 156
Holloway, David Pierson, 156
Holloway, William Judson, 307
Holman, Rufus Cecil, 156
Holman, William Steele, 156
Holmes, Adoniram Judson, 156
Holmes, Charles Horace, 157
Holmes, David, 157, 296
Holmes, Elias Bellows, 157
Holmes, Gabriel, 157, 304
Holmes, Isaac Edward, 157
Holmes, John, 157
Holmes, Oliver Wendell Jr., 44 (box), 48, 53
Holmes, Otis Halbert, 157
Holmes, Pehr Gustaf, 157
Holmes, Robert Denison, 308
Holmes, Sidney Tracy, 157
Holmes, Uriel, 157
Holsey, Hopkins, 157
Holshouser, James Eubert Jr., 305
Holt, Hines, 157
Holt, Homer Adams, 318
Holt, Joseph, 34
Holt, Joseph Franklin III, 157
Holt, Marjorie Sewell, 157
Holt, Orrin, 157
Holt, Rush D., 157
Holt, Rush Dew, 157
Holt, Thomas Michael, 305
Holt, William Elmer, 298
Holten, Samuel, 157
Holton, Abner Linwood Jr., 317
Holton, Hart Benton, 157
Holtzman, Elizabeth, 157
Holtzman, Lester, 157
Honda, Michael M., 157
Honeyman, Nan Wood, 157
Hood, George Ezekial, 157
Hook, Enos, 157
Hook, Frank Eugene, 157
Hooker, Charles Edward, 157
Hooker, James Murray, 157
Hooker, Warren Brewster, 157
Hooks, Charles, 157
Hooley, Darlene, 157
Hooper, Ben Walker, 313
Hooper, Benjamin Stephen, 157
Hooper, Joseph Lawrence, 157
Hooper, Samuel, 157
Hooper, William Henry, 157

Hoover, Herbert Clark, 13, 27 (box), 27, 34, 42, 44 (box)
Hoover, Lou Henry, 9 (box)
Hope, Clifford Ragsdale, 157
Hopkins, Albert Cole, 157
Hopkins, Albert Jarvis, 157
Hopkins, Benjamin Franklin, 157
Hopkins, David William, 157
Hopkins, Francis Alexander, 157
Hopkins, George Washington, 157
Hopkins, Harry Lloyd, 34
Hopkins, James Herron, 157
Hopkins, Larry Jones, 157
Hopkins, Nathan Thomas, 157
Hopkins, Samuel, 157
Hopkins, Samuel Isaac, 157
Hopkins, Samuel Miles, 157
Hopkins, Stephen Tyng, 157
Hopkinson, Joseph, 157
Hoppin, William Warner, 309
Hopwood, Robert Freeman, 157
Horan, Walter Franklin, 157
Horn, Henry, 157
Horn, Joan Kelly, 157
Horn, Steve, 157
Hornbeck, John Westbrook, 157
Horner, Henry, 286
Hornor, Lynn Sedwick, 157
Horr, Ralph Ashley, 157
Horr, Roswell Gilbert, 157
Horsey, Outerbridge, 157
Horsford, Jerediah, 157
Horton, Frank Jefferson, 157
Horton, Frank Ogilvie, 157
Horton, Henry Hollis, 313
Horton, Thomas Raymond, 158
Horton, Valentine Baxter, 158
Hoskins, George Gilbert, 158
Hosmer, Craig, 158
Hosmer, Hezekiah Lord, 158
Hostetler, Abraham Jonathan, 158
Hostetter, Jacob, 158
Hostettler, John, 158
Hotchkiss, Giles Waldo, 158
Hotchkiss, Julius, 158
Houck, Jacob Jr., 158
Hough, David, 158
Hough, William Jervis, 158
Houghton, Alanson Bigelow, 158
Houghton, Amory Jr., 158
Houghton, Sherman Otis, 158
Houk, George Washington, 158
Houk, John Chiles, 158
Houk, Leonidas Campbell, 158
House, John Ford, 158
Houseman, Julius, 158
Houston, Andrew Jackson, 158
Houston, David Franklin, 34
Houston, George Smith, 158, 276
Houston, Henry Aydelotte, 158
Houston, John Mills, 158
Houston, John Wallace, 158
Houston, Robert Griffith, 158
Houston, Samuel, 158, 312, 313
Houston, Victor Stewart Kaleoaloha, 158
Houston, William Cannon, 158
Houx, Frank L., 319
Hovey, Alvin Peterson, 158, 286

Ten Eyck, Egbert, 246
Ten Eyck, John Conover, 246
Ten Eyck, Peter Gansevoort, 246
Tener, John Kinley, 246, 308
Tenerowicz, Rudolph Gabriel, 246
Tenney, Samuel, 246
Tenzer, Herbert, 246
Terral, Thomas Jefferson, 278
Terrell, George Butler, 246
Terrell, James C., 246
Terrell, Joseph Meriwether, 246, 284
Terrell, William, 246
Terry, Charles Laymen Jr., 282
Terry, David Dickson, 246
Terry, John Hart, 246
Terry, Lee, 246
Terry, Nathaniel, 246
Terry, William, 246
Terry, William Leake, 246
Test, John, 246
Tewes, Donald Edgar, 246
Thacher, Thomas Chandler, 246
Tharp, William, 282
Thatcher, George, 246
Thatcher, Maurice Hudson, 246
Thatcher, Samuel, 246
Thayer, Andrew Jackson, 246
Thayer, Eli, 246
Thayer, Harry Irving, 246
Thayer, John Alden, 246
Thayer, John Milton, 246, 298
Thayer, John Randolph, 247
Thayer, Martin Russell, 247
Thayer, William Wallace, 307
Theaker, Thomas Clarke, 247
Thibodeaux, Bannon Goforth, 247
Thibodeaux, Henry Schuyler, 289
Thill, Lewis Dominic, 247
Thistlewood, Napoleon Bonaparte, 247
Thom, William Richard, 247
Thomas, Albert, 247
Thomas, Benjamin Franklin, 247
Thomas, Charles, 282
Thomas, Charles Randolph, 247
Thomas, Charles Randolph, 247
Thomas, Charles Spalding, 247, 279
Thomas, Christopher Yancy, 247
Thomas, Clarence, 46 (box), 51–52, 54
Thomas, Craig, 247
Thomas, David, 247
Thomas, Elbert Duncan, 247
Thomas, Francis, 247, 292
Thomas, George Morgan, 247
Thomas, Henry Franklin, 247
Thomas, Isaac, 247
Thomas, James, 292
Thomas, James Houston, 247
Thomas, Jesse Burgess, 247
Thomas, John, 247
Thomas, John Chew, 247
Thomas, John Lewis Jr., 247
Thomas, John Parnell, 247
Thomas, John Robert, 247
Thomas, John William Elmer, 247
Thomas, Lera Millard, 247
Thomas, Lot, 247
Thomas, Ormsby Brunson, 247
Thomas, Philemon, 247

Thomas, Phillip Francis, 39, 247, 292
Thomas, Richard, 247
Thomas, Robert Lindsay, 247
Thomas, Robert Young Jr., 247
Thomas, William Aubrey, 247
Thomas, William David, 247
Thomas, William Marshall, 247
Thomason, Robert Ewing, 247
Thomasson, William Poindexter, 247
Thompson, Albert Clifton, 247
Thompson, Benjamin, 247
Thompson, Bennie G., 247
Thompson, Charles James, 247
Thompson, Charles Perkins, 247
Thompson, Charles Winston, 247
Thompson, Chester Charles, 247
Thompson, Clark Wallace, 247
Thompson, Fountain Land, 247
Thompson, Frank Jr., 247
Thompson, Fred, 247
Thompson, George Western, 247
Thompson, Hedge, 247
Thompson, Hugh Smith, 311
Thompson, Jacob, 39, 247
Thompson, James, 247
Thompson, James Robert, 286
Thompson, Joel, 247
Thompson, John, 247
Thompson, John, 247
Thompson, John Burton, 248
Thompson, John McCandless, 248
Thompson, Joseph Bryan, 248
Thompson, Melvin Ernest, 284
Thompson, Michael, 248
Thompson, Philip, 248
Thompson, Philip Burton Jr., 248
Thompson, Philip Rootes, 248
Thompson, Richard Wigginton, 39, 248
Thompson, Robert Augustine, 248
Thompson, Ruth, 248
Thompson, Smith, 39, 45 (box), 54
Thompson, Standish Fletcher, 248
Thompson, Theo Ashton, 248
Thompson, Thomas Larkin, 248
Thompson, Thomas Weston, 248
Thompson, Tommy George, 39, 319
Thompson, Waddy Jr., 248
Thompson, Wiley, 248
Thompson, William, 248
Thompson, William George, 248
Thompson, William Henry, 248
Thompson, William Howard, 248
Thomson, Alexander, 248
Thomson, Charles Marsh, 248
Thomson, Edwin Keith, 248
Thomson, John, 248
Thomson, John Renshaw, 248
Thomson, Mark, 248
Thomson, Meldrim Jr., 301
Thomson, Vernon Wallace, 248, 319
Thone, Charles, 248, 299
Thorington, James, 248
Thorkelson, Jacob, 248
Thornberry, William Homer, 248
Thornberry, William M. "Mac," 248
Thornburgh, Jacob Montgomery, 248
Thornburgh, Richard Lewis, 27 (box), 39, 309

Thornton, Anthony, 248
Thornton, Daniel Isaac J., 280
Thornton, John Randolph, 248
Thornton, Raymond Hoyt Jr., 248
Thorp, Robert Taylor, 248
Thorpe, Roy Henry, 248
Throckmorton, James Webb, 248, 314
Throop, Enos Thompson, 248, 303
Thropp, Joseph Earlston, 248
Thruston, Buckner, 248
Thune, John, 248
Thurman, Allen Granberry, 248
Thurman, John Richardson, 248
Thurman, Karen Loveland, 248
Thurmond, James Strom, 248, 311
Thurston, Benjamin Babcock, 248
Thurston, John Mellen, 248
Thurston, Lloyd, 248
Thurston, Samuel Royal, 248
Thye, Edward John, 248, 295
Tiahrt, Todd, 248
Tibbatts, John Wooleston, 248
Tibbits, George, 248
Tibbott, Harve, 248
Tiberi, Patrick J. "Pat," 248
Tichenor, Isaac, 249, 315
Tiemann, Norbert Theodore, 299
Tiernan, Robert Owens, 249
Tierney, John F., 249
Tierney, William Laurence, 249
Tiffin, Edward, 249, 306
Tift, Nelson, 249
Tilden, Daniel Rose, 249
Tilden, Samuel Jones, 7, 50, 303
Tillinghast, Joseph Leonard, 249
Tillinghast, Thomas, 249
Tillman, Benjamin Ryan, 249, 311
Tillman, George Dionysius, 249
Tillman, John Newton, 249
Tillman, Lewis, 249
Tillotson, Thomas, 249
Tilson, John Quillin, 249
Timberlake, Charles Bateman, 249
Timmerman, George Bell Jr., 312
Tincher, Jasper Napoleon, 249
Tingley, Clyde, 302
Tinkham, George Holden, 249
Tipton, John, 249
Tipton, Thomas Foster, 249
Tipton, Thomas Weston, 249
Tirrell, Charles Quincy, 249
Titus, Obadiah, 249
Tobey, Charles William, 249, 301
Tobin, Maurice Joseph, 39, 294
Tod, David, 306
Tod, John, 249
Todd, Albert May, 249
Todd, John Blair Smith, 249
Todd, Lemuel, 249
Todd, Paul Harold Jr., 249
Todd, Thomas, 54
Tolan, John Harvey, 249
Toland, George Washington, 249
Toll, Herman, 249
Tollefson, Thor Carl, 249
Tolley, Harold Sumner, 249
Tomlinson, Gideon, 249, 280
Tomlinson, Thomas Ash, 249

Subject Index

African Americans
  cabinet members, 26, 28
  members of Congress, 60, 64–65, 378–379
  number of black members of Congress, 1947–2005 (box), 64
  presidential candidates, 10
  slaves in House apportionment, 57–58
  Supreme Court justices, 50–51
Age
  average by Congress, 61 (box)
  members of Congress, 59, 60–61
  presidents, 1, 12
  Supreme Court justices, 47–48
Agriculture, backgrounds in
  members of Congress, 61
  presidents, 12
Agriculture Department, U.S., 24 (box)
Appointments. See Nominations and appointments
Articles of Confederation, 23, 57, 59, 60
Asian Americans
  cabinet members, 26
  members of Congress, 60
Assassination attempts, 2–3, 12 (box)
Attorneys general. See also Cabinet
  Clinton nominations, 27, 28
  history, 24 (box)
  later Supreme Court justices, 47

Blacks. See African Americans
Businesspeople in Congress, 61

Cabinet
  appointment process, 27
  diversity, 26
  executive departments, 2005, 24–25 (box)
  function, role, 26–27
  holdovers, 27 (box)
  member biographies, 29–40
  member facts, 27–28
  members, by administration, 327–349
  members later president, vice president, 27–28
  members later Supreme Court justices, 47
  origin, development, 23–26
  other officials joining, 25–26

presidential style, 1945–2005, 25–26
service records, 28
vice president's role, 17
Catholics
  members of Congress, 62
  presidents, 6 (box), 10
  Supreme Court justices, 46 (box)
Chief justices. See also Supreme Court justices
  age, 47–48
  cabinet role, 23
  list, 42 (box)
Citizenship
  House, Senate qualifications, 59–60
  presidential qualification, 1
Civil War
  and presidential nominees, 4–7
  and Supreme Court, 43
Columbia University Law School, 44
Commerce Department, U.S., 24 (box)
Congress, members of. See also
  Congress, U.S.; Congressional-executive relations; House of Representatives, U.S.; Senate, U.S.
  African Americans, 60, 64–65
  age, 59, 60–61
  average age, 1949–2005 (box), 61
  biographies, 69–269
  chamber shifts, 68
  committee chairs since 1947, 386–374
  eligibility for federal office, 60
  former presidents, 68
  Hispanics, 60, 65
  incumbents, 60, 66–68
  later presidents, 58 (box)
  later Supreme Court justices, 45–46
  later vice presidents, 18, (box)
  minorities, 60
  occupational background, 61
  occupations, 109th Congress, 62 (box)
  as presidential candidates, 9–10
  prestige, 60
  qualifications, 59–60
  religious affiliations, 61–62
  service records, 67 (box)
  term length, 59
  term limits, 59
  turnover, 60, 65–68
  voting individually, 59

women, 60, 62–64, 65, 375–377
Congress, U.S. See also Congress, members of; Congressional-executive relations; House of Representatives, U.S.; Senate, U.S.
  constitutional structure, 57–60
  membership turnover, 60, 65–68
  sessions, 1789–2005, 352–358
Congressional-executive relations
  cabinet history, 23–26
  membership turnover in Congress, 65–68
  party affiliations, Congress and the presidency, 350–351
  over Supreme Court nominations, 41–42, 49 (box)
  vice president's role, 15, 17, 19–20
Constitution, U.S. See also specific amendments
  cabinet history, 23
  presidential disability, succession, 2–3 (box), 15
  presidential election, 1–4
  presidential qualifications, 1
  qualifications for Congress, 59–60
  signers as Supreme Court justices, 41
  structure of Congress, 57–60
  Supreme Court qualifications, 41
  term limits, 59 (box)
  vice president's role, 15–16, 17
Council of National Defense, 25

Deaths
  presidents, 12, 27 (box)
  vice presidents, 16
Defense Department, U.S., 24 (box)
Democratic Party
  African American members of Congress, 65
  congressional turnover, 60, 65–68
  governorships, 1950–2004, 272 (box)
  members' occupations, 109th Congress, 62 (box)
  military background of candidates, 4, 6–7
  nonpartisan Supreme Court appointments, 42
  party affiliations in Congress, presidency, 1789–2005, 350–351
  swing state candidates, 7
Disability
  presidents, 2–3 (box), 15, 16, 17

451